W9-APH-517

COMPOSITION
in Four Keys
INQUIRING INTO THE FIELD

• Art   • Nature   • Science   • Politics

Mark Wiley
California State University, Long Beach

Barbara Gleason
The City College of New York

Louise Wetherbee Phelps
Syracuse University

MAYFIELD PUBLISHING COMPANY
Mountain View, California
London • Toronto

Copyright © 1996 by Mayfield Publishing Company

All rights reserved. No portion of this book may be reproduced
in any form or by any means without written permission of the
publisher.

Library of Congress Cataloging-in-Publication Data

Wiley, Mark.
    Composition in four keys : inquiring into the field   / Mark Wiley,
Barbara Gleason, Louise Wetherbee Phelps.
       p.   cm.
    Includes index.
    ISBN 1-55934-265-X
    1. English language—Composition and exercises—Study and
teaching.   2. English language—Rhetoric—Study and teaching.
I. Gleason, Barbara.   II. Phelps, Louise Wetherbee.
III. Title.
PE1404.W53   1995
808'. 042'07—dc20   95-20821
                                      CIP

Manufactured in the United States of America
10 9 8 7 6 5 4 3 2 1

Mayfield Publishing Company
1280 Villa Street
Mountain View, California 94041

Sponsoring editor, James Bull; production editor, April Wells-
Hayes; manuscript editor, Robert Hartwell Fiske; text and
cover designer, Donna Davis; illustrators, Willa Bower and
Robin Mouat; art director, Jeanne M. Schreiber; manufacturing
manager, Amy Folden. The text was set in 10.5/13 Berkeley
Book by Clarinda/Atlantic and printed on 50# Ecolocote by
Malloy Lithographing, Inc.

Acknowledgments and copyrights continue at the back of the
book on pages 594–597, which constitute an extension of the
copyright page.

This book is printed on acid-free, recycled paper.

 Preface

Many colleges and universities have already established (or are in the process of establishing) courses or course sequences in theories and practices of teaching writing. However, because of the heterogeneity of the field, an introductory course poses difficult pedagogical problems for teachers and students alike. These problems arise primarily from deciding what material should be covered and to what depth, and how this material might be presented to readers with little or no background knowledge. Although we expect that this anthology will be used chiefly in graduate and undergraduate courses, the readers we have imagined for it are developing scholars and established scholars who want to learn more about composition. *Composition in Four Keys* therefore introduces readers to this complex interdisciplinary field by inviting them to take on the role of active inquirers and to construct the field by developing an understanding—through use—of the map that we offer.

The book is divided into five parts. The four major sections—Nature, Art, Science, and Politics—reflect issues, debates, practices, and assumptions salient primarily in the 1970s and 1980s, but Part 4 (the key of Politics) ends with work done in the early 1990s. Part 5 offers alternative organizational schemes that serve as bases for comparing these four keys. We believe these four categories will be immediately intelligible to readers unfamiliar with the field because most people already associate certain concepts with nature, art, science, and politics. The book builds on this immediate recognition and uses the keys as heuristics both to organize the field and to generate further inquiry. As readers work through the material, these heuristics will function as powerful tools for interpreting and placing scholarship and research. Moreover, the keys allow for inquiry beyond the limits of a single course.

A general introduction, called "Mapping Composition and Rhetoric," explains our approach and its rationale. Each of the five parts begins with an introductory essay, and each article is prefaced with a brief headnote. In addition, the book includes a number of boxed "inquiries," practical activities to enable inquiry and to initiate readers into the scholarly conversations and practices of the discipline. We have also attempted to build in flexibility. The book can be read in any order, although we recommend that you read the general introduction first and not read Part 5 until after generously sampling the first four parts.

Inventing a genre to reflect an evolving interdisciplinary field is not only a risky scholarly venture, but a risky financial one, too. We are grateful to Mayfield Publishing for taking a chance and for supporting us throughout the long process of trying to articulate what we wanted when we did not often know in the beginning exactly what that was. We want to thank Tom Broadbent, Uyen Phan, Pamela Trainer, and April Wells-Hayes. We especially want to recognize Jim Bull's unflagging efforts—and patience—in steering this project through to its present form.

We have subjected the developing manuscript to extensive review and would like to acknowledge and thank those who have collaborated with us in making this book more informed than it might have been without their insightful and productive comments. We thank Richard Haswell, James Kinneavy, Cheryl Glenn, Theresa Enos, and especially James Zebroski, who reviewed three versions of this book. We would also like to thank Cheryl Geisler, Janice Lauer, and Peter Elbow for timely suggestions regarding selections of individual articles.

We particularly want to honor those who have given us so much throughout our extended "composing process": Susan Marron for her needed humor and constant encouragement; Ed Quinn for his careful reading and constructive comments as well as for his invaluable moral support. And we owe a special thank you to Fred Phelps for the moral support and technical assistance he provided.

Finally, this project would not exist without the work of our first "readers"—those first seminar participants at the University of Southern California in the spring of 1986. We also acknowledge the subsequent work and responses of our graduate students at California State University, Long Beach; City College of the City University of New York; and Syracuse University.

We hope you will use this book in the spirit in which it is offered. It is not only a way of discovering where we have been as a field of study but an invitation and a sincere hope that you—our readers—will chart directions for future growth that none of us can foresee.

Contents

v

Introduction: Mapping Composition and Rhetoric

To readers, students, and scholars new to composition and rhetoric, encountering the literature of the field for the first time may feel something like landing in the middle of a large, unfamiliar city and having to make sense of it. Without a map and maybe a guidebook to navigate on their own, our hypothetical strangers must rely on the advice of knowledgeable city dwellers for information about what's worth seeing. The exploratory process is a hit-or-miss affair for the visitors though they may manage to visit a few "interesting" sites based on the advice (and biases) of their more knowledgeable informants.

The "territory" of composition is at first encounter a vast maze of texts that defy easy passage. The newcomer has, on a larger scale, the typical dilemma of anyone beginning to read an unknown text on unfamiliar ideas and topics. In order to comprehend, research tells us, readers need a prior context that makes individual sentences or details meaningful by relating them to an organized whole. But, paradoxically, new readers can't form such a framework until they already have some specific, well-understood building blocks from which to construct it. (This vicious circle is known in studies of reading and interpretation as the "hermeneutical circle" [see Kinneavy].) The expanse of texts that greets the new scholar of rhetoric and composition has no obvious principle of order. Explorers discover a sprawling exuberance, bewildering variety, ill-defined edges and overlaps with other fields. No wonder they often long for some simple scheme to organize this material and plot a path through their reading: a map of the territory of composition studies. But they quickly find that there is no simple, knowledgeable guide to which they can appeal. Rather than a commonly shared framework, they find an array of competing proposals to frame the study and teaching of writing.

One reason is that twentieth-century composition and rhetorical studies have been defined and practiced from the start as multidisciplinary. To conjoin these in a modern discipline, scholars have drawn on many traditions and methods, forming alliances and interdisciplinary configurations with all types of academic fields—the arts, sciences, and professions. Studies on writing and rhetoric are also influenced intellectually by the practices they examine, for example, teaching and learning in schools, writing in nonacademic settings, and political rhetoric. This multidisciplinarity has spawned a multifaceted and loosely structured academic field, encompassing various practical and theoretical activities that cover a wide range of interests, subject matters, methodologies, goals, and affiliations. The beginner in the field risks being overwhelmed by the sheer mass and variety of texts and by the lack of an intelligible method to find significant patterns in this material.

Then, you might wonder, how *do* those encountering composition and rhetoric for the first time figure out what the field is all about? More constructively, how *can* newcomers to the field read with active, engaged understanding? And how might we, as scholars and teachers, ease and support that process?

A Method of Structured Inquiry

This book grew from our own efforts to find practical solutions to this puzzle, first as teacher (Phelps) and graduate students (Gleason and Wiley) together, then as colleagues teaching at different institutions. Our answer is a structured inquiry: a practical experiment that encourages you, as new readers and students of composition and rhetoric, to construct the meanings and implications of texts and arguments in this field through your own vigorous investigation and debates.

As we envision the process, most often you will want to multiply the effectiveness of your inquiries by working collectively in some kind of face-to-face learning community, of which a formal class is only one example. Some, however, may by choice or necessity read, write, and study largely on their own, treating the texts in this anthology and beyond as a "virtual" community—or perhaps networking electronically with other readers in cyberspace. Through your own inquiry and the intellectual exchanges within your learning communities, we intend our book to model and engage you in the scholarly process itself, alongside and with the authors of the texts you are reading.

To begin your studies, we offer a map to organize what you read by means of four categories, or **keys**. This map is intended to be heuristic—an exploratory tool rather than a definitive claim—that can serve as a provisional framework for reading with immediate, if partial, understanding. By means of your own experiments in applying and testing the limits of this scheme, you will gradually make it more complex and qualified; complement it with other ways of reading and interpreting texts and arguments; define its strengths and limitations; maybe abandon it and invent your own maps. It is this probing, critical, reflective process of mapping, not the categories of the map itself, that should enable users of this book to learn how to make their own sense of composition and rhetoric.

Because we devised the four keys based on pragmatic and rhetorical considerations like how people talk about writing, what they argue about and with whom, what associations they join, or how they practice what they preach, using them will teach you more than the content and conceptual divisions of the field. You will learn about its scholarly processes: how a field's ideas and intellectual structure develop dynamically by means of the activities (empirical, conceptual, practical, and discursive) and the argumentation of its scholars and students. As you observe and participate in the interactions among scholars and trace their activities and arguments through texts, you will become increasingly conscious of scholarship itself as a rhetoric and a form of writing.

The four keys of our map are named **Nature, Art, Science**, and **Politics**. Although "key" is itself a metaphor with many interpretations (unlocking, for example), we are thinking primarily of the musical sense, in which one may be said to think or write or teach tonally in a particular key. We are indebted to the philosopher Susanne K. Langer for this metaphor, which she first used to describe a major shift in the mode and tenor of philosophic thinking in the twentieth century. But we've expanded the idea to imagine not one great shift (as from major to minor) but multiple keys in which different voices in rhetoric and composition compose the field. We chose four that seemed to emerge in the language and debates of the crucial decades (mainly, the late 1970s and 1980s) when scholars and teachers of writing began to search for ways to articulate a new discipline of written language—or, as some saw it, to revive an ancient one grounded in the tradition of Western rhetoric. Because these debates make highly explicit the terms, arguments, perspectives, ideals, ideologies, tensions, and topics that converged to characterize this field, we limited the time frame for article selections largely to this period, with a few scattered earlier ones and a few that take us into the early 1990s. Later, we will mention some other bases for selection.

Notice that we have been referring to the field by a number of slightly variant names, most of them pairing composition and rhetoric. Just as there is no single definitive framework, or paradigm, governing studies in contemporary composition and rhetoric, so there is no single agreed-on way to name the field. Of course, these two uncertainties are related. Different names correlate to some extent with divergent frameworks, which in turn represent different conceptions of the history of the field, along with competing goals, research traditions, contemporary sources of influence, teaching practices, and so on. In particular, naming expresses different conceptions of the relationships, historical and intellectual, between composition and rhetoric. (For two different interpretations, see Gage, and Phelps.)

In this book, we will understand composition as always paired with rhetoric in the field you are studying, but we will not take a position on their specific relationship since that is a debatable question among the four keys (and, indeed, among your editors). For convenience, however, we will often (as in our title) use the word *composition* for short.

The Nature of the Keys

The four keys, insofar as they derive from the discourse of this formative period, are inductive and pragmatic rather than strict logical categories with precisely controlled meanings and no overlap. They reflect and express communities of interest and difference among people who identified themselves as doing work in "composition" or "rhetoric"; who associated in departmental life, conventions, or publication sites; and who thought of themselves as engaged in a common enterprise. These teachers and scholars of writing talked about their ideas and named themselves as members of groups sharing scholarly interests and informing traditions, in opposition to others who were proposing alternative ideas and traditions, in a period when these arguments competed to shape and define an emerging discipline. We have included articles that use terms suggestive of each key; the "art" of writing is one instance, and the teaching of writing as a "natural" process is another. You, in using the four keys, are therefore mapping the rhetorical scene of composition as that scene was constructed through the arguments and analyses of those involved. And with these scholars, you can debate concepts, premises, ideologies, philosophies, and activities associated, however loosely, with these heuristic groupings called keys.

From another perspective, though, the four keys work for the purposes of this book because they are cultural (Western) *commonplaces*. (For a discussion of the historical evolution of the rhetorical commonplaces or, "topoi," see D'Angelo.) It may seem confusing to readers, initially, that we offer no minimal guidelines or definitions to help you narrow down the meanings of these terms. But this is a deliberate strategy appropriate to the nature of the keys as loose groupings rather than ideological definitions (though you may use them to arrive at such constructions). As cultural commonplaces, these keys are particularly rich in complexity, contradiction, and multiple meanings. Readers can (like the authors they are reading) immediately draw on these associations and resonances to identify intelligible patterns of commonality and difference. Precisely because the keys carry a lot of historical and connotative baggage, they provide newcomers with already articulated modes to help organize and interpret primary texts in composition. The concepts of Nature, Art, Science, and Politics should quickly become "good enough" to start sorting out some of the tonal and ideological differences that we are calling keys. Don't worry if your initial understanding of the keys shows many of the features of what the Russian psychologist Lev Vygotsky called pseudoconcepts—terms that, as you begin to acquire them, are both overly rich and sketchy, overgeneralized, or vague (Vygotsky 62–69). Gradually, you can sharpen and clarify how they may be useful in your own writing and thinking. (At the end of this introduction, we list some of the features to look for, from the most concrete language cues to the underlying philosophical assumptions.)

At this point, you might want to test our map—and our claim about your knowledge of commonplaces—by trying the following experiment.

> Think for a minute about what you already know or associate with each of these terms: Nature, Art, Science, and Politics. You might brainstorm a list of associations individually or do so in a group. In the following examples, try to match each passage with one of the keys you have identified as Nature, Art, Science, or Politics. After you have read and discussed your reasons for the ways you have identified these passages, you can find the sources for them at the end of this introduction.[1] If you want, you can then read each article in full.

EXAMPLE 1

Writers who wish to be read must often adapt their discourse to meet the needs and expectations of an addressed audience. They may rely on past experience in addressing audiences to
guide their writing, or they may engage a representative of that audience in the writing
process. The latter occurs, for instance, when we ask a colleague to read an article intended for
scholarly publication. Writers may also be required to respond to the intervention of others—
a teacher's comments on an essay, a supervisor's suggestions for improving a report, or the insistent, catalyzing questions of an editor. Such intervention may in certain cases represent a
powerful stimulus to the writer, but it is the writer who interprets the suggestions—or even
commands—of others, choosing what to accept or reject. Even the conscious decision to accede to the expectations of a particular addressed audience may not always be carried out; unconscious psychological resistance, incomplete understanding, or inadequately developed
ability may prevent the writer from following through with the decision—a reality confirmed
by composition teachers with each new set of essays.

EXAMPLE 2

The themes of this paper were formulated during the course of a participant observation
project in an urban magnet school on the west coast. The study site drew children from social
and ethnic groups from across this urban community. The children were from Anglo, Asian,
Black, Hispanic, Middle Eastern and mixed ethnicities. The school's 79 primary (K–3) grade
children were separated into three "home classrooms": a kindergarten, a first/second grade,
and a second/third grade. Beginning in January of the school year, all of the primary grade
school children moved throughout the school day among the three teachers' classrooms. The
kindergarten "home" teacher, Margaret, was responsible for language arts instruction for all
the children throughout the data collection periods.

Since this project focused on young children's use of talk, pictures, and written text, I used
inductive analysis procedures to develop categories describing the children's use of these varied media. Inductive procedures involve, first, segmenting data into similar units of behavior;
second, comparing those units; and third, composing descriptors to specify how those units
vary. Those descriptors become the coding categories (see Bogdan & Biklen, 1982). . . .

EXAMPLE 3

Moreover, Hirsch seeks to require mastery not merely of Standard English, but of a particular
style of writing Standard English, a style encapsulated in the maxims of Strunk and White's
well-known manual, which he recommends. His argument for the cognitive superiority of a
clear, concise style of Standard English, like the humanists' argument for the cognitive characteristics of literate style, fails to notice that this style is socially situated. Hirsch's preferred verbal style, and the humanists' literate style, both appear upon further analysis to be the
preferred style and thought patterns of academics, not necessarily of all literate people. In
short, Hirsch's candidate for privileged ideology of literacy is not as context-free as he claims:
it is an academic ideology of literacy.

EXAMPLE 4

What characterizes much excellent writing is precisely this special quality of lively or heightened semantic presence. It's as though the writer's mental activity is somehow alive with her
meaning.

When a writer is particularly fluent, she has the gift of doing less internal rehearsal. The acts of figuring out what she wants to say, finding the words, and putting them down somehow coalesce into one act—into that integrative meaning-making/language-finding act which is characteristic of speech. But even beginners (or writing teachers) can achieve this liveliness and presence when they engage in freewriting or spontaneous writing. It is this semantic presence which often makes freewriting seem peculiarly lively to read. One of the best directions for coaching freewriting is to tell oneself or one's students to "talk onto the paper."

In our own experiences with these and similar passages, the keys prove to have immediately comprehensible meanings in "common sense" derived from Euro-American cultural contexts. It's not important whether readers place these passages within the keys as we, the editors, expect. What's interesting (and revealing about commonplaces) is the reasons readers give and the patterns of tacit knowledge that quickly become evident in discussing those reasons.

The experiment is intended to let you test the principles we have been developing for using this book most effectively. To summarize:

- *We envision our readers as proactive, creative, inquiring, curious—which is to say, as trying on the role of scholars in rhetoric and composition and treating the authors as their potential colleagues.*

Some of our readers (for example, new teachers of writing who are reading this anthology to get some background in composition theory) may be surprised to find that it is not a how-to book. Countless textbooks and increasing numbers of trade books are intended to instruct teachers "practically" how to teach. (In fact, readers of this book may want to survey both textbooks and how-to texts, using the four keys experimentally to describe and compare them.) But our book has a different purpose: to introduce novice scholars to the literature of composition and rhetoric and to help them find—and learn to create—organizing patterns to make its discourse intelligible. We believe that even readers who have different goals in learning about composition and rhetoric will benefit from hypothesizing themselves as future scholars because that will engage them—like students of writing—in designing and practicing inquiry as a learning mode. Our approach also expresses an unusual view of the relations between the teaching of writing as a "practice" and the disciplinary knowledge developed by empirical, historical, and theoretical investigations. We believe that teaching itself can be scholarly and should not be dominated by externally generated theories although it should be informed and stimulated by such work. That is why we invite teachers, along with other readers of this anthology, to identify themselves from the beginning collegially as members of the "community of scholars" represented by the authors of these texts. Readers of all backgrounds and purposes should find it enlightening and empowering to address these authors as fellow inquirers and students of writing and rhetoric.

- *We imagine our audience for this book as typically collective.*

Far more important than the individual keys, the map, or even the mapping process, is you, the inquirers. We assume you are capable, highly motivated thinkers who will form learning communities and thereby direct your own individual learning in cooperation with others so inclined. Actually, the first experimenters with the keys of this book were such a group: graduate students, teachers of writing, and assorted visitors in a seminar on composition and rhetoric led by Louise Phelps, with Mark Wiley and Barbara Gleason as participants. Our hypothesis—that these newcomers could join and make contributions to the community of scholars by engaging in structured investigations with no conclusions preset by the teacher—was confirmed and in fact resulted in our composing this collection together after many years of experimenting independently with its ideas and pedagogical philosophy.[2]

Although the book can be read and used by an individual, mapping is most powerful as a tool when it is practiced by a group of different thinkers, with different purposes, backgrounds, and patterns of interpretation, who can divide up the work of researching and reading and can debate their findings. We imagine, for example, a graduate or even an advanced undergraduate class taking up these inquiries together, perhaps working in small groups that change from time to time. But we also welcome other audiences who might be novice readers in composition and rhetoric: teachers, public reading groups, scholars in related disciplines pursuing common interests, or faculty engaged in writing-across-the-curriculum initiatives who want to learn more about scholarship in writing.

In imagining such nontraditional reading collectives, some of the limitations of cultural commonplaces reveal themselves and (in what we hope will be a characteristic move in your studies of this material) can be turned into opportunities. We are counting on readers to be English-speaking persons acquainted with the Western tradition through cultural exposure. If this is not the case, you and your colleagues will be able to probe cultural differences in understandings of these terms and perhaps to propose and alert one another to alternative rubrics based on different commonplaces—schemes that might either reinterpret or challenge the beliefs and assumptions underlying the debates of this period. For example, Native American, African American, Latino or Hispanic, Asian, and various specific immigrant groups all have contributed alternate rhetorical traditions that influence American writing. Is it possible to account for these influences within the four keys, or must they be transformed, discarded, or supplemented?

- *The map is not the territory. But believing in it is a useful game.*

We offer this map as a descriptive tool, but it is only one way of mapping the territory. It is not the territory itself (see Bateson). Exactly what the possible relations are between a map (labels, patterns) and the things and relations it maps or categorizes is a difficult philosophical matter that we will consider in Part 5. For the moment, we simply offer a caution. In asking you to experiment with the keys as a system for noticing things, for describing, for comparing or contrasting different texts, authors, and groups of ideas, we are inviting you to "believe" in the keys as a hypothesis, not accept them as gospel. Peter Elbow calls this playing the "believing game." It involves consciously suspending or "bracketing" skepticism or doubt while you thoroughly explore and test the map against the materials reprinted in this book and, we hope, against other examples as well. But testing is a two-way street and inevitably generates doubt about the map itself as you discover that it doesn't quite fit the territory. Our invitations to inquiry in each part will often include challenges to provoke and keep track of such observations. In Part 5, we provide alternative maps in order for you to play the "doubting game" with our map itself, marshaling this evidence of inadequacy and oversimplification and comparing underlying principles for constructing maps.

An Approach to Using This Book

How then, exactly, can you use this anthology as a whole, and its mapping system, to learn about the field of rhetoric and composition and to enter it as a participant?

We invite you to set up a dialectic that exploits the very paradox that we pointed out earlier as a hermeneutical circle. That means you are asked to work back and forth constantly between the map and the texts: using the texts to help you define the keys, using the keys to understand the texts. You will identify features in the texts that are collected in each part in order to develop provisional definitions for each key and to contrast and analyze its relationship to other keys within the mapping scheme. Simultaneously, or dialectically, you will employ the keys to bring order to the apparent chaos of ideas and positions in these sample texts, interpreting or "placing" them on the map in order to understand what they say and what is at stake in their arguments. As you proceed, we will frequently suggest comparisons and other experiments, activities, or questions in the introductions; we will also encourage you to test the keys against other materials—books, articles, curriculum guides, teaching materials, and so on.

Specifically, we suggest that you divide responsibilities among those in your learning community to work through each section by hypothesizing pragmatic features and conceptual content to characterize each key and then testing and refining your hypotheses against the (inevitably messier) content of the texts and the frequently inconsistent or questionable alignment of authors with keys. We recommend strongly that you begin with the most mundane, concrete, pragmatic, or rhetorical observations: for example, where the work is published and for what audience; what sources are cited; what topics are commonly addressed; or what kinds of student writing, if any, are favored. From here, you can work up cautiously to ideological differences and make inferences about grounding premises and attitudes: for example, beliefs about ways of knowing (philosophy and research method) or some of the principles that give the key its name (like postulating composition studies as a science).

You may wonder what has governed the selection of articles given that we have pictured the field as so unbounded and internally diverse. We make no claim for comprehensiveness—that would be absurd in any volume of this sort. We regard the texts here simply as a sampling, chosen to be sufficiently varied, eclectic, and representative to allow you to use the four keys to construct a holographic and tentative sense of the whole. As noted earlier, we narrowed the pool of potential choices by drawing primarily from a period in composition and rhetoric when its discourse flowered in richness and diversity, becoming very explicit about intellectual purposes and differences in the project of defining composition studies and rhetoric as a unified discipline. There is much we want you to gain from the mapping experiment, including a critical appreciation of maps and mapping, but with respect to grasping the range of the field, these are our goals:

> When you finish (or even as you are working through the inquiries here), you should be able to read texts outside the anthology with some understanding and sense of familiarity with issues being debated; to recognize divergence from these categories (and therefore their incompleteness); and to be able to modify your understandings and your maps to account for materials that do not fit easily within the scheme. You should be prepared by your work on this anthology to extend your further inquiries in many directions: into the past of composition and rhetoric, for example; into in-depth analysis and close readings of work in the field; into other, closely related disciplinary studies evoked and cited in these materials; and, most important, into the work of the 1990s and beyond.

Given these goals, we made no attempt to select work thought to be the "best" in composition; to choose those most heavily cited or written by the most well-known or well-published scholars and researchers; or to include the most up-to-date information and ideas on a topic. Instead, we tried to compose a set of materials that express something of the range of concerns, topics and themes, debates, genres, and styles to be found in composition during its emergent period. Of course, having practiced with many others the same inquiry you are undertaking, we looked for texts that would give the richest and most diverse clues to the features that typify and characterize the differences we have named keys. We juggled many other considerations and made difficult tradeoffs. For example, we sought at least some recognizable names and texts that might conventionally be associated with each key and tried to represent a number of the major publishing venues and genres in which work identified with composition and rhetoric has appeared. And we tried in each part to provide some texts that will challenge the most stereotypical definitions of the key: for instance, by their introduction of unexpected themes or their openness to alternative interpretations.

Our **Inquiries** in each part will point you to some of these dissonances and keep you on your toes in drawing conclusions about each key. So you will find yourself examining the political premises implicit in an article selected for Nature, or realizing that some rhetoricians see no incompatibility between Art and Science. As you proceed with your investigations, someone will be sure to question the placement of pieces within a particular part. Why does it belong here and not there? Why not in both places? Are the keys really mutually exclusive? You will also find yourselves arguing with one another about where to place outside readings. In some cases, they don't seem to fit anywhere in the keys. This is especially likely if you try applying the map to very recent publications, conference presentations, or curricular materials and practices.

One strategy we recommend is to create a **wild card** category for whatever doesn't seem to fit any of the keys and seems in fact "off the map." We periodically will be asking questions about these misfits; for example, do they seem to introduce new ideas or extend ideas already identified, or do they suggest new keys to add to or replace those named? Some of these misfits may cause you to question the relevance of this mapping scheme to some work in the field. Or they may lead you to identify a strong minority theme or tradition that explains a misfit.

As you become comfortable with two or more keys, you will be comparing and contrasting one key with another, playing out differences and similarities, and continually thinking of new questions. Do they have a temporal relationship, or did they all spring into being at once? Whether they name antecedents or not, do they have a history? Is it possible to identify some contemporary intellectual or cultural crisis or transformation that is broad enough to affect all the keys? Can the field be read through the lens of one key, or does this negate the value of the keys as a mapping system? And so on.

The four key parts can be read and sampled in any order—remembering the proviso that Part 5 is best read later. We offer some context for each key in part introductions, but our focus is on providing invitations to inquiries—projects and activities—interspersed throughout the introduction. These invitations are developed from the list of features on page 11 and are intended as an aid for participants who may want to further their exploration of the keys and pursue issues, themes, or topics beyond the selections provided here. (There is more here than can be "covered" in a semester or quarter class, but then again we hope you, as scholars, will not conceive of inquiry as necessarily cut up into ten- or fifteen-week units.)

As you work on understanding the materials of this book through the keys while trying to characterize and define the features of the keys themselves, you will necessarily **indwell**, or live inside each key and the map, until—even if you try not to—you come to believe in their reality. As you do, there's a great temptation to declare your allegiance to one of the keys. In your group, you may even reproduce the divisions and differences of belief and attitude that motivated the authors you are reading, and which, as recent publications show, continue to matter to the field today even as others are raising new questions and perhaps creating new keys. Recognizing that these investments in what you are reading are part of the believing game and that they can be productive and fun, we suggest that you remember to play believing as a game, reserving strong commitment and considered judgments until you have explored all the keys.

At the same time, don't neglect the frequent clues from your investigations that this map as a construct has important limitations and blind spots as a way of describing and accounting comprehensively for the writings and practices of composition and rhetoric. We anticipate—and will deliberatively provoke—much

Features of the Keys

You may find the concepts on the following list useful for hypothesizing about the four keys. We have arranged them here (roughly) from the concrete to the abstract.

Allies and enemies (those contemporary in the field)

Heroes and villains (for example, philosophers, rhetoricians, figures in history, critics outside the field)

Favored audiences

Disciplines drawn on as authorities and sources

Traditions appealed to

Typical topics and problems with a view of what is problematic or at issue

Approved pedagogy, including topics taught and pedagogical style and technique

Types of student writing favored

Sites of writing (encompasses developmental age and place; for example, high school, elementary school, workplace)

Significant concepts and terms

Characteristic style (language—vocabulary, syntax)

Favored genre and channel (for example, journal articles, anthologies, textbooks, curriculum guides, conference presentations)

Favored publication outlets (journals, publishers, and so on)

Formats for references (bibliographies, notes, and so on)

Technologies of interest

History

Relation to rhetoric

Method of inquiry

Epistemology

Explicit theories and metadiscourses about the discipline

Definitions of the field, principled inclusions and exclusions

We will use these terms (though not exhaustively) to generate invitations to inquire in introductions to other parts of the book. Throughout your reading, we suggest that you select from and add to the terms useful to your own investigations.

discussion of the limits and frustrations of this map. But again we recommend that you develop a critical assessment of it by fully and carefully working through the four keys before looking at Part 5, where we have included some other scholars' maps for reading and interpreting composition. At that point, not only should you be ready to appreciate and experiment with alternatives, but you will also have a base for making comparisons and judgments about their value in different circumstances, for different purposes. That is to say, at this point, we will invite you to play the "doubting game" with our map itself and with rival representations of the divisions and debates of composition and rhetoric.

A final declaration of principle: In every way possible, this book has been designed to entrust you with a great deal of responsibility for your own learning, both individually and collectively. But you are also responsible for the learning of others,

Inquiries

1. Participants might embark on this reading project by sharing tasks with others in doing outside reading in journals and anthologies. They could form enough groups not only to read as much of the composition and rhetoric literature as possible but also for each group to focus on a particular key. One goal could be to write a joint annotated bibliography charting a semester's reading and writing (or however long participants work on this project). You might also include in these bibliographies texts that do not fit easily into the conceptual scheme presented here.

Reading groups can record ideas and arguments regarding what goes into each key and maybe keep notes on reservations and issues raised by the fact that each article, even if it fits, does not fit perfectly, has things in it that fall outside the keys altogether, may contradict others apparently in the same key, and so forth.

2. Again, if you are working with a group or a class, you might consider inviting individuals within the group to "become experts." Here, one reader takes responsibility for reading as much as possible by one author and then informs the group about the possible range of concerns for this particular scholar or researcher. Experts can note where their scholars may migrate to other keys or do work that can't be adequately placed within the four identified here. Shifts in a given scholar's thinking can also be remarked on, including how earlier and later work may or may not form a coherent pattern when read within one of the keys.

This same idea about becoming an expert can also be applied to topics and themes instead of to particular writers. One could, for instance, become an expert on style and explore how style is treated by various individuals across the keys. Readers will no doubt think of other activities that groups can perform in helping one another become experts.

beyond yourself and your circle of friends. Through your inquiries, as with other groups we have taught or who have participated in using the keys, we confidently expect you to expand the possibilities of our mapping scheme, to challenge it and invent others, to represent it in fresh and revealing ways (as some of our students have, with graphs and charts), and to surprise us with the marvelous unpredictability of what you discover. Learners teaching scholars and becoming colleagues in spirit or in fact—that is our ultimate dream. Have fun!

NOTES

1. The four passages are from the following articles in this volume: Example 1 is from Lisa Ede and Andrea Lunsford, "Audience Addressed/Audience Invoked: The Role of Audience in Composition Theory and Pedagogy"; Example 2 is from Anne Haas Dyson, "Negotiating among Multiple Worlds: The Space/Time Dimensions of Young Children's Composing"; Example 3 is from Patricia Bizzell, "Arguing about Literacy"; and Example 4 is from Peter Elbow, "The Shifting Relationships between Speech and Writing."

2. Under Louise Phelps's guidance, Larry Ferrario, Barbara Gleason, and Mark Wiley composed a panel on "ideologies" in composition for the 1987 Conference on College Composition and Communication. In the interim between that CCCC presentation and the decision to do this anthology, the present editors have substituted "key" for "ideology" because the latter term too readily provokes reactions oriented toward politics. Since these keys serve as cultural commonplaces (as we have been arguing), they include politics but are not limited to it. The use of the word *keys* is an editorial decision and does not necessarily reflect the views of other participants in that first seminar.

WORKS CITED

Bateson, Gregory. "Form, Substance, and Difference." *Steps to an Ecology of Mind.* New York: Ballantine Books, 1972. 448–66.

D'Angelo, Frank J. "The Evolution of the Analytic Topoi: A Speculative Inquiry." *Essays on Classical Rhetoric and Modern Discourse.* Eds. Robert Connors, Lisa Ede, and Andrea Lunsford. Carbondale: Southern Illinois UP, 1984. 50–68.

Elbow, Peter. "Preface 4: The Doubting Game and the Believing Game." *PRE/TEXT 3* (1982): 339–51.

Gage, John T. "On 'Rhetoric' and 'Composition.'" *An Introduction to Composition Studies.* Eds. Erika Lindemann and Gary Tate. New York: Oxford UP, 1991. 15–32.

Kinneavy, James L. "The Relation of the Whole to the Part in Interpretation Theory and in the Composing Process." *The Territory of Language: Linguistics, Stylistics, and the Teaching of Composition.* Ed. Donald McQuade. Carbondale: Southern Illinois UP, 1986. 292–312.

Langer, Susanne K. *Philosophy in a New Key: A Study in the Symbolism of Reason, Rite, and Art.* 1942. 3rd ed. Cambridge: Harvard UP, 1957.

Phelps, Louise Wetherbee. "Composition Studies." *Encyclopedia of Rhetoric.* Ed. Theresa Enos. Garland (forthcoming, 1995).

Vygotsky, Lev Semenovich. *Thought and Language.* Ed. and trans. Eugenia Hanfmann and Gertrude Vakar. 1962. Cambridge: MIT Press, 1984.

Part One

Nature

"Natural" Development: Teacher, Student, Scholar

MARK WILEY

In 1986, I was in my penultimate semester of taking courses in the Rhetoric, Linguistics, and Literature doctoral program at the University of Southern California. The diversity of interests of the composition and rhetoric faculty provided students with multiple perspectives on theories of writing and teaching writing. Ross Winterowd was battling the English department, arguing that it should be devoted to literacy studies and the teaching of writing and reading informed with principles from classical rhetoric. Lawrence Green was pursuing scholarship in classical rhetoric. Marilyn Cooper and Michael Holzman, drawing on the work of Foucault and Freire among others, were arguing that writing (and literacy in general) were fundamentally social activities, and Louise Phelps was intensively engaged in building theories of writing and literacy by drawing on a range of intellectual traditions and disciplines from American pragmatism to European text linguistics, hermeneutics, and phenomenology; from physics and biology to psychology and literary theory.

Those participating in Phelps's seminar therefore brought to bear on the material a mix of backgrounds, perspectives, and interests, including often unrecognized preconceptions and biases. The structure of the course, however, allowed us the opportunity to pool our knowledge and apply it to primary sources in composition. By using the three commonplaces of Nature, Art, and Science, we were encouraged to explore from the ground up what those who studied composition and rhetoric claimed about themselves and their work. The fourth key we created did not actually function as the other keys did because it became our "wild card" category for everything that did not fit the other three.

I mention this fourth nonkey because it reminded participants that this map when put into practice—as a map—would broadly sort the field in intelligible ways but would not necessarily do justice to the work of a given individual or to a body of work. The wild card acknowledged idiosyncrasy as well as ongoing change in the field, so seminar participants could make their best case for including articles in any one key, with those arguments serving as the bases for differentiating one key from another. But at the same time, in the process of arguing and constructing our map, we were forced to be aware of our own blind spots about work we could not account for, whether work by individual scholars or work reflecting different traditions or larger movements within the field. Consequently, we did not have to make the field stretch to fit our categories. But we could explore how far we could stretch these keys to fit our developing sense of what composition was about.

Though the intellectual work we were doing in that seminar was significant for our individual growth as scholars, equally important in hindsight were the noticeable psychological and social shifts we experienced in how we approached our seminar tasks. That shifting is roughly intelligible when viewed through William Perry's map for intellectual and ethical development. For my present purpose, I am reducing to three positions Perry's nine-celled scheme. In the first stage, students just entering college tend to be dogmatic in their thinking. There is a right and wrong answer to all questions. As students are exposed to multiple views, each supported by convincing arguments, dogmatism gives way to relativism. What one believes is right and wrong depends on one's perspective and context. In the last stage, however, individuals make a conscious commitment to one belief system or another for reasons that they can articulate. Although seminar participants were not first-year college students, we did initially use the keys as hard and fast categories, like bins into which we could toss particular scholars we were reading: This is a writer in the Art key because she advocates . . . , which is what Art people do. Or this person should be in Nature because he thinks that . . .

We also tended to see Nature and Art as opposed to each other. In other words, we foregrounded each key's distinctions from one another and, at first, ignored their similarities. As we pursued our investigations, though, we began to see overlaps in concerns between and among keys. Freewriting when used as a technique in Nature pedagogy, for example, meant something quite different than when it might be used as a heuristic in a writing class informed by concepts we associated with Art. These differences, we reasoned, stemmed from systematically differing conceptions of the purposes of a writing course, the functions of writing, ways of teaching and learning how to write, the writer's role in the composing process, and relationships between thought and language in both its spoken and written forms.

To further complicate matters, some scholars we were reading could sound like Nature advocates in one article and proponents of Art or Science in other publications. James Moffett and James Britton are notable examples. As the semester progressed, some students in the class became committed to one key more than to another. It became very difficult to maintain "objectivity" and to avoid any personal stance toward and eventual commitment to what we were hypothesizing each key stood for. The degree of commitment seemed to coincide with the prior interests and values each person brought to the seminar plus the amount of time and effort spent on reading and writing about scholarship in a, by now, favored key.

In hindsight in our seminar debates, in the interests we were pursuing and in the positions we were staking out for ourselves, we were replicating what was happening in the emerging field of composition and rhetoric. We were dramatizing the emergent differences we understood, which were also products of our taking courses from the several faculty members in the Rhetoric program. As we mapped the field using the keys, we were enacting a rite of initiation into the discipline because we were consciously composing its scope and complexity; its partial history and intellectual traditions; its enduring themes; its ongoing debates and interests; its key players; and its possible future directions.

The seminar forced me first to explore, then to question, and eventually to reconsider my assumptions about writing, teaching, and learning to write as well as about the place of the writer in the academy and in the culture. My previous training in literature and my reactions against that training along with my decision to pursue a Ph.D. in rhetoric and composition led me to form an early allegiance to what I saw and valued in Nature—its emphasis on the primacy of the writer. The scholarship and research I was reading in the other keys seemed to displace the authority of the writer and the authority for teaching writing onto impersonal systems of inquiry and instruction that required highly specialized knowledge to master and apply. I felt then, while reading the literature in the key of Art particularly, that the actual person doing the writing was less important than the purpose of the writing and what it looked like when it was finished. What I interpreted in reading outside the key of Nature was consequently being influenced by what I believed was true and valuable in my favored key.

My resistance to whatever I read that challenged my previous beliefs was increased further by some of the current work we were finding that did not map well in our three keys. I interpreted this recent work emphasizing the social dimension of composing as a reaction against the focus on the psychology of the individual writer. And though these arguments for the social aspects of composing were convincing, I still could not completely accept this shift. I used myself as an example: My experience teaching writing had led me to believe that for any real growth to occur, each student had to struggle with his or her ideas and their significance; each had to commit time and disciplined effort to their writing, which meant that they had to believe and take pride in what they were doing. In short, they had to take the locus of control for their writing away from their teacher and internalize it for themselves. (I now think this is what Moffett means by "authentic authoring.")

Another factor that prevented me from wholeheartedly embracing the turn to the social was that I identified my own struggle with learning how to write as a scholar in composition with my students' struggle to learn how to write in the academy. My struggle could certainly be argued as arising from the juxtaposition of the academic program I was working in with the new field I was trying to enter. Yet it was also clear to me that the conflicts I experienced were idiosyncratic, based on my experiences, concerns, goals, values, and prejudices. Though all graduate students felt degrees of anxiety and insecurity, feelings arising from a social context, those feelings were still experienced in unique ways. I felt no other choices were open to me but to submit to the authority of the phenomenal reality I experienced.

In forming my individual identity within this larger field, it seemed important not only to discover what I believed and valued but also to argue my position in terms of what—and who—I was against. The origins of my "differences" with other views expressed in composition and rhetoric stemmed as much from my autobiography (as I was constructing it) as from the competing positions then being staked out and debated publicly. As a developing scholar, it was consequently necessary for me to learn that the personal can merge easily with the public, but it was just as necessary for me to learn that the relationship between the two realms was tenuous, that in many instances it was wiser to put distance between the personal and the public. For example, I might have taken personally another seminar participant's argument against a practice advocated by Peter Elbow. Not because the argument was wrong: The objections to Elbow's practices could have been quite reasonable; rather, what was "wrong" in Elbow I interpreted to mean was wrong in the values I cherished and in how I was teaching my students to write. Criticisms of Elbow were therefore criticisms I projected onto my teaching and the role I imagined for myself as a teacher of writing.

The distance I needed therefore was to create a critical space within which I could separate what I valued from my need to value it. I could create that space by placing the themes and practices I valued in Nature within a larger historical frame in order to scrutinize the tacit intellectual and cultural assumptions that sanctioned and made persuasive the work of scholars I placed within this key. The other two keys we were working with—Art and Science—had clearly identifiable intellectual traditions; in contrast, this was not the case with Nature since these scholars—with the exception of Ann Berthoff—made scant reference to a larger history within which their work could be placed and understood. The themes that preoccupied me in Nature were personal power and authority and the role they played in a writer's development. Those twin themes eventually became the focus of my dissertation. Though I saw connections to versions of continental romanticism, I saw a more fruitful line of inquiry in American transcendentalism, specifically in the work of Ralph Waldo Emerson. Based on my reading in the key of Nature, I first tried to characterize what sort of power and authority were crucial to the developing writer in that key. I then found parallels in Emerson's work and in my dissertation argued that his concerns regarding the relationship among language, power, and authority resonated in the work of several compositionists—Elbow, Macrorie, and Berthoff certainly—but also in Bartholomae (see his essay in Politics).

My use of this map then forced me to look at my own interest in writing and teaching from several perspectives, with the challenges that those perspectives raised complicating what I understood to be true at the time. In trying to resolve the dissonance I experienced, I had to let go of my allegiance to Nature. In attempting to transcend the frame I was operating within, I had to use the keys as critical levers to move my thinking from where it "naturally" wanted to go. I have continued to rethink primary issues that first aroused my curiosity. The focus on the power and authority of the writer has since metamorphosized into political interpretations of those terms. I encourage you to do such comparisons of themes and issues you discover in Nature as well as in the other keys and beyond. Your course of reading will surely not be mine. See where it leads you.

Inquiries

1. Try to identify oppositions or areas of tension or conflict in Nature. Then see if one term or concept is favored over another. Here are two possible oppositions:

SPONTANEOUS   PROCESS
planned   product

Explore the consequences of privileging one term over the other. This activity can be applied to individual selections in this chapter. For example, note that Bissex sets up an opposition between the organic development of the writer and the assembly-line process of education. Attempt to tease out the conceptual and practical implications of this oppositional pair. Where does the organic metaphor break down or produce contradictions?

2. Compose a brief argument in the following way:

Although Bruffee's essay can reasonably be placed in Nature because _____ , it could also be argued that it belongs in Art because _____ .

Try the same method with Phelps's essay, but substitute Science for Art. Alternatively, substitute "it does not belong in any of these four keys because _____ .

3. Here is Ken Macrorie on voice:

> There is nothing so good as *feeling* to control actions. Lots of talk flying around these days about developing intellectual control, but to learn to tap feelings so they control actions and words is far more useful. If you find the feeling that belongs to a piece of writing you want to create—your feeling toward the subject and the persons you are writing to—then the composing may be accomplished almost without your help, and it will be true in tone, and compelling. (149)

> Finding the right voice will help you write better than you ever thought yourself capable of writing.

> Finding a true voice gives a piece of writing unity. (151)

In addition to Macrorie, scholars such as Peter Elbow, Donald Murray, and Toby Fulwiler are famous for their concern with voice. But is it clear what voice means? Is Macrorie using voice in the same way as Elbow and Murray, for instance? Is Moffett's advocacy of "inner speech" a recommendation that students tap into their inner voices? Are there any connections between the pedagogical functions of freewriting and Britton's concept of "shaping at the point of utterance"?

Investigate the degree of emphases and variations in the way voice is used across the keys. Does voice mean the same as and function similarly to "ethos" in Art? How is voice interpreted in Politics, and what is significant about challenges to it? How might voice be treated in Science?

4. Several scholars associated with Nature, such as Donald Graves, Lucy McCormick Calkins, and Peter Medway, have taught or worked in elementary

schools. Study the ideal of the typical "student" in each key, and explore the degree to which each key focuses attention on different ages of language learning from preliteracy to adults. One way to investigate this question is to note the frequency of studies published in journals of elementary-, secondary-, or college-level teaching. How old are the writers and learners studied in journals like *Research in the Teaching of English*? Are these writers and learners represented as typical? Are there differences in how each key attends to different age levels and in how they imagine and value children versus adults? Work in Nature is often associated with romanticism. Do you see any link with romantic depictions of the child?

5. Consider various dimensions of the "personal" as it appears in certain contexts and as it is valued in this key as well as across the keys. The personal can show up, for example, in types of assigned writing preferred, or in writing appreciated, by readers, or it can show up in the ways that teachers' work in the classroom is posed against or related to research or theory. Consider some recent titles of journal articles: "Rediscovering the Essay"; "The Exploratory Essay: Enfranchising the Spirit of Inquiry in College Composition"; "A Common Ground: The Essay in the Academy"; "Freedom, Form, Function: Varieties of Academic Discourse"; and the title of an anthology—*The Politics of the Essay: Feminist Perspectives*. Is there any connection between the "essay" as genre and the place of the personal in academic and public writing? How might each key treat this particular genre? Are there relationships between advocacies of the essay and defenses of the author, the validity of personal experience, and ways we might think of writing as transformative?

6. In reflecting on Jeanette Harris's book *Expressive Discourse*, Peter Elbow writes:

> When I first discovered . . . that she wanted to get rid of expressive discourse as a category in our discipline, I was intrigued—even attracted. Not just because I don't find the word "expressive" particularly central to my own lexicon, nor just because I too sometimes wonder what the word means, but most of all, quite frankly, because I find these days that the term is mostly used as a stick to beat me over the head with. (84)

Try to complete this argument: Those favoring other keys have mapped Nature as "neo-Romantic," "vitalist," or "expressivist." These various labels construct a stereotype of Nature as ——————. Yet those so labeled don't necessarily accept these stereotypes and view their own positions as more complicated. For example, many (Elbow, Berthoff, Murray) qualify their position by ——————.

In your argument try to challenge or complicate the stereotype, and explain how you are going to do so.

WORK CITED

Perry, William, Jr. *Forms of Intellectual and Ethical Development in the College Years: A Scheme.* New York: Holt, Rinehart and Winston, 1968.

SUGGESTED READINGS

Voice

Coles, William E., Jr. *The Plural I: The Teaching of Writing.* New York: Holt, 1978.

Fulwiler, Toby, ed. *The Journal Book.* Portsmouth: Boynton/Cook, 1987.

Macrorie, Ken. *Telling Writing.* Rev. 2nd ed. Rochelle Park: Hayden Book Co., 1976.

Yancey, Kathleen Blake, ed. *Voices on Voice: Perspectives, Definitions, Inquiry.* Urbana: NCTE, 1994.

Uses of the Child

Calkins, Lucy McCormick. "Children Write—and Their Writing Becomes Their Textbooks." *Language Arts* 55 (1978): 804–10.

Graves, Donald H. *Writing: Teachers and Children at Work.* Portsmouth: Heinemann Educational Books, 1983.

Phelps, Louise Wetherbee. "Literacy and the Limits of the Natural Attitude." *Composition as a Human Science.* New York: Oxford UP, 1988. 108–30.

Rico, Gabrielle. "The Childhood Origins of Natural Writing." *Writing the Natural Way.* Los Angeles: J.P. Tarcher, 1983. 50–62.

The Essay

Bridwell-Bowles, Lillian. "Freedom, Form, Function: Varieties of Academic Discourse." *College Composition and Communication* 46 (1995): 46–61.

Joeres, Ruth-Ellen Boetcher, and Elizabeth Mittman, eds. *The Politics of the Essay: Feminist Perspectives.* Bloomington: Indiana UP, 1993.

Spellmeyer, Kurt. "A Common Ground: The Essay in the Academy." *College English* 51 (1989): 262–76.

Winterowd, W. Ross. "Rediscovering the Essay." *Journal of Advanced Composition* 8 (1988): 146–57.

Zeiger, William. "The Circular Journey and the Natural Authority of Form." *Rhetoric Review* 8 (1990): 208–19.

Critiques and Defenses of Expressivism

Burnham, Christopher. "Expressive Rhetoric: A Source Study." *In Defining the New Rhetorics.* Ed. Theresa Enos and Stuart Brown. Newbury Park: Sage, 1993. 154–70.

Elbow, Peter. "Some Thoughts on *Expressive Discourse:* A Review Essay." *Journal of Advanced Composition* 11 (1991): 83–93.

Faigley, Lester. "Competing Theories of Process: A Critique and a Proposal." *College English* 48 (1986): 527–42.

Fishman, Stephen, and Lucille Parkinson McCarthy. "Is Expressivism Dead?" *College English* 54 (1992): 647–61.

Harris, Jeanette. *Expressive Discourse.* Dallas: Southern Methodist UP, 1990.

natural process of discourse
experiences ; perception

I, You, and It

James Moffett

Moffett's essay was published first in College Composition and Communication 16
(1965): 243–48. It has been republished in Active Voice: A Writing Program Across
the Curriculum. *2nd edition. Portsmouth, NH: Boynton/Cook. 1992. 196–203.*

Consider, if you will, those primary moments of experience that are necessarily the raw stuff of all discourse. Let us suppose, for example, that I am sitting in a public cafeteria eating lunch. People are arriving and departing, passing through the line, choosing tables, socializing. I am bombarded with smells of food, the sounds of chatter and clatter, the sights of the counter, the tables, the clothing, the faces, the gesticulations and bending of elbows. But I am not just an observer; I am eating and perhaps socializing as well. A lot is going on within me—the tasting and ingesting of the food, reactions to what I observe, emotions about other people. I am registering all these inner and outer stimuli. My perceptual apparatus is recording these moments of raw experience, not in words but in some code of its own that leads to words. This apparatus is somewhat unique to me in the way it selects and ignores stimuli and in the way it immediately connects them with old stimuli and previously formed conceptions. It is difficult to separate this sensory recording from the constant stream of thoughts that is going on simultaneously and parallel to the sensory record but may often depart from it. This verbal stream is the first level of discourse to be considered. The subject is *what is happening now,* and the audience is oneself.

Suppose next that I tell the cafeteria experience to a friend sometime later in conversation. For what reason am I telling him? Would I tell it differently to someone else? Would I tell it differently to the same person at another time and in different circumstances? These are not rhetorical questions but questions about rhetoric. The fact that my account is an unrehearsed, face-to-face vocalization, uttered to *this* person for *this* reason at *this* time and place and in *these* circumstances determines to an enormous degree not only the overall way in which I abstract certain features of the ongoing panorama of the cafeteria scene but also much of the way I choose words, construct sentences, and organize parts. Compare this discourse with the third stage, when my audience is no longer face to face with me, but is farther removed in time and space so that I have to write a letter or memo to him. Informal writing is usually still rather spontaneous, directed at an audience known to the writer, and reflects the transient mood and circumstances in which the writing occurs. Feedback and audience influence, however, are delayed and weakened. Written discourse must replace or compensate for the loss of vocal characteristics and all physical expressiveness of gesture, tone, and manner. Compare in turn now the changes that must occur all down the line when I write about this cafeteria experience in a discourse destined for publication and distribution to a mass, anonymous audience of present and perhaps unborn people. I cannot allude to things and ideas that only my friends know about. I must use a vocabulary, style, logic, and rhetoric that anybody in that mass audience can understand and respond to. I must name and organize what happened during those moments in the cafeteria that day in such a way that this mythical average reader can relate what I say to some primary moments of experience of his own. In other words, whether this published discourse based on the cafeteria luncheon comes out as a fragment of autobiography, a short story, a humorous descriptive essay, or a serious theoretical essay about people's behavior in public places, certain necessities frame the discourse and determine a lot of its qualities before the writer begins to exercise his personal options.

These four stages of discourse—inner verbalization, outer vocalization, correspondence, and formal writing—are of course only the major markers of a continuum that could be much more finely calibrated. This continuum is formed simply by increasing the distance, in all senses, between speaker and audience. The audience is, first, the speaker himself, then another person standing before him, then someone in another time and place but having some personal relation to the speaker, then, lastly, an unknown mass extended over time and space. The activity necessarily changes from thinking to speaking to writing to publishing. (Thinking as inner speech is at least as old as Bergson and William James and as new as Piaget and Vygotsky.) For me no discussion of language, rhetoric, and composition is meaningful except in this context, for there is no speech without a speaker in some relation to a spoken-to and a spoken-about.

Starting with our cafeteria scene again, I would like to trace it as a subject that may be abstracted to any level I would wish. Please understand that by "subject" I mean some primary moments of experience regardless of how dimly they may appear in the discourse. There are four stages in the processing of raw phenomena by the human symbolic apparatus, although, again, one may recognize many gradations in between. This continuum can best be represented by verb tenses, which indicate when events occurred in relation to when the speaker is speaking of them. Suppose I represent the cafeteria scene first as *what is happening,* which would be the lowest level of verbal abstraction of reality: the order and organization of events would correspond most closely to phenomenal reality, and my verbal-

ization of them would be the most immediate and unpondered that is possible. That is, my symbolic representation in this case would entail the least processing of matter by mind. If next I treat the events at the cafeteria as *what happened,* the subject will necessarily partake a little more of my mind and a little less of the original matter. Although the order of events will still be chronological, it is now my memory and not my perceptual apparatus that is doing the selecting. Some things will stick in my mind and some will not, and some things I will choose to retain or reject, depending on which features of this scene and action I wish to bring out. Of the details selected, some I will dwell upon and some I will subordinate considerably. Ideas are mixed with material from the very beginning, but the recollection of a drama—a narrative, that is—inevitably entails more introduction of ideas because this is inherent in the very process of selecting, summarizing, and emphasizing, even if the speaker refrains from commenting directly on the events.

Suppose next that I speak of my cafeteria experience as *what happens.* Obviously, if we consider it for a moment, the difference between *what happened* and *what happens* is not truly a time difference, or at least we must realize that what we are calling a time difference is actually a difference in the level to which I choose to abstract some primary moments of experience. I am now treating my once-upon-a-time interlude at the cafeteria as something that recurs. I have jumped suddenly, it seems, from narrative to generalization. Actually, as we have said, ideas creep in long before this but are hidden in the processing. Now they must be more explicit, for only by renaming the experience and comparing it with other experiences can I present it as what happens. No primary moments of experience recur. What we mean is that we as observers see similarities in different experiences. Only the human mind, capable of sorting and classifying reality, can do this. What I do, for example, is make an analogy between something in the cafeteria experience and something I singled out of a number of other experiences. I summarize a lot of little formless dramas into pointed narratives and then I put these narratives into some classes, which I and others before me have created. In this third stage of processing, then, the cafeteria scene will become a mere example, among several others, of some general statement such as "The food you get in restaurants is not as good as what you get at home," or "People don't like me," or "Americans do not socialize as readily with strangers in public places as Italians do," or "The arrivals and departures within a continuous group create changes in excitation level comparable to the raising and lowering of electric potential in variously stimulated sensory receptors." It is apparent that these sample generalizations could all have contained the cafeteria experience as an example but vary a great deal in their abstractness, their range of applicability, their objectivity or universal truth value, and their originality.

The transition from a chronological to an analogical discourse is of enormous importance in teaching. The student must forsake the given order of time and replace it with an order of ideas. To do this he must summarize drastically the original primary moments of experience, find classes of inclusion and exclusion, and rename the moments so that it becomes clear how they are alike or different. Most students fail to create original and interesting classes because they are unwittingly encouraged to borrow their generalizations from old slogans, wise saws, reference books, and teachers' essay questions, instead of having to forge them from their own experience. Many students leave out the illustrations completely and offer only their apparently sourceless opinions. Others, reluctant to leave the haven of narrative, tell several anecdotes and never show how they are related. But these are failures of teachers, not of students. Proper writing assignments can lead the students to good generalizations.

In what I will call the last stage of symbolizing a subject, you may wonder why I still refer to the cafeteria, since none of that experience appears any longer in the discourse, which is now a highly theoretical essay. That is deceptive; it is behind the discourse, buried in the processing and so combined with other experiences, and so renamed, that we do not recognize it any more. The "subject" seems to be a theory, some combining and developing of generalizations. This stage is telling *what will, may,* or *could happen.* Some general assertions previously arrived at by analogical thinking are now plugged into each other in various ways according to the rules of formal logic. Suppose we take some generalizations about the behavior of Americans and the behavior of Italians and the behavior of South Sea islanders and we transform and combine these statements in such a way as to come out with an anthropological conclusion that was not evident in any of the original moments of experience nor even in the generalizations about them. It took manipulations of logic to show the implications of the earlier statements. To go beyond this stage is to enter the realm of mathematical equations. What will, may, or could happen is a high-level inference entailing tautology, verbal equations. My own essay is an example of stage-four abstraction. I am setting up a series of equations among "levels of abstraction," "distance between speaker, listener, and subject," verb tenses, human faculties, and kinds of logic. I will then conclude a theory about composition curriculum by combining generalizations about what happens in discourse with what happens in the learning process of people. What enables me to do this is that something fundamental to the operation of our nervous system underlies all these man-made conceptions.

I have traced separately, and grossly, two abstractive progressions—one in which the speaker's audience becomes more remote and diffused over time and space, and another in which the speaker's subject becomes less and less matter and more and more idea. Each relation—and of course the two must be taken together—entails certain necessities, and shifts in these relations entail changes all down the line, from the organization of the whole discourse to individual word choice. As we move through the progressions, perception gives way to memory and memory to ratiocination; chronology gives way to analogy and analogy to tautology. But each faculty and kind of logic depends on the one before. In view of what we know now about abstractive processes and the cognitive and verbal growth of children, this order seems pedagogically sound to me. In other words, the necessities inherent in devising a rhetoric for an increasingly remote audience and in abstracting moments of experience to higher and higher symbolic levels are precisely the limitations which should shape our writing assignments.

According to Piaget, and Vygotsky agrees with him, the early egocentric speech of the child becomes gradually "socialized" and adapts itself to other people. At the same time his mental outlook decenters; that is, he gradually yields up his initial, emotionally preferred vantage point, and expands his perspective so as to include many other points of view. Of course, both these kinds of growth never really stop. The movement is from self to world, from a point to an area, from a private world of egocentric chatter to a public universe of discourse. Cognitively, the young person passes through, according to Jerome Bruner, three phases—the enactive, the iconic, and the symbolic. First he knows things by manipulating them with his hands, then he begins to classify and interpret the world by means of image summaries, and finally he can carry out logical operations in his head modeled on his earlier physical manipulations. Most teachers have always known that in some way the child should move from the concrete to the abstract, but the whole notion of an abstraction scale has never been clear and still requires more study. I have found the communication engineers' definition of coding to be very helpful in all this: Coding is the substitution of one set of events for another. What I call the processing of matter by mind is in fact the substitution of inner events for outer events. These inner events are neural, and we don't yet know very much about them. We can be sure, however, that as the child's nervous system develops, these neural operations become more complicated. A series of writing assignments is a series of thinking assignments and therefore a sequence of internal operations.

As a model for a composition course, imagine the trinity of discourse—first, second, and third persons—to be a single circle that separates into three overlapping circles which move out until they merely touch. The discourse unity of somebody talking to somebody else about something is what we must never lose, but we can create phases, not by decomposing composition into analytical elements but by gradually pushing the persons apart. Language and rhetoric are variable factors of each other and of shifting relations among persons. We abstract not only from something but for someone. Rhetoric, on the other hand, is to some extent dictated by the abstraction level we have chosen; in drama and narrative one appeals mainly by concrete recognitions, and in exposition and argumentation mainly by one's classes and logical justice. So the rationale of our composition course lies in some crossing of the two progressions I have sketched. This is not only possible but will spiral the curriculum. For example, we ask the student to tell what happened in four different rhetorics—to himself as he spontaneously recalls a memory, to a friend face to face, to someone he knows in a letter, and to the world at large in formal writing. Generalizations and theories can be dealt with first in interior monologues, then in dialogues, in letters and diaries, and only at the end in essays. The student is never assigned a subject, only a form and the forms are ordered according to the preceding ideas, as they seem to apply to individuals.

Specifically, I would have the student write in this order: all kinds of real and invented interior monologues, dramatic monologues, dialogues, plays, letters, diaries, fragments of autobiography, eye-witness accounts, reporters-at-large (modeled on those in *The New Yorker*), case studies, first- and third-person fiction, essays of generalization and essays of logical argumentation. Many teachers may feel that such a program slights exposition in favor of so-called personal or creative writing. In the first place, one doesn't learn exposition just by writing it all the time. An enormous amount of other learning must take place before one can write worthwhile essays of ideas; that is in the nature of the whole abstraction process. All writing teaches exposition. Furthermore, I cannot conceive a kind of discourse which does not contain ideas; even in concrete description, contrasts, similarities, and notions of causality and progression are strongly implicit.

Monologues, dialogues, letters, diaries, and narratives may either contain explicit ideas or be shaped by ideas. What do we mean by a *pointed* narrative? What are Socratic dialogues about? And why do we have students digging for meaning in literary works of imagination if they are not full of ideas? The issue is not idea writing versus other kinds of writing but rather which *form* the ideas are presented in. All modes must be taught. The panic to teach exposition is partly responsible for its being taught so badly. Teachers do not feel they can take the time to let a student abstract from the ground up. But if they do not, he will never learn to write exposition.

There are several corollaries of the program I am proposing. Since it attempts to exercise the student in all possible relations that might obtain between him and an audience and a subject, one corollary is that he not be allowed to get stuck with one audience or at one range of the abstractive spectrum. It is essential that he address someone besides the English teacher and get some kind of feedback other than red marks. As one solution, I suggest that he be accustomed to write to the class peers as being the nearest thing to a contemporary world at large. Compositions should be read in class, and out of class, reacted to and discussed. One must know the effects of one's rhetoric on someone who does not give grades and does not stand as an authority figure. I suggest also the performance and publication of student works as frequently as possible. Monologues, dialogues, letters, and diaries give the student the opportunity both to address a real or invented person outside the classroom and to adopt a voice not his own.

What most frequently freezes the student at one end of the abstractive spectrum is too much writing about reading. Perhaps because of the great influence of college essay exams and of literary exegesis, composition courses often boil down to "how to write about books." This is a narrow notion of exposition. Abstracting about someone else's already high abstraction, whether it be a book

or a teacher's essay question, means that certain essential issues of choice about selecting and treating material and creating classes are never permitted to come up for the student. When I assign a topic such as "loyalty" or "Irony in A. E. Housman," all I am asking the student to do is to find illustrations for my classifications. By doing half of his work for him, I am impoverishing his education. Rather than assign literary exegesis, I would have him write in the forms he reads. As practitioner he will naturally be a better literary critic than a student who only analyzes. Rather than assign book reports and essays on books, I would encourage the student to incorporate into his essays of generalization illustrations and ideas drawn from his reading and to mix these with his own experiences and observations; in other words, get *him* to create the classes into which he can fit people and actions drawn from both books and life. There is a real place for reading in a composition course, not as subject matter to write about but as a source of experience and as a repertory of discourse. After all, reading provides some excellent primary moments of experience.

From the perceptual level on up the student should be forced in effect to confront all the right issues of choice. Only in this way will he develop the faculties necessary to produce the ideas of exposition. On the same grounds, I am leery of asking the student to read about writing. I have spent a lot of time unteaching the dicta of composition texts and manuals of advice. Trial and error best develops judgment and taste, if this trial and error process is keyed in with the student's learning schedule. Explanations and definitions of good style, technique, and rhetoric create more problems than they solve. The issue here is not only one of cognitive development but of psychological independence. We must give students an emotional mandate to play the symbolic scale, to find subjects and shape them, to invent ways to act upon others, and to discover their own voice.

addressing process oriented writing — invention techniques

spontaneity

Shaping at the Point of Utterance

James Britton

This essay originally appeared in Reinventing the Rhetorical Tradition. *Ed. Aviva Freedman and Ian Pringle. Ottawa: The Canadian Council of Teachers of English, 1980. 61–65. It is also reprinted in* Prospect and Retrospect: Selected Essays of James Britton. *Ed. Gordon Pradl. Montclair: Boynton/Cook, 1982. 139–45.*

The two words, "spontaneity" and "invention" as we ordinarily use them must surely have something in common: an element of surprise, not only for those who encounter and respond to the act or expression, but also for those who originate it. I want to suggest here that rhetoricians, in their current concern for successive drafts and revision processes in composing, may be underestimating the importance of "shaping at the point of utterance," or the value of spontaneous inventiveness. It is my claim, in fact, that a better understanding of how a writer shapes at the point of utterance might make a major contribution to our understanding of invention in rhetoric.

In all normal speech we do, almost of necessity, shape as we utter. Syntactically, we launch into a sentence and hope somehow to reach closure. We had a Director at the Institute of Education where I once worked who was a very powerful speaker, but also a great "um"-er and "ah"-er. As you listened to him it would go something like this: "It seems to me, Mr. Chairman—ah—in spite of the difficulties Professor X has raised—ah—that what we most need—ah—in the present circumstances—ah—and—ah—at this moment in time—ah—is some way to bring to a conclusion this intolerably long sentence." Listening, we could tell precisely at what point he foresaw his total structure, the point at which he "took it on the run."

What is not so easily demonstrated is that the shaping as we speak applies not only to syntactic

but also to semantic choices. When we start to speak, we push the boat out and trust it will come to shore somewhere — not *anywhere,* which would be tantamount to losing our way—but somewhere that constitutes a stage on a purposeful journey. To embark on a conversational utterance is to take on a certain responsibility, to stake a claim that calls for justification: and perhaps it is the social pressure on the speaker to justify his claim that gives talk an edge over silent brooding as a problem-solving procedure. Heinrich von Kleist, the early 19th Century German writer, puts this point boldly in an essay he called, "On the Gradual Fabrication of Thought While Speaking":

> Whenever you seek to know something and cannot find it out by meditation, I would advise you to talk it over with the first person you meet. He need not be especially brilliant, and I do not suggest that you *question* him, no: *tell* him about it. . . . Often, while at my desk working, I search for the best approach to some involved problem, I usually stare into my lamp, the point of optimum brightness, while striving with utmost concentration to enlighten myself. . . . And the remarkable thing is that if I talk about it with my sister, who is working in the same room, I suddenly realize things which hours of brooding had perhaps been unable to yield. . . . Because I do start with some sort of dark notion remotely related to what I am looking for, my mind, if it has set out boldly enough, and being pressed to complete what it has

begun, shapes that muddled area into a form of new-minted clarity, even while my talking progresses.

As teachers, we are likely to have similar evidence from much nearer home: how often have we had a student come to us with his problem, and in the course of verbalizing what that problem is reach a solution with no help from us?

Then what about writing? First it must be said that students of invention in writing cannot afford to rule out of court evidence regarding invention in speech: there must be some carry-over from expression in the one medium to expression in the other. Shaping at the point of utterance is familiar enough in the way young children will spin their yarns to entertain an adult who is willing to provide an audience. (A ten-minute tape-recorded performance by a five-year-old boy winds up: "So he had ten thousand pounds, so everyone loved him in the world. He buy—he buyed a very fast racing car, he buyed a magic wand, he buyed everything he loved, and that's the end of my story what I told you." A five-year-old sense of closure!) There is ample evidence that spontaeous invention of this kind survives, and may even appear to profit from, the process of dictating, where parent or teacher writes down what the child composes orally. That it is seriously inhibited by the slowing down of production when the child produces his own written script is undeniable. But it is my argument that successful writers adapt that inventiveness and continue to rely on it rather than switching to some different mode of operating. Once a writer's words appear on the page, I believe they act primarily as a stimulus to *continuing*—to further writing, that is—and not primarily as a stimulus to *re*-writing. Our experiments in writing (Britton et al, 1973, p. 35) without being able to see what we had written suggested that the movements of the pen capture the movement of our thinking, and it is a serious obstacle to further composition not to be able to reread, to "get into the tramlines" again. An eight-year-old Newcastle schoolboy wrote about his own writing processes: "It just comes into your head, it's not like thinking, it's just there. When you get stuck you just read it through and the next bit is there, it just comes to you." I think many teachers might regard the outcome of such a process as mere "fluency," mere verbal facility, and not the sort of writing they want to encourage. It is my argument that highly effective writing may be produced in just that spontaneous manner, and that the best treatment for empty verbalism will rarely be a course of successive draft making.

"It just comes into your head, it's not like thinking": it seems that Barrett Mandel would agree with the eight-year-old, for he calls his recent article on writing, "Losing One's Mind: Learning to Read, Write and Edit." I quote his views here because they are in part an attempt to make room for the process of shaping at the point of utterance. He sets out the three steps that occur in his own writing process: "(1) I have an idea about something I want to write; (2) I write whatever I write; (3) I notice what I've written, judge it, and edit it, either a lot or a little" (1978, p. 363). And his claim is that the relationship between (1) and (2) is not one of cause and effect; rather, "step one *precedes* writing and *establishes a frame of mind in which writing is likely to occur*" (1978, p. 363). "It is the *act of writing* that produces the discoveries," he claims, and, by way of explanation, "words flow from a pen, not from a mind; they appear on the page through the massive co-ordination of a tremendous number of motor processes. . . . More accurately, I *become* my pen; my entire organism becomes an extension of this writing implement. Consciousness is focused in the point of the pen" (1978, p. 365).

So far, so good, but since Mandel goes on to approve of his colleague, Janet Emig's, description of writing as "a form of cognition" it seems to me a little perverse to propose (by his title, "Losing One's Mind") a mindless form of cognition. "Freeing one's mind" would be more appropriate, the freedom being that of ranging across the full spectrum of mental activity from the autistic pole to the reality-adjusted pole, as Peter McKellar (1957, p. 5) has described it. Or, as we might speculatively describe it today, right brain and left brain in intimate collaboration.

I want to associate spontaneous shaping, whether in speech or writing, with the moment by moment interpretative process by which we make sense of what is happening around us; to see each as an instance of the pattern-forming propensity of man's mental processes. Thus, when we come to write, what is delivered to the pen is in part already shaped, stamped with the image of our own ways of perceiving. But the intention to *share,* inherent in spontaneous utterance, sets up a demand for further shaping.

Can we go deeper than this, penetrate beyond the process of drawing upon our own store of interpreted experience? Perl and Egendorf believe we must if we are to provide a full account of writing behaviour. In an article they call "The Process of Creative Discovery," they speak of a new line of philosophical enquiry, the "philosophy of experiencing," and quote from the writings of Eugene Gendlin (1962) "Many thinkers since Kant," they suggest, "have claimed that all valid thought and expression are rooted in the wider realm of pre-representational experience" (1979, p. 121). "Experiencing," or pre-representational experience, "consists of continuously unfolding orders rather than finished products" (1979, p. 122); in Gendlin's words, it is "the felt apperceptive mass to which we can inwardly point" (quoted in Perl, Egendorf, 1979, p. 122). It is fluid, global, charged with implicit meanings—which we alter when by expressing them we make them explicit. D. W. Harding, psychologist and literary critic, explores a similar distinction in his book, *Experience into Words:* "The emergence of words or images as part of our total state of being is an obscure process, and their relation to the non-verbal is difficult to specify. . . . The words we choose (or accept as the best we can find at the moment) may obliterate or slightly obscure or distort fine features of the non-verbal background of thinking . . . a great deal of speaking and writing involves the effort to be a little more faithful to the non-verbal background of language than an over-ready acceptance of ready-made terms and phrases will permit" (1963, pp. 170–72). Perl and Egendorf comment on that effort as they observe it in their students: "When closely observed, students appear to write by shuttling back and forth from their sense of what they wanted to say to the words on the page and back to address what is available to them inwardly" (1979, p. 125). This is in essence the process they call "retrospective structuring," and its near inevitability might be suggested by comparing writing with carving: the sculptor with chisel in hand must both cut and observe the effect of his cut before going on. But retrospective structuring needs to be accompanied by what the authors call "projective structuring," shaping the material in such a way that the writer's meaning carries over to the intended reader. It is in this aspect of writing that "discovery," or shaping at the point of utterance, tends to break down: a mistaken sense of a reader's expectations may obstruct or weaken the "sense of what they wanted to say"—or in Harding's terms "obliterate . . . fine features of the non-verbal background of thinking." Observing unskilled writers, Perl and Egendorf comment: "What seems particularly unskilled about the way these students write is that *they apply prematurely a set of rigid, critical rules for editing* to their written products" (1979, p. 127). "Prematurely" might be taken to mean at first draft rather than at second or third, but I think this does less than justice to the authors' meaning. Minor editing—for spelling, for example—is better left, we can agree, to a rereading stage. What is at issue here is a more important point: that too restricted a sense of a reader's expectations may result in "projective structuring" coming to dominate the shaping at the point of utterance, to the exclusion or severe restriction of the "retrospective structuring," the search for a meaning that in its expression satisfies the writer.

Such a conclusion would gain general support from a neat little study by Mike Rose, a study he calls "Rigid Rules, Inflexible Plans and the Stifling of Writing." A case study of five fluent writers and five with "writer's block" leads him to conclude that "the non-blockers operate with fluid, easily modified, even easily discarded rules and plans, that are often expressed with a vagueness that could almost be interpreted as ignorance. There lies the irony. The students that offer the least precise rules and plans have the least trouble composing" (1978, unpublished paper).

What I have suggested, then, is that shaping at the point of utterance involves, first, drawing upon interpreted experience, the results of our moment by moment shaping of the data of the senses and the continued further assimilation of that material in search of coherence and pattern (the fruits of our contemplative moments); and, secondly, seems to involve by some means getting behind this to a more direct apperception of the felt quality of "experiencing" in some instance or instances; by which means the act of writing becomes itself a contemplative act revealing further coherence and fresh pattern. Its power to do so may depend in part upon the writer's counterpart of the social pressure that listeners exert on a speaker, though in this case, clearly, the writer himself is, in the course of the writing, the channel through which that pressure is applied.

I must now add the much more obvious point that in the initial stages of learning to write a child must draw upon linguistic resources gathered principally through speaking and listening, and apply those resources to the new task of writing. Some children, however, will also be familiar with some forms of the written language derived from stories that have been read to them. A four-year-old, for example, dictated a fairy story of his own composition in which he said, "The king went sadly home for he had nowhere else to go," a use of "for" that can hardly have been learned from listening to speech. Thus the early writer shuttles between internalised forms of the written language and his general resources recruited through speech: that he should maintain access to the latter is important if he is to embark on the use of writing to fulfil a range of different purposes. His progress as a writer depends thereafter, to a considerable degree, on his increasing familiarity with forms of the written language, the enlargement of his stock of "internalised" written forms through reading and *being read to*. (The process of recreating the rhythms of the written language from his own reading must derive from that apprenticeship to an adult's reading.) To put it simply, if rather crudely, I see the developed writing process as one of hearing an inner voice dictating forms of the written language appropriate to the task in hand.

If it is to work this way, we must suppose that there exists some kind of *pre-setting mechanism* which, once set up, continues to affect production throughout a given task. The difficulties many writers feel in "finding a way in" or in "finding one's own voice" in a particular piece of writing, as well as the familiar routine of running through what has been written in order to move on, seem to me to supply a little evidence in favour of such a "pre-setting mechanism." Beyond that I can offer only hints and nudges. There is, for example, the phenomenon of metric composition. Read aloud a passage in galloping iambics and most listeners are enabled to compose spontaneously in that rhythm; young children's facility in picking up pig-Latin or dog-Latin is probably another example of the same sort of process. And by way of explanation, there is Kenneth Lashley's longstanding notion of a "determining tendency" in human behaviour: "The cortex must be regarded as a great network of reverberatory circuits constantly active. A new stimulus, reaching such a system, does not excite an isolated reflex path but must produce widespread changes in the pattern of excitation throughout a whole system of already interacting neurons" (1961, p. 194). Such a determining tendency, he argues, is related to an individual's *intention*. In this and other respects the notion parallels Michael Polanyi's (1969, p. 146) description of focal and subsidiary awareness. Applying that to the writing process, a writer is subsidiarily aware of the words and structures he is employing and focally aware of an emergent meaning, the meaning he intends to formulate and convey. And it is the focal awareness that guides and directs the use made of the means, of which he is subsidiarily aware. In similar fashion, a reader's attention is not focused upon the printed marks: he attends *from* them to the emerging meaning. To focus on the words would be to inhibit the handling of meaning by writer or reader. "By concentrating on his fingers," says Polanyi, "a pianist can paralyse himself; the motions of his fingers no longer bear then on the music performed, they have lost their meaning" (1969, p. 146).

Painting in oils, where one pigment may be used to obliterate another, is a very different process from painting in water-colours, where the initial process must capture immediately as much as possible of the painter's vision. Do modes of discourse differ in production as sharply as that? And does our present concern with pre-planning, successive drafting and revision suggest that in taking oil-painting as our model for writing we may be underestimating the value of "shaping at the point of utterance" and hence cutting off what might prove the most effective approach to an understanding of rhetorical invention?[1]

Note

I am grateful to Geoffrey Summerfield of York University and Frank Smith of the Ontario Institute for Studies in Education who introduced me to the articles by Heinrich von Kleist and Kenneth Lashley respectively.

Works Cited

1. James Britton, Tony Burgess, Nancy Martin, Alex McLeod and Harold Rosen, *The Development of Writing Abilities*, 11-18, Schools Council Research Studies, Macmillan Education, 1975, p. 35.

2. Barrett J. Mandel, "Losing One's Mind: Learning to Write and Edit," *College Composition and Communication*, December, 1978, pp. 363-5.

3. Peter McKellar, *Imagination and Thinking*, Cohen and West, 1957, p. 5.

4. Sondra Perl & Arthur Egendorf, "The Process of Creative Discovery: Theory, Research, and Implications for Teaching" in Donald McQuade, ed., *Linguistics, Stylistics and the Teaching of Composition*, Studies in Contemporary Language No. 2, Department of English, University of Akron, 1979, pp. 121-27.

5. Eugene Gendlin, *Experiencing and the Creation of Meaning*, Free Press, 1962.

6. D. W. Harding, *Experience into Words*, Chatto and Windus, 1963, pp. 170-2.

7. Mike Rose, "Rigid Rules, Inflexible Plans, and the Stifling of Writing: A Cognitivist Analysis of Writer's Block", unpublished paper, 1978, Department of English, University of California, Los Angeles.

8. Kenneth Lashley, "The Problem of Serial Order in Behavior," in Sol Saporta, ed., *Psycholinguistics: A Book Of Readings*, Holt, Rinehart and Winston, 1961, p. 194.

9. Michael Polanyi, *Knowing and Being*, Routledge and Kegan Paul, 1969, p. 146.

Growing Writers in Classrooms

Glenda L. Bissex

This essay is reprinted from Language Arts *58 (1981): 785–91.*

I live on a hilltop in Vermont, three miles above a town of some 2,000 souls. Living with nature while being engaged in education has shaped my understanding of learning, and so I write about learning as growth.

Organisms, whether plants or animals, bean seeds or tadpoles, grow through orderly processes toward internally determined forms. Growth occurs through interactions between an organism and its environment. The organism provides its growth processes and its structure; the environment provides the nourishment to activate and sustain those processes, enabling the organism to grow to its potential form.

Manufacture is different from growth. A manufacturer takes inert raw materials and imposes upon them an externally determined form to fulfill the manufacturer's purposes. Children are not raw materials, teachers are not manufacturers, and schools are not factories, although some people talk and act as though they were. The industrial model of schools can be seen, for example, in a striving for the uniformity of mass production—homogeneous grouping, all children reading "at grade level"—and in an emphasis on the technology of teaching rather than educative relationships.

Studies of how children learn to speak have shown us some growth processes of language, processes children bring to their subsequent literacy learning. Without benefit of a programmed text, even very young children learn systematically, not randomly or by mere imitation. This is evident when children overgeneralize rules, as in regularizing past tenses ("They goed away") and plurals

("He has four foots"). Preschoolers' invented spellings, which are unconventional but consistent across children, are likewise rule-governed. For instance, nasals before consonants are unrepresented (DUP = *dump*) since that nasal is not articulated as a separate speech segment. Without instruction in sound-letter relationships, these young spellers abstract relationships from the letter names they know, leading them to many conventional consonant spellings but also to such inventions as H for "ch" (PKHR = *picture*).

Children learn to talk by interacting with an environment that provides rich information about language: they learn by speaking, being spoken to, asking questions and listening to speech. From models of older speakers they learn the values and functions of speech; they receive feedback, support, and encouragement. The first of three principles of language growth I will describe and relate to learning to write is that *children learn to talk by talking, in an environment that is full of talk.*

Some people believe that children all learn to speak because speech is somehow "natural" for us as humans while writing (and with it, of course, reading) is not "natural." But children who have grown up in isolation from human society—the wild boy of Aveyron in the last century and Genie most recently—have not grown up speaking. The capacity for speech may be innately human, but it develops only in a speech environment.

Although written language arose later than speech in the history of mankind and is not yet universal, it was preceded by drawing, another form of writing down meanings, of representing graphically what we know. Our use of an alphabetic writing system may lead us to forget that there have been in human cultures writing systems that did not represent speech sounds but were closer to drawing. Children in our culture remind us of this connection as they take one of their first steps toward literacy, differentiating writing from drawing.

I was taught much about the naturalness and forcefulness of the urge to write among children growing up in a literate society by my undergraduate Education students at Johnson State College. I asked them to write their autobiographies as writers, reaching as far back into childhood as they could. The earliness and vividness of their memories astonished me:

> I started writing as soon as I could hold a pencil. I can remember sitting up in my high-chair with the tray up, working on my homework, like my brothers and sisters. I would yell to mother, "Is PTO right?" And she would say, "Yes, I guess so." I would say, "Yes, PTO is right," and go on pretending to do my homework. The only word I thought I could spell right was PTO, which I later learned wasn't even a word.

> I can remember wanting to learn to write so badly! I would watch my brothers and sister as they scribbled nonsense on paper. They looked so official, so grown up. I would imitate their grandeur. I quite often played "restaurant" where I would "write" orders on paper and hand it in to the "chef."

> My writing career began at an early age. When I was a pre-schooler, I would study my older brother's school papers. The thing that intrigued me most was the letter C, which the teacher used to indicate that the paper was correct. I worked on making my own C's. I practiced them in orange crayon all over the bathroom walls in our house.

> I remember, before school years, doing a lot of scribbling, although this scribbling meant nothing to my family. I can recall being able to read the whole thing. As the family giggled and thought how "cute" it was, I would sit in my chair and read my scribbles.

> Since I can remember, I wrote. I remember taking crayons and writing on the walls and my mother

would yell at me because it was scribbling. But would it be funny if I wrote a word; she probably wouldn't have yelled at me then. I really remember wanting to express with my pencil, pen, or whatever, but I couldn't, no one understood!

> When I became aware of letters I was amazed, and I learned to write words. I remember my teachers making me always write in pencil because I'd have to erase my errors. I always wished it could have been in pen so I could just keep writing without stopping.

Just as children learn to talk by talking in an environment that is full of talk, children learn to write by writing in an environment full of writing and writings. In the classrooms of Vermont Writing Program teachers, children of all ages are learning to write by writing every day in environments that are full of writing in progress as well as finished products. Teachers write, often at the same time as their students do. They share their writing problems or drafts with their students and may ask for their help as an audience, as critical listeners or readers. Through writing conferences, modeled and guided by their teachers, students become eager to share their writings with one another. They know they are writing to produce reading, not exercises for the teacher or "dummy runs." They come to understand, through the power of their own experience, that text conveys, above all, meanings.

Which brings me to a second principle of language development that also holds true for writing: *Children learn language among people who respond to their meanings before their forms.* We are eager to attach meanings to babies' first speech sounds. We do not immediately correct a beginning speaker's misarticulations; in fact we sometimes imitate them. We do not insist that beginning speakers talk in complete sentences, but may expand their one or two word sentences to check if we have understood their unverbalized meanings. How differently some beginning writers are treated in classrooms!

One youngster had his own "dictionary" in which the teacher recorded words he needed to have spelled for his writing. He had been writing at home for over a year and was already spelling a good many words conventionally, so I was surprised to find the word *dog*—one of the first words he'd learned—in his dictionary. When I asked him if he didn't know it already, he said, "Yes, but I didn't know how to make the *g*." While at home he had written at length and in a variety of forms, at school he wrote one sentence on the few lines beneath his picture the way the other kids did. As he must have seen it, writing at school meant writing correctly formed letters in correctly spelled words on the lines. Instead, he spent much of his time elaborating his drawings, for which there weren't expectations of correctness.

In contrast, beginning writers in Vera Milz's classroom (1980) write notes to their teacher, to each other and to penpals—all of whom respond to their messages. They write journals whose content their teacher responds to in writing at the end of each week. They write books that their classmates read. They know they are writing messages— meanings—and their skills grow through constant practice within a literate environment rich with information about print and through the genuine motivation of being understood.

Children learn language—written or spoken— among people who respond to meaning before form. That is the principle of writing conferences such as this one from a primary classroom in Vermont. Tiffany reads her story aloud to Amy. The story tells about mice chasing another mouse. Echoing a question her teacher asks in writing conferences, Amy leads off with, "Tiffany, where did you get the idea?"

Tiffany: I just thought about it. I got it from writing some stories on a piece of paper.

Amy: Why don't you tell what happened to the other mice?

Tiffany: That's a good idea.

Amy: 'Cause how would I know that? They ran after him. What did they do after that?

Tiffany: I guess they just ran back 'cause they knew he was too far away to catch him.

A little while later, she adds to her story: "The other mice were running back to have a drink."

In a high school classroom, Jeanne is finishing reading to Martha a draft of her piece about someone in a hospital:

. . . This was the toughest part of the visit because there wasn't much to say, and everything they did say was due to the fact that they forced their words out. Very soon the talk would die and her visitors would stare at the ceiling till someone suggested that they leave. A procession left the room, and just like everyone and everything else at the hospital, it too traveled slowly.

Now satisfied with their departure but joyed with the thought that they cared enough to visit her, she looked around her dull brown cell and wondered when she could get out, back into the real world.

Martha asks, "Are you talking about your own experience?"

The writer, Jeanne, answers: "Slightly my own experience, and then a couple of weeks ago my mom was in the hospital and a lot of my own feelings came out just walking down the hall to visit her. I didn't like it at all."

Martha: I kind of think you have two purposes: one being how different people change when they talk to people in the hospital, and then that it's a really scarey thing—that they want to get it over with fast. Well, I'm trying to decide which one is the purpose. Which one do you mean?

Jeanne: I don't know. Maybe a little bit of both. I was looking mostly at the personality changes 'cause when I went down you just sit there and you're really quiet. You try to say something and it's always, you know, "Well, how's it going?" and you really don't care. You're just down there to be nice and polite.

Martha: Do you mean to say—is your focus on the patient or on the visitor?

These writing conferences did not just "happen"; they were guided by teachers who put first things first and trained their students to do the same. Once Jeanne and Tiffany have revised their pieces in response to their readers' questions about content, they are ready for an editing conference where they will work on form—spelling, punctuation, and such.

Good writers have been found to focus first on meaning, while poor writers, conceiving of good writing as correct writing, focus from the start on correctness and neatness, on avoiding errors. Their premature corrections, according to Sondra Perl (1979), break the flow of their writing and thinking without making substantial improvement. Of course correctness is desirable, but placing it before meaning confuses the means with the ends of writing—like hitting the right notes but missing the music.

Good writers, seeing personal value in writing, write spontaneously outside of school and thus get additional practice. At home or at school they have models of writers and an interested audience that responds to the content of their writing. Poor writers, on the other hand, view writing as an externally imposed task. They do not see adults writing, and their teacher audience at school "corrects" their writing rather than responding to its message (Birnbaum 1980). Children can be taught to be poor writers or good writers. The role of the teacher is crucial, especially for children who have less opportunity to learn to write at home.

Finally, *language grows from being telegraphic and context-embedded toward being elaborated and explicit.* Children start speaking not single words but one- and then two-word sentences. "Car" may mean "I hear a car," "sweater chair," "my sweater is on that chair." Generally the most concrete and significant words are stated, while the rest of the meaning may reside in the context shared by the speaker and the listener; for example, they both hear the car. Soon after children begin using telegraphic sentences, more and more of the deleted elements appear on the surface—are stated rather than assumed.

We see the same process as children begin writing. In invented spellings, more and more of the omitted speech sounds become represented: from H to HS to HAOS for *house.* Text often develops in the same way, as seen in some writings by first graders in September:

Jamie drew a monster (labeled MSTR) standing beside his cave (CAV). He chose the most important and concrete words to write; the deleted words emerged when he told his teacher his paper said "This monster lives in a cave."

On the first day of school Jennifer drew a house and wrote H. The next week both her drawing and writing were elaborated: a house (HS) with a smoking chimney and a lawn in front on which stood two smiling figures, Mary (M) and ME. She told her teacher it said, "I am at my friend Mary's house."

An eight-year-old with a learning problem who is also in this classroom shows the same pattern of development. The first day of school he drew a square green wagon with a large wheel (labeled WE) and dictated, "My wagon has wheels." The next week he drew a pelican (PLEN) in wavy water (WTR) with a dock (DC) at one edge of it: "I saw a pelican in Florida near the dock." Toward the end of September his sentence was fully represented in writing: THE FIS IS IN THE WTR.

Teachers who grow writers in their classrooms also regard pieces of writing as growing things to be nurtured rather than as objects to be repaired or fixed. These first grade writings were nurtured by a teacher who provided an hour every day for children to write on subjects they chose, who listened to each child read what she or he had written and then responded to it, who repeatedly encouraged children to figure out spellings for themselves, who typed their favorite writings into books for other children to read and for the authors to see their own words in conventional spellings, who collected each child's writings in a folder so the parents, the child and she, the teacher, could see the child's progress.

Once their sentences become explicit and elaborated in writing, children need help in making explicit their meanings on a larger scale, as happened dramatically through a third grade whole-class writing conference. Tanya chose to read to the class the first piece she had written in September. In order to minimize interruptions during writing, the teacher had told her students to put down the letters they knew in a word if they didn't know the spelling or couldn't figure it all out; thus "h,n," represents Hunger Mountain.

I went on a hike to h,n, and I had a picnic the food was fruit and meat and I like it and it was fun my frend Jenny went with me. We camt out. The end

Her classmates and teacher asked a lot of questions about what she'd written:

Which Jenny?

You should say where you camped out.

It doesn't make sense "the food was."

What was the weather like?

What did you have to drink?

Did you walk from your house to Hunger Mountain, or did you drive there?

The teacher then asked Tanya, "If you went back to work on it, what parts would you work on?" "I think I need to work on *all* of it," said Tanya. And she did. The next day she wrote her second draft, a much fuller version:

I went on a hike up to hongger montain. I went by car. I had fun climming up hongger montain. When I got up on top I met my freind Jenny Adams. I ask what was she doing here. She said "That her father drove her" I was glad she was here. We had supper and after we went to bed in the morning we had breakfast and after that are parnets came and pit use up and took use home. I ask Jenny's Father and mother if she could stay other night her parnets said 'yes' I was glad that she could The end.

The writing problems of adult literacy students as well, Elsasser and John-Steiner (1977) observe, come from failures to transform compact inner speech into elaborated written language that is comprehensible to readers who do not share the writer's context.

Language—both spoken and written—develops from being telegraphic and context-embedded toward being elaborated and explicit. It is learned among people who attend to meaning before form. And it is learned in a language environment, not merely by imitation but by re-creation—by constructing and testing rules. That is, children learn language not just as little mimics but as little scientists. Each child needs to make sense for himself of how language works. That seems to be how language grows.

When we try to manufacture what must be grown, we are in trouble. The self-regulating systems of growing things, interacting with their environments, create the energy for growth. Manufacture requires new, external energy. When both teachers and learners are cut off from their natural energy sources, we have to "motivate" learners and combat teacher "burn out"—acknowledgements of our educational energy crisis.

When teaching is seen as control rather than nurturance, it is not surprising that students are seen as and become "irresponsible," for they are not being responded to; they are being "made into" something. They are raw materials for our educational technology—materials to be ground down to uniformity so they can be "efficiently" processed according to the designs of publishers, test makers, and curriculum committees.

As Robert White (1952, p. 363) has said

the task of rearing and guiding children can best be represented by the metaphor of raising plants. This should be encouraging, because raising plants is one of mankind's most successful activities. Perhaps the success comes from the fact that the husbandman does not try to thrust impossible patterns on his plants. He respects their peculiarities, tries to provide suitable conditions, protects them from the more serious kinds of injury—but he lets the plants do the growing. He does not poke at the seed in order to make it sprout more quickly, nor does he seize the shoot when it breaks the ground and try to pull open the first leaves by hand. Neither does he trim the leaves of different kinds of plants in order to have them all look alike. The attitude of the husbandman is appropriate in dealing with children. It is the children who must do the growing.

Works Cited

Birnbaum, June. "Why Should I Write? Environmental Influences on Children's Views of Writing," *Theory into Practice* 19 (1980): 202–210.

Elsasser, Nan and John-Steiner, Vera, "An Interactionist Approach to Advancing Literacy." *Harvard Educational Review* 47 (1977): 355–369.

Milz, Vera E. "First Graders Can Write: Focus on Communication." *Theory into Practice* 19 (1980): 179–185.

Perl, Sondra. "The Composing Processes of Unskilled College Writers." *Research in the Teaching of English* 13 (1979): 317–336.

White, Robert W. *Lives in Progress.* New York: Dryden Press, 1952.

addressing cognitive psychologists

imagination: spontaneity

The Intelligent Eye and the Thinking Hand

Ann E. Berthoff

This essay appeared in The Making of Meaning: Metaphors, Models, and Maxims for Writing Teachers. *Montclair: Boynton/Cook, 1981. 61–67. In that volume Berthoff notes that "The Intelligent Eye" was a paper read at a conference co-sponsored by the New York College English Association and the Department of English, Skidmore College, October 1980. The conference was called "The Writer's Mind: Writing as a Mode of Thinking." Conference proceedings were later published and included Berthoff's essay. (See* The Writer's Mind: Writing as a Mode of Thinking. *Ed. Janice Hays, Phyllis Roth, Jon Ramsey, and Robert Foulke. Urbana: NCTE, 1983. 191–96.)*

It is inspiriting to participate in a conference of teachers addressing themselves unabashedly to mind, not problem-solving; daring to speak of *the writer's mind,* not competence or performance; of *writing as a mode of thinking,* not as verbal communication. It is a pleasant change to find the emphasis on *mind* rather than on information processing or signal detectability or protocol analysis. To speak of mind could represent an unembarrassed recognition of the fact that everything we deal with in composition theory is fundamentally and unavoidably philosophical. I believe that it is only by being philosophical that rhetoric can "take charge of the criticism of its own assumptions." That was the way I. A. Richards put it in 1936 in *The Philosophy of Rhetoric,* a book that we composition teachers should return to, if only to rinse our minds of the effects of another book, curiously called *The Philosophy of Composition.* Let me say right away that what Professor Hirsch means by "philosophy," though obscure, is in any case not what Dr. Richards meant or what, in my opinion, teachers of composition should concern themselves with: *The Philosophy of Composition* gives philosophy, to say nothing of composition, a bad name.

Professor Hirsch has, interestingly enough, chosen as an epigraph for his book a statement of Herbert Spencer, the English father of Positivism. Positivist presuppositions are everywhere to be found in current rhetorical theory, and they are the chief cause of all our woe. Let me offer a polemical summary. Positivism is a philosophy whose epistemology is fundamentally associationist. The positivist notion of critical inquiry is a naïve misconception of scientific method—what is sometimes called "scientism." Positivists believe that empirical tests yield true facts and that's that; they do not understand that scientists test hypotheses. Underlying all positivist methods and models is a notion of language as, alternately, a set of slots into which we cram or pour our meanings or as a veil that must be torn asunder to reveal reality directly, without the distorting mediation of form. (If that sounds mystical, it's because if you scratch a positivist, you'll find a mystic: neither can tolerate the concept of mediation.) I believe that we should reject this false philosophy, root and branch, and in doing so it is important to realize that we are in excellent company.

We can count as allies, among others, Susanne K. Langer, William James, C. S. Peirce, and I. A. Richards. Mrs. Langer, in the first volume of *Mind: An Essay on Human Feeling* (the very title is important), explains how it is that psychologists have de-

nature of writing / looks @ writing as process of mind / mind as speculation / mind as "idea"

veloped no sound theories of mind: when they have seen that to ask, "What is mind?" leads to a futile search for metaphysical quiddities, instead of reconceiving the critical questions that would yield working concepts, they have worshipped the "idols of the laboratory." These are physicalism, mathematization, objectivity, methodology, and jargon. Any teacher who has been intimidated by the false philosophy of such books as Professor Hirsch's should read Dr. Langer's critique every morning before breakfast. And, in resisting the positivists, we will have an ally in William James, a great psychologist by virtue of being a great philosopher. (Alfred North Whitehead listed him as one of the four greatest of all times because of his understanding of the importance of experience.) James, in his typically lively *Talks to Teachers,* warns his audience not to expect insight into the nature of such aspects of thought as attention, memory, habit, and interest to be forthcoming from what he calls the "brass instrument" psychologists. I am just old enough to have studied psychology at a time when those brass instruments were still around, albeit in glass cases lining the walls of the laboratory. Brass instruments were used to measure such phenomena as the fatigue your finger suffered as you tapped it over three hundred fifty-eight times; after you'd had a bit of cane sugar, the psychologist would watch to see the effects on the tapping. If he was very venturesome, he might record the subject's verbal response, though there was no brass instrument to help him in that case. The brass instrument psychologists are with us still, though the instrumentation has changed. Cognitive psychologists carry out their investigations in a clinical atmosphere and feed their data to hungry computers; it could be that psycholinguists wear white coats as they set about discovering the secrets of how the mental encyclopedia is organized by asking such questions as, "What bird is most typical?" The new brass instrument psychologists, like the old, are concerned with what can be factored, plotted, and quantified, and that does not include the things we want to know about—the composing process or the writer's mind or modes of learning and their relationship to kinds of writing.

Our most important ally in rejecting positivism is C. S. Peirce, the philosopher who first conceptualized the structure and function of the sign and invented semiotics (including the term itself). Peirce had an amused contempt for psychologists, who were, in the main, ignorant of logic. He scorned the notion that the study of meaning was of a kind with the study of natural phenomena. In one of his calmer moments, he declared: "Every attempt to import into psychics the conceptions proper to physics has only led those who made it astray."

And, to conclude this short list of allies, there is I. A. Richards, who memorably wrote in *Speculative Instruments:* "The Linguistic Scientist . . . does not yet have a conception of the language which would make it respectable. He thinks of it as a code and has not yet learned that it is an organ—the supreme organ of the mind's self-ordering growth." Note the "yet": Dr. Richards, who died last year at 86, always included it in even the gloomiest of his assessments of the state of rhetoric. Our field continues to suffer incursions of those who have no intention of conceiving language as "the supreme organ of the mind's self-ordering growth" and I am not yet sure that we should emulate his patience.

The reason for impatience is simply that we might very well lose the advantage that the novel effort to think about mind could give us. Unless we think philosophically about thinking, what's likely to happen with *mind* is what has already happened with *process:* it will be used and manipulated within the framework of positivist assumptions and thus will not help us develop a pedagogy appropriate to teaching the composing process. To be able to use mind as a speculative instrument, we will have to become authentic philosophers—and quick.

If we are to avail ourselves of that incomparable resource, the minds of our students, we will have to know what we're looking for, to have some philosophically sound idea of the power the mind promises. I believe that for teachers of composition, such a philosophy of mind is best thought of as a theory of imagination. If we can reclaim imagination as the forming power of mind, we will have the theoretical wherewithal for teaching composition as a mode of thinking and a way of learning.

Reclaiming the imagination is necessary because the positivists have consigned it to something called "the affective domain," in contradistinction to "the cognitive domain." You can see the false philosophy at work there, importing conceptions appropriate to neurology and biochemistry into psychics: certainly, there are areas and domains in the brain, but to use the term *domain* about modes of mental operation is to create the same kind of confusion as when the word *code* is used to designate both linguistic form and brain function. The false philosophy cannot account for imagination as a way of knowing or a means of making meaning because it understands imagination as ancillary or subordinate, not as fundamental and primordial. Imagination has famously been defined as "the living power and prime agent of all human perception." Coleridge here, as in so many other instances, is our best guide in developing a philosophy of rhetoric. (Condescension to him on the part of the New Rhetoricians is ridiculous and the allegation that those who believe as he did in the natural powers of mind—"vitalists," we've been called—are therefore opposed to method is an ignorant and self-serving charge.) The imagination is the shaping power: perception works by forming—finding forms, creating forms, recognizing forms, interpreting forms. Let me read you what Rudolf Arnheim, in his superb book *Visual Thinking,* lists as the operations involved in perception: "active exploration, selection, grasping of essentials, simplification, abstraction, analysis and synthesis, completion, correction, comparison, problem-solving, as well as combining, separating, putting in context." Doesn't that sound like an excellent course in writing?

To think of perception as *visual thinking* helps make the case for observation in the composition classroom, not for the sake of manufacturing spurious "specifics" and vivid detail about nothing much, but because perception is the mind in action. Thinking begins with perception; the point is nicely caught in the title of R. L. Gregory's book on perception, *The Intelligent Eye*. A journal of observations—the "dialectical notebook" I've described in *Forming/Thinking/Writing* in which students re-cord observations and observe their observations—affords students the experience of mastery because it exercises powers we do not have to teach, the natural power of forming in *perception* and the natural power of *conception,* concept formation, which in so many ways is modeled on the activities of "the intelligent eye." Observation of observation becomes the model of thinking about thinking, of "interpreting our interpretations" (Kenneth Burke), of "arranging our techniques for arranging" (I. A. Richards). The consciousness represented in such circular formulations is not *self* consciousness but an awareness of the dynamic relationship of the *what* and the *how,* of the reflexive character of language, of the dialectic of forming. The consciousness of consciousness, which is encouraged by looking and looking again, is at the heart of any critical method.

Once we give some thought to imagination, "the living power and prime agent of all human perception," we can see how it is that visualizing, making meaning by means of mental images, is the paradigm of all acts of mind: *imagining* is forming par excellence, and it is therefore the emblem of the mind's power. Students who learn to look and look again, to observe and to observe their observations, are discovering powers they have not always known are related in any way to the business of writing. If we trust "the intelligent eye," we can teach our students to find in perception an ever-present model of the composing process; they will thereby be reclaiming their own imaginations.

Shaping is as important an emblem as visualizing of that forming, which is the work of the active mind. The artist at work—especially the sculptor—is surely the very image of imagination as the creation of form, though artists often prefer to speak of their creative activity as a matter of finding form: Michelangelo famously spoke of liberating the form in the stone. The popular doctrine of art as, simply, the "expression" of "emotion" leaves out of account forming, shaping, and thus cannot contribute to a theory of imagination. As an antidote, let me quote a passage from the autobiography of Barbara Hepworth, the British sculptor: "My left hand is my thinking hand. The right is only a motor hand. This holds the hammer. The left hand, the thinking hand, must be relaxed, sensitive. The rhythms of thought pass through the fingers and grip of this hand into the stone." I like the echo in Mrs. Langer's title, *Mind: An Essay on Human Feeling,* of Dame Barbara's phrases, "my thinking hand" and "rhythms of thought," and I leave it to you to consider the implications of the fact that neither the philosopher nor the artist considers it paradoxical to speak of thinking and feeling as a single activity of forming. (And I leave it to you to consider that both are women.)

That single activity of forming can be carried out in two modes, and no theory of imagination can be sound which does not recognize them both. What we call them is a matter of some interest since our pedagogy will be guided, sometimes surreptitiously, by what we take as the implications of the terms. I have been arguing that the positivist differentiation of cognitive and affective is wrongheaded and misleading: indeed, it is the root cause of the widespread failure to get from so-called personal writing to so-called expository writing, from informal to formal composition—even from so-called "pre-writing" to writing. This false differentiation creates an abyss, which rhetoricians then spend their time trying to bridge by scotch-taping together topics and places and modes of discourse, by one or another innovative strategy, heuristic model, or methodological breeches buoy. A theory of imagination can help us solve the problem of the abyss by removing the problem: there is no abyss if composing is conceived of as forming and forming as proceeding by means of abstraction. I will conclude by suggesting how we can differentiate two modes of abstraction, but let me note briefly why it is that current rhetorical theory manifests no understanding of forming as abstraction.

That fact must be correlated with the fact that though it's defunct elsewhere, General Semantics is alive and kicking in the midst of any assembly of rhetoricians. For General Semantics, abstraction is the opposite of reality: Cow[1], Cow[2], Cow[3] are real, but *cow* or *cows* are not real; they are words and they are "abstract." Now, General Semanticists have never understood that Laura, Linda, Louise—all

cows of my acquaintance—are also abstract: the smellable, kickable, lovable, milkable cow is there: it is recalcitrant, in Kenneth Burke's sense of that term and the dairy farmer's; it is part of the triadicity of the sign relationship, in Peirce's terms; but this actual cow, this cow as *event,* as Whitehead would say, is known to us in the form provided by the intelligent eye—and the intelligent ear and the intelligent nose. That form—that percept—is a primordial abstraction. Abstraction is not the opposite of reality but our means of making sense of reality in perception and in all that we do with symbolic forms.

Forming is a single activity of abstraction: once we have the genus, we can then develop the definition dialectically by recognizing the two kinds of abstraction. There is the *discursive* mode, which proceeds by means of successive generalization, and the *nondiscursive* or *presentational* mode, which proceeds by means of "direct, intensive insight." These are Mrs. Langer's terms; they derive from Cassirer and they are, I think, both flexible and trustworthy. The discursive mode is familiar because it is what rhetoric chiefly describes: generalization is at the heart of all discourse, and of course it is central to concept formation. But it is not the only mode of abstraction: we do not dream or perceive or create works of art by generalizing. One of the chief reasons that composition theory is stymied is the dependence on a brass instrument manufactured by General Semantics, *the ladder of abstraction.* Rhetoricians continually use it to explain how we climb from the positive earth to the dangerous ether of concept. But it's that metaphoric ladder itself that's dangerous. We could rename it *the ladder of degrees of generality* to avoid the misleading notion that all abstraction proceeds by means of generalizing, but the ladder metaphor is inappropriate even to the generalizing central to concept formation, because, as Vygotsky points out, conceptualizing is "a movement of thought constantly alternating in two directions": only Buster Keaton could handle that ladder!

When we see a chair, we do not do so by a process of conscious generalizing; when the artist creates or finds the form by means of which feelings and thoughts are to be represented, he (or she) does so not by generalizing but by symbolizing insight—by *imagining*. In perception and in art, forming is primarily nondiscursive, but the point should be made explicitly that both modes of abstraction function in all acts of mind. We can save the term *imagination* to name only the nondiscursive, but having reclaimed it, I think there is much to be said for using it as a speculative instrument to focus on what it means to say that composing is a process of making meaning. The emblems I've discussed—"the intelligent eye" and "the thinking hand"—are images of imagination in the larger sense, that is, as the forming power of mind.

A Curious Triangle and the Double-Entry Notebook; or, How Theory Can Help Us Teach Reading and Writing

Ann E. Berthoff

This essay is also from The Making of Meaning *(1981): 41–47. Berthoff notes that this essay first appeared in the Winter 1981 issue of* Focus: Teaching English Language Arts, *a journal published by the Southeastern Ohio Council of Teachers of English and the Department of English, Ohio University.*

*C*riticism is a tricky word, as tricky as any we depend on when we talk about how to teach reading and writing. I suggest that we think of criticism as the point where theory and practice meet: Criticism is knowing what you're doing and thereby how to do it. Criticism is method; it is practicing what you preach. One reason the teaching of English is stymied is that the sense of method as theory brought to bear on practice has been lost. Theory is considered as either irrelevant, because it's abstract, or important, for precisely the same reason. The result is that instead of guidance for our pedagogy, we have, on the one hand, recipe-swapping ("I tried this last week and it worked—never mind why.") and, on the other, abstruse collocations of "data" concerning such ill-defined concepts as "syntactical maturity." If teachers have no interest in theory, it becomes the province of social scientists, psycholinguists, behavioral and cognitive psychologists, or anybody else who can be funded to do "research." Criticism in the classroom could make researchers of all teachers: research in our field ought to mean studying the relationship of the *what* and the *how*.

By assuring a place for criticism in the classroom, we are reclaiming method. Becoming critical, developing a method, is the best way, I think, for teachers and students to learn from one another. If we are all continually discovering, recognizing what it is we are doing, we'll have many more ways of finding out how to do it. In other words, criticism in the classroom could help us get rid of rigid lesson plans so that we would be able to take advantage of what John Donne called "emergent occasions." We could get rid of study questions, refusing to order textbooks that include them; refusing the Instructor's Manual that has the answers, asking for a refund of the money added onto the cost of the textbook so that the manual could be "provided free of charge." Out would go prefabricated units and tests and assignments. A ritual bonfire of those pink and yellow markers used to make pastel islands out of "important passages" would close this introductory phase of criticism in the classroom. We would then be free to undertake what I. A. Richards considered central to all learning, "the continuing audit of meaning."[1]

It is often argued that we should encourage spontaneous response to literature rather than intervening with theory and abstract questions. I want to suggest in the following comment that our pedagogical choices are not limited to fostering un-thinking "gut" reactions or encouraging anxious answers from our students about why they "feel" as they do, or tirelessly asking, "What is the author trying to say?" The essential significance of criti-cism in the classroom is that it enables us to teach reading for meaning and writing as a way of mak-ing meaning.

Criticism requires a theory of language that can account for meaning, which does not set it aside as a "mentalistic" matter or treat it as "the semantic component," a spark plug that you insert in the language machine. How we think of language will, of course, determine how we think of literature. If we think of language as a set of slots to be filled, literature will be simply a fancy set of such slots; and we will teach, alternately, the slots and the slotted: "form" and "content." If our idea of lan-guage is that it is simply a "communication medium," then our energies in the literature class will go to finding "the message" that's being sent over the wires. If language is a veil that obtrudes between us and reality, there will be no way to sug-gest revisions or reconsiderations of one or another attempt to pierce it, boring or wild as the foray might be.

If we are to teach our students to read for meaning—to construe and interpret and appreciate literary texts—the meaning of *meaning* most useful to us is that it is a means: speaking and writing, lis-tening and reading all engage us in the making of meaning by means of language. If we can learn to think of language not as a tool, a single-purpose facilitator, but as an instrument that lets us see in many different ways—as both microscope and telescope, X-ray and radar—then we can better discover how to make room at the center of all our courses for interpretation, for the study of meaning.

When we read critically, we are reading for meaning—and that is not the same thing as reading for "message." Meanings are not things, and finding them is not like going on an Easter egg hunt. Mean-ings are relationships: they are unstable, shifting, dynamic; they do not stay still nor can we prove the

authenticity or the validity of one or another mean-ing that we find. But that does not imply a neces-sary solipsism; it doesn't mean that the only thing we can say is, "To me it means X—and that's that!" Rather, when teachers and students, in construct-ing and construing, cultivate the attitude that the philosopher C. S. Peirce called a "contrite fallibil-ism," the need for making a careful case to support our interpretations becomes evident. Isn't that what we want to teach? If students see that we can't prove we're absolutely correct, interpretations not being amenable to that kind of demonstration, then the task of making the best possible case gains an authenticity it might have lacked. If we aren't gods who have perfect knowledge, we are none-theless powerful creatures who can describe and define; argue and tell stories, encouraging, per-suading, entertaining: *rhetoric* is what we have in-stead of *omniscience*.

Before turning to the practical aspects of meth-od, let me suggest how we might keep in mind the nature of meaning as a means, a way to remember that meaning is dynamic and dialectical, that it de-pends on context and perspective, the setting in which it is seen and the angle from which it is seen. The model I'm thinking of is a triangle, but of a radically different sort from the familiar "triangle of discourse," which looks like this:

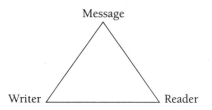

Sometimes, *speaker/reality/audience* are at the three points, with *language* or *text* occupying the field en-closed. In this model there is no way of telling the relationship of *message* to either its sources or to the speaker or the form in which it is expressed. As we know, "messages" are continually sent in the real world without being understood, but there is noth-ing in this model to explain why, or what we, as teachers of reading and writing, might do about failures of "communication."

The triangle I'm suggesting as a model helps on that score; it looks like this:

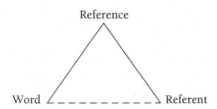

This diagram represents the "sign," or what I've been calling the "meaning relationship." What the word stands for—the referent—is known in terms of the reference. The dotted line stands for the fact that there is no immediate, direct relationship between words and things (including other words); we interpret the word or symbol by means of the idea it represents to us. It takes an idea to find an idea. We know reality *in terms of* our ideas of reality. This curious triangle with the dotted line can help us remember that what we know, we know by means of mediating form. The triangle represents mediation, the interdependence of interpreter (what he already knows), the symbol (image or word), and the import or significance it has. Ironically, by not being quite a triangle, this triangle represents the *triadicity* of meaning relationships. It can help us keep in mind that we must include the beholder, the interpreter, in our account of texts; that texts require contexts and that contexts depend on perspective.[2]

If criticism is supported by such a theory of language as mediating form, what are the pedagogical implications? How can the curious triangle help us teach reading and writing? First of all, it can clarify how being conscious of what we are doing is the way to find out how to do it. Critical awareness is consciousness of *consciousness* (a name for the active mind). Minding the mind, being conscious of consciousness, is not the same sort of thing as thinking about your elbows when you're about to pitch a baseball; nor is it *self*-consciousness. Con-

sciousness in meaning-making activity always involves us in interpreting our interpretations; thinking is a matter of "arranging our techniques of arranging"; criticism is a matter of coming to "know our knowledge." These circular formulations (they can make you dizzy at first) are, like the triangle with the dotted line, emblems of the fact that we can't get under the net of language. The point is that we can learn to take advantage of that fact, making the raising of consciousness about the making of meaning our chief strategy in teaching the circularity of all knowledge and in developing a "pedagogy of knowing."[3]

And, second, the curious triangle can help us focus on ways to bring students to see texts as the intermediary form of a process of making meaning that began in mysterious and unknowable ways, unfolding in sometimes predictable ways and sometimes in surprising ways, and which continues as texts are construed and reconstructed. (The faddish term for this process is *deconstruction*, but that word suggests to me *demolition*, the breaking down of analysis without the synthesis that constitutes the other aspect of critical response.) Students can learn to see texts as mediating forms by studying evidence of the process by which they came into being. Reading in the notebooks of poets and novelists; seeing the rough drafts of a single poem; tracing the growth and development of a story from a scribbled note, a single image, a pair of terms; watching the meanings shift and change in the course of revising—all such study of literary work in progress will help make the point of "technique as discovery," in a well-known phrase.[4] It's a good idea too, I think, to cultivate the habit of watching and listening to rehearsals and practice sessions of musicians and dancers, of watching artists at work. There is as much to be learned in the studio and the practice room about the composing process, the making of meaning, as there is in the library.

The most useful way to raise consciousness of texts as intermediary forms and to develop a method of critical reading is, simply put, to have students write continuously in a double-entry notebook, which I will shortly describe. Writing in the literature class is usually limited to taking notes on lectures and composing critical appreciations, critical essays, or book reports. But writing can help develop a critical method of reading by, first of all, providing for students an example of a text coming into being—their own. And, second, by encouraging habits of reflective questioning in the process of reading, chiefly by means of interpretive paraphrase, writing can help students replace the nonquestion, "What is the author trying to say?" with the critical question, "How does it change the meaning when I change the text and put it this way?" The double-entry notebook, by offering the chance to practice interpreting in such a way that whatever is learned about reading is something learned about writing, can teach that how we construe is how we construct. *Languaging,* as some like to say, is our means of making meaning.

I ask my students (all of them: freshmen, upper-classmen, teachers in graduate seminars) to furnish themselves with a notebook, spiral-bound at the side, small enough to be easily carried around but not so small that writing is cramped. (School teachers who have tried this idea tell me, however, that their students insist on a notebook that will fit into the back pocket of their jeans.) What makes this notebook different from most, perhaps, is the notion of the double entry: on the right side reading notes, direct quotations, observational notes, fragments, lists, images—verbal and visual—are recorded; on the other (facing) side, notes about those notes, summaries, formulations, aphorisms, editorial suggestions, revisions, comment on comment are written. The reason for the double-entry format is that it provides a way for the student to conduct that "continuing audit of meaning" that is at the heart of learning to read and write critically. The facing pages are in dialogue with one another.

The double-entry notebook is for all kinds of writing, creative or critical; any assignment you can think up can be adapted so that it can teach dialectic, another name for the continuing audit.[5] Suppose you want your students in the seventh grade (or the eleventh: in between, *self*-consciousness tends to overpower conscientization) to read some nature poems. The writing assigned could be a

record of ten minutes of observation and meditation carried out daily over a week—descriptions and speculations in response to a seashell, a milkweed pod, a chestnut burr, or any natural object (the odder the better) that can serve as "text": *reading the book of nature* is probably the oldest writing assignment in the world. Each day should begin with rereading the notes from the day before and writing a recapitulation on the facing page. At the week's end, two paragraphs are assigned: (1) a description of the object, based on the right-hand side entries; (2) a comment on the process of observing and interpreting, based on the left-hand side—but in either case, the writer is free to move back and forth from notes to recapitulation.

But assignments need not be so highly structured: any writing assignments that encourage students to look and look again will be teaching critical reading and critical thinking. Perception is one of the best models for the process of making meaning. A few strategies like transformation or a simple heuristic such as, "What is it the opposite of?" can be quickly learned and put to use by all students, no matter what their level of proficiency. Designing a poster to advertise a play, for instance, could be a process of constructing that would use the right-hand page for notes on lettering, visual design, suggestions of scenes to be depicted, and so forth. The left-hand page could be a rough sketch or instructions to the artist. This is not an "affective" pleasantry but an exercise in translating, the most basic form of interpretation. Writing mini-versions of novels and plays exercises the powers of generalizing, summary and definition.[6] Expanding or expatiating or parodying is an excellent way to practice drawing out implications. Thus working towards narrative from photographs in Edward Steichen's *Family of Man* can teach as much about the strategies of characterization as students would get in fifty pages of study questions about how Hardy makes his characters plausible.

The essential point of the double-entry notebook is that meaning is being made from the first: the reason that we find it so hard to move from personal writing to expository writing in our teaching is that we do not always define what they have in

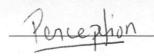
common. The chief pedagogical use of the curious triangle with the dotted line is to remind us that students, in whatever they write and with whatever they read, are interpreting and composing: they are making meaning.

Notes

1. Richards, one of the founders of modern literary criticism, is the only critic to have devoted his time principally to elucidating the ways in which theory and practice can be mutually beneficial. English teachers at all levels have more to learn from him than from anyone else, I believe. *Speculative Instruments* (N.Y.: Harcourt, 1955) and *How to Read a Page* (N.Y.: Norton, 1942; rpt. 1965) are good places to begin.

2. The "triadic" triangle comes from *The Meaning of Meaning,* C. K. Ogden and I. A. Richards (N.Y.: Harcourt, 1946). For an interesting discussion of the two triangles and "triadicity," see Walker Percy, *The Message in the Bottle* (N.Y.: Farrar, Straus, Giroux, 1975). I have tried to suggest some of the pedagogical implications of triadicity in "Towards a Pedagogy of Knowing," *Freshman English News* (Spring 1978). (See pages 48–60.)

3. "Pedagogy of knowing" and "conscientization" are terms of critical importance (they are both theoretical and practical) in the thinking of Paulo Freire, from whose work in literacy training we all can learn. *Education for Critical Consciousness* (N.Y.: Seabury Press, 1973) is a good introduction.

4. The essay with this title by Mark Schorer is an important document in modern criticism. It appeared in the first issue of the *Hudson Review* (1948) and has been widely reprinted.

5. *Dialogue* and *dialectic* are cognate: I call it a "dialectical notebook" in my textbook, *Forming/Thinking/Writing: The Composing Imagination* (Hayden, 1978), where it is described in some detail.

6. Morris Sagoff's *ShrinkLits* (N.Y.: Workman, 1980) offers some amusing examples.

Teaching the Other Self:
The Writer's First Reader

Donald M. Murray

This essay appeared in College Composition and Communication 33 *(1982):* 140–47.

We command our students to write for others, but writers report they write for themselves. "I write for me," says Edward Albee. "The audience of me." Teachers of composition make a serious mistake if they consider such statements a matter of artistic ego alone.

The testimony of writers that they write for themselves opens a window on an important part of the writing process. If we look through that window we increase our understanding of the process and become more effective teachers of writing.

"I am my own first reader," says Isaac Bashevis Singer. "Writers write for themselves and not for their readers," declares Rebecca West, "and that art has nothing to do with communication between person and person, only with communication between different parts of a person's mind." "I think the audience an artist imagines," states Vladimir Nabakov, "when he imagines that sort of thing, is a room filled with people wearing his own mask." Edmund Blunden adds, "I don't think I have ever written for anybody except the other in one's self."

The act of writing might be described as a conversation between two workmen muttering to each other at the workbench. The self speaks, the other self listens and responds. The self proposes, the other self considers. The self makes, the other self evaluates. The two selves collaborate: a problem is spotted, discussed, defined; solutions are proposed, rejected, suggested, attempted, tested, discarded, accepted.

This process is described in that fine German novel, *The German Lesson,* by Siegfried Lenz (Hamburg, Germany: Hoffman Und Campe Verlag, 1968; New York: Hill and Wang, 1971), when the narrator in the novel watches the painter Nansen at work. "And, as always when he was at work, he was talking. He didn't talk to himself, he talked to someone by the name of Balthasar, who stood beside him, his Balthasar, who only he could see and hear, with whom he chatted and argued and whom he sometimes jabbed with his elbow, so hard that even we, who couldn't see any Balthasar, would suddenly hear the invisible bystander groan or, if not groan, at least swear. The longer we stood there behind him, the more we began to believe in the existence of that Balthasar who made himself perceptible by a sharp intake of breath or a hiss of disappointment. And still the painter went on confiding in him, only to regret it a moment later."

Study this activity at the workbench within the skull and you might say that the self writes, the other self reads. But it is not reading as we usually consider it, the decoding of a completed text. It is a sophisticated reading that monitors writing before it is made, as it is made, and after it is made.

The term "monitor" is significant, for the reading during writing involves awareness on many levels and includes the opportunity for change. And when that change is made then everything must be read again to see how the change affects the reading.

The writer, as the text evolves, reads fragments of language as well as completed units of language, what isn't on the page as well as what is on the page, what should be left out as well as what should be put in. Even patterns and designs—sketches of possible relationships between pieces of information or fragments of rhetoric or language—that we do not usually consider language are read and discussed by the self and the other self.

It is time researchers in the discipline called English bridge the gulf between the reading researcher and the writing researcher. There are now many trained writing researchers who can collaborate with the trained researchers in reading, for the act of writing is inseparable from the act of reading. You can read without writing, but you can't write without reading. The reading skills required, however, to decode someone else's finished text may be quite different from the reading skills required to chase a wisp of thinking until it grows into a completed thought.

To follow thinking that has not yet become thought, the writer's other self has to be an explorer, a map-maker. The other self scans the entire territory, forgetting, for the moment, questions of order or language. The writer/explorer looks for the draft's horizons. Once the writer has scanned the larger vision of the territory, it may be possible for him (or her) to trace a trail that will get the writer from here to there, from meaning identified to meaning clarified. Questions of order are now addressed, but questions of language still delayed. Finally, the writer/explorer studies the map in detail to spot the hazards that lie along the trail, the hidden swamps of syntax, the underbrush of verbiage, the voice found, lost, found again.

Map-making and map-reading are among man's most complex cognitive tasks. Eventually the other self learns to monitor the always changing relationship between where the writer is and where the writer intended to go. The writer/explorer stops, looks ahead, considers and reconsiders the trail and the ways to get around the obstacles that block that trail.

There is only one way the student can learn map-reading—and that is in the field. Books and lectures may help, but only after the student writer has been out in the bush will the student understand the kind of reading essential for the exploration of thinking. The teacher has to be a guide who doesn't lead so much as stand behind the young explorer, pointing out alternatives only at the moment of panic. Only after the writer/explorer has read one map and made the trip from meaning intended to meaning realized, will the young writer begin to trust the other self and have faith that it will know how to read other trails through other territories.

The reading writer—the map-maker and map-reader—reads the word, the line, the sentence, the paragraph, the page, the entire text. This constant back-and-forth reading monitors the multiple complex relationships between all the elements in writing. Recursive scanning—or reviewing and previewing—during revision is beginning to be documented by Sondra Perl, Nancy Sommers, and others. But further and more sophisticated investigation will, I believe, show that the experienced writer is able, through the writer's other self, to read what has gone before and what may come afterward during the writing that is done before there is a written text, and during the writing that produces an embryonic text.

I think we can predict some of the functions that are performed by the other self during the writing process.

- The other self tracks the activity that is taking place. Writing, in a sense, does not exist until it is read. The other self records the evolving text.

- The other self gives the self the distance that is essential for craft. This distance, the craftsperson's step backwards, is a key element in writing that is therapeutic for the writer.

- The other self provides an evolving context for the writer. As the writer adds, cuts, or reorders, the other self keeps track of how each change affects the draft.

- The other self articulates the process of writing, providing the writer with an engineering history of the developing text, a technical resource that records the problems faced and the solutions that were tried and rejected, or not yet tried, and the ones that are in place.

- The other self is the critic who is continually looking at the writing to see if, in the writer's phrase, "it works."
- The other self also is the supportive colleague to the writer, the chap who commiserates and encourages, listens sympathetically to the writer's complaints and reminds the writer of past success. The deeper we get into the writing process the more we may discover how affective concerns govern the cognitive, for writing is an intellectual activity carried on in an emotional environment, a precisely engineered sailboat trying to hold course in a vast and stormy Atlantic. The captain has to deal with fears as well as compass readings.

We shall have to wait for perceptive and innovative research by teams of reading and writing researchers to document the complex kind of reading that is done during the writing process. But, fortunately, we do not have to wait for the results of such research to make use of the other self in the teaching of writing.

The other self can be made articulate. It has read the copy as the copy was being created and knows the decisions that were made to produce the draft. This does not mean that they were all conscious decisions in the sense that the writer articulated what was being done, but even instinctive or subconscious editorial decisions can be articulated retrospectively.

Many teachers of writing, especially those who are also teachers of literature, are deeply suspicious of the testimony of writers about their own writing. It may be that the critic feels that he or she knows more than the writer, that the testimony of writers is too simple to be of value. But I have found in my own work that what students and professional writers say about their own writing process is helpful and makes sense in relation to the text.

Writing is, after all, a rational act; the writing self was monitored by the reading self during the writing process. The affective may well control or

stimulate or limit the cognitive, but writing is thinking, and a thinking act can, most of the time, be recreated in rational terms. The tennis pro may return a serve instinctively, but instinct is, in part, internalized consciousness, and if you ask the pro about that particular return the experienced player will be able to describe what was done and why. If the player thought consciously at the time of the serve, the ball would sail by. The return was a practiced, learned act made spontaneous by experience, and it can be described and explained after the fact.

This retroactive understanding of what was done makes it possible for the teacher not only to teach the other self but recruit the other self to assist in the teaching of writing. The teacher brings the other self into existence, and then works with that other self so that, after the student has graduated, the other self can take over the function of teacher.

When the student speaks and the student and the teacher listen, they are both informed about the nature of the writing process that produced the draft. This is the point at which the teacher knows what needs to be taught or reinforced, one step at a time, and the point at which the student knows what needs to be done in the next draft.

Listening is not a normal composition teacher's skill. We tell and they listen. But to make effective use of the other self the teacher and the student must listen together.

This is done most efficiently in conference. But before the conference, at the beginning of the course, the teacher must explain to the class exactly why the student is to speak first. I tell my students that I'm going to do as little as possible to interfere with their learning. It is their job to read the text, to evaluate it, to decide how it can be improved so that they will be able to write when I am not there. I point out that the ways in which they write are different, their problems and solutions are different, and that I am a resource to help them find their own way. I will always attempt to underteach so that they can overlearn.

I may read the paper before the conference or during the conference, but the student will always speak first in the conference. I have developed a repertoire of questions—what surprised you? what's working best? what are you going to do next?—but I rarely use them. The writing conference is not a social occasion. The student comes to get my response to the work, and I give my response to the student's response. I am teaching the other self.

The more inexperienced the student and the less comprehensible the text, the more helpful the writer's comments. Again and again with remedial students I am handed a text that I simply can not understand. I do not know what it is supposed to say. I can not discover a pattern of organization. I can not understand the language. But when the writer tells me what the writer was doing, when the other self is allowed to speak, I find that the text was produced rationally. The writer followed misunderstood instruction, inappropriate principles, or logical processes that did not work.

Most students, for example, feel that if you want to write for a large audience you should write in general terms, in large abstractions. They must be told that that is logical, but it simply doesn't work. The larger the audience, the more universal we want our message to be, the more specific we must become. It was E. B. White who reminded us, "Don't write about Man, write about *a man*."

When the teacher listens to the student, the conference can be short. The student speaks about the process that produced the draft or about the draft itself. The teacher listens, knowing that the effective teacher must teach where the student is, not where the teacher wishes the student was, then scans or re-scans the draft to confirm, adjust, or disagree with the student's comments.

One thing the responsive teacher, the teacher who listens to the student first, then to the text, soon learns is that the affective usually controls the cognitive, and affective responses have to be dealt with first. I grew used to this with students, but during the past two years I have also worked with professionals on some of the best newspapers in the country, and I have found that it is even more true of published writers. Writers' feelings control the environment in which the mind functions. Unless the teacher knows this environment, the teaching will be off target.

In conference, for example, the majority of men have been socialized to express a false confidence in their writing. The teacher who feels that these men are truly confident will badly misread the writer's other self. The behavior of women in conference is changing, but not fast enough. Most women still express the false modesty about their accomplishments that society has said is appropriate for women. Again the teacher must recognize and support the other self that knows how good the work really is.

I am constantly astonished when I see drafts of equal accomplishment, but with evaluations by the writers that are miles apart. One student may say, "This is terrible. I can't write. I think I'd better drop the course." And right after that on a similar paper a student says, "I never had so much fun writing before. I think this is really a good paper. Do you think I should become a writer?"

Many students, of course, have to deal first with those feelings about the draft—or about writing itself. The teacher in conference should listen to these comments, for they often provide important clues to why the student is writing—or avoiding writing—in a particular way.

The instructor who wishes to teach the other self must discuss the text with that other self in less despairing or elated tones. Too often the inexperienced conference teacher goes to the polar extreme and offers the despairing student absolute praise and the confident student harsh criticism. In practice, the effective conference teacher does not deal in praise or criticism. All texts can be improved, and the instructor discusses with the student what is working and can be made to work better, and what isn't working and how it might be made to work.

After the student learns to deal with his or her defensiveness toward criticism of a working draft, the student can move on to more cognitive matters. At first the students, and the ineffective writing teacher, focus on the superficial, the most obvious problems of language or manuscript preparation. But the teacher, through questioning, can reorient the student to the natural hierarchy of editorial concerns.

These questions, over a series of conferences, may evolve from "What's the single most important thing you have to say?" to "What questions is the reader going to ask you and when are they going to be asked?" to "Where do you hear the voice come through strongest?"

The students will discover, as the teacher models an ideal other self, that the largest questions of content, meaning, or focus have to be dealt with first. Until there is a clear meaning the writer can not order the information that supports that meaning or leads towards it. And until the meaning and its supporting structure are clear the writer cannot make the decisions about voice and language that clarify and communicate that meaning. The other self has to monitor many activities and make sure that the writing self reads what is being monitored in an effective sequence.

Sometimes teachers who are introduced to teaching the other self feel that listening to the student first means that they can not intervene. That is not true. This is not a do-your-own-thing kind of teaching. It is a demanding teaching; it is nothing less than the teaching of critical thinking.

Listening is, after all, an aggressive act. When the teacher insists that the student knows the subject and the writing process that produced the draft better than the teacher, and then has faith that the student has an other self that has monitored the producing of the draft, then the teacher puts enormous pressure on the student. Intelligent comments are expected, and when they are expected they are often received.

I have been impressed by how effectively primary students, those in the first three grades in school, have a speaking other self. Fortunately this other self that monitors the writing process has been documented on tape in a longitudinal study conducted in the Atkinson, New Hampshire, schools by Donald Graves, Lucy Calkins and Susan Sowers at the University of New Hampshire. There the other self has been recorded and analyzed. The most effective learning takes place when the other self articulates the writing that went well. Too much instruction is failure-centered. It focuses on error and unintentionally reinforces error.

The successful writer does not so much correct error as discover what is working and extend that element in the writing. The writer looks for the voice, the order, the relationship of information that is working well, and concentrates on making the entire piece of writing have the effectiveness of the successful fragment. The responsive teacher is always attempting to get the student to bypass the global evaluations of failure—"I can't write about this," "It's an airball," "I don't have anything to say"—and move into an element that is working well. In the beginning of a piece of writing by a beginning student, that first concern might well be the subject or the feeling that the student has toward the subject. The teacher may well say, "Okay. This draft isn't working, but what do you know abut the subject that a reader needs to know?"

Again and again the teacher listens to what the student is saying—and not saying—to help the student hear that other self that has been monitoring what isn't yet on the page or what may be beginning to appear on the page.

This dialogue between the student's other self and the teacher occurs best in conference. But the conferences should be short and frequent.

"I dunno." the student says. "In reading this over I think maybe I'm more specific."

The teacher scans the text and responds, "I agree. What are you going to work on next?"

"I guess the ending. It's sorta goes on."

"Okay. Let me see it when it doesn't."

The important thing is that only one or two issues are dealt with in a conference. The conference isn't a psychiatric session. Think of the writer as an apprentice at the workbench with a master workman, a senior colleague, stopping by once in a while for a quick chat about the work.

We can also help the other self to become articulate by having the student write, after completing a draft, a brief statement about the draft. That statement can be attached on the front of the draft so the teacher can hear what the other self says and respond, after reading that statement and the draft, in writing. But I have found this procedure far less effective than the face-to-face conference, where the act of listening is personal, and where the teacher can hear the reflection and the pause as well as the statement and where the teacher can listen with the eye, reading the student's body language as well as the student's text.

The other self develops confidence through the experience of being heard in small and large group workshops. The same dynamics take place as have been modeled in the conference. The group leader asks the writer, "How can we help you?" The other self speaks of the process or of the text. The workshop members listen and read the text with the words of the other self in their ears. Then they respond, helping the other self become a more effective reader of the evolving text.

The papers that are published in workshops should be the best papers. The workshop members need to know how good writing is made, and they need to know how good writing can be improved. I always make clear that the papers being published in workshops are the best ones. As the other self speaks of how these good papers have been made and how they can be improved, the student being published has that student's most effective writing process reinforced. You can hear the other self becoming stronger and more confident as it speaks of what worked and as it proposes what may work next. The other workshop members hear an effective other self. They hear how a good writer reads an evolving draft. And during the workshop sessions their other selves start to speak, and they hear their own other selves participate in the helpful process of the workshop.

The teacher must always remember that the student, in the beginning of the course, does not know the other self exists. Its existence is an act of faith for the teacher. Sometimes that is a stupendous act

of faith. Ronald, his nose running, his prose stalled, does not appear to have a self, and certainly not a critical, constructive other self. But even Ronald will hear that intelligent other self if the teacher listens well.

The teacher asks questions for which the student does not think there are answers: Why did you use such a strong word here? How did you cut this description and make it clearer? Why did you add so many specifics on Page 3? I think this ending really works, but what did you see that made you realize that old beginning was the new ending?

The student has the answers. And the student is surprised by the fact of answers as much as by the answers themselves. The teacher addresses a self that the student didn't know existed, and the student listens with astonishment to what that other self is saying—"Hey, he's not so dumb." "That's pretty good, she knows what she's doing."

The teacher helps the student find the other self, get to know the other self, learn to work with the other self, and then the teacher walks away to deal with another Ronald in another course who does not know there is another self. The teacher's faith is built on experience. If Ronald had another self, then there is hope for Edith.

What happens in the writing conference and the workshop in which the other self is allowed to become articulate is best expressed in the play, *The Elephant Man*, by Bernard Pomerance, when Merrick, the freak, who has been listened to for the first time in his life, says, "Before I spoke with people, I did not think of all those things because there was no-one to think them for. Now things come out of my mouth which are true."

Liberatory Writing Centers: Restoring Authority to Writers

Tilly Warnock and John Warnock

This essay is from Writing Centers: Theory and Administration. *Ed. Gary Olson. Urbana: NCTE, 1984. 16–23.*

In conceptualizing the modern writing center as a "liberatory lab," the authors assert the center as a means of instruction that frees both the student and the instructor from the bondage of rigid and stifling pedagogies. In such centers, students take responsibility for their own learning and engage in revision—not only revision of writing but also of the world and of themselves.

In many writing centers writing is taught with a focus on meaning, not form; on process, not product; on authorial intention and audience expectation, not teacher authority or punitive measures; on holistic and human concerns, not errors and isolated skills. This kind of teaching, which arises "naturally" out of the writing center situation, proves to have great practical advantages if the center director's goal is truly to teach writing. What is practical about writing centers—cost and time efficient as well as effective—is their "philosophical commitment to individuation through conference teaching," the "one tenet fundamental to all of the most successful writing laboratories." The commitment to individuation rather than to mass production, to growth from within rather than to packaging from without, results in the practical advantage that students learn to conceive ideally, to play with "as if" and the future tenses, to imagine how they might "rewrite" themselves and their worlds. Students learn the practical skills of learn-ing to live in the face of determinate and indeterminate meaning; they learn to revise.

Writing centers and laboratories have continued to flourish despite the disenchantment with the liberal assumptions that spawned them. We wish to argue that though centers may have liberal origins, they continue to grow because they are *liberatory*.[1] The revision from liberal to liberatory seems analogous to broader shifts in our conceptions of writing—from product to process and to performance, from text-centered to reader-centered and context-based. These revisions of terms in composition theory and practice seem in turn analogous to movements being documented in individual and cultural consciousness, shifts Susanne K. Langer designates as the pervasive "key change" of the modern period, evident in fields as various as physics, art, science, religion, and literature. The change she documents in *Philosophy in a New Key* is to a view that recognizes content as symbolic forms, not as truth in an absolute sense, or, in Kenneth Burke's terms, language as performance, as symbolic action, not language as objective reference. The relationship between symbolic action and liberation is made explicit by Ernst Cassirer: "It is symbolic thought which overcomes the natural inertia of man and endows him with a new ability to constantly reshape his human universe."[2]

As writing teachers, our actions are usually felt to be restricted to the symbolic realm. This is often understood as "merely" the symbolic realm, an assumption reflected in our students' expectation that we ought to respond only to their "style" or "form," not to "what they say." This kind of disenfranchisement is often accepted by teachers, particularly those outside the language arts—if, indeed, it is possible to speak of a teacher actually functioning outside the language arts. But the notion of symbolic action becomes a good deal less restrictive when we give emphasis to symbolic action as an *action*. We do not speak of "mere" action. Action is real, a source of power. For Cassirer and for many others, among them Plato and Kenneth Burke, symbolic action is what is most real. Langer's "key change" is a recognition of this reality, this power.

Teachers, particularly in the liberal arts, sometimes speak of developing students' abilities to re-shape their human universes. Teachers in writing centers know, as lecturers and teachers of graduate seminars may not, that these abilities turn out to be not skills in the usual sense, but attitudes that invite revision—revision of the self ("internal revision" as Donald Murray calls it), revision of the language by which the self comes to terms with the universe, revision of the methods which put these terms into action, and finally revision of the world which in turn defines the self. Not all writing centers are liberatory, of course, nor are all actions taken in centers, even by the most liberated of teachers. We want to propose some of the revisions entailed in shifts from the liberal to the liberatory.

THE REVISION OF THE INSTRUCTOR

The first revision concerns the instructor. Writing teachers must first see themselves as writers; they must write so that they can understand writing from the inside out and learn to respect the variety of writing processes, attitudes, readers, and contexts. But this is not all. A liberal understanding, as we are using this term, might take this variety as a sanction for relativism. But a liberatory understanding recognizes also that authority derives from a personal struggle with this variety, a struggle which must be undertaken by each author and which each author is *entitled* to undertake for

him- or herself. Thus, the image of the teacher as writer results in a revision of the teacher's relationship with students, for students in liberatory centers also become authors of and authorities on their own texts. Teachers in a writing center usually do not stand—and if they do, certainly not at the head of their classes—parceling out information at their own discretion, according to their timetable or lesson plan. Writing center teachers often sit comfortably and alertly among their students, listening to papers being read aloud and discussed. Being a writer, having the same relation to "the writing problem" as the students, this sort of teacher does not demand writing formulated according to his or her authority, but instead works with students *in* the process of writing.

Writing center faculty are usually called staff, not faculty, and though the shift in terms may be intended to indicate the less prestigious status of people who work there, certain liberatory tendencies are also implied. A liberatory center staff is composed of part-time, nontenured instructors, graduate students, peer tutors, and tenured faculty. In the center it is impossible to distinguish among the various ranks; in fact, it is often impossible to distinguish between the faculty and the students. Neither age, dress, nor posture will indicate the distinctions; furthermore, the staff are officially students in many cases, and liberatory staff are—significantly—students in their attitudes. The teacher, who listens to students talk about and read papers on issues on which they are authorities, can learn not just new information, not just new symbolic forms, but new relationships to the problems of writing. The teacher is not a traditional teacher-evaluator but a person who assists writers by listening and reading, by helping students imagine an audience, form intentions, and realize them. Writing center teachers honor their own ignorance, and this attitude allows them to act with poise, confident in what they know and others know, and confident that they themselves can revise. Writing center teachers are ready to learn and to listen, empowered with a critical consciousness which comes from understanding language as symbolic action, as having the power to revise the self and the world.

THE REVISION OF THE STUDENT

Teachers know that once students develop a critical consciousness toward their own writing, they will very likely have developed such consciousness toward the context for that writing, the world they live in, and thus will be able to *happen to*. However, students may not always, and usually do not at first, come to the center to learn to *happen to* their worlds. They may want at first only to be rescued: "Would somebody proofread this for me?" "How can I pass this course?" But teachers in liberatory centers know that it is cruel to rescue those who will only be thrown back into the same waters again. If students are not taught to swim, or at least float on their own, they cannot "happen" to water. In liberatory centers, then, it is not enough to provide students with what some call "survival skills." The strongest swimmers will not plunge in if they have no place they want to go or think they can get to, and thus they will not survive.

In addition to this attention to motives and purposes, the liberatory teacher realizes that learning to write is also a matter of writing. William Stafford argues for "the value of an unafraid, face-down, flailing, and speedy process in using the language":

> Writers are persons who write; swimmers are (and from teaching a child I know how hard it is to persuade a reasonable person of this)—swimmers are persons who relax in the water, let their hands go down, and reach out with ease and confidence.[3]

Writers can become people who move themselves and the waters that sustain them. The teacher's task becomes redefined further as a new definition of "student" develops in the liberatory center.

The most serious problem most writers have is having no place they want to get to *as writers*. They want, or think they want, any number of things: cars, money, passing grades, correct and complete writing the first time around. But real writing has nothing to do with any of these things, including the last one. In nonliberatory centers, writing is at best a means to an end that is entirely independent of writing: make enough money and you can hire someone to write for you; or write it correctly and completely the first time and then you will not waste any more valuable time than is absolutely necessary on this worthless writing course.

Of course, teachers in liberatory centers do not set out to change the values of students as such nor, of course, do students come to have their values changed. But such teachers do often find that the best and perhaps the only way to change student writing is to help students revise their attitudes towards themselves as writers and towards writing. A crucial part of the change is to restore to students the sense of their own authority and responsibility. In traditional teaching, the students' sense of their own authority in learning is irrelevant, even counterproductive, because students must feel themselves void of knowledge in order to accept that which is being given or driven into them. Liberatory learning requires that learners feel confident enough about themselves that they listen to others and evaluate what they learn, transforming some of what they hear into their own purposes, revising their own views in light of the new learning, rejecting what they do not value or believe might have value for them in the future.

More specifically, if the center is to encourage students to assume authorship of their texts and their lives, students must decide whether or not they will attend the center. Classroom teachers may encourage attendance, and adjunct relationships between the center and regular classes may be helpful, but the philosophy of liberatory learning requires that students take responsibility for themselves. Thus, students take an assertive role in deciding what happens to them and to their texts when they come to the center. They determine when they will come, what they will do, whether or not they will return. In short, students evaluate their own learning processes.

Students often need to adjust to this freedom. They bring to the centers the kind of unliberated consciousness that asks only to have their papers proofread, corrected, rewritten by someone other than themselves, to be acceptable to someone other than themselves. This is crucial because writing center staff cannot do that for them—ethical considerations prevent it, if nothing else. So the staff must create a situation that helps to give a sense of options and authority to the writer.

The new role for students in liberatory writing centers allows them to speak what they think, to ask for what they want and need, to give to others, to wait and see. It allows them to draw on their expertise gained gradually in the process of living and interacting with others. Students who say they cannot write will not also say they do not know what they think, and they therefore will be willing to listen to another student's draft and give their opinions. The student can act out familiar life roles that are not permitted in regular classes, where the student is often defined as the one who does not know, who does not even know what is good for him or her. The traditional student role prescribes particular postures, voice tones, politeness rituals, even specific eye contact routines. It entails the attitude of passive receptivity that lacks all wonder and delight. Students are asked to wait in regular classes, but not to wait and learn; they are asked to wait until teachers get to where they want to go, until they "cover" what was planned. Students in regular classes even have to wait until the end of class. In liberatory centers, students wait, listen, and learn, but they also act and determine their own actions, symbolic and otherwise. They read their drafts aloud to others and listen to responses, often conflicting responses, and decide what they will have to do on the basis of the responses. They do not follow criticism obediently, but act on their own critical consciousness.

THE REVISION OF STUDENT-FACULTY RELATIONSHIPS

The context of a liberatory center is fundamental to the revisions of "faculty" and "student" and their relationships to each other. In centers, students come and go at will, and they even determine the use of time and materials in the center. In fact, they bring the materials, their own writing, which immediately establishes their authority.

Traditional spatial relationships are also revised in liberatory centers. One reason that staff and students cannot be distinguished is that they do not maintain the conventional distance; people move closer, then back, turn away, even stare at each other—as people do in their everyday interactions. Chairs are usually arranged around a table, ideally a round table, and teachers and students alike feel free to sit on desks, to imagine other functions for equipment and space and time than are dictated by the constraints of the traditional setting.

If we were to accept the problematic metaphor of the learning place as marketplace, we could say that the writing center is a buyer's market, with different goods and different rates of exchange than those that characterize the regular class. Although traditional classes do not exist without students, the pretense is that the teacher and the course are permanent while the students are changeable and even expendable.

Power relationships are fluid in liberatory centers, and every effort is exerted to identify victimizing actions. Students and staff are both writers, confronting the same kinds of problems; students and staff are allies. They both develop critical consciousnesses, the capacity to entertain seriously each other's viewpoint, confident that other views can be accepted, rejected, or modified. The understanding of language as symbolic action allows for revision because language is regarded as a performance, not a reference to an absolute truth that cannot be revised because it emanates from a source of incontestable power. Critical consciousness is not power itself (such as is sometimes claimed for knowledge), but it is the necessary condition of power. When language is defined as symbolic action, it becomes a playground for experimenting with ideas, roles, and expectations. It also is an arena for action in which all things are not possible (not all actions are possible all of the time), in which necessities are recognized, and in which revision is defined as an action that changes according to people, purposes, and places, and writing is defined as, among other things, process, product, performance, problem-solving, and thinking. In general, writing is defined as the ability to read a particular situation critically and to decide what kind of symbolic action will work best, given the specific context and motives.

THE WRITING CENTER AS "OUTSIDER"

Liberatory centers are risk-taking operations, just as liberatory learning is risky business for individuals who allow for revision in themselves. These centers usually exist on the fringes of the academic establishment, often in unused classrooms, old barracks, and basements. Salaries for staff are often low and granted on a year-to-year, even semester-to-semester, basis. The primary materials of the center are the students' own messy texts. The body of knowledge is the students themselves. But despite those obvious signs of "decay," labs flourish and students know where the real action is. Voices are loud, and laughter and tears are frequent. It is these characteristics of the liberatory center scene that nourish liberatory learning because in such contexts faculty and textbooks are not the authorities: students are their own authors.

While we do not suggest that centers must remain in condemned buildings or that staff salaries must remain low, it is probably a mistake for centers to seek integration into the established institution. We are suggesting that the liberatory center remain on the fringes of the academic community, in universities or public schools, in order to maintain critical consciousness. This does not mean a lack of involvement; it means, in fact, active involvement but with a critical distance to assess and evaluate in the light of a theory of liberatory learning. This critical stance is revolutionary and revisionary, as Cassirer explains in his discussion of a child's first awareness of language as symbolic form:

> With the first understanding of the symbolism of speech a real revolution takes place in the life of the child. From this point on his whole personal and intellectual life assumes an entirely different shape.

Roughly speaking, this change may be described by saying that the child passes from a more subjective to a more objective state, from a merely emotional attitude to a theoretical attitude. . . . [T]he child himself has a clear sense of the significance of a new instrument for his mental development. He is not satisfied with being taught in a purely receptive manner but takes an active share in the process of speech which is at the same time a progressive objectification.[4]

This power of revision comes with the understanding of language as symbolic action. This understanding comes to communities and to cultures, as well as to individuals, and the understanding comes, in revised forms, many times. The function of our schools and universities is too often to contradict such consciousness, causing students to deny the revisionary power in and of themselves. Centers are in a unique position to restore that power, that authorial nature, to students and staff.

Notes

1. The notion of "liberatory learning" is today associated most closely with Paolo Friere. See his *Pedagogy of the Oppressed* (New York: Seabury, 1970), and *Pedagogy in Process* (New York: Seabury, 1978). "Critical consciousness" is that consciousness which enables a people to see themselves as agents in their society, not just "knowers" but also "doers." The notion is explained, and practical ways of "teaching" it are proposed, by Ira Shor, *Critical Thinking and Everyday Life* (Boston: South End Press, 1980). An analogous notion is "cultural literacy" as this term is developed by C. A. Bowers, *Cultural Literacy for Freedom* (Eugene, Oregon: Elan Publishers, 1974). The argument that conventional composition classes serve the interests of the establishment is made by Richard Ohmann, *English in America* (New York: Oxford University Press, 1976). Recent articles discussing the teaching of writing and language in terms relevant to our discussion of liberatory learning are Kay Fiore and Nan Elsasser, "'Strangers No More': A Liberatory Learning Curriculum," *College English* 44 (February 1982): 115–18; Richard Ohmann, "Reflections on Class and Language," *College English* 44 (January 1982): 1–17; John J. Rouse, "Knowledge, Power, and the Teaching of English," *College English* 40 (January

1979): 473–91; and Gerald Graff, "The Politics of Composition: A Reply to John Rouse," *College English* 41 (April 1980): 851–56.

2. Ernst Cassirer, *An Essay on Man: An Introduction to the Philosophy of Human Culture* (New Haven: Yale University Press, 1944), 62. Kenneth Burke's philosophy of symbolic action may be seen as a rhetorical revision of Cassirer's notion.

3. William Stafford, *Writing the Australian Crawl: Views on the Writer's Vocation* (Ann Arbor: University of Michigan Press, 1978), 22–23.

4. Cassirer, *An Essay on Man,* 131.

Nature – must get self out of way of natural process of writing of language

How to Get Power through Voice

Peter Elbow

This selection is excerpted from chapter 26 of Writing with Power: Techniques for Mastering the Writing Process. *New York: Oxford UP, 1981. 304–13.*

People often lack any voice at all in their writing, even fake voice, because they stop so often in the act of writing a sentence and worry and change their minds about which words to use. They have none of the natural breath in their writing that they have in speaking because the conditions for writing are so different from the conditions for speaking. The list of conditions is awesome: we have so little practice in writing, but so much more time to stop and fiddle as we write each sentence; we have additional rules of spelling and usage to follow in writing that we don't have in speaking; we feel more culpable for our written foolishness than for what we say; we have been so fully graded, corrected, and given feedback on our mistakes in writing; and we are usually trying to get our words to conform to some (ill-understood) model of "good writing" as we write.

Frequent and regular freewriting exercises are the best way to overcome these conditions of writing and get voice into your words. These exercises should perhaps be called compulsory writing exercises since they are really a way to *compel* yourself to keep putting words down on paper no matter how lost or frustrated you feel. To get voice into your words you need to learn to get each word chosen, as it were, not by you but by the preceding word. Freewriting exercises help you learn to stand out of the way.

In addition to actual exercises in nonstop writing—since it's hard to keep writing *no matter what* for more than fifteen minutes—force yourself simply to write enormous quantities. Try to make up

for all the writing you haven't done. Use writing for as many different tasks as you can. Keep a notebook or journal, explore thoughts for yourself, write to yourself when you feel frustrated or want to figure something out.

Practice revising for voice. A powerful exercise is to write short pieces of prose or poetry that work without any punctuation at all. Get the words so well ordered that punctuation is never missed. The reader must never stumble or have to reread a phrase, not even on first reading—and all without benefit of punctuation. This is really an exercise in adjusting the breath in the words till it guides the reader's voice naturally to each pause and full stop.

Read out loud. This is a good way to exercise the muscle involved in voice and even in real voice. Good reading out loud is not necessarily dramatic. I'm struck with how some good poets or readers get real voice into a monotone or chant. They are trying to let the words' inner resonance come through, not trying to "perform" the words. (Dylan Thomas reads so splendidly that we may make the mistake of calling his technique "dramatic." Really it is a kind of chant or incantation he uses.) But there is no right way. It's a question of steering a path between being too timid and being falsely dramatic. The presence of listeners can sharpen your ear and help you hear when you chicken out or overdramatize.

Real voice. People often avoid it and drift into fake voices because of the need to face an audience. I have to go to work, I have to make a presentation,

[handwritten annotations: "this is an interesting topic — I feel a 'fake voice' is frequently a problem I see in students' essays"]

I have to teach, I have to go to a party, I have to have dinner with friends. Perhaps I feel lost, uncertain, baffled—or else angry—or else uncaring—or else hysterical. I can't sound that way with all these people. They won't understand, they won't know how to deal with me, and I won't accomplish what I need to accomplish. Besides, perhaps I don't even know *how* to sound the way I feel. (When we were little we had no difficulty sounding the way we felt; thus most little children speak and write with real voice.) Therefore I will use some of the voices I have at my disposal that will serve the audience and the situation—voices I've learned by imitation or made up out of desperation or out of my sense of humor. I might as well. By now, those people think those voices are me. If I used my real voice, they might think I was crazy.

For real voice, write a lot without an audience. Do freewritings and throw them away. Remove yourself from the expectations of an audience, the demands of a particular task, the needs of a particular interaction. As you do this, try out many different ways of speaking.

But a certain *kind* of audience can help you toward real voice even though it was probably the pressures of audience that led you to unreal voices in the first place. Find an audience of people also committed to getting power in their writing. Find times when you can write in each other's presence, each working on your own work. Your shared presence and commitment to helping each other will make you more powerful in what you write. Then read your rough writing to each other. No feedback: just welcoming each other to try out anything.

Because you often don't even know what your power or your inner self sounds like, you have to try many different tones and voices. Fool around, jump from one mood or voice to another, mimic, play-act, dramatize and exaggerate. Let your writing be outrageous. Practice relinquishing control. It can help to write in settings where you never write (on the bus? in the bathtub?) or in modes you never use. And if, as sometimes happens, you know you are angry but somehow cannot really feel or inhabit that feeling, play-act and exaggerate

it. Write artificially. Sometimes "going through the motions" is the quickest way to "the real thing."

Realize that in the short run there is probably a conflict between developing real voice and producing successful, pragmatic writing—polished pieces that work for specific audiences and situations. Keeping an appropriate stance or tone for an audience may prevent you from getting real voice into that piece of writing. Deep personal outrage, for example, may be the only authentic tone of voice you can use in writing to a particular person, yet that voice is neither appropriate nor useful for the actual document you have to write—perhaps an official agency memo or a report to that person about his child. Feedback on whether something works as a finished piece of writing for an audience is often not good feedback on real voice. It is probably important to work on both goals. Work on polishing things and making sure they have the right tone or stance for that audience. Or at least not the wrong one: you may well have to play it safe. But make sure you also work on writing that *doesn't* have to work and doesn't have to be revised and polished for an audience.

And yet you needn't give up on power just because a particular writing situation is very tricky for you. Perhaps you must write an essay for a teacher who never seems to understand you; or a report for a supervisor who never seems able to see things the way you do; or a research report on a topic that has always scared and confused you. If you try to write in the most useful voice for this situation—perhaps cheerful politeness or down-to-business impersonality—the anger will probably show through anyway. It might not show clearly, readers might be unaware of it, yet they will turn out to have the kind of responses they have to angry writing. That is, they will become annoyed with many of the ideas you present, or continually think of arguments against you (which they wouldn't have done to a different voice), or they will turn off, or they will react condescendingly.

To the degree that you keep your anger hidden, you are likely to write words especially lacking in voice—especially dead, fishy, fake-feeling. Or the process of trying to write in a non-angry, down-to-business, impersonal way is so deadening to you that you simply get bored and sleepy and devoid of energy. Your mind shuts off. You cannot think of anything to say.

In a situation like this it helps to take a roundabout approach. First do lots of freewriting where you are angry and tell your reader all your feelings in whatever voices come. Then get back to the real topic. Do lots of freewriting and raw writing and exploration of the topic—writing still in whatever style comes out. Put all your effort into finding the best ideas and arguments you can, and don't worry about your tone. After you express the feelings and voices swirling around in you, and after you get all the insights you can while not having to worry about the audience and the tone, then you will find it relatively easy to revise and rewrite something powerful and effective for that reader. That is, you can get past the anger and confusion, but keep the good ideas and the energy. As you rewrite for the real audience, you can generally use large chunks of what you have already written with only minor cosmetic changes. (You don't necessarily have to write out *all* the anger you have. It may be that you have three hundred pages of angry words you need to say to someone, but if you can get *one* page that really opens the door all the way, that can be enough. But if this is something new to you, you may find you cannot do it in one page—you need to rant and rave for five or ten pages. It may seem like a waste of time, but it isn't. Gradually you will get more economical.)

By taking this roundabout path, you will find more energy and better thinking. And through the process of starting with the voices that just happen and seeing where they lead, often you will come to a *new* voice which is appropriate to this reader but also rings deeply. You won't have to choose between something self-defeatingly angry that will simply turn off the reader or something pussyfooting, polite, and full of fog—and boring for you to write.

A long and messy path is common and beneficial, but you can get some of the benefits quicker if you are in a hurry. Just set yourself strict time limits for the early writing and force yourself to write without stopping throughout the early stages. When I have to write an evaluation of a student I am annoyed at, I force myself to write a quick freewriting letter to the student telling him everything on my mind. I make this uncensored, extreme, exaggerated, sometimes even deliberately unfair—but very short. And it's for the wastepaper basket. Having done this, I can turn to my official evaluation and find it much easier to write something fair in a suitable tone of voice (for a document that becomes part of the student's transcript). I finish these two pieces of writing much more quickly than if I just tried to write the official document and pick my way gingerly through my feelings.

Another reason people don't use real voice is that it makes them feel exposed and vulnerable. I don't so much mind if someone dislikes my writing when I am merely using an acceptable voice, but if I use my real voice and they don't like it—which of course is very possible—that hurts. The more criticism people get on their writing, the more they tend to use fake voices. To use real voice feels like bringing yourself into contact with the reader. It's the same kind of phenomenon that happens when there is real eye contact and each person experiences the presence of the other; or when two or more people stop talking and wait in silence while something in the air gets itself clear. Writing of almost any kind is exhibitionistic; writing with real voice is more so. Many professional writers feel a special need for privacy. It will help you, then, to get together with one or more others who are interested in recovering their power. Feeling vulnerable or exposed with them is not so difficult.

Another reason people don't use their real voice is that it means having feelings and memories they would rather not have. When you write in your real voice, it often brings tears or shaking—though laughter too. Using real voice may even mean finding you *believe* things you don't wish to believe. For all these reasons, you need to write for no audience and to write for an audience that's safe. And you need faith in yourself that you will gradually sort things out and that it doesn't matter if it takes time.

Most children have real voice but then lose it. It is often just plain loud: like screeching or banging a drum. It can be annoying or wearing for others. "Shhh" is the response we often get to the power of our real voice. But, in addition, much of what we say with real voice is difficult for those around us to deal with: anger, grief, self-pity, even love for the wrong people. When we are hushed up from those expressions, we lose real voice.

In addition, we lose real voice when we are persuaded to give up some of our natural responses to inauthenticity and injustice. Almost any child can feel inauthenticity in the voices of many TV figures or politicians. Many grown-ups can't hear it so well—or drown out their distrust. It is difficult to get along in the world if you hear all the inauthenticity: it makes you feel alone, depressed, hopeless. We need to belong, and society offers us membership if we stop hearing inauthenticity.

Children can usually feel when things are unfair, but they are often persuaded to go along because they need to belong and to be loved. To get back to those feelings in later life leads to rage, grief, aloneness and—since one has gone along—guilt. Real voice is often buried in all of that. If you want to recover it, you do well to build in special support from people you can trust so you don't feel so alone or threatened by all these feelings.

Another reason people don't use real voice is that they run away from their power. There's something scary about being as strong as you are, about wielding the force you actually have. It means taking a lot more responsibility and credit than you are used to. If you write with real voice, people will say "You did this to me" and try to make you feel responsible for some of their actions. Besides, the effect of your power is liable to be different from what you intended. Especially at first. You cause explosions when you thought you were just asking for the salt or saying hello. In effect I'm saying, "Why don't you shoot that gun you have? Oh yes, by the way, I can't tell you how to aim it." The standard approach in writing is to say you mustn't pull the trigger until you can aim it well. But how can you learn to aim well till you start pulling the trigger? If you start letting your writing lead you to real

voice, you'll discover some thoughts and feelings you didn't know you had.

Therefore, practice shooting the gun off in safe places. First with no one around. Then with people you know and trust deeply. Find people who are willing to be in the same room with you while you pull the trigger. Try using the power in ways where the results don't matter. Write letters to people that don't matter to you. You'll discover that the gun doesn't kill but that you have more power than you are comfortable with.

Of course you may accept your power but still want to disguise it. That is, you may find it convenient, if you are in a large organization, to be able to write about an event in a fuzzy, passive "It has come to our attention that . . ." kind of language, so you disguise not only the fact that it was an action performed by a human being with a free will but indeed that *you did it*. But it would be incorrect to conclude, as some people do, that all bureaucratic, organizational, and governmental writing needs to lack the resonance of real voice. Most often it could do its work perfectly well even if it were strong and clear. It is the *personal, individualistic,* or *personality-filled* voice that is inappropriate in much organizational writing, but you can write with power in the impersonal, public, and corporate voice. You can avoid "I" and its flavor, and talk entirely in terms of "we" and "they" and even "it," and still achieve the resonance of real voice. Real voice is not the sound of an *individual personality* redolent with vibes, it is the sound of *a meaning* resonating because the individual consciousness of the writer is somehow fully behind or in tune with or in participation with that meaning.

I have stressed the importance of sharing writing without any feedback at all. What about asking people to give you feedback specifically on real voice? I think that such feedback can be useful, but I am leery of it. It's so hard to know whether someone's perception of real voice is accurate. If you want this feedback, don't get it early in your writing development, make sure you get it from very different kinds of people, and make sure not to put too much trust in it. The safest method is to get them to read a piece and then ask them a week later what they remember. Passages they *dislike* often have the most real voice.

But here is a specific exercise for getting feedback on real voice. It grows out of one of the first experiences that made me think consciously about this matter. As an applicant for conscientious objector status, and then later as a draft counselor, I discovered that the writing task set by Selective Service was very interesting and perplexing. An applicant had to write why he was opposed to fighting in wars, but there was no right or wrong answer. The draft board would accept any reasons (within certain broad limits); they would accept any style, any level of skill. Their only criterion was whether *they* believed that the *writer* believed his own words. (I am describing how it worked when board members were in good faith.)

Applicants, especially college students, often started with writing that didn't work. I could infer from all the arguments and commotion and from conversations with them that they were sincere but as they wrote they got so preoccupied with theories, argument, and reasoning that in the end there was no conviction on paper. When I gave someone this feedback and he was willing to try and try again till at last the words began to ring true, all of a sudden the writing got powerful and even skillful in other ways.

The exercise I suggest to anybody, then, is simply to write about some belief you have—or even some experience or perception—but to get readers to give you this limited, peculiar, draft-board-like feedback: where do they really believe that you believe it, and where do they have doubts? The useful thing about this exercise is discovering how often words that ring true are not especially full of feeling, not heavy with conviction. Too much "sincerity" and quivering often sounds fake and makes readers doubt that you really believe what you are saying. I stress this because I fear I have made real voice sound as though it is always full of loud emotion. It is often quiet.

In the end, what may be as important as these specific exercises is adopting the right frame of mind.

Look for real voice and realize it is there in everyone waiting to be used. Yet remember, too, that you are looking for something mysterious and hidden. There are no outward linguistic characteristics to point to in writing with real voice. Resonance or impact on readers is all there is. But you can't count on readers to notice it or to agree about whether it is there because of all the other criteria they use in evaluating writing (e.g., polished style, correct reasoning, good insights, truth-to-life, deep feelings), and because of the negative qualities that sometimes accompany real voice as it is emerging. And you, as writer, may be wrong about the presence or absence of real voice in your writing—at least until you finally develop a trustworthy sense of it. You have to be willing to work in the dark, not be in a hurry, and have faith. The best clue I know is that as you begin to develop real voice, your writing will probably cause more comment from readers than before (though not necessarily more favorable comment).

If you seek real voice you should realize that you probably face a dilemma. You probably have only one real voice—at first anyway—and it is likely to feel childish or distasteful or ugly to you. But you are stuck. You can either use voices you like or you can be heard. For a while, you can't have it both ways.

But if you do have the courage to use and inhabit that real voice, you will get the knack of resonance, you will learn to expand its range and eventually make more voices real. This of course is the skill of great literary artists: the ability to give resonance to many voices.

It's important to stress, at the end, this fact of many voices. Partly to reassure you that you are not ultimately stuck with just one voice forever. But also because it highlights the mystery. Real voice is not necessarily personal or sincere. Writing about your own personal concerns is only one way and not necessarily the best. Such writing can lead to gushy or analytical words about how angry you are today: useful to write, an expression of strong feelings, a possible *source* of future powerful writing, but not resonant or powerful for readers as it stands. Real voice is whatever yields resonance, whatever makes the words bore through. Some writers get real voice through pure fantasy, lies, imitation of utterly different writers, or trance-writing. It may be possible to get real voice by merging in your mind with another personality, pretending to be someone else. *Shedding* the self's concerns and point of view can be a good way to get real voice—thus writing fiction and playing roles are powerful tools. Many good literary artists sound least convincing when they speak for themselves. The important thing is simply to know that power is available and to figure out through experimentation the best way for you to attain it.

Nature – cognitive processes

The Shifting Relationships between Speech and Writing

Peter Elbow

This essay is from College Composition and Communication 36 (1985): 283–303.

> Paradoxes . . . beset the relationships between the original spoken word and all its technological transformations. . . . [I]ntelligence is relentlessly reflexive, so that even the external tools that it uses to implement its workings become "internalized," that is, part of its own reflexive process. (Ong, *Orality*, 81)[1]

We have seen interesting work in recent years on the nature of speech and writing and the mentalities associated with each. The insights from these investigations are extremely valuable, but a dangerous assumption is sometimes inferred from them: that speech and writing are distinctly characterizable media, each of which has its own inherent features and each of which tends to foster a particular cognitive process, or "mentality."[2] I am interested in the cognitive processes associated with speech and writing, but instead of saying that each medium has a particular tendency, I will argue that each medium can draw on and foster *various* mentalities. This essay is a call for writers and teachers of writing to recognize the enormous choice we have and to learn to take more control over the cognitive effects associated with writing. This essay is in three parts—each showing a different relationship between speech and writing.

I. THE TRADITIONAL VIEW: INDELIBLE WRITING, EPHEMERAL SPEECH

Obviously writing is more indelible or permanent than speech. Speech is nothing but wind, waves of temporarily squashed air, waves that begin at once to disperse, that is, to lose their sound. Writing, on the other hand, stays there—"down in black and white." Once we get it on paper it takes on a life of its own, separate from the writer. It "commits us to paper." It can be brought back to haunt us: read in a different context from the one we had in mind—read by any audience, whether or not we know them or want them to see our words.

Where the *intention* to speak usually results automatically in the *act* of speech, writing almost always involves delay and effort. Writing forces us not only to form the letters, spell the words, and follow stricter rules of correctness (than speech); we must also get into the text itself all those cues that readers might need who are not present to us as we write, who don't know the context for our words, and who don't know us or how we speak. In addition to this "contextualizing," we must capture onto the page some substitute for all those vocal and visual cues for listeners that we give without effort or attention in speaking. We can take nothing for granted in writing; the text has to say it all.

In the effort to do all these things as we write, how can we help but pause and reflect on whether what we are engaged in putting down is really right—or even if it is, whether it is what we really wanted to say? If we are going to take the trouble to write something down, then, we might as well get it right. *Getting it right,* then, feels like an inherent demand in the medium itself of writing.

Research (see Tannen, "Oral and Literate Strategies") shows that speech tends to carry more "phatic" messages than writing—messages about the relationship between the speaker and the listener or between the speaker and his material (e.g., "I know you're my friend"), even when the ostensible function of the spoken words is purely substantive or informational. Thus writing tends to carry a much higher proportion of "content" messages to absent readers—more permanent messages which are judged for validity and adequacy, not just accepted as social interchange.

This feeling that we must get things right in writing because written words are more indelible than speech is confirmed when we look to the *history* of speech and writing. The development of writing as a technology seems to have led to the development of careful and logical thinking—to a greater concern with "trying to get it *really* right" (see Ong, *Orality,* and his other works; Goody, *Domestication;* Havelock, *Plato*). Ong claims that the development of writing gave us a new "noetic economy," that is, a wholly new relationship to words and knowledge—new habits of shaping, storing, retrieving, and communicating what we know.[3]

We see a parallel argument about the teaching of writing. That is, leading theorists tell us that the poor thinking we see in many of our students stems from their not yet having made that great developmental leap from oral language strategies to written or literate language strategies (Lunsford, "Cognitive Development"; Shaughnessy, *Errors.*) Obviously, students can think better when they can examine their thoughts more self-consciously as a string of assertions arranged in space. The technology of indelible writing permits students in a sense to step out of the flux of time: to detach themselves from oral discourse, from the context in which words are uttered and first thought about, and from

the tendency in speech to rely on concrete and experiential modes of discourse. As Havelock emphasizes, writing helps to separate the knower from the known.

This contrast between the two media is reinforced when we turn to the story of how we learn to speak and to write as individuals. We learn speech as infants—from parents who love us and naturally reward us for speaking at all. Our first audience works overtime to hear the faintest intention in our every utterance, no matter how hidden or garbled that meaning may be. Children aren't so much criticized for getting something wrong as praised for having anything at all to say—indeed they are often praised even for emitting speech as pure play with no message intended.

What a contrast between that introduction to speech and the introduction to writing which most children get in school. Students can never feel writing as an activity they engage in as freely, frequently, or spontaneously as they do in speech. Indeed, because writing is almost always a requirement set by the teacher, the act of writing takes on a "required" quality, sometimes even the aspect of punishment. I can still hear the ominous cadence in my ears: "Take out your pens." Indeed, in the classic case of school punishment the crime is speech and the punishment is writing ("I will not talk in class. I will not talk in class."). Do some teachers still insist, as some of mine did, that ink must be used? The effect was to heighten our sense of writing as indelible, as the act of making irrevocable choices—as though there were something wrong about changing our minds.

I don't want to imply gradgrindish conditions which may no longer be widespread. But the school setting in which most of us learn to write and have most of our writing experiences till we leave school is just one more reason why we experience writing as more indelible than speech—and why we experience writing as inherently a medium for *getting it right.*[4]

But we need to turn this accustomed picture upside down.

II. *SPEECH* AS INDELIBLE, WRITING AS EPHEMERAL

As Roland Barthes says, "it is ephemeral speech which is indelible, not monumental writing. . . . Speech is irreversible: a [spoken] word cannot be retracted. . . ." ("Death of the Author"). Precisely because speech is nothing but temporary crowdings in air molecules, we can never revise it. If we speak in the hearing of others—and we seldom speak otherwise—our words are heard by listeners who can remember them even (or especially) if we say something we wish they would forget. Once we've said (as a joke), "I've never liked that shirt you gave me," or (in a fight), "Well damn it, that *is* a woman's job," or even (in a seminar, without thinking about what our colleagues might think of us), "I've never been able to understand that poem"—or once Jesse Jackson refers to Jews in public as "hymies"—once any of these words are spoken, none can be undone.

Speech is inherently more indelible than writing also because it is a more vivid medium. When we speak, listeners don't just see our words, they see us—how we hold and move ourselves. Even if we only hear someone over the phone or on the radio—perhaps even someone we've never met—still we experience the texture of her talk: the rhythms, emphases, hesitations, and other tonalities of speech which give us a dramatized sense of her character or personality. And if we *don't* reveal ourselves more through our speech than our writing, that too is taken as a revelation: someone will say, as of Gary Hart, "he seems a bit cool and aloof."

But perhaps you will reply that *casual speech* is more ephemeral than writing. Yet there are plenty of occasions when we are trying as hard as we can to "get it right" in speech—because our speech is "a speech," or an "oral report," or discourse to strangers; or for some reason we feel we are being carefully judged for our speech, as in a job interview. Perhaps casual speech is more common in our culture—or in literate or print cultures—than in others. In oral cultures such as the Homeric Greek, the Anglo-Saxon, and the Native American, there was scorn for anyone who spoke hasty un-planned words. Perhaps we fall into the assumption that speech is ephemeral because we live in a blabbing culture.

In short, our sense of speech as ephemeral and writing as indelible stems not so much from the nature of speech and writing as media but from how and where they are most often used. (And researched. See Schafer, "Spoken and Written," for a corrective view.) Our paradigm for speech is casual conversation among trusted friends; our paradigm for writing is more formal discourse to a little-known audience or an audience that is likely to judge us on our utterance.

So far from speech being ephemeral, then, the problem with speech is that it isn't ephemeral enough. What we need is a mode of discourse that really *is* ephemeral—we need the luxury of being able to utter everything on our minds and not have anyone hear it until *after* we decide what we really mean or how we want to say it. Interestingly enough, the most indelible medium of all is also the most ephemeral: writing.

However indelible the ink, writing can be completely evanescent and without consequences. We can write in solitude—indeed we seldom write otherwise—we can write whatever we want, we can write as badly as we want, and we can write one thing and then change our mind. No one need know what we've written or how we've written it. In short, writing turns out to be the ideal medium for *getting it wrong*. (This evanescence of writing is enormously enhanced by the new electronic media where words are just electrical or magnetic impulses on a screen or a disk.)

Perhaps there's nothing new in the idea of writing as ephemeral. Perhaps the phrase from Barthes has tempted me into that Gallic weakness for trying to phrase the obvious as a scandal. In the days of parchment, people wrote to last, but now we are flooded with ephemeral temporary documents.[5]

But though we float on a rising tide of ephemeral writing, our writing habits and instincts are dominated by the old assumption that writing is indelible. That is, most people, even when they are writing a draft that no one will read, nevertheless write by habit *as though readers were going to see it.*

Do I exaggerate? Plenty of people experiment or make a mess as they write. Yet what do most people do when they are writing along and they suddenly wonder whether they really believe what they are about to write, or whether it holds up on examination, or even whether it is well phrased? Most people stop writing and don't resume writing till they have figured out what they want to say. This *feels* like a reasonable and normal way to behave, but notice the assumption it reveals: that the function of writing is to record what we have *already* decided—not to figure out *whether* we believe it. If we were speaking, we would be much more likely to speak the train of thought as it comes to mind even though we're not sure of our final opinion—as a *way* of making up our minds. It is almost as though we fear, as we write, that someone might at any moment swoop down and read what we have just written and see that it is rubbish.

Thus writing for most people is dominated by the experience of not writing: of elaborate planning beforehand to decide what to write and frequent pausing in midcourse to search for the right word or the right path. This nonwriting behavior is not surprising since *planning* is probably stressed more than anything else in advice to writers. (This advice is stressed not only in traditional textbooks but in recent ones such as Linda Flower's.) But because of my own difficulties in writing, I have come to notice the enormous cognitive and linguistic leverage that comes from learning to avoid the mentality dominated by the indelibility of writing and learning instead to exploit the ephemeral or "under" side of writing. It feels very different to put down words not as commitment but as trial, or as Barthes and some of the deconstructionists say, as play, *jouissance,* or the free play of language and consciousness. Thinking is enriched. Writing in this mode can produce an *immersion in discourse itself* that doesn't occur when we sit and think—an immersion in language that can entice us into ideas and perceptions we could not get by planning.

Exploiting the ephemeral quality of writing is often a matter of exploiting chaos and incoherence. Often I find I cannot work out what I am trying to say unless I am extremely disorganized, frag-

mented, and associative, and let myself go down contrary paths to see where they lead. (Note that what one is *trying to say* is more than what one *has in mind*—see Perl on "felt sense" in "Understanding Composing.") I can't be that incoherent when I start off trying to write it right. I can't even be that incoherent in speech. My listeners are too impatient for sense, for my main point. (Now I know why I often close my eyes when talking about something difficult: it is an instinctive attempt to blot out the audience and their implicit demand that I be clear and come to the point.) So when trying to write it right, and even in speaking, I must usually settle for the short run of *some* coherence—making *some* sense—and abandon the thread (only it's not really a thread because it's so broken) of the long-run, incipient, more complex meaning which has been tickling the back of my mind. But when I write in the ephemeral and fully exploratory mode for myself alone, I can usually find that meaning by inviting myself to wander around it and finally stumble into it. Thus whereas the commonsense view is that planning is more appropriate to writing than to speaking, the opposite is also true: we badly need arenas for *nonplanning* in our discourse, and speech is too constricting. For nonplanning we need private writing.

We think of the mind's natural capacity for chaos and disorganization as the *problem* in writing—and before we finish any piece of indelible public writing, of course, that incoherence must be overcome. But what a relief it is to realize that this capacity for ephemeral incoherence is valuable and can be harnessed for insight and growth. The most precious thing in this kind of writing is to find one contradicting oneself. It guarantees that there will be some movement and growth in one's thinking; the writing will not just be a record of past thoughts or prejudices. (Good teachers, in commenting on student papers, have learned to see contradictions in the text as positive opportunities for mental action and growth, not just as problems.)

But even when we have the safety of knowing that our words are private and ephemeral and that we will revise them into coherence, we often feel

there is something dangerous about letting ourselves write down what is wrong or doubtful or un-
gainly, or even just something we are not sure we
believe. To do so seems to violate a taboo that derives from a magical sense that writing is indelible
even if no one else ever sees the words. We stop
and correct our words or crumple up the sheet because it feels as though if we leave the wrong words
there, they will somehow pollute us. Words on paper will "take"—debilitate the mind. Yet we cannot
exploit the ephemerality of language unless we are
willing to take the risk.

But why not use the *mind* for all this ephemeral
work? Would God have given us a mind if he'd
wanted us to waste all this paper writing down
what's wrong or badly put? But that internal thinking process lacks a dimension which writing provides. When we just think inside our heads, the
cycle of language is incomplete; we are prey to obsession. The thoughts, sentences, images, or feelings that play in our heads continue to play round
and round. But when we write down those
thoughts or feelings, the sterile circle is often broken: they have a place on paper now; they evolve
into another thought or even fade away. Writing is a
way to get what is inside one's head outside, on paper, so there's room for more.[6] (Of course speaking
too can have this same function—"getting things
out"—but sometimes the presence of a listener is a
hindrance.)

I come here to what I most want to emphasize:
the *mentalities* related to speech and writing. Ong
and the others emphasize how the use of writing
enhances logical, abstract, and detached thinking.
True enough. But there is a very different kind of
good thinking which we can enhance by exploiting
the underside of writing as ephemeral. And like the
effect Ong speaks of, this kind of thinking is not
just an occasional way of considering things but a
pervasive mode of cognitive functioning. I'm talking about the mentality that gradually emerges
when we learn how to put down what's in mind
and invite that putting down to be *not* a committing ourself to it but the opposite, a letting go of the
burden of holding it in mind—a letting go of the
burden of having it shape our mind. Having let it

go, our mind can take on a different shape and go
on to pick up a different thought.

In this way writing can function as a prosthesis
for the mind—a surrogate mind instead of just a
mouthpiece for the mind. For the mind is a structure of meaning and so too is a piece of writing.
The mind, as a structure of meaning, can grow and
develop through stages and so too can a piece of
writing. Thus writing provides us with two organisms for thinking instead of just one, two containers instead of just one; the thoughts can go back
and forth, richen and grow. We think of writing as
deriving meaning from the mind that produces it,
but when all goes well the *mind* derives meaning
from the text it produces. (Organization, or meaning, or negative entropy, can flow in both directions.)

I don't mean to sound too mysterious here. I am
just talking about the common phenomenon of
people's ideas developing and changing as a result
of their thinking. It often happens as people live
and talk and write over months and years. But in
truth, people tend to stay stuck in their points of
view. They are prevented from growing until they
get out of or move past the structure of meaning
that *is* their mind. Ong might say that indelible,
careful writing enhances such growth. Yes, that's
true when all goes well. But the crucial mental
event in growth is often the *abandonment* of a position we hold. Ephemeral writing is usually better
than careful writing at helping us abandon what we
start out thinking. (See Elbow, *Teachers,* Appendix
essay.)

Thus the potentiality in writing that I want to
highlight here does not just involve generative
techniques for getting first drafts written quicker,
but rather a genuine change in mentality or consciousness. The original development of writing
long ago permitted a new mentality that fostered
thinking that was more careful, detached, and logical. But along with it and the indelibility that
makes writing valuable came also a mentality that
tends to lock us into our views once we have carefully worked them out in writing. In contrast, the
cultivation of writing as ephemeral fosters the *opposite* mentality whereby we use discourse (and writ-

ing in particular) not so much to express what we think but rather to develop and transform it.

Before going on to Section III, I should emphasize that the opposite claims in the first two sections—that writing is both *more* and also *less* indelible than speech—do not really undercut each other. My celebration of writing as ephemeral in no way diminishes the fact that writing is also the best medium for being careful, for getting things right, for "quality." I am unrepentant about insisting that we can have it both ways—if we learn how.

We need writing to help domesticate our minds (the title of Goody's book about the development of literacy is *The Domestication of the Savage Mind*), but we also need writing as a way to unleash some cognitive savagery—which is often lacking in a "literate" world too often lulled into thinking that picking up a pencil means planning and trying to get things right. And speech, being a social medium, seldom leads us to the conceptual wilderness we sometimes need.

For not only is there no theoretical contradiction between the two functions of writing, it turns out that they enhance or reinforce each other. People can be *more* careful and get their final drafts *righter* when they spend some of their time unhooking themselves from the demands of audience and inviting themselves to get it wrong. And contrarily, people can be more fruitful in the mentality of nonsteering when they know they will turn around and shift consciousness—impose care and control and try for indelibility—before their text goes to the real audience.

III. WRITING AS SIMILAR TO SPEECH

Having indicated two ways in which speech and writing are *different* or *opposite* from each other, finally I want to argue how they are or can be essentially similar. I will proceed by focusing on a series of features characteristic of speech, and argue in each case why we should seek to foster them in writing.

To exploit the speech-like qualities of writing as we teach is a way of teaching to strength: capitalizing on the oral language skills students already possess and helping students apply those skills immediately and effortlessly to writing—a way of helping with the crucial process Ong calls the "internalization of the technology of writing."

(1) In informal speech situations we can utter our words spontaneously—comfortably, naturally, unselfconsciously—with full attention on our meaning and no attention on how we actually *form* the signs or symbols that convey our meaning. We can come close to achieving this situation in writing through the use of "spontaneous writing" or "freewriting": writing in which we put down whatever words come to mind—without regard to the conventions of forming words and without regard to the quality of the writing. We don't give the writing to an audience—or if we do, the audience merely "listens" to it for the meaning and doesn't respond (see Elbow, *Power*, 13–19). The work of Graves and Calkins shows how much we have tended to overestimate the amount of special knowledge or control of the medium people need for fluent and comfortable writing.

Speech is usually social and communal, writing solitary. But we can make writing communal too by having people write together and to each other in ways that are worth spelling out in more detail below.[7]

(2) Speech usually responds to a particular occasion and fits a particular context. It's not usually meant to last or be recorded—it's for a particular audience which is right there when the discourse is uttered and hears it right away. We can make all this happen in writing if we have students write in class or in small groups—particularly if they write about some issue or situation in which they are involved—and have them immediately share with each other what they write. The audience is right there and known; the writing is part of the context and the interaction of a particular group on a particular day. In speech, when something isn't clear, the audience asks for clarification right away. We can invite this naturally to happen in response to writing.

(3) In speech, the response—immediate, of course—is usually a *reply* to *what* has been said, not

an *evaluative comment* on *how* it was said. And the reply is almost invariably an invitation to the speaker to reply to the reply. We can make this happen too in our teaching (though students often need coaching to get out of the assumption that the only way to respond to a text is to criticize it).

For of course the point of speech is often not to be a final or definitive statement but rather to keep the discourse going and produce more discourse in response—to sustain an ongoing dialogue or discussion. We can easily give writing this quality too by making our course a forum for constant writing-in-response-to-each-other's-writing, that is, by stressing the ways in which writing naturally functions as an invitation to future writing or a reply to previous writing—which is how most writing in the world· actually occurs. Paradoxically, it turns out that if we invite much of the writing in a course to be more temporary and speech-like (that is, if we relax some of the pretense of chirographic, i.e., formal, definitiveness), students often manage to achieve *higher* levels of text-like definitiveness or indelibility on the fewer pieces where we stress revision and transcendence of local context.

For obviously I am not arguing that we should exploit similarities to speech in *all* the writing we ask of students. Many of our assignments should stress indelibility—stress the need for tight, coherent, final drafts which are statements that could survive outside the context of local author and local audience. We can decide on how much writing to treat in one mode or the other depending on the students we are teaching. For example, if the course is for weak students who are scared or uncomfortable in their writing, I would go quite far in exploiting speech similarities.

Thus the teaching practices I have just described *could* be called condescending strategies: ways to manage the writing context so as to *relax* temporarily some of the inherent difficulties in writing as a medium.[8] But I wish to go on now to stress how writing of the very highest quality—writing as good as any of us could possibly hope to achieve—not only can but should have many of the essential qualities somewhat misguidedly labelled "inherent in speech."

(4) The best writing has *voice*: the life and rhythms of speech. Unless we actively train our students to *speak onto paper,* they will write the kind of dead, limp, nominalized prose we hate—or *say* we hate. We see the difference most clearly in extreme cases: experienced teachers learn that when they get a student who writes prose that is so tied in knots that it is impenetrable they need only ask the student to *say* what she was getting at and the student will almost invariably speak the thought in syntax which is perfectly clear and lively, even if sometimes inelegantly colloquial. If the student had known enough to "speak the thought onto paper" and then simply cleaned up the syntax, the writing would have been much better than her best "essay writing."

(5) Excellent writing conveys some kind of involvement with the audience (though sometimes a quiet non-obtrusive involvement). This audience involvement is most characteristic of oral discourse. The best writing has just this quality of being somehow a piece of two-way communication, not one-way—of seeming to be an invitation to the audience to respond, or even seeming to be a reply to what the audience had earlier thought or said. This ability to connect with the audience and take its needs into account is *not* lacking in most students—contrary to much recent received opinion. Students use this social skill quite spontaneously and well in much of their speech to a present audience, but they naturally enough neglect to use it in much of their writing since the audience is less clear to them. We can easily help students transfer to writing their skill in connecting with an audience by having them write more often in a local context to a limited and physically present audience (as when they talk).

I am speaking here to what I see as a growing misconception about the inability of adolescents to "decenter": a dangerous tendency to make snap judgments about the level of a student's cognitive development on the basis of only a text or two—texts which are anything but accurate embodiments of how the student's mind really operates. Teachers and researchers sometimes describe the weakness of certain student writing as stemming from an inability to move past oral language strategies and a dependence on local audience and context.[9] But in reality the weakness of those pieces of writing should often be given the *opposite* diagnosis: the student has drifted off into writing to *no one in particular.* Often the student need only be encouraged to use *more* of the strategies of oral discourse and the discourse snaps back into good focus, and along with it usually comes much more clarity and even better thinking.

(6) Commentators like to distinguish speech from writing by saying that speech is reticent: it invites listeners to fill in meanings from their involvement in the context and their knowledge of the speaker. Good writing, on the other hand (so this story goes), must make all the meanings explicit, must "lexicalize" or "decontextualize" all the meanings, and not require readers to fill in. But here too, this talk about the inherent nature of speech and writing is misguided. It is precisely a quality that distinguishes certain kinds of good writing that it makes readers *contribute to* or *participate in* the meanings, not just sit back and receive meanings that are entirely spelled out.

Deborah Tannen, a speech researcher, illuminates this confusion ("Oral and Literate," 89):

> If one thinks at first that written and spoken language are very different, one may think as well that written literature—short stories, poems, and novels—are the most different from casual conversation of all. Quite the contrary, imaginative literature has more in common with spontaneous conversation than with the typical written genre, expository prose.

> If expository prose is minimally contextualized—that is, the writer demands the least from the reader in terms of filling in background information and crucial premises—imaginative literature is maximally contextualized. The best work of art is the one that suggests the most to the reader with the fewest words. . . . The goal of creative writers is to encourage their readers to fill in as much as possible. The more the readers supply, the more they will believe and care about the message in the work.

Although we can *maximize* the unstated only in imaginative literature, nevertheless, I believe it is unhelpful to go along with Tannen's oversimple contrast between imaginative and expository writing. Surely it is the mark of really good essays or expository writing, too, that they bring the reader *in* and get him or her to fill in and participate in the meanings, and thereby make those written meanings seem more real and believable. (I think of the expository writing of writers like Wayne Booth, Stephen Gould, or Lewis Thomas.) And even to the degree that imaginative literature is different from expository prose, we must not run away from it as a model for what gives goodness to good expository prose.

If we accept uncritically the assumption that "cognitive development" or "psychological growth" consists of movement from concrete "oral" modes to abstract "literate" modes, we are left with the implication that most of the imaginative literature we study is at a lower developmental and cognitive level than most of the expository writing turned in by students. I'm frightened at the tendency to label students cognitively retarded who tend to exploit those oral or concrete strategies that characterize so much good literature, namely narration, description, invested detail, and expression of feeling. I'm not trying to deny the burden of Piaget, Bruner, etc., etc., namely, that it is an important and necessary struggle to learn abstract reasoning, nor to deny that teaching it is *part* of our job as teachers of writing. Again I claim both positions. But there is danger in *over*emphasizing writing as abstract and non-speech-like. (Even Bruner makes a similar warning in his recent work "Language, Mind.")

(7) Commentators on orality and literacy tend to stress how speech works in time and writing in space. Ong is eloquent on the evanescence of speech because it exists only as sound and thus is lost in the unstoppable flow of time. In speech, past and future words *do not exist* (as they would do if they were part of a text): the only thing that exists is that fleeting present syllable that pauses on the tongue in its journey to disappearance. Speech and oral cultures are associated with narration—which takes time as its medium. Writing and literate

cultures are associated with logic—which exists outside of time.

This is an important distinction and people like Ong are right to exploit its remarkably wide ramifications, but there is a danger here, too. In truth, writing is also essentially time-bound. Readers are immersed in time as they read just as listeners are when they hear. We cannot take in a text all at once as we can a picture or a diagram. We see only a few written words at a time. It is true that if we pause in our reading, we can *in a sense* step outside the flow of time and look back to earlier sections of the text, or look forward to later sections; I don't mean to underestimate the enormous contrast here with speech where such "back-" or "forward-scanning" is impossible. Nevertheless the essential process of reading a text is more like listening than looking: the essential phenomenology involves being trapped in time and thus unable to take in more than a few words at a time.

This point is not just theoretical. The problem with much poor or needlessly difficult writing is the way it pretends to exist as it were in space rather than in time. Such writing is hard to read because it demands that we have access all at once to the many elements that the writer struggled to get into the text. The writer forces us repeatedly to stop and work at finding explanations or definitions or connections which he *gave,* it is true, or *will* give in a few pages, but which he does not bring to our minds now when we need them. (It often feels to the writer as though he's *already* given us the material we need when we are reading page two—even though we don't get it till page six—because he's *already* written page six when he rewrites page two.) Poor writers often assume that because they are making a document rather than a talk, they are *giving us a thing in space* rather than *leading us on a journey through time,* and that therefore they can pretend that we can "look at the whole thing."[10]

One of the marks of good writers, on the other hand, is their recognition that readers, like listeners, are indeed trapped in the flow of time and can take in only a few words at a time. Good writers take this as an opportunity, not just a problem. The drama of movement through time can be embodied in thinking and exposition as naturally as in stories. And the ability to engage the reader's time sense is not a matter of developing some wholly new skill or strategy, it is a matter of developing for writing that time-bound faculty we've all used in all speaking.

(8) By reflecting on how writing, though apparently existing in space, is essentially speech-like in that it works on readers in the dimension of time, we can throw important light on the peculiar *difficulties of organizing or structuring a piece of writing.*

In thinking about organization in writing we are tempted to use models from the spatial realm. Indeed our very conception of organization or structure tends to be spatial. Our *sense,* then, of what it means to be well organized or well structured tends to involve those features which give coherence to space—features such as neatness, symmetry, and non-redundancy. Giving good organization to something in time, however, is a different business because it means giving organization or structure to something of which we can grasp only one tiny fraction at any moment.

A thought experiment. Imagine a large painting or photograph that looks well organized. Imagine next an ant crawling along its surface. How would we have to modify that picture to make it "well organized" for the ant? Since he cannot see the picture all at once, we would have to embed some tiny, simplified reductions or capsule "overviews" of the whole picture at periodic points in his path—especially where he starts and finishes. Otherwise he could never make sense of the barrage of close-up details he gets as he crawls along; he would have no overall "big picture" or gestalt into which to integrate these details. But if we should make such modifications we would make the picture much "messier" from a visual point of view.

The plight of our ant points to the interesting work in composition theory and cognitive science about "chunking" and short- and long-term memory and the magic number seven. (In effect, the ant needs the visual information "chunked" for him.) Because language is time-bound, its meanings cannot actually enter our minds through our eyes—its meanings must detour through memory. If eyes were enough, "chunking" would be much easier, for as gestalt psychology has shown, vision as a cognitive process involves the making of gestalts, i.e., automatic chunking. (See G. A. Miller's classic essay, "The Magical Number Seven.")

Thus the test of good organization in writing—as in speech—is not whether the text *looks* neat when diagrammed in an outline or some other visual scheme, but whether it produces an *experience* of structure and coherence for the audience in time. But how is this effect achieved? The issue is complex, but I would suggest that certain common features of speech help discourse function as coherent in time—and thus are helpful for creating the sense of good structure in a text. We are more likely in speaking than in writing to give the quick forward- and backward-looking structural aids that readers need when they are trapped in the flow of time. When we are speaking we are less likely to put our heads down and forget about the structural needs of our audience because our audience is right there before us.

Discourse is sometimes given coherence by the use of cyclical or spiral patterns characteristic of speech—or a kind of wave-like repetition in which new material is introduced only after some allusion (however brief) to the past material needed for understanding the new material. This is the archetypal back-and-forth movement of waves on a beach which Auerbach (*Mimesis*) relates to the rhythm of Old Testament poetry—or the homely "mowing long grass" pattern of movement where repeatedly you push the mower forward four feet and back two feet, so each piece of ground is covered twice: there is always a quick summary before going forward.[11]

Oddly enough, *lists* (that feature of oral and epic poetry) are remarkably effective ways to give structure to discourse in time. As researchers into document design have noticed, written texts are often much more coherent to readers when a connected chain of statements is reshaped into a main statement and a *list* of supporting or following items. Lists have an interesting cognitive characteristic: as we take in each item we tacitly rehearse our sense of what that item is an instance *of*. Thus, a list is a

way of increasing unity and also giving readers a re-iterated sense of the main point without having to repeat it explicitly for them.

Discourse is sometimes given coherence in time by the use of recurring phrases, metaphors, images, or resonant examples (not merely decorative or illustrative but structural) which "chunk" or function as micro-summaries. Such recurring miniature units are characteristic of oral discourse (and music). A phrase can continue to ring in the reader's ear or an image continue to appear in the mind's eye while trapped in the underbrush of prose, and thus give structure or coherence to an experience in time.

The big picture problem is really a problem of how to get readers to hold in mind a *pattern* or *relationship* among elements while having to focus attention on only one of those elements. Imagine an essay with three major points or sections (as with the present essay). If we think of it "structurally" or "from above"—that is, spatially—we see three emphases or focuses of attention, as so many paintings and photographs are organized triangularly. But what holds the picture together is the fact that in the realm of vision we can focus on one of the three main areas yet simultaneously retain our view of the other two and our sense of how they relate to the one we are looking at. With an essay, on the other hand, we can read *only* one small part at a time, and so it is hard to experience the *relationship* or *interaction* of the three parts.

Thus the problem of structure in a temporal medium is really the problem of how to *bind time*. Whereas symmetry and pattern bind space (and also bind smaller units of time—in the form of rhythm), they don't manage very well to hold larger units of time together. What binds larger units of time? Usually it is the experience of anticipation or tension which then builds to some resolution or satisfaction. In well-structured discourse, music, and films (temporal media) we almost invariably see a pattern of alternating dissonance-and-consonance or itching-and-scratching. Narrative is probably the most common and natural way to set up a structure of anticipation and resolution in discourse.

But how do we bind time with patterns of anticipation and resolution in *essays or expositiory writing?*[12] Here the tension or itch that binds the words is almost always the experience of some *problem* or *uncertainty,* that is somehow conveyed to the reader. Unless there is a felt question—a tension, a palpable itch—the time remains unbound. The most common reason why weak essays don't hang together is that the writing is all statement, all consonance, all answer: the reader is not made to experience any cognitive dissonance to serve as a "net" or "set" to catch all these statements or answers. Without an itch or a sense of felt problem, nothing holds the reader's experience together—however well the text itself might summarize the parts. (This is a common problem in the essays of students since they so often suppose that essays are only for telling, not for wondering.) I wish workers on coherence and cohesion would focus more on the ways in which writers convey a sense of felt problem or itch. Surely that does more to hold texts together than repeated words or phrases.

If it seems as though I'm trying to fiddle with our sense of structure in texts, I must plead guilty. For I think that we often call texts well structured when they are merely "neat" or symmetrical, but really don't *hold* together: we "look through" our temporal experience of the text to a projected outline of the meanings. Particularly as academics, we are trained to read this way. Other readers—"popular" or informal readers—often do not notice that atemporal neatness and so feel such texts as incoherent. Yet on the other hand such readers are sometimes *satisfied* with the structure of texts that are less "neat"—we would call them sprawling—because the writer has been able to string those sprawling elements together experientially in time.

Have I gone too far? Obviously this is a tangled matter. For we yearn for neatness, economy, and spatial structure in our texts: poor writing is often poor because of the lack of these features. The problems of structure in writing are subtly difficult. Because of the confusion introduced into our very notion of structure by the pervasive metaphor of space, I suspect that we are still waiting for the help we need in showing us simple and valid models of

good structure in time. If we want to explain the structure of well-ordered expository writing, we probably would do well to look to studies of the structure of music and film and poetry. (See, for example, Meyer and Zuckerkandl on music.)

Yet we mustn't plead ignorance too fast. As speakers, everyone has had extensive experience organizing discourse in time to make it coherent to listeners. (I admit that coherent speech is rare—but not as rare as coherent writing. And it is true that we speak in dialogue more often than in monologue—but we have had more experience with monologue than with writing.) Thus, continual experience with speaking of all sorts—even experience in not being understood and then clarifying our meaning—has built up for all speakers extensive intuitive skill at organizing discourse in time.

Thus we do well to exploit these intuitive, time-oriented speech skills when we try to organize our writing (particularly expository or conceptual writing where organizational problems are most difficult). When we tell ourselves to "be careful about organization" or to "give good structure" to our text, we tend to think in terms of building blocks laid out in space, and thus we often fail to give our readers an experience of coherence and clarity (however neatly we pattern our blocks). If, on the other hand, we think of our structural problem as that of trying to speak a long monologue so it is coherent to listeners in time, we are more likely to invoke crucial temporal organizational skills at two levels:

(a) In the large, overall structure of our text, we are more likely to "tell the story" as it were of our thinking. This doesn't usually mean turning it into actual narrative (although that needn't be ruled out as the most natural and effective structure for thinking), but rather saying, "Where does this thinking *start?* Where is it *going?* And where is it trying to *get to?*" Our attempt to speak a monologue will get us to find the larger *movement* of thought and help us intuitively to appeal to the faculty of hearing and memory, not visual schematics.

(b) In the smaller structures of our text, we are even more likely to appeal directly to hearing if we think of ourselves as speaking a monologue, and this will help us naturally chunk shorter sequences of information or thinking (from one to several paragraphs) into "heard" units which will cohere and thus be more easily understood and remembered.

So here again my point is that in order to make writing good we should try to make it like speech. When we structure speech we naturally exploit our time sense, our hearing, and our memory; and we naturally build in patterns of tension and resolution, not just arrangement of parts.

(9) A final reason why writing needs to be like speech. Perhaps it is fanciful to talk of speech having a magic that writing lacks—call it presence, voice, or *pneuma*—but the truth is that we tend to experience meaning somehow more *in* spoken words than written ones. (Socrates and Husserl make this point: See Searle, "The Word Turned Upside Down.")

This vividness of speech is illustrated in academic conferences where people speak written papers out loud. Because we are listening to *writing* presented orally, we may notice in a curiously striking way how it seldom seems as semantically "inhabited" or "presenced" as speech.

Of course most of us can convey *more* meaning by reading a written essay out loud than by trying to give a speech from notes—more precisely, clearly, and quickly too. Yet the moment-to-moment language of a recited essay (even if more precise) is almost invariably less "full of meaning" than the language of our actual live speech (even if that speech has some stumbling and lack of precision). In short, writing seems to permit us to get *more* meaning into words (get more said more quickly), but speech helps get our meanings integrated more *into* our words.

But why should it be that we seem to experience the meaning more in spoken words than written words? Is it just because spoken words are *performed* for us and so we get all those extra cues from seeing the speaker, hearing how she speaks—all those rhythms and tonalities? That is important, but there's something else that goes deeper: in listening to speech we are hearing mental activity going on—live; in reading a text we are only encountering the record of completed mental events. It's not that the audience has to *receive* the words while the mental activity is going on, but that the language has to be *created* while the mental activity is going on: the language must embody or grow out of live mental events. The important simultaneity is not between meaning-making and hearing, but between meaning-making and the production or emergence of language. The crucial question for determining whether discourse achieves "presence" is whether the words produced are *an expression of something going on* or *a record of something having gone on.*

To speak is (usually) to give spontaneous verbal substance to mental events occurring right at that moment in the mind. Even when we are stuck or tongue-tied we seldom remain silent for long: Billy Budd is the exception. Usually we say something about our inability to figure out what to say. To write, however, is usually to *rehearse* mental events inside our heads before putting them down. (Someone's speech usually sounds peculiar if he rehearses his words in his head before speaking them.)

My hypothesis, then, is that when people produce language *as* they are engaged in the mental event it expresses, they produce language with particular features—features which make an audience feel the meanings very much *in* those words. Here then is an important research agenda for discourse analysis: what are the language features that correlate with what people experience as the semantic liveness of speech? (See Halpern, "Differences," for a start at this job.)

Such research would have very practical benefits for writing theory, since of course writing *can* be as alive as speech. What characterizes much excellent writing is precisely this special quality of lively or heightened semantic presence. It's as though the writer's mental activity is somehow there in the words on the page—as though the silent words are somehow alive with her meaning.

When a writer is particularly fluent, she has the gift of doing less internal rehearsal. The acts of figuring out what she wants to say, finding the words, and putting them down somehow coalesce into one act—into that integrative meaning-making/language-finding act which is characteristic of speech. But even beginners (or writing teachers) can achieve this liveliness and presence when they engage in freewriting or spontaneous writing. It is this semantic presence which often makes freewriting seem peculiarly lively to read. One of the best directions for coaching freewriting is to tell oneself or one's students to "talk onto the paper."

Of course we cannot usually produce a carefully-pondered and well-ordered piece of writing by talking onto paper. In any piece of writing that has been a struggle to produce, there is often a certain smell of stale sweat. And freewriting or spontaneous speech may be careless or shallow (the meaning is *in* the words but the *amount* of meaning is very small). But if we learn to talk onto paper and exploit the speech-like quality possible in writing, we can have the experience of writing words with presence, and thereby learn what such writing *feels* like—in the fingers, in the mouth, and in the ear. This experience increases our chances of getting desirable speech qualities into the writing we revise and think through more carefully.

IV. CONCLUSION

I have argued three contrary claims: writing is essentially unlike speech because it is more indelible; writing is essentially unlike speech because it is more ephemeral; and writing is essentially *like* speech. My goal is to stop people from talking so much about the inherent nature of these media and start them talking more about the different ways we can *use* them. In particular I seek to celebrate the flexibility of writing as a medium, and to show that we need to develop more control over ourselves as we write so that we can *manage* our writing process more judiciously and flexibly. Let me end with three images for the writer (one to match each claim)—and with each image a mentality.

First, I see the writer clenched over her text, writing very slowly—indeed pondering more than writing—trying to achieve something permanent and definitive: questioning everything, first in her mind before she writes the phrase, then after she sees it on paper. She is intensely self-critical, she tries to see every potential flaw—even the flaws that some unknown future reader might find who is reading in an entirely different context from that of her present audience. She is using the "new" technology of indelible writing that Ong and others speak of and thereby enhancing her capacity for careful abstract thinking by learning to separate the knower from the known. She is learning the mentality of detachment.

Second, I see the writer in a fine frenzy: scribbling fast, caught up in her words, in the grip of language and creation. She is writing late at night—not because of a deadline but because the words have taken over: she wants to go to bed but too much is going on for her to stop. She has learned to relinquish some control. She has also learned to let herself write things she would never show to anyone—at first anyway. By exploiting the ephemeral underside of writing, she learns to promote the mentality of wildness with words—the mentality of discourse as play. And perhaps most important, she has learned to promote the mentality of involvement in her words rather than of detachment or separation. But because that involvement is so totally *of the moment,* she knows she may well write a refutation tomorrow night of what she is writing tonight. She writes to explore and develop her ideas, not just express them.

Third, I see the writer at her desk conjuring up her audience before her in her mind's eye as she writes. She is looking *at* them, speaking *to* them—more aware of the sound of her spoken words in her ear than the sight of her written words on paper. She is the writer as raconteur, the writer with the gift of gab. She is not "composing" a text or "constructing" a document in space—she is "uttering" discourse in time; she is not "giving things" to her readers, she is leading readers on a mental journey. She is a bit of a dramatist, using discourse as a way to *do* things to people. She is involved with her discourse through being involved with her audience. Often her audience is a genuine community and her writing grows out of her sense of membership in it.

Is one of these modes of writing better? I don't believe so. Yet in the end I think there *is* a single best way to write: to move back and forth among them. And I believe there is a particular mentality which the technology of writing is peculiarly suited to enhance (as speech is not), namely *the play of mentalities.* We can learn to *be* all three writers imaged above. Writing can show us how to move back and forth between cognitive processes and mentalities which at first may seem contradictory, but which if exploited will heighten and reinforce each other.

Notes

1. For quotations and references I give an abbreviated title and page number for works listed in the bibliography at the end. I am grateful for feedback by colleagues here at Stony Brook, the Breadloaf School of English, and the Penn State Conference on Rhetoric and Composition—where I read earlier drafts of this paper.

2. See Walter Ong, *Orality and Literacy,* 1982, for a powerful summary of his extensive work in this area and his wide-ranging citations to others working in it. For welcome warnings about stereotyping the mentalities associated with orality and literacy, see Cooper and Odell, "Sound in Composing"; Harste, "Assumptions"; Scribner and Cole, *Psychology of Literacy;* Heath, "Oral and Literate Traditions"; and Robinson, "Literacy." A number of the essays in Kroll and Vann, *Exploring Speaking-Writing Relationships,* e.g. O'Keefe, also warn against oversimplifying the contrast between speech and writing as media.

3. Ong focuses on the development of writing, but it is important to stand back and take a longer perspective. That is, the biggest boost to careful thinking came earlier with the birth of *language itself*—original spoken language. "As long as we carry intuitive belief without a symbolic representation, we are one with it and cannot criticize it. But once we have formulated it, we can look at it objectively and learn from it, even from its rejection." (Karl Popper, cited in Kroll and Vann, *Exploring Speaking-Writing Relationships,* p. 151.) See also Vygotsky, *Thought and Language,* on the effect of language itself as a "second signalling system."

4. It may be, however, that many of the effects we are tempted to ascribe to literacy are really effects of schooling. See Gere, "Cultural Perspectives"; Olson, "Languages of Instruction"; and Scribner and Cole, *Psychology of Literacy.*

5. Literate people like to complain that the telephone and other electronic media have almost destroyed writing by permitting people to do most of their business orally and refrain from writing unless there is some pressing need for "hard" (i.e. indelible) copy. But I suspect that more people write more now than ever before. Engineers are estimated to spend from a quarter to a third of their working time involved in some kind of writing. See Faigley et al, "Writing After College." The spread of radios and phonographs raised fears that people would no longer go to concerts or play musical instruments: the opposite has occurred.

6. This somatic perspective heightens the paradoxes. Writing is the external, indelible medium—yet is the most easily changed. Thinking is the most internal and changeable medium—yet from another point of view it is the most intractable to change: try removing or changing a thought you don't like. Speech, chameleon-like, is in the middle.

7. In enumerating these characteristics of speech I am drawing on Tannen, "Oral and Literate"; see also Emig, "Writing as a Mode of Learning." In describing some ways to provide speech conditions in a writing class, I am drawing on a discussion with members of the fall 1983 teaching practicum at Stony Brook—for whose help I am grateful.

8. I don't really grant this point, however. Though these procedures are particularly suitable for basic students, they are also the kinds of writing that occur in many workplace settings (for example with a research team, an investigative committee, or any other working group whose members communicate to each other in letters, queries, and rough position papers). Sometimes people who talk about the "inherent difference" between speaking and writing get carried away and ignore the brute fact that much of the writing in the world—perhaps even most of it—takes place in a strongly social or communal context: the writing is in response to an earlier discourse and gives rise to subsequent discourse and is asked for and read by particular people whom the writer knows—people who share a common context and set of assumptions with the writer.

9. See Lunsford, "Cognitive Development," and Shaughnessy, *Errors.* Instead of just talking about "oral interference" as a problem, I would also use the term in the positive sense: oral skills and habits can "run interference" for writing—knocking down some of the obstacles that make writing difficult.

10. This is particularly a problem in certain technical documents and reports, and it is interesting to see how canny readers of such genres have learned to accommodate to

the bad treatment they receive: they "read" such documents as though they were looking at a diagram rather than reading a text—namely, by quickly scanning through it, perhaps more than once, trying to develop an overview and a sense of perspective which they know the writer does not provide. Being trained and consenting to read in this way, in a sense they perpetuate the problem.

11. Theorists of style in general and of cohesion and coherence in particular talk about this phenomenon at the sentence or syntactic level (see Joseph Williams, *Style*), but I'm not sure that there's enough recognition of it at the level of the whole. See, however, the reference to beginning work on the "macrotheme-rheme" problem in Witte and Faigley's "Coherence, Cohesion."

12. We should recognize how often good essays or books are actually held together by being stories: "here is the story of my thinking," or "here is a ride on the train of my thought," or even just, "this and this and this, and here is the moral."

Works Cited

Note: For two rich bibliographies on the relation between speech and writing, see the Kroll and Vann volume noted below, and the annotated bibliography by Sarah Liggett in the recent *CCC*: 35 (October, 1984), 334–44.

Auerbach, Erich. *Mimesis*. Tr. W. Traske. Berne, 1946.

Barthes, Roland. "Death of the Author." In *Image, Music, Text*. New York: Hill and Wang, 1977.

Bruner, Jerome. *Studies in Cognitive Growth*. Cambridge, MA: Harvard University Press, 1966.

———. "Language, Mind, and Reading." In *Awakening Literacy*. Ed. Hillel Goelman, Antoinette Obeng, and Frank Smith. Exeter, NH: Heineman Educational Books, 1984.

Calkins, Lucy. *Lessons from a Child on the Teaching and Learning of Writing*. Exeter, NH: Heinemann Educational Books, 1983.

Cooper, Charles, and Lee Odell. "Considerations of Sound in the Composing Process of Published Writers." *RTE,* 10 (Fall, 1976), 103–115.

Elbow, Peter. *Writing Without Teachers*. New York: Oxford University Press, 1973.

——— *Writing With Power*. New York: Oxford University Press, 1981.

Emig, Janet. "Writing as a Mode of Learning." *CCC,* 28 (May, 1977), 122–128. Reprinted in *The Writing Teacher's Sourcebook*. Ed. Gary Tate and Edward P. J. Corbett. New York: Oxford University Press, 1981.

Faigley, L., et al. "Writing After College: A Stratified Survey of the Writing of College-Trained People," Writing Program Assessment Technical Report No. 1, University of Texas, Austin, 1981.

Gere, Anne Ruggles. "A Cultural Perspective on Talking and Writing." In Kroll and Vann, *Exploring Speaking-Writing Relationships*.

Goody, Jack. *The Domestication of the Savage Mind*. Cambridge, England: Cambridge University Press, 1977.

Graves, Donald. *Writing: Teachers and Children at Work*. Exeter, NH: Heinemann Educational Books, 1983.

Halpern, Jeanne, "Differences Between Speaking and Writing and Their Implications for Teaching," *CCC,* 35 (October, 1984), 345–357.

Harste, Jerome C., Virginia A. Woodward, Carolyn L. Burke, "Examining our Assumptions: A Transactional View of Literacy and Learning," *RTE,* 18 (February, 1984), 84–108.

Havelock, Eric A. *Preface to Plato*. Cambridge, MA: Belknap Press of Harvard University Press, 1963.

Heath, Shirley Brice. "Oral and Literate Traditions." *International Social Science Journal,* 36 (1984), 41–57.

Kroll, Barry M., and Roberta J. Vann (ed.). *Exploring Speaking-Writing Relationships*. Urbana, IL: National Council of Teachers of English, 1981.

Lunsford, Andrea. "Cognitive Development and the Basic Writer." *CE,* 41 (September, 1979), 38–46.

Meyer, Leonard B. *Emotion and Meaning in Music*. Chicago: University of Chicago Press, 1956.

Miller, George. "The Magical Number Seven Plus or Minus Two: Some Limits on our Capacity for Processing Information." *Psychological Review,* 63 (March, 1956), 81–97.

Olson, D. R. "The Languages of Instruction: The Literate Bias of Schooling." In *Schooling and the Acquisition of Knowledge*. Ed. R. C. Anderson, R. J. Siro, and W. E. Montague. Hillsdale, NJ: Lawrence Erlbaum, 1977.

Ong, Walter J. *Orality and Literacy*. New York: Methuen, 1982.

Perl, Sondra. "Understanding Composing." *CCC,* 31 (December 1980), 363–369.

Robinson, Jay L. "The Users and Uses of Literacy." In *Literacy of Life: The Demand for Reading and Writing*. Ed. Richard W. Bailey and Robin Melanie Fosheim. New York: Modern Language Association, 1983.

Schafer, John C. "The Linguistic Analysis of Spoken and Written Texts." In Kroll and Vann, *Exploring Speaking-Writing Relationships*.

Scribner, Sylvia, and Michael Cole. *The Psychology of Literacy*. Cambridge, MA: Harvard University, Press, 1981.

———. "Unpackaging Literacy." In *Variations in Writing: Functional and Linguistic-Cultural Differences.* Ed. Marcia Farr Whiteman. Hillsdale, NJ: Lawrence Erlbaum Assocs., 1981, 71–87.

Searle, John. "The Word Turned Upside Down." *The New York Review of Books,* 27 October 1983, 74–79.

Shaughnessy, Mina P. *Errors and Expectations: A Guide for the Teacher of Basic Writing.* New York: Oxford University Press, 1977.

Tannen, Deborah. "Oral and Literate Strategies in Spoken and Written Discourse." In *Literacy for Life: The Demand for Reading and Writing.* Ed. Richard W. Bailey and Robin Melanie Fosheim. New York: Modern Language Association, 1983.

Vygotsky, Lev. *Thought and Language.* Cambridge, MA: MIT Press, 1962.

Williams, Joseph M. *Style: Ten Lessons in Clarity and Grace.* Glenview, IL: Scott Foresman and Co., 1981.

Williams, Joseph M., and Rosemary L. Hake. "Style and Its Consequences: Do as I Do, Not as I Say." *College English,* 43 (September, 1981), 433–451.

Witte, Stephen, and Lester Faigley. "Coherence, Cohesion, and Writing Quality." *CCC,* 32 (May, 1981), 189–204.

Zuckerkandl, Victor. *Sound and Symbol: Music and the External World.* New York: Pantheon Press, 1956, reprinted 1976.

Collaborative Learning and the "Conversation of Mankind"

Kenneth A. Bruffee very influential essay

Kenneth A. Bruffee, "Collaborative Learning and the 'Conversation of Mankind,'" College English, November 1984. Copyright 1984 by the National Council of Teachers of English. Reprinted with permission. The argument of this article is more fully developed in Collaborative Learning: Higher Education, Independence, and the Authority of Knowledge *(Johns Hopkins UP, 1993).*

There are some signs these days that collaborative learning is of increasing interest to English teachers.[1] Composition teachers seem to be exploring the concept actively. Two years ago the term appeared for the first time in the list of topics suggested by the Executive Committee of the Conference on College Composition and Communication for discussion at the CCCC annual convention. It was eighth or ninth on a list of ten items. Last year it appeared again, first on the list.

Teachers of literature have also begun to talk about collaborative learning, although not always by that name. It is viewed as a way of engaging students more deeply with the text and also as an aspect of professors' engagement with the professional community. At its 1978 convention the Modern Language Association scheduled a multi-session forum entitled "Presence, Knowledge, and Authority in the Teaching of Literature." One of the associated sessions, called "Negotiations of Literary Knowledge," included a discussion of the authority and structure (including the collaborative classroom structure) of "interpretive communities." At the 1983 MLA convention collaborative practices in reestablishing authority and value in literary studies were examined under such rubrics as "Talking to the Academic Community: Conferences as

Institutions" and "How Books 11 and 12 of *Paradise Lost* Got to Be Valuable" (changes in interpretive attitudes in the community of Miltonists).

In both these contexts collaborative learning is discussed sometimes as a process that constitutes fields or disciplines of study and sometimes as a pedagogical tool that "works" in teaching composition and literature. The former discussion, often highly theoretical, usually manages to keep at bay the more troublesome and problematic aspects of collaborative learning. The discussion of classroom practice is less fortunate. What emerges there is that many teachers are unsure about how to use collaborative learning and about when and where, appropriately, it should be used. Many are concerned also that when they try to use collaborative learning in what seem to be effective and appropriate ways, it sometimes quite simply fails.

I sympathize with these experiences. Much the same thing has happened to me. Sometimes collaborative learning works beyond my highest expectations. Sometimes it doesn't work at all. Recently, though, I think I have been more successful. The reason for that increased success seems to be that I know a little more now than I did in the past about the complex ideas that lie behind collaborative learning. This essay is frankly an attempt to encourage other teachers to try collaborative learning and to help them use collaborative learning appropriately and effectively. But it offers no recipes. It is written instead on the assumption that understanding both the history and the complex ideas that underlie collaborative learning can improve its practice and demonstrate its educational value.

The history of collaborative learning as I know it can be briefly sketched. Collaborative learning began to interest American college teachers widely only in the 1980s, but the term was coined and the basic idea first developed in the 1950s and 1960s by a group of British secondary school teachers and by a biologist studying British post-graduate education—specifically, medical education. I myself first encountered the term and some of the ideas implicit in it in Edwin Mason's still interesting but now somewhat dated polemic entitled *Collaborative Learning* (London: Ward Lock Educational Co., 1970), and in Charity James' *Young Lives at Stake: A Reappraisal of Secondary Schools* (London: Collins, 1968). Mason, James, and Leslie Smith, colleagues at Goldsmith's College, University of London, were committed during the Vietnam era to democratizing education and to eliminating from education what were perceived then as socially destructive authoritarian social forms. Collaborative learning as they thought of it emerged from this largely political, topical effort.

The collaborative forms that Mason and his colleagues proposed to establish in education had already been explored and their educational value affirmed, however, by the earlier findings of M. L. J. Abercrombie. Abercrombie's *Anatomy of Judgment* (Harmondsworth: Penguin, 1964) culminated ten years of research on the selection and training of medical students at University College, University of London. The result of her research was to suggest that diagnosis, the art of medical judgment and the key element in successful medical practice, is better learned in small groups of students arriving at diagnoses collaboratively than it is learned by students working individually. Abercrombie began her study by observing the scene that lay people think is most typical of medical education: the

group of medical students with a teaching physician gathered around a ward bed to diagnose a patient. She then made a seemingly slight but in outcome enormously important change in the way that scene is usually played out. Instead of asking each individual member of the group of students to diagnose the patient on his or her own, Abercrombie asked the whole group to examine the patient together, discuss the case as a group, and arrive at a consensus, a single diagnosis that they could all agree to. What she found was that students learning diagnosis this way acquired good medical judgment faster than individuals working alone (p. 19).

For American college teachers the roots of collaborative learning lie neither in radical politics nor in research. They lie in the nearly desperate response of harried colleges during the early 1970s to a pressing educational need. A decade ago, faculty and administrators in institutions throughout the country became aware that, increasingly, students entering college had difficulty doing as well in academic studies as their native ability suggested they should be able to do. Of course, some of these students were poorly prepared academically. Many more of them, however, had on paper excellent secondary preparation. The common denominator among both the poorly prepared and the seemingly well-prepared was that, for cultural reasons we may not yet fully understand, all these students seemed to have difficulty adapting to the traditional or "normal" conventions of the college classroom.

One symptom of the difficulty these students had adapting to college life and work was that many refused help when it was offered. The help colleges offered, in the main, were tutoring and counseling programs staffed by graduate students and other professionals. These programs failed because undergraduates refused to use them. Many solutions to this problem were suggested and tried, from mandated programs that forced students to accept help they evidently did not want, to sink-or-swim programs that assumed that students who needed help but didn't seek it out didn't belong in college anyway. One idea that seemed at the time among the most exotic and unlikely (that is, in the jargon of the 60s, among the most "radical") turned out in the event to work rather well. Taking hints about the social organization of learning given by John Bremer, Michael von Moschzisker, and others writing at that time about changes in primary and secondary education, some college faculty members guessed that students were refusing help because the kind of help provided seemed merely an extension of the work, the expectations, and above all the social structure of traditional classroom learning (*The School Without Walls* [New York: Holt, 1971], p. 7). It was traditional classroom learning that seemed to have left these students unprepared in the first place. What they needed, it seemed, was help that was not an extension of but an alternative to traditional classroom teaching.

To provide that alternative some colleges turned to peer tutoring. Through peer tutoring teachers could reach students by organizing them to teach each other. And peer tutoring, it turned out, was just one way of doing that, although perhaps the most readily institutionalized way. Collectively, peer tutoring and similar modes such as peer criticism and classroom group work could be sensibly classified under the convenient term provided by our colleagues in Britain: collaborative learning. What the term meant in practice was a form of indirect teaching in which the teacher sets the problem and organizes students to work it out collaboratively. For example, in one type of collaborative learning, peer criticism (also called peer evaluation), students learn to describe the organizational structure of a peer's paper, paraphrase it, and comment both on what seems well done and what the author might do to improve the work. The teacher then evaluates both the essay and the critical response. In another type of collaborative learning, classroom group work, students in small groups work toward a consensus in response to a task set by the teacher, for example, a question about a play, a poem, or another student's paper. What distinguished collaborative learning in each of its several types from traditional classroom practice was that it did not seem to change what people learned (a supposition that now seems questionable) so much as it changed the social context in which they learned it. Students' work tended to im-

prove when they got help from peers; peers offering help, furthermore, learned from the students they helped and from the activity of helping itself. Collaborative learning, it seemed, harnessed the powerful educative force of peer influence that had been—and largely still is—ignored and hence wasted by traditional forms of education.[2]

More recently, those of us actively interested in collaborative learning have begun to think further about this practical experience. Recent developments in philosophy seem to suggest a conceptual rationale for collaborative learning that yields some unexpected insights into pedagogical practice. A new conception of the nature of knowledge provides direction that we lacked earlier as we muddled through, trying to solve practical problems in practical ways. The better we understand this conceptional rationale, it seems, the more effective our practice of collaborative learning becomes.

In the hope that this experience will prove true for others, the following three sections outline the rationale of collaborative learning as I currently understand it and the relation of that rationale to classroom practice. The final section outlines some as yet not fully worked out implications both of collaborative learning as a practice and of some aspects of its conceptual rationale. Practice and rationale together, I will argue there, have the potential to challenge fairly deeply the theory and practice of traditional classroom teaching.

CONVERSATION AND THE NATURE OF THOUGHT AND KNOWLEDGE

In an important essay on the place of literature in education published some twenty years ago, "The Voice of Poetry in the Conversation of Mankind," Michael Oakeshott argues that what distinguishes human beings from other animals is our ability to participate in unending conversation. "As civilized human beings," Oakeshott writes,

> we are the inheritors, neither of an inquiry about ourselves and the world, nor of an accumulating body of information, but of a conversation, begun in the primeval forests and extended and made more articu-

late in the course of centuries. It is a conversation which goes on both in public and within each of ourselves. . . . Education, properly speaking, is an initiation into the skill and partnership of this conversation in which we learn to recognize the voices, to distinguish the proper occasions of utterance, and in which we acquire the intellectual and moral habits appropriate to conversation. And it is this conversation which, in the end, gives place and character to every human activity and utterance. (*Rationalism in Politics* [New York: Basic Books, 1962], p. 199)

Oakeshott argues that the human conversation takes place within us as well as among us, and that conversation as it takes place within us is what we call reflective thought. In making this argument he assumes that conversation and reflective thought are related in two ways: causally and functionally. That is, Oakeshott assumes what the work of Lev Vygotsky and others has shown, that reflective thought is public or social conversation internalized (see, for example, Vygotsky, *Mind and Society* [Cambridge, Mass.: Harvard University Press, 1978]). We first experience and learn "the skill and partnership of conversation" in the external arena of direct social exchange with other people. Only then do we learn to displace that "skill and partnership" by playing silently ourselves, in imagination, the parts of all the participants in the conversation. As Clifford Geertz has put it,

> thinking as an overt, public act, involving the purposeful manipulation of objective materials, is probably fundamental to human beings; and thinking as a covert, private act, and without recourse to such materials [is] a derived, though not unuseful, capability. . . . Human thought is consumately social: social in its origins, social in its functions, social in its form, social in its applications.[3]

Since what we experience as reflective thought is related causally to social conversation (we learn one from the other), the two are also related functionally. That is, because thought is internalized conversation, thought and conversation tend to work largely in the same way. Of course, in thought

some of the limitations of conversation are absent. Logistics, for example, are no problem at all. I don't have to take the A train or Eastern Airlines flight #221 to get together with myself for a chat. And in thought there are no differences among the participants in preparation, interest, native ability, or spoken vernacular. Each one is just as clever as I can be, or just as dull. On the other hand, in thought some of the less fortunate limitations of conversation may persist. Limitations that may be imposed, for example, by ethnocentrism, inexperience, personal anxiety, economic interests, and paradigmatic inflexibility can constrain my thinking just as they can constrain conversation. If my talk is narrow, superficial, biased, and confined to cliches, my thinking is likely to be so too.

Still, it remains the case that according to this concept of mental activity many of the social forms and conventions of conversation, most of the grammatical, syntactical and rhetorical structures of conversation, and the range, flexibility, impetus, and goals of conversation are the sources of the forms and conventions, structures, impetus, range and flexibility, and the issues of reflective thought.

The relationship I have been drawing here between conversation and thought illuminates the source of the quality, depth, terms, character, and issues of thought. The assumptions underlying my argument differ considerably, however, from the assumptions we ordinarily make about the nature of thought. We ordinarily assume that thought is some sort of given, an "essential attribute" of the human mind. The view that conversation and thought are causally related assumes not that thought is an essential attribute of the human mind but that it is instead an artifact created by social interaction. We can think because we can talk, and we think in ways we have learned to talk. As Stanley Fish has put it, the thoughts we "can think and the mental operations [we] can perform have their source in some or other interpretive community."[4] The range, complexity, and subtlety of our thought, its power, the practical and conceptual uses we can put it to, and the very issues we can address result in large measure directly from the degree to which we have been initiated into what Oakeshott calls the potential "skill and partnership" of human conversation in its public and social form.

To the extent that thought is internalized conversation, then, any effort to understand how we think requires us to understand the nature of conversation; and any effort to understand conversation requires us to understand the nature of community life that generates and maintains conversation. Furthermore, any effort to understand and cultivate in ourselves the kind of thought we value most requires us to understand and cultivate the kinds of community life that establish and maintain conversation that is the origin of that kind of thought. To think well as individuals we must learn to think well collectively—that is, we must learn to converse well. The first steps to learning to think better, therefore, are learning to converse better and learning to establish and maintain the sorts of social context, the sorts of community life, that foster the sorts of conversation members of the community value.

This principle has broad applicability and has implications far beyond those that may be immediately apparent. For example, Thomas Kuhn has argued in *The Structure of Scientific Revolutions,* (2nd ed.: Chicago: University of Chicago Press, 1970) that to understand scientific thought and knowledge we must understand the nature of scientific communities. Scientific knowledge changes not as our "understanding of the world" changes. It changes as scientists organize and reorganize relations among themselves (pp. 209–10). Carrying Kuhn's view and terminology further, Richard Rorty argues in *Philosophy and the Mirror of Nature* (Princeton: Princeton University Press, 1979) that to understand any kind of knowledge we must understand what he calls the social justification of belief. That is, we must understand how knowledge is established and maintained in the "normal discourse" of communities of knowledgeable peers.[5] Stanley Fish completes the argument by saying that these "interpretive communities" are the source of our thought and of the "meanings" we produce through the use and manipulation of symbolic structures, chiefly language. Fish suggests further, reflecting Erving Goffman's conclusion to *The*

Presentation of Self in Everyday Life ([New York: Doubleday Anchor, 1959], pp. 252–53), that interpretative communities may also be in large measure the source of what we regard as our very selves (Fish, p. 14). Our feelings and intuitions are as much the product of social relations as our knowledge.

EDUCATIONAL IMPLICATIONS: CONVERSATION, COLLABORATIVE LEARNING AND "NORMAL DISCOURSE"

The line of argument I have been pursuing has important implications for educators, and especially for those of us who teach English—both literature and composition. If thought is internalized public and social talk, then writing of all kinds is internalized social talk made public and social again. If thought is internalized conversation, then writing is internalized conversation re-externalized.[6]

Like thought, writing is related to conversation in both time and function. Writing is a technologically displaced form of conversation. When we write, having already internalized the "skill and partnership" of conversation, we displace it once more onto the written page. But because thought is already one step away from conversation, the position of writing relative to conversation is more complex than the position of thought relative to conversation. Writing is at once two steps away from conversation and a return to conversation. We converse; we internalize conversation as thought; and then by writing, we re-immerse conversation in its external, social medium.

My ability to write this essay, for example, depends on my ability to talk through with myself the issues I address here. And my ability to talk through an issue with myself derives largely from my ability to converse directly with other people in an immediate social situation. The point is not that the particular thing I write every time must necessarily be something I have talked over with other people first, although I may well often do just that.

What I have to say can, of course, originate in thought, and it often does. But my thought itself is conversation as I have learned to internalize it. The point, therefore, is that writing always has its roots deep in the acquired ability to carry on the social symbolic exchange we call conversation.

The inference writing teachers should make from this line of reasoning is that our task must involve engaging students in conversation among themselves at as many points in both the writing and the reading process as possible, and that we should contrive to ensure that students' conversation about what they read and write is similar in as many ways as possible to the way we would like them eventually to read and write. The way they talk with each other determines the way they will think and the way they will write.

To organize students for these purposes is, in as general a way as I can put it, to organize collaborative learning. Collaborative learning provides a social context in which students can experience and practice the kinds of conversation valued by college teachers. The kind of conversation peer tutors engage in with their tutees, for example, can be emotionally involved, intellectually and substantively focused, and personally disinterested. There could be no better source than this of the sort of displaced conversation—writing—valued by college teachers. Similarly, collaborative classroom group work guided by a carefully designed task makes students aware that writing is a social artifact, like the thought that produces it. Writing may seem to be displaced in time and space from the rest of a writer's community of readers and other writers, but in every instance writing is an act, however much displaced, of conversational exchange.

Besides providing a particular kind of conversation, collaborative learning also provides a particular kind of social context for conversation, a particular kind of community—a community of status equals: peers. Students learn the "skill and partnership" of re-externalized conversation, writing, not only in a community that fosters the kind of conversation college teachers value most, but also in a community that approximates the one most students must eventually write for in everyday life, in business, government, and the professions.

It is worthwhile to digress a moment here to establish this last point. In most cases people write in business, government, and the professions mainly to inform and convince other people within the writer's own community, people whose status and assumptions approximate the writer's own.[7] That is, the sort of writing most people do most in their everyday working lives is what Richard Rorty calls "normal discourse." Normal discourse (a term of Rorty's coinage based on Thomas Kuhn's term "normal science") applies to conversation within a community of knowledgeable peers. A community of knowledgeable peers is a group of people who accept, and whose work is guided by, the same paradigms and the same code of values and assumptions. In normal discourse, as Rorty puts it, everyone agrees on the "set of conventions about what counts as a relevant contribution, what counts as a question, what counts as having a good argument for that answer or a good criticism of it." The product of normal discourse is "the sort of statement that can be agreed to be true by all participants whom the other participants count as 'rational'" (p. 320).

The essay I am writing here is an example of normal discourse in this sense. I am writing to members of my own community of knowledgeable peers. My readers and I (I presume) are guided in our work by the same set of conventions about what counts as a relevant contribution, what counts as a question, what counts as having a good argument for that answer or a good criticism of it. I judge my essay finished when I think it conforms to that set of conventions and values. It is within that set of conventions and values that my readers will evaluate the essay, both in terms of its quality and in terms of whether or not it makes sense. Normal discourse is pointed; it is explanatory and argumentative. Its purpose is to justify belief to the satisfaction of other people within the author's community of knowledgeable peers. Much of what we teach today—or should be teaching—in composition courses is the normal discourse of most academic, professional, and business communities. The rhetoric taught in our composition textbooks comprises—or should comprise—the conventions of normal discourse of those communities.[8]

Teaching normal discourse in its written form is central to a college curriculum, therefore, because the one thing college teachers in most fields commonly want students to acquire, and what teachers in most fields consistently reward students for, is the ability to carry on in speech and writing the normal discourse of the field in question. Normal discourse is what William Perry describes as discourse in the established contexts of knowledge in a field, discourse that makes effective reference to facts as defined within those contexts. In a student who can integrate fact and context together in this way, Perry says, "we recognize a colleague."[9] This is so because to be conversant with the normal discourse in a field of study or endeavor is exactly what we mean by being knowledgeable—that is, knowledge-able—in that field. Not to have mastered the normal discourse of a discipline, no matter how many "facts" or data one may know, is not to be knowledgeable in that discipline. Mastery of a knowledge community's normal discourse is the basic qualification for acceptance into that community.

The kind of writing students find most useful to learn in college, therefore, is not only the kind of writing most appropriate to work in fields of business, government, and the professions. It is also the writing most appropriate to gaining competence in most academic fields that students study in college. What these two kinds of writing have in common is that they are both written within and addressed to a community of status equals: peers. They are both normal discourse.

This point having, I hope, been established, the nature of the particular kind of community that collaborative learning forms becomes clearer. Collaborative learning provides the kind of social context, the kind of community, in which normal discourse occurs: a community of knowledgeable peers. This is one of its main goals: to provide a context in which students can practice and master the normal discourse exercised in established knowledge communities in the academic world and in business, government, and the professions.

But to say this only raises a host of questions. One question is, how can student peers, who are not members of the knowledge communities they hope to enter, who lack the knowledge that constitutes those communities, help other students enter them? The first, more concrete answer to this question is that no student is wholly ignorant and inexperienced. Every student is already a member of several knowledge communities, from canoeing to computers, baseball to ballet. Membership in any one of these communities may not be a resource that will by itself help much directly in learning to organize an essay or explicate a poem. But pooling the resources that a group of peers brings with them to the task may make accessible the normal discourse of the new community they together hope to enter. Students are especially likely to be able to master that discourse collaboratively if their conversation is structured indirectly by the task or problem that a member of that new community (the teacher) has judiciously designed.[10] To the conversation between peer tutors and their tutees in writing, for example, the tutee brings knowledge of the subject to be written about and knowledge of the assignment. The tutor brings sensitivity to the needs and feelings of peers and knowledge of the conventions of discourse and of standard written English. And the conversation is structured in part by the demands of the teacher's assignment and in part by the formal conventions of the communities the teacher represents, the conventions of academic discourse and standard English.

Such conversation among students can break down, of course, if any one of these elements is not present. It can proceed again if the person responsible for providing the missing element, usually but not always the teacher, is flexible enough to adjust his or her contribution accordingly. If, for example, tutees do not bring to the conversation knowledge of the subject and the assignment, then the teacher helps peer tutors see that their most important contribution may be to help tutees begin at the very beginning: how to go about making sufficient acquaintance with the subject matter and how to set out to clarify the assignment. If tutors lack sensitivity to language and to the feelings and needs of their peers, tutees must contribute by making those feelings and needs more clearly evident. If the task or assignment that the teacher has given is unclear or too difficult or too simpleminded to engage students effectively, then the teacher has to revise it. Throughout this process the teacher has to try to help students negotiate the rocks and shoals of social relations that may interfere with their getting on with their work together.

What students do when working collaboratively on their writing is not write or edit or, least of all, read proof. What they do is converse. They talk about the subject and about the assignment. They talk through the writer's understanding of the subject. They converse about their own relationship and, in general, about relationships in an academic or intellectual context between students and teachers. Most of all they converse about and as a part of writing. Similarly, what students do when working collaboratively in small groups in order to read a text with understanding—a poem, a story, or another student's paper—is also to converse. They converse in order to reach consensus in answer to questions the teacher has raised about the text. They converse about and as a part of understanding. In short, they learn, by practicing it in this orderly way, the normal discourse of the academic community.

COLLABORATIVE LEARNING AND THE AUTHORITY OF KNOWLEDGE

The place of conversation in learning, especially in the humanities, is the largest context in which we must see collaborative learning. To say that conversation has a place in learning should not of course seem peculiar to those of us who count ourselves humanists, a category that includes all of us who teach literature and most of us who teach writing. Furthermore, most of us believe that "class discussion" is one of the most effective ways of teaching. The truth, however, is that despite this belief the person who does most of the discussing in most of our discussion classes is the teacher.

This tends to happen because behind our enthusiasm for discussion lies a fundamental distrust of it. The graduate training most of us have enjoyed—or endured—has taught us, in fact, that collaboration and community activity is inappropriate and foreign to work in humanistic disciplines such as English. Humanistic study, we have been led to believe, is a solitary life, and the vitality of the humanities lies in the talents and endeavors of each of us as individuals. What we call discussion is more often than not an adversarial activity pitting individual against individual in an effort to assert what one literary critic has called "will to power over the text," if not over each other. If we look at what we do instead of what we say, we discover that we think of knowledge as something we acquire and wield as individuals relative to each other, not something we generate and maintain in company with and in dependency upon each other.[11]

Only recently have humanists of note, such as Stanley Fish in literary criticism and Richard Rorty in philosophy, begun to take effective steps toward exploring the force and implications of knowledge communities in the humanistic disciplines, and toward redefining the nature of our knowledge as a social artifact. Much of this recent work follows a trail blazed two decades ago by Thomas Kuhn. The historical irony of this course of events lies in the fact that Kuhn developed his notion about the nature of scientific knowledge after first examining the way knowledge is generated, established, and maintained in the humanities and social sciences. For us as humanists to discover in Kuhn and his followers the conceptual rationale of collaborative learning is to see our own chickens come home to roost.

Kuhn's position that even in the "hard" sciences knowledge is a social artifact emerged from his attempt to understand the implications of the increasing indeterminacy of knowledge of all kinds in the twentieth century.[12] To say that knowledge is indeterminate is to say that there is no fixed and certain point of reference, no Arnoldian "touchstone" against which we can measure truth. If there is no such absolute referent, then knowledge must be a thing people make and remake. Knowledge must be a social artifact. But to call knowledge a social artifact, Kuhn argues, is not to say that knowledge is merely relative, that knowledge is what any one of us says it is. Knowledge is maintained and established by communities of knowledgeable peers. It is what together we agree it is, for the time being. Rorty, following Kuhn, argues that communities of knowledgeable peers make knowledge by a process of socially justifying belief. Collaborative learning models this process.

This then is a second and more general answer to the question raised in the preceding section. How can student peers, who are not themselves members of the knowledge communities they hope to enter, help other students to enter those communities? Isn't collaborative learning the blind leading the blind?

It is of course exactly the blind leading the blind if we insist on the Cartesian model of knowledge: that to know is to "see," and that knowledge is information impressed upon the individual mind by some outside source. But if we accept the premise that knowledge is an artifact created by a community of knowledgeable peers constituted by the language of that community, and that learning is a social and not an individual process, then to learn is not to assimilate information and improve our mental eyesight. To learn is to work collaboratively to establish and maintain knowledge among a community of knowledgeable peers through the process that Richard Rorty calls "socially justifying belief." We socially justify belief when we explain to others why one way of understanding how the world hangs together seems to us preferable to other ways of understanding it. We establish knowledge or justify belief collaboratively by challenging each other's biases and presuppositions; by negotiating collectively toward new paradigms of perception, thought, feeling, and expression; and by joining larger, more experienced communities of knowledgeable peers through assenting to those communities' interests, values, language, and paradigms of perception and thought.

If we accept this concept of knowledge and learning even partially and tentatively, it is possible to see collaborative learning as a model of the way that even the most sophisticated scientific knowledge is established and maintained. Knowledge is the product of human beings in a state of continual negotiation or conversation. Education is not a process of assimilating "the truth" but, as Rorty has put it, a process of learning to "take a hand in what is going on" by joining "the conversation of mankind." Collaborative learning is an arena in which students can negotiate their way into that conversation.

COLLABORATIVE LEARNING AND NEW KNOWLEDGE

Seen this way, collaborative learning seems unexceptionable. It is not hard to see it as comfortable, not very surprising, not even very new. In discovering and applying collaborative learning we seem to be, if not exactly reinventing the wheel, certainly rediscovering some of the more obvious implications of that familiar and useful device. Collaborative learning, it seems, is no new thing under the sun. However much we may explore its conceptual ramifications, we must acknowledge the fact that people have always learned from their peers and doggedly persist in doing so whether we professional teachers and educators take a hand in it or not. In Thomas Wolfe's *Look Homeward Angel* Eugene Gant records how in grammar school he learned to write (in this case, form the words on a page) from his "comrade," learning from a peer what "all instruction failed" to teach him. In business and industry, furthermore, and in professions such as medicine, law, engineering, and architecture—where to work is to learn or fail—collaboration is the norm. All that is new in collaborative learning, it seems, is the systematic application of collaborative principles to that last bastion of hierarchy and individualism, the American college classroom.

This comfortable view, while appropriate, may yet be deceptive. If we follow just a bit further the implications of the rationale for collaborative learning that I have been outlining here, we catch a glimpse of a somewhat startling educational scene. Take, for example, the principle that entering an existing knowledge community involves a process of negotiation. Followed to its logical conclusion this principle implies that education is not a rite of passage in which students passively become initiated into an institution that is monolithic and unchanging. It implies that the means by which students learn to negotiate this entry, collaborative learning, is not merely a better pedagogy, a better way of initiating new members into existing knowledge communities. And it implies that collaborative learning as a classroom practice models more than how knowledge is established and maintained. The argument pursued here implies, in short, that in the long run collaborative learning models how knowledge is generated, how it changes and grows.

This way of thinking about collaborative learning is somewhat speculative, but it is nevertheless of considerable interest and importance to teachers of English. If, as Rorty suggests, knowledge is a social artifact, if knowledge is belief justified through normal discourse, then the generation of knowledge, what we call "creativity," must also be a social process. It too must involve discourse. But the discourse involved in generating knowledge cannot be normal discourse, since normal discourse maintains knowledge. It is inadequate for generating new knowledge. Knowledge-generating discourse is discourse of quite another kind. It is, to use Rorty's phrase, abnormal discourse.

In contrast to normal discourse, abnormal discourse occurs between coherent communities or within communities when consensus no longer exists with regard to rules, assumptions, goals, values, or mores. Abnormal discourse, Rorty says, "is what happens when someone joins in the discourse who is ignorant of" the conventions governing that discourse "or who sets them aside." Whereas normal discourse produces "the sort of statement which can be agreed to be true by all participants whom the other participants count as 'rational,'" "the product of abnormal discourse can be anything from nonsense to intellectual revolution." Unlike the participants in normal discourse who sound "rational" to the others in the community, a person speaking abnormal discourse sounds "either 'kooky' (if he loses his point) or 'revolutionary' (if he gains it)" (pp. 320, 339).

The importance of abnormal discourse to the discussion of collaborative learning is that abnormal discourse serves the function of helping us—immersed as we inevitably are in the everyday normal discourse of our disciplines and professions—to see the provincial nature of normal discourse and of the communities defined by normal discourse. Abnormal discourse sniffs out stale, unproductive knowledge and challenges its authority, that is, the authority of the community which that knowledge constitutes. Its purpose, Rorty says, is to undermine "our reliance upon the knowledge we have gained" through normal discourse. We must occasionally undermine this reliance because normal discourse tends to "block the flow of conversation by presenting [itself] as offering the canonical vocabulary for discussion of a given topic" (pp. 386–387).

Abnormal discourse is therefore necessary to learning. But, ironically, abnormal discourse cannot be directly taught. "There is no discipline that describes" abnormal discourse, Rorty tells us, "any more than there is a discipline devoted to the study of the unpredictable or of 'creativity'" (p. 320). What we can teach are the tools of normal discourse, that is, both practical rhetoric and rhetorically based modes of literary criticism such as the taxonomy of figures, new-critical analysis, and deconstructive criticism.[13] To leave openings for change, however, we must not teach these tools as universals. We must teach practical rhetoric and critical analysis in such a way that, when necessary, students can turn to abnormal discourse in order to undermine their own and other people's reliance on the canonical conventions and vocabulary of normal discourse. We must teach the use of these tools in such a way that students *can* set them aside, if only momentarily, for the purpose of generating new knowledge, for the purpose, that is, of reconstituting knowledge communities in more satisfactory ways.

It is just here that, as I mentioned at the beginning of this essay, we begin to move beyond our earlier suppositions about what people learn through collaborative learning. Defining knowledge as a social artifact established and maintained through normal discourse challenges the authority of knowledge as we traditionally understand it. But by changing what we usually call the process of learning—the work, the expectations, and the social structure of the traditional classroom—collaborative learning also changes what we usually call the substance of learning. It challenges the authority of knowledge by revealing, as John Trimbur has observed, that authority itself is a social artifact. This revelation and the new awareness that results from it makes authority comprehensible both to us as teachers and to our students. It involves a process of reacculturation. Thus collaborative learning can help students join the established knowledge communities of academic studies, business, and the professions. But it should also help students learn something else. They should learn, Trimbur says, "something about how this social transition takes place, how it involves crises of identity and authority, how students can begin to generate a transitional language to bridge the gap between communities" (private correspondence).

Challenging the traditional authority of knowledge in this way, collaborative learning naturally challenges the traditional basis of the authority of those who teach. Our authority as teachers always derives directly or indirectly from the prevailing conception of the authority of knowledge. In the pre-Cartesian world people tended to believe that the authority of knowledge lodged in one place, the mind of God. In that world teachers derived their authority from their godliness, their nearness to the mind of God. In Cartesian, Mirror-of-Nature epistemology, the authority of knowledge has had three alternative lodgings, each a secular version of the mind of God. We could believe if we chose that the authority of knowledge lodged in some touchstone of value and truth above and beyond ourselves, such as mathematics, creative genius, or the universals of sound reasoning. We could believe that the authority of knowledge lodged in the mind of a person of genius: a Wordsworth, an Einstein, or a Freud. Or we could believe that the authority of knowledge lodged in the nature of the object objectively known: the universe, the human mind, the text of a poem.

Our authority as teachers, accordingly, has had its source in our nearness to one of these secular versions of the mind of God. In the first case we derive our authority from our identification with the "touchstone" of value and truth. Thus, for some of us, mathematicians and poets have, generally speaking, greater authority than, say, sociologists or literary critics. According to the second alternative we derive our authority from intimacy with the greatest minds. Many of us feel that those who have had the good fortune to study with Freud, Faraday, or Faulkner, for example, have greater authority than those who studied with their disciples; or, those who have studied the manuscripts of Joyce's fiction have greater authority than those who merely studied the edited texts. According to the third alternative, we derive our authority as teachers from being in direct touch with the objective world. Most of us feel that those whose knowledge is confirmed by hands-on laboratory experimentation have greater authority than those whose knowledge is based on a synthesis of secondary sources.

Because the concept that knowledge is socially justified belief denies that the authority of knowledge lodges in any of these places, our authority as teachers according to that concept has quite another source as well. Insofar as collaborative learning inducts students into established knowledge communities and teaches them the normal discourse of those communities, we derive our authority as teachers from being certified representatives of the communities of knowledgeable peers that students aspire to join, and that we, as members of our chosen disciplines and also members of the community of the liberally educated public at large, invite and encourage them to join. Teachers are defined in this instance as those members of a knowledge community who accept the responsibility for inducting new members into the community. Without successful teachers the community will die when its current members die, and knowledge as assented to by that community will cease to exist.

Insofar as collaborative learning helps students understand how knowledge is generated through abnormal discourse, however, our authority as teachers derives from another source. It derives from the values of a larger—indeed, the largest possible—community of knowledgeable peers, the community that encompasses all others. The interests of this largest community contradict one of the central interests of local communities such as professional disciplines and fields of study: to maintain established knowledge. The interest of the larger community is to resist this conservative tendency. Its interest is to bridge gaps among knowledge communities and to open them to change.

The continued vitality of the knowledge communities we value—in particular the community of liberally educated people and its sub-communities, the scholarly and professional disciplines—depends on both these needs being met: to maintain established knowledge and to challenge and change it. As representatives and delegates of a local, disciplinary community, and of the larger community as well, teachers are responsible for the continued vitality of both of the knowledge communities we value. Responsible to both sets of values, therefore, we must perform as conservators *and* agents of change, as custodians of prevailing community values *and* as agents of social transition and reacculturation.

Because by giving students access to the "conversation of mankind," to return to Oakeshott's phrase, collaborative learning can serve both of these seemingly conflicting educational aims at once, it has an especially important role to play in studying and teaching English. It is one way of introducing students to the process by which communities of knowledgeable peers create referential connections between symbolic structures and "reality," that is, by which they establish knowledge and by doing so maintain community growth and coherence. To study adequately any text—student theme or play by Shakespeare—is to study an entire social symbolic process, not just part of it. To

study and teach English is to study and teach the social origin, nature, reference, and function of symbolic structures.

The view that knowledge is a social artifact, furthermore, requires a reexamination of our premises as students of English and as teachers. To date, very little work of this sort has been done. One can only guess what might come of a concerted effort on the part of the profession as a whole. The effort might ultimately involve "demystifying" much that we now do as humanists and teachers of the humanities. If we bring to mind, for example, a sampling of important areas of current theoretical thought in and allied to literary criticism, we are likely to find mostly bipolar forms: text and reader, text and writer, symbol and referent, signifier and signified. On the one hand, a critique along the lines I have been following here might involve examining how these theories would differ if they included the third term missing from most of them. How would a psychoanalytically oriented study of metaphor differ, for example, if it acknowledged that psychotherapy is fundamentally a kind of social relationship based on the mutual creation or recreation of symbolic structures by therapist and patient? How would semiotics differ if it acknowledged that all "codes" are symbolic structures constituting language communities and that to understand these codes requires us to examine and understand the complex social symbolic relations among the people who make up language communities? How would practical rhetoric look if we assumed that writer and reader were not adversaries but partners in a common, community-based enterprise? How would it look if we no longer assumed that people write to persuade or to distinguish themselves and their points of view and to enhance their own individuality by gaining the acquiescence of other individuals? How would it look if we assumed instead that people write for the very opposite reason: that people write in order to be accepted, to join, to be regarded as another member of the culture or community that constitutes the writer's audience?

Once we had reexamined in this way how English is studied professionally, we could on the other hand also undertake to reexamine how English is taught as well. If we did that, we might find ourselves taking issue with Stanley Fish's conclusion that to define knowledge as a social artifact generated by interpretive communities has no effect whatsoever on the way we read and teach literature and composition. My argument in this essay suggests, on the contrary, that some changes in our pedagogical attitudes and classroom practices are almost inevitable. These changes would result from integrating our understanding of social symbolic relationships into our teaching—not just into what we teach but also into how we teach it. For example, so long as we think of knowledge as a reflection and synthesis of information about the objective world, then to teach *King Lear* seems to involve providing a "correct" text and rehearsing students in "correct" interpretations of it. "Correct" here means the text and the interpretations that, as Fish puts it, seem "obvious and inescapable" within the knowledge community, within the "institutional or conventional structure," of which we happen to be members (p. 370).

But if we think of knowledge as socially justified belief, then to teach *King Lear* seems to involve creating contexts where students undergo a sort of cultural change. This change would be one in which they loosen ties to the knowledge communities they currently belong to and join another. These two communities would be seen as having quite different sets of values, mores, and goals, and above all quite different languages. To speak in one community of a person asking another to "pray you undo this button" (V, iii) might be merely to tell a mercantile tale, or a prurient one, while in another community such a request could be both a gesture of profound human dignity and a metaphor of the dissolution of a world.

Similarly, so long as we think of learning as reflecting and synthesizing information about the objective world, to teach expository writing is to provide examples, analysis, and exercises in the traditional modes of practical rhetoric—description, narration, comparison-contrast—or examples, analysis, and exercises in the "basic skills" of writing, and to rehearse students in their proper use. But if we think of learning as a social process, the process of socially justifying belief, then to teach expository writing seems to involve something else entirely. It involves demonstrating to students that they know something only when they can explain it in writing to the satisfaction of the community of their knowledgeable peers. To teach this way, in turn, seems to require us to engage students in collaborative work that does not just reinforce the values and skills they begin with, but that promotes a sort of reacculturation.[14]

The argument I have been making here implies, in short, that students and teachers of literature and writing must begin to develop awareness and skill that may seem foreign and irrelevant to our profession at the present time. Organizing collaborative learning effectively requires doing more than throwing students together with their peers with little or no guidance or preparation. To do that is merely to perpetuate, perhaps even aggravate, the many possible negative efforts of peer group influence: conformity, anti-intellectualism, intimidation, and leveling-down of quality. To avoid these pitfalls and to marshal the powerful educational resource of peer group influence requires us to create and maintain a demanding academic environment that makes collaboration—social engagement in intellectual pursuits—a genuine part of students' educational development. And that in turn requires quite new and perhaps more thorough analyses of the elements of our field than we have yet attempted.

Notes

1. I am indebted for conversation regarding substantive issues raised in this essay to Fellows of the Brooklyn College Institute for Training Peer Tutors and of the Asnuntuck Community College Institute in Collaborative Learning and Peer-Tutor Training, and to Peter Elbow. Both Institutes were supported by grants from the Fund for the Improvement of Postsecondary Education. I am particularly grateful to Peter Hawkes, Harvey Kail, Ronald Maxwell, and John Trimbur for reading the essay in early drafts and for offering suggestions for improvement. The essay is in many ways and at many levels a product of collaborative learning.

2. The educative value of peer group influence is discussed in Theodore M. Newcomb and Everett K. Wilson, eds., *College Peer Groups* (Chicago: Aldine, 1966).

3. *The Interpretation of Cultures* (New York: Basic Books, 1971), pp. 76–77, 360. In addition to "The Growth of Culture and the Evolution of Mind," also relevant in the same volume are "The Impact of the Concept of Man" and "Ideology as a Cultural System," parts four and five.

4. *Is There a Text in This Class?: The Authority of Interpretive Communities* (Cambridge, Mass.: Harvard University Press, 1980), p. 14. Fish develops his argument fully in part 2, pp. 303–371. On the distinction between "interiority" or "inwardness" and "internalization," see Stephen Toulmin, "The Inwardness of Mental Life," *Critical Inquiry,* 6 (1979), 1–16.

5. I have explored some of the larger educational implications of Rorty's argument in "Liberal Education and the Social Justification of Belief," *Liberal Education,* 68 (1982), 95–114.

6. I make a case for this position in "Writing and Reading as Collaborative or Social Acts," in Janice N. Hays, et al, eds., *The Writer's Mind: Writing as a Mode of Thinking* (Urbana, Ill.: National Council of Teachers of English, 1983), pp. 159–169. In the current critical climate the distinction between conversation and speech as sources of writing and thought is important to maintain. Deconstructionist critics such as Paul de Man argue (e.g., in his *Blindness and Insight* [Minneapolis: University of Minnesota Press, 1983]), following Derrida, that writing is not displaced speech but a primary act. This argument defines "writing" in a much broader sense than we are used to, to mean something like "making public" in any manner, including speech. Hence deconstructionist "writing" can be construed as a somewhat static conception of what I am here calling "conversation": a social act. So long as the conversational, hence social, nature of "writing" in the deconstructionist sense remains unrecognized, the aversion of deconstructionist criticism to the primacy of speech as embodying the phenomenological "metaphysics of presence" remains circular. The deconstructionist argument holds that privileging speech "centers" language in persons. But "persons" are fictions. The alternative proposal by deconstruction, however, that writing is "free play," invites centering once again, since the figure of play personifies language. The deconstructionist critique has thus yet to acknowledge sufficiently that language, and its products such as thought and the self, are social artifacts constituted by "interpretive communities."

7. Some writing in business, government, and the professions may of course be like the writing students do in school for teachers, that is, for the sake of practice and evaluation. Certainly some writing in everyday working life is done purely as performance to please superiors in the corporate or department hierarchy, tell them what they already know, and demonstrate to them the writer's proficiency *as* a writer. It may be true, therefore, that learning to write to a person who is not a member of one's own status and knowledge community, that is, to a teacher, has some practical everyday value. But the value of writing of this type is hardly proportionate to the amount of time students normally spend on it.

8. A textbook that acknowledges the normal discourse of academic disciplines and offers ways of learning it in a context of collaborative learning is Elaine Maimon, et al., *Writing in the Arts and Sciences* (Boston: Little, Brown, 1981).

9. "Examsmanship and the Liberal Arts," in *Examining in Harvard College: A Collection of Essays by Members of the Harvard Faculty* (Cambridge, Mass.: Harvard University Press, 1963). Quoted from Kenneth A. Bruffee, *A Short Course in Writing* (Boston: Little, Brown, 1980), p. 221.

10. For examples and an explanation of this technique, see my *A Short Course in Writing,* cited above, and "CLTV: Collaborative Learning Television," *Educational Communication and Technology Journal,* 30 (1982), 26–40. Also see Clark Bouton and Russell Y. Garth, eds., *Learning in Groups* (San Francisco: Jossey-Bass, 1983).

11. I discuss the individualistic bias of our current interpretation of the humanistic tradition in "The Structure of Knowledge and the Future of Liberal Education," *Liberal Education,* 67 (1981), 181–185.

12. I trace briefly the history of the growing indeterminacy of knowledge and its relevance to the humanities in "The Structure of Knowledge," cited above.

13. Christopher Norris defines deconstruction somewhat simplistically but usefully for most purposes as "rhetorical questioning" (*Deconstruction: Theory and Practice* [London: Methuen, 1982], p. 21).

14. I suggest some possible curricular implications of the concept of knowledge as socially justified belief in "Liberal Education and the Social Justification of Belief," cited above. See also Clifford Geertz, *Local Knowledge* (New York: Basic Books, 1983), pp. 14–15, 161; Richard M. Rorty, "Hermeneutics, General Studies, and Teaching," *Synergos: Selected Papers from the Synergos Seminars,* George Mason University, 2 (Fall 1982), 1–15; and my "Learning to Live in a World out of Joint: Thomas Kuhn's Message to Humanists Revisited," *Liberal Education,* 70 (1984), 77–81.

Collaborative Learning
and Composition: Boon or Bane?

Donald C. Stewart

This selection is from Rhetoric Review 7 *(1988): 58–83.*

Four times during this past year, my attention has been drawn forcibly to the fact that, in our discipline, another major ideological shift is underway. A letter from a friend who characterized the 1987 CCCC meetings for me; Andrea Lunsford's announcement of the theme for the 1988 CCCC meetings—"Language, Self, and Society"; the first paragraph of Geoffrey Chase's "Accommodation, Resistance and the Politics of Student Writing" in the February, 1988, issue of *College Composition and Communication;* and a summary of David Bartholomae's speech to be given this June at the University of San Francisco's Literacy Conference all tell us implicitly that the era of the cognitive psychologists is waning; the era of the social constructionists is just beginning.[1]

I do not wish to suggest, of course, that social constructionism and, more specifically, collaborative learning, a practical manifestation of it in composition teaching, have suddenly appeared in our world like hitherto undetected nubulae. Kenneth Bruffee, in particular, has been espousing the benefits of collaborative learning for nearly two decades. My point is that, for the first time, this emphasis is now commanding the attention of a large number of composition theorists and practitioners. Any movement which attains that level of visibility inevitably invites close scrutiny.

I cannot offer a definitive study of collaborative learning and social constructionism—that would be far too large a task for this paper—but I do want to respond to some of the published remarks of its

most currently visible proponents, especially Bruffee, indicating thereby some serious reservations I have about various aspects of this movement. For convenience and expediency, I have organized my remarks around the following six questions:

1. What is collaborative learning?
2. What is the history of this movement?
3. Upon what philosophical and theoretical bases does it rest?
4. How does it work in the classroom?
5. What is good about it?
6. What's wrong with it?

John Trimbur provides the most succinct yet complete answer to the first question I have yet found:

Collaborative learning is a generic term, covering a range of techniques that have become increasingly visible in the past ten years, practices such as reader response, peer critiques, small writing groups, joint writing projects, and peer tutoring in writing centers and classrooms. The term refers to a method of conducting the business at hand—whether a freshman composition course or a workshop for writing teachers. By shifting initiative and responsibility from the group leader to the members of the group, collaborative learning offers a style of leadership that actively involves the participants in their own learning. (87)

Trimbur also directs his readers to Kenneth Bruffee's definition of collaborative learning as "a form of indirect teaching in which the teacher sets the problem and organizes the students to work it out collaboratively" ("Collaborative Learning" 638).

Trimbur says the movement emerged in the 1960s when students challenged the university's *in loco parentis* doctrine, demanded a greater role in determining the scope and content of their education, and demonstrated suspicion of authority in general. He cites the development of free universities, teach-ins, anti-war study groups, and consciousness raising groups among women, minorities, and those in the counter-culture, all reflecting a felt need for "community, self-organization, mutual aid, and nonauthoritarian styles of leadership and decision making. If much of what appeared to be subversive in the sixties degenerated during the Me Decade of the seventies into narcissistic self-realization fads, the antiauthoritarian values and communal ethos of the sixties nonetheless initiated critical thinking about social relations in higher education" (90).

Another factor contributing to the development of collaborative learning was the appearance of nontraditional students through open-admissions programs. Its methods proved to be particularly appealing to students who were not prepared intellectually or socially for life in academic communities. "Learning in groups," Kurt Lewin and Paul Grabbe point out, "is often more effective than learning individually because learning involves more than simply acquiring new information. It also involves the acceptance of new habits, values, beliefs, and ways of talking about things" (90).[2]

Collaborative learning also has a history in such programs as the writing fellow and science mentor program at Brown, peer tutoring programs at Harvard and Yale, and learning communities at Rollins and Stony Brook.

In addition to the social and political forces already cited, authoritarian educational and academic traditions contributed to the emergence of collaborative learning. Trimbur notes that it emerged as a critique of current traditional rhetoric

which grounded authority in the teacher and the text and thus was congenial to English teachers brought up under the aegis of the New Criticism. Collaborative learning emphasizes process and challenges the authority of the text and teacher, and, in workshop practices, essentially defines the text as a product of the interaction of reader and writers. Students under the old system were perpetually frustrated by the difficulty of writing for both present and past teachers, primarily to approximate what they perceived to be the ideal theme. He identifies James Moffett and Peter Elbow as among the most visible opponents of this authoritarian tradition in the classroom.

Bruffee provides some additional history for this movement. He traces its inception to British secondary school teachers and a medical educator who found that her students improved their diagnostic skills by collaborating rather than trying to work individually. The key documents are Edwin Mason's *Collaborative Learning* and M. L. J. Abercrombie's *Anatomy of Judgment*.

American teachers, says Bruffee, were motivated in the early 1970s by a "pressing educational need": the difficulty of both poorly and apparently well-prepared high school students to adapt "to the traditional or 'normal' conventions of the college classroom" ("Collaborative Learning" 637). A key symptom was students' refusal to seek or accept help offered by the colleges and universities. "What they needed, it seemed, was help that was not an extension of but an alternative to traditional classroom teaching" ("Collaborative Learning" 637). The answer: collaborative learning. It didn't change what students learned; it changed the social context in which they learned it. "Collaborative learning, it seemed, harnessed the powerful educative force of peer influence that had been—and largely still is—ignored and hence wasted by traditional forms of education" ("Collaborative Learning" 638).

Philosophically, the collaborative classroom can be described as a critique of the teacher-centered classroom. In the latter, authority is vested in a teacher who disseminates knowledge to students. In the former, authority is vested in the subject and in the social interaction of the learners. The sources for the philosophical and theoretical insights that inform the work of proponents of this movement are varied, but some appear consistently in the literature about the movement. Trimbur says that John Dewey is the source of the idea that there is an organic connection between experience and education and the recognition that one simply couldn't do away with authority in the classroom: it had to be relocated. Abercrombie, already cited, is the source of the insight that students in groups learned to apply knowledge acquired but not yet assimilated sufficiently that they could make use of it in solving problems. From Mason comes the term *collaborative learning,* the insight that traditional learning fostered a destructive competitiveness rather than cooperation, and the assertion that "collaborative learning not only represents a more humane way to organize teaching and learning . . . [but that] knowledge itself is a social construct, produced by collaborative activity" (Trimbur 93). This concept, "that knowledge is a social artifact, generated and authorized by the assent of members of knowledge communities" (Trimbur 94), is reinforced and amplified by Thomas Kuhn in the history of science, Richard Rorty in philosophy, and Clifford Geertz in anthropology.

Invoking Kuhn, Rorty, Michael Oakeshott, and Lev Vygotsky, Bruffee argues that

reflective thought is public or social conversation internalized. . . . To the extent that thought is internalized conversation, then, any effort to understand how we think requires us to understand the nature of conversation, and any effort to understand conversation requires us to understand the nature of community life that generates and maintains conversation. Furthermore, any effort to understand and cultivate in ourselves the kind of thought we value most requires us to understand and cultivate the kinds of community life that establish and maintain conversation that is the origin of that kind of thought. To think well as individuals we must learn to think well collectively—that is, we must learn to converse well. The first steps to learning to think better, therefore, are learning to converse better and learning to establish

and maintain the sorts of social context, the sorts of community life, that foster the sorts of conversation members of the community value. ("Collaborative Learning" 639–40)

From this position Bruffee moves easily to the assertion that writing is internalized conversation re-externalized.

One should also acknowledge the movement's indebtedness to Brazilian educator Paulo Freire, who sees traditional education as a domesticating force. It conditions students to live passively within oppressive and alienating structures. He and his disciples propose conscientization, "a method of resistance where learners are no longer passive recipients of knowledge but rather knowing subjects whose learning leads them to a deepening awareness of the social forces and relations of power that shape their immediate experience" (Trimbur 93).

Without attempting to be rigorously systematic, let me cite a few other examples of philosophical and theoretical positions taken by Bruffee which have caught my attention forcibly.[3] For example, citing *The Organizer's Manual,* which emerged from the Kent State anti-Vietnam War strike, he says that "in such ways as these, people have begun to create, outside classrooms, structures in which learning is integral with human interdependence and private inner experience and feeling" ("Way Out" 462).

Following an analysis of three "classic" failures in collaborative learning—he cites the flawed experiments reported by Jarrold Zacharias, Peter Elbow, and Martin Duberman—Bruffee asks, "Is it not true that it is only in infancy (and in our infantile moments as adults) that we are concerned exclusively to please ourselves? When we work maturely and at our best, do we not work to please those we want to please, which usually, but seldom exclusively, includes ourselves?" I will return to those questions later in this paper.

From Clifford Geertz's *Local Knowledge,* Bruffee derives the position that "humanistic scholarship and liberal education must be modernized. To do this, he says [reference to Geertz], humanists will need to develop 'a critical consciousness' that leaves behind what he calls 'the epistemological complacency of traditional humanism' (23, 44). In its place, we must learn to conceive 'of cognition, emotion . . . whatever'—entities we normally think of as strictly individual, internal, and mental affairs—'as themselves, and directly social affairs'" (Geertz 153; "Social Construction" 775).

Taking issue with a particular aspect of cognitive terminology, Bruffee says:

> A third assumption we make when we talk in cognitive terms about what we do is that the individual self is the matrix of all thought: "I think, therefore I am." A great idea is the product exclusively of a single great mind. Each of us studies to make knowledge "our own." And so on. In contrast, social construction assumes that the matrix of thought is not the individual self but some community of knowledgeable peers and the vernacular language of that community. That is, social construction understands knowledge and the authority of knowledge as community-generated, community-maintaining, symbolic artifacts. Indeed, some social constructionists go so far in their nonfoundationalism as to assume, along with the sociologist Erving Goffman for example, that even what we think of as the individual self is a construct largely community-generated and community-maintained. ("Social Construction" 777)

Two more illustrations will suffice to give a fair representation of the positions taken by Bruffee and, I presume, those who share his enthusiasm for social constructionism and collaborative learning. "Much of what we teach today—or should be teaching—in composition courses is the normal discourse of most academic, professional, and business communities. The rhetoric taught in our composition textbooks comprises—or should comprise—the conventions of normal discourse of those communities" ("Collaborative Learning" 643). This, together with his mention of Elaine Maimon's text on writing in the various disciplines, I take to be an implicit endorsement of writing-across-the-curriculum programs.

Aware of the fact that some will question him about issues of genius and creativity, Bruffee turns to Richard Rorty and the position that since normal knowledge does not generate new knowledge, creativity is the product of "abnormal discourse" and involves a different social process. He says that as we learn that knowledge is socialized belief, we learn also that authority is a social construct. Thus, the student who learns the conversation of mankind, learns how communities maintain knowledge and belief; he also learns how to challenge the status quo, to sniff out the stale and no longer viable, and so forth.

In practice, most of the collaborative learning about which I have read occurs in small groups or in one-to-one sessions in which peers tutor one another. The small-group work, usually four to six students, goes best when the teacher sets a problem and then asks students to work it out. Without this kind of direction, groups often will flounder and not work productively. One could say that they work best when students recognize the problem to be attacked as one which merits their effort and attention in the same way, for example, that the problem of preparing for an examination draws them together outside the classroom.

At this point it is only fair to point out what is right with collaborative learning. I see several virtues in it and in the social constructionist theory which supports it: (1) its attempt to do away with the sterile and nonproductive authoritarianism of the traditional classroom; (2) its effort to involve students meaningfully and significantly in their learning; (3) its potential humaneness, especially when students are nourished both socially and intellectually by the groups in which they work; (4) its recognition of the role social forces play in the very nature of language and learning. These are powerful and commendable virtues.

Unfortunately, neither collaborative learning nor the social constructionist theory that supports it is the educational panacea which its advocates imply. I have a great many problems with this movement and wish, therefore, to discuss them in some detail for the rest of this paper.

In the first place, those writing about this movement strike me as a bit naive historically. For example, they give an incomplete picture of the history of authoritarianism in the traditional classroom.

Doubtless, one could invoke the entire history of the American and English schoolmaster as stern, humorless, and frequently brutal disciplinarian, one who believed that learning was pounded rather than coaxed into students and who could not tolerate any challenge to his authority. I am more interested, however, in a particularly American manifestation of this phenomenon at the university level. To what school and what person, one should ask, can we trace the concept of the college professor as a classroom dictator intimidating students with his forbidding demeanor and encyclopedic knowledge? It is absurd to suggest that one school and one individual are totally responsible, but, as I have pointed out elsewhere, I think it impossible to overestimate the influence of the Harvard English Department in the late nineteenth century and of its emperor, George Lyman Kittredge. Much as "Kitty's" students have tried to gloss over the fact, and none worked harder at it than Rollo Walter Brown, the man's classroom arrogance and bullying were legendary. He *dominated* his students. His knowledge was encyclopedic, and he rarely withheld his scorn from those who did not share his passion for information. His admirers, of course, defended the rigor and thoroughness of his scholarship.[4] His critics, however, were not so charitable. In *Intellectual America,* published in 1941, Oscar Cargill lashed out in a scathing indictment of Kittredge, his mentor, Francis Child, three of Kittredge's most famous students, and the influence of the Harvard department in general. He said that Child's magnum opus, *The English and Scottish Popular Ballads,* had been "inordinately praised in academic circles" and described it as "a monument to the simple credulity of a good man in the current dogma of Primitivism" (522). Child's assumptions about the creation of ballads were subsequently discredited by Louise Pound. Kittredge he called "the most influential of all the Aryanizers," a man who dominated Harvard's English Department and American literary education from 1894 to 1936. He blamed Kittredge for turning doctoral dissertations into a "device for killing the last spark of sensibility in the future teacher of literature" and for sending his clones out to dominate English departments across the country. The major scholarly work of three of Kittredge's pupils, John Matthews Manly, John S. P. Tatlock, and Karl Young, he characterized as pedantry, "a multiplication of zero by nothing." The problem was compounded, as he saw it, by the fact that "the students of Kittredge and his disciples are legion—they are spread not only throughout the institutions of higher learning, but through their offspring and through their text-books they exercise still a dominant influence upon the secondary schools" (523). Harsh as Cargill's remarks may seem, I do not think he greatly overstated the case.

Equally revealing is the attitude Kittredge's students had toward him. They groveled. I have been told that O. J. Campbell, while at Michigan, used to tell a story about a lecture on Shakespeare that he gave in Cambridge. Kittredge and his daughter were sitting on the front row, and after the talk, she turned to him and said, "Well now, Papa, I thought that was rather a good speech. Don't you think there was something in it?" Turning to her, that perpetually fierce and arrogant expression on his face, Kittredge held the thumb and index finger of his right hand about a quarter of an inch apart and said, "About that much!" And Campbell loved it!

This tradition, the authoritarianism of Kittredge and his disciples, infected American higher education for nearly seven decades. It was a tradition that the early initiators of collaborative learning were fully justified in opposing.

There was another authoritarian tradition, however, much more benevolent and far more humane, than that represented by the monarch of Harvard and his disciples. While Kittredge was browbeating his students, Fred Newton Scott of Michigan, a man of equally vast learning and linguistic competence (Scott's undergraduate transcript alone shows 69 hours of language: Latin, Greek, French, German, Italian, and Sanskrit; he later became proficient in Russian), was gathering his students around a table, leading them gently with probing questions, and, in the words of the students who admired and loved him, "teaching us to educate ourselves." Where Scott's influence prevailed, there were communities of scholars, led by a teacher whose authority was unquestioned but never abused. In Scott's classrooms students did learn to think for themselves, to create, in the language of the social constructionists, their own knowledge.[5] Had it been the prevailing influence in American higher education, the need to break away from the authoritarian classroom might never have been felt in such a pressing way.

We do not know what Kittredge thought of Scott, although his career paralleled that of the man from Michigan with whom he was in frequent contact at MLA meetings, but we do get a tiny glimpse of Scott's perception of Kittredge, tucked away in a very brief and obscure diary entry, made December 28, 1911, while Scott was attending the MLA meetings in Chicago. He had gone to the University Club to hear Kittredge's Smoker Talk on New Pedants. "Kittredge seemed to be unusually self conscious at one moment as if he felt that everyone knew he had chosen this topic in order to divert attention from his own pedantry, and patronisingly imperious at the next as if he must act the part of the great Kittredge fallen among barbarians. This probably does him injustice, but strangely he was not wholly in accord with the environment, and might have been considered as having continually on his lips the words, 'You ask me why, though ill at ease, within this region I subsist.'"

There is a second historical gap which I find in the literature of the social constructionists. As I pointed out in a review in this journal (Fall 1987) of Karen Burke LeFevre's *Invention as a Social Act,* she tells only part of the story of the 1960s. I do not question her assertion that "romantic individualism was particularly evident in the late sixties' emphasis on self-expression, epitomized in the battles of the intuitively good flower child from the country, straight from Rousseau, against the contaminated urban forces of organized bureaucracy" (18), but that was only part of the picture. A number of us were seizing the occasion to encourage students to find their own voices, to escape from the pasteurized and pedestrian prose they had been conditioned to produce in the traditional classroom. Both the Rohman-Wlecke study on pre-writing and Robert Zoellner's monograph on the applications of

behavioral psychology to composition teaching gave some impetus to this effort. Today, these studies are neither remembered nor their significance acknowledged by the collaborative writing advocates.

A third example of historical naiveté exhibited by proponents of this movement is their obvious and, perhaps, excusable ignorance of World War II history. I suspect that most were born either during or after that war and thus have only book knowledge of it. Those of us who lived during that period and were old enough to be interested in what was going on remember what ugly connotations attended the word *collaborator.* In the occupied countries, this was a person who assisted the Nazis, even to the point of betraying his or her countrymen. Like *appeasement, collaborator* is a word which was relatively innocuous before the war, obscene during and after it. I find it a curious irony that *collaboration* now has such favorable connotations for some English teachers.

A second large area of difficulty I have with this movement is its rather flexible definition of the word *collaboration,* specifically its lack of a clear distinction between *influence* and *collaboration.* When collaboration means groups of people working together to solve some problem or produce a written document, I understand the term clearly. All of us are familiar with the teams of scientists who regularly collaborate, with television script writers who combine their efforts to produce a variety of shows. I am even willing to acknowledge the fact that collaboration is a much larger part of our lives than we have previously recognized, as Bruffee and the people he cites frequently are fond of pointing out. However, there is a point beyond which I will not go. For example, when we say that we are influenced by someone, or that such and such a composer is influenced by his predecessors, even in the sense in which T. S. Eliot used the word in "Tradition and the Individual Talent," are we asked to extend *collaboration* to mean the effects of absorbed learning? How does one account for the originality of genius? How does the genius transcend the influences that have molded him? Bruffee feels that Rorty accounts for this phenomenon in his discussion of "abnormal discourse." The person who has learned the conversation of mankind, we are told, learns how to challenge the status quo, to sniff out the stale and no longer viable. How? This is a completely unsatisfactory explanation of Mozart's ability to transcend the influence of Haydn, of Beethoven's to transcend Mozart, of Brahms' to transcend Beethoven. Nor does it explain a Newton or an Einstein.[6] I will readily concede that each man had fully absorbed mathematical learning from the previous two or three centuries, but what enabled him to develop the revolutionary insights which synthesized and transcended that previous learning? I find it very difficult to call such an effort a collaboration.

As a matter of fact, writers are particularly sensitive to the question of influence. Historically, we have honored them because they rose above the conventions of their time to create new art forms. In some cases they rebelled angrily at the notion that their work was an extension of those who influenced them. Hemingway's *Torrents of Spring,* for example, is a loud and angry assertion by the author that he is not Sherwood Anderson's boy, that his work must be measured by a different yardstick.

A third area that troubles me is the pedagogical limitations of collaborative writing. I found Bruffee's statement about what should be taught in the composition classroom appallingly limited. "Much of what we teach today—or should be teaching—in composition courses," he says, "is the normal discourse of most academic, professional, and business communities. The rhetoric taught in our composition textbooks comprises—or should comprise the conventions of normal discourse of those communities" ("Collaborative Learning" 643). This goal is too limited, much too limiting, and, in some ways positively wrong-headed. The normal discourse of many of our academic and professional communities is a disgrace. This is a point which has been made repeatedly over the past forty years by professional writers who are appalled at academic jargon.

The most obvious targets are educationists and ial scientists. They provide abundant examples of writing whose purpose is to impede genuine communication with every resource the writer can muster. In 1947 Samuel Williamson gave us all a demonstration lesson in writing like a social scientist. Saying that he was "still convalescing from overexposure some time ago to products of the academic mind," he offered, in a spirit of savage irony, six rules for writing like a social scientist:

1. *Never use a short word when you can think of a long one.* His illustrations: use "currently" instead of "now"; "sufficiency" instead of "enough"; "termination" instead of "end."

2. *Never use one word when you can use two or more.* By a series of steps he demonstrates how "probably" can be extended to "available evidence would tend to indicate that it is not unreasonable to suppose."

3. *Put one-syllable thought into polysyllabic terms.* Illustration: Instead of saying that "musicians out of practice can't hold jobs," report that "the fact of rapid deterioration of musical skill when not in use soon converts the unemployed into the unemployable."

4. *Put the obvious in terms of the unintelligible.* You can join the guild (in social constructionists' terms you are a member of this discourse community) when you can parlay "Each article sent to the cleaner is handled separately" into "Within the cleaning plant proper the business of the industry involves several well-defined processes, which, from the economic point of view, may be characterized simply by saying that most of them require separate handling of each individual garment or piece of material to be cleaned."

5. *Announce what you are going to say before you say it.* Illustration of what he calls the "contortionist" wind-up: "Perhaps more important, therefore, than the question of what standards are in a particular case, there are the questions of the extent of observance of these standards and the methods of their enforcement." As one would expect, Williamson advises completing one's training by saying what one has said after one

has said it. This particular rule also covers both the introductions and conclusions not only to the ubiquitous five-paragraph essay but to most doctoral dissertations in education.

6. *Defend your style as "scientific."* Scorn clear, simple English, says Williamson, as popular or journalistic.

He concludes with the observation that such writing has long been excused as "the academic mind." He says it should be characterized instead as "intellectual laziness and grubby-mindedness."

About a decade later, Malcolm Cowley took his shot at social scientists in an article which appeared in *The Reporter:* "Sociological Habit Patterns in Linguistic Transmogrification." Like Williamson, Cowley was on a search and destroy mission and in no mood to take prisoners. Generalizing about the writing of the social scientists, he said that their language "has to be learned almost like Esperanto. It has a private vocabulary which, in addition to strictly sociological terms, includes new words for the commonest actions, feelings, and circumstances. It has the beginnings of a new grammar and syntax, much inferior to English grammar in force and precision. So far as it has an effect on standard English, the effect is largely pernicious" (41). His prime example is an extended passage from an article by Norman Green in the 1956 *American Sociological Review.* Cowley calls it Green's "contribution to comparative linguistics":

> In effect, it was hypothesized that certain physical data categories including types and densities, land use characteristics, and ecological location constitute a scalable content area. This could be called a continuum of residential desirability. Likewise, it was hypothesized that several social data categories, describing the same census tracts, and referring generally to the social stratification system of the city, would also be scalable. This scale could be called a continuum of socio-economic status. Thirdly, it was hypothesized that there would be a high positive correlation between the scale types on each continuum.
>
> This relationship would define certain linkages between the social and physical structure of the city.

It would also provide a precise definition of the commonalities among several spatial distributions. By the same token, the correlation between the residential desirability scale and the continuum of socio-economic status would provide an estimate of the predictive value of aerial photographic data relative to the social ecology of the city.

What does the man mean? He means that "rich people live in big houses set farther apart than those of poor people. By looking at an aerial photograph of any American city, we can distinguish the richer from the poorer neighborhoods." If you say it that way, however, you will be excluded from Mr. Green's discourse community.

A decade and a half later social psychologists Peter Madden and Lloyd Engdahl gave their professional colleagues a view from the inside of the language peculiar to their community. They created the "EMPTI Guide to Swollen Prose," an acronym for "The Engdahl-Madden Psychological Terms Inventory." "The EMPTI," they say, "was created to serve as an aid in the writing of professional-sounding psychological reports and articles. Properly used, EMPTI provides an economical, concise survey of terms which describe most human situations. Authors will find EMPTI quite useful in adding bulk and a professional veneer to their writing and a hearty supplement to any original ideas the writer may have. Words may be added to each column as they occur to the user. If applied liberally, the terms in this inventory will help assure that future psychological writing contains as many EMPTI phrases as previous contributions to the literature" (99).

They provide three columns of words and then direct the writer to select any term from the first column and combine it randomly with terms selected from the next two columns. Following their directions, one creates such phrases as the following: "conflicting cognitive integration"; "extrinsic developmental equilibrium"; "undifferentiated synergistic integration."

To the charge that I have chosen only the worst possible examples of writing in these discourse communities, I must plead not guilty. When writers in three different decades see this pattern, and when it confirms my own experience, I do not think it is at all atypical.

Now, do we want to teach our students majoring in the social sciences to write such rubbish? Bruffee will say, no, of course not. These are excesses. But they are not. They are the norms of these communities, which is why it is often so difficult to read what they write. As Will Durant pointed out in the preface to *The Story of Philosophy,* academics, in their opposition to "popularizing" a field, aren't reacting against popularizing. They are reacting against an attempt to make their knowledge intelligible to the general public.

On another front Bill Lutz and his NCTE Committee on Public Doublespeak continue to offer yearly examples of linguistic outrage, perpetuated by people who have learned very well the normal discourse of their communities. Readers will recall that part of the Doublespeak Award went one year to President Reagan and his description of the MX Missile as a "peacemaker." That particular euphemism showed us how well he had absorbed the language of that particular discourse community. In fact, I believe he had absorbed it so completely that he had lost the power to analyze it objectively. For that reason, I do not believe that one develops the insights to criticize the language in which one is immersed from social collaboration.

Teaching students the normal discourse of various other academic disciplines has some additional drawbacks. Unlike the discourse of the social sciences which deliberately obfuscates, it is merely faceless and dreary. When I encounter this kind of writing in biology, geology, engineering, and business textbooks, I feel sympathy for the students required to study them. Even more troubling to me, however, are our colleagues in composition who are obsessed with the idea that the end of writing instruction should be teaching students to write effective arguments. The emphasis in these books is on thesis statements, orderly presentation of proof, and logic. I have no quarrel with the value of such training, as *part* of a composition program. But those who believe that logic and orderly presentations alone can carry an argument should re-read

Richard Weaver's essay on the *Phaedrus* in *The Ethics of Rhetoric.* As Weaver points out, Plato there says that dialectic may establish the truth of a proposition, but impassioned rhetoric is needed to persuade men to accept it. This is a point clearly understood by Lewis Lapham, editor of *Harper's Magazine,* who tells those wishing to submit long pieces to his magazine that they "should be construed as topical essays on all manner of subjects (politics, the arts, crime, business, etc.) *to which the author can bring the force of passionately informed statement* [italics mine]" (*Writer's Market,* 1988, 294). I would much prefer teaching a student to meet Lapham's standards rather than the requirements of a particular type of academic discourse.

The basic fact is that most students can learn what they need to know about any discipline's discourse on the job. We writing teachers should be teaching them to be lucid and literate, in powerful and convincing ways. That may often require them to do battle with the language of the disciplines which they choose.[7]

I have another set of pedagogical problems with this movement. How do these people define good writing? And what criteria do they give students in groups who are commenting on the work of their peers? When Bruffee says that "students learn to describe the organizational structure of a peer's paper" ("Collaborative Learning" 638), I want to ask, "How?" More important, what are they taught about organization? In what ways does that background dictate the nature of their evaluations of peers' work? This is a critical issue in this whole method, and these people glide over it as blithely as ice skaters on a pond.

Here are my concerns. Students, regardless of their preparation, do not come to us as great vacuums to be filled. They come with some ideas of structure, most likely that nonfiction is to be written in five-paragraph essays. If they have been freed from that, they have probably been exposed to academic discourse and its neurotic fascination with topic sentences, development, and conclusion. I suspect that good writing means to them the paragraph as defined by Alexander Bain in 1866 and still taught in 1988. I suspect it means use of the modes of discourse, conventional patterns of arrangement, and limited stylistic options. After all, one has to pay attention to the kinds of textbooks that sell the most copies: handbooks and extremely conventional and outdated rhetorics. I doubt that they are told that this kind of writing is also unread except by those who are in a professional field and obliged to deal with it. I seriously doubt that students in this situation would come up with something as radical as Grammar B, but even if a student did, his or her peers would probably reject it as inappropriate.[8]

My concerns on this subject, voiced time and time again, are that most writing teachers do not have a sense of the history of this profession and of writing instruction in American colleges in particular. They have got to learn where their ideas about paragraph structure, topic sentences, usage, general theme organization, and so forth, came from, what contexts they apply to, and how to teach students the really fundamental things like choice of good subjects, inventional strategies for developing information on those subjects, flexible and varied organizational patterns, and necessary editing skills.

When Ken Bruffee advocates teaching students the language of their academic disciplines, I fear that they are learning stuff that really has no life beyond the classroom or, at best, the obscure professional journals which accept it. Students in this kind of situation understand, as do academicians accumulating bibliographies against the day of tenure reckoning, that what they produce is never to be read for its intrinsic worth as writing. Supposedly, that is a problem corrected in the collaborative situation, but it cannot be, in a real sense, unless students in these groups are prepared to accept a wide variety of texts accommodated to a wide variety of contexts.

The students' notion that in the writing classroom one doesn't have to write anything real is a central problem in composition pedagogy. Robert Zoellner articulated it beautifully in 1969, but most of those reading his monograph in *College English* simply became angry and ceased to pay attention to what he was saying. He had violated the constraints

of the discourse community in which he was writing, and he knew it, but he hoped, as one always does, that his readers would be capable of recognizing a highly original and provocative contribution to composition research. Most did not. I still regard that response as one of this profession's most egregious mistakes, an error it never rectified.

A fourth difficulty I have with the collaborative writing people and the social constructionists is the problem of ethics. Here, although I regret singling out a single individual, I take issue with some remarks that appear in Karen Burke LeFevre's *Invention as a Social Act*. They occur in the chapter entitled "Implications of a Social Perspective":

> Or consider the case of an engineering student who tells a writing tutor that his advisor will not allow him to draw certain conclusions in his thesis because the agency sponsoring the research would discover that the work was essentially completed and would cut off funding. It would be beside the point for the tutor to suggest that this student try free-writing or tagmemics to come up with new material for his conclusion. (134)

Given the constraints in a situation like this, LeFevre asks:

> What is a writing teacher or tutor to do? That is difficult to say. We can help writers to articulate their concerns and their perceptions of the constraints they face. We can talk about ways they might test the accuracy of their perceptions, or work around their constraints, or discuss problems with those responsible for creating and enforcing certain rules and policies. The writers and their supervisors may or may not try to change the status quo. What we cannot do is act as if these problems do not exist, as if people's jobs are not at stake, as if invention means asking the journalist's five W's and an H without taking into account the very real implications that these choices have for writers in their social contexts. (134)

I cannot speak for others, but I find the moral relativism of such remarks disquieting. What, indeed, is a writing teacher to do in such a situation? I understand that in this case a degree is at stake. In another it will be a job. But the point is that in this example, those exercising the constraints are behaving *illegally and immorally*. They should be exposed. The student should write the report indicating that the research was complete. If that report is suppressed by those protecting government grant money and, I hasten to add, exploiting taxpayers, the student should appeal it all the way to the president of his university and if he finds no satisfaction there, he should take his major professor to court. This is a humanistic dilemma. Does one choose the ethically right or the morally expedient course of action? English teachers with a good background in Greek philosophy, particularly in Plato's works, know the answer to that question. And yes, one can pay the price for doing the right thing. But that is what makes us humanists, or at least, should. The basic character of the good humanist is forged in the crucible of such morally difficult decisions.

Let us move on to another set of problems posed by the collaborative learners and social constructionists. From what I have read so far, I am not convinced that they have examined fully the political implications of what they propose. The rhetoric they value is well suited to a society that needs managing—China for example. The United States is not ready for that yet. In our history we have championed the trail blazer, the pioneer, the self-sufficient person. The advancing frontier is still too close to us historically for our society to change its attitudes fundamentally.

It has also occurred to me that the social constructionist movement may be a reaction against the excesses of individualism—the cult of personality so obnoxious in Nazi Germany or Stalin's Russia or the moral anarchism of the past several decades. Social constructionism emphasizes human cooperation because it asserts that humans acquire their identities from groups and that their knowledge is a product of belief. But if individualism has its excesses, so can social constructionism: the police state, the group mentality to the point at which it eliminates "non-social" types such as the Jews in Nazi Germany.

One also senses in this movement a reaction against the reactionary and occasionally rampant individualism of exploitative capitalism. But social construction, in its worst phases, represents the economic inflexibility of totalitarian states in the modern world. Individualism under capitalism is not a bad thing per se; it is bad when it gives free rein to greed, power-seeking, and vicious and unethical competitiveness.

While there is no doubt a deep humanitarian impulse motivating those who champion this movement, I fear that they are blind to its potentially darker side. For example, if all knowledge is socially constructed, if the individual really doesn't exist but is the product of a social context, then we have laid the groundwork for Orwell's *1984* or, even more likely, Huxley's *Brave New World*. There, if any place, one finds socially adjusted people! My point is that this movement, if it takes a wrong turn, leads to totalitarian societies in which the individual is completely subjected to and subjugated by the will of the group.

Finally, and this may be the most damning criticism of all, I find collaborative learning and social constructionism unsound psychologically. I would be far more comfortable if I were to find in the bibliography of just one of these people Isabel Briggs Myers' *Gifts Differing*, a study of human personality types which has its bases in Jung's work. Her book opens, from the social constructionist point of view, on an extremely discordant note:

> It is fashionable to say that the individual is unique. Each is the product of his or her own heredity and environment and, therefore, is different from everyone else. From a practical standpoint, however, the doctrine of uniqueness is not useful without an exhaustive case study of every person to be educated or counselled or understood. Yet *we cannot safely assume that other people's minds work on the same principles as our own. All too often, others with whom we come in contact do not reason as we reason, or do not value the things we value, or are not interested in what interests us.*
>
> The merit of the theory presented here is that it enables us to *expect* specific personality differences in particular people and to cope with the people and the differences in a constructive way. Briefly, the theory is that much seemingly chance variation in human be-

havior is not due to chance; it is in fact the logical result of a few basic, observable differences in mental functioning. (1, italics mine)

The author then goes on to identify sixteen distinctive personality types. She finds major differences between introverts and extraverts, between individuals who perceive their world through the senses and those who perceive through intuition; between individuals who come to conclusions through thinking instead of feeling; and between those who develop a judging opposed to a perceptive attitude toward the outer world. What makes her theory of personality types so intriguing are the various combinations of these traits and the extent to which dominant processes are complemented and partially balanced by auxiliary processes.

My own guess is that a good many of the people who are attracted to social constructionism and collaborative learning are what Myers-Briggs calls ESFJ types. Here is her characterization of such people:

Value, above all, harmonious human contacts.

Best at jobs dealing with people and in situations where needed cooperation can be won by good will.

Friendly, tactful, sympathetic, able almost always to express the feelings appropriate to the moment.

Sensitive to praise and criticism, and anxious to conform to all legitimate expectations.

Judgment outwardly directed, liking to have things decided and settled.

Persevering, conscientious, orderly even in small matters, and inclined to insist that others be the same.

Idealistic and loyal, capable of great devotion to a loved person or institution or cause.

Thinking-judgment may occasionally help in appreciating and adapting to points made by a thinker, but is never permitted to oppose feeling aims.

She says further, "All their mental processes seem to operate best by contact. Van der Hoop says, 'Their thoughts take shape while being expressed' (J. H. Van der Hoop. *Conscious Orientation*. New York: Harcourt Brace, 1939.)."

There are some other personality types, however, with whom the ESFJ is going to have considerable difficulty. One, in particular, caught my attention: the Introverted Intuitive Types. Here are their characteristics:

Driven by their inner vision of the possibilities.

Determined to the point of stubbornness.

Intensely individualistic, though this shows less in INFJs, who take more pains to harmonize their individualism with their environment.

Stimulated by difficulties, and most ingenious in solving them.

Willing to concede that the impossible takes a little longer—but not much.

More interested in pioneering a new road than in anything to be found along the beaten path.

Motivated by inspiration, which they value above everything else and use confidently for their best achievements in any field they choose—science, engineering, invention, political or industrial empire-building, social reform, teaching, writing, psychology, philosophy, or religion.

Deeply discontented in a routine job that offers no scope for inspiration.

Gifted, at their best, with a fine insight into the deeper meanings of things and with a great deal of drive. (112, italics mine)

Again, quoting Van der Hoop's work, admittedly dated but still very convincing, she provides this further information about this particular personality type:

Such children are not very amenable to influence from their environment. They may have periods of uncertainty and reserve, after which they suddenly become very determined, and if then they are opposed, they may manifest an astonishing self-will and obstinacy. As a result of the intensely spontaneous activity within, they are frequently moody, occasionally brilliant and original, then again reserved, stubborn and arrogant.

In later life, also, it is a persistent characteristic of people of this type, that while on the one hand they possess great determination, on the other hand they find it very difficult to express what they want. Although they may have only a vague feeling about the way they want to go, and of the meaning of their life, they will nevertheless reject with great stubbornness anything that does not fit in with this. They fear lest external influences or circumstances should drive them in a wrong direction, and they resist on principle. (48)

One other point of interest derived from this most interesting book, to which I have not done even partial justice, is that the majority of people are extraverts but, curiously enough, many of the college students she studied were introverts. Her student population was taken from prestigious Eastern schools, a good time ago, however, and very likely does not reflect the balance of personality types found in the modern public university.

Now, what has all this to do with the collaborative learners and the social constructionists? A number of things, but let me outline the major points. I feel very strongly that this movement fails to recognize its inherent groupiness. Bruffee has said that the social perspective no longer assumes that "people write to persuade or to distinguish themselves and their points of view and to gain the acquiescence of other individuals." Instead, it assumes "that people write in order to be accepted, to join, to be regarded as another member of the culture or community that constitutes the writer's audience." Only an extravert could make such assertions. It totally fails to account for the creation of a work like Swift's *A Modest Proposal*. It totally fails to come to terms with a writer like William Manchester who, in doing the research on John Kennedy's assassination, expressed his complete distaste for committee and collaborative efforts which he found time-consuming, time-wasting, and completely frustrating.

In reporting on and evaluating the success of his efforts to establish writing-across-the-curriculum programs, Toby Fulwiler, apparently without realizing the depth of the personality problem he is confronting, observes these distinctions in responses to his program. "We learned right away that writing workshops cannot inspire or transform unmotivated, inflexible, or highly-suspicious faculty members" (115). I find this language absolutely wonderful. Note the terms used to characterize those who don't adapt: "unmotivated," "inflexible," "highly-suspicious." If ever there was a case of the extraverted personality describing the introverted, this is it. He goes on:

> Some people seem to be constitutionally uncomfortable with workshop-style activities which require a lot of participant risks, such as reading aloud one's own writing to colleagues or generating consensus ideas or writing in a personal journal. . . . Such people often attend with good intentions, but cannot adapt the informal workshop style to their own learning and teaching styles. One person, for example, from mathematics could not identify with any activity that encouraged multiple drafts as the route to good writing: he always wrote well in one draft and could not understand why others could not also. I believed that he spoke truly about his own writing process, but his vocal resistance was such that many in the workshop found him difficult to work with and I had a hard time being patient with his intolerance. The mode of writing and learning we presented in our model did not match his model at all. (115–16)

Exactly. Fulwiler has just described a classic confrontation between the ESFJ and INTJ types described earlier. How appropriate that the man giving him the most trouble was a mathematician! One might also ask Fulwiler this question: Had the man with whom he had so much difficulty been conducting the workshop and attempting to gain acceptance of *his* learning style, might not Fulwiler himself have become resistant, difficult to work with, and taxing to the patience of the workshop leader?

I do not wish to belabor this point much longer, but it is essential that we grasp the ironic egocentricism of the social constructionists and collaborative learners when they characterize the behavior of radically different personality types as "inflexible," "stubborn," and "infantile." The history of social, scientific, musical, and literary innovation is a history of people who were light years ahead of their times and who decided that their contemporaries could go to hell; they would do their thing and let the rest catch up. To describe such behavior as infantile is the fundamental mistake of the E personality judging the I.

Psychologist Erich Fromm addressed this problem some years ago in his discussion of the creative attitude. He says that the sense of self, the sense by which one experiences himself as the true center of his world, is what it means to be original. "To feel a sense of self, a sense of identity, is a necessity for every human being. We would become insane unless we had such a sense of self" (50). He continues with the observation that the sense of "I as we" is characteristic of a *primitive* society. "As man proceeds in the process of evolution and emerges as an individual, his sense of identity becomes separated from that of the group" (50).

Then, in a direct challenge to the social constructionist point of view he says:

> There is a great deal of misunderstanding about this sense of self. There are some psychologists who believe that the sense of self is nothing but a reflection of the social role which is ascribed to him, nothing but the response to expectations others have about him. Although it is true that, empirically speaking, this is the kind of self most people in our society experience, *it is nevertheless a pathological phenomenon, the result of which is deep insecurity and anxiety and a compulsion to conform.* (50, italics mine)

In a passage much more congenial to social constructionists and collaborative learners, however, Fromm says that a person "must break out of his person. He has to give up holding on to himself as a thing and begin to experience himself only in the process of creative response; paradoxically enough, if he can experience himself in this process he loses himself. He transcends the boundaries of his own

person, and at the very moment when he feels 'I am' he also feels 'I am you, I am one with the whole world'" (50–51). Perhaps this is the kind of collaboration social constructionists seek.

What can we now say in summing up our impressions of social constructionism and collaborative learning? I find much to admire in both. Their recognition of the importance of the human community in shaping our perceptions of the world and our use of language is one which cannot be idly dismissed. Their attempts to engage students in creating their own knowledge and learning to solve problems constructively and cooperatively is certainly preferable to teaching them how to compete in ever more vicious ways. But we must remember that this movement, like that of the cognitive psychologists which has just preceded it, like the revival of classical rhetoric and the new experiments with invention, voice, and free writing, is not the writing teacher's panacea. It will work with certain students in certain contexts.[9] It most certainly will not work with a number of students in a number of contexts. Teachers should assimilate as much of this theory and method as is congenial to their own teaching styles and which they can employ usefully in their classrooms. It should become yet one more resource in assisting a teacher in composition instruction, surely one of the most difficult teaching tasks confronted by any person who makes pedagogy his or her vocation. Composition teachers, like writers, need a tremendous variety of resources on which to draw. Collaborative learning, when employed judiciously, is one that can prove useful.

I hope it will be apparent that I am not trying to be reactionary or obstructionist. Instead, I have offered this long list of my reservations about collaborative learning and the philosophical and theoretical underpinnings upon which it rests, admittedly sharply critical at times, so that its advocates will be able to ponder them and perhaps escape the intellectual hubris which always characterizes particular philosophical or educational movements in the hour of their ascendancy.

Notes

1. I do not want to give the impression that I am ignoring pervasive and powerful writing-across-the-curriculum programs which have been in full swing for some time. I see them at the very least as complementary to and, more accurately, part of the collaborative writing movement. Writing across the curriculum is much concerned with discourse communities and the way individuals function within them.

   I also do not wish to give the impression that I think the work of the cognitive psychologists was a passing fad which will be largely ignored in the future. No such thing. I am suggesting, however, that whereas for the past ten years or so the cognitive psychologists have held center stage, they now find themselves giving it up to the social constructionists and collaborative learners. There is, of course, strong evidence that the cognitive psychologists are very much aware of this shift of gravity in our profession and are seeking to accommodate themselves to it. For example, reports coming out of the Center for the Study of Writing, a joint enterprise involving faculty at Carnegie Mellon and the University of California at Berkeley, imply a linking of the cognitive psychologists and social constructionists. Technical Report Number 1 from this group, "Research in Writing: Past, Present, and Future," jointly authored by Sarah Warshauer Freedman, Anne Haas Dyson, Linda Flower, and Wallace Chafe, openly states as one of its objectives, "Building a Social-Cognitive Theory." I cannot speak for others who may have read it, but I have two problems with this paper: (1) it is historically naive, implying as it does that very little of significance in composition research happened before 1970; (2) by linking cognitive psychology and social constructionism, it compounds the problems endemic to both.

2. It continually amuses me to read about the "appearance" of nontraditional students through open admissions programs initiated around 1970. I have always felt that Mina Shaughnessy's *Errors and Expectations* received such an immediate and enthusiastic response among segments of our profession, not so much because of its sensitive and intelligent assessment of nontraditional students and their problems, but because it offered immediate practical assistance to college teachers, primarily in the East, who were baffled by this new "animal" in their classroom. Those of us teaching in the middle of the country were quite familiar with nontraditional students, having had them in our classrooms for decades and having devised a number of strategems for assisting them. University of Kansas teaching assistants who date back to 1952 still have in their files a paper called "The Wolverian," a quintessential nontraditional student document.

3. One can find a much more rigorous and systematically worked-out presentation of these philosophical and theoretical issues in chapters 3–6 of Karen Burke LeFevre's *Invention as a Social Act.*

4. See, in addition to Brown's, the essays by John Livingston Lowes and Elizabeth Jackson.

5. Eloquent testimonies to Scott's wisdom and benevolence have been provided by Helen Ogden Mahin and Ray Stannard Baker. In a letter to me, October 10, 1983, Harold Allen, who once had the opportunity to see Scott in action, made these observations: "The class met in a large room in Angell Hall. Its seven or eight members sat around a huge round table, along with Professor Scott. . . . Scott presided with warm—not austere—dignity. He looked, of course, like a professor 'of the old school,' with that carefully trimmed Van Dyke, but his manner was not austere. There was a rather free give-and-take in the discussion, and he invited class reactions, but he never quite relinquished his role as the professor, the mentor, the guide, the leader."

6. Discussion of this issue always brings to mind one of Wordsworth's greatest lines in *The Prelude.* As a student in his quarters at Cambridge he says that

   . . . from my pillow, looking forth by light
   Of moon or favouring stars, I could behold
   The antechapel where the statue stood
   Of Newton with his prism and silent face,
   The marble index of a mind for ever
   Voyaging through strange seas of Thought, alone.

   This, of course, is precisely the conception of genius that the social constructionists are laboring so hard to discredit. For the time being, however, I prefer Wordsworth's to theirs.

7. Her failure to acknowledge these serious deficiencies in the normal discourse of several academic communities seriously undermines a central assumption in Catherine Pastore Blair's "Only One of the Voices: Dialogic Writing Across the Curriculum" in the April, 1988, issue of *College English.*

8. Reference is to a term coined by Winston Weathers in *An Alternate Style.* Grammar B includes such strategies as lists, collages, montages, double-voices, crots, etc. It is an extension of the options in Grammar A, the more conventional manner in which most writing is done.

9. I should point out that it will also work for certain professionals in certain contexts. For example, Andrea Lunsford and Lisa Ede have collaborated successfully on several articles because they have for one another, as my

Spanish-speaking friends say, *simpathia*. They like each other personally, they respect each other's intelligence and creativity, and they like working together.

Thomas Thompson, in an article entitled "Writing for Television" in James Collins' *The Western Writer's Handbook,* is pragmatic about collaboration. If you want to write for television, he says, "you must suffer the indignity of sharing your copy with ten to twenty other people, each of whom has an idea of how to write it much better than you do. Television is a group process, as opposed to novel writing which is a pretty individual affair" (33).

Works Cited

Abercrombie, M. L. J. *Anatomy of Judgment.* Harmondsworth: Penguin, 1960.

Baker, Ray Stannard. *Native American.* New York: Scribner's, 1941.

Blair, Catherine Pastore. "Only One of the Voices: Dialogic Writing Across the Curriculum." *College English* 50 (1988): 383–89.

Brown, Rollo. "'Kitty' of Harvard." *Atlantic Monthly* Oct. 1948: 65–69.

Bruffee, Kenneth. "Collaborative Learning and the 'Conversation of Mankind.'" *College English* 46 (1984): 635–52.

———. "Social Construction, Language, and the Authority of Knowledge: A Bibliographical Essay." *College English* 48 (1986): 773–90.

———. "The Way Out." *College English* 33 (1972): 457–70.

Cargill, Oscar. *Intellectual America.* New York: Macmillan, 1941.

Chase, Geoffrey. "Accommodation, Resistance, and the Politics of Student Writing." *College Composition and Communication* 39 (1988): 13–22.

Cowley, Malcolm. "Sociological Habit Patterns in Linguistic Transmogrification." *The Reporter* 20 Sept. 1956: 41–43.

Freedman, Sarah Warshauer, et al. "Research in Writing: Past, Present, and Future." Technical Report No. 1. U of California/Carnegie Mellon U: Center for the Study of Writing, 1987.

Fromm, Erich. "The Creative Attitude." *Creativity and Its Cultivation.* Ed. Harold H. Anderson. New York: Harper, 1959. 44–54.

Fulwiler, Toby. "How Well Does Writing Across the Curriculum Work?" *College English* 46 (1984): 237–42.

Geertz, Clifford. *Local Knowledge.* New York: Basic Books, 1983.

Jackson, Elizabeth. "The Kittredge Way." *College English* 4 (1943): 483–87.

Kuhn, Thomas. *The Structure of Scientific Revolutions.* 2nd ed. Chicago: U of Chicago P, 1970.

LeFevre, Karen Burke. *Invention as a Social Act.* CCCC Studies in Writing and Rhetoric. Carbondale: Southern Illinois UP, 1987.

Lowes, John Livingston. "George Lyman Kittredge." *American Scholar* 10 (1941): 469–71.

Madden, Peter, and Lloyd Engdahl. "The EMPTI Guide to Swollen Prose." *Psychology Today* June 1973: 99.

Mahin, Helen. "Half Lights." *The Fred Newton Scott Anniversary Papers.* Chicago: The U of Chicago P, 1929. 1–3.

Mason, Edwin. *Collaborative Learning.* New York: Agathon, 1972.

Myers, Isabel Briggs, with Peter B. Myers. *Gifts Differing.* Palo Alto: Consulting Psychologist's P, 1980.

Rohman, D. Gordon, and Albert O. Wlecke. *Pre-Writing: The Construction and Application of Models for Concept Formation in Writing.* Cooperative Research Project No. 2174, U.S. Department of Health, Education, and Welfare. East Lansing: Michigan State University, 1964.

Rorty, Richard. *Philosophy and the Mirror of Nature.* Princeton: Princeton UP, 1979.

Thompson, Thomas. "Writing for Television." *The Western Writer's Handbook.* Ed. James L. Collins. Boulder: Johnson Books, 1987. 33–42.

Trimbur, John. "Collaborative Learning and Teaching Writing." *Perspectives on Research and Scholarship in Composition.* Ed. Ben W. McClelland and Timothy R. Donovan. New York MLA, 1985. 87–109.

Weathers, Winston. *An Alternate Style.* Rochelle Park, NJ: Hayden, 1980.

Weaver, Richard. "The *Phaedrus* and the Nature of Rhetoric." *The Ethics of Rhetoric.* Chicago: Regnery, 1953. 3–26.

Williamson, Samuel. "How to Write Like a Social Scientist." *Saturday Review of Literature* 4 Oct. 1947: 17, 27, 28.

Zoellner, Robert. "Talk-Write: A Behavioral Pedagogy for Composition." *College English* 30 (1969): 267–320.

Rhythm and Pattern in a Composing Life

Louise Wetherbee Phelps

Phelps's essay appears in Writers on Writing. *Ed. Tom Waldrep. Vol. 1. New York: Random House, 1985. 241–57.*

An experience, a very humble experience, is capable of generating and carrying any amount of theory (or intellectual content), but a theory apart from an experience cannot be definitely grasped even as a theory.

—JOHN DEWEY

When I perform I'm transformed into something else. Once you start to touch on yourself you touch other people. But it has to have fire. It has to have meaning. It has to have living—all the things that I've gone through and that I'm sure everyone else has.

—DWIKE MITCHELL, JAZZ PIANIST

THE MUSIC IN MY HEAD

Sometime early in my marriage I discovered the tune in my head. My husband informed me that I had an irritating habit—quite unconscious—of tapping my feet or hands incessantly, especially while reading. Following the rhythm back into my mind, I found the tune there, or rather many tunes. Occasionally I sit down at the piano and find it at my fingertips, but mostly it just runs along quietly below my thoughts and sets my foot swinging. Recently, I read in Howard Gardner's account of musical intelligence that according to Roger Sessions my tune marks me a composer:

As [Sessions] explains it, a composer can be readily identified by the fact that he constantly has "tones in his head"—that is, he is always, somewhere near the surface of his consciousness, hearing tones, rhythms,

and larger musical patterns. While many of these patterns are worth little musically and may, in fact, be wholly derivative, it is the composer's lot constantly to be monitoring and reworking these patterns.

Composing begins at the moment when these ideas begin to crystallize and to assume a significant shape.[1]

Whatever little talent I might have as a musician is exploited only in the pleasure of playing the piano and listening to music. But I am another kind of composer, with a different and predominant tune in my head—the music of my worded thoughts. Like the musician, I lead a composing life, and the sounds and images of language in my head crystallize periodically into texts. This essay is about the rhythms and patterns of my composing life, and how my writer's imagination works and elaborates them constantly toward finished discourse.

I have been struck for a long time by the embedding of so-called "composing processes" in the continuous language experience of the literate person. Every human being is immersed in a sea of discourse that permeates the cellular membranes of the self with a ceaseless flow of talk, writing, and verbal thought. These currents form the semiotic environment or cultural context for my understanding and using language in a given instant. In this great interchange of symbolic energy I experience myself distinctively as a central source of language, through the symbolizing function of my human brain, which continually transforms my experience into a personal stream of verbal activity. That ongoing process of symbolization forms the innermost context for my specific language experiences and the situational matrix for all my composing activities.

Composing, as distinct from the practical literacy of signing one's name or writing a grocery list, or from the fluent spontaneous improvisation of conversation, is a process of channeling and consciously working some of this dynamic linguistic material into discursive form. Being a verbal composer by nature, choice, and training, I am attuned to the discursive possibilities in my inner and outer language, which appears to me tacitly as intrinsically composable, inviting craft to shape and elaborate it as wood or stone invites the sculptor's hand. This situation engenders distinguishable composing acts, not when I pick up a pen, but whenever I direct my mind attentively toward a particular event, thought, or utterance as potentially textual and begin to play with it and work it over in composing ways. At any moment in my daily round—fixing dinner, playing ping-pong, listening to music, talking with friends—such moments of composing attention may crystallize in my consciousness as images, fragments of text, shadowy patterns: sometimes transient, merging smoothly back into the verbal background; sometimes fixing themselves in notes or talk or memory; sometimes pursued effortfully throughout long periods of sustained composition.

But I may also be composing without knowing it. Much of my language and thought is not consciously oriented to text, yet later I will perceive, use, and refer to it as a precursor of achieved writing. More significantly, like other nervous activity much of my ongoing composing process is submerged below consciousness and only occasionally and partially rises to the level of intensity where it can be felt. Even less often does it result in observable language behavior. But in my life as a writer part of the stream of my language is continually being directed in all these ways toward multiple, vaguely anticipated or possible textual events, some of which are gradually discriminated from their matrix and realized as individual entities. I see

this enlarged, holistic "composing process" as the primary reality to be explained.

This is quite a different perspective from that of most empirical research, which takes discrete, time-limited composing events to be the molecular elements of literacy and does not really try to account for their contextual source in the verbal life stream of the individual. If you try to extend the model for that purpose, it quickly breaks down. My composing life is a texture of discursive ideas that cannot easily be referred to in particular texts. Looking ahead, I cannot fully identify which strands of my composing will result in texts, and how they will get braided or separated into specific bundles of written language. Looking back from the finished text, I cannot clearly trace its history; its beginnings and sources are fuzzy, its development entangled with the threads of other compositions. Because my texts are relatively long (up to book length, some of them), deeply felt and thought through; because I write slowly, often painfully, and develop ideas discontinuously over long stretches; and perhaps because I am composing theories of discourse that depend on a reflective understanding of my own language experience, my personal life, work, and writing intersect in changing but always intimate ways.

The peculiar reflexivity of being a writing theorist means that I am always examining my own composing with a detached and ironic eye. What I am trying to do here—a beginner's effort—is to intensify that self-reflective attitude to approach the level and quality of phenomenological description, which involves not only intuiting, analyzing, and describing particulars of composing in their full concreteness, but also attempting to attain insight into the essence of the experience.[2] A primary obstacle to this goal is the conceptual baggage I carry—the labels, concepts, distinctions, and assumptions I have absorbed from existing rhetorical or composing theory and the teaching tradition. In order to clarify my intuitions and open myself patiently to the truth of my own experiences, I need to bracket or hold in abeyance two aspects of my composing that carry a heavy burden of such prejudices. Formulating and maintaining those brackets has been the most difficult and rigorous task in composing this account, requiring constant vigilance. As in perceiving one of those ambiguous visual figures, my mind slips constantly even now into a different gestalt.

The first bracket involves postponing the question of how specific composing activities attach themselves to particular texts so that I experience them as coherent and bounded events. This bracket is implied in the distinction I took as a premise, between composing episodes and a composing life. The naive common-sense conception of "writing a paper" so powerfully dominates one's consciousness that only by trying to set it aside can I feel clearly, and thus articulate, the slow, deep rhythms and texture of the composing life. Ultimately, this decision leads me to conceive composing events as constructed from a more diffuse and confused experience—as much the products of a composing life as the texts themselves. More immediately, it requires me to observe and describe my composing from a middle distance, close enough for detail but not zoomed in to the molecular level of, say, protocols, which follow thought and inscription minute by minute over brief intervals. What is grasped from middle distance is called by psychologists "molar activity," meaning events perceived at a normative level where, though dispersed in time and space, they cohere holistically and acquire names such as walking the dog or going on a diet.

The second bracket suspends consideration of the temporal nature of composing experience, even as molar activity, because of the irresistible association of sequence with the history of particular texts. When dealing with such an integral yet intricately interlaced tissue as a composing life, one cannot grasp it through componential analysis, which involves cutting up a whole into its irreducible atomic elements, examining them in isolation, and determining rules of combination and transformation. Rather, I want to abstract from the ongoing vital process itself the dynamic principles that govern its continuities and change. Hence the unit of analysis here is a stretch of experience—approximately three summer months—sliced at convenient junctures from the continuum of my composing life, during which I studied introspectively these processes and their patterns. Those which I can identify as textually pointed present a dense, busy pattern of simultaneous and interconnected intellectual work.

Here are some of the more distinct activities, in no particular order: writing a prospectus for a book of philosophical essays; reading for and planning three remaining essays for that book; much professional and personal reading that is less textually directed; imagining a graduate course on literacy development and a writing course to be taught next year; writing an abstract for a convention paper; preparing and giving two lectures for a seminar on rhetoric and composition; making notes for future projects of various kinds; preparing a commentary on a pair of essays; working on this account. I talked with family and friends, wrote letters, journals, notes, abstracts, outlines, essays, kept a reading journal, filled three daybooks with notes on my composing, elaborated all these in further notes, annotations and commentary, sketches and maps, drafts, on the computer screen. In the chaos and multiplicity of these composing activities I discern finally an underlying simplicity in my composing life: two deeply rooted impulses whose conjunctions and opposition construct its fundamental rhythm.

Quite late in the composing work on this essay, in a marginal notation to my daybook, I wrote the charged phrase "resistance to form." There followed quickly a wave of annotations whereby I gathered together under this rubric dozens of diverse and hitherto unrelated behaviors, observations, and reflections. These words signal my first clear intuition of a motive underlying the fluctuations of surface patterns in my composing, almost immediately suggesting a dialectic of opposing and complementary impulses: the *generative,* a desire to link information and feeling into more and more densely connected and layered networks; and the *discursive,* a drive to formulate meaning in precisely articulated, highly textualized, and rhetorically addressed sequences of meaning.

My composing nature motivates me powerfully to formulate knowledge and feeling in the discursive order of written language. But this drive encounters at every step the pressure of the generative impulse to wait, to postpone form indefinitely: instead to remain open to the inexhaustibly changing patterns of connection within the stream of experience. My notes, journals, discourse maps, drafts, inscriptions of all kinds short of finished texts—all these display an extraordinary resistance to order, hierarchy, selection, definition: they are scrawled in every direction on the page, in layers of inserts and annotations, in various colors, with an impatient illegibility. I feel compulsively reluctant to follow the conventions of outlining, to write or think in terms of thesis statements; I proliferate redundant words and phrases rather than choose one form over another and, especially on my computer screen, multiply and juxtapose alternate versions of whole stretches of text.

Yet in the very abundance of these wild and anarchic scribblings there is an insistent desire to articulate distinctions, find the precise and true word and image, develop lines of thought that can arrow through the jumble of ideas toward some satisfying closure. In one place I write in my notebook of the danger in outlines of thinness—loss of depth and richness of meaning; in the next breath I write of the danger of muddle and disorder in my loosely scripting ways, in the piles of paper that rise around the house in little puddles concentrated around couch, chair, desk, bed. Between these two (I write finally) I am drawn back and forth irresistibly, as in breathing. The push and pull of generative and discursive impulses is not just a brute force struggle; they enact a true dialectic rhythm. Without the generative urge the drive toward form would be empty; without the possibility of writing them out these patterns of understanding would remain mute and unrealized.

It is tempting to suggest here such classic oppositions as metaphor and metonymy, or to invoke the specialized functions of right and left hemispheres—staples of composition theory. I will acknowledge these cultural resonances and their undoubted channeling of my thought even as I insist on bracketing these theoretical constructs along with others. I am trying here to train and to rely on

my own introspection, largely via the medium of a daybook always at hand, repeatedly reread and examined, annotated, expanded in separate notes, elaborated in layer upon layer of reflections. Here is the direct source of the distinctions drawn so far, and the basis for pursuing them further.

The deeply figured interplay of motives that I have described runs along below the rhythms that play across the surface of my everyday composing mind: the ebb and flow of power and fluency; highs and lows of feeling; repetition of themes, breaks in continuity, turns of feeling; the symmetries and contrasts of form. From these patterns I want to abstract three "moments" of composing as action. Much earlier than my intuition of the dialectic of generative and discursive impulses, I recognized "generating," "structuring," and "focusing" as the three most distinctive molar experiences of my composing life. The trouble was that their meaning as concepts shifted constantly (even throughout the drafting of this essay), largely because it is so hard to detach these notions from the temporal evolution of a given text in "stages" (i.e., the planning, organizing, drafting, revising, editing sequence we attribute to composing events). By rigorously striving for the suspension of textual particularity and temporality I succeeded in conceiving these as abstract, unordered phases or "moments"—composing ways of the mind in the sense that David Sudnow describes the ways of the hand in playing jazz piano.[3] I am using "moments" in the phenomenological sense, not as temporal points (though they have complex temporal implications) but as contextual elements of a concrete experience that can be conceived separately only by abstraction. They may be thought of to begin with as attitudes or modes of attention in terms of which I think composingly, with characteristic feeling tones, objects, purposes, textual expression, pace, structure, and problems.

Through abstraction and contrastive analysis these moments will appear at first pure and distinct attitudes, but even at this point they must be defined relationally. Their complex interpenetrations and mutual affordances will unfold as the description proceeds, until finally I must remove the brackets and deal with events of concrete textuality. For now I will put their relation in this tentative formulation: *generating* is the moment of connectivity, an open-ended exchange between myself and the ideational environment; *focusing* is the moment of tunnel vision, single-mindedly coming to grips with meaning at the fine-grained levels of textuality, sacrificing many latent possibilities for the lesser actuality; *structuring* is the work that mediates these modes, translating open radial patterns into closed, linear, teleological ones.

GENERATING

Throughout my daybooks I have tried repeatedly to capture the feeling of the generative moment. It is not a cool, cerebral experience but a joyous state of physical excitement and pure power felt in the stomach and rising up in the chest as a flood of energy that pours out in rapid, explosive bursts of language. It is a pleasantly nervous state, like the feeling of the gymnast ready to mount the apparatus who is tuned tautly and confidently to the powers and capabilities of her own body. Ideas compel expression: I write in my daybook of their force shooting and sparking through my fingers onto the paper.

The generative power both draws on and affects everything in my environment. It means being wide open to stimuli from every direction and source. In this state any experience, no matter how trivial, may suddenly seem strikingly relevant, funneling into the expanding connective web of my thought. My mind transforms everything around me—the concentration of an Olympic athlete, the spareness of a Japanese house, the self-consciousness of an adolescent son—into ideas for writing about writing. When most intense this attitude makes the entire stream of daily life nutritive, to the point of overstimulation. The transforming power of the generative state is generous, contagious, unselective in what it affects, ideas touching each other off like firecrackers almost simultaneously. Ultimately composing power spills over from writing to other dimensions of my life, creating everywhere possibilities for action, order, transformation.

The essence of the generative moment is experiencing the human power to connect. The small power of my composing is perhaps a very shadowy expression of the unity of being that is felt in profound religious experience—what Freud called the oceanic feeling. It is by nature both an enormous and a diffuse power, because it understands or presents everything I know in terms of (ultimately) everything else I know or learn. Nothing is excluded and therefore nothing is selected or directed—except, as we shall see, through the mediation of the structuring moment. Hence to be in the high generative state is to be uncritical, naive, playful, and unfocused. Typically I might wake up from a dream, rush out of the shower, or return from my hour-long commute with my head crammed with inchoate ideas, fragments of phrases, titles, vague patterns that I try quickly to capture in free, telegraphic, idiosyncratic text and, often, little icons—sketches, diagrams, lists. This brings me to what I call the observables of my composing, a technology of physical forms, formats, tools, places, and ways of inscription.

Technology creates an external memory without which I could not compose because of the transience of the word music in my head. I store in this safety net traces of the vast verbal matrix from which my texts will emerge: in a homely image, like the French stockpot simmering on the back of the stove, to which nutritious bits of bones and meat are regularly added, forming a base for various stews, sauces, soups, and other dishes.

My basic stockpots are two more or less continuous notebooks, one called "The Third Basket" and the other "Reading Journal." The Third Basket takes its name from Sir Isaiah Berlin, who wrote that human questions fall into three baskets: the empirical, for questions whose answers depend on data; the formal, for questions whose answers require calculation (deduction); and the third basket, for everything else, including questions of ordinary life, art, craft, and philosophy.[4] The Third Basket is mainly a dated journal where I write down any thinking that seems to point toward texts, typically philosophical writing about discourse. Near the beginning I simply list, and periodically update, titles or key words that trace the course of my projected writing. I have added other sections at times, on teaching or large projects, but my journal works best when I throw everything into one pot. Although apparently a sequence of pages, it is actually constructed in layer upon layer of annotation, producing an enormous, inchoate mass of observations and commentary; any page may contain ideas that end up in four or five different texts. Recently I have been working on systematizing these layers through ink colors and tags written in margins and on facing pages. I try to keep the Reading Journal physically independent, but it has the same texture of notes upon notes: paraphrase, quotation, commentary, and response merging into text planning—more about what I am going to write than what I've read.

This prediscursive, partly iconic analogue to my memory presents similar problems of tagging, filing, and retrieving information. I am peculiarly incapable of detail memory and find myself having to read and sort through both my journals and subsequent notes repeatedly in order to produce a particular text, going back to this chaotic source even though I have made a long series of abstracts and outlines that are supposed to reduce and organize it. I sometimes wonder if I am relying more heavily than most people on the global, fuzzy, holographic aspect of memory, as represented in notebooks that, like a radio set, can only be tuned in all at once. If I do not work continuously on a piece of writing, most of it disappears from my head and I must rely on my notebooks, not so much to remember what I planned, but to stimulate a new, similar but not identical train of thought. This method (not really a choice, but my nature) is undoubtedly slow and inefficient, but it also holds off the premature closure of form and keeps my mind more flexible to adapt to new information. To think freshly it is often useful, even necessary, to forget what I (or someone else) has already thought. I thus notice in my composing a texture of recognition and surprise, innovation and continuity, which marks the reinvention in different terms of half-forgotten themes. Over a writing life this texture is how I come to know and project my identity as a theorist and composer.

How do I make up my stockpot and what are the ingredients? Basically I am always generating patterns of two kinds: patterns that connect events and objects and abstractions in the world I am writing about, and patterns of discursivity. Searching for such patterns is not a matter of applying "heuristics" in the textbook sense. Over the years I have acquired heightened sensitivity to abstract connections of ideas in my field and to discourse patterns generally, constantly enhanced by studying writers I admire, students' work and my own. Like other composers, I have a conceptual style, a habit of noticing certain kinds of connections and constructing them discursively in typical ways. Probably the coherence of my work as a theorist depends as much on these preferences (which have many cultural roots) as on specific content. For example, I often develop a distinction that is mediated by a third term. I almost always turn a straightforward analysis or description of something in the world into a self-reflexive and ironic consideration of thinking and writing about it. I am fascinated by the particle-wave-field distinction in two interpretations. First, setting in motion an apparently static object and, its reverse, freezing a flux in space or time so as to perceive it as a simultaneous whole. Second, the precipitation of a perceptually real "particle" from a dance of energy through the interaction of an observer. The reader can discern some of these patterns in this discourse; over the years I have become self-conscious of their appearance and learned to recognize and elaborate them deliberately.

My power of creativity is subject to a natural ebb and flow accompanied by extreme swings of mood. I have described the flow, a state of high excitement; the ebb is an affliction of spirit that I have not learned to accept easily. I call it a slump, to suggest the inexplicable alternation of slumps and streaks in the baseball player's season, defined as a sustained period of discouragement, depression, confusion, loss of confidence and competence. Typically, I went through one long slump this summer of several weeks, much of it spent worrying futilely because I could not restore my energy and work when I needed to. I wrote in my daybook:

"listless, lethargic, no ideas, no new ideas, all ideas seem worthless. Nothing connects or reminds or leads anywhere." (I knew, of course, that it would pass; but that was an intellectual conviction, not truly felt.) I marveled at the descriptions I had written earlier of the generative moment; later, when I had passed out of the slump I could not remember how it felt or how one could ever feel that way.

Trying to exorcise that feeling, I looked for explanations and, finding no rational ones, blamed myself for sloth and a failure of will. After a while I discovered that there is a natural rhythm to creativity that cannot be altered simply by will power. When I chart the ebb and flow of generativity in my composing life, there are broad, slowly changing tides representing my power to compose over a period of time, and little waves and swells day to day, minute to minute. I am particularly susceptible to the ebb of creative energy in transition periods between work activities that are differently paced.

At the same time, this intense lethargy is not arbitrary, because whatever its mysterious source it becomes attached to genuine intellectual and ethical problems that have to be worked through. The most profound of these has to do with the abstract nature of philosophical writing and a related dependence of my work on analogies to work in other disciplines.

The abstractness of writing philosophically about discourse and teaching is a constant threat to the experiential richness of connectivity that constitutes the generative moment. Abstractions empower connection because they relate concrete experiences and feelings through concepts; but they also empty those realities of their content. I write over and over again in the daybooks about my fear of losing the richness behind the abstraction and forgetting its concrete meaningfulness. When this happens, the codings in my journals and notes—lists of comparisons, titles, fragments of text—suddenly appear to be nothing but words, and I can't imagine how I could ever have expected to flesh them out in consecutive text. They are empty, thin, sparse (I complain to myself); the problem is not too few connections but too many,

too vague, too general. In contrast, when my concepts are charged with generative power they carry a penumbra of concrete possibility layered down to my own actual experience of discourse or teaching or growth. This structure supports and anticipates the detailed working out of a concept and constitutes an image of achievement for eventual text, like those which athletes project with closed eyes to set in their muscles the patterns they are about to enact. When I lose that image, my ability to write is paralyzed and I must restore it by reexploring the relationship between my abstraction and the realities it represents or derives from. (At least, I console myself, I cannot deliberately write abstractions false to my experience.)

One reason for losing this contact is that I draw many ideas for understanding problems in my own field by analogy with other disciplines. This necessitates adapting concepts and terms to a new technical use and producing connected step-by-step arguments. It means that work starts at a high level of abstraction, relying on a strong intuition of relevance that is based on my own experience but has not been directly referred to it. An example is my application (in the lecture to the Purdue Seminar in Rhetoric and Composition) of concepts drawn from the analysis of women's ethical development to composition as a field. After drawing together a number of points about the status of the discipline, I was inspired in reading Carol Gilligan's *In a Different Voice* to interpret these in a developmental framework, specifically to see composition as experiencing the same developmental crises and espousing the same "ethic of care" as the women she describes.[5] The typical work of composing following this intuition involves analyzing and following out the implications of the concept rather than illustrating or detailing the experience it is based on. Thus my musings explore the various ways that philosophical discourse makes itself real to readers while trying to make sure I myself do not lose the sense of experience that charges my concepts and analogies with meaning—a problem that is not solved by giving examples in some simple sense.

FOCUSING

Focusing is the mood or mode of fierce concentration that funnels thought from its diffuse matrix into fully discursive form. Literally, it is the attitude necessary for me to draft a single text per se, as distinct from producing written thought in fragments and clusters unattached or only loosely attached to possible discourse. Here it is necessary to explain what I mean by fully discursive, and how text differs from the writing of daily life—a kind of deposit or trace of the constantly composing mind.

Text creates the virtual experience of a train of thought for a reader or audience to whom it is addressed in a situation defined by occasion and purpose. It does not, like the composing life reflected in my notebooks and their extensions, simply go on indefinitely; it has distinct scope as an episode. Thus it begins, moves, ends. As I have suggested, composing is the tension between the effort to turn mental life into event and the correlative resistance to the closure of form as false to experience. For me, to produce text as event it seems necessary to construct it eventfully: on a single impulse held with intense concentration from beginning to end of the inscription process.

Here is what I imagine, desire, project as I write—discursive form in the large. It is patterned in many ways, but gathering up all these patterns is a great sweep or movement to carry the reader irresistibly through the text from start to close. I conceive it most often as a path I must find, and create for the reader, through a nonlinear network of patterns. As a path it reveals the topography of thought as felt, with a distinctive rhythm, pace, points of intensity and relaxation, surprising turns—an experience something like skiing a particular trail. The point of departure is crucial, and my most difficult task in focusing is to find my way onto a path that feels right and flows smoothly. I am constructing something here entirely different structurally from the verbal matrix—what I call the "narrative line" for a given text.

Two decision points fix my intention to focus. The first is a resolve to plan, and the second to write out (draft and complete) a particular text, defined as particular by title, audience, occasion, and a process of collecting relevant material that has gradually accumulated in my various storehouses of composing ideas. Each stage of intent has a textual analogue: at the planning point, setting up a folder to contain any further writings for this definitely anticipated text, separating these sharply from the notebooks (I will use these now as a stimulus and source of plans); at the drafting point, titling and numbering a page as first in a consecutive sequence. No matter how many times I throw away that page, I will always begin again by titling the whole piece and (usually) identifying or titling an introduction.

By the time the second decision is made, I have put myself in the focused state, usually gradually and at considerable cost. By definition focusing excludes composing in the usual diffuse daily ways since it requires attending exclusively to one text and (because of the difficulty in holding concentration) producing it as rapidly and continuously as possible. (In the case of very long texts, this is a severe problem, only partly alleviated by chunking them into parts.) I describe this process in the notebooks as one of closing down, shutting out stimulation, tightening and screwing down my attention through an exertion of will, sinking deep into a trance of concentration. It is a self-contained, inward, absorbed state. When the composing is difficult or the text long I work almost continuously for days if possible (to the degree my family and circumstances will tolerate it), resisting interruption and scheduling meals and rest around the rhythms of my thought and writing. During such a period I must deliberately avoid intellectual stimulation such as reading, which might throw me into a generative state, incompatible with focusing because it destroys my control over the connectivity of my understanding.

The primary means of control, or the top level, is a set of patterns that has emerged, usually tentatively and somewhat confusedly, from the verbal matrix and structuring process. This includes a rather unstable anticipation of the narrative line that will eventually dominate the text. All these patterns together constitute what I think of as the harmony of the text, within and against which I improvise a melody, the spinning out of ideas from word to phrase to sentence to paragraph. I call changes in the harmony "deep revision" and in the melody "shallow revision," the latter including both language and content (inseparable at this microscopic level). As in the improvisation of jazz, the melody is the most labile and free element of what is created; harmonic changes, that is, restructuring the conceptual patterns, are less drastic and frequent; the most enduring, and in discourse, least definable, qualities are the rhythm of thought and the identity or essence of intention that persists through all the changes.

I am going to say little of the actual improvisation, the detail of drafting, because it must be described at a closer distance than the molar one I have chosen. Broadly, it is a recurrent cycling between maps or abstractions of meaning, freely written loose approximations, and carefully formed text, which involves a pulsing of attention between a participatory and a critical focus. In the first case I indwell my language and experience my meaning as intention. In the second, I withdraw to a critical distance and experience the text as reader. Control, the essence of the focused moment, depends on this critical eye to make two comparisons and judgments. On the one hand, I must compare an image of achievement (the shadowy anticipations and projections of my intention) to the meaning I actually read back out of the text. More profoundly, I must test my meaning for its truth, by going back to memory or verbal matrix and reexperiencing in imagination the truth that I claim. Whereas the generative moment suspended both tests to allow imagination free play, the moment of focusing sternly demands of me both a faithful clarity of language and a rigorous integrity of conceptualization.

My resistance to form derives partly from the impossibility of satisfying this discursive ideal, which cannot capture through its linear, teleological, sharply articulated disciplines the holistic network of understanding and feeling that is elaborated partially in my notebooks and more generally by the composing life. My exquisitely

poignant awareness of this inadequacy creates the pain of the focusing moment, which at times intensifies to the point of blocking. Blocking (quite distinct from the slump that marks the low ebb of generativity) occurs when the critical function overwhelms the power of the patterning imagination to control and yet free the forming impulse to improvise text. It creates a negative force of inertia and fear that results in my making repetitive formulations of alternate choices—the same idea in different language, different orders or patterns for a sequence of ideas—and feeling unable to choose among them. The resistance to form that is productive in generating is destructive in this instance, reaching its height at the second decision point when, writing a title and the first sentence that is not free-floating but addressed, I balk at committing myself to event. Not only must I give up the fluid dynamic of my composing life for the controlled path of text, but I must enter into a relationship only dimly apprehended up to now, a dialogue with another whose demands make themselves felt most intensely at the beginning of text.

I can overcome blocking with patience and blind faith, slogging through the repetitions until finally I break out of the vicious circle and begin improvising fluently. As I proceed I encounter another problem, particularly when the focusing moment must be sustained over days or weeks. Such concentration is a fragile thing that must be selfishly protected from the interruptions of daily life. What I am doing as I write is to stabilize and intensify my holistic sense of the controlling patterns in my text until they are both so simple and so compelling that I can pack them like suitcases with layers of richly textured development. Once such a texture is laid down, it becomes accessible to craft, and it is relatively easy to prune, sharpen, and heighten impact through editing.

If I lose concentration before I gain this degree of control, I usually have to begin again on a new impulse. I am always surprised, therefore, to realize how differently a text would have developed had circumstances varied slightly: how unexpected and dependent on chance is its actual content. This is my compensation for the discipline of form, the manifestation of the suppressed generative moment in improvisation. Composing even in focusing must remain for me an open system, as John McDermott remarked about modern art:

> Order is maintained, but at the service of novelty. The future is anticipated not as a codification of our intention, rather as a harbinger of surprise. Indeed, intention itself emerges with clarity only when we are far into the creative process, and is often retrospectively reconstructed when our work takes a surprising turn.[6]

STRUCTURING

In the process of describing the generative and focused moments, I have gradually disclosed the role of structuring and opened the way to understanding how the composing event crystallizes in relation to text from my composing life. The essence of the structuring moment is *work,* the working of weblike patterns of meaning into discursive ones. Here let me reintroduce, or rather recognize, the aspect of temporality in the nature of each moment. The generative moment is a rhythm of ebb and flow that underlies composing at any temporal point, but is most quintessentially realized when I am able to relax into this productive state over a time of my life, often a vacation with lots of personal reading, varied experiences, a change of place, a renewal of relationships. During such a time no pressure compels me toward focusing, and my composing energies disperse themselves fruitfully in many directions, attached loosely to shifting and shadowy potential texts. In contrast the focused moment is sharply delineated within my life as an intensive episode during which my composing mind is concentrated exclusively on one text in a purposeful, determined movement toward completion.

In one sense structuring enters into both these moments. Structuring may be defined more specifically as the process by which discursive features arise and persist in clusters of ideas, so that looking backward from an actual text I perceive that text as having evolved from a few key words through notes, lists, outlines, sketches, and other pre-texts to its drafts and final form. From this perspective focusing appears as a refined mode or final stage of structuring, during which such features as sequenced, grammatical sentences, cohesive devices, paragraph indentation, and so on are introduced or stabilized. On the other hand, in the generative mode what I create are connections that are the seeds or material of structures. What I want to think about now is how these patterns develop simultaneously but at varying pace toward focusing moments, through a differentiation of the verbal matrix.

My composing life produces a verbal stream that is partially captured in a dynamic matrix of written materials (for which the Third Basket and Reading Journal can stand). This production of written thought continues at all times except when I am focusing, when it becomes the object and source of further writing. In fact, the typical activity of my composing life is not a pure generative state (rare) or focusing (relatively short and intense) but a sort of normative structuring work that goes on intermittently through the medium of my notebooks. When I look at these chronologically, I discover a series of generative points each representing a high point of creative energy, followed by the working out of these ideas in increasingly discursive ways. Frequently the first move in this process is to title a possible text. Titles function as nodes or hooks on which to hang my ideas; and my constant titling changes represent the fine-tuning of a discursive intention. This work differentiates the matrix into pattern clusters (although they still intermingle up to the moment of focusing), some of which ultimately devolve into individual texts.

A particularly clear example of such differentiation occurred this summer when I worked simultaneously and interactively on the plans for a book prospectus and for three of the essays in the book. I perceived this work as a process of discovering principles by which I could sort many closely related ideas into piles of strands and braid them into distinct essays—in the case of the prospectus, combine them. This work went on at the same time as, and indeed by virtue of, my creation of new patterns, not simply connecting ideas but connecting them in discursive ways. This means that they began to acquire such features as these: discrimination of segments or parts; order; hierarchy; holistic unity (keyed often to a title); specific relations such as opposition or similarity. As I worked on the three essay plans, eventually through a focusing mode tied to writing the prospectus, I noticed that the work proceeded by decision points in the same sense that I spoke of in focusing, except that here the decision applied to the whole matrix rather than a single text. Each decision point was a choice that opened other choices and led to experiments with their structural implications and possibilities. For example, I might decide to collect many ideas under the notion of theme and variation or hermeneutical interpretation, or to relate them through dynamic principles such as a pendulum swing or sudden reversal.

Eventually this structuring work moved from notebook (verbal matrix) to folders (in the case of planning the essays, no further than this first decision point in focusing). As structuring progressed I tended to focus more and more urgently on the narrative line, that is, a plan that would set in motion (and address to a reader) the various distinctions and relations I had sketched out. I displayed distinct preferences for particular designs and rhythms, often dissolving a knot in my thinking by turning to a favorite one. Choices such as these examples have a strong aesthetic motive: a distinction mediated by a third term; parallelism or symmetry; analogies; and surprising turns and moves within a drama of thought.

REFLECTION

An ironic reversal has occurred in this effort to describe the three moments of my composing life as the mediated relation of generative and discursive impulses. In articulating my composing life I reveal composing events to be not raw experience but constructs of anticipation and memory that are precipitated from the continuity of my composing life just as texts are from the verbal matrix. The very notion of a "composing process" seems para-doxically dependent on that of fully deployed text. In my experience the event appears to be constructed by making focusing the temporal center for a pattern of decision points that is only fully realized in memory, but unfolds through anticipation. Thus prospectively, I differentiate the matrix through structuring and gradually, moving toward the point of separation or birth, create intentionality; retrospectively, I revise memory to reflect more cleanly and coherently the historical evolution of an achieved text—here is where it began, this is when I realized . . ., this goes back to. . . .

In the same way reflection layers yet another moment into the melange of thought and language—the moment of self-consciousness embodied in this essay. Through reflection I reconstruct and rationalize the composing life in order to understand how it shapes my being as theorist, teacher, person. I discover in doing so how intimately tangled are my composing energies, my work, and my personal growth, daily life, and relationships. The composing life seems sometimes to me a burden, almost a geas; in the focusing moment particularly it is fiercely self-absorbed and narrowing, asserting its imperatives in competition with the pleasures and responsibilities of family and public life and forcing me to agonizing choices. In compensation, there is a symbiotic relation between my composing life and the experience that it interprets, because the power to connect not only feeds on the vitality of life but illuminates and changes its possibilities. My work as a theorist ultimately develops that symbiosis, relating the composing of meanings through writing to the ways individuals grow and develop in personal contexts.

The use of language to compose meaning must, like any universal human act, have both great commonalities and incredible idiosyncrasy and individuality. For theorists of discourse, reflections such as we write here on our own composing experiences clearly have subjective value and indeed are simply intensifications, as I have described, of a sustained attitude and habit. Intensifying to this level of description tears away the conventional sedimentations that frame my composing behavior and leads to understandings that change it—for example I am newly aware of the ethical nature of conflicts that had appeared technical or psychological. But I also think there is an objective value in these accounts, because they at once reveal a human practice, in which literacy or composing always grows out of and expresses a life and a personal identity, and remind us unforgettably of the endless multiplicity of the concrete activity of making meanings, which in the end is what the teacher or the composer must confront. As Clifford Geertz puts it, in an old African proverb, "Wisdom comes out of an ant heap."[7]

Notes

1. Howard Gardner, *Frames of Mind: The Theory of Multiple Intelligences* (New York: Basic Books, 1983), p. 101.

2. See Herbert Spiegelberg, *The Phenomenological Movement: A Historical Introduction,* 3rd ed., rev. and enl. (The Hague: Martinus Nijhoff, 1982), pp. 681–719, on essentials of the phenomenological method.

3. David Sudnow, *Ways of the Hand: The Organization of Improvised Conduct* (Cambridge, Mass.: Harvard University Press, 1978).

4. Isaiah Berlin, *Concepts and Categories: Philosophical Essays,* ed. Henry Hardy (New York: Viking, 1979), pp. 1–11.

5. Carol Gilligan, *In a Different Voice: Psychological Theory and Women's Development* (Cambridge, Mass.: Harvard University Press, 1982).

6. John McDermott, *The Culture of Experience: Philosophical Essays in the American Grain* (New York: New York University Press, 1976), p. 90.

7. Clifford Geertz, *Local Knowledge: Further Essays in Interpretive Anthropology* (New York: Basic Books, 1983), p. 91.

Part Two

Art

Putting It Together:
The Art of Composition

BARBARA GLEASON

What is the nature of language? What is the relationship between mind and language? Between language and its referents? Although these broadly conceived questions are currently being confronted in a wide range of disciplines, they have a distinctive resonance in the key of Art, where language is a central concern. A valuable heuristic for coming to grips with language in this key is Kenneth Burke's concept of "terministic screens": "Even if any given terminology is a *reflection* of reality, by its very nature as a terminology it must be a *selection* of reality; and to this extent it must function also as a *deflection* of reality" (Burke 45). The first part of the project we are engaging in might usefully be understood as one of articulating the key of Art as a terministic screen.

The second half of this project involves an imposition of that screen on the field of composition. By way of epistemological strategy, you might bear in mind the distinctions between a terministic screen, the key of Art in this case, and the body of scholarship we are examining. At issue is how the key of Art serves to guide and shape a reader's attention.

In order to write about the key of Art, I have constructed my own set of terms as the structural basis for this essay. My list is necessarily short, limited by the constraints of my own writerly purpose and the format of this book. These terms are *rhetoric, transaction, invention, form,* and *style.*

Rhetoric

What is rhetoric? Who uses the term in the field of composition, and how does it apply to the key of Art? If we begin with Aristotle, whose influence in this key is still pervasive, we discover that "rhetoric may be defined as the faculty of observing in any given case the available means of persuasion" ("Rhetoric," Bizzell and Herzberg 153). Expressing a commonly held assumption among contemporary composition professionals, Timothy Crusius argues that "composition is no longer

Inquiry

What does *art* mean to you? A set of central terms for understanding the key of Art can be found in some of the words from the titles in this section: art, rhetoric, reading, transaction, discourse community, teaching, and audience. Comparing this list with several of the words in the Nature titles—growing, liberatory, self, voice, integrity—suggests that for each key there exists a common "language," that is, a symbolic means of articulating shared assumptions, expectations, and goals. In Kenneth Burke's definition of rhetoric, this symbolism establishes a sense of *identification,* leading to *cooperation* among those using the shared language (Burke, *Rhetoric* 43; Coe).

After examining the titles and quickly skimming through some of the pages in this section, try creating a set of terms you believe to be central for characterizing the key of Art. If possible, show your list to another person engaged in "reading" composition in this key. To what degree do your lists overlap? How are they different? How might the differences be accounted for?

what it once was for the ancient world—the art of persuasion . . . for us, rhetoric is the art of written discourse" (Crusius 1).

This shift to written discourse referred to by Crusius—often keyed by the term *new rhetoric*—retains two fundamental assumptions of classical rhetoric: first, that language can be separated from immediate experience and examined as an artifact; and, second, that language forms and strategies can be described, codified, and then used by individuals to develop expertise in language use. These assumptions might well be considered "first principles" for the key of Art even though they are controversial among the full range of composition scholars. At issue is whether or not developing writers actually do benefit from learning about language forms and strategies, and, if so, how best to teach these forms and strategies in a writing class. The eddies of this controversy whirl most forcefully among the keys of Nature, Politics, and Art. Since scientists—both in linguistics and in composition—also examine, describe, and analyze language, teachers working in the key of Art may well value scientific studies of language.

In order to grasp the vastly complex scholarship in rhetorical theories from the Pre-Socratics to twentieth-century rhetoricians, you might begin with Edward P. J. Corbett's *Classical Rhetoric for the Modern Student,* a chapter of which appears in this section, and then move on to an admirably comprehensive and carefully edited collection, *The Rhetorical Tradition: Readings from Classical Times to the Present* by Patricia Bizzell and Bruce Herzberg. What becomes apparent as one wanders through this landscape is that there are multiple approaches to theorizing rhetoric and several contexts of application, the writing classroom being only one.

In their 1962 textbook, *Rhetoric: Principles and Usage,* Richard E. Hughes and P. Albert Duhamel provide one of the earliest applications of Aristotelian rhetoric to writing pedagogy. Hughes and Duhamel make a distinction between two kinds of rules (or principles): those of the artist and those of the scientist: "The study of any art, like the study of any science, requires the mastery of certain basic principles. There is, however, a profound difference between the validity of such principles. The principles of physics, for example, are . . . . The principles of rhetoric are. . . ."

How might Hughes and Duhamel have completed these last two statements? How does this distinction between different sorts of principles help distinguish between the key of Art and the key of Science?

Within the recent history of composition, classical rhetoric has enjoyed a significant revival. This renewed interest in classical rhetoric has been accompanied by an increased interest in the work of Chaim Perelman, Stephen Toulmin, Kenneth Burke, and Richard Weaver, all of whom are cited repeatedly in the 1960s and 1970s issues of *College Composition and Communication* and *College English.* A problem that has never been adequately addressed within composition is how *this* renaissance squares with *another* rhetorical tradition, one first referred to by Daniel Fogarty in 1959 as "current traditional rhetoric." Current traditional rhetoric, often characterized as principally concerned with written products, highly constrained views of discourse form (for example, the five-paragraph essay), correct usage, and style (Young), is the tradition that composition scholars and teachers have been collectively reacting against since the 1960s. More succinctly, current traditional rhetoric has long been—and continues to be—the nemesis of all composition professionals.

In point of fact, however, a number of current traditional rhetoric's features (emphasis on form and style, for instance) would seem to suggest an overlapping with the key of Art. And since both traditions are informed by theories of rhetoric, albeit different theories of rhetoric, we might wonder whether the key of Art is an elaboration of current traditional rhetoric rather than a fundamentally opposed approach.

Transaction

One approach to distinguishing between current traditional rhetoric and the key of Art is to consider the "communication triangle" as it might appear from the standpoint of each tradition.

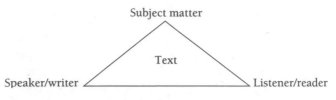

The Communication Triangle
(Reprinted from Edward P. J. Corbett, Classical Rhetoric for the Modern Student, *3rd ed. New York: Oxford UP, 1990. 5.)*

In any given writing situation, certain elements of this communication model achieve greater or lesser significance, depending on the genre, the writer's purpose, and the writing and reading contexts. For example, text may be fore grounded in a poem while audience may achieve greater prominence in a political speech (Winterowd 25–34). Of particular interest to our examination of the key of Art is how the communication triangle has been defined, redefined, and theorized by various scholars. James Kinneavy notes that his work and the work of two other major discourse theorists—James Britton and James Moffett—"is rooted in the basic semiotic structure of the communication triangle" (40). Andrea Lunsford and Lisa Ede address this issue as it bears on concepts of audience in "Audience Addressed/Audience Invoked." As your reading in the key of Art expands and deepens, you might consider how the communication triangle appears (or is represented as appearing) at particular historical moments in the history of composition (for example, the 1960s versus the 1980s).

Contemplating various versions of the rhetorical situation (as represented in the communication triangle) opens up the composing process to the idea of transactions among writer, text, context, and reader. Building on classical rhetoric, a transactional model of writing incorporates reading and a more distinctively social cast to what is sometimes represented as a private and necessarily solitary act. In her transactional theory of reading literature, Louise Rosenblatt provides a description of her view of transaction: "'The poem' comes into being in the live circuit set up between the reader and 'the text.' As with the elements of an electric circuit, each component of the reading process functions by virtue of the presence of the others" (14). A transactional model of writing, then, incorporates both rhetoric and reading theory into a model in which writing is viewed as a dynamic interplay of transactional experiences between writer and text, reader and text, writer and reader, and relevant environments. Ross Winterowd invokes a transactional model (with a side glance at Burke's pentad) when he characterizes a "discourse act, written or spoken, . . . [as] *the projection of a SEMANTIC INTENTION through a STRUCTURE to an AUDIENCE in a SCENE*" (286).

Invention

In contemporary writing classrooms, instructors generally provide students with strategies for discovering or "inventing" ideas. Teachers may prefer expressive strategies such as journal writing and free writing on the one hand or more formal heuristics on the other, for example, the Burkean pentad of *act, agent, agency, scene,* and *motive*—a dramatistic set of topics that can aid a writer in exploring and analyzing a writing subject, or the tagmemic grid of differing perspectives: a topic can be viewed as particle (a set of features), wave (a process), or field (a system of interlocking components). (For a more detailed explanation, see Richard Young's discussion of the tagmemic heuristic in his essay "Concepts of Art and the Teaching of Writing" in this section.)

Teachers and scholars identified with the key of Art have shown a keen interest in formal heuristics, though this is less true today than it was in the past. In her 1970 essay entitled "Heuristics and Composition," Janice Lauer presents a case for composition professionals' turning to psychologists' studies of how people use problem-solving strategies (heuristics) in order to better understand invention as a phase of the composing process. In a passionate response to Janice Lauer's advocacy of heuristics, Ann Berthoff argues against problem solving and the use of formal heuristics as a basis for writing pedagogy. Berthoff finds it preferable for student writers to begin by exploring their own experiences rather than analyzing social problems or controversies.

In this widely cited debate, Lauer and Berthoff square off on issues such as "studying the methods and rules of discovery and invention" versus attending first to "natural resources of mind"; and "investigating beyond the field of English" versus "English teachers . . . daring to raise their own fresh questions about the nature of learning and knowing and . . . daring, furthermore, [to] answer some of those questions."

Ultimately, we might wonder whether the positions of Lauer and Berthoff can be bridged successfully or whether these positions are in fact diametrically opposed and incompatible. Given that this dialogue occurred in the early 1970s, we might speculate about its role in the development of composition as an academic discipline. Why would composition professionals engage so heatedly in a debate about differing perspectives on mind, creativity, and composing? Why the conflict over relying on "experts" from other fields? What was at stake for composition teachers and scholars?

Form

Since form appears as a topic in a number of essays throughout this section, one might reasonably infer that form is a principal focus within the key of Art. Why form has assumed such a prominent role within this key—a more prominent role than, say, in the key of Nature—is a question well worth pursuing. Reading Mina Shaughnessy, Edward Corbett, James Porter, and Richard Coe, we come away with

Inquiry

> Imagine yourself as a writing teacher who structures journal writing and free writing into a class as primary activities for student writers. Then, imagine that you are presenting formal heuristics (for example, the Burkean pentad) for students to practice using with various writing topics. What might motivate you to use journal writing or free writing on the one hand or the more formal heuristics on the other? To what degree might your decision depend pragmatically on working within a writing program curriculum, teaching a specific class, or using a particular writing assignment? To what degree might your decision reveal your own assumptions about writing and about learning to write?

a list of terms that are themselves suggestive of different traditions and epistemologies: *outline, organization, arrangement, frame, framework, structure, disposition, system, order.* What different associations are suggested, for instance, by *outline* versus *arrangement*? In fact, the people who use these terms may or may not be addressing the same issues or even thinking of form in the same ways. More radically, we might consider whether or not terms such as *outline, arrangement,* and *structure* even refer to the same phenomenon.

One distinction commonly made is that of organic form versus mechanical form. Samuel Taylor Coleridge has described these two views:

> The form is mechanic when, on any given material, we impress a pre-determined form. . . .
> The organic form, on the other hand, is innate; it shapes as it develops itself from within and the fulness of its development is one and the same with the perfection of its outward form. (Raysor Vol. I, 198)

Ann Berthoff builds on this distinction as well as other concepts and theories advanced by Coleridge to develop her theory of writing, which contrasts sharply with theories associated with the key of Art. (See Berthoff's "The Intelligent Eye and the Thinking Hand" in the Nature section.) Whereas professionals identified with nature are generally less inclined to view form as a primary topic, art-oriented scholars tend to address form more directly as an issue. Moreover, scholars associated with art often focus on specific ways in which form can generate meaning (for example, form as a method of invention) and can be understood as rhetorical (for example, choices about form can be audience oriented). (See Coe, "An Apology for Form; or, Who Took the Form Out of the Process?" in this section; D'Angelo; Larson.)

Style

Richard Young's distinction between art as imaginative acts and art as craft ("Concepts of Art") indicates how awareness of language form (both at the discourse and sentence levels) plays a prominent role in at least one view of art—that

One approach to teaching essay form is to present students with a sample structure that can then be used for a particular writing assignment. In his textbook *The Versatile Writer,* for example, Donald Stewart outlines the five parts of a classical oration: (1) the introduction, (2) the narration or statement of facts, (3) the argument, (4) the refutation, and (5) the conclusion. Each of these parts is further elaborated on; in his description of the narration or statement of facts, for instance, Stewart emphasizes that there is always a persuasive dimension to any ordering and presentation of facts. In a subsequent chapter, Stewart offers several alternative patterns and organizational strategies.

What is the potential value of presenting novice writers with an essay structure such as the one described here and then inviting them to incorporate that structure into their writing? What objections to this teaching practice might be raised? What assumptions about writing and writing development underlie this teaching strategy?

of art as craft. To pursue this line of thinking further, we might ask questions such as the following: Are writers helped or hindered by conscious knowledge of sentence style and grammatical structures? Is the language play that many expert writers engage in essentially spontaneous and subconscious or deliberate and consciously controlled? Still at issue is whether or not developing writers should attend to stylistic concerns in first-year college writing courses and, in fact, what *attending to stylistic concerns* means for contemporary students— many of whom speak and write English as a second dialect or language. One objection that might be raised is that this sort of self-conscious composing may be too inhibiting during early phases of writing development. Knowing some of the different ways in which style is understood and how writers develop awareness and control of style may enable teachers to make informed decisions in this area. One writing theorist who has long advocated language play and focus on style is Richard Lanham. In *Style: An Anti-Textbook, Revising Prose,* and *Analyzing Prose,* Lanham formulates a pedagogy that centers on crafting written language.

In her essay appearing in this section, Mina Shaughnessy argues that "objectifying a statement so as to 'work' on it is the distinctive opportunity of writing" and that "the central goal of any writing class is . . . to lead the student to an awareness of his power to make choices (semantic, syntactic, organizational) that bring him closer to his intended meanings." Shaughnessy further asserts that the ability to craft prose frees writers by increasing their options and thus enhances the pleasure of writing. In an exploration of his own development as a writer, Joseph Comprone bears witness to Shaughnessy's thesis, describing an early focus on crafting written

Some composition professionals find that an explicit focus on language structures and stylistic concerns can be pedagogically naive or wrongheaded, needlessly restrictive, or—in worst-case scenarios—a highly charged form of authoritarianism. Compare the views expressed by Mina Shaughnessy to those articulated by John Rouse in "The Politics of Composition" (in the Politics section). Would you locate their differences in the ways in which they view students? In their beliefs about the goals of writing instruction? In their theories of writing and writing development?

prose and the benefits accrued later on: "My early years as a writer emphasized craft over expression of thought; my later years in formal education began to foreground thought and background craft. But most important to me was the fact that neither ever left the other alone" (75).

Conclusion

In constructing a terministic screen for the key of Art, I have deliberately excluded a number of terms that others may deem important or even essential (for example, *discourse analysis, interpretation, text*). As you become immersed in the experience of interpretation, you may easily come away with different ways of seeing this key or with different ways of reading the composition scholarship. A potential value of these varying interpretations rests with their power to reveal conflicts or tensions inherent to this key.

A deeper understanding of the key of Art can be achieved in part by turning from interpreting texts to reflecting on direct experiences of writing and teaching. In the context of your own individual perceptions and experiences, what issues or topics seem particularly salient yet are not addressed by the authors in this section? How, for example, do feminine and masculine perspectives play into the key of Art? And how well are women and feminist issues represented in scholarship that we associate with the key of Art?

To take another example, how does the key of Art account for the literacies of various social and ethnic groups and of different cultures? Is the apparent bias toward a Western intellectual tradition in this key best explained by history and accidents of circumstance or is it inherent in the key itself? For a look at scholarly writing that was considered but ultimately not included in this section, see Cheryl Glenn's "Rhetoric

1. The goals of writing instruction in the key of Art generally tend to be socially oriented, for example, participating in a liberal arts curriculum and involvement of citizens in a democracy. Critical pedagogy, radical pedagogy, and other teaching approaches associated with the key of Politics also aim for students to become active participants in their communities.

Ira Shor, author of *Critical Teaching and Everyday Life* (Boston: South End, 1980) and other scholarly works on critical pedagogy, comments on "liberating education" in a 1986 interview:

> Liberating education can encourage students to become active citizens who take seriously their role in constructing a humane democracy. . . . It invites students to first be critical of the kind of society that we are in rather than simply swallowing myths or being obedient to authority. And secondly, it invites them to take responsibility, to remake and reconstruct the society that they critically analyze.
> —FROM "A CONVERSATION WITH IRA SHOR" BY RACHEL MARTIN, 1986)

In what respects might writing pedagogy in the keys of Art and Politics overlap? How might teaching in the key of Art and teaching in the key of Politics be distinguished from each other?

2. Consider how the specific elements in the discourse model shown here would be foregrounded and backgrounded within the keys of Nature, Art, Science, and Politics. In which key might we expect to find greater emphasis on the writer? On context? On reader?

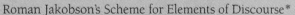

Roman Jakobson's Scheme for Elements of Discourse*

context

(speaker/writer)　　message　　*(listener/reader)*

addresser————————————————addressee

contact *(voice/page)*

code

From Thomas E. Sebeok, ed. Style in Language. Cambridge: MIT Press, 1960. 353.

in *The Book of Margery Kempe*," Carolyn Matalene's "Contrastive Rhetoric: An American Writing Teacher in China," and Keith D. Miller's "Composing Martin Luther King, Jr." How might including these works have altered this particular representation of the key of Art? To what extent would such readings have angled this key toward the key of Politics?

WORKS CITED

Berthoff, Ann E. "The Problem of Problem Solving." *College Composition and Communication* 22 (1970): 237–42.

Bizzell, Patricia, and Bruce Herzberg, eds. *The Rhetorical Tradition: Readings from Classical Times to the Present.* Boston: Bedford Books of St. Martin's P, 1990.

Burke, Kenneth. *Language as Symbolic Action: Essays on Life, Literature, and Method.* Berkeley: U of California P, 1966.

Coe, Richard M. "Defining Rhetoric—and Us." *Journal of Advanced Composition* 10.1 (1990): 39–52.

Comprone, Joseph. "Composition, Intellectual Life, and the Process of Writing as Public Knowing." *Writers on Writing,* Volume I. Ed. Tom Waldrep. New York: Random House, 1985. 71–85.

Crusius, Timothy W. *Discourse: A Critique and Synthesis of Major Theories.* New York: MLA, 1989.

D'Angelo, Frank J. *A Conceptual Theory of Rhetoric.* Cambridge: Winthrop, 1976.

Eisner, Elliot W., and David J. Flinders. "Research and Criticism: A Case for Separate But Equal." *Research in the Teaching of English* 28 (1994): 341–57.

Fogarty, Daniel. *Roots for a New Rhetoric.* New York: Teacher's College, 1959.

Glenn, Cheryl. "Rhetoric in *The Book of Margery Kempe.*" *College English* 54 (1992): 540–53.

Hughes, Richard E., and Duhamel, P. Albert *Rhetoric: Principles and Usage.* Englewood Cliffs: Prentice Hall, 1962.

Kinneavy, James. "A Pluralistic Synthesis of Four Contemporary Models for Teaching Composition." *Reinventing the Rhetorical Tradition.* Ed. Aviva Freedman and Ian Pringle. Ottawa: The Canadian Council of Teachers of English, 1980. 37–52.

Lanham, Richard. *Style: An Anti-Textbook.* New Haven: Yale UP, 1974.

———. *Revising Prose.* New York: Scribners, 1979.

———. *Analyzing Prose.* New York: Scribners, 1983.

Larson, Richard. "Toward a Linear Rhetoric of the Essay." *College Composition and Communication* 22 (1971): 140–46.

Lauer, Janice. "Heuristics and Composition." *College Composition and Communication* 21 (1970): 396–404.

Martin, Rachel. "A Conversation with Ira Shor." *Literacy Research Center* 2 (Spring 1986): 1, 6–7.

Matalene, Carolyn. "Contrastive Rhetoric: An American Writing Teacher in China." *College English* 47 (1985): 789–808.

Miller, Keith D. "Composing Martin Luther King, Jr." *PMLA* 105 (1990): 70–82.

Raysor, T. M., ed. *Coleridge's Shakespearean Criticism.* 2 vols. 2nd ed. London: Dent, 1960.

Rosenblatt, Louise M. *The Reader, The Text, The Poem: The Transactional Theory of the Literary Work.* Carbondale: Southern Illinois UP, 1978.

Stewart, Donald. *The Versatile Writer.* Lexington: D. C. Heath, 1986.

Winterowd, W. Ross. *Composition/Rhetoric: A Synthesis.* Carbondale: Southern Illinois UP, 1986. 281–97.

Young, Richard. "Paradigms and Problems: Needed Research in Rhetorical Invention." *Research on Composing: Points of Departure.* Eds. Charles R. Cooper and Lee Odell. Urbana: NCTE, 1978.

SUGGESTED READINGS

Rhetoric

Connors, Robert J., Lisa S. Ede, and Andrea A. Lunsford, eds. *Essays on Classical Rhetoric and Modern Discourse*. Carbondale: Southern Illinois UP, 1984.

Enos, Theresa, and Stuart C. Brown, eds. *Professing the New Rhetorics: A Sourcebook*. Englewood Cliffs: Prentice Hall, 1994.

Freedman, Aviva, and Ian Pringle, eds. *Reinventing the Rhetorical Tradition*. Ottawa: Canadian Council of Teachers of English, 1980/1984.

Glenn, Cheryl. "Remapping Rhetorical Territory." *Rhetoric Review* 13 (1995): 287-303.

Reynolds, John Frederick, ed. *Rhetorical Memory and Delivery: Classical Concepts for Contemporary Composition and Communication*. Hillsdale: Lawrence Erblaum, 1993.

Welch, Kathleen. *The Contemporary Reception of Classical Rhetoric*. Hillsdale: Lawrence Erblaum, 1990.

Transaction

Horner, Winifred Bryan, ed. *Composition and Literature: Bridging the Gap*. Chicago: Chicago UP, 1983.

Newkirk, Thomas, ed. *Only Connect: Uniting Reading and Writing*. Upper Montclair: Boynton/Cook, 1986.

Petersen, Bruce T., ed. *Convergences: Transactions in Reading and Writing*. Urbana: NCTE, 1986.

Invention

Cicero, Marcus Tullius. *On Invention*. Trans. H. M. Hubbell. Cambridge: Harvard UP, 1949.

Covino, William. *The Art of Wondering: A Revisionist Return to the History of Rhetoric*. Portsmouth: Boynton/Cook, 1988.

Crowley, Sharon. *The Methodical Memory: Invention in Current-Traditional Rhetoric*. Carbondale: Southern Illinois UP, 1990.

Young, Richard E., Alton L. Becker, and Kenneth L. Pike. *Rhetoric: Discovery and Change*. New York: Harcourt, 1970.

Form

Biber, Doug. *Variation across Speech and Writing*. New York: Cambridge UP, 1991.

D'Angelo, Frank. "Aims, Modes, and Forms of Discourse." *Teaching Composition: 12 Bibliographical Essays*. Rvd. ed. Ed. Gary Tate. Fort Worth: Texas Christian UP, 1987. 131–54.

Slevin, James F. "Genre Theory, Academic Discourse, and Writing Within Disciplines." *Audits of Meaning: Festschrift in Honor of Ann E. Berthoff*. Ed. Louise Z. Smith. Englewood Cliffs: Boynton/Cook, 1988. 3–16.

Style

Christensen, Francis. "A Generative Rhetoric of the Sentence." In his *Notes Toward a New Rhetoric: Six Essays for Teachers*. New York: Harper and Row, 1967. 1–17.

Daiker, Donald A., Andrew Kerek, and Max Morenberg, eds. *Sentence Combining: A Rhetorical Perspective*. Carbondale: Southern Illinois UP, 1985.

McQuade, Donald A. *The Territory of Language: Linguistics, Stylistics, and the Teaching of Composition*. Carbondale: Southern Illinois UP, 1986.

O'Hare, Frank. *Sentencecraft: An Elective Course in Writing*. Lexington: Ginn and Co., 1975.

Introduction to *Classical Rhetoric for the Modern Student*

Edward P. J. Corbett

The excerpts reprinted here are taken from the Introduction to Classical Rhetoric and the Modern Student. *3rd ed. New York: Oxford UP, 1990. 3–30. Corbett's textbook was originally published in 1965.*

Rhetoric is the art or the discipline that deals with the use of discourse, either spoken or written, to inform or persuade or motivate an audience, whether that audience is made up of one person or a group of persons. Broadly defined in that way, rhetoric would seem to comprehend every kind of verbal expression that people engage in. But rhetoricians customarily have excluded from their province such informal modes of speech as "small talk," jokes, greetings ("Good to see you"), exclamations ("What a day!"), gossip, simple explanations ("That miniature calculator operates on dry-cell batteries"), and directions ("Take a left at the next intersection, go about three blocks to the first stoplight, and then . . ."). Although informative, directive, or persuasive objectives can be realized in the stop-and-go, give-and-take form of the dialogue, rhetoric has traditionally been concerned with those instances of formal, premeditated, sustained monologue in which a person seeks to exert an effect on an audience. This notion of "an effect on an audience"—a notion that gets at the very essence of rhetorical discourse—is implicit in such definitions as Marie Hochmuth Nichols's: "a means of so ordering discourse as to produce an effect on the listener or reader"; Kenneth Burke's: "the use of language as a symbolic means of inducing cooperation in beings that by nature respond to symbols"; or Donald Bryant's: "the function of adjusting ideas to people and of people to ideas." The classical rhetoricians seem to have narrowed the particular effect of rhetorical discourse to persuasion. Aristotle, for instance, defined rhetoric as "the faculty of discovering all the available means of persuasion in any given situation." But when one is reminded that the Greek word for *persuasion* derives from the Greek verb "to believe," one sees that Aristotle's definition can be made to comprehend not only those modes of discourse that are "argumentative" but also those "expository" modes of discourse that seek to win acceptance of information or explanation.

But whether we are seeking, as the eighteenth-century Scottish rhetorician George Campbell put it, "to enlighten the understanding, to please the imagination, to move the passions, or to influence the will," we must adopt and adapt those strategies that will best achieve our end. *Strategies* is a good rhetorical word, because it implies the *choice* of available resources to achieve an end. It is no accident that the word *strategy* has military associations, for this word has its roots in the Greek word for *army*. Just as a general will adopt those resources, those tactics, which are most likely to defeat the enemy in a battle, so the marshaller of language will seek out and use the best argument, and the best style to "win" an audience. . . .

A BRIEF EXPLANATION OF CLASSICAL RHETORIC

Although modern students may often have heard the term *rhetoric* used, they probably do not have a clear idea of what it means. Their uncertainty is understandable, because the word has acquired many meanings. Rhetoric may be associated in their minds with the writing of compositions and themes or with style—figures of speech, flowery diction, variety of sentence patterns and rhythms—or with the notion of empty, bombastic language, as implied in the familiar phrase "mere rhetoric." Maybe tucked away somewhere in their consciousness is the notion of rhetoric as the use of language for persuasive purposes.

What all these notions have in common is that rhetoric implies the use or manipulation of words. And, indeed, a look at the etymology of the word *rhetoric* shows that the term is solidly rooted in the notion of "words" or "speech." The Greek words *rhēma* ("a word") and *rhētor* ("a teacher of oratory"), which are akin, stem ultimately from the Greek verb *eirō* ("I say"). Our English noun *rhetoric* derives from the Greek feminine adjective *rhetorikē*, which is elliptical for *rhetorikē technē* ("the art of the rhetor or orator"). English got its word immediately from the French *rhétorique*.

This investigation of the etymology of the term brings us somewhat closer to the original meaning of rhetoric: something connected with speaking, orating. From its origin in fifth-century Greece through its flourishing period in Rome and its reign in the medieval *trivium*, rhetoric was associated primarily with the art of oratory. During the Middle Ages, the precepts of classical rhetoric began to be applied to letter-writing, but it was not until the Renaissance, after the invention of printing in the fifteenth century, that the precepts governing the spoken art began to be applied, on any large scale, to written discourse.

Classical rhetoric was associated primarily with persuasive discourse. Its end was to convince or persuade an audience to think in a certain way or to act in a certain way. Later, the principles of rhetoric were extended to apply to informative or expository modes of discourse, but in the beginning, they were applied almost exclusively to the persuasive modes of discourse.

Rhetoric as persuasive discourse is still very much exercised among us, but modern students are not likely to have received much formal training in the art of persuasion. Frequently, the only remnant of this training in the schools is the attention paid to argumentation in a study of the four forms of discourse: Argumentation, Exposition, Description, and Narration. But this study of argumentation usually turns out to be an accelerated course in logic. For the classical rhetorician, logic was an ancillary but distinct discipline. Aristotle, for instance, spoke of rhetoric as being "an offshoot" or "a counterpart" of logic or, as he called it, dialectics. The speaker might employ logic to persuade the audience, but logic was only one among many "available means of persuasion." So those who study argumentation in classrooms today are not really exposed to the rich, highly systematized discipline that earlier students submitted to when they were learning the persuasive art.

Although classical rhetoric has largely disappeared from our schools, there was a time when it was very much alive. For extended periods during its two-thousand-year history, the study of rhetoric was the central discipline in the curriculum. Rhetoric enjoyed this eminence because, during those periods, skill in oratory or in written discourse was the key to preferment in the courts, the forum, and the church. One of the reasons why the study—if not the practice—of rhetoric has declined in our own times is that in an industrial, technological society like our own, there are avenues to success other than communication skills. Part of the folklore of America is that in the years from about 1870 to 1910, some barely literate men became millionaires—some of whom, ironically, later founded libraries and endowed universities.

One fact that emerges from a study of the history of rhetoric is that there is usually a resurgence of rhetoric during periods of social and political upheaval. Whenever the old order is passing away and the new order is marching—or stumbling—in, a loud, clear call goes up for the services of the person skilled in the use of spoken or written words. One needs only to hearken back to such historical events as the Renaissance in Italy, the Reformation in England, and the Revolution in America to find evidence of this desperate reliance, in times of change or crisis, on the talents of those skilled in the persuasive arts. As Jacob Burckhardt has pointed out in *The Civilization of the Renaissance in Italy,* the orator and the teacher of rhetoric played a prominent role in the fifteenth-century humanistic movement that was casting off the yoke of the medieval church. After Henry VIII broke with Rome, the Tudor courts of England resounded with the arguments of hundreds of lawyers engaged to fight litigations over confiscated monastic properties. Students of the American Revolution need recall only Tom Paine's incendiary pamphlets, Patrick Henry's rousing speeches, Thomas Jefferson's daring Declaration of Independence, and Hamilton's and Madison's efforts to sell constitutional democracy in the *Federalist Papers* to be convinced that in time of change or upheaval, we rely heavily on the services of those equipped with persuasively eloquent tongues or pens. Something of the same kind of rhetorical activity is raging today among the nationalists fighting for independence in African and Asian countries. More recently in our own country, we witnessed the furious rhetorical activity, expressed in both words and physical demonstrations, in the civil-rights movement of the 1960s. . . .

THE FIVE CANONS OF RHETORIC

Inventio is the Latin term (*heuresis* was the equivalent Greek term) for "invention" or "discovery." Theoretically, an orator could talk on any subject, because rhetoric, as such, had no proper subject matter. In practice, however, each speech that the orator undertook presented a unique challenge. He had to find arguments that would support whatever case or point of view he was espousing. According to Cicero, the speaker relied on native genius, on method or art, or on diligence to help find appropriate arguments. Obviously, that individual was at a great advantage who had a native, intuitive sense for proper arguments. But lacking such an endowment, a person could have recourse either to dogged industry or to some system for finding arguments. *Inventio* was concerned with a system or method for finding arguments.

Aristotle pointed out that there were two kinds of arguments or means of persuasion available to the speaker. First of all, there were the non-artistic or non-technical means of persuasion (the Greek term was *atechnoi pisteis*). These modes of persuasion were really not part of the art of rhetoric; they came from outside the art. The orator did not have to *invent* these; he had merely to use them. Aristotle named five kinds of non-artistic proofs: laws, witnesses, contracts, tortures, oaths. Apparently, the lawyer pleading a case in court made most use of this kind of proof, but the politician or the panegyrist could use them too. The representatives today, for instance, who are trying to persuade the citizens to adopt a sales tax quote statistics, legal contracts, existing laws, historical documents, and the testimony of experts to bolster their case. They do not have to invent these supporting arguments; they already exist. True, there is a sense in which they have to find such supporting arguments. They have to be aware that they exist, and they have to know what departments or records to go in order to discover them. . . .

The second general mode of persuasion that Aristotle spoke of included artistic proof—"artistic" in the sense that they fell within the province of the art of rhetoric: *rational* appeal (*logos*), *emotional* appeal (*pathos*), and *ethical* appeal (*ethos*). In exercising the rational appeal, the speaker was appealing to the audience's reason or understanding. The speaker is "arguing," in other words. When we argue, we reason either *deductively* or *inductively*—that is, we either draw conclusions from affirmative or negative statements (e.g., No man can attain perfect happiness in this life; John is a man; therefore John cannot attain perfect happiness in this life) or make generalizations after observing a number of analogous facts (e.g., Every green apple that I bit into had a sour taste. All green apples must be sour). In logic, the deductive mode of arguing is commonly referred to by the term that Aristotle used, the *syllogism*. In rhetoric, the equivalent of the syllogism was the *enthymeme*. The rhetorical equivalent of *full induction* in logic is the *example*. Since the next chapter will provide an elaborate explanation of syllogism, enthymeme, induction, and example, we will not dwell on them here.

A second mode of persuasion is the emotional appeal. Since people are by nature rational animals, they should be able to make decisions about their private and public lives solely by the light of reason. But they are also endowed with the faculty of free will, and often enough their will is swayed more by their passions or emotions than by their reason. Aristotle expressed the wish that rhetoric could deal exclusively with rational appeals, but he was enough of a realistic to recognize that a person is often prompted to do something or accept something by his or her emotions. And if rhetoric was, as he defined it, the art of discovering "all the available means of persuasion," then he would have to give a place in his *Rhetoric* to an investigation of the means of touching the emotions. Accordingly, he devoted the major portion of Book II of his *Rhetoric* to an analysis of the more common human emotions. This was the beginning of the science of human psychology. If the orator was to play upon people's emotions, he must know what those emotions were and how they could be triggered off or subdued.

A third mode of persuasion was the ethical appeal. This appeal stemmed from the character of the speaker, especially as that character was evinced in the speech itself. A person ingratiated himself or herself with an audience—and thereby gained their trust and admiration—if he or she managed to create the impression that he or she was a person of intelligence, benevolence, and probity. Aristotle recognized that the ethical appeal could be the most potent of the three modes of persuasion. All of an orator's skill in convincing the intellect and moving the will of an audience could prove futile if the audience did not esteem, could not trust, the speaker.

For this reason politicians seeking election to public office take such great care to create the proper image of themselves in the eyes of the voters. It was for this reason also that Cicero and Quintilian stressed the need for high moral character in the speaker. Quintilian defined the ideal orator as "a good man skilled in speaking." In his *Nicomachean Ethics,* Aristotle explored the *ēthos* proper for the individual; in his *Politics,* the *ēthos* proper for individuals living together in a society.

The method that the classical rhetoricians devised to aid the speaker in discovering matter for the three modes of appeal was the *topics. Topics* is the English translation of the Greek word *topoi* and the Latin word *loci*. Literally, *topos* or *locus* meant "place" or "region" (note our words *topography* and *locale*). In rhetoric, a topic was a place or store or thesaurus to which one resorted to find something to say on a given subject. More specifically, a topic was a general head or line of argument which suggested material from which proofs could be made. To put it another way, the topics constituted a method of probing one's subject to discover possible ways of developing that subject. Aristotle distinguished two kinds of topics: (1) the special topics (he called them *idioi topoi* or *eidē*); (2) the common topics (*koinoi topoi*). The special topics were those classes of argument appropriate to particular kinds of discourse. In other words, there were some kinds of arguments that were used exclusively in the law courts; some that were confined to the public forum; others that appeared only in ceremonial addresses. The common topics, on the other hand, were a fairly limited stock of arguments that could be used for any occasion or type of speech. Aristotle named four common topics: (1) more and less (the topic of degree); (2) the possible and the impossible, (3) past fact and future fact; (4) greatness and smallness (the topic of size as distinguished from the topic of degree).

The second part of rhetoric was *dispositio* (Greek, *taxis*), which may be translated as "disposition," "arrangement," "organization." This was the division of rhetoric concerned with the effective and orderly arrangement of the parts of a written or spoken discourse. Once the ideas or arguments are discovered there remains the problem of selecting, marshalling, and organizing them with a view to effecting the end of the discourse.

In the simplest terms, one might say that any discourse needs a beginning, a middle, and an end; but this division is self-evident and not much help. Rhetoricians spelled out the division of a discourse more specifically and functionally. Aristotle held that there were really only two essential parts of a speech: the statement of the case and the proof; but he was ready to concede that in practice orators added two more parts: an introduction and a conclusion. Latin rhetoricians, like the author of the *Ad Herennium,* further refined these divisions, recognizing six parts: (1) the introduction *(exordium);* (2) the statement or exposition of the case under discussion *(narratio);* (3) the outline of the points or steps in the argument *(divisio);* (4) the proof of the case *(confirmatio);* (5) the refutation of the opposing arguments *(confutatio);* (6) the conclusion *(peroratio).*

Such a division may strike writers as being arbitrary, mechanical, and rigid. Two things may be said in defense of this conventional pattern. It did set forth clear principles of organization, and inexperienced writers need nothing so much as simple, definite principles to guide them in arrangement of material. Then too the rhetoricians allowed for some adjustments in this scheme. Accepting the Aristotelian notion of the "available means of persuasion," they acknowledge that on some occasions it was expedient to omit certain parts altogether (for instance, if one found it difficult to break down the opposing arguments, it might be advisable to omit the stage of *confutatio)* or to re-arrange some of the parts (for instance, it might be more effective to refute the opposing arguments *before* advancing one's own arguments).

Unquestionably, there is a close interrelation between *inventio* and *dispositio,* and in many rhetoric books these two divisions were treated under one head. Disposition was looked upon as just another aspect of invention; *inventio* was the originative aspect, and *dispositio* was the organizing aspect. As one may learn from the history of rhetoric in the Appendix, Peter Ramus and his followers, like

Francis Bacon, wanted to relegate invention and disposition to the province of logic and to limit rhetoric to considerations of style, memory, and delivery. . . .

The third part of rhetoric was *elocutio* (Greek, *lexis* or *hermēneia* or *phrasis).* The word *elocution* means something quite different to us from what it meant to the classical rhetorician. We associate the word with the act of speaking (hence, the elocution contest). This notion of speaking is, of course, implicit in the Latin verb from which this word stems, *loqui,* "to speak" (cf. Greek, *legein,* "to speak"). We have a number of English words based on this Latin verb: *loquacious, colloquial, eloquence, interlocutor.* It was after the revival of interest in delivery in the second half of the eighteenth century that the word *elocution* began to take on its present meaning. But for the classical rhetorician, *elocutio* meant "style."

Style is a difficult concept to define, although most of us feel we know what it is. Famous definitions of style, like Buffon's "style is the man," Swift's "proper words in proper places," Newman's "style is a thinking out into language," and Blair's "the peculiar manner in which a man expresses his conceptions," are apt, but they are just vague enough to tease us out of thought and just general enough to give us a sense for style without giving us a clear definition of it. None of the major rhetoricians attempted to give a definition of style, but most of them had a great deal to say about it; in fact, some of the Renaissance rhetorics were devoted exclusively to a consideration of style.

One of the points that elicited a great deal of discussion was the classification of styles. Various terms were used to name the kinds of style, but there was fundamental agreement about three levels of style. There was the *low* or *plain* style *(attenuata, subtile);* the *middle* or *forcible* style *(mediocris, robusta);* and the *high* or *florid* style *(gravis, florida).* Quintilian proposed that each of these styles was suited to one of the three functions that he assigned to rhetoric. The plain style was most appropriate for instructing *(docendi);* the middle for *moving (movendi);* and the high for *charming (delectandi).*

All rhetorical considerations of style involved some discussion of *choice of words,* usually under such heads as correctness, purity (for instance, the choice of native words rather than foreign words), simplicity, clearness, appropriateness, ornateness.

Another subject of consideration was the *composition or arrangement of words* in phrases or clauses (or, to use the rhetorical term, *periods*). Involved here were discussions of correct syntax or collocation of words; patterns of sentences (e.g., parallelism, antithesis); proper use of conjunctions and other correlating devices both within the sentence and between sentences; the euphony of sentences secured through the artful juxtaposition of pleasing vowel and consonant combinations and through the use of appropriate rhythmical patterns.

A great deal of attention was paid, of course, to *tropes* and *figures* (Greek, *schēmata,* hence the English term *schemes,* which was often used in place of *figures*). Since the concept of tropes and schemes is very complex, it is better that we defer any definition and illustration of these terms to the appropriate section of the text.

Also involved in considerations of style were arguments about (1) the functional vs. the embellishing character of style; (2) Asianism vs. Atticism; (3) the written style vs. the spoken style; (4) economy of words vs. copia of words. These points of discussion are rather peripheral matters, but it is remarkable how much time and energy the rhetoricians devoted to such controversies.

The fourth part of rhetoric was *memoria* (Greek, *mnēmē*), concerned with memorizing speeches. Of all the five parts of rhetoric, *memoria* was the one that received the least attention in the rhetoric books. The reason for the neglect of this aspect of rhetoric is probably that not much can be said, in a theoretical way, about the process of memorizing; and after rhetoric came to be concerned mainly with written discourse, there was no further need to deal with memorizing. This process did receive, however, some attention in the schools of rhetoric set up by the sophists. The orator's memory was trained largely through constant practice (just as professional actors today acquire an amazing facility in memorizing a script), but the rhetors did suggest various mnemonic devices that facilitated the memorizing of speeches. The courses that one sometimes sees advertised in newspapers or magazines—"I Can Give You a Retentive Memory in Thirty Days"—are modern manifestations of this division of rhetoric.

The fifth division of rhetoric was *pronuntiatio* (Greek, *hypokrisis*) or delivery. As in the case of *memoria,* the theory of delivery was conspicuously neglected in the rhetoric texts until the elocutionary movement began about the middle of the eighteenth century. But most rhetoricians would acknowledge the importance of effective delivery in the persuasive process. When Demosthenes, the greatest of the Greek orators, was asked what he considered to be the most important part of rhetoric, he replied, "Delivery, delivery, delivery." Despite the neglect of delivery in the rhetoric books, a great deal of attention was devoted to this aspect in the Greek and Roman schools of rhetoric. Skill in delivery can best be acquired, of course, not by listening to theoretical discussions of this art but by actual practice and by analyzing the delivery of others. Understandably enough, discussions of delivery, as well as of memory, tended to be even more neglected in rhetoric texts after the invention of printing, when most rhetorical training was directed primarily to written discourse.

Involved in the treatment of delivery was concern for the management of the voice and for gestures *(actio).* Precepts were laid down about the modulation of the voice for the proper pitch, volume, and emphasis and about pausing and phrasing. In regard to action, orators were trained in gesturing, in the proper stance and posture of the body, and in the management of the eyes and of facial expressions. What this all amounted to really was training in the art of acting, and it is significant that all the great orators in history have been great "hams."

There is no denying the importance of delivery in effecting the end that one sets for oneself. Many speeches and sermons, however well prepared and elegantly written, have fallen on deaf ears because of inept delivery. Writers lack the advantage a speaker enjoys because of their face-to-face contact with an audience and because of their vocal delivery; the only way in which writers can make up for this disadvantage is by the brilliance of their style.

THE THREE KINDS OF PERSUASIVE DISCOURSE

All rhetoricians distinguished three kinds of orations, and this tripartite classification is well-nigh exhaustive. First, there was *deliberative* oratory, also known as *political, hortative,* and *advisory,* in which one deliberated about public affairs, about anything that had to do with politics, in the Greek sense of that term—whether to go to war, whether to levy a tax, whether to enter into an alliance with a foreign power, whether to build a bridge or a reservoir or a temple. More generally, however, deliberative discourse is that in which we seek to persuade someone to do something or to accept our point of view. . . . According to Aristotle, political oratory was always concerned about the *future* (the point at issue is something that we will or will not do); its special topics were the *expedient* and the *inexpedient;* and its means were *exhortation* and *dehortation.*

Second, there was *forensic* oratory, sometimes referred to as *legal* or *judicial* oratory. This was the oratory of lawyers in the courtroom, but it can be extended to cover any kind of discourse in which a person seeks to defend or condemn someone's actions. (Richard Nixon's famous "Checkers" speech before a nationwide television audience can be considered as an example of forensic rhetoric; and Newman's *Apologia Pro Vita Sua* is another example of forensic discourse.) Forensic oratory, according to Aristotle, was concerned with *past* time (court trials are always concerned with actions or crimes that took place in the past); its special topics were *justice* and *injustice;* and its means were *accusation* and *defense.*

Third, there was *epideictic* oratory. This species has had a variety of other titles: *demonstrative, declamatory, panegyrical, ceremonial.* It is the oratory of display, the kind of oratory exemplified in the *Gettysburg Address* and in the old-fashioned Fourth of July speeches. In this kind of discourse, one is not so much concerned with persuading an audience as with pleasing it or inspiring it. *Ceremonial* discourse—the term we use in this text—is the most "literary" and usually the most ornate of the three kinds of discourse. Aristotle had to strain to fit a proper time-province to this form of oratory, but in the interests of neatness he laid it down that ceremonial oratory was concerned primarily with the *present.* Its special topics were *honor* and *dishonor,* and its means were *praise* and *blame.* The ancients made no provision in their rhetorics for sermons or homiletics. But later, when rhetoric was studied in a Christian culture, the art of preaching was usually considered under the head of epideictic oratory—even though preachers are also concerned with people's past and future actions.

THE RELEVANCE AND IMPORTANCE OF RHETORIC FOR OUR TIMES

The kind of complicated, formalized system of rhetoric described in the previous sections may seem to be remote from the concerns and needs of contemporary society. Indeed, some exercises that students in Greek and Roman schools were subjected to are totally dispensable. Practices and principles should not be retained simply because they are venerable with age. They should be retained only if they prove relevant and useful.

Let it be said, first of all, that rhetoric is an inescapable activity in our lives. Every day, we either use rhetoric or are exposed to it. Everyone living in community with other people is inevitably a rhetorician. A parent constantly uses rhetoric on a child; a teacher, on his or her students; a salesperson, on customers; a supervisor, on workers. During every half hour that we spend in front of a television set, we are subjected three or four times to somebody's efforts to get us to buy something. During election time, we are bombarded by candidates' appeals for our vote. Even when we are driving on the streets and highways, our eyes are constantly assaulted by sales pitches on huge billboards.

Advertising may be the most ubiquitous example of an activity that practices what Aristotle preached. But many other fields of endeavor in modern life rely on rhetoric too. The diplomat is a traveling rhetorician with portfolio. The public-relations agent is a practitioner of ceremonial rhetoric, that variety of rhetoric that seeks to reflect credit on a person or an institution. Law is such a many-faceted profession today that many lawyers never get a chance to practice the forensic brand of rhetoric in the courtroom; but even those lawyers whose principal function is to prepare briefs for the Clarence Darrows of the courtroom can be said to be engaged in the *inventio* and *dispositio* aspects of rhetoric. Insurance agents and sales personnel of various kinds practice deliberative rhetoric, often very effectively, every day. Preachers, press-agents, senators and representatives, counsellors, union leaders, business executives, lobbyists are as actively exercising their rhetorical skills today as they ever were.

There are some forms of rhetoric practiced today that we regard with suspicion, even disdain. One of these is propaganda. The term *propaganda* was once a neutral word, signifying the dissemination of truth. But because some people have used propaganda for unscrupulous purposes, *propaganda* has taken on decidedly unfavorable connotations. Closely allied to this disreputable form of rhetoric is demagoguery. The names of the most successful of the twentieth-century demagogues are etched so deeply into our memories that they need not be specified here. These were the exploiters of specious arguments, half-truths, and rank emotional appeals to gain personal advantage rather than to promote the public welfare. Another variety of dangerous rhetoric is brainwashing. A definitive analysis of this diabolical technique has yet to be written, but a beginning has been made in the terrifying final chapters of George Orwell's novel *1984*. Another term has been taken from Orwell's novel to designate another dangerous form of rhetoric, *doublespeak*—a deliberate attempt to use language in such a way as to deceive or confuse listeners or readers. A good argument for an intensive study of rhetoric is that citizens might thereby be put on their guard against the onslaughts of these vicious forms of persuasion.

If "rhetoric" is such a pervasive activity in contemporary society, it behooves us to be aware of the basic strategies and principles of this ancient art. If nothing else, a knowledge of this art will equip us to respond critically to the rhetorical efforts of others in both the oral and written forms. As originally conceived, rhetoric was primarily a synthetic art—an art for "building up," for "composing," something. But rhetoric can also be used as an analytical art—an art for "breaking down" what has been composed. As such, it can make us better readers. As Malcolm Cowley once pointed out, the New Criticism of writers like Cleanth Brooks and Robert Penn Warren represented an application of rhetorical principles to the close reading of poetic texts. Mortimer Adler's *How to Read a Book* presented a rhetorical technique for the reading of expository and argumentative prose. Wayne C. Booth, in his book *The Rhetoric of Fiction,* has shown us the subtle operations of rhetoric in such narrative forms as the short story and the novel. And a knowledge of rhetoric can help us to respond critically and appreciatively to advertisements, commercials, political messages, satires, irony, and doublespeak of all varieties.

Rhetoric can also assist us in becoming more effective writers. One of the chief values of rhetoric, conceived of as a system for gathering, selecting, arranging, and expressing our material, is that it represents a *positive* approach to the problems of writing. Students have too often been inhibited in their writing by the negative approach to composition—don't do this, beware of that. Classical rhetoric too had its negative prescriptions, but, in the main, it offered positive advice to help writers in the composition of a specific kind of discourse directed to a definite audience for a particular purpose. Rhetoric cannot, of course, tell us what we must do in any and every situation. No art can provide that kind of advice. But rhetoric can lay down the general principles that writers can adapt to fit a particular situation. At least, it can provide writers with a set of procedures and criteria that can guide them in making strategic decisions in the composition process.

Students may fear that an elaborately systematized approach to composition will inhibit rather than facilitate writing. There is no denying that formula can retard and has retarded inventiveness and creativity. But to admit that formula *can* inhibit writers is not to admit that it invariably does. Almost every one of the major English writers, from the Renaissance through at least the eighteenth century—Chaucer, Jonson, Shakespeare, Milton, Dryden, Pope, Swift, Burke—had been subjected to an intensive rhetoric course in their grammar school or university. If one cannot claim that the study of rhetoric made them great writers, one might yet venture to say that the study of rhetoric did not prevent them from becoming great writers and might even have made them better writers than they would have been on genius alone.

Lest any false hopes be raised, however, let it be affirmed that this adaptation of classical rhetoric offers no magic formula for success in writing.

Students will have to work hard to profit from the instruction offered in this book, for it is not all easy to understand, and what is learned must be applied.

The road to eloquence is a hard road and a lonely road, and the journey is not for the fainthearted. But if, as we are told, the ability to use words to communicate thoughts and feelings is our most distinctively human accomplishment, there can be few satisfactions in life that can match the pride a person feels when he or she has attained mastery over words. As Quintilian said, "Therefore let us seek wholeheartedly that true majesty of expression, the fairest gift of God to man, without which all things are struck dumb and robbed both of present glory and the immortal acclaim of posterity; and let us press on to whatever is best, because, if we do this, we shall either reach the summit or at least see many others far beneath us."

Some New Approaches toward Teaching[1]

Mina P. Shaughnessy

Shaughnessy's essay was originally published in A Guide for Teachers of College English. *New York: Office of Academic Development, CUNY, 1970. The version reprinted here is from the* Journal of Basic Writing 13 (1994): 103–16.

TEACHING BASIC WRITING

I

The term "basic writing" implies that there is a place to begin learning to write, a foundation from which the many special forms and styles of writing rise, and that a college student must control certain skills that are common to all writing before he takes on the special demands of a biology or literature or engineering class. I am not certain this is so. Some students learn how to write in strange ways. I recall one student who knew something about hospitals because she had worked as a nurse's aide. She decided, long before her sentences were under control, to do a paper on female diseases. In some way this led her to the history of medicine and then to Egypt, where she ended up reading about embalming—which became the subject of a long paper she entitled "Post-mortem Care in Ancient Egypt." The paper may not have satisfied a professor of medical history, but it produced more improvement in the student's writing than any assignments I could have devised.

Perhaps if students with strong enthusiasms in special fields were allowed to exercise themselves in those fields under the guidance of professors who felt responsible for the writing as well as the reading of students, we could shorten the period of apprenticeship. But clearly this is not the way things are, and students who need extra work in writing are therefore placed in courses called Basic Writing, which are usually taught by English teach-ers who, as specialists themselves, are inclined to assume that the best way to teach writing is to talk about literature. If such talk will stimulate the stu-dent to write, however, then it will serve most stu-dents at least as well as mummies, for the answer to improved writing is writing. Everything else— imaginative writing texts, thoughtfully designed as-signments, elaborate rationales for teaching writing this way or that—is merely part of the effort to get writing started and to keep it going.

There are many views on the best way to do this and there is some damning evidence piled up against some of the ways that once seemed right. Since English teachers are often considered both the victims and the perpetuators of these appar-ently mistaken approaches, it becomes important for them to try once in a while to think away every-thing except the facts and insights that their experi-ences with students as writers have given them.

The following pages are my effort to do this.

II

Writing is the act of creative reading. That is, it is the encoding of speech into lines of print or script that are in turn decoded into speech by a reader. To understand the nature of writing, and therefore the way writing can be learned, it is nec-essary to understand the connections and distinc-tions between speech, writing, and reading and to identify the skills that are implied in the ability to write.

For most people, speech is easy and writing is difficult; the one is inevitable, the other acquired, generally under conditions that seem to violate rather than use the natural learning abilities of people. Because of this violation, learning to write requires almost as much undoing as doing, whether one is involved with those skills implied in the encoding process itself (handwriting, spelling, and punctuation) or those skills that are carried over from speech to the page (making and ordering statements).

Beyond these two types of skills, there is an additional opportunity in writing that distinguishes it both as a skill and as a product: the opportunity to objectify a statement, to look at it, change it by additions, subtractions, substitutions or inversions, the opportunity to take time for as close and economical a "fit" as possible between the writer's meaning and the record of that meaning on the page. The typescript of a taped discussion is not, therefore, writing in this sense; it is, rather, a repetition on the page of what was spoken. And the goal in writing is not simply to repeat speech but to overcome certain disadvantages that the medium of sound imposes upon speech. (In speech, time says when you are finished; in writing, you say when you are finished.)

Writing thus produces a distinctive circuitry in which the writer continually feeds back to himself (as writer and reader) and acts upon that feedback at any point and for as long a time as he wishes before his statement is finally put into circulation. This opportunity for objectifying a statement so as to "work" on it is the distinctive opportunity of writing, and the central goal of any writing class is therefore to lead the student to an awareness of his power to make choices (semantic, syntactic, organizational) that bring him closer and closer to his intended meaning. Ideally, this opportunity should free the writer because it increases his options; it should give him pleasure because it sharpens his sense of what to say and thereby his pleasure in saying it; and it should make him feel comfortable with so-called mistakes, which are simply stages in the writing process. Unfortunately, the fact that writing can by its very nature produce a more precise and lasting statement than speech has led teachers to expect (and demand) a narrow kind of perfection which they confuse with the true goal in writing, namely, the "perfect" fit of the writer's words to his meaning. Teachers, in other words, have not only ignored the distinctive circuitry of writing—which is the only source of fullness and precision—but have often shortcircuited the writing activity by imposing themselves as a feedback. Students, on the other hand, have tended to impose upon themselves (even when bluebook essays do not) the conditions of speech, making writing a kind of one-shot affair aimed at the teacher's expectations. Students are usually surprised, for example, to see the messy manuscript of pages of famous writers. "You should see how bad a writer Richard Wright was," one of my students said after seeing a manuscript page from *Native Son*. "He made more mistakes than I do!" Somehow students have to discover that the mess is *writing;* the published book is *written.*

A writing course should help the student learn how to make his own mess, for the mess is the record of a remarkable kind of interplay between the writer as creator and the writer as reader, which serves the writer in much the same way as the ear serves the infant who is teaching himself to speak. No sooner has the writer written down what he thinks he means than he is asking himself whether he understands what he said. A writing course should reinforce and broaden this interplay, not interrupt it, so that the student can use it to generate his own criteria and not depend upon a grade to know whether he has written well. The teacher can help by designing writing situations that externalize the circuitry principle. The teacher and the class together can help by telling the writer what they think he said, thereby developing an awareness of the possibilities for meaning or confusion when someone else is the reader.

But if the student is so well-equipped to teach himself to write and the teacher is simply an extension of his audience, why does he need a teacher at all? The answer is, of course, that he doesn't absolutely need a teacher to learn to write, that, in fact, remarkably few people have learned to write through teachers, that many alas, have learned to write in spite of teachers. The writing teacher has but one simple advantage to offer: he can save the student time, and time is important to students who are trying to make up for what got lost in high school and grade school.

To help in even this limited way, a teacher must know what skills are implied in the ability to write what is called basic English and he must understand the nature of the difficulties students seem to have with each of them. The following list is a move in that direction.

Handwriting. The student has to have enough skill at writing to take down his own dictations without getting distracted by the muscular coordination writing requires. If a student has done very little writing in high school, which is often the case, he may need to exercise his writing muscles. This is a quantitative matter—the more of anything he copies, the better the coordination. Malcolm X's exercise of copying the dictionary may not be inspiring enough for many students, but if a student keeps copying something, his handwriting will begin to belong to him. Until then, he is likely to have his problems with handwriting mistaken for problems with writing.

Spelling and Punctuation. To write fluently, a student must feel reasonably comfortable about getting the words and punctuation down right, or he must learn to suspend his concern over correctness until he is ready to proofread. If he is a bad speller, chances are he knows it and will become so preoccupied with correctness that he will constantly lose his thought in order to find the right letters, or he will circumlocute in order to avoid words he can't spell. A number of students enter our classes every semester so handicapped by misspelling and generally so ineffectively taught by us that they are almost certain not to get out of basic writing. It is a problem neither we nor the reading teachers have willingly claimed, but it presses for a solution. The computer, which seems to hold great promise for misspellers, is still a laboratory. The Fidel chart, so successfully used by Dr. Gattegno in

teaching children and illiterate adults to read, has not yet been extensively tried in college programs such as ours.[2]

Students are generally taught to think of punctuation as the scribal translation of oral phrasing and intonation. Some students have, in fact, been taught to put commas where they breathe. As a translation of voice pauses and intonations, however, punctuation is quite crude and almost impossible to learn. Commas can produce as long a pause as a period, and how much time does a semi-colon occupy? Most students solve the problem by working out a private punctuation system or by memorizing a few "rules" that often get them into more trouble than they are worth (like always putting a comma before "and").

In the end, it is more economical for the student to learn to translate punctuation marks into their conventional meaning and to recognize that while there are stylistic choices in punctuating, even these choices are related to a system of signs that signal grammatical (or structural) information more accurately than vocal spacing and intonation. The marks of punctuation can in fact be studied in isolation from words, as signals that prepare a reader for certain types of constructions. Whether these constructions are given their grammatical names is not important, but it is important that a student be able to reconstruct from a passage such as the following the types of constructions he—and other readers—would expect:

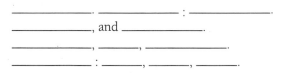

Sentence fragments, run-ons, and comma splices are mistranslations of punctuation marks. They can occur only in writing and can be understood once the student understands the structures they signal. This suggests that punctuation marks should not be studied in isolation from the structural units they signal. For example, when the student is experimenting with the ways in which information can be added to a subject without creating a new sentence (adjectival functions), it is a good time to look at the serial comma, the appositional commas, and the comma in the nonrestrictive clause.

Making Sentences. An English-speaking student is already a maker of statements that not only sound like English but sound like him. Because he has spoken so many more years of sentences than he has written, however, there is a gap between what he can say and what he can write. Sometimes the writing down of sentences is in fact such a labor that he loses his connection with English and produces a tangle of phrases he would never speak. Such a student does not need to learn how to make statements but how to write them at least as well as he speaks them. Other students with foreign language interferences may have to work on English sentence structure itself, but even here their speech is doubtless ahead of their pens. Learning to write statements, therefore, is at first a matter of getting the ear to "hear" script. Later, when the writer wants to exploit the advantages that writing has over speech, the advantage of polishing and perfecting, he may write things he would not be likely to say, but this happens after his pen has caught up with his voice. Students who have little confidence in their voice, or at least in the teacher's response to that voice, have often gone to a great deal of trouble to superimpose another voice upon their writing—sometimes it represents the student's version of a textbook voice; sometimes it is Biblical; sometimes it is a business letter voice—but almost always it seems to keep the writer from understanding clearly what he wants to say. The following sentence, which seems to be a version of the textbook voice, illustrates the kind of entanglement that can result:

> In a broad sense admittance to the SEEK program will serve as a basis of education for me in terms of enlightenment on the tedious time and effort which one must put into all of his endeavors.

A student will usually not abandon this acquired voice until he begins to recognize his own voice and sees that it is safe to prefer it.

There is another skill with sentences which affects the quality of a student's theme as well as his sentences. It involves his ability to "mess" with sentences, to become sensitive to the questions that are embedded in sentences which, when answered, can produce modifications within the sentence or can expand into paragraphs or entire essays. It involves his awareness of the choices he has in casting sentences, of styles in sentences. As Francis Christensen has illustrated in *Notes Toward a New Rhetoric,*[3] the sentence is the microcosm. Whatever the writer does in the sentence when he modifies is in principle what he does in paragraphs and essays. The principle of coordination and subordination can be learned there. The foundation of a paragraph, a chapter, a book is there. It is tempting to say that a student who knows his way around the sentence can get any place in writing. And knowing his way means working on his own sentences, not so much to polish them as to see how much of his meaning they can hold.

But for many students, putting sentences on a page seems a little like carving something on stone: an error cannot be ignored or skimmed over as it can be in speech. It is there forever. "Everything has to be exactly right," explained one of my students, "and that makes me nervous." The page disconnects the student from his product, which will appear alone, before strange eyes, or worse, before the eyes of an English teacher who is a specialist at finding mistakes. To make matters worse, most students feel highly mistake-prone about sentences. They half remember prohibitions about beginning with certain words, but they aren't certain of which words or why (probably the result of lessons on sentence fragments). In short, they feel they are about to commit a verbal sin but they aren't certain what sin is. In such a situation, it seems safer to keep still. It is not unusual to have students at the beginning of the semester who sit through several class periods without writing a word, and when they explain that they don't know how to begin, they are not saying they don't have an idea. They are saying they are not certain which are the "safe" words to begin with.

Students who become observers of sentences and experimenters with sentences lose their fear of them. This experimentation can take many forms. Sentences can be examined as if they were separate compositions. A sentence such as the following by Richard Wright can be written on the board without reference to its context:

> Those brave ones who struggle against death are the ones who bring new life into the world, even though they die to do so, even though our hearts are broken when they die.

Students can talk about the way the sentence is built; they can try to imitate it or change it; or they can try to build a paragraph by expanding some part of it.

There is a kind of carpentry in sentence making, various ways of joining or hooking up modifying units to the base sentence. Suffixes added to make adjectives or adverbs, prepositions, -wh words like where, when, who, which, etc., the double commas used in appositional constructions—all of these can be seen as hooking devices that preserve us from the tedium of Dick-and-Jane sentences. As a form of sentence-play, students can try to write 50- or 100-word sentences that contain only one independent clause. Once discovering they can do it, they usually lose their inhibitions about "real" sentences. Some even move from carpentry to architecture. This sentence was written by a student who was asked in an exam to add information to the predicate of the sentence: "The problem will be solved."

> The problem will be solved with the help of the Almighty, who, except for an occasional thunderstorm, reigns unmolested, high in the heavens above, when all of us, regardless of race or religious differences, can come together and study this severe problem inside out, all day and all night if necessary, and are able to come to you on that great gettin' up morning and say, "Mrs. Shaughnessy, we do know our verbs and adverbs."

Ordering Sentences. Order is an arrangement of units that enables us to see them as parts of something larger. The sense of orientation that results from this arrangement creates a pleasure we call understanding. Perhaps because writing isolates a reader from everything except the page, whereas speech is supported by other gestures and by the right of the audience to query and disagree, we seem to be more tolerant of "disorder" (no clear pattern) in speech than in writing. The talker is not, therefore, committed to knowing where he is going in quite the way that a writer is although he often gets someplace in a way that turns out to have order to it. The writer, however, puts himself on the line, announcing where he is going to go before he sees how he is going to get there. He has to move in two directions at the same time—ahead, point by point toward a destination he has announced but never been to, and down, below the surface of his points to see what they are about. Sometimes, having decided on or having been given an over-all arrangement (or plan) that seems a sensible route to where he is going, the writer hesitates to leave the security of this plan to explore the parts of his paper. Result: a tight, well-ordered but empty paper. At other times, the writer stops to explore one point and never gets back because he cannot get control over the generating force of sentences, which will create branches off branches off branches unless the writer cuts them off. Result: a wilderness.

The skill of organizing seems to require a kind of balance between the demand that a piece of writing get someplace along a route that is sufficiently marked for a reader to follow and the demand that there be freedom for the writer to explore his subject and follow where his questions and inventions take him. The achievement of this balance produces much of the "mess" in writing. Often, however, teachers stress the "administrative" aspects of writing (direction and procedure) over the generative or even assume that the generative is not a part of the organizing skill. This assumption in turn seems to lead to the formulation of organizational patterns in isolation from content (pyramids, upside-down pyramids, etc.) and the efforts to get students to squeeze their theme materials into these patterns. I do not mean to say that restrictions or limits in writing are necessarily inhibiting. They can be both stimulating and liberating, as the sonnet illustrates. But the restrictions I speak of here merely hint at forms they are unable to generate, leaving the reader with the feeling that there is a blank to be filled in but with no sense of how to do it.

Because of this isolation of form from content, students have come to think of organization as something special that happens in themes but not in themselves, daily, as they think or talk. They do not notice that they usually "talk" a better-organized paper than they write, that they use illustrations, anticipate questions, repeat thematic points more effectively in conversation than in writing, whereas the conscious effort to organize a theme often cuts them off from the real content of the theme, giving them all the organizational signposts but no place to go. In talking, they are evolving order; in writing, they often feel they must impose it.

This is not to say that developing a paper is as easy as talking but simply that the difficulty lies not in fitting an amount of raw content into a prefabricated frame but in evoking and controlling the generating power of statement. Every sentence bears within it a new set of possibilities. Sometimes the writer chooses to develop these possibilities; sometimes he prefers to let them lie. Sometimes he decides to develop them fully; at other times, only slightly. Thus each step in the development of a base or thesis statement must inevitably send the writer into a wilderness of possibilities, into a fecundity as dense and multiform as thought itself. One cannot be said to have had an idea until he has made his way through this maze. Order is the pattern of his choices, the path he makes going through

The initial blocking out of a paper, the plan for it, is a kind of hypothesis which allows the writer to proceed with his investigation. Any technique of organization, however, that ignores the wilderness, that limits the freedom of the writer to see and make choices at every step, to move ahead at times without knowing for certain which is north and south, then to drop back again and pick up the old path, and finally to get where he is going, partly by conscious effort but also by some faculty of intel-

lection that is too complex to understand—any technique that sacrifices this fullest possible play of the mind for the security of an outline or some other prefabricated frame cuts the student off from his most productive thinking. He must be allowed something of a frontier mentality, an over-all commitment, perhaps, to get to California, but a readiness, all along the way, to choose alternative routes and even to sojourn at unexpected places when that seems wise or important, sometimes, even, to decide that California isn't what the writer really had in mind.

The main reason for failure in the writing proficiency test at City College, a test given to all upper classmen, has not been grammar or mechanics but the inability to get below the surface of a topic, to treat a topic in depth. The same problem arises in blue-book essays. It is the familiar complaint of students: "I can't think of anything more to say." They are telling us that they do not have access to their thoughts when they write. A part of this difficulty may be related to the way they have learned to write. And a part of the answers may lie in our designing assignments that make the student conscious of what the exploration of an idea is and how this exploration relates to organization.

Grammatical Correctness. Correctness involves those areas of a dialect where there are no choices. (The "s" on the present tense 3rd person singular is correct in standard English; the use of a plural verb with the subject "none" is a choice; the comparison "more handsome" is a choice but "more intelligenter" is incorrect.) Native speakers of a dialect are not concerned with correctness; they unconsciously say things the correct way. Non-native speakers of a dialect must consciously acquire the "givens" if they want to communicate without static in that dialect. This is a linguistic fact that seems at the outset to put speakers of a nonstandard dialect at a disadvantage. But it is a strange logic that says having access to one dialect is better than having access to two, particularly when we know that every dialect or language system sets limits on the ways we can perceive and talk about the world.

Unfortunately, this is not the way speakers of other dialects have been encouraged to think about their dialects, with the result that writing classes and writing teachers seem to put them at a disadvantage, creating either an obsessive concern with correctness or a fatalistic indifference to it. The only thing that can help the student overcome such feelings is to help him gain control over the dialect. It is irresponsible to tell him that correctness is not important; it is difficult to persuade him after years of indoctrination to the contrary that "correctness" plays a subordinate role in good writing; but it is not impossible to give him the information and practice he needs to manage his own proofreading.

The information will inevitably be grammatical, whether the terminology of grammar is used or not. But it is more important to remember that the student who is not at home with standard English has most likely had several doses of grammar already and it hasn't worked. For reasons that he himself doesn't quite understand, the explanations about things like the third-person "s" or the agreement of subject and verb haven't taken. He is not deliberately trying to make mistakes but for some reason they keep happening. What he often does not realize, and what the teacher has to realize is that his difficulties arise from his mastery of one language or dialect, and that changing to another often involves at certain points a loss or conflict of meaning and therefore difficulty in learning, not because he is stubborn or dumb or verbally impoverished but because he expects language to make sense. (The student, for example, who finally told me he couldn't use "are" to mean something in the present because it was too stiff and formal and therefore faraway, and the Chinese student who could not make a plural out of sunrise because there is only one sun, were both trying to hold on to meaning, as Will James, the cowboy author, was when, he continued to use "seen" for the past tense because it meant seeing farther than "saw.")

These are obviously grammatical matters, but this does not mean they require the traditional study of grammar. The question of what they do require is widely debated. Certainly it should be apparent that teachers working with students who have black dialect or Spanish or Chinese or some other language background should be familiar with the features of those languages that are influencing their students' work in Standard English. This should be part of the general equipment of us all as teachers. And the new insights that come from the linguists should also be ours. But none of this information will be of much use if we simply make pronouncements about it in class. Students cannot be expected to get more help from memorizing two grammatical systems instead of one, and the diagrams in transformational grammar are still diagrams. The acquisition of new information will not automatically make us better teachers. To make this happen, we need to develop a sharp sense of the difference between talking and teaching. We need to design lessons that highlight the grammatical characteristics of a dialect so that the student can discover them for himself. (It is one thing to tell a student about the "s" in the third-person present singular; it is another for him to discover the power of that schizophrenic letter which clings so irrationally to its last verb to mark its singularity while it attaches itself to nouns to mark their plurality, and then, confusing things further, acquires an apostrophe and marks the singular possessive.) We need to devise ways of practicing that the student enjoys because he is able to invent rather than memorize answers. We need, finally, to teach proofreading as a separate skill that uses the eye in a different way from reading and places the burden of correctness where it belongs—at the end of (rather than during) the writing process. To do things for the student that he can do himself is not generosity but impatience. It is hard work for a teacher not to talk, but we must now be very industrious if we want our students to learn what we have to teach.

III

I have been speaking about the skills that seem basic to writing, but basic writing courses that prepare students for college writing are actually concerned with a rather special kind of prose called exposition, a semi-formal analytical prose in which the connections between sentences and paragraphs surface in the form of conjunctive adverbs and transitional sentences. More simply, it means the kind of writing teachers got B's and A's for in college, a style whose characteristics they have now internalized and called a standard.

Teachers of basic writing are thus responsible for helping their students learn to write in an expository style. They must also give them practice in writing to specification (i.e., on a special topic or question and in a certain form) since many assignments require it. The question of how to reach such objectives and at the same time give each student a chance to discover other things about writing and about his individual powers as a writer troubles many teachers and creates many different "positions." Where, for example, on the following list, ranging from highly controlled to free assignments, is it best to begin a course in basic writing:

1. paraphrase

2. summary

3. exegesis of a passage

4. theme in which topic sentence and organizational pattern are given

5. theme in which topic sentence is given (includes the examination question which is usually an inverted topic sentence)

6. theme in which subject is given

7. theme in which form is given—description, dialogue, argument, etc.

8. theme in which only the physical conditions for writing are given—journal, free writing, etc.

Teachers take sides on such a question, some insisting that freedom in anything, including writing, cannot exist until there is control and that this comes through the step by step mastery of highly structured assignments; others insist that students must begin not with controls but with materials— the things they have already seen or felt or imagined—and evolve their own controls as they try to translate experience into writing. Meanwhile students confuse the issue by learning to write and not learning to write under almost all approaches. I prefer to start around #7, with description. But

then, I have to remember the student who started a research paper on mummies before she could manage her sentences. "Positions" on curriculae and methods are somehow always too neat to say much about learning, which seems to be sloppy. They tend to be generalizations about students, not about the nature of the skills that have to be mastered, and the only generalization that seems safe to make about students is the ones they persistently make about themselves—that they are individuals, not types, and that the way to each student's development is a way the teacher has never taken before. Everything about the teacher-student encounter should encourage a respect for this fact of individuality even though the conditions under which we must teach in large institutions often obscure it. Books do have to be ordered and teachers do have to make plans. But perhaps the plans need not be so well-laid that they cannot go awry when the signals point that way. A teacher must know deeply what it is he is teaching—what is arbitrary or given and what is built upon skills the student already possesses. This is his preparation. But he cannot know about his student until both meet in the classroom. Then teaching becomes what one student described as "simply two people learning from each other."

In the confusion of information on methods and curriculae that comes to us from publishers—and from each other—it is probably important to emphasize this single truth.

Notes

1. Reprinted by permission from *A Guide for Teachers of College English.* New York: Office of Academic Development, CUNY, 1970.

2. Caleb Gattegno, *Teaching Reading with Words in Color,* Educational Solutions, Inc., New York, 1968.

3. Francis Christensen, *Notes Toward a New Rhetoric,* New York, Harper & Row, 1967.

The Rhetorical Transaction of Reading

W. Ross Winterowd

Winterowd's essay was first published in College Composition and Communication *27 (1976): 185–91. The version reprinted here is taken from* Composition/Rhetoric: A Synthesis. *Carbondale: Southern Illinois UP, 1986. 265–72.*

The writer projects his meanings, intentions, and so forth onto the page in the form of raw information, black squiggles against a white background. The reader processes this information to reconstruct the writer's meanings, intentions, and so forth. To concentrate on the page and what can be found there, however, will inevitably bring about a serious misunderstanding of the rhetorical transaction of reading.

It goes without saying that all composition teachers are, *ipso facto,* reading teachers; therefore, it should be useful to understand the relationship between reading and rhetoric. Indeed, such an understanding will have practical consequences in the classroom.

To explore this relationship, we will merely survey rhetoric from the standpoint of reading theory. Our question will be, simply, how does reading theory bear on the concepts of *logos* (logical arguments), *ethos* (arguments based on the character of the speaker), and *pathos* (arguments based on the nature of the audience), which constitute the classical department of invention, on arrangement or form *(dispositio),* and on style? We will use these categories loosely, as a method of organization and as a heuristic.

THE MEANING OF "MEANING"

We will equate *logos* with what might be called "pure" meaning, which includes information (a term that will be defined hereafter), logical

consistency, and reference. Indeed, this extension does not seriously warp Aristotle's intention but merely expands it. From the standpoint of reading theory, what is the meaning of "pure meaning"?

The page itself, with its black squiggles against a white background, contains no meaning, only information from which meaning can be derived. The information on the page is arranged in a series of interrelated *cue systems:* graphophonic, syntactic, and semantic.[1] Take the following example:

(1) We flew to New York in a _____.

If we are beginning or inefficient readers we can "sound the sentences out" to make the correspondence between the printed marks (graphemes) and the meaningful sounds which they represent (phonemes). Of course, efficient readers go directly from grapheme to meaning, without the mediation of sound,[2] like this:

GRAPHEME → MEANING

Only the inefficient or beginning readers need the mediation of sound, like this:

GRAPHEME → PHONEME → MEANING

Furthermore, the syntactic system of the language determines that the blank can be filled only by a Noun Phrase, just as the syntactic system of the language determines the contrast in meaning between

(2) Man bites dog.

and

(3) Dog bites man.

Finally, the semantics of the language and the semantic "field" of the sentence (as well as our knowledge of the world) allow us to predict with some certainty that the blank will be filled by either *plane* or *jet*. Notice the increasing improbability and strangeness of the following:

(4) We flew to New York in a plane/jet.
(5) We flew to New York in a balloon.
(6) We flew to New York in a carrot.

Information, of course, is not meaning, but we can use information to construct meaning; in fact, that is precisely what we do in the reading process.

In regard to *pathos,* the reader is the audience for written discourse, and meaning is not "down there" on the page, but "up here" in the reader's mind. In processing the information on the page to derive meaning, the reader employs three "systems": eyesight, short-term memory, and long-term memory. The short-term memory is a screening device which keeps the long-term memory from being continually flooded with information to process. It is axiomatic that the short-term memory can process only *seven-plus-or-minus-two* bits of information at one time. A bit of information is a "chunk" of some kind that reduces uncertainty by one-half. If I am holding a playing card from an ordinary deck and ask you to guess the suit, you might ask me, "Is it black?" When I answer, "No," you have received one bit of information. You now ask, "Is it a heart?" I answer, "No," and you are certain that the card is a diamond. Two bits of information were all that you needed to achieve certainty.[3]

How many bits of information are there in the sentence *Man bites dog*? That question is, of course, impossible to answer, for we can view every horizontal and vertical line, every curve and every serif as a bit of information. Obviously, if we used all of the information there is in the sentence, we could

never derive meaning, for our short-term memories impose the seven-plus-or-minus-two limit on us. Somehow, we obviously chunk our information, and under no circumstances do we use all of the plethora of information that is available on the printed page.

The construction of meaning, then, takes place in the mind of the reader. The meaning constructed is curiously independent of the information from which it is derived; at this point, you can probably explain to me or to someone else the meaning of what I have written so far, but in doing so you will probably use none of the exact sentences or even phrases that I have written. You will translate the meaning you have derived into information that can be reprocessed for meaning.

If I *write* the sentence

(7) I stopped the auto, shut off the engine, and opened the bonnet.

and you *tell* me that the sentence means

(8) /I stopped the *car,* shut off the *motor,* and opened the *hood.*/

you have obviously not misread, for you have gained meaning and have translated that meaning into another information system.

The importance of this concept is obvious. If, for instance, a speaker of the urban black dialect reads

(9) My father is at home.

and *says*

(10) /My father be at home./

he or she has not misread but has gained the meaning from the sentence and has translated that meaning into his or her own dialect.

Consider that the graphophonic correspondence is tenuous at best, as the following demonstrates: *tough, through, though.* Consider, further, the following renditions of *Cuba is rather close:*

(11) /Cuber is rathuh close./
(12) /Cuba is rahther close./
(13) /Cuba's rather close./

Even though these examples are only loose attempts to give written approximations of some American dialects, it should become apparent that dialect *per se* has nothing to do with reading ability.

In the construction of meaning from the information provided by print, the mind of the reader is obviously all-important. This is embarrassingly self-evident. If I had trouble in reading *Principia Mathematica,* I would certainly not go to Evelyn Wood to improve my reading ability but would go to the math department for a few courses. The reader brings his or her totality of experience and knowledge to bear in the reading process; thus, reading is partly a mechanical skill—the ability to use the cue system efficiently. But, even more important, it is a rhetorical transaction in which the pathetic factor is supreme.

We have drawn a correspondence between *logos* and the information on the page and between *pathos* and the use of that information by the reader. (Perhaps the correspondence is too rough, but I think not.) However, we have still not totally accounted for meaning—as the following sentence makes clear:

(14) Could you raise the window?

As it stands, it is ambiguous. Namely, we wonder if it is an inquiry or a request. In other words, does (15) or does (16) capture the intention

(15) I *inquire* of you, "Could you raise the window?"
(16) I *request* of you, "Could you raise the window?"

Presumably, (15) would result in an answer of "yes" or "no," but (16) would result, probably, in the hearer's raising the window. Sentences, in other words, are *intended*—as statements, warnings, exhortations, requests, and so on. Intention implies a writer. In other words, the concept of *ethos* enters our account of meaning.

Reading theory has almost nothing to say that bears on *ethos.* In fact, at this point, rhetoric can fill out a gap in reading theory. Equally important to the function of *ethos* in meaning is speech-act theory.[4] To develop an adequate account of speech-act theory in regard to reading would demand a separate essay, but a brief sketch will provide a hint of the connections.

The speech act is composed of *utterance act,* making speech sounds or writing graphemes; *propositional act,* in which reference and predication take place, as when I predicate "yawn" of "Norma" in *Norma yawns;*[5] *illocutionary act,* which is actually the speaker's intention to state, warn, promise, dare, etc.; *perlocutionary act,* which is the effect of the sentence, as when I utter *Norma yawns,* you may take the sentence as a statement, a warning that you'd better liven up the party, an insult that implies your conversation is dull, and so on.[6]

Clearly, you cannot interpret a sentence until you know how it is intended. Intention (or motive) suggests a writer, and the intentional fallacy is not a fallacy but a necessity.

In the foregoing, of course, I have not done justice to reading or speech-act theory. Both are rich bodies of thought—and data—that I feel composition teachers should be thoroughly familiar with. But what I would like to do now is to construct a rough model of reading as a rhetorical transaction—simply, a writer influencing the beliefs, actions, attitudes, etc. of an audience through the medium of the printed page.

The page itself is a meaningless bit of opacity covered by not particularly attractive designs. The reader comes to the page with the ability to process these designs for meaning—that is, with the mechanical ability to read—and with a whole world of ideas, attitudes, cultural sets, and so on—with everything, in short, that constitutes the human mind. If the page is from, say, *PMLA* and the reader has made a lifelong career of literary scholarship, the reading task will probably be fairly simple, as it would not be for a Ph.D. in mathematics who had very little experience in the world of literature. It is a fact, however, that in one sense the reading of all texts is equally easy (or equally difficult), provided that the reader is familiar with all of the vocabularies used; namely, the process of reading as the use of the cue system is constant throughout all materials. But reading is the derivation of meanings; therefore, a number of factors make reading more or less difficult for the "good" reader: familiarity with the concepts developed in the text; the accessibility of the syntax employed by the author;[7] cultural biases in the text; the clarity of the print; and so on.

In the process of reading, the reader must construct, more or less clearly, a concept of intention and hence supply a writer. Take the following example. These lines

(17) Lift receiver.
Deposit coin.
Listen for dial tone.
Dial number.

are found in (1) a phone booth and (2), with the title "AT&T," in a paperback volume entitled *Now Poetry*. In the first instance, they are a set of instructions; in the second instance, they are an esthetic object, perhaps a satire or a spoof. To translate this concept into the jargon of speech-act theory, the perlocutionary act is the reader's discovery of the illocutionary act. In irony, of course, intention is the fulcrum upon which the weight of the work can be swung.

There is, then, a correspondence between current theories of reading and classical notions of invention. The rhetorician is quite at home as a teacher of composition or as a teacher of reading.

ARRANGEMENT: ATTACK SKILLS AND DISPOSITIO

Though I seriously doubt that there is any such thing as speed reading in the popular sense of that term, there certainly are (1) different reading purposes and (2) more or less efficient ways to process the information on the page to derive meaning.

The most efficient way to derive meaning from a text is to get a general idea of what "it's all about" through scanning, after which the general outline can be "impleted" with details. This would imply that the most efficient way to read a book or an article is to scan two or three times and then to return for close reading. Kenneth Goodman says that efficient readers *sample,* to get a notion of the meaning of a text; then they *predict* what the meaning will be; next they *test* this prediction; and then they *con-*

firm or *disconfirm* it.[8] The sampling-predicting-testing-confirming process can operate at the sentence level or beyond.

This principle is richly suggestive about organization in writing. Suppose that the intention of the writer is to facilitate the reader's understanding of the piece. In that case, the organization will demand a very general statemental outline of the essay, chapter, or whatever, followed by paragraphs or sections that systematically "implete" the general concepts in the outline; paragraphs will start with a clearcut topic sentence, and subsequent sentences will fill in the details, as in the subordinate-sequence paragraphs that Francis Christensen describes.[9] (You will notice that I have not followed my own advice in this essay.)

Of course, it is not the purpose of all writing to be optimally readable. The desire for a given rhetorical effect might well dictate a "surprise ending" or an inverted order, in which the essay proceeds from details to more and more broad generalities.

Nor should all reading be "efficient." In my engagement with a novel, I seldom want to lose the sequacious richness of the development in order to read efficiently.

I would like, however, to suggest a pedagogical gimmick. I think that we are seldom very helpful in our attempts to teach students how to organize. If we point out that efficient reading demands an inexorable movement from the general to the specific, in the whole essay and in the individual paragraphs, we will have set up a formal principle which is coherent and simple. Once the essay has been written according to this plan, what are the permutations that rearrangements can bring about, and what will be their rhetorical effects? Explorations of this kind can demonstrate that form has consequences.

STYLE AS ACCESSIBILITY

It is axiomatic that some sentences are easier to read than others. For instance, the grammar of the language allows us to place the particle either before or after the Noun Phrase object of the verb, thus:

(18) She turned *off* the light.

(19) She turned the light *off*.

Notice what happens with the following, however:

(20) She tore down the shed which he put up.

(21) She tore the shed which he put up down.

Or even more horrendously:

(22) She tore down the shed which fouled up the view when the sun came down.

(23) She tore the shed which fouled the view when the sun came down up down.

Clearly, some structures are easier to process for meaning than others. (That is just one of the points regarding heavy nominalization.) This is a facile statement which can be taken too broadly; for instance, evidence indicates that passive is as easy to process as active, depending on the context.[10] Nonetheless, it is a fact that syntax can stand in the way of efficient reading.

We have seen that efficient readers process meaning from graphemes, without the intervention of phonemes. In other words, efficient reading demands that we *not* make the grapheme-phoneme correspondence. However, it is a fact that some writings virtually force this correspondence upon us. I refer, of course, to poetry, in which rhyme, meter, alliteration, assonance, and so on, reify the graphophonic correspondence that, as efficient readers, we have been able to ignore. Even in everyday expository prose, sound patterns tend to make the graphophonic system visible, whereas in efficient reading it should be invisible or transparent. In the last sentence, the alliteration of "everyday expository" turns those words into phonic phenomena.

Just as syntax and the graphophonic system should be "invisible" or "transparent" for efficient reading, so should the semantic system. This is merely a truism in one sense; the moment we stop to ask "I wonder what that word means?" efficiency in reading ceases, and, in a sense, the semantic cue system is reified. Or to state the point another way: in reading, we are merely processing language; when we must ask for a definition, we have shifted our concern to metalanguage, that is, to language about language.

In regard to the semantics of nonliterary and literary discourse, I can think of no better discussion than Philip Wheelwright's "The Logical and the Translogical."[11] Wheelwright's point in general is that nonliterary discourse uses a relatively firm semantic base. That is, the terms do not tend to shift their meanings, and they have little or no iconographic quality. In literary language, a term is quite likely to have the nature of a variable, taking the value that the reader assigns it in his or her attempt to get at the meaning of a work. And the literary term is likely to have both an imagistic and a strictly semantic value: "the marriage of true minds," "time's winged chariot," "bare ruined choirs," "a woman lovely in her bones." The nonliterary term is also, of course, frequently an image, but the imagistic quality is normally subordinate to what might be called the cognitive or referential quality.

In regard to the cue system, we can think of the Coleridgean image of a frost-covered window pane. We can see through the pane to the outside world, but we can also contemplate the frost patterns as objects of delight.

This is the point regarding style as accessibility. In efficient reading, the graphophonic, syntactic, and semantic cue systems have no visibility; they are clear panes of glass that allow us to see meaning through them.

LITERATURE AS "MERE" RHETORIC

But, of course, a pane of glass, regardless of how Windexed, is nonetheless a pane of glass. It reflects and diffuses. Even when not frost-covered, it presents a visual experience for anyone who is interested in looking. Whether the pane of glass is "there" or not depends on the intention (and attention) of the viewer. Under any and all circumstances, you can look either through it or at it. You can contemplate the designs of the frost or the shadowy forms that reveal themselves beyond the frost.

"Pure" literature—and, of course, there is no such thing—is an object of contemplation. It is the frost-covered window, and we are interested in the frost.

The moments when we can contemplate frost with intensity and satisfaction, however, are rare and fleeting. Suddenly the frost patterns become mountains or faces or snowscapes, and suddenly we become aware of the shapes in the world beyond the windowpane. We are out of the realm of purity and into the realm of experience, memory, hope, desire.

When we read, we are also in the realm of experience, memory, hope, desire. We are human beings reading, not reading machines. Which means that "pure" literature exists only at the imaginary interface between contemplation and the act of reading.

For when we read, we continually try to grasp intention; in so doing, we supply an author. We cannot escape from the rhetorical, pathetic, intentional fallacy.

The meaning is meaningful only in terms of our own beings. We are caught inexorably in the affective fallacy, and there is no escape. Across the cryptic neatness of the page, a writer is contacting a reader.

A poem can never be an artifact, for in language, an artifact is merely data, information; and information is meaningless. Surely no one would argue that a true poem is meaningless.

But there is a supreme irony about literature. The poem invites us to contemplate it *as if it were* an artifact. This we can never do, for poems are to be read.

Reading theory leads me to conclude that literature is "mere" rhetoric.

Notes

1. Kenneth S. Goodman, "Psycholinguistic Universals in the Reading Process," *Psycholinguistics and Reading,* ed. Frank Smith (New York: Holt, Rinehart and Winston, 1973).

2. Frank Smith, *Understanding Reading* (New York: Holt, Rinehart and Winston, 1971), 204–10; Frank Smith, "Decoding: The Great Fallacy," *Psycholinguistics and Reading.*

3. Smith, *Understanding Reading,* 12–26.

4. J. L. Austin, *How to Do Things with Words* (New York: Oxford University Press, 1962); John Searle, *Speech Acts* (Cambridge: Cambridge University Press, 1969).

5. Searle, 22–26.

6. As Searle (p. 25) explains: "Correlated with the notion of illocutionary acts is the notion of the consequences or *effects* such acts have on the actions, thoughts, or beliefs, etc. of hearers. For example, by arguing I may *persuade* or *convince* someone, by warning him I may *scare* or *alarm* him, by making a request I may *get him to do something,* by informing him I may *convince him (enlighten, edify, inspire him, get him to realize).*" The italicized expressions above denote perlocutionary acts.

7. More about this later.

8. Goodman, "Psycholinguistic Universals in the Reading Process."

9. "A Generative Rhetoric of the Paragraph," *Notes Toward a New Rhetoric* (New York: Harper & Row, 1967).

10. Dan I. Slobin, *Psycholinguistics* (Glenview, Ill.: Scott, Foresman 1971), 33–38.

11. *Critical Theory Since Plato,* ed. Hazard Adams (New York: Harcourt Brace Jovanovich, 1971). The essay is Chapter 4 of *The Burning Fountain: A Study in the Language of Symbolism* (Bloomington: Indiana University Press, 1954).

The Phenomenology of Error

Joseph M. Williams

Williams's essay appeared in College Composition and Communication 32 *(1981):* 152–68.

I am often puzzled by what we call errors of grammar and usage, errors such as *different than, between you and I,* a *which* for a *that,* and so on. I am puzzled by what motive could underlie the unusual ferocity which an *irregardless* or a *hopefully* or a singular *media* can elicit. In his second edition of *On Writing Well* (New York, 1980), for example, William Zinsser, an otherwise amiable man I'm sure, uses, and quotes not disapprovingly, words like *detestable vulgarity* (p. 43), *garbage* (p. 44), *atrocity* (p. 46), *horrible* (p. 48); *oaf* (p. 42), *idiot* (p. 43), and *simple illiteracy* (p. 46), to comment on usages like *OK, hopefully,* the affix *-wise,* and *myself* in *He invited Mary and myself to dinner.*

The last thing I want to seem is sanctimonious. But as I am sure Zinsser would agree, what happens in Cambodia and Afghanistan could more reasonably be called horrible atrocities. The likes of Idi Amin qualify as legitimate oafs. Idiots we have more than enough of in our state institutions. And while simply illiteracy is the condition of billions, it does not characterize those who use *disinterested* in its original sense.[1]

I am puzzled why some errors should excite this seeming fury while others, not obviously different in kind, seem to excite only moderate disapproval. And I am puzzled why some of us can regard any particular item as a more or less serious error, while others, equally perceptive, and acknowledging that the same item may in some sense be an "error," seem to invest in their observation no emotion at all.

At first glance, we ought to be able to explain some of these anomolies by subsuming errors of grammar and usage in a more general account of defective social behavior, the sort of account constructed so brilliantly by Erving Goffman.[2] But errors of social behavior differ from errors of "good usage": Social errors that excite feelings commensurate with judgments like "horrible," "atrocious," "oaf(ish)," and "detestable" are usually errors that grossly violate our personal space: We break wind at a dinner party and then vomit on the person next to us. We spill coffee in their lap, then step on a toe when we get up to apologize. It's the Inspector Clouseau routine. Or the error metaphorically violates psychic space: We utter an inappropriate obscenity, mention our painful hemorrhoids, tell a racist joke, and snigger at the fat woman across the table who turns out to be our hostess. Because all of these actions crudely violate one's personal space we are justified in calling them "oafish"; all of them require that we apologize, or at least offer an excuse.

This way of thinking about social error turns our attention from error as a discrete entity, frozen at the moment of its commission, to error as part of a flawed transaction, originating in ignorance or incompetence or accident, manifesting itself as an invasion of another's personal space, eliciting a judgment ranging from silent disapproval to "atrocious" and "horrible," and requiring either an explicit "I'm sorry" and correction, or a simple acknowledgment and a tacit agreement not to do it again.[3]

To address errors of grammar and usage in this way, it is also necessary to shift our attention from error treated strictly as an isolated item on a page, to error perceived as a flawed verbal transaction between a writer and a reader. When we do this, the matter of error turns less on a handbook definition than on the reader's response, because it is that response—"detestable," "horrible"—that defines the seriousness of the error and its expected amendment.

But if we do compare serious nonlinguistic gaffes to errors of usage, how can we not be puzzled over why so much heat is invested in condemning a violation whose consequence impinges not at all on our personal space? The language some use to condemn linguistic error seems far more intense than the language they use to describe more consequential social errors—a hard bump on the arm, for example—that require a sincere but not especially effusive apology. But no matter how "atrocious" or "horrible" or "illiterate" we think an error like *irregardless* or a *like* for an *as* might be, it does not jolt my ear in the same way an elbow might; a *between you and I* does not offend me, at least not in the ordinary sense of offend. Moreover, unlike social errors, linguistic errors do not ordinarily require that we apologize for them.[4] When we make *media* a singular or dangle a participle, and are then made aware of our mistake, we are expected to acknowledge the error, and, if we have the opportunity, to amend it. But I don't think that we are expected to say, "Oh, I'm sorry!" The objective consequences of the error simply do not equal those of an atrocity, or even of clumsiness.

It may be that to fully account for the contempt that some errors of usage arouse, we will have to understand better than we do the relationship between language, order, and those deep psychic forces that perceived linguistic violations seem to arouse in otherwise amiable people.[5] But if we cannot yet fully account for the psychological source of those feelings, or why they are so intense, we should be able to account better than we do for the variety of responses that different "errors" elicit. It is a subject that should be susceptible to research. And indeed, one kind of research in this area has a long tradition: In this century, at least five major surveys of English usage have been conducted to determine how respondents feel about various matters of usage. Sterling Leonard, Albert Marckwardt, Raymond Crisp, the Institute of Education English Research Group at the University of Newcastle upon Tyne, and the *American Heritage Dictionary* have questioned hundreds of teachers and editors and writers and scholars about their attitudes toward matters of usage ranging from *which* referring to a whole clause to split infinitives to *enthuse* as a verb.[6]

The trouble with this kind of research, though, with asking people whether they think *finalize* is or is not good usage, is that they are likely to answer. As William Labov and others have demonstrated,[7] we are not always our own best informants about our habits of speech. Indeed, we are likely to give answers that misrepresent our talking and writing, usually in the direction of more rather than less conservative values. Thus when the editors of the *American Heritage Dictionary* asks its Usage Panel to decide the acceptability of *impact* as a verb, we can predict how they will react: Merely by being asked, it becomes manifest to them that they have been invested with an institutional responsibility that will require them to judge usage by the standards they think they are supposed to uphold. So we cannot be surprised that when asked, Zinsser rejects *impact* as a verb, despite the fact that *impact* has been used as a verb at least since 1601.

The problem is self-evident: Since we can ask an indefinite number of questions about an indefinite number of items of usage, we can, merely by asking, accumulate an indefinite number of errors, simply because whoever we ask will feel compelled to answer. So while it may seem useful for us to ask one another whether we think X is an error, we have to be skeptical about our answers, because we will invariably end up with more errors than we began with, certainly more than we ever feel on our nerves when we read in the ways we ordinarily do.

In fact, it is this unreflective feeling on the nerves in our ordinary reading that interests me the most, the way we respond—or not—to error when we do not make error a part of our conscious field of attention. It is the difference between reading for typographical errors and reading for content.

When we read for typos, letters constitute the field of attention; content becomes virtually inaccessible. When we read for content, semantic structures constitute the field of attention; letters—for the most part—recede from our consciousness.

I became curious about this kind of perception three years ago when I was consulting with a government agency that had been using English teachers to edit reports but was not sure they were getting their money's worth. When I asked to see some samples of editing by their consultants, I found that one very common notation was "faulty parallelism" at spots that only by the most conservative interpretation could be judged faulty. I asked the person who had hired me whether faulty parallelism was a problem in his staff's ability to write clearly enough to be understood quickly, but with enough authority to be taken seriously. He replied, "If the teacher says so."

Now I was a little taken aback by this response, because it seemed to me that one ought not have to appeal to a teacher to decide whether something like faulty parallelism was a real problem in communication. The places where faulty parallelism occurred should have been at least felt as problems, if not recognized as a felt difficulty whose specific source was faulty parallelism.

About a year later, as I sat listening to a paper describing some matters of error analysis in evaluating compositions, the same thing happened. When I looked at examples of some of the errors, sentences containing alleged dangling participles, faulty parallelism, vague pronoun reference, and a few other items,[8] I was struck by the fact that, at least in some of the examples, I saw some infelicity, but no out-and-out grammatical error. When I asked the person who had done the research whether these examples were typical of errors she looked for to measure the results of extensive training in sentence combining, I was told that the definition of error had been taken from a popular handbook, on the assumption, I guess, that that answered the question.

About a year ago, it happened again, when a publisher and I began circulating a manuscript that in a peripheral way deals with some of the errors I've mentioned here, suggesting that some errors are less serious than others. With one exception, the reviewers, all teachers at universities, agreed that an intelligent treatment of error would be useful, and that this manuscript was at least in the ballpark. But almost every reader took exception to one item of usage that they thought I had been too soft on, that I should have unequivocally condemned as a violation of good usage. Unfortunately, each of them mentioned a different item.

Well, it is all very puzzling: Great variation in our definition of error, great variation in our emotional investment in defining and condemning error, great variation in the perceived seriousness of individual errors. The categories of error all seem like they should be yes-no, but the feelings associated with the categories seem much more complex.

If we think about these responses for a moment we can identify one source of the problem: We were all locating error in very different places. For all of us, obviously enough, error is in the essay, on the page, because that is where it physically exists. But of course, to be in the essay, it first has to be in the student. But before that, it has to be listed in a book somewhere. And before that in the mind of the writer of the handbook. And finally, a form of the error has to be in the teacher who resonated or not—to the error on the page on the basis of the error listed in the handbook.

This way of thinking about error locates error in two different physical locations (the student's paper and the grammarian's handbook) and in three different experiences: the experience of the writer who creates the error; in the experience of the teacher who catches it; and in the mind of the grammarian—the E. B. White or Jacques Barzun or H. W. Fowler—who proposes it. Because error seems to exist in so many places, we should not be surprised that we do not agree among ourselves about how to identify it, or that we do not respond to the same error uniformly.

But we might be surprised—and perhaps instructed—by those cases where the two places occur in texts by the same author—and where all three experiences reside in the same person. It is, in fact, these cases that I would like to examine for a moment, because they raise such interesting questions about the experience of error.

For example, E. B. White presumably believed what he (and Strunk) said in *Elements of Style* (New York, 1979) about faulty parallelism and *which* vs. *that:*

> Express coordinate ideas in similar form. This principle, that of parallel construction, requires that expressions similar in content and function be outwardly similar. (p. 26)
>
> *That, which. That* is the defining or restrictive pronoun, *which* the non-defining or non-restrictive . . . The careful writer . . . removes the defining *whiches,* and by so doing improves his work. (p. 59)

Yet in the last paragraph of "Death of a Pig,"[9] White has two faulty parallelisms, and according to his rules, an incorrect *which:*

> . . . the premature expiration of a pig is, I soon discovered, a departure which the community marks solemnly on its calendar . . . I have written this account in penitence and in grief, as a man who failed to raise his pig, and to explain my deviation from the classic course of so many raised pigs. The grave in the woods is unmarked, but Fred can direct the mourner to it unerringly and with immense good will, and I know he and I shall often revisit it, singly and together, . . .

Now I want to be clear: I am not at all interested in the trivial fact that E. B. White violated one or two of his own trivial rules. That would be a trivial observation. We could simply say that he miswrote in the same way he might have mistyped and thereby committed a typographical error. Nor at the moment am I interested in the particular problem of parallelism, or of *which* vs. *that,* any more than I would be interested in the particular typo. What I **am** interested in is the fact that no one, E. B. White least of all, seemed to **notice** that E. B. White had made an error. What I'm interested in here is the noticing or the not noticing by the same person who stipulates what should be noticed, and why anyone would surely have noticed if White had written,

> I knows me and him will often revisit it, . . .

Of course, it may be that I am stretching things just a bit far to point out a trivial error of usage in one publication on the basis of a rule asserted in another. But this next example is one in which the two co-exist between the same covers:

> *Were* (sing.) is, then, a recognizable subjunctive, & applicable not to past facts, but to present or future non-facts. (p. 576)
>
> Another suffix that is not a living one, but is sometimes treated as if it was, is *-al* . . . (p. 242)
>
> —H. W. Fowler. *A Dictionary of Modern English Usage.* Oxford, 1957.

Now again, Fowler may have just made a slip here; when he read these entries, certainly at widely separate intervals, the *was* in the second just slipped by. And yet how many others have also read that passage, and also never noticed?

The next example may be a bit more instructive. Here, the rule is asserted in the middle of one page:

> In conclusion, I recommend using *that* with defining clauses except when stylistic reasons interpose. Quite often, not a mere pair of *that's* but a threesome or foursome, including the demonstrative *that,* will come in the same sentence and justify *which* to all writers with an ear. (p. 68)

and violated at the top of the next:

> Next is a typical situation which a practiced writer corrects for style virtually by reflex action. (p. 69)
>
> —Jacques Barzun. *Simple and Direct.* New York, 1976.

Now again, it is not the error as such that I am concerned with here, but rather the fact that after Barzun stated the rule, and almost immediately violated it, no one noticed—not Barzun himself who must certainly have read the manuscript several times, not a colleague to whom he probably gave the manuscript before he sent it to the publisher, not the copy editor who worked over the manuscript, not the proof reader who read the galleys, not Barzun who probably read the galleys after them, apparently not even anyone in the reading public, since that *which* hasn't been corrected in any of the subsequent printings. To characterize this failure to respond as mere carelessness seems to miss something important.

This kind of contradiction between the conscious directive and the unreflexive experience becomes even more intense in the next three examples, examples that, to be sure, involve matters of style rather than grammar and usage:

> Negative constructions are often wordy and sometimes pretentious.
>
> 1. wordy Housing for married students is not unworthy of consideration.
>
>   concise Housing for married students is worthy of consideration.
>
>   better The trustees should earmark funds for married students' housing. (Probably what the author meant)
>
> 2. wordy After reading the second paragraph you aren't left with an immediate reaction as to how the story will end.
>
>   concise The first two paragraphs create suspense.

The following example from a syndicated column is not untypical:

> Sylvan Barnet and Marcia Stubbs. *Practical Guide to Writing*. Boston, 1977, p. 280.

Now Barnet and Stubbs may be indulging in a bit of self-parody here. But I don't think so. In this next example, Orwell, in the very act of criticising the passive, not only casts his proscription against it in the passive, but almost all the sentences around it, as well:

> I list below, with notes and examples, various of the tricks by means of which the work of prose construction is habitually dodged . . . *Operators* or *verbal false limbs.* These save the trouble of picking out appropriate verbs and nouns, and at the same time pad each sentence with extra syllables which give it an appearance of symmetry . . . the passive voice is wherever possible used in preference to the active, and noun constructions are used instead of gerunds . . . The

range of verbs if further cut down . . . and the banal statements are given an appearance of profundity by means of the *not un* formation. Simple conjunctions are replaced by . . . the ends of sentences are saved by . . .

> —"Politics and the English Language"

Again, I am not concerned with the fact that Orwell wrote in the passive or used nominalizations where he could have used verbs.[10] Rather, I am bemused by the apparent fact that three generations of teachers have used this essay without there arising among us a general wry amusement that Orwell violated his own rules in the act of stating them.

And if you want to argue (I think mistakenly) that Orwell was indulging in parody, then consider this last example—one that cannot possibly be parodic, at least intentionally:

> Emphasis is often achieved by the use of verbs rather than nouns formed from them, and by the use of verbs in the active rather than in the passive voice.
>
> —*A Style Manual for Technical Writers and Editors,* ed. S. J. Reisman. New York, 1972. pp. 6–11.

In this single sentence, in a single moment, we have all five potential locations of error folded together: As the rule is stated in a handbook, it is simultaneously violated in its text; as the editor expresses in the sentence that is part of the handbook a rule that must first have existed in his mind, in his role as writer he simultaneously violates it. And in the instant he ends the sentence, he becomes a critical reader who should—but does not—resonate to the error. Nor, apparently, did anyone else.

The point is this: We can discuss error in two ways: we can discuss it at a level of consciousness that places that error at the very center of our consciousness. Or we can talk about how we experience (or not) what we popularly call errors of usage as they occur in the ordinary course of our reading a text.

In the first, the most common way, we separate the objective material text from its usual role in uniting a subject (us) and that more abstract "content" of the object, the text, in order to make the sentences and words the objects of consciousness. We isolate error as a frozen, instantiated object. In the second way of discussing error, a way we virtually never follow, we must treat error not as something that is simply on the surface of the page, "out there," nor as part of an inventory of negative responses "in here," but rather as a variably experienced union of item and response, controlled by the intention to read a text in the way we ordinarily read texts like newspapers, journals, and books. If error is no longer in the handbook, or on the page, or in the writer—or even purely in the reader—if instead we locate it at an intersection of those places, then we can explain why Barzun could write—or read—one thing and then immediately experience another, why his colleagues and editors and audience could read about one way of reflexively experiencing language and then immediately experience it in another.

But when I decided to intend to read Barzun and White and Orwell and Fowler in, for all practical purposes, the way they seem to invite me to read— as an editor looking for the errors they have been urging me to search out—then I inform my experience, I deliberately begin reading, with an intention to experience the material constitution of the text. It is as if a type-designer invited me to look at the design of his type as he discussed type-design.

In short, if we read any text the way we read freshman essays, we will find many of the same kind of errors we routinely expect to find and therefore do find. But if we could read those student essays unreflexively, if we could make the ordinary kind of contract with those texts that we make with other kinds of texts, then we could find many fewer errors.

When we approach error from this point of view, from the point of view of our pre-reflexive experi-

ence of error, we have to define categories of error other than those defined by systems of grammar or a theory of social class. We require a system whose presiding terms would turn on the nature of our response to violations of grammatical rules.

At the most basic level, the categories must organize themselves around two variables: Has a rule been violated? And do we respond? Each of these variables has two conditions: A rule is violated or a rule is not violated. And to either of those variables, we respond, or we do not respond. We thus have four possibilities:

1a. A rule is violated, and we respond to the violation.

1b. A rule is violated, and we do not respond to its violation.

2a. A rule is not violated, and we do not respond.

2b. A rule is not violated, and we do respond.

	[+ response]	[− response]
[+ violation]		
[− violation]		

Now, our experiencing or noticing of any given grammatical rule has to be cross-categorized by the variable of our noticing or not noticing whether it is or is not violated. That is, if we violate rule X, a reader may note it or not. But we must also determine whether, if we do not violate rule X, the same reader will or will not notice that we have violated it. Theoretically, then, this gives us four possible sets of consequences for any given rule. They can be represented on a feature matrix like this:

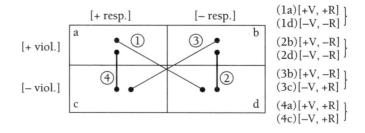

That is, the first kind of rule, indicated by the line marked①, is of the following kind: When violated, [+V], we respond to the violation, [+R]. When it is not violated, [−V], we do not respond, [−R]. Thus the same rule results in combinations of features indicated by (a-d). Rule type② is characterized by a rule that when violated, [+V], we do not notice, [−R]. But when we do not violate it, [−V], we do not notice it either, [−R]. Thus the single rule combines features indicated by (b-d). The other rules follow the same kind of grid relationships. (As I will point out later, the problem is actually much more complex than this, but this will do as a first approximation.)

I do not assert that the particular items I will list as examples of these rules are universally experienced in the way indicated. These categories are based on personal responses, and it is possible that your responses are quite different than mine. But in fact, on the basis of some preliminary research that I shall report later, I would argue that most readers respond in the ways reflected by these categories, regardless of how they might claim they react.

The most obviousest set of rules be those whose violation we instantly notes, but whose observation we entirely ignore. They are the rules that define bedrock standard English. No reader of this journal can fail to distinguish these two passages:

> There hasn't been no trainees who withdrawed from the program since them and the Director met to discuss the instructional methods, if they met earlier, they could of seen that problems was beginning to appear and the need to take care of them immediate. (+V, +R)

> There haven't been any trainees who have withdrawn from the program since they and the Director met to discuss the instructional methods. If they had met earlier, they could have seen that problems were beginning to appear and that they needed to take care of them immediately. (−V, −R)

Among the rules whose violation we readily note but whose observance we do not are double negatives, incorrect verb forms, many incorrect pronoun forms, pleonastic subjects, double comparatives and superlatives, most subject-verb disagreements, certain faulty parallelisms,[11] certain dangling modifiers,[12] etc.

The next most obvious set of rules are those whose observation we also entirely ignore, but whose violation we ignore too. Because we note neither their observation nor their violation, they constitute a kind of folklore of usage, rules which we can find in some handbook somewhere, but which have, for the most part, lost their force with our readers. For most readers, these two passages differ very little from one another; for many readers, not at all:

> Since the members of the committee had discussed with each other all of the questions which had been raised earlier, we decided to conduct the meeting as openly as possible and with a concern for the opinions of everyone that might be there. And to ensure that all opinions would be heard, it was suggested that we not limit the length of the meeting. By opening up the debate in this way, there would be no chance that someone might be inadvertently prevented from speaking, which has happened in the past. (+V, −R)

> Because the members of the committee had discussed with one another all the questions that had been raised earlier, we decided to conduct the meeting in a way that was as open as possible and concerned with the opinion of everyone who might be there. To ensure that all opinions would be heard, someone suggested that we not limit the length of the meeting. By opening up the debate in this way, we would not take the chance that someone might be inadvertently prevented from speaking, something which has happened in the past. (−V, −R)

I appreciate the fact that some readers will view my lack of sensitivity to some of these errors as evidence of an incorrigibly careless mind. Which errors go in which category, however, is entirely beside the point.[13] The point is the existence of a *category* of "rules" to whose violation we respond as indifferently as we respond to their observance.

A third category of rules includes those whose violation we largely ignore but whose observance we do not. These are rules which, when followed, impose themselves on the reader's consciousness either subliminally, or overtly and specifically. You can sense the consequence of observing these rules in this next "minimal pair":

I will not attempt to broadly defend specific matters of evidence that one might rest his case on. If it was advisable to substantially modify the arguments, he would have to re-examine those patients the original group treated and extend the clinical trials whose original plan was eventually altered. (+V, −R)

I shall not attempt broadly to defend specific matters of evidence on which one might rest one's case. Were it advisable substantially to modify the arguments, one should have to re-examine those patients whom the original research group treated and extend the clinical trials the original plan of which was eventually altered. (−V, +R)

I appreciate that many of you believe that you notice split infinitives as quickly as you notice a subject-verb error, and that both should be equally condemned in careful prose. At the end of this paper, I will try to offer an argument to the contrary—that in fact many—not all—of you who make that claim are mistaken.

The exceptions are probably those for whom there is the fourth category of error, that paradoxical but logically entailed category defined by those rules whose violation we note, and whose observance we also note. I think that very few of us are sensitive to this category, and I think for those very few, the number of items that belong in the category must, fortunately, be very small. Were the number of items large, we would be constantly distracted by noticing that which should not be noticed. We would be afflicted with a kind of linguistic hyperesthesia, noticing with exquisite pleasure that every word we read is spelled correctly, that every subject agrees with its verb, that every article precedes its noun, and so on. Many of us may be surprised when we get a paper with no mispelled words, but that pleasure does not derive from our noticing that each word in turn is correctly spelled, but rather in the absence of mispelled words.

In my own case, I think I note equally when an infinitive is split, and when it is not. In recent months, I also seem to be noticing when someone uses *that* in the way that the "rule" stipulates, and I notice when a writer uses *which* in the way which the "rule" prohibits. I hope I add no more.

I suspect that some readers put into this category the *regardless/irregardless* pair, *media* as a singular and as a plural, perhaps *disinterested/uninterested*. I offer no pair of contrasting examples because the membership of the category is probably so idiosyncratic that such a pair would not be useful.

Now in fact, all this is a bit more complicated than my four categories suggest, albeit trivially so. The two-state condition of response: [+/−], is too crude to distinguish different qualities of response. Responses can be unfavorable, as the ordinary speaker of standard English would respond unfavorably to

Can't nobody tell what be happening four year from now.

if it appeared in a text whose conventions called for standard English. A response can be favorable, as in the right context, we might regard as appropriate the formality of

Had I known the basis on which these data were analyzed, I should not have attempted immediately to dissuade those among you whom others have . . .

(We could, of course, define a context in which we would respond to this unfavorably.)

Since only the category of [+response] can imply a type of response, we categorize favorable and unfavorable response, [+/−favorable], across only [+response]. This gives us four more simple categories:

[+violate, −favorable]
[−violate, +favorable]
[+violate, +favorable]
[−violate, −favorable]

The first two I have already illustrated:

[+v, −f]: He knowed what I meaned.
[−v, +f]: Had I known the basis on which . . . I
should not etc.

This leaves two slightly paradoxical categories, which, like Category IV: those rules whose violations we notice and whose observations we notice too, are populated by a very small number of items, and function as part of our responses only idiosyncratically. In the category [−violate, −favorable], I suspect that many of us would place *It is I,* along with some occurrences of *whom,* perhaps.

The other paradoxical category, [+violate, +favorable] is *not* illustrated by *It's me,* because for most of us, this is an unremarked violation. If it elicits a response at all, it would almost invariably be [−favorable], but only among those for whom the *me* is a bête noir. In fact, I can only think of one violation that I respond to favorably: It is the *than* after *different(ly)* when what follows is a clause rather than a noun:

> This country feels differently about the energy crisis than it did in 1973.

I respond to this favorably because the alternative,

> This country feels differently about the energy crisis from the way it did in 1973.

is wordier, and on principles that transcend idiosyncratic items of usage, I prefer the two less words and the more certain and direct movement of the phrase. My **noticing** any of this, however, is entirely idiosyncratic.

As I said, though, these last distinctions are increasingly trivial. That is why I refrain from pursuing another yet more finely drawn distinction: Those responses, favorable or unfavorable, that we consciously, overtly, knowingly experience, and those that are more subliminal, undefined, and unspecific. That is, when I read

> It don't matter.

I know precisely what I am responding to. When most of us read a *shall* and a shifted preposition, I suspect that we do not consciously identify those

items as the source of any heightened feeling of formality. The response, favorable or unfavorable, is usually less specific, more holistic.

Now what follows from all this? One thing that does not follow is a rejection of all rules of grammar. Some who have read this far are undoubtedly ready to call up the underground grammarians to do one more battle against those who would rip out the Mother Tongue and tear down Civilized Western Values. But need I really have to assert that, just because many rules of grammar lack practical force, it is hardly the case that none of them have substance?

Certainly, how we mark and grade papers might change. We need not believe that just because a rule of grammar finds its way into some handbook of usage, we have to honor it. Which we honor and which we do not is a problem of research. We have to determine in some unobtrusive way which rules of grammar the significant majority of careful readers notice and which they do not. One way to do this research is to publish an article in a journal such as this, an article into which have been built certain errors of grammar and usage. The researcher would then ask his readers to report which errors jumped out at them **on the first reading.** Those that you did not notice should then not be among those we look for first when we read a student's paper.

One curious consequence of this way of thinking about error is that we no longer have to worry about defining, rejecting, quibbling over the **existence** of a rule. We simply accept as a rule anything that anyone wants to offer, no matter how bizarre or archaic. Should anyone re-assert the 19th-century rule against the progressive passive, fine. Upon inspection it will turn out that the rule belongs in the category of those rules whose violation no one notices, and whose observation no one notices either. As I said, it may be that you and I will find that for any particular rule, we experience its violation in different ways. But that is an empirical question, not a matter of value. Value becomes a consideration only when we address the matter of which errors we **should** notice.

Done carefully, this kind of classification might also encourage some dictionary makers to amend their more egregious errors in labeling points of usage. The *AHD,* for example, uses "non-standard" to label

> . . . forms that do not belong in any standard educated speech. Such words are recognized as nonstandard not only by those whose speech is standard, but even by those who regularly use non-standard expressions.

The *AHD* staff has labeled as non-standard, *ain't, seen* as the past tense of *see,* and *don't* with a singular subject. It has also labeled as non-standard *irregardless, like* for *as, disinterested* for *uninterested,* and *see where,* as in the construction, I *see where . . .* Thus we are led to believe that a speaker who would utter this:

> I see where the President has said that, irregardless of what happens with the gasoline shortage, he'll still be against rationing, just like he has been in the past. He seems disinterested in what's going on in the country.

would be just as likely to continue with this:

> I ain't sure that he seen the polls before he said that. He don't seem to know that people are fed up.

Indeed, we would have to infer from this kind of labeling that a speaker who said "I ain't sure he seen . . ." would also be sensitive to mistakes such as *disinterested* for *uninterested* or *like* for *as.* In matters such as this, we see too clearly the very slight scholarly basis upon which so much of this labeling rests.

Finally, I think that most of this essay is an exercise in futility. In these matters, the self-conscious report of what should be counted as an error is certainly an unreliable index to the unself-conscious experience. But it is by far a more satisfying emotion. When those of us who believe ourselves educated and literate and defenders of good usage think about language, our zealous defense of "good writing" feels more authentic than our experience of the same items in unreflective experience of a text. Indeed, we do not experience many of them at all. And no matter how wrong we might discover we are about our unreflective feelings, I suspect we could be endlessly lectured on how we do not respond to a *less* in front of a count noun, as in *less people,* but we would still express our horror and disgust in the belief that *less* is wrong when used in that way. It simply feels more authentic when we condemn error and enforce a rule. And after all, what good is learning a rule if all we can do is obey it?

If by this point you have not seen the game, I rest my case. If you have, I invite you to participate in the kind of research I suggested before. I have deposited with the Maxine Hairston of the University of Texas at Austin (Austin, Texas 78712), a member of the Editorial Board of this journal, a manuscript with the errors of grammar and usage that I deliberately inserted into this paper specifically marked. How can I ask this next question without seeming to distrust you? If you had to report right now what errors you noticed, what would they be? Don't go back and reread, looking for errors, at least not before you recall what errors you found the first time through. If you would send your list (better yet, a copy of the article with errors noted on first reading circled in red) to Professor Hairston, she will see that a tally of the errors is compiled, and in a later issue will report on who noticed what.

If you want to go through a second time and look for errors, better yet. Just make clear, if you would, that your list is the result of a deliberate search. I will be particularly interested in those errors I didn't mean to include. There are, incidentally, about 100 errors.

Notes

1. I don't know whether it is fair or unfair to quote Zinsser on this same matter:

   > OVERSTATEMENT. "The living room looked as if an atomic bomb had gone off there," writes the inexperienced writer, describing what he saw on Sunday morning after a Saturday night party that got out of hand. Well, we all know that he's exaggerating to make a droll point, but we also know that an atomic bomb didn't go off there, or any other bomb except maybe a water bomb. . . . These verbal high jinks can get just so high—and I'm already well over the

limit—before the reader feels an overpowering drowsiness. . . . Don't overstate. (p. 108)

2. Erving Goffman, *Frame Analysis: An Essay on the Organization of Experience.* (New York: Harper and Row, 1974).

3. Some social errors are strictly formal and so ordinarily do not require an apology, even though some might judge them "horrible": a white wedding gown and a veil on a twice-divorced and eight-month pregnant bride, brown shoes with a dinner jacket, a printed calling card.

4. Some special situations do require an apology: When we prepare a document that someone else must take responsibility for, and we make a mistake in usage, we are expected to apologize, in the same way we would apologize for incorrectly adding up a column of figures. And when some newspaper columnists violate some small point of usage and their readers write in to point it out, the columnists will often acknowledge the error and offer some sort of apology. I think William Safire in *The New York Times* has done this occasionally.

5. Two other kinds of purely linguistic behavior do arouse hostile feelings. One kind includes obscenities and profanities. It may be that both are rooted in some sense of fouling that which should be kept clean: obscenities foul the mouth, the mouth fouls the name of a deity. The other kind of linguistic behavior that arouses hostility in some includes bad puns and baby talk by those who are too old for it. Curiously, Freud discusses puns in his *Wit and the Relation to the Unconscious* (under "Technique of Wit") but does not in "The Tendencies of Wit" address the faint sense of revulsion we feel at a bad pun.

6. Sterling Leonard, *Current English Usage,* English Monograph No. 1 (Champaign, Ill.: National Council of Teachers of English. Chicago, 1932); Albert H. Marckwardt and Fred Walcott, *Facts About Current English Usage,* English Monograph No. 7 (Champaign, Ill.: National Council of Teachers of English. New York, 1938); Raymond Crisp. "Changes in Attitudes Toward English Usage," Ph.D. dissertation, University of Illinois, 1971; W. H. Mittins, Mary Salu, Mary Edminson, Sheila Coyne, *Attitudes to English Usage* (London: Oxford University Press, 1970); *The American Heritage Dictionary of the English Language* (New York: Dell, 1979). Thomas J. Cresswell's *Usage in Dictionaries and Dictionaries of Usage,* Publication of the American Dialect Society, Nos. 63-64 (University, Alabama: University of Alabama Press 1975), should be required reading for anyone interested in these matters. It amply demonstrates the slight scholarly basis on which so much research on usage rests.

7. William Labov, *The Social Stratification of English in New York City* (Washington, D.C.: Center for Applied Linguistics, 1966), pp. 455–81.

8. Elaine P. Maimon and Barbara F. Nodine, "Words Enough and Time: Syntax and Error One Year After," in *Sentence Combining and the Teaching of Writing,* eds. Donald Daiker, Andrew Kerek, Max Morenberg (Akron, Ohio: University of Akron Press, 1979) pp. 101–108. This is considered a dangling verbal: *For example, considering the way Hamlet treats Ophelia, there is almost corruptness in his mind.* Clumsy yes, but *considering* is an absolute, or more exactly, metadiscourse. See footnote 12. This is considered a vague pronoun reference: *The theme of poisoning begins with the death of old King Hamlet, who was murdered by his brother when a leperous distillment was poured into his ear while he slept.* Infelicitous, to be sure, but who can possibly doubt who's pouring what in whose ear (p. 103)? Counting items such as these as errors and then using those counts to determine competence, progress, or maturity would seem to raise problems of another, more substantive, kind.

9. *Essays of E. B. White* (New York: Harper and Row, 1977), p. 24.

10. Orwell's last rule: *Break any of these rules sooner than say anything outright barbarous,* does not apply to this passage. Indeed, it would improve if it had conformed to his rules:

> I list below, with notes and examples, various of the tricks by means of which a writer can dodge the work of prose construction . . . such writers prefer wherever possible the passive voice to the active, and noun constructions instead of gerunds . . . they further cut down the range of verbs . . . they make their banal statements seem profound by means of the *not un*-formation. They replace simple conjunctions by . . . they save the ends of sentences . . .

Should anyone object that this is a monotonous series of sentences beginning with the same subject, I could point to example after example of the same kind of thing in good modern prose. But perhaps an example from the same essay, near the end, will serve best (my emphasis):

> When *you* think of a concrete object, *you* think wordlessly, and then, if *you* want to describe the thing *you* have been visualizing, *you* probably hunt about till *you* find the exact *words that* seem to fit it. When *you* think of something abstract *you* are more inclined to use words from the start, and unless *you* make a conscious effort to prevent it, the existing dialect will come rushing in and do the job for you . . .

Nine out of ten clauses begin with *you,* and in a space much more confined than the passage I rewrote.

11. Virtually all handbooks overgeneralize about faulty parallelism. Two "violations" occur so often in the best prose that we could not include them in this Category I. One is the kind illustrated by the E. B. White passage: the coordination of adverbials . . . *unerringly and with immense good will.* The other is the coordination of noun phrases and WH-clauses: *We are studying the origins of this species and why it died out.* Even that range of exceptions is too broadly stated, but to explain the matter adequately would require more space than would be appropriate here.

12. Handbooks also overgeneralize on dangling constructions. The generalization can best be stated like this: When the implied subject of an introductory element is different from the overt subject of its immediately following clause, the introductory element dangles. Examples in handbooks are always so ludicrous that the generalization seems sound:

> Running down the street, the bus pulled away from the curb before I got there.

> To prepare for the wedding, the cake was baked the day before.

Some handbooks list exceptions, often called absolutes:

> Considering the trouble we're in, it's not surprising you are worried.

> To summarize, the hall is rented, the cake is baked, and we're ready to go.

These exceptions can be subsumed into a more general rule: When either the introductory element *or* the subject of the sentence consists of meta-discourse, the introductory element will not always appear to dangle. By meta-discourse I mean words and phrases that refer not to the primary content of the discourse, to the reference "out there" in the world, the writer's subject matter, but rather to the process of discoursing, to those directions that steer a reader through a discourse, those filler words that allow a writer to shift emphasis *(it, there, what),* and so on, words such as *it is important to note, to summarize, considering these issue, as you know, to begin with, there is,* etc. That's why an introductory element such as the following occurs so often in the prose of educated writers, and does not seem to dangle (meta-discourse is in bold face):

> To succeed in this matter, **it is important** for you to support as fully as possible . . .

> Realizing the seriousness of the situation, **it can be seen that** we must cut back on . . .

As I will point out later, the categories I am suggesting here are too broadly drawn to account for a number of finer nuances of error. Some violations, for example, clearly identify social and educational background:

> He didn't have no way to know what I seen.

But some violations that might be invariably noted by some observers do not invariably, or even regularly, reflect either social or educational background. Usages such as *irregardless, like* for *as, different than,* etc. occur so often in the speech and writing of entirely educated speakers and writers that we cannot group them with double negatives and non-standard verb forms, even if we do unfailingly respond to both kinds of errors. The usage note in the *American Heritage Dictionary* (Dell Paperback Edition, 1976; third printing, November, 1980) that *irregardless* is non-standard and "is only acceptable when the intent is clearly humorous" is more testimony to the problems of accurately representing the speech and writing of educated speakers. On February 20, 1981, the moderator on *Washington Week in Review,* a Public Broadcasting System news program, reported that a viewer had written to the program, objecting to the use of *irregardless* by one of the panelists. To claim that the person who used *irregardless* would also use *knowed* for *knew* or an obvious double negative would be simply wrong. (I pass by silently the position of *only* in that usage note. See footnote 13, item 9.) The counter-argument that the mere occurrence of these items in the speech and writing of some is sufficient testimony that they are not in fact educated is captious.

13. Here are some of the rules which I believe belong in this Category II: (1) Beginning sentences with *and* or *but;* (2) beginning sentences with *because* (a rule that appears in no handbook that I know of, but that seems to have a popular currency); (3) *which/that* in regard to restrictive relative clauses; (4) *each other* for two, *one another* for more than two; (5) *which* to refer to a whole clause (when not obviously ambiguous); (6) *between* for two, *among* for more than two. These next ones most readers of this journal may disagree with personally; I can only assert on the basis of considerable reading that they occur too frequently to be put in any other category for most readers: (7) *less* for *fewer;* (8) *due to* for *because;* (9) the strict placement of *only;* (10) the strict placement of *not only, neither,* etc. before only that phrase or clause that perfectly balances the *nor.* The usage of several disputed words must also suggest this category for most readers: *disinterested/uninterested, continuous/continual, alternative* for more than two. Since I have no intention of arguing which rules

should go into any category, I offer these only as examples of my observations. Whether they are accurate for you is in principle irrelevant to the argument. Nor is it an exhaustive list.

14. The rules that go into Category III would, I believe, include these. Again, they serve only to illustrate. I have no brief in regard to where they **should** go. (1) *shall/will,* (2) *who/whom,* (3) unsplit infinitives, (4) fronted prepositions, (5) subjunctive form of *be,* (6) *whose/of which* as possessives for inanimate nouns, (7) repeated *one* instead of a referring pronoun *he/his/him,* (8) plural *data* and *media,* singular verb after none.

Concepts of Art and the Teaching of Writing

Richard E. Young

This version of Young's essay is from The Rhetorical Tradition and Modern Writing. *Ed. James J. Murphy. New York: MLA, 1982. 130–41. In Murphy's anthology, he explains that Young's essay is revised from a version titled, "Arts, Crafts, Gifts, and Knacks: Some Disharmonies in the New Rhetoric." This earlier version was published in* Reinventing the Rhetorical Tradition. *Eds. Aviva Freedman and Ian Pringle. Ottawa: The Canadian Council of Teachers of English, 1980. "Arts" also appeared in* Visible Language *14 (1980), a special issue on the "Dynamics of Writing." Ed. Peter Wason.*

. . . *glamour* and *grammar* or, in French, *grimoire* and *grammaire* were originally the same word and thus combined, even in the vocabulary, the magical and rationalistic aspects of speech.

JACQUELINE DE ROMILLY[1]

I

To understand recent developments in the teaching of writing, we must see them as reactions to an earlier rhetoric. Hence I would like to begin with a series of statements by the nineteenth-century rhetorician John Genung, whose textbooks, most notably *The Practical Elements of Rhetoric,* helped establish the paradigm that has dominated the teaching of rhetoric in the United States for nearly a century. "Rhetoric," he says,

is literature, taken in its details and impulses, literature in the making. . . . it is concerned, as real authorship must be, not with a mere grammatical apparatus or with Huxley's logic engine, but with the whole man, his outfit of conviction and emotion,

imagination and will, translating himself, as it were, into a vital and ordered utterance.[2]

Genung argues, however, that in spite of rhetoric's theoretical concern with the entire process of making literature, any practical treatment of the subject must exclude those acts we would call creative, particularly those associated with the genesis of the composing process:

All the work of origination must be left to the writer himself; the rhetorical text-book can merely treat of those mental habits and powers which give firmness and system to his suggestive faculty. . . .[3]

Genung makes a similar point in explaining what he means by "practical rhetoric." Certain rhetorical elements, he says,

though very real and valuable, are not practical because the ability to employ them cannot be imparted by teaching. They have to exist in the writer himself, in the peculiar bent of his nature. (*Practical Elements,* p. xi)

Since the "work of origination" cannot be taught, he argues, a practical rhetoric must be limited to the conventions and mechanics of discourse—for example, to the modes and structures of discourse, the characteristics of various genres, the norms of style and usage—which are valuable primarily in organizing, editing, and judging what has already been produced by more mysterious powers. "Literature is of course infinitely more than mechanism," he says,

> but in proportion as it becomes more, a text-book of rhetoric has less business with it. It is as mechanism that it must be taught; the rest must be left to the student himself. (*Practical Elements*, p. xii)

For Genung, then, the ability to write with skill requires both a creative gift and a mastery of the craft, but the discipline of rhetoric is of necessity concerned only with craft since only craft can be taught.[4]

By way of contrast, consider this statement by Gordon Rohman, written fifteen years ago, when serious challenges to Genung's position were appearing with increasing frequency:

> Writing is usefully described as a process, something which shows continuous change in time like growth in organic nature. Different things happen at different stages in the process of putting thoughts into words and words onto paper. . . . we divided the process at the point where the "writing idea" is ready for the words and the page: everything before that we called "Pre-Writing," everything after "Writing" and "Re-Writing." . . . what sort of "thinking" precedes writing? By "thinking," we refer to that activity of mind which *brings forth* and develops ideas, plans, designs, not merely the entrance of an idea into one's mind; an active, not a passive enlistment in the "cause" of an idea; conceiving, which includes consecutive logical thinking but much more besides; essentially the imposition of pattern upon experience.[5]

For Genung, rhetoric was a body of information about the forms and norms of competent prose and their uses in the later stages of the composing process—the rhetoric of the finished word. For Rohman, rhetoric does include the craft of writing, but it also includes—and assigns primary importance to—that effort of origination that Genung ar-

gued lay beyond the boundaries of a practical rhetoric. "Students," Rohman says, "must learn the structure of thinking that leads to writing since there is no other 'content' to writing apart from the dynamic of conceptualizing" (p. 107).

In these statements by Genung and Rohman we can see the century-old tradition of school rhetoric and what has become the principal argument against it. This argument, which emphasizes the importance of what Rohman calls the "dynamic of conceptualizing" and "creative discovery," is for many the distinctive feature of what is now commonly referred to as the "new rhetoric." W. E. Evans and J. L. Walker describe the difference between the two positions this way:

> While traditional rhetoric was concerned with skill in expressing preconceived arguments and points of view, the new rhetoric is concerned with the exploration of ideas. . . . The new rhetoric, in short, is based on the notion that the basic process of composition is discovery. . . .[6]

Much of the recent work of rhetoricians has been devoted to finding ways of teaching the process of discovery and of making it a part of a rhetoric that is not only new but practical.

II

Yet the new rhetoric is not nearly so homogenous as this characterization suggests, for we can discern in the developments to which we give that name two apparently irreconcilable positions. And the difference between them is as important theoretically and pedagogically as the difference between the new and the older rhetoric.

Frank D'Angelo has appropriately called one of these positions the "new romanticism."[7] Though we lack the historical studies that would permit us to generalize with confidence, the position seems not so much an innovation in the discipline as a reaffirmation of the vitalist philosophy of an old romanticism enriched by modern psychology. It maintains that the composing process is, or should be, relatively free of deliberate control, that intellect is no better guide to understanding reality than nonlogical processes are, and that the act of composing is a kind of mysterious growth fed by what Henry James called "the deep well of unconscious cerebration."[8] Above all, it insists on the primacy of the imagination in the composing process. "The mystery of language," says James Miller, an advocate of this position,

> is, in large part, the mystery of the processes of the imagination. . . . For too long the assumption has been made that language used by an individual originates in the orderly processes of his rational mind, in his reason, in his faculty of systematic logic. Instruction in language-use has therefore been largely aimed at this logical faculty, in the belief that the teaching of orderly processes will result in good writing. The result, though, has too often been not good writing but dead writing, obedient to all the inhibitions and restraints drilled into the reason, but generally dehumanized and unreadable.[9]

The new romanticism presents the teacher of composition with a difficult problem: that is, how does one teach a mystery? William Coles makes the point well when he says that

> the teaching of writing as writing is the teaching of writing as art. When writing is not taught as art, as more than a craft or a skill, it is not writing that is being taught, but something else. . . . On the other hand, art because it is art, cannot be taught.[10]

Like Genung, Coles believes that the art of composing, as opposed to the craft, cannot be taught; but unlike Genung, he does not on that basis regard a concern with the creative process as impractical: "What is wanted, then, for the teaching of writing as writing, is a way of teaching what cannot be taught, a course to make possible what no course can do" (Coles, p. 111).

The solution to the dilemma is to change the role of the teacher. Teachers are no longer to be purveyors of information about the craft of writing; instead, they must become designers of occasions that stimulate the creative process. Or to put it another way, what Jerome Bruner calls the "expository mode" of teaching is to be replaced by the "hypothetical mode."[11] In contrasting the traditional "classroom of correction" with the new "creative classroom," James Miller says that the latter would be "a place where language would be surrounded not by dogma but by mystery—the mystery of creation. . . ." And, he continues, "the teacher would be free, and would not be telling, but would be exploring with the students alert for the spontaneous, the intuitive, the innovative."[12] Such a situation need not be devoid of rigor, a frequently heard accusation against the new romanticism. For example, Coles establishes a kind of apprentice-master relationship with his students, encouraging them to emulate his own tough-minded intellectual probing and linguistic precision.[13] They learn to be good stylists, in the broadest sense of that term, by observing and trying to imitate the way a good stylist works. If, as the new romantics maintain, the art of writing cannot be taught, the teacher can nevertheless present students with situations in which it can be learned more easily.

The primary disagreement between the new romantics and those representing the second position, whom we might call, for want of a better term, the "new classicists," is a disagreement about what constitutes an art. For the new romantics, art contrasts with craft; the craft of writing refers to skill in technique, or what Genung called "mechanics," a skill that can be taught. Art, however, is associated with more mysterious powers that may be enhanced but that are, finally, unteachable. Art as magic, as glamour.

For the new classicists, art means something quite different: it means the knowledge necessary for producing preconceived results by conscious, directed action. As such, it contrasts not with craft but with knack, that is, a habit acquired through repeated experience. An art, for the new classicist, results from the effort to isolate and generalize what those who have knacks do when they are successful. The distinction is apparent in the opening sentences of Aristotle's *Rhetoric:*

> . . . all men . . . endeavor to criticize or uphold an argument, to defend themselves or accuse. Now, the majority of people do this either at random or with a familiarity arising from habit. But since both these

ways are possible, it is clear that matters can be reduced to a system, for it is possible to examine the
reason why some attain their end by familiarity and
others by chance; and such an examination all would
at once admit to be the function of art.[14]

In the *Rhetoric* we find a clear instance of what
R. G. Collingwood called the "technical theory of
art"—art as grammar.[15]

Aristotle pursues the distinction between knack
and art in the *Metaphysics,* where he argues that art
arises from experience, emerging as we become
aware of the causes of success in carrying out a particular activity. Both those who have a knack and
those who have an art can carry out that activity,
but, he says, we view artists "as being wiser not in
virtue of being able to act, but of having the theory
for themselves and knowing the causes."[16]

One crucially important implication of this difference, he maintains, is that the artist can teach
others to carry out the activity, while those who
merely have a knack cannot:

> . . . it is a sign of the man who knows and of the man
> who does not know, that the former can teach, and
> therefore we think art more truly knowledge than ex-
> perience is; for artists can teach, and men of mere ex-
> perience cannot. (*Metaphysics* I.a.1; p. 690)

Aristotle is no doubt the most appropriate
spokesman for the technical theory of art, but it is
apparent today in the work of rhetoricians such as
Richard Weaver, Edward Corbett, Richard Hughes,
Albert Duhamel, Ross Winterowd, Francis Christensen, and those of us working on tagmemic
rhetoric. As this list suggests, one need not be an
Aristotelian to embrace the theory.

III

Specifically, what is it that the new classicists
teach? The question is worth answering in detail,
partly to clarify their conception of art and to dispel
misconceptions, which abound, and partly to elaborate on what is in practice a fundamental difference between the two groups of rhetoricians. But a
detailed answer also suggests that there may be a
basis for accommodation between art as grammar
and art as glamour.

What is taught? The answer is, essentially,
"heuristics" and whatever is necessary to make
them clear and meaningful to the user. Heuristic
procedures must not be confused with rule-
governed procedures, for if we confuse the two, we
tend to reject the use of explicit techniques in
composing since few rule-governed procedures are
possible in rhetoric. A rule-governed procedure
specifies a finite series of steps that can be carried
out consciously and mechanically without the aid
of intuition or special ability and that if properly
carried out always yields a correct result. For example, the procedure for making valid inferences in
syllogistic reasoning is rule-governed. But a heuristic procedure provides a series of questions or operations whose results are provisional. Although
more or less systematic, a heuristic search is not
wholly conscious or mechanical; intuition, relevant
knowledge, and skill are also necessary. A heuristic
is an explicit strategy for effective guessing. Heuristics are presently available for carrying out many
phases of composing, from the formulation of
problems to various kinds of editing; some of these
procedures are part of our heritage from ancient
times, some have been developed within the last
twenty years in response to the call for a process-
oriented rhetoric.

The use of heuristic procedures implies certain
assumptions about the processes they are designed
to facilitate. First, their use implies a generic
conception of the process. To use a heuristic appropriately writers must see the situation they
are confronting at the moment as a specific variant
of the *kind* of situation for which the procedure
was designed; they must behave as though in some
sense they have been there before. If they regard
each situation as unique, they have no reason
to believe that a technique that was useful once
will be useful again. Second, the use of heuristic
procedures implies that some, though not necessarily all, phases of the process the writer is trying
to control can be carried out deliberately and rationally. That kind of control is a condition for using a heuristic procedure, at least while it is being

learned and before it becomes a habitual way of thinking.

If the creative process has generic features, if some of its phases can be consciously directed, and if heuristic procedures can be developed as aids, then it can be taught. To be more precise, certain aspects of the creative process can be taught. We cannot teach direct control of the imaginative act or the unanticipated outcome, but we can teach the heuristics themselves and the appropriate occasions for their use. And this knowledge is important, for heuristic procedures can guide inquiry and stimulate memory and intuition. The imaginative act is not absolutely beyond the writer's control; it can be nourished and encouraged.

These generalizations about heuristics and the technical theory of art become clearer if we recall Francis Christensen's generative rhetoric of the sentence, a technique that uses form to produce ideas.[17] After a close examination of the practice of modern writers who have a knack for good prose—Hemingway, Steinbeck, Faulkner, and others—Christensen identified four principles operating in the production of what he called "cumulative sentences." First, we make a point by adding information to the noun and the verb, which serve as a base from which the meaning will rise. Second, the modifiers usually follow the base clause instead of preceding it or being embedded in it. Third, complexity and precision arise from various levels of generality in the modifiers. Finally, density and richness are the result of the number of modifiers used.

Heuristic procedures enable the writer to bring principles such as these to bear in composing by translating them into questions or operations to be performed. If we were to invent a procedure based on these principles, it might look something like this: study what is being observed, write a base clause about it, and then try piling up at the end of the clause analogies, details, and qualities that serve to refine the original observation. If the writer observes well and has reasonable control of the language and the heuristic—and is lucky—the result can be a sentence like, "He dipped his hands in the bichloride solution and shook them, a quick shake,

fingers down, like the fingers of a pianist above the keys" (Christensen, p. 9).

"In composition courses," Christensen says, "we do not really teach our captive charges to write better—we merely *expect* them to. And we do not teach them to write better because we do not know how to teach them to write better" (p. 3). What can we give students if we are interested in having them write elegant and original sentences of this type? One answer is Christensen's four principles and the heuristic derived from them, along with examples, practice, and whatever else is necessary to use them effectively.

Consider another example, from tagmemic rhetoric.[18] The conception of the creative process in tagmemic rhetoric draws heavily on the extensive psychological literature on creativity and problem solving—on the work of Graham Wallas, John Dewey, George Miller, and Leon Festinger in particular. Although the process of original inquiry may seem mysterious and beyond analysis, certain kinds of activity do recur from instance to instance. The process begins with a feeling of difficulty or confusion. If the feeling is insistent, an effort is made to understand its origins, to formulate it as a problem, and to explore data associated with the problem. This exploratory activity often leads to the intuition of one or more possible solutions that are then evaluated for adequacy. If one of these solutions proves adequate, the process is complete; if not, the inquirer may abandon the effort or recycle through various phases of the process. Interspersed are periods of unconscious activity, most notably between the exploration of problematic data and the intuition of possible solutions. Notice that this conception does not insist on the primacy of reason nor does it repudiate nonrational activity; instead it assumes a subtle and elaborate dialectic between the two. In the conscious phases of the process, heuristics can be used—for example, a heuristic can be used for exploring problematic data.

A very young child, when presented with an interesting and enigmatic object, will touch it, taste it, smell it, shake it, and so on—all in an effort to understand it. More mature minds, when confronted with problems, do not abandon physical manipulation but rely more heavily on its intellectual equivalent. We manipulate symbols, instead of things, which immensely increases the range, subtlety, and efficiency of exploration. We compare, contrast, classify, segment, reorder, shift focuses of attention, and so on. By these means, we try to coax intuitions of reasonable solutions.

I am concerned here not only with what we do when engaged in intellectual explorations but also with what we can do to increase our control over it to make it more effective than it might otherwise be. The answer offered by tagmemic rhetoric is a heuristic based on principles of tagmemic linguistics, a linguistic theory developed primarily by Kenneth Pike. These principles, Pike maintains, are universal invariants that underlie all human experience and are characteristic of rationality itself.[19] For example, one such principle states that to describe any unit of experience adequately we must know its contrastive features; otherwise we could not distinguish it from other units. We must also know how it can vary without losing its identity; otherwise we could not recognize it again. And we must know its distribution in various systems, since all units exist in contexts. A knowledge of such contexts enables us to discuss roles; make definitions, predictions, and assumptions about appropriateness of occurrence; and in general perceive the systemic relationships that are part of the unit's identity.

A heuristic exploiting this principle might also ask us to change our mode of perception of the same unit, viewing it as a static, sharply defined particle, as a wave of activity, and as a field of relationships. In each mode we are asked to note the unit's contrastive features, variations, and distributions. In this way we are led through a set of complementary lines of inquiry that direct our attention to features of the unit we might otherwise overlook, help us bring to bear information that we already have in our memories, and identify what we do not yet know. "Discovery," Jerome Bruner observes, ". . . favors the well-prepared mind."[20] The exploratory procedure can be seen as a way of moving the mind out of its habitual grooves, of shaking it loose from a stereotypic past that wants to be retrieved, of helping the writer get beyond the superficial to levels tapped by the romantic's muse.[21]

The great danger of a technical theory of art—of art as grammar—is and has been a tendency to overrationalize the composing process. Techniques tend to multiply beyond utility, and what begins with an effort to develop a teachable art ends with an excessively complex and hence impractical methodology. Whenever writers carry out an activity repeatedly and successfully, it seems possible to generalize about what they are doing and to invent heuristics that enable others to improve their ability to carry out the same activity. In their preoccupation with analysis and method, those holding the theory may ignore our nonrational powers, devising strategies for carrying out processes better dealt with by the unaided mind. But a more adequate understanding of the history of rhetoric and the nature of skillful composing, coupled with careful testing of proposed heuristics for effectiveness, would go far toward curbing unneeded proliferation. Overrationalization is a danger, but it is not an inevitable consequence of the theory.

IV

I have been arguing that two conflicting conceptions of art are discernible in that conglomeration of developments we call the "new rhetoric." The conflict, however, is not new. Jacqueline de Romilly has explored it in the rhetorics of Gorgias, Plato, Aristotle, Longinus, and others; it is clearly apparent in the work of the new rhetoricians of the eighteenth century and romantics like Coleridge in the century that followed. It reemerges every time we think seriously about the discipline. "After all," de Romilly remarks, "it amounts to a struggle between the spell of the irrational and the desire to master it by means of reason. . . ."[22]

The durability of these two fundamental conceptions of rhetorical art and the effectiveness of the pedagogical methods based on them suggest that in some sense both are true, in spite of their seeming incompatibility. We can respond to this conflict by partisan denial of one of the truths, as many have done, though the price of partisanship strikes me as excessively high. Or we can cultivate a Keatsian negative captivity and live with the conflict, exploiting one or the other of the conceptions as it suits our needs as teachers. Such a strategy is not necessarily an evasion of intellectual responsibility; "both-and" may well be, for the moment, a more appropriate response than "either-or." As Niels Bohr once observed, the opposite of a correct statement is an incorrect statement, but the opposite of a deep truth may well be another deep truth.[23] The conflict might well be mitigated if curriculum planners remembered Alfred North Whitehead's argument that education properly moves in a cycle from romantic freedom through an emphasis on precise analysis and intellectual discipline and finally to generalization, the application of principles and techniques to the immediate experiences of life.[24]

Or we can respond by considering the possibility that behind art as glamour and art as grammar there may be a more adequate conception of rhetorical art that does not lead us to affirm the importance of certain psychological powers at the cost of denying the importance of others. If we choose this last course of action, we might begin with a scholarly investigation of the role of heuristic procedures in the rhetorical process, since they call into play both our reason and our imagination.

Notes

1. Jacqueline de Romilly, *Magic and Rhetoric in Ancient Greece* (Cambridge: Harvard Univ. Press, 1975), p. v.

2. John Franklin Genung, *The Working Principles of Rhetoric* (Boston: Ginn, 1901), p. vii.

3. John Franklin Genung, *The Practical Elements of Rhetoric* (Boston: Ginn, 1892), p. 8; hereafter cited in text. Compare Genung's more detailed statement:

   The first stage [of composing], the finding of material by thought or observation, is the fundamental and inclusive office of invention, the distinctive power that we designate in the popular use of the term. Herein lies obviously the heart and center of literary production; it is what the writer finds, in his subject or in the world of thought, that gauges his distinction as an author. Yet this is, of all processes, the one

least to be invaded by the rules of the text-book. It is a work so individual, so dependent on the peculiar aptitude and direction of the writer's mind, that each one must be left for the most part to find his way alone, according to the impulse that is in him. (p. 217)

4. For a discussion of this argument and evidence that it was shared by many of Genung's contemporaries, see Albert Kitzhaber, "Rhetoric in American Colleges: 1850–1900," Diss. Univ. of Washington 1953, pp. 156–67.

5. D. Gordon Rohman, "Pre-Writing: The Stage of Discovery in the Writing Process," *College Composition and Communication,* 16 (1965), 106; hereafter cited in text.

6. William H. Evans and Jerry L. Walker, *New Trends in the Teaching of English in Secondary Schools* (Chicago: Rand McNally, 1966), pp. 53–54.

7. Frank J. D'Angelo, *A Conceptual Theory of Rhetoric* (Cambridge, Mass.: Winthrop, 1975), p. 159.

8. Henry James, *The Art of the Novel* (New York: Scribners, 1947), pp. 22–23.

9. James E. Miller, Jr., *Word, Self, Reality: The Rhetoric of Imagination* (New York: Dodd Mead, 1972), pp. 3–4.

10. W. E. Coles, Jr., "The Teaching of Writing as Writing," *College English,* 29 (1967), 111; hereafter cited in text.

11. For a discussion of the distinction, see Jerome S. Bruner, *On Knowing: Essays for the Left Hand* (New York: Atheneum, 1965), p. 83.

12. James E. Miller, Jr., "Everyman with Blue Guitar: Imagination, Creativity, Language," *ADE Bulletin,* No. 43 (Nov. 1974), p. 42.

13. William E. Coles, Jr., *The Plural I: The Teaching of Writing* (New York: Holt, 1978).

14. Aristotle, *The "Art" of Rhetoric,* trans. John Henry Freese, Loeb Classical Library (Cambridge: Harvard Univ. Press, 1959), I.i.1–3; p. 3.

15. R. G. Collingwood, *The Principles of Art* (New York: Oxford Univ. Press, 1958), p. 3.

16. Aristotle, *Metaphysics,* trans. W. D. Ross, in *The Basic Works of Aristotle,* ed. Richard McKeon (New York: Random, 1941), I.a.1; p. 690.

17. Francis Christensen, "A Generative Rhetoric of the Sentence," in *Notes toward a New Rhetoric: Six Essays for Teachers* (New York: Harper, 1967), pp. 1–22.

18. For a composition text based on the principles of tagmemics, see Richard E. Young, Alton L. Becker, and Kenneth L. Pike, *Rhetoric: Discovery and Change* (New York: Harcourt, 1970).

19. A convenient summary of the principles can be found in Kenneth L. Pike, "Beyond the Sentence," *College Composition and Communication,* 15 (1964), 129–35.

20. Bruner, *On Knowing,* p. 82.

21. For a discussion and illustration of this particular heuristic, see Richard Young, "Methodizing Nature: The Tagmemic Discovery Procedure," *Retrospectives and Perspectives: A Symposium in Rhetoric,* ed. Turner S. Kobler, et al. (Denton: Texas Women's Univ. Press, 1978), pp. 30–39.

22. de Romilly, *Magic and Rhetoric,* p. 85.

23. Niels Bohr, "Discussions with Einstein on Epistemological Problems in Atomic Physics," *Atomic Physics and Human Knowledge* (New York: Wiley, 1958). Bohr comments that

> in the Institute in Copenhagen, where through those years a number of young physicists from various countries came together for discussions, we used, when in trouble, often to comfort ourselves with jokes, among them the old saying of the two kinds of truth. To the one kind belong statements so simple and clear that the opposite assertion obviously could not be defended. The other kind, the so-called "deep truths," are statements in which the opposite also contains deep truth. Now, the development in a new field will usually pass through stages in which chaos becomes gradually replaced by order; but is not least in the intermediate stage where deep truth prevails that the work is really exciting and inspires the imagination to search for a firmer hold. (p. 66)

24. Alfred North Whitehead, "The Rhythm of Education" and "The Rhythmic Claims of Freedom and Discipline," *The Aims of Education and Other Essays* (New York: Free Press, 1967).

Rhetoric in the American College Curriculum: The Decline of Public Discourse

S. Michael Halloran

Michael Halloran's essay was published in PRE/TEXT 3 (1982): 245–69.

Richard Young has popularized the term "current-traditional rhetoric" for the theory and pedagogy that until recently dominated the wasteland of freshman composition.[1] The term "current-traditional rhetoric" seems to me an odd one. First, it's an oxymoron of sorts: what's current is almost by definition not traditional. More importantly, current-traditional rhetoric bears very little resemblance to the rhetorical tradition. The question I'd like to address in this essay is, How did we get from the rhetorical tradition to current traditional rhetoric? This is an enormous question to which I don't pretend to have a complete answer. What I'm going to develop here is in effect a brief for an argument that I hope eventually to develop more fully.

First I'll offer some definitions and then spend some time trying to say what the teaching of rhetoric was like in the 17th and 18th century American colleges. Then I'll try to identify some important aspects of a change that took place during the 19th century, the change that produced current-traditional rhetoric. Finally, I want to suggest an important deficiency of current-traditional rhetoric which the recent revival of rhetoric in English departments has so far failed to address. As my title suggests, this deficiency has to do with something I call public discourse.

By rhetoric, I mean the art of effective communication.[2] As an art, rhetoric stands somewhere between a purely intuitive knack and an exact science; it provides techniques together with principles to govern their use, but it cannot say with total confidence that a given technique will achieve a desired effect. As an art of communication, rhetoric deals with the symbols—chiefly words—through which humans make and exchange meaning. As an art of effective communication, rhetoric focuses upon the adaptation of symbols to the demands of particular audiences, purposes, and situations.

By the rhetorical tradition, I mean a tradition of teaching and practice in the art of effective communication that flourished in classical Greece and Rome, survived in attenuated form through the middle ages, and revived in the Renaissance.[3] Its fullest expression was in the works of Cicero and Quintilian. Aristotle was its principal theorist, but the tradition was defined most importantly not by its theory, but rather by its cultural ideal—the orator.[4] The rhetorical tradition portrayed the orator as a person who embodies all that is best in a culture and brings it to bear on public problems through eloquent discourse. Quintilian wrote of the good man skilled in speaking; Cicero of the *doctus orator,* the learned speaker. Both of them referred to a civic leader who understood all the values of his culture and used artful speech to make those values effective in the arena of public affairs. The purpose of education in the rhetorical tradition was to prepare such leaders.

As an art of effective communication, then, the tradition of classical rhetoric gives primary emphasis to communication on public problems, problems that arise from our life in political communities. The many other sorts of problems that might be addressed through an art of communication—problems of business and commerce, of self-understanding and personal relationships, of scientific and philosophical investigation, of aesthetic experience, for example—are in the tradition of classical rhetoric subordinate. This point of emphasis is central to the argument of this essay. My thesis is that rhetoric in the sense of an art of public discourse flourished in American colleges of the 18th century and died out during the 19th. I argue further that the revival of rhetoric in the field of English composition has thus far failed to address the need for a revival of public discourse. I call attention to the history of rhetoric in American colleges because I believe we have lost something that is worth trying to recover.

The rhetoric that was imported to the first American college (Harvard, founded in 1636) was in effect a much truncated version of classical rhetoric. One historian of rhetoric has characterized it as decadent.[5] Samuel Eliot Morison, looking not just at rhetoric but at the whole of Puritan culture, suggests that its thinness was not decadence or even anemia, but leanness appropriate to the conditions of frontier life.[6] In his view the Puritans brought to the new world as much of European Humanism as was likely to survive in an environment that directed one's attention relentlessly to the most basic material things—food and shelter. And it is true that while the rhetorical doctrine of 17th century Harvard was a pale shadow of classical rhetoric, it would later become a full revival of the tradition of Cicero and Quintilian.

There are two important respects in which 17th century American rhetoric was anti-classical. The first is that it made a sharp distinction between substance and form in discourse. What was called "rhetoric" dealt exclusively with what we might call the surface features of discourse. It had to do with variations of word order and with metaphors of various kinds, or as they were known in the rhetorical theory of the time, figures and tropes. The purpose of this rhetoric was simply to provide a pleasing surface for argumentative structures derived from other fields of study, such as theology, philosophy, and natural science. The more-or-less standard definition for rhetoric at this time was the art of ornamenting discourse.[7] Its parts were style and delivery, and it placed heaviest emphasis on style. The classical tradition, by contrast, had seen rhetoric as an art of persuasion, of moving an audience to act or think or feel in a particular way. The stylistic ornaments were simply means to this end, and they were understood as much more closely wedded to the substance and purpose of discourse.

The rhetoric I have characterized was of course not invented by the Puritan founders of Harvard College. What they imported was the rhetoric of Peter Ramus, or more properly of Omer Talon, Ramus's disciple in the program of curricular reform he undertook at the University of Paris during the 16th century.[8] A question one might reasonably ask is whether this art of ornamenting discourse can rightly be considered a rhetoric in the sense I have given to that term. In what sense is this an art of effective communication? Where is the notion of adaptation to the demands of audience, purpose, and situation? The answer, I believe, is that Ramistic rhetoric must be grounded in a highly stereotyped understanding of rhetorical situations. Standards of propriety are relatively simple and rigid, so they need not be considered explicitly. Ramistic rhetoric is thus suitable for a homogeneous and stable society, or at least for a society that wants to be homogeneous and stable. It adopts what might be called the verbal technology of traditional rhetoric, but rejects its sense of culture as complex and evolving. Later, this fragment of classical rhetoric would grow into the full tradition, and it would support the growth of a more complex and dynamic body politic.

The second anti-classical aspect of the rhetoric taught in the early years at Harvard was its relative indifference to communication in the vernacular. Both texts and classroom exercises were in Latin. Speaking English was prohibited, even in informal conversation, though scholars doubt that students observed the rule meticulously.[9] But in the curriculum, the language of social and political affairs had no place. The practical end of higher education in early colonial times seems to have been to produce mastery in the classical languages—first Latin, then Greek, finally Hebrew, which was at the time thought to be the original of all languages. The three classical tongues were understood as the key to all learning, both human and divine. A student was supposed to be more or less fluent in Latin and in command of the rudiments of Greek before being admitted to Harvard. The actual standard of performance was somewhat below this ideal, and one explanation of the simplified rhetorical doctrine in use is that it served as a sort of advanced grammar to shore up instruction in Latin.[10] The schemes and tropes of rhetoric according to this view simply elaborated the principles behind the grammatical paradigms.

In any event, no formal attention was paid to the students' ability to communicate effectively in their native language. This "classical" emphasis was in reality alien to the classical tradition. Quintilian's program for the formation of the ideal orator had placed considerable emphasis on Greek, a language that was to the students he had in mind foreign (though by no means dead), but his educational goal was to produce mastery in the artful use of Latin, the language of everyday political and social affairs.[11] Much of his theory and pedagogy focused minutely on style and strategy in Latin. An equivalent program for students at 17th century Harvard would have subordinated the study of classical languages to the study of English. An equivalent rhetoric would have said much about style and strategy in English, would have concentrated on making students artful in the language of everyday political and social affairs. There was, of course, a great deal of "spillover" from the study of rhetoric in Latin to the practice of discourse in English. It would be difficult to make sense of a Puritan sermon except as a deliberate application of Ramistic rhetoric. But the notion that one achieves eloquence in the vernacular not by studying and working in the vernacular, but as a by-product of work in foreign languages—this curious notion which on its face seems to respect the classics is in fact a clear violation of classical educational and rhetorical thinking.[12]

During the 18th century, the rhetoric taught at Harvard and at the newer colleges such as William and Mary (1693) and Yale (1700) gradually took on a more fully classical flavor. Classical texts that had been unavailable on this side of the Atlantic during the 17th century were imported. During the second decade of the 18th century, the works of Cicero and Quintilian began to appear in college libraries, and by mid-century De Oratore was widely known. It was, for example, required reading for students at what is now the University of Pennsylvania.[13] From Cicero and Quintilian, students would learn to understand rhetoric as an art of moving an audience through eloquent speech, not merely of ornamenting discourse according to tacit and stereotypic notions of propriety.

This broadening view of rhetoric can be seen in the theses listed for disputation at Harvard commencements. Throughout the 17th and into the 18th century, thesis lists regularly included definitions of rhetoric as the art of ornamenting discourse, and dividing it into the standard Ramistic parts: style and delivery. But a 1748 thesis states that rhetoric has four parts: invention, arrangement, style, and delivery.[14] This approximates the full classical understanding of rhetoric, omitting only the canon of memory. This four part division of rhetoric means that by 1748 the art is understood to include deciding what to say and what order to put it in, as well as the specific verbal flourishes to use and matters of voice and gesture. Rhetoric had in effect been redefined as an art of adapting knowledge to specific occasions and audiences, which was essentially what Cicero and Quintilian had understood it to be.

The emergence of the full classical idea of rhetoric is also reflected in the increasing emphasis given in the curriculum to the English language. At least one English language treatise on rhetoric had been available in the Harvard College library by 1683—John Smith's *The Mysterie of Rhetorique Unveiled.*[15] This was simply a conventional Ramistic rhetoric of tropes and figures with illustrations taken mainly from the Bible. An English translation of the Port Royal *Art of Speaking,* which presented something much closer to the full classical doctrine, was available at Harvard by 1716 and at Yale by 1722.[16] When John Ward's *A System of Oratory* appeared in 1759, it was very quickly taken up by colleges in America and remained the dominant text until 1780. Ward's *System* relied heavily on Quintilian and Cicero, and is regarded by some scholars as the fullest expression of classical rhetoric ever to appear in the English language. It is worth noting that this work enjoyed far greater popularity in American colleges than in its native England.[17]

The new emphasis on English was reflected in faculty appointments and college exercises as well as in the books in use. Pennsylvania appointed a professor of "English and oratory" in 1753, and by 1768 he needed an assistant. Timothy Dwight, who would later become president of Yale, was appointed in 1776 to teach "rhetoric, history, and the belles lettres" in English. Harvard adopted a tutorial plan that included "composition in English, Rhetoric, and other Belles Lettres" in 1766. Both Harvard and Yale instituted public speaking exercises in English during the 1750s. Prior to that time these very important exercises, in which all students were supposed to perform in order to achieve a degree, had been done exclusively in the classical languages. The new emphasis on English was also expressed in the student literary and debate societies that sprang up in great numbers during the 18th century.[18] From the beginning, English was the standard language of these groups, in contrast to the long-standing tradition that serious intellectual discourse was to be conducted in Latin. Some of the societies had explicit rules against speaking Latin.

The shift to English meant that learning could more readily be brought to bear on problems in the world of practical affairs, the world defined by the English language. And the growing interest of students in public affairs can be read in this list of questions disputed publicly at Harvard commencements:

In 1729, Is unlimited obedience to rulers taught by Christ and his apostles?

In 1733, Is the voice of the people the voice of God?

In 1743, Is it lawful to resist the Supreme Magistrate, if the Commonwealth cannot otherwise be preserved? (Samuel Adams argued the affirmative.)

In 1743, 1747, 1761, and 1762, Does Civil Government originate from compact?

In 1758, Is civil government absolutely necessary for men? (John Adams argued the affirmative.)

In 1759, Is an absolute and arbitrary monarchy contrary to right reason?

In 1765, Can the new prohibitary duties, which make it useless for the people to engage in commerce, be evaded by them as faithful subjects? (Here is a headlong leap from the abstract world of philosophy and political theory, to the concrete world of affairs.)

In 1769, Is a just government the only stable foundation of public peace?

Again in 1769, Are the people the sole judges of their rights and liberties?

In 1770, Is a government tyrannical in which the rulers consult their own interest more than that of their subjects?

Again in 1770, Is a government despotic in which the people have no check on the legislative power?[19]

Other colleges exhibited a similar interest in the application of learning to public issues. At the 1770 commencement of the College of New Jersey, James Witherspoon defended in Latin the thesis that the law of nature obliged subjects to resist tyrannical kinds; Witherspoon was the son of the college president. Two years later, president John Witherspoon would defend the students' inclination to speak on political subjects, declaring himself proud of "the spirit of liberty [which breaths] high and strong" among students and faculty.[20] He would himself serve as a member of the New Jersey Constitutional ratifying convention and hold other public offices, all the while carrying on his duties as the head of the faculty at what is now Princeton University.

Up to this point I've tried to show that rhetoric in the college curriculum evolved toward a full expression of the classical tradition, starting with a sharply truncated version of it in the 17th century. But there are two major respects in which the whole college curriculum in America was directly in line with the tradition of classical rhetoric from the very beginning.

In the first place, rhetoric was treated as the most important subject in the curriculum. Typically, it was taught throughout all four years, and in many cases lecturing on rhetoric was a stated responsibility of the college president. The original statutes at Harvard, for example, required the president to lecture on rhetoric each Friday morning. The first theory of rhetoric developed by an American was contained in the lectures on eloquence delivered by John Witherspoon during the time he was president of Princeton.[21] When Timothy Dwight became president of Yale, he continued to lecture on rhetoric and belles lettres, and one of his first official acts as president was to engage in a formal debate with the senior students; the topic was whether the Old and New Testaments are the Word of God.[22] Rhetoric was emphasized so heavily because it was understood as the art through which all other arts could become effective. The more specialized studies in philosophy and natural science and the classical languages and literatures would be brought to a focus by the art of rhetoric and made to shed light on problems in the world of social and political affairs. The purpose of education was to prepare men for positions of leadership in the community, as it had been for Cicero and Quintilian.

The second respect in which the American college curriculum was from the beginning rhetorical is that it made oral communication primary. The most common classroom procedure was oral disputation. A student would be appointed to defend a thesis taken from assigned reading material against counterarguments made by the instructor and other students. Originally the form of the disputation was strictly syllogistic, in line with late medieval practice. During the 18th century the forensic form, which demanded more fully elaborated discourse ranging beyond the limits of strictly logical appeal, became more and more common.[23] The evolution of the forensic disputation was an important aspect of the increasingly Ciceronian emphasis of the colleges during this period. While the older syllogistic disputation had been rhetorical in the prominence it gave to orality, it had been anti-rhetorical in the formal limits it had placed on discourse. In addition to these classroom exercises, students periodically gave declamations and orations publically—that is, in forums open to the entire college and to people in the surrounding community.

Written examinations did not come into use until well into the 19th century. Instead, a three week period of "visitation" was held each June, during which students seeking a degree or promotion had to make themselves available for oral examination by "all Commers [sic]" in all the subjects for which they were responsible. The exams were essentially disputations similar in form to the classroom exercises: the student was expected to defend assigned theses against whatever counter-argument a visitor chose to make. A student could be held back for a year by the judgment of "any three of the visitors being overseers of the Colledge [sic]."[24] (The specific system described here, known as "sitting solstices," was prescribed at Harvard. I cannot say how closely examination systems at other colleges approximated the details of this one, but as late as 1842, Francis Wayland, President of Brown, speaks of oral examinations as standard in all American colleges. He advocates the adoption of written examinations, and the only example he can offer of a place where such a system is in use is Cambridge University in England.[25])

Students were expected to hand in written copies of their formal oral performances, and we can assume that their tutors paid some attention to the quality of this written work. The growth in the 18th century of a concern for the students' work in English seems to have included a growing focus on written as well as oral composition. But what the students composed were speeches, not term papers or essays. They wrote primarily as a means of preparing and documenting an oral performance. This can be a tricky issue, since the term "composition" has in our own time come to apply almost exclusively to written work. In elementary and high-school, we speak of students "doing a composition," and the term most commonly refers to the thing he or she hands in to the teacher, the sheet of paper with words inscribed on it. In more enlightened circles, "composition" is now understood as referring to a process rather than a sheet of paper, but it is still a process of producing written material. From this perspective, then, a debate held in 1794 at Princeton might look like evidence that writing was in competition with orality for primacy in the curriculum; the question was, "Whether debating or composition be more improving."[26] I believe, however, that the real issue was not writing vs. speech, but formally composed oratory vs. the new form of extemporaneous debate, which had been introduced in the Phi Beta Kappa chapters at William and Mary in 1778, and Harvard in 1785. Orality was still the primary medium and the first concern of the curriculum.

The only primarily written exercise that I am aware of was the requirement at Harvard that candidates for the MA degree write a "Synopsis, or Compendium" of one of the arts. Samuel Eliot Morison believes that this was not so much a demonstration of the candidate's scholarly accomplishment as a convenient means by which the college acquired elementary texts for use by undergraduates.[27]

This is not to say that students didn't write much in the course of their studies. My guess is that they wrote considerably more than many undergraduates of today, but the nature of their writing tasks was rather different. Much of it was sheer copying for purposes that today are served by the Xerox machine and printing press. For example, a student's first task upon being admitted to Harvard was to write out his own copy of the college laws, which he and the President would then sign as a kind of contract.[28] During the course of his studies, he would keep a series of "paper books" into which he would copy remarkable passages from his reading. He would write copious summaries and analyses of reading material—the cost of books would have made our modern ways of textual notation quite extravagant. He may have done less than the modern student does of what we would consider original composition, and the great bulk of that was intended for oral delivery.

What were the effects of all this emphasis on oral communication? First and perhaps most obviously, a certain readiness of mind and speech, and a zest for rhetorical encounters. Here is what one scholar has to say about the practice of disputation. (The quotation refers to disputation as a medieval practice, but in context it is a comment on 17th century English colleges, which were the original from which Harvard and Yale took the practice of syllogistic disputation.)

> The method became very successful under favorable circumstances, and was not the dry-as-dust, tedious, and stifling affair that pleaders for the perfections of the so-called Renaissance have pictured it. Public disputing, by the twelfth century (Aquinas and others), had become the highly developed art of quickly and logically defining one's thoughts as well as the thoughts of an opponent while face to face with him that taught a student to defend any topic or proposition against attack. The method brought into play all the excitement of a contest, the triumphant ecstasy of winning, or the disgrace of defeat, [here perhaps is the source of Jim McKay's famous opener for the ABC Wide World of Sports] that emphasized the value of what had been learned and the importance of an alert wit together with constant readiness to use it. The method was possible only within the limits of a closed system of knowledge as deduced from the same set of principles, thoroughly agreed upon as principles, and rarely scrutinized for their own sake.[29]

I think it's worth dwelling for a moment on the apparent absence among students of the 18th century of that much studied modern phenomenon called "communication anxiety."[30] We all suffer from it to some degree, and I recall seeing somewhere a report of a study allegedly demonstrating that the most common of all neurotic fears is the fear of speaking before an audience. A fair amount of energy in modern speech pedagogy seems to go into the simple task of getting students to the point where they can stand before a group of people and utter sentences. Yet American students of the eighteenth century so relished the opportunity to speak that every college had one or more literary and debate societies, all of them entirely student originated and governed, most of them highly active and successful. My own guess it that these students were no less subject to "communication anxiety" than students today, but that speaking mattered to them in a way it does not on most 20th century campuses. And this was simply a natural result of the overwhelming emphasis given to rhetoric in their curriculum.

The speaking emphasized was public in two senses. First, it dealt importantly with public problems. I've already quoted some of the more overtly political questions that were disputed at Harvard commencements during the 18th century. Similar issues were debated in classroom and public exercises at other colleges. The point was that learning in philosophy and literature and the other subjects was understood as bearing directly upon the nature of the commonwealth. A primary emphasis of the curriculum was, in the phrase of the Harvard college charter of 1650, "all good literature," writings worth preserving for their moral significance, the light they could shed on the life of the body politic.[31] Morison makes a point about his own alma mater that holds equally of the other colleges of the late 18th century: "it was the classics that made Harvard men of that day effective in politics and statesmanship. In Plutarch's lives, the orations of Cicero and Demosthenes, and ancient history, young men saw a mirror of their own times; in Plato's Dialogues and Aristotle's Politics they learned the wisdom to deal with men and events. The classical pseudonyms with which our Harvard signers of the great Declaration signed their early communications to the press were not mere pen-names chosen by chance, but represented a very definite point of view that every educated man recognized."[32] Simply stated, their point of view was that public life is the great topic of both learning and discourse. It informed the works of Cicero and Quintilian and John Ward, and thereby the lectures of John Witherspoon and Timothy Dwight and the other men who transmitted the rhetorical tradition to American students.

The second sense in which the speaking emphasized in 18th century colleges was public had to do with audience. As a student advanced through the four years of the curriculum, more and more of his speaking was done in forums open to anyone who chose to attend. On regular ceremonial occasions, the more advanced students were required to speak and dispute before audiences that included at least some dignitaries of the local community. (I say they were "required" to do this, but I have seen no evidence that the students regarded the duty as onerous.) The ordeal of "sitting solstices," remember, was open to "all Commers," and the students' performance was judged not by the tutors with whom they lived and studied, but by those of the visitors "being overseers of the Colledge"—a position equivalent to trustee in a modern college. On commencement day, every student who was to receive a degree would deliver at least one oration or dispute a question—by the latter half of the 18th century, the old style syllogistic disputations were commonly assigned to the duller students, while the forensic disputations and orations were given to the bright ones.[33] Every student had to be prepared to speak in a fully public forum. The common ground upon which he stood with his audience was simply membership in the commonwealth.

At the end of the 18th century, then, rhetoric at American colleges was the classical art of oral public discourse. It stood very near if not precisely at the center of pedagogical concern. It provided students with an art, and more importantly with copious experience and with a tacit set of values bearing directly on the use of language in managing public affairs.

Within a century the picture had changed drastically. While the classical idea of rhetoric had not disappeared altogether, it had gone into a severe eclipse from which it has not yet emerged, if indeed it ever will. The most obvious changes were the move to a primary focus on written rather than oral communication, the demotion of rhetoric to a minor place in the curriculum, and the detachment of classical learning from the general concerns of rhetoric. Insofar as the rhetoric then emerging as dominant had a theory, it was the theory that Young and others characterize as current-traditional rhetoric—i.e., emphasis on the written product rather than the process of composition or of communication; classification of discourse into the four so-called modes (description, narration, exposition, argumentation); concentration on correctness of usage and certain stylistic qualities, without much reference to the invention of substance for discourse.[34]

How can we explain this radical departure from the tradition of classical rhetoric? The only serious attempt I am aware of points to the emergence at the beginning of the 19th century of certain vitalistic assumptions about the human mind and the creative act, assumptions commonly associated with romanticism.[35] In my own view this explanation is at best only partly satisfactory. It may account for the emphasis of current-traditional rhetoric on products rather than processes and the consequent absence of any treatment of invention. But I don't think it explains the new theory's tendency toward downright obsession with correctness of usage and purity of style, or the demotion of rhetoric to its new, low estate. Further, this explanation treats rhetoric more-or-less in isolation; a full explanation must portray it in the larger contexts of curriculum and culture. While I don't pretend to offer a full explanation of the rise of current-traditional rhetoric in this essay, I want to sketch three points that will have to figure prominently in such an account. The first is a development within the tradition of rhetorical studies itself; the other two have to do with the context within which rhetoric was studied.

First is the emergence of the concept of belles lettres. The term "belles lettres" was adopted into the English language during the first third of the 18th century by way of three French men of letters whose works were translated into English and achieved some currency. They are Rene Rapin, Dominique Bonheurs, and Charles Rollin.[36] All three authors used the term belles lettres to name a broad category subsuming at a minimum history, poetry, and rhetoric (meaning the theory and practice of persuasive oral discourse). Rapin included philosophy as well, and Rollin included the study of languages as well as the other four parts. The English version of Rollin's works added physics to the list, perhaps because physical science was still understood as having a loose connection with philosophy. Thus, by 1740, "belles lettres" had come into English as a generalized term for learning in philosophy, history, languages, poetry, rhetoric, and—perhaps—natural science. Common synonyms were "fine learning" and "polite literature."[37] But as it very shortly came to be used in English, belles lettres was somewhat less generalized and more vague than the original French term had been. Both Adam Smith and Hugh Blair gave lectures on rhetoric *and* belles lettres; the two terms were made coordinate, whereas in French belles lettres had subsumed rhetoric. Neither Smith nor Blair drew any clear distinction between the two notions, but in Blair's *Lectures*, which were to become the most widely used rhetoric text in America during the early 19th century, the addition of belles lettres to rhetoric seemed to consist in a new concern with poetry and the aesthetic experience as well as with oratory and persuasion.[38] In America the term was likewise made coordinate with terms it had originally subsumed. Timothy Dwight was appointed at Yale to teach "rhetoric, history, and the belles lettres." The 1766 Harvard tutorial plan uses the term in what looks like its original sense— "Composition in English, Rhetoric, and other Belles Lettres"—but by 1819 George Ticknor is named professor of "French and Spanish Languages and Belles lettres." This chair would one day pass to Bliss Perry, under whom it would become a professorship of English literature.[39]

The emergence of this notion of belles lettres as something connected in an at best vaguely specified way with rhetoric had two crucial effects: first, it destabilized the boundaries of rhetoric—or, perhaps better, it distracted the gaze of rhetoricians from their central concern with public discourse; second, it encouraged a new interest in the purely aesthetic qualities of discourse. The old notion of "good literature," upon which the Harvard curriculum had been founded, valued texts for their moral and political significance. Samuel Eliot Morrison claims that the term "good literature" as used in the Harvard charter of 1650 is simply a literal translation of the Ciceronian concept of "bonae litterae."[40] I have not been able to find where in the works of Cicero or any other Roman author a concept of "bonae litterae" is developed at length, but the idea squares perfectly with the thinking of Quintilian, Cicero's most ardent and theoretically significant admirer. In the tenth book of the *Institutio Oratoria* he develops a literary canon, and the criteria for selection make it more a canon of bonae litterae than of belles lettres. It was their contribution to social morality that made poetic and oratorical and philosophical texts worth preserving. The 18th century notion of belles lettres called attention to the purely aesthetic qualities of texts, thus laying the groundwork for development of the modern notion of literary studies, in which the primary qualification for inclusion in the canon is a work's aesthetic merit.[41]

There was perhaps a precedent for belles lettres in the 17th century curriculum of Cambridge University, the model from which Harvard drew its original plan of studies. This was the so-called "studia leviora," light pursuits deemed suitable for men who came to college not to be serious scholars, but rather to "gett such learning as may serve for delight and ornament and such as the want wherof would speake a defect in breeding rather then Scholarship."[42] Under this heading we find some English poetry, English translations of classical works, and more recent works in Latin that students might read strictly for pleasure. Harvard made no formal allowance for the pursuit of studia leviora, and in fact tried to enforce a more strict scholarly standard than Cambridge on the use of Latin among students and faculty. The growth of the literary and debate societies during the 18th

century was motivated partly by the students' own desire to read and discuss critically works that would have been included in the studia leviora. Thus, "polite literature" was tolerated as a minor pursuit at English universities of the 17th century, and flourished as what we would call an extracurricular activity at American colleges of the 18th century. During the 19th century it achieved full status in the curriculum, eventually displacing rhetoric as the primary concern of what became the Department of English.

The second point to be taken into account in tracing the development of current-traditional rhetoric is specialization of the curriculum during the 19th century. The original system of instruction at Harvard and the other early Colleges was tutorial—a single tutor would take responsibility for an entering class, which throughout the 17th and into the 18th century might number no more than ten or a dozen boys.[43] Under the close supervision of the president, the tutor was responsible for directing the entire course of studies, and for overseeing the students' moral and spiritual development, during the next four years. Under such a system the boundaries between subjects in the curriculum wouldn't count for very much, since every teacher dealt with the whole curriculum. He told the students what books to read and at what time, how to read them, what sorts of notes to take and analyses to write.

During the second half of the 18th century, professorships associated with particular subjects began to be established, and by the 1840s the typical college faculty consisted of a few professors, each one responsible for a certain "department" of the curriculum, each one assisted by a few tutors.[44] In part, this institutionalizing of boundaries between subjects was simply a bow to the necessity created by expanding enrollments; more students needed more teachers, and a larger faculty called for some division of labor. But the process was fed by the influence of the German universities where American teachers were going to study, then returning and bringing with them new ideals of specialized scholarship and learning for its own sake rather than for the public use to which the rhetorical tradition would direct it. The inclination toward specialization became an avalanche with the institution of the elective system during the last half of the 19th century. By the turn of the 20th century, virtually every major college in America had given up the fully prescribed curriculum, and undergraduate students were being encouraged to emulate their professors by specializing in some particular discipline. More importantly, the students' readiness for advancement or for a degree was no longer judged by the broad and public standard of "sitting solstices." Instead, professors in specialized disciplines gave marks for narrowly circumscribed things called "courses." A student read Horace or Dante or Shakespeare for a fixed period of time, and then demonstrated his mastery of that body of reading to an expert in the field. The task of relating specialized knowledge to more general and public concerns dropped out of sight.

While many of the early professorships established at American colleges were in rhetoric, the rhetorical tradition was a natural casualty of the specializing tendency.[45] As Aristotle pointed out centuries ago, rhetoric is by its very nature an inexact and unspecialized faculty (Rhetoric 1, 4). The rhetorical tradition was not so much a body of specialized knowledge as a way of tying together and focusing the specialized knowledge provided by other fields of study. To the degree that specialized knowledge pursued for its own sake became an ideal in American colleges, rhetoric would necessarily fall from the elevated position it had once held.

The third point I want to focus on is a subtle but profound shift in the way colleges perceived their social function. Harvard was founded because the Puritans "dread[ed] to leave an illiterate ministry to the churches when our present ministers shall lie in the dust."[46] Their eyes were fixed on the needs of the community. Students were to be educated for positions of leadership not so much for their own personal advantage, but because the community had need of them. During the 19th century, this emphasis shifted. A college education came to be understood as a means by which students could pursue their own advancement in so-

ciety.[47] This was particularly true of the newer institutions specializing in science and engineering; applied scientific knowledge was frequently connected with the interests of farmers and merchants and mechanics.[48] But even in the older institutions that remained committed to the notion of classical or liberal education, the value of that education tended to shift. As early as 1819, Edward Tyrrell Channing gave expression to this shift in his inaugural lecture as the third Boylston Professor of Rhetoric at Harvard: "We look back to the best ages of those commonwealths, when society, letters, and all the liberal arts were advanced the farthest, and we find eloquence the favorite and necessary accomplishment of all who were ambitious of rising in the world."[49] His eyes were fixed upon the individual. Rather than providing leaders for the community, education was becoming an opportunity provided by the community for the individual.

A consequence of this shift was an increased emphasis on evaluation of the student's achievements. So long as the college served to provide leaders for the community, the issue of rigorous evaluation was not terribly crucial. If a man who was not particularly well qualified somehow got admitted to the baccalaureate degree, no real harm or injustice had been done, since the community—the church or the body politic—had its own means of judging the quality of men. But when higher education came to be understood as an opportunity for individual advancement, the degree became something more like a certificate of qualification, and the institution had to concern itself with "quality control." Together with the steady growth in numbers of students, the new emphasis on rigorous evaluation produced the shift to writing as the primary medium in which students exercised their mastery of subject matter. A paper took up far less classroom time than a disputation or an oration, and it could be subjected to the most meticulous scrutiny.[50]

My claim, then, is that the shift from the 18th century revival of Ciceronian rhetoric to current-traditional rhetoric was shaped by three factors in addition to the rise of romantic vitalism:

1. the evolution of the concept of belles lettres as a concern of rhetorical theory and pedagogy;

2. the steady specialization of knowledge and the curriculum;

3. a shift in the social function of colleges toward emphasis on providing opportunities for individual advancement. There are no doubt other aspects of this change, and they deserve serious attention because the demise of the rhetorical tradition was a significant event in our educational and cultural history.

I hope I'm not just being nostalgic in believing that, while many of the changes that took place in American colleges during the 19th century were laudable, something of real value was lost in the eclipse of the rhetorical tradition by current-traditional rhetoric. Part of it is being regained and even improved upon by the developments that are finally robbing the current-traditional paradigm of its currency. I'm thinking primarily of research into the composing process, which has recovered the ancient idea of rhetoric as an art, an imprecise but still enormously helpful methodizing of a task we must otherwise accomplish by trial and error.

But there is one aspect of the rhetorical tradition that so far as I can tell remains quite dead—its focus on public discourse. I suggested toward the beginning of this paper that a rhetoric is defined not just by its theory, but by the sorts of rhetorical problems it gives most emphasis to. The rhetorical tradition gave primary emphasis to public discourse, and subordinated the many other sorts of rhetorical problems people must deal with to the public arena; it was in essence a rhetoric of citizenship. In its mature form, current-traditional rhetoric gave primary emphasis to expository essays of the sort students would have to write in their other courses; at its worst, it was a series of unhelpful lessons in how to get through college. The new rhetoric that has been developing over the past two decades or so retains some of this emphasis on the discourse of academic disciplines, and it has added

a concern for rhetorical problems of self-understanding and personal relationships, and of business, commerce, and industry. It addresses students under three aspects of their identity: personal, intellectual-academic, and professional. It does not address students as political beings, as members of a body politic in which they have a responsibility to form judgments and influence the judgments of others on public issues. In the college as in the pre-college curriculum, English remains separate from social studies, the arts of discourse from the arts of citizenship.

In fall of 1981, when the U.S. Senate was considering President Reagan's proposal to sell the Awacs air defense system to Saudi Arabia, James Reston of the New York Times wrote half wistfully, half cynically of "The Forgotten Debate." What we had a right to expect of the President and Congress, in Reston's view, was a serious debate on the issues of Middle East foreign and defense policy, a debate that would convince us that "these devilish questions are being decided in the national interest by serious people in a serious way . . . and not fiddled by backdoor deals and personal tradeoffs."[51] Such a debate might even have enabled some ordinary citizens to form their own intelligent views on these matters, though this was more than Reston would hope for.

There was a time when politicians engaged in serious debate on such matters, debate that helped to shape reasonable and sound opinion on matters of public policy. When Daniel Webster debated the nature of the Constitution with Hayne and later with Calhoun, his arguments and those of his opponents were printed and the copies read and discussed in general stores and barber shops around the country. Webster had learned the art of rhetoric at Dartmouth. I believe that the vitality of the classical rhetorical tradition in the colleges of the 18th and early 19th centuries helped to maintain a standard of public discourse far superior to what we have in politics today. I think further that as rhetorical studies begin to regain some of their antique vitality and prominence, we might well turn some of our attention to the discourse of public life.

Notes

Earlier versions of this paper were read at Carnegie-Mellon University and Mercyhurst College. Among the many people who offered helpful comments, I would like especially to thank Profs. Richard Leo Enos and David Kaufer of Carnegie-Mellon, and Prof. George Garrelts of Mercyhurst.

1. Richard E. Young, "Paradigms and Problems: Needed Research in Rhetorical Invention," in Charles R. Cooper and Lee Odell, *Research on Composing: Points of Departure* (Urbana, Ill.: NCTE, 1978), pp. 29–47.

2. I have extrapolated this definition from the discussion of classical and contemporary rhetoric and in Richard E. Young, Alton L. Becker, and Kenneth L. Pike, *Rhetoric: Discovery and Change* (New York: Harcourt, 1970), pp. 1–9. I believe it is sufficiently general to avoid commitment to any particular system of rhetoric, yet sufficiently precise to avoid making the term mean everything, and thus nothing.

3. For a compact historical survey, see Edward P. J. Corbett, "Survey of Rhetoric," in *Classical Rhetoric for the Modern Student* (New York: Oxford Univ. Press, 1965), pp. 535–68; for a more complete yet still compact overview, see George A. Kennedy, *Classical Rhetoric and its Christian and Secular Tradition from Ancient to Modern Times* (Chapel Hill: Univ. of North Carolina Press, 1980.

4. See S. M. Halloran, "On the End of Rhetoric, Classical and Modern," *College English*, 36 (Feb. 1975), 621–31, and "Tradition and Theory in Rhetoric," *Quarterly Journal of Speech*, 62 (Oct. 1976), 234–41.

5. Warren Guthrie, "The Development of Rhetorical Theory in America I," *Speech Monographs*, 13 (1946), 14–22.

6. Samuel Eliot Morison, *The Intellectual Life of Colonial New England* (New York: New York Univ. Press, 1956).

7. This definition appears in William Dugard, *Rhetorices Elementa*, a standard text at Harvard throughout the 17th and into the 18th century. This same definition appears in lists of commencement theses at both Harvard and Yale. See Guthrie, op. cit.; Guthrie, "Rhetorical Theory in Colonial America" in Karl R. Wallace, ed., *History of Speech Education in America: Background Studies* (New York: Appleton, 1954), pp. 48–59; Porter Gale Perrin, *The Teaching of Rhetoric in the American Colleges before 1750*, Diss. Univ. of Chicago, 1936.

8. Guthrie, "The Development of Rhetorical Theory in America I," pp. 16–18. See also Perry Miller, *The New England Mind: the Seventeenth Century* (Boston: Beacon, 1939; rpt. 1961), pp. 300–62.

9. Samuel Eliot Morrison, *Harvard College in the Seventeenth Century* (Cambridge: Harvard, 1936), p. 85.

10. Guthrie, "The Development of Rhetorical Theory in America I," p. 21.

11. See Quintilian, *On the Early Education of the Citizen-Orator* (*Institutio Oratoria* Book I, and Book II, ch. 1–10) trans. John Selby Watson, ed. James J. Murphy (Indianapolis: The Bobbs-Merril, 1965). Morison notes that the *Institutio Oratoria* was unavailable at Harvard during the 17th century (*Harvard College in the Seventeenth Century*, p. 172).

12. The idea nonetheless flourished well into the 20th century. Bliss Perry, Harvard's first formally designated professor of English literature wrote in 1935 that the best way to form students in English composition is to require them to learn Latin and Greek and to drill them in translation. *And Gladly Teach: Reminiscences* (Boston: Houghton Mifflin, 1935), pp. 254–55.

13. Guthrie, "The Development of Rhetorical Theory in America, 1635–1850 II," *Speech Monographs*, 14 (1947), 38–54; Guthrie, "Rhetorical Theory in Colonial America," p. 54.

14. Perrin, p. 53.

15. Guthrie, "The Development of Rhetorical Theory in America, 1635–1850 I," p. 19.

16. Guthrie, "The Development of Rhetorical Theory in America, 1635–1850 II," p. 38.

17. For an analysis of Ward's work and its influence, see Douglas Ehninger, "John Ward and His Rhetoric," *Speech Monographs*, 18 (151), 1–16.

18. David Potter, "The Literary Society," in Wallace, ed., *History of Speech Education in America: Background Studies*, pp. 238–58.

19. Samuel Eliot Morison, *Three Centuries of Harvard 1636–1936* (Cambridge: Harvard Univ. Press 1936), pp. 90–91.

20. Ralph Ketcham, *James Madison: A Biography* (New York: Macmillan, 1971), pp. 37–38.

21. John Witherspoon, *Lectures on Moral Philosophy and Eloquence* (Philadelphia: Woodward, 1810). Guthrie identifies Witherspoon's Lectures as the "first complete American rhetoric" in his "Rhetorical Theory in Colonial America." See also: Wilson B. Paul, "John Witherspoon's Theory and Practice of Public Speaking," *Speech Monographs*, 16 (1949), 272–89; Wilbur Samuel Howell, *Eighteenth-Century British Logic and Rhetoric* (Princeton: Princeton Univ. Press, 1971), pp. 671–91.

22. Barbara Miller Solomon, Introduction to Timothy Dwight, *Travels in New England and New York,* ed.

Barbara Miller Solomon (Cambridge: Harvard Univ. Press, 1969), xvii–xviii.

23. George V. Bohman, "Rhetorical Practice in Colonial America," in Wallace, ed., *History of Speech Education in America: Background Studies,* pp. 60–79.

24. Morison, *Harvard College in the Seventeenth Century,* pp. 67–68.

25. Francis Wayland, *Thoughts on the Present Collegiate System in the United States* (New York: Arno Press and The New York Times, 1842; rpt. 1969), pp. 93–99.

26. Potter, "The Literary Society," in Wallace, ed., *History of Speech Education in America: Background Readings,* p. 250.

27. Morison, *Harvard College in the Seventeenth Century,* p. 148–50.

28. Morison, 81.

29. Harris Francis Fletcher, *The Intellectual Development of John Milton II* (Urbana: Univ. of Illinois Press, 1961), pp. 231–32.

30. For a recent example of the research, see Malcolm R. Parks, "A Test of the Cross-Situational Consistency of Communication Apprehension," *Communication Monographs,* 47 (Aug. 1980), 220–32.

31. Morison, *Harvard College in the Seventeenth Century,* p. 5.

32. Morison, *Three Centuries of Harvard 1636–1936,* p. 136.

33. Bohman, "Rhetorical Practice in Colonial America," pp. 70–71.

34. Young, "Paradigms and Problems: Needed Research in Rhetorical Invention," pp. 30–33.

35. Hal Rivers Weidner, *Three Models of Rhetoric: Traditional, Mechanical and Vital,* Diss., Univ. of Michigan, 1975.

36. The English language versions of their works are: Rene Rapin, *The Whole Critical Works of Monsieur Rapin, in Two Volumes . . . Newly Translated into English by Several Hands* (London, 1706); Dominique Bonheurs, *The Art of Criticism: or, The Method Of making a Right Judgment Upon Subjects of Wit and Learning* (London, 1705); Charles Rollin, *The Method of Teaching and Studying the Belles Lettres, or An Introduction to Languages, Poetry, Rhetoric, History, Moral Philosophy, Physicks, &c.* (London, 1734). The significance of these works for the history of rhetoric in English is discussed in Howell, *Eighteenth-Century British Logic and Rhetoric,* pp. 519–35.

37. See, for example, Alexander Jamieson, *Grammar of Rhetoric and Polite Literature,* which was used as a text at Amherst, Bowdoin, Wesleyan and Yale during the early part of the 19th century. Samuel Eliot Morison uses the term "polite literature" as a synonym for bonae litterae and associates the notion with the interests of well-to-do young men who came to college not for serious scholarly pursuits but to acquire the outward marks of gentility. (*The Founding of Harvard College,* Cambridge: Harvard Univ. Press, 1936, p. 56; *The Intellectual Life of Colonia New England,* p. 32). In my own view, conflating "good literature" and "polite literature" misses a subtle but important distinction.

38. Note, for example, the emphasis given to the development of taste in Hugh Blair, *Lectures on Rhetoric and Belles Lettres,* ed. David Potter (Carbondale: Southern Illinois Univ. Press, 1783; rpt. 1965). This emphasis is even more pronounced in some of the later rhetorics that were influenced by Blair. Samuel P. Newman, *A Practical System of Rhetoric* (Portland: Shirley and Hyde, 1827) devotes two of its five chapters to the notion of taste; Newman's *System* is probably the first rhetoric of written composition, and perhaps also the first textbook in the modern sense of that curiously redundant term, written by an American.

39. Perry's intellectual memoire, *And Gladly Teach,* offers a case study in the displacement of the rhetorical tradition by modern literary studies. He started his career as teacher of rhetoric and oratory at Williams College during the 1880s, then moved to Princeton where he taught courses in both literature and rhetoric and eventually was appointed Holmes Professor of English Literature and Belles Lettres. Of this chair, he writes that it "freed me, after many years, from the claims of Oratory" (p. 160), though as a younger man he seems to have felt a real affection for the study of rhetoric and oratory. After a time as editor of *The Atlantic Monthly,* he joined the faculty at Harvard, becoming in 1906 its first formally designated Professor of English Literature.

40. Morison, *The Founding of Harvard College,* p. 248.

41. My account of the relationship between rhetoric and belles lettres conflicts with the view developed in Howell, pp. 441 ff. Howell portrays the matter in fairly neat, categorical terms: classical rhetoric "limit[ed] itself to persuasive popular discourse as exemplified by political, forensic and ceremonial speeches"; the new rhetoric of the late eighteenth century "expand[ed] its interests to include learned and didactic discourses and perhaps even the forms of poetry." I believe that this view misrepresents both classical and "new" rhetoric. With the exception of Aristotle, classical rhetoricians were not much inclined to limit the compass of rhetoric, though they did tend to subordinate other forms of discourse to "persuasive popular discourse." In the long term the issue raised by eighteenth century

rhetoricians was not simply whether rhetoric should expand its purview, but what kind(s) of discourse should dominate its field of interest. The relevant question about a rhetorical tradition is not whether it does or does not profess to account for a given form of discourse, but what importance it attaches to that form relative to others.

42. Richard Holdsworth, "Directions for a Student in the Universitie," in Fletcher, *The Intellectual Development of John Milton* II, 623–64. The significance of Holdsworth's "Directions" for understanding the original Harvard plan of study is discussed in Morison, *The Founding of Harvard College,* pp. 62–74.

43. Morison, *Harvard College in the Seventeenth Century,* pp. 50–53; *Three Centuries of Harvard 1636–1936,* pp. 90.

44. Wayland, *Thoughts on the Present Collegiate System in the United States,* pp. 25–26.

45. The transformation of one of the early professorships is told in Ronald F. Reid, "The Boylston Professorship of Rhetoric and Oratory, 1806.1904. A Case Study of Changing Concepts of Rhetoric and Pedagogy," *Quarterly Journal of Speech,* 45 (Oct. 1959), 239–57.

46. "New England's First Fruits" in Morison, *The Founding of Harvard College,* p. 432.

47. This view is apparent throughout Wayland's *Thoughts on the Present Collegiate System in the United States.*

48. Stephen Van Rensselaer announced the founding of one of the earliest American schools of engineering thus: "I have established a school . . . for the purpose of instructing persons, who may choose to apply themselves, in the application of science to the common purposes of life. My principal object is, to qualify teachers for instructing the sons and daughters of farmers and mechanics . . . in the application of experimental chemistry, philosophy and natural history, to agriculture, domestic economy, the arts and manufactures." Samuel Rezneck, *Education for a Technological Society: A Sesquicentennial History of Rensselaer Polytechnic Institute* (Troy, N.Y.: Rensselaer Polytechnic Institute, 1968), p. 3. The specific reference to daughters as well as sons is worth noting. At that time (1824), the liberal arts colleges were exclusively and emphatically male.

49. Edward T. Channing, *Lectures Read to the Seniors in Harvard College,* ed. Dorothy I. Anderson and Waldo W. Braden (Carbondale: Southern Illinois Univ. Press, 1856; rpt. 1968), p. 2.

50. This is the rationale of Wayland's brief for written examinations in *Thoughts on the Present Collegiate System in the United States.*

51. James Reston, "The Forgotten Debate," New York *Times,* Oct. 18, 1981, sect. 4, p. 21.

Audience Addressed/Audience Invoked: The Role of Audience in Composition Theory and Pedagogy

Lisa Ede and Andrea Lunsford

This essay is from College Composition and Communication 35 (1984): 155–71. *Ede and Lunsford's essay was reprinted in* The Writing Teacher's Sourcebook. *Eds. Gary Tate and Edward P. J. Corbett. 2nd ed. New York: Oxford UP, 1988. 169–84. It also appears in the third edition of* The Writing Teacher's Sourcebook, 1994. 243–57.

One important controversy currently engaging scholars and teachers of writing involves the role of audience in composition theory and pedagogy. How can we best define the audience of a written discourse? What does it mean to address an audience? To what degree should teachers stress audience in their assignments and discussions? What is the best way to help students recognize the significance of this critical element in any rhetorical situation?

Teachers of writing may find recent efforts to answer these questions more confusing than illuminating. Should they agree with Ruth Mitchell and Mary Taylor, who so emphasize the significance of the audience that they argue for abandoning conventional composition courses and instituting a "cooperative effort by writing and subject instructors in adjunct courses. The cooperation and courses take two main forms. Either writing instructors can be attached to subject courses where writing is required, an organization which disperses the instructors throughout the departments participating; or the composition courses can teach students how to write the papers assigned in other concurrent courses, thus centralizing instruction but diversifying topics."[1] Or should teachers side with Russell Long, who asserts that those advocating greater attention to audience overemphasize the role of "observable physical or occupational characteristics" while ignoring the fact that most writers actually create their audiences. Long argues against the usefulness of such methods as developing hypothetical rhetorical situations as writing assignments, urging instead a more traditional emphasis on "the analysis of texts in the classroom with a very detailed examination given to the signals provided by the writer for his audience."[2]

To many teachers, the choice seems limited to a single option—to be for or against an emphasis on audience in composition courses. In the following essay, we wish to expand our understanding of the role audience plays in composition theory and pedagogy by demonstrating that the arguments advocated by each side of the current debate oversimplify the act of making meaning through written discourse. Each side, we will argue, has failed adequately to recognize 1) the fluid, dynamic character of rhetorical situations; and 2) the integrated, interdependent nature of reading and writing. After discussing the strengths and weaknesses of the two central perspectives on audience in composition—which we group under the rubrics of *audience addressed* and *audience invoked*[3]—we will propose an alternative formulation, one which we believe more accurately reflects the richness of "audience" as a concept.*

AUDIENCE ADDRESSED

[handwritten: actual ppl writing to]

Those who envision audience as addressed emphasize the concrete reality of the writer's audience; they also share the assumption that knowledge of this audience's attitudes, beliefs, and expectations is not only possible (via observation and analysis) but essential. Questions concerning the degree to which this audience is "real" or imagined, and the ways it differs from the speaker's audience, are generally either ignored or subordinated to a sense of the audience's powerfulness. In their discussion of "A Heuristic Model for Creating a Writer's Audience," for example, Fred Pfister and Joanne Petrik attempt to recognize the ontological complexity of the writer-audience relationship by noting that "students, like all writers, must fictionalize their audience."[4] Even so, by encouraging students to "construct in their imagination an audience that is as nearly a replica as is possible of *those many readers who actually exist in the world of reality,*" Pfister and Petrik implicitly privilege the concept of audience as addressed.[5]

Many of those who envision audience as addressed have been influenced by the strong tradition of audience analysis in speech communication and by current research in cognitive psychology on the composing process.[6] They often see themselves as reacting against the current-traditional paradigm of composition, with its a-rhetorical, product-oriented emphasis.[7] And they also frequently encourage what is called "real-world" writing.[8]

Our purpose here is not to draw up a list of those who share this view of audience but to suggest the general outline of what most readers will recognize as a central tendency in the teaching of writing today. We would, however, like to focus on one particularly ambitious attempt to formulate a theory and pedagogy for composition based on the concept of audience as addressed: Ruth Mitchell and Mary Taylor's "The Integrating Perspective: An Audience-Response Model for Writing." We choose Mitchell and Taylor's work because of its theoretical richness and practical specificity. Despite these strengths, we wish to note several potentially significant limitations in their approach, limitations which obtain to varying degrees in much of the current work of those who envision audience as addressed.

In their article, Mitchell and Taylor analyze what they consider to be the two major existing composition models: one focusing on the writer and the other on the written product. Their evaluation of these two models seems essentially accurate. The "writer" model is limited because it defines writing as either self-expression or "fidelity to fact" (p. 255)—epistemologically naive assumptions which result in troubling pedagogical inconsistencies. And the "written product" model, which is characterized by an emphasis on "certain intrinsic features [such as a] lack of comma splices and fragments" (p. 258), is challenged by the continued inability of teachers of writing (not to mention those in other professions) to agree upon the precise intrinsic features which characterize "good" writing.

Most interesting, however, is what Mitchell and Taylor *omit* in their criticism of these models. Neither the writer model nor the written product model pays serious attention to invention, the term used to describe those "methods designed to aid in

---

*A number of terms might be used to characterize the two approaches to audience which dominate current theory and practice. Such pairs as identified/envisaged, "real"/fictional, or analyzed/created all point to the same general distinction as do our terms. We chose "addressed/invoked" because these terms most precisely represent our intended meaning. Our discussion will, we hope, clarify their significance; for the present, the following definitions must serve. The "addressed" audience refers to those actual or real-life people who read a discourse, while the "invoked" audience refers to the audience called up or imagined by the writer.

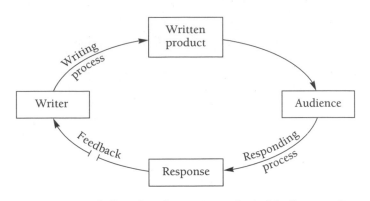

Figure 1. Mitchell and Taylor's "General Model of Writing" (p. 250)

retrieving information, forming concepts, analyzing complex events, and solving certain kinds of problems."[9] Mitchell and Taylor's lapse in not noting this omission is understandable, however, for the same can be said of their own model. When these authors discuss the writing process, they stress that "our first priority for writing instruction at every level ought to be certain major tactics for structuring material because these structures are the most important in guiding the reader's comprehension and memory" (p. 271). They do not concern themselves with where "the material" comes from—its sophistication, complexity, accuracy, or rigor.

Mitchell and Taylor also fail to note another omission, one which might be best described in reference to their own model (Figure 1). This model has four components. Mitchell and Taylor use two of these, "writer" and "written product," as labels for the models they condemn. The third and fourth components, "audience" and "response," provide the title for their own "audience-response model for writing" (p. 249).

Mitchell and Taylor stress that the components in their model interact. Yet, despite their emphasis on interaction, it never seems to occur to them to note that the two other models may fail in large part because they overemphasize and isolate one of the four elements—wrenching it too greatly from its context and thus inevitably distorting the com-

posing process. Mitchell and Taylor do not consider this possibility, we suggest, because their own model has the same weakness.

Mitchell and Taylor argue that a major limitation of the "writer" model is its emphasis on the self, the person writing, as the only potential judge of effective discourse. Ironically, however, their own emphasis on audience leads to a similar distortion. In their model, the audience has the sole power of evaluating writing, the success of which "will be judged by the audience's reaction: 'good' translates into 'effective,' 'bad' into 'ineffective.'" Mitchell and Taylor go on to note that "the audience not only judges writing; it also motivates it" (p. 250),[10] thus suggesting that the writer has less control than the audience over both evaluation and motivation.

Despite the fact that Mitchell and Taylor describe writing as "an interaction, a dynamic relationship" (p. 250), their model puts far more emphasis on the role of the audience than on that of the writer. One way to pinpoint the source of imbalance in Mitchell and Taylor's formulation is to note that they are right in emphasizing the creative role of readers who, they observe, "actively contribute to the meaning of what they read and will respond according to a complex set of expectations, preconceptions, and provocations" (p. 251), but wrong in failing to recognize the equally essential role writers play throughout the composing process not only as creators but also as *readers* of their own writing.

As Susan Wall observes in "In the Writer's Eye: Learning to Teach the Rereading/Revising Process," when writers read their own writing, as they do continuously while they compose, "there are really not one but two contexts for rereading: there is the writer-as-reader's sense of what the established text is actually saying, as of this reading; and there is the reader-as-writer's judgment of what the text might say or should say. . . ."[11] What is missing from Mitchell and Taylor's model, and from much work done from the perspective of audience as addressed, is a recognition of the crucial importance of this internal dialogue, through which writers analyze inventional problems and conceptualize patterns of discourse. Also missing is an adequate awareness that, no matter how much feedback writers may receive after they have written something (or in breaks while they write), as they compose writers must rely in large part upon their own vision of the reader, which they create, as readers do their vision of writers, according to their own experiences and expectations.

Another major problem with Mitchell and Taylor's analysis is their apparent lack of concern for the ethics of language use. At one point, the authors ask the following important question. "Have we painted ourselves into a corner, so that the audience-response model must defend sociologese and its related styles?" (p. 265). Note first the ambiguity of their answer, which seems to us to say no and yes at the same time, and the way they try to deflect its impact:

> No. We defend only the right of audiences to set their own standards and we repudiate the ambitions of English departments to monopolize that standard-setting. If bureaucrats and scientists are happy with the way they write, then no one should interfere.
>
> But evidence is accumulating that they are not happy. (p. 265)

Here Mitchell and Taylor surely underestimate the relationship between style and substance. As those concerned with Doublespeak can attest, for example, the problem with sociologese is not simply its (to our ears) awkward, convoluted, highly nominalized style, but the way writers have in certain instances used this style to make statements otherwise unacceptable to lay persons, to "gloss over" potentially controversial facts about programs and their consequences, and thus violate the ethics of language use. Hence, although we support Mitchell and Taylor when they insist that we must better understand and respect the linguistic traditions of other disciplines and professions, we object to their assumption that style is somehow value free.

As we noted earlier, an analysis of Mitchell and Taylor's discussion clarifies weaknesses inherent in much of the theoretical and pedagogical research based on the concept of audience as addressed. One major weakness of this research lies in its narrow focus on helping students learn how to "continually modify their work with reference to their audience" (p. 251). Such a focus, which in its extreme form becomes pandering to the crowd, tends to undervalue the responsibility a writer has to a subject and to what Wayne Booth in *Modern Dogma and the Rhetoric of Assent* calls "the art of discovering good reasons."[12] The resulting imbalance has clear ethical consequences, for rhetoric has traditionally been concerned not only with the effectiveness of a discourse, but with truthfulness as well. Much of our difficulty with the language of advertising, for example, arises out of the ad writer's powerful concept of audience as addressed divorced from a corollary ethical concept. The toothpaste ad that promises improved personality, for instance, knows too well how to address the audience. But such ads ignore ethical questions completely.

Another weakness in research done by those who envision audience as addressed suggests an oversimplified view of language. As Paul Kameen observes in "Rewording the Rhetoric of Composition," "discourse is not grounded in forms or experience or audience; it engages all of these elements simultaneously."[13] Ann Berthoff has persistently criticized our obsession with one or another of the elements of discourse, insisting that meaning arises out of their synthesis. Writing is more, then, than "a means of acting upon a receiver" (Mitchell and Taylor, p. 250); it is a means of making meaning for writer *and* reader.[14] Without such a unifying, balanced understanding of language use, it is easy to overemphasize one aspect of discourse, such as audience. It is also easy to forget, as Anthony Petrosky cautions us, that "reading, responding, and composing are aspects of understanding, and theories that attempt to account for them outside of their interaction with each other run the serious risk of building reductive models of human understanding."[15]

AUDIENCE INVOKED

[handwritten: audience would be a fiction] *[handwritten: those you would like to address]*

Those who envision audience as invoked stress that the audience of a written discourse is a construction of the writer, a "created fiction" (Long, p. 225). They do not, of course, deny the physical reality of readers, but they argue that writers simply cannot know this reality in the way that speakers can. The central task of the writer, then, is not to analyze an audience and adapt discourse to meet its needs. Rather, the writer uses the semantic and syntactic resources of language to provide cues for the reader—cues which help to define the role or roles the writer wishes the reader to adopt in responding to the text. Little scholarship in composition takes this perspective; only Russell Long's article and Walter Ong's "The Writer's Audience Is Always a Fiction" focus centrally on this issue.[16] If recent conferences are any indication, however, a growing number of teachers and scholars are becoming concerned with what they see as the possible distortions and oversimplifications of the approach typified by Mitchell and Taylor's model.[17]

Russell Long's response to current efforts to teach students analysis of audience and adaptation of text to audience is typical: "I have become increasingly disturbed not only about the superficiality of the advice itself, but about the philosophy which seems to lie beneath it" (p. 221). Rather than detailing Long's argument, we wish to turn to Walter Ong's well-known study. Published in *PMLA* in 1975, "The Writer's Audience Is Always a Fiction" has had a significant impact on composition studies, despite the fact that its major emphasis is on fictional narrative rather than expository writing. An analysis of Ong's argument suggests that teach-

ers of writing may err if they uncritically accept Ong's statement that "what has been said about fictional narrative applies ceteris paribus to all writing" (p. 17).

Ong's thesis includes two central assertions: "What do we mean by saying the audience is a fiction? Two things at least. First, that the writer must construct in his imagination, clearly or vaguely, an audience cast in some sort of role. . . . Second, we mean that the audience must correspondingly fictionalize itself" (p. 12). Ong emphasizes the creative power of the adept writer, who can both project and alter audiences, as well as the complexity of the reader's role. Readers, Ong observes, must learn or "know how to play the game of being a member of an audience that 'really' does not exist" (p. 12).

On the most abstract and general level, Ong is accurate. For a writer, the audience is not *there* in the sense that the speaker's audience, whether a single person or a large group, is present. But Ong's representative situations—the orator addressing a mass audience versus a writer alone in a room—oversimplify the potential range and diversity of both oral and written communication situations.

Ong's model of the paradigmatic act of speech communication derives from traditional rhetoric. In distinguishing the terms audience and reader, he notes that "the orator has before him an audience which is a true audience, a collectivity. . . . Readers do not form a collectivity, acting here and now on one another and on the speaker as members of an audience do" (p. 11). As this quotation indicates, Ong also stresses the potential for interaction among members of an audience, and between an audience and a speaker.

But how many audiences are actually collectives, with ample opportunity for interaction? In *Persuasion: Understanding, Practice, and Analysis,* Herbert Simons establishes a continuum of audiences based on opportunities for interaction.[18] Simons contrasts commercial mass media publics, which "have little or no contact with each other and certainly have no reciprocal awareness of each other as members of the same audience" with "face-to-face work groups that meet and interact continuously over an extended period of time." He goes on to note that: "Between these two extremes are such groups as the following: (1) the *pedestrian audience,* persons who happen to pass a soap box orator . . . ; (2) the *passive, occasional audience,* persons who come to hear a noted lecturer in a large auditorium . . . ; (3) the *active, occasional audience,* persons who meet only on specific occasions but actively interact when they do meet" (pp. 97–98).

Simons' discussion, in effect, questions the rigidity of Ong's distinctions between a speaker's and a writer's audience. Indeed, when one surveys a broad range of situations inviting oral communication, Ong's paradigmatic situation, in which the speaker's audience constitutes a "collectivity, acting here and now on one another and on the speaker" (p. 11), seems somewhat atypical. It is certainly possible, at any rate, to think of a number of instances where speakers confront a problem very similar to that of writers: lacking intimate knowledge of their audience, which comprises not a collectivity but a disparate, and possibly even divided, group of individuals, speakers, like writers, must construct in their imaginations "an audience cast in some sort of role."[19] When President Carter announced to Americans during a speech broadcast on television, for instance, that his program against inflation was "the moral equivalent of warfare," he was doing more than merely characterizing his economic policies. He was providing an important cue to his audience concerning the role he wished them to adopt as listeners—that of a people braced for a painful but necessary and justifiable battle. Were we to examine his speech in detail, we would find other more subtle, but equally important, semantic and syntactic signals to the audience.

We do not wish here to collapse all distinctions between oral and written communication, but rather to emphasize that speaking and writing are, after all, both rhetorical acts. There are important differences between speech and writing. And the broad distinction between speech and writing that Ong makes is both commonsensical and particularly relevant to his subject, fictional narrative. As our illustration demonstrates, however, when one turns to precise, concrete situations, the relationship between speech and writing can become far more complex than even Ong represents.

Just as Ong's distinction between speech and writing is accurate on a highly general level but breaks down (or at least becomes less clear-cut) when examined closely, so too does his dictum about writers and their audiences. Every writer must indeed create a role for the reader, but the constraints on the writer and the potential sources of and possibilities for the reader's role are both more complex and diverse than Ong suggests. Ong stresses the importance of literary tradition in the creation of audience: "If the writer succeeds in writing, it is generally because he can fictionalize in his imagination an audience he has learned to know not from daily life but from earlier writers who were fictionalizing in their imagination audiences they had learned to know in still earlier writers, and so on back to the dawn of written narrative" (p. 11). And he cites a particularly (for us) germane example, a student "asked to write on the subject to which schoolteachers, jaded by summer, return compulsively every autumn: 'How I Spent My Summer Vacation'" (p. 11). In order to negotiate such an assignment successfully, the student must turn his real audience, the teacher, into someone else. He or she must, for instance, "make like Samuel Clemens and write for whomever Samuel Clemens was writing for" (p. 11).

Ong's example is, for his purposes, well-chosen. For such an assignment does indeed require the successful student to "fictionalize" his or her audience. But why is the student's decision to turn to a literary model in this instance particularly appropriate? Could one reason be that the student knows (consciously or unconsciously) that his English teacher, who is still the literal audience of his essay, appreciates literature and hence would be entertained (and here the student may intuit the assignment's actual aim as well) by such a strategy? In Ong's example the audience—the "jaded" school-teacher—is not only willing to accept another role but, perhaps, actually yearns for it. How else to escape the tedium of reading 25, 50, 75 student papers on the same topic? As Walter

Minot notes, however, not all readers are so malleable:

> In reading a work of fiction or poetry, a reader is far more willing to suspend his beliefs and values than in a rhetorical work dealing with some current social, moral, or economic issue. The effectiveness of the created audience in a rhetorical situation is likely to depend on such constraints as the actual identity of the reader, the subject of the discourse, the identity and purpose of the writer, and many other factors in the real world.[20]

An example might help make Minot's point concrete.

Imagine another composition student faced, like Ong's, with an assignment. This student, who has been given considerably more latitude in her choice of a topic, has decided to write on an issue of concern to her at the moment, the possibility that a home for mentally-retarded adults will be built in her neighborhood. She is alarmed by the strongly negative, highly emotional reaction of most of her neighbors and wishes in her essay to persuade them that such a residence might not be the disaster they anticipate.

This student faces a different task from that described by Ong. If she is to succeed, she must think seriously about her actual readers, the neighbors to whom she wishes to send her letter. She knows the obvious demographic factors—age, race, class—so well that she probably hardly needs to consider them consciously. But other issues are more complex. How much do her neighbors know about mental retardation, intellectually or experientially? What is their image of a retarded adult? What fears does this project raise in them? What civic and religious values do they most respect? Based on this analysis—and the process may be much less sequential than we describe here—she must, of course, define a role for her audience, one congruent with her persona, arguments, the facts as she knows them, etc. She must, as Minot argues, *both* analyze and invent an audience.[21] In this instance, after detailed analysis of her audience and her arguments, the student decided to begin her essay by emphasizing what she felt to be the genuinely admirable qualities of her neighbors, particularly their kindness, understanding, and concern for others. In so doing, she invited her audience to see themselves as *she* saw them: as thoughtful, intelligent people who, if they were adequately informed, would certainly not act in a harsh manner to those less fortunate than they. In accepting this role, her readers did not have to "play the game of being a member of an audience that 'really' does not exist" (Ong, "The Writer's Audience," p. 12). But they did have to recognize in themselves the strengths the student described and to accept her implicit linking of these strengths to what she hoped would be their response to the proposed "home."

When this student enters her history class to write an examination she faces a different set of constraints. Unlike the historian who does indeed have a broad range of options in establishing the reader's role, our student has much less freedom. This is because her reader's role has already been established and formalized in a series of related academic conventions. If she is a successful student, she has so effectively internalized these conventions that she can subordinate a concern for her complex and multiple audiences to focus on the material on which she is being tested and on the single audience, the teacher, who will respond to her performance on the test.[22]

We could multiply examples. In each instance the student writing—to friend, employer, neighbor, teacher, fellow readers of her daily newspaper—would need, as one of the many conscious and unconscious decisions required in composing, to envision and define a role for the reader. But *how* she defines that role—whether she relies mainly upon academic or technical writing conventions, literary models, intimate knowledge of friends or neighbors, analysis of a particular group, or some combination thereof—will vary tremendously. At times the reader may establish a role for the reader which indeed does not "coincide[s] with his role in the rest of actual life" (Ong, p. 12). At other times, however, one of the writer's primary tasks may be that of analyzing the "real life" audience and adapting the discourse to it. One of the factors that makes writing so difficult, as we know, is that we have no recipes:

each rhetorical situation is unique and thus requires the writer, catalyzed and guided by a strong sense of purpose, to reanalyze and reinvent solutions.

Despite their helpful corrective approach, then, theories which assert that the audience of a written discourse is a construction of the writer present their own dangers.[23] One of these is the tendency to overemphasize the distinction between speech and writing while undervaluing the insights of discourse theorists, such as James Moffett and James Britton, who remind us of the importance of such additional factors as distance between speaker or writer and audience and levels of abstraction in the subject. In *Teaching the Universe of Discourse,* Moffett establishes the following spectrum of discourse: recording ("the drama of what is happening"), reporting ("the narrative of what happened"), generalizing ("the exposition of what happens") and theorizing ("the argumentation of what will, may happen").[24] In an extended example, Moffett demonstrates the important points of connection between communication acts at any one level of the spectrum, whether oral or written:

> Suppose next that I tell the cafeteria experience to a friend some time later in conversation. . . . Of course, instead of recounting the cafeteria scene to my friend in person I could write it in a letter to an audience more removed in time and space. Informal writing is usually still rather spontaneous, directed at an audience known to the writer, and reflects the transient mood and circumstances in which the writing occurs. Feedback and audience influence, however, are delayed and weakened. . . . *Compare in turn now the changes that must occur all down the line when I write about this cafeteria experience in a discourse destined for publication and distribution to a mass, anonymous audience of present and perhaps unborn people.* I cannot allude to things and ideas that only my friends know about. I must use a vocabulary, style, logic, and rhetoric that anybody in that mass audience can understand and respond to. I must name and organize what happened during those moments in the cafeteria that day in such a way that this mythical average reader can relate what I say to some primary moments of experience of his own. (pp. 37–38; our emphasis)

Though Moffett does not say so, many of these same constraints would obtain if he decided to describe his experience in a speech to a mass audience—the viewers of a television show, for example, or the members of a graduating class. As Moffett's example illustrates, the distinction between speech and writing is important; it is, however, only one of several constraints influencing any particular discourse.

Another weakness of research based on the concept of audience as invoked is that it distorts the processes of writing and reading by overemphasizing the power of the writer and undervaluing that of the reader. Unlike Mitchell and Taylor, Ong recognizes the creative role the writer plays as reader of his or her own writing, the way the writer uses language to provide cues for the reader and tests the effectiveness of these cues during his or her own rereading of the text. But Ong fails adequately to recognize the constraints placed on the writer, in certain situations, by the audience. He fails, in other words, to acknowledge that readers' own experiences, expectations, and beliefs do play a central role in their reading of a text, and that the writer who does not consider the needs and interests of his audience risks losing that audience. To argue that the audience is a "created fiction" (Long, p. 225), to stress that the reader's role "seldom coincides with his role in the rest of actual life" (Ong, p. 12), is just as much an oversimplification, then, as to insist, as Mitchell and Taylor do, that "the audience not only judges writing, it also motivates it" (p. 250). The former view overemphasizes the writer's independence and power; the latter, that of the reader.

RHETORIC AND ITS SITUATIONS[25]

If the perspectives we have described as audience addressed and audience invoked represent incomplete conceptions of the role of audience in written discourse, do we have an alternative? How can we most accurately conceive of this essential rhetorical element? In what follows we will sketch a tentative model and present several defining or constraining statements about this apparently

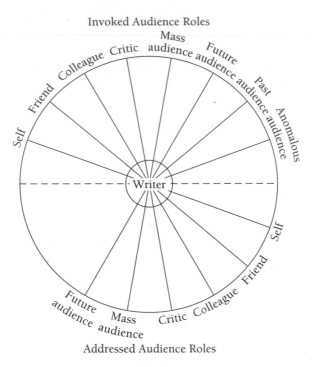

Figure 2. The Concept of Audience

slippery concept, "audience." The result will, we hope, move us closer to a full understanding of the role audience plays in written discourse.

Figure 2 represents our attempt to indicate the complex series of obligations, resources, needs, and constraints embodied in the writer's concept of audience. (We emphasize that our goal here is *not* to depict the writing process as a whole—a much more complex task—but to focus on the writer's relation to audience.) As our model indicates, we do not see the two perspectives on audience described earlier as necessarily dichotomous or contradictory. Except for past and anomalous audiences, special cases which we describe paragraphs hence, all of the audience roles we specify—self, friend, colleague, critic, mass audience, and future audience—may be invoked or addressed.[26] It is the writer who, as writer and reader of his or her own text, one guided by a sense of purpose and by the particularities of a specific rhetorical situation, establishes the range of potential roles an audience may

play. (Readers may, of course, accept or reject the role or roles the writer wishes them to adopt in responding to a text.)

Writers who wish to be read must often adapt their discourse to meet the needs and expectations of an addressed audience. They may rely on past experience in addressing audiences to guide their writing, or they may engage a representative of that audience in the writing process. The latter occurs, for instance, when we ask a colleague to read an article intended for scholarly publication. Writers may also be required to respond to the intervention of others—a teacher's comments on an essay, a supervisor's suggestions for improving a report, or the insistent, catalyzing questions of an editor. Such intervention may in certain cases represent a powerful stimulus to the writer, but it is the writer who interprets the suggestions—or even commands— of others, choosing what to accept or reject. Even the conscious decision to accede to the expectations of a particular addressed audience may not always be carried out; unconscious psychological resistance, incomplete understanding, or inadequately developed ability may prevent the writer from following through with the decision—a reality confirmed by composition teachers with each new set of essays.

The addressed audience, the actual or intended readers of a discourse, exists outside of the text. Writers may analyze these readers' needs, anticipate their biases, even defer to their wishes. But it is only through the text, through language, that writers embody or give life to their conception of the reader. In so doing, they do not so much create a role for the reader—a phrase which implies that the writer somehow creates a mold to which the reader adapts—as invoke it. Rather than relying on incantations, however, writers conjure their vision—a vision which they hope readers will actively come to share as they read the text—by using all the resources of language available to them to establish a broad, and ideally coherent, range of cues for the reader. Technical writing conventions, for instance, quickly formalize any of several writer-reader relationships, such as colleague to colleague or expert to lay reader. But even comparatively local semantic decisions may play an equally essential role. In "The Writer's Audience Is Always a Fiction," Ong demonstrates how Hemingway's use of definite articles in *A Farewell to Arms* subtly cues readers that their role is to be that of a "companion in arms . . . a confidant" (p. 13).

Any of the roles of the addressed audience cited in our model may be invoked via the text. Writers may also invoke a past audience, as did, for instance, Ong's student writing to those Mark Twain would have been writing for. And writers can also invoke anomalous audiences, such as a fictional character—Hercule Poirot perhaps. Our model, then, confirms Douglas Park's observation that the meanings of audience, though multiple and complex, "tend to diverge in two general directions: one toward actual people external to a text, the audience whom the writer must accommodate; the other toward the text itself and the audience implied there: a set of suggested or evoked attitudes, interests, reactions, conditions of knowledge which

may or may not fit with the qualities of actual readers or listeners."[27] The most complete understanding of audience thus involves a synthesis of the perspectives we have termed audience addressed, with its focus on the reader, and audience invoked, with its focus on the writer.

One illustration of this constantly shifting complex of meanings for "audience" lies in our own experiences writing this essay. One of us became interested in the concept of audience during an NEH Seminar, and her first audience was a small, close-knit seminar group to whom she addressed her work. The other came to contemplate a multiplicity of audiences while working on a textbook; the first audience in this case was herself, as she debated the ideas she was struggling to present to a group of invoked students. Following a lengthy series of conversations, our interests began to merge: we shared notes and discussed articles written by others on audience, and eventually one of us began a draft. Our long distance telephone bills and the miles we travelled up and down I-5 from Oregon to British Columbia attest most concretely to the power of a co-author's expectations and criticisms and also illustrate that one person can take on the role of several different audiences: friend, colleague, and critic.

As we began to write and re-write the essay, now for a particular scholarly journal, the change in purpose and medium (no longer a seminar paper or a textbook) led us to new audiences. For us, the major "invoked audience" during this period was Richard Larson, editor of this journal, whose questions and criticisms we imagined and tried to anticipate. (Once this essay was accepted by *CCC*, Richard Larson became for us an addressed audience: he responded in writing with questions, criticisms, and suggestions, some of which we had, of course, failed to anticipate.) We also thought of the readers of *CCC* and those who attend the annual CCCC, most often picturing you as members of our own departments, a diverse group of individuals with widely varying degrees of interest in and knowledge of composition. Because of the generic constraints of academic writing, which limit the range of roles we may define for our readers, the

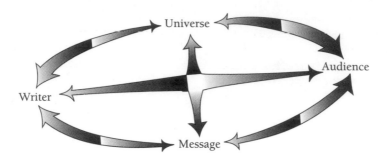

Figure 3. Corbett's Model of "The Rhetorical Interrelation-ships" (p. 5)

audience represented by the readers of *CCC* seemed most vivid to us in two situations: 1) when we were concerned about the degree to which we needed to explain concepts or terms; and 2) when we considered central organizational decisions, such as the most effective way to introduce a discussion. Another, and for us extremely potent, audience was the authors—Mitchell and Taylor, Long, Ong, Park, and others—with whom we have seen ourselves in silent dialogue. As we read and reread their analyses and developed our responses to them, we felt a responsibility to try to understand their formulations as fully as possible, to play fair with their ideas, to make our own efforts continue to meet their high standards.

Our experience provides just one example, and even it is far from complete. (Once we finished a rough draft, one particular colleague became a potent but demanding addressed audience, listening to revision upon revision and challenging us with harder and harder questions. And after this essay is published, we may revise our understanding of audiences we thought we knew or recognize the existence of an entirely new audience. The latter would happen, for instance, if teachers of speech communication for some reason found our discussion useful.) But even this single case demonstrates that the term *audience* refers not just to the intended, actual, or eventual readers of a discourse, but to *all* those whose image, ideas, or actions influence a writer during the process of composition. One way to conceive of "audience," then, is as an overdeter-

mined or unusually rich concept, one which may perhaps be best specified through the analysis of precise, concrete situations.

We hope that this partial example of our own experience will illustrate how the elements represented in Figure 2 will shift and merge, depending on the particular rhetorical situation, the writer's aim, and the genre chosen. Such an understanding is critical: because of the complex reality to which the term audience refers and because of its fluid, shifting role in the composing process, any discussion of audience which isolates it from the rest of the rhetorical situation or which radically overemphasizes or underemphasizes its function in relation to other rhetorical constraints is likely to oversimplify. Note the unilateral direction of Mitchell and Taylor's model (p. 5), which is unable to represent the diverse and complex role(s) audience(s) can play in the actual writing process—in the creation of meaning. In contrast, consider the model used by Edward P. J. Corbett in his *Little Rhetoric and Handbook*.[28] This representation, which allows for interaction among all the elements of rhetoric, may at first appear less elegant and predictive than Mitchell and Taylor's. But it is finally more useful since it accurately represents the diverse range of potential interrelationships in any written discourse.

We hope that our model also suggests the integrated, interdependent nature of reading and writing. Two assertions emerge from this relationship. One involves the writer as reader of his or her own work. As Donald Murray notes in "Teaching the Other Self: The Writer's First Reader," this role is critical, for "the reading writer—the map-maker and map-reader—reads the word, the line, the sentence, the paragraph, the page, the entire text. This constant back-and-forth reading monitors the multiple complex relationships between all the elements in writing."[29] To ignore or devalue such a central function is to risk distorting the writing process as a whole. But unless the writer is composing a diary or journal entry, intended only for the writer's own eyes, the writing process is not complete unless another person, someone other than the writer, reads the text also. The second assertion thus emphasizes the creative, dynamic duality of the process of reading and writing, whereby writers create readers and readers create writers. In the meeting of these two lies meaning, lies communication.

A fully elaborated view of audience, then, must balance the creativity of the writer with the different, but equally important, creativity of the reader. It must account for a wide and shifting range of roles for both addressed and invoked audiences. And, finally, it must relate the matrix created by the intricate relationship of writer and audience to all elements in the rhetorical situation. Such an enriched conception of audience can help us better understand the complex act we call composing.

Notes

1. Ruth Mitchell and Mary Taylor, "The Integrating Perspective: An Audience-Response Model for Writing," *CE,* 41 (November, 1979), 267. Subsequent references to this article will be cited in the text.

2. Russell C. Long, "Writer-Audience Relationships: Analysis or Invention," *CCC,* 31 (May, 1980), 223 and 225. Subsequent references to this article will be cited in the text.

3. For these terms we are indebted to Henry W. Johnstone, Jr., who refers to them in his analysis of Chaim Perelman's universal audience in *Validity and Rhetoric in Philosophical Argument: An Outlook in Transition* (University Park, PA: The Dialogue Press of Man & World, 1978), p. 105.

4. Fred R. Pfister and Joanne F. Petrik, "A Heuristic Model for Creating a Writer's Audience," *CCC,* 31 (May, 1980), 213.

5. Pfister and Petrik, 214; our emphasis.

6. See, for example, Lisa S. Ede, "On Audience and Composition," *CCC,* 30 (October, 1979), 291–295.

7. See, for example, David Tedlock, "The Case Approach to Composition," *CCC,* 32 (October, 1981), 253–261.

8. See, for example, Linda Flower's *Problem-Solving Strategies for Writers* (New York: Harcourt Brace Jovanovich, 1981) and John P. Field and Robert H. Weiss' *Cases for Composition* (Boston: Little Brown, 1979).

9. Richard E. Young, "Paradigms and Problems: Needed Research in Rhetorical Invention," in *Research on Composing: Points of Departure,* ed. Charles R. Cooper and Lee Odell (Urbana, IL: National Council of Teachers of English, 1978), p. 32 (footnote # 3).

10. Mitchell and Taylor do recognize that internal psychological needs ("unconscious challenges") may play a role in the writing process, but they cite such instances as an "extreme case (often that of the creative writer)" (p. 251). For a discussion of the importance of self-evaluation in the composing process see Susan Miller, "How Writers Evaluate Their Own Writing," *CCC,* 33 (May, 1982), 176–183.

11. Susan Wall, "In the Writer's Eye: Learning to Teach the Rereading/Revising Process," *English Education,* 14 (February, 1982), 12.

12. Wayne Booth, *Modern Dogma and the Rhetoric of Assent* (Chicago: The University of Chicago Press, 1974), p. xiv.

13. Paul Kameen, "Rewording the Rhetoric of Composition," *Pre/Text,* 1 (Spring-Fall, 1980), 82.

14. Mitchell and Taylor's arguments in favor of adjunct classes seem to indicate that they see writing instruction, wherever it occurs, as a skills course, one instructing students in the proper use of a tool.

15. Anthony R. Petrosky, "From Story to Essay: Reading and Writing," *CCC,* 33 (February, 1982), 20.

16. Walter J. Ong, S. J., "The Writer's Audience Is Always a Fiction," *PMLA,* 90 (January, 1975), 9–21. Subsequent references to this article will be cited in the text.

17. See, for example, William Irmscher, "Sense of Audience: An Intuitive Concept," unpublished paper delivered at the CCCC in 1981; Douglas B. Park, "The Meanings of Audience: Pedagogical Implications," unpublished paper delivered at the CCCC in 1981; and Luke M. Reinsma, "Writing to an Audience: Scheme or Strategy?" unpublished paper delivered at the CCCC in 1982.

18. Herbert W. Simons, *Persuasion: Understanding, Practice, and Analysis* (Reading, MA: Addison-Wesley, 1976).

19. Ong, p. 12. Ong recognizes that oral communication also involves role-playing, but he stresses that it "has within it a momentum that works for the removal of masks" (p. 20). This may be true in certain instances, such as dialogue, but does not, we believe, obtain broadly.

20. Walter S. Minot, "Response to Russell C. Long," *CCC,* 32 (October, 1981), 337.

21. We are aware that the student actually has two audiences, her neighbors and her teacher, and that this situation poses an extra constraint for the writer. Not all students can manage such a complex series of audience constraints, but it is important to note that writers in a variety of situations often write for more than a single audience.

22. In their paper on "Student and Professional Syntax in Four Disciplines" (unpublished paper delivered at the CCCC in 1981), Ian Pringle and Aviva Freedman provide a good example of what can happen when a student creates an aberrant role for an academic reader. They cite an excerpt from a third year history assignment, the tone of which "is essentially the tone of the opening of a television travelogue commentary" and which thus asks the reader, a history professor, to assume the role of the viewer of such a show. The result is as might be expected: "Although the content of the paper does not seem significantly more abysmal than other papers in the same set, this one was awarded a disproportionately low grade" (p. 2).

23. One danger which should be noted is a tendency to foster a questionable image of classical rhetoric. The agonistic speaker-audience relationship which Long cites as an essential characteristic of classical rhetoric is actually a central point of debate among those involved in historical and theoretical research in rhetoric. For further discussion, see: Lisa Ede and Andrea Lunsford, "On Distinctions Between Classical and Modern Rhetoric," in *Classical Rhetoric and Modern Discourse: Essays in Honor of Edward P. J. Corbett,* ed. Robert Connors, Lisa Ede, and Andrea Lunsford (Carbondale, IL: Southern Illinois University Press, 1984).

24. James Moffett, *Teaching the Universe of Discourse* (Boston: Houghton Mifflin, 1968), p. 47. Subsequent references will be mentioned in the text.

25. We have taken the title of this section from Scott Consigny's article of the same title, *Philosophy and Rhetoric,* 7 (Summer, 1974), 175–186. Consigny's effort to mediate between two opposing views of rhetoric provided a stimulating model for our own efforts.

26. Although we believe that the range of audience roles cited in our model covers the general spectrum of options, we do not claim to have specified all possibilities. This is particularly the case since, in certain instances, these roles may merge and blend—shifting subtly in character. We might also note that other terms for the same roles might be used. In a business setting, for instance, colleague might be better termed co-worker; critic, supervisor.

27. Douglas B. Park, "The Meanings of 'Audience,'" *CE,* 44 (March, 1982), 249.

28. Edward P. J. Corbett, *The Little Rhetoric & Handbook,* 2nd edition (Glenview, IL: Scott, Foresman, 1982), p. 5.

29. Donald M. Murray, "Teaching the Other Self: The Writer's First Reader," *CCC,* 33 (May, 1982), 142.

Kairos: A Neglected Concept in Classical Rhetoric

James L. Kinneavy

"Kairos" was first presented as a conference paper in Washington, D.C., in October 1983. The conference was entitled "Classical Rhetoric and the Teaching of Composition." The version presented here comes from Rhetoric and Praxis: The Contribution of Classical Rhetoric to Practical Reasoning. *Ed. Jean Dietz Moss. Washington, D.C.: The Catholic University of America Press, 1986. 79–105.*

HISTORY OF *KAIROS* AND CONTEMPORARY PARALLELS

This volume of essays is an attempt to show the relevance of some important concepts of classical rhetoric to modern composition. Anyone in the field of rhetoric has undoubtedly already encountered the concepts being discussed by the other contributors; practical reasoning, *topoi*, enthymeme, *aitia*, and *telos* hardly need justification in such a symposium. But *kairos* is not listed in Lanham's *A Handlist of Rhetorical Terms*,[1] nor in the four volumes of the *Dictionary of the History of Ideas*,[2] nor in the two volumes of *The Great Ideas: A Syntopicon*,[3] which accompanies the Great Books of the Western World series. Yet a strong case can be made for the thesis that *kairos* is the dominating concept in sophistic, Platonic, and, in a sense, even in Ciceronian rhetoric. This essay is an attempt to reassert its importance for a contemporary theory of composition.

The second part of the essay will be an extended definition of *kairos,* but provisionally it might be defined as the right or opportune time to do something, or right measure in doing something. Often the two notions are joined; thus, the righteous anger justified in a war situation would be exces-sive and improper in a family dispute: the *kairos* would not be right. Before expanding and clarifying this definition, it might be worthwhile to give a brief sketch of the history of the notion and an explanation for its neglect by many rhetoricians, both historical and contemporary.

Although the word does not occur in Homer, it already occurs in Hesiod (seventh century B.C.), whose statement "Observe due measure, and proportion [*kairos*] is best in all things"[4] became a proverb. It is a critical concept in the poetry of Pindar (fl. fifth century B.C.), where the meaning of due or proper measure is given more emphasis than it had been in either Hesiod or Theognis.[5] The notion of *kairos* was embodied in several of the maxims attributed to the Seven Sages of Greece, particularly "Nothing in excess" and "Seal your word with silence and your silence with the right time," both of which were sometimes specifically linked with Solon.[6] It seems clear that with the influence of Hesiod, Pindar, and some of the sayings of the Seven Sages, the concept of *kairos* had become a part of the educational ideals of early Greece. As Levi says, "To the Socratic 'Know thyself,' the pre-Socratic ethic juxtaposed its own 'Know the opportunity,' *kairon gnothi.*"[7]

The pre-Socratic prominence of *kairos* in Greek thought can particularly be seen in the Pythagorean school. Rostagni has analyzed this aspect of Pythagorean thought more than anyone else. He states that to Pythagoreans this maxim was inscribed, "The most important thing in every action is *kairos*."[8] Untersteiner states this in another way: for the Pythagoreans, *kairos* was "one of the laws of the universe."[9] Pythagoras and his school gave further complexity to the concept of *kairos*, linking it closely with the basis of all virtue, particularly justice, and consequently with civic education. Indeed, several of the Pythagoreans made the mastery of *kairos* to be the essence of philosophy.[10] Others considered it a faculty on a par with the soul and the intellect.[11]

The sophists Prodicus, Antiphon, Hippias, and probably also Protagoras used the concept of *kairos* in their philosophical and rhetorical systems. But, as Untersteiner has thoroughly demonstrated, it was Gorgias who made *kairos* the cornerstone of his entire epistemology, ethics, aesthetics, and rhetoric. Gorgias and some of the other sophists carried the implications of the relativism of different situations to such lengths that Plato countered with the stability and permanence of his world of ideas. Yet even Plato did not dispense with *kairos*, particularly in rhetoric. And Plato also used *kairos* as the foundation on which to construct his theory of virtue as a mean between two extremes, the theory developed still further by Aristotle.

With Gorgias and Plato, the concept of *kairos* undoubtedly reached its apogee. Aristotle, interested more in the art of rhetoric than in the act of rhetoric, gave *kairos* considerably less prominence than did Plato. Among Hellenistic thinkers, the concept was not nearly so important as it had been in Hellenic times, although some Stoic philosophers used the notion in discussing the ethics of suicide, cannibalism, and other actions under certain circumstances.[12]

But in Stoicism, particularly Latin Stoicism, the concept of *kairos* merged with that of *prepon* (propriety or fitness), as Max Pohlenz has shown in his admirable study of this latter concept.[13] In this guise, *kairos* is the dominating concept in both Cicero's ethics and his rhetoric. Consequently, it is not inaccurate to say that *kairos*, with the related concept of *prepon*, was a major influence in much of classical rhetoric in antiquity, particularly with the Pythagoreans, the sophists, Plato, and Cicero.

However, although the Ciceronian notion of propriety persisted throughout the medieval and Renaissance periods, the residual influence of *kairos* is almost a negligible chapter in the history of rhetoric since antiquity, partly because of the overwhelming influence of Aristotelian rhetoric in this history. This partially explains the absence of *kairos* in the dictionaries and handbooks of rhetoric that I alluded to earlier.

Three Italian scholars in this century are mainly responsible for the recognition that *kairos* played such an important role in Greek rhetoric and thought generally. In 1922 Augusto Rostagni wrote a monograph-size article entitled (in English) "A New Chapter in Rhetoric and Sophistry."[14] He carefully traced the history of the notion and particularly demonstrated the dominating influence of the Pythagorean school, especially on Gorgias and Plato. In the next two years Doro Levi published two additional articles on *kairos*, one specifically on the importance of the concept in Plato's philosophy.[15] In 1948 Mario Untersteiner published his innovative and controversial study, *The Sophists,* in which he analyzed in great detail the influence of *kairos* in sophistic thought, especially in that of Gorgias. The final voice that has called the attention of the twentieth century to *kairos* has been that of the German theologian Paul Tillich, who made the concept of *kairos*, as it is presented in the New Testament, one of the foundation ideas of his entire theology. His works include at least five major statements on *kairos*.[16] Although Tillich does not address the issue of *kairos* from a rhetorician's point of view, his ideas, I will attempt to show, can be applied to the matter of teaching composition.

These major scholars have been calling our attention to *kairos* for more than sixty years, but few rhetoricians have given them much attention. Yet I am firmly convinced that rhetoric desperately needs the notion of *kairos*. I have made several pleas for its reincorporation into the systematic study of composition because I see it as a dominant motif in disciplines related to our own. The concept of situational context, which is a modern term for *kairos,* is in the forefront of research and thought in many areas.[17] The phrase "rhetorical situation" has almost become a slogan in the field of speech communications since Lloyd Bitzer's article on the subject appeared in 1964.[18] I have argued that the relevance of the immediate situation is at the heart of Freudian dream analysis; that Kenneth Burke's pentad is an attempt to erect the major dimensions of a situation; that the "emic," as opposed to the "etic," approach of the tagmemic linguistics of Kenneth Pike has a similar emphasis; that the ethnomethodology approach in modern anthropology is a movement in exactly the same direction; that the hermeneutic forestructure of Heidegger, the prejudices of Gadamer, and the demythologizing movement of Bultmann are evidences of the same insistence on situational and cultural context in philosophy and theology; that the strong critical reaction against the near autonomy of the text in literary criticism has resulted in different emphases on the individuality of the reader's response in such different writers as Jacques Derrida, Edward Said, Stanley Fish, and Josue Harari; and that the current theories in pragmatics, of Bobrow and Norman, of Minsky, and of Schank all stress the importance of the unique background of the interpreter to the business of interpreting anything.[19] Even in composition theory itself, the necessity of a cultural and informational background has been stressed by E. D. Hirsch.[20]

All of these voices saying ultimately the same thing ought to convince us that some consideration in any rhetorical theory must be given to the issue raised by the concept of *kairos*—the appropriateness of the discourse to the particular circumstances of the time, place, speaker, and audience involved.

If this is so, it may be that modern treatments of situational context can learn something from the handling of the same topic in antiquity. I would argue that they can, particularly in the ethical and educational realms. Consequently, it may be worthwhile to analyze the notion of *kairos* in an attempt to isolate its various components in the hope that the concept of *kairos* can contribute something of value to modern composition theory.

THE COMPLEX CONCEPT OF *KAIROS* IN GREEK RHETORIC

This brief historical survey has already suggested that *kairos* is a complex concept, not easily reduced to a simple formula. I would like to analyze the various factors of the concept, considering in sequence the two fundamental elements embodied in five major areas in which the concept was relevant. In the analysis, I am following the findings of Rostagni, Levi, Untersteiner, and Tillich, although I have some qualifications about the last three, qualifications that will become clear in the sequel.

The Basic Concept: Two Components

The two basic elements of the concept are already seen in Hesiod and continue unabated through Cicero. They are the principle of right timing and the principle of a proper measure. Usually they are joined in a single concept, although individual occurrences of the term may focus on one or the other aspect. In the sense of "right" time, *kairos* may be opposed to the more routine *chronos,* although this opposition is not consistent in Hellenic, Hellenistic, and New Testament Greek.[21] Sometimes *kairos* can be viewed as neutral and a "good time" (*eukairos*), as opposed to a time without *kairos* (*akairos*).[22]

The second element is more elusive. The propriety of the concept of *kairos* is sometimes quite explicit, as in the proverb derived from Hesiod, "Observe good measure, and proportion [*kairos*] is best in all things," but other times it is only implicit. An example of this is the *locus classicus* of the rhetorical use of the notion of *kairos* in Plato. This occurs in the *Phaedrus* after Socrates has carefully constructed all of the basic dimensions of an ideal rhetoric. He summarizes his conclusions and then adds another dimension:

Since it is in fact the function of speech to influence souls, a man who is going to be a speaker must know how many kinds of souls there are. Let us, then, state that they are of this or that sort, so that individuals also will be of this or that type. Again, the distinctions that apply here apply as well in the cases of speeches: they are of this or that number in type, and each type of one particular sort. So men of a special sort under the influence of speeches of a particular kind are readily persuaded to take action of a definite sort because of the qualitative correlation that obtains between speech and soul; while men of a different sort are hard to persuade because, in their case, this qualitative correlation does not obtain. Very well. When a student has attained an adequate grasp of these facts intellectually, he must next go on to see with his own eyes that they occur in the world of affairs and are operative in practice; he must acquire the capacity to confirm their existence through the sharp use of his senses. If he does not do this, no part of the theoretical knowledge he acquired as a student is as yet of any help to him. But it is only when he has the capacity to declare to himself with complete perception, in the presence of another, that here is the man and here the nature that was discussed theoretically at school—here, now present to him in actuality—to which he must apply *this* kind of speech in *this* sort of manner in order to obtain persuasion for *this* kind of activity—it is when he can do all this and when he has, in addition, grasped the concept of propriety of time [*kairos*]—when to speak and when to hold his tongue [*eukairos* and *akairos*], when to use brachylogy, piteous language, hyperbole for horrific effect, and, in a word, each of the specific devices of discourse he may have studied—it is only then, and not until then, that the finishing and perfecting touches will have been given to his science.[23]

In this passage Plato indicates the primacy of the notion of *kairos* to his rhetorical system. It is the capstone that gives meaning to the entire substructure of the art. The notion of propriety is only implicit, however, even though the translation uses the words "propriety of time" to translate *kairos*. Yet the translation is quite accurate since the concept of propriety undergirds the entire passage.

But the component of propriety and measure in rhetoric is much richer than just a sense of the adaptation of the speech to the audience. In order to read into the notion of *kairos* its full connotations, even in rhetoric, it is necessary to establish its rich dimensions. In addition to the rhetorical, they embrace ethical, educational, epistemological, and aesthetic levels, all of which are linked to each other.

The Ethical Dimension of *Kairos*

One of the most significant ethical components of *kairos* had to do with its close relation to justice, particularly in the Pythagoreans. Justice was defined as giving to each *according to merit,* that is, generously to those who had worked hard and parsimoniously to those who had shirked. Justice, therefore, was determined by circumstances: justice was *kairos.*[24] This combination was omnipresent in Pythagoras, according to Rostagni: "All of his [Pythagoras's] teachings, his influence as founder of a school and as expert and custodian of minds—everything is based on the combined principles of *kairos* and *dikaion* [justice]."[25]

This facet of *kairos,* which is linked with the word in its earliest historical occurrences in Hesiod, Theognis, and later, especially in Pindar. Gorgias, Antisthenes, and other sophists continued this ethical facet of *kairos,* although some of them also skirted dangerously with the extreme relativism that a notion of situational determinism could carry with it. Isocrates and others, for example, accuse Gorgias of carrying situational ethics to the point of complete relativism,[26] although Untersteiner and Rostagni dispute this accusation.[27]

Plato and Socrates were seriously concerned with the relativism implicit in such a situational ethic, and Plato's ethic is an attempt to provide an alternative. Yet, curiously, Plato's ethic is also grounded on the notion of *kairos.* Plato used the concept of proper measure and right time—the two fundamental components of the concept of *kairos*—to construct the doctrine of virtue as the mean between two extremes (excess and deficiency). This doctrine is further developed by

Aristotle and emerges as the classic Greek doctrine of virtue.[28]

More than any one strand of *kairos,* this aspect is continued in the Latin concept of propriety, especially in Cicero. It is the basis of his entire ethical treatise on duties—according to one scholar, possibly the single most influential book, other than the Bible, in Western civilization.[29]

Any application of *kairos* to the teaching of composition can not ignore the ethical dimension of the notion.

The Epistemological Dimension of *Kairos*

A common epistemological thread is woven into the meaning of *kairos* from Pindar and Bacchylides, writing poetry in the fifth century B.C., through the Pythagoreans, Gorgias, and Plato, and is still found in the modern extrapolations of the concept made by Tillich, the twentieth-century theologian. At the risk of simplifying, let me provisionally say that *kairos* brings timeless ideas down into the human situations of historical time. It thus imposes value on the ideas and forces humans to make free decisions about these values. Let us flesh these ideas out with a little history.

Pindar and, to a lesser extent, Bacchylides felt that it was the task of the poet to make known the divine revelation to man. Pindar claims that his poems are from the gods, through the Muses.[30] Although the gods provide the message and the stimulus to create, the poet must incorporate his god-given wisdom (*sophia*) in the work of his own crafting.[31] And Pindar felt that his contribution to the craft of poetry was his ability to single out the critical moment of a story (the *kairos*) and weave a short poem around it. He tells the story of Orestes in twenty-four lines, whereas his predecessor, Stesichorus, filled two books with the same story.[32] The divine ideas thus acquire a human value.[33]

Gorgias takes a more strident view of this process. The transcendent divine ideas take no account of the facts of human existence. To apply to man, the divine ideas must become immanent in human life through *kairos.* This can be achieved when the writer enters into the "psychological situation of whoever has perpetrated the deed [being written about], trying to understand its individual character."[34] This, for Gorgias, can come about only through the deceptions of persuasive rhetoric and poetry.[35]

It is very clear that in Plato's system, rhetorical thought becomes effective only at the moment of *kairos,* as the lengthy passage from the *Phaedrus* quoted above amply illustrates. And I have already called attention to the significance of the notion of *kairos* in Plato's ethic. In both rhetoric and ethic, Plato's world of ideas is brought down to earth by the notion of *kairos.*

Tillich has taken these Greek ideas and has drawn from them some theological, historical, and philosophical corollaries. Although I seriously disagree with some of his conclusions, his contrast of the two philosophical tendencies in Western thought, *kairos* and *logos,* is a valuable addition to the epistemological sketch here being attempted. Tillich distinguishes *logos* thinking as characterized by an emphasis on timelessness, on form, on law, on stasis, on method; he finds it the dominant pattern of Western thought, from Plato and Aristotle through most of the Church Fathers, on to Descartes and Kant. Opposing this trend is *kairos* thinking, characterized by an emphasis on time, on change, on creation, on conflict, on fate, and on individuality. He cites Jakob Boehme, Duns Scotus, Luther, and the late Romantics as instances of this minority approach to Western thought.[36] He argues for the importance of the *kairos* approach because it brings theory into practice, it asserts the continuing necessity of free decision, it insists on the value and norm aspects of ideas, it champions a vital and concerned interest in knowledge because knowledge always is relevant to the situational context, and it provides a better solution to the problem of uniting idea and historical reality than the solution of either Hegel or Marx.[37] Tillich contends that Hegel sacrificed freedom by making historical reality follow the logical norms of ideality, and he maintains that Marx capitulated to relativism and sacrificed real knowledge by subordinating idea to historical situation.[38] He argues for the union of freedom and fate in *kairos* and for a less rigid notion of unchanging idea, a notion of a dynamic idea.[39]

One critic of Tillich argues that Tillich's concept of *kairos* is at least partially indebted to the Marxist concern for historical consciousness.[40] It certainly is closely allied to Walter Benjamin's notion of the importance of being aware of the "now-time," the revolutionary possibilities inherent in the moment, the "state of emergency" in which we live, the potentials for change inherent in the historical situation.[41]

The Rhetorical Dimension of *Kairos*

I already established the rhetorical dimension of *kairos* in Platonic rhetoric in the *Phaedrus* quotation cited earlier to illustrate the implicit sense of right measure in *kairos*. Plato was responding to the sophistic concept of rhetoric in the *Phaedrus*. He did repudiate the sophistic basis of probability and some of the sophistic conceptions of mechanical structure and organization, but he did not repudiate the thoroughly Gorgian idea of *kairos* as being the cornerstone of rhetoric. Untersteiner has fully developed this aspect of sophistic rhetoric, particularly in Gorgias.[42] Rostagni sees a heavy Pythagorean influence on Gorgias and Antithenes in their notions of rhetoric, persuasion, and the close affinity these have to *kairos*.[43]

The Aesthetic Dimension of *Kairos*

Levi begins his article on *kairos* in Plato with this statement, "The concept of *kairos*, as we have often observed, is both an ethical and an aesthetic concept."[44] He goes on to point out that throughout Greek thought the ethical and the aesthetic are consistently intertwined. Indeed, he devotes half of his article to an analysis of the beautiful in Plato and to its relationship to the good. The common basis of Plato's ethics and aesthetics is the concern for "right measure;" this had formed the popular and the philosophic basis for these areas throughout Greek history.[45] And "right measure" is intimately connected with *kairos*, as we indicated

earlier. Plato had summarized the relation of the beautiful to the good and to the proportionate near the end of the *Timaeus*: "Everything that is good is fair, and the fair is not without proportion; and the animal which is to be fair must have due proportion."[46]

More even than Plato, however, Gorgias had asserted the necessity of *kairos* for a theory of aesthetics, a topic that has been given considerable attention by Untersteiner.[47] And, in discussing Pindar's epistemology of *kairos*, we saw that it was difficult to separate it from his theory of poetry. Finally, the residue of *kairos* in Cicero, the notion of propriety, is at the basis of his entire theory of style, particularly in the *Orator*.

The Civic Educational Dimension of *Kairos*

The educational implications of the various dimensions of *kairos* are obvious, and they were not lost on the Greeks. On this issue, three considerations, central to my general thesis, must be made. Throughout the period that we have been considering, *kairos* was closely aligned with education. We have only to remind ourselves of the early maxims of Hesiod and Solon on the topic. In addition, we know that Pythagoras had oriented his training in education to civic education, to training for public affairs, for life in the polis.[48] Iamblichus in his *Life of Pythagoras* states: "They say that he would have been the inventor of all civic education [*politike paideia*]."[49] The constant theme of all of his speeches was virtue, with *kairos* the determining principle in each case.[50] For the Greeks, the importance of the city was the common bond of humanity that it afforded those living together and the strangers who visited them. In fact, the origins of the concept of "humanity" are traced by Fritz Wehrli to this idea, grounded in the existence of the polis.[51] Since freedom and the ability to persuade and be persuaded are the essence of the polis, it is not surprising to see the education to the life of the polis grounded in persuasion and to see this closely related to the notion of *kairos*. Gorgias, for instance, relates the sense of *philanthropia* to persuasion, which was, as we have noted, for him necessarily grounded in *kairos*.[52]

Probably the most obvious connection of *kairos* to civic education, however, is a symbolic one. Since the Greeks deified many of their ideals, it is not surprising that Kairos was also a god. The usual representation of Kairos was as an ephebe, a young man attending the two years of required civic and military education, at the end of which rite of passage he came into manhood (*ephebeia*).[53] The young athletic man was characterized by a striking hair style, a lock at the front with short hair behind. The presence of the forelock, says Delling, "confirms the fact that even religiously Kairos originally had the character of decision, since the lock of hair is a symbol that one must take the favourable opportunity by the forelock."[54] Kairos, the god, was thus symbolically linked to the public education program that prepared the young man for initiation into citizenship—the program, incidentally, dominated by rhetoric.

KAIROS AND THE CONTEMPORARY COLLEGE COMPOSITION SCENE

As we have seen, *kairos* has distinct educational overtones in addition to its rich ethical, epistemological, aesthetic, and rhetorical tonalities. The problem in applying this rich concept to college composition is the danger of losing some of its essential complexity. Yet the attempt should be worthwhile. Indeed, it may lend a unity to several separate movements. What is required, if we are to be faithful to our historical analysis, is to devise a college composition program that will have ethical, epistemological, rhetorical, aesthetic, and political dimensions involving something like a notion of contemporary practical relevance to the young women and men of today. Can we write such a program? I believe that we can. And, to make this more than just an exercise in imaginative antiquarianism, I believe it will be significantly superior to the vast majority of composition programs in existence in the colleges of this country at the present time.

The Situational Context: College Composition as Rite of Passage

In an article I once wrote for *Freshman English News,* I claimed that college composition particularly, and the college experience generally, was the basic rite of passage for the most influential segment of the American populace, incorporating all of the components of Van Gennep's anthropological study.[55] I stand by the same argument today. The college experience is students' initiation into adulthood. The major decisions of their lives are usually made in these four years; they face financial, religious, philosophical, emotional, educational, and political crises, threats to the values of their family, their hometown, their church, etc. The god Kairos is a proper symbol for them: they must make decisions that will stay with them the remainder of their lives. And, lest the women feel slighted, I might point out that when Kairos was transferred to Italy, he graciously consented to a sex change because the Latin word for occasion was *occasio,* a feminine noun. As a result, she was a feminine goddess in Latin, with as long a history as her masculine counterpart had had in Greek.[56]

Students' decisions during college involve the values that will dictate the contours of their lives. Within this broad scene of decision making, let us look at the areas in which *kairos* will have a say. One caution before wandering into the separate areas: a college composition program need not be just a freshman composition program. Indeed, many of the major universities of the country are viewing the composition program as a vertical sequence of skills that must be monitored from the freshman year to the senior year—otherwise, as the Harvard experience has taught us, the skills may deteriorate.[57] For this reason, I am going to address a program that may span the four years of college—not just a freshman composition program. It is up to the individual school to make up its own mind about the sequencing of the components of its composition program. Some elite institutions may not require a freshman year; others may require monitoring at each year

	Composing	Interpreting
Universal History		
		Dilthey, Von Ranke, Hegel, Gadamer
Cultural Context		
		Heidegger, Bultmann, Jonas, Dilthey
Situational Context		
	Sophists, Plato, Aristotle, Burke, Britton, Kinneavy	Schleiermacher, Hirsch, Bitzer, Pratt, Tillich
Text		
	D'Angelo, Moffet, McCrimmon	Luther, many critics
Paragraph		
	Christensen	
Sentence		
	Christensen, Morenberg, et al.	Ricoeur, Genette
Word		
Morpheme		
Phoneme		
	Structural linguists	

Figure 5-1. Levels of Emphasis in Composition Programs *Source: James L. Kinneavy, "The Relation of the Whole to the Part in Composition and in Interpretation Theory," in* Linguistics, Stylistics, and the Teaching of Composition, *ed. Donald McQuade (Akron, Ohio: Language and Style, 1979).*

with a required course. Some may not find it necessary to require any course at all. But the same basic skills should result from all programs—assuming that we are sending our students out into the personal, political, and career worlds of their choice.

Kairos: Its Epistemological Consequences

What happens when *kairos,* that is, situational context, dominates a composition program? Figure 5–1, Levels of Emphasis in Composition Programs, may clarify this issue. The diagram attempts to show the various levels that may be chosen as the central point of emphasis in composing and in interpretation, the other side of the composing process, as Friedrich Schleiermacher pointed out.[58] In composition, the dominant emphasis in this country today is still the text. The "theme" is the god of the composition teacher, just as the literary text is the god of his literary counterpart, the new critic, still the prevailing power in most English departments. We are literary and rhetorical protestants. I am urging us to move to the next bracket of the figure, situational context, where, as has been shown earlier, Plato and the sophists and Aristotle and Kenneth Burke and James Britton recommend a program based on the current life situation of the writer.

An even worse level of emphasis would be to concentrate on levels below the text. Some composition programs, such as the sentence combining program of Daiker, Kerek, and Morenberg, do just that.[59] And some remedial programs that focus only on grammar represent similar dangerous concentrations.

For the average student in the typical four-year, private or public institution, what should an emphasis on situational context mean? It ought to mean that the student do at least some writing in the area of his or her interests, that is, his or her major, regardless of what it is: physics, mathematics, English, accounting, etc. This means that some sort of writing across the curriculum ought to be incorporated into every composition program that purports to respect the situational context of the student's personal interests and career choices. Writing across the curriculum might be handled in the courses of the student's major, as happens in the program at Michigan and elsewhere, or it may be carried out in a centralized English or rhetoric department, as happens at Maryland and Texas and Brigham Young, for example. But it should be handled somewhere.

This conclusion does not rule out other types of writing, such as those traditionally pursued in required literary courses, but it at least gives coordinate legitimacy to courses in writing across the curriculum.

The obligation to write about a specific subject matter forces the student to take general rhetorical principles and apply them to a particular field. It satisfies Tillich's criteria of historical relevance, interest in the subject, and free decision, but it does not solve the value and ethical issues raised by the concept of kairos.

Kairos: Its Ethical Consequences

Let us therefore turn to the ethical consequences of informing a composition program by the notion of kairos. If a writing program is to have an ethical dimension, it must take into account the value system of the situational context of the writer and reader. Consequently, the writing in a computer science department must not just be about the mechanics of creating better programs or better computers; it must look at the values implicit in the discipline of computer science and at the place of the computer scientist as a person and as a scientist in the world determined by those values.

A kairos program will demand, therefore, that the student write some papers about the ethical concerns of his or her personal interests and career choices. Consequently, there will have to be a humanistic component to such a program. It cannot simply be a course in what is traditionally called "technical writing," although it should include such writing.

The ethical consequences of emphasizing the life situation of the student in writing entail both individual and social affairs. The student should be asked to inquire into the aspects of his or her discipline that will morally affect the student's decisions in the present and in the foreseeable future. Such inquiries are not usual in the present university structure. Physicists leave it up to the philosophers or theologians in an institution to teach ethics, even the ethics of science. This would be all right if we could be assured that all students were being asked to write about their own discipline in such a class. The ethics issue parallels the rhetorical issue—it must be done somewhere. In any case, physicists eventually have to make moral decisions; no one can abrogate his or her own responsibilities and leave morality to philosophers or theologians.

Kairos: Its Social Consequences

The ethical issues have already hinted at the social issues; it is questionable if there is any ethic in a social vacuum anyway. Consequently, the next dimension of a writing program based on situational context must frame the social context of the writer and the reader. This dimension is an echo of the civic education component of Greek education and of the awareness of the historical-consciousness emphasis of Tillich.

Let me illustrate this dimension by an incident that happened recently. I was teaching a course in freshman composition, and I had asked the students to read an essay by Lt. Colonel Donald Gilleland entitled "The Perils of a Nuclear Freeze," which I had photocopied from that month's issue of *Vital Speeches*.[60] Several of the students were quite impressed by Lt. Colonel Gilleland's strong statements that the United States would not drop the first bomb in a nuclear war. They were concerned that Russia would, and consequently accepted Gilleland's main thesis. One student, discussing her analysis of the speech in a conference with me, was totally taken aback when I informed her that the only nation that had ever dropped a nuclear bomb in war was the United States: she had never heard of Nagasaki or Hiroshima. This student obviously did not have the historical consciousness to write on the topic.

Such ignorance of history is frightening. It is this sort of lack of fundamental information that led me to suggest to the President's Commission on Excellence in Education that all high school seniors be required to write an extemporaneous essay on a current political topic as a graduation requirement and that all colleges require a similar essay as an entrance examination.

In any case, a serious writing program should include in it some writing by the students on the political issues relevant to their own disciplines and on the political scene generally. This is one of the fundamental purposes of both public and private education. Societies invest in education for some social return on their investment.

Sometimes society may not like the return it gets. The social and political consciousness of college students during the 1960s was not the social return that many parents expected on their investment. But at least the students had, precisely because of their personal stake in the war, a sense of historical consciousness. It would be desirable if they had it without the necessity of the rhetoric of a war.

Kairos: Its Rhetorical Consequences

Sometimes the word "rhetoric" is used in the general sense of effectiveness, or a general study of techniques of composition, and sometimes it is used in the rather specific sense of the type of persuasion seen in political speeches, legal pleas in a courtroom, advertisements, and religious sermons. Thus far in this essay I have not felt it important to distinguish between these two uses. However, in this section I will restrict my use of the term to the latter meaning, the historical meaning of rhetoric that distinguishes it from poetry on the one hand and scientific or expository prose on the other. The distinctions are implicit in the liberal arts tradition where grammar (the study of literature) is distinguished from logic and dialectic, and all three of these from rhetoric (persuasion in this narrower sense). Up to now, no consideration has been given to the specific kind or kinds of writing that should be expected in a writing program. Most of the implications have been in the direction of expository writing. Normally students in physics or accounting would be expected to write informative or demonstrative prose about physics or accounting. And even student inquiries into the moral aspects of computer sciences or chemistry or geology would be exploratory or dialectical. All of these would be in the area of expository writing.

Most of the university courses giving some attention to writing emphasize expository writing. In a few courses some attention is given to the belletristic (creative writing, drama, some journalism). But few courses consciously pay attention to the persuasive as distinct from the other two. (Advertising and, in seminaries, sermon writing may be the only exception.) This alienation of rhetoric from the university at large has had some unfortunate consequences. In the first place, it has had the effect of breaking up the major connection of the humanities to the daily life of the average citizen of the state. Rhetoric, more than literature and more than science (the grammar and logic of the traditional arts), was the linking bridge of the humanities to the average citizen. By alienating rhetoric from the academy, the university has lost its major contact with real life, in the view of the populace. This partly explains the university rebellions in this century in France, Germany, and in this country. The academic can become, well, academic.

Secondly, the alienation of rhetoric from the university has produced a new exemplar of the teacher since the Renaissance. The reduction of the training of the student writer to an expertise in expository writing (demonstrative, informative, and exploratory prose) has narrowed the conceived audience to peers or superiors and separated the student's ethical and moral responsibilities from scientific concerns. Once scientist/teachers no longer feel that it is their duty to address the populace in rhetorical genres, and once they are able to pursue their scholarly interests untrammeled by the intervention of religious or moral beliefs, they can perform amorally in the laboratory and in the classroom, as mere scientist/teachers.

Such scientist/teachers can pass on to intermediaries, political or journalistic or marketing, the responsibility of using the objects of their scientific research, since they are no longer responsible to the populace directly. And such scientist/teachers will turn out similar scientist/students.

Yet it does seem immoral for a discipline as a whole to disavow the responsibility for its creations. Computer scientists, chemists, philosophers, journalists, novelists, and engineers, *as social groups,* have a responsibility for the abuses to which society puts their products, just as they also have a right to the plaudits that follow their successes. It is precisely the chemist or the computer scientist personally who can most accurately foresee the benefi-

cial and harmful uses to which their inventions may be put. Each profession as a subculture has a rhetorical obligation to alert the culture as a whole to new benefits and also to new dangers.

This informative and rhetorical function of the profession should be taught the practitioners of that métier. In a practical vein this means that the politics, the ethics, and the rhetoric of a profession ought to be a part of the curriculum of any discipline. And the rhetoric of the discipline means the ability to address the populace in persuasive language that will be listened to. And this persuasive language will often have to be intensive, even impassioned, audienced based and biased, and stylistically appropriate to a given subculture. We don't teach our majors this kind of prose.

Consequently, it is not enough to teach the practitioners of a given craft how to communicate with each other in the jargon of their own department. They must also be taught the common language of humanity in its full rhetorical scales. This means that all disciplines should incorporate a training in the persuasive techniques of rhetoric. Thus, at least some geologists, some pharmacists, some civil engineers, some political theorists, etc., should engage in the impassioned and simple prose that affects the multitude. Training these future professionals to write only expository prose is training them to ignore their political and ethical responsibilities.[61]

It should be fairly palpable by this time that the rhetorical consequences of a *kairos* theory of composition are not unconnected with the ethical and political consequences discussed earlier.

The critical element in applying *kairos,* or situational context, to any discussion of composition problems was made by Plato in his discussion of the place of *kairos* in rhetorical theory. The theory is only theory until it has been applied to a concrete situation with unique circumstances. For this reason it is desirable, in rhetorical (and scientific and literary) writing, to enable the students to find a realistic audience, apart from the teacher, if this is at all possible.

Real publication of the students' papers, in any local or state or national medium, directed to real audiences for specific purposes, is ideal for any composition program. I once had all of the pharmacists in Austin worried about the implementation of a legislative bill mandating the public display of generic prices for drugs because some of my students were working on a paper in this field and had contacted enough of the local druggists to arouse concern. (It helped that the state agency was also involved in investigating the same issue.) Campus publication in the school newspaper is also a wonderful stimulant. Even class publication, with everyone reading everyone else's paper, is a good technique. There is no more immediate application of the principle of *kairos* than establishing a real audience distinct from the classroom situation.

Kairos: Its Aesthetic Consequences

I wish I knew more about the subtle connections among the ethical, the rhetorical, and the aesthetic in Greek thought. I wish I really understood more than I do what the Greeks meant by beautiful/goodness (*kalokagathia*), that peculiar Greek combination of the beautiful and the good. If I did, I feel fairly certain that my aesthetic corollary of the idea of *kairos* would be more complex and more interrelated with the remainder of this essay than what I am going to suggest. I am not going to apologize for this segment of a *kairos* program, but I do feel that it could be stronger.

It seems clear that a *kairos* program of composition ought to have an aesthetic component. Levi, in particular, insisted on the aesthetic element in *kairos*. It is an educational commonplace that the aesthetic sense in the Greeks was fostered, among other sources, by the study of Homer and later by the study of the other great literary giants of Greek thought. If we are to take a cue from the Greeks to foster a sense of *kairos,* then we might do well to train to *kairos* by a study of literature.

Such a study would certainly incorporate the aesthetic into the composition program. It could be a part of the composition program in two different ways: students could study great literature and write about it, or they could try to write original literary pieces of their own. Both of these approaches

have traditionally been a part of composition programs. The aesthetic might also be served by having students write about other fine arts, such as drama, dance, music, sculpture, and painting. The advantage of literature over these other fine arts is that students bring to literature a sophistication in language that permits a richer and more complex aesthetic experience.

This represents the final dimension of a *kairos* program in composition. I believe that it has its own internal defense: the ethical, the epistemological, the rhetorical, the educational, and the aesthetic foundations have a validity of their own. But two other arguments might be adduced to buttress this "kairotic" unity.

The first has already been implied. Because *kairos* has much in common with situational context, the general arguments for the importance of situational context in anthropology, in hermeneutics (literary, biblical, legal, and philosophical), in linguistic pragmatics, in speech communication, in tagmemics, in poststructuralist literary criticism, in Freud, in Kenneth Burke, and in E. D. Hirsch apply to rhetorical studies as well.[62]

The second argument has not yet been broached. Because the concept of the program that was delineated includes an emphasis on expository prose, on rhetorical prose, and on a study of literature, the program can be said to include the three kinds of thinking represented by the traditional liberal arts: grammar, rhetoric, and logic/dialectic. The writing of expository prose sharpens scientific thinking; persuasive prose sharpens rhetorical thinking; and literary analysis sharpens aesthetic thinking. The university is supposed to train students in these three basic kinds of thinking, and it is this emphasis that makes the program a continuation of the long history of the liberal arts tradition. A *kairos* program is a liberal arts program in the historic sense of the term.

The wholesomeness of the student who was scholar, and rhetorician, and aesthete is a wholesomeness we cannot dispense with. Fragmented scholars, whether teachers or students, are irresponsible scholars, as capable of turning out iniquitous monsters as beneficent marvels.

Notes

1. Richard A. Lanham, *A Handlist of Rhetorical Terms: A Guide for Students of English Literature* (Berkeley, Calif.: University of California Press, 1969). *Kairos* is mentioned in Heinrich Lausberg, *Handbuch der literarischen Rhetorik: Eine Grundlegung der Literaturwissenschaft* (Munich: Max Heuber Verlag, 1960), but not in Henri Morier, *Dictionnaire de poétique et de rhétorique* (Paris: Presses Universitaires de France, 1961).

2. Philip P. Wiener, ed., *Dictionary of the History of Ideas: Studies of Selected Pivotal Ideas* (New York: Scribner's, 1973).

3. Mortimer J. Adler, ed., *The Great Ideas: A Syntopicon of Great Books of the Western World,* No. 2 of *Great Books of the Western World,* ed. Ribert Maynard Hutchins (Chicago, Ill.: Encyclopaedia Britannica, Inc., 1951). *Kairos* is not even mentioned in the large article on "Time," nor in the bibliographic references.

4. Henry George Liddell and Robert Scott, comps., *A Greek-English Lexicon,* revised by Sir Henry Stuart Jones and Robert McKenzie (Oxford: At the Clarendon Press, 1968), p. 859.

5. Doro Levi, "Il *Kairos* Attraverso la letteratura Greca," *Rendiconti della Reale Accademia Nazionale dei Lincei. Classe di scienza Morali,* RV, vol. 32 (1923), pp. 266 [260–281]. Henceforth referred to as "*Kairos.*"

6. Ibid., p. 274.

7. Ibid., p. 275.

8. Augusto Rostagni, "Un Nuovo Capitolo nella Storia della Retorica e della Sofistica," *Studi Italiani di filologia classica,* N.S., vol. 2, 1–2 (1922), p. 165 [148–201]. He finds this statement in Iamblichus, *Life of Pythagoras,* p. 49. I am using an unpublished translation of Rostagni's article by Philip Sipiora, p. 29.

9. Mario Untersteiner, *The Sophists,* trans. Kathleen Freeman (Oxford: Basil Blackwell, 1954), p. 110.

10. Ibid., p. 82.

11. Levi, "*Kairos,*" p. 275.

12. A. A. Long, *Hellenistic Philosophy: Stoics, Epicureans, Sceptics* (London: Gerald Duckworth and Co., Ltd., 1974), p. 206.

13. Max Pohlenz, "*To Prepon:* Ein Beitrag zur Geschichte des griechischen Geistes," *Nachrichten von der Gesellschaft der Wissenschaften zu Goettingen, Philologisch-historische Klasse, Heft I* (1933), pp. 54–55 [53–92]. Reprinted, *Kleine Schriften,* ed. Heinrich Dorrie (Hildesheim: G. Olms, 1965), vol. 2, pp. 100–139.

14. Rostagni, see note 8.

15. Levi, see note 5 for the general article; "Il Concetto di Kairos e la Filosofia di Platone," *Accademia Nazionale dei Lincei, Roma. Classe di Scienze Morali, Storiche, Critichee Filologiche,* Rendiconti vol. 33 (1924), pp. 93–118. Henceforth referred to as "Concetto."

16. See Paul Tillich, "Kairos and Logos," in *The Interpretation of History,* trans. N. A. Rasetzki and Elsa Talmey (New York: Scribner's, 1936). Henceforth referred to as "Kairos." See also "Kairos and Kairoi," *Systematic Theology* (Chicago, Ill.: The University of Chicago Press, 1963), vol. 2, pp. 369–372; "Kairos I," *Der Widerstreit von Raum und Zeit: Schriften zur Geschichtsphilosophie, Gesammelte Werke,* VI, pp. 10–28; "Kairos II, Ideen zur Geisteslage der Gegenwart," VI, pp. 29–41; and "Kairos und Utopie," VI, pp. 149–165.

17. James L. Kinneavy, "The Relation of the Whole to the Part in Interpretation Theory and in the Composing Process," in *Linguistics, Stylistics, and the Teaching of Composition,* ed. Donald McQuade (Akron, Ohio: Language and Style, 1979), pp. 1–23. Henceforth referred to as "Relation."

18. Lloyd F. Bitzer, "The Rhetorical Situation," *Philosophy and Rhetoric* I (1968): 1–14.

19. On Freudian dream analysis, see Kinneavy, "Relation," p. 17; and p. 22, note 80, for many references. My other arguments are developed in James L. Kinneavy, "Contemporary Rhetoric," in *The Present State of Scholarship in Historical and Contemporary Rhetoric,* ed. Winifred Bryan Horner (Columbia, Mo.: University of Missouri Press, 1983), pp. 174–177 [167–213].

20. E. D. Hirsch, Jr., "Culture and Literacy," *Journal of Basic Writing* 3 (Fall/Winter 1980): 27–47.

21. See James Barr, *Biblical Words for Time,* 2nd ed. (London: S.C.M. Press, 1969), pp. 20–21.

22. See Plato, *Phaedrus,* trans and intro. by W. C. Helmbold and W. G. Rabinowitz (Indianapolis, Ind.: The Bobbs-Merrill Co., Inc., 1958), pp. 272a.

23. Ibid., pp. 271d–272b.

24. Rostagni, p. 163.

25. Ibid., p. 168.

26. Untersteiner, pp. 198–199.

27. Ibid., pp. 155–156, 204.

28. This argument for the *kairos* origin of the doctrine of the mean is drawn from Levi, "*Kairos,*" pp. 277–279; see also Rostagni, p. 164.

29. A. E. Douglas, "Cicero the Philosopher," in *Cicero,* ed. T. P. Dorey (New York: Basic Books, Inc., 1965), p. 149.

30. C. M. Bowra, *Pindar* (Oxford: At the Clarendon Press, 1964), p. 5, cites Olympia XI, line 10, Olympia IX,

lines 100–104, and Olympia II, lines 86–88, to support this point.

31. Ibid., p. 21.

32. Gilbert Norwood, *Pindar* (Berkeley, Calif.: Univ. of California Press, 1945). pp. 168–172.

33. Untersteiner, p. 111.

34. Ibid., p. 104.

35. Ibid., pp. 108–114.

36. Tillich, "Kairos," pp. 127–129.

37. Ibid., pp. 130–131, 134, 136–139, 143–148.

38. Ibid., pp. 152–157.

39. Ibid., pp. 157–164.

40. Raymond F. Bulman, "Theonomy and Technology," in *Kairos and Logos: Studies in the Roots and Implications of Tillich's Theology,* ed. John J. Carey (Cambridge, Mass.: North American Paul Tillich Society, 1978), p. 240.

41. Walter Benjamin, *Illuminations,* trans. Harry Zoln, ed. Hannah Arendt (New York: Schocken Books, 1969), pp. 257–262.

42. Untersteiner, pp. 119–120, 194–205.

43. Rostagni, pp. 160–168.

44. Levi, "Concetto," p. 93.

45. Ibid., pp. 110–114.

46. Plato, *Timaeus,* trans. Benjamin Jowett, 87c.

47. Untersteiner, pp. 185–194.

48. Rostagni, p. 188.

49. Quoted in Rostagni, p. 71.

50. Ibid., p. 193.

51. Fritz R. Wehrli, "Vom antiken Humanitätsbegriff," *Theoria und Humanitas: Gesammelte Schriften zur antiken Gedankenwelt* (Zurich: Artemis Verlag, 1972), pp. 12–14.

52. Untersteiner, p. 115.

53. G. Delling, "Kairos," in Gerhard Kittell, ed. *Theological Dictionary of the New Testament,* trans. and ed. Geoffrey W. Bromiley (Grand Rapids, Mich.: William B. Eerdmans Publishing Co., 1964–1976), vol. 3, p. 457.

54. Delling, p. 457.

55. James L. Kinneavy, "Freshman English: An American Rite of Passage," *Freshman English News* 7 (1977): 1–3.

56. See Arthur Bernard Cook, "Appendix A: Kairos," in *Zeus: A Study in Ancient Religion* (Cambridge: At the University Press, 1925), vol. 2, pt. 2, pp. 862–863. This article is a delightful history of the god/goddess over eighteen centuries, as Cook remarks, p. 867.

57. The summary report by Derek C. Bok, "Harvard University: The President's Report," *Harvard University Gazette,* vol. 73, no. 24, March 17, 1978, p. 5 [Insert, pp. 1–12].

58. Friedrich Schleiermacher, cited in Hans-Georg Gadamer, *Truth and Method,* trans. G. Barden and J. Cumming (New York: The Seabury Press, 1964), p. 167.

59. See Donald Daiker, Andrew Kerek, Max Morenberg, "Sentence Combining and Syntactic Maturity in Freshman English," *College Composition and Communication* 19 (February 1978): 36–41.

60. Vol. 49, June 15, 1983, pp. 514–517.

61. These remarks on rhetoric have been drawn from an article I wrote that appeared in the Winter 1983 edition of the *ADE Bulletin,* published by the Modern Language Association.

62. See notes 18 through 20 for the references.

Intertextuality and the Discourse Community

James E. Porter

Porter's essay was published in Rhetoric Review 5 (1986): 34–47.

At the conclusion of Eco's *The Name of the Rose,* the monk Adso of Melk returns to the burned abbey, where he finds in the ruins scraps of parchment, the only remnants from one of the great libraries in all Christendom. He spends a day collecting the charred fragments, hoping to discover some meaning in the scattered pieces of books. He assembles his own "lesser library . . . of fragments, quotations, unfinished sentences, amputated stumps of books" (500). To Adso, these random shards are "an immense acrostic that says and repeats nothing" (501). Yet they are significant to him as an attempt to order experience.

We might well derive our own order from this scene. We might see Adso as representing the writer, and his desperate activity at the burned abbey as a model for the writing process. The writer in this image is a collector of fragments, an archaeologist creating an order, building a framework, from remnants of the past. Insofar as the collected fragments help Adso recall other, lost texts, his experience affirms a principle he learned from his master, William of Baskerville: "Not infrequently books speak of books" (286). Not infrequently, and perhaps ever and always, texts refer to other texts and in fact rely on them for their meaning. All texts are interdependent: We understand a text only insofar as we understand its precursors.

This is the principle we know as intertextuality, the principle that all writing and speech—indeed, all signs—arise from a single network: what Vygotsky called "the web of meaning"; what poststructuralists label Text or Writing (Barthes, *écriture*); and what a more distant age perhaps knew as *logos.* Examining texts "intertextually" means looking for "traces," the bits and pieces of Text which writers or speakers borrow and sew together to create new discourse.[1] The most mundane manifestation of intertextuality is explicit citation, but intertextuality animates all discourse and goes beyond mere citation. For the intertextual critics, Intertext is Text—a great seamless textual fabric. And, as they like to intone solemnly, no text escapes intertext.

Intertextuality provides rhetoric with an important perspective, one currently neglected, I believe. The prevailing composition pedagogies by and large cultivate the romantic image of writer as free, uninhibited spirit, as independent, creative genius. By identifying and stressing the intertextual nature of discourse, however, we shift our attention away from the writer as individual and focus more on the sources and social contexts from which the writer's discourse arises. According to this view, authorial intention is less significant than social context; the writer is simply a part of a discourse tradition, a member of a team, and a participant in a community of discourse that creates its own collective meaning. Thus the intertext *constrains* writing.

My aim here is to demonstrate the significance of this theory to rhetoric, by explaining intertextuality, its connection to the notion of "discourse community," and its pedagogical implications for composition.

THE PRESENCE OF INTERTEXT

Intertextuality has been associated with both structuralism and poststructuralism, with theorists like Roland Barthes, Julia Kristeva, Jacques Derrida, Hayden White, Harold Bloom, Michel Foucault, and Michael Riffaterre. (Of course, the theory is most often applied in literary analysis.) The central assumption of these critics has been described by Vincent Leitch: "The text is not an autonomous or unified object, but a set of relations with other texts. Its system of language, its grammar, its lexicon, drag along numerous bits and pieces—traces—of history so that the text resembles a Cultural Salvation Army Outlet with unaccountable collections of incompatible ideas, beliefs, and sources" (59). It is these "unaccountable collections" that intertextual critics focus on, not the text as autonomous entity. In fact, these critics have redefined the notion of "text": Text *is* intertext, or simply Text. The traditional notion of the text as the single work of a given author, and even the very notions of author and reader, are regarded as simply convenient fictions for domesticating discourse. The old borders that we used to rope off discourse, proclaim these critics, are no longer useful.

We can distinguish between two types of intertextuality: iterability and presupposition. Iterability refers to the "repeatability" of certain textual fragments, to citation in its broadest sense to include not only explicit allusions, references, and quotations within a discourse, but also unannounced sources and influences, clichés, phrases in the air, and traditions. That is to say, every discourse is composed of "traces," pieces of other texts that help constitute its meaning. (I will discuss this aspect of intertextuality in my analysis of the Declaration of Independence.) Presupposition refers to assumptions a text makes about its referent, its readers, and its context—to portions of the text which are read, but which are not explicitly "there." For example, as Jonathan Culler discusses, the phrase "John married Fred's sister" is an assertion that logically presupposes that John exists, that Fred exists, and that Fred has a sister. "Open the door" contains a practical presupposition, assuming the presence of a decoder who is capable of being addressed and who is better able to open the door than the encoder. "Once upon a time" is a trace rich in rhetorical presupposition, signaling to even the youngest reader the opening of a fictional narrative. Texts not only refer to but in fact *contain* other texts.[2]

An examination of three sample texts will illustrate the various facets of intertextuality. The first, the Declaration of Independence, is popularly viewed as the work of Thomas Jefferson. Yet if we examine the text closely in its rhetorical milieu, we see that Jefferson was author only in the very loosest of senses. A number of historians and at least two composition researchers (Kinneavy, *Theory* 393–49; Maimon, *Readings* 6–32) have analyzed the Declaration, with interesting results. Their work suggests that Jefferson was by no means an original framer or a creative genius, as some like to suppose. Jefferson was a skilled writer, to be sure, but chiefly because he was an effective borrower of traces.

To produce his original draft of the Declaration, Jefferson seems to have borrowed, either consciously or unconsciously, from his culture's Text. Much has been made of Jefferson's reliance on Locke's social contract theory (Becker). Locke's theory influenced colonial political philosophy, emerging in various pamphlets and newspaper articles of the times, and served as the foundation for the opening section of the Declaration. The Declaration contains many traces that can be found in other, earlier documents. There are traces from a First Continental Congress resolution, a Massachusetts Council declaration, George Mason's "Declaration of Rights for Virginia," a political pamphlet of James Otis, and a variety of other sources, including a colonial play. The overall form of the Declaration (theoretical argument followed by list of grievances) strongly resembles, ironically, the English Bill of Rights of 1689, in which Parliament lists the abuses of James II and declares new powers for itself. Several of the abuses in the Declaration seem to have been taken, more or less verbatim, from a *Pennsylvania Evening Post* article. And the most memorable phrases in the Declaration seem to be least Jefferson's: "That all men are created equal" is a sentiment from Euripides which Jefferson copied in his literary commonplace book as a boy; "Life, Liberty, and the pursuit of Happiness" was a cliché of the times, appearing in numerous political documents (Dumbauld).

Though Jefferson's draft of the Declaration can hardly be considered his in any exclusive sense of authorship, the document underwent still more expropriation at the hands of Congress, who made eighty-six changes (Kinneavy, *Theory* 438). They cut the draft from 211 lines to 147. They did considerable editing to temper what they saw as Jefferson's emotional style: For example, Jefferson's phrase "sacred & undeniable" was changed to the more restrained "self-evident." Congress excised controversial passages, such as Jefferson's condemnation of slavery. Thus, we should find it instructive to note, Jefferson's few attempts at original expression were those least acceptable to Congress.

If Jefferson submitted the Declaration for a college writing class as his own writing, he might well be charged with plagiarism.[3] The idea of Jefferson as author is but convenient shorthand. Actually, the Declaration arose out of a cultural and rhetorical milieu, was composed of traces—and was, in effect, team written. Jefferson deserves credit for bringing disparate traces together, for helping to mold and articulate the milieu, for creating the all-important draft. Jefferson's skills as a writer was his ability to borrow traces effectively and to find appropriate contexts for them. As Michael Halliday says, "[C]reativeness does not consist in producing new sentences. The newness of a sentence is a quite unimportant—and unascertainable—property and 'creativity' in language lies in the speaker's ability to create new meanings: to realize the potentiality of language for the indefinite extension of its resources to new contexts of situation. . . . Our most 'creative' acts may be precisely among those that are realized through highly repetitive forms of behaviour" (*Explorations* 42). The creative writer is the creative borrower, in other words.

Intertextuality can be seen working similarly in contemporary forums. Recall this scene from a recent Pepsi commercial: A young boy in jeans jacket, accompanied by dog, stands in some desolate plains crossroads next to a gas station, next to which is a soft drink machine. An alien spacecraft, resembling the one in Spielberg's *Close Encounters of the Third Kind,* appears overhead. To the boy's joyful amazement, the spaceship hovers over the vending machine and begins sucking Pepsi cans into the ship. It takes *only* Pepsi's, then eventually takes the entire machine. The ad closes with a graphic: "Pepsi. The Choice of a New Generation."

Clearly, the commercial presupposes familiarity with Spielberg's movie or, at least, with his pacific vision of alien spacecraft. We see several American clichés, well-worn signs from the Depression era: the desolate plains, the general store, the pop machine, the country boy with dog. These distinctively American traces are juxtaposed against images from science fiction and the sixties catchphrase "new generation" in the coda. In this array of signs, we have tradition and counter-tradition harmonized. Pepsi squeezes itself in the middle, and thus becomes the great American conciliator. The ad's use of irony may serve to distract viewers momentarily from noticing how Pepsi achieves its purpose by assigning itself an exalted role through use of the intertext.

We find an interesting example of practical presupposition in John Kifner's *New York Times* headline article reporting on the Kent State incident of 1970:

> Four students at Kent State University, two of them women, were shot to death this afternoon by a volley of National Guard gunfire. At least 8 other students were wounded.
>
> The burst of gunfire came about 20 minutes after the guardsmen broke up a noon rally on the Commons, a grassy campus gathering spot, by lobbing tear gas at a crowd of about 1,000 young people.

From one perspective, the phrase "two of them women" is a simple statement of fact; however, it presupposes a certain attitude—that the event, horrible enough as it was, is more significant because two of the persons killed were women. It might be going too far to say that the phrase presupposes a sexist attitude ("women aren't supposed to be killed in battles"), but can we imagine the phrase "two of them men" in this context? Though equally factual, this wording would have been considered odd in 1970 (and probably today as well) because it presupposes a cultural mindset alien from the one dominant at the time. "Two of them women" is shocking (and hence it was reported) because it upsets the sense of order of the readers, in this case the American public.

Additionally (and more than a little ironically), the text contains a number of traces which have the effect of blunting the shock of the event. Notice that the students were not shot by National Guardsmen, but were shot "by a volley of . . . gunfire"; the tear gas was "lobbed"; and the event occurred at a "grassy campus gathering spot." "Volley" and "lobbed" are military terms, but with connections to sport as well; "grassy campus gathering spot" suggests a picnic; "burst" can recall the glorious sight of bombs "bursting" in "The Star-Spangled Banner." This pastiche of signs casts the text into a certain context, making it distinctively American. We might say that the turbulent milieu of the sixties provided a distinctive array of signs from which John Kifner borrowed to produce his article.

Each of the three texts examined contains phrases or images familiar to its audience or presupposes certain audience attitudes. Thus the intertext exerts its influence partly in the form of audience expectation. We might then say that the audience of each of these texts is as responsible for its production as the writer. That, in essence, readers, not writers, create discourse.

THE POWER OF DISCOURSE COMMUNITY

And, indeed, this is what some poststructuralist critics suggest, those who prefer a broader conception of intertext or who look beyond the intertext to the social framework regulating textual produc-

tion: to what Michel Foucault calls "the discursive formation," what Stanley Fish calls "the interpretive community," and what Patricia Bizzell calls "the discourse community."

A "discourse community" is a group of individuals bound by a common interest who communicate through approved channels and whose discourse is regulated. An individual may belong to several professional, public, or personal discourse communities. Examples would include the community of engineers whose research area is fluid mechanics; alumni of the University of Michigan; Magnavox employees; the members of the Porter family; and members of the Indiana Teachers of Writing. The approved channels we can call "forums." Each forum has a distinct history and rules governing appropriateness to which members are obliged to adhere. These rules may be more or less apparent, more or less institutionalized, more or less specific to each community. Examples of forums include professional publications like *Rhetoric Review, English Journal,* and *Creative Computing;* public media like *Newsweek* and *Runner's World;* professional conferences (the annual meeting of fluid power engineers, the 4C's); company board meetings; family dinner tables; and the monthly meeting of the Indiana chapter of the Izaak Walton League.

A discourse community shares assumptions about what objects are appropriate for examination and discussion, what operating functions are performed on those objects, what constitutes "evidence" and "validity," and what formal conventions are followed. A discourse community may have a well-established *ethos;* or it may have competing factions and indefinite boundaries. It may be in a "pre-paradigm" state (Kuhn), that is, having an ill-defined regulating system and no clear leadership. Some discourse communities are firmly established, such as the scientific community, the medical profession, and the justice system, to cite a few from Foucault's list. In these discourse communities, as Leitch says, "a speaker must be 'qualified' to talk; he has to belong to a community of scholarship; and he is required to possess a prescribed body of knowledge (doctrine). . . . [This system] operates to constrain discourse; it establishes limits and regularities. . . . who may speak, what may be spoken, and how it is to be said; in addition [rules] prescribe what is true and false, what is reasonable and what foolish, and what is meant and what not. Finally, they work to deny the material existence of discourse itself" (145).

A text is "acceptable" within a forum only insofar as it reflects the community episteme (to use Foucault's term). On a simple level, this means that for a manuscript to be accepted for publication in the *Journal of Applied Psychology*, it must follow certain formatting conventions: It must have the expected social science sections (i.e., review of literature, methods, results, discussion), and it must use the journal's version of APA documentation. However, these are only superficial features of the forum. On a more essential level, the manuscript must reveal certain characteristics, have an *ethos* (in the broadest possible sense) conforming to the standards of the discourse community: It must demonstrate (or at least claim) that it contributes knowledge to the field, it must demonstrate familiarity with the work of previous researchers in the field, it must use a scientific method in analyzing its results (showing acceptance of the truth-value of statistical demonstration), it must meet standards for test design and analysis of results, it must adhere to standards determining degree of accuracy. The expectations, conventions, and attitudes of this discourse community—the readers, writers, and publishers of *Journal of Applied Psychology*—will influence aspiring psychology researchers, shaping not only how they write but also their character within that discourse community.

The poststructuralist view challenges the classical assumption that writing is a simple linear, one-way movement: The writer creates a text which produces some change in an audience. A poststructuralist rhetoric examines how audience (in the form of community expectations and standards) influences textual production and, in so doing, guides the development of the writer.

This view is of course open to criticism for its apparent determinism, for devaluing the contribution of individual writers and making them appear merely tools of the discourse community (charges

which Foucault answers in "Discourse on Language"). If these regulating systems are so constraining, how can an individual merge? What happens to the idea of the lone inspired writer and the sacred autonomous text?

Both notions take a pretty hard knock. Genuine originality is difficult within the confines of a well-regulated system. Genius is possible, but it may be constrained. Foucault cites the example of Gregor Mendel, whose work in the nineteenth century was excluded from the prevailing community of biologists because he "spoke of objects, employed methods and placed himself within a theoretical perspective totally alien to the biology of his time. . . . Mendel spoke the truth, but he was not *dans le vrai* (within the true)" (224). Frank Lentricchia cites a similar example from the literary community. Robert Frost "achieved magazine publication only five times between 1895 and 1912, a period during which he wrote a number of poems later acclaimed . . . [because] in order to write within the dominant sense of the poetic in the United States in the last decade of the nineteenth century and the first decade of the twentieth, one had to employ a diction, syntax, and prosody heavily favoring Shelley and Tennyson. One also had to assume a certain stance, a certain world-weary idealism which took care not to refer too concretely to the world of which one was weary" (197, 199).

Both examples point to the exclusionary power of discourse communities and raise serious questions about the freedom of the writer: chiefly, does the writer have any? Is any writer doomed to plagiarism? Can any text be said to be new? Are creativity and genius actually possible? Was Jefferson a creative genius or a blatant plagiarist?

Certainly we want to avoid both extremes. Even if the writer is locked into a cultural matrix and is constrained by the intertext of the discourse community, the writer has freedom within the immediate rhetorical context.[4] Furthermore, successful writing helps to redefine the matrix—and in that way becomes creative. (Jefferson's Declaration contributed to defining the notion of America for its discourse community.) Every new text has the potential to alter the Text in some way; in fact, every text admitted into a discourse community changes the constitution of the community—and discourse communities can revise their discursive practices, as the Mendel and Frost examples suggest.

Writing is an attempt to exercise the will, to identify the self within the constraints of some discourse community. We are constrained insofar as we must inevitably borrow the traces, codes, and signs which we inherit and which our discourse community imposes. We are free insofar as we do what we can to encounter and learn new codes, to intertwine codes in new ways, and to expand our semiotic potential—with our goal being to effect change and establish our identities within the discourse communities we choose to enter.

THE PEDAGOGY OF INTERTEXTUALITY

Intertextuality is not new. It may remind some of Eliot's notion of tradition, though the parameters are certainly broader. It is an important concept, though. It counters what I see as one prevailing composition pedagogy, one favoring a romantic image of the writer, offering as role models the creative essayists, the Sunday Supplement freelancers, the Joan Didions, E. B. Whites, Calvin Trillins, and Russell Bakers. This dashing image appeals to our need for intellectual heroes; but underlying it may be an anti-rhetorical view: that writers are born, not made; that writing is individual, isolated, and internal; not social but eccentric.

This view is firmly set in the intertext of our discipline. Our anthologies glorify the individual essayists, whose work is valued for its timelessness and creativity. Freshman rhetorics announce as the writer's proper goals personal insight, originality, and personal voice, or tell students that motivations for writing come from "within." Generally, this pedagogy assumes that such a thing as the writer actually exists—an autonomous writer exercising a free, creative will through the writing act— and that the writing process proceeds linearly from writer to text to reader. This partial picture of the process can all too readily become *the* picture, and our students can all too readily learn to overlook vital facets of discourse production.

When we romanticize composition by overemphasizing the autonomy of the writer, important questions are overlooked, the same questions an intertextual view of writing would provoke: To what extent is the writer's product itself a part of a larger community writing process? How does the discourse community influence writers and readers within it? These are essential questions, but are perhaps outside the prevailing episteme of composition pedagogy, which presupposes the autonomous status of the writer as independent *cogito*. Talking about writing in terms of "social forces influencing the writer" raises the specter of determinism, and so is anathema.

David Bartholomae summarizes this issue very nicely: "The struggle of the student writer is not the struggle to bring out that which is within; it is the struggle to carry out those ritual activities that grant our entrance into a closed society" (300). When we teach writing only as the act of "bringing out what is within," we risk undermining our own efforts. Intertextuality reminds us that "carrying out ritual activities" is also part of the writing process. Barthes reminds us that "the 'I' which approaches the text is already itself a plurality of other texts, of codes which are infinite" (10).

Intertextuality suggests that our goal should be to help students learn to write for the discourse communities they choose to join. Students need help developing out of what Joseph Williams calls their "pre-socialized cognitive states." According to Williams, pre-socialized writers are not sufficiently immersed in their discourse community to produce competent discourse: They do not know what can be presupposed, are not conscious of the distinctive intertextuality of the community, may be only superficially acquainted with explicit conventions. (Williams cites the example of the freshman whose paper for the English teacher begins "Shakespeare is a famous Elizabethan dramatist.") Our immediate goal is to produce "socialized writers," who are full-fledged members of their discourse community, producing competent, useful discourse within that community. Our long-range goal might be "post-socialized writers," those who have achieved such a degree of confidence, authority, power, or achievement in the discourse community so as to become part of the regulating body. They are able to vary conventions and question assumptions—i.e., effect change in communities—without fear of exclusion.

Intertextuality has the potential to affect all facets of our composition pedagogy. Certainly it supports writing across the curriculum as a mechanism for introducing students to the regulating systems of discourse communities. It raises questions about heuristics: Do different discourse communities apply different heuristics? It asserts the value of critical reading in the composition classroom. It requires that we rethink our ideas about plagiarism: Certainly *imitatio* is an important stage in the linguistic development of the writer.

The most significant application might be in the area of audience analysis. Current pedagogies assume that when writers analyze audiences they should focus on the expected flesh-and-blood readers. Intertextuality suggests that the proper focus of audience analysis is not the audience as receivers per se, but the intertext of the discourse community. Instead of collecting demographic data about age, educational level, and social status, the writer might instead ask questions about the intertext: What are the conventional presuppositions of this community? In what forums do they assemble? What are the methodological assumptions? What is considered "evidence," "valid argument," and "proof"? A sample heuristic for such an analysis—what I term "forum analysis"—is included as an appendix.

A critical reading of the discourse of a community may be the best way to understand it. (We see a version of this message in the advice to examine a journal before submitting articles for publication.) Traditionally, anthologies have provided students with reading material. However, the typical anthologies have two serious problems: (1) limited range—generally they overemphasize literary or expressive discourse; (2) unclear context—they frequently remove readings from their original contexts, thus disguising their intertextual nature. Several recently published readers have attempted to provide a broader selection of readings in various forums, and actually discuss intertextuality. Maimon's *Readings in the Arts and Sciences,* Kinneavy's *Writing in the Liberal Arts Tradition,* and Bazerman's *The Informed Writer* are especially noteworthy.

Writing assignments should be explicitly intertextual. If we regard each written product as a stage in a larger process—the dialectic process within a discourse community—then the individual writer's work is part of a web, part of a community search for truth and meaning. Writing assignments might take the form of dialogue with other writers: Writing letters in response to articles is one kind of dialectic (e.g., letters responding to *Atlantic Monthly* or *Science* articles). Research assignments might be more community oriented rather than topic oriented; students might be asked to become involved in communities of researchers (e.g., the sociologists examining changing religious attitudes in American college students). The assignments in Maimon's *Writing in the Arts and Sciences* are excellent in this regard.

Intertextual theory suggests that the key criteria for evaluating writing should be "acceptability" within some discourse community. "Acceptability" includes, but goes well beyond, adherence to formal conventions. It includes choosing the "right" topic, applying the appropriate critical methodology, adhering to standards for evidence and validity, and in general adopting the community's discourse values—and of course borrowing the appropriate traces. Success is measured by the writer's ability to know what can be presupposed and to borrow that community's traces effectively to create a text that contributes to the maintenance or, possibly, the definition of the community. The writer is constrained by the community, and by its intertextual preferences and prejudices, but the effective writer works to assert the will against those community constraints to effect change.

The Pepsi commercial and the Kent State news article show effective uses of the intertext. In the Kent State piece, John Kifner mixes picnic imagery ("grassy campus gathering spot," "young people") with violent imagery ("burst of gunfire") to dramatize the event. The Pepsi ad writers combine two unlikely sets of traces, linking folksy depression-era American imagery with sci-fi imagery "stolen" from Spielberg. For this creative intertwining of traces, both discourses can probably be measured successful in their respective forums.

CODA

Clearly much of what intertextuality supports is already institutionalized (e.g., writing-across-the-curriculum programs). And yet, in freshman comp texts and anthologies especially, there is this tendency to see writing as individual, as isolated, as heroic. Even after demonstrating quite convincingly that the Declaration was written by a team freely borrowing from a cultural intertext, Elaine Maimon insists, against all the evidence she herself has collected, that "Despite the additions, deletions, and changes in wording that it went through, the Declaration is still Jefferson's writing" (*Readings* 26). Her saying this presupposes that the reader has just concluded the opposite.

When we give our students romantic role models like E. B. White, Joan Didion, and Lewis Thomas, we create unrealistic expectations. This type of writer has often achieved post-socialized status within some discourse community (Thomas in the scientific community, for instance). Can we realistically expect our students to achieve this state without first becoming socialized, without learning first what it means to write within a social context? Their role models ought not be only romantic heroes but also community writers like Jefferson, the anonymous writers of the Pepsi commercial—the Adsos of the world, not just the Aristotles. They need to see writers whose products are more evidently part of a larger process and whose work more clearly produces meaning in social contexts.

Notes

1. The dangers of defining intertextuality too simplistically are discussed by Owen Miller in "Intertextual Identity," *Identity of the Literary Text,* ed. Mario J. Valdés and Owen Miller (Toronto: U of Toronto P, 1985), 19–40. Miller points out that intertextuality "addresses itself to a plurality of concepts" (19).

2. For fuller discussion see Jonathan Culler, *The Pursuit of Signs* (Ithaca: Cornell UP, 1981), 100–16. Michael Halliday elaborates on the theory of presupposition somewhat, too, differentiating between exophoric and endophoric presupposition. The meaning of any text at least partly relies on exophoric references, i.e., external presuppositions. Endophoric references in the form of cohesive devices and connections within a text also affect meaning, but cohesion in a text depends ultimately on the audience making exophoric connections to prior texts, connections that may not be cued by explicit cohesive devices. See M. A. K. Halliday and Ruqaiya Hasan, *Cohesion in English* (London: Longman, 1976).

3. Miller cautions us about intertextuality and *post hoc ergo propter hoc* reasoning. All we can safely note is that phrases in the Declaration also appear in other, earlier documents. Whether or not the borrowing was intentional on Jefferson's part or whether the prior documents "caused" the Declaration (in any sense of the word) is not ascertainable.

4. Robert Scholes puts it this way: "If you play chess, you can only do certain things with the pieces, otherwise you are not playing chess. But those constraints do not in themselves tell you what moves to make." See *Textual Power* (New Haven: Yale UP, 1985), 153.

Works Cited

Barthes, Roland. *S/Z.* Trans. Richard Miller. New York: Hill and Wang, 1974.

Bartholomae, David. "Writing Assignments: Where Writing Begins." *fforum.* Ed. Patricia L. Stock. Upper Montclair, NJ: Boynton/Cook, 1983.

Bazerman, Charles. *The Informed Writer.* 2nd ed. Boston: Houghton Mifflin, 1985.

Becker, Carl. *The Declaration of Independence.* 2nd ed. New York: Random, Vintage, 1942.

Bizzell, Patricia. "Cognition, Convention, and Certainty: What We Need to Know about Writing." *PRE/TEXT* 3 (1982): 213–43.

Culler, Jonathan. *The Pursuit of Signs.* Ithaca: Cornell UP 1981.

Dumbauld, Edward. *The Declaration of Independence.* 2nd ed. Norman: U of Oklahoma P, 1968.

Eco, Umberto. *The Name of the Rose.* Trans. William Weaver. San Diego: Harcourt Brace Jovanovich, 1983.

Fish, Stanley. *Is There a Text in This Class?* Cambridge: Harvard UP, 1980.

Foucault, Michel. *The Archaeology of Knowledge and the Discourse on Language.* Trans. A. M. Sheridan Smith. New York: Harper & Row, 1972.

Halliday, M. A. K. *Explorations in the Functions of Language.* New York: Elsevier, 1973.

Halliday, M. A. K., and Ruqaiya Hasan. *Cohesion in English.* London: Longman, 1976.

Kifner, John. "4 Kent State Students Killed by Troops." *New York Times* 5 May 1970: 1.

Kinneavy, James L. *A Theory of Discourse.* Englewood Cliffs: Prentice-Hall, 1971.

———. et al. *Writing in the Liberal Arts Tradition.* New York: Harper & Row, 1985.

Kuhn, Thomas S. *The Structure of Scientific Revolutions.* 2nd ed. Chicago: U of Chicago P, 1970.

Leitch, Vincent B. *Deconstructive Criticism.* New York: Cornell UP, 1983.

Lentricchia, Frank. *After the New Criticism.* Chicago: U of Chicago P, 1980.

Maimon, Elaine P., et al. *Readings in the Arts and Sciences.* Boston: Little, Brown, 1984.

———. *Writing in the Arts and Sciences.* Cambridge: Winthrop, 1981.

Miller, Owen. "Intertextual Identity." *Identity of the Literary Text.* Ed. Mario J. Valdés and Owen Miller. Toronto: U of Toronto P, 1985, 19–40.

Scholes, Robert. *Textual Power.* New Haven: Yale UP, 1985.

Williams, Joseph. "Cognitive Development, Critical Thinking, and the Teaching of Writing." Conference on Writing, Meaning, and Higher Order Reasoning, University of Chicago, 15 May 1984.

Appendix: Forum Analysis

Background

Identify the forum by name and organizational affiliation.

Is there an expressed editorial policy, philosophy, or expression of belief? What purpose does the forum serve? Why does it exist?

What is the disciplinary orientation?

How large is the forum? Who are its members? Its leaders? Its readership?

In what manner does the forum assemble (e.g., newsletter, journal, conference, weekley meeting)? How frequently?

What is the origin of the forum? Why did it come into existence? What is its history? Its political background? Its traditions?

What reputation does the forum have among its own members? How is it regarded by others?

Discourse Conventions

Who Speaks/Writes?

Who is granted status as speaker/writer? Who decides who speaks/writes in the forum? By what criteria are speakers/writers selected?

What kind of people speak/write in this forum? Credentials? Disciplinary orientation? Academic or professional background?

Who are the important figures in this forum? Whose work or experience is most frequently cited?

What are the important sources cited in the forum? What are the key works, events, experiences that it is assumed members of the forum know?

To Whom Do They Speak/Write?

Who is addressed in the forum? What are the characteristics of the assumed audience?

What are the audience's needs assumed to be? To what use(s) is the audience expected to put the information?

What is the audience's background assumed to be? Level of proficiency, experience, and knowledge of subject matter? Credentials?

What are the beliefs, attitudes, values, prejudices of the addressed audience?

What Do They Speak/Write About?

What topics or issues does the forum consider? What are allowable subjects? What topics are valued?

What methodology or methodologies are accepted? Which theoretical approach is preferred: deduction (theoretical argumentation) or induction (evidence)?

What constitutes "validity," "evidence," and "proof" in the forum (e.g., personal experience/observation, testing and measurement, theoretical or statistical analysis)?

How Do They Say/Write It?

Form

What types of discourse does the forum admit (e.g., articles, reviews, speeches, poems)? How long are the discourses?

What are the dominant modes of organization?

What formatting conventions are present: headings, tables and graphs, illustrations, abstracts?

Style

What documentation form(s) is used?

Syntactic characteristics?

Technical or specialized jargon? Abbreviations?

Tone? What stance do writers/speakers take relative to audience?

Manuscript mechanics?

Other Considerations?

An Apology for Form; or, Who Took the Form Out of the Process?

Richard M. Coe

"An Apology" appeared in College English *49 (1987): 13–28.*

Form . . . is an arousing and fulfillment of desires. A work has form in so far as one part of it leads a reader to anticipate another part, to be gratified by the sequence.

(BURKE, *Counter-Statement* 124)

Desire is the presence of an *absence*.

(KOJEVE 134)

Translated into terms of the composition class, "form" becomes "organization" and brings with it . . . the most dismal stuff that students and teachers must deal with. And yet, the concept of form in discourse is utterly fascinating, for it concerns the way in which the mind perceives infinitely complex relationships. The way, indeed, in which the mind constructs discourse.

(WINTEROWD 163)

I. HISTORY, POLITICS, AND THEORY

At this point in the history of our profession, the conflicts within the fold of the faithful (i.e., among adherents of "the process approach" to teaching composition) are far more significant than the opposition between process and "product" approaches. Which process emphasis one chooses matters a great deal, not only to the type of success students may achieve but also to such relationships as those between writing and humanistic education, between writers as individuals and writing as process. Certain conceptions of process (and of the relationship between form and process) prevent us from realizing the full potential of process approaches to composition.

Historically, the process approach must be understood as antithesis. At the Dartmouth Conference and elsewhere, practitioners such as John Dixon, D. Gordon Rohman, Ken Macrorie, Stephen Tchudi, Donald Graves, Donald Murray, et al. spoke and wrote from their own experiences, but also in response to a traditional way of teaching writing—proffering an antidote, if you will, to the inadequacies of that traditional approach. Their emphases, as always in an antithetical situation, were defined to some significant extent by what they were opposing. To reach a clearer understanding of writing as process, we must sublate (i.e., simultaneously transcend and conserve) this antithesis.

Before distinguishing types of process approaches, it is important to clarify the distinction between process writing and what preceded it. These days, it has become commonplace to juxtapose process writing with a so-called "product approach." Rather than defining what the traditional approach is, this inadequate and derogatory title shifts our attention to what it is not (i.e., not process). Properly termed, what the past two decades saw was a conflict between a (traditional) *formal* approach and a (renewed) *process* approach. To sublate the antithesis and avoid the simplistic

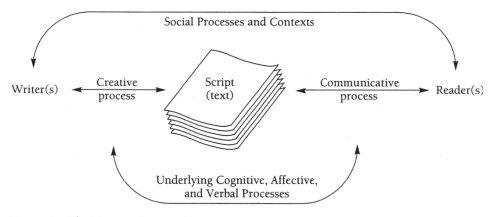

Figure 1. The Process Approach

choice, we must clarify the relationship between form and process, define the place of forms in the process.

Although it dabbled occasionally (and inaccurately) in process—what else is outlining?—the traditional formal approach essentially taught good form. It answered, formally, the question, "What is good writing?" Because it radically dichotomized form from "content," its answer emphasized structure: sentence structure, paragraph structure, essay structure, even the proper structures for term papers, business letters, resumes—all that Winterowd calls "dismal stuff." If the proper forms were defined, they could be described and exemplified for students. After students wrote, they could be shown where their writing failed to match the ideal forms. And then, the formalists hoped, students would correct their writing to create a better match.

Unfortunately, most students failed to do this because the formalists told them only *what* to do, not also *how* to do it. Until a few decades ago, however, this was not a major social problem because such students also failed to stay in school. Although the data vary from country to country and region to region, we may safely say that only after World War II do even half the students who start grade one complete high school. But then radical changes in the nature of work and other social realities led to declining drop-out rates and increasing post-secondary enrollment, creating a need for a pedagogy that would work with students who used to disappear before senior high school—and thus forming a historical opening for process approaches (Coe, "Literacy 'Crises'"). For any process approach, by definition, concerns itself with one or more of the *hows* formalists traditionally ignore: *how* writers create; *how* writers think, feel, and verbalize to enable writing; *how* writers learn while writing; *how* writing communicates with readers; and *how* social processes and contexts influence the shaping and interpreting of texts.[1]

There is not one process approach; there are many. All share an emphasis on process, and any process approach inevitably involves intervening in the creative process, if only by recontextualizing it. But writing comprises many processes, and the strongest pedagogical conflict is between those who emphasize writing as a learning process and those who emphasize writing as a communicative process (see Fig. 1; cf. Perelman 471–72, Faigley 527–28).

Those concerned with process writing as a means of learning tend to emphasize underlying mental processes and techniques for destructuring invention, for enabling unconscious processes (e.g., freewriting). Those concerned with writing as a process with worldly uses tend to emphasize communicative process and techniques for structuring invention, for enabling conscious planning (e.g., heuristics, nutshelling). Although there are certainly senses in which both emphases deal with writing as social, these are very different senses, and the treatment of form also differs radically between these two emphases, which I shall call Expressionist and New Rhetorical.[2]

Behind the traditional conception of form lies a long-dead metaphor—one so dead we fail to notice it—inherited from such conservative neo-Classicists as Samuel Johnson. In this metaphor, form is a *container* to be filled (hence the term *content*). If the metaphor is to make sense, our conception of the matter with which we fill forms must be sufficiently "liquid" (i.e., independent of form) to accept the out-lines imposed by the shape of the form. This is not Cicero's conception of form, but it is Samuel Johnson's, which is why he can speak of language as a dress thought puts on. For neo-Classicists, ideas exist first; then we dress them in (socially conventional) words and forms. (It is highly significant that most New Critics, neo-Romantics when they deal with literature, adopt this neo-Classical conception of form when they must teach composition.)

Although advocates of Expressionist process writing are radical neo-Romantics, and thus more consistent with what was and probably still is the majority approach to literature, they continue to operate in terms of a form/content dichotomy. For them, however, form grows organically to fit the shape of the subject matter. Thus there is little need to teach form except as an afterthought (along with punctuation) late in both the teaching and writing processes. Thus the Expressionist process approach and the traditional formal approach are indeed opposites: where the traditional approach ignores content to teach form, Expressionist process writing enables content, allowing form to develop organically. Interestingly, Ken Macrorie's pragmatic description of "good form" represents the same stylistic values (and often the same particulars) as does Strunk and White's; but *Telling Writing* presents them as secondary, to be dealt with during revision, while in *The Elements of Style* they are virtually the whole ball of wax. And the very act of enabling content, of encouraging student writers to write about what concerns them, does create the potential of writing as a liberating *social* act of self-discovery (cf. Schultz).

In *The Philosophy of Rhetoric,* I. A. Richards urges us to "avoid some traditional mistakes—among them the use of bad analogies which tie us up if we take them too seriously." Some of these bad analogies, Richards asserts,

> are notorious; for example, *the opposition between form and content.* . . . These are wretchedly inconvenient metaphors. So is that other which makes language a dress which thought puts on. We shall do better to think of meaning as though it were a plant that has grown—not a can that has been filled or a lump of clay that has been moulded. (12, emphasis added)

Richards reminds us that implicit in the form/content opposition is the "dead" neo-Classical metaphor which makes form a container. If form is like a container, then form and "content" are relatively independent: a can can hold peas (or marbles) quite as well as beans, and pouring your peas (or marbles) from one can to another does not affect their substance. Like clay, "content" is malleable, capable of adapting to any mold without changing its essential nature.

These metaphors are "inconvenient," Richards argues, because they lead us to misconceive the relation of form to (what we should *not* call) "content." There is no meaning without form: information is *formed* matter (which becomes meaningful in relation to contexts). When you *transform* a message into a new form, as when you translate a poem, you have re*form*ulated it, thus to some extent changing the meaning. Information is made by putting data (i e , subject matter) *in formation,* by forming. What neo-Classical formalists called "content" is unknowable in its formlessness; it becomes substantive and knowable only when formed. (And this formed matter becomes meaning-full only when someone relates it to some context—but that is another issue.)

Richards' assertion, perhaps controversial when made in 1936, is now thoroughly confirmed by research in cognitive psychology, information theory, and other such disciplines. As Richards argued, perception itself is humanly impossible until

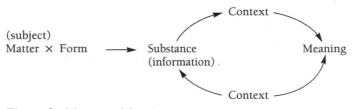

Figure 2. Matter to Meaning

sensory input has been formed (i.e., coded, juxtaposed with mental schema that allow us to perceive pattern in the thousands of "bits" of input that would otherwise overwhelm our mental capacities). As the information theorists would have it:

$$\text{Noise} \times \text{Code} \longrightarrow \text{Information}$$

Broadly, then, we can define form in terms of its function in a process of forming. This definition is purposively tautological: whatever is used to inform—to impose pattern on noise, cosmos on chaos—is form. Even when we define form narrowly (as rhetorical forms, patterns of development, and so on), we should retain this process conception of form, which reminds us of function.

In composition, as elsewhere, the formalists promulgated a falsely static sense of form. They ignored, rather than refuted, Richards. Meanwhile, the conception we need to sublate the static form/content dichotomy awaited us in the New Rhetoric: the theory we find in Richards and, especially, Kenneth Burke: later from practitioners such as Francis Christensen and Ann Berthoff come practical applications to teaching composition.

Frank D'Angelo summarized the concept this way in *A Conceptual Theory of Rhetoric:*

> Following Aristotle's system I take form to be closely related to the formal principle, i.e., one of the causes of a mode of being which produces discourse. . . . Patterns of development are not only organizational, they . . . also . . . serve a heuristic function. . . . They are . . . dynamic organizational processes, symbolic manifestations of underlying mental processes, and not merely conventional static patterns. (56–57)

In this conception form is both generative and constraining—or, better said, generative because constraining. Form is empty, an absence. But this emptiness has shape (i.e., form). In human beings, at least, this emptiness creates a desire to find what might fill it—which is at least part of what Burke means in "Definition of Man" when he wryly defines us as "rotten with perfection" (*Language* 16 ff.).

Another aspect of Burke's point—Burke's significant points are never singular—reminds me of Donald Murray (the writer, *not* the theoretician of writing) describing invention as knowing how to sit waiting under the lightning. Murray recounted how various wordings of a particular subject struck him until, recognizing the last as a poem, he wrote it out ("Talking to Yourself"; cf. Murray's essay in Waldrep's collection).

I take his report of the process as exceptionally significant because it sublates his own theory. Somehow, Murray recognized a particular set of words *as a poem.* His selection of this version as poem was also, inevitably, a rejection/deflection of other versions (as non-poem or, at least, as inferior poem). And his recognition could only have occurred because Murray had within his mind a schema for poem, an abstract (i.e., empty) formal idea of *poem*—a "perfection" through which Murray is "rotten," far beyond his willingness to admit, *with the social.* For since this poem was later recognized by an editor (hence published) and by readers, I take it that Murray's schema of poem is shared, not idiosyncratic.

In short, we have here a shared form "provided by language," a cultural form, a social structure enabling the creative process. That Murray, like many writers, finds it useful to ignore the place of cultural/social structures in his writing process is neither here nor there—it certainly does not imply that teachers of writing should ignore the impact of such structures on the creative process.

Form, in its emptiness, is heuristic, for it guides a structured search. Faced with the emptiness of a form, a *human* being seeks matter to fill it. Form becomes, therefore, a motive for generating information. Like any heuristic, it motivates a search for information of a certain type: when the searchers can anticipate what shape of stuff they seek, generation is less free, but much more efficient; by constraining the search, form directs attention. (Heuristics, in this sense, are distinct from *un*structuring discovery techniques such as freewriting.)

Consider, for example, the form we entitle "the five-paragraph essay." In my more cynical moments, I suspect that the better part of several generations of students have been socialized to believe that, at least in school, there are three reasons for (and/or three examples of) anything. Although the five-paragraph essay originates as an exercise in using the Classical *proposition + partition* to structure an essay, and although there is no reason whatsoever why it should not sometimes contain two or four or more body paragraphs, students who have memorized the form almost inevitably generate three.

In my less cynical moments, I recognize the good in this: left on their own, many of these same students would discover only one reason or example. Thus even this static school form has some liberal value. My main point here, however, is that the form, *because it contains three* **empty** *slots,* motivates students to continue inventing until they have discovered subject matter to fill three slots. (For a broader critique of formal tyranny in school essays, see Fort.)

In this respect, any form is like the forms we are often served by various bureaucracies (e.g., income tax forms). They move us to consider certain types of things, to search for particular information and, generally, to find something (if only "N/A") to fill every slot. And the other side of this mundane example is the sense in which all heuristics, not just the tagmemic grid but also the Pentad and the journalists' 5Ws, are empty forms whose shaped emptinesses motivate writers to generate appropriate information.

Rhetorical structures are in this sense the social memory of standard responses to particular types of rhetorical situations and subject matter.[3] Like language, form is thus social. One function of discourse communities is to provide, prescribe, and prefer forms. Learning conventional forms, often by a tacit process of "indwelling," is a way of learning a community's discourse, gaining access, communicating with that community. For a form implies a strategy of response, an attitude, a way of sorting factors, sizing up situations. If a text, as Burke would have it, dances an attitude, then forms are attitudes frozen in synchronicity. Insofar as a form is socially shared, adopting the form involves adopting, at least to some extent, the community's attitude, abiding by its expectations.

Readers who make up the community use these same forms to focus their attention, to anticipate as they approach and move through a text, as they use the text to reinvent meanings. Recognizing forms—both of the whole text (sonnet, editorial, term paper) and of parts within the text (definition, example, instructions)—is an important aspect of reading. Readers' abilities to recognize—even (or perhaps especially) subliminally—various kinds of formal patterns of development allow them to "process" text (i.e., to understand it) efficiently. Those who fail to recognize forms, perhaps because they are from another culture or subculture, not part of the community, often misinterpret function, hence meaning.

Writers' abilities to use formal patterns particular readers will recognize allow them to communicate accurately and effectively. In general, communication is most likely to succeed, to generate understanding rather than misunderstanding, when writer(s) and reader(s) know and use the same forms.[4] (For writers, "use" may mean reproducing *or varying* the form; in either case, recognition enables reading.)

Conventional forms, as they function in both creative and communicative processes, are a major part of what makes those processes social. And, to continue along these Burkean lines, inasmuch as an attitude is an incipient action, i.e., a potential action waiting for an activating situation, so forms are suasive, rhetorical insofar as by shaping our attitudes they guide our responses to situations.

Thus an example somewhat more interesting than the five-paragraph essay or a bureaucratic form is the form that allows us to "know" there are two sides to a question or issue even before we know what the question or issue is. The apparent motive behind this form is usually to get someone who is seeing only one side to look for another. In that sense, this is a generative form. Perhaps because it fits so neatly with binary dualism and other reductionist tendencies in modern Western culture, however, it is also a constraining form that allows us to feel fulfilled after we have discovered *only* two sides: how else can we explain several decades during which otherwise intelligent Westerners looked at the Middle East and saw *only* two sides? And, worse, this form becomes the basis of Golden Mean dualism, which allows us to know that both extremes are wrong and the liberal middle correct even before we know what the issue is. (What is the Golden Mean in the conflict between rapist and victim?)

As this example indicates, form is cultural, not neutral. The sense in which conventional forms are culture-bound is most apparent: but other sorts of forms; such as those discussed by D'Angelo (*Conceptual Theory* 38–60) or those Burke calls progressive and repetitive (*Counter-Statement* 124–25), vary more from culture to culture than most of us realize.

A form may be generative insofar as it motivates a search for more information; but any form also biases the direction of the searching and constrains against the discovery of information that does not fit the form. A particular message may be very difficult (if not impossible) to communicate within the parameters of a conventional form. Literary history is filled with examples of writers who needed to invent new forms to communicate new messages. More mundanely, certain messages are hard to squeeze into a business letter, for example, because

they exceed the maximum effective length of that form (i.e., two typewritten pages). A pedagogically significant example is the standard formal technique for achieving focus, which often constrains against what a student writer has set out to say (Coe, "If Not to Narrow"). Form can, in this sense, be ideological: when a particular form constrains against the communication of a message contrary to the interests of some power elite, it serves an ideological function. Insofar as form guides function, formal values may carry implicit moral/political values.

As this series of examples indicates, the nature of form is variable. If you accept the notion of form I am putting forth, one implication is that we need to study form—and forming—much more carefully and in many more contexts than we have: form as organic, as construct; as flexible, as rigid; as generative, as constraint; as an instrument of creation and meaning; as the social penetrating the personal. In order to emphasize the essential nature of form, I have in this essay been conflating distinctions that would distinguish various types of forms. For the unity is logically prior to the partition. That unity grasped, however, we do need better insights into the various functions of distinct formal principles. And while remembering Burke's warning "not to confine the explanation [of form] to *one* principle, but to formulate sufficient principles to make an explanation possible" (*Counter-Statement* 129), we could certainly do worse than to start from his discussion of progressive (syllogistic and qualitative), repetitive, conventional, and minor or incidental form.

Even without awaiting further study, we can draw certain implications from the general thesis argued here. As humanists, we should be able to explain (especially to our students) the relation of forms to functions. As rhetoricians, we should explicitly invent forms to meet new needs, new functions, as Young, Becker, and Pike formally invented Rogerian persuasion. As writing teachers we need a more articulated understanding than do writers of how form functions in the writing process.

That brings me to "Monday morning."

	Synchronic Patterns	Progressive Patterns
Report Patterns	Description	Narration
Explanatory Patterns	Comparison/contrast Classification and division Definition Analogy and exemplification	Process-analysis Causal explanation Logical progression

Figure 3. Basic Patterns of Arrangement

II. MONDAY MORNING

If you agree with the New Rhetorical conception of form asserted here, what should you do on Monday morning?

1. You should help students learn those forms socially necessary for effective communication within the society in which they live. (This is comparable to teaching them Standard English so that they have functional access to professional jobs, power, etc.)

2. You should help them learn—and invent—forms that allow them to understand and communicate what they want to understand and communicate, what it is in their interests to understand and communicate.

3. You should help students grasp this New Rhetorical conception of form and learn how to think critically about form—but, let me add immediately, not by pontificating about form; rather by creating processes that allow them to experience both the constraining and generative powers of forms.

Learning socially significant forms—and understanding how they function, how to use them appropriately—is a key to success (sometimes even to survival) in a discourse community. This is per-haps particularly so in schools, for schools serve in part to teach such forms, or at least to weed out those who do not know them. As Frances Christie argues,

> Those who fail in schools are those who fail to master the genres of schooling: the ways of structuring and of dealing with experience which schools value in varying ways. (24; cf. Heath)

So it matters that we continue to teach the basic forms which constitute a condition of access to professional discourse, and hence to professional communities, in modern societies. But it also matters that we discuss these forms, as any others, in terms of their functions in various writing processes (cf. Figure 1 above): how they serve (or limit) the creative process, how they enable (or disable) communication, how they structure what happens in our minds, how they mesh with social processes.

Like other rhetorical factors, form should be taught in context, in terms of appropriateness and effectiveness. When teaching such standard forms as the thesis paragraph (i.e., thesis statement + partition used to prefigure the argument), it matters that we explain the importance of this form in academic (and other professional) discourse, make clear why it predominates in certain types of dis-

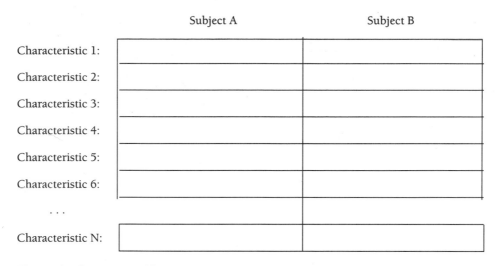

Figure 4. Comparison/Contrast

course (academic, scientific, professional—and textbooks). We should validate (and limit) this form by showing that it makes a certain type of critical reading easier because proofs can be evaluated more easily if readers know in advance what they purportedly prove, because information can be taken in more efficiently if one knows in advance the outline of what is to be learned. In this way, we should put whatever forms we teach in functional rhetorical context.

Though we might wish to emphasize patterns relevant to our students' educational, professional and humane purposes, we can begin with the standard formal *patterns of development,* largely on the hypothesis that they correspond with basic patterns of thought (cf. D'Angelo, *Conceptual Theory* 28–29, 42–47, 53–59; Berthoff 38–45). The main innovation is to treat the formal patterns as representing mental functions and to place them functionally within the creative process.

I start with narration and description, modes in which the structure of the text is ordinarily shaped to a significant extent by the chronology of the story being narrated or the arrangement of what is being described. Studies in contrastive rhetoric demonstrate that even narrative and description are not simple reflections of reality; on the contrary, they vary significantly from one culture to another. (To cite just one example, place is very important in the stories of aboriginal Australians, but it is stated near the end; when those stories are translated for Anglo Australians, the translators generally move the statement of place to the beginning, where English narrative form demands it.) There is, nonetheless, a sense in which the arrangements of narrative and description are shaped by the structure of their subject matter to a greater extent than are the arrangements of more abstract modes. The cognitive task of arrangement is, therefore, easier in these modes, and so I do start with them.

Thence I follow traditional pedagogy to comparison/contrast, the thought structure of which may be represented by the grid in Figure 4. Obviously, this structure focuses attention, hence invention, toward a particular task (i.e., toward comparing and contrasting). Students instructed to compare and contrast generate different substance than would students instructed to, say, describe and exemplify. Thus teaching this pattern of development teaches a heuristic technique; already the formalists' static conception of form is sublated. (Is not the grid in Figure 4 just as much a heuristic as the tagmemic grid?)

But there are further implications because two distinct rhetorical forms can be used to communicate comparison/contrast. In the half-and-half format, composition moves vertically down the grid: Subject A is described first, then Subject B is compared and contrasted. In the alternating characteristics format, composition moves horizontally: each characteristic of Subject A is compared and/or contrasted with Subject B before the next characteristic is raised.

How boring! No, because even in a case such as this the choice of rhetorical format may significantly affect the substance of what gets invented. Ask a writer who has used the half-and-half format to reformulate using the alternating characteristics format, and the message will sometimes change. First, the close juxtaposition of each comparison/contrast point often leads writers to notice that they have left something out. Second, and more significantly, when the rhetorical format forces close juxtaposition, writers sometimes decide that an example, or even the point, is not so strong as they thought. For an instance of what happened to one student's literary critical essay when she was assigned to reformulate it in this way, (see Coe, *Form* 238–41).

A more interesting exercise of the same type involves the juxtaposition of two rhetorical forms that serve the same general purpose. For instance, one can juxtapose Classical and Rogerian persuasion. It quickly grows obvious to students that the choice of a form for persuasion affects both tone and substance. I effect the juxtaposition this way:

1. First, I ask students to pair themselves with someone with whom they can agree on a thesis for a persuasive writing. Each pair must submit a single thesis statement.

2. Working in pairs, using Aristotle's *topoi,* brainstorming, and whatever other invention techniques they wish, each pair of students invents as many arguments as they can in support of their chosen thesis.

3. One student of each pair elects to try the Classical form, the other to try the Rogerian form. Each chooses an appropriate audience, i.e., a group of potential readers who would (a) initially disagree with the thesis, and (b) effectively be addressed by whichever form that student has elected. (Note that the exercise is inevitably artificial here: in real world writing situations, writers generally know the audience first, choose an appropriate form second—and the nature of the audience is usually an important factor in the invention of arguments.)

4. Each student submits a brief audience analysis, outlining the relevant knowledge, beliefs, and vested interests of the chosen audience. On the basis of this audience analysis, each selects arguments from those the pair has invented, adds any others that might be suggested by the nature of the audience, and writes a persuasion using the elected format.

5. The persuasions are read and criticized (in terms of how well they are likely to persuade the chosen audiences). They are then revised.

6. To discover how audience and form have influenced the tone and substance, we do comparison/contrast of persuasions written from the same corpus of invented arguments to support the same thesis.

Quite a number of birds get hit by this one assignment: learning to work with another writer, at least through the stage of invention; developing the ability to empathize with and analyze an audience; learning two rhetorical forms for organizing persuasion; learning something about the relationship between audience and rhetorical structure; developing some control of tone and understanding of the relationship between audience and tone; and learning something, hands on, about the relationship between form and substance.

It is important that students understand composition *as a forming process.* As Ann Berthoff argues,

Composing is like an organic process, not an assembly line on which some prefabricated parts are fitted together. However, plants and animals don't just "grow" mystically, developing from seed to flower and fully framed creatures, without plan or guidance or system. All organic processes are forms in action: the task of the composer is to find the forms that find forms; the structures that guide and encourage growth; the limits by means of which development can be shaped. [This] method of composing . . . is a way of making meanings by using the forms provided by language to re-present the relationships we see. (153)

The curriculum and pedagogy championed by Berthoff exemplifies this emphasis. For pedagogical examples, see *forming/thinking/writing* (50–62, on classifying, and 94–100, on defining); cf. Berthoff, "The Intelligent Eye and the Thinking Hand," in Hays et al.

In North America, at least, Francis Christensen is the best-known early proponent of teaching what I call *generative form.* First on the level of the sentence, then on the level of the paragraph, and posthumously (through his followers) on the level of the whole piece of writing, Christensen taught form as "generative rhetoric." If one teaches students the form of the cumulative sentence, replete with "loose" or free modifiers, he argued, the students will generate the material to fill "empty" modifier slots in their sentences. Thus their writing will acquire what Christensen termed "texture": details, examples, reasons, qualifiers, etc. Comparable lessons on the paragraph level will motivate them to generate that form of texture writing teachers have traditionally called good or full "development." (For pedagogical examples and detailed discussion, see Christensen's articles on generative rhetoric and his *Rhetoric Program,* the cited articles by Grady, D'Angelo, Nold and Davis, and Shaughnessy's chapter, "Beyond the Sentence," in *Errors and Expectations.*)

Taking this lesson one step further, I will argue that a new form often must be created in order to express a radically new idea—and that knowing a form with which an idea can be articulated improves the likelihood of thinking that idea. Teaching a new form is a pedagogy often used to encourage a new *form of discourse.* Before reading Richards, I used to call this, "New Forms for New Content." Oppressed social groups often find it necessary to invent new forms because the socially dominant forms will not readily carry their ideas. Several examples of this kind of formal invention can be found in the work of feminists.

There is, for instance, the formula for constructive criticism, synthesized by U.S. feminists from humanistic psychology and Mao Zedung's essay on criticism/self-criticism, that I find tremendously useful in my composition classes. The formula, simply, is:

When you _____, I feel/think _____, so I wish you would _____ instead.

When you tell me my writing is "incoherent, ungrammatical and confused," *I feel* stupid, discouraged, and angry, *so I wish you would* make more specific and constructive criticisms *instead.*

This formula has two virtues: (a) it encourages constructive criticism (rather than blaming criticism) by helping to keep criticism specific, making it clear that a particular action (not the whole person) is being criticized, focusing attention on the effect of the criticized action and forcing the critic to indicate what can be done about the criticism; and (b) by providing an appropriate structure, the formula makes it easier for people to express criticisms. Indeed, if one looks at feminist assertiveness training, one sees that providing appropriate forms is one of the most important techniques for enabling a new kind of communication.

This same principle can be applied to teaching the standard rhetorical patterns of development. I have done so frequently, especially when asserting that the traditional cause-to-effect pattern should be complemented with instruction in causal explanation by constraints. Explanation by constraints focuses more attention on context as a possible locus of cause and motive, thus improving students' ability to think and communicate about organized complexity (e.g., about human motives, human societies, ecosystems).[5] A similar argument can be made that while the standard forms of Western thought are effective for thinking about stasis and essences, teaching the form of reasoning and communication embodied by the Hegelian/Marxist dialectic (or even the Taoist/Zen Buddhist dialectic) helps people think and communicate more effectively about process and change.

Though the kind of instruction I am describing is in a significant sense formal and sublates certain aspects of traditional formal curricula, it is worlds (or, more accurately, levels) away from traditional static formalism. For it places form in the context of various processes: creative, communicative, mental, social, and learning. Thus formalism is not rejected, but subordinated to process. And we create a kind of process approach that encompasses and transforms formalism, rather than simply opposing it.

What I am advocating is that we teach this New Rhetorical kind of process writing. That in part through theory, but mostly through hands-on practice, we help our students develop an awareness of form as simultaneously constraining and generative that will empower them to understand, use, and even invent new forms for new purposes.[6]

Notes

1. There is, of course, a sense in which this distinction between mental and social processes is false, for our minds are themselves social as well as individual. The metaphor that equates mind with brain misleads us into locating our minds "in" our heads; but while the brain is a crucial locus of mind, we would avoid many errors if we made a radical epistemological shift and began thinking of our minds as open systems, as structures and flows of information that pass through our brains. Cf. Bateson (esp. 478–88 and 494–505). Burke makes a similar point when he locates motives.

2. In evoking this antithesis, I use Berlin's terms, in part because I think they are significantly accurate, in part to avoid a proliferation of terminologies. My point, however, does not depend upon his analysis. Indeed, I disagree with parts of Berlin's analysis and recognize that any analysis of this nature reduces the complex variety of what is actually happening—that is how it achieves clarity and defines the core of the issue. But I think it is fair to assert that the two major influences on classroom practice, at least in North America, were the traditional formal approach and the Expressionist process approach.

   The traditional formal approach avoided questions of substance by defining "content" as outside the field of composition, i.e., either as unteachable art (as in "inspiration") or as the proper concern of other disciplines ("content" courses, as contrasted with "skills" courses). The Expressionist process approach, taking its cue from the derivation of *education* (to lead out, to draw forth), also avoided questions of substance but by placing "content" within students; this process approach begins by removing constraints, creating contexts and processes through which students can express themselves, can articulate (hence, on another level, discover) what *they* want to say, can *ex-press* what is presumably already "inside" them.

   The differences in the ways the two process approaches deal with the social aspect of process writing is consistent with their respective conceptions of form. The New Rhetorical treatment of form is radically distinct from either the traditional formal approach or the Expressionist process approach.

3. Cf. Burke's assertion that "critical and imaginative works are answers to questions posed by the situation in which they arose," that we should think of "any work of critical or imaginative cast" as "the adopting of various strategies for the encompassing of situations. These strategies size up the situations, name their structure and outstanding ingredients, and name them in a way that contains an attitude towards them. . . . The symbolic act is the *dancing of an attitude*" (*Philosophy* 3, 8–9). The point I am making about rhetorical forms is Burke's point generalized—as the forms are generalized texts. Forms are synchronic structures that function as generalized memories of (diachronic) processes. For an application this conception of form to the interpretation of literature (and architecture), see Wayne's *Penshurst*.

4. De Beaugrande coins the term "frame defense" to argue that a text may be "rejected or simply not understood" if it conflicts with a reader's informational or situational frame (168). Hypothetically, I would apply this notion to formal frames as well. Cf. Kinsch's argument that readers structure information within a knowledge frame they bring to the text and Goffman's notion of "primary frames" (21–39). Burke, of course, has made various comparable analyses earlier, although without using the same terminology.

5. The essence of this argument is that the cause-to-effect pattern of development taught in traditional composition courses overestimates the extent to which occurrences are explainable as the result of prior events that actively "caused" them and underestimates the sense in which certain types of occurrences are better explained as responses or adaptations to contexts. The theory of evolution is an excellent example of an idea invented because its inventor stopped looking for "causes" and

started looking at contexts. The increasing tendency in various practical and academic disciplines to discuss causation in terms of "parameters," "restraints" and "constraints" indicates increasing awareness that contextual factors are crucial for explaining events and decisions shaped by organized complexity. Contextual factors are qualitatively different from mechanistic causes, but it is difficult to emphasize, communicate or even think about that qualitative difference while using the cause-to-effect pattern of development. See especially Coe "Closed System Composition," "Rhetoric 2001," and "Causation" in *Form and Substance* (300–20). Cf. Bateson (399–410), the discussion of scenic factors in Burke's *Grammar* (esp., xv–vii, 3–7, 127–70), and of order and hierarchy in Burke's *Rhetoric* (Part III).

6. Since the social nature of invention is currently a major topic of discussion, I should note that this article began as a long talk at the 1985 Wyoming Conference on Freshman and Sophomore English, became a short paper at the 1986 Conference on College Composition and Communication and a long paper at the 4th International Conference on the Teaching of English. The constructive criticism received at those conferences, as well as from several correspondents, was critical to the social process of inventing/reinventing the article. Important points would have been left out or left implicit (and thus open to misunderstanding) were it not for these constructive critics, especially Erica Bauermeister, Russell Hunt, Karen Burke Lefevre, Nan Johnson, Jim Reither, and one anonymous referee.

By way of clarifying another aspect of invention as a social process (i.e., the sense in which the jargons of discourse communities serve as terministic motives), I should note that I have largely evaded a number of jargons, including those of structuralism, semiotics, psycholinguistics, and information theory. I have made the judgment that, in this case, demonstrating those parallels by using the jargon would confuse rather than aid my communication; I presume that readers familiar with those discourses will recognize the parallels.

Works Cited

Bateson, Gregory. *Steps to an Ecology of Mind.* New York: Ballantine, 1972.

Berlin, James A. "Contemporary Composition: The Major Pedagogical Theories." *College English* 44 (1982): 765–77.

Berthoff, Ann E. *forming/thinking/writing.* Rochelle Park, NJ: Hayden, 1978.

Burke, Kenneth. *Counter-Statement.* 1931. Berkeley: U of California P, 1968.

———. *A Grammar of Motives.* 1945. Berkeley: U of California P, 1969.

———. *Language as Symbolic Action.* Berkeley: U of California P, 1966.

———. *A Rhetoric of Motives.* 1950. Berkeley: U of California P, 1969.

———. *The Philosophy of Literary Form.* 1941. New York: Vintage, 1957.

Christensen, Francis. *The Christensen Rhetoric Program.* New York: Harper, 1966.

———. "A Generative Rhetoric of the Paragraph." *College Composition and Communication* 16 (1965): 144–56.

———. "A Generative Rhetoric of the Sentence." *College Composition and Communication* 14 (1963): 155–61.

Christie, Frances. "Language and Schooling." *Language, Schooling and Society.* Ed. Stephen Tchudi. Upper Montclair, NJ: Boynton, 1985. 21–40.

Coe, Richard M. "Closed System Composition." *ETC., A Review of General Semantics* 32 (1975): 403–12.

———. *Form and Substance.* New York: Wiley: Scott, 1981.

———. "If Not to Narrow, Then How to Focus." *College Composition and Communication* 32 (1981): 272–77.

———. "Literacy 'Crises': A Systemic Analysis." *Humanities in Society* 4 (1981): 363–78.

———. "Rhetoric 2001." *Freshman English News* 3.1 (1974): 1–13.

D'Angelo, Frank. *A Conceptual Theory of Rhetoric.* Cambridge, MA: Winthrop, 1975.

———. "A Generative Rhetoric of the Essay." *College Composition and Communication* 25 (1974): 388–96.

De Beaugrande, Robert. *Text, Discourse, and Process: Toward a Multidisciplinary Science of Texts.* Norwood, NJ: Ablex, 1980.

Faigley, Lester. "Competing Theories of Process: A Critique and a Proposal." *College English* 48 (1986): 527–42.

Fort, Keith. "Form, Authority, and the Critical Essay." *College English* 33 (1971): 629–39.

Goffman, Erving. *Frame Analysis.* New York: Harper, 1974.

Grady, Michael. "A Conceptual Rhetoric of the Composition." *College Composition and Communication* 22 (1971): 348–54.

———. "On Teaching Christensen Rhetoric." *English Journal* 61 (1972): 859+.

Hays, Janice N., et al., eds. *The Writer's Mind: Writing as a Mode of Thinking.* Urbana: NCTE, 1983.

Heath, Shirley Brice. *Way with Words: Language, Life, and Work in Communities and Classrooms.* Cambridge, Cambridge UP, 1983.

Kinsch, Walter. "On Modeling Comprehension." *Literacy, Society, and Schooling.* Ed. Suzanne de Castell, Allan Luke, and Kieran Egan. Cambridge, UK: Cambridge UP, 1986.

Kojeve, Alexandre. *Introduction to the Reading of Hegel.* Tran. J. H. Nichols, Jr. New York: Basic, 1969.

Macrorie, Ken. *Telling Writing.* 3rd ed. Rochelle Park, NJ: Hayden, 1980.

Murray, Donald M. "Talking to Yourself: The Reason Writers Write." Opening Sess. Wyoming Conference on Freshman and Sophomore English. Laramie, 24 June 1985.

Nold, Ellen W., and Brent E. Davis. "The Discourse Matrix." *College Composition and Communication* 31 (1980): 141–52.

Perelman, Les. "The Context of Classroom Writing," *College English* 48 (1986): 471–79.

Richards, I. A. *The Philosophy of Rhetoric.* London: Oxford, 1936.

Shaughnessy, Mina. *Errors and Expectations.* New York: Oxford, 1977.

Shultz, John. "Story Workshop." *Research on Composing.* Ed. Charles Cooper and Lee Odell. Urbana: NCTE, 1978. 151–87.

Strunk, William, and E. B. White. *The Elements of Style.* New York: Macmillan, 1959.

Waldrep, Tom, ed. *Writers on Writing.* New York: Random, 1985.

Wayne, Don E. *Penshurst: The Semiotics of Place and the Poetics of History.* Madison: U of Wisconsin P, 1984.

Winterowd, W. Ross, ed. *Contemporary Rhetoric.* New York: Harcourt, 1975.

Young, Richard, Alton Becker, and Kenneth Pike. *Rhetoric: Discovery and Change.* New York: Harcourt, 1970.

Instructional Practices:
Toward an Integration

Janice M. Lauer

Lauer's article was published in Focuses 1 (Spring) 1988: 3–10.

Composition teaching has taken at least two directions in its effort to avoid a pedagogy restricted to grammatical rules and skills, modes of discourse as ends, and stylistic prescriptions. Two alternative pedagogies have been advocated— teaching writing as an art and nurturing natural processes (Young). As extreme and exclusive positions, however, they do not provide the most effective means of helping students to develop as writers who strive dialogically to forge new understanding in a range of discourse communities. I want to argue here that integrating these two pedagogies together with two others, imitation and practice, offers a more stimulating and supportive context in which students can learn to write and write to learn.

Each of these four teaching approaches offers important advantages to students and requires certain teaching skills. Teaching writing as an *art* gives students practical strategies and rhetorical knowledge to guide them during their writing and to accompany them beyond the classroom, when the instructor and peers will no longer be present to motivate and respond to their natural processes at work. Art stresses the value of using "plans up front," which help engender confidence and independence (Perkins 190–219). Teaching writing as an art requires that the teacher study the processes and acts of effective writers in order to develop or make use of helpful heuristics which will facilitate these acts. Such teaching is most effectively done using the environmental mode of instruction in

which students are situated to use strategies collaboratively in solving genuine writing problems.

Natural process pedagogy emphasizes the role of what David Perkins calls "plans down deep" (162–89) and highlights the importance of attitude and cognitive style in individual writers. This pedagogy involves motivating students and giving them responses to their developing texts. Consequently, instructors engaged in natural process pedagogy need the ability to set compelling contexts and to be sensitive to individual differences in order to find "zones of proximal development" for inexperienced writers.

Practice, especially in classroom writing workshops and writing centers, insures that writers learn to apply their art appropriately in a variety of situations and that they develop habits as writers. Engaging students in intelligent practice requires the patience to cope with approximate texts, a tolerance of mistakes, and a willingness to withhold evaluation as portfolios expand.

The use of *imitation* expands students' awareness of effective processes and good prose. For the teacher or writing center director, it entails searching for models that exemplify processes as well as products, providing exemplars that students can emulate, and modeling the struggles and satisfactions in the instructor's own writing.

Integrating these instructional practices requires a strong commitment to work toward a creative pedagogy that fits one's students and one's own teaching style. No one way of integration exists; it requires time, dedication, and study on the part of the instructor and/or tutors. At least two kinds of evidence support this goal of integration: empirical and historical.

George Hillocks' recent meta-analysis of experimental research on five focuses and three modes of instruction demonstrates that some improvement in writing was achieved by students in classes using each of these four pedagogies: inquiry skills (art and practice), sentence combining (art and practice), criteria (art and imitation), models (imitation), and free writing (natural process and art). The only focus that produced negative results was grammatical instruction. His study also concludes that both the environmental mode of instruction (which includes art) and natural process pedagogy had more positive influences on student writing than did presentational instruction. Since each of these pedagogies accounted for a portion of improvement, how much more development could be fostered by combining the best features of each so that their strengths could complement each other. Integrated, they offer a way of situating students in richer contexts for reaching and sharing new understanding.

Each of the four pedagogies also has an impressive historical pedigree in rhetoric. Most classical rhetoricians speak of their importance in educating a maker and sharer of meaning, but rank their relative merits differently.

Aristotle highlights *art,* defining it in the *Metaphysics* as principles or theories gleaned from expert performance that explain the nature of this performance and serve as a source of strategies to guide communicators. Aristotle considers art to be a type of practical knowledge in the communicator and a set of principles in a discipline (499–500). This kind of "practical" knowledge, which is designed for performance, contrasts with scientific knowledge, which exists for its own sake. He begins his treatise on rhetoric by classifying it as an art:

> All men attempt to discuss statements and to maintain them, to defend themselves and to attack others. Ordinary people do this either at random or through practice and from acquired habit. Both ways being possible, the subject can be plainly handled systematically, for it is possible to inquire the reason *why* some speakers succeed through practice and others spontaneously; and everyone would agree that such an inquiry is the function of an art. (19)

Here Aristotle posits a dynamic relationship between good performance and art. Art's principles and strategies are not formulated in a vacuum—they are drawn from observation and analysis of effective communicators. Moreover, Aristotle explains that the possessor of an art is a mastercraftsman who has an advantage over the mere performer. the handicraftsman, because the mastercraftsman understands what he is doing and therefore can teach others. He not only models good performance but also can explain it (*Metaphysics* 499–500).

Aristotle cautions that an art is not a formula which guarantees success. The communicator, the rhetor, can only discover the means of "coming as near such success as the circumstances of each particular case allow" (*Rhetoric* 9–10). In other words, discoursers have to learn to apply appropriately their repertoire of strategies to genuine rhetorical situations. This concept of situatedness is an important concomitant of art. A dynamic interaction exists between art and act, the right time or the appropriate situational context. Art supplies principles that apply across many situations. *Kairos* grounds those principles in individual circumstances (see Kinneavy for a discussion of *Kairos*). Each discourse context holds for the rhetor both the old and the new. A successful communicator is one who learns by practice and imitation to choose wisely from an artistic repertoire for a particular occasion. In writing as art, writers do not face every task totally unprepared; they have strategies to help them reach new understanding in each case, but their art must be resituated.

The Roman treatise *Rhetorica and Herennium,* which influenced education to the Renaissance, contends that all four instructional practices are necessary. It maintains that art reinforces talent and develops natural advantages, making the strongly talented exceptional and the average stronger (28–29). It explains, however, that theory (art) without continuous practice is of no avail. It also advocates the use of models to illustrate the skillful application of principles.

In Cicero's *De Oratore,* Crassus, echoing Isocrates, discusses the relative merits of these four pedagogies, privileging natural ability:

> This is then my opinion . . . that in the first place natural talent is the chief contributor to the virtue of oratory; and indeed in those writers on the art, of whom Antonius spoke just now, it was not the principles and method of oratory that were wanting, but inborn capacity. . . . I do not mean that art cannot in some cases give polish,—for well I know that good abilities may through instruction become better, and that such as are not of the best can nevertheless be, in some measure, quickened and amended. (81)

Crassus has some disdain for unenlightened practice used alone: "most students . . . merely exercise their voices (and that in the wrong way) . . . and whip up their rate of utterance, and revel in a flood of verbiage. This mistake is due to their having heard it said that it is by speaking that men as a rule become speakers" (103). Antonius also emphasizes the pre-eminent role of natural ability:

> Since . . . three things are necessary to discovery of arguments, first acuteness, secondly theory, or art, as we may call it if we like, and thirdly painstaking, I must needs grant pride of place to talent, though talent is itself roused from lethargy by painstaking, painstaking, I repeat, which is always valuable. . . . Indeed between talent and painstaking there is very little room left for art. (305–07)

Quintilian comments on Antonius' position: "Some would have it that rhetoric is a natural gift though they admit that it can be developed by practice. So Antonius in the *de Oratore* of Cicero styles it a *knack derived from experience,* but denies that it is an art" (I: 327–29). Quintilian then takes issue with this view:

> [Certain persons] make it their boast that they speak on impulse and owe their success to their native

powers. . . . Further, owing to their contempt for method, when they are meditating on some future effusion, they spend whole days looking at the ceiling in the hope that some magnificent inspiration may occur to them, or rock their bodies to and fro, booming inarticulately as if they had a trumpet inside them. . . . The least unreasonable of them devote their attention not to the actual case but to their purple patches, in the composition of which they pay no attention to the subject-matter, but fire off a series of isolated thoughts just as they happen to come to hand. . . . Nonetheless they do occasionally strike out some good things. . . . Why not? and if we are to be satisfied with this sort of thing, then goodbye to any theory [art] of rhetoric. (I: 281–83)

Quintilian argues instead for an integration of the four approaches: "Without natural gifts . . . rules [art] are useless. Gifts, on the other hand, are of no profit in themselves unless cultivated by skillful teaching, persistent study, and continuous and extensive practice" (I: 19). He maintains that "the average orator owes much to nature while the perfect orator owes more to education" (I: 349). For Quintilian, art is a "power reaching its ends by a definite path, that is, by ordered methods" and is based on examination and practice (I: 345). About the art of invention he asserts: "We owe a debt of gratitude to those who have given us a short cut to knowledge. For thanks to them the arguments discovered by the genius of earlier orators have not got to be hunted out and noted down in detail" (II: 269). He cautions, however, against an excessive reliance on art, calling those who have only book knowledge of the topics "possessors of a dumb science" because "the discovery of arguments was not the result of the publication of text-books. . . . The creators of the art were the orators" (II: 269–70). He ridicules those who plod through entire lists of topics "knocking at the door of each with a view to discovering whether they may chance to serve to prove our point" (II: 269). He does not, however, rule out methodical invention, but reserves it for learners (II: 269–70), recommending that communicators develop a sense of appropriateness by applying strategies in real situations, not in practice exercises.

What happened to this integrated view of instruction in discourse? At least two major complex developments have brought us to a condition of exclusion and extreme emphasis on one or the other type of pedagogy. First, the concept of art changed. Second, different periods valorized one or the other of these instructional practices.

When Aristotle or Quintilian speak of the art of rhetoric, they refer to principles and strategies for invention, arrangement, and style. But in the medieval period, as Richard McKeon has explained, the concept of art is narrowed because the art of invention is gradually driven out of rhetoric to play an underground role in the formation of the scholastic and scientific methods. During this period, another curious development occurs: art and natural ability start to polarize, almost reify, into two positions. The first is that of Aquinas, who treats art as a body of formal principles, intellectualizing the art and changing its orientation to subject matter and to problems of inquiry and understanding. The second is that of Bonaventure, who considers art as knowledge in the artist, leading to a preoccupation with the relationship between morals and eloquence and to a view of rhetoric as virtue (189).

By the Renaissance, the concept of art has become ambiguous. On the one hand, according to Sister Miriam Joseph, the Aristotelian meaning still prevails: "The Elizabethan literary critics and poets, no less than the rhetoricians and logicians, insisted on the importance of precepts and theory in the creation of literature. . . . Art . . . is assumed to rest on a body of precepts derived from nature" (7). On the other hand, Ramus narrows the scope of rhetorical art, transferring invention and arrangement to dialectic and reducing the art of rhetoric to style. The Ramian texts do more than narrow the scope of art; they distort it. Walter J. Ong examines the complex meanings of "method" that Ramus inherits, shrinks, and transmits, showing that Ramus changes the concept of art from that of action guided by principles and strategies to that of a rigid method of analysis. The student produces discourse not by learning and applying principles and strategies but by analyzing and imitating texts. This transformation manifests itself in Ramus' discussion of invention as a part of dialectic. Ong translates Ramus as saying:

> Logical analysis is the process by which a given example of discourse already composed is examined in terms of the laws of the art, the question is extracted, then the invention studied, and the place from which the argument was drawn looked for. This is the analysis of invention. (263–64)

Ong explains that

> analysis, for Ramus, is thus at root a way of operating didactically upon a text. It belongs not to an art but to *usus* or exercise, and is complemented by *genesis* or composition, for, once the schoolboy has broken down a sample of discourse—written discourse, for analysis is here growing out of the humanist approach to language through the written word—he can assemble the parts in configurations of his own, which according to Ramus, is what one does in composing. (264)

Moreover, instead of explaining principles and strategies in terms of their nature, purpose, and appropriateness in different contexts, the Ramian treatises print geometric models of logic, schemes, and tropes, stripped of context.

In the eighteenth century Hugh Blair reiterates this reduction of art, proclaiming: "With respect to [invention], I am afraid it is beyond the power of art to give any real assistance. Art cannot go so far as to supply a speaker with arguments . . . though it may be of considerable use in assisting him to arrange and express those which his knowledge of the subject has discovered" (117). Blair emphasizes natural processes. "Whether nature or art contribute most to form an orator, is a trifling inquiry. In all attainments whatever, nature must be the prime agent" (129). In the nineteenth century, Richard Whately skeptically describes the prevailing view:

> Many, perhaps most persons, are inclined to the opinion that Eloquence, either in writing or speaking, is either a natural gift, or at least, is to be acquired by mere practice, and is not to be attained or improved

by any system of rules. And this opinion is favoured not least by those . . . whose own experience would enable them to decide very differently; and it certainly seems to be in great deal practically adopted. (287)

CURRENT PRACTICES

At the present time, three divergent conceptions of art have emerged: 1) art as natural process, 2) art as heuristics, and 3) art as prescription. The first is the opposite of the classical conception. William Stafford describes art as "an interaction between object and beholder. . . . One doesn't learn how to do art, but one learns that it is possible by a certain adjustment of consciousness to participate in art—it's a natural activity for one not corrupted by mechanical ways" (48). John Barth expresses a similar view of art and its consequences for teaching:

Given the inclination and the opportunity, those with any aptitude for it at all surely hone what skills they have, in the art of writing as in any other art, craft, skill. It gets learned . . . first, by paying a certain sort of attention to the experience of life as well as merely undergoing it; second, by paying a certain sort of attention to the works of their great and less great predecessors in the medium of written language, as well as merely reading them; third, by practicing that medium themselves, usually a lot; . . . and fourth, by offering their apprentice work for discussion and criticism by one or several of their impassioned peers, or by some more experienced hand, or both. (36)

For Barth art has turned into natural processes, imitation, and practice to the exclusion of the classical concept of art.

The second contemporary meaning of art is articulated by those who advocate the use of heuristics to guide composing. *Heuristics* for them has the same meaning as the classical concept of art: "explicit strategies for effective guessing. Heuristic procedures are not to be confused with rule-governed procedures . . . there are few rule-governed procedures possible in rhetoric. . . . A heuristic procedure provides a series of questions or operations whose results are provisional. Al-

though explicit and more or less systematic, heuristic search is not wholly conscious or mechanical; intuition, relevant knowledge, and skill are also necessary" (Young 57). The purpose and value of these heuristics is discussed by Christina Murphy in a recent dialogue:

Allowing students to wander through rhetorical mazes unassisted in search of insights into the riddles of compositional strategies and outcomes that have already been demystified and resolved seems largely an inefficient practice. . . . Strategies of inquiry free many students to understand in the fullest sense what the creative process at the heart of composition is all about. (14)

The third view of art is a rule-governed one whose roots go back to Roman times. From the Roman period to the Renaissance, technical rhetorics appeared, crowded with topics that had been endlessly subdivided and with lengthy prescriptions for parts of the discourse. These bloated and mechanistic versions of art were perpetuated by the encyclopedic treatises of the medieval period and deteriorated into the lists of the Renaissance. Learning hundreds of directives for invention, arrangement, and style became an end, not a means. Such a version of art prevails today in text books, particularly handbooks, which present rules of style and arrangement as invariant, true for any context or type of discourse. Classrooms based on this version of art teach isolated prescriptions, formulae like the five-paragraph theme and the features of good style.

In addition to the existence of divergent conceptions of art, another force is contributing to a lack of integration in our current instructional practices: an overemphasis on one or the other of the four types of instruction. Some champions of natural process assert its preeminence to the exclusion of art, considering a knowledge of principles and strategies not only ineffective but obstructive to writers. Cy Knoblauch and Lil Brannon claim:

Teaching, from this vantage point, no longer stresses giving people a knowledge they did not previously possess, but instead involves creating supportive environments in which a competence they already have can be nurtured to yield increasingly mature performance. . . . Progress toward excellence is a function of increasing experience more than objective understanding of principles. . . . Highlighting "strategies" . . . seems more distracting than helpful. (4, 15, 37)

An overreliance on imitation can be seen in the dominance of collections of readings in composition classrooms. Although some instructors use these collections interactively with the other pedagogies, a high percentage of teachers devote the majority of class time to reading and analyzing essays, with the assumption, as Gordon Rohman expresses it, "that if we train students how to recognize an example of good prose (the rhetoric of the finished word), we have given them a basis on which to build their own writing abilities" (17). Practice too has its zealots, who base their pedagogy on the maxim: "a theme a day keeps illiteracy away." Finally, overenthusiasm for art can be seen in instructors who present heuristics as ends to be mastered rather than as means to meaningful discourse, who proliferate heuristics so that learning then consumes writers' energies, who lecture on strategies rather than encourage collaborative engagement in using them purposefully, or who convert heuristics into formulae that are claimed to guarantee good writing.

These overemphases obscure the goal of integration that I argue for here—classrooms or writing centers that draw on the strengths of each of the four instructional practices: setting motivating contexts in which writers can raise and answer their own compelling questions, offering students guiding strategies, engaging students collaboratively in writing in a range of discourse communities, and presenting models of students, teachers, and professional writers planning and revising texts.

Works Cited

Aristotle. *Metaphysics*. Great Books of the Western World. Ed. Robert Hutchins. Chicago: Encyclopedia Britannica, 1952.

———. *The Rhetoric and The Poetics of Aristotle*. Trans. W. Rhys Roberts. New York: Modern Library, 1954.

Barth, John. "Writing: Can It be Taught?" *New York Times Book Review* 16 June 1985: 1, 36–37.

Blair, Hugh. *Lectures on Rhetoric and Belles Lettres: The Rhetoric of Blair, Campbell, and Whately*. Ed. James L. Golden and Edward Corbett. New York: Holt, 1968.

Cicero. *De Oratore*. Trans. E. W. Sutton. Cambridge: Harvard UP, 1942.

Hillocks, George. "What Works in Teaching Composition: A Meta-analysis of Experimental Treatment Studies." *American Journal of Education*. 93 (1984): 133–70.

Kinneavy, James. "The Relationship of the Whole to the Part in Interpretation Theory and in the Composing Process." *Linguistics, Stylistics, and the Teaching of Composition*. Ed. Donald McQuade. Akron, OH: L & S Books, 1979. 292–312.

Knoblauch, C. H., and Lil Brannon. *Rhetorical Tradition and the Teaching of Writing*. Upper Montclair, NJ: Boynton/Cook, 1984.

McKeon, Richard. "Rhetoric in the Middle Ages." *The Province of Rhetoric*. Ed. Joseph Schwartz and John Rycenga. New York: Ronald, 1965, 172–212.

Miriam Joseph, Sister. *Rhetoric in Shakespeare's Time*. New York: Harcourt, 1962.

Murphy, Christina, and Bonnie Dickinson. "If You Meet the Buddha with a Rosetta Stone: A Dialogue on Strategies of Inquiry and The New Rhetoric." *Freshman English News* 14 (1985): 13–18.

Ong, Walter J. *Ramus: Method and the Decay of Dialogue*. Cambridge: Harvard UP, 1958.

Perkins, David *The Mind's Best Work*. Cambridge: Harvard UP, 1981.

Quintilian. *The Institutio Oratoria of Quintilian*. Trans. H. E. Butler. Vols. I and II. Cambridge: Harvard UP, 1920.

Ramus, Peter. *The Logike of the Moste Excellent Philosopher P. Ramus, Martyr: Translated by Roland MacIlmaine (1574)*. Ed. Catherine Dunn. Northridge, CA. San Fernando Valley State College, 1969; Dudley Fenner. *The Artes of Logike and Rhetorike, plainelie set foorth in the Englishe tounge*. Ed. Robert Pepper. Gainesville, FL: Scholars' Facsimiles, 1966.

Rhetorica ad Herennium. Trans. Harry Caplan. Cambridge: Harvard UP, 1954.

Rohman, D. Gordon, and Albert Wlecke. *Pre-Writing: The Construction and Application of Models for Concept Formation in Writing*. U. S. Office of Education Cooperative Research Project No. 2174. East Lansing: Michigan State UP, 1964.

Stafford, William. *Writing the Australian Crawl.* Ann Arbor: The U of Michigan P, 1978.

Whately, Richard. *Elements of Rhetoric: The Rhetoric of Blair, Campbell, and Whately.* Ed. James L. Golden and Edward P. J. Corbett. New York: Holt, 1968.

Young, R. E. "Arts, Crafts, Gifts, and Knacks: Some Disharmonies in the New Rhetoric." *Reinventing the Rhetorical Tradition.* Ed. A. Freedman and I. Pringle. Urbana, IL: NCTE, 1980. 53–60.

Part Three

Science

How are these people
Studying writing?

Research methods :
what the research makes
them think of writing?

Science and Composition: Concepts, Controversies, and Correlations

BARBARA GLEASON

In contrast to Nature, Art, and Politics, the key of Science offers far more indirect arguments about pedagogy, foregrounding instead the themes of inquiry and knowledge. Moreover, rather than debating pedagogical approaches or theories of learning per se, composition professionals working within this key most often argue about research methods, research conclusions, and objects of inquiry. This is not to say, however, that scientific studies are not invoked as evidence for particular pedagogical approaches or even that composition professionals who view themselves as scientists hold no strong views about teaching and learning. They generally do. It is in fact important for us as readers of scientific reports and arguments to be as aware of researchers' assumptions and theories as we are of their findings and conclusions. In reading Janet Emig's 1971 case study of twelfth graders' composing processes, for instance, we discover Emig not just investigating composing but *advancing the relatively new theory that writing is a process.* Careful readings of the other research studies in this section will reveal each author's initial questions, premises, or hypotheses to be important indicators of these researchers' theories about writing, writing development, or teaching.

In addition to invoking questions about research methods, objects of inquiry, and knowledge, science has lent prestige, authority, and credibility to composition as a newly emerging field. Why composition might have *needed* enhanced credibility is in fact itself a question well worth pursuing. Scholars examining the history of English education have turned for answers to the influence of the Cold War on public perceptions of education, the 1957 launching of Sputnik, and the subsequent increase in federal funding for science and English education (Applebee; North). For a more specific focus on composition, one might consider the rise of junior colleges and of open admissions policies during the 1960s and 1970s, with a consequent need for mass assessment of writing, both to place students in and out of remedial courses and to test for "minimal competency"—all of which yields most readily to quantification, or what some call the "language" of science.

Simultaneously, science has proved to be a divisive force in our field, heavily implicated in, to take just one example, a researcher–teacher hierarchy that privileges the researcher's knowledge over the teacher's. The extent to which teachers should rely on scientific studies of writing, language, literacy, and learning has always been at issue—but this was articulated most forcefully in the 1980s, when Ann Bertfhoff published her now classic essay "The Teacher as Researcher" in Dixie Goswami and Peter Stillman's *Reclaiming the Classroom: Teacher Research as an Agency for Change.* Although the issue of epistemic authority may seem an obvious one to contemporary readers, this was far from being the case in 1963, the year in which the first major overview of scientific research in composition appeared in print. Not coincidentally, 1963 is also the year in which the modern field of composition is often said to have begun (North 15).

Surveying scientific research in composition became the charge of an ad hoc committee appointed by the Executive Committee of the National Council of Teachers of English in 1961. This committee stated its aim as one of "review[ing] what is known and what is not known about the teaching and learning of composition and the conditions under which it is taught, for the purpose of preparing a publication of a special scientifically based report on what is known in this area" (Braddock et al. 1). In their review of studies on written composition, the committee limited their sample to "research employing 'scientific methods,' like controlled experimentation and textual analysis" (1). This extensive survey resulted in a meta-analysis of 504 research studies, reported in *Research in Written Composition* by Richard Braddock, Richard Lloyd-Jones, and Lowell Schoer (1963), and ultimately in a newly formed journal, *Research in the Teaching of English.* Particularly noteworthy about both Braddock et al. and *Research in the Teaching of English* (in its early years) is the virtual equating of empirical research—and especially experimental methods—with science.

In the process of separating out the terms *science, research,* and *empirical,* it eventually becomes apparent that as a heuristic for examining composition the key of Science encompasses more than just research (for example, the rhetoric of science, the uses of scientific research) and that research is not necessarily limited to empirical methods. Yet, the association between science and empirical research remains inordinately strong. In his sequel to Braddock et al. (1963), George Hillocks, Jr. (1986) does not refer to *science* at all but does include in his meta-analysis of research in composition *only* empirical studies. Although Hillocks states clearly that he has excluded historical, literary, and theoretical inquiries, no rationale for this decision is provided. Readers are left to their own interpretations, one of which may be that empirical research weighs in as more authoritative or more compelling than other forms of research, and, in conjunction with this, the notion that the only knowledge that really counts is that which is scientific—an idea sometimes referred to as *scientism.*

Reading the Braddock et al. report, we might well be led to speculate on why these authors concentrated so heavily on research methods rather than research questions or the content of these reports as Charles Cooper and Lee Odell advocate doing in *Research on Composing* (1978). In their introduction, Braddock et al. tell us that "today's research in composition, taken as a whole, may be compared to chemical research as it emerged from the period of alchemy." How might this statement be interpreted, and how might it tie in to the authors' concern with research methods?

A close reading of scientific research and of arguments about science in this section—as well as in the composition scholarship generally—will reveal a good deal of variance both in understandings of what science is and in attitudes toward science. This situation is complicated by the fact that many composition scholars enter the field with a humanities-oriented background, a choice often made quite deliberately and for very specific reasons. As readers in the key of Science, therefore, it is important for us to become sensitive to the beliefs and epistemological leanings of the authors whose work we are examining, whether it involves reporting on scientific studies, discussing methods, or arguing about science and its role in composition.

One fairly prominent model of science (referred to in the composition literature by Anne Ruggles Gere as the "standard view") is formulated as follows: The aims of scientific investigation are description, explanation, and prediction; appropriate objects of inquiry are empirical, which is most often taken to mean available to sense perception; research methods are systematic enough to be replicated by other scientists (traditionally, experimental methods involving statistics have been preferred though this is less true today); and the ultimate vision of success is the accumulation of knowledge over time. Given this description, we might ask how this—the standard view of science—would play out in the context of composition research. What would be considered appropriate objects of inquiry, research methods, and aims of composition scientists? Ruth Ray articulates the standard view of science as it appears in the context of composition:

> In summary, composition researchers working under the scientific model construct hypotheses about writing and writing behavior; collect data, such as written texts and protocols, in as controlled a manner as possible; analyze and describe these data; attempt to verify their findings through similarly controlled studies; and work to generalize from these studies in order to create profiles or models of teaching and writing. (5)

Keeping in mind that the idea of standard science is itself open to multiple interpretations, readers might try classifying the research studies in this section as either *inside* or *outside* the bounds of the standard view of science. Specifically, would the work of Emig, Flower, Freedman, Dyson, Geisler, Moss, Sternglass, and Haswell be classifiable as standard science? This exercise in taxonomy does not necessarily imply a value judgment if we can bracket for now questions about the usefulness, desirability, or validity of this particular model.

If the standard model of science offers only one view, we might with some justification inquire about alternatives. In his widely read critique of scientific thinking, *The Structure of Scientific Revolutions* (1962), Thomas Kuhn argues that within scientific communities there exist shared ideological, epistemological, and methodological assumptions that can, at various points in time, achieve a high degree of stability and thus appear as "normal science" or become so destabilized that a "paradigm shift" occurs. In the field of linguistics, for example, the replacement of descriptive linguistics by Chomsky's theory of transformational grammar exemplifies this sort of eclipse in the thinking of scientists, with established objects of inquiry, research methods, and theories all called into question by new ways of imagining the field. The relevance of Kuhn's analysis to research and theory in composition has been widely discussed by scholars such as Maxine Hairston, Patricia Bizzell, Anne Ruggles Gere, Robert Connors, and Ruth Ray. *Indeed, this entire issue of what constitutes science within composition might arguably be construed as the major controversy within this key.* Debates about research methods, objects of inquiry, and even language may all spin out from this central issue.

A second prominent controversy revolves around questions about the status of science in composition. Is composition a scientific discipline, or should composition aspire in this direction? How might the concerns of legitimizing a newly forming academic field within academia play a role in this controversy? And how might applications for funding from one's own institution, from the government, and from private foundations affect the practices and the language of composition professionals? Robert Connors suggests that the apparent popularity of Thomas Kuhn's theories—as evidenced by the generous sprinkling of his terms throughout the composition scholarship—sends a *"tacit message . . . that composition studies should be a scientific or prescientific discipline"* (5). In her response to Maxine Hairston's emphasis on empirical research as an important form of evidence in composition (1978 address at the Convention on College Composition and Communication), Patricia Bizzell has argued *against* "empirical evidence" (or science) as a principal basis for composition theory and research, and *for* self-consciousness of language and the ways in which language situates us historically as primary sites for inquiry. As you read through this section, you may find it productive to construct each author's possible response to questions about whether or not composition is, or is becoming, a science and about the role of empirical evidence in the evolution of composition as a discipline.

Related to the issue of what constitutes science in composition are a host of questions about objects of inquiry. Should researchers arrive at a consensus on just what phenomena they should be investigating? Or to formulate the question more broadly, how important might it be to develop a conceptually unified approach

Inquiry

In his *A Conceptual Theory of Rhetoric,* Frank D'Angelo draws on the ideas of Martin Steinmann to set up a distinction between art and science, describing "rhetoric as an art (the ability of a person to write or speak effectively) and rhetoric as a science (a theory or body of information about rhetoric)" (2). Notice that this extremely broad definition of science makes no reference to any particular research method or aim beyond that of developing theory.

How would this definition accord with your own pre-established ideas about science? Which authors in this section might be most inclined to accept D'Angelo's definition of science?

D'Angelo goes on to propose that rhetoric is "the science which attempts to discover general principles of oral or written discourse" and that "composition is essentially the art of applying these principles in writing" or in the teaching of writing (3).

How might particular researchers whose work is represented in this section respond to this analysis? In what respects is this an argument between the key of Art and the key of Science? Try assuming the stance of Linda Flower and John Hayes or of any other composition researcher in formulating a response to D'Angelo. If you are working with other readers of this text, you might construct dialogues that you share for purposes of discussion.

such as the one Stephen B. Witte outlines in "Toward a Model for Research in Written Composition"? In making his case for a consensus among researchers, Witte proposes four specific areas of research: producing written texts, written products, decoding written products, and pedagogy.

We might also consider the role of objects of inquiry in determining whether or not a particular investigation *is scientific.* For instance, would a phenomenological investigation of mental acts involved in writing or reading, as exemplifed by Louise Phelps's "Rhythm and Pattern in a Composing Life" (included in the Nature section), count as science given that mental acts are not available to sense perception and are therefore often not considered "empirical"? Ultimately, it will be important to reflect on how influential objects of inquiry are in defining the academic field of composition, and to consider this: *If the field is not defined by its objects of inquiry, just what is it that does define this or any academic field?*

Prior to 1963, as Braddock et al. inform us, the most favored objects of empirical research were writing products (frequency counts of errors or of linguistic features; rating compositions) and comparative studies of teaching methods. During the 1960s and even more so in the 1970s, the composing process or acts of writing became a principal focus of research. We learned from researchers such as

Inquiry

Why a researcher selects particular research methods and objects of inquiry is sometimes less than obvious, even to the researcher. What influenced Linda Flower and John Hayes to use protocol analysis as a research method? And why have they focused so intensively on the composing process? To take another example, Beverly Moss chose to use ethnographic methods in her study of language in a church. Why ethnography, and why the focus on church events?

Talk to two different researchers in any discipline about how they go about determining what to study and which research methods to use. During your investigation, inquire about the order of these two decisions. Does the researcher become expert in using a particular methodology and then find something to study? Or does the researcher begin by identifying some phenomenon or problem and *then* identify methodologies that are appropriate for the particular objects being studied?

If you are working with a group of people who are learning about the composition field, consider sharing your findings and asking for others' responses to what you've discovered.

Sondra Perl and Nancy Sommers of the importance of *recursiveness* (backward and forward looping) as a principle of composing, and our consciousness about writing apprehension as an important issue was raised by researchers such as Mike Rose and Roy Fox. George Hillocks, Jr., provides an admirably comprehensive overview of composing process research.

Certain composition scholars, including Louise Phelps (1988), have claimed that the 1960s' and 1970s' interest in writing as process encapsulated a rejection not only of empirical research on writing products but also of a highly product-oriented approach to writing instruction. At least in this instance, ideas about teaching and objects of empirical research correlated rather closely. That is, process-oriented pedagogies came to the fore just as composing process research overcame the long-established tradition of investigating writing products.

In your reading of the research reports and essays representing the key of Science in this section, you might bear in mind possible correspondences between ongoing arguments about pedagogy or writing program curricula on the one hand and objects of research on the other. In so doing, you may wish to consider the extent to which scientific research influences debates about teaching and learning and, conversely, the ways in which debates about pedagogy affect scientists' research agendas. Underlying these questions, an even more fundamental issue can be found: the various roles that science has played in the evolution of our field—with respect to both establishing a scholarly discipline and influencing classroom practices.

Inquiries

Having read through the essays and reports representing the key of Science in this section, you may well come away with questions about the basis for our editorial choices. How well do these selections portray the body of scientific research and science-related issues in composition? What research methods, objects of inquiry, research goals, or issues are *not* represented? One approach to grasping the totality of this section is to articulate its thematic structure by outlining the authors' objects of inquiry, research methods, and research aims, and then identifying important absences. Another approach is to begin reading more widely in the composition field. The following inquiries suggest ways into and out of this process of reflective reading.

1. In 1973, Mina Shaughnessy wrote an essay entitled "Open Admissions and the Disadvantaged Teacher" in which she commented on the ways in which science was being used at her college:

> Unfortunately, the debate about Open Admissions has been and is being carried on in the language of those who oppose it: in the alphabet of numbers, the syntax of print-outs, the transformations of graphs and tables, the language, in particular of a prestigious group of social scientists who perceive through their language truths that even they seem, at times, unwilling to hear, much as scientists of another kind in another era were led inexorably by the dictates of their language to an atomic arsenal (*College Composition and Communication* [1973]:401–04).

What does Shaughnessy appear to be saying about the prestige and the politics of scientific language in educational environments? What exactly is the nature of Shaughnessy's critique, and why might she have felt that it was important for her to publish this critique in a national journal?

2. After examining the scientific research in composition, you may well be wondering about potential relationships between conducting and reading research on the one hand and theorizing pedagogy on the other. For answers to such questions, you might begin by turning to the scholarship on teaching that draws deliberately on scientific research. This scholarship includes books written directly to teachers on issues of writing program curriculum and classroom teaching as well as books written directly to an audience of writing students.

Among the many books for teachers that you might choose to examine are the following:

Marie Wilson Nelson. *At the Point of Need: Teaching Basic and ESL Writers.* Forward by Nancy Martin. Portsmouth: Heinemann, 1991.

Marjorie Montague. *Computers, Cognition, and Writing Instruction.* Albany: SUNY Press, 1990.

(continued)

Inquiries

(continued)

Eleanor Kutz, Suzy Q Groden, and Vivan Zamel. *The Discovery of Competence: Teaching and Learning with Diverse Student Writers*. Portsmouth: Heinemann, 1993.

Examples of composition textbooks informed by scientific research include the following:

William Strong. *Sentence Combining: A Composing Book,* 2nd ed. New York: Random House, 1981.

Patrick Hartwell, with Robert H. Bentley. *Open to Language: A New College Rhetoric*. New York: Oxford UP, 1982.

Linda Flower. *Problem-Solving Strategies for Writing*. New York: Harcourt Brace Jovanovich, 1981.

After reviewing a sampling of these types of books—both those written for teachers and those written for students—try formulating and then addressing questions about relationships between scientific research and teaching theory and practice.

WORKS CITED

Applebee, Arthur. *Tradition and Reform in the Teaching of English: A History*. Urbana: NCTE, 1974.

Berthoff, Ann. "The Teacher as REsearcher." In *Reclaiming the Classroom: Teacher Research as an Agency for Change*. Eds. Dixie Goswami and Peter R. Stillman. Upper Montclair: Boynton/Cook, 1987.

Bizzell, Patricia. "Thomas Kuhn, Scientism, and English Studies." *College English* (1979): 764–71.

Braddock, Richard, Richard Lloyd-Jones, and Lowell Schoer. *Research in Written Composition*. Urbana: NCTE, 1963.

Connors, Robert. "Composition Studies and Science." *College English* (1983): 1–20.

Cooper, Charles R., and Lee Odell. *Research on Composing*. Urbana: NCTE, 1978.

D'Angelo, Frank. *A Conceptual Theory of Rhetoric*. Cambridge: Winthrop, 1975.

Fox, Roy. "Treatment of Writing Apprehension and Its Effects on Composition." *Research in the Teaching of English* 14 (1980): 39–49.

Gere, Anne Ruggles. "Empirical Research in Composition." In *Perspectives on Research and Scholarship in Composition*. Ben W. McClelland and Timothy R. Donovan. New York: MLA Press. 110–24.

Goswami, Dixie, and Peter R. Stillman, eds. *Reclaiming the Classroom: Teacher Research as an Agency for Change*. Upper Montclair: Boynton/Cook, 1987.

Hairston, Maxine. "The Winds of Change: Thomas Kuhn and the Revolution in the Teaching of Writing." *College Composition and Communication* (1982): 78–86.

Hillocks, George Jr. *Research on Written Composition*. Urbana: NCTE, 1986.

Kuhn, Thomas. *The Structure of Scientific Revolutions,* 2nd ed. Chicago: U of Chicago P, 1970.

North, Stephen M. *The Making of Knowledge in Composition: Portrait of an Emerging Field.* Upper Montclair: Boynton/Cook, 1987.

Perl, Sondra. "Understanding Composing." *College Composition and Communication* (1980): 363–69.

Phelps, Louise Wetherbee. *Composition as a Human Science: Contributions to the Self-Understanding of a Discipline.* New York: Oxford UP, 1988.

Ray, Ruth. *The Practice of Theory: Teacher Research in Composition.* Urbana: NCTE, 1993.

Rose, Mike. *Writer's Block: The Cognitive Dimension.* Carbondale: Southern Illinois UP, 1984.

Sommers, Nancy. "Revision Strategies of Student Writers and Experienced Adult Writers." *College Composition and Communication* (1980): 378–88.

Witte, Stephen D. "Toward a Model for Research in Written Composition." *Research in the Teaching of English* (1980): 73–81.

SUGGESTED READINGS

Beach, Richard, and Lillian S. Bridwell, eds. *New Directions in Composition Research.* New York: The Guilford Press, 1984.

Jolliffe, David, ed. *Advances in Writing Research, Volume Two: Writing in Academic Disciplines.* Norwood: Ablex, 1988.

Lauer, Janice M. and J. William Asher. *Composition Research: Empirical Designs.* New York: Oxford UP, 1988.

Mosenthal, Peter, Lynne Tamor, and Sean A. Walmsley. *Research on Writing: Principles and Methods.* New York: Longman, 1993.

Odell, Lee, and Dixie Goswami, eds. *Writing in Nonacademic Settings.* New York: The Guilford Press, 1985.

Lynn: Profile of a Twelfth-Grade Writer

Janet Emig

This selection is chapter four (pages 45–73) from Emig's research report (no. 13) for the NCTE. We have not included the appendix that provides the data from this case study. Composing Processes *was published in 1971. A version of this study appears in Emig's collection of essays* The Web of Meaning: Essays on Writing, Teaching, Learning, and Thinking. *Ed. Dixie Goswami and Maureen Butler. Upper Montclair: Boynton/Cook, 1983. 61–96.*

CONTEXT

The community in which Lynn lives is one of the few truly cross-cultural districts within Chicago. The local couplet, like the area, runs "From the mill/To Pill Hill." The mills are the steel mills of South Chicago; near them live, often on relief, blacks and newly arrived Mexicans and Puerto Ricans. "Pill Hill" is the residential area where many Jewish doctors, dentists, and professors live. Between lie several miles of small brick bungalows owned by second generation Polish- and Serbian-Americans. The school district has this approximate ethnic distribution: 16 percent black, 20 percent Polish and Serbian, 24 percent Mexican and Puerto Rican, 40 percent Jewish.

Lynn lives on "Pill Hill," the oldest of four children of a Jewish lawyer. Her mother is a high school history teacher at the same high school Lynn attends (this fact may at least partially explain Lynn's sophistication, hovering near cynicism, about teachers and their ways revealed in her interviews). Her brother is three years younger; her sisters, six and eight-and-a-half years younger. All four of Lynn's grandparents were born in Europe.

Lynn's high school has a proud academic tradition: until recently, in addition to the five tracks common in other Chicago high schools, it had a special Century Club—the top 100 in each class of approximately 550 students. Many senior members of the Century Club, like Lynn, take advanced placement courses and actual college courses at a nearby city junior college; in fact, Lynn's schedule, with its spaced classes and free time, more closely resembles the schedule of a college freshman than that of a high school senior.

In addition to being in the top five percent of her class academically, Lynn is coeditor of the yearbook and a study hall monitor. If her conversation gives an accurate index, by far the most important extracurricular activity, however, is her work as officer of the Midwest Jewish Youth Institute.

Personally, Lynn is very vivacious as well as a very perceptive girl, attuned to herself and her world. She proved an exceptionally interesting subject because of her self-knowledge and her ability to verbalize the process of her thinking and writing.

Prewriting and Nature of Stimulus

For Lynn the length of prewriting period differs markedly for her three pieces, two essays and a poem. The prewriting period for "Profile of a Smile" . . . is extremely brief—three minutes—probably because this session represents the first the investigator conducts; and in her anxiety she unintentionally hurries the process. It is the first for the subject as well, and their mutual apprehensions tend to reinforce one another. Also, the investigator presents the writing of the first piece as an exercise—in a sense, as if it were a pilot for writing to come—rather than as an integral part of the investigation. Finally, the investigator really supplies the stimulus:

> It can be, you know, well you can have a description of your feelings about the testing on Saturday or you said something about having a new job. Your impressions of the new job.*

Lynn readily accepts this suggestion—"Yeah, the job would probably be a pretty good idea"—and immediately sets about planning: "Now there are a number of ways I could approach it."

The second session is taken up with Lynn's giving her writing autobiography.† At its close the investigator gives the stimulus for the second piece of writing: "Write about a person, idea, or event that especially intrigues you." Lynn immediately produces three possible subjects:

> Is that such as say, I could talk about taking a bus ride downtown . . . you know, I might be able to get something interested [sic], interesting, I was thinking about this . . . tonight we're going to have a bridge game at my house and I've invited two boys that I've both been dating and neither knows that the other's going out with me, that should be interesting. Also, I notice all these queer people on the bus going, like today, these two old ladies got on, they were straight out of *Arsenic and Old Lace,* they had very tall, very spare looking, they must have been in their sixties, their skirts were halfway to their ankles, they looked like something out of the 1930's and they, I thought they were very interesting, occasionally I see like, I think old people are very interesting, to watch them, and see what they do, little kids too . . . I might be

able to get something, just from, some of the people I work with or some of the people who come into the store I could, take one of them.

At the beginning of the next session, which does not occur until two weeks later because of a holiday in the intervening week, Lynn adds two new possible subjects, Snoopy and her grandmother:

> Last week I had said how I noticed how I always think old people on the bus and everything were very interesting. And my grandmother stayed with us for the weekend and it sort of struck me that she was a lot older than she used to be and I thought this might be an interesting topic. I could write about that, it's probably the best of the lot.

Note that two of the possible four topics involve Lynn: her grandmother and the two boys; that the fields of discourse in these cases would be the two categories of *self* and *human relationships;* and that the mode if she wrote about either might well be the *reflexive.* The other two subjects of the old ladies on the bus and Snoopy could be handled at a greater distance, with less self-involvement. Lynn chooses Snoopy, the cardboard dog. Why?

Both at the beginning and at the end of the third session Lynn speaks about why she decides against writing about the boys and about her grandmother. One ostensible reason for not writing about the boys is that such a "story" would be too limited in audience appeal: that it would please only girls who read such magazines as *Seventeen.* A second is that the subject is trite: "Oh, I'm sure everybody has had a boyfriend at some time in their life. . . . It's easy to get trite when you're talking about [boys]." Lynn's ostensible reason for not writing about her grandmother is that her grandmother's visit to their home is now two weeks away and no longer fresh in her memory. When the investigator asks her if there are other reasons, Lynn says "the Snoopy thing" is "easier" to write about:

> To write about my grandmother one thing that really struck me was when she would sit down in a chair she would sort of almost fall into it and my mother would sort of watch her when she was going up the

---

*Unless otherwise noted, the quotations in this chapter come from transcripts of the interviewer's taped sessions with Lynn.

†Because of a scheduling problem, Lynn's second and third sessions were reversed in content from the ordering described on page 30.

Profile of a Smile

After a few days of desperate searching, having just quit my job at Woolworth's sweat shop, I walked into a warm-looking yellow-and-orange dress shop on East Randolph. My anticipations of a cosy atmosphere were dispelled when I was greeted by a wall of frigid air from the hard-working air conditioner.

I was directed by a frigid sales-lady to the hard-working manager at his desk in the back. The first thing that struck me about Mr. Hobeck was his resemblance to the next-door neighbor on the old Burns and Allen television series. I spent the rest of the interview trying to remember that character's name, but could only come up with the fact that he sold Goodyear tires. Mr. Hobeck had the friendly smile of a practiced salesman which I was not going to let fool me, because those smiles often had the words "we're

not hiring" right behind them. The first clue that all this affability was not put-on came when he said that they were hiring summer help. Throughout the interview, which lasted some time and involved a personal questionaire and a rather complicated mathematics test, Mr. Hobeck's smile remained a constant.

This smile has not once left his face in the two weeks I have worked with him and I have thought of three possible causes. The first one is that Mr. Hobeck suffers from a peculiar disease that will not let the muscles of his face turn into a frown. The second is that he is a man of extreme endurance and superior salesmanship which forces him to smile in all situations. The last, and most probable, is that he is a person who really enjoys his work and lets this show through to others.

stairs because they don't have stairs at her house, and this had never occurred to me before that she was rather old. And it would be kind of hard to formulate an entire theme. If I would have perhaps seen her again this week or, I didn't see too many old people on the buses going downtown either which would have given me some insight. No, this is the easiest thing to write about.

The interesting question here is to define what for Lynn is an "easy" subject and what is a "hard" one. Clearly, an "easy" one is a nonpersonal subject, one that does not demand interacting with her feelings, one that is *not* reflexive.

There is evidence from her writing autobiography that this is a fair, if partial, interpretation. At the beginning of her account of high school writing, Lynn says:

I found that if I could write about a specific incident, and use, specific facts, I was doing a lot better than if I just had to write about like my ambitions . . . I'm sure we had to do a composition on that theme, ah

. . . it was very hard, it still is very hard for me to write about abstract things like feelings about something, I do a lot better when I have facts.

Note she defines feelings as "abstract things."

Later in the same session, the investigator asks Lynn why she thinks she feels more comfortable writing about facts rather than feelings. At first she claims she has no idea and changes the subject; later she admits that she finds expressing her feelings painful:

I've always . . . I've always had trouble talking to people about, my feelings on something. I can quote from other people I can . . . talk about, ahm . . . I can talk about facts more easily than I can talk about abstract things . . . when . . . I was at this Institute, one of the kids kept saying, 'Lynn, you know, you're a great kid but you know it doesn't come out in our discussion group because you seem to be talking in clichés, you never seem to be talking about yourself, about your own feelings, you seem to be giving examples all the

Today
* I wish the world were black and white
And white and black,
And laid out neatly
In checkerboard boxes.
The grays ~~are confusing~~.
(~~confuse me~~)

Today I wish ~~that world were~~ there was hate and
(But more love) love
And nothing
In between.

For today I am in the grays,
And hate and love are so mixed up
In this giant mixmaster of life
That I am afraid to choose;
A wrong choice.

"I set before thee the Blessing
And the Curse"
I don't know which is which.

But lacking that
I think he is afraid to love,
For he's been hurt before.

First Draft "Simplicity, Please"

time,' I don't know why this is, I could, get some sort of explanation, rather I'm sure, but I don't know.

The investigator then asks if Lynn writes about her feelings when an audience, such as teachers or peers, are not involved: the purpose of the question is to try to discover if Lynn ever engages in private self-sponsored writing, such as diary or journal writing. Lynn then describes two occasions when she has written because she "felt very strongly about something." In both cases, she says she has written these pieces because "there was nobody I could talk to."

Lynn is clearly discomfited by her difficulty in expressing feelings, both in speaking and in writing. She is almost vehement about trying to avoid clichés in her writing, the clichés that her perceptive friend in the quotation above identifies as a defense against the expression of actual emotion. One way of interpreting Lynn's effort to eliminate clichés is as a struggle to find feeling and to express it in her writing.

That her grandmother is moving toward death deeply distresses Lynn; she has difficulty examining her feelings about it, even at the distance of writing about the old ladies on the bus—clearly surrogates for her grandmother. In choosing Snoopy, the

> Simplicity, Please
>
> Today I wish the world were black and white
> And white and black,
> And laid out neatly
> In checkerboard boxes.
> The grays are confusing.
>
> Today I wish that there was ~~love~~ hate and ~~hate~~ love,
> (But more love)
> And nothing
> In between.
> (But especially love.)
>
> For today I am in the grays,
> And love and hate are so mixed up
> In the giant Mixmaster
> That I am afraid to choose
> A wrong choice.
>
> "I set before thee the Blessing
> "And the" Curse."
> I don't know which is which.

Final Draft

cardboard dog, she chooses the subject of the four least requiring emotions from her, although the decision makes her feel guilty.

To suggest that fear of feeling is the sole, or even the predominant, reason for Lynn's choice of topics is not just; her own behavior reveals that the factor of time—more specifically, the amount of time available to her for musing during the prewriting period—strongly affects her choice of subject matter. The relatively swift response which the design of this study requires and her own schedule, too full of distractions, both obviate against her choosing a subject that requires time and quiet.

She is not wholly unwilling to write about the two boys or her grandmother; in fact, for her third piece of writing she says, "I might be able to write on one of these other two topics I was talking about." She chooses poetry rather than the short story as her form "because short stories involve a good plot and I find it hard to invent plots and poetry would be easier."

Her poem "Simplicity, Please" deals, in its original version, with one of the two boys. . . . The question here is why she again chooses the subject of the boy over that of her grandmother. Once more, the factor of time seems significant. At the last session, during which Lynn describes the background to the poem, she says that she first began thinking about the matter in April, four months earlier. The subject of the boy has had a chance to ripen, to deepen; the subject of her grandmother has not.

Lynn's accounts of the prewriting periods of all three pieces lead to the following hypothesis: The length of the prewriting period available affects the choice of subject matter. If, according to the writer's perception, the period is curtailed by his own schedule or by others, he usually does not elect to work on a topic or problem he regards as cognitively or psychically complex. Rather, he chooses one he perceives as more "programmable"—that is, one that corresponds with some kind of schema he has already learned or been taught, and one he has internalized. For Lynn, as for most older secondary students in American schools, this schema is for some kind of extensive expository writing that does not require the deep personal engagement of the writer.

The linguist Leon A. Jakobovits suggests that "stale art" is algorithmic—that is, it is produced by a known algorithm, "defined as a computational device that specifies the order and nature of the steps to be followed in the generation of a sequence."[1] One could say that the major kind of essay too many students have been taught to write in American schools is algorithmic, or so mechanical that a computer could readily be programmed to produce it: when a student is hurried or anxious, he simply reverts or regresses to the only program he knows, as if inserting a single card into his brain.

PLANNING

The length of time Lynn spends upon the initial planning for the two prose pieces is quite brief; for the poem, nonexistent. The reason for Lynn's spending only three minutes planning how she will approach "Profile of a Smile" may be attributable to the circumstances under which she and others have been asked to write in school. This may account also for the brevity of the prewriting period.

What happens, however, when Lynn is relatively unrestricted in the time she can spend contemplat-

ing and planning a piece of prose? If her approach to "Terpsichordean Greetings" is representative, she spends whatever additional time she has or is given in contemplation, but not in planning. Rather, she still does her planning, as with "Profile of a Smile," immediately before writing.

There are other similarities in her planning for these two pieces. For both, as was shown above, she considers several organizational options—three, in each case. For both, as was also shown above, she considers a personal approach—that is, writing in the reflexive mode—then decides to write extensively, and impersonally, instead.

For both, her planning is oral, not written. Why this absence of written prefiguring? First, both are relatively short pieces of writing (289 and 279 words respectively); and as the pilot study in chapter 1 demonstrates, able students engage in very little written prefiguring for pieces of 500 words or fewer. By not planning in any written form, Lynn proceeds like her peers who participated in the pilot study. As she puts it in her writing autobiography:

> I've never done outlines for compositions which, might help me, sometimes . . . if in this, course when I was a sophomore, I would write down two or three points and I'd put them in what order, like one two three four and then I'd put two where four was, and things like that.

and

> Planning, I've never really done much, really. I plan it more in my head and then put it down.

For both pieces of writing she attempts to project the scope of the whole piece and, indeed, does. What she says she will include in "Terpsichordean Greetings," for example, she does include; . . . and in the order she describes:

> This morning I had an idea to write about this thing we got from my sister who is on vacation with our cousins. She sent us from, it might have been Disneyland, a two-foot-high cut-out of Snoopy, the Peanuts dog dancing, and my mother set it up in the

Terpsichordean Greetings

One of the last things someone would expect to find in a livingroom with walnut-paneled, book-lined walls would be a very large cardboard statue of Snoopy, the Peanuts dog. But in our livingroom anything is possible. He dances with an expression of utter bliss on his face, his arms held open in greeting directly in the path of anyone entering the front door.

Since he is unavoidable, all visitors to our house must register some sort of reaction. My girlfriend Barbara, who also holds her arms open in greeting to the world, embraced Snoopy in all his cardboard cuddliness and cooed, "Isn't he sweet?" The cardboard did not hug her back. My youngest sister does not lavish affection on him although they do carry on some rather interesting, if one-sided, conversations about their mutual enemy, the cat.

Friends of my parents pretend that they don't see Snoopy, politely ignoring what they consider sloppy housekeeping on my mother's part. On the contrary, it was she who put him there, and when she proudly draws attention to his presence the women coo like Barbara and think, "How quaint" and their husbands mutter an embarrassed, "Well, isn't that nice."

The only person who gave a completely sincere reaction was my current beau Marc who stalked into the house, stopped, curled his lip, gave Snoopy his best Jonathan Brewster stare and haughtily said "How gauche can you get!" Alas, poor Marc, you and all the others will never observe Snoopy's credo "To dance is to live; to live is to dance." There are very few dancers in my world.

middle of the living room so you see it when you walk in the front door. And I thought it might be interesting to write about people's reactions to it, there have been quite a few. And I was thinking of, I had two extremes in mind. This one boy when he walked in the door sort of curled up his nose at it, and I could just hear him thinking, my how gauche can you get. (laughs) And one of my girl friends came and she picked up the thing and she said, "Oh I love Snoopy," and she hugs it, this piece of cardboard. (laughs) Those are two extremes and my mother had a suggestion, well what about the adults who walk in and pretend not to see it, and that might be interesting.

Lynn's approach to "Simplicity, Please," the only poem in this sample, differs in one major way from her approaches to her prose pieces in that she engages in no planning, oral or written, for the poem. In this respect, her practice—or nonpractice—matches that of the professional poets cited in chapter 1. Since many poems, particularly lyric poems,

have fewer than 500 words, perhaps the factor of length is more significant than the factor of genre in accounting for the absence of planning.

STARTING

For Lynn, starting to write presents a paradox. Her *decision* to begin is a swift, and seemingly painless, one. Her *enactment* of a first sentence, however, is an arduous, even a tortuous, matter; and the actual time expended upon its formulation with both prose pieces is as long as that spent on any sentence—ten minutes for "Terpsichordean Greetings," seven for "Profile of a Smile."

For "Profile of a Smile," after a digression designed to assure the investigator and/or herself that she is intelligent (an evaluation the investigator had already made independently), Lynn says simply, "I think I'll start chronologically. Should I sort of read what I'm writing?" For "Terpsichordean Greetings," once she has established the scope of the piece, she begins:

> . . . this Snoopy [thing] might be interesting if I could think of enough examples. You know, I think I'm right about that? Now, did you want me to start writing?

In a personal letter to the investigator, the psychologist Jerome Bruner once commented that he was awed at the ease with which his children, then in high school, began writing. They simply sat down, and began. Bruner ends his paragraph: "Writing is for me no ordinary task."

For many adult professional writers, as for Bruner, starting to write represents so awesome a moment that they experience blocks, deterrents that can last, as in the case of Rilke, twenty years or more. Why does Lynn begin so matter-of-factly?

The reason seems linked to the reason for her choosing the subject of Snoopy, the cardboard dog, over that of her grandmother. The time allocated for her writing, by adults whom she is dutiful and disciplined enough to want to please, does not allow her to behave otherwise. She is not permitted to have blocks, as adults are. One can readily imagine what would have happened to Lynn if she had said to one or more of the teachers she describes in her writing autobiography, "I'm sorry; I have a block and can't write today." Or "Please give me another topic; I just can't write on this one." Or "I need more time if I'm to deal with this subject the way I want and feel."

As with the choice of topic, too, her own schedule does not permit her to have blocks. Along with being an extremely amiable girl, Lynn is extremely efficient and well-organized: in fact, no form of American society requires for success from its members more cognitive and psychic versatility and organization than the American high school—and Lynn, assuredly, is one of the successful ones. Lynn must fit widely disparate activities into a limited number of hours, even during her summer vacation: there is no time for mooning or moping or any form of temperament. Writing is a task to be done like any other, and one simply gets on with it.

With all three pieces, Lynn begins at the beginning: at no time, even with the poem, does she proceed from a Valeryian "ligne donée," a word, phrase, or clause that will ultimately appear in other than the initial position. This initial left-to-right thrust of composing—this "marching-through-Georgia" effect—holds for the over-all rhetorical organization of the pieces. Once into the piece, certain recursive movements, certain pendulum actions, occur; but Lynn enters the material once and once only, from a given vantage; and she does not go outside again to consider another route in.

COMPOSING ALOUD: A CHARACTERIZATION

Certain general statements can be made about Lynn's process of writing as she composes aloud. The first is that her dealings with smaller segments of discourse like the sentence and her dealings with a total piece of writing resemble one another. Both, obviously, involve the selection and arrangement of elements—lexical, syntactic, imagaic. Less obviously, there are in the parts as in the whole the same discernible portions of projecting, formulating, and reformulating.

The second is that Lynn, like the professional writers discussed by Richard Ohmann, has characteristic ways "of deploying the transformational apparatus of a language."[2] She, too, relies heavily upon "a very small amount of grammatical apparatus."[3]

Third, there seem to be certain stylistic principles operating to affect, even govern, Lynn's choices of transforms. Indeed, Lynn seems to follow some sort of "program" of style, a program whose origins can be partially traced. This program affects not only her dealings with syntax, but with lexis, rhetoric, and imagery as well.

Finally, the composing does not occur as a left-to-right, solid, uninterrupted activity with an even pace. Rather, there are recursive, as well as anticipatory, features; and there are interstices, pauses involving hesitation phenomena of various lengths and sorts that give Lynn's composing aloud a certain—perhaps a characteristic—tempo.

Projecting—Anticipating

With both prose pieces, Lynn anticipates major later portions of discourse. With "Profile of a Smile," after she refers to the smile of the manager, she foresees, essentially, the rest of her description:

Yeah, I can sort of wrap it up here by saying like, 'Throughout the interview which involved the math test blah, blah, blah'—ah, 'he still remained sunny,' and then I can just say, 'after having worked there for two week's he's still smiling and for anyone to have a phony smile for that long, he's either got terrific endurance, or he's sincere.' Then I could end it right there.

Very early in the composing of "Terpsichordean Greetings," Lynn anticipates her use of Snoopy's motto which will eventually become the second-to-last sentence in her twelve-sentence essay:

. . . something about 'it is hard to describe the utter bliss that is on this dog's face' if you've ever seen the picture of the dancing where they have 'to live is to dance, to dance is to live.'

A short while later, she speaks about the motto once again, this time in conjunction with her friend Barbara:

She [Barbara] remembered the motto that, uhm, the Snoopy sweatshirts have, this same picture of Snoopy.

In fact, it is accurate to suggest that for Lynn almost all major elements that fuse to form both essays seem present, from a very early moment in the composing process, within the foreconsciousness of the writer. (The significant exception may be Lynn's finest act of rhetoric—the last sentence of "Terpsichordean Greetings.")

Kinds of Transformational Operations

How does Lynn build a sentence? Here she is engaged in constructing the second sentence of "Terpsichordean Greetings":

*He dances in front**
He dances
He dances in front of the living room
He dances (sixteen-second pause)
He dances with an expression of utter bliss on his face, I could say "smack in the middle of the" (three-second pause)
He dances with an expression of utter bliss on his face directly in the path of anyone—yes, this is going to be good—*entering the front door* . . . Now I think I can put something else in that sentence about 'He dances' (rereads silently)
I might make it, "He dances with an expression of utter bliss on his face, his arms held open in greeting, directly in the path, et cetera"

If this sentence is divided into Christensen's "levels," it can be set out as follows:

1 He dances
  2 with an expression of utter bliss on his face (Prepositional phrase)
    3 his arms held open in greeting (Absolute)
      4 directly in the path of anyone (Prepositional phrase)
        5 entering the front door (Verb cluster)

As with many other sentences in these pieces, the architectonics of this sentence involves many major forms of transforming operations. One could say that the essential, or base, operation is that of a right-branching addition: that the movement of the sentence is essentially left-to-right.

But there are also recursive, and endocentric, features: first the adverb *smack* is inserted; later the noun absolute *his arms held open in greeting* is inserted prior to *directly in the path.*

There are exact grammatical substitutions: the single adverb *smack* is replaced by the single adverb *directly.*

There is an expansion: the juxtaposed prepositional phrases *in front of the living room* become the juxtaposed prepositional phrases *plus* the participial phrase *entering the front door.*

Lynn does not employ all transforming operations with equal frequency. There are favored

---

*Italic type denotes what Lynn wrote.

operations; for example, embeddings involving the construction of the appositive and of compound adjectives. The combining of two bases into compound adjectives is one of the few transforming actions that occurs in slow and externalized motion.

In "Profile of a Smile," for example, Lynn describes the shop:

> It was all yellow and everything as you walk into this (ten-second pause) you know. It was yellow and orange. Could I hyphenate yellow and orange if I want? (writing) . . . It will make the construction better. *I walked into a warm-looking yellow-and-orange dress shop on East Randolph.*

Here is the movement from base sentences to predicate adjective to pre-noun compound adjectives:

> The shop was yellow.
> The shop was orange.
> The shop was yellow and orange.
> The yellow-and-orange dress shop.

Lynn is aware not only of using, but of overusing, this construction. Referring to the compound adjective *yellow-and-orange,* she says, "I love my hyphenated adjectives." Referring to the double compound *book-lined, walnut-paneled,* she says more critically, "I don't like the construction. I use it too much, I think."

Style

There seems to be in Lynn's writing the operation of a "program" in style: that is, there seems to be a series of stylistic principles that direct Lynn's choices among options. Thanks to a revelation in her writing autobiography, one can discern the source of this "program" that directs many, if not most, of Lynn's choices. Near the end of her autobiography, Lynn refers to a three-part directive reiterated many times by her otherwise forgettable eleventh-grade teacher:

> one thing last year in our English course she said, "your writing should be clear concise and memorable," those were our key words

That these words affect her explicitly is seen as she composes aloud "Profile of a Smile." She refers to this teacher as she shortens *he did the Goodyear tires commercial* to *he sold Goodyear tires:*

> I had an English teacher who was always telling us to be concise, and she loved Melville who was anything but concise. But I guess I'm no Melville so I'll have to make it concise.

Analysis of what Lynn does as she composes aloud reveals that her behavior can be interpreted as efforts to enact the first two parts of this directive (Lynn seems, sensibly, to treat the third part—the production of memorable prose—as overambitious), according to her own operational definitions of these abstractions.

Not only do Lynn's efforts to be clear and concise affect her dealings with syntax; they affect as well her dealings with (1) lexical, (2) rhetorical, and (3) imagaic components.

(1) For example, in "Profile of a Smile" Lynn can be seen revising earlier elements to prevent exact lexical repetition. In the first paragraph, she changes *shop* in the first sentence to *store:* "Just make this 'store,' in the sentence before, because I think 'shop' would sound better." In the second paragraph she uses the store manager's name in the fourth sentence because "[I've] already said 'manager.' " It is as if Lynn is heeding the implicit, misguided directive: "One way of achieving clarity is not to use the same word twice if a synonym or antecedent can be found."

(2) Despite her efforts to achieve concision, Lynn produces, as noted above, a number of grammatically intricate sentences—and these worry her. Her concern takes the form of attempting consciously at times a short and relatively untransformed sentence. Lynn says, as she composes the sentence *But in our living room anything is possible,* "just make a short sentence to relieve after all of that,"—"that" being the first intricate sentence of "Terpsichordean Greetings."*

---

*Another explanation for the short sentence could be sheer fatigue: transforming the former sentence, a first sentence, has taken a great deal of energy; and Lynn is giving herself a respite.

(3) Lynn tries to arrange subtle and imaginative transitions through patterns of imagery. In fact, she is so concerned with shaping such transitions that she is willing to sacrifice both her overall plan for the piece and verisimilitude to achieve them.

As she works on the imagaic transition achieved by the double use of *frigid* and *hard-working* at the beginning of "Profile of a Smile," she realizes she is changing the nature of her essay: "This isn't turning out to be, this isn't turning out as a character. . . . " But she continues shaping the transition. Later, she sacrifices verisimilitude:

> Now I could lie a little and say "it was a complicated mathematics test and Mr. H_____'s smile remained a constant." I'll do that. It sounds better even though it's not true.

Such shaping of transitions can be regarded as a response to her teacher's three-part directive since it is clear that the succinctness achieved through imagaic transitions is yet another means of achieving concision.

OTHER OBSERVED BEHAVIORS

Observed behaviors, as noted in chapter 3, can be divided into silent activities and vocalized hesitation phenomena. The three kinds of silent activity are physical writing, silent reading, and "unfilled" pauses. Vocalized hesitation phenomena or filled pauses consist of filler sounds, expressions of feelings and attitudes, digressions, and repetition of elements.

Silent Activities

By examining Appendix B, which indicates at what points Lynn is actually putting pen or pencil to paper, one can note that there is no regular pattern of when scribal activity occurs in relation to oral composing. . . . At times Lynn writes an element at the same time she first utters it; at times she writes the element after she has uttered it a number of times. At times the element is just a word or a phrase; at times she waits, then writes a fairly long complex sentence straight through—for ex-

ample, the eleventh sentence of "Terpsichordean Greetings."

Scribal activity seems also to function as an intrusive form of "noise" in the composing process. At one point Lynn notes as she is writing, "I forgot what I was going to say." At another, she forgets to write down the phrase, *of my parents,* which she has already spoken; and she makes the comment, "I think faster than I write." If oral anticipating thrusts the discourse forward, as Bruner suggests, the physical act of writing may be said, on the other hand, to pull it back.

Reading is for Lynn another kind of hesitation phenomena. This activity usually occurs when Lynn comes to the end of a group of sentences she regards as a paragraph:

> I want to read this part over again; I think I might start a new paragraph.
> I will read the whole thing through, the whole paragraph.

and

> . . . I'm reading over that last paragraph. I have to think of a better ending.

Lynn's behaviors here suggest that her operational definition of a paragraph is "that segment of discourse at the end of which I pause and read." In his article "A Discourse-Centered Rhetoric of the Paragraph," Paul C. Rodgers, Jr., notes what he finds as the only universal characteristic of paragraphs:

> About all we can usefully say of *all* paragraphs at present is that their authors have marked them off for special considerations as *stadia of discourse,* in preference to other stadia, other patterns, in the same material. 'At this point,' the writer tells us with his indentation, 'a major stadium of discourse has just been completed. Rest for a moment, recollect and reconsider, before the next begins.'[4]

If one were to continue the quotation on the basis of Lynn's paragraphing behavior, it might read:

> . . . 'Rest for a moment, recollect and consider' just as I the writer did when I was composing.

Once again, the data suggest that later reader behavior parallels the behavior of the original reader, the writer himself, as he composed.

Vocalized Hesitation Phenomena

Lynn seldom fills pauses with filler sounds: both her spontaneous speech and her "composing" speech are usually free of [m], [3], and [e]. On two occasions when she uses "Hmm," the syllable qualifies as an interjection rather than as a filler sound.

At times she employs morphemes of low semantic content. There are instances of the use of "et cetera," "blah, blah, blah," and "such-and-such" to fill pauses. Each seems to serve a different function. "Et cetera" occurs at the end of a segment and suggests there, as it conventionally does, that the material to follow will be treated as the material that preceded. "Blah, blah, blah" is a semantically empty surrogate for a meaningful morpheme that will fill the given spaces within the utterance later. The single instance of "such-and-such" is a substitute for "Woolworth's," a name Lynn cannot for the moment remember because her attention seems focused on a more immediate composing problem. A more characteristic set of "fillers" Lynn employs is the use of phrases of low semantic content. Commonly used are "let's see," "something about," "still can't think," "How can I phrase that?"

Statements revealing one's attitudes toward his own skills and abilities while composing, as during other activities, can be arranged along a continuum from self-congratulation to self-denigration (intervening "stages" would be self-acceptance, neutrality, ambivalence, self-criticism).

If Lynn's statements about herself as she writes the two pieces of prose (she makes none toward herself as poet) are placed along this continuum, a few qualify as self-congratulatory (3); many as self-accepting (12); almost none as neutral or ambivalent (1); some as self-critical (8); and none as self-denigrating.

Lynn is not often self-congratulatory; but occasionally her ingenuity in solving an immediate writing problem delights her: "Now this gives me

a tie-in to relate to different people's reactions. Hmm, that's pretty clever"; and " 'Alas'—oh, this is good!" Her most frequent comments indicate self-acceptance and willingness to try. There are three main verbal indices for this category: "Yeah," "Okay," and "I can." Lynn demonstrates here at the same time tentativeness and commitment, a polarity of traits often present in creative activity: "It might be too complex but I'll see what I come up with" and "This is sort of a digression but I think it's okay because it brings in a sort of different point."

She is self-questioning somewhat less frequently. A few of the questions are clearly directed to the investigator; when this is the case and the question trivial, the investigator responds nondirectively:

L: Could I hyphenate yellow and orange if I want?
I: If you want.

When she abandons an option, she is occasionally forceful in her displeasure—"No, no, no"; but her displeasure with herself is mild as it is rare—for example, "But I don't like it [the title] so much."

The profile Lynn gives through these comments, then, is that of an extremely poised, assured, and open writer, occasionally skeptical about what she has done or what she plans to do, but never so negative about a specific piece of work nor of her ability in general that she stops trying in disgust or defeat. Her ego-strength seems great enough for her to believe that she can complete any assigned writing task, not only adequately but skillfully enough to please herself and her evaluator, whoever the evaluator may be.

Lynn proceeds as if what she writes will find an audience—and one wider than a single teacher or investigator. Note her use of *everyone* in the following sentence: "I don't know if everyone who reads this would get the implication." She also seems to consider it part of her writing task to pique and maintain the interest of her readers. She chooses not to write a story about her current social difficulties with one of two young men: "that wouldn't be too interesting to anyone else." Later, she enlarges the scope of the possible audience for her story:

> It might be interesting to write something just to earn money for it but they're not that interesting really, they have a limited audience appeal. This magazine [*Seventeen*] is aimed at high school aged girls and those are the only people who'd be interested in this sort of a story.

Clearly, Lynn wants, and expects, to be read.

Earlier, it was shown that Lynn's major objective as she wrote was to enact her eleventh grade teacher's directive, to be clear, concise, and memorable. All three parts of this directive really emanate from a concern for the reader. That Lynn tries so assiduously to heed them is probably the best index of her profound concern for her reader.

Of the two possible kinds of self-imposed interruptions to the writing process, blocks and digressions, we have already seen that Lynn does not experience blocks because she does not attempt over-difficult tasks. Lynn does, however, experience digressions, which can be defined either as a diversion initiated by the writer to take him temporarily away from a writing problem or as a nonproductive effort at anticipation.

There are essentially two types of digressions Lynn engages in: the first, extrinsic and ego-enhancing; the second, discourse-related. Here is a series of ego-enhancing digressions; the first two appear in the first session; the third, in the third session:

1. When I walked into the store for the first time, I'd never heard of the place and I went looking for the manager and he . . . said, 'How are you?' and 'You look very bright.'

2. Now this is really getting off the track but I think it was very interesting. The test was, it was like a standardized test. It was printed out and with multiple choice answers but the questions were so ridiculous . . . like 'If something was selling three for eighty-eight' or something like that. You know, 'how much would one thing be,'

you know, simple math problems. But they had really stupid questions, I thought they were stupid. . . . They would have a list of proverbs. . . . I got all of those wrong, but I got all of the math questions right so I got the job. Let's see how can I phrase it about the proverbs?

3. The thing about our living room, there are more books and magazines there than, that's no, really not so many books because there are boxes of books in the basement. . . . There are magazines galore.

Lynn's third digression, for example, is to assure the investigator that she comes from a literate household, or at least from one in which there are not only books but "magazines galore." The purpose of the first digression is to show the investigator that others find her bright, with the implicit causal question, "Therefore why shouldn't you?" The second is a little more complex. Lynn seems to need to confess to the investigator that she did not do well on a verbal test (the proverbs test), perhaps so that there is no feeling she is involved in the inquiry under the false pretenses of being a highly able verbal student. At the same time, she also needs reassurance that the test itself was stupid, or at least misleading. She not only gives herself this reassurance; but she fuses the difficult verbal test with a mathematics test in which she did well, to neutralize its effect.

In addition to this kind of digression, the motivation of which Lynn seems unaware, there are others where she seems to understand why she makes a certain writing decision: "I find it hard to do dialogue because all my characters end up speaking like me which is not really good because that's not how they talk."

Her final digression is to explain an allusion, not unlike a footnote in "The Waste Land":

> gave Snoopy his best Jonathan Brewster, now I don't know if you, Jonathan Brewster is the Frankenstein nephew in *Arsenic and Old Lace*. He [Marc] played him in a play, it was excellent.

As this section reveals, Lynn engages in very few digressions unrelated to the writing of the two prose pieces. When she does, her usual purpose seems to be to win the approval of, or to inform, the investigator.

An example of a digression which might be defined as a nonproductive anticipation is Lynn's dealings with the family cat in "Terpsichordean Greetings." She has just finished formulating the sentence, *Even my youngest sister does not lavish affection on him, although she does carry on some rather interesting, if one-sided, conversations about their mutual enemy, the cat.* The cat stimulates his own chain of associations:

> Now I could talk about what the cat does. Perhaps the cat realizes that Snoopy is a dog and therefore dislikes him, or perhaps she's jealous that people seem to pay more attention to him when they walk in the door. But she sort of gives it a whack with a paw when she walks by. My father pretends to hate the cat. He will fake a kick when he walks by and stamp his foot. That's sort of what the cat's doing to Snoopy.

At last she realizes how far she has moved from her consideration of human reactions to Snoopy. She says, laughing, "That's an entirely different story. I think I can just drop the cat."

Lynn does not seem to be victimized by the irrelevant as some writers are. She sees clearly that she has moved away from the subject of her piece and that the material generated does not belong. Matter-of-factly, she does "just drop the cat" and move back to her prior material and organization.

The Tempo of Composing

Composing aloud as a process consists of the alternation of actual composing behaviors (the selection and ordering of elements) and of all hesitation phenomena the writer employs. Hesitations can consist of a single behavior of the sort noted in the section above or of a series of aligned behaviors, in various combinations. For example, the following sequence

> *the Peanuts dog* (pause) just make a short sentence to relieve after all of that

consists of scribal activity + unfilled pause + "empty" phrase.

Another way of putting the matter is that a hesitation extends from one piece of composing behavior to the next. The hesitation may be very brief, of several seconds' duration, or very long, of several minutes' duration.

With what, if anything, does the length of hesitation correlate? The recent work of two verbal behaviorists provides a double hypothesis to examine with the data. The first is the general conclusion presented by the psychologist Frieda Goldman-Eisler that for spontaneous speech "hesitation pauses precede a sudden increase of information, estimated in terms of transition probabilities."[5] The second is the assumption that George A. Miller tests experimentally and reports in "Some Psychological Studies of Grammar": "the more complicated a grammatical transformation the longer it will take people to perform it."[6]

If composing aloud can be characterized in ways comparable with spontaneous speech, the following two hypotheses may obtain:

1. In composing aloud, a specialized form of verbal behavior, hesitation pauses precede a sudden increase of information as represented by grammatical transformations of varying complexity;

2. The writer requires longer pauses to perform more complex transformations.

Unfortunately, an analysis of the data yields only the grossest distinctions in the time Lynn requires for performing given transformations. For example, the appositives in the two prose pieces with one exception take an imperceptible amount of time—that is, less than a second. Left-branching additions, such as *Since he is unavoidable,* require, on the other hand, an average of twenty seconds to perform. No accurate statements can be made about other transforming operations Lynn performs because of the grossness of the study. Assuredly, a study of a finer calibration with more careful recording techniques would be useful in ascertaining if some kind of hierarchy can be established for transforming operations performed during composing aloud, for a single writer or for a given group of writers.

REFORMULATING; STOPPING; CONTEMPLATING THE PRODUCT

Reformulating, stopping, and contemplating the product are treated here in a single section because in Lynn's process of writing they take up so little chronological and psychological time that they almost coalesce into a single barely occurring experience.

Partially because of the design and the conduct of this inquiry—but, seemingly, far more because of her attitude toward revising—Lynn does not really reformulate any of the three pieces she writes. There are several features of the design and Lynn's attitudes toward the sessions that may explain, at least in the cases of the two prose pieces, why she does not. Of prime importance is the fact that the design does not explicitly provide for reformulation, an activity which requires quiet, if not solitude; leisure; and some separation in time from the act of writing.

The investigator neither states nor suggests that Lynn revise, nor does she make a direct offer for Lynn to take her piece away so that she can reformulate. Lynn, perhaps consequently (and perhaps like the investigator), treats the sessions as self-contained units to which she allocates, roughly, ninety minutes per session, and in which she devotes her energy to the central writing act. And although there are no verbal data to corroborate the investigator's intuitions on this matter, Lynn behaves as if the investigator, like herself, has a view of the writing process as a no-nonsense, no-dawdle task to which one devotes a given amount of time, and no more.

Lynn's attitudes toward reformulating seem to emanate from her experiences with school writing. In her writing autobiography Lynn makes clear why she "never took it on myself to rewrite a composition":

> Partly because it seemed to be punishment work we were just said [sic], if you have more than so many

mistakes, you have to rewrite your composition and it has to be in by Friday after, and . . . she never would . . . our English teachers never re-r——, I mean, maybe she talked to me about my composition I don't remember but I never remember any suggestions which inspired me, to rewrite something, so that there was any change in the, so that it was any better, the only changes seemed to be technical ones.

First, although it is clear from her responses that Lynn understands the term *revise,* she never uses it herself. Rather, as in the statement above, she speaks instead of *rewriting.* As usual, Lynn is careful in her choice of words. Lynn's operational definition of rewriting seems to be the act of "correcting" errors in the accidents of discourse—spelling, punctuation, titling, and the like. Such essences as organization of the whole and tone are, seemingly, left undisturbed. There is only a superficial, a surface realignment or correcting the trivial.

Lynn does not voluntarily reformulate because, simply and understandably, she equates reformulation with "punishment work." Also, she does not reformulate because her teachers do not "inspire" her to. What does this word mean coming from a girl who does not seem to ask for inspiration from any other teaching she experiences? She seems to mean first that her teachers, on the whole, write evaluative comments that do not deal with what she is really trying to say; and that they are not really interested in reading and evaluating any reformulation she might attempt. She is in effect accusing them of oversimplification (the equation of reformulating with the "correction" of trivia); and casualness, if not cynicism, in evaluation (they demand correction of trivia, but they will not read and reevaluate a serious effort to recast essences).

Influence of Teachers

The influence of her teachers upon these three pieces of Lynn's writing can, of course, only be inferred. A major source of the investigator's information about the teaching of writing Lynn has experienced is what Lynn says she remembers about such teaching. Also, with Lynn, the investigator is fortunate in having a subject who saved some of her writing from fourth grade forward, including a folder from her tenth grade English class which contained the total output of her assigned writing for that year. The investigator, then, has had an opportunity to see Lynn's composition work for a full school year with all written emendations and evaluations made by her teacher for that year.

One way of approaching the matter of influence is to note what Lynn worries about as she writes; then, to try to find possible origins for her worries in previous school experiences she describes. As she composes aloud, Lynn's energies seem divided between dealing with the actual stuff of discourse and with the amenities. During the writing sessions, she deals explicitly five times with amenities: three concern spelling; one, legibility; one, titling. Once she asks how to spell a word, *terpsichordean:* "Is it 'terps *e*' or '*i*'?" When the investigator does not respond, she spells it correctly with an *i*. Once she asks whether or not she should hyphenate a compound adjective. When the investigator says, "If you wish," Lynn does hyphenate *yellow-and-orange*. In the three pieces of writing Lynn misspells only one word; and she knows it is misspelled: "I forgot how to spell 'questionnaire.' " (Lynn spells it with one *n*.)

Lynn's handwriting is always legible. That she strives for legibility is evident from this comment about an insertion: "Now where can I write that so that it can be legible?"

Lynn, then, is very aware of the amenities of writing, particularly spelling and handwriting. Was she trained to be aware of these? Lynn's first memory of writing in school is that "it seemed to me going through my notebooks from grammar school that all we did was spelling. I had pages on pages of spelling exercises, and really didn't do too much writing at all." The first "theme" she remembers writing is "a composition about ah . . . something about some poor child who never got anything for Christmas and they got a musical teddy bear and they were very happy." She remembers writing

the story on the board; in relating the incident she pauses, then breaks off her account with a rather abrupt "That's about all I can remember from third or fourth grade." But later in the session she remembers more, much more: she remembers what made the composition of the musical teddy bear so painfully memorable that it stayed in the forefront of her consciousness for eleven years while all other writing experiences of the same period dropped away:

> I remember writing this composition about the musical teddy bear on the board; our district superintendent was coming in that day and I, my teacher thought it was very good and I spelled *musical* wrong, and she was very embarrassed, that's why I remember the composition, just because of that incident.

Lynn makes five other comments about spelling while presenting her writing autobiography. Her own point of view about her teachers' stress, or obsession, is summed up in one sentence: "They seem to have this thing about spelling."

There are powerful reasons from her past school experiences for her wanting to write legibly, too. For a full school year she was punished for not writing Palmer style:

> In sixth grade I remember we had a teacher who'd give us two grades on a composition, this I thought was horrible, one on composition, and another on your handwriting, and this counted as much, I used to get "E's" on my composition, "E" for excellent, and "F-plus" on my handwriting because it tended to be rather ornate, I had all these little curlicues attached on it, and I have it here, it's really a riot when I look at it now.

The whole matter of "technical correctness," as Lynn aptly calls it, has loomed large not only in her life but in her friends' lives. In fact, she attributes her selection as subject in my investigation to her department chairman's preoccupation with correctness:

> This one girl was in my class, and we had another—I don't know what you could call these courses, you could call them orthodox classes where we just were

corrected practically on technical errors, she was getting "B's" again instead of "A's" although I thought her writing was much better than most of the kids in our class. That's possibly why I was picked for this program, this girl . . . could have done it as well but the teacher who . . . liked all these technically correct papers and that's what I turned in so, that's why she liked me.

A last amenity Lynn has clearly been taught: that every piece of writing, no matter what its length or significance, must have a title. Her last act with all three pieces of writing is to supply, reluctantly, a title. "Now, title, 'terpsichordean' means to dance, you could say 'Terpsichordean Greetings' but I don't like it so much." [She writes it at the top of the page] "Is it 'terps e' or 'i'?"

For her first piece the following exchange occurs:

L: Do I have to title it?

I: Whatever you wish.

L: I could get something . . . on 'Profiles of Courage' and make it 'Profiles,' 'Profiles and Smiles,' or something like that. [As she writes it down], Why not?

With her usual self-awareness, Lynn knows she is hostile toward giving themes titles yet conditioned since grammar school toward using them:

> I could never think of an ending, and also the title, this principal of our grammar school had gotten this idea that she didn't want kids writing compositions like my trip to the zoo, and title it like that, so we would write, say, about our trip to the zoo, and maybe it would turn out that we would write only about a polar bear we saw, so the title of the composition would be ahm . . . something about the ice-cream-colored bear, you know, or we would, would get rather imaginative titles, hence when I got into high school I didn't want to put titles on my compositions, you saw last week I really didn't want to put a title on it.

The principal's concern seems to be with the limitation of subject, but note for Lynn the stress becomes one of titling.

Along with one "thing" about spelling, and another about titling, Lynn's teachers also seem to have "this business" about length. Within the forty-five minutes Lynn spends recounting her writing autobiography, she alludes nine times to the length of pieces of writing, with eight of these related to teacher directives. Again, it is the third-grade teacher, Lynn's first teacher of writing, who first gives Lynn limitations in length:

> So she had us writing, we were limited, in about third grade we were limited to about fifty words.

But other elementary teachers also ask her to observe comparable limitation:

> All through grammar school we were still limited to this, sixty-word business.

In her writing sessions with the investigator, Lynn makes many comments that reveal her concern with length; it is as if she has spent her writing life in school learning to respond only to Madison Avenue contests of twenty-five-words-or-less.

It is not surprising that one of the peripheral skills Lynn has developed in the course of her schooling is the ability to judge, with high accuracy, the number of words comprising any given segment of discourse. "I really don't think I need any sort of a tie-in right here because I'm definitely talking about the manager even though I have this business of about twenty-five words about Burns and Allen." It is probably not accidental, either, that her two prose pieces are almost identical in length, with 289 words in one and 279 words in the other.

Finally, the investigator's policy of nonintervention as Lynn writes makes her anxious, and angry, only once. She asks, "Now how long should this be?" When the investigator doesn't immediately answer her question, she asks:

> Which would you rather see, or aren't you going to say anything, you're just going to sit there nodding your head?

One can only conclude that some of Lynn's preoccupations as she writes have been conditioned by teachers who clearly had as their motto: "The good student writer is the polite student writer."

Lynn worries about elements, as well as amenities, of discourse. She alludes to three "problems" (her words) in her writing—one lexical, one lexical-syntactic, and one rhetorical. First, she is extremely concerned with avoiding the trite expression—what she calls a "cliché phrase." Examples are "striking resemblance," "one of those people who has found his place," and "one of the last things." (She notes no "cliché phrases" in her poem, although an adult evaluator might.) She does not always decide to eliminate these from writing. Although she changes "striking resemblance" to "plain resemblance" (really, a semantic shift), she decides to retain "who has found his place" because it fits into the conversational style she has set for her piece ("the composition is written sort of in a telling manner"); and "one of the last things" because "[it's] sort of a cliché phrase but it's okay."

Along with worrying about triteness, Lynn worries about being "flowery" or "corny"—both terms synonyms, apparently, for pretentious or sentimental. She makes fewer allusions to this stylistic hazard, however. She does decide against using "anticipations were dispelled" with the comment, "I'm always afraid of being too corny because there are some kids in my class who write [like that]."

She repeatedly demonstrates she is attuned to words—their appropriate idiom and their connotative aura: "some word like 'premonition,' only without those fearful overtones"; " 'dispelled' sounds as though you had a number of things which are scattered"; "something about 'entrance,' but 'entrance' isn't good because that's like entering school"; and "now a look that is threatening. What's that called?" Lynn never finds "sneer," the word she is probably seeking; and she finally compromises with "stare" (note the allophonic nearness to "sneer").

Lynn also demonstrates an awareness of the relations of ordinates and their enclosing superordinates, a phase of what might be regarded as the logic of language. For example, she changes *picked Snoopy up* to *embraced Snoopy* because "she had to pick him up to embrace him."

CONCLUSION

Lynn seems to write with greater ease in the extensive than in the reflexive mode. There seem to be both personal and curricular reasons. Personally, she seems a girl reserved about her feelings, although open, even volatile, about ideas. It could even be said she reveals a certain fear of feeling. Also, the curriculum she has experienced in composition, both in elementary and in secondary school, has provided her with very few school-sponsored opportunities for engaging in reflexive writing, as her writing autobiography and a review of her theme folders confirm.

Lynn's view of the composing process is that it is essentially and centrally the act of the first discursive writing. For this inquiry, at least, she devotes very little time to prewriting, projecting, and reformulating activities, while her energy and concentration upon the task of composing aloud are great.

Although the assigning of causality is especially hazardous in matters of teaching and learning, Lynn seems susceptible to the teaching of composition she has experienced. Her view of what portion of the composing process is most important matches the views of her teachers who do not provide school time for the earlier, and later, portions. She worries about what her teachers have stressed, especially the accidents of spelling, handwriting, and length. She tries, often with great skill, to translate directives of high abstractness into sets of behaviors she can enact.

At the same time, there is the inescapable impression that Lynn is more sophisticated than her teachers, both as to the level of her stylistic concerns and to the accuracy and profundity of her analysis of herself as a writer.

Notes

1. Leon A. Jakobovits, "Rhetoric and Stylistics: Some Basic Issues in the Analysis of Discourse," *College Composition and Communication* (December 1969), p. 325.

2. Richard Ohmann, "Generative Grammars and the Concept of Literary Style," *Word* (1964), p. 431.

3. *Ibid.*, p. 433.

4. Paul C. Rodgers, Jr., "A Discourse-centered Rhetoric of the Paragraph," *College Composition and Communication* (February 1966), p. 5.

5. Frieda Goldman-Eisler, "Discussion and Further Comments," *New Directions in the Study of Language,* ed. Eric H. Lenneberg, p. 120.

6. George A. Miller, "Some Psychological Studies of Grammar," *Readings in the Psychology of Language,* ed. Leon A. Jakobovits and Murray S. Miron, p. 212.

Studies student during writing process,
Examines pre-writing, composition : revision,
(of which there is none) tempo, hesitations
writing influences,
attempts to make conclusions about
writing process f/ these actions

From questions researcher poses, it becomes
apparent she believes writing process is a
result of training by teachers and molded
by necessity of circumstances or conditions

A Cognitive Process Theory of Writing

Linda Flower and John R. Hayes

Flower and Hayes's essay originally appeared in College Composition and Communication *32 (1981): 365–87.*

There is a venerable tradition in rhetoric and composition which sees the composing process as a series of decisions and choices.[1] However, it is no longer easy simply to assert this position, unless you are prepared to answer a number of questions, the most pressing of which probably is: "What then are the criteria which govern that choice?" Or we could put it another way: "What guides the decisions writers make as they write?" In a recent survey of composition research, Odell, Cooper, and Courts noticed that some of the most thoughtful people in the field are giving us two reasonable but somewhat different answers:

> How do writers actually go about choosing diction, syntactic and organizational patterns, and content? Kinneavy claims that one's purpose informing, persuading, expressing, or manipulating language for its own sake—guides these choices. Moffett and Gibson contend that these choices are determined by one's sense of the relation of speaker, subject, and audience. Is either of these two claims borne out by the actual practice of writers engaged in drafting or revising? Does either premise account adequately for the choices writers make?[2]

Rhetoricians such as Lloyd Bitzer and Richard Vatz have energetically debated this question in still other terms. Lloyd Bitzer argues that speech always occurs as a response to a rhetorical situation, which he succinctly defines as containing an exigency (which demands a response), an audience, and a set of constraints.[3] In response to this "situation-driven" view, Vatz claims that the speaker's response, and even the rhetorical situation itself, are determined by the imagination and art of the speaker.[4]

Finally, James Britton has asked the same question and offered a linguist's answer, namely, that syntactic and lexical choices guide the process.

> It is tempting to think of writing as a process of making linguistic choices from one's repertoire of syntactic structures and lexical items. This would suggest that there is a meaning, or something to be expressed, in the writer's mind, and that he proceeds to choose, from the words and structures he has at his disposal, the ones that best match his meaning. But is that really how it happens?[5]

To most of us it may seem reasonable to suppose that all of these forces—"purposes," "relationships," "exigencies," "language"—have a hand in guiding the writer's process, but it is not at all clear how they do so or how they interact. Do they, for example, work in elegant and graceful coordination, or as competitive forces constantly vying for control? We think that the best way to answer these questions—to really understand the nature of rhetorical choices in good and poor writers—is to follow James Britton's lead and turn our attention to the writing process itself: to ask, "but is that really how it happens?"

This paper will introduce a theory of the cognitive processes involved in composing in an effort to lay groundwork for more detailed study of thinking processes in writing. This theory is based on our work with protocol analysis over the past five years

285

and has, we feel, a good deal of evidence to support it. Nevertheless, it is for us a working hypothesis and springboard for further research, and we hope that insofar as it suggests testable hypotheses it will be the same for others. Our cognitive process theory rests on four key points, which this paper will develop:

1. The process of writing is best understood as a set of distinctive thinking processes which writers orchestrate or organize during the act of composing.

2. These processes have a hierarchical, highly embedded organization in which any given process can be embedded within any other.

3. The act of composing itself is a goal-directed thinking process, guided by the writer's own growing network of goals.

4. Writers create their own goals in two key ways: by generating both high-level goals and supporting sub-goals which embody the writer's developing sense of purpose, and then, at times, by changing major goals or even establishing entirely new ones based on what has been learned in the act of writing.

1. Writing is best understood as a set of distinctive thinking processes which writers orchestrate or organize during the act of composing.

To many this point may seem self-evident, and yet it is in marked contrast to our current paradigm for composing—the stage process model. This familiar metaphor or model describes the composing process as a linear series of stages, separated in time, and characterized by the gradual development of the written product. The best examples of stage models are the Pre-Write/Write/ReWrite model of Gordon Rohman[6] and The Conception/Incubation/Production model of Britton *et al.*[7]

Stage Models of Writing

Without doubt, the wide acceptance of Pre-Writing has helped improve the teaching of composition by calling attention to planning and discovery as legitimate parts of the writing process. Yet many question whether this linear stage model is really an accurate or useful description of the composing process itself. The problem with stage descriptions of writing is that they model the growth of the written product, not the inner process of the person producing it. "Pre-Writing" is the stage before words emerge on paper; "Writing" is the stage in which a product is being produced; and "Re-Writing" is a final reworking of that product. Yet both common sense and research tell us that writers are constantly planning (pre-writing) and revising (re-writing) as they compose (write), not in clean-cut stages.[8] Furthermore, the sharp distinctions stage models make between the operations of planning, writing, and revising may seriously distort how these activities work. For example, Nancy Sommers has shown that revision, as it is carried out by skilled writers, is not an end-of-the-line repair process, but is a constant process of "re-vision" or re-seeing that goes on while they are composing.[9] A more accurate model of the composing process would need to recognize those basic thinking processes which unite planning and revision. Because stage models take the final product as their reference point, they offer an inadequate account of the more intimate, moment-by-moment intellectual process of composing. How, for example, is the output of one stage, such as pre-writing or incubation, transferred to the next? As every writer knows, having good ideas doesn't automatically produce good prose. Such models are typically silent on the inner processes of decision and choice.

A Cognitive Process Model

A cognitive process theory of writing, such as the one presented here, represents a major departure from the traditional paradigm of stages in this way: in a stage model the major units of analysis are *stages* of completion which reflect the growth of a written product, and these stages are organized in a *linear* sequence or structure. In a process model, the major units of analysis are elementary mental *processes,* such as the process of generating ideas. And these

[handwritten margin notes: "this seems to be" "what "science"" "are done" "determining" "what" "is done" "that" "they can" "to better" "understand" "of how" "writing" "is done"]

processes have a *hierarchical* structure . . . such that idea generation, for example, is a sub-process of Planning. Furthermore, each of these mental acts may occur at any time in the composing process. One major advantage of identifying these basic cognitive processes or thinking skills writers use is that we can then compare the composing strategies of good and poor writers. And we can look at writing in a much more detailed way.

In psychology and linguistics, one traditional way of looking carefully at a process is to build a model of what you see. A model is a metaphor for a process: a way to describe something, such as the composing process, which refuses to sit still for a portrait. As a hypothesis about a dynamic system, it attempts to describe the parts of the system and how they work together. Modeling a process starts as a problem in design. For example, imagine that you have been asked to start from scratch and design an imaginary, working "Writer." In order to build a "Writer" or a theoretical system that would reflect the process of a real writer, you would want to do at least three things:

1. First, you would need to define the major elements or sub-processes that make up the larger process of writing. Such sub-processes would include planning, retrieving information from long-term memory, reviewing, and so on.

2. Second, you would want to show how these various elements of the process interact in the total process of writing. For example, how is "knowledge" about the audience actually integrated into the moment-to-moment act of composing?

3. And finally, since a model is primarily a tool for thinking with, you would want your model to speak to critical questions in the discipline. It should help you see things you didn't see before.

Obviously, the best way to model the writing process is to study a writer in action, and there are many ways to do this. However, people's after-the-fact, *introspective analysis* of what they did while writing is notoriously inaccurate and likely to be influenced by their notions of what they should have done. Therefore we turned to *protocol*

analysis, which has been successfully used to study other cognitive processes.[10] Unlike introspective reports, thinking aloud protocols capture a detailed record of what is going on in the writer's mind during the act of composing itself. To collect a protocol, we give writers a problem, such as "Write an article on your job for the readers of *Seventeen* magazine," and then ask them to compose out loud near an unobtrusive tape recorder. We ask them to work on the task as they normally would—thinking, jotting notes, and writing—except that they must think out loud. They are asked to verbalize everything that goes through their minds as they write, including stray notions, false starts, and incomplete or fragmentary thought. The writers are not asked to engage in any kind of introspection or self-analysis while writing, but simply to think out loud while working like a person talking to herself.

The transcript of this session, which may amount to 20 pages for an hour session, is called a protocol. As a research tool, a protocol is extraordinarily rich in data and, together with the writer's notes and manuscript, it gives us a very detailed picture of the writer's composing process. It lets us see not only the development of the written product but many of the intellectual processes which produced it. The model of the writing process presented in Figure 1 attempts to account for the major thinking processes and constraints we saw at work in these protocols. But note that it does *not* specify the order in which they are invoked.

The act of writing involves three major elements which are reflected in the three units of the model: **the task environment, the writer's long-term memory, and the writing processes.** The task environment includes all of those things outside the writer's skin, starting with the rhetorical problem or assignment and eventually including the growing text itself. The second element is the writer's long-term memory in which the writer has stored knowledge, not only of the topic, but of the audience and of various writing plans. The third element in our model contains writing processes themselves, specifically the basic processes of **Planning, Translating, and Reviewing,** which are under the control of a Monitor.

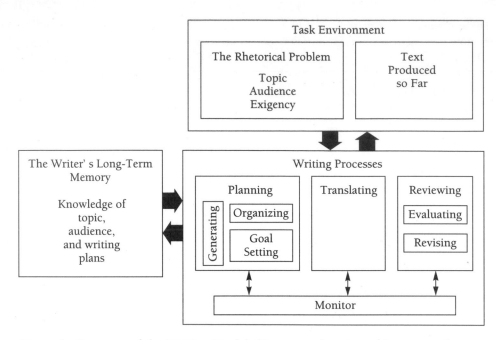

Figure 1. Structure of the Writing Model. (For an explanation of how to read a process model, see note 11.)

This model attempts to account for the processes we saw in the composing protocols. It is also a guide to research, which asks us to explore each of these elements and their interaction more fully. Since this model is described in detail elsewhere,[11] let us focus here on some ways each element contributes to the overall process.

Overview of the Model

The Rhetorical Problem

At the beginning of composing, the most important element is obviously **the rhetorical problem** itself. A school assignment is a simplified version of such a problem, describing the writer's topic, audience, and (implicitly) her role as student to teacher. Insofar as writing is a rhetorical act, not a mere artifact, writers attempt to "solve" or respond to this rhetorical problem by writing something.

In theory this problem is a very complex thing: it includes not only the rhetorical situation and au-

dience which prompts one to write, it also includes the writer's own goals in writing.[12] A good writer is a person who can juggle all of these demands. But in practice we have observed, as did Britton,[13] that writers frequently reduce this large set of constraints to a radically simplified problem, such as "write another theme for English class." Redefining the problem in this way is obviously an economical strategy as long as the new representation fits reality. But when it doesn't, there is a catch: people only solve the problems they define for themselves. If a writer's representation of her rhetorical problem is inaccurate or simply underdeveloped, then she is unlikely to "solve" or attend to the missing aspects of the problem. To sum up, defining the rhetorical problem is a major, immutable part of the writing process. But the way in which people choose to define a rhetorical problem to themselves can vary greatly from writer to writer. An important goal for research then will be to discover how this process of representing the problem works and how it affects the writer's performance.

The Written Text

As composing proceeds, a new element enters the task environment which places even more constraints upon what the writer can say. Just as a title constrains the content of a paper and a topic sentence shapes the options of a paragraph, each word in the growing text determines and limits the choices of what can come next. However, the influence that the growing text exerts on the composing process can vary greatly. When writing is incoherent, the text may have exerted too little influence; the writer may have failed to consolidate new ideas with earlier statements. On the other hand, one of the earmarks of a basic writer is a dogged concern with extending the previous sentence[14] and a reluctance to jump from local, text-bound planning to more global decisions, such as "what do I want to cover here?"

As we will see, the growing text makes large demands on the writer's time and attention during composing. But in doing so, it is competing with two other forces which could and also should direct the composing process; namely, the writer's knowledge stored in long-term memory and the writer's plans for dealing with the rhetorical problem. It is easy, for example, to imagine a conflict between what you know about a topic and what you might actually want to say to a given reader, or between a graceful phrase that completes a sentence and the more awkward point you actually wanted to make. Part of the drama of writing is seeing how writers juggle and integrate the multiple constraints of their knowledge, their plans, and their text into the production of each new sentence.[15]

The Long-Term Memory

The writer's long-term memory, which can exist in the mind as well as in outside resources such as books, is a storehouse of knowledge about the topic and audience, as well as knowledge of writing plans and problem representations. Sometimes a single cue in an assignment, such as "write a persuasive . . . ," can let a writer tap a stored representation of a problem and bring a whole raft of writing plans into play.

Unlike short-term memory, which is our active processing capacity or conscious attention, long-term memory is a relatively stable entity and has its own internal organization of information. The problem with long-term memory is, first of all, getting things out of it—that is, finding the cue that will let you retrieve a network of useful knowledge. The second problem for a writer is usually reorganizing or adapting that information to fit the demands of the rhetorical problem. The phenomena of "writer-based" prose nicely demonstrates the results of a writing strategy based solely on retrieval. The organization of a piece of writer-based prose faithfully reflects the writer's own discovery process and the structure of the remembered information itself, but it often fails to transform or reorganize that knowledge to meet the different needs of a reader.[16]

Planning

People often think of planning as the act of figuring out how to get from here to there, i.e., making a detailed plan. But our model uses the term in its much broader sense. In the **planning** process writers form an internal *representation* of the knowledge that will be used in writing. This internal representation is likely to be more abstract than the writer's prose representation will eventually be. For example, a whole network of ideas might be represented by a single key word. Furthermore, this representation of one's knowledge will not necessarily be made in language, but could be held as a visual or perceptual code, e.g., as a fleeting image the writer must then capture in words.

Planning, or the act of building this internal representation, involves a number of subprocesses. The most obvious is the act of **generating ideas**, which includes retrieving relevant information from long-term memory. Sometimes this information is so well developed and organized *in memory* that the writer is essentially generating standard written English. At other times one may generate only fragmentary, unconnected, even contradictory thoughts, like the pieces of a poem that hasn't yet taken shape.

When the structure of ideas already in the writer's memory is not adequately adapted to the current rhetorical task, the sub-process of **organizing** takes on the job of helping the writer make meaning, that is, give a meaningful structure to his or her ideas. The process of **organizing** appears to play an important part in creative thinking and discovery since it is capable of grouping ideas and forming new concepts. More specifically, the organizing process allows the writer to identify categories, to search for subordinate ideas which develop a current topic, and to search for superordinate ideas which include or subsume the current topic. At another level the process of organizing also attends to more strictly textual decisions about the presentation and ordering of the text. That is, writers identify first or last topics, important ideas, and presentation patterns. However, organizing is much more than merely ordering points. And it seems clear that all rhetorical decisions and plans for reaching the audience affect the process of organizing ideas at all levels, because it is often guided by major goals established during the powerful process of **goal-setting.**

Goal-setting is indeed a third, little-studied but major, aspect of the **planning** process. The goals writers give themselves are both procedural (e.g., "Now let's see—a—I want to start out with 'energy'") and substantive, often both at the same time (e.g., "I have to relate this [engineering project] to the economics [of energy] to show why I'm improving it and why the steam turbine needs to be more efficient" or "I want to suggest that—that—um the reader should sort of what what should one say—the reader should look at what she is interested in and look at the things that give her pleasure . . .").

The most important thing about writing goals is the fact that they are *created* by the writer. Although some well-learned plans and goals may be drawn intact from long-term memory, most of the writer's goals are generated, developed, and revised by the same processes that generate and organize new ideas. And this process goes on throughout composing. Just as goals lead a writer to generate ideas, those ideas lead to new, more complex goals which can then integrate content and purpose.

Our own studies on goal setting to date suggest that the act of defining one's own rhetorical problem and setting goals is an important part of "being creative" and can account for some important differences between good and poor writers.[17] As we will argue in the final section of this paper, the act of developing and refining one's own goals is not limited to a "pre-writing stage" in the composing process, but is intimately bound up with the ongoing, moment-to-moment process of composing.

Translating

This is essentially the process of putting ideas into visible language. We have chosen the term **translate** for this process over other terms such as "transcribe" or "write" in order to emphasize the peculiar qualities of the task. The information generated in **planning** may be represented in a variety of symbol systems other than language, such as imagery or kinetic sensations. Trying to capture the movement of a deer on ice in language is clearly a kind of translation. Even when the **planning** process represents one's thought in words, that representation is unlikely to be in the elaborate syntax of written English. So the writer's task is to translate a meaning, which may be embodied in key words (what Vygotsky calls words "saturated with sense") and organized in a complex network of relationships, into a linear piece of written English.

The process of **translating** requires the writer to juggle all the special demands of written English, which Ellen Nold has described as lying on a spectrum from generic and formal demands through syntactic and lexical ones down to the motor tasks of forming letters. For children and inexperienced writers, this extra burden may overwhelm the limited capacity of short-term memory.[18] If the writer must devote conscious attention to demands such as spelling and grammar, the task of translating can interfere with the more global process of planning what one wants to say. Or one can simply ignore some of the constraints of written English. One path produces poor or local planning, the other produces errors, and both, as Mina Shaughnessy showed, lead to frustration for the writer.[19]

In some of the most exciting and extensive research in this area, Marlene Scardamalia and Carl Bereiter have looked at the ways children cope with the cognitive demands of writing. Well-learned skills, such as sentence construction, tend to become automatic and lost to consciousness. Because so little of the writing process is automatic for children, they must devote conscious attention to a variety of individual thinking tasks which adults perform quickly and automatically. Such studies, which trace the development of a given skill over several age groups, can show us the hidden components of an adult process as well as show us how children learn. For example, these studies have been able to distinguish children's ability to handle idea complexity from their ability to handle syntactic complexity; that is, they demonstrate the difference between seeing complex relationships and translating them into appropriate language. In another series of studies Bereiter and Scardamalia showed how children learn to handle the translation process by adapting, then eventually abandoning, the discourse conventions of conversation.[20]

Reviewing

As you can see in Figure 1, reviewing depends on two sub-processes: evaluating and revising. Reviewing, itself, may be a conscious process in which writers choose to read what they have written either as a springboard to further translating or with an eye to systematically evaluating and/or revising the text. These periods of planned reviewing frequently lead to new cycles of planning and translating. However, the reviewing process can also occur as an unplanned action triggered by an evaluation of either the text or one's own planning (that is, people revise written as well as unwritten thoughts or statements). The sub-processes of revising and evaluating, along with generating, share the special distinction of being able to interrupt any other process and occur at any time in the act of writing.

The Monitor

As writers compose, they also monitor their current process and progress. The monitor functions as a writing strategist which determines when the writer moves from one process to the next. For example, it determines how long a writer will continue generating ideas before attempting to write prose. Our observations suggest that this choice is determined both by the writer's goals and by individual writing habits or styles. As an example of varied composing styles, writers appear to range from people who try to move to polished prose as quickly as possible to people who choose to plan the entire discourse in detail before writing a word. Bereiter and Scardamalia have shown that much of a child's difficulty and lack of fluency lies in their lack of an "executive routine" which would promote switching between processes or encourage the sustained generation of ideas.[21] Children for example, possess the skills necessary to generate ideas, but lack the kind of monitor which tells them to "keep using" that skill and generate a little more.

Implications of a Cognitive Process Model

A model such as the one presented here is first and foremost a tool for researchers to think with. By giving a testable shape and definition to our observations, we have tried to pose new questions to be answered. For example, the model identifies three major processes (**plan, translate, and review**) and a number of sub-processes available to the writer. And yet the first assertion of this cognitive process theory is that people do not march through these processes in a simple 1, 2, 3 order. Although writers may spend more time in planning at the beginning of a composing session, planning is not a unitary stage, but a distinctive thinking process which writers use over and over during composing. Furthermore, it is used at all levels, whether the writer is making a global plan for the whole text or a local representation of the meaning of the next sentence. This then raises a question: if the process of writing is not a sequence of stages

(Plan) Ok, first day of class . . . . . just jot down a possibility.

(Translate)   *Can you imagine what your first day of a college English class will be like?*

(Review) I don't like that sentence, it's lousy—sounds like theme talk.

(Review) Oh Lord—I get closer to it and I get closer—

(Plan) Could play up the sex thing a little bit

(Translate)   *When you walk into an English class the first day you'll be
interested, you'll be thinking about boys, tasks, and professor—*

(Review) That's banal—that's awful.

Figure 2. An Example of Embedding

but a set of optional actions, how are these thinking processes in our repertoire actually orchestrated or organized as we write? The second point of our cognitive process theory offers one answer to this question.

2. The processes of writing are hierarchically organized, with component processes embedded within other components.

A hierarchical system is one in which a large working system such as composing can subsume other less inclusive systems, such as generating ideas, which in turn contain still other systems, and so on. Unlike those in a linear organization, the events in a hierarchical process are not fixed in a rigid order. A given process may be called upon at any time and embedded within another process or even within another instance of itself, in much the same way we embed a subject clause within a larger clause or a picture within a picture.

For instance, a writer trying to construct a sentence (that is, a writer in the act of **translating**) may run into a problem and call in a condensed version of the entire writing process to help her out (e.g., she might generate and organize a new set of ideas, express them in standard writing English, and review this new alternative, all in order to further her current goal of translating. This particular

kind of embedding, in which an entire process is embedded within a larger instance of itself, is known technically in linguistics as recursion. However, it is much more common for writers to simply embed individual processes as needed—to call upon them as sub-routines to help carry out the task at hand.

Writing processes may be viewed as the writer's tool kit. In using the tools, the writer is not constrained to use them in a fixed order or in stages. And using any tool may create the need to use another. Generating ideas may require evaluation, as may writing sentences. And evaluation may force the writer to think up new ideas.

Figure 2 demonstrates the embedded processes of a writer trying to compose (translate) the first sentence of a paper. After producing and reviewing two trial versions of the sentence, he invokes a brief sequence of planning, translating, and reviewing— all in the service of that vexing sentence. In our example the writer is trying to translate some sketchily represented meaning about "the first day of class" into prose, and a hierarchical process allows him to embed a variety of processes as sub-routines within his overall attempt to translate.

A process that is hierarchical and admits many embedded sub-processes is powerful because it is flexible: it lets a writer do a great deal with only a few relatively simple processes—the basic ones being **plan, translate,** and **review.** This means, for

Science theorists use research to answer ?'s about composing

instance, that we do not need to define "revision" as a unique stage in composing, but as a thinking process that can occur at any time a writer chooses to evaluate or revise his text or his plans. As an important part of writing, it constantly leads to new planning or a "re-vision" of what one wanted to say.

Embedding is a basic, omni-present feature of the writing process even though we may not be fully conscious of doing it. However, a theory of composing that only recognized embedding wouldn't describe the real complexity of writing. It wouldn't explain *why* writers choose to invoke the processes they do or how they know when they've done enough. To return to Lee Odell's question, what guides the writers' decisions and choices and gives an overall purposeful structure to composing? The third point of the theory is an attempt to answer this question.

3. Writing is a goal-directed process. In the act of composing, writers create a hierarchical network of goals and these in turn guide the writing process.

This proposition is the keystone of the cognitive process theory we are proposing—and yet it may also seem somewhat counter-intuitive. According to many writers, including our subjects, writing often seems a serendipitous experience, an act of discovery. People start out writing without knowing exactly where they will end up; yet they agree that writing is a purposeful act. For example, our subjects often report that their writing process seemed quite disorganized, even chaotic, as they worked, and yet their protocols reveal a coherent underlying structure. How, then, does the writing process manage to seem so unstructured, open-minded, and exploratory ("I don't know what I mean until I see what I say") and at the same time possess its own underlying coherence, direction, or purpose?

One answer to this question lies in the fact that people rapidly forget many of their own local working goals once those goals have been satisfied. This is why thinking aloud protocols tell us things retrospection doesn't.[22] A second answer lies in the nature of the goals themselves, which fall into two

distinctive categories: process goals and content goals. Process goals are essentially the instructions people give themselves about how to carry out the process of writing (e.g., "Let's doodle a little bit." "So . . . , write an introduction." "I'll go back to that later."). Good writers often give themselves many such instructions and seem to have greater conscious control over their own process than the poorer writers we have studied. Content goals and plans, on the other hand, specify all things the writer wants to say or to do to an audience. Some goals, usually ones having to do with organization, can specify both content and process, as in, "I want to open with a statement about political views." In this discussion we will focus primarily on the writer's content goals.

The most striking thing about a writer's content goals is that they grow into an increasingly elaborate network of goals and sub-goals as the writer composes. Figure 3 shows the network one writer had created during four minutes of composing. Notice how the writer moves from a very abstract goal of "appealing to a broad range in intellect" to a more operational definition of that goal, i.e., "explain things simply." The eventual plan to "write an introduction" is a reasonable, if conventional, response to all three top-level goals. And it too is developed with a set of alternative sub-goals. Notice also how this network is hierarchical in the sense that new goals operate as a functional part of the more inclusive goals above them.

These networks have three important features:

1. They are created as people compose, throughout the entire process. This means that they do not emerge full-blown as the result of "pre-writing." Rather, as we will show, they are created in close interaction with ongoing exploration and the growing text.

2. The goal-directed thinking that produces these networks takes many forms. That is, goal-setting is not simply the act of stating a well-defined end point such as "I want to write a two-page essay." Goal-directed thinking often involves describing one's starting point ("They're not going to be disposed to hear what I'm saying"), or laying out a plan for reaching a goal ("I'd better explain things

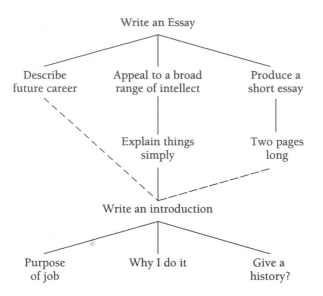

Figure 3. Beginning of a Network of Goals

simply"), or evaluating one's success ("That's banal—that's awful"). Such statements are often setting implicit goals, e.g., "Don't be banal." In order to understand a writer's goals, then, we must be sensitive to the broad range of plans, goals, and criteria that grow out of goal-directed thinking.

Goal-directed thinking is intimately connected with discovery. Consider for example, the discovery process of two famous explorers—Cortez, silent on his peak in Darien, and that bear who went over the mountain. Both, indeed, discovered the unexpected. However, we should note that both chose to climb a long hill to do so. And it is this sort of goal-directed search for the unexpected that we often see in writers as they attempt to explore and consolidate their knowledge. Furthermore, this search for insight leads to new, more adequate goals, which in turn guide further writing.

The beginning of an answer to Odell's question, "What guides composing?" lies here. The writer's own set of self-made goals guide composing, but these goals can be inclusive and exploratory or narrow, sensitive to the audience or chained to the topic, based on rhetorical savvy or focused on producing correct prose. All those forces which might "guide" composing, such as the rhetorical situation,

one's knowledge, the genre, etc., are mediated through the goals, plans, and criteria for evaluation of discourse actually set up by the writer.

This does not mean that a writer's goals are necessarily elaborate, logical, or conscious. For example, a simple-minded goal such as "Write down what I can remember" may be perfectly adequate for writing a list. And experienced writers, such as journalists, can often draw on elaborate networks of goals which are so well learned as to be automatic. Or the rules of a genre, such as those of the limerick, may be so specific as to leave little room or necessity for elaborate rhetorical planning. Nevertheless, whether one's goals are abstract or detailed, simple or sophisticated, they provide the "logic" that moves the composing process forward.

3. Finally, writers not only create a hierarchical network of guiding goals, but, as they compose, they continually return or "pop" back up to their higher-level goals. And these higher-level goals give direction and coherence to their next move. Our understanding of this network and how writers use it is still quite limited, but we can make a prediction about an important difference one might find between good and poor writers. Poor writers will frequently depend on very abstract, undeveloped

top-level goals, such as "appeal to a broad range of intellect," even though such goals are much harder to work with than a more operational goal such as "give a brief history of my job." Sondra Perl has seen this phenomenon in the basic writers who kept returning to reread the assignment, searching, it would seem, for ready-made goals, instead of forming their own. Alternatively, poor writers will depend on only very low-level goals, such as finishing a sentence or correctly spelling a word. They will be, as Nancy Sommers student revisers were, locked in by the myopia in their own goals and criteria.

Therefore, one might predict that an important difference between good and poor writers will be in both the quantity and quality of the middle range of goals they create. These middle-range goals, which lie between intention and actual prose (cf., "give a brief history" in Figure 3), give substance and direction to more abstract goals (such as "appealing to the audience") and they give breadth and coherence to local decisions about what to say next.

Goals, Topic, and Text

We have been suggesting that the logic which moves composing forward grows out of the goals which writers create as they compose. However, common sense and the folklore of writing offer an alternative explanation which we should consider, namely, that one's own knowledge of the topic (memories, associations, etc.) or the text itself can take control of this process as frequently as one's goals do. One could easily imagine these three forces constituting a sort of eternal triangle in which the writer's goals, knowledge, and current text struggle for influence. For example, the writer's initial planning for a given paragraph might have set up a goal or abstract representation of a paragraph that would discuss three equally important, parallel points on the topic of climate. However, in trying to write, the writer finds that some of his knowledge about climate is really organized around a strong cause-and-effect relationship between points 1 and 2, while he has almost nothing to say about point 3. Or perhaps the text itself attempts to take control,

e.g., for the sake of a dramatic opening, the writer's first sentence sets up a vivid example of an effect produced by climate. The syntactic and semantic structure of that sentence now demand that a cause be stated in the next, although this would violate the writer's initial (and still appropriate) plan for a three-point paragraph.

Viewed this way, the writer's abstract plan (representation) of his goals, his knowledge of the topic, and his current text are all actively competing for the writer's attention. Each wants to govern the choices and decisions made next. This competitive model certainly captures that experience of seeing the text run away with you, or the feeling of being led by the nose by an idea. How then do these experiences occur within a "goal-driven process"? First, as our model of the writing process describes, the processes of **generate** and **evaluate** appear to have the power to interrupt the writer's process at any point—and they frequently do. This means that new knowledge and/or some feature of the current text can interrupt the process at any time through the processes of **generate** and **evaluate**. This allows a flexible collaboration among goals, knowledge, and text. Yet this collaboration often culminates in a revision of previous goals. The persistence and functional importance of initially established goals is reflected by a number of signs: the frequency with which writers refer back to their goals; the fact that writers behave consistently with goals they have already stated; and the fact that they evaluate text in response to the criteria specified in their goals.

Second, some kinds of goals steer the writing process in yet another basic way. In the writers we have studied, the overall composing process is clearly under the direction of global and local *process* goals. Behind the most free-wheeling act of "discovery" is a writer who has recognized the heuristic value of free exploration or "just writing it out" and has chosen to do so. Process goals such as these, or "I'll edit it later," are the earmarks of sophisticated writers with a repertory of flexible process goals which let them use writing for discovery. But what about poorer writers who seem simply to free associate on paper or to be obsessed with perfecting the current text? We would argue that often they too are working under a set of implicit process goals which say "write it as it comes," or "make everything perfect and correct as you go." The problem then is not that knowledge or the text have taken over, so much as that the writer's own goals and/or images of the composing process put these strategies in control.[23]

To sum up, the third point of our theory—focused on the role of the writer's own goals—helps us account for purposefulness in writing. But can we account for the dynamics of discovery? Richard Young, Janet Emig, and others argue that writing is uniquely adapted to the task of fostering insight and developing new knowledge.[24] But how does this happen in a goal-directed process?

We think that the remarkable combination of purposefulness and openness which writing offers is based in part on a beautifully simple, but extremely powerful principle, which is this: *In the act of writing, people regenerate or recreate their own goals in the light of what they learn.* This principle then creates the fourth point of our cognitive process theory.

4. Writers create their own goals in two key ways: by generating goals and supporting sub-goals which embody a purpose; and, at times, by changing or regenerating their own top-level goals in light of what they have learned by writing.

We are used, of course, to thinking of writing as a process in which our *knowledge* develops as we write. The structure of knowledge for some topic becomes more conscious and assertive as we keep tapping memory for related ideas. That structure, or "schema," may even grow and change as a result of library research or the addition of our own fresh inferences. However, writers must also generate (i.e., create or retrieve) the unique goals which guide their process.

In this paper we focus on the goals writers create for a particular paper, but we should not forget that many writing goals are well-learned, standard ones stored in memory. For example, we would expect many writers to draw automatically on those goals

associated with writing in general, such as, "interest the reader," or "start with an introduction," or on goals associated with a given genre, such as making a jingle rhyme. These goals will often be so basic that they won't even be consciously considered or expressed. And the more experienced the writer the greater this repertory of semi-automatic plans and goals will be.

Writers also develop an elaborate network of working "sub-goals" as they compose. As we have seen, these sub-goals give concrete meaning and direction to their more abstract top-level goals, such as "interest the reader," or "describe my job." And then on occasion writers show a remarkable ability to regenerate or change the very goals which had been directing their writing and planning: that is, they replace or revise major goals in light of what they learned through writing. It is these two creative processes we wish to consider now.

We can see these two basic processes—creating sub-goals and regenerating goals—at work in the following protocol, which has been broken down into episodes. As you will see, writers organize these two basic processes in different ways. We will look here at three typical patterns of goals which we have labeled "Explore and Consolidate," "State and Develop," "Write and Regenerate."

Explore and Consolidate

This pattern often occurs at the beginning of a composing session, but it could appear anywhere. The writers frequently appear to be working under a high-level goal or plan to explore: that is, to think the topic over, to jot ideas down, or just start writing to see what they have to say. At other times the plan to explore is subordinate to a very specific goal, such as to find out "what on earth can I say that would make a 15-year-old girl interested in my job?" Under such a plan, the writer might explore her own knowledge, following out associations or using more structured discovery procedures such as tagmemics or the classical topics. But however the writer chooses to explore, the next step is the critical one. The writer pops back up to her top-level goal and from that vantage point reviews the information she has generated. She then consolidates it, producing a more complex idea than she began with by drawing inferences and creating new concepts.

Even the poor writers we have studied often seem adept at the exploration part of this process, even to the point of generating long narrative trains of association—sometimes on paper as a final draft. The distinctive thing about good writers is their tendency to return to that higher-level goal and to review and consolidate what has just been learned through exploring. In the act of consolidating, the writer sets up a *new goal* which replaces the goal of explore and directs the subsequent episode in composing. If the writer's topic is unfamiliar or the task demands creative thinking, the writer's ability to explore, to consolidate the results, and to regenerate his or her goals will be a critical skill.

The following protocol excerpt, which is divided into episodes and sub-episodes, illustrates this pattern of **explore and consolidate.**

Episode 1 a, b

In the first episode, the writer merely reviews the assignment and plays with some associations as he attempts to define his rhetorical situation. It ends with a simple process goal—"On to the task at hand"—and a reiteration of the assignment.

> (1a) Okay—Um . . . Open the envelope—just like a quiz show on TV—My job for a young thirteen to fourteen teenage female audience—Magazine—*Seventeen.* My job for a young teenage female audience—Magazine—*Seventeen.* I never have read *Seventeen,* but I've referred to it in class and other students have. (1b) This is like being thrown the topic in a situation—you know—in an expository writing class and asked to write on it on the board and I've done that and had a lot of fun with it—so on to the task at hand. My job for a young teenage female audience—Magazine—*Seventeen.*

Episode 2 a, b, c, d

The writer starts with a plan to explore his own "job," which he initially defines as being a teacher and not a professor. In the process of exploring he develops a variety of sub-goals which include plans to: make new meaning by exploring a contrast; present himself or his persona as a teacher; and affect his audience by making them reconsider one of their previous notions. The extended audience analysis of teen-age girls (sub-episode 2c) is in response to his goal of affecting them.

At the end of episode 2c, the writer reaches tentative closure with the statement, "By God, I can change that notion for them." There are significantly long pauses on both sides of this statement, which appears to consolidate much of the writer's previous exploration. In doing this, he dramatically extends his earlier, rather vague plan to merely "compare teachers and professors"—he has regenerated and elaborated his top-level goals. This consolidation leaves the writer with a new, relatively complex, rhetorically sophisticated working goal, one which encompasses plans for a topic, a persona, and the audience. In essence the writer is learning through planning and his goals are the creative bridge between his exploration and the prose he will write.

Perhaps the writer thought his early closure at this point was too good to be true, so he returns at 2d to his initial top-level or most inclusive goal (write about my job) and explores alternative definitions of his job. The episode ends with the reaffirmation of his topic, his persona, and, by implication, the consolidated goal established in Episode 2c.

> (2a) Okay lets see—lets doodle a little bit—Job—English teacher rather than professor—I'm doodling this on a scratch sheet as I say it.—ah—(2b) In fact that might be a useful thing to focus on—how a professor differs from—how a teacher differs from a professor and I see myself as a teacher—that might help them—my audience to reconsider their notion of what an English teacher does. (2c)—ah—English teacher—young teen-age female audience—they will all have had English—audience—they're in school—they're taking English—for many of them English may be a favorite subject—doodling still—under audience, but for the wrong reasons—some of them will have wrong reasons in that English is good because its

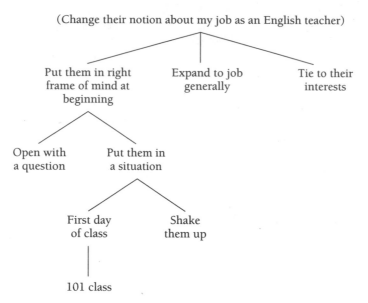

Figure 4. Writer Developing a Set of Sub-Goals

tidy—can be a neat tidy little girl—others turned off of it because it seems too prim. By God I can change that notion for them. (2d) My job for a young teenage female audience—Magazine—*Seventeen.*—ah—Job—English teacher—guess that's what I'll have to go—yeah—hell—go with that—that's a challenge—rather than—riding a bicycle across England that's too easy and not on the topic—right, or would work in a garden or something like that—none of those are really my jobs—as a profession—My job for a young teenage female audience—Magazine—*Seventeen.* All right—I'm an English teacher.

State and Develop

This second pattern accounts for much of the straightforward work of composing, and is well illustrated in our protocol. In it the writer begins with a relatively general high-level goal which he then proceeds to develop or flesh out with subgoals. As his goals become more fully specified, they form a bridge from his inital rather fuzzy intentions to actual text. Figure 4 is a schematic representation of the goals and sub-goals which the writer eventually creates.

Episode 3 a, b, c

The episode starts with a sub-goal directly subordinate to the goal established in Episode 2 (change their notion of English teachers). It takes the pattern of a search in which the writer tries to find ways to carry out his current goal of "get [the audience?] at the beginning." In the process he generates yet another level of sub-goals (i.e., open with a question and draw them into a familiar situation). (A note on our terminology: in order to focus on the overall structure of goals and sub-goals in a writer's thinking, we have treated the writer's plans and strategies all as sub-goals or operational definitions of the larger goal.)

Notice how the content or ideas of the essay are still relatively unspecified. The relationship between creating goals and finding ideas is clearly reciprocal: it was an initial exploration of the writer's ideas which produced these goals. But the writing process was then moved forward by his attempt to flesh out a network of goals and sub-goals, not just by a mere "pre-writing" survey of what he knew about the topic. Episode 3c ends in an effort to test one of his new goals against his own experience with students.

(3a) All right—I'm an English teacher. I want to get at the beginning—I know that they're not going to be disposed—to hear what I'm saying—partly for that reason and partly to put them in the right, the kind of frame of mind I want—I want to open with an implied question or a direct one and put them in the middle of some situation—then expand from there to talk about my job more generally . . . and try to tie it in with their interest. (3b) So one question is where to begin—what kind of situation to start in the middle of—probably the first day of class. . . . They'd be interested—they'd probably clue into that easily because they would identify with first days of school and my first days are raucous affairs—it would immediately shake-em up and get them to thinking a different context. (3c) Okay—so—First day of class—lets see.—Maybe the first 101 class with that crazy skit I put on—that's probably better than 305 because 101 is freshmen and that's nearer their level and that skit really was crazy and it worked beautifully.

Write and Regenerate

This pattern is clearly analogous to the explore and consolidate pattern, except that instead of planning, the writer is producing prose. A miniature example of it can be seen in Figure 2, in which the writer, whose planning we have just seen, attempts to compose the first sentence of his article for *Seventeen*. Although he had done a good deal of explicit planning before this point, the prose itself worked as another, more detailed representation of what he wanted to say. In writing the sentence, he not only saw that it was inade-

quate, but that his goals themselves could be expanded. The reciprocity between writing and planning enabled him to learn even from a failure and to produce a new goal, "play up sex." Yet it is instructive to note that once this new plan was represented in language—subjected to the acid test of prose—it too failed to pass, because it violated some of his tacit goals or criteria for an acceptable prose style.

The examples we cite here are, for the purposes of illustration, small and rather local ones. Yet this process of setting and developing sub-goals, and—at times—regenerating those goals is a powerful creative process. Writers and teachers of writing have long argued that one learns through the act of writing itself, but it has been difficult to support the claim in other ways. However, if one studies the process by which a writer uses a goal to generate ideas, then consolidates those ideas and uses them to revise or regenerate new, more complex goals, one can see this learning process in action. Furthermore, one sees why the process of revising and clarifying goals has such a broad effect, since it is through setting these new goals that the fruits of discovery come back to inform the continuing process of writing. In this instance, some of our most complex and imaginative acts can depend on the elegant simplicity of a few powerful thinking processes. We feel that a cognitive process explanation of discovery, toward which this theory is only a start, will have another special strength. By placing emphasis on the inventive power of the writer, who is able to explore ideas, to develop, act on, test, and regenerate his or her own goals, we are putting an important part of creativity where it belongs—in the hands of the working, thinking writer.

Notes

1. Aristotle, *The Rhetoric,* trans. Lane Cooper (New York: Appleton-Century-Crofts, 1932), Richard Lloyd-Jones, "A Perspective on Rhetoric," in *Writing: The Nature, Development and Teaching of Written Communication,* ed.

C. Frederiksen, M. Whiteman, and J. Dominic (Hillsdale, N.J.: Lawrence Erlbaum Associates, in press).

2. Lee Odell, Charles R. Cooper, and Cynthia Courts, "Discourse Theory: Implications for Research in Composing," in *Research on Composing: Points of Departure,* ed. Charles Cooper and Lee Odell (Urbana, IL: National Council of Teachers of English, 1978), p. 6.

3. Lloyd Bitzer, "The Rhetorical Situation," *Philosophy and Rhetoric,* 1 (January, 1968), 1–14.

4. Richard E. Vatz, "The Myth of the Rhetorical Situation," in *Philosophy and Rhetoric,* 6 (Summer, 1973), 154–161.

5. James Britton et al., *The Development of Writing Abilities, 11–18* (London: Macmillan, 1975), p. 39.

6. Gordon Rohman, "Pre-Writing: The Stage of Discovery in the Writing Process," *CCC,* 16 (May, 1965), 106–112.

7. See Britton et. al., *The Development of Writing Abilities,* pp. 19–49.

8. Nancy Sommers, "Response to Sharon Crowley, 'Components of the Process,'" *CCC,* 29 (May, 1978), 209–211.

9. Nancy Sommers, "Revision Strategies of Student Writers and Experienced Writers," *CCC,* 31 (December, 1980), 378–388.

10. John R. Hayes, *Cognitive Psychology: Thinking and Creating* (Homewood, Illinois: Dorsey Press, 1978); Herbert A. Simon and John R. Hayes, "Understanding Complex Task Instruction," in *Cognition and Instruction,* ed. D. Klahr (Hillsdale, N.J.: Lawrence Erlbaum Associates, 1976), pp. 269–285.

11. John R. Hayes and Linda S. Flower, "Identifying the Organization of Writing Processes," in *Cognitive Processes in Writing: An Interdisciplinary Approach,* ed. Lee Gregg and Erwin Steinberg (Hillsdale, N.J.: Lawrence Erlbaum Associates, 1980), pp. 3–30. Although diagrams of the sort in Figure 1 help distinguish the various processes we wish our model to describe, these schematic representations of processes and elements are often misleading. The arrows indicate that *information* flows from one box or process to another; that is, knowledge about the writing assignment or knowledge from memory can be transferred or used in the planning process, and information from planning can flow back the other way. What the arrows *do not mean* is that such information flows in a predictable left to right circuit, from one box to another as if the diagram were a one-way flow chart. This distinction is crucial because such a flow chart implies the very kind of stage model against which we wish to argue. One of the central premises of the cognitive process theory presented here is that writers are constantly, instant by instant, orchestrating a battery of cognitive processes as they integrate planning, remembering, writing, and rereading. The multiple arrows, which are conventions in diagramming this sort of model, are unfortunately only weak indications of the complex and active organization of thinking processes which our work attempts to model.

12. Linda S. Flower and John R. Hayes, "The Cognition of Discovery: Defining a Rhetorical Problem," *CCC,* 31 (February, 1980), 21–32.

13. Britton et al. *The Development of Writing Abilities,* pp. 61–65.

14. Sondra Perl, "Five Writers Writing: Case Studies of the Composing Process of Unskilled College Writers," Diss. New York University, 1978.

15. Linda S. Flower and John R. Hayes, "The Dynamics of Composing: Making Plans and Juggling Constraints," in *Cognitive Processes in Writing: An Interdisciplinary Approach,* ed. Lee Gregg and Erwin Steinberg (Hillsdale, N.J.: Lawrence Erlbaum Associates, 1980), pp. 31–50.

16. Linda S. Flower, "Writer-Based Prose: A Cognitive Basis for Problems in Writing," *College English,* 41 (September, 1979), 19–37.

17. Flower, "The Cognition of Discovery," pp. 21–32.

18. Ellen Nold, "Revising," in *Writing: The Nature, Development, and Teaching of Written Communication,* ed. C. Frederiksen *et al.* (Hillsdale, N.J.: Lawrence Erlbaum Associates, in press).

19. Mina Shaughnessy, *Errors and Expectations* (New York: Oxford University Press, 1977).

20. Marlene Scardamalia, "How Children Cope with the Cognitive Demands of Writing," in *Writing: The Nature, Development and Teaching of Written Communication,* ed. C. Frederiksen *et al.* (Hillsdale, N.J.: Lawrence Erlbaum Associates, in press). Carl Bereiter and Marlene Scardamalia, "From Conversation to Composition: The Role of Instruction in a Developmental Process," in *Advances in Instructional Psychology,* Volume 2, ed. R. Glaser (Hillsdale, N.J.: Lawrence Erlbaum Associates, in press).

21. Bereiter and Scardamalia, "From Conversation to Composition."

22. John R. Hayes and Linda Flower, "Uncovering Cognitive Processes in Writing: An Introduction to Protocol Analysis," in *Methodological Approaches to Writing Research,* ed. P. Mosenthal, L. Tamor, and S. Walmsley (in press).

23. Cf. a recent study by Mike Rose on the power of ineffective process plans, "Rigid Rules, Inflexible Plans, and the Stifling of Language. A Cognitivist's Analysis of Writer's Block," *CCC*, 31 (December, 1980), 389–400.

24. Janet Emig, "Writing as a Mode of Learning," *CCC*, 28 (May, 1977), 122–128; Richard E. Young, "Why Write? A Reconsideration," unpublished paper delivered at the convention of the Modern Language Association, San Francisco, California, 28 December 1979.

? What guides the processes by which we write? Ultimate answers — or the decisions writer makes as he writes

goals · subgoals

Have their question, create model of writer & no fixed order to parts of process, - examine ea. part of process for answer — look @ protocols for direction

The questions asked here reflect author's belief that, rather than knowledge being gained through writing, recursive actions of writing continually bring writer back to generating process & thus writer discovers more ideas, etc.

The Registers of Student and Professional Expository Writing: Influences on Teachers' Responses

Sarah Warshauer Freedman

(handwritten: this title makes no sense)

Freedman's article was published in New Directions in Composition Research. *Eds. Richard Beach and Lillian S. Bridwell. New York: Guilford Press, 1984. 334–47.*

Would teachers evaluate expository prose written by professional writers as better than that written by college students? The answer to this question seems obvious. Professional writers are generally thought to be more skillful as writers than college students (Atlas, 1979; Flower & Hayes, 1980; Sommers, 1980). Thus, teachers who are thought to value such skill should prefer professionals' essays to those of college students. The real answer, however, is not so clear-cut. I found that when I asked professional writers and college students to produce essays under similar conditions (assigned topic, 45-minute time limit) and that when teachers judged these essays, thinking they all had been written by students, the teachers did not evaluate the professional essays as better across the board.

Two explanations for this unexpected finding seem plausible. First, professionals, given a constrained writing situation, may not be able to demonstrate their skill and thus may not produce better essays than many students. Atlas (1979), Flower and Hayes (1980), and Sommers (1980) found that professionals, even on constrained, assigned tasks, exhibited different problem-solving and revision strategies than did the nonexpert student. However, no one has examined in detail differences in the quality of the essays that these two groups produce. It may be the case that professionals' essays do not deserve to be judged as better across the board. A second conceivable explanation for the finding that teachers in general did not give higher ratings to professional essays has to do with the teachers. If the professionals wrote superior essays, teachers, when blind to whose writing they are judging, may not value the generally more skillful professional writing because something within the essays biases them. For example, Markham (1976) has demonstrated that handwriting features may bias raters. And Hake and Williams (1981) have found that syntactic style and black English vernacular may be sources of bias. Certainly, professionals who assume a student role might write in ways that could bias raters.

These two explanations, one focusing on the writer and the other on the evaluator, are not mutually exclusive. Evidence from two sources, the patterns of the teachers' judgments and the essays themselves, lends support to both. However, most of the evidence supports the second explanation—that the teachers often did not value the greater skill demonstrated by the professional.

For this study, I first had 64 college students write essays. Each wrote on one of eight expository topics, with eight students writing on each topic. Half of the topics asked students to compare and contrast two quotations; the other topics asked them to argue their opinion on a current controversial topic. A sample of each type of topic follows:

1. A Founding Father said: "Get what you can, and what you get hold: 'Tis the Stone that will turn all your Lead into Gold." A contemporary writer said: "If it feels good, do it." What do these two statements say? Explain how they are alike and how they are different.

2. Do you think the drinking age in California should or should not be lowered to 18? Give reasons for the position you take.[1]

I chose the expository mode since this is the mode most commonly taught in college-level required writing classes and is the mode most frequently called for in proficiency and placement essay tests.

The students were enrolled in required writing classes at four San Francisco-area colleges ranging in type from highly select private schools to open-admissions public schools. Thus, the student writers exhibited a wide range of abilities.

I next recruited eight professional writers from different parts of the United States, each to write on one of the eight topics. Initially, all eight agreed to write; only five completed the task. Although I agreed to keep the identities of these writers confidential, the following information indicates their caliber. All have published books and articles, and all have had extensive experience teaching composition at the college level. One is a novelist and poet; one is a literary scholar and the author of a freshman rhetoric text and has directed a freshman composition program at a major university; one is an eminent researcher on composition; another has authored a bestselling text on teaching writing and is a literary scholar.

Four experienced college writing teachers, who also were experienced with holistic rating, evaluated the essays. First, all four teachers rated each essay with a four-point holistic scale. They judged each essay independently and read the essays in topic sets. In each set, there were the eight student essays on the topic and one professional essay if it was available. The professional essay was always placed at the end of the set so that it would not influence how the raters reacted to the student essays. I feared that if the professional essays were placed early and were too good, they might raise the raters' expectations to unrealistic heights for the subsequent student essays. If no professional essay was available, an extra student essay was included in the set so that the raters would be reading the same number of essays in every set. After the holistic ratings were completed, two raters evaluated each essay with an analytic rating scale.[2] The scale, modeled after Diederich's (1974), contained six categories: voice, development, organization, sentence structure, word choice, and usage. The two raters independently gave each paper a score of 1 to 6 in each of the categories, so that the highest summed analytic score a paper could receive from each rater was 36 and the lowest was 6.

The patterns of the teachers' judgments for the students and for the professionals proved quite different. First, I will examine the scores the teachers gave the different groups on the two rating scales, and then I will look at differences in their reliability as they rated the two groups of essays.

On the holistic scale, the teachers rated reliably. According to Cronbach's alpha, the reliability of the differences in papers was high ($\alpha = .84$) and the consistency of differences between readers was low ($\alpha = .20$) for ratings with the holistic scale. On this scale, the teachers did not give the professionals much better scores than they gave the students. The average score given a professional on a four-point holistic scale was 2.65; the average score given a student was 2.24. According to a t test, the difference in the mean holistic score for the professional versus the student groups was insignificant ($t = 1.19$). Although professional holistic scores were slightly better on the average, students received the three highest holistic scores.

On the analytic scale the professionals fared better. The averaged summed analytic score given the professionals as 30.2; the average for the students was 19.5. According to a t test, the difference in the mean analytic score for the professional versus the student groups was significant at the .02 level of confidence ($t = 2.43$). Whereas on the holistic scale students received the three highest scores, on the analytic scale professionals received the three highest scores. Since the professional papers would receive consistently higher scores when rated analytically than when rated holistically, those professionals who received the same ratings as the students on the holistic scale could expect to receive ratings higher than their student counterparts on the analytic scale.

Table 17–1 compares the analytic scores for each professional paper with the range of analytic scores for the student papers that received holistic scores identical with the professionals'. In the table, the scores are summed across both raters. So, for the holistic rating, across four raters, with the top score given by each rater being a 4, a paper could receive a high holistic score of 16 if it received a 4 from all four raters. And on the analytic scale, a paper could receive as many as 36 points from each of two raters for a maximum of 72 points. Notice, in Table 17–1, that the professional papers that received a summed holistic score of 9 received summed analytic scores of 55 and 59; the student papers receiving a holistic score of 9 were given analytic scores between 34 and 54. Actually, only one of these students received a 54; the others received scores below 49. The other holistic/analytic comparisons in Table 17–1 bear out the discrepancy between students' and professionals' holistic and analytic scores.

A breakdown of the analytic scale by categories revealed that the professionals had received outstanding scores on voice, sentence structure, word choice, and usage. But they were not judged so consistently high on the categories of development and organization. The boost in the analytic scores came primarily from high scores in the more technical, style-oriented categories (sentence structure, word choice, and usage) and from the style/personality category (voice). It is interesting that the directions to the raters regarding the voice category instructed them to give a high score to anyone who wrote with a distinctive voice or personality; the directions did not include anything about liking that voice or personality. So it was possible for a rater to give a high score to a paper with a distinctive voice even if the rater disliked the voice that was there.

Table 17–1. Professional versus Student Scores

Holistic Score	Analytic Score Range	
	Professional	Student
4	—	22–28
5	—	12–38
6	—	31–42
7	—	26–42
8	—	24–47
9	55–57	34–54
10	59	27–55
11	67	37–57
12	—	39–49
13	—	43–58
14	64	52
15	—	47–56

This breakdown of scores on the analytic scale shows that the raters gave the professionals credit for their technique (sentence structure, word choice, and usage) and for the presence of a voice.

In another study I had average-quality student essays revised to be either weaker or stronger in development, organization, sentence structure, and mechanics (Freedman, 1977, 1979a, 1979b). I then presented the revised essays to raters to see how strength or weakness in the different categories would influence their holistic scores. I found that the traits of an essay that contribute most to a rater's holistic judgment are development and organization as opposed to sentence structure and mechanics. In the present study, the raters' lower judgments of the professional essays in the development and organization categories of the analytic scale indicate that they would be inclined to give lower holistic scores. These low analytic and holistic scores led me to suspect that either the development and organization were inadequate in the professional essays, and thus had caused the lowered scores, or that something else within these essays had caused the raters to rate them low in these areas. Certainly, these two analytic categories and the holistic scale provided a convenient channel through which the raters could indicate bias, since these parts of the rating system allowed more subjectivity than the other parts.

The following reliability pattern also supports the conclusion that some factors common in the professional essays but not in the student essays had led raters to respond differently, and sometimes in a negative way, to the professional essays. As I noted earlier, the four raters were very reliable when rating the 64 student essays holistically; that is, they agreed well with one another on holistic scores for the student papers. However, about the professional essays, the raters disagreed violently with one another. The four holistic scores for each of the five professional essays are shown in Table 17–2. For every essay, there was at least one two-point disagreement, and two essays (1P and 5P) received the lowest score possible from one rater and the highest score possible from another.

In contrast, the scores for five randomly selected student papers in Table 17–2 demonstrate the raters' usual reliable pattern. Notice that in four out of five cases (1S, 2S, 3S, and 5S) three of the four raters gave identical scores, with one rater just one point off from the other three. In only one case (4S) was there a two-point discrepancy, and then the two agreeing raters gave scores in the middle. For the professionals the two-point discrepancies followed a different pattern. In all cases when raters agreed (2P, 3P, 4P, and 5P), their scores were higher

than the other raters', indicating perhaps that these other, lower scores should have been higher and were given because the raters were inappropriately biased. Only one of the raters, rater 3, liked all of the professional essays, giving them all scores of 3 or 4. Rater 1 generally was displeased, giving all the professionals scores of 1 or 2. The other two raters gave the professionals the whole range of scores, liking some essays and disliking others, but not agreeing on the essays they liked and the ones they disliked. Some qualities in the professional essays seemed to attract attention, enough attention to jar the raters and make them all, except rater 3, give low holistic scores on some occasions.

The holistic/analytic scale differences combined with this odd reliability pattern at least indicate that the raters generally responded to the professional essays differently from the way they responded to the student essays. Because something within the essays produced erratic scoring and probably some biased responses from most raters, my next step was to analyze the student and professional essays in order to account for the scoring. Others who have examined the differences between student and professional prose have counted the frequency of occurrence of particular linguistic features in student writing and published professional prose (e.g., Hunt, 1965; Christensen, 1967). Since the teachers in this study gave the professionals lower scores for development and organization, I was not as interested in syntactic features as in the larger features of the text that might have influenced the teachers' judgments. So I examined the

Table 17–2 Holistic Scores—Individual Raters

Rater	Professional Essays					Student Essays				
	1P	2P	3P	4P	5P	1S	2S	3S	4S	5S
1	1	2	1	2	1	3	1	2	2	3
2	2	4	3	1	4	3	1	1	2	3
3	4	4	3	3	4	3	1	2	1	4
4	3	4	2	3	2	2	2	2	3	3

essays as a literary critic, looking for major differences in development and organization as well as for differences in style or approach that might have biased the raters. I also informed my observations with work in discourse analysis in linguistics.

As I began my critical examination of the essays, I found that the professional essays were well developed but that their organizational patterns were, at times, unconventional. Since essay length may be considered a rough measure of development, it is interesting to note that the professional essays averaged 694 words. The number of words averaged 416 for the two top-scoring student essays on each topic for which there was a professional essay. Interestingly, essay length usually correlates strongly and positively with raters' scores (e.g., Nold & Freedman, 1977; Grobe, 1981).

However, what stood out more than either the development or the organization was an obvious difference in the tone of the sets of texts. The professionals' writing seemed more informal and casual than the students'. The professionals did not distance themselves from their readers; rather, they tried to establish closeness with their informality. One important marker of this informality was the professionals' frequent use of the first-person pronoun "I," with four out of five using the first person throughout their papers and with three of the five beginning their essays with the focus on themselves. The first words of these three essays were:

1P. I feel most strongly that . . .

2P. First, I want to answer . . .

3P. You've asked me to comment on . . . and I've made a goodfaith effort to do so.

Students, by contrast, tend to begin differently. The following openers are typical of the top-ranked student essays:

1S. Different assumptions underlie the two quotes presented.

2S. The two statements from topic B are spoken from two different points of view . . .

3S. In recent years a great controversy has been raised concerning abortions.

Certainly, students use the first-person pronoun, even to open their papers. But they generally do so only in response to the demand of a topic asking whether or not they agree with a particular point of view, and then they are quick to depersonalize. An example:

> I agree with the court's decision, although it may lead to many problems. Mercy killing is a question which is, in most instances throughout history, handled by individual decisions.

Besides the use of the first-person pronoun, the professionals conveyed a familiar tone by seeming actually to speak to the reader directly. The third professional writer (3P) begins directly with a statement to "you," the reader. The one writer who did not use the first-person pronoun spoke to the reader inside parenthetical remarks, which he punctuated with dashes: "In a commercial civilization—and American civilization is just that—language is, more often than not used deceitfully. . . ." As a matter of fact, four of the five made frequent use of the dash in this way, while the fifth writer put long segments of discourse in parentheses. Interestingly, these punctuation conventions usually are associated with less formal, more personal forms, such as the letter. Every professional writer used one or more of these punctuation devices to establish informality and familiarity. I could find no instances when high-scoring student writers attempted to establish familiarity with the reader in these ways. Hayes and Flower (1979) and Atlas (1979) both noted that their experts wrote in a more personal style than their novices, and Atlas identified these differences "especially in the personalization of the opening paragraph" (p. 18).

By applying the concept of speech registers to written language, one can see why the professional writers may have chosen such an informal style. Speech registers are marked in three key ways: by their context, by the relationship between the speaker and the hearer, and by their linguistic form.[3] An example of a speech register is nurse–patient talk in a hospital. The social context is the hospital; the nurse is in a superior role to the patient, who is often helpless and dependent on the nurse; and the linguistic features typical of baby talk are rampant in the nurse's speech as he or she addresses the patient with a line such as: "Did we have our dinner tonight?" Writers, it seems, parallel speakers by writing in certain social contexts (e.g., the school), establishing certain role relationships with their readers (e.g., inferior student writer to superior teacher), and marking their prose linguistically to indicate the register they are using (e.g., the professionals' already described marks of informality, which they perhaps used to indicate that they were not subordinate to their readers).

In comparing the student and professional prose written within the context of this study, I believe that the professionals' display of informality and the students' usual formality can be traced back to their natural or usual registers. The normal context for professional prose is the nonschool world. The professionals' role is usually superior to that of his or her readers, who consist of uninformed strangers whom the professional expects to inform. The professional writes to this audience about deeply held beliefs and novel ideas. For students, on the other hand, the normal writing context is the school. The student generally writes for a teacher-reader and is in a subordinate role to the teacher since the teacher will evaluate the prose and instruct the student. The student writer is necessarily in a subordinate role to the teacher-evaluator, who possesses all the power and most of the knowledge. Rarely is the student's audience wider than the teacher, and then it commonly includes only other members of a writing class. When writing, the student, as a subordinate, must use linguistic forms that show respect, deference, and the proper degree of formality. Just as the student cannot assume that it is all right to call the teacher by his or her first name, the student cannot presume to establish too much closeness or be too informal with the teacher-reader. So the students in this study wrote formally as they usually do for school writing.

But the professionals were unused to writing as subservient students and could not easily assume this role. They knew they were at least the peers of their readers and thus felt free to write informally and casually. Some even seemed to be rubbing in

their status, writing too casually. The professionals' prose took on the tone of a friendly letter, full of dashes, addressed to a reader of equal or lower status.

The teacher-readers in this study, expecting prose from student subordinates, may well have reacted against the professionals' too familiar tone. In the context of this study and of other school writing, students who write informally do so because they do not know what the appropriate formality level is for the occasion or because they do not know how to show the appropriate degree of formality as they write. As a matter of fact, students who write too formally may be trying to achieve the proper formality level, but like students who write too informally, they do not know how to achieve the level they desire, and so they write gobbledegook that seems to parody academic prose.

A second striking difference between the student and professional essays in this study was that three of the five essays by professionals were marked by an initial defiance of the task that ended in acceptance of the task. One of the professionals who began his essay defiantly said, "First I want to answer 'damned if I know.' Then 'who cares?'" In the third paragraph, he made a transition to his acceptance: "What is more interesting to me than the answer is the reasoning I'm forced to go through to achieve my considered indifference. For the issue is full of things to which I am not indifferent." And with the beginning of the fourth paragraph, he writes more conventionally, "First of all it is clear to me that drinking is a problem in our society." This initial defiance resulted in what the teachers may have judged as weak organization, but the organization of such essays was not weak once the defiant first section had ended.

Students usually accept assigned tasks without rebelling on paper, but the few times that they take a defiant stance in an essay they generally carry through with their defiance adamantly. And in doing so, they expect to be penalized by the teacher-reader. The initial defiance on the part of the professionals seemed to occur when they felt alienated by their topics and by the situation. The defiance did not take the form of a diatribe from which they could not recover; rather, the professionals seemed not to be able to write without first overcoming their honest alienation. Some reacted to the time limitation and to the overwhelming initial alienation they felt by expressing their feelings on paper as they tried to cope with the constraints of the writing situation and to find something within the topic that was personally meaningful, to discover an honest approach. Most students do not go through this process of establishing a serious commitment to the topic, especially when writing an in-class assigned essay, and so they would never show such a step on paper. The initial musings of the professionals on paper did seem inappropriate content to be included in a polished essay. Since the musings were so unconventional and were inappropriate to a finished product, some raters may have penalized the professional writers for them. And since some of the writers honestly admitted their hostility toward the task, this admission easily could have been comprehended as a student's overstepping his or her role instead of as a struggle by a professional to cope with a difficult situation.

Searle's (1969) differentiation between two types of questions, "real questions" and "exam questions," may clarify why the professionals were compelled to find meaning in these topics. "In real questions S [speaker] wants to know (find out) the answer; in exam questions S wants to know if H [hearer] knows" (p. 66). In the context of the present study, S is the teacher who assigns the topic—or, in Searle's terms, asks the question—and H is the student or professional who receives the topic and then responds to it. When a teacher in a classroom assigns an essay topic, he or she is assigning an "exam" question. In this case, the teacher wants to know not what the student knows, but how well the student knows how to write. And as Horner (1979) has noted, students interpret such topics as "exam" topics. In the real world, when professional writers assign themselves a topic, they generate "real" questions to which their readers presumably do not know the answers. The professionals in this study seem to have approached their teacher-assigned "exam" questions as though they were "real" questions. The raters did not expect the writers to answer

"real" questions; rather, they expected them to answer "exam" questions. And all five writers, whether they were initially alienated by their topic or liked their topic, wrote as though the topics posed "real" rather than "exam" questions.

A third general difference between the two sets of papers surfaced in the level of emotional commitment the professionals exhibited toward the topics. Once they accepted the task, they wrote with passion, with feeling, and with definiteness. This emotional commitment may stem from the fact that the topics were or became "real" to the professionals. One professional attacked the author of a quotation about which he was writing as "the self-assured, moralizing, and to me, pompous sort of person who delights in highly generalized pronouncements to an audience. . . ."Another said about politicians and advertisers, "Both groups of language-mongers twist words and phrases—and communication distortion be damned!—to achieve their desired ends." Another author concluded his argument in favor of abortion with, "But niceness about the idea that the embryo is a sacred life—at any point during gestation—is a sentimental fastidiousness that we cannot as a society afford—not if we intend to have a society fit to live in for our children's children." The professionals did not argue irrationally. They wrote emotionally and definitely because they were able to develop a commitment to their assigned topics and because their role as an authority demands this style. Although the teachers should not have penalized the professionals for writing definitely, they may have, since they would not expect students to exercise such authority. Students mitigate their statements or give the expected cliché-like responses. Professionals typically make unexpected points and offer strong, decisive statements about these points.

A fourth and final difference that marked the professional essays was that the writers exhibited evidence of varied and broad experience with the world. One of the writers used many scholarly references to lend support to his opinions—Forrester, Schumacher, Mills, and Rawls. Another referred to Aristotle. Scholarly reading formed a significant part of the professionals' personal experience. Even the examples from personal experience that the professionals brought to the task were, at times, different in kind from the examples the students brought. Because the teacher-readers had less experience, the scholarly allusions and personal experiences marked the writer as more powerful and statusful than the reader. The evaluators, thinking the professionals were students, could not believe the extent of the scholarly experiences that the professionals displayed.

In some manifestation, all four of these distinctive markers of professional written discourse—familiarity with audience, task defiance/acceptance, commitment to topic, and scholarly experience—could have influenced some teachers to evaluate a given essay more negatively than they should have. By examining the role relationship between the reader and writer, one sees a plausible explanation for why the teacher-readers sometimes reacted negatively to the professional writers' essays. With all four markers, the professionals violated their expected student roles: they were threateningly familiar, some defied the task, they wrote too definitely about novel ideas, and they displayed a literally unbelievable amount of knowledge. Although the teachers may have been justified in penalizing the writers for an inappropriately familiar tone and for the task defiance, they might have overreacted to these features. This may have caused them to react against the other features of definiteness and knowledge, and thus sometimes not to give credit to the professionals for what they had done well (e.g., development).

Whenever writers violate their expected roles, their readers are prone to react negatively, just as hearers do when speakers violate their roles. Such violations can even cause miscomprehension. Searle (1969) discusses how our social roles "infect" the ways in which our speech acts are comprehended. He explains how only someone in authority over someone else can issue a command. If the speaker does not have authority over the hearer, a command will not be comprehended as such. Likewise, if a reader (teacher) does not perceive the writer (student or professional) to have authority and if a reader takes authority, much of

the writer's language can be misinterpreted and misevaluated. The teachers thought they were rating student papers, papers written by writers who were their subordinates. Since the professionals did not write as subordinates, the teachers could well have miscomprehended the intent of the writers and evaluated the papers in a biased way. For example, the informal dashes might have signaled to the evaluator that the writer lacked knowledge about the expected expository form. Indeed, in an informal discussion after the ratings, one rater accused one of the professionals, who had used quite a few scholarly references in his piece, of "obnoxious name-dropping." I doubt that the rater, an advanced graduate student, would have entertained this thought, much less expressed it, had he been aware that the essay was written by one of his most admired professors rather than by the lowly student whom he understood to be dropping names.

The writing and rating situations in this study were admittedly special and unusual. Teachers usually know whose writing they are reading, and professional writers usually do not write solely to be evaluated. Nevertheless, the results of the rating and the analysis of the essays bring up some issues for writing teachers to consider.

First, teachers may have biased responses to prose, especially when we feel that our role as an authority has been threatened. Like the professionals in this study, students probably overstep their roles from time to time when they write. As teachers we may tend to overreact to this overstepping, taking it as a threat to our authority, misunderstanding the writer's intent, and thus penalizing the student unfairly. Teachers must guard against this source of bias when evaluating student writing, especially since shows of authority are marks of professional prose.

Second, one of the problems that many students exhibit when they write is a lack of force, a lack of commitment to their topics. I do not believe that most of us take into account how much the teacher–student role relationship militates against the student's ability to write with force and authority. The amount of force a student can show is most likely directly related to the student's power over the topic and the audience. The more the student thinks he or she knows as opposed to what the audience knows, the more forceful the student will be able to be. As teachers we must remember that part of a strong self-concept and force comes from knowledge. Students must become intimate with and committed to their topics. We should teach students to become flexible enough to develop commitments even to topics that at first may seem uninteresting, as the professionals in this study did. Most important of all, once we ask for and get forceful writing, we must be careful not to show bias and penalize the writer inadvertently for what may appear to be a student's overstepping of his or her role. As teachers, we must be secure enough to help our students, as they advance, become better, yes better, writers than we ourselves are.

Notes

1. All topics are detailed in Freedman (1977, pp. 73–75, 198–200). The balanced design for assigning a particular topic to a given student is also elaborated there (pp. 76–77, 201).

2. The complete design for the rating system can be found in Freedman (1977, pp 80–88, 204).

3. This concept of speech register is derived from the work of Bloch (1974, 1975) and Olson (1980).

Works Cited

Atlas, M. *Writer insensitivity to audience: Causes and cares.* Paper presented at annual meeting of American Educational Research Association, San Francisco, 1979.

Bloch, M. Symbols, song, dance and features of articulation. *Archives Europeans de Sociologie,* 1974, 15, 51–81.

Bloch, M. (Ed.). *Political language and oratory in pretraditional society.* London: Academic Press, 1975.

Christensen, F. *Notes toward a new rhetoric: Six essays for teachers.* New York: Harper & Row, 1967.

Diederich, P. B. *Measuring growth in English.* Urbana, Ill.: National Council of Teachers of English, 1974.

Flower, L., & Hayes, J. R. The cognition of discovery: Defining a rhetorical problem. *College Composition and Communication,* 1980, 31, 21–32.

Freedman, S. *Influences on the evaluators of student writing.* Unpublished doctoral dissertation, Stanford University, 1977. Freedman, S. How characteristics of student essays influence teachers' evaluations. *Journal of Educational Psychology,* 1979, 71, 328–338. (a)

Freedman, S. Why teachers give the grades they do. *College Composition and Communication,* 1979, 30, 161–164. (b)

Grobe, C. Syntactic maturity, mechanics, and vocabulary as predictors of quality ratings. *Research in the Teaching of English,* 1981, 15, 75–85.

Hake, R., & Williams, J. Style and its consequences: Do as I do, not as I say. *College English,* 1981, 43, 433–451.

Hayes, J. R., & Flower, L. *Writing as problem solving.* Paper presented at meeting of American Educational Research Association, San Francisco, 1979.

Horner, W. Speech-act and text-act theory: "Theme-ing" in freshman composition. *College Composition and Communication,* 1979, 30, 165–169.

Hunt, K. *Grammatical structures written at three grade levels* (Research Report No. 3). Urbana, Ill.: National Council of Teachers of English, 1965.

Markham, L. Influences of handwriting quality on teacher evaluation of written work. *American Educational Research Journal,* 1976, 13, 277–283.

Nold, E., & Freedman, S. An analysis of readers' responses to essays. *Research in the Teaching of English,* 1977, 11, 164–174.

Olson, O. On the language and authority of textbooks. *Journal of Communication,* 1980, 30, 186–196.

Searle, J. *Speech notes: An essay in the philosophy of language.* London: Cambridge University Press, 1969.

Sommers, N. Revision strategies of student writers and experienced adult writers. *College Composition and Communication,* 1980, 31, 378–388.

Asked ? – Would teachers evaluate professional & student writers similarly (would prof. rank better) In study they did not. Then ask why? Study essays. What do answers say about the essay and about ways teachers evaluate?

Negotiating among Multiple Worlds: The Space/Time Dimensions of Young Children's Composing

Anne Haas Dyson

Dyson's research was published in Research in the Teaching of English 22 *(1988):* 355–90.

Abstract

This article discusses the developmental sense of children's seemingly disorganized texts. It is based on a two-year study of eight primary-grade children attending an urban magnet school. The study focused on interrelationships between the children's creation of written, imaginative worlds and their use of other symbolic media (drawing and talk) and other people (particularly peers). Collected data included the children's drawn and written products, audiotapes of their talk, and handwritten observations. A series of data analyses revealed the multiple worlds within which the children worked: the imaginary worlds formed from varied media, the ongoing peer social world, and the wider experienced world. Tensions among these worlds, with their different space/time dimensions, were evident in both the children's talk and their texts (e.g., shifts of time frames and points of view). The author thus argues that children's developmental challenge is not simply to create a unified, "disembedded" text world but to differentiate and coordinate multiple worlds.

Writing Example 1

Once there was a cowboy. I hated the cowboy a lot. Do You LIke cowboy's? but I like YOu alot. Sometimes I LIke The cowboy. TueSdaYs I LiKe The cowboy. The End. [text accompanying a drawing of a cowboy]

Writing Example 2

Once there was a girl. I like the girl. I Hate the Girls Brother a Lot. The End [text accompanying a drawing of a crying little boy and a frowning girl]

These products, by 6-year-old Mitzi, illustrate what is often described as the "primitive collections of random ideas" produced by young children (Perera, 1984, p. 217). Here are not the unified text worlds of the adult writer, worlds whose space/time structures are unified through linguistic markers of tense and person (Bruner, 1986). Rather, Mitzi appears to be moving among worlds, from an imaginary, observed past to a conversational, involving present, influenced perhaps by the pictorial world (the drawn cowboy) and her memories of the daily world she shared with her baby brother (whom she loved, "but not always").

Most studies of young writers like Mitzi have not explored the sense of children's unstable worlds, except to label them as such. Rather, they have documented the increasingly unified and coherent nature of children's text worlds—the texts' "disembeddedness" or freedom from outside symbolic or social ties (Donaldson, 1978; Olson, 1977). Thus, the developmental questions about young children's writing have revolved around how children's text-producing processes change (Graves, 1983), how their narratives or nonnarratives are structured over time, and how comfortable children are in story or expository frames, or poised conversationally and "expressively" between the two (King & Rentel, 1981; Newkirk, 1987).

In the project reported in this article, I adopted a different, although not incompatible, perspective. I followed Mitzi and seven of her primary-grade peers over a two-year period, observing them as they composed imaginary worlds. I focused on the interrelationships between children's creation of written *text worlds* and their use of or response to forces outside those worlds but within the situational context of the classroom—particularly *other symbolic media* (drawing and talk) and *other people* (particularly peers). Rather than focusing on how the children's written messages became disembedded, I examined how their use of writing was embedded within a network of supportive symbolic and social relationships.

Based on the project's findings, I argue here that children's major developmental challenge is not simply to create a unified text world but to move among multiple worlds, carrying out multiple roles and coordinating multiple space/time structures. That is, to grow as writers of imaginary worlds and, by inference, other sorts of text worlds as well, children must differentiate, and work to resolve the tensions among, the varied symbolic and social worlds within which they write—worlds with differing dimensions of time and space. And it is our own differentiation of these competing worlds that will allow us as adults to understand the seemingly unstable worlds, the shifts of time frames and points of view, that children create.

The Theoretical Frame: Learning to Negotiate among Multiple Worlds

Surface appearances to the contrary, there is sense and order to children's apparently disorganized texts. To discover that sense, though, we must take a long view, a developmental view, considering children's past and future efforts, and a broad view considering the symbolic and social forces that surrounded and shaped those texts.

To elaborate, children's first writing efforts are typically intermingled with drawing and talk, resulting in multimedia creations. Depending on the child's intentions, a label—"cowboy"—could be the written tip of an imaginary world (Dyson, 1983) or the seedling of an essay on cowboys or, more likely in Mitzi's case, on brothers (Newkirk, 1987). As writers, children's developmental challenge is to deliberately structure a "web of meaning"—to write a world (Vygotsky, 1962, p. 100). To shape that world, children must differentiate the boundaries between the written, drawn, and spoken symbol systems (Harste, Woodward, & Burke, 1984; Dyson, 1986). And, if it is to be a fictional world, they must distinguish as well between the imaginary world they are creating, the experienced world they are transforming, and the ongoing social world in which they are acting (Scarlett & Wolf, 1979).

At the same time, the boundaries between these symbolic and social worlds must be permeable; the text world is nestled within the larger symbolic and social world in which the author lives (Geertz, 1983). That image of embedded worlds arises from the work of both sociolinguists interested in literary discourse (Nystrand, 1982; Polanyi, 1982; Rader, 1982; Tannen, 1985) and literary theorists themselves (Booth, 1961; Barthes, 1974; Rosen, n.d.)

These scholars suggest that literary artists play with space/time structures, operating within multiple worlds. They shape an imaginary world in time past, but they aim as well to induce in their readers an anticipatory stance toward that world—their readers should wonder what *will* happen as they are drawn into the sounds and images evoked by the printed words (Rader, 1982). Thus, authors must find vantage points from which they can both energize the characters moving within their imaginary worlds and engage their readers in the real world: authors, like storytellers, face "the problems of finding a place to stand in order to report the goings on in another world while carrying out one's role as a competent and trustworthy member of society" (Polanyi, 1982, p. 169).

To illustrate the challenges inherent in the negotiation among these worlds, I refer to Mitzi's first piece. At a developmentally earlier time, Mitzi might have written "This is a cowboy," using her written text as a commentary on her drawn picture. But, in the presented piece, Mitzi marked her written world as independent of her accompanying visual art: the drawn cowboy was a present time representation of a figure from the indefinite past—"Once there was a cowboy." As suggested by her second piece, Mitzi's ambivalence about the cowboy reflected her ongoing ambivalence about boys in general and her brother in particular: the symbolic world reflected Mitzi's evaluation of her experienced world (Labov & Waletsky, 1967). And, as will be illustrated, her beckoning in of likeable "you's" reflected her efforts to use her text world, as all authors do, to connect with her ongoing social world.

Thus, to grow as creators of written worlds, children must indeed form a "verbal object isolated from the traffic of daily existence" (Britton, 1984, p. 322). And yet, their own role as creators of such a world must be to move in multiple worlds—now the real world director of the unfolding imaginary plot; now, deep in that imaginary world, an actor speaking a character's words, feeling a character's emotion; then inside a remembered world, a reflective storyteller reliving past experiences; and then, a socially astute communicator, adjusting words and phrases to ease interaction with real-world readers; simultaneously a painter of word pictures, a musician finding the contours and rhythms of word notes. Experiencing the tension between these worlds may lead to resolutions, as children find new ways of drawing on these symbolic and social resources to capture sensory experiences and social interactions within the flat spaces and colorless squiggles of written text.

Descriptions of children's progressively more organized written texts are accumulating (e.g., King & Rentel, 1981; Perera, 1984; Newkirk, 1987). To complement such studies, I focus on the sophisticated symbolic and social processes that may result in seemingly (and, for some children, increasingly) *disorganized* texts. Specifically, I intend to illustrate the tensions created when children attempt to capture pictured and oral experiences in written forms, to create an ongoing social relationship with others through a symbolic world, and to render an experienced world in an imaginary form. And I aim as well to illustrate that those tensions may result in disorganization—texts with shifts of time frames and author stances. That is, the "random" and "unorganized" flow of children's texts may be, at least in part, the result of children's developing realization of the multiple functions of literary texts and their simultaneous struggle to effect those functions through the cultural tools of writing conventions (c.f., Langer, 1986, p. 4).

In the following sections, I first summarize the study, including the series of data analyses, upon which this argument is based. Next, I illustrate, drawing upon all eight case study children's work, the sorts of symbolic and social tensions that were evident in their efforts; I then present a brief summary of one case, Mitzi's, in order to illustrate how these tensions might arise and then, ultimately, be resolved over time. Finally, I consider the significance of this theoretical perspective—this view of children as operating within multiple worlds—for the developmental issues regarding children's text worlds (i.e., the role of "narratives," "non-narratives," and "expressive" writing).

THE DATA BASE

The themes of this paper were formulated during the course of a participant observation project in an urban magnet school on the west coast. The study site drew children from social and ethnic groups from across this urban community. The children were from Anglo, Asian, Black, Hispanic, Middle Eastern, and mixed ethnicities. The school's 79 primary (K–3) grade children were separated into three "home classrooms": a kindergarten, a first/second grade, and a second/third grade. Beginning in January of the school year, all of the primary grade school children moved throughout the school day among three teachers' classrooms. The kindergarten "home" teacher, Margaret, was responsible for language arts instruction for all children throughout the data collection periods.

Margaret's language arts program centered around journals (books composed of construction paper and alternating blank and lined paper). From January through May, the children drew and wrote in their journals between two and five times weekly. During journal time, Margaret circulated, talking to the children about their ideas and the mechanics of production and, in the kindergarten, acting as scribe for their dictations. Margaret allowed time for each child to share two or three entries from their completed journals with the class.

While Margaret was only intermittently available to any individual child, she allowed them ongoing symbolic and social sources of support. Symbolically, the children could lean on drawing and on talking to help form and convey their ideas. Socially, they could lean on each other—they were free to ask each other questions and to comment on each other's work.

I observed the hour-long language arts periods in Margaret's kindergarten and first/second grade classes an average of twice a week from January through May 1985 (year 1). I began again in February 1986, observing through May 1986 (a teacher strike necessitating a February, rather than January, starting date). During 1986 (year 2), I was aided by two research assistants; we each observed twice weekly in the first/second and second/third grade classrooms.

The first few weeks of each year were spent observing each class as a whole and establishing our role as friendly, reactive adults (Corsaro, 1981). We then gathered holistic, descriptive data: audiotapes of the children's talk, photocopies of their drawn and written products, and notes on observed behaviors; audiotapes were transcribed and integrated with the notes after each observation was completed, producing an annotated transcript of each observation.

While data were gathered on all children, eight—four kindergartners and four first graders—were chosen as case studies during year 1. All case study children had attended kindergarten at the magnet school, and thus, by the end of the project's second year, they had been together for two or three years. They were familiar with the journal activity, with Margaret, and with each other.

The case study children were all judged by Margaret to be within the range of "normal" both academically and emotionally, although they varied in social and artistic style. (These differences will be illustrated in the case study excerpts; articles documenting these differences are available in Dyson 1986, 1987a). Table 1 provides the age, gender, and ethnicity of each child. As this is case study research, the children were not randomly selected to "represent" any particular subpopulation of children. Diversity in case study selection was considered essential in order to detect categories and patterns of behaviors that would yield a comprehensive description and interpretation of children's symbolizing behaviors.

Each focal child was observed completing one journal entry (a picture/text set generally defined by the child as "my story") at least once per month; such an observation generally took one or two days in the kindergarten and early first grade and could take as long as two weeks in the second grade, when entries were longer. (Longer entries were primarily due to the child's incorporation of several pages of writing and pictures in one "story.")

In all, we collected approximately 60 hours of audiotaped data in year 1, approximately 84 hours in year 2. We also collected 246 journal entries produced by the case study children; Margaret provided an additional 100 entries produced by the kindergarten case study children in the fall of year 1 before data collection began. (Generally, the first graders did not do extended writing in the fall, before they began language arts class with Margaret.) Table 2 provides the distribution of products collected.

In the following section I provide an overview of the data analysis procedures used to examine this large set of collected data. I focus particularly on those procedures that led to the differentiation of the varied space/time structures—the multiple worlds—within which the children worked. As will be illustrated, my own identification of these worlds seemed to roughly parallel the children's process of differentiation. As I moved from the kindergarten through the first and second

Table 1 Age, Gender, and Ethnicity of Focal Children

	Age[a]	Gender	Ethnicity
Kindergarteners			
Maggie[b]	5;0	Female	Anglo
Regina	6;0	Female	Black
Jesse	5;6	Male	Anglo
Rueben	5;10	Male	Hispanic
First graders			
Sonia	6;2	Female	Hispanic
Mitzi[c]	6;3	Female	Anglo
Jake	6;5	Male	Mixed (Black/Anglo)
Manuel	7;3	Male	Mixed (Hispanic/Anglo)

[a]Age as of January 1, 1985 (given in Years; Months).

[b]During 1985, Christopher, a kindergartener, was a focal child; Maggie was a "back up": she was observed, although less intensively, and all her journal entries were collected. During 1986, Christopher withdrew temporarily from the school, and so Maggie became a regular case study participant, Christopher a back up.

[c]During the observations from February through May 1986, Mitzi was in the second/third grade classroom; all other children were in the first/second grade room.

grade data, the analysis procedures became increasingly more complex to accommodate the increasingly complex behavior of the children themselves.

Data Analysis: Identifying Multiple Worlds

Since this project focused on young children's use of talk, pictures, and written text, I used inductive analysis procedures to develop categories describing the children's use of these varied media. Inductive procedures involve, first, segmenting data into similar units of behavior; second, comparing those units; and, third, composing descriptors to specify how those units vary. Those descriptors become the coding categories (see Bogdan & Biklen, 1982). By using such categories as an organizational scheme—a specialized vocabulary—for describing each case study child's composing, I aimed to understand how the children's use of these varied media changed over time.

This formal analysis process took place in four separate phases: analysis of the kindergarten data collected in year 1 (Dyson, 1986), the first grade data collected in year 1 (Dyson, 1987a), the first and second grade data collected in year 2, and finally, further analyses of all collected products. The products were further analyzed in order to provide additional support for behavior patterns (i.e., the existence of space/time tensions) qualitatively identified during the construction of the case studies—in Erickson's words, "to persuade the reader that the event described [in the qualitative narratives] was *typical*" of the data set (1986, p. 150). For the sake of clarity, then, product analysis procedures

Table 2 Number of Journal Entries Collected from Focal Children

	Grade			
	K		1st	2nd
Child	Preobservation[a]	Observation		
Maggie	25 (22.9)	13 (22.6)	9 (40.4)	
Regina	21 (19.0)	14 (27.4)	16 (24.0)	
Jesse	27 (15.1)	19 (21.8)	21 (14.0)	
Reuben	27 (19.7)	21 (19.8)	21 (22.4)	
Sonia			10 (18.2)	9 (29.1)
Mitzi			22 (20.2)	17 (49.2)
Jake			14 (22.9)	20 (50.7)
Manuel[b]			8 (17.8)	12 (22.6)
Totals	100 (19.0)	67 (22.9)	121 (22.5)	58 (37.9)

Note: The figures in parentheses indicate the average number of words per entry.

[a]These products were collected by the classroom teacher before the project formally began.

[b]Manuel's entire second grade journal comprised one story; he, however, divided the story into "parts" that could be "finished" (as in "I finished that part."). Therefore "parts" rather than "entries" are entered for second grade.

will be described during the presentation of case study excerpts.

For all phases of data analysis, the written products and annotated transcripts were organized into composing events. An event included all behaviors centered around the production of one journal entry. Next, the transcripts and products were analyzed in order to develop the coding categories, resulting in three sets of categories. Two sets focused on the children's talk (language functions, message topics), one (meaning elements) on each symbolic medium used.

The *function* categories described how the children used language to represent real and imaginary situations, to monitor and direct their own behavior (including their drawing and writing behaviors), to seek information, to express their feelings and attitudes, and to manage social relationships. The *meaning elements* coding system described the "meanings" the children expressed in different media, including in the talk used to represent their imaginary worlds, the completed pictures, and the content of their written products; categories included objects, actors, actions, placement in time (past, present, future) and space, and motorsensory qualities (direction, force, speed, volume). (For illustrations of these categories, see Dyson, 1986.)

The coding system that developed most extensively throughout the data analysis process was that focused on the *topics* of the children's representational talk. That talk occurred primarily during drawing for the kindergarteners and during drawing and writing for the first and second graders. To develop the coding system, I identified distinguishing properties or characteristics of the children's talk—differences in what they were talking about. The major categories of this system are summarized below.

Relevancy: Involvement in One's Own World

Differences were noted in the relevancy of the children's talk to the ongoing journal activity. During the analysis of the kindergarten data, I distinguished between *task involved* and *non-task involved* talk. Only talk that was perceived as directly relevant to the child's ongoing journal entry was considered "task involved."

Of the task involved talk, differences were noted in the degree of symbolic involvement in the task. A child might focus on his or her *own feelings and actions,* commenting on procedures or process ("I'm gonna made a bird in that nest."). In contrast, a child might enter the boundaries of the imaginary world, focusing on the *actions or state of the depicted figures and events* ("And she's looking at her egg . . ." [said while drawing]).

Of the talk focused on the depictions, differences were noted in the nature of the time frame created. A child might create a *static* time frame, in which the depicted figures do not move through time, as in the sort of time frame typically associated with a picture or a slide. Or a child might create a *dynamic* time frame, in which the depicted figures or events do move through time, as in a movie.

In analyzing the first grade data set, I identified two additional categories that reflected the nature of the children's involvement with their symbolic worlds. As a group, the first graders not only discussed the actions of the depicted figure or event; they also focused notably on the specific *figure or event being rendered* (i.e., the referent). This talk initially occurred primarily during drawing, as opposed to writing. For example, in kindergarten, Regina talked about what "this little girl" in the picture "is doing." In the first grade, she talked about what the little girl "is" like or "can" do. She even commented on which of those characteristics would be incorporated into her written text ("She's [the pictured girl] just in the Brownies, but I'm not gonna say that she's in the Brownies."). The little girl being depicted was clearly separate from the depiction itself.

The final differentiated category included talk focused on the *symbolic vehicle itself,* separate from the imagined or depicted experience. That is, the children engaged in metasymbolic talk about the qualities of the drawn or written symbols. For example, they discussed how "soft" colors were, how punctuation worked, how syntactically "good" certain phrases sounded.

Relevancy: Involvement in Others' World

Beyond the changes in the "task involved" category noted above, analyzing the first grade data set led to the abandonment of the simplistic distinction between task involved and non-task involved talk and the formation of two additional categories for coding topic. First, the children frequently entered into the task of a peer, commenting on the peer's actions or even entering the peer's imaginary world. That is, their talk was *other's task involved* and could be coded for degree of symbolic involvement and for the type of time frame governing that talk (e.g., a child could stretch a peer's world forward in time or elaborate on a point in time).

Relevancy: Involvement in the Real World

The children's comments on each other's work often led to talk that was *task related,* the second new topic category. This talk was outside the boundaries of the particular imaginary worlds the children were creating but clearly related to those worlds. It included talk about the referent category of the figures and/or events being depicted (e.g., Mitzi's picture of a teen-age mother led to a general discussion of teen-age mothers) and talk about thematically related experiences (e.g., Mitzi's beach story led to Sonia's talk about her own beach experience). The children's talk about the broader background of concepts and experiences upon which their entries drew linked those entries more closely to both the children's past experiences and to their ongoing intellectual lives.

Certainly the observed kindergarteners talked about peers' work and related topics, but the initial research focus was the composing of individuals. The first and second graders engaged in more extended talk about the content of each others' imaginary worlds than did the kindergarteners; they thus forced a broadening of this study of writing development to include not only other symbolic media, but also the children's developing relationships with each other and, more broadly, with the world around them.

In sum, then, the data analysis categories suggested the multiple worlds within which the children moved: the imaginary worlds formed from varied symbolic media—drawing, talking, writing; the ongoing social world; and the wider experienced world of people, places, objects, and events. To become a meaningful object, a world apart, a written text must be separate from and intimately linked with such other worlds. As will be illustrated in the next section, over time the observed young composers often found themselves caught on the symbolic and social boundaries that define written worlds, and, as they wrestled with these borders, they sometimes left their footprints in their texts.

MOVEMENT AMONG MULTIPLE WORLDS: ILLUSTRATION AND DISCUSSION OF THE CASE STUDIES

In constructing each case study, I wrote a narrative account of each composing event observed, basing that description primarily on the coded and annotated transcripts. The case studies highlighted differences among the children, as each had a unique way of interacting with symbolic and social materials. The children differed in how extensively they crossed symbolic boundaries to interweave drawing and talk to encode "meanings" (e.g., actors, actions, time) (Dyson, 1986). And they differed in how and how extensively they crossed social boundaries, involving other people in their own activities (Dyson, 1987a). All, however, grappled with the coordination of space/time structures and with finding their own place to stand amidst these varied worlds. These conflicts among multiple worlds were evident in the kindergarteners' dictating and in their subsequent independent writing as first graders.

In this section, I draw on all cases to illustrate these common struggles and their possible resolutions, focusing first on tensions among the differing (but overlapping) symbolic space/time structures of children's imaginary worlds and, then, on those among the imaginary, ongoing social, and wider experienced worlds. In addition, I provide summary data from the product analyses.

Tensions among the Symbolic Worlds of Drawing, Talking, and Writing

Domination of Text by Visual Media: Art Notes

Many of the children's first texts were inextricably linked to the space/time structures of their pictures; these texts pointed to the pictures with deictic expressions and/or progressive verbs ("This little girl is looking . . ."). I labeled such texts "Art Notes" to suggest their dependence upon pictures. In year 1, 63 percent of all kindergarteners' products were Art Notes; in year 2, 18 percent of these same children's products were Art Notes. In year 1, 19 percent of the first graders' products were Art Notes, while in year 2, these children produced far fewer, only 7 percent. (Art Note coding procedures will be described below.)

Art Notes were typically non-narrative (non-chronologically ordered), but they were not, in the context of this activity, precursors to exposition (cf. Newkirk, 1987). In addition, while an Art Note was dependent upon the child's picture, it did not necessarily capture the meanings—the imaginary world—the child had created while drawing and talking. Creating an Art Note could highlight the space/time dimensions of pictures, talk, and written text.

For example, in the kindergarten and the first grade, Regina talked liberally while drawing. She elaborated on the characteristics of her drawn figures, reported any past actions leading up to their current pictured state, and predicted future actions. Her imaginary worlds thus had static time frames—they were frozen in the present, although pressing against the past and future. Art Notes were one way of reducing these bulging imaginary worlds into written texts.

For instance, in the first grade, Regina drew a little girl who was holding up her dress because "she fell into the mud puddle" and "had some stuff on her shoes, and she doesn't want her dress to get all dirty—that stuff on her stockings." Her text was an Art Note:

Writing Example 3

This is a girl She has something on her leg's but she doesn't know that it was on her but she will know it.

When Regina reread her text, she became quite concerned: "It [the text] can't say that," she explained. The girl could not be unaware of the mud on her legs "because she's going like that [holding up her dress]." Thus, the difficulty in coordinating the time frames of the picture and the written text led to an evaluation and revision of that text. Regina adjusted her entry to read that the girl "know now that it was on her legs" (rather than "doesn't know") and that "she will not like it" (rather than "will know it").

The Juxtaposition of Media Influences

Children who, unlike Regina, created dynamic time frames during drawing could not solve their text creation problems with a simple Art Note. For example, Jesse's pictures were the scenes of orally dramatized adventures that, once accomplished, he did not refer to in present tense. To illustrate, Jesse had drawn a small splotch, a "motorcycle guy," and then traced the path of a wild motorcycle race. As his marker wound around the page, he commented on the action:

"Errrrrrrrrrrrrrrrrrrrrrrrrrr [the sound of a motorcycle being driven]. And he falls off, and he hurts himself, and he gets back up."

To an adult reader, Jesse's subsequent text is jarring—it begins as an Art Note (the pictured splotch is labeled in present tense) but then changes abruptly to the past tense, as the previously narrated action is reported:

Writing Example 4

This is a motorcycle guy.
And then the motorcycle guy won.

The combined influence of told experiences and drawn pictures could lead to written texts that juxtaposed past, present and future time frames. While writing the following text, Jake "copied [his story] offa the picture":

Writing Example 5

Once there WAs a three head bubble car on a jet that is running out of gasoline. Then the bubble CAr is going to Crash. But the jet is going to blow up be cause it is out of gasoline.
the end

Jake begins, written language-like fashion, in past tense. He then describes the current actions of the pictured vehicles and anticipates future destructive actions. Those actions were in fact accomplished in his present-tense, narrative talk during drawing, when frantic squiggles were drawn around the vehicles. (However, the pictured bubble car, which is headed towards a door, does not actually contact that door—although it is clearly "going to.")

Footprints in the Texts

Based on the observed behaviors of Regina, Jake, Jesse, and their peers, I inferred that tensions among the overlapping space/time structures created through drawing, talk, and written texts contributed to the unexpected (from an adult perspective) tense shifts in the children's work; such tense shifts occurred in 36% of all collected products. In addition, such tensions appeared to lead to written texts, like Jesse's and Jake's, that were story-like and, yet, not technically "narratives": in these texts, movement was implied but not actually accomplished.

To document the frequency of this phenomenon, a research assistant and I analyzed all written products. From our viewpoint as adult readers, we judged whether narrative movement was absent, implied, or actually accomplished in each text (i.e., there were two temporally-ordered, independent clauses presenting action or a character's reaction [adapted from Labov & Waletsky, 1967]). As we reflected on the basis for our judgements, we turned to media metaphors: a text with no movement suggests a slide, a text with accomplished movement suggests a movie, while one with implied movement suggests a frame lifted from a movie—it has linguistic sprockets. Most typically, these sprockets were tense shifts that implied accomplished movement (as in Jesse's shift from the existing motorcycle guy to the race that *was* won) or imminent movement (as in Jake's establishment of the "once-upon-a-time" bubble car facing impending disasters).

These categories of movement are emic, that is, designed to reveal changes in this data set. After refining these categories, we each independently coded the 346 products and discussed all products with discrepant coding. To judge our consistency as judges, we coded and then determined interrater reliability for a random selection of 50 products, drawn from all eight cases; we agreed in our judgement of 92% of the products. The results of our analysis are presented in Table 3.

The product analysis, unlike the case studies, does not consider the intentions of individual children and, indeed, masks individual variation. Nonetheless, the analysis does suggest that the qualitative excerpts taken from the cases are indicative of space/time tensions that appeared frequently in the children's work. Although the children were primarily concerned with creating imaginative worlds—worlds that existed through their deliberate symbolic efforts—the majority of their texts did not contain narrative movement, as here defined. However, while approximately 2/3 of the first graders' texts produced in year 1 contained no movement, in year 2 approximately 2/3 of the then second graders' texts at least implied movement.

Resolving Tensions through Manipulation of Symbolic Resources

To this point, I have illustrated that the symbolic resources these young composers leaned upon, drawing and talking, also posed challenges.

Table 3 Presence of Movement in Children's Texts

Grade[a]	Percent of Products		
	No Movement	Implied Movement	Movement
K 1985			
preobs.[b]	65	20	14
obs.	43	22	34
1st 1986	45	28	27
1st 1985	65	19	17
2nd 1986	27	26	47
Total Percent	51	23	26
Number of Products	174	79	91

[a]"K 1985" and "1st 1986" refer to the products collected from Maggie, Regina, Jesse, and Reuben. "1st 1985" and "2nd 1986" refer to the products collected from Sonia, Mitzi, Jake, and Manuel.

[b]Two texts were eliminated as they were copied from the chalkboard due to the direction of a substitute teacher.

At the same time, however, those resources could be drawn upon in new ways to resolve these very challenges. For example, the order of drawing and then writing could be changed or more than one picture/text set could be incorporated into one journal entry, thereby breaking through the space/time limitations posed by a picture frame.

This latter resolution appeared in year 2 and was used by all four second graders and, in the last month of school, by one first grader; its use was initially prompted by a long text that spilled over onto another lined page. Generally, scenes depicted in each sequenced picture were described or dramatized in an accompanying text; these texts might be linked through adverbials (*next, then, all of a sudden*). Sonia juxtaposed pictures for her first (and only) written narrative that extended beyond 2 temporally-related actions, although she did not actually link her texts. Presented without her pictures and her accompanying talk, the written text seems disjointed:

Writing Example 6

Happy Birthday Sonia
"Today is your birthday,"
said Mom. The lights were
turned on. [accompanying picture of balloons and swirls of crepe paper]
"Let's eat the spaghetti. m-m-m"
said everybody. "Mom, can we have the ice cream?"
"Yes, cleanup kids". "Mom can we watch
the TV?" "Yeees". [accompanying picture of three little girls sitting at a huge table that is spread with birthday food]
"What will we watch?" "I don't know.
"What is on?" Too close for comfort.
"Who wants to watch that?"
"I don't know" but I do" [accompanying picture of little girl watching television]
"Play time," said Sonia. "What will
we play?" Let's play house". [accompanying picture of two little girls lying flat on either side of a mattress; this page is meant to be funny—and is, I think—as, actually, it's time for bed]

As Sonia's text also illustrates, a child's use of written "talk" could also support narrative movement. That talk could be similar to the dramatic dialogue certain children used during drawing, or, as in Sonia's text it could be more written language-like (i.e., "said-[character]" constructions). All of the case study children made use of dialogue, a particularly helpful strategy, as, even within one picture frame, the passage of time could be captured as characters exchanged talk.

Regina, in the first grade, illustrated dramatically the potential power of written dialogue. The elaborate talk surrounding her drawings was described earlier (see discussion of Example 3). Regina first produced written texts containing narrative movement by abandoning those imaginary worlds constructed through pictures and speech and by turning to written language-like dialogues.

For example, during one event Regina talked elaborately, in present tense, about "Candy Land," which she was drawing; in this land,

> When it rains, people are—they come outside. Some people on this side, um that side [of the drawn candy house], they want lemonade. On this side, they want chocolate sprinkles on this side. . . .

And so Regina drew raindrops of lemonade and chocolate sprinkles. However, when she went to write, a new scene was constructed:

Writing Example 7

> I found the Candy House where my Friends lived. It's us said them. Hi I said. Can I come in? Yes they said. Come in. We have three dogs. Wow wee I said.

All four of Regina's first grade narratives involved dialogue and incorporation of new meanings (new information beyond that included in her talk during drawing). Regina thus appeared to develop her texts linearly, in striking contrast to her development of imaginary worlds during drawing and talking, when she alternately recalled the past, anticipated the future, and described the present. Her linear "what next" strategy (Bereiter & Scardamalia, 1982) is generally considered young children's simplest strategy for text construction (Graves, 1983;

Harris & Wilkinson, 1986). Yet, that strategy clearly had a role in the growth of Regina and her peers as composers, as manipulators of time and space.

The children's writing was progressively less influenced by drawing and accompanying talk (for similar observations, see Rosen & Rosen, 1974; Graves, 1983; Newkirk, 1987). During year 2, the second graders—Mitzi, Jake, Manuel, and less often, Sonia—subordinated both drawing and writing to a meaning, a potential message, that may have been stimulated by a personal memory, a story from a book or the television, or even a story that had evolved during drawing but, through frequent repetition, gained independence. This subordination was particularly critical for children who did not use talk extensively during drawing to construct an imaginary world; these children often had great difficulty finding a verbal story in a picture and frequently voiced, in less direct ways, Sonia's explicit plea: "Do you see anything in this story [picture]?"

These new overriding meanings had an existence, however hazily, separate from the drawn and the written depictions. This existence was reflected in the children's talk, during both drawing and writing, about the figure or event being rendered: the symbolic tool of talk became the mediator between the more differentiated space/time structures of pictures and written texts. So, second grader Manuel, for example, studied both his picture and his written text, as he worried about whether or not his readers would understand his story. Implicitly, Manuel was acknowledging that both his story and his readers' stories were mediated by, realized in and through, his symbols (Iser, 1974). This brings us to children's use of written texts to participate in the social world around them, a topic of the following section.

Tensions among the Symbolic, Ongoing Social, and Experienced Worlds

To this point, I have examined the tensions arising from crossing symbolic borders, particularly those that arose in the observed activity as children worked to render their drawn and, often, spoken

worlds in (at least compatible) written worlds. But there were other worlds being moved among as well, worlds which contributed not only to shifting time frames within written texts but also to shifts in children's roles as authors—in the personal stances they adopted toward their text worlds.

As documented in the previous section, over time the children's work became less oriented around their pictures. Art Notes like "This little girl is happy" or "The ghost is flying around the house" became much less common. At the same time, as authors, the children became progressively more involved in both their ongoing social world and the wider experienced world. As will be illustrated, these role changes were reflected in their talk, as it evidenced this increased interest in their peers' activity and in how their peers' and their own journal entries related to the way the world worked. Changes in the children's roles—as well as the children's ambivalence about their roles—were also reflected in their texts. I turn first to those texts.

Footprints in the Texts

To document these tracings of children's role changes, a research assistant and I, regularly joined by an additional assistant, studied the written products. As adult readers, we identified the roles or stances children appeared to be taking vis-a-vis their written worlds, refining categories initially developed during construction of the case studies. In our judgment, a child might assume the role of *commentator* on the pictured world (reflected in an Art Note), *observer* of a world forming within the text itself (reflected in a third person stance in a text that was not an Art Note), or *actor* within that world (reflected in a first person stance in a non-Art Note text).

At times, children appeared to abruptly change stances, as in Mitzi's texts at the beginning of this article; such texts were classified as shifting between two different stances. For example, Mitzi's texts were coded Observer/Actor (i.e., she shifted from an observer of an imagined cowboy to an actor who hated that cowboy).

In our analysis, we followed the procedures described for coding narrative movement; inter-rater

Table 4 Personal Stance in Children's Texts

| Grade[a] | Percent of Products | | | | | |
	Art Notes	Art Notes/ Observer	Art Notes/ Actor	Observer/ Actor	Observer	Actor
K 1985						
preobservation[b]	67	16	5	0	5	6
observation	57	37	0	0	6	0
1st 1986	18	9	6	0	46	20
1st 1985	19	15	2	24	20	20
2nd 1986	7	5	3	16	28	42
Total Percent	38	17	3	6	19	16
Number of Products	130	58	12	22	67	33

[a]"K 1985" and "1st 1986" refer to the products collected from Maggie, Regina, Jesse, and Reuben. "1st 1985" and "2nd 1986" refer to the products collected from Sonia, Mitzi, Jake, and Manuel.
[b]These products were collected by the classroom teacher before the project formally began.

reliability for a random selection of 50 products was 94 percent. The results of our analysis are presented in Table 4.

Table 4 illustrates this group of children's movement away from commentator roles and, also, their relatively late adoption of roles as actors in their own imaginary, written worlds, a finding consistent with Harprin's findings on British children (cited in Perera, 1984); texts coded as embodying the actor role doubled between the first and second grade. Even children like Jesse, who dramatized—was an actor within—his drawn worlds, generally remained outside his written worlds: as an author, he moved first from a role as commentator on pictures to an observer of actions. Jesse's "motorcycle guy" (Example 4) is illustrative: Jesse begins by commenting on his picture ("This is a motorcycle guy") and then becomes an observer reporting a past action ("And then the motorcycle guy won.")

As will be illustrated in both the following case study excerpts and Mitzi's case summary, the children did not only mark their existence within their written worlds through the use of "I"; they left their mark less explicitly through revealing the internal worlds (the thoughts and feelings) of their characters. In Bruner's words, the children evidenced emerging abilities to "construct two landscapes simultaneously," for the imaginary world consists of both the landscape of actors and actions described in story grammars and the "landscape of consciousness: what those involved in the action know, think, or feel, or do not know, think, or feel" (1986, p. 14).

The children's movement into their written worlds seemed related to the decreasing influence of drawing. And, simultaneously, it seemed supported by the children's use of those text worlds to move within the wider world, including the ongoing social world of the classroom.

The Written Texts' Role in the Social World

Over time, the children's written texts played an increasingly larger social role within the life of the classroom (for an extended discussion of the social life in this room and literacy's role in that life, see Dyson, in press). The children could quite literally bring the social life of the classroom into their written texts. Dialogue, already noted as a strategy for creating dynamic movement in texts, was also a way of incorporating social interaction into the texts themselves. Another was the fictionalization of self and peers.

For example, in the first grade Jake engaged in dramatic play with his friends while he drew, creating elaborate oral adventures. However, during writing, he "copied offa the picture," and thus his texts described his pictures (see Example 5). During the second grade, Jake began to engage in interactive dramatic play during *writing,* and moreover, he brought that play into his texts. With this support from peers (and from talk), he broke through the time constraints of a picture frame; further, he evidenced more awareness of the boundaries of the imaginary world being shaped in written words:

Jake has been writing a story in which Manuel meets Buck Rogers:

Jake: Uh, Manuel! You get to see Buck Rogers!

Manuel: What!

Jake: Buck Rogers

Manuel: Oh. *You mean in your story.* [emphasis added]

Jake: Yeah. Buck Rogers, twenty-first century person.

. . . [omitted data]

[to Marcos, Manuel's brother] You wouldn't see your brother again, ever again Marcos. *You would never see him in a story again.* [emphasis added]

Marcos: I wouldn't

Jake: In my stories, uh uh. Cause that would be the last. Eepoof! Nothing.

Manuel: Oh God. Oh, well, it's been fun having adventures with you. Um, but I'm gonna get blown to pieces.

. . .

Jake: You might get your butt saved by Buck Rogers. You want your butt saved by Buck Rogers?

Manuel: What I want is my body saved. I don't wanna die. I don't wanna—

. . .

Jake: You want your whole body saved by Buck Rogers?

In Jake's story, Buck does teach Manuel how to take on the bad guys—Manuel's existence in the text world is secured.

Jake's apparent discovery that texts could be used to socially interact with his peers led to more elaborate but also more unstable worlds. Jake-the-observer telling about a world abruptly became Jake-the-actor in the thick of things. And, as he did so, the time frame governing that world typcally changed as well: his "once-upon-a-time" worlds often became the sites of present tense encounters:

Writing Example 8

Once there was a boy that is named manuel. manuel is going to fly the fastest jet and I am going to fly the jet too. But Manuel's headquarters is going to blow up But I am OK But I don't know about manuel but I am going to find manuel. But When I find him I like him. But I think I see him. He is in the jet. Manuel are you OK? Yes, I am OK. you are being attacked. I will shoot the bad guys out of the universe. OK yes shoot them now. the end

Jake's example suggests a connection between the role written texts played in the children's social lives and the degree to which the children entered into those texts, a connection suggested, in different ways, by all of the case studies, including Mitzi's. With their feet in both their ongoing social world and the imaginative text world, their texts certainly could be unstable. The children were quite literally both creating a relationship between characters in their texts and sustaining a relationship with friends in their social worlds. In time, though, those others may become distanced readers, not interested peers sitting right beside them.

Tension between the Experienced and the Symbolic World

Over time the children became increasingly concerned about the relationship of their written worlds to the experienced world. From the beginning of the project, certain children sometimes wrote what seemed to be texts about personal experiences. But, without consulting the child authors, it was impossible to judge whether or not the texts actually were "real"—reports of parties, long walks, the existence of siblings, a move to a new house, were upon inquiry, "fake," to use Sonia's descriptor. And texts that were framed as "unreal" were sometimes quite real—"Once upon a time there was a girl Which is Me." In the context of this activity, the children generally viewed their writing as "pretend." However, they were concerned about the validity of these "pretend" worlds. The kindergarteners might say indignantly, "That's not what a _____ looks like"; the more experienced first and second graders were just as apt to voice "That's not true" about a peer's text—and, on occasion, even raised the most sophisticated objection of all, "That wouldn't happen!"

As they moved between their imaginary and real worlds, the children confronted developmentally taxing issues for young children: What is "true"? How true does "not true" have to be"? (Piaget, 1929; Applebee, 1978). Manuel was explicit about these issues, even in the first grade; in an attempt to end a long, loud argument about the possibility of a bomb making a volcano, he said, "Well, anyway, it's a pretend story. In real life, it may [not] be true."

The following interaction between Mitzi and Sonia also illustrates this tension between the experienced and the real world:

Writing Example 9 (included in transcript excerpts)

Mitzi has used "Snoopy stickers" to create a picture of the cartoon character Snoopy and a small bear at the beach. She then writes:

> Once there was a bear. And there was Snoopy too. They were

She stops and comments:

> *Mitzi:* OK, there'll be a little tiny sister.

Sonia overhears her:

> *Sonia:* They were sisters?
>
> *Mitzi:* Yeah.
>
> *Sonia:* Snoopy isn't a girl.
>
> *Mitzi:* I know. Sister AND brother.

Mitzi completes her text:

> [They were] sister and brother. And they were at the beach. **Snoopy is a boy** and the bear was the girl. The End. [emphasis added]

Mitzi's text seems disjointed. She temporarily changes her role as writer, a change too sophisticated for our role coding system. She abandons her observational perch by the imaginary world, set in the indefinite past, to make a "real" world observation about Snoopy.

Truth in imaginary worlds depends primarily upon capturing the quality of human experiences or "psychic reality" (Bruner, 1986, p. 14). The children typically captured the quality of experiences in their pictures; by second grade, the children's drawn characters could register such qualities as surprise, wickedness, fear, sadness, joy. However, as discussed in the previous section, capturing their own peer relationships in their texts could help provide this quality, this insight into the internal world of characters.

In addition, the children could comment directly on the quality of the imaginary world or on an element of that world. Such comments on, or evaluations of, experiences occurred primarily in the talk surrounding the children's texts. But, occasionally, those statements were tacked on, as in the following story by Jake; notice his role change from the observer of a past and imaginary jet to an actor sharing the present with that jet and expressing his amazement at its existence:

Writing Example 10

> Once upon a time
> there was helicopter that was the
> fastest helicopter in the world.
> But the helicopter
> can fly in two seconds.

I can't believe
that it can. [emphasis added]

Means of Resolving Tensions among Symbolic, Social, and Experienced Worlds

In general, the children's behaviors during journal time, as well as in their written texts, reflected the *discovery of,* more than the *resolution of,* the tensions illustrated in this section. As the children's texts became more involved with their ongoing and experienced worlds, new complications arose. The children's social world—their use of fictionalized self and peers, their use of dialogue—could destabilize as well as enrich their written worlds. In addition, the children's increasing attention to the relationship between their texts and their real world experiences raised new issues for them, particularly about fictional reality. The children had to find ways of rendering the meanings—the essence—of their experienced worlds more directly in written forms.

The first textual signs of the evaluation of experience—other than "I like _____ "—was the use of certain graphic conventions; these graphics, including exclamation points or playful spellings ("OOOOOOOOOOOOOoh!!!!!!!!!"), mimic the ability of the voice to convey the perceived quality of experience (Cook-Gumperz & Gumperz, 1981).

Even fluent, adolescent writers may be far from skilled in embedding the quality of an experience in textual description and narration of actors and their actions (Dixon & Stratta, 1986). Yet certain focal children did evidence emerging skill. For example, in the kindergarten, Maggie had often been silly with her texts (e.g., reading them in a falsetto voice), but her texts themselves had not been funny. Late in the first grade year, though, she began to find them quite funny ("I can't believe what I'm writing. This is so funny.").

One funny text was a story about two friends, Alice and Lacey. Maggie orally elaborated upon her written characters: "Alice and Lacey are the real people. They're real names. Anyone could be them." These "anyones" had a common experience, particularly common for Maggie—they were consistently late to school: as she put it in her text, "as usual they Got a tarDy tag again." The "as usual"

reflects the resigned but slightly amused stance Maggie herself often adopted.

Such fictionalization of experiences and their qualities, which will be further illustrated in Mitzi's case summary, seems critical. It is the controlled meshing of the experienced and the imaginary world that ultimately allows authors and readers to connect—that allows their social interaction to occur: Authors evaluate their own life experiences through writing—and readers draw on their "repertoires of conceptions about human plights" to experience the sights and sounds cued by print (Bruner, 1986, p. 34, drawing upon the work of Barthes, 1974, and Iser, 1974).

In the preceding pages, I have pulled apart the many worlds children operate in as writers—worlds that are in fact inextricably linked. I have highlighted these texts where certain space/time structures protruded out awkwardly—an unexpected "Do you like cowboys?" or "I can't believe that it can." These seemingly disorganized texts, when viewed within the context of individual children's case histories, suggested the theoretical frame presented here, this frame of multiple worlds. In the next section of this article, I pull these worlds together again by summarizing the case history of Mitzi.

MITZI: AN ILLUSTRATIVE CASE

Mitzi, like all the case study children, grappled with the coordination of space/time structures. Her ways of negotiating among worlds changed dramatically over the two years of observation, so her case serves especially well to illustrate the process of learning to negotiate among multiple worlds. However, since this was case study research—and thus the unit of concern was the individual, not the group—Mitzi does not serve in any way to represent "group norms." As noted earlier, the case study children were selected precisely because they varied as symbolizers and socializers. Thus, each case differed in particular ways from all other cases. Nonetheless, each contributed to the theoretical perspective on writing development presented here, this concept of multiple worlds. It is this broad perspective—this way of making sense of child behavior—that is illustrated by the particular experiences of each unique child, including Mitzi.

Mitzi was a tall, slender child with a low, soft voice and a straightforward manner. Throughout the two years of observation, her behaviors consistently reflected her involvement with her friends and her family. However, the relationship of Mitzi's journal entries to her ongoing social life in school and to her wider experienced world, including her family, changed over time, as did the relationship among the drawing, talking, and writing behaviors leading to and surrounding those entries.

First Grade

During year 1, Mitzi's written texts appeared only superficially related to her drawings. In this way, Mitzi's texts differed from those of other first grade cases, whose texts included at least partial Art Notes. Mitzi's texts, in contrast, directly presented her feelings about people—real, imaginary, or simply unspecified ("I like you."). Mitzi generally began a journal entry by drawing a picture of a little girl against a background. While drawing, she did talk with her peers, but, unlike certain other children's talk, Mitzi's talk was not directly involved in her ongoing drawing. She talked about her family and friends—whom she liked and whom she hated.

After drawing, Mitzi quickly produced a written entry. As in the texts opening this report, most of Mitzi's entries began with a "once-there-was" opening, followed by a label for the drawn entity. Next came a statement of her own feelings (or, perhaps, "yours") about that entity. Thus, as indicated by Table 5, Mitzi's texts, like those of all first grade cases, were primarily non-narrative; 86 percent contained no movement through time. And, in over half (59 percent) of her texts, she shifted her own stance as author from an observer of an imaginary world set in the past to an actor in a present time world, as in the following example:

Writing Example 11

Once There was a girl
She might like You.

Table 5 Mitzi's Written Products

	Percent of Products	
	Grade	
Product Descriptor	1	2
Movement		
No movement	86	41
Implied movement	0	6
Movement	14	53
Stance		
Art Notes/Actor	0	6
Observer/Actor	59	29
Observer	18	18
Actor	23	47
Inclusion of Others		
"You"	36	6
Names of peers and family members	23	53
Number of Products	22	17

She liveds under a rainbow
I like you.   The End

While the process of producing written texts was no doubt eased by Mitzi's repetitive "I likes," her products were not simply texts of convenience. They reflected the symbolic and social resources that she leaned upon for help. During drawing, Mitzi did not create elaborate stories—the picture provided only a figure or an object to be labeled. And, as noted above, Mitzi's talk during journal time centered on relationships. Thus, Mitzi's texts seemed to grow primarily from her general concerns with relationships. In fact, in one event, Mitzi abandoned her typical "once-upon-a-time" frame and brought her text directly into her ongoing social life:

Writing Example 12 (included in transcript excerpt)

While completing a piece in her journal, Mitzi has been talking about her upcoming birthday/slumber party with Sonia. Sonia frequently seeks reassurance from Mitzi about their friendship, as the following conversation suggests:

> *Sonia:* Where am I going to sleep?
>
> *Mitzi:* Me and Bessie are gonna sleep up on the top [of Mitzi's bunk bed].
>
> *Sonia:* Oh. Who's gonna sleep on the bottom? Your brother. Where am I gonna sleep, Mitzi?
>
> *Mitzi:* You're gonna sleep in my sleeping bag.

Mitzi immediately begins writing a new journal entry; this entry includes the names of all the children invited to her party:

> [Text] I like Sally. And I like Sonia too. And I like Elizabeth
>
> [Bessie] and I like Sarah. The End.

Sonia does not dismiss the significance of this text:

> *Sonia:* Mitzi, you love me. (very pleased)
>
> *Mitzi:* I said *like,* not I *love.* (firmly)

Mitzi's texts related in a similarly unadorned way to her feelings about her family. Since these references to family often followed imaginative openings, they resulted in texts that mixed fantasy and reality, as in the following example (see also Example 2):

Writing Example 13 (included in transcript)

Mitzi has worked intensively on a large, carefully detailed picture of a mean-looking witch. She is quite pleased with her drawing, remarking that it is her "favorite story." She now begins to write:

> Once there was a witch.
>
> She is my mom.

Jenni and Bessi, who are sitting nearby, attend to Mitzi's rereading of her story:

> *Jenni:* I have a witch mother.
>
> *Mitzi:* What?
>
> *Jenni:* I have a real witch mother. My mother's a friend of a witch.
>
> *Mitzi:* A bad one?
>
> *Jenni:* No, a good one/bad one.

Mitzi may be feeling uneasy about referring to the witch as her mother, for she now writes:

> I love my mom

Bessie and Jenni seem to be concerned about Mitzi's text as well:

> You shouldn't share it [with the class].
>
> *Mitzi:* She's a bad witch. (pointing to her picture)
>
> *Jenni:* Then you're a bad girl.

Perhaps a little girl who writes that her own mother is a witch is a bad girl indeed, from Jenni's point of view. Mitzi seems to interpret Jenni's statement similarly:

> *Mitzi:* No, I'm not. I might not even like my mom, or I love my mom.

At this point, Mitzi draws a conversation bubble next to her drawn witch and writes:

> I am bad.

In this example, the varied worlds Mitzi moved among as a writer were quite visible. There was the present two-dimensional "story" of the carefully drawn witch and overlapping "once-there-was" world she began to shape with written words; these symbolic worlds were embedded within the ongoing peer social world and, also, within her wider experienced world, for her current feelings about her mom pulled in the world beyond the classroom walls.

However, in this example, Mitzi's text is related to her social life in less direct ways than in previous examples. Mitzi's social relationship with her friends was mediated by the written world she created (and they re-created), a world both separate from and yet embedded in their shared world, and this created world affected others' behaviors toward her just as did the more direct "I like Sonia." In both Examples 12 and 13, however, the reactions of her friends seemed to have highlighted for Mitzi both the text world itself (e.g., "*like* not I *love*") and the social world within which it exists. Indeed, spontaneous peer response served a similar role in all eight cases (for an elaboration of the role of peers, see Dyson 1987c).

Despite Mitzi's consistent combining of "once-there-was" openings and references to apparently real and present-time others, she was not oblivious to the inherent conflict between truth in imaginary and real worlds. Indeed, while the observed children as a group argued about the truth quality of pictures and texts, this issue of fictional truth was a particularly consistent theme in Mitzi's case. She regularly voiced her concern about whether or not *other children's* journal entries were "true." She even accused Jake once of "lying" in his story. In the second grade, though, Mitzi became more concerned about *her own* combining of social, experienced, and imaginary worlds. She developed more sophisticated ways of moving among those space/time structures and, in addition, found new ways of coordinating symbolic media to create her imaginary worlds.

Second Grade

Before beginning her second grade journal, Mitzi organized a table of contents:

Writing Example 14

1. Me and my friend
2. Me and my dream
3. Me and My
4. Me and My

While I had inferred Mitzi's concern about human relationships in the first grade, no such inference was necessary in the second. As Mitzi said, "It's going to be me me me me me and and and." When her friends Bessie and Jenni described their stories as being about bunnies and cats respectively, Mitzi noted, "Mine are about people."

Although Mitzi's concerns remained the same, her composing behaviors changed. To begin, Mitzi's use of drawing changed, as did, to varying degrees, that of all second grade focal children. Rather than beginning her journal entries by drawing, Mitzi drew after finishing her written text; drawing became a way of illustrating her ideas. Mitzi's abandonment of the initial drawing phase may have been interrelated with her abandonment of her repetitive text routine as well. Rather than building affective statements around her drawn fig-

ures, in the second grade she frequently relied upon personal experiences or fictionalized personal experiences for her text.

Interwoven with this change in the use of the drawing was continued change in Mitzi's use of writing to participate in her ongoing peer social life and to evaluate her experiences in the wider world. Mitzi's relationships were now not only mediated by but often embedded in her imaginary worlds. Rather than straightforward "I like you" statements, Mitzi incorporated peers and family members into her texts as characters who then could interact with a fictionalized "I"; 53% of her texts now contained the names of peers and/or family members, compared with 23% in the first grade (see Table 5). Thus Mitzi, like all second grade focal children, used the narrative form to dynamically play out her relationships with others, and thus her texts, like theirs, often moved through time (see Table 5). In addition to incorporating her relationships into her texts, Mitzi, again like all second grade focal children, began to spontaneously share her text with her peers, as the ability of the texts to entertain others became socially more important.

These social behaviors described above are illustrated in the following example. In this example Mitzi appears to use talk about the soon-to-be rendered world to both plan her written imaginary world and to engage her real world friend Jenni:

Writing Example 15 (included below)

Mitzi has begun writing:

Me and My Dream
I had a dream and My dream was a Big Nightmare and
This is My Nightmare. Once there was a boy

Mitzi stops and erases *boy*. She turns to Jenni:

Now this is going to be a true dream.

. . .

This is a nightmare I once had and the girl was you.

Jenni: Yeah?

Mitzi: And you really hated me.

Jenni: No wonder it's a nightmare.

The ideas discussed with Jenni appear in Mitzi's completed story, which vacillates between the past and the present:

> I had a dream and My dream was a BiG NiGht-Mare. and This is My NiGhtMare. Once there was a Girl and her name was Jenni and she hated me. But I do not know why. and she had a magic bulb. her bulb was a very powerful bulb. It was so powerful it turned Me into a Powerful bulb and now she has Two Powerfull Bulbs. The one that is Me is even Powerfuller than the other one. The End.

As soon as she finishes her text, Mitzi turns to Jenni:

> OK, want me to read this to you? It's very funny.

Incorporating real others into imaginary worlds highlighted the relationship between the experienced, the ongoing social, and the symbolic worlds, and more particularly, the issue of truth in fiction. In Example 15, Mitzi used the concepts of "magic" and "dreaming" to incorporate the real-world Jenni into a non-real world: "This is a true dream." Mitzi's accompanying picture fleshed out the fanciful quality of that dream. In the text, Jenni is simply Jenni with a magical bulb; in the picture, Jenni has witch-like nose and hands and is saying, "He, He, He"; the bulbs look like crystal balls. Mitzi had thus produced a "funny" imaginary world that included Jenni; this world reflected Mitzi's love/hate experiences with a variety of significant others, including Jenni; Mitzi used her imaginary entry about Jenni to engage her friend in the ongoing social world they shared.

In order to meld the imaginary and the real world in comfortable ways—without the use of dreams and magic—one must contextualize the essence of a real experience in an imaginary one. And, as suggested in the writing sample above, Mitzi was beginning to do this. Ambivalent emotions—the liking and hating of her first grade texts—were no longer her personal reactions to depicted or, occasionally, real figures. Rather, they were more firmly embedded in a drama (Jenni hated her and turned her into a bulb). Indeed, all four second grade focal children produced at least some texts that conveyed the internal world of their characters. In Mitzi's case, those emotions evolved from simply liking and hating to include sharing secrets and suffering betrayal, as in the following imaginative story. In the text, entitled "How My Life Was," Mitzi had a twin sister. (In real life, her friend Jenni had a twin brother.)

Writing Example 16

> I said to my sister one day that I was going to run away. My sister screamed, "Oh no." My mother and father ran down the stairs. "What happened" they said. My sister was beginning to say that I was going to run away When I ran across the room and covered her Mouth. The End. [In the accompanying picture are two little girls, one labeled "me," the other, "my twin."]

Throughout the second grade observation, Mitzi grappled with the relationship between her standard "once-there-was" openings and real-world experiences and with that between the real experiences of "I" and the essence of those experiences as retold by a fictive "I." Example 16, written in mid-April, was Mitzi's first imaginative piece that did not have a variation of "once-there-was" as an opening—above the piece Mitzi wrote "not true" in small letters. Although Mitzi continued to mark imaginative stories "not true," she had become both more flexible and more conventional about openings and about her texts in general. She no longer began true written texts about friends or family with "once there was," and she began her imaginative texts in varied ways and, also, consistently wrote them in past tense.

In the final observed event of year 2, Mitzi wrote a deceptively simple text about cats. Of all the pieces in her first and second grade journals, this was the first imaginary text containing narrative movement in which she was an *observer*, rather than an *actor*. Certainly kindergarteners and first graders produced texts coded similarly—what was distinctive about this text was the sophisticated manipulation of worlds it involved. As will be illustrated, Mitzi clearly separated the imaginary from the real world: "They're my made-up cats," she told Yahmya.

Further, her text, assisted by the picture, conveyed something of the quality of the cats' experience—their abrupt surprise, tragic for the birds. Mitzi had first conveyed such qualities when she became a character in a drama: in this text, however, Mitzi was no longer the "I" in the thick of things but the distant creator of a logical if fanciful world. Finally, the content of this distant world provided a social link to Jenni, who was fascinated by and consistently wrote about cats. In the following excerpt, Mitzi's sophisticated movement among the imaginary, social, and experienced world is reflected in her talk:

Writing Example 17

Mitzi's friends have been writing about cats, and, on this day, Mitzi wants to write about cats too. Since, days earlier, she wrote the title for the entry, she knows that the story has to have something to do with "The Surprise Party."

> *Mitzi:* Jenni, what can I write about? Um, I'm thinking about cats. It's gonna be a surprise party about cats. What should I write about? You're good, you're good at that. You're good at this [i.e., writing about cats], Jenni. Jenni you're good at that! (pause) I know! A bird that'll go and kill a cat!

Yahmya does find this surprising.

> *Yahmya:* A vulture?

> *Mitzi:* No! They're my made-up cats. Once I made up some cats. Once I made up some cats. And there were some birds. Birds! And they eat' em too.

> *Yahmya:* They eat CATS?

> *Mitzi:* Mm mmm.

When Mitzi finally begins writing, however, she writes about cats that eat birds. Perhaps Yahmya's critique of the reverse situation has made her reconsider. After writing her piece, Mitzi begins drawing a tree and soon realizes that she needs "dead birds down here" under her tree.

> *Jenni:* Cats?

> *Mitzi:* Yeah—listen:

Once there was a bunch of cats. Then all of a sudden there came a flock of birds. This was a BIG surprise to the cats. At once the cats started to kill them.

Mitzi read "the cats started to kill them," although she has actually written "they started to kill them." The confusion with Yahmya and now with Jenni over who was killing whom—and her own change of plans—may have led to this change in the text. (Later, she will erase *they* and substitute *the cats*.)

> *Darius:* Meow, meow, meow.

Jenni suggests a strategy for avoiding a page full of dead birds:

> *Jenni:* You can put some flying away up here.

Mitzi pauses and then has yet another thought:

> *Mitzi:* No, I know what I'm going to do.

Mitzi then adds "and eat them" to the last line of her text, eliminating the need for dead birds. She draws one bird; it's crying as it hovers near the tree.

In this event, Mitzi produced a carefully coordinated picture and story that combined to tell a sensible, imaginary tale to her interested, inquisitive friends. The text seems written from the point of view of the cats, but the picture depicts the internal feelings of the lone surviving bird. As the event illustrates, Mitzi had progressed from "I like you" journal entries surrounded by social talk to written worlds in which characters liked, hated, were surprised and saddened, betrayed and befriended.

THEORETICAL IMPLICATIONS: THE MULTIPLE WORLDS OF CHILD WRITERS

In this report, I have examined how eight primary grade children composed imaginary worlds, emphasizing changes in that composing over two years of observation. The observed children's text worlds were, as a group, gradually less governed by drawing and any accompanying talk: to oversimplify, as authors of imaginary worlds, the group moved from a tendency to comment on pictures, to a tendency to observe scenes and, finally, to act within dynamic worlds. At the same time, however, their composing behaviors suggested that their use of writing became progressively more involved with their ongoing social and their wider experienced worlds: the children specifically shared and discussed their *written* messages and the relationship of those messages to the wider world rather than to only their pictures (e.g., "That's not true" occurred along with "That doesn't look like a . . ."). Indeed, generic characters gave way to named ones, who were often fictionalized peers and family members.

The focal children's unexpected oral and textual excursions into varied space/time structures (unexpected shifts of tense and author role, movement realized in talk but only implied in text) suggested that these young authors wrestled with and, at time, got caught on the borders between differing symbolic and social space/time structures, differing worlds. To help resolve these tensions, the children found new ways to use the resources offered by these worlds (e.g., sequencing pictures to capture narrative movement; incorporating talk—dialogue—into their texts; fictionalizing self, peers, and experiences to meld the ongoing social, the wider experienced, and the evolving symbolic world in new ways).

In different classrooms, under different instructional contexts, children might have different symbolic and social resources and, thus, the specific nature of their behaviors might be different. However, while the specific behaviors of the focal children cannot be generalized, the social and symbolic tensions identified—and the theoretical perspective they gave rise to—seem potentially generalizable; this perspective is, as discussed throughout this article, consistent with scholarship in both literary discourse and child language development. Thus, I have argued here that the developmental challenge of writing imaginary texts is the working out of the writer's relationship to both self and others in past, present, and future time and space. Writers, while centered on the evolving text world, carry our multiple roles and coordinate multiple space/time structures.

Certainly the dynamic relationships between text and contexts have been a focus of ethnographic studies of particular groups (e.g., Heath, 1983; Cochran-Smith & Schiefflin, 1984; Shuman, 1986). For the most part, however, the developmental literature has stressed how young writers' texts gain *freedom from,* as opposed to how young writers use texts to make connections with, the worlds surrounding those products (among the exceptions, Gundlach, McLane, Stott, & McNamee, 1985).

Yet, there is potential theoretical power to adding contextual depth to our examination of young children's writing, that is, to considering not only how children organize textual worlds but also how they simultaneously manipulate the surrounding worlds. In the following sections, I consider the implications of this perspective for current questions about the developmental roles of narrative, non-narrative and expressive writing.

Narrative versus Non-narrative Writing: Redrawing the Boundaries

First, a recent developmental issue has centered around whether or not young children's earliest writing is predominantly narrative. Although narratives are often assumed to be the earliest extended writing produced by young children (Perera, 1984), this is not necessarily the case, as illustrated by observations reported here and elsewhere (Sowers, 1979; Newkirk 1987). However, *narrative's* opposite—*non-narrative*—seems to be used synonomously with *exposition,* with conveying information about the real world; and it is used antonymously with *story.*

In the currently reported project, the children's observed writing, though multifunctional, was predominantly playful and imaginative. Yet their *written* imaginative texts were not necessarily narratives, even though all focal children spontaneously *told* narratives. Further, from the children's point of view, the essential writing issue did not appear to be whether to write a narrative or non-narrative, but what sort of stance or role to adopt vis-a-vis—their relationship as authors to—the social, experienced, and symbolic worlds. For example they wrestled with whether their text worlds were "real" or "not real" and—in a more sophisticated vein—with how to comfortably exist within a "might-be-even-if-it-isn't" world.

In open-ended tasks such as the observed journal activity, children's early school writing may tend to be non-narrative, but that does not necessarily imply a relative absence of writing that is, at least in spirit, "story"—that is, of imaginary worlds. Both narrative and non-narrative forms figure into children's growth as creators of imaginative texts.

Thus, this project suggests that *narrative* and *non-narrative* may not be the most meaningful higher-level categories for investigating children's writing growth (for related views, see Rosen & Rosen, 1974, and Bissex, 1980). Rather than categories related to form, those related to children's purposes and to their stances may provide more insight.

Expressive Writing: From One Stance to Many

The issue of stance or role leads to a second developmental issue. This issue centers on Britton's concept of expressive writing, writing produced by the relaxed, conversational "speaker" (Britton, 1970; Britton, Burgess Martin, McLeod & Rosen, 1975). Britton hypothesizes that such writing should be particularly helpful for young children. First, expressive writing allows children to draw on "the knowledge of worlds and structure . . . built up in speech," while gradually internalizing written language structures (Britton et al., 1975, p. 82). Second, expressive writing is "close to self," in part perhaps because it is a relatively undifferentiated genre and thus does not require writers to clothe their voices in formal structures; expressive writing, therefore, should allow children to develop a "working relationship" between their language and their experiences (Britton, 1982, p. 97).

Since Britton first developed his theory, researchers have documented children's ability to write for a range of functions, many, like listing, decidedly unlike speech (e.g., Bissex, 1980; Dyson, 1983; Harste, Woodward, & Burke, 1984; Newkirk, 1987). Further, they have documented "oral" literacy (Scollon & Scollon, 1981; Tannen, 1982), and

well-read (to) children are now viewed as developing written language registers much earlier than previously supposed (Purcell-Gates, 1986; Teale & Sulzby, 1986). These findings have led to a questioning of the developmental role of expressive writing (e.g., Bissex, 1980; Newkirk, 1987).

In the observed classroom, the focal students relied on talking and, also, drawing to develop their meanings. But they relied on written language as well as oral language features to render and develop their meanings in written text. Certain children, like Manuel, used primarily a written language register in his stories (see Dyson, 1987b). The role of expressive writing seems to be a variable one, dependent no doubt on the knowledge of oral and written language the child can and chooses to draw upon and the overriding function of the writing.

In addition, "expressive" writing may itself need refinement as a concept. Children's "undifferentiated" writing did not seem due to only an "expressive" or conversational stance. Rather the children's writing suggested a struggle with the multiple stances inherent in writing and, more specifically, in imaginative writing: the children could be observers or actors in the imaginary, the ongoing social, or the broader world—or even commentators on other symbolic forms.

One aspect of the expressive writing concept did figure clearly into the observed children's development as imaginative writers: the adoption of a stance "close to self." In varied ways, all four of the first/second grade children began synthesizing their varied roles as writers by making their stories "close to self," particularly by embodying themselves, their friends, and/or their experiences as elements within their imaginative worlds. Bringing writing "in close" appeared to be a powerful way of finding firmer ground upon which to act, feel, and move forward within the imaginative world, while maintaining connections with the ongoing social world, the wider experienced world, and their own renderings of experiences in other symbolic media.

In Britton's terms, the children were working out their relationship with experience through language. But there was more than one relationship involved. The observed children were finding how their relationships to others and to the wider world could be mediated through texts, working toward a clearer writing voice or, in Halliday's words, an integrated "personality—a role complex" (1978, p. 15). And, as suggested by Mitzi's last stories, the children will find this written self a "useful mask . . . In the end, of course, the mask resembles our own faces, but with no need to say 'I'" (Muschg, 1987, p. 28).

IN CONCLUSION

This article has offered an interpretive frame for viewing school children's growth as creators of imaginative worlds, a frame that will need to be explored within the instructional contexts of other classrooms. Within this frame, children are viewed as gradually differentiating the multiple social and symbolic worlds within which authors of imaginary prose create. Such a view of child writers suggests that writing development does not depend only on children's discovery of cognitive and linguistic strategies for creating coherent written texts. Rather, these strategies themselves may depend on children's discovery that writing can help authors create coherence in their worlds beyond the texts.

For, while I have focused on imaginative writing, the development of any use of written language no doubt involves the discovery of a stance—of "how one [who uses language in a particular way] is situated with respect to others and toward the world" (Bruner, 1986, p. 136). This complex process cannot be understood through focusing only on text worlds with beginnings, middles, and ends. For, if those text worlds are to figure into the lives of children, those worlds must offer children ways of understanding their own experiences and of connecting with others. That is, text worlds are suspended—embedded—within a web of multiple worlds.

Note

Support for this work was provided in part by the Spencer Foundation and by the Office of Educational Research and Improvement/Department of Education (OERI/ED). However, the opinions expressed herein do not necessarily reflect the position or policy of the OERI/ED and no official endorsement by the OERI/ED should be inferred.

I thank my research assistants, Mary Gardner, Mark McCarvel, Jim Slagel, and, especially, Carol Heller who has assisted throughout all phases of this research. I thank also the children's teacher, who has graciously shared her children with me.

Works Cited

Applebee, A. N. (1978). *The child's concept of story.* Chicago: University of Chicago Press.

Barthes, R. (1974). *S/Z.* New York: Hill and Wang.

Bereiter, C., & Scardamalia, M. (1982). From conversation to composition: The role of instruction in a developmental process. In R. Glaser (Ed.) *Advances in instructional psychology,* Vol 2. (pp. 1–64). Hillsdale, NJ:Erlbaum.

Bissex G. (1980). *Gyns at wrk: A child learns to read and write.* Cambridge, MA: Harvard University Press.

Bogdan, R., & Biklen, S. K. (1982). *Qualitative research for education: An introduction to theory and methods.* Boston, MA: Allyn & Bacon.

Booth, W. C. (1961.) *The rhetoric of fiction.* Chicago: The University of Chicago Press.

Britton, J. (1970). *Language and learning.* Harmondsworth, Middlesex, England: Penguin Press.

Britton, J. (1982). Writing to learn and learning to write. In G. Pradl (Ed.), *Prospect and retrospect: Selected essays of James Britton* (pp. 94–111). Upper Montclair, NJ: Boynton-Cook.

Britton, J. (1984). Viewpoints; The distinction between participant and spectator role language in research and practice. *Research in the Teaching of English, 18,* 320–331.

Britton, J., Burgess, T., Martin, N., McLeod, A., & Rosen, H. (1975). *The development of writing abilities 11–18.* London: Macmillan.

Bruner, J. (1986). *Actual minds, possible worlds.* Cambridge, MA: Harvard University Press.

Cochran-Smith, M., & Schieffelin, B. (1984). Learning to read culturally: literacy before schooling. In H. Goelman, A. A. Oberg, & F. Smith (Eds.), *Awakening to literacy* (pp. 3–23). Exeter, NH: Heinemann.

Cook-Gumperz, J., & Gumperz, J. (1981). From oral to written culture: The transition to literacy. In M. Farr Whiteman (Ed.), *Variation in writing: Functional and linguistic-cultural differences* (pp. 89–110). Hillsdale, NJ: Erlbaum.

Corsaro, W. A. (1981). Entering the child's world: Research strategies for field entry and data collection in a preschool setting. In J. Green & C. Wallat (Eds.), *Ethnography and language in educational settings* (pp. 117–146). Norwood, NJ: Ablex.

Dixon, J., & Stratta, L. (1986). *Writing narrative—and beyond.* Upper Montclair, NJ: Boynton/Cook.

Donaldson, M. (1978). *Children's minds.* New York: Norton.

Dyson, A. H. (1983). The role of oral language in early writing processes. *Research in the Teaching of English, 17,* 379–409.

Dyson, A. H. (1986). Transitions and tensions: Interrelationships between the drawing, talking, and dictating of young children. *Research in the Teaching of English, 20,* 379–409.

Dyson, A. H. (1987a). Individual differences in beginning composing: An orchestral vision of learning to compose. *Written Communication, 4.*

Dyson, A. H. (1987b). Research currents: The emergence of children's written voices. *Language Arts, 64.*

Dyson, A. H. (1987c). The value of "Time off Task": Young children's spontaneous talk and deliberate text. *Harvard Educational Review, 57,* 396–420.

Dyson, A. H. (in press). Unintentional helping in the primary grades: Writing in the children's world. In B.A. Rafoth & D.L. Rubin (Eds.), *The social construction of written communication.* Norwood, NJ: Ablex.

Erickson, F. (1986). Qualitative methods in research on teaching. In M.C. Wittrock (Ed.), *Handbook of research on teaching* (pp. 119–161). New York: Macmillan.

Geertz, C. (1983). *Local knowledge.* New York: Basic Books.

Graves, D. (1983). *Writing: Teachers and children at work.* Exeter, NH: Heinemann.

Gundlach, R., McLane, J. B., Stott, F. M., & McNamee, G. D. (1985). The social foundations of children's early writing development. In M. Farr (Ed.) *Advances in writing: Vol. 1 Children's early writing development.* Norwood, NJ: Ablex.

Halliday, M. A. K. (1978). *Language as social semiotic.* Victoria, Australia: Edward Arnold.

Harris, J., & Wilkinson, J. (1986). *Reading children's writing: A linguistic view.* London: Allen & Unwin.

Harste, J. C., Woodward, V. A., & Burke, C. L. (1984). *Language stories and literacy lessons.* Portsmouth, NH: Heinemann.

Heath, S. B. (1983). *Ways with words: Language, life, and work in communities and classrooms.* New York: Cambridge University Press.

Iser, W. (1974). *The implied reader.* Baltimore: Johns Hopkins University Press.

King M. L., & Rentel, V. (1981). *How children learn to write: A longitudinal study* Columbus, OH: Ohio State University.

Labov, W., & Waletsky, J. (1967). Narrative analysis: Oral versions of personal experience. In *Essays on the verbal and visual arts, Proceedings of the 1966 spring meetings of the American Ethnological Society* (pp. 12–44). Seattle: University of Washington Press.

Langer, J. A. (1986). *Children reading and writing: Structures and strategies.* Norwood, NJ: Ablex.

Muschg, A. (1987, February 1). Staying alive by learning to write. *New York Times Book Review, 25,* 27–28.

Newkirk, T. (1987). The non-narrative writing of young children. *Research in the Teaching of English, 21,* 121–145.

Nystrand, M. (1982). The structure of textual space. In M. Nystrand (Ed.), *What writers know: The language, process, and structure of written discourse* (pp. 75–86). New York: Academic Press.

Olson, D. (1977). From utterance to text. *Harvard Educational Review, 47,* 257–279.

Perera, K. (1984). *Children's writing and reading: Analysing classroom language.* Oxford, England: Basil Blackwell.

Piaget, J. (1929). *The child's conception of the world.* New York: Basic Books.

Polanyi, L. (1982). Literary complexity in everyday storytelling. In D. Tannen (Ed.), *Spoken and written language: Exploring orality and literacy.* Norwood, NJ: Ablex.

Purcell-Gates, V. (1986). *Expectations of sentence-level features of written narrative by well-read-to kindergartners and second graders.* Unpublished doctoral dissertation. University of California, Berkeley.

Rader, M. (1982). Context in written language: The case of imaginative fiction. In D. Tannen (Ed.), *Spoken and written language: Exploring orality and literacy.* Norwood, NJ: Ablex.

Rosen, C., & Rosen, H. (1974). *The language of primary school children.* Hardmonsworth, Middlesex, England: Penguin Education.

Rosen, H. (n.d.). *Stories and meaning.* Upper Montclair, NJ: Boynton-Cook.

Scarlett, W. G. and Wolf, D. (1979). When it's only make-believe: The construction of a boundary between fantasy and reality in storytelling. *New Directions in Child Development, 6,* 29–40.Scollon, R., & Scollon, S. B. K. (1981). *Narrative, literacy, and face in inter-ethnic communication.* Norwood NJ: Ablex.

Shuman, A. (1986). *Storytelling rights: The uses of oral and written texts by urban adolescents.* New York: Cambridge University Press.

Sowers, S. (1979). Young writers' preference for non-narrative modes of composing. Paper presented at the Boston University Conference on Language Development.

Tannen, D. (1982). *Spoken and written language: Exploring orality and literacy.* Norwood, NJ: Ablex.

Tannen, D. (1985). Relative focus on involvement in oral and written discourse. In D. R. Olson, N. Torrance, & A. Hildyard (Eds.), *Literacy, language, and learning: The nature and consequences of reading and writing* (pp. 124–147). Cambridge, England: Cambridge University Press.

Teale, W., & Sulzby, E. (Eds.) (1986). *Emergent literacy: Writing and reading.* Norwood, NJ: Ablex.

Vygotsky, L. S. (1962). *Thought and language.* Cambridge, MA: Massachusetts Institute of Technology Press.

Research and Recommendations for Computers and Composition

Gail E. Hawisher

This essay is reprinted from Critical Perspectives on Composition Instruction. *Eds. Gail E. Hawisher and Cynthia L. Selfe. New York: Teachers College Press, 1989. 44–69.*

In extolling the educational worth of computers in general, Papert (1981) stated, "[Computers] will change work and play, but the most important change will not come through what the computers can do for us, but through their effect on how people learn" (p. 99). In the same article, he noted that the "computer presence . . . will perhaps even reverse the order [of learning language skills] in that mastery of writing may develop faster once it starts, than mastery of speech" (p. 100). Papert's predictions are noteworthy, not because we, as writing teachers and researchers, necessarily believe them, but rather because of the optimism they reflected in 1981 for the promise of this strange new tool in fostering learning and literacy.

This enthusiasm was not restricted to mathematicians or to others whom we commonly associate with technology. In his 1984 foreword to *Computers and Composing,* Corbett argued that English teachers must rise to the challenges of electronic communication and that "after only a week of hands-on experience with this wondrous machine, [he] acquired a keen sense of its potency and its potential" (p. xii). Our students, too, told us of the wonders of word processing, and our own writing on the machine suggested the credibility of their opinions. Thus, those of us who taught with computers and studied the influence of computers on writers and their products approached our research with high expectations. It is no surprise,

then, that in our ebullience, we sometimes expected so much of computers and word processing that our research became "technocentric," a term Papert used in a 1987 article in the *Educational Researcher.*

According to Papert (1987), technocentrism is analogous to Piaget's notion of egocentrism; that is, just as a child has difficulty in moving beyond the self in comprehending phenomena, so those of us caught up in technocentrism have difficulty in "decentering" the computer in our research. Furthermore, he maintains that technocentrism manifests itself in such research questions as "What is *the* effect of *the* computer on cognitive development?" (p. 23). Humanists, he goes on to assert, are especially susceptible to technocentrism because of the awe and misunderstanding with which we often approach technology. Thus misconceptions are likely to lead us to ask such questions as "What is *the* effect of the computer on *the* writing process?"

I shall return to Papert's notion of technocentrism and its application to our field of research, but first I shall review the kinds of inquiry into computers and composition with which we, as a profession, have been engaged for the past several years. I do not wish to criticize early studies but rather to sort out what we have learned so that new research can add to an accumulating knowledgebase in assessing the value of word processing for writing and for teaching writing. After presenting

337

an overview of 42 studies conducted since 1981, I discuss some directions that researchers might profitably pursue in the future.

OVERVIEW

Research into computers and composition over the past several years has concentrated on the effects of word processing on students and other writers, on the processes in which writers engage as they write, and on the products writers create with the aid of computers. Few studies have examined how computers affect and interact with the cultural context or learning environment in which they are used—either for writing or for instruction. Many of the investigations dealing with the school setting, however, both acknowledge and emphasize that change or lack of change in writers' behavior or products cannot be attributed to computers alone; the writing instruction students receive is also important in shaping the influence of computers. Several investigations are concerned not with instruction but rather with how computers facilitate experienced and professional writers' work.

Selection Criteria

Several criteria were applied in choosing the 42 studies reported here. First, the studies are either published pieces, national conference papers from 1981 onwards, or dissertations listed in *Dissertation Abstracts International* for the same period of time. In the case of dissertations, abstracts were used to identify studies before the full text was subsequently examined. Second, each of the studies regards computers as tools for writing rather than as intact instructional delivery systems. Although heuristic and invention software, text analysis programs, and drill and practice courseware might well influence writers and their products, they were not the focus of this overview. Third, the research reported here includes more than surveys of students' or other writers' attitudes toward working with computers. Although surveys can provide significant information on writers' reported use of word processing and its perceived influence on

writing habits and processes, these 42 studies all relied on additional methods of inquiry. When surveys were included, the researchers' aim was to corroborate findings from other methods of study and observation. Fourth, research that was basically an informal inquiry or that did not specify a particular methodology was not selected for this review. (For a review of this earlier, exploratory research, see Hawisher, 1986b.)

Research Design

Studies in word processing over the past several years can be classified into two categories: those that employ primarily quantitative methods of inquiry and those that rely largely on qualitative techniques. The qualitative studies can be divided further into case studies and ethnographies. When we look at the research design of the studies reviewed here, 26 can be termed comparative (or quantitative) and 16 naturalistic (or qualitative). Twelve of the qualitative investigations were classified as case studies and four as ethnographies. (See Tables 4.1 and 4.2 [pages 340–343].)

When we examine the quantitative and qualitative research with regard to the characteristics of the sample, the context or setting for the study, and the results of the study, some interesting patterns emerge. I shall first review the comparative investigations and then discuss the case studies and ethnographies.

EXAMINATION OF RESEARCH

Comparative Studies

By far the most common population of interest for the quantitative studies was students of some sort. Of the 26 comparative studies (refer to Table 4.1), seven examined samples of undergraduate college students, eight focused on secondary school students, and eight on elementary students. Only three of the comparative studies reviewed here looked at writers outside the school context— two studies conducted by Haas and Hayes with the same sample of 15 faculty and staff and Gould's investigation of 10 IBM researchers. In terms of setting, then, we can say that the majority of the quantitative studies focused on the effects of word processing used in school to teach writing rather than to facilitate writing outside the academic context.

Almost all of these quantitative studies conducted in the school setting described the instruction as *process-oriented*. That is, writing is viewed as an *activity* in which writers engage in prewriting, composing, and revising of multiple drafts. The activity also includes "conferencing," that is, teacher and student conferring between drafts and/or peer evaluation. Although two of the quantitative studies excluded peer evaluation from the research design for fear that it would make judging the influence of word processing more difficult (e.g., Cirello, 1986; Hawisher, 1986a, 1987), the majority regarded peer interaction as integral to a process-based environment. It would seem, then, that most of these studies were not only sensitive to the role instruction plays in combination with word processing but also created a setting in which the pedagogy was grounded in theory and research.

Most of the comparative studies also tried to control for the potentially biasing effects of teacher differences. These attempts usually took the form of having the same instructor, often the researcher, teach all treatment groups. If the instructor were biased toward one of the treatments, however, this method would exert little control. Hillocks (1986) stipulated for the studies in his meta-analysis of empirical research in writing from 1963 to 1982 that there be twice as many instructors as treatments. To control for teacher bias, in other words, the studies that focused on students writing with and without computers needed four instructors, with the two treatments then counterbalanced over four classes. Only a few of the studies conformed to this criterion (e.g., Coulter, 1986; Hawisher & Fortune, 1988; Sommers, 1986; Wetzel, 1985). Many researchers contented themselves with using one instructor for both treatment groups, and some neglected to report the number of instructors.

For the most part, then, these comparative studies explored how word processing in combination with a process-oriented teaching methodology influenced writers' processes and products. Two of the studies (i.e., Duling, 1985; Miller, 1984) looked at the word processor only as a revision tool; that is, the students produced all first drafts by hand and only revised at a computer. Harris's (1985) case study of college students is similar in that students could produce their first drafts in any fashion they pleased; they were required only to revise with word processing. Increasingly, however, studies in word processing seem to be moving away from exclusive emphasis on revision and instead examine how writers *compose* with computers, how they plan, generate, and evaluate text either on-screen or in some combination with hard copy.

This new emphasis on the interaction of computers with composing processes other than revision is especially true of an investigation (e.g., Haas, 1986) outside the instructional context, with writers who are experienced at word processing rather than novices who are learning a system. In fact, if we look at the earliest study among the 26—Gould's (1981) pioneering investigation of IBM researchers—and Haas's (1986) study of Carnegie-Mellon faculty and staff, we can trace the direction in which research in computers and writing seems to be moving and follow the rapid advancements which have been made in technology. The first part of Haas's study, which she conducted with Hayes (see Haas & Hayes, 1986b), is actually a replication of Gould's early study. The second part, however, departs from Gould's methods: whereas Gould in 1981 used videotapes to look at writers composing, planning, and rereading with a line editor and examined the variables of time, length, quality, and frequency of revision, Haas in 1986 used think-aloud protocols to examine how the processes of planning and rereading interact with composing at an advanced workstation with a large-screen monitor and mouse, as well as their interaction with a standard personal computer. Thus, as research in composition has refined methods borrowed from cognitive psychology, we see more and more of this same sort of analysis in studies of computers and composition.

Table 4.1 Comparative Studies

	Design				Tools		Context			
	Sample	Number	Duration: Weeks	Word-Processing Package	Computer	Description of Instruction	# Instructors	Composed at Computers	Attitudes	Errors
Beesley (1986)	6th graders	23	18	BSW 1982	Apple	Process oriented	1	Y	X	X
Burnett (1984)	Gr. 1–5 low achievers	10	8	BSW 1982	Apple	Process oriented	•	Y	X	—
Cirello (1986)	Gr. 10 basic writers	30	20	BSW 1982	Apple	Process w/o peer review	1	Y	—	—
Coulter (1986)	1st year college	62	16	•	•	•	6	Y	—	—
Daiute (1986)	7th & 9th graders	57	36	CATCH	Apple	Process-centered workshop	1	Y/N	—	X
Dalton & Hannafin (1987)	Gr. 7 low achievers	80	36	FreeWriter	Apple	Process oriented	•	N	X	—
Deming (1987)	College basic writers	24	10	BSW	Apple	Process oriented	1	Y	—	—
Duling (1985)	9th graders	20	36	Scripsit StoryWriter	TRS 80 PET	Engl. curr. of lit. & writing	1	N	—	X
Gould (1981)	IBM researchers	10	—	EDIT REDIT	IBM mainframe	—	—	Y	—	—
Haas (1986)	Experienced academics	8	—	EMACS* MINCE	Andrew mainframe	—	—	Y	—	—
Haas & Hayes (1986)	Experienced academics	15	—	EMACS* MINCE	Andrew mainframe	—	—	Y	—	—
Hawisher (1986, 1987)	1st year college	20	16	Volkswriter	IBM	Process w/o peer review	1	Y/N	X	—
Hawisher & Fortune (1988)	College basic writers	40	16	WordStar	Zenith	Process oriented	4	Y	—	—
Juettner (1987)	11th & 12th graders	19	16	Magic Window	Apple	Comb. trad. & process oriented	2	Y	X	—
Kaplan (1986)	5th graders	56	5	SELECT	DRC Rainbow	Conference process approach	2	Y	—	—
King, Birnbaum, & Wageman (1984)	College basic writers	10	16	BSW 1982	Apple	Remedial tutoring	1	Y/N	X	—
Kurth (1987)	10th & 11th graders	28	12	Word-Perfect	Apple IBM	Process oriented	1	Y	X	X
Levin, Riel, Rowe, & Boruta (1985)	6th graders	10	36	Writer's Assistant	Apple	Process oriented	1	•	X	X
Miller (1984)	6th graders	28	5	BSW 1982	Apple	•	2	N	X	—
Moore (1987)	4th & 5th graders	204	16	BSW	Apple	Process oriented	12	Y	X	—
Pivarnik (1985)	Gr. 11 basic writers	76	36	WordStar	TRS 80	Process oriented	1	Y	—	—
Posey (1986)	College basic writers	13	14	BSW	Apple	Process-centered workshop	1	Y	X	—
Sommers (1986)	College students	79	16	BSW Homework AppleWriter	Apple	Process oriented	6	Y/N	X	—
Wetzel (1985)	3rd–5th graders	36	10	BSW 1984	Apple	Tchrs. used rsrchr's scripts	8	Y	—	—
Woodruff, Lindsay, Bryson, & Joram (1986)	Gr. 8, avg. & enriched	16	1	icon-driven word proc.	ICON	—	•	Y	X	X
Woolley (1985)	5th graders	120	2	BSW	Apple	Process oriented	2	Y	—	—

Y = yes   N = no   N/Y = yes & no   • = information not given   X = examined   — = not a concern of study   *with mouse

Table 4.1 Continued

Quality	Syntax	Processes	Revision	# Words	Cognitive Skills	Assessment	Revision	Interview	Surveys	Protocols	Journals	Positive Attitudes	Fewer Errors	Improved Quality	Increased Revision	Increased Fluency	Increased Length	Noteworthy
X	—	—	X	X	—	H	Observation	X	X	—	—	Y	Y	N	Y	—	N	Revision analysis focused on writing of 6 students
X	X	—	—	—	—	H&A	—	X	—	—	—	Y	—	Y	—	Y	—	Experiment replicated 9 times with different students
X	X	—	—	X	—	H	Researcher's criteria	—	X	—	X	—	—	N/Y	Y	Y	Y	Significant improvement on 2 of 3 writing tasks
X	—	—	X	—	X	H	Bridwell (1980)	—	—	—	—	—	—	N	N	—	—	No significant correlation between time spent in writing and quality, revision frequency, or cognitive gain
X	—	—	X	X	—	H	Faigley & Witte (1981)	—	—	—	—	—	Y	N/Y	—	—	—	Also looked at effect of computer prompt for revision
X	—	—	X	—	—	A	Observation	X	—	—	—	Y	—	Y	Y	—	—	All post-tests handwritten
X	—	—	X	—	—	H	Faigley & Witte (1981)	—	X	—	—	—	—	N	Y	—	—	WP group made significantly more microstructure revisions
X	X	—	X	X	—	H	Bridwell (1980)	—	—	—	—	—	Y	N	N	—	N	All 1st drafts handwritten
X	—	X	X	X	—	H	Videotapes	—	—	—	—	—	—	N	Y	—	Y	Word processor was line editor, not screen editor
—	—	X	X	—	—	—	protocols	X	—	X	—	—	—	—	—	—	—	Looked at planning and rereading; less planning in computer condition
X	—	—	—	X	—	A	—	—	—	—	—	—	—	N/Y	—	—	Y	Highest quality writing produced at work-station with larger screen
X	—	X	X	—	—	A	Faigley & Witte (1981)	—	—	—	X	Y	—	N	N	—	—	Same students wrote 4 essays with and without computers
X	—	—	—	X	X	H&A	—	—	—	—	—	—	—	N	—	—	Y	Few differences between the 2 groups in kinds of thinking prized in college
—	X	—	—	X	X	—	—	X	X	—	—	Y	—	—	—	N	Y	Researcher tracked schemata students developed for using WP
X	—	—	X	X	—	II	Faigley & Witte (1981)	—	—	—	—	—	—	Y	N	—	Y	Experimental group wrote longer & better pieces in a revision-centered instructional environment with WP
X	—	—	X	—	—	A	Checklist	X	X	—	X	Y	—	Y	—	—	Y	All female students
—	—	—	X	X	—	—	Researcher's criteria	—	X	—	—	Y	Y	—	N	—	N	Use of spelling checker probably accounted for fewer errors of WP group
—	—	—	X	X	—	—	—	X	X	—	—	Y	Y	—	—	—	N	Students made and corrected more surface errors with WP
X	—	—	—	—	—	H	—	—	X	—	—	—	—	N	—	—	N	All first drafts handwritten
X	—	—	X	X	—	H	Faigley & Witte (1981)	X	X	—	—	Y	—	Y	Y	—	Y	Revision analysis focused on writing of 8 students
X	—	—	—	—	—	H	—	—	—	—	—	—	—	Y	—	—	—	A second writing sample supported initial results
X	—	X	X	—	—	H	•	X	X	—	X	Y	—	N	Y	—	—	Writing posttests were handwritten
X	—	X	X	—	—	H	Faigley & Witte (1981)	—	—	—	—	Y	—	Y	Y	—	—	Revision analysis focused on writing of 4 students
X	—	—	—	—	—	H	—	—	—	—	—	—	—	N	—	—	—	Significant positive correlation between typing speed and quality of writing
X	X	X	X	X	X	H	•	X	X	X	—	N/Y	Y	N	—	—	Y	Study focused on how students' cognitive ability affected use of WP
X	—	—	—	—	—	H&A	—	—	Y	—	—	—	—	N	—	—	—	Students in experimental group wrote at computer for 16 45-min. periods

H = holistic A = analytic

Table 4.2 Case Studies and Ethnographies

Case Studies	Design				Tools		Context	
	Sample	Number	Duration: # Weeks	Word-Processing Package	Computer	Setting	Number of Instructors	Description of Instruction
Bessera (1986)	College basic writers	6	•	DEC type	Mainframe	Private room and computer lab	1	Process oriented
Bridwell, Johnson, & Brehe (1986)	Published graduate students	8	10	WordStar	IBM	Working at computers/lab	—	—
Bridwell, Sirc, & Brooke (1985)	College students	5	10	WordStar	IBM	Working at computers/lab	1	Business writing class
Catano (1985)	Novelists	2	52	Brown Univ. system	Mainframe IBM	Working at computers/lab	—	—
Collier (1982, 1983)	Nursing students	4	6	AES	AES-C20	Classroom; also computer lab	1	•
Daiute (1984, 1985)	12-year-olds	8	5	CATCH	Apple	•	•	•
Flinn (1985)	6th graders	8	36	Milliken word processor	Apple	Classroom with computers	4	National Writing Project classes
Harris (1985)	College students	6	•	•	•	Writing center or micro-computer lab	•	•
Lutz (1983, 1987)	Professional or experienced writers	7	—	MTS	Mainframe	•	—	—
Nichols (1986)	College basic writers	5	7–10 days	BSW 1982	Apple	Private room in library and computer lab	1	No composition instruction during study
Schipke (1986)	Professional writers	2	12 hrs over many months	Scripsit OASYS 64	TRS 80 NB1	Home office	—	—
Selfe (1985)	College students	8	16	•	•	Computer lab	—	—
Ethnographies								
Curtiss (1984)	High school seniors	53	18	BSW 1982 AppleWriter	Apple	Computer lab classroom	1	Process oriented
Dickinson (1986)	1st & 2nd graders	21	32	•	Apple	Classroom with one computer	1	Process oriented
Herrmann (1985, 1987)	High school students	8	36	BSW 1982	Apple	Classroom with computers	1	Process oriented
Reid (1985)	4th graders	a class	28	Milliken's Writing Workshop	Apple	Classroom, hall, and lab	1	2 days of writing per week

Y = yes   N = no   N/Y = yes & no   • = information not given   X = examined   — = not a concern of study

Table 4.2 Continued

Composed with Computers	Interview	Keystroke	Assessment	Survey	Revision	Protocols	Journals	Observation	Video/Audio Tapes	Themes
Y	X	X	H	X	X	Retrospective	X	X	X	Students did not demonstrate increased prewriting with computers
Y/N	X	X	—	—	—	—	X	—	X	Researchers identified 3 kinds of writers whose adaptation to computer composing varied with their style. Writers produced longer texts for final draft
Y	X	X	—	X	Bridwell (1980)	X	—	—	X	Writer, computer, and task all interrelated in determining how WP will be used by individuals
Y	X	—	—	—	—	—	—	X	—	Writers reported that WP seemed to facilitate their collection of information and to stimulate creativity
N	X	—	X	—	Collier (1982)	X	—	—	X	Although students seemed to revise more frequently, they did not revise more successfully
Y	X	—	H	—	Faigley & Witte (1981)	—	—	X	—	After using CATCH, a WP program with revision prompts, most students revised more and corrected more errors, but few produced texts that were rated higher
Y	X	X	—	—	Bridwell (1980)	X	X	X	X	Children revised larger chunks of text at computers; pen and paper writers focused instead on surface features
N	X	—	—	—	Faigley & Witte (1981)	—	X	X	—	Fewer macrostructure changes were made with computers. It should be noted that 1st drafts not necessarily written on computer
Y	X	X	—	—	Faigley & Witte (1981)	—	—	X	X	Both professionals and experienced writers made many more revisions at computers
Y	X	—	—	—	X	X	—	—	—	Writers used the system to do more of the same of what they were doing without WP; longer texts with WP
Y	X	—	—	—	X	X	X	X	—	WP helped professional writers carry out their established practices and routines with greater efficiency
Y/N	—	—	—	X	—	X	—	X	X	Individuals' attitudes toward WP and the ease with which they could adapt their writing habits to computers determined how they used WP
Y/N	X	—	X	X	X	—	X	X	—	51 of the 53 students came to value WP as a tool for creating quality writing
Y	X	—	—	—	—	—	X	X	X	Talk between students at computer more likely to focus on style and content than on production of acceptable handwritten text, a common concern for these students without computers
Y/N	X	—	—	—	X	—	X	X	X	Computers seemed to reinforce differences in both socioeconomic and academic standing that already existed among students
Y	X	—	—	X	—	—	—	X	X	Computer seemed to act as catalyst in transforming writing from a private to public activity

The results from these quantitative studies are many and varied (refer to Table 4.1). Students seem to have positive attitudes toward writing and word processing after working with computers; students exhibit finished products that have fewer mechanical errors than those written with traditional tools; and many students write longer pieces with word processing than with traditional methods. We find conflicting results when we examine two variables: revision and quality. Slightly more studies found an increase in revision as found no increase in revision, and fewer studies found improvement in quality as found no improvement. These findings suggest that writers' predispositions as revisers or nonrevisers are more significant in predicting behavior than the influence of the machine and the ease with which writers revise with word processing. Quality of writing, similarly, does not seem to be tied to computer usage.

There is some indication that basic writers may profit more from a word-processing environment than other students. Of the 24 comparative studies that examined quality, 10 found improvement. (All these studies employed trained raters and presented inter-rater reliability coefficients or percentages of agreement.) Yet, of the eight dealing with basic or developmental writers, five reported improved writing with word processing in samples ranging from elementary (e.g., Burnett, 1984) to secondary school (e.g., Cirello, 1986; Dalton & Hannafin, 1987; Pivarnik, 1985) to college (e.g., King, Birnbaum, & Wageman, 1984). When I examined research directed at this group of writers in a 1986 review (Hawisher, 1986b), I found that all three studies of basic writers reported improvement in students' writing. At that time I suggested that further investigation was warranted with regard to the possible benefits a computers-and-writing curriculum might provide to students deficient in writing skills. By freeing basic writers from the laborious task of writing by hand, computers might be especially promising tools for low-achieving students.

To test this hypothesis, a colleague and I (see Hawisher & Fortune, 1988) conducted a study in which trained raters assessed essays produced with

and without word processing by first-year college basic writers. Results from this study indicated that regardless of whether students wrote at computers or with pen-and-paper and regardless of whether they were male or female, improvement both in quality and in the kinds of thinking prized in the college setting was minimal. Although we continue to believe that the medium might well make a difference for some groups of writers, our investigation failed to advance this conclusion for first-year basic writers. Another study appearing since the review (e.g., Deming, 1987) also found no significant differences in the writing of this student population. Contradictory results are beginning to emerge with basic writers as they have earlier with other student populations.

Why some studies and not others found that unskilled writers made greater progress in writing with word processing than with conventional tools is perplexing. Two studies, one finding improvement in students' writing (i.e., Dalton & Hannafin, 1987) and another citing no improvement (i.e., Posey, 1986), required students in the experimental group to complete post-tests by hand rather than with word processing. These procedures seem especially demanding for students who have difficulty composing in the first place. To teach basic writers how to write with a new tool and then to deprive them of this tool when testing their writing is also likely to confuse results from the research. If we eliminate these studies from consideration and examine the three remaining that were directed at older students (i.e., King, Birnbaum & Wageman, 1984; Pivarnik, 1985; Cirello, 1986), we find that Pivarnik's and Cirello's investigations extended beyond one semester and that both reported writing improvement with word processing.

It may be that one semester is simply not long enough to encourage discernible growth in writing with computers, especially when dealing with word-processing novices. This last explanation, however, fails to account for the success of the ten female students in the semester study by King et al. (1984). It also doesn't seem to apply to those studies of competent students that reported increased success with word processing (e.g., Kaplan, 1986;

Moore, 1987; Sommers, 1986), although one study citing improvement (i.e., Daiute, 1986) was conducted over an academic year. Investigations into computers and their influence on the quality of students' writing continue to yield conflicting results regardless of the population of interest.

Case Studies

When we turn to the kinds of subjects examined in the case studies, differences appear in the targeted samples as well as in the focus of the research. Although some studies looked at elementary pupils, secondary school students, and college undergraduates, we find an additional emphasis on professional writers. In fact, four of the twelve investigations relying on case study methodology dealt with published writers. In these, as in those case studies examining the educational setting, the major research questions were the following:

How do writers adapt their strategies to computer writing?

Do writers' habits change with the technology?

How do writers regard writing with computers after working with them over a given period of time?

A general theme of these studies is similar to one drawn from the comparative studies; that is, a writer's or student's particular habits and strategies for composing seem to take precedence over the influence of the machinery. While most writers adapt easily to a computer and find word processing an asset to their writing, they bring their routines and patterns of writing with them. If they weren't extensive revisers before word processing, they probably will not become extensive revisers as a result of learning word processing even when revision strategies are part of the instruction. As Nichols (1986) pointed out in his case study of basic writers, "writers [use] the system mostly to do more of the same" of what they were doing with conventional methods (p. 90). Some don't even do more of the same. Although Bridwell, Sirc, and Brooke

(1985) suggest that one of their subjects was interested in reformatting as a pen-and-paper composer and expanded this interest as a computer composer, two of the undergraduates they studied seemed to use the system to avoid revising; that is, they interacted with their first drafts less intensely, printing out clean copy with few changes as final drafts.

One of the more intriguing hypotheses generated by the case study research is Catano's (1985) suggestion that the two novelists he studied used the computer to collect information and create meaning in such a way that word processing seemed to foster synthesis of their ideas. If, indeed, word processing can be used to help *students* interact with their texts in ways that encourage higher order thinking skills, we need to find out how. Seldom, however, are we able to study students intensely for a full year, the length of time Catano observed the two novelists.

Several of the case studies reported here also analyzed writing products quantitatively (e.g., Bridwell, Johnson & Brehe, 1986; Bridwell, Sirc & Brooke, 1985; Collier, 1983; Daiute, 1984, 1985; Flinn, 1985; Harris, 1985; Lutz, 1983, 1987; Nichols, 1986; Schipke, 1986). In general, their findings are congruent with the results of the comparative studies; that is, texts tend to be longer with word processing and students' final products exhibit fewer mechanical errors. Again, when revision and quality are examined, the results are mixed. It should be noted, however, that far fewer of the qualitative studies tried to assess writing quality (e.g., Collier, 1983; Daiute, 1984, 1985; and Curtiss, 1984) and that, excepting Daiute's studies, the judging of the writing was informal, with no checks for reliability or rater agreement.

Ethnographic Studies

If case studies can be considered careful, naturalistic examinations of individuals, then ethnographies are their counterpart for examining a culture. Context, which includes the social situation in which the activity of writing takes place and by which it is shaped, is integral to an ethnographic perspective. The ethnographies presented here all deal with the culture of the school and classroom. Two of the studies looked at how elementary school students interact with a computer in a classroom context, and the other two examined students and computers in a high school setting. Some of Dickinson's (1986) findings from a first- and second-grade combined class are provocative. While students did their paper-and-pencil writing silently and privately at their desks, writing at a computer seemed to create a collaborative social organization in which considerable talk related to the writing took place. Moreover, the conversation among students seemed to focus on content and style, whereas collaborate efforts with pencil and paper often became bogged down in talk over handwriting. These studies of young children who have not yet developed writing strategies with pencil and paper offer us a fresh perspective on how writers may use word processing when they are not trying to adapt old strategies to a new technology. Reid's (1985) ethnographic study of fourth graders also notes that computers seemed to transform writing from a private to public activity. This theme corresponds to Selfe and Wahlstrom's (1986) observations of the kinds of interactions that occurred among writers in a college computer writing lab. Herrmann's (1985) ethnographic study of high school students, on the other hand, indicated that the presence of computers exacerbated differences among the eight students she studied in both their socioeconomic standing and their academic standing. Can we find ways to reverse this potentially harmful influence by regarding it as a challenge rather than as a verdict? These ethnographies, then, in elucidating the subtle influences of computers in social interactions among students and teachers, suggest the importance of the cultural context in shaping writers' work with word processing. The success or failure of students' encounters with word processing and writing might well depend on the context into which computers are introduced.

Some General Observations

Observations concerning both the quantitative and qualitative research reported here seem appro-priate. When we look to the description of the context in which the research was conducted, there is often a decided lack of detail. Ironically, the quantitative studies seem to present a more complete description in this area, perhaps because the instructional context was often regarded as part of the treatment and, therefore, in keeping with the conventions of empirical research, discussed in detail. The qualitative studies present rich detail in researchers' descriptions of their naturalistic observations and interviews but often fail to describe adequately the full environment and social milieu by which the activity of writing might well have been shaped.

Another flaw of several of the studies is their failure to include and describe the word-processing package. Only three of the studies omitted the specific computer and word-processing software, but the majority did not report the capabilities and idiosyncratic workings of the software. For example, the early *Bank Street Writer* (1982) forces writers to leave an insert mode in order to edit, certainly a maneuver which is antithetical to a recursive writing process. *WordStar* uses an abundance of control characters to perform operations, decidedly differing from other programs with their greater reliance on function keys. Some programs facilitate the moving of text by allowing writers to highlight the targeted segment and reinsert it somewhere else very quickly; other programs make this block movement of text tedious and cumbersome. My point is that different programs might well facilitate some writing strategies to the exclusion of others, but we can't infer this without a description of the features of the word-processing package.

A final general comment has to do with whether writers are composing at a computer or entering prewritten text. A great many more of the studies in this review seem to be focusing on writers' composing at computers than in the past. Most would agree that to use a word processor as merely a transcription tool limits its capacity to influence composing processes. Moreover, composing at computers has come to mean a combination of hard-copy and screen-related activities. Bridwell, Sirc, and Brooke (1985), for example, in their case studies of undergraduates define computer composing as "whatever [the writers] did while they were working with the word-processing systems, even though several of them continued to use paper for planning and some drafting" (p. 179). Some researchers (e.g., Lutz, 1983, 1987)—mistakenly, I think—took pains to limit or prevent writers from printing out drafts during composing sessions, thinking that hard copy was the province of pen-and-paper composing rather than computer composing. The longer we as writers and researchers work with computers, however, the more we realize that the screen often leads to reading difficulties and that intermittent printings of a draft allow us to compensate for having "screens-full" rather than "pages-full" of text (see Chapters 1 and 2 of this volume; Haas & Hayes, 1986a).

RECOMMENDATIONS

The foregoing review and discussion leads to a consideration of future directions of research to add to our accumulative knowledge in computers and composition. I would like to make several recommendations as to how we might approach research projects and whom we might study, and speculate on different contexts for this research. I then discuss the computer as a research tool.

Research Approaches

Build upon Previous Research. Qualitative studies often provide rich description, revealing patterns and themes that can then be studied through quantitative methods. This is normally the way in which some perceive qualitative and quantitative research as intersecting. Seldom, however, do we see this relationship in research practice with computers and composition. For example, in their case studies of experienced writers, Bridwell, Johnson, and Brehe (1986) observed writers devoting more time to pausing and planning than had been reported in other studies for writing in general. This prewriting or planning often took the form of writers pausing or jotting notes to themselves while they were writing at computers. These notes were sometimes metacomments, suggesting directions for organization and bearing scant resemblance to

the final written products. Certainly, the way writers adapt this planning and note jotting to computer writing bears further investigation. One wonders, for example, if these organizational promptings differ when writers compose at computers compared with conventional methods.

As mentioned earlier, Christina Haas (1986) has begun to examine this phenomenon of planning on computers with the experienced writers she studied. Although Haas's experiment is small in scale and more of an attempt to replicate Gould's (1981) study than to experiment with some of the insights gleaned from an earlier qualitative study, it illustrates, I think, a pattern that could be followed as we establish our field of research. Studies should build upon one another. As we conduct our research, we must be aware of what has gone before us and how new research can confirm or contradict but, nevertheless, extend our emerging knowledge base.

Let us consider how to extend our investigations. In the two studies discussed above, Bridwell and her colleagues (1986) looked at planning as it manifests itself in written notes and pauses at the machine, whereas Haas (1986) concentrated on how this planning manifests itself in verbal protocols. Another investigation might examine how experienced word-processing writers use the bottom of their screens, or splitscreens that contain two or more files, or the special note options of some word processors—or, for that matter, hard copy for their interspersed planning. . . . If experienced writers can indeed use these features effectively, then perhaps we want to introduce these methods to students in instructional settings to examine how they integrate note-taking with computer composing. Some note-taking strategies might help students move back and forth between the conventions of standard printed text and the virtual text of a computer. . . .

Design a Series of Studies. In writing of composition research in general, Hillocks (1986) discusses the need for a series of studies to examine a range of variables. Citing the work of Carl Bereiter, Marlene Scardamalia, and their colleagues at the Ontario Institute for Studies in Education (OISE) and Linda Flower, John Hayes, and their colleagues at Carnegie-Mellon University (CMU), Hillocks suggests that these researchers are noteworthy for their systematic research agendas. Both OISE and CMU have contributed important studies for computers and composition as well. (Refer to Haas, 1986; Haas & Hayes, 1986a; Woodruff et al., 1986, in Table 4.1.) Lillian Bridwell, Donald Ross, and their colleagues at the University of Minnesota have also been active in carrying out such research with word processing. (Refer to Bridwell, Johnson, & Brehe, 1986; Bridwell, Sirc, & Brooke, 1985, in Table 4.2.) More recently at CMU, Christine Neuwirth, Christina Haas, and John Hayes have mapped out a series of seven studies with computers, as part of a funded grant from the Fund for the Improvement of Postsecondary Education (FIPSE). The proposed studies (Neuwirth, Haas, & Hayes, 1986) systematically explore three elements of the writing process: planning, revising, and reviewing. They are noteworthy in that each is prefaced with such statements as "If Study 1.1 obtains the expected results . . . we will then conduct Study 1.2" (p. 10). In this way, each of the studies builds upon the previous ones and, when completed, should prove valuable to the field of computers and composition. As Hillocks (1986) suggests, more researchers need to engage in a systematic series of studies designed to add to an emerging knowledge base.

Use a Longitudinal Approach. A definite need also exists for longitudinal studies with writers and word processing. When one scans the research presented in Tables 4.1 and 4.2, it becomes apparent that the majority of studies took place over a relatively short duration of time. The longest study lasted for one full year (i.e., Catano, 1985), and several were conducted over an academic year (e.g., Daiute, 1986; Dickinson, 1986; Duling, 1985; Flinn, 1985; Herrmann, 1985; Levin et al., 1985; Pivarnik, 1985). But some were carried out over exceedingly short periods of time (e.g., Collier, 1983; Daiute, 1984, 1985; Miller, 1984; Nichols, 1986; Woodruff et al., 1986; Woolley, 1985) ranging from one to six weeks. One (i.e., Harris, 1985) didn't report the duration of the

study. Since most of these investigations were also concerned with how the computer interacted with the writing processes of inexperienced computer-users, one wonders how much of the influence of word processing was captured over these short periods. New research might be directed, instead, to examining inexperienced users of word processors over their four-year period in college. This sort of longitudinal approach might suggest emerging patterns of composing that we have as yet not observed.

Research Population

Focus on Experienced Student-Users of Word Processors. Up to now most of our research with students has focused on inexperienced users of word processors out of necessity; few students worked extensively with word processing prior to their experience in our classes. This situation is changing. At Illinois State University, for example, where all first-year students are taught their required writing course at computers, advanced writing classes are often comprised of students who have composed with computers for three years or more. This new group of student computer composers bears investigation.

Focus on Experienced Writers Who Are Proficient at Word Processing. Another recommendation is to do more studies of experienced writers who use word processing all the time for their composing. Several years ago few writers could perhaps be so categorized, but today we have burgeoning numbers of computer composers. Schipke (1986), in her research of a free-lance science writer and a speech writer, adds considerably to Catano's (1985) study of experienced writers who are unskilled in word processing. Schipke notes that the ways these experienced writers used word processing varied considerably with the knowledge they possessed over their topic. Additional studies might shed light on whether word processing does indeed contribute to stimulating creative thought, as the professional writers in Catano's (1985) study suggest.

Research Contexts

Interaction of Computers and Classroom Activities. For the instructional context, we need to examine how computers interact with the activities of the classroom. Preliminary evidence (Selfe & Wahlstrom, 1986; Dickinson, 1986) suggests that computers foster collaboration among writers, transforming the process of writing from a private to a public act (Reid, 1985) for both young students and adults. These initial studies have been surveys or qualitative investigations. Another way of approaching this question might be to compare classroom activities that occur in process-centered, computer-equipped classrooms with activities in process-centered, conventional classrooms. During classroom observations, researchers would code activities, using similar categories as those outlined by Applebee (1981) in his description of writing in secondary schools. Applebee (1981) lists writing without composing, and informational, personal, and imaginative uses of writing as types of writing activities that might occur in a classroom. Added to this list might be other precisely defined categories to describe the amount of time each class period devotes to teacher presentation, student presentation, group work (with and without computers), and writing (with and without computers). These data would then be analyzed to determine similarities and differences in several composition classes taught with and without computers. The types of work assigned outside of class would also be examined. Such an approach would allow us to assess the kinds of collaboration that occur among students and teachers, as well as to determine the types of learning activities that instructors tend to rely on in computer-assisted and conventional writing classes.

Introduction of Computers into English Curricula. Little research has been completed that examines how computers interact with the departmental English program or the larger school curriculum as a whole. In other words, one might hypothesize that when computers are introduced into writing classes, the entire school is affected, regardless of whether the change is at the elementary, secondary, or college level. During writing-across-the-curriculum workshops at Illinois State for faculty from throughout the university, one question arises frequently: "Now that all students prepare in their composition classes on computers, can we expect them to write and revise their work for us with word processing?" Thus teachers in other classes not only begin to request students to complete class work with computers but also expect them to revise assignments readily. Teachers believe they can set higher standards than previously and have them met by students. Although these particular attitudinal changes are all to the good, no systematic research of which I am aware has investigated such phenomena.

Other changes occur as well. With the introduction of computers comes the need to prepare teachers to work with new technology through workshops and in-service opportunities. Social structures within schools begin to change, with those teachers who "know" technology receiving perhaps more admiration or, sometimes, a heavier workload. In addition, teachers themselves can prepare materials faster with computers and modify them easily from year to year. In other words, the introduction of computers into English curricula is a contextual change that encourages and brings about alterations in the political, social, and educational structures of an entire system. Research that attempts to identify the influences of computers on an English department or an entire school is sorely needed.

The Computer as a Research Tool

The advantages of using the computer as a research tool have been noted elsewhere (Bridwell, Johnson, & Brehe, 1986). For the first time we have a tool with an enormous memory for recording writers' generating and revising of text. Using public-domain macro software at Illinois State University, we have developed a keystroke-monitoring program that captures all keystrokes writers make in a given session, thus providing a record of their composing and revising. Lutz (1983, 1987) and Flinn (1985) also report using keystroke-capturing programs for their research. A sophisticated program developed by the University of Minnesota team seems especially promising. In addition to capturing keystrokes, it offers a built-in record of the time writers spend in composing as well as in pausing. It also allows for a playback of text that researchers can then use for retrospective protocols; that is, writers describe what they were thinking as their text scrolls before them at the same rate of speed with which they produced it. (See Bridwell, Nancarrow, & Ross, 1984, for a more complete description of the program.) Given the advantages of such records, it is surprising that we don't see more research conducted with these programs.

One of the problems, I believe, is that while keystroke programs enable computers to collect enormous amounts of data, these data must still be analyzed by human beings. One paragraph with all its revisions often yields a full page or more of data, and these data increase exponentially with several drafts of a paper. Thus a three-page, double-spaced draft might well yield ten pages of data, which then must be compared with the writer's actual text to understand what was generated and revised. The keystroke printout alone is undecipherable in terms of seeing change in relation to the writer's text. Thus, although we now have the technology to help with in-process revision data collection, we still lack an expedient tool to aid in analysis.

More time and energy should be spent in developing programs that are easily decipherable by trained text analysts. We envision a program that prints the real text in one column with the changes in a second column, at least allowing a ready scanning and comparison of keystroke printout and text. The computer could also be programmed to record changes that involve larger segments of text along with appropriate function keys, rather than concentrating on individual keystrokes. We have learned through our research that although writers seem to make more typographical errors initially (Bridwell, Sirc, & Brooke, 1985), they quickly correct them, and final texts tend to exhibit fewer sur-

face errors with word processing (Daiute, 1986; Duling, 1985; Levin et al., 1985; Woodruff et al., 1986). Therefore, we might concentrate on developing programs that focus on chunks of text, since in good writers' writing, larger revised segments often contain meaningful changes (Faigley & Witte, 1981).

Although the development of additional research programs requires careful planning between researchers and programmers, the time devoted to this endeavor would be well spent in facilitating research efforts. Ideally, of course, it would be helpful if technology could also be enlisted to analyze some of the changes, but this eventuality seems distant in terms of the computer's current capability to process natural language. In any event, we need to develop computers as research tools. We have only begun to tap the potential of technology and its possible contribution to research.

CONCLUSION

What have we learned from our research of the past several years? Is it, as Papert (1987) suggests of computer research in general, technocentric? Perhaps, but we are also slowly but surely building a research base that relies less on a technocentric perspective than on a view informed by the interaction of technology with the culture in which it exists. Even though a review of the titles of some of the more recent studies reveals a technocentric emphasis, the quantitative studies, as well as the qualitative, often consider context. Moreover, several of the studies, such as that by Woodruff et al. (1986), are asking complex questions such as how does cognitive development in students interact with and affect their use with computers. Notice the emphasis here is on *students* rather than on *computers*. It is worth remembering, I think, that most of the studies cited here were begun an average of three or more years ago. None of these studies, for example, looked at writers interacting with the Macintosh with its icon system and highly developed graphic capabilities.

When I reviewed 24 studies in computers and writing in 1986 (see Hawisher, 1986b), few of the patterns noted here were evident. Instead the results seemed to be confusing and contradictory—as they still are to a great extent today. But in the past couple of years there has been a coming together of findings that begin to form a research base; students appear to write longer texts that demonstrate fewer mechanical errors at computers, and they exhibit positive attitudes toward writing with computers. These positive attitudes toward computer composing, moreover, tend to contribute to a spirit of cooperation rather than competitiveness within a classroom. This resulting change in social interactions among students and instructors might be capable of creating an improved classroom culture, if we can act upon it.

Kuhn (1970), whom both Kinneavy (1980) and Hairston (1982) cited in describing the preparadigm stage of rhetoric and composition, also has something to say that applies to our research in computers and composition. Kuhn notes that when a field is establishing itself, its research is inconclusive and that the same ground is covered repeatedly. Studies in word processing and writing are only now emerging from this preparadigm stage of development. It will be interesting to see how we pursue our research in computers and composition during the next several years. As Papert (1987) has suggested for computer research and as Purves and Purves (1986) have argued in discussing the study of writing in general, we must give culture—along with technology—its due.

Note

I would like to thank James Raths, University of Vermont, for calling my attention to many of the studies reported here and for his invaluable assistance in reading drafts of this chapter.

Works Cited

Applebee, A. N. (1981). *Writing in the secondary school: English and the content areas.* Urbana, IL: National Council of Teachers of English.

Beesley, S. M. (1986). The effects of word processing on elementary students' written compositions: Processes, products, and attitudes. (Doctoral dissertation, Indiana University, 1986). *Dissertation Abstracts International, 47,* 4006A.

Beserra, W. C. (1986). Effects of word processing upon the writing processes of basic writers. (Doctoral dissertation, New Mexico State University, 1986). *Dissertation Abstracts International, 48,* 34A.

Bridwell, L. S. (1980). Revising strategies in twelfth grade students' transactional writing. *Research in the Teaching of English, 14,* 197–222.

Bridwell, L. S., Nancarrow, P. R., & Ross, D. (1984). The writing process and the writing machine: Current research on word processors relevant to the teaching of composition. In R. Beach & L. S. Bridwell (Eds.), *New directions in composition research* (pp. 381–398). New York: Guilford.

Bridwell, L. S., Johnson, P., & Brehe, S. (1986). Composing and computers: Case studies of experienced writers. In A. Matsuhashi (Ed.), *Writing in real time: Modelling production processes* (pp. 81–107). Norwood, NJ: Ablex.

Bridwell, L. S., Sirc, G., & Brooke, R. (1985). Revising and computing: Case studies of student writers. In S. Freedman (Ed.), *The acquisition of written language: Revision and response.* Norwood, NJ: Ablex.

Burnett, J. H. (1984). Word processing as a writing tool of an elementary school student (a single-case experiment with nine replications). (Doctoral dissertation, University of Maryland, 1984). *Dissertation Abstracts International, 47,* 1183A.

Catano, J. (1985). Computer-based writing: Navigating the fluid text. *College Composition and Communication, 36,* 309–316.

Cirello, V. J. (1986). The effect of word processing on the writing abilities of tenth grade remedial writing students. (Doctoral dissertation, New York University, 1986). *Dissertation Abstracts International, 47,* 2531A.

Collier, R. M. (1982). *The influence of computer-based text editors on the revision strategies of inexperienced writers.* (ERIC Document Reproduction Service No. ED 266 719)

Collier, R. M. (1983). The word processor and revision strategies. *College Composition and Communication, 35,* 149–155.

Corbett, E. P. J. (1984). Foreword. In J. W. Halpern & S. Liggett (Eds.), *Computers and composing: How the new technologies are changing writing.* Carbondale, IL: Southern Illinois University Press.

Coulter, C. A. (1986). Writing with word processors: Effects on cognitive development, revision and writing quality. (Doctoral dissertation, University of Oklahoma, 1986). *Dissertation Abstracts International, 47,* 2551A.

Curtiss, D. H. (1984). The experience of composition and word processing: An ethnographic, phenomenological study of high school seniors. (Doctoral dissertation, Boston University, 1984). *Dissertation Abstracts International, 45,* 1021A.

Daiute, C. (1984). Can the computer stimulate writers' inner dialogues? In W. Wresch (Ed.), *The computer in composition instruction* (pp. 131–139). Urbana, IL: National Council of Teachers of English.

Daiute, C. (1985). Do writers talk to themselves? In S. Freedman (Ed.), *The acquisition of written language: Revision and response* (pp. 133–159). Norwood, NJ: Ablex.

Daiute, C. (1986). Physical and cognitive factors in revising: Insights from studies with computers. *Research in the Teaching of English, 20,* 141–159.

Dalton, D. W., & Hannafin, M. J. (1987). The effects of word processing on written composition. *Journal of Educational Research, 80,* 338–342.

Deming, M. P. (1987). The effects of word processing on basic college writers' revision strategies, writing apprehension, and writing quality while composing in the expository mode. (Doctoral dissertation, Georgia State University, 1987). *Dissertation Abstracts International, 48,* 2263A.

Dickinson, D. K. (1986). Cooperation, collaboration, and a computer: Integrating a computer into a first-second grade writing program. *Research in the Teaching of English, 20,* 141–159.

Duling, R. A. (1985). Word processors and student writing: A study of their impact on revision, fluency, and quality of writing. (Doctoral dissertation, Michigan State University, 1985). *Dissertation Abstracts International, 46,* 3535A.

Faigley, L., & Witte, S. (1981). Analyzing revision. *College Composition and Communication, 32,* 400–414.

Flinn, J. Z. (1985). Composing, computers, and contexts: Case studies of revision among sixth graders in national writing project classrooms. (Doctoral dissertation, University of Missouri-St. Louis, 1985). *Dissertation Abstracts International, 46,* 3636A.

Gould, J. D. (1981). Composing letters with computer-based text editors. *Human Factors, 23,* 593–606.

Haas, C. (1986, May). *Computers and the writing process: A comparative protocol study.* Paper presented at the 1986 Conference on Computers and Writing, Pittsburgh, PA.

Haas, C., & Hayes, J. R. (1986a). What did I just say? Reading problems in writing with the machine. *Research in the Teaching of English, 20* (1), 22–35.

Haas, C., & Hayes, J. R. (1986b). *Pen and paper vs. the machine: Writers composing in hard copy and computer conditions.* Pittsburgh, PA: Carnegie-Mellon Technical Report No. 16.

Hairston, M. (1982). The winds of change: Thomas Kuhn and the revolution in the teaching of writing. *College Composition and Communication, 33,* 76–88.

Harris, J. (1985). Student writers and word processing: A preliminary evaluation. *College Composition and Communication, 36,* 323–330.

Hawisher, G. E. (1986a). The effects of word processing on the revision strategies of college students. (Doctoral dissertation, University of Illinois, 1985). *Dissertation Abstracts International, 47,* 876A.

Hawisher, G. E. (1986b). Studies in word processing. *Computers and Composition, 4,* 6–31.

Hawisher, G. E. (1987). The effects of word processing on the revision strategies of college freshmen. *Research in the Teaching of English, 21,* 145–159.

Hawisher, G. E. (1988). Research update: Writing and word processing. *Computers and Composition, 5,* 7–23.

Hawisher, G. E., & Fortune, R. (1988, April). *Research into word processing and the basic writer.* Paper presented at the annual meeting of the American Educational Research Association, New Orleans, LA.

Herrmann, A. (1985). Using the computer as a writing tool: Ethnography of a high school writing class. (Doctoral dissertation, Teachers College, Columbia University, 1985). *Dissertation Abstracts International, 47,* 02A. (University Microfilms No. DA8602051)

Herrmann, A. (1987). An ethnographic study of a high school writing class using computers: Marginal, technically proficient, and productive learners. In L. Gerrard (Ed.), *Writing at century's end: Essays on computer-assisted composition* (pp. 79–91). New York: Random House.

Hillocks, G., Jr. (1986). *Research on written composition: New directions for teaching.* Urbana, IL: National Council of Teachers of English.

Juettner, V. W. (1987). The word processing environment and its impact on the writing of a group of high school students. (Doctoral dissertation, The University of Arizona, 1987). *Dissertation Abstracts International, 48,* 635A.

Kaplan, H. (1986). Computers and composition: Improving students' written performance. (Doctoral dissertation,

University of Massachusetts, 1986). *Dissertation Abstracts International, 47,* 776A.

King, B., Birnbaum, J., & Wageman, J. (1984). Word processing and the basic college writer. In T. Martinez (Ed.), *The written word and the word processor* (pp. 251–266). Philadelphia, PA: Delaware Valley Writing Council.

Kinneavy, J. L. (1980). *A theory of discourse* (2nd ed.). Englewood Cliffs, NJ: Prentice-Hall.

Kuhn, T. (1970). *The structure of scientific revolutions* (2nd ed.). Chicago: University of Chicago Press.

Kurth, R. (1987). Using word processing to enhance revision strategies during student writing activities. *Educational Technology, 27,* 13–19.

Levin, J., Riel, M., Rowe, M., & Boruta, M. (1985). Muktuk meets jacuzzi: Computer networks and elementary school writers. In S. Freedman (Ed.), *The acquisition of written language: Response and revision* (pp. 160–171). Norwood, NJ: Ablex.

Lutz, J. A. (1983). A study of professional and experienced writers revising and editing at the computer and with pen and paper. (Doctoral dissertation, Rensselaer Polytechnic Institute, 1983). *Dissertation Abstracts International, 44,* 2755A.

Lutz, J. A. (1987). A study of professional and experienced writers revising and editing at the computer and with pen and paper. *Research in the Teaching of English, 21,* 398–421.

Miller, S. K. (1984). Plugging your pencil into the wall: An investigation of word processing and writing skills at the middle school level. (Doctoral dissertation, University of Oregon, 1984). *Dissertation Abstracts International, 45,* 3535A.

Moore, M. A. (1987). The effect of word processing technology in a developmental writing program on writing quality, attitude towards composing, and revision strategies of fourth and fifth grade students. (Doctoral dissertation, University of South Florida, 1987). *Dissertation Abstracts International, 48,* 635A.

Nichols, R. (1986). Word processing and basic writers. *Journal of Basic Writing, 5,* 81–97.

Neuwirth, C., Haas, C., & Hayes, J. R. (1986). *Does word processing improve students' writing? A critical appraisal and proposed assessment.* Unpublished manuscript. Carnegie-Mellon University, Pittsburgh, PA.

Papert, S. (1981). Society will balk, but the future may demand a computer for each child. In G. Hass (Ed.), *Curriculum planning: A new approach* (4th ed., pp. 99–101). Boston: Allyn and Bacon.

Papert, S. (1987). Computer criticism vs. technocentric thinking. *Educational Researcher, 16,* 22–30.

Pivarnik, B., (1985). The effect of training in word processing on the writing quality of eleventh grade students. (Doctoral dissertation, University of Connecticut, 1985). *Dissertation Abstracts International, 46,* 1827A.

Posey, E. J. (1986). The writer's tool: A study of microcomputer word processing to improve the writing of basic writers. (Doctoral dissertation, New Mexico State University, 1986). *Dissertation Abstracts International, 48,* 39A.

Purves, A. C., & Purves, W. C. (1986). Viewpoints: Cultures, text models, and the activity of writing. *Research in the Teaching of English, 20,* 174–197.

Reid, T. R. (1985). Writing with microcomputers in a fourth grade classroom: An ethnographic study. (Doctoral dissertation, Washington State University, 1985). *Dissertation Abstracts International, 47,* 817A.

Schipke, R. C. (1986). Writers and word processing technology: Case studies of professionals at work. (Doctoral dissertation, University of Pennsylvania, 1986). *Dissertation Abstracts International, 47,* 1226A.

Selfe, C. (1985). The electronic pen: Computers and the composing process. In J. Collins & E. Sommers (Eds.), *Writing on-line: Using computers in the teaching of writing* (pp. 55–66). Upper Montclair, NJ: Boynton/Cook.

Selfe, C. L., & Wahlstrom, B. J. (1986). An emerging rhetoric of collaboration: Computers, collaboration, and the composing process. *Collegiate Microcomputer, 4,* 289–296.

Sommers, E. (1986). The effects of word processing and writing instruction on the writing processes and products of college writers. (Doctoral dissertation, State University of New York at Buffalo). *Dissertation Abstracts International, 47,* 2064A.

Wetzel, K. A. (1985). The effect of using the computer in a process writing program on the writing quality of third, fourth, and fifth grade pupils. (Doctoral dissertation, University of Oregon). *Dissertation Abstracts International, 47,* 76A.

Woodruff, E., Lindsay, P., Bryson, M., & Joram, E. (1986, April). *Some cognitive effects of word processors on enriched and average 8th grade writers.* Paper presented at the annual meeting of the American Educational Research Association, San Francisco, CA.

Woolley, W. C. (1985). The effects of word processing on the writing of selected fifth-grade students. (Doctoral dissertation, The College of William and Mary, 1985). *Dissertation Abstracts International, 47,* 82A.

The Need for Interdisciplinary Studies on the Teaching of Writing

George Hillocks, Jr.

Hillocks's essay was published in Rhetoric Review 7 (1989): 257–72.

The main question asked by Braddock, Lloyd-Jones, and Schoer in 1963 was, "What procedures of teaching and learning composition are most effective?" At the end of their summary of research, they raised a set of 24 questions they regarded as "untouched" but important for composition research. Their final question ("Of what does skill in writing really consist?") may be the most important but least well answered of these questions. These two questions, taken together, are, in my opinion, still the most pressing questions for those interested in the teaching and learning of writing.

However, today, with substantial advances in our knowledge about composing processes and the teaching of writing, these two questions subsume a host of other questions about the features of effective texts, the kinds and uses of knowledge in the composing process, and the effects of different modes and foci of instruction on that knowledge and the processes of composing.

Our increased knowledge demands that we ask increasingly more precise and complex questions. At the same time, many of these questions are related and may be usefully examined together. For example, we know that task-oriented, student-led small group discussions can result in improved writing for the participants. Students practice strategies orally in small groups. They can then apply them independently in their writing in new situations. However, we do not know very much about what happens in group discussion that re-

sults in learning the strategies or failure to learn them. We do not know how prior knowledge affects the course of group discussion or how knowledge changes as the result of discussion. And we do not know as much as we need to know about the strategies themselves and how they are used in the composing process. These questions are probably most fruitfully addressed together in a series of related studies which use appropriate methods of research, including rhetorical and textual analyses, case studies, psychometric techniques, and experimental designs. Because the questions we ask are divergent, they will require divergent methodologies. If we want to know whether or how well an instructional method works, we will need "controlled experimental studies." If we want to examine how and why it works or fails to work, we will need ethnographic and observational methods.

What's more, the key questions are located in a variety of fields of inquiry from philosophy, rhetoric, text analysis, and linguistics to anthropology, cognitive psychology, instruction and measurement. Further, any given question approached from a single field is likely to lead to, if not involve from the outset, questions in related fields. And, I suspect that any question so conceived that it does not involve more than a single field may not be worth pursuing. In short, a serious program of research on teaching composition will require multi-disciplinary approaches: combinations of philosophical analysis and psychometrics, of observational methods and experimental designs, of case studies and surveys, and so forth. Despite the obvious need for broad-based, interdisciplinary approaches, several writers recommend that we narrow the base, that we jettison quantitative methods and turn to qualitative methods.

One of the more recent of these recommendations comes from William Irmscher. He claims that composition specialists have been rejected by the literature specialists in English departments, that "they are underpaid," and that "some are being shunted into administrative positions that may pay generously, but carry no job security or academic standing." He concludes this lament with the question, "If composition specialists have not yet acquired the academic respectability they seek, why not?"

"Part of the answer," he says, "lies in the nature of research on composition." (Irmscher does not tell us what the other part of the answer is.) He traces the "direction of present research efforts" to *Research in Written Composition* by Braddock, Lloyd-Jones, and Schoer and to the founding of *Research in the Teaching of English*. He claims that "research in composition has become identified with one kind of research—controlled experimental studies producing statistical evidence" (82). The problem with such research, he says, quoting Hagstrum's 1964 review of Braddock, Lloyd-Jones, and Schoer, is there is very little promise that "without rigorous antecedent thought, the 'scientific' method applied to composition will yield better results in the future than it has in the past" (83).

Irmscher quotes another of Hagstrum's observations: "Reason and experience—those most indispensable tools of intellectual progress in any field are insulted and ultimately weakened when we run to the laboratory for proof of the obvious." In reference to "most research on composition," Irmscher claims that after struggling "through the prose and the statistics and the diagrams, one discovers that the investigator has complicated the familiar and obfuscated the obvious" (83). He continues, "To Braddock, Hillocks, and the tradition they represent, much of the research on composition lacks rigorous procedure. To others it lacks rigorous thought."

There is some truth in these charges against quantitative research. A great deal of quantitative research "lacks rigorous thought." That lack of rigorous thought is reflected in poor design. Often even the treatments studied are not fully explained. Often experimental variables are confounded so that two or more explanations of change are possible. For example, in one study students in one experimental group revised systematically after conferring with teachers. Was the improvement in test scores due to the conference, the revision, or the combination? Often the studies do not systematically exclude bias. Such problems with experimental research in composition have been enumerated by Braddock, Lloyd-Jones, and Schoer, Wesdorp, and Hillocks (*Research on Written Composition*). Those who engage in quantitative research would identify such problems as problems in design. What Irmscher and Hagstrum do not realize is that problems in design reflect a lack of rigorous thought in thinking through what is to be examined and how it is to be examined. Such problems lie not within the methodology but with the researcher who may not take the time to think through the problem and its design or have the resources to carry out adequate designs.

The second charge, that quantitative research only provides "proof of the obvious" or "obfuscates the obvious" or "contains no surprises" (Larson), is probably as common as it is facile. Such comments come after the results are in, and as we all know, hindsight is always 20-20.

But when is a result obvious before we have it in hand? Perhaps we would be willing to bet that the results are obvious when the variables tested seem silly: the size of paper and its effect on the quality of writing; the repetition of lists of real and nonsense words in the hope of enabling students to concentrate on words in context and thus improve both reading and writing; an attempt in two days to teach students to evaluate their own writing using abstract, largely unexplained criteria such as "coherence"; teaching a heuristic involving over 60 questions to guide invention and thereby improve writing.

In all of these cases there were no significant differences between the experimental and control groups. We will be disposed to cluck happily that we "knew" it all along. But when we say we "knew it," we are, after all, talking about probabilities. There is very little that we know with absolute certainty. We say that we are fairly certain that the size of writing paper will not affect the quality of writing. When the results show no significant differences, we say it was "obvious." We "knew" it all along. But would we say, with the same certainty, that the heuristic of 60 questions would have no effect? I think not. Experienced teachers might guess that 60 questions are too many to hold in mind, that even trying to recall them from long term memory might disrupt the composing process. But if we had to bet on paper size *or* the heuristic as more likely to affect writing quality, most of us would put money on the heuristic.

Many rhetoricians put money on the specification of the rhetorical situations in writing assignments and prompts for both instruction and assessment as a way of improving writing. This was something we thought we knew. It seemed logical in terms of rhetorical theory. Several studies (Brossell; Metviner; Kahn and Johannessen), however, suggest that such specification may hinder high school students and college freshmen. That is, students with prompts which do not specify all elements of the rhetorical situation tend to write better essays than do those for whom all elements are specified. This finding makes sense despite rhetorical theory, when we consider the idea of cognitive overload. In the performance of any task, if we have too much to hold in mind, too many distractions, we cannot perform as well. Is this finding "obvious"? It only becomes "obvious" when we see the evidence *and* have a plausible explanation which allows us to see why the result may be as it is.

The problem of what is "obvious" appears to lie more with the individual critic's beliefs than with the research method. What may be obvious to some people will not be obvious to others. However, when we make decisions that affect other people, even if only in the relatively limited ways we can expect teaching to affect others, I believe we have a moral obligation to base our decisions on the best arguments available, whether they be philosophical, empirical, or experiential. I say *argument* because even if the decision is based upon one's own experience, that experience must have been examined and questioned carefully. The propositions of policy resulting from personal experience must be subject to thoughtful change with the garnering of more experience. From that point of view we should accept nothing as "obvious." Rather, we must ask with what degree of confidence we can accept a proposition or conclusion. What is the evidence?

But we must ask more than what the evidence is. We must ask what the *question* is and what means are appropriate for gathering the evidence. When Irmscher recommends that we in English departments find a "comfortable identity" by preferring "case-study and ethnographic inquiry to controlled group studies involving comparisons" and by "depend[ing] less on generalizations about all cases than on insights about particular cases . . ." (86), he places severe restrictions on researchers.[1] He automatically disallows very important questions of the kind Toulmin poses in *The Uses of Argument,* crucial questions about the nature and effect of current practices in schools and colleges (e.g., Applebee's, *Contexts*), all questions about the relative effectiveness of instruction, all questions about the composing process which require rigorous inference-making (Bereiter and Scardamalia), and many more. He even seems to disallow cross-cultural studies and even ethnographic studies of contrasting cases and groups. Such restrictions are crippling. There are simply too many questions which cannot be answered through "case-study and ethnographic inquiry" into "particular cases."

On the other hand, it would be equally foolish to restrict ourselves to "controlled group studies involving comparisons." Those researchers who are most productive use a variety of methods. Take Arthur Applebee for example. Applebee has written books on the history of English teaching, on children's stories, on practices in teaching writing, on methods of teaching writing, and on the assessment of writing (e.g., *Writing: Trends Across the Decade*). These books involve historical, survey, rhetorical, case-study, ethnographic, psychometric, statistical sampling methods, and statistical inference comparable to that in controlled comparison studies. It seems to me that we are better off for all that work.

Researchers who engage in programs of research (a series of studies related to one or more central questions) tend to use a variety of methods. One of Judith Langer's recent books, for example, uses case studies, test analyses, and statistical inference in making many different kinds of comparisons among the groups studied. The research team of Bereiter and Scardamalia use a combination of observation, interviews, questionnaires, text analysis, and a wide variety of experimental designs.

Most important, in a program of research, access to a variety of research methods allows us to address a variety of related questions, such that the evidence from one source may support or question the evidence from another. Let me illustrate this point from some of my own research-in-progress.

For a number of years, I have been interested in the analysis and teaching of what I call "basic writing or discourse tasks" and their extended versions. I am certain I have not identified all such basic discourse tasks, and I remain tentative about the three I think I have identified. They are narrative, argument, and analytic definition. I call them *basic* for three reasons. First, each can be defined by the presence or absence (though not necessarily the order) of distinctive, minimal features. For example, following Toulmin's analysis, an argument consists of a claim, datum, warrant, and so forth. Following Stein and Glenn, one kind of story consists of a setting and an episode. The episode consists of an initiating event, an attempt, a result, a reaction, and so forth. A basic analytic definition places a definiendum in a class and differentiates it from other phenomena in the same or contingent classes through the use of criteria, examples, and contrast. Second, each can be embedded, almost as building blocks, within one of the other discourse tasks. For example, an argument that someone is guilty of first degree murder is likely to include both a definition of first degree murder and a narrative. Similarly,

Aristotle's *Nichomachean Ethics* is a complex combination of argument, definition, and minimal narrative. Third, each can appear with only minimal features in a few clauses or in an extended version in which the basic features recur in linked or nested patterns.

What are the research methods for developing these ideas? Certainly not "controlled group studies involving comparisons." But just as certainly, not "case-study or ethnographic inquiry." Although I am fairly certain Mr. Irmscher would not disbar it, I am not sure what to call it. Reflection, text-analysis, definition, comparison/contrast? All of the above?

How can I extend this research? One method is through extensive and intensive text analysis. I need to ask whether or not the features of these three basic tasks account adequately for extended discourse (say, a newspaper story, an essay in a scholarly journal, a human interest story). My first step might be to examine a text, label its parts, and determine the relationships among those parts. If that proved satisfactory, I might engage in formal content analysis to determine whether more than one analyst would make comparable judgments about the text.

There are other interesting questions as well. For example, would people of various ages, social groups, and educational levels make the same distinctions that I have tried to draw? That is, would they discriminate basic narrative from argument and definition, and so on? Further, which features of basic narratives or arguments are most salient for them? One study by McCann indicates that when the presence of the features of argument is systematically varied, even sixth graders rate the arguments with most features as the best. At the same time, while sixth graders appear to recognize the features suggested by Toulmin, they do not produce them in their own written arguments. Such studies can contribute not only to general discourse theory but to our understanding of the development of discourse knowledge.

Let me turn to the teaching/learning phase of this research. My meta-analysis of composition studies indicates that the most effective mode of instruction involves students in small group discussion in which they practice using particular strategies to solve problems of a kind they will later address in their writing. Over a series of studies, this mode of instruction is significantly more effective than the other three modes examined (Hillocks, *Research in Written Composition*). In that analysis I called the most effective mode of instruction *environmental* because the teacher, the materials and problems, and the students seemed to have more balanced roles than in the other modes. One other mode I called *presentational* because the teacher and materials presented information to students who appeared to be passive receptors. Goodlad calls this mode of instruction *frontal teaching* and claims that it increasingly dominates classrooms in the United States from third grade on.

In addition, the meta-analysis examined the foci of instruction in the treatment studies. One of these is model pieces of writing. Generally speaking, in such treatments teachers ask students to read and analyze the models. Then they ask them to write compositions in which they use the features of the models studied. For example, a treatment might ask students to read and analyze orally a series of "descriptive" passages. The following assignment asks students to write a description.

A second focus is what I call *inquiry*. Any study placed in this category presented students with a set of data and asked them to examine it using one or more of the strategies used in conducting an inquiry (Hillocks, "Inquiry and the Composing Process"). One such strategy is observing phenomena closely and translating those sensory perceptions into language. In this focus of instruction, students might observe a series of phenomena and voice or write their observations before writing a full descriptive piece comparable to that in the focus on models.

The meta-analysis shows the focus on inquiry to be significantly more effective than the focus on models. However, while the meta-analysis provided comparisons of these two modes and foci across a variety of studies, it does not compare them directly. Therefore, I designed a "controlled group study involving comparisons," four groups

in fact and multiple comparisons (Hillocks, "Mode and Focus of Instruction"). Two groups use the presentational mode and two the environmental. One of each of these focuses on models, and one of each focuses on inquiry. The following four groups result: (1) presentational/models; (2) presentational/inquiry; (3) environmental/models; (4) environmental/inquiry. In the presentational groups, teachers led all discussions and presented analyses and guidelines for writing. In environmental groups students worked frequently in small groups without the direct supervision of the teacher but with specified problems, materials, and guidelines.

Since the particular writing task involved was that of extended definition, students in the *models* groups read and analyzed extended definitions. In the *inquiry* groups, they read and examined scenarios which illustrate closely related concepts. For example, one set of scenarios was concerned with freedom of speech, another with courageous action. In examining the scenario, students had to decide whether the particular speech act was allowable and stipulate the rule (or criterion) by which they decided. A later task involved students in generating scenarios *and* criteria for defining other concepts.

The study involved a total of twelve teachers and twenty-four classes in four schools. Each teacher taught two treatments, one to each of two classes. The pretests and posttests asked students to write a definition of one of five concepts not studied in class: freedom of religion, child abuse, accomplice in crime, police brutality, and loyalty. These were coded, then scored using an open-ended primary trait scale that scored each new example and criterion, as well as statements of class and differentiate which were scored only once.

The results supported the hypotheses derived from the meta-analysis. The environmental-inquiry treatment was significantly stronger than the others. The presentational-models treatment was significantly weaker than the others. However, all groups made advances. When we examined the sub-scales for examples and criteria, we found that the presentational-model groups made *no gains in the use of criteria*. *Gains for those students were confined to the use of examples.* The environmental-inquiry groups, however, made significant gains in the use of both examples and criteria.

This combination of results very strongly suggests that when students work in small groups devising criteria for discriminating closely related phenomena, they are later better able to do so independently, even when working with new definienda. This finding is in keeping with the more general finding from the meta-analysis that indicates that when students use various strategies in small group problem solving activities, they become better able to use the same strategies independently in relation to new writing tasks.

Although a number of studies outside the field of writing instruction (Johnson and Johnson; Slavin) indicate powerful effects for small group, collaborative learning, only one study, to my knowledge, examines the actual operation of student-led small group discussions. Freedman reports that small groups in two teachers' classes differ by function on such features as time-on-task and strategies used to accomplish a task. She claims that their study "corroborates" my findings that "problem solving interaction provides an intrinsically rich environment for learning" (145). It is useful to have an independent, ethnographic study confirm the results of quantitative comparison group studies. Their findings suggest the value of partnership between quasi-experimental research and case study or ethnographic research. The former can provide estimates of differences among or between groups. The latter can provide specific information about what happens during the instructional process, information which is crucial to developing a sound theoretical understanding of how the instruction works.

Freedman indicates that the collaborative thinking groups she studied are characterized by the task of having to "find, or make something as a group collaboratively, and the group output is presented, in some way, to the entire class" (140). She identifies a variety of patterns in how students accomplish these tasks: dividing "the task into smaller components," making suggestions about possible solutions, using the suggestions "to build ideas collaboratively," and ensuring that suggestions and ideas are "legitimate" matches for the question posed in the task (140).

Because of my interest in how students learn specific strategies or thinking skills which appear to be transferable to new situations, it has been necessary for my research assistants and me to ask very specific questions about how students deal with specific tasks. One of our current studies examines student responses to one of the tasks used in the inquiry groups discussed above. Because we wish to discover how students learn in the group discussions, we have needed a means of discovering what they already know. A measure of what students already know or can do should enable us to track changes in declarative and procedural knowledge through the group discussions. Further, tasks constituting the measure of prior knowledge must be parallel to the tasks addressed in student groups.

In this case, the task is to devise a set of criteria for defining courageous action. We examine student ability to do this in two ways: (1) through a written composition and (2) through response to a set of ten scenarios, most of which describe actions which may or may not be considered courageous, depending on the criteria brought to bear on them. The scenarios were initially developed as a teaching device (Hillocks, "Processes in Composing") on the basis of criteria used by Aristotle for discriminating true courageous action from seeming courageous action. These include the ideas that a courageous action must involve but overcome fear, be freely chosen, be deliberate, be noble, and so forth.

We devised at least three scenarios for each criterion and one each to illustrate true courageous action and cowardice. These were submitted to about thirty ninth and thirty twelfth graders who were asked to decide whether or not the action was courageous and to explain in writing "why each action is or is not courageous." The responses were scored to reveal which criteria students brought to bear in making their decisions. These results were submitted to Rasch model analysis (Wright and Masters) to determine the comparability of the scenarios. The scenarios were revised, added to, and retested. From the pool of items, judged to be comparable in terms of "difficulty" and the concept illustrated, we selected two sets of ten items.

One set was used as a test of prior knowledge. The second was used as the task for small group discussion. So far these have been used for pilot studies in three classes. In each of the classes, following a brief lesson on criteria based on a definition of friendship and led by the teacher, at least two groups of the students discussed the scenarios, one group worked on the scenarios independently, and one or two groups discussed their own compositions about courage. (We will ignore the latter in this paper.) Students with different tasks were separated into different rooms to avoid contamination. All group discussions were audio-recorded and transcribed for analysis. The analysis of this pilot data is nearly complete at this writing. What we find is that while students working independently on scenarios make virtually no change in their use of criteria, those working in groups make very marked changes.

Students in most cases (but not all) make use of a three-stage process, the first stage of which may be partly dictated by the assignment. In that stage students share their opinions about whether the action is courageous. Usually, this is a very brief stage. However, on occasions, when the difference in opinion is pronounced, this stage is longer, with students presenting their reasons at a rapid pace. Whether the stage is brief and cool or extended and heated, it usually gives way to a period of addressing the salient features of the scenario. This stage usually gives way to using knowledge of those features, often in contrast to features of other scenarios, to develop a rule or criterion. This third stage is often highly collaborative with one or more students making initial suggestions about a possible statement of criterion. Other students provide emendations until some consensus is reached. In some groups, one other collaborative strategy appears—that of extension. That is, one student begins to state a criterion, and another continues the statement, usually specifying it more, as though both had had the same idea initially.

Let us look at one group's talk about one of the scenarios, the sixth one in the sequence, based on

Aristotle's idea that people (soldiers) highly trained and with superior equipment may only seem to be courageous. Most students working independently on this item decide that the action is courageous because of the risk involved. Most of those who decide it is not, are not able to devise adequate statements of criteria. The sixth scenario follows along with two and five to which the students contrast the sixth.

Scenario 6: On Monday the fire had started on the oil derrick far out at sea. By Wednesday the men working on the derrick had been rescued, but the fire was out of control. "Red" Granger and his men were called in to fight the dangerous fire. "Red" and his men had fought many oil fires. They had the training and experience to put out the fire. Are "Red" and his men courageous when they fight the fire?

Scenario 2: Out of the corner of his eye, the Secret Service agent spotted a gun aimed at the President. Instantly, he threw himself in the line of fire, taking the bullet meant for the President. Was the agent's act of jumping in front of the bullet courageous?

Scenario 5: Joseph Wadsworth came from a family of military men. Both his father and grandfather had been soldiers. He had no interest in being in the military, but he was afraid that his family would be upset if he did not join the military. He joined the service and volunteered to fight in Vietnam. Is Joseph courageous when he joins the service and volunteers to fight?

After a reading of scenario #6, the discussion proceeds:

Scott: God, all these contradict the other ones.

Keith: Yeah.

Scott: Six contradicts the one with the agent, the security agent.

Keith: I don't think they're courageous because they're experienced, but they're not actually putting themselves at risk. They're just doing another job. It's not actual . . .

Scott: What did we have for number 2?

Keith: Yes.

Scott: Yes. Then this one has to be yes. It's a job.

Keith: No, not necessarily.

Amy: No, it's different. You're not putting yourself in front of a bullet.

Keith: Yeah. Chances are that some people are going to die in car wrecks every day. Just because you get in a car doesn't mean you're courageous.

Scott: But really, it's their job to do something like that. And you have to be courageous to take a job like that in the first place.

Sue: He has fought many oil fires it says.

Amy: Yeah, that guy was going in front of many bullets. *[sarcastic]*

Sue: This emphasizes their training and their fighting many of them. The other one was just like I saw them out of the corner of my eye.

Amy: So this one is not courageous. They have the experience, so they're not doing anything out of the ordinary.

Keith: Yeah, even if the bullet doesn't kill him, he's pretty sure he's going to get hurt. These, they might go in there and not get hurt at all.

Amy: Right.

Scott: Yeah but in number 5 when a person goes to Vietnam or something like that and after he stays there a course of time, he's well trained in that too. Does that make him not courageous any more?

Amy: No, he's not courageous to begin with because of the reason we gave.

Scott: No, I mean if a person was in Vietnam for a year . . .

Amy: No, we're still saying that he could still do something that would be courageous. We're talking about *[unclear]*

Scott: I was getting into death. I don't want to get into death. When I get into death, I don't know what I'm talking about, man. I'll be rattling off stuff.

Keith: I think anybody goes over there and they're well trained and stuff like that.

Scott: Yeah, like for a course of time.

Sue: Ok, this one is . . .

Scott: They've mostly seen everything that has to be seen.

Sue: A courageous person will . . . Same as number 4?

Amy: No

Scott: Let's read the book when it comes out.

Amy: He's not really in that much danger because of his training.

Keith: I think they're a little bit courageous, but they're not.

Amy: But it's their job and they're being trained for it, so they're being trained for it. And they put out similar fires too.

Keith: They're not facing certain death or certain harm or whatever.

Sue: Something they are trained and familiar with? *[asking about criterion phrasing]*

Keith: Yeah.

Sue: What would you say, "A person is not courageous when they are trained and familiar with . . ."?

Amy: A situation.

Sue: Usually a fatal situation?

Amy: No, they're trained.

Keith: So it's not going to be a fatal situation to them.

Amy: Yeah, they're going to know how to take steps to make it . . .

Sue: Ok, what if you say, "A person is not courageous when they're trained and familiar with a usual situation"?

Keith: Well, it's usual for them. I think that's the big thing.

Amy: It's something they're used to.

Sue: So should I write that?

Keith: Yeah.

In this discussion the period of sharing lasts for about ten lines. Initially, however, Scott sets the stage for examining salient features when he suggests that "six contradicts the one with the agent." Amy points out the salient difference: "You're not putting yourself in front of a bullet." Scott disagrees, "You have to be courageous to take a job like that in the first place." Sue, Amy, and Keith contrast the salient differences. Scott refers to scenario 5 to bolster his position. For a few lines the discussion goes off track. But Sue, who is the group recorder, brings it back, asking if they should use the same criterion as they had used for scenario 4. From this point, the students try to boil down the salient features into an abstract criterion. For several lines the students focus on essential words, until Sue says, "Something they are trained and familiar with?" Here, she is clearly asking about phrasing the criterion.

From this point on Amy, Sue, and Keith develop the final statement by extending and rephrasing the ideas of the others. Sue finally writes, "A person is not courageous when they are trained and familiar with a usually fatal situation." Although Aristotle might have been more elegant in his statement, he would probably agree. And even though Scott did not participate in phrasing the final version, he forced the comparisons which helped the others clarify their thinking. In short, all students in the group have participated in using strategies necessary to generating an effective extended definition.

The point of all this is to illustrate how ethnographic research like that of Sarah Freedman and her team and observational studies such as the one outlined above are not antipathetic to controlled experimental or quasi-experimental research. Nor is one method subservient to the other. Qualitative and various kinds of quantitative research need to be used in productive symbiotic relationships. At a time when research into the nature of the teaching and learning of literacy continues to explode, researchers need every tool available and those yet to be invented. Those who back themselves into the corner of a "comfortable identity" do themselves, and perhaps the field, a disservice. What we need is a perhaps *uncomfortable* but certainly exciting

identity which allows us to approach problems from a variety of research perspectives.

Note

Irmscher appears not to be aware that one of the basic tenets of quantitative research is that generalizations do *not* apply to *all cases*. Good quantitative researchers always present several indicators of the extent to which generalizations apply to a particular sample.

Works Cited

Applebee, A. N. *The Child's Concept of Story: Ages Two to Seventeen.* Chicago: U of Chicago P, 1978.

————. *Contexts for Learning to Write: Studies of Secondary School Instruction.* Norwood, NJ: Ablex, 1983.

————. Applebee, A. N., J. Langer, and I. Mullis. *Writing: Trends Across the Decade, 1974–1984.* Princeton: ETS, 1984. NAEP Report 15-W-01.

Bereiter, C., and M. Scardamalia. *The Psychology of Written Composition.* Hillsdale, NJ: Lawrence Erlbaum, 1987.

Braddock, R., R. Lloyd-Jones, and C. Schoer. *Research in Written Composition.* Champaign, IL: NCTE, 1963.

Brossell, G. "Rhetorical Specification in Essay Examination Topics." *College English* 45 (1983): 165–73.

Freedman, S. W., and J. Bennett. *Peer Groups at Work in Two Writing Classrooms.* Center for the Study of Writing at Berkeley and Carnegie Mellon. 1987. Berkeley: Final Report Draft: Project 5 (Study 2).

Goodlad, J. I. *A Place Called School: Prospects for the Future.* New York: McGraw-Hill, 1984.

Hagstrum, J. H. Review of *Research in Written Composition. College English* 26 (1964): 53–56.

Hillocks, G., Jr. "Inquiry and the Composing Process: Theory and Research." *College English* 44 (1982): 659–73.

————. "Mode and Focus of Instruction: Teaching Procedural and Declarative Knowledge for Writing." Paper, annual meeting AERA, 1987.

————. "Processes in Composing: Invention to Product." Unpublished manuscript, 1979.

————. *Research on Written Composition: New Directions for Teaching.* Urbana: ERIC Clearinghouse on Reading and Communication Skills and The National Conference on Research in English, 1986.

Irmscher, W. F. "Finding a Comfortable Identity." *College Composition and Communication.* 38 (1987): 81–87.

Johnson, D. W., and R. T. Johnson. "Conflict in the Classroom: Controversy and Learning." *Review of Educational Research* 49 (1979): 51–70.

Kahn, E., and L. Johannessen. "Does the Assignment Make a Difference? Four Variations of a Writing Task and Their Effects on Student Performance." University of Chicago: Unpublished manuscript, 1982.

Langer, J. A. *Children Reading and Writing: Structures and Strategies.* Norwood, NJ: Ablex, 1986.

Larson, R. L. Review of *Research on Written Composition: New Directions for Teaching. College Composition and Communication* 38 (1987): 207–11.

McCann, T. M. "Student Argumentative Writing Knowledge and Ability at Three Grade Levels." University of Chicago: Unpublished manuscript, 1986.

Metviner, E. S. "Rhetorically Based and Rhetorically Deficient Writing: The Effects of Purpose and Audience on the Quality of Ninth Grade Students' Compositions." *DAI* 41 (1981): 3977-A.

Slavin, R. E. *Cooperative Learning.* New York: Longman, 1983.

Stein, N. L., and C. G. Glenn. "An Analysis of Story Comprehension in Elementary School Children." In *New Directions in Discourse Processing.* Vol. 2. Ed. R. O. Freedle. Norwood, NJ: Ablex, 1979. 53–120.

Toulmin, S. E. *The Uses of Argument.* Cambridge: Cambridge UP, 1958.

Wesdorp, H. *SCO Rapport: De Didactiek van Het Stellen: Een Overzicht van Het Onderzoek naar de Effecten van Diverse Instructie—Variabelen of de Stelvaardigheid.* Amsterdam: U of Amsterdam, 1982.

Wright, B. D., and G. N. Masters. *Rating Scale Analysis.* Chicago: MESA P, 1982.

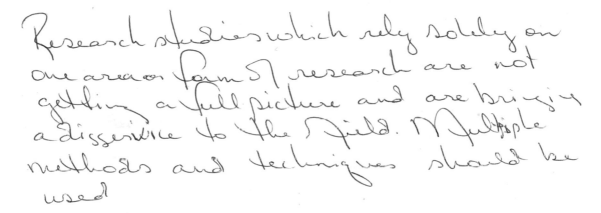

Research studies which rely solely on one area or form of research are not getting a full picture and are bringing a disservice to the field. Multiple methods and techniques should be used

Textual Research and Coherence: Findings, Intuition, Application

Richard H. Haswell

This essay appeared in College English *51 (1989): 305–19.*

Periodically, researchers discover a promising and disquieting fact, that merely to describe the texts of student and professional writers is to question the textbooks of English teachers. R. D. Meade and W. G. Ellis found that writers for *The English Journal* and *The Saturday Review of Literature* order over half of their paragraphs by methods not mentioned in composition textbooks. Richard Braddock found that similar high-brow writers begin 87% of their paragraphs without a topic sentence. Paul Roberts found they use the pronoun "this" 70% of the time with no specific nominal as antecedent, Francis Christensen that they begin more than three-fourths of their sentences with (of all things) the subject, Kellogg Hunt that they begin nearly a tenth of them with a "But," an "Or," or an "And." And periodically, as these textual revisionists did, the researchers publish their discoveries, often in the form of a comparison of professional and student writing, hoping to civilize if not the textbooks at least the teachers who are still setting up some of the more outdated idols in the classroom—the idol of the Initial Topic Sentence, for instance, or of the Buried Coordinating Conjunction.

"Idol" is a strong word and no doubt overstates the case. But in one particular way the situation calls for it. Teacher eidolons do not immediately vanish upon exposure. Twenty or more years have passed since the publication of the above findings, twenty years of biennial teaching-assistant turnover

and of triennial textbook revision, and it seems that not many teachers or textbooks have much revised their ways with topic sentences, sentence openers, or any other of the targets of the researchers. Even though I am thinking of "idols" more in the context of Francis Bacon than Edgar Rice Burroughs, the textual revisionists might well prefer the language of Fowler, who called such stubborn precepts "superstitions" and "fetishes."

Look at the active verb. A goodly amount of research into usage seems to recommend that teachers be not so active in ridding the passive from student writing. Between 10% and 15% of the main verbs in even the vigorous writing of *Time Magazine* and *The New York Times* are passive (Warfel). In popular scientific writing the figure averages around 12% (Hopkins), in social-service agency reports and memos from 20% to 54% (Odell and Goswami). Even developmental trends argue that a substantial use of the passive is a sign of mature writing, and Hunt's figure rises steadily from 2% for 4th graders to 9% for 12th graders. Yet as the textual evidence continues to come in (my own research—which I will describe in a minute—finds competent writers in business and industry producing impromptu a rate of around 15%), handbooks and teachers continue to recommend a virtual excommunication of the passive, as for example Kathleen Kiefer and Charles R. Smith have done in their computer text-analysis for college writers, which admonishes writers when passives approach 5%. The iconoclasts apply their numbers, but the icon will not break.

RESISTANCE TO EMPIRICAL TEXTUAL STUDIES

This is not to say that all resistance to the findings of revisionist textual research is reactionary or simple-minded. If a few teachers adhere to the old commandments because they do not understand or have not read the research, or if some textbook writers adhere to the old religion because they find it sells, there are still many more members of the profession who question the methodology of textual studies on quite reasonable grounds. So reasonable, in fact, that currently the person who risks being called outdated or uninformed is the one who dares to argue, as I am going to argue, that textual research has its value to the profession.

Using a maneuver probably as old as idol-worship itself, the new resistance turns the tables on the textual researchers, accusing them of erecting idols—and idols as legion as the ones they hoped to topple. To mention only the most brazen, they are accused of worshipping the gods of Numbers, fondly imagining that if one measures only traits that can be measured, the reality measured will not be trivial; of Linearity, taking two features to be half as effective as four of the same features; of the Eighth Day, endowing a-rhetorical zombies, such as t-units, with animation and then ordering them to replace rhetorical realities, such as sentences; of Truth-in-Analysis, trusting that atomistic breakdown will reveal living anatomy; of Universal Transference, holding faith that one writing context or group of writers is identical to another; of Immaculate Surfaces, preaching that the effect of a purpose (a product) fully expresses the purpose; of the Sterile Laboratory, believing that, after most of the context of writing has been sliced off to create a controlled design for testing, writing will still be alive to be tested. Even without swelling the list with the train of minor idols—of Skills-the-Only-God, Mysteries-of-Probability-Statistics, Truth-in-Jargon, Truth-in-Exactness, Faith-in-Gim-

mickry—it is clear that more often than any other kind of research in composition, comparative textual studies have been attacked on the crucial issue of validity, by Carl Bereiter and Marlene Scardamalia, Dwight L. Burton, Robert Connors, Janet Emig, Donald Graves, George Hillocks, Jr., Michael Holzman, and Stephen North.

The attack does not stop with validity. Even were a textual study proved fully valid, its findings still might lack the ultimate sanction: pertinence to teaching. The actual rules for in-print use of the passive may be too complex for marginal comment on student essays, or too sophisticated even for college students to learn, or too barbaric aesthetically for teachers to endorse. These issues of feasibility and teachability and taste are not directly addressed by comparison of texts. There are other important issues, but for the moment it is enough to recognize the severity of the situation. The notion of a "continuum" from basic research to application, say researchers Bereiter and Scardamalia, is "now largely discredited" (23). "Mountains of data and findings," says North, a critic of researchers, lie inert, a "sleeping giant," or possibly "a monster" that ought never be awakened (196). The situation is not just a matter of the textbook and the statistical print-out calling one another black. It is the question of whether a certain kind of composition research, indeed whether a wealth of research findings of many different methodologies, can be used.

I think the findings can, and should. I am both a researcher and a teacher of composition and am aware of how difficult it is for one part of me to talk to the other. But what I know as a researcher does sometimes change what I do as a teacher. My argument here sets forth one such time when findings toppled a pedagogical idol. It was not a conversion, since it led to a position doubly heretical, but a reversal of vision nonetheless. My argument asks some strange questions. Can the research lack validity but the findings still have value? Can the findings fail to address teaching issues but still change teachers? I will not deny that the direct way from research to application has been discredited, but I will argue—it is perhaps more of a narrative than an argument—that the way may still be traversed, with credit to both researcher and teacher and with benefit to the student. I will, however, stop short of predicting revision of handbook precepts, though my argument points in that direction. Handbooks may never change.

AN IDOL AND SOME FINDINGS

Over the years *Hodge's Harbrace College Handbook* has found little reason to modify its stand on transitional devices, or what researchers now call explicit cohesive ties: "Sentences linked by transitional devices such as pronouns, repeated key words, transitional expressions, or parallel structure help create a unified paragraph" (365). It is hard to think of a pronouncement more orthodox. When E. K. Lybbert and D. W. Cummings surveyed hand-book advice on coherence twenty years ago, they found exactly the same ingredients. And the degree to which *Harbrace* still reflects common practice of teachers can be demonstrated handily. Take two sentences from a student paragraph, described by Anita Bostroff as "apparently incoherent" (280), and give them, embedded in the original paragraph if need be (see below, 312), to English teachers for rewriting.

> Success sounds like a lot of hard work. Successful people delight in taking challenges and surmounting them elegantly.

In my department, 30 of 34 teachers responded by adding "But" or "however" to the second sentence.

Were I an editor of *Harbrace,* I would be pleased. As a teacher, I recognize a reflex editorial gesture once long my own. As a teacher/researcher, I now believe that the *Harbrace* precept misrepresents the issue, that the emendation of the teachers misleads the student, that we are in the presence of the false god of Manifest Transitions.

I say as a teacher/researcher because my new belief reflects one of those changes in teaching prompted by research findings, in this case a finding of my own. I was studying writing development during the college years, analyzing a sample of essays written by 18, 19, and 20-year-old undergrad-

uates. The essays represented regular academic progress and a normal range of writing skill at a land-grant university. For comparison I had essays written under the same conditions—same topics, same time constraints—by nonacademics: employees from a wide range of occupations in business and industry, college graduates, thirty years old or older. I was analyzing both sets by M.A.K. Halliday and Ruqaiya Hasan's standard research scheme of cohesive ties (synopses of the complex scheme are provided by Witte and Faigley 190–95, and by Myers 53–55).

The results were unexpected in terms of the *Harbrace* precept. The older writers had not used more synonyms or parallelism than had the students. The rate at which the employees had used ties of "reference" (pronouns, demonstratives, and comparatives) actually declines, a statistically significant drop. The rate of repeated words also drops, as does that of logical connectors like "for example" and "however." All told, the older writers had used fewer of the four transitional devices recommended by *Harbrace* (the research is reported in Haswell, "Change in Undergraduate"). Incidentally, they had been identified by their supervisors as especially "competent" writers on the job, and their essays had been rated substantially better than the student essays by a group of college English teachers who at the time were requiring their students to buy and use the *Harbrace Handbook,* teachers who might have been startled, as I certainly was, to see evidence that the solution to incoherence in student writing may not be to stuff it with more pronouns, parallelism, repeated key words, or transitional markers.

AN INTUITION

On second thought, I felt not so much startlement as the proverbial shock of recognition, both a recognizing and a re-cognition. Let's call it a moment of intuition. Granted, it did not take place in a moment, and it was not simple. It combined my notions about language, personal preference in style, hours of reading student writing, frustrations in responding to that writing, and disappointments and successes in getting improvement. It emerged from the wholly intuitive only gradually.

I think my first conscious understanding was that the finding made sense theoretically. Twenty-five years ago, when I first began teaching, the story would have been different, for then language theory had a limited grasp of coherence. Analysis was largely confined to single linkages between sentences. Today discourse analysis has told us that writing coheres by an awesome density and diversity and redundance of "structures of expectation," not one-plied but multiple-layered and nested. Discourse connects new and old information via many sub-strata: given and new, topic and comment, frame and insert, deemphasis and salience, foreground and ground. It unifies its larger stretches with rhetorical and psychological and logical patterns, nonfictional plots which theorists are only beginning to name and classify. Reaching even further outward, into what theorists call "coherence" (as distinguished from cohesion), it attaches itself to cultural maps of all sorts (call them "frames," "scripts," "schemata," or "modules"), appropriates their conventional organization, and thereby structures its own text. In the other direction, it uses all the sub-sentence ways that language coheres: syntactic relationships such as modification, case relationships such as instrumentality, semantic relationships such as shared features. The old terrain embraced by the researcher's term "explicit cohesion" or the handbook's term "transitions," east of "coherence" and west of the sentence, turns out to be a rather small country indeed. (For good bibliographies and a fuller account of the current theory, see Phelps; Witte and Faigley.)

It occurred to me that with such a supply of ways to help discourse flow, better writers may have a lower rate of a certain device simply because they are inclined toward variety. They may be disinclined toward the orthodox devices of pronouns, repeated words, synonyms, and logical transitions because these means are explicit, stated, whereas other means are tacit, operating in invisible chunks around the words and thereby quickening pace and reducing short-term memory load. The theory also made sense to me because it agreed with my taste for prose that moves rapidly and cleanly. Both the researcher's theory and the teacher's aesthetics shared the same system, a concept of what might be called cohesive efficiency or elegance.

SOME APPLICATIONS

Gradually, my diagnosis of writing, student and professional, began to shift. The orthodox precept that more is better in cohesion had beguiled me into looking for a debilitating scarcity of transitional devices. Now I began to see instances of debilitating abundance as well. I returned to my research sample and, with the help of the statistical print-out, located examples by the score. Take the repetition of key words. Students sometimes triple the average rate of the competent employees.

> As one gets older his spectrum of **beauty** increases. A 35 **year old** man might think that **girls** from 17–45 **years old** are **beautiful.** He still likes **girls** in his own **age group** but also **girls** of younger **age.** Society brings this on. **Girls** from 17–25 are usually considered the most **beautiful.** Then as one ages, she is supposed to get less **beautiful.** So the guy **35 years old** should **think younger girls** are **more beautiful.**

Repeats, highlighted here, make up every third word (some with precursors in the preceding paragraph). It is easy to size up the paragraph as wordy, but a bit shocking to comprehend that wordiness as a form of cohesion. Since all coherence entails the carrying forward of old information, explicit cohesion not needed to maintain flow is nothing but excessive repetition. To replace repetitions with synonyms usually does not solve the problem, especially when the synonyms are too exact to add any useful new information (as "guy" in the last sentence above).

Demonstratives, I now saw, are often just another and sometimes longer form of identical or synonymous ties.

> **The** three reasons mentioned in **this** paper describe why conceptions of human beauty are harmful. Because of **this** our society needs to evaluate **these** conceptions and not place as much emphasis on them.

A quick revision shows how all but one of the demonstratives (in bold) are unnecessary: "These three reasons describe why conceptions of human beauty are harmful and should be re-evaluated and de-emphasized."

Notice that "our" and "them" are also revised out. An abundance of pronouns is sometimes another warning that cohesion has passed from useful redundance to true wordiness.

> Manufacturers make a killing in profit with the young generation of today. Jeans for example may cost 10 dollars for **them** to make and **they** sell **them** at around 30 dollars. Teens know that **they** are getting ripped off, so why don't **they** stop buying **them?**

I now saw why often the solution to problems in pronoun reference is not to clarify the antecedence but to eliminate the pronouns. The second sentence alone can read, "Jeans cost 10 dollars to make and sell for around 30."

The disappearance of the "for example" in this revision leads to the logical transitional marker (in bold below), the prodigal son of composition teachers.

> *The conceptions for "right" and "proper"* are different for different age levels. **For instance** our society looks upon crying as a childish, emotional act. **Therefore,** it is *proper* for a *child* to *cry* **but** when an adult, especially a male *cries,* it doesn't seem *right* to most *people*. **Thus** *the adult* holds back his *emotions* to fit in the *unwritten rules* of *"proper"* and *"right"* of *our society*.

Since the content is already structured logically, the "For instance" and "Therefore" can be removed without loss in readability. I was especially surprised to find how often such markers did little more than signal the presence of that stifled, walking-under-water style of excessive cohesion.

All the other explicit cohesion in this last example is italicized to contrast with the opposite style, something not illustrated in *Harbrace:* writing with an efficient scarcity of explicit cohesion. Here is a paragraph from an employee essay rated better than 116 of the 128 undergraduate essays.

> As *this* young teenage girl turns 14, 15, 16 years of age, the momentum of the peer group changes focus slightly, and the quality of *friendships* becomes an important aspect of *their* lives. *It* might be poems to a very close *friend* saying how much their *friendship* means. Or increased exploration of the tenuous, exciting, frustrating world of the boy-girl relationships. The values have shifted center somewhat. The outward appearance of clothes and wardrobe are *more* balanced with how *they* perceive *that* person to be: a friend I know I can trust, one I can share a secret with, one who can listen to what I'm saying and understand where I'm coming from.

All of the explicit ties between t-units are italicized. There are no logical transitions. In the previous student example, explicit cohesion accounts for a third of the words, here for less than a tenth. Now I could guess how this paragraph, as complex as any cited above, can still cohere: with implicit ties. Ties of collocation associate propositions, "co-locating" them within some cultural basket, as the words "momentum," "changes," "becomes," "increased," and "shifted" articulate the first half of the paragraph because they encode our contemporary belief in a period of rapid maturation following puberty. Unstated logical schemes and other conventional orderings of ideas map equally large stretches, as where the concepts "turns" and "exploration" and "balanced" convey a pattern of Eriksonian personality development well enough known to need no explicit sign-posts. Within t-units, linkage is achieved with great efficiency. In the first two sentences, two pre-nominal series establish the frame of maturation ("14, 15, 16 years of age" and "tenuous, exciting, frustrating world"). In the last sentence, a final free modifier re-defines something outward ("a friend") in terms of a miniature narrative proceeding by steps inward ("trust . . . share . . . listen . . . understand").

I now had a precept of my own: when possible, cohesive elegance uses unstated structures of expectation to avoid those explicit ties that add words without adding new information. Since then the precept has been reinforced by the studies of other teachers and researchers. Betty Bamberg, Jeanne Fahnestock, Gary Sloan, and Robin Bell Markels have also stressed the function of implicit cohesion. Fahnestock says, "The fact that the semantic relationship between a pair of clauses can be articulated though it goes unmarked by a transition word is a fundamental principle of coherence" (402), and notes that a common pattern is "the paragraph which leaves most of the continuative relations between sentences implicit and marks sentences only to emphasize or to signal the discontinuative" (410). Sloan found in professional published essays only 29% of t-units linked by explicit transitional markers and only 7% needing obligatory explicit markers: "the writers I liked best stuck mainly to unobtrusive markers and used markers sparingly" (174). Fahnestock's "mainly" and Sloan's "most," of course, point out the danger of enforcing any precept of implicit cohesion too absolutely. An important corollary is illustrated by my employee essays. At one point they used explicit cohesion much more often than did the students: between paragraphs. Employees connected the first sentence of one paragraph to the last sentence of the previous with coherence of the *Harbrace* sort 95% of the time, students 61%. But still I found cohesive elegance an idea that not only made sense of the analysis sheet but as well proved practicable in the classroom, across the desk, and in the margin.

Imagine a teacher faced with our original example of "apparently incoherent" student writing.

> Success sounds like a lot of hard work. Successful people delight in taking challenges and surmounting them elegantly.

We now see that the traditional reflex emendation, inserting a "however" or "but," corrects the problem of flow but adds words. We also see that implicit structures connecting the two sentences already abound in the original version. In accordance with the discourse analyst's "rule of antecedence," the student has placed old information from the first sentence (success, hard work) first in the second sentence. She has reduced the frame drawn by the first sentence (success as hard work) by the insert of the second (a particular kind of person involved in success). Familiar cultural plots unify the movement from sentence one to sentence two—from illusion ("sounds like") to truth, predicament ("lot") to escape, rags ("work") to riches, obstacles ("hard") overcome, pressure han-

dled by grace ("elegantly"). Any one of these structures, already intuited by the student, readily suggests alternate revisions.

> Success can be a lot of hard work—or a delight in surmounting challenges elegantly.

> It is the unsuccessful who think success a lot of hard work. Challenges can be surmounted with elegance and delight.

> Real success, not the hard work some imagine, is delight in surmounting challenges elegantly.

Implicit cohesion serves even better for revision of extended passages. Here is the student's original paragraph.

> Success sounds like a lot of hard work. Successful people delight in taking challenges and surmounting them elegantly. Weights of money, prestige and desire are often attached to our notions of success. In a social environment it is easy to select the better. The one flashing his teeth in every direction and making gross comments is not successful, for example.

I have found that college juniors and seniors especially seem impressed by the contrast between a version relying heavily on *Harbrace's* explicit devices:

> Success sounds like a lot of hard work. Successful people, however, delight in taking challenges and surmounting them elegantly. These real winners do not attach weights of money, prestige, and desire to their notion of success as, on the other hand, others sometimes do. In a room full of people, the two types are easy to select. The one flashing his teeth in every direction and making gross comments, for example, is not successful.

and one relying on implicit devices:

> True success, not the hard work one imagines at first, comes with a delight in surmounting challenges elegantly. Weights of money, prestige, and desire drop away, and a certain composure grows. The man flashing his teeth in every direction and making gross comments has not arrived.

The readiness of older college students to appreciate these revisions began to clarify other findings of my research. One particularly complex pattern became apparent. From entering freshman to beginning junior, a trend of a decline in rate of logical transitions, identical ties and reference ties combines with a statistically significant growth in areas that provided the employees with structures for implicit cohesion: the logical complexity of top-level organizational patterns, the incidence of three-or-more-item series, the amount and complexity of both free and bound modification, and the length of sentences (Haswell, "Change" and "Organization"). Undergraduates may be instinctively shifting toward the kind of cohesive elegance preferred by competent older writers. Because this complex shift is more pronounced with juniors than with sophomores, perhaps due to the time it takes for students to absorb the necessary cultural frames, I now have a rough curricular approach to coherence, de-emphasizing it altogether with underclassmen, emphasizing tactics of cohesive elegance with older students. Although I have no handbook precept to back me up, I am enforcing a rhetorical truth which I imagine college students will find congenial because they have been learning it already on their own.

THEORETICAL PROBLEMS WITH COHESION RESEARCH

This narrative of my journey from research to application has tried to answer realistically a very real question: Can quantified research convince a teacher to change teaching habits, a teacher who has been trained in a humanistic discipline and who must face daily the sincere interrogation of the classroom, who is inherently skeptical of numbers, and who, in fact, has engaged in enough number research to be familiar with its problems and self-deceptions? If the narrative offers a qualified yes to this question, it has done so by insisting, no doubt doggedly, on the concrete and practical, relating how one research finding helped one teacher diagnose Friday's batch of student writing, offer hard solutions to hard writing problems, and refurbish curricular sequence. It is important to recognize this focus on the pragmatic because the minute the

focus shifts to the theoretical, the journey swerves toward an ideological bog.

Begin again with the finding: in the impromptu essays of my undergraduates, an explicit cohesive tie (repeated word, synonym, pronoun, comparative, demonstrative, or logical transition) occurs on the average every 8.0 words; in the employee essays, every 9.6 words. How can one take such an observation as a sanction for pedagogical action? Is it not more a sanctification?

Ideologically, cohesion researchers stand particularly vulnerable to the new charges of idolatry in quantified textual studies. Their trust in Numbers has spawned a pandemonium of analytical measures. Some researchers count ties only between sentences, some only between t-units, some within t-units. Some calculate frequency as ties per word, others as ties per t-unit, words per tie, percent of all words, percent of all ties, or partial correlation with total words. All these rates assume a Linearity of cohesion to length of writing, which in fact is unlikely, a convenient figment (Haswell, "Length of Text"). The ties themselves undoubtedly are partly figments, creations of the researchers' Eighth Day. This is obviously so with implicit semantic ties like collocation, where special knowledge in the rater/reader is needed to make the connections, but so too with other kinds of ties. How do readers understand the link between the word "differ" and a previous "differently"? One may see it as a synonym, another as a repetition, another as a member of a subordinate/superordinate set with the verb naming a specific act of the general state named by the adverb. And what if "differently" occurs so far previous that it coheres for some readers but not for others? The Immaculate Surface hides a quicksand of unmeasured intentions.

And if Truth-in-Analysis begins to look more like numerology than numbers, any belief in Universal Transference looks like a desperate worship of dismembered parts of Osiris tumbling in the tide. Comparison of findings from different studies simply does not recommend much trust in the methodology so far developed by workers in cohesion. At SUNY–Buffalo Charles R. Cooper and his associates found the very best freshman essays (holistically rated) with twice the density of cohesion as the very worst; across state at Canisius College, Jerome L. Neuner found no difference in density. Odell and Goswami report social-service administrators producing logical transitions at half the rate of Witte and Faigley's worst freshman writers and one-seventh the rate of their best freshman writers, and together (as Sandra Stotsky points out, "Types of Lexical Cohesion" 439–40) these same freshmen generate one collocation tie about every t-unit while professional popular-science writers, according to the count of Robert Morris Hopkins, generate about one tie every third t-unit. V. M. Rentel and colleagues found that frequency of ties in primary-grade narratives increases with age of writer, Jill Fitzgerald and Dixie Lee Spiegel that it decreases—and somehow both conclude that coherence improves with schooling.

Right now cohesion research is a mess. Normally when experimental context is not replicated or much controlled—as in most social-science research and in nearly all textual studies in composition—common trends in findings across diverse studies may be especially meaningful, but in cohesion research (of all places) it is hard to find such coherence. A few generalizations can be pieced together. Widely dispersed studies seem to agree that very short papers at the bottom of holistic ratings have shorter lengths of chains of ties, that at least up to the first year of college better writers produce a greater ratio of synonyms over repeats, and that, progressing from the early grades on beyond college, writers rely more and more on collocation. But these are exceptions. The broad picture is one of mutual unsupport. If six studies appear to back my finding that better writing uses fewer explicit ties, half a dozen appear to contradict it. It seems that within the Sterile Laboratory of hypothesis testing, context control, and cohesion count, the main finding so far has been a self-generated sterility. Where does one go from there?

The question is theoretical. One goes from there. The findings do not remain with the research. They enter, freely and shamelessly, the laboratory of the teacher, selected by intuition and changed back into hypotheses to be tested by a new context. It should not be forgotten that replicability, probability, validity, and reliability describe methods, not assertions. A research finding, as any other human notion, may be right even if totally ungrounded. A teacher may discover in a nonsignificant finding of a seriously flawed study an idea that triggers insight, makes sense, feels right, proves useful. This fact, it should be emphasized, does not argue against rigor in research. Researchers are bound and will be bound to improve their methodology—to tie empirical studies together with common rating systems and replications, to set hypotheses in sounder and more precise theory. But in the meanwhile, a teacher is free to use current findings when they work. Experimental researchers do not err by increasing the rigor of their methods but by tending to assume, as Stephen North explains, more sanction than their present methods warrant. But then critics of the researchers tend to confine the implications of the research to less than they deserve, especially overlooking their potential pragmatic impact.

PRAGMATIC IMPACT OF COHESION RESEARCH

"Truth must of necessity be stranger than fiction," said Basil, placidly. "For fiction is the creation of the human mind, and therefore is congenial to it."

G. K. Chesterton, *The Club of Queer Trades*

It is worth asking how this impact can happen. "One of the reasons teachers have rejected research information for so long," writes Donald H. Graves in an attack on textual studies, "is that they have been unable to transfer faceless data to the alive, inquiring faces of the children they teach the next morning" (918). But a difference of 1.6 words per explicit tie is not faceless. With a glance at the writing of students, it will help the teacher see times where flow occurs with unusual ease and elegance, where ideas move with energy and efficiency because they are backed by structures of thinking and feeling implicitly shared by reader and writer. A second look at it will show the teacher the actual faces of students frustrated by the effort of connecting ideas that seem to stall and involute like a nightmare of mirrors. A number is no more faceless than any other piece of language. Braddock's 87% of paragraphs without an initial topic sentence (regardless of reliability) can picture a student stalled in the middle of a paragraph by premature consolidation of ideas. Christensen's 32% of professionally written words in free modification (regardless of sample error) can envision a writer whose scant repertoire of syntax is sapping his desire to express complex truths. The regular occurrence of the passive in print (regardless of transferability) can limn the very furrows on the brow of a student who has been untaught the one structure she needs to get naturally to her next sentence. Anyone else's findings, researched or not, textual or not, are empty and faceless until rediscovered.

"Experimental inquiry," counters North, "is not geared to produce discoveries" (150). The criticism, one of the most common and most damning leveled against formal research, hits home well enough in the way that experimenters, having discovered something, then insert it as a hypothesis into the machinery of methodology for testing, for validation. In the way that researchers operate otherwise, nothing could be further from the truth. Discovery is the very pith and materialization of research. Just because the machine cranks out the hypothesis flattened into a statistic and stamped with a probability figure does not alter the original observation's status as discovery. Experimental inquiry is geared to produce nothing but discoveries, albeit in a certain form. It is also geared to precipitate discoveries. Especially in comparative textual studies, where hypotheses tend to be loose, the systematic means of analysis consistently—the temptation is to say inevitably—produces discoveries. On undertaking my study, I hypothesized that students change in their writing during college, but I was surprised, upon the application of Halliday and Hasan's system, to find their rates of cohesion declining. North figures 1,500 formal research studies in composition since 1963 (Hillocks adds 500 more). Can one be found that does not describe some point where results surprised the researcher? More to the point, even if the results were totally expected by the experimenter, potentially they may surprise any number of readers.

The notion of research as only a machine for validation assumes a simple flow of knowledge from input to output. Nothing could be more misleading. Research is helical. Not only are new puzzles generated, old puzzles are reconstituted. Why should competent writers produce both fewer explicit ties and longer essays than did my undergraduate population? If the answer is that they unconsciously relied on ingrained cultural structures, then suddenly Ann Matsuhashi's enigmatic discovery that both students and skilled writers pause less before scribing a collation tie than a repeat tie gains new meaning, as does Marion Crowhurst's finding of a decrease in logical transitions of cause from Grade 4 to Grade 12, or Lyman B. Hagen's 25-year-old curiosity that professional magazine writers produced fewer transitional phrases per word than freshmen, who produced fewer than seventh graders, who produced fewer than third graders. Complaints that researchers always end their studies with a plea for more research oversimplify the plea. It is more than an admission that composition research currently resides in a pre-paradigmatic field where little holds, or a confession that results were incomprehensible, or a plug for future grants. It is a piece of history, an account not only of research findings but also of researcher findings, moments of startlement and intuition which beg for revision of thought.

For teachers the pragmatic impact lies in this edgy, helical nature of systematic research. Research does not have—nor will it ever have, no matter how refined—a methodology to sanction pedagogical action by validating "truths." But it does have a methodology to question "truths." Whether it studies written products or writer processes or ethnographic contexts or hermeneutical meanings, it forces a stringent and uncustomary system of looking at the subject. With an alien perceptional set it breaks more familiar or conventional sets. We need not conceive of "truth," as Chesterton's detective Basil Grant does, as standing somewhere beyond "creations of the human mind" to see his point that fictions may be more or less "congenial" to that mind. The harshest criticism of research detectives takes their procedural orientations as fiction-making, but even so, their fictions—their idols, if you will—may be useful in making us aware of our own set orientations, which by the same criticism must be acknowledged equally as idols. I have little assurance about my difference of 1.6 as a universal truth. Other systems of cohesion analysis will define the difference by other figures, other samplings of writers might divest it of statistical significance, other writing tasks might erase the contrast between student and employee writing altogether. But I am sure about the pedagogical insights 1.6 led me to. And I am not sure I would have been led to them in any other way.

A research datum is both something uncovered and something recovered, in part a finding like the unearthing of a potsherd, allowed by techniques of systematic chance and open to rejection and contemplation, in part an observation like any other human observation, fabricated out of imaginative experience and open to abuse and use. The double nature makes the datum more valuable than were it only one or the other, either just another fragment of a hard fact to number and throw on a shelf or just someone else's inkling about writing. This is why systematic research studies have a history of failing to change the ways of teachers and a special potential for changing those ways. Precise numbers and statistical procedures dazzle, yet discover connections the habituated eye cannot see. Inquiry methodology lies open to charges of invalidity and unreliability, yet attacks the non-logic of conventional response. A mechanical and inhuman ("faceless") system takes over human sight, yet gives it unsuspected insights on itself. Measurement disfigures the nature of intuition, yet reveals sham laws, undeceives the credulous, and persuades the incredulous. Partaking of that unsettling ambiguity of any act of breaking set, where force is needed to unseat force, idol to bring down idol, research is easy to fault, hard to interpret, risky to apply, liberating when it works.

Writing research may be in its infancy, pre-paradigmatic, currently with a deep-seated suspicion toward it among writing teachers (see Chapman), and with a life more useful for teachers in the future. But its essential iconoclasm already inheres, even in its most willful and ridiculed preoccupations, as in these textual inventories cluttering the back room of cohesion. A few teachers, with a distaste for ambiguity and a yearning for the idols of status quo, may never be changed by research, brought no matter how close to their faces. That is no reason to shield others from its revisionist light.

Works Cited

Bamberg, Betty. "What Makes a Text Coherent?" *College Composition and Communication* 34 (1983): 417–29.

Bereiter, Carl, and Marlene Scardamalia. "Levels of Inquiry in Writing Research." *Research on Writing: Principles and Methods.* Ed. Peter Mosenthal, Lynne Tamor, and Sean A. Walmsley. New York: Longman, 1983. 3–25.

Bostroff, Anita. "Coherence: 'Next to' Is Not 'Connected To.'" *College Composition and Communication* 32 (1981): 278–94.

Braddock, Richard. "The Frequency and Placement of Topic Sentences in Expository Prose." *Research in the Teaching of English* 8 (1974): 287–302.

Burton, Dwight L. "Research in the Teaching of English: The Troubled Dream." *Research in the Teaching of English* 7 (1973): 160–89.

Chapman, David W. "Conflict and Consensus: How Composition Scholars View their Discipline." *ADE Bulletin* 87 (1987): 1–3.

Christensen, Francis, and Bonniejean Christensen. *Notes Toward a New Rhetoric: 9 Essays for Teachers.* 2nd ed. New York: Harper & Row, 1978.

Connors, Robert. "Composition Studies and Science." *College English* 45 (1983): 1–20.

Cooper, Charles R., Roger Cherry, Barbara Copley, Stefan Fleischer, Rita Pollard, and Michael Sartisky. "Studying the Writing Abilities of a University Freshman Class: Strategies from a Case Study." *New Directions in Composition Research.* Ed. Richard Beach and Lillian S. Bridwell. New York: Guilford, 1984. 19–52.

Crowhurst, Marian. "Cohesion and Narration at Three Grade Levels." *Research in the Teaching of English* 21 (1987): 185–201.

Emig, Janet. "Inquiry Paradigms and Writing." *College Composition and Communication* 33 (1982): 64–75.

Fahnestock, Jeanne. "Semantic and Lexical Coherence." *College Composition and Communication* 34 (1983): 400–16.

Fitzgerald, Jill, and Dixie Lee Spiegel. "Textual Cohesion and Coherence in Children's Writing." *Research in the Teaching of English* 20 (1986): 263–80.

Graves, Donald H. "Research Update: A New Look at Writing Research." *Language Arts* 57 (1980): 914–17.

Hagen, Lyman B. "An Analysis of Transitional Devices in Student Writing." *Research in the Teaching of English* 5 (1971): 190–201.

Halliday, M. A. K., and Ruqaiya Hasan. *Cohesion in English*. London: Longman, 1976.

Haswell, Richard H. "Change in Undergraduate and Post-Graduate Writing Performance: Quantified Findings." ERIC: 1986. ED 269 780.

———. "Length of Text and the Measurement of Cohesion." *Research in the Teaching of English* 22 (1988): 428–33.

———. "The Organization of Impromptu Essays." *College Composition and Communication* 37 (1986): 402–15.

Hillocks, Jr., George. "Criticisms of Experimental Studies." *Research on Written Composition: New Directions for Teaching*. Urbana: NCTE, 1986. 95–98.

Hodges, John C., and Mary E. Whitten. *Harbrace College Handbook*. 9th ed. San Diego: Harcourt, 1982.

Holzman, Michael. "Scientism and Sentence-Combining." *College Composition and Communication* 34 (1983): 73–79.

Hopkins, Robert Morris. "Popular Scientific Discourse: A Rhetorical Model for Teaching Writing and Reading." Diss. U of Missouri, 1969.

Hunt, Kellogg W. *Grammatical Structures Written at Three Grade Levels*. Urbana: NCTE, 1965.

Kiefer, Kathleen, and Charles R. Smith. "Improving Student's Revising and Editing: The Writer's Workbench System." *The Computer in Composition Instruction: A Writer's Tool*. Ed. William Wresch. Urbana: NCTE, 1984. 65–82.

Lybbert, E. K., and D. W. Cummings. "On Repetition and Coherence." *College Composition and Communication* 20 (1969): 35.

Markels, Robin Bell. *A New Perspective on Cohesion in Expository Paragraphs*. Carbondale, IL: Southern Illinois UP, 1984.

Matsuhashi, Ann. "Pausing and Planning: The Tempo of Written Discourse Production." *Research in the Teaching of English* 15 (1981): 113–34.

McCulley, George A. "Writing Quality, Coherence, and Cohesion." *Research in the Teaching of English* 19 (1985): 269–82.

Meade, Richard A., and W. Geiger Ellis. "The Use of Writing of Textbook Methods of Paragraph Development." *Journal of Educational Research* 65 (1971): 74–76.

Myers, Miles. *The Teacher-Researcher: How to Study Writing in the Classroom*. Urbana: ERIC Clearinghouse on Reading and Communication Skills and NCTE, 1985.

Neuner, Jerome L. "Cohesive Ties and Chains in Good and Poor Freshman Essays." *Research in the Teaching of English* 21 (1987): 92–105.

North, Stephen M. "The Experimentalists." *The Making of Knowledge in Composition: Portrait of an Emerging Field*. Upper Montclair, NJ: Boynton/Cook, 1987. 141–96.

Odell, Lee, and Dixie Goswami. "Writing in a Non-Academic Setting." *Research in the Teaching of English* 16 (1982): 201–23.

Rentel, V. M., and M. L. King, B. Pettegrew, and C. Pappas. "A Longitudinal Study of Coherence in Children's Written Narratives." ERIC: 1982. ED 237 989.

Phelps, Louise Wetherbee. "Dialectics of Coherence: Toward an Integrative Theory." *College English* 47 (1985): 12–29.

Roberts, Paul. "Pronomial 'This': A Quantitative Analysis." *American Speech* 27 (1952): 171–78.

Sloan, Gary. "The Frequency of Transitional Markers in Discursive Prose." *College English* 46 (1984): 158–79.

Stotsky, Sandra. "On Learning to Write About Ideas." *College Composition and Communication* 37 (1986): 276–93.

———. "Types of Lexical Cohesion in Expository Writing: Implications for Developing the Vocabulary of Academic Discourse." *College Composition and Communication* 34 (1983): 430–40.

Warfel, Harry R. "Frequency of the Passive Voice." *College English* 15 (1953): 129.

Witte, Stephen P., and Lester Faigley. "Coherence, Cohesion, and Writing Quality." *College Composition and Communication* 32 (1981): 189–204.

Toward a Sociocognitive Model of Literacy: Constructing Mental Models in a Philosophical Conversation

Cheryl Geisler

Geisler's study appeared in Textual Dynamics of the Professions: Historical and Contemporary Studies of Writing in Professional Communities. *Eds. Charles Bazerman and James Paradis. Madison: U of Wisconsin P, 1991. 171–90.*

A writer writes. A reader reads. The effort to understand these apparently simple acts and the relationship between them has motivated numerous research agenda in recent years. Reading research, writing research, composition studies, rhetorical theory, anthropology, critical theory, sociolinguistics, cognitive science, literary studies—each of these terms invokes an affiliation, a national conference, and a set of epistemic beliefs that have all been pressed into the service of explaining these peculiarly human acts.

Against this backdrop, the goal of synthesizing a sociocognitive model of literacy has received increasing attention (Langer, "Musings . . ."). If achieved, such a model would allow researchers to consider human acts such as reading and writing along two dimensions that have often been seen at odds: the axis of individual cognition and the axis of social interaction. Although such a goal is clearly beyond the scope of any individual study, the results presented here move in that direction. In particular, they suggest that experts at advanced philosophical argument use acts of reading and writing to construct and act upon *socially configured mental models*. The presence of such mental models, I will argue, indicates that a purely conversational model of literacy may be missing the point of

why individuals propose and maintain written interaction in the first place.

DESIGN: READING AND WRITING ABOUT PHILOSOPHY

The study reported here examined the practices of four individuals asked to read and write about the ethical issue of paternalism. Two were disciplinary insiders: professional philosophers familiar with ethical philosophy, both men. Expert 1 had recently completed his Ph.D. and had accepted a position at a prestigious university. Expert 2 was still working on his degree. Two were disciplinary outsiders: second-semester freshmen at a private university who had not yet taken an introductory freshman philosophy course, both women. Novice 1 was an engineering student who had received an A in her humanities course the previous semester. Novice 2 was a design student who had received a B in her writing course the previous semester.[1]

All four participants were asked to complete the same reading/writing task: they were asked to read eight articles on the ethical issue of paternalism and to write an original essay defining paternalistic interference and describing the conditions, if any, under which it could be justified. They were told that the intended readers were to be "well-educated people who may at some time in their lives have to deal with the issue of paternalism." The philosophers were solicited through contacts with the philosophic community and worked on the project as consultants. The freshmen were solicited through advertising on campus and completed the work as regular student employment.

Paternalistic interference is an issue for ethical philosophers because it appears to violate widespread assumptions about individual rights and yet occasionally to be justified. John Stuart Mill claimed that the individual had exclusive rights to make decisions regarding his or her own welfare. This "harm principle" has become the starting point for many ethicists' discussions on the nature of rights. Paternalism is a problem in these discussions because it involves the interference by one person in the affairs of another for his or her own good; it thus appears to violate the harm principle. Nevertheless few would argue that it cannot be justified in some cases: parents' paternalism toward children; teachers' paternalism toward students; government paternalism toward the mentally incompetent. In an effort to define the boundaries between justified and unjustified action, ethical philosophers have offered conflicting definitions of paternalistic interference and conflicting specifications of the conditions under which it can be justified.

The two expert philosophers described here were both familiar with Mill's harm principle and with the general discussion of individual rights. Neither, however, was familiar with the issue of paternalism or the particular literature they were given at the start of the project. The two novice freshmen were unfamiliar with the technical issues of ethics, but both readily recognized that they had been subject to the paternalism of parents and school.

All participants worked on the task at their own rate for between 30 and 60 hours spread over 10 to 15 weeks during the spring of 1985. Data were collected during this time in three ways: First, participants were asked to verbalize their thoughts into a tape recorder whenever they worked on the project, producing "think-aloud" protocols (Newell and Simon; Ericsson and Simon). Second, participants were asked to keep all of the writing they produced. And third, participants were interviewed between working sessions concerning what they had accomplished and what they were hoping to accomplish on the task. The resulting transcripts and texts amounted to over 750,000 words.

FRAMEWORK FOR ANALYSIS: A HYBRID MODEL OF LITERACY

The departure point for the data analysis was a hybrid sociocognitive model of literacy combining aspects of Scribner and Cole's model of literacy practice and Heritage's model of conversational turn-taking. These two models take complementary sociocognitive perspectives on human action. By combining them, we achieve a hybrid model of some theoretical power.

Along the cognitive axis of the hybrid model, we locate the cognitive components suggested by Scribner and Cole's model of literacy practice. Scribner and Cole proposed this model to account for their observations of the Vai, a West African tribe with literacy in three different scripts. Their research indicated that individuals literate in each of these scripts showed different patterns of cognition. The model they put forward emphasized the effects of social context on the three cognitive components examined in this study: activities, knowledge representations, and goals.[2]

While the first and last of these cognitive components are familiar to researchers on reading and writing, the middle component of knowledge representation merits some introduction. Researchers in cognitive science now generally believe that knowledge representations in the form of mental models play a central role in defining expertise (Glaser; Johnson-Laird). A mental model is an abstraction from everyday, often spatial or visual, perception that allows people to think about a situation without the clutter of unnecessary details or the cumbersome (and sometimes impossible) requirement of actually manipulating physical objects. An example of a mental model that nearly everyone uses are the "mental maps" with which we plan shopping trips and give visitors directions.

Researchers investigating particular domains of expertise have found that individuals who are good at something—baseball (Chiesi, Spilich, and Voss), radiology (Lesgold), chess (Chase and Simon), social science (Voss, Greene, Post, and Penner), physics (Larkin), geometry (Anderson, Greeno, Kline, and Neves)—make use of mental models that are even more abstracted from everyday experience than mental maps. Where most of us would see blurs and blobs in an X-ray, for example, a student of radiology sees isolated organs, muscles, and bones; a skilled radiologist sees even more abstract "systems."

As of yet, we have little understanding of the special mental models that may be used by those expert at advanced literacy practices in academic fields such as philosophy. Some suggestive remarks have been made, however, by researchers centered at the Ontario Institute for Studies in Education (OISE). In a much-cited article on the relationship between speech and writing, Olson has claimed that literacy depends on decontextualized features of language. In speaking, he argues, we attend to the intentions of the speaker, to what is meant; in writing, on the other hand, our attention must shift to the meaning of the language itself, to what is actually said. In a similar vein, Bereiter and Scardamalia have argued that learning to write means learning to move away from dependence on conversational input from an interlocutor. Although these claims have implications for the kinds of knowledge representations that experts in fields such as philosophy might be expected to construct, these implications have not yet been investigated.

Along the second, social axis of literacy, the hybrid model locates the turn-taking sequence described by conversation analyst John Heritage (*Garfinkel and Ethnomethodology*). According to Heritage, conversational participants build, maintain, and shift contexts through the mechanism of three-turn sequences. In the first turn, a speaker proposes a given context by using the first part of an adjacency pair such as a greeting, question, or invitation. In the next turn, a second speaker responds with one of the following: the preferred response (an acknowledgement, acceptance, or answer); a dispreferred response plus some account for it ("Oh, that would be nice, but I've already made plans"); a completely unexpected response (staring the first speaker in the eye and not returning the greeting). Finally, in an optional third turn, the first speaker can repair any contextual misunderstandings indicated by the second speaker's response.

Applied to the uses of reading and writing in philosophy, this conversational sequence suggests a mechanism by which social context can be created and sustained through written language. A written text can be seen as one philosopher's proposal. The writing of a new text can be seen as the other philosopher's response. Through a series of such written interactions, the context of a philosophical conversation can be built, maintained, or shifted. Applied in this way, Heritage's conversational model refines the many suggestions that have been made concerning the conversational nature of literacy (Bartholomae; Bazerman, "A Relationship between Reading and Writing"; Bizzell; Bruffee; Latour and Woolgar; McCloskey).

The analysis in this study used the hybrid model of literacy in a two-stage procedure. At the first level, the text, protocol, and interview data were analyzed to provide information concerning the three cognitive components suggested by Scribner and Cole. Here my questions concerned the way the *readers*, reading texts that represent previous conversational turns, became *writers*, taking a turn of their own. What activities did they engage in? What knowledge representations did they construct and manipulate? What goals did they have?

At the second level of analysis, the descriptive data were examined for evidence of the ways in which the individuals made use of their reflexive awareness of the social dimension. If we assume that written interactions can be appropriately described as conversational, we can then ask how the philosophers' cognitions exhibited characteristics that are peculiarly conversational. The

	Materials Consulted	Materials Produced	Sequencing Principle
READING	articles	notes	order of words in articles
REFLECTING	articles notes	notes	on-the-fly
ORGANIZING	notes	linear order of topics	on-the-fly
DRAFTING	notes articles outline	continuous draft intended for product	outline
REVISING	draft	annotations to draft	order of words in draft

Figure 7.1 Definitions of Categories Used to Segment the Activities of Each Participant

undeveloped state of sociocognitive theory prevents us from being definitive about what would constitute an answer to this question; nevertheless, the implications seem to be at variance with the OISE position. As we have already noted, Olson seems to argue that advanced literacy involves *moving away* from conversation. The sociocognitive model we have constructed following Heritage leads us to expect some movement *toward* it. Untangling these expectations was one of the major goals for this second level of analysis.

The design of this study as a comparison of expert and novice cognitions plays a crucial role in working toward answers to questions at both levels of analysis. Using the hybrid model, we can view expert/novice studies as comparisons of organizations along the cognitive axis at what we assume are qualitatively different places along the social axes. That is, we assume the experts are effective participants in the conversation of the disciplines of philosophy whereas the novices are not. We can use the data from novices, then, to highlight the significant cognitive characteristics that accompany effective conversational participation. In this way, the novice practices serve a heuristic function in helping us to pick out significant features of expert practice.[3]

FIRST-LEVEL RESULTS: DESCRIPTIONS OF LITERACY PRACTICE

Activities

We begin our description of the cognitive literacy practices of the four participants with an examination of their activity structures. To determine how the participants sequenced their activities, I coded the think-aloud protocols using a set of categories developed inductively from the data. These five-categories—reading, reflecting, organizing, drafting, and revising—were defined as particular constellations of (a) the materials consulted, (b) the materials produced, and (c) the sequencing principle guiding attention. Specific definitions are given in figure 7.1.

Once the protocols were coded, I examined the way participants distributed these activities over 100 percent of their working time. The results of this analysis indicate that all four participants used the same activity structure to complete the task. All began by reading, followed with a period of reflecting, moved to organizing, and then finally to drafting interspersed with revising. The only major departure from this sequence occurred with

Novice 1 who divided her working time into two halves, the first concerned with the definition of paternalism and the second with its justification. Within each half, however, the sequencing from reading to drafting/revising occurred, albeit in a more abbreviated form the second time round.[4]

Knowledge Representations

The knowledge representations used by the participants were examined using a construct developed from the interview data, the construct of authorship. Like many professionals, we began this study with the assumption that authorship was an important attribute of the texts on paternalism. We had even taken care to choose articles by authors who cross-referenced each other. The interview data caused us to reexamine this assumption. In particular, the two novices did not talk about the articles as having authors. In fact, one of them regularly referred to the collection of articles as "the book" and, on occasion, described herself as checking what "the book said" about an issue. On the other hand, the experts both regularly spoke in terms of the authors they were reading.

To analyze participants' use of the construct of authorship, I examined the protocol data for the presence of *author mentions*, which were defined to include:

- names of specific authors (e.g., "Childress")

- nominals standing for an aggregate of authors (e.g., "these guys");

- nominals standing for roles of authors (e.g., "a moral philosopher");

- pronouns standing in for any of the above ("she"; "they").

The results of this examination showed that the novices attended to authorship an average of 3.5 times in each 1000 words of think-aloud protocol. The experts, on the other hand, attended to authorship at least twice as often in the case of Expert 1 and almost four times as often in the case of Expert 2.

Final Texts

To examine what participants saw as the desired goal of their task, I analyzed the final texts they produced using a modified version of Langer's system for the analysis of structure (*Children Reading and Writing;* see Appendix). The product of this analysis is a complex tree diagram in which each T-unit of a text forms a node that can either be subordinated or coordinated to other nodes in the tree.[5] In addition to this structural analysis, a cross-check was made of the texts for the presence of author mentions.

On a global level, several generalizations can be made concerning the differences between the expert and novice texts. To begin with, experts' texts are longer (1280, 1680, 2930, and 6010 words[6]). In addition, they show an advantage in both the number of T-units (70, 93, 121, and 271) and the average length of the T-units (18, 18, 24, and 22 words/T-unit). Finally, they show greater subordination (11, 11, 19, and 16 levels) and contain a greater number of author mentions (0, 12, 44, and 74 author mentions).

A review of the individual texts makes clear the source of these global differences. The expert texts follow a similar pattern. Major sections present the terms of definition and justification given by the task. Subordinate to them, secondary units present cases of paternalism and approaches to these cases. Further, in both expert texts, author mentions are almost exclusively associated with the secondary units presenting approaches. That is, both experts used authorship attribution to define what we call an "approach" which, in turn, is the major structure of their final texts.

In addition, the experts organized their presentation of approaches similarly. Each began with an approach he considered faulty. Then, through a critique, he eliminated that approach. The order in which the approaches were characterized and eliminated was determined by how faulty the approach was. Very wrong approaches were dealt with early; more complex and harder to refute approaches were dealt with later. Then, after all the elimination was done, the resulting approach, the main path taken

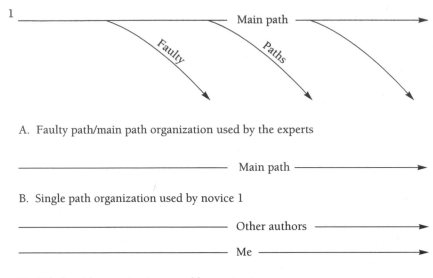

A. Faulty path/main path organization used by the experts

B. Single path organization used by novice 1

C. Side-by-side organizations used by novice 2

Figure 7.2. Organizing Structures in Participant's Texts

by the expert himself, was left as the only remaining alternative. This organization can be visualized in terms of a set of faulty and main paths through an issue as shown in diagram A of figure 7.2.[7]

Units 5 through 8 of Expert 2's text can serve as an example of this faulty path/main path organization. Unit 5, dealing with the approach taken by Dworkin, is a typical faulty path, containing both a characterization of Dworkin's approach (52–53) and a critique that eliminates that approach (54–60):

(52) The prominence of such examples as these in the discussion of the moral status of paternalism suggests to Dworkin (source one above) the following "rough" definition of paternalism (pg. 7):

(53) D1: "Paternalism is the interference with a person's liberty of action justified by reasons referring exclusively to the welfare, good, happiness, needs, interests, or values of the person being coerced."

(54) The definition D1 is faulty in several respects, and is not made any better by Dworkin's admission that it is "rough." (55) First, as it stands, if the definition is right, there can be no unjustified (i.e. wrong) paternalistic action for D1 says paternalism is justified. (56) Doubtless this is part of the "roughness." (57) Perhaps what Dworkin intends is something more like the following:

(58) D1: "Paternalism is interference with a person's liberty of action of such a sort that if justified at all it is justified exclusively by its positive bearing on the welfare, good, happiness, needs, interests or values of the person's being coerced."

(59) But this will still not work, as can be seen from Example 3 above. (60) In the case of the drug laws, potential buyers who can't buy because the product is not on the market are not coerced at all though they are the ones whose benefit is intended.

The units following this one deal similarly with the approaches taken by Buchannon and Carter, by Gert and Culver, and by Childress. The ordering is keyed to how faulty Expert 2 considered the approach. With Dworkin, whom he dealt with first, the approach is highly flawed and the critique is intended to be devastating. With Childress, whose approach he dealt with last, the approach is plausible and his critique is more pro forma:

(94) I will have more to say of this shortly. (95) For now it is enough to point out that plausible definitions satisfying this requirement are in the field. Here, for instance, is Childress' definition (pg. 17, source 3):

> (97) D5: "Paternalism is nonacquiescence in a person's wishes, choices and actions for that person's own benefit."

(98) The definition is not without flaw ([99] surely he means "or" and not "and," [100] and "nonacquiescence" is even fuzzier than "paternalism") (101) but it illustrates the point.

Although the novices used similar terms of definition and justification to structure the major units of their texts, their secondary units point to significant differences. In her secondary units, Novice 1 used a typological organization. In the first major section she enumerated the factors important to defining paternalism (7 units); in the second, she enumerated the conditions for justification (7 units). Although her protocols suggest she was aware of disagreements between authors, her final text neither includes specific authors' names nor indicates any difference in approach among them. Thus, in contrast to the faulty path/main path structure used by the experts, her text seems to represent the issue of paternalism as a single main path with everybody on it (see diagram B in figure 7.2).

Novice 2 organized the secondary units of her text with greater awareness of disagreements. Unlike Novice 1, she had an abiding and continuing personal disagreement with all of the authors she read. From her protocols and interviews, we know that she had seen her own family disregard her grandfather's wishes not to be placed on a respirator and she was convinced that this had been wrong. Thus, based on a family experience, she was fundamentally opposed to paternalistic interference. In her text, she was careful to state her position by giving her own definition of paternalism and her own approach to justification.

What is interesting to note, however, is that her claims stand in ambiguous relationships to the claims of the authors she is opposing. She does not, for example, make clear how her own definition of paternalism relates to other definitions she reviews earlier. Is it in agreement? Is it in disagreement? Is it a qualified agreement? She is not clear.

Further, even when she is more careful to specify that her claim about justification is in disagreement, she still fails to articulate the grounds for her differences. Instead, she simply characterizes the opinion of others and then gives her own as a contrast:

(68) If we accept the following descriptions of Rosemary Carter, Bill is considered incompetent. (69) There is a group of people who we as a society label as being incompetent, therefore justifying paternalistic acts toward them. (70) These people are described and labelled as the following: those who are unable to understand or practice satisfactorily the basic requirements of survival, and so whose lives would be at worst in constant peril, and at best grossly unhappy, if not for the intervention of others. (71) Those suffering from mental retardation, below a certain level, and those suffering from certain kinds of insanity are included in this class.

(72) Rosemary Carter's description of competence as a means for justification also speaks for both James Childress and Gerald Dworkin, with the following exceptions: . . .

(77) Altogether, these people tend to describe the same conditions for justification, but in a different manner with different examples. (78) While these conditions for justification are accepted by some of today's society, I feel that paternalism can be justified under only one condition, that of prior consent. (79) The conditions of mental retardation, and insanity do not give justification for paternalistic actions. (80) These persons should have the right to incorporate their views and feelings into medical decisions. (81) After all these people do have the ability to communicate to certain extents. (82) Why should the views of these people be carelessly disposed of.

Structurally, what is lacking here is the critique used so extensively by both experts. Instead of an argument structure that eliminates other authors' approaches on the way to validating her own, Novice 2 simply presents the two approaches side by side, and distinguishes between them on the basis, not of truth, but of authorship: Here is what others believe: here is what I believe (figure 7.2, diagram C).

Summary

Before proceeding to the results of the second-level analysis, we can summarize the first-level descriptions as follows:

1. The literacy practices of the two experts in this study appear to be aimed at producing positions on the issue of paternalism by characterizing and critiquing approaches taken by other authors. To achieve this goal, both experts read, reflected on what they read, organized their thoughts, and wrote and revised a draft. Throughout their working time, they attended to the authorship of claims and, in their final texts, they used authorship as the defining attribute of the approaches they characterized and critiqued.

2. Like the experts, the two novices in this study appeared to use literacy practices to create positions on the issue of paternalism. To do so, they read the articles, reflected on what they had read, organized their thoughts, and wrote and revised a draft.

3. Unlike the experts, however, the novices did not seem to represent their knowledge as a series of approaches distinguished by authorship. What they did instead, however, varied.

4. Novice 1 developed a knowledge representation consisting of positions on each of a number of subissues. We know from the protocols that the majority of her reflecting time was spent identifying these subissues and figuring out her position on them. Her final text presents these positions, but it does not explicitly identify them as her own. Nor

does it distinguish her positions from positions taken by other authors. Consonant with her goal, she did not attend to the authorship of claims with anywhere near the frequency of either of the experts.

5. Perhaps driven by her personal experience, Novice 2, on the other hand, developed a knowledge representation in which authorship played some role. Her final text carefully distinguishes between her own position and the position taken by the authors she disagreed with. This structure remains different from that employed by the experts, however, because it does not indicate the relationship between the position she takes and the position she's opposing. Indeed, during most of her reflecting time, Novice 2 tried to construct her own position with little attention given to the positions of the authors she had read. Thus, despite the presence of some author mentions in her final text, she did not attend to authorship in her working time at any greater rate than did Novice 1.

SECOND-LEVEL RESULTS: SOCIALLY CONFIGURED MENTAL MODELS

Turning to the second-level analysis, we can now ask how the expert cognitions described above were shaped by their participation in a philosophical conversation. Although the descriptive data of this study cannot support a definitive answer to this important question, they do suggest a possible hypothesis for future research. Specifically, I will argue that the expert cognitions seemed to involve the construction and manipulation of socially configured mental models—knowledge representations shaped by attributes of the social axis, but which depart in systematic ways from standard conversation.[8]

To begin the case for socially configured mental models, we return to evidence from the knowledge representation data. There we found that, indeed, experts' practices were configured by at least one attribute of the social axis: the authorship of claims. Further, insofar as attention to authorship indicates

	Conversational Practice	Literacy Practice
Turn 1:	Proposes context	Writes
Turn 2:		Reads Reflects Organizes
	Responds	Drafts/revises
Turn 3:	Repairs misunderstandings	

Figure 7.3 Comparison of the Activity Structures of Conversational Practice and Literacy Practice

an awareness of other interlocutors, these practices appear to be somewhat conversational. Here we have evidence, then, that advanced literary practices in philosophy *are* configured by social context, just as the model of written conversation would suggest.

Other evidence warns us, however, against assuming these practices are isomorphic with those of standard conversation. The first evidence comes from the data on activity structure. As shown in figure 7.3, the participants in this study structured their activities in four-part sequences of reading, reflecting, organizing, and drafting/revising. Standard conversation, by contrast, is structured as two-part interchanges with an optional third turn for repairs. Assuming that reading is the equivalent of the first speaker's conversational turn and drafting/revising is the equivalent of the second speaker's response, we see that these participants' literacy practices involved two activities that are not found in standard conversation: reflecting and organizing. Their literacy practices, then, appear to have opened up a reflective space for cognition that simply would be unavailable to oral interlocutors.

The kind of mental work that the experts may have been accomplishing in this additional reflective space is further suggested by the final texts they produced. In several respects, these texts reflect mental models of written interaction that are not isomorphic with those of standard conversation. To begin with, they are made

up of "approaches" that are only indirectly related to other authors' actual claims. For example, Expert 1 did not assume a one-to-one isomorphism between the set of claims made by Dworkin and the approaches he discussed in his own argument. Instead, once he had characterized and dismissed the definition Dworkin actually gave, he went on to consider what Dworkin might have meant:

> Perhaps what Dworkin intends is something more like the following: . . . (59) But this will still not work. . . .

If Expert 1's goal were simply to respond to previous interlocutors, then discussing what Dworkin might have said makes little sense. But if his intention were to construct a mental model made up of a wide range of approaches, then this abstraction is a sensible inventional strategy.

The abstract nature of the experts' mental models is also suggested by the way they organized their texts. As noted earlier, both experts arranged their discussions of approaches in descending order of faultiness: more faulty approaches were discussed first; less faulty approaches discussed later. This written practice differs from standard conversation in two ways. First, conversational interlocutors rarely take on the burden of creating a spontaneous single response to multiple previous speakers' first turns. Instead, they respond to claims locally as they arise, one at a time. Second, on those few occasions when they do address multiple prior claims, the linear ordering is ad hoc—indeed, if meaningful, we assume that it arises from cognitions outside of the current conversation ("I see you've been giving this some thought"). Thus, the experts' mental models appear to be consolidated and linearized in ways that are unpredicted and almost inconceivable accomplishments within the constraints of standard face-to-face interaction.

The final evidence concerning the abstract nature of the experts' mental models concerns the conventions by which they treat previous authors. Basically, the authors in these written interactions were treated differently than interlocutors in standard conversations: personal attributes and social affiliations are off-limits; actual intentions are irrelevant.[9] For example, Expert 1 did not argue against Dworkin's approach on the grounds that he was a "Reaganite conservative"—even though his protocol shows that he thought so. Nor did Expert 2, when attributing an approach to Buchannon and Carter, consider whether these two authors liked each other or, indeed, whether they had ever met. These personal considerations, important in everyday conversation, were inappropriate according to the conventions of written interaction these experts followed.

Furthermore, authors' rights to the third-turn repairs, so common in standard conversation, were restricted in these written interactions. As mentioned earlier, Heritage suggests that third-turn repairs are always an option for first-turn speakers who feel they have been misinterpreted. Thus, in oral conversations, we routinely expect to be able to say, "No, that is not what I meant to say. What I really meant was . . . ." Authors, however, are not routinely extended this right. Thus, for example, Dworkin could not reply to Expert 1's critique by saying that he didn't *really* mean what he wrote. Miswritings, unlike misspeakings, are not good grounds for repairing intersubjective knowledge. Of course, authors have many other ways they can repudiate misinterpretations of their work or repudiate previous positions, but, as Olson points out, these rely on conventions for what words mean rather than on independent evidence of what the

author actually intended. In fact, these conventions of interpretation are so widely available that third-turn repairs may be made by someone other than the original author—a freedom less often assumed by third parties in oral interactions.

Taken together, this evidence suggests that our philosophers were creating special mental models that, like those used in so many other domains, departed in characteristic ways from everyday practice—in this case, the practice of standard conversation. Although they were configured by some of the attributes of everyday conversation and might even be taken as identical by those less than expert, the mental models of advanced literacy in philosophy appear to be different. By expanding their activity structure, abstracting approaches, consolidating and linearizing their responses, and accepting restrictions on their right of repair, the philosophers in these literacy interactions were able to produce knowledge beyond that which is ordinarily possible in everyday conversation.

CONCLUDING REMARKS: TOWARD A SOCIOCOGNITIVE MODEL

Thus far, I have argued that the expertise of advanced literacy practices exhibited by the philosophers studied here can best be characterized as the construction and manipulation of special socially configured mental models. In closing, I would now like to consider some of the implications this claim has for a sociocognitive model of literacy.

According to the hybrid model with which this study began, social and cognitive practices are arrayed along two intersecting dimensions of human action. As it now stands, this two-dimensional model cannot account for mental representations that depart from standard conversational practice: The individual cognitions suggested by Scribner and Cole were assumed to be directly embedded in the social practices of everyday conversation outlined by Heritage. To accommodate the existence of abstract mental constructs, we must amend this model in at least one of two ways.

First, we might say that advanced literacy practices are embedded in *different* social contexts than those of standard conversation. That is, we might assume that those who make use of advanced reading and writing propose and maintain specialized contexts for their interpretation. Learning to read and write, then, would mean learning to function in these specialized contexts, learning the rules of new discourse communities such as the community of philosophers.

Some precedents already exist for arguing that departures from standard conversation define specialized contexts. In schools, for example, teachers ask questions for which they already have the answers; thus they reserve for themselves the unusual right to bring a turn-taking sequence to a close or extend it until the correct answer is reached (Mehan). In news interviews and interrogations, questioners systematically withhold acknowledgements of the truth or newsworthiness of respondents' answers; they thus simultaneously maintain the required institutional indifference and acknowledge the role of the overhearing audience (Heritage, "Analyzing News Interviews"). Whenever such unusual practices are invoked, according to Heritage *(Garfinkel and Ethnomethodology),* participants know they are operating in specialized contexts.

The trouble with amending our model to allow for alternative social contexts is that the novices in this study showed less, not more, evidence of being in everyday conversation. If learning to read and write in philosophy required moving toward more specialized contexts, then we would expect novices to show greater, not fewer, signs of conversational practice. In this study, however, we saw evidence of the reverse: it was the novices, not the experts, who were operating in a world without interlocutors.

A second way of amending the hybrid model of literacy is suggested by my use of the concept of "mental models." Mental models in all domains characteristically exhibit a specific duality of reference: they *both* move away from everyday practice and remain rooted there. In radiology, for example, mental models of the body both surpass what we can do with ordinary understanding and have implications for everyday treatment. In effect, they create a new plane of understanding by projecting

and abstracting from everyday entities while, at the same time, remaining connected to those entities. Indeed, it is this ability to go beyond mundane reasoning while speaking to it which justifies the social expense of developing expertise.

In professions like philosophy, we see a similar duality: written interactions are both rooted in the everyday practices of conversation and go beyond them. In this study, for example, both philosophers felt impelled to discuss their ideas with colleagues as well as work on them in the privacy of their office. Like most academics and researchers, they accompany their writing with conversation—in the hallways, on the phone, and at conferences. Mental models like those described above may be the mechanism by which they are able to overlay abstract cognitions on everyday conversational practices.

We can amend our hybrid model, then, by projecting outward from the social and cognitive axes to hypothesize a new kind of practice that both extends and refers back to standard conversational practices. The suggestion is that by opening up the activity structure of oral conversation, literacy in philosophy provides experts with the reflective space necessary to construct socially configured mental models. These mental models create, in effect, a new plane of intersubjective knowledge, a third dimension of culturally shared abstractions. Such a three-dimensional model of literacy would help us explain not only how ways of thinking inconceivable in oral conversation are interwoven with and supported by distinctive social practices, but also why—throughout history—people have considered reading and writing to be their link with a more timeless wisdom of the ages.

Appendix: Analysis of Structure

The analysis of text structure was carried out in four phases. In the first phase, texts were divided into T-units.

In the second phase, this list of T-units was divided into rhetorical units linked by: (a) explicit connecting phrases such as conjunctions, comparatives, demonstratives, enumeratives, and various linking phrases; (b) anaphoric links or any transition from the indefinite to the definite article; (c) intended parallel structures; (d) some connecting punctuation; and (e) narrative schemata.

In the third phase, the structure of each rhetorical unit was diagrammed as a series of subordinations and coordinations in which each T-unit was attached to one of the rightmost nodes of the developing tree. T-units were coordinated if they served the same function, were in some standard relationship to one another, concerned the same superordinate T-unit, or elaborated upon a multi-T-unit entity rather than a single T-unit. They were subordinated if one was an elaboration of the other.

In the fourth phase, rhetorical units were joined together into an integrated tree.

Notes

Research presented here was supported by a grant from the Fund for the Improvement of Post-Secondary Education to the author and David S. Kaufer, Christine Neuwirth, and Preston Covey at Carnegie Mellon University. Some of the material in this paper was originally presented at the 1987 annual convention of the American Educational Research Association in Washington, D.C., and has further benefitted from discussions with S. Michael Halloran, Nancy Nelson Spivey, Charles Bazerman, Sister Barbara Sitko, and Mark Stein.

1. Gender and expertise were inextricably mixed in these case studies. Both experts were men; both novices were women. Although we will focus on expertise rather than gender in our interpretations, it is important to realize that academic expertise may be more comfortable to men than to women. Belenky, Clinchy, Goldberger, and Tarule, for instance, have suggested that women may prefer a style of "connected knowing" that prizes identification rather than the distance of "separate knowing" commonly prized in philosophical argument.

2. The fourth component, technology, actually combines cognitive and social concerns and was not included in the initial hybrid model.

3. The status of the novice data, considered independently of the experts, is beyond the scope of this article. See, however, North for one treatment.

4. A comparison of the percentage of working time given by the participants to each of the five activities indicates the following: All four participants gave the greatest percentage of their time to reading (37% average) through the articles on paternalism. All gave the smallest percentage of time to organizing topics into a linear structure (5% average). The participants varied in the percentage of time given to revising and reflecting. Novice 2 and Expert 1 revised extensively; Novice 1 and Expert 2 revised for proportionately less time. Novice 1, Novice 2, and Expert 1 spent about the same percentage of time reflecting; Expert 2 spent proportionately more time.

Interesting differences between the experts and novices occurred with respect to drafting. Even though all participants spent about the same percentage of their time in reading and organizing, both philosophers took a smaller percentage of their time to draft (29% and 32% for the novices vs. 17% and 13% for the experts). Since both experts completed the task in less time than both novices, the difference in the actual time spent drafting was even greater. The experts also delayed drafting longer than the novices. The two novices began drafting about 35% of the way through their work. The two experts, by contrast, began drafting at 61% and 76% of the way through their work.

5. Reliability checks on sample texts revealed 100% agreement among six raters (who apply a coding scheme to data) on T-unit segmentation, 89% agreement between two raters on the location of a T-unit attachment, and 87% agreement between two raters on the type of attachment.

6. Statistics are ordered: Novice 1, Novice 2, Expert 1, Expert 2.

7. An example of what is involved in teaching students to construct the faulty path/main path organization is found in Kaufer, Geisler, and Neuwirth.

8. The argument made here extends an observation by Bazerman ("Physicists Reading Physics") on the existence of special-purpose reading schemata among professional physicists.

9. The difference between authors and everyday people has also been commented on by Foucault (121–22).

Works Cited

Anderson, John R., J. G. Greeno, P. J. Kline, and D. M. Neves. "Acquisition of Problem Solving Skills." In *Cognitive Skills and Their Acquisition,* ed. J. R. Anderson, 191–230. Hillsdale, N.J.: Erlbaum, 1981.

Bartholomae, David. "Inventing the University." In *When a Writer Can't Write: Studies in Writer's Block and Other Com-*

posing Process Problems, ed. Mike Rose, 134–65. New York: Guilford Press, 1985.

Bazerman, Charles. "Physicists Reading Physics: Schema-Laden Purposes and Purpose-Laden Schema." *Written Communication* 2 (January 1985): 3–23.

Bazerman, Charles. "A Relationship between Reading and Writing: The Conversational Model." *College English* 41 (February 1980): 656–61.

Belenky, Mary Field, Blythe McVicker Clinchy, Nancy Rule Goldberger, and Jill Mattuck Tarule. *Women's Ways of Knowing: The Development of Self, Voice, and Mind.* New York: Basic Books, 1986.

Bereiter, Carl, and Marlene Scardamalia. "From Conversation to Composition: The Role of Instruction in Developmental Processes." In *Advances in Instructional Psychology, Vol. 2,* ed. R. Glaser, 1–64. Hillsdale, N.J.: Erlbaum, 1982.

Bizzell, Patricia. "College Composition: Initiation into the Academic Discourse Community." *Curriculum Inquiry* 12 (1982): 191–207.

Bruffee, Kenneth A. "Collaborative Learning and the 'Conversation of Mankind.'" *College English* 46 (November 1984): 635–52.

Chase, William G., and Herbert A. Simon. "The Mind's Eye in Chess." In *Visual Information Processing,* ed. W. G. Chase, 215–81. New York: Academic Press, 1973.

Chiesi, H. L., G. J. Spilich, and J. F. Voss. "Acquisition of Domain Related Knowledge in Relation to High and Low Domain Knowledge." *Journal of Verbal Learning and Verbal Behavior* 18 (1979): 257–74.

Ericsson, K. Anders, and Herbert A. Simon. *Protocol Analysis.* Cambridge: MIT Press, 1984.

Foucault, Michel. "What Is an Author?" *Language, Countermemory and Practice.* Ed. Donald Bouchard. Trans. Donald Bouchard and Sherry Simon. Ithaca: Cornell University Press, 1977.

Glaser, Robert. "Education and Thinking: The Role of Knowledge." *American Psychologist* 39 (1984): 93–104.

Heritage, John. "Analyzing News Interviews: Aspects of the Production of Talk for an Overhearing Audience." In *Handbook of Discourse Analysis, Vol. 3: Genres of Discourse,* ed. T. A. van Dijk, 95–117. New York: Academic Press, 1984.

Heritage, John. *Garfinkel and Ethnomethodology.* Cambridge: Polity Press, 1984.

Johnson-Laird, P. N. "Mental Models in Cognitive Science." *Cognitive Science* 4 (1980): 71–115.

Kaufer, David, Cheryl Geisler, and Christine Neuwirth. *Arguing from Sources: Exploring Issues through Reading and Writing.* San Diego, Calif.: Harcourt Brace Jovanovich, 1989.

Langer, Judith A. *Children Reading and Writing: Structures and Strategies.* Norwood, N.J.: Ablex Press, 1986.

Langer, Judith A. "Musings . . . A Sociocognitive View of Language Learning." *Research in the Teaching of English* 19 (1985): 325–27.

Larkin, Jill. "Understanding, Problem Representations, and Skill in Physics." In *Thinking and Learning Skills, Vol. 2: Research and Open Questions,* ed. S. F. Chipman, J. Segal, and R. Glaser, 141–59. Hillsdale, N.J.: Erlbaum, 1985.

Latour, Bruno, and Steve Woolgar. *Laboratory Life: The Social Construction of Scientific Facts.* Beverly Hills: Sage, 1979.

Lesgold, Alan. "Human Skill in a Computerized Society: Complex Skills and Their Acquisition." *Behavior Research Methods, Instruments, and Computers* 10 (1984): 79–87.

McCloskey, Donald N. *The Rhetoric of Economics.* Madison: University of Wisconsin Press, 1985.

Mehan, Hugh. *Learning Lessons: Social Organization in the Classroom.* Cambridge: Harvard University Press, 1979.

Newell, Allen, and Herbert A. Simon. *Human Problem Solving.* Englewood Cliffs, N.J.: Prentice Hall, 1972.

North, Stephen M. "Writing in Philosophy Class: Three Case Studies." *Research in the Teaching of English* 20 (1986): 225–62.

Olson, David. "From Utterance to Text: The Bias of Language in Speech and Writing." *Harvard Educational Review* 47 (1977): 257–81.

Scribner, Sylvia, and Michael Cole. *The Psychology of Literacy.* Cambridge: Harvard University Press, 1981.

Voss, J. F., T. R. Greene, T. A. Post, and B. C. Penner. "Problem Solving Skill in the Social Sciences." In *The Psychology of Learning and Motivation: Advances in Research Theory, Vol. 17,* ed. G. H. Bower, 165–213. New York: Academic Press, 1983.

Ethnography and Composition:
Studying Language at Home

Beverly J. Moss

This essay is from Methods and Methodology in Composition Research. *Eds. Gesa Kirsch and Patricia A. Sullivan. Carbondale: Southern Illinois UP, 1992. 153–71.*

When, as a graduate student, I was faced with the task of choosing an area of research and—more specifically—a research question that would lead to a dissertation, I was, to say the least, a little intimidated. I realized that much of the research I had read seemed to have no real connection to me and where I came from, that a large gap existed between the people I knew and the people being described in that research. Much research in composition studies focused on novice and expert writers and on how one group (usually people from backgrounds similar to mine) didn't measure up to another group (expert writers, usually white, middle-class students). I knew then that I needed my scholarly life to have some real connection to my personal life, that I needed a bridge between what I saw as a rather large gap between academic research and real problems that affected the people where I came from.

So where did that discovery get me? It got me interested in the work of Shirley Brice Heath. In a very concrete way, Heath's work on communities in the Piedmont Carolinas touched me. As I read *Ways with Words*, I realized that I was reading about people and communities I knew. I was born and raised in the Piedmont Carolinas, and most of my relatives still live in that area. Heath's work validated my desire to do research that connected with me, and I became more and more interested in examining language use outside the classroom because I

was convinced, as were Heath and others, that finding out what students did outside class was the key to helping them succeed in school.

Next, I needed a research problem and a method. Enter divine inspiration (literally). I was sitting in church one morning listening to the sermon when I was struck not only with what the minister was saying but how and why he was saying it and how the congregation reacted to it. The beginnings of a research project were stirring. More and more studies were being done on language use in the home and the work place, but I realized that various community institutions also played a prominent role in the lives of our students. In the African American community, one of the most prominent institutions is the church. While Heath had included the church in the study of Trackton and Roadville, it was only a minor part of her study. This community institution deserves more attention than it has received because its literate practices are powerful in the lives of its members, shaping, in part, their identities and ways of thinking, acting, and engaging in everyday discourse. So why not study literacy in the African American church?

The only way that I could even think about examining literacy in the African American church was through ethnography. This was the only research method I had been introduced to that allowed a researcher to tell a story about a community—a story told jointly by the researcher and the members of the community. In addition, this method allowed for, even demanded, that context be a part of the data. Ultimately, ethnography allowed me to be part of the research project in more than some abstract "researcher" way. It allowed me to take pictures of the community (through fieldwork) and be in the picture at the same time, something that other research methods frown upon.

However, this ethnographic project presented me with challenges and methodological questions: What did I, as a composition scholar, need to learn about ethnography in order to do the project? And what special problems did I face because I had chosen to do an ethnography in a community of which I was a member? These two questions are the central questions behind this essay. I first describe the goals of ethnography, including the principles that inform good ethnographic studies, and then I address the particular issues associated with studying one's own community, using my study of the African American church as illustration.

CONDUCTING AN ETHNOGRAPHY: MAKING THE STRANGE FAMILIAR

Ethnography is a qualitative research method that allows a researcher to gain a comprehensive view of the social interactions, behaviors, and beliefs of a community or social group. In other words, the goal of an ethnographer is to study, explore, and describe a group's culture (Agar 12–14; Spradley 3–10; Zaharlick and Green 205–6). Ethnographers tend to focus on the daily routines in the everyday lives of the communities being studied. They study what members of a community do, what they say, what they know, and what their physical artifacts are (Spradley 54). It is through examining such ordinary, daily routines of a community that ethnographers are able to accomplish their ultimate goal: to describe a particular community so that an outsider sees it as a native would and so that the community studied can be compared to other communities. Only through such careful comparisons can re-

searchers start to develop a global picture of cultural groups.

Hymes, in "What Is Ethnography?" identifies three modes of ethnographic inquiry: comprehensive-oriented ethnography, topic-oriented ethnography, and hypothesis-oriented ethnography. Comprehensive-oriented ethnography seeks to document or describe a total way of life. Few ethnographers claim to have done totally comprehensive ethnographies. Time and space generally do not allow for describing everything about a community. Topic-oriented ethnography narrows the focus to one or more aspects of life known to exist in a community (see Heath's *Ways with Words* and Shuman's *Storytelling Rights*). Comprehensive and topic-oriented ethnographies lead to hypothesis-oriented ethnography, which can be done only when one has a great deal of general ethnographic knowledge about a community (Hymes, "What Is Ethnography?" 22–23). The mode of inquiry may influence the type of data collected, how data are collected, how long an ethnographer stays in the field, and what role she plays in the community being studied.

While ethnography in general is concerned with describing and analyzing a culture, ethnography in composition studies is generally topic oriented and concerned more narrowly with communicative behavior or the interrelationship of language and culture. Hymes describes this kind of ethnography as ethnography of communication ("Models of Interaction"; *Foundations*). Saville-Troike explains that ethnography of communication "is directed, on the one hand, at the description and understanding of communicative behavior in specific cultural settings, but it is also directed toward the formulation of concepts and theories upon which to build a global metatheory of human communication" (2). Given its goals and methods, it is not hard to see why ethnography has gained in popularity in composition research. This methodology not only allows for but emphasizes the context that contributes to acts of writing and written products. That is, ethnographers who study writing, literacy, and so on, study writing as it occurs in its specific cultural setting. A study that ignores the social context of language use is not an ethnography.

Ethnographers look to several principles to inform the research and guide them through its various stages. First, good ethnographies are theoretically driven, and due to the interdisciplinary nature of the field, composition scholars may make use of more than one theoretical perspective. The theoretical orientation of an ethnographer may not always be a conscious choice or even be made explicit, but it is usually evident. Ethnography is generally associated with a "phenomenological-oriented paradigm which embraces a multicultural perspective because it accepts multiple realities" (Fetterman 15). This or any other theoretical perspective necessarily orients researchers, leading them to focus on one aspect of cultural phenomena rather than another. For instance, a cognitive theory might orient a researcher to focus on what members of a social group say and do as a way of finding out what they think and what they believe. This researcher looks to make "cognitive maps and taxonomies." On the other hand, researchers who are influenced by cultural ecology or Marxist theory may focus on material resources within a community to determine social behavior patterns. The theoretical perspective that ethnographers adopt influences research questions, tools and techniques of data collection and analysis, and the conceptual framework of the study.

Because of the decisions ethnographers have to make before they even enter the field, such as choosing theoretical perspectives, they do not enter communities with blank slates. They gather some information on the history of the community (if appropriate), the participants, and the language. In spite of this previous knowledge, however, one important feature of ethnography is the open-mindedness of the ethnographer. While an ethnographer may begin with a set of research questions, new questions should emerge and old questions be reshaped as data are collected and analyzed. As much as possible, research questions and hypotheses are context-dependent and, therefore, should emerge from the social situation being studied.

At the root of most ethnographic research is the native's perspective (the emic perspective), usually accessible to ethnographers through fieldwork. Ethnographers allow the participants (along with artifacts from the community) to define the community for them. The object of ethnography is to provide what Geertz refers to as a "thick description" of the culture being studied (10–14). That thick description is based on how the members make meaning and explain and interpret social actions in their own communities; in short, how they define culture. One can gain such data only by immersing oneself in the community being studied.

An important prerequisite to this immersion is for ethnographers to negotiate both access into the community and the role the ethnographers will take on. How access to a community is gained can influence the ease or difficulty with which ethnographers can collect data. Just as there is no cookbook recipe for how to do ethnography, there is no best way to gain access to a community (Walters). There are countless ways to enter a community, and these depend on such variables as the type of community (village, school, bar, church, and so forth), the focus of the ethnography, the length of time the ethnographer plans to invest in the study, the relationship of the ethnographer to the community, and the role the ethnographer will play in the community. For many ethnographers, the first step toward gaining access is to have a contact person within the community who will introduce the ethnographer to or identify the key person(s) from whom the ethnographer must seek permission to conduct the study (if permission is needed). Ethnography in a school may require permission from several levels, from parents to a state board of education. An ethnography of shoppers in a mall may require no permission.

Once access is gained, the role the ethnographer takes in the community must be negotiated with participants and may determine the kind of data an ethnographer can collect. The goal in negotiating a role is to interfere as little as possible with the daily routines in the community. The teacher who studies his or her own classroom will run into difficulty here because the daily routines depend, in large part, on him or her. Since participant observation is the major data gathering technique in ethnography, the ethnographer's role in the community influences the level of participant observation in the field. Spradley explains that "the participant observer enters a social situation with two purposes: to engage in activities appropriate to the situation and to observe the activities, people, and physical aspects of the situation" (55). Holy stresses that actively participating allows the researcher to fully experience actions of the community, and that observation alone cannot be the main process through which data are gathered (22–29).

With a community or social situation located, a research question and mode of inquiry identified, a theoretical perspective and conceptual framework in mind, access to the community gained, and one's role negotiated, the ethnographer is ready to begin fieldwork, the major method of data collection for the ethnographer. The goal of fieldwork is to collect as much data as possible, data that will yield an understanding of the complex relationships that exist in a community. Fieldwork is characterized by participant observation, formal and informal interviews of informants, photographs, audio and video recordings of daily occurrences in a community, gathering of physical artifacts that are a part of the daily routine of a community (e.g., written documents produced and used in a community), and on rare occasions questionnaires distributed to members. Not all of these methods will be used in every ethnography, and no ethnography makes use of only one of these methods. However, participant observation and formal and informal interviews have traditionally yielded the richest fieldnotes. Through these methods, the ethnographer usually has her or his greatest contact with informants, and from these informants, the ethnographer gains an emic perspective (insider's view) of the culture. Zaharlick and Green go so far as to argue that "the members of the social group (e.g., classroom) become formal and informal collaborators in the research. That is, the researcher needs the support and cooperation of those members of the social group who hold 'cultural knowledge' about the meaning of the events, actions, objects, and behav-

iors the ethnographer observes as well as the beliefs, values, and attitudes of members of the group" (214). Any patterns or impressions that the ethnographer recognizes and forms throughout the ethnography are tested by comparing one source of information with other sources in order to eliminate alternative explanations and arrive at a valid interpretation (Fetterman 89). The ethnographer checks her notes against informants' explanations and vice versa to determine whether informants do what they say they do and to see if the ethnographer has recorded notes accurately. This verification is referred to as triangulation, a concept that is essential to every ethnography and that provides validity to data analysis (see also Grant-Davie, this volume, for a discussion of validity, reliability, and interpretation).

Data analysis consists of recognizing patterns and relationships that emerge from the fieldwork. Because of the cyclical nature of ethnography, data analysis takes place throughout the study. Early analysis can help the ethnographer become more focused and may contribute to refined research questions. The ethnographer who waits until all the data have been collected (anywhere from months to years) to start data analysis runs the risk of being totally overwhelmed by the amount of data collected as well as finding out too late that she has focused on one aspect of the community while patterns in the data indicate that she should have focused on another. The ethnographer develops a coding scheme that illuminates these patterns and turns them into categories. It is by establishing these categories that the ethnographer begins to make meaning of a community for an outsider. One of the flexibilities of ethnography is that data can be analyzed and reported in various ways. While ethnography is qualitative, qualitative and quantitative methods can often be combined (Jacobs). Depending upon the type of data collected and the focus of the ethnography, an ethnographer can make use of no statistics at all or use some of the most sophisticated statistical analyses available.

When the analysis (the process) is complete, the ethnographer's final step is to write the ethnography (the product). According to Van Maanen, how an ethnography is presented depends on several factors, such as the nature of the ethnographic study (comprehensive-oriented, topic-oriented, or hypothesis-oriented), its purpose, its audience (policy makers, other ethnographers, members of the community), and its style (critical, literary, realistic, impressionistic) (quoted in Zaharlick and Green 221). Linda Brodkey adds that in writing ethnographies, "The controversy specifically raised by ethnographic narratives is whether data are interpreted or analyzed, or, put another way, whether the researcher or the research methodology is telling the story" (26). She argues that we must recognize the role of narrative in all ethnographic reports, that "the single most important lesson to be learned from ethnographic fieldwork is that experience is not—indeed, cannot be—reproduced in speech or writing, and must instead be narrated" (26).

STUDYING ONE'S OWN COMMUNITY: MAKING THE FAMILIAR STRANGE

When ethnographers study a community as outsiders, they must spend a significant amount of time gaining access to the community and learning the rules of the community well enough to gather and eventually analyze the data. In contrast, ethnographers who study their own community may already have access to almost all facets of that community's life, most likely have roles in the community that existed before the study, and consciously or subconsciously know the rules of behavior within the community. In composition studies, where ethnography is becoming valued as a way to explore problems in the field, more researchers are studying communities with which they have some prior experience and/or of which they are members. For example, a growing number of researchers are conducting ethnographies of their own classrooms or, as in my case, of social organizations to which they belong.

Are there special problems for ethnographers in composition who study their own communities?

Consider the following excerpt from Gloria Naylor's *Mama Day*:

> Look what happened when Reema's boy—the one with the pear-shaped head—came hauling himself back from one of those fancy colleges mainside, dragging his notebooks and the tape recorder and a funny way of curling up his lip and clicking his teeth, all excited and determined to put Willow Springs on the map. . . . And then when he went around asking us about 18 & 23, there weren't nothing to do but take pity on him as he rattled on about 'ethnography,' 'unique speech pattern,' 'cultural preservation'. . . . He was all over the place—What 18 & 23 mean? What 18 & 23 mean? And we told him the God-honest truth: it was just our way of saying something . . . but he done still made it to the conclusion that 18 & 23 wasn't 18 & 23 at all—was really 81 & 32, which just so happened to be the lines of longitude and latitude marking off where Willow Springs sits on the map. And we were just so damned dumb that we turned the whole thing around. . . . The people who ran the type of schools that could turn our children into raving lunatics—and then put his picture on the back of the book so we couldn't even deny it was him—didn't mean us a speck of good. . . . Naw, he didn't really want to know what 18 & 23 meant, or he woulda asked. . . . On second thought, someone who didn't know how to ask wouldn't know how to listen. (5–7)

If Reema's boy really wanted to know what "18 & 23" meant, he would have found out how to ask and who to ask (a function of fieldwork), as Naylor's narrator illustrates later in this opening section of *Mama Day*. The issue for Reema's boy was not only that he did not know how to ask (a problem any ethnographer may have), but that he assumed that by virtue of being born and raised in this community, he automatically had access to all facets of the community. As this quotation illustrates, he was mistaken. He also assumed that no matter how he approached people and "asked questions," he would gain the information for which he was searching. Again, he was mistaken. And finally, because he thought he had all the answers to his questions, he never realized that he was asking the wrong questions. It is important that Naylor portrays the ethnographer as a member of this community, not as a stranger. His preexisting relationship with the members of the community sets up, rightly or not, expectations for both the researcher and community. Community expectations for ethnographers who study their own communities must be addressed, as must the researchers' own expectations.

This previous example comes from fiction; yet, it is not an unreal situation. When Seteney Shami, an Arab anthropologist, conducted an ethnography in her native town, she had an experience similar to that of Reema's boy. She comments on the value she attached to data she received early on from older informants: "Having heard many of the stories before, I was neither interested nor stimulated. I was laying too much emphasis on getting what I wanted to hear and dismissing what they were telling me as somehow not being data, because it was not new" (120). Shami's previous experience in her community affected her judgment about what is important. In *Arab Women in the Field,* Soraya Altorki and Camilla Fawzi El-Solh point out, on the one hand, that some researchers believe ethnographers studying their own communities may be able to discern patterns and attach meanings to them more quickly and with less difficulty than outsiders. On the other hand, Altorki and El-Solh (7–9) and others (Ablon 70; Cassell 412–26; Aguilar 21) point out that insiders may also be more vulnerable to value conflicts because they are unable to maintain a safe emotional distance from the communities they research.

The move to study one's own community raises a number of questions: (1) What role does an ethnographer's degree of membership in a community play in successfully carrying out the study? (2) How does the role of the researcher affect the preexisting established relationships in this community; specifically, how does her or his role affect how he or she is perceived by the community and how he or she perceives the community? (3) Will the ethnographer make assumptions about what certain behaviors signify or how meaning is established in this community based on previous knowl-

edge or on the actual data collected? (4) Would an outsider attach more significance to observed patterns than the insider, based on the degrees of distance? (5) What issues might an insider face when writing up the ethnography? These are just a few questions that I faced when doing my study of the African American church and that I will address in the remaining pages of this essay.

There are, of course, degrees of membership in a community. For instance, we may hold membership in the larger society (e.g., American society) as well as specific social institutions (e.g., the African American church, college composition teachers) and small groups (Ohio State University English professors). Within any of these communities, a member may be a more actively involved, full-fledged member than others who may operate on the boundaries of a community. Generally, the smaller the community, the fuller the degree of membership; and the degree of membership and size of the community influence the various stages of the ethnography. For instance, I collected ethnographic data in three African American churches in Chicago. Because I was a member of the African American church community, I was familiar in a general sense with how these fairly traditional African American churches operated. I knew how to enter this community and act in a manner that signaled my membership. However, I had little knowledge of two of the three churches. I needed someone within those churches to introduce me to the minister. Yet, in the third church, which I had been attending for more than two years, I needed no intermediary, no introductions. I just went in to see the minister and told him about my study. The third minister was far more accessible than the first two; he volunteered a great deal of references to me in my interviews and let me have free audiocassettes of his sermons (usually sold by the church). In the first two churches, I had to make my own tapes (one church did not record its services) or buy the tapes of the services (the other church recorded and sold tapes of its services). This difference in level of familiarity with the specific churches and the level of familiarity with African American churches in general influenced how I gained access to the churches and ministers and gathered data.

As I suggest in the second question, ethnographers must be concerned with how their previous roles and their new roles (that of researcher) will affect their perceptions of the community as well as the community's perception of them. Will informants talk more openly because they know the ethnographers, or less openly? Will they assume that the ethnographers already know everything about the community because of their membership? Will the ethnographers be more judgmental or attach more value to certain acts because of their knowledge of the community or their preexisting relationships with members of that community?

Obviously, Reema's boy was not a hit in Willow Springs when he came back to town running around with his tape recorder and notebooks. He consistently reinforced these skeptical feelings in the community because he was perceived as asking senseless questions and not really listening to the answers people gave him. Novelist Zora Neale Hurston, a trained cultural anthropologist who collected folktales in her community, initially ran into similar problems when she began her study. She explains that she returned to Eatonville from Barnard and began to ask people in her best "Barnardese" if they knew any folktales (49). She got virtually no response from these people whom she had known most of her life. When Hurston realized that she was then perceived as an outsider because of her Barnardese and her newly acquired urban manners, she was able to revise her approach. She went back into Eatonville some time later and reacclimated herself to the ways of her community and fit in to their way of life. She was then perceived as the insider she originally had been and was able to collect more folktales than she could use.

While Reema's boy and Hurston contributed to their community's perception of them, sometimes ethnographers have no control over how they are perceived. When I was interviewing three ministers (one whose church I was studying and two visiting ministers), they constantly relied on shared knowledge among the four of us about African American preaching and assumed a great deal of knowledge on my part. During the interview one of these ministers said to me in reference to a point he was making, "you know what I mean, you've grown up in southern black churches." I was put in the position of having to answer either "yes" and assume I did know what he was referring to (that was basically true) or saying "no, could you tell me what you mean" (or some variation). The problem with saying yes is that I may have assumed mistakenly; also, my object was to get the informants to be as explicit as possible. However, if I had said no, the informants may have questioned whether or not I was really a member of this community. If they questioned my community membership, it may have affected the easy relationship we had already established, due in part to my being a southern African American woman who had grown up in and gone to African American churches all her life. I chose to signal that I indeed did know what this minister meant and let the ministers continue to talk, which they did for two and one-half hours. At another point, one minister's expectations and perception led to great anxiety on my part. During an interview in the early stages of fieldwork, this minister explained that because of my joint memberships in the African American community, the African American church community, and the academic community, I had the knowledge and the opportunity to raise African American language to the high status it deserves, especially in the eyes of the academy. I found this minister's expectations overwhelming and a little scary. Consequently, for awhile, I found myself thinking about how skilled these ministers were with language instead of describing their language use.

Of course, my perceptions and expectations of the community also posed potential problems. I expected to find a great deal of similarity in the churches because they were, after all, three African American inner-city churches with well-educated African American male ministers and fairly well-educated congregations. I expected the smallest church, which was Pentecostal, to be like many southern African American Pentecostal churches, "stay in all day Sunday holy rollers." However, through my fieldwork, I found that, while there were similarities among the three churches, each church had its own distinct personality, and that the Pentecostal church was the most sedate church of the three churches studied. I learned the hard way that I shouldn't have so many expectations. My membership in the African American church community at large and in specific churches did not provide me with knowledge about every African American church and about all denominations.

There are other concerns for ethnographers who study their own communities: they must learn to think of all patterns that occur in the communities as important and informative. There is a tendency for insiders to overlook patterns because they are not unique or strange or new (as Shami did). After my first two weeks of fieldwork in the first church, I recognized that I had fallen into the same trap as Shami had. I reviewed my two weeks' worth of fieldnotes, which took less than an hour. Obviously, something was wrong. I knew I should have more than the few pages of fieldnotes. However, as I reviewed them again and reflected on why I had written some things down and not others, I found I had been looking for events that stood out. Since so much of what was happening during the church service was not new to me, I had either assumed that many of the routine events were unimportant or hadn't even noticed certain events. When I reminded myself and was reminded by my adviser that the routine "stuff" was the most important data, I then had to train myself to pay attention to as much detail as possible and to assume that everything was important until I had enough data and had done enough analysis to know otherwise.

Ethnographers may also have a tendency to rely on their own knowledge for a great deal of data. This is not to say that they must ignore everything they know about the community, but they must find a way to make explicit that implicit knowledge that is in their heads and that comes from membership (they cannot rely solely on that knowledge). Ethnographers must be careful to actually listen to and see the community, rely on informants, and draw conclusions from actual data collected during the study; basically, ethnographers should not be

major informants. Triangulation is one of the keys to success here. For teachers who study their own classrooms, familiarity with their community is problematic because they are major informants in their own studies (see, for example, Herrmann's "Using the Computer"). How might teachers achieve triangulation? Videotaping may help here, or having another participant observer in the classroom might be most useful. Another key is to gather as much data as possible from as many different sources as possible (see also Ruth Ray's chapter on teacher research in this volume).

What do ethnographers do when faced with the issues raised above? Taylor and Dorsey-Gaines, in *Growing Up Literate,* remind us that, as outsiders, we must "deal on a daily basis with our own ethnocentrism and mental baggage. Reflection and introspection are continuous processes which must take place throughout the study" (xv). As insiders, we too must deal with our own ethnocentrism and the mental baggage we carry, precisely because of our memberships in the communities we study. And we must also be prepared to deal with the mental baggage and expectations of the other members of the community. That critical reflection and introspection which Taylor and Dorsey-Gaines speak of takes on greater importance than usual for ethnographers examining their own classrooms or neighborhoods. I contributed to my own introspection and reflection in two ways: I constantly asked myself questions such as, Where is my evidence for this or that claim? or Did I assume something? or Did my informants say or do this? And I discussed my findings with people who were familiar with ethnography and composition research but who were not members of the community I was studying. The latter proved to be a most valuable tool because I found myself looking to the data for answers to the questions that these outsiders would raise.

The final challenge that ethnographers face is writing the ethnography. When they are writing about their own communities, this challenge can be problematic. Most likely, ethnographers who write about communities that they aren't members of will have little, if any, contact with those communities once the ethnography is completed. However, ethnographers who write about communities to which they belong may spend unlimited amounts of time in or may indeed live in those communities. Consequently, they may face certain pressures: What pictures do their ethnographies paint of the communities? Have they been as accurate and fair as possible? Have they been overly critical? Not critical enough? How will the communities react to their studies? I faced all these questions in my study. I did not want to be unfair to any of the churches and ministers I studied. Like most ethnographers, I developed a strong sense of loyalty to the community I studied; I did not want anyone in the community to be dissatisfied with what I had written. I also knew that once the study was completed, I wanted to go back to these churches, particularly the one I had been attending, as a regular parishioner. At the same time, I wanted to be rigorous and thorough. These feelings led to anxiety as I was writing, yet they must be faced in the same way that getting through fieldwork and analysis are faced, through introspection, reflection, and triangulation. Most important, of course, ethnographers must be responsible to the community.

Many of the issues I have raised may, of course, concern ethnographers who are strangers to the communities they are studying. However, these issues seem to be paramount for the insider who has to make the "familiar strange." If those of us who study our own communities do not want to be caught in Reema's boy's shoes, that is, being denied by our own communities, then we must be aware of and prepared to deal with the baggage that membership brings. What kept me from being in Reema's boy's shoes was my willingness to learn as much about ethnography as I could before and during the study. Those of us who study our own communities have an obligation to understand as much as we can about ethnography. This knowledge will make us aware that our role in a community may provide us with insights that others do not have, but it can also blind us, just as it did Reema's boy. The goal of any ethnographer, whether insider or outsider, must be to guard against blindness, to drive instead toward increased insight into the ways in which language communities work. That is the excitement and the challenge of ethnography.

Note

I would like to thank Lisa Ede, Marcia Farr, Kay Halasak, Andrea Lunsford, and Carole Clark Papper for their comments on various drafts of this essay.

Works Cited

Ablon, Joan. "Field Methods in Working with Middle Class Americans: New Issues of Values, Personality and Reciprocity." *Human Organization* 36 (1977): 69–72.

Agar, Michael. *Speaking of Ethnography.* Newbury Park, CA: Sage, 1986.

Aguilar, John L. "Insider Research: An Ethnography of a Debate." *Anthropologists at Home in North America: Methods and Issues in the Study of One's Own Society.* Ed. Donald A. Messerschmidt. Cambridge: Cambridge UP, 1981. 15–26.

Altorki, Soraya, and Camilla Fawzi El-Solh. Introduction. *Arab Women in the Field.* Ed. Soraya Altorki and Camilla Fawzi El-Solh. Syracuse: Syracuse UP, 1988. 1–24.

Brodkey, Linda. "Writing Ethnographic Narratives." *Written Communication* 4 (1987): 25–50.

Cassell, Joan. "The Relationship of Observer to Observed in Peer Group Research." *Human Organization* 36 (1977): 412–16.

Fetterman, David. *Ethnography Step by Step.* Newbury Park, CA: Sage, 1989.

Geertz, Clifford. *The Interpretation of Cultures.* New York: Basic, 1973.

Heath, Shirley Brice. *Ways with Words: Language, Life, and Work in Communities and Classrooms.* Cambridge: Cambridge UP, 1983.

Herrmann, Andrea. "Using the Computer as a Writing Tool: Ethnography of a High School Writing Class." Diss. Columbia Teachers College, 1985.

Holy, Ladislav. "Theory, Methodology and the Research Process." *Ethnographic Research: A Guide to General Conduct.* Ed. Roy F. Ellen. New York: Academic, 1984.

Hurston, Zora Neale. *I Love Myself When I am Laughing . . . and Then Again When I am Looking Mean and Impressive: A Zora Neale Hurston Reader.* Ed. Alice Walker. Old Westbury: Feminist, 1979.

Hymes, Dell. *Foundations in Sociolinguistics.* Philadelphia: U of Pennsylvania P, 1974.

————. "Models of the Interaction of Language and Social Life." *Directions in Sociolinguistics: The Ethnography of Communication.* Ed. John J. Gumperz and Dell Hymes. New York: Holt, 1972. 35–71.

————. "What Is Ethnography?" *Children In and Out of School: Ethnography and Education.* Ed. Perry Gilmore and Allan A. Glathorn. Washington: Center for Applied Linguistics, 1982. 21–32.

Jacobs, Evelyn. "Combining Ethnographic and Quantitative Approaches: Suggestions and Examples from a Study in Puerto Rico." *Children In and Out of School: Ethnography and Education.* Ed. Perry Gilmore and Allan A. Glathorn. Washington: Center for Applied Linguistics, 1982. 124–47.

Moss, Beverly J. "The African-American Sermon as a Literacy Event." Diss. U of Illinois at Chicago, 1988.

Naylor, Gloria. *Mama Day.* New York: Tichnor, 1988.

Saville-Troike, Muriel. *The Ethnography of Communication.* New York: Basil Blackwell, 1982.

Shami, Seteney. "Studying Your Own: The Complexities of a Shared Culture." *Arab Women in the Field.* Ed. Soraya Altorki and Camilla Fawzi El-Solh. Syracuse: Syracuse UP, 1988. 115–38.

Shuman, Amy. *Storytelling Rights.* Cambridge: Cambridge UP, 1986.

Spradley, James. *Participant Observation.* New York: Holt, 1980.

Taylor, Denny, and Catherine Dorsey-Gaines. *Growing Up Literate: Learning from Inner City Families.* Portsmouth, NH: Heinemann, 1988.

Walters, Keith. "Initiation Rites and Responsibilities." Unpublished essay, 1990.

Zaharlick, Amy, and Judith Green. "Ethnographic Research." *Handbook of Research in Teaching the English Language Arts.* Ed. James Flood, et al. New York: Macmillan, 1991. 205–25

Writing Development as Seen through Longitudinal Research: A Case Study Exemplar

Marilyn S. Sternglass

Sternglass's research was published in Written Communication *10 (1993): 235–61.*

On the basis of data collected for the past 3½ years in a longitudinal study of writing and learning projected to last for 5 years, it is possible to begin to present insights about writing development of urban college students that can be gleaned from this type of research. In this study, students from three different writing levels at the City College of the City University of New York (CUNY) were interviewed twice each semester, were asked to provide copies of the papers they wrote in all their courses, and were observed in one of their classes each semester. Using the information gathered thus far as a general contextual background, I will present a case study of one student who started at the first level of basic writing to illustrate the richness and complexity of analysis available through the compilation of data in a longitudinal study examining academic and personal histories.

The writing samples I collected were written for a variety of instructors in a wide range of disciplines and because I have no oral protocol materials, I recognize that my analysis of the writing itself will be text based. But because I have interviewed the students in the study twice each semester over a wide range of academic and personal topics, I have a fuller and richer picture of their development as "whole persons" as well as writers than have had researchers who have studied the composing process over shorter periods of time and without such detailed personal histories. I knew all the students in the study because I was their instructor in their composition courses in the fall of 1989 when the study began. The students in the study were from three classes in the composition program: English 1 (the first basic writing level), English 2 (the second basic writing level), and English 110 (freshman composition).

The observational reports of the instructional settings, although not as extensive as those collected by such researchers as Langer and Applebee (1987) or Walvoord and McCarthy (1990), present another aspect of the learning contexts in which students operated. These observational reports describe classroom settings and tasks in which I had no role. Instructors were unaware that any students in their classes were part of the study until one of my research assistants asked permission to sit in on a class and requested course materials. These reports, then, reflect instructional settings and curricula planned solely by the teachers themselves.

Such "snapshots," when combined, can provide more diverse, more complete, and more revealing portraits of how individuals respond at discrete times and over longer periods of time to the demands of the academic environment than do accounts from other kinds of studies, which can be artificial and isolated from real contexts.

WRITING TO LEARN STUDIES

One of the central issues in examining the relationship between writing and learning has to do with how learning has been defined. Some studies define learning as recall (primarily of facts), others as the ability to organize and synthesize information, and still others as the ability to apply information to the creation of new knowledge. Examining these different notions of learning through a longitudinal study can help determine whether they may be developmental as well as related to the type of writing task that is called for.

Reviewing a series of earlier studies, Langer and Applebee (1987) concluded that "any manipulation or elaboration of material being studied tends to improve later *recall*, but the type of improvement is very closely tied to the type of manipulation" (p. 92, emphasis added). In their own study of 9th- and 11th-grade students over 3 years, Langer and Applebee found that note taking and responding to study questions facilitated the remembering of discrete facts and that analytic writing fostered better understanding of concepts and relationships between ideas, although students' ability to recall particular information from the source text was more focused and thus more limited (pp. 130–131).

Newell and Winograd (1989), in a reexamination of the data collected in Newell's (1984) study, concluded that both responding to questions and writing analytic essays enabled students "to *recall* the overall organizing frames of the original passages more often than when they engaged in notetaking" (p. 210, emphasis added). Recall of gist was best fostered by analytic writing (p. 211). Newell and Winograd also found that note taking was least effective for recall, suggesting that simply "translating" information in prose passages into lists of facts does not lead to the building of relationships among ideas (p. 206).

The relationship between writing and learning has frequently been examined from a cognitive perspective. Spear (1983) has argued that "cognitive development follows a hierarchical sequence of stages [which] suggests that a curriculum can be sequentially organized to promote cognitive development" (p. 47). Schumacher and Nash (1991) also believe that the different kinds of cognitive operations writers engage in different types of writing tasks account for the different kinds of learning (p. 69).

These studies examined discrete academic tasks with little knowledge of the writers, except for their level of prior knowledge about the topic being addressed in the reading passage. Such limited background information about the writers makes it difficult to assess the basis of their reasoning because of lack of information about what Brandt (1992) calls "cultural resources" (p. 350). From an ethnmethodological view, Brandt offered a wider definition of prior knowledge than simply background information. She defined it as "methods of experiencing, methods by which a person 'rounds out' an isolated event so that it can appear sensible, typical, normal, or whole" (p. 329). This approach led her to define a sense-making model as one that "can capture wider cultural considerations that writers attend to, considerations that arise from sources other than a particular writer–reader relationship or the rhetorical exigencies of a particular occasion" (p. 330). Longitudinal studies have the ability to provide insight into the effects of wider cultural considerations.

Because a number of studies have compared the various writing tasks related to learning (note taking, responding to questions, and essay writing) and the findings suggest that analytic writing is the strongest contributor to learning, especially if learning is thought of as the ability to discover new ideas, it seems appropriate to move beyond these studies to examine how learning through writing develops over time in relation to the complex changes in individual students' lives as well as in relation to the academic demands placed on them.

LONGITUDINAL STUDIES

Only a few longitudinal studies of writing have been carried out over the past 30 years, although currently such studies are being conducted or are projected at the University of Dayton, the University of Washington, the University of Oklahoma, and Harvard University. Most of the previous longitudinal studies of writing were carried out in elementary schools or secondary schools, some following the same population over time and others studying different individuals representing different grade levels. Only two studies followed the same groups of students over several years. Loban (1963) examined language learning of the same group of elementary students, and Perry (1968) followed a group of students over their 4 years of college in terms of their intellectual and ethical development. Other studies examined writing development of students with different individuals representing each level (Britton, Burgess, Martin, McLeod, & Rosen, 1975; Freedman & Pringle, 1980; Hays, 1983; Wilkinson, Barnsley, Hanna, & Swan, 1980).

Although these studies provide useful categories for examining writing development, none combined the approaches brought together in this study: (a) examining writing and learning on a true longitudinal basis, i.e., following the same students; (b) studying a multicultural urban college population; (c) examining the relationship between writing and learning in a number of different disciplines; and (d) taking into consideration nonacademic factors that influence academic performance.

Other longitudinal studies of college students have looked at large populations from a statistical perspective to examine issues related to student performance. The study most directly related to this study was carried out by Lavin, Alba, and Silberstein (1981). Lavin et al. followed for 5 years the progress of the first three cohorts of students who entered the CUNY campuses after the implementation of open admissions in 1970. Their research was purely quantitative, examining such issues as numbers of credits earned and grade point

averages. In their analysis of the data, Lavin et al. (1981) distinguished between what they termed "dropouts" and "persisters" and between "regular" and "open admissions" students (p. 128). The students in my study who began their work in basic writing classes seem equivalent to Lavin's open admissions cohort, and those who started at the regular freshman composition level are equivalent to those labeled regular. In my study, I can, of course, follow only those students who remain at the college and who agree to remain in my study (like Lavin's persisters), but I have tried to learn what has happened to those who have left the college (the dropouts). (Of the 53 students who started in my study, 24 are still enrolled in the college, 7 have transferred to other institutions of higher education, and 4, who brought transfer credits to the college, have graduated. Thus, of the original 53 students, 35 are either continuing their education or have completed their college work.)

OVERVIEW OF THE STUDY

Population of the Study

In the fall term of 1989, students in one section each of English 1, English 2, and English 110, all of which I taught, were asked to participate in this longitudinal study. Students in English 1 and English 2 were placed at these levels on the basis of their performance on the Writing Assessment Test. Students in English 110 had multiple routes into the course: initial placement on the basis of the Writing Assessment Test, enrollment after one or two semesters of basic writing or after one, two, or three semesters of English as a second language (ESL), or as transfer students who had not satisfactorily completed the English composition requirement. Although ESL students were not specifically recruited for the study, they were represented in both the English 2 and English 110 classes. Of the total 53 students in the original classes, 21 were African-American, 26 Latino, 4 Asian, and 2 White. Thirty were males and 23 were females. Twenty-five were born outside the continental United States, including 3 born in Puerto Rico.

Interviews

Each semester I have interviewed students twice, asking them the same series of questions at the beginning of each semester and varying the questions at the end of each term. For example, at the beginning of each semester I have asked students what they considered their easiest and their most difficult courses and the reasons why each fell into that category. As students progressed from the basic courses in writing and mathematics to the courses in their disciplines, the responses to these questions indicated the relationship between level of difficulty and level of interest in its effect on selection of a student's major.

Because this study focuses on the relationship between writing and learning, each semester students were asked whether they believed that having to write something about the materials they were studying helped them to understand these materials better. Students' responses to this question reveal that over time they came to use a range of reading and writing strategies including rewriting their classroom and textbook notes in order to analyze the material and construct generalizations, organizing research materials in ways that permitted them to support their major positions, and becoming more concerned with expressing their own ideas in ways that would garner academic approval (Sternglass, 1993).

The educational and social histories of the students emerged through an initial demographic questionnaire and the subsequent interviews. It was not surprising that in an urban, inner-city public college like City College, many of the students in the study are in the first generation of their families to attend college, but it was also not uncommon to find students with siblings who either already attend college or plan to. So, although most of the students' parents have not had higher education, there is clearly an "education ethic" that is strong in many of the families. Such a finding suggests that students who are considered to be high risk because of their economic and educational backgrounds may in fact be a select population who have been encouraged by their families to achieve professional and financial success as have previous generations of immigrants and individuals from poor economic straits. Thus this study will not claim to make broad generalizations about the writing and learning processes of urban, high-risk college students in general, but it will attempt to account for the kind of progress that is possible for students of this background. The City College, justly famous for educating immigrant populations in the 1920s and 1930s in New York City, seems to be fulfilling that same role now for both minority and new immigrant groups in the city.

Other questions revealed that almost all students at the City College have some kind of outside employment, ranging from 4 to 40 hours per week. As students have advanced in their academic majors, they have begun to tell me that they are attempting to cut back on their working hours, even though this may mean economic hardship for them, because they recognize that they need more time for their schoolwork. Over these 3½ years, students have shared aspects of their personal lives with me, telling me of illnesses or deaths in their families that interfered with their ability to do their schoolwork, of loves lost and loves found, of recognition that partying must give way to studying, and increasingly, of their determination to succeed in their work.

I have often asked myself what makes the students who continue to participate in the study take the trouble to come to see me twice a semester, to bring me their papers from their courses, and to allow my graduate assistant to visit their classes? One factor, I believe, is that those who are being academically successful have been more likely to continue in the study. I have not been able to offer these students any tangible rewards, I have not been able to pay them, and I have not been able to offer them credits to participate in the study, as has been done at other institutions. I have frequently been asked to write letters of recommendation for them for various purposes. But, most of all, my impression is that my relationship with them represents a kind of continuity for them in the college, a relationship with an individual who has known them from the beginning of their academic careers and who is clearly proud of their accomplishments.

Class Observations

Beginning with the second year of the study, a graduate assistant visited, with the student's and the instructor's permission, one class for each of the students each semester. In the second year of the study, students, particularly those who had started at basic skills levels, were still taking required courses including those in the core curriculum. Observations were made of the writing courses, the core courses, and some introductory courses in the students' major fields. By the third and fourth years of the study, observations were made of more advanced courses in the varying disciplines.

Writing Tasks

Because the students in the study started at a variety of levels in their writing classes, it is possible to follow their progression through the writing curriculum from the point at which each started. Larson (1991) has noted the value of collecting papers in chronological order over time: "[A] portfolio of writings gathered over a student's academic career, from freshman to senior year, may be examined by faculty for evidence of changes in the way the student thinks, reacts to problems, assesses data, or chooses values" (p. 138).

In addition to having at least the freshman composition course in common, the students were all required to follow the core curriculum requirements of the college. Students' majors then determined the amount and kind of writing that was required of them in the college. I have collected papers from courses in philosophy, psychology, nursing, education, communication, geology, womens' studies, and art. Little or no writing has been required in the science or engineering courses that many of our students take.

Method of Analysis

The papers I have collected from the students were written for a wide range of courses. Some of the papers were copied after the instructors returned them so I have a record of the instructor's

response. In some instances, students who wrote their papers on a word processor simply printed out an extra copy for me when they prepared the paper. Except for the first semester when all of the students were enrolled in one of the levels of composition that I taught, I had no relationship with the instructors or the courses the students were enrolled in. Thus the papers present an unbiased picture of the actual kinds and amounts of writing assigned in a wide range of courses.

Because I had no access to the composing processes involved in the preparation of the students' papers, my analysis must be a textual one. Studies of development in writing have made use of different analytic schemes in recent years. Cognitive development has been used to analyze student writing, most frequently using Piaget's (1955) model of conceptual growth, especially the movement from concrete to abstract thinking (Lunsford, 1980) or Perry's model (Hays, 1983). More recently Rose (1988) has critiqued such approaches, arguing that to assess ability to handle academic tasks is not the same thing as to assess cognitive development.

With the increased interest in assessing student writing through analyses of portfolios, Larson (1991) designed a set of categories for examining student writing over a longer period of time than one semester and over a range of academic courses. Larson and his colleagues developed an approach to evaluate the new curriculum for general education at Lehman College of the City University of New York through an examination of student portfolios. Although the general education curriculum at Lehman and the core curriculum at City College are not identical, course content and types of tasks assigned are similar enough to warrant using Larson's categories for the analysis of my students' writing. Larson and his colleagues adapted the concept of speech act and applied it to written texts, calling their adaptation "act of discourse" (p. 142). They defined an act of discourse as

a specific kind of action performed by a writer in addressing a reader or readers to meet the specific requests, wishes, interests, or possible needs of these readers: for example, summarizing data, reporting and analyzing a sequence of events, defining a problem, setting forth criteria for judging an item and applying them to that item (such as a work of art), analyzing the structure of a text, and so on. . . . We looked for the acts by which writers seek to add to their reader's knowledge, alter readers' beliefs, evoke feelings, change attitudes, prompt judgments, lead their readers to action, encourage readers to follow out a line of inquiry or speculation, assist readers in understanding the personalities or motives of the writer, and so on. (pp. 142–143)

Using these acts as the basis for analysis of the student writing in my study is appropriate because they cover the range of writing assignments students encounter as they progress from introductory to more advanced courses.

One set of categories that Larson and his colleagues constructed for the analysis of the academic papers they collected dealt with "the kinds of acts we are identifying as representative of those assigned, invited, or considered valuable in academic writing in our program" (p. 142). A student's ability to carry out the implied cognitive and analytic functions of the more complex tasks will thus reveal the student's ability to use textual knowledge to move beyond recall and repetition of facts to analysis and synthesis and to the creation of new knowledge (new to the student even if not new to the discipline).

Larson's set of categories for the "acts of discourse" are as follows:

1. Narrative, with or without commentary, of events in the writer's life.

2. Descriptive representation (it may include some narrating) of persons, objects, or conditions directly observed by the writer, *not* part of autobiographic writing (where the focus is on the writer's self).

3. Analysis of the reporting or argument in a piece or pieces of writing by a person or persons other than the student compiling the portfolio.

4. Presentation of the student's own views on a conceptual (e.g. philosophic) or historical issue—a question difficult to resolve and to which there can be two or more possible answers.

5. Analysis and recommendation concerning a problem: in the world outside of college (in the larger society or in a particular institution) on which action must be taken.

6. Presentation of essential data about a historical period, social condition, political structure, and so on.

7. Analysis of the data presented concerning that historical period, social condition, or political structure, to suggest what the data tell the student (what the data "mean") and whether in those data any interpretive problems or problems requiring action arise.

8. Summary of the "research" findings of others, along with evaluation of what subsequent research is needed.

9. Analysis/interpretation of all or part of a work of art (literature, music, sculpture, film). (pp. 143–144, emphasis in original)

Examination of these "acts of discourse" reveals that students' ability to recall information would be demonstrated through Categories 1, 2, 3, 6, and the first part of Category 8, whereas texts that fulfill the acts of Categories 4, 5, 7, 9, and the second part of Category 8 would provide evidence that students are moving toward learning as analysis and synthesis and the creation of new knowledge.

CASE STUDY OF LINDA—ENGLISH 1

Linda is an African-American female student majoring in nursing. She attended elementary school at an air force base in West Germany (as it was called then) while her father was in military service. She attended junior high school in Brooklyn and graduated from Washington Irving High School in New York City. She was 2 months short of age 19 when she started City College immediately after her high school graduation. Her father has a college degree and her mother a high school degree. She receives financial support from her parents and relatives and was "unemployed" (her word) when the study began.

The analysis of Linda's writing in her first 3½ years at the City College examines her changing views on the role of women in society. When examining Linda's writing, it is important to keep in mind that she started college as a basic writing student, placed in the lowest level of basic writing on the basis of her performance on the college's Writing Assessment Test. Brandt (1992) has asked whether we can "treat all texts as accounts of their authors' reasoning processes if authors lack the know-how to display those processes fully or accessibly in public, written language" (p. 350). "On the other hand," Brandt goes on to argue, "composition studies would benefit from assuming more competence on the part of the people typically studied. Rather than looking for flaws in [students'] reasoning, we might look instead for the grounds of their reasoning" (p. 350). For a less experienced writer like Linda, then, it seems reasonable to try to understand the basis for the positions she develops, and to understand that she may not yet be able to articulate fully the reasons for her positions.

Courses in English composition, psychology, world humanities, social sciences, and women's studies provided Linda with opportunities to write about the role of women in society. Two descriptions of her mother, both falling within Larson's Category 2, the first written during her first semester at the college in English 1 (Excerpt A) and the second written in a Psychology of Women course in her fourth year at the college (Excerpt B), show her changing understanding of her relationship with her mother.

Excerpt A

My mother has to know every move I make and [is] always hunting me down no matter where I go and it's really annoying. She tells me she's only looking out for my best intrest [sic] and I yell at her and tell her I don't need her looking out for me. She seems hurt, but she'll get over it. (Fall 1989)

Excerpt B

Up to this point D_____ [her mother] is satisfied with what she done [sic] with her life. She admits that she wish [sic] that she could've done more. She's happy that her children are getting an [sic] higher education and didn't stray away, such as using drugs or getting impregnated early or becoming a high school dropout. D_____ doesn't believe that things would've been different if she was a man and she would not prefer to be a man in a million lifetimes!!!!

Even though my mother never received a Bachelor's or a Master's Degree, doesn't mean that she's stupid. My mother is my best friend and confidant. She's a true gem and a fabulous woman and I thank god every day for her being here. . . . (Fall 1992)

In Excerpt A, Linda has expressed an immediate desire for independence. The picture Linda presented of her mother reflected only Linda's point of view and, although the writing was ostensibly about her mother, it came close to being a narrative of Linda's experience (Larson's Category 1) with only one small commentary, "She tells me she's only looking out for my best intrest [sic]," which Linda rejected. Both narrative and descriptive writings of Larson's Categories 1 and 2 require no basis for examination of the views of others. This piece of writing illustrates recall of discrete facts, but there is little attempt to express causal relationships, as her linking of ideas with "ands" throughout the excerpt demonstrates.

By her fourth year, in Excerpt B, Linda's writing reflected an understanding that her mother had only been trying to protect her from what she perceived as potentially dangerous influences in their community. Linda herself came to gradually adopt these values and by her fourth year at college, she was able to see her mother's protectiveness as a positive rather than a negative trait (Linda herself was born before her parents married). Linda had come to reevaluate her mother's relationship to her on the basis of her life experience and the readings she had encountered over the years between Excerpt A and Excerpt B.

Linda's writing here also reflected a growing awareness that people are frequently valued on the basis of their level of education, hence her spirited defense of her mother who had only a high school degree. She noted her mother's satisfaction with being a woman but simultaneously acknowledged her mother's admission that she wished she could have done more with her life. From her writing, Linda can be seen to have made a decision that her own life would be more accomplished.

In this writing, Linda's most complex grammatical structure occurred in the sentence in which she introduced a subordinating conjunction of contrast, "even though," when she described her mother's lack of higher education. Other than in that sentence of contrast, Linda's sentences still joined ideas with the conjunction "and," thus not identifying relationships among the ideas. It can be seen then, as Brandt has pointed out, that a writer may be capable of having reasons for the views that he or she expresses even if he or she does not yet have the rhetorical sophistication to present them with appropriate conceptual linkages. Linda's writing also continued to suggest, even into her fourth year at the college, that grammatical features of writing were not yet automatic for her.

The changes in Linda's attitude about the role of women in society evolved as she began to read texts about women's experiences and was required to write papers about them. In her second semester, Linda read a text in a psychology course that depicted a female third-year medical resident being denied the opportunity to assist the Chief Surgeon of Cardiology in a bypass heart operation. Linda was asked to apply concepts from her psychology course to an analysis of this situation. Her response (Excerpt C), falling in Larson's Category 3, illustrates an early attempt to analyze events. It also reflects her increasing awareness of the difficulties qualified women have in being taken seriously and treated fairly:

Excerpt C

In the concept of *Social Comparison,* Dr. Harmon stated that his collegues [sic] would not allow a woman in their establishment. Seeing that he did not have enough physical evidence to support his reasons of rejection, Dr. Harmon used the opinions of his fellow co-workers to back his actions. In social comparison, we tend to be influenced by our peer's objections if there isn't enough physical evidence present. (Spring 1990)

Still tied very directly to the language of the definitions provided in her psychology course, Linda was trying, in Excerpt C, to apply the concepts she was studying to the materials presented to her. This practice of staying very close to original text language is a common strategy for less confident writers in early attempts at analysis. Linda reflected her ability to understand the relationship between the ideas in the source text and the concepts being applied. Such tasks did not yet offer opportunities for original interpretations.

The psychology course Linda was taking was a special extended section that covered the normal material of a one-semester course in two semesters. (Such bridge courses were designed to assist students identified as basic readers and writers in their early academic endeavors.)

During the first semester of her second year, the difficulty of her courses increased dramatically. Linda commented to me that she knew that "writing makes or breaks you." She was beginning to discover that courses that allowed her to write papers offered her more opportunities to succeed than those that evaluated students on the basis of short-answer or multiple-choice tests. Writing papers gave her opportunities to explore her ideas, and frequently instructors would allow her to rewrite papers for possible higher grades. When she encountered those kinds of environments in her courses, she had a greater likelihood of succeeding.

In telling me about an upper-level psychology course she was taking that semester, Linda said, "The more I wrote, the more I understood what I was writing about." The professor told my research assistant that he was aware that the students felt a lot of pressure from this course because it combined material that had previously been in two three-credit courses (November 1, 1990), quite the opposite situation from her previous psychology course that had permitted two semesters to cover one semester's usual course work. This upper-level course is required for nursing students.

Because Linda had moved entirely out of remedial courses at that point, she was aware that there was a "big shift in the regular courses," and she wished that she had been better prepared in her earlier composition courses. The readings in her World Humanities course were very demanding. But her most difficult course was chemistry, and as a nursing major, she knew she had to understand the subject thoroughly (October 4, 1990). (Linda received a "D" in the chemistry course and retook it in a later semester, passing with a "C.")

Opportunities for writing about women's role in society began to occur frequently in Linda's courses. The issue of whether women should feel guilty if they decide not to have children was explored first by Linda in her freshman composition course in her second year (Excerpt D) and then again in a paper for a women's studies course in her third year (Excerpt E).

Excerpt D

I want to talk about a topic which is not talked about often—childless women. Believe me, there are women out there who do not want children just as much as women who do. Childless women aren't as equally respected as their maternal counterparts. They are considered selfish women who are not doing their duty. They are also considered not to be total women.

First of all, why are women considered selfish just because they don't want any kids? Women should be able to choose in wehter [sic] they want to have children or not. Nobody has the right to force a woman or berate her because she doesn't have any offsprings [sic]. (Fall 1990)

Excerpt E

Women were always the individual that one didn't concern themselves over. Women are perceived as unintelligent, obedient and docile creatures. They were never encouraged by their society to strive. They were berated if they didn't accomplish what God created for them to do. That is, to become a good servant to her man, bear babies and keep house.

She was never one that society encouraged to succeed in life. She was considered too time-consuming, ignorant and slow to become an educated individual. (Fall 1991)

As Excerpt D reveals, Linda presented her view on a historical issue (Larson's Category 4) without analyzing the causes of the attitude of the society. She maintained that no one had the right to force a woman to have children, but she was limited in her argument to stating that women should have the right to choose to bear children or not. She did not seem ready to offer reasons for this position or valid alternative paths that women might take.

In Excerpt D, Linda had stopped joining ideas within sentences with the word "and," but she had replaced this stylistic feature with short, separate sentences, achieving the same effect of simple linkage. She showed how women were judged but provided no defense against these judgments (in other words, no reasons why the judgments should be changed). Thus the view on the historical issue remained undefended.

In the second writing, Excerpt E, a year later, Linda reflected an understanding of how societal attitudes toward women had attempted to shape the decisions women made. Women were now understood by Linda to have been stereotyped as too ignorant and slow to pursue their own accomplishments, a position she clearly rejected. Although she had moved beyond the position of Excerpt D, a presentation of her views, to an attempt to analyze the causes of the stereotyping (Larson's Category 5), she was not yet able to make recommendations about how the problem could be remedied. Although she did not use the word *stereotype* in this or later writings, this concept came to play an important role in her analysis of women's roles in society.

In Excerpt E, Linda began to link ideas within sentences more clearly than she had in previous writings. By presenting several ideas in sequence within individual sentences, Linda demonstrated her awareness that the ideas were related to each other. For example, when she sarcastically stated what some believe "God created [women] to do," she listed the roles that traditionally had been identified with the tasks of subservient women. She went on to note that women had been denied educational opportunities because of the value judgments that had been made about their qualifications. Even though Linda did not yet possess the academic language to express these ideas fully, it is clear that the reading she has done has prepared her to identify reasons for her objection to the assumption that all women should bear babies, a step she could not have taken a year earlier.

Between these two writings, Linda had taken two semesters of a World Civilization course. In the second semester, she wrote a paper (Excerpt F) about one of the female characters in Dickens's *Hard Times* in which she presented data about the social conditions within a historical period (Larson's Category 6):

Excerpt F

One positive note is that Louisa had the opportunity to have an equal education as her male counterpart. Women in this society had to either work in the factories or hopefully be born into a wealthy family. A solid education was not freely given to women. (Fall 1991)

Because of her increasing awareness of the attitudes of society toward women, Linda had begun to be aware of the importance of education and the independence it could provide for women. Linda had recognized that women in the past either had to work in factories or depend on men for support. Such a recognition may account, in part, for her later defense of her mother's intelligence despite her lack of higher education.

In Excerpt F, Linda continued to produce simple sentences, but she was starting to make judgments about the materials she had been reading. She understood the stark choices that confronted women in the 19th century and she was able to see Louisa's opportunities for education as a positive force in an otherwise bleak situation.

In her third year, Linda took a women's studies course and began to look at the "male-dominated" culture in a way that examined both sides of issues. Linda felt that writing was making her more interested in the materials in her courses and that research made her feel more involved, better informed. She said, "The something extra you've learned, you can keep in your brain" (September 23, 1991).

Linda's women's studies instructor encouraged her students to present their views on current problems in the society (Category 5 in Larson's set). Linda wrote:

Excerpt G

I, overall, have shown [in this paper] just a microcosm of women's problems from assorted viewpoints. Women have suffered so much in this world of ours. Unfortunately, women's cries go unanswered. As human beings, we should teach our society to understand the plight of women's hardships just as we thoroughly study the plights of others. People should be taught about women and their struggle to cope in a rampantly sexist society. Showing people daily experiences of what women go through will not only open their eyes, but it will give them a better sense of understanding the women who incorporate their lives. Today nothing could be more vital for a woman and also a man. Once we establish a basis of equilibrium between the sexes, the better the future will start to hold for them. (Fall 1991)

No longer satisfied to see women treated as victims, Linda had adopted a more assertive tone, arguing that when all individuals, men and women, were educated about the status of women in the society, both groups would benefit. Through education, she noted, all members of the society should be made aware of the constraints that affect women's lives and opportunities.

In Excerpt G, Linda began to establish causal relationships between ideas. The writing moved from a recognition that women's cries were unanswered to an identification of the reasons why this situation existed. She argued that when people were educated to "what women go through," they would not only come to understand the problems of women, but they might come to see the benefits of a more equal society for all. Thus she had moved beyond an analysis of the problem to a recommendation for solving it, fulfilling the second part of Larson's Category 5.

As evidence to support the notion that a sexist society currently exists, earlier in the paper (Excerpt H), Linda had analyzed the significance of the most widely read fairy tales and children's stories from her perspectives as both a woman and an African-American, here fulfilling Larson's Category 9 (analysis of a work of art, here a literary work):

Excerpt H

Take our classics like Little Red Riding Hood, Sleeping Beauty, Snow White and Cinderella. These young, virginal, fair-haired, white-skinned women who were considered epitomes of beauty were always the scared, gentle, feminine, shy, and quiet types. They were never strong women who could protect themselves. A man was always present to save "screaming damsels from distress." Women in these stories were never encouraged to bond as a strong group. Instead, they are pitted against each other with strong and disturbing hatred which lead to the demise of the other female. (Fall 1991)

In a clear and confident voice, Linda went beyond her previous assertions about the rights of women to be considered as equals to assert several problems in the literature that young women have been nurtured on: (a) that all heroines are depicted as weak and helpless, (b) that heroines are invariably White, and (c) that women are pictured as "pitted against each other" rather than in supportive relationships. These insights demonstrated a level of reflection and analysis beyond her earlier writings and showed that she had increasingly identified herself as an able African-American woman who would accept none of these stereotypical descriptions for herself.

In Excerpt H, Linda analyzed evidence from the fairy tales to reveal how stereotypes are formed. She also pondered the significance of how women are depicted as behaving destructively toward each other. Although she drew no conclusions in this section of her paper, her tone revealed her contempt for these characterizations.

By the end of her third year, Linda was able to recognize the media's role in stereotyping women. In a review of the film "Thelma and Louise" (Excerpt I, in Larson's Category 9, interpretation of a work of art, here a film) for a women's studies

course, Linda compared the way women are conventionally portrayed to the roles undertaken by the characters Thelma and Louise:

Excerpt I

This is a movie that gave me a good feeling. This film was seriously a breath of fresh air for me and probably alot [sic] of other women. When I first saw this movie in the city, I didn't know what to expect, a typical T&A [she seemed reluctant to write out the vulgar phrase, "tits and ass"] film where women were just floating objects of sexuality? No, it wasn't that. It was a film that let women know that they, too, had the right to let their hair down and explore the darkened mysterious roads of America's heartlands. (Spring 1992)

Recognizing how women had been stereotyped from fairy tales to 19th-century British literature to contemporary films, in Excerpt I, Linda explored her growing awareness of the need for women to assert the right to their individuality. The writing tasks pushed her increasingly from narration and description to analysis and synthesis. They led her finally to offer her own assessments of the materials she encountered and to create new insights for herself.

As Excerpt I reveals, Linda's writing allowed her to express her opinions about issues, but she had not yet mastered an academic presentation. Her language in this excerpt was more lyrical than in any of her earlier writing, perhaps reflecting the fact that she felt comfortable enough in this course to express herself more freely. Linda has told me that she writes creative pieces on her own and has done so since high school, but she has not yet shared any of those pieces with me.

Linda's progression in writing about the role of women in society was not matched by her overall performance at the college. She struggled with some of the science requirements for the nursing program, and in the courses that required analyses of abstract concepts, like philosophy, or analysis of complex texts like World Humanities and World Civilization, Linda floundered. She accounted for some of her difficulties by describing the teaching she received as presenting material that was "over [our] heads" (Philosophy 101). She failed the philosophy course and retook it in the fall of 1992 when she told me that her new instructor was "breaking things down which is helpful," but "It's too deep for me. Every time I leave that class, my brain hurts" (September 17, 1992).

When the first semester of the World Civilization course was partly a Black history class and dealt with issues like the then ongoing Persian Gulf War that engrossed her (September 23, 1991), Linda did well, but in the second semester course, the professor gave multiple-choice exams on which she was not successful. She did well on her papers and wrote extra papers for extra credit, trying to improve her grade (February 24, 1992). She passed the course with a "C." In these difficult courses, then, when writing was a component of evaluation, Linda was sometimes able to make up for her weaknesses in the examinations that demanded factual knowledge or subtle interpretation.

Linda was less confident and less successful in her ability to analyze the complex literary works she was reading in her World Humanities course. In an attempt to summarize how it was that Macbeth became king, Linda revealed confusion about the actual events in the play, thus demonstrating that writing alone was not helping her to recall factual information correctly from readings that she seemed not to be able to handle either independently or with the amount of support offered in the classroom lectures and discussions. She wrote:

Excerpt J

In the play *Macbeth* by William Shakespeare, Macbeth wanted to become king. In order to become king, Macbeth had to get rid of Banquo who was in line to become king. One night when Banquo and his son Fleon [sic] were travelling the roads, some thieves came upon them. Banquo was killed but Fleon escaped somewhere else. Since that event happened, Macbeth was given the title of king. (Fall 1990)

The instructor noted in the margin the actual facts of Macbeth's ascension to the throne to clarify the information for Linda. It is likely that her difficulty with reading the play limited what she felt confident writing about. Carolyn Burke has spoken of "levels of challenge" and "levels of frustration" in reading. If the works in the World Humanities course represented the level of frustration for Linda, writing alone could not overcome these difficulties for her. Much more support in the classroom would be essential, and instructors might pay heed to Vygotsky's (1978) "zone of proximal development" (p. 86), the concept that students should be presented with materials that they can handle with the assistance of a competent professional person. Her classroom instruction seemed not to be providing adequate assistance for her needs.

In this paper, Linda attempted no analysis or interpretation of the play. She seemed to sense that she was having so much difficulty understanding it that she could not move beyond an attempt at description.

By the end of the second year, Linda recognized that she had to work harder, that as she got deeper into her courses, she had to study harder. She was starting to do "a lot of deep thinking, especially about ethics [in the nursing course]." She saw that issues were complicated and that there was not necessarily "a right way." She said, "Writing helps teachers discover more about a person—how mature a person is and what the student is learning" (May 29, 1991). Linda was thinking of how her writing increased her instructors' awareness of her learning, but it was, of course, demonstrating to her also what knowledge she had gained and with what level of maturity she could handle that knowledge.

Linda's commitment to the field of nursing grew over her years at the college. She was in a supportive environment where her instructors made certain that students understood all the points being discussed in the class and elicited examples from the students' experiences and everyday life to help them make connections to the ideas being developed (class observation, March 2, 1992).

Encouraged by such support in her nursing courses, Linda was beginning to see the issues surrounding the profession of nursing. Analyzing one of the central issues of concern to her, she wrote (in Category 5 of Larson's set):

Excerpt K

Overall, if the [nursing] shortage had its advantages, its [sic] been on the salaries. The main thing here is that many hospitals will become self-satisfied once the shortage eases. Many people will forget about rewarding good nursing; then enrollments will drop again and the shortage cycle will start all over again. (Spring 1991)

Implicit here was Linda's recognition that the law of supply and demand would determine the ways in which nursing professionals would be valued. She seemed ready to recommend that the society recognize its needs for qualified nurses and not repeat the mistakes of previous years.

Linda reflected further on the consequences of nursing shortages in a small group paper she wrote with four other classmates:

Excerpt L

The concept of nursing shortage entails much more than just a lack of staff. It incorporates patient care or lack thereof, staff retention, nurse burnout, the definition of nursing roles, education, and interstaff conflicts. Unless many of these suggested solutions [proposed earlier in the paper] are put into practice, the many problems plaguing the nursing profession will continue and may even worsen, having a profound effect on direct patient care. (Spring 1991)

Here, with her classmates, Linda moved to Larson's Category 8, analyzing data related to a particular social condition (nursing shortage) to reflect on the implications of this problem. In particular, increasingly identifying herself as a nursing professional, Linda exhibited empathy not only for those within her profession but also for those affected most directly by her profession, the patients.

DISCUSSION OF THE CASE STUDY

Linda has not become a proficient writer thus far in her college experience, but she has grown in her ability to reflect on the ideas she has been exposed to in her courses and to question the assumptions of the society around her. As a woman and as an African-American, Linda has used the information she has studied in her courses to reassess the potential roles of women in the society. She has become aware of the roadblocks that may stand in her way. But her writing and her interviews reveal a dedication to her profession and a respect for herself that has strengthened her commitment to obtaining an education that will give her choices and opportunities that she recognizes were denied to her mother.

An analysis of her writing reveals that Linda has been given assignments over her first 3½ years at the college that were intended to give her opportunities to carry out many of the acts of discourse in Larson's scheme. In her first-year courses, Linda's writing remained primarily descriptive (Excerpt A), but in her psychology course she attempted an analysis of an experience using concepts from the course (Excerpt C). Her ability to handle analysis was very limited at this point, and she was unable to translate the concepts into her own language.

In her second year, Linda was able to identify an issue about which she felt strongly (Excerpt D), but she failed to provide reasons to support her position. The readings in the freshman composition course were not thematically structured, so no knowledge base was built in any area. In her World Humanities course, she reverted to description (Excerpt J) when the readings were inaccessible to her. On the other hand, the nursing course gave Linda an opportunity to examine issues in more depth (Excerpt K) so that she was able to analyze a problem and offer possible solutions. Excerpt L, written for that same course in a group writing, analyzed the implications of nursing shortages in a more sophisticated way than had appeared in the earlier writings.

In Linda's third year, her writing was strongly enhanced by her commitment to the topics she was reading about in her women's studies classes. In Excerpts E and G, she demonstrated that she could provide reasons to support her views when the material she was working with was accessible to her. In Excerpts H and I, she was able to analyze the impact of stereotyping of women in fairy tales and films.

In her fourth year, Linda's paper about her mother (Excerpt B) did not demonstrate the levels of analysis that she had shown herself capable of handling in other papers. It may be that the topic was too personal, and she did not wish to subject her mother to such scrutiny.

When this analysis of Linda's writing over the years is combined with a presentation of her overall academic progress at the college, it can be seen that Linda flourishes in settings that engage her deeply and that support her efforts to work out her perspectives through writing. But in environments where the materials are too conceptually complex for her, and the instructional settings neither provide sufficient support nor encourage writing as a means of working through issues, Linda is not as successful.

Writing helps students like Linda, but writing alone is not a sufficient teaching tool. Instructional support must be offered on an ongoing basis for students whose reading and writing processes require continual assistance and development.

WHAT CAN LONGITUDINAL STUDIES TELL US ABOUT WRITING DEVELOPMENT?

Longitudinal studies have several advantages over short-term studies for analyzing writing development. Although this particular study does not have composing process data, there is compensation for that lack in the other kinds of data that have been accumulated: interviews with the students twice each semester over 3½ years, so far; collection of papers written in a range of courses at a variety of levels; observation of instructional settings in composition courses, core curricula courses, and courses in students' majors.

When a longitudinal study follows groups of students who started their college experience at different levels of writing development, as this one has done, it is possible to examine whether those

groups that started at the lower levels "catch up" with those who started at a traditional level by the time all the groups have completed their academic programs. Furthermore, the writing of students within each group can be compared to determine what intragroup differences there may be and what effect academic majors have on writing development. In addition, an examination of the writing progress of each level of students provides an opportunity to compare the writing progress of students within groups as well as between groups.

The effect on writing development of different disciplines can also be assessed. Previous studies of writing development have suggested that writing in the humanities fosters analytic development (Hays, 1983), but there has been little examination of the effects of writing in other disciplines.

Longitudinal studies that take into consideration the contextual factors of the lives of students can account for the ease or difficulty that individual students may have in accomplishing their academic goals. For example, all too frequently the students in my study have told me that their arduous hours of outside employment have interfered with their ability to carry out academic tasks as rigorously as they would like to. This kind of information should not be offered as an excuse for less proficient accomplishment, but it could suggest to instructors that, on occasion, some flexibility in deadlines might make significant differences in students' performance.

There are several instructional implications that can be seen from these first years of data collection in my longitudinal study. For example, as Linda's case study demonstrates, as soon as students move out of composition programs into core curriculum courses or courses required for their major, it is assumed that they can handle tasks that require analysis of conceptually difficult reading materials and the writing of complex papers. It seems reasonable to suggest, then, that the composition courses, beginning at the lowest levels of basic writing, should provide students with opportunities to practice analysis and synthesis even as they are mastering rhetorical forms and grammatical structures.

Designers of core curricula can sequence materials within courses and between courses that will assist students in handling increasingly complex texts. All such courses should foster writing as exploration as well as analysis to assist students in comprehending and analyzing these texts. Students need to be encouraged to take risks in their writing so that new insights may emerge. Emphasis needs to be placed on providing instructional support in the core courses, especially in institutions where student populations have likely not had rigorous demands placed on them before they came to college.

It is, of course, impossible to generalize about the value of a longitudinal study to understand the role of writing development through the examination of one case study. But this case study does reveal aspects of how writing affects learning that have not been considered in earlier studies.

In this article, then, I have attempted to place the case study of one student within the larger context of her academic institution and her life experiences. From the snapshots of her life and her academic progress, it is possible to see that longitudinal studies have the ability to provide insights about writing development that are not accessible through other research methods.

Note

Support for this longitudinal study has been provided by the Professional Staff Congress-City University of New York Research Foundation, the National Council of Teachers of English Research Foundation, and Paul Sherwin, the Dean of Humanities of the City College of New York. Special thanks to my research assistants, David Marshall, Tara Cunningham, and Esther Bohm. I also wish to thank Roger Cherry for his many helpful suggestions and editorial comments on earlier drafts.

Works Cited

Brandt, D. (1992). The cognitive as the social: An ethnomethodological approach to writing process research. *Written Communication, 9,* 315–355.

Britton, J., Burgess, T., Martin, N., McLeod, A., & Rosen, H. (1975). *The development of writing abilities: 11 to 18.* Urbana, IL: National Council of Teachers of English.

Freedman, A., & Pringle, I. (1980). Writing in the college years: Some indices of growth. *College Composition and Communication, 31,* 311–324.

Hays, J. N. (1983). The development of discursive maturity in college writers. In J. N. Hays, P. A. Roth, J. R. Ramsey, & R. D. Foulke (Eds.), *The writers mind* (pp. 127–144). Urbana, IL: National Council of Teachers of English.

Langer, J. A., & Applebee, A. N. (1987). *How writing shapes thinking: A study of teaching and learning* (Research Report No. 22). Urbana, IL: National Council of Teachers of English.

Larson, R. L. (1991). Using portfolios in the assessment of writing in the academic disciplines. In P. Belanoff & M. Dickson (Eds.), *Portfolios: Process and product* (pp. 137–149). Portsmouth, NH: Boynton/Cook-Heinemann.

Lavin, D. E., Alba, R. D., & Silberstein, R. A. (1981). *Right versus privilege: The open admissions experiment at the City University of New York.* New York: Free Press.

Loban, W. (1963). *The language of elementary school children* (Research Report No. 1). Champaign, IL: National Council of Teachers of English.

Lunsford, A. A. (1980). The content of basic writers' essays. *College Composition and Communication, 31,* 278–290.

Newell, G. E. (1984). Learning from writing in two content areas: A case study/protocol analysis. *Research in the Teaching of English, 18,* 265–287.

Newell, G. E., & Winograd, P. (1989). The effects of writing on learning from expository text. *Written Communication, 8,* 196–217.

Perry, W. (1968). *Forms of intellectual and ethical development in the college years, a scheme.* New York: Holt, Rinehart & Winston.

Piaget, J. (1955). *The language and thought of the child.* New York: Meridian.

Rose, M. (1988). Narrowing the mind and page: Remedial writers and cognitive reductionism. *College Composition and Communication, 39,* 267–297.

Schumacher, G. M., & Nash, J. G. (1991). Conceptualizing and measuring knowledge change due to writing. *Research in the Teaching of English, 25,* 67–96.

Spear, K. I. (1983). Thinking and writing: A sequential curriculum for composition. *Journal of Advanced Composition, 4,* 47–63.

Sternglass, M. S. (1993, April). *When I write something, it goes more into my brain.* Paper presented at the annual meeting of the Conference on College Composition and Communication, San Diego, CA.

Vygotsky, L. S. (1978). *Mind in society: The development of higher psychological processes* (M. Cole, V. John-Steiner, S. Scribner, & E. Souberman, Eds.). Cambridge: Harvard University Press.

Walvoord, B. E., & McCarthy, L. P. (1990). *Thinking and writing in college: A naturalistic study of students in four disciplines.* Urbana, IL: National Council of Teachers of English.

Wilkinson, A., Barnsley, G., Hanna, P., & Swan, M. (1980). *Assessing language development.* Oxford: Oxford University Press.

Part Four

Politics

The (Re)Turn
to the Political

MARK WILEY

> . . . [F]or leftist teachers and educational theorists, what seems to make pedagogy radical is the informing sense that schooling is a political event, preshaped by the pressures and limits of the dominant culture. From this perspective, the politics called for in radical pedagogy appear to be self-evident, a matter of politicizing the classroom by raising to consciousness the ways schooling and other cultural practices articulate race, class, nationality, gender, sexual orientation, and so on to mark and legitimatize differences in an unequal social order. (194)

This citation appears in John Trimbur's review essay published in *College English* in 1994. It is Trimbur's way of characterizing "radical pedagogy." By 1994, his characterization of these practices appears to be a commonplace. But let me set up a dialectic with Trimbur's description by juxtaposing Maxine Hairston's question and response concerning the politics of radical pedagogy that appear in her essay "Diversity, Ideology, and Teaching Writing" (*CCC*, 1994; included in this chapter).

> But how did all this happen? Why has the cultural left suddenly claimed writing courses as their political territory?
>
> There's no simple answer, of course. Major issues about social change and national priorities are involved, and I cannot digress into those concerns in this essay. But my first response is, "You see what happens when we allow writing programs to be run by English departments." (p. 533).

When we were debating what should and should not be in this chapter, we recognized that many of the articles that seemed overtly "political" appeared in journals with increasing frequency from the mid-1980s onward. Some might call this period the "political turn" in composition and rhetoric. Though seemingly slow to begin influencing work in the field, post-structuralist, post-modern, neo-Marxist, and feminist themes appear more consistently in the composition and rhetoric

Inquiry

Survey the table of contents of back issues of *College English, College Composition and Communication, Language Arts, Rhetoric Review, Journal of Advanced Composition, Pre/Text*, and *Journal of Basic Writing*. Note the titles of articles, and skim some of them in order to detect shifts or trends in the focus of work published between the 1970s and the present.

literature during this time. If we use the journals as a gauge of scholarly interests, then Politics—the fourth key—apparently emerged later in the field than the other three. Trimbur's description of the "politicized" classroom and Hairston's resistance to that political turn is one site among several others where the drama of turning political is, at this writing, being enacted. By initiating a dialogue about politics in composition and rhetoric, I want to pose the question of *when* it emerged as precisely the problem, for in trying to answer questions about the *when,* we invariably get to questions about the *why.* As readers pursue possible answers, they can begin exploring the scope and ramifications of politics in the field.

It is perhaps a truism now that composition and rhetoric took a social turn during the 1980s. In that period, scholarship and research focused increasingly on the social dimensions and contexts of language use, and the keys of Nature, Art, and Science seemed to reflect that turn as well. Yet, though the political always involves the social, the social does not necessarily entail the political. Why did the turn to the social usher in the political? Or perhaps a more productive way of posing the same question is, Why did composition's growing awareness of the social dimensions of language translate into concerns regarding the politics of writing instruction? Let me construct a series of possible explanations to account for this emergence of the political.

One story about composition and rhetoric might read this way: First-generation compositionists were primarily concerned with the relationship between language and mind as mediated by texts. So they looked chiefly to cognitive science and to linguistics, to text discourse analysis, to literary theories, and to classical rhetoric for their ideas and working concepts in order to explain how thought eventually winds up as text. However, in mining these other disciplines and traditions, certain anomalies could not be ignored. By investigating classical rhetoric, scholars could see the relation between the "well wrought" text and the social situation (or scene) within which that text made sense. Texts could not be separated from their contexts, and therefore examining various scenes of writing opened up a range of functions for writing and the roles writers might play. Instead of students in a composition class producing the English department's idealized version of the "perfect" text, they could produce texts that perform actions in the world. A composition course might then provide rhetorical training for students to prepare them to be effective citizens in a democratic society (see Halloran's essay in this volume).

Inquiry

Explanations of change usually begin with the work of the field and ask how those doing it discovered some limitations or problems. Another way, however, to approach change in the keys of composition is to look to those external contexts that created new conditions making politics, or a new conception of politics, more visible or important. Consider what social events (American, global) and economic or political or cultural changes might have influenced composition's definition of and interest in the political in the 1960s and 1970s versus the 1980s and 1990s. (Or, conversely, try to identify the historical continuity between these periods.)

Another story could also be told if "mind" is our key term. The relationship of thought to language led to considerations of how, to put it rather baldly, ideas get into our heads. The emphasis on the social nature of language led scholars to examine the material sources for our thinking. This social materialist orientation toward cognition gathered momentum through the influence of Lev Vygotsky's theories concerning the place of "mind in society." Vygotsky postulated that all higher mental activity originates in the social sphere. The fact that Vygotsky's thinking arose within a Marxist context (whether scholars wanted to recognize this fact or not) directed attention toward the relation between individual thought and larger social and ideological systems within which our thinking is embedded. Scholars such as Richard Ohmann in "Use Definite, Specific, Concrete Language" were pointing out the materialist bases of language (and by extension, thought) as well as how composition courses themselves served class interests (see *English in America*).

The emergence of politics can also be accounted for if we take language as our protagonist where it plays a primary role in the symbolic meaning-making activity of literacy. As the gaze of scholarship and research moved away from the scene of classroom instruction toward other scenes of practice, differences in how individuals and groups acquired, used, and were taught to use language became evident. The literacy research of Shirley Brice Heath and Scribner and Cole placed in stark relief cultural variations regarding types of literacy and how it is used and valued in different sociocultural contexts.

But now stand back a minute and consider what I have just done. I have used familiar categories to suggest (albeit in a necessarily simplistic way) how the political emerged from within this social turn. I have used *text, mind,* and *language* (or *literacy*) to generate my accounts. Yet I have been offering these accounts from a perspective outside the key of Politics. In fact, when viewing my explanations from within this key, I have not been offering any account of the political at all. Once I start looking at my hypothetical explanations from a political perspective, my "key"

Inquiries

1. In "Inventing the University," Bartholomae says that

[i]f writing is a process, it is also a product; and it is the product, and not the plan for writing, that locates a writer on the page, that locates him in a text and a style and the codes or conventions that make both of them readable" (465).

Reflect on Bartholomae's insistence that writing is a product. What does he mean by "product"? How might his meaning differ from the way those in Nature and Art talk about the writing process and its products? How does Bartholomae's understanding of the product of writing possibly shift the way writing is taught compared to Art and Nature? What does happen to the product versus process debate in the key of Politics?

2. Smitherman-Donaldson refers to the resolution passed in 1974 by the Conference on College Composition and Communication. That resolution reads:

We affirm the students' right to their own patterns and varieties of language—the dialects of their nurture or whatever dialects in which they find their own identity and style. Language scholars long ago denied that the myth of a standard American dialect has any validity. The claim that any one dialect is unacceptable amounts to an attempt of one social group to exert its dominance over another. Such a claim leads to false advice for speakers and writers, and immoral advice for humans. A nation proud of its heritage and its cultural and racial variety will preserve its heritage of dialects. We affirm strongly that teachers must have the experiences and training that will enable them to respect diversity and uphold the right of students to their own language. (3)

This political statement weaves together the multicultural and the moral. Think about not only why, in Smitherman-Donaldson's words, the "goal" of the resolution "was not realized" but about what has happened to language policies in the writing class since this resolution was first approved. Consider language issues related to ESL students and their writing but also think about some of the issues raised in Villanueva, Jr.'s autobiographical reflections concerning contrastive rhetoric and possible influences on the various ways students use their languages. Is there a place in the writing class for variations in rhetorical form and for experimenting with different discourses? Does your understanding of "multiculturalism," for instance, include tolerance for nonconventional stylistic forms in student texts?

3. As you reflect on language issues related to genres and writing styles, try to explain what might justify differences in such styles as Susan Miller's and Peter Elbow's. What might each say about the other's way of arguing?

4. In the anthology *Composition and Resistance,* James Berlin justifies the use of cultural studies in the composition class by arguing that those who do such work

> make students aware of the cultural codes—the various competing discourses—that attempt to influence who they are. Our larger purpose is to encourage students to resist and to negotiate these codes—these hegemonic discourses—in order to bring about more personally humane and socially equitable economic and political arrangements. (50)

In the same anthology, Jay Rosen and Joseph Harris want to use their writing course on media criticism to help students "become critics," to help them "begin to resist the power of discourses, to transform their rules" (66–67).

Explore some of the recent work arguing for including cultural studies in the composition class. As you research these pedagogies, examine not only descriptions of them but defenses and critiques. See if you can identify roles student writers are asked to assume in representative pedagogies across these keys. What are the implications of these various roles for what students understand about writing and its functions?

5. The writing across the curriculum movement has also helped focus questions concerning the function of writing at various institutional sites. Conflicts between using writing to learn and learning to write in the disciplines may reflect enduring themes articulated differently in these keys (see Kirscht et al.). Consider how the scene of writing might determine its function. What, for instance, is the relevance of some of the political conflicts you have identified with writing that occur both within and outside the academy?

organizing terms are transformed. *Mind,* for instance, is meaningful only within some disciplinary context where certain ways of thinking and speaking about it are privileged over others. Also neglected are analyses of external sociocultural, political, and economic changes and their effects on disciplinary concerns.

James Berlin might say that my account fails to recognize its own rhetoricality. In "Rhetoric and Ideology," he asserts that "[a] rhetoric can never be innocent, can never be a disinterested arbiter of the ideological claims of others because it is always already serving certain ideological claims" (477). In his argument, Berlin substitutes the grounds for meaningful discourse

> in a way that situates rhetoric within ideology, rather than ideology within rhetoric. . . . [I]nstead of rhetoric acting as the transcendental recorder or arbiter of competing ideological claims, rhetoric is regarded as always already ideological. This position means that any examination of a rhetoric must first consider the ways its very discursive structure can be read so as to favor one version of economic, social, and political arrangements over other versions.

Consequently, some might want to argue that the turn to politics was not new at all, but rather a "return." One could argue that composition and rhetoric emerged precisely in response to a political exigency. Because of a host of social, economic, and political forces in the 1950s and 1960s, students who previously might not have considered enrolling in college did so. Open admissions policies of the 1960s and 1970s accelerated this shift in population, forcing changes in writing instruction because these "new" students brought with them a variety of socio-cultural experiences and linguistic backgrounds that defied conventional wisdom about how students learned to write. When seen from within the key of politics, Mina Shaughnessy's *Errors and Expectations* was a politically sensitive response to meet the needs of basic writers as those needs were institutionalized by the open admissions policy at City College in New York.

Accounts explaining why the key of Politics emerged in the mid-1980s are contingent on definitions of the political. If you see politics as the sort of radical pedagogy described by Trimbur, then perhaps for you the political emerges later in composition than the other three keys. If you define the political differently, you may see other beginnings and points of intersection that move the political from the background to the fore of the field's interests—regardless of whether those interests were explicitly acknowledged earlier. As you read through this chapter and consider composition in the key of Politics, note not only new themes and concerns but any recurring themes encountered in other keys that have been somehow transformed or used for differently conceived ends.

WORKS CITED

Berlin, James. "Rhetoric and Ideology." *College English* 50 (1988): 477–94.

Heath, Shirley Brice. *Ways With Words: Language, Life, and Work in Communities and Classrooms.* Cambridge: Cambridge UP, 1984.

Ohmann, Richard. "Use Definite, Specific, Concrete Language." *College English* 41 (1979): 390–97.

——. *English in America: A Radical View of the Profession.* New York: Oxford UP, 1976.

Scribner, Sylvia, and Michael Cole. *The Psychology of Literacy.* Cambridge: Harvard UP, 1981.

Shaughnessy, Mina P. *Errors and Expectations: A Guide for the Teaching of Basic Writing.* New York: Oxford UP, 1977.

Trimbur, John. "The Politics of Radical Pedagogy: A Plea for 'A Dose of Vulgar Marxism.'" *College English* 56 (1994): 194–206.

Vygotsky, Lev S. *Mind in Society: The Development of Higher Psychological Processes.* Eds. Michael Cole, Vera J. Steiner, Sylvia Scribner, and Ellen Souberman. Cambridge: Harvard UP, 1978.

SUGGESTED READINGS

Language Issues

Allen, Michael. "Writing Away from Fear: Mina Shaughnessy and the Uses of Authority." *College English* 41 (1980): 857–75.

Bleich, David. "Genders of Writing." *Journal of Advanced Composition* 9 (1989): 10–25.

Butler, Melvin, ed. "Students' Right to Their Own Language." Urbana: NCTE, 1974.

Daniels, Harvey A., ed. *Not Only English: Affirming America's Multicultural Heritage.* Urbana: NCTE, 1990.

Pedagogical Issues

Berlin, James A., and Michael J. Vivion, eds. *Cultural Studies in the English Classroom.* Portsmouth: Boynton/Cook, 1992.

Bizzell, Patricia. "The Politics of Teaching Virtue." *ADE Bulletin* 103 (1992): 4–7.

Cooper, Marilyn M., and Michael Holzman. *Writing as Social Action.* Portsmouth: Boynton/Cook, 1989.

Fox, Thomas. "Repositioning the Profession: Teaching Writing to African American Students." *Journal of Advanced Composition* 12 (1992): 291–303.

Hurlbert, C. Mark, and Michael Blitz, eds. *Composition & Resistance.* Portsmouth: Boynton/Cook, 1991.

Phelps, Louise Wetherbee. "The Politics of Teaching Virtue." *ADE Bulletin* 103 (1992): 13–20.

Institutional, Disciplinary, and Cultural Issues

Crowley, Sharon. "A Personal Essay on Freshman English." *PRE/TEXT* 12 (1991): 155–76.

Flannery, Kathryn T. "Concepts of Culture: Cultural Literacy/Cultural Politics." *Farther Along: Transforming Dichotomies in Rhetoric and Composition.* Eds. Kate Ronald and Hephzibah Roskelly. Portsmouth: Boynton/Cook, 1990. 86–100.

Gunner, Jeanne. "The Fate of the Wyoming Resolution: A History of Professional Seduction." *Writing Ourselves into the Story: Unheard Voices from Composition Studies.* Eds. Sheryl I. Fontaine and Susan Hunter. Carbondale: Southern Illinois UP, 1993. 107–22.

Holbrook, Sue Ellen. "Women's Work: The Feminizing of Composition." *Rhetoric Review* 9 (1991): 201–29.

Kirscht, Judy, Rhonda Levine, and John Reiff. "Evolving Paradigms: WAC and the Rhetoric of Inquiry." *College Composition and Communication* 45 (1994): 369–80.

Schilb, John, and Patricia Harkin, eds. *Contending With Words: Composition and Rhetoric in a Postmodern Age.* New York: MLA, 1991.

Sledd, James. "Why the Wyoming Resolution Had to Be Emasculated: A History and a Quixotism." *Journal of Advanced Composition* 11 (1991): 261–81.

Slevin, James. "The Politics of the Profession." *Introduction to Composition Studies.* Eds. Erika Lindemann and Gary Tate. New York: Oxford UP, 1991. 135–59.

The Politics of Composition

John Rouse

This selection is from College English *41 (1979): 1–12.*

Of all school subjects, English is surely the most controversial. How the young should be instructed in their use of language is an issue that agitates multitudes, for language learning is the process by which a child comes to acquire a specific social identity. What kind of person should we help bring into being? So important has English become in socializing the young that it is now compulsory through all the twelve years of early schooling and sometimes beyond. And every vested interest in the community is concerned with what is to happen during those years, with how language training is to be organized and evaluated, for the continued survival of any power structure requires the production of certain personality types. The making of an English program becomes, then, not simply an educational venture but a political act.

We have an interesting illustration of this in Mina Shaughnessy's recent work, *Errors and Expectations* (New York: Oxford University Press, 1977), which describes a writing program for open admissions students in the City University of New York. With open admissions large numbers of young people formerly considered unsuited for higher learning or incapable of it, particularly blacks and hispanics, now gained entrance to college. The essays they wrote during their first weeks in class, Shaughnessy tells us, "stunned the teachers who read them." Here were teachers "trained to analyze the belletristic achievements of the centuries marooned in basic writing classrooms with adult students who appeared by college standards to be illiterate" (p. 3). And marooned there without a suitable guide or even textbook. So Shaughnessy has supplied in this book a guide, a sort of frontier map as she describes it, to the basic writing wilderness. But the overriding need to socialize these young people in a manner politically acceptable accounts, I think, for her misinterpretations of student work and her disregard of known facts of language learning.

Consider her reading of one paper, the first example of student writing she offers. This paper, we are told, illustrates the "disintegration" of a student who so fears making mistakes that he cannot get going. For these are young people who know they leave behind a trail of errors as they write, and usually they can think of little else. So this student, inhibited by fear, has made ten abortive attempts to get going with the first essay assignment, including these:

Start 1

Seeing and hearing is something beautiful and strange to infant.

Start 3

I agree that seeing and hearing is something beautiful and stronge to a infants. A infants heres a strange sound such as work mother, he than acc

Start 8

I agree and disagree that seeing and hearing have a different quality for infants than for grownups, because to see and hear for infants its all so new and mor appreciate, but I also feel that a child parent appreciate the sharing

424

Start 10

I disagree I fell that seeig and hearing has the same quality to both infants and parents. Hearing and seeing is such a great quality to infants and parents, and they both appreciate, just because there aren't that many panters or musicians around doesn't mean that infants are more sensitive to beautiful than there parents. (pp. 7–8)

But surely these failures do not illustrate the student's fear of making errors but rather his desperate effort to find *something* to say about the assigned topic. His thought moves from paraphrase through agreement to disagreement—and this last position pays off, it provides the most words.

But not enough to satisfy Shaughnessy, who wants a developed essay contrasting the ways children and adults see the physical world. Now there's a task likely to leave any of us stammering for words. In this program young people are not asked to write about matters that engage them deeply, that draw on their experience and knowledge of life, they are asked to write about "trends in kidnapping" or "City X and the tree crisis." No wonder they seem inarticulate or unthinking.

They must feel a considerable anxiety. Any writing task involves anxiety, of course—we always wonder if the words will come, if the ideas will make good sense. But our interest in the project keeps us going until finally we have created from out of ourselves and our material an essay, perhaps, that might interest others. And once more we feel at peace with ourselves. But here the students are cut off by these topics from their own resources, and their anxiety level must rise. What *can* I say? Notice how in his desperation this student is willing to take any position, to agree or disagree or both at once—any position that will supply the needed words and satisfy the demand of authority. Here with this first writing assignment begins a training in that amorality so useful to authority everywhere.

Authority needs people concerned with the smooth transmission of messages, not with their meaning. People who will carry out their assigned functions without raising troublesome questions about the human consequences of their work, about

the moral meaning of what they do. And here are all these young students ready for training. So far, without their success, cut off from the interests that would sustain them, they welcome with relief the suggestion that first they must learn to use language correctly. They now demand prescriptive teaching, Shaughnessy tells us, they demand grammar (p. 11). That should do it. That's something specific and factual we can get hold of. We will learn to write and we will succeed by learning the "rules and principles of language." After having resisted just such instruction all their school years, they now declare themselves ready, even eager, to toe the line. Of course the inadequacy of traditional grammar as a description of the language is well-known in the profession, but no matter—it still retains a useful disciplinary value. It helps train young people to be concerned with the rules laid down by authority, even when those rules do not fit the situation. Language training is always behavior training.

And so Shaughnessy will oblige them by teaching grammar. Yet there may still be some resistance at first because "the effort to perceive forms rather than meanings . . . goes against the grain" (p. 129), so the instructor must make the reason for stressing grammar clear. If you know the rules you can correct your errors. Now comes the customary machine metaphor: How can you repair a motor if you don't know how it works? (p. 137). As though a living language is like a machine that must be kept in repair, its purpose fulfilled in the smooth functioning of the mechanism. But like everyone who opts for this approach to writing instruction, Shaughnessy is soon entangled in endless complications. There are at least four grammatic concepts the students must know in order to correct their errors, she tells us: sentence, inflection, tense, and agreement—and knowing these means knowing person, number, mood, prepositional phrases, modifying clauses, adverbial modifiers, auxiliary verbs, and much more. The student who writes "He watches the car moves" probably

is unaware that the second verb is non-finite and therefore has no tense so that the rule governing the choice of a finite verb does not apply. (p. 133)

Is that clear, everyone? If not, Shaughnessy will make it clear with a simple rule. But there are so many exceptions to this simple rule that five more rules are needed to account for them, and a lesson on all this requires pages of exercises (pp. 137–152). All so that students can learn to proofread their papers and correct their errors. And proofreading itself, they learn, "is an indispensible aid to the mastery of grammar" (p. 155). So the system turns back on itself in a closed circle, there is no escape: proofreading is not so much for the clarification of meaning as for the learning of rules!

Shaughnessy knows that teaching grammar as a method of teaching writing has no support whatever in research evidence. But that's only because grammar has not been taught properly, you see, the lessons "have traditionally ended up with exercises in workbooks, which, by highlighting the feature being studied, rob the student of any practice in seeing that feature in more natural places" (p. 155). This bit of sophistry cannot disguise the fact that most of Shaughnessy's own exercises would fit nicely into a traditional grammar text like *Warriner's Handbook*. But what her argument lacks in substance it gains in political appeal. Consider those teachers "trained to analyze the belletristic achievements of the centuries marooned in basic writing classrooms." They can now turn to the mysteries of grammar, they can still be the expositors of an esoteric knowledge. They can still be authorities. Shaughnessy is satisfying here a powerful need.

And at the same time she offers them a certain freedom. They are free in this program to ignore modern linguistic scholarship, free to invent their own grammar as they go along, perhaps

> a Rube Goldberg grammar, full of borrowed and makeshift parts, unsupported by any overarching theory, untransferable to any book or even another classroom, but for reasons never researchable somehow able to do the job at the particular moment. (p. 156)

For on the basic writing frontier, where little is known about how young people like these learn language skills, we must invent English composition anew out of our own understanding of students and language (p. 120). In other words, teachers must be free to ignore evidence or theory, free to rely on their own intuition or insight. Oh, how we love to hear that! But what effect does this have on students? They are not free in this program, they are learning the rules laid down by authority—rules that may be invented on the spot to fit the occasion. They are being trained to follow authority, however willful or arbitrary. They must sense this in the dynamics of the lesson—how do they feel about it?

My young friend Eileen invited me to visit her at school, so next day I went. By the time I found her classroom the grammar lesson was already underway, the teacher standing at the chalkboard before the rows of children, illustrating the mysteries of the sentence: verb, adverb, predicate, pronoun, determiner, noun phrase. After a time I glanced over at Eileen. She sat there at her desk, resting her head in one hand propped up by an arm while she doodled with the other hand in restless indifference. The training begins this early, in third grade.

Shaughnessy has reviewed a great mass of student work, and she has found that many of the errors these young people make in their writing can be traced to nonstandard speech habits. Yet that does not account for all their errors, she points out, perhaps not even for the most serious ones. Because whether their speech is standard or not, all students face the same difficult task: learning to use patterns of language in their writing that are not used in ordinary talk (p. 51). And these young people, unlike their middle-class predecessors, have had little experience with the patterns of the formal code used in writing, they write as they do because they are beginners. This formulation, this insistence that writing is so different from speech that it constitutes a separate code or dialect, will involve Shaughnessy in serious misconceptions about language training. And it leaves unanswered the question, Why are these students unprepared for the elaborations of formal writing? Why after all these years of schooling are they still only beginners?

One answer could be this: Because they still rely on a restricted code learned in their family and neighborhood, the schools having failed to teach them an elaborated *speech* code and the habits of mind that go with it. This formulation has been developed by Basil Bernstein in his *Class, Codes and Control* (1971; 2nd ed. London: Routledge and Kegan Paul, 1975), where he describes these two speech forms and how they are learned. A restricted code relies on context to give its statements meaning, on common experience. It is for all of us the language of intimacy, a language in which little need be made explicit because so much is understood. When Bernstein speaks of it a sense of loneliness may come over us, we long once more for the warmth and heartfelt communion remembered from our most satisfying relationships. But a child who has only that code is at a disadvantage in school, where the whole educational enterprise is for more explicitness and for the mind that takes nothing for granted. Schools in the industrial society take people away from their familiar, intimate places and require them to make their meanings plain to everyone, to work with an elaborated code. Usually the middle-class child has learned those speech forms and habits of mind needed for success in school and the outside world, where verbal explicitness matters, but the lower-class child may not have been socialized in the same advantageous way.

Bernstein illustrates this difference by describing two families. In one the children must do as they are told because they must learn to take their places in a pattern; no other reason than the pattern is given as explanation. A boy who plays with dolls is told, "Little boys do not play with dolls." If he persists then his mother gives him a drum and says, "Here, play with this." In the family pattern his position is that of a child, a boy, perhaps the first, and he must act accordingly. So his roles are gradually made apparent to him in rules and categories. In the other family, however, the mother says, "Why do you want to play with the doll—they are so boring—why not play with the drum?" She speaks to the child as to an individual with decisions to make, she invites him to think about the situation. Where the first child might challenge the authority of the parent, the second child learns to question the reasons given by the parent. He might say, on

another occasion, "Why do you always have a headache when I want to play?"

Or consider what happens when the family goes to visit a grandfather who is unwell and so has not been shaving. The child does not want to kiss him. On the way one mother says to the child, "Children kiss their Grandpa." If the child objects, the mother might say, "He's not well—I don't want none of your nonsense." The other mother says, however, "I know you don't like kissing Grandpa, but he is unwell, and he is very good to you, and it makes him happy." She recognizes the child's intent explicitly and relates it to the wishes of another. Also, she encourages the child to make an independent judgment, as though there is a choice. If the child makes an objection or raises a question, more explanation is given. So the mother lays out the situation for the child, who learns the rule in an individualized and interpersonal context. Given the situation and the explanation, the child opts for the rule—*achieves* the rule, so to speak. Control in this family is personal, and based on verbally elaborated meanings rather than on power (although power remains, of course, the real basis of authority). And the child, not having been assigned a role, must learn to make one and find a place through verbal interaction with others. The value of such learning in a highly differentiated, success-oriented culture is evident.

Those children who have been led by their family experience to strive towards their own role and position have a sense of uniqueness, of separation from others: each has in mind what "I think" as against what "you think." So they learn to make their meanings explicit—to reach conclusions, give reasons for them, and relate both to the experience of others. And these habits of mind are expressed in the structure of their sentences, in an elaborated speech code. Schooling is for them the further development of a social identity already welling-established. But those children who have been assigned their roles by adults have a sense of sameness, of oneness with others in their position; each has in mind what "we think" as against what "they think." So they learn to rely on implicit meanings—to make unqualified assertions, omit reasons, and assume common experience. And these habits of mind are expressed in the structure of their sentences, in a restricted speech code. Such children have learned all the language options used by others for logical modification and stress—they know, for example, the connectives used for relating ideas—but their family experience does not elicit them. Whole orders of learning are unavailable in the family where control is positional, and schooling requires of these children a fundamental change in the way they look at things, in their very identity.

That Shaughnessy is working with students limited to a restricted speech code is evident from the observations she makes about their writing habits. They put down ideas without giving evidence or reasons, she tells us—for they have not yet learned to communicate with the anonymous reader, who expects evidence and reasons to be made explicit (p. 187). They often fail to name the object or person or idea they write about, making vague references instead to "it" and "they" and "thing" (p. 199). The connections between their statements are usually implicit, they assume the reader understands what is going on in the writer's mind and therefore needs no introductions, transitions, or explanations (p. 240). So limited is their way with words that their encounters with school language have generally been humiliating, and the pleasures of peer and neighborhood talk still have a strong hold on them (p. 10). In short, their writing shows that even after twelve years of training many have "never successfully reconciled the worlds of home and school" (p. 3).

Shaughnessy's explanation is rather more simple than Bernstein's: These students lack experience with the patterns of language used in writing, she tells us, they are "unfamiliar with certain features of the code that governs formal English" (p. 45). That's why they've always had trouble in school. So obviously they must learn those forms and patterns they don't know, they must be given exercises and pattern practice with logical connectives, for example, so that they learn how to use words like *although, unless,* and *because* (p. 30). In this way, through sentence-combining and other exercises,

they will learn how ideas are logically connected, they will learn the syntactic choices open to them. In fact, the value of writing and then correcting the errors lies in discovering that language is influenced by rules and patterns that can be learned (p. 76). Where Bernstein is concerned with social interaction and the habits of mind and speech it produces, Shaughnessy confines herself to the rules and patterns of written expression. And doing so, insisting that writing be considered a thing apart, soon involves her in various misconceptions about language training.

For example, she believes that these students should learn how to punctuate a sentence by learning how to analyze it grammatically. They come to class unaware of "the role that grammatical structure plays in determining which of the many pauses in speech get marked and which get ignored," they need to learn about relative clauses and appositional forms and participial phrases and all the rest. What modern punctuation does, she tells us, is to "sharpen the sense of structure in a sentence . . . by showing how certain words, phrases, or clauses within the sentence are related" (p. 24). But that is *not* the case. Although writing may be more formal and more elaborate in its structural patterns than speech, it derives from speech and is punctuated to indicate the pitch and pause of spoken language. In *A Dictionary of Modern American Usage* (New York: Random House, 1957), Bergan Evans remarks that commas, together with colons and semicolons,

> were once used to show the grammatical relationships between different parts of a sentence. This is no longer true. In the United States today we use a comma to reflect a speech device, which sometimes shows grammatical relationship but sometimes does not. Anyone who learns to hear a comma can use it correctly ever after. (p. 102)

Teaching punctuation, then, would mean teaching students how to listen to written sentences, and how to test their own sentences by ear.

Further, Shaughnessy believes that unless students learn rules and patterns they cannot improve their work. They cannot, for example, add to their vocabulary of connectives unless they can explain the relationships between sentences and parts of sentences (p. 54). Of course students already have these connectives, she tells us, but they don't really *know* them, they don't have a cognitive grasp of them—they can't tell us, for example, that logical connectives fall into six categories that represent six types of logical relationships (p. 34). By this dubious line of reasoning Shaughnessy justifies what she calls the analytic method. Students will learn to improve their work by analyzing it according to the rules and patterns of formal writing—they will learn to dismember the body of language and label the parts as they would dismember a dead specimen in a laboratory. Finding some anomalous part, some error, they will substitute another form as dictated by the rules. So these students practice their "finger exercises," as Shaughnessy calls them, their manipulations of dead sentences, in order to get this cognitive grasp of form. In this method *rationality* is a key concept; form will be rationalized according to rules that are grasped cognitively. Shaughnessy often speaks as though students will write not so much to express their individual meaning as to learn rules and patterns—as though they need only regularize their forms and meaning will take care of itself. Yet most syntactic errors do not result from ignorance of forms but rather from inconsistencies in thought, and we improve our sentences by testing their meaning and their sound.

But whatever its shortcomings, the analytic method is useful as a form of control. Here are students whose language and loyalties are different from those of teachers trained in the belletristic achievements of the centuries. And partly because of this, because of their restricted code and their group loyalties, they have not done well academically in the past and so pose a threat to any teacher's sense of competence. Moreover, unlike their middle-class predecessors, they are apt to challenge not the reasons given by authority but authority itself. They are, in short, difficult. The analytic method is an assertion of authority in the face of this threat, it demands that students show themselves willing to learn the rules and patterns of behavior set for them. And Shaughnessy will remind them that other

teachers, other authorities, expect them to get right—that, it seems, is the principal reference of the word *expectations* in her title (p. 240).

The system of control in the Shaughnessy classroom, then, is positional—the same control that has limited these students to their restricted code. Here they have their assigned place in a pattern, they are BWs (as Shaughnessy calls them). Here the teacher lays down the rules that BWs (basic writers) are to follow, and moves them on from one language form to another in a relatively impersonal way, not from one personally achieved meaning to another. Those students who fail the program two or three times may then be placed in a class where more personal controls are used, where they interact with each other in small groups (p. 83), but those with a memory for this sort of information and a willingness to submit themselves to this training learn their grammar and pass on.

During a final examination students were asked to add adverbial modifiers to "The problem will be solved," and Shaughnessy gives us one of the responses in order to show that students can learn to elaborate sentences by her method. But notice first that this passage owes its life to a form that Shaughnessy has said is not a suitable model, namely the sermon:

> The problem will be solved with the help of the Almighty, who, except for an occasional thunderstorm, reigns unmolested, high in the heavens above, when all of us, regardless of race or religious difference, can come together and study this severe problem inside out, all day and night if necessary, and are able to come to you on that great gettin' up morning and say, "Mrs. Shaughnessy, we do know our verbs and adverbs." (p. 132)

Is this submission with a cheerful smile? "Mrs. Shaughnessy, we do know our verbs and adverbs."

Shaughnessy speaks of these students as "egocentric"—they write as though for themselves alone without taking the reader into account, without developing or explaining their thought. But Bernstein has shown that speakers of a restricted code are *not* egocentric but rather sociocentric and context-dependent, they rely on common experience to make their meanings clear. If they are to learn an elaborated code they must become, in fact, more "egocentric"—they must move from what *we* know to what *I* know. They must learn that language is a way of presenting your separate and individual experience to others, of making your subjective intent explicit. The person who says "I think" raises the egocentric premise of the interaction like a flag, inviting not affirmation but rather an equally individualistic response from the listener. Each must make personal meanings explicit. And through such interaction the self becomes verbally differentiated, and the unique character of the individual, implicit in the restricted code, now becomes a matter of special concern. In short, the move to an elaborated code is a move toward identity as an organizing concept within experience.

We might suppose, then, while working with these young people, that in poetic fictions—in stories and poems—we have a valuable means of moving with them toward the identity question. For the poetic fiction engages each of us in a personal experience, it invites an individual response to a particular view of life, and it establishes a context of feeling and thought within which questions can be raised about the way we live. It invites the "I think" response.

And further, it invites the verbal expression of feeling. Those who have only a restricted code have learned a language with few personal qualifications, and so they tend to communicate their feelings, Bernstein suggests, either by nonverbal means or by broad declarative statements. So feeling tends to be as undifferentiated as the language. But a poetic fiction quickens feeling and helps us develop in the complexity and subtlety of our emotional response. It clarifies and makes explicit the emotions by illustrating them in specific life situations—for what an emotion is called depends very much on the context in which feeling occurs and how one acts in response to it. A poetic fiction, giving us context and action, is itself the naming of an emotionally significant situation. And young people, caught up in this experience, talking about the emotions and ideas it

engenders in them, clarify their own feeling and thought. By making these reactions explicit so that others may know them, they come to know themselves. And new words, new language patterns, are learned and remembered because they are being used within an ordering of feeling that requires them and gives them significance.

How does Shaughnessy use a poem or story? To engage the feeling and thought of these young people with issues important to them? No. Rather, she uses it to give them training in the "perception of structure" and the "recognition of thought patterns" (p. 250). Consider her lesson on a structural feature of Richard Wright's *Black Boy*. The student is to take one of those lists that Wright includes in his text (for example, the list of childhood superstitions), examine it carefully, note what precedes and what follows it, and then formulate a general statement about it. Next, the student goes on to write a paper in which this general statement is explained, illustrated, and related to the rest of the book. The sample lesson given to demonstrate this procedure outlines Shaughnessy's own insightful reading of the passage, and is certainly a good lesson of its kind—the kind likely to suit those teachers trained to analyze the belletristic achievements of the centuries. But what is most interesting about this analytic approach to *Black Boy* is what it leaves out.

Not a word here about the young woman who whispered secretly to him the story of Bluebeard, deepening his sense of life and leaving him desperately serious. Nothing about Uncle Hoskins murdered by white men who wanted his saloon. Nothing about the boy's discovery that his kind lived in fear without knowing the possibilities of feeling, without genuine passion. Or about the pain of his isolation as he began to think and speak differently from others, who would look at him doubtfully, suspiciously, wondering why a boy would want to write a story. Nothing about his refusal to surrender himself to authority and live in a world where one's self has no meaning because authority and tradition are meaning enough. Or about his trying to learn good English from grammar books but finding that novels gave him a better sense of language. Or about his reading current novels for their point of view, because they looked on American life with a critical eye. Nothing about how it was from stories, from

> out of the emotional impact of imaginative constructions of heroic or tragic deeds, that I felt touching my face a tinge of warmth from an unseen light; and in my leaving [the South] I was groping toward that invisible light, always trying to keep my face so set and turned that I would not lose the hope of its faint promise, using it as my justification for action. (*Black Boy,* [New York: Harper, 1945], p. 283)

And nothing about what he learned as a black boy in the white man's world. Not a word about that.

Much of the pain he felt, and makes us feel, came from his willful struggle to move on from a life dominated by authority and tradition toward an individual life, his own identity—the same move that many of these young people are making, perhaps without being aware of it. And he has given us a powerful statement of the part poetic fictions can play in this move, of how they can be a criticism of life suggesting new possibilities of being. But Shaughnessy has not heard him. She is too busy with the book's structure, with how one part links to another, with what she calls "a grammar of passages"—and doesn't the heart sink, hearing that? What this life might say to these young people, what it might make them feel and think, hardly seems important. The book has become an object of structural study, like a monument that memorializes some action done some time ago, and is no longer an experience that might become justification for another action.

The analytic method entails for these students, then, a considerable denial of self—and we have an indication of that in some of their own writing. A striking example is provided when Shaughnessy explains how students, needing a word unfamiliar to them, may substitute another phonetically similar, as for example in these sentences:

> Coming to writing class *stifle* not only our will to write but your drive to think. . . .

> . . . our students must also make an effort to make the necessary *transgressions* to fulfill their needs.

School increases the childrens ability to *withhold* meaning. (p. 191)

These mistakes are like those Richard Nixon often made in his time of troubles, when he said things like, "Looking back over these past fears—ah, five years. . . ." Both had their truth. And perhaps what these students have written has its truth.

When the grammar lesson in Eileen's third grade class finally came to an end, the teacher said, "Now I'll read a story." Eileen looked up hopefully. The story was about a teacher, Mrs. Lavender, and her class at the end of the school year, and how the children hated to leave her but wanted to move on, and what they told the other children who would be in her class next year, and. . . . A story that could have gone on and on, without point, without end. Eileen turned away in restless indifference. But then the teacher, glancing up at the wall clock and closing her book, said, "Well, it's time for gym: line up!" And the children got up and went cheerfully to their places along the wall.

Near the end of her book Shaughnessy tells us what that first essay assignment was—the one which elicited a student's ten abortive attempts to get started. The class was given a passage that described a scene between a father and his child. The child is watching and enjoying some birds when the father intervenes to teach him their names. And this illustrates, the author believes, how the child's direct way of experiencing the world through his senses gives him a capacity to enjoy beauty—a capacity lost to the adult, who accepts society's way of classifying things and knows the world through objective analysis. The students were asked if they agreed or disagreed with the author (p. 242). We could hardly have a neater symbolic expression of Shaughnessy's own dilemma and the theme of her book than we have in this first essay assignment.

For Shaughnessy is herself that adult who intervenes to teach these young people the names of things and give them a method of objective analysis. And this for the purpose, I think, of socializing them to accept "society's way of classifying things." Her constant emphasis on order, on structure, on form implies that these young people lead formless, unstructured, disordered lives, impulsive and emotional. We may prefer the moving expressiveness of their personal writing, she tells us, but we must recognize that such writing is not analytical and does not conform to the conventions of academic prose (p. 239). She is right, but her emphasis seems to be on conforming to convention. The dilemma that engages her is that of choosing which to place first, the individual or society, and she has resolved it here in favor of society. The students responding to this assignment are, in effect, commenting on the very situation in which they now find themselves, for they must deny their subjective individuality and learn objective analysis, as that child learns it from his father. The tension implicit in this situation must have been felt throughout the course, as we can feel it throughout this book.

As we feel it during the lesson on *Black Boy,* when Shaughnessy demonstrates how one analyzes a text objectively. Yet this story must arouse intense feeling in many of these young people, who would see there an oppressive world still very much like their own, from which they must break away in order to possess themselves. But Shaughnessy denies feeling. She has chosen *Black Boy,* I think, because it deals with her own dilemma and can be used to give practice in subduing one's feelings in the interest of doing one's duty. Training in the analytic method is training in self-control, even self-denial.

Having taken as her task the socializing of these young people, Shaughnessy concerns herself with rules and patterns, develops a program using positional controls, with authority and rationality as key concepts. Here the order of doing becomes very important, as students are led from sentence to paragraph to essay, from narration to description to comparison and on through the rhetorical forms in a thoroughly rationalized sequence. So they learn to conform with the demands of a social mechanism that moves independently of their feeling and thought. An alternative to this, yet one giving a rigorous training in composition, would be a program using personal controls and stressing the making of individual judgments, so that students move through a sequence of their own created meanings. But that would require a context in which feeling is so aroused by an issue that it demands expression. Shaughnessy is well aware that language skills are best learned in such a context, but these students have already lost too much time, she tells us, they need to apply their minds directly to the mastery of language forms, they need the analytic method in order to catch up (p. 218). So the expression of creative power in the making of judgments will become important later, it seems, when those who have demonstrated their willingness to subdue themselves have learned the correct forms and been properly socialized.

A composition program, then, can help produce a personality type acceptable to those who would maintain things as they are, who already have power. Usually we are unaware of the degree to which this political concern enters into the organization and evaluation of teaching, we are thinking not about politics but about our professional responsibility. Yet students are allowed into our classrooms, as we are allowed into them, only because certain political accommodations have been made. The very determination of who is capable of benefitting from our teaching can be a political matter, as the open admissions policy demonstrates—for that policy resulted from political pressure by various power groups, including those teachers whose jobs would otherwise have been eliminated because of declining enrollments. Shaughnessy has shown here an astute political instinct. The program she describes is one suitable for processing large numbers of young people in a way eminently acceptable to those who matter, who have power.

The distribution of speech forms reflects the distribution of power, Bernstein remarks. Those who can only teach their children a restricted code belong to a social class far removed from the major decision-making areas of the social structure, they have limited access to those specialized roles that require and teach an elaborated code. The difficulties we have with these young people, then, lie not in their language itself, certainly not in any lack of grammar, but rather in their social experience, in the habits of feeling and thought they have learned. What should be the context of social experience in our classrooms? What should be the values implicit there? The answers we give will express not only our views of teaching but also of what society should be. Any decision about language teaching is a moral and political decision.

elaborated speech code vs restricted

elaborated → "proper written language"
            ego centric
            capable of questioning and
                determining things for themselves
                feeling thru language
restricted → improper grammar, structure
            relies on society/ outside for
                decision making cues
            feelings - nonverbal

Shaughnessy calls for grammar & rules
            training for students w/ writing
            problems

Rouse calls for program which would
            teach "personal controls" and
            "stress making individual judgements"
            thereby being able to "move
            through a sequence of their own
            created meanings"
Shaughnessy's method maintains the structure
            which keeps the power in the hands of
            those of opportunity

"Strangers No More": A Liberatory Literacy Curriculum

Kyle Fiore and Nan Elsasser

This essay originally appeared in College English 44 *(1982): 115–28. It has been reprinted in* Perspectives on Literacy. *Eds. Eugene Kintgen, Barry Kroll, and Mike Rose. Carbondale: Southern Illinois UP, 1988. 286–99.*

College of the Bahamas
November 17, 1979

Dear Kyle, Pat and Larry,

I think our basic writing curriculum works! After ten weeks of discussing reading and writing about the generative theme of marriage, students have actually begun to use their newly won knowledge and skills for their own purposes. Last night we were reviewing for the final—a test designed, administered and graded by the College English Department—when Louise, one of my students, broke in to say that no test could measure what she had learned over the semester! Another student nodded in agreement. She said, "We've learned about marriage, men, and women. We've learned to write. We've learned about ourselves." Perfect Freirian synthesis! As if that weren't reward enough for one night, Eurena suggested that the class—all women—summarize and publish their knowledge. Then everyone jumped in. Our review of dashes and semicolons was forgotten as the class designed its first publication. It's hard to believe that in September these women had difficulty thinking in terms of a paragraph—now they want a manifesto! I'll keep you posted.

    Love, Nan

Nan Elsasser's letter elated us. That semester she had been experimenting with a remedial English program we had designed[1] in the spring of 1978. We had first come together just after Christmas, drawn to each other by the desire to share our classroom frustrations, our successes, our gripes, over a common pitcher of beer. Trading stories with one another, we discovered we were four teachers in search of a curriculum. Standard English textbooks and traditional curricula did not fit our students at the University of Albuquerque and the University of New Mexico. Chicanos, Blacks, Anglos, and Native Americans, they had enrolled in our courses to gain writing skills which would help them succeed in college and carve a place for themselves in society. Once they arrived, however, our students found themselves strangers in a strange world. A wide gulf stretched between the classroom curriculum and their own knowledge gained in the barrios of Albuquerque and the rural towns and pueblos of New Mexico. Confronted by a course that negated their culture, many failed to master the skills they sought. Others succeeded by developing a second skin. Leaving their own customs, habits, and skills behind, they participated in school and in the world by adapting themselves to fit the existing order. Their acquisition of literacy left them not in control of their social context, but controlled by it.

We were troubled. We wanted our students to be able to bring their culture, their knowledge, into the classroom. We wanted them to understand and master the intricacies of the writing process. And we wanted them to be able to use writing as a means of intervening in their own social environment. Sparked by our common concerns, we decided to create a curriculum which would meet our goals. As we cast about for theories and pedagogies, we discovered the work of Lev Vygotsky and Paulo Freire. These scholars intrigued us because they believe writing involves both cognitive skills and social learnings. Their approaches parallel and complement each other. Vygotsky explores students' internal learning processes. Frieire emphasizes the impact of external social reality.

Vygotsky's work clarifies the complex process of writing.[2] He postulates that learning to write involves the mastery of cognitive skills and the development of new social understandings. According to Vygotsky, we categorize and synthesize our lives through inner speech, the language of thought. In inner speech, a single word or phrase is embroidered with variegated threads of ideas, experiences, and emotions. The multileveled, personal nature of inner speech is illustrated by a woman student's response to a word association exercise: *sex: home, time, never, rough, sleep.*

Vygotsky explains that to transform the inner speech symbols to written text, this woman must consciously step outside the shorthand of her thoughts and mentally enter the social context she shares with her reader. Only from this common perspective can she begin to unfold the mystery of her thoughts to create written prose.

Focusing on the learner's environment, Freire discusses the social and political aspects of writing. A designer of liberatory or revolutionary literacy programs, Freire maintains that the goal of a literacy program is to help students become critically conscious of the connection between their own lives and the larger society and to empower them to use literacy as a means of changing their own environment. Like Vygotsky, Freire believes the transformation of thought to text requires the conscious consideration of one's social context. Often, Freire says, students unaware of the connections between

their own lives and society personalize their problems. To encourage students to understand the impact of society on their lives, Freire proposes students and teachers talk about generative themes drawn from the students' everyday world. Investigating issues such as work or family life from an individual and a socio-historical perspective, students bring their own knowledge into the classroom and broaden their sense of social context.

For example, one woman beaten by her husband may think she has simply made a bad choice and must bear her lot with dignity. Another woman may think her husband would stop if she could live up to his expectations. When they talk with each other and other women, these two discover that brutality is a social phenomenon; it is widespread in the community. As they read, they learn that many aspects of their problem are rooted in the social realm and can best be attached by pressing for legal changes, battered women's shelters, more responsive attitudes on the part of the police. Through continued discussion, these women realize how they can use literacy to win those changes by swearing out complaints in court, sending petitions to public officials, or writing newspaper articles and letters to the editor.

We decided to base our curriculum on Vygotsky's theory and Freire's pedagogy. Vygotsky's theory of inner speech would enable students to understand the writing process. Freire's pedagogy would encourage them to bring their culture and personal knowledge into the classroom, help them understand the connections between their own lives and society, and empower them to use writing to control their environment.

As advanced literacy teachers in traditional universities, we realized we could not use a pure Freirian approach. Designed for teachers in revolutionary settings, Freire's basic literacy programs do not consider the time constraint of semesters or the academic pressure of preparing students to meet English department standards. However, we thought it would be possible to combine Freire's goal of increasing students' critical consciousness with the teaching of advanced literacy skills. As Freire wrote in *Pedagogy in Process* (New York: Seabury, 1978), "The best way to accomplish those things that are impossible today is to do today whatever is possible" (p. 64).

That spring we met every Saturday at each other's houses. Spurred on by coffee and raised glazed doughnuts, we talked about the advanced literacy techniques we were using and explored ways to link those techniques with Vygotsky's and Freire's work. We designed word association exercises to Vygotsky's theory of inner speech. We charted ways to fit rhetorical forms in a Freirian investigation. We finished in May. That same month Nan Elsasser won a Fulbright to teach advanced literacy at the College of the Bahamas. She would be the first to try our curriculum. The next fall Elsasser kept us abreast of her experiment by mail. In the pages that follow we have summarized her letters and combined them with copies of student papers to create a first-person account of our curriculum in process.

THE COLLEGE OF THE BAHAMAS: AN EXPERIMENT IN POSSIBILITIES

Arriving in the Bahamas before the semester begins, I have a few days to learn about the college.

Located on the island of New Providence, the College of the Bahamas is a two-year community college offering daytime and evening classes. Over ninety percent of the students at the College are black Bahamians. Many work by day, attend school by night. Two-thirds of these students are women.

The language skills class I am to teach is the first in a series of four English courses offered by the college prep program. All of these courses are taught along traditional lines. To practice grammar students change tenses, add punctuation, or fill in blank spaces in assigned sentences. To demonstrate reading ability they answer multiple choice or true-false questions on short paragraphs. A colleague tells me the year before forty-five to sixty percent of the students failed to meet English department standards. She also shows me a College of the Bahamas study demonstrating no significant correlation between grades in English and grades in other academic subjects. Her revelations strengthen my determination to try out our curriculum.

I get to class early on the first night, worried my students' traditional expectations will make them leary of a new approach. Checking my roster, I discover all my students are women (later, I learn women make up two-thirds of the college's student body). I start class by introducing myself and describing the problems I've encountered teaching English traditionally. Telling the women we'll be using an experimental approach, I stress this experiment will succeed only if we can pick topics, discuss material, and evaluate results together. I admit class will lack coherency at times, and one student asks if they will be able to pass the standardized English exam given at the end of the semester. I say I think so, but that she is free to transfer if she wants a more traditional approach. She leaves; but the rest stay.

To establish a sense of common ground, I ask my students about their work and former schooling. Half of them clerk in banks. The others type or run computers. Collectively, these women represent the first generation of Bahamian women to enter the business world and go to college. They have an average of six years of education behind them. Recalling her early school days, one woman speaks of days spent copying poems from a colonial primer. Another recounts the times she stayed home to care for the younger ones while her mother went to sell her wares at the straw market. They all remember problems with writing.

So they can begin to understand the cause of their problems, we spend the next three weeks investigating the complexities of going from inner speech to finished written product. We begin with a series of word association exercises designed to illustrate Vygotsky's theory. Comparing their responses to trigger words such as *sex, home, work,* the women start to see that even at this most basic level they categorize and store information in various ways. Some students list contrasting affective responses. Others jot down visual images. One woman divides the inner speech word into subtopics, like an outline: "job: where you would like to work, type boss, what specific field." Contrasting their different ways of organizing and listing thoughts, students gain a strong sense of why they need to elaborate their thoughts in writing. To end the session, we each transform our private lists to public prose.

To continue our study of the transformations involved in writing clear, explicit prose, I look for a topic which will stress the value of personal knowledge, break down the dichotomy between personal and classroom knowledge, and require explicit elaboration. As a newcomer to the island, I ask them to advise me "What You Need to Know to Live in the Bahamas." I introduce this assignment by talking about writing as an interaction between process and product, personal and social points of view, concrete and abstract knowledge. A student writing a recipe for conch salad needs concrete knowledge about preparing conch combined with the abstract knowledge of an audience as people with some shared assumptions as well as some lack of common ground.

The women have a number of problems with this assignment, evidencing what Freire calls the inability to step outside immediate contextual realities and incorporate broader points of view. Some students write very brief suggestions. Others write in the first person or list topics of interest, but don't include concrete information. Still others complain they are stymied trying to figure out what I'd like to do. Though she knows I am a stranger to the island, the woman writing me a recipe for conch salad assumes conch is a familiar food. Yet another woman constructs an imaginary audience to help herself focus on the assignment: "What You Need to Know to Live in the Bahamas. A Young married couple on Vacation. Leisure Activities. Whatever your taste in holiday diversion you'll never be at loss for something to do in the Bahamas. . . ."

This assignment extends over several sessions. Students write and rewrite their essays. During this time we develop the basic procedure we'll use to investigate a generative theme. First, we discuss the topic at hand (e.g., "What You Need to Know to Live in the Bahamas"). Then one student volunteers a thesis statement related to the topic. Other women help narrow and sharpen this statement and develop an essay outline. Students use these outlines as guidelines for their rough drafts. I reproduce the

drafts, and we read and comment on them. After prolonged discussion, each woman rewrites her draft to meet the questions we've raised.

In moving from the discussion of inner speech to writing about the Bahamas, students take on more and more responsibility for the class. While in writing they are still trapped by their personal perspectives, in discussions they begin to critique and respond to one another's views. Gradually they start to investigate their environment. Before, they passively received knowledge. Now, they pursue it.

Freire states that students caught by their own subjectivity can break through personal walls and move to a collective social perspective through investigating generative themes. Such themes must be selected carefully so that they encourage students to write for a broader, more public audience and empower them to use writing to change their lives. Freire advises teachers searching for themes to involve themselves intimately in their students' culture and minutely observe all the facets of their daily lives, recording "the way people talk, their style of life, their behavior at church and work" (*Pedagogy of the Oppressed* [New York: Seabury, 1970], p. 103). Analyzing these observations with a team of other educators, the teacher will discern meaningful generative themes.

A stranger, unaccompanied by a "literacy team," I can't follow Freire's advice, and in my ignorance I turn to my students for help. We discuss generative themes, and they each select three issues from their daily lives that they would like to talk, read, and write about for the semester. When they bring in their suggestions, I list them on the board. We debate them briefly and they vote, picking marriage for their generative theme. This theme affects their lives economically, socially, and emotionally. Ninety percent of these women have been raised by two parents in traditional Bahamian homes. Seventy-five percent are now mothers. Two-thirds of these mothers are single parents totally responsible for their children's physical and emotional well-being.

Having chosen their theme, the women break into groups. They discuss the areas of marriage they want to investigate and construct an outline of subtopics, including *housework, divorce, sexuality,* and *domestic violence.* With these subtopics in hand, I start to hunt for reading materials. I look for articles which bridge the distance between students' lives and society. We'll use these articles as a basis for dialogues about individual problems, common experiences, and the larger social world.

My search of the college library yields nothing on contemporary Bahamian marriage. Writing back to the United States for articles, culling my old *Ms.* magazines, and hounding the local newsstand, I collect a packet which fits our course outline. Initial reading assignments come from popular magazines: an article on wife beating from *New Woman,* one entitled "Why Bad Marriages Endure" from *Ebony.* As students' reading skills and knowledge increase, we will use more advanced texts, such as *Our Bodies Ourselves* (2nd ed., New York: Simon and Schuster, 1976), and *The Longest War: Sex Differences in Perspective* by Carol Tavris and Carole Offir (New York: Harcourt Brace Jovanovich, 1977). At the end of the semester we will read *Nectar in a Sieve* (New York: New American Library, 1971), a novel by Kamala Markandaya about peasant marriage in India.

For the rest of the semester we spend about one week co-investigating each subtopic of our marriage theme. I introduce each subject by handing out a related article. To help the women understand new information, I discuss the concepts I think unfamiliar, e.g., the historical concept of Victorian as a set of sexual attitudes. After reading and talking about the articles, we develop a thesis statement following the procedure we devised when writing essays on the Bahamas. When discussing articles and writing critiques students do not follow the traditional liberal arts criteria. Their criticism is not bound by the authors' intent or opinion, nor do they consider all articles equally valid. Rather, they judge the reading by whether or not it connects with their personal perspectives and tells them about marriage as a socioeconomic institution. They find much of value in *Our Bodies Ourselves.* They dismiss poet Judith Viorst as a spoiled middle-class housewife.

During our investigation students pass through three distinct phases as they hone their abilities to examine, critique, and write about marriage. They elaborate their own experience more skillfully, and they perceive stronger links between their own lives and the larger social context. They reach outside their own experience to seek new sources of knowledge. Finally, they become critically conscious of the way society affects their lives, and they begin to use writing as a means of intervening in their own social environment.

In the early weeks many women have trouble discerning the connections between their personal life and their social context. They analyze problems using concrete knowledge drawn from experience. They argue by anecdote. To encourage them to broaden their outlook, I ask for a definition of marriage as a social institution. In response, they describe what marriage should be ("communication," "love," "fidelity"), or they recite personal experiences ("men can come and go as they please, women cannot"; "men neglect their financial responsibilities"; "men have sweethearts"; "men are violent"). Posing questions targeting a social definition of marriage, I elicit broader, abstract responses: "legal procedure," "age requirements," "union between man and woman," "religious sanctioning of sex." Looking over this list, they ask me to throw out their earlier, more personal definitions.

Next, they construct lists of the positive and negative aspects of marriage as a social institution. These lists display a mixture of personal experiences, idealistic yearnings, and social traits.

Positive	Negative
Safe from rape and break-ins	Sex against our will
Not coming home to an empty house	Security sours relationships
Community approval of the relationship	Loss of freedom

Comparing these lists, the women start to talk about the social aspects of marriage. They conclude that the major benefit of marriage is security and social approval; its major shortcoming, a loss of freedom. Even after our extended dialogue, in their essays on "The Worst or Best Things about Marriage," women either write empty generalizations or briefly recount their own experience.

The Worst Thing About Marriage
by Rosetta Finlay

The worst thing about marriage is security. Whenever a couple is married they tend to become too sure of themselves. One would say, "All is well." I already have whom I want so I don't have to say I love you anymore; I don't have to show that' I care as much. We don't have sex as often and you can go out with the boys while I go out with the girls.

This is where one would find time to go out of the home and look for the missing links in his marriage. That's when all the problem arises as soon as this happens, there's no end to problems.

The Best Thing About Marriage
by Eurena Clayton

I enjoyed being with my husband when we were dating and the things we did together drew us closer. After we got married my husband's business prevents us from doing as many things as we used to do together. Usually when we have a spare chance we take off on trips which we simply enjoy together. The feeling of not having to bother with the every day responsibilities is a great burden lifted for that period. We find ourselves taking in the movies, theatre, tennis, golfing or simply sightseeing.

There are special occasions such as anniversary or birthday which are always remembered. Sometimes for no reason you receive a beautiful gift which is always appreciated and thoughtful.

In order to achieve one's goal in life it is safe to pool both resources.

I suggest revisions for these essays, reproduce them, and pass them out. Students critique each other's papers, and each woman rewrites her piece. This time a number of students expand their essays through elaboration. However, at this stage no one goes beyond her own experience without writing platitudes, and few maintain a consistent focus throughout the entire paper. The woman writing this third draft has expanded and improved her mechanics and drawn clearer contrasts in her conclusion. She still reverts to an unrelated generality.

Draft III
By Rosetta Finlay

The worst thing about marriage is emotional security. When a couple is married, they tend to become too sure of themselves. One will say, "All is well I already have whom I want so I don't have to look nice anymore; I don't have to say I love you anymore; I don't have to show that I care as much; we don't have sex as often and you can go out with the boys while I go out with the girls."

Marriage shouldn't be taken so much for granted there's always improvement needed in every marriage. Marriage is like a job e.g.—one has a job everything is routine; you have a steady salary; steady hours nine o'clock in the morning to five o'clock in the evening; go to work every day and perform the duties your job position requires.

Marriage is very similar e.g.—one has a steady companion; cook every day; keep the house and laundry clean; have babies and bring them up. Apart from doing the house chores there's the chauffeuse part to be done and the office work.

I personally think that there is a lot more to be done if you want to have a successful marriage. Therefore if more interest is taken in these areas, marriage would be much better than what it is today.

In the sessions that follow, students evidence similar problems with the reading assignment. The article is about battered wives. Although they can read the words, the women have difficulty distinguishing major ideas from details. Where in writing they recounted personal experiences, now in reading they focus on anecdotes. They underline when, where, or how hard Frank hit Marlene, as opposed to the main concept this example illustrates.

To sharpen the contrast between a main idea and an illustration I ask them to list causes of domestic violence on the board. Then we start to talk about the difference between causes and anecdotes. It takes students several sessions to learn to select main points correctly on their own. During these sessions they also begin to gain a better grasp of the connections between their own lives and the forces of society.

I am reminded as I consider my students that teaching and learning are part of a single process. To present something in class is not to teach it. Learning happens when students make cognitive transformations, expanding and reorganizing the knowledge in their cerebral filing systems. Only then can they assimilate and act upon ideas.

By the end of Phase One the women have made several such transformations. They have an idea of their individual differences and a sense of the common ground they share. Although they still rely on personal experience as a source of knowledge, they are beginning to recognize how the outside society affects their lives. This awareness has improved their writing. They use more detail. They separate ideas and events into paragraphs. They sustain a third-person perspective with greater skill. They clarify generalizations with examples.

A "Typical" Bahamian Marriage
by Rosetta Finlay

"For richer, for poorer, for better, for worse, in sickness and in health, until death do us part." God has commanded his children to join in the holy matrimony and obey these rules. Unfortunately, the majority of the Bahamian marriages tend to focus more on the negative, than the positive aspects of marriage. A Typical Bahamian Marriage will begin with both, the male and female being in love with each other, so much in love that the husband will help with the house chores, such as washing the dishes, doing the laundry, taking out the garbage and making breakfast. It will even get to the point where the husband will stay up at night with their first child. Every Sunday the family will go to church and have dinner together. Later in the evening the husband and wife will go to the movies or a special function.

Week days, both the husband and wife will go out to work, usually they both work. After work the wife rushes home to prepare the dinner. The bills are paid by both the husband and wife's salary put together and if possible, a little is saved. For some period of time, the wife will satisfy her husband's need such as, sharing sex, understanding and the house chores.

Then all of a sudden, for an unknown reason the husband changes.

He will start staying out X amount of hours and stop putting his share of monies towards the bills. Comes home and take out his frustration on his wife and children by, snapping at children and beating his wife. He does not even want to spend any time at home to help with the house chores or baby sit. He only comes home to change, if he is questioned about money it will end in a fight. Then he will leave home for another day or two.

The wife, is now in a situation where she does not have enough money to pay the bills and support the children, no husband to lean on and protect the family. She does not have any where to go, because he keeps telling her that she cannot go without him. Getting a divorce in the Bahamas is completely out of the question. So she will have to, "grin and bear it" until death.

By mid-semester most women have entered Phase Two. We pause to take stock of our work. Looking back over their gains, women are sparked with pride. They begin seizing more control in class and start to generate their own theories on the writing mechanics. One night we tackle the problem of pronoun agreement. While aware they often switch back and forth in writing from *they* to *you, she/he,* and *I,* students have little success self-editing for pronouns because we don't know the cause of this problem. Then one woman comments she has no trouble writing general points in the third person. However, she says when she illustrates these points or gives advice, she starts mentally addressing a particular person and slips into a second-person referent. Examining several essays, classmates confirm her observation; as a result, they begin to catch and correct these errors.

Women also start to discover punctuation rules. Although I have not stressed punctuation as such, they observe patterns in the reading, and they hypothesize the rules themselves. While working on the use of logical connectors like *however* and *similarly,* a student asks if the first sentence always ends in a semicolon followed by the connector, a comma, and another sentence. After consulting with each other and essays, other students incorporate this rule in their writing.

During this phase students also break away from their total dependence on personal experience. They become more confident about gaining knowledge from class dialogues and reading. One night we debate whether or not women "ask for" rape. Remembering how reading about wife beating changed our stereotypes, one student asks for additional materials on rape. Others second her request. Spurred on by their own curiosity, they assail excerpts from Susan Brownmiller's *Against Our Will* and discuss how her theories and statistics destroy or reinforce their personal myths and beliefs.

Encouraged by their confidence and advancing skills, I begin to introduce the idea of rhetorical forms: cause and effect, definition, comparison and contrast. Rather than concentrating on these forms explicitly, we employ them as a means of pondering, exploring, and writing about various facets of marriage. When looking at the social forces that perpetuate wife beating, we cover cause and effect. To illustrate the relationships between wife beating and rape, we use comparison and contrast. The outline students construct for this topic clarifies the social similarities and differences between these two forms of violence.

Comparison and Contrast on Rape and Wife Beating

Comparison

brutality to women

—by men

—at night

—police take male side

—society reluctant to believe women

—female shame

Contrast

—husband vs. stranger

—predictability

—sentence more severe for rape

—provocation

In their essays comparing and contrasting rape and wife beating, the women bring together cognitive skills and social realizations. They now write from a unified perspective with more coherence, fewer sentence fragments, and more complex sentence structure. They combine information gained from discussions and reading with their personal knowledge to create a solid argument by crisp, focused examples.

Comparison and Contrast of Rape and Wife Beating by Rosetta Finlay

In 1973 over half a million rapes were estimated by F.B.I. along with 14,000 wife abuse complaints in New York alone reached the family courts during a comparable period that same year. Rape and wife beating are common crimes done by men in our society.

Unfortunately, the women of our society have to turn to the law who are men for help. Very seldom a female will win a rape case to get protection from the law on a wife abuse complaint. Calling the police will not help, not when they ask you questions like, "Are there any witnesses to this assault?" "Look lady he pays the bills, doesn't he?" Only to conclude with "What he does in his house is his business." and "Why don't you two kiss and make up." They really don't act any different when called upon a rape assault not when they say things like, "well things certainly seem to be in order here now." "What was the problem?" "What were you wearing, were your pants tight?" On the other hand the female in wife abuse must think about her dependency upon her husband, when she thinks about taking her complaint to family court, eg:—who will pay the bills? In most cases the female doesn't work and what will she do without him, where will she turn after not working for years? This is where the female is trapped and cannot win.

Despite the trapping situation the women of our society have decided to fight against that to bring more rights and evidence for the female, for instance Judge Oneglia who as a lawyer specializes in marital problems, recommends that the female should get out of the house, go to a friend or neighbor, and cause as much disturbance as possible. The more witnesses the better. As in a rape case the victim must produce pictures or evidence of (bruises or semen) to corroborate the rape victim's testimony, another prohibits the introduction in court of evidence concerning a rape victim's previous sexual conduct.

The women in society have formed groups and organizations to fight and protect themselves from wife abuse and rape, for instance they have decided to get together with other women in their neighborhood or apartment building and establish a whistle signal. In cases where the female lives alone she should list only her first initial in the telephone directory and also keep all outside doors and windows dead bolt locked mostly used in a rape case. In a wife abuse case the women of our society have recommended to call a special meeting to discuss the problem inviting representatives from the police, clergy and social service agencies to participate. Hopefully, this would contribute to cut down on rape and wife abuse.

In Phase Three students begin to use writing as a means of intervening in their own social environment. A few weeks before the end of the semester the women decide to share the knowledge they have gained about marriage with the world outside classroom by publishing an open "Letter to Bahamian Men" in the island newspapers. Writing this manifesto takes four weeks. In addition to class time, we meet together on Sundays and put in hours of extra work. We start by writing individual letters. We discuss these letters in class, then outline a collective letter.

A. Introduction
  1. Role of women in Bahamian society
  2. Oppression of women in marriage
B. Women victims of men's inconsiderate actions
C. Men's financial neglect of the family
D. Men's lack of help at home
E. Men's lack of responsibility for their children
F. Men's failure to satisfy women sexually
G. Conclusion: recommendations for Bahamian men

After considering the concerns each woman mentioned in her first letter, I assign each one a particular topic to develop. I organize the topics into a text, leaving gaps where I think there is a need for further work. From this point on my role is limited to copying, cutting and pasting. Equipped with her own copy, each woman begins to edit her epistle. They go line by line, spending over an hour on each page. Students silent all semester defend their contributions vehemently. They argue over punctuation, style, and semantics. They debate whether to separate the list of men's inconsiderate actions with colons, semicolons, or full stops. One woman thinks a reference to *gambling* too colloquial. Another questions the use of *spend* vs. *squander.*

They consider their audience's viewpoint, calculating the effect of their words. They discuss whether to blame the issue of sweethearts on the men or the sweethearts themselves. One student observes that since the letter confronts the wrongs men perpetrate on women, it would be a tactical error to criticize other women. They finally compromise by using the term *extra-marital affairs.* Wanting to state their case clearly yet not run the risk of censorship, they rewrite the paragraph on sex several times. The final letter appears in both Nassau daily papers.

Bahamian Women Deserve a Change

Dear Bahamian Men:

The social, spiritual and economic growth of Bahamian society depends on men as well as women. For a very long time there has been a downward trend in male support of their wives and children. In the typical Bahamian marriage both the male and the female begin by thinking that they are in love, so much in love that the husband will help with the household chores. The husband will even stay up all night with their first child. Every Sunday the family will go to church and have dinner together. Later in the evening the husband and wife might go to a movie or a special function. Week days both the husband and wife will go to work. After work the wife rushes home to prepare dinner. The bills are paid by putting together both the husband and wife's salaries and if possible, a little is saved. For some time all will go very well in the home. Then all of a sudden, for some unknown reason, the husband begins to change.

We are a group of women who have all been victims of men's inconsiderate actions. We would like to focus on the punishment, deprivation, discourtesy, mental anguish and death of the soul for which Bahamian men are responsible: Punishment because some women are beaten by their husband: Deprivation because husbands give wives less and less to survive on each month: Discourtesy because extramarital affairs disturb the home. Mental anguish is humiliation of the mind, for whose mind can be at ease in such a situation! Death of the soul deteriorates the whole body, for women are made to feel they serve no purpose.

These problems arise when the men begin to neglect their homes. The main problems between men and women in the Bahamas are: child raising, housekeeping, finances, and sex. Men are the root of most of these problems.

In most cases the male salary is more than the females. Despite this fact, the majority of Bahamian men neglect the financial upkeep of their families in some way or the other. Because of this, the greater part of the financial burden which includes savings, school fees, groceries, utilities, and even mortgages have been left to women. The male finds other things to do with his salary. Some men wait for the women to remind them about their bills. Others expect the women to pay all the bills. How can the female be expected to do all of this with a salary that is less than the males?

For centuries women have been solely responsible for housework. So men still think that a woman's place is in the home. Men expect women to work all day, come home and cook, wash dishes, clean house, wash clothes, prepare dinner and get the children ready for bed while they sit around and watch. It used to be that women did not work and were solely dependent on their husbands for support. Since women are now working and helping their husbands with most of the financial upkeep, there is no reason why the men can't be a part when it comes to housework. It is both the male's and the female's place to share the responsibilities of the home.

It takes two to produce a child and so it should be two to see to the upbringing of the child. Fathers do not spend sufficient time in the home. The most important stages in a child's life, the most cherished and once in a life time moments are when the child says his first word, makes his first step, and claps his hands for the first time. Fathers being around the home when moments like the above mentioned take place are important in children's lives. Here in the Bahamas fathers have failed to be real fathers, and children have been left totally dependent on their mothers. Having children and not supporting them is not a good way to prove one's manhood. A child should have both parents' care and attention. But before men see that their children are well taken care of they prefer to spend money on their own pleasure. Why be responsible for another life coming into the world if men don't care if the children are properly fed, have proper clothing to wear, and get a proper education?

Men tend not to realize the necessity in satisfying their partners when making love. Unfortunately, they are mainly concerned with the fulfillment of their desires. They come home at the most tiresome hours of the night, hop in bed and expect us to respond without any love or affection. Most Bahamian men don't take the time to caress women's bodies before having sex. Therefore, the instant they get into bed—if they're in the mood—women are expected to perform. However, when women are in the mood, they don't respond. This leaves women dissatisfied and angry.

Our recommendations to Bahamian men in relation to the above are as follows:

a. That men join in family worship at least twice a month.
b. That men stop putting most of the financial burden on women. 75% of the household responsibilities should be handled by men.
c. That men at least buy their children's groceries, pay school fees and buy clothes.
d. That men take their children out for recreation at least once a week.
e. That men do an equal share of the housework.
f. That men do not allow extra-marital affairs to damage or destroy their marriages.
g. That men make more effort to sexually satisfy their wives. Talk about the things that please

them. Caress their women until they're ready for sex. Try not to climax until the women are ready.

Men, there is definitely room for improvement in love, affection and communication. Try it.

Sincerely,
English 016-06

Comparing this "Open Letter to Bahamian Men" with women's earlier essays on "Rape and Battered Wives," "The Worst Things in a Marriage," and life in the Bahamas demonstrates how, through the investigation of a generative theme, students can advance their reading and writing skills, recognize links between their own lives and the larger society, and develop ways of using their newfound writing skills to intervene in their own environment.

At the end of the semester all these women passed the College-administered English exam. Most received "B" grades on the essay component. Further, they decided to continue meeting throughout the next spring in order to read about women in other countries, broaden their under-

standings, and write a resource book for Bahamian women.

The success of this pedagogical experiment demonstrates that advanced literacy teachers can modify Freire's pedagogy to fit the needs of their students and the demands of the college. Through this approach students will achieve literacy in the truest, most profound sense: they will understand "their reality in such a way that they increase their power to transform it" (Darcy de Olivera and Rosiska de Olivera, *Guinea-Bissau Reinventing Education* [Geneva: Institute of Cultural Action, 1976], p. 48).

Notes

1. The curriculum described in this article was developed by Nan Elsasser, Kyle Fiore, Patricia Irvine, and Larry Smith.

2. See, especially, *Thought and Language* (Cambridge, Mass.: MIT Press, 1962). We would like to thank Vera John-Steiner for sharing with us her knowledge of and commitment to the theories of L. S. Vygotsky.

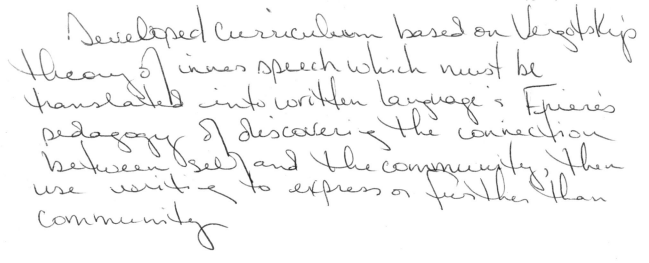

Developed curriculum based on Vygotsky's theory of inner speech which must be translated into written language; Freire's pedagogy of discovering the connection between self and the community, then use writing to express or further than community

The Language of Exclusion: Writing Instruction at the University

Mike Rose

Rose's essay is from College English 47 (1985): 341–59.

"How many '*minor* errors' are acceptable?"

"We must try to isolate and define those *further* skills in composition . . ."

". . . we should provide a short remedial course to patch up any deficiencies."

"Perhaps the most striking feature of this campus' siege against illiteracy . . ."

"One might hope that, after a number of years, standards might be set in the high schools which would allow us to abandon our own defensive program."

These snippets come from University of California and California state legislative memos, reports, and position papers and from documents produced during a recent debate in UCLA's Academic Senate over whether a course in our freshman writing sequence was remedial. Though these quotations—and a half dozen others I will use in this essay—are local, they represent a kind of institutional language about writing instruction in American higher education. There are five ideas about writing implicit in these comments. Writing ability is judged in terms of the presence of error and can thus be quantified. Writing is a skill or a tool rather than a discipline. A number of our students lack this skill and must be remediated. In fact, some percentage of our students are, for all intents and purposes, illiterate. Our remedial efforts, while currently necessary, can be phased out once the literacy crisis is solved in other segments of the educational system.

This kind of thinking and talking is so common that we often fail to notice that it reveals a reductive, fundamentally behaviorist model of the development and use of written language, a problematic definition of writing, and an inaccurate assessment of student ability and need. This way of talking about writing abilities and instruction is woven throughout discussions of program and curriculum development, course credit, instructional evaluation, and resource allocation. And, in various ways, it keeps writing instruction at the periphery of the curriculum.

It is certainly true that many faculty and administrators would take issue with one or more of the above notions. And those of us in writing would bring current thinking in rhetoric and composition studies into the conversation. (Though we often—perhaps uncomfortably—rely on terms like "skill" and "remediation.") Sometimes we successfully challenge this language or set up sensible programs in spite of it. But all too often we can do neither. The language represented in the headnotes of this essay reveals deeply held beliefs. It has a tradition and a style, and it plays off the fundamental tension between the general education and the research missions of the American university. The more I think about this language and recall the contexts in which I've heard it used, the more I realize how caught up we all are in a political-semantic web that restricts the way we think about the place of writing in the academy. The opinions I have been describing are certainly not the only ones to be heard. But they are strong. Influential. Rhetorically effective. And profoundly exclusionary. Until we seriously rethink it, we will misrepresent the nature of writing, misjudge our students' problems, and miss any chance to effect a true curricular change that will situate writing firmly in the undergraduate curriculum.

Let us consider the college writing course for a moment. Freshman composition originated in 1874 as a Harvard response to the poor writing of *upper*classmen, spread rapidly, and became and remained the most consistently required course in the American curriculum. Upper division writing courses have a briefer and much less expansive history, but they are currently receiving a good deal of institutional energy and support. It would be hard to think of an ability more desired than the ability to write. Yet, though writing courses are highly valued, even enjoying a boom, they are also viewed with curious eyes. Administrators fund them—often generously—but academic senates worry that the boundaries between high school and college are eroding, and worry as well that the considerable investment of resources in such courses will drain money from the research enterprise. They deny some of the courses curricular status by tagging them remedial, and their members secretly or not-so-secretly wish the courses could be moved to community colleges. Scientists and social scientists underscore the importance of effective writing, yet find it difficult—if not impossible—to restructure their own courses of study to encourage and support writing. More than a few humanists express such difficulty as well. English departments hold onto writing courses but consider the work intellectually second-class. The people who teach writing are more often than not temporary hires; their courses are robbed of curricular continuity and of the status that comes with tenured faculty involvement. And the instructors? Well, they're just robbed.

The writing course holds a very strange position in the American curriculum. It is within this setting that composition specialists must debate and defend and interminably evaluate what they do. And

how untenable such activity becomes if the very terms of the defense undercut both the nature of writing and the teaching of writing, and exclude it in various metaphorical ways from the curriculum. We end up arguing with words that sabotage our argument. The first step in resolving such a mess is to consider the language institutions use when they discuss writing. What I want to do in this essay is to look at each of the five notions presented earlier, examine briefly the conditions that shaped their use, and speculate on how it is that they misrepresent and exclude. I will conclude by entertaining a less reductive and exclusionary way to think—and talk—about writing in the academy.

BEHAVIORISM, QUANTIFICATION, AND WRITING

A great deal of current work in fields as diverse as rhetoric, composition studies, psycholinguistics, and cognitive development has underscored the importance of engaging young writers in rich, natural language use. And the movements of the last four decades that have most influenced the teaching of writing—life adjustment, liberal studies, and writing as process—have each, in their very different ways, placed writing pedagogy in the context of broad concerns: personal development and adjustment, a rhetorical-literary tradition, the psychology of composing. It is somewhat curious, then, that a behaviorist approach to writing, one that took its fullest shape in the 1930s and has been variously and severely challenged by the movements that followed it, remains with us as vigorously as it does. It is atomistic, focusing on isolated bits of discourse, error centered, and linguistically reductive. It has a style and a series of techniques that influence pedagogy, assessment, and evaluation. We currently see its influence in workbooks, programmed instruction, and many formulations of behavioral objectives, and it gets most of its airplay in remedial courses. It has staying power. Perhaps we can better understand its resilience if we briefly survey the history that gives it its current shape.

When turn-of-the-century educational psychologists like E. L. Thorndike began to study the teaching of writing, they found a Latin and Greek-influenced school grammar that was primarily a set of prescriptions for conducting socially acceptable discourse, a list of the arcane do's and don'ts of usage for the ever-increasing numbers of children—many from lower classes and immigrant groups—entering the educational system. Thorndike and his colleagues also found reports like those issuing from the Harvard faculty in the 1890s which called attention to the presence of errors in handwriting, spelling, and grammar in the writing of the university's entering freshmen. The twentieth-century writing curriculum, then, was focused on the particulars of usage, grammar, and mechanics. Correctness became, in James Berlin's words, the era's "most significant measure of accomplished prose" (*Writing Instruction in Nineteenth-Century American Colleges* [Carbondale: Southern Illinois University Press, 1984], p. 73).

Such particulars suited educational psychology's model of language quite well: a mechanistic paradigm that studied language by reducing it to discrete behaviors and that defined language growth as the accretion of these particulars. The stress, of course, was on quantification and measurement. ("Whatever exists at all exists in some amount," proclaimed Thorndike.[1]) The focus on error—which is eminently measurable—found justification in a model of mind that was ascending in American academic psychology. Educators embraced the late Victorian faith in science.

Thorndike and company would champion individualized instruction and insist on language practice rather than the rote memorization of rules of grammar that characterized nineteenth-century pedagogy. But they conducted their work within a model of language that was tremendously limited, and this model was further supported and advanced by what Raymond Callahan has called "the cult of efficiency," a strong push to apply to education the principles of industrial scientific management (*Education and the Cult of Efficiency* [Chicago: University of Chicago Press, 1962]). Educational gains were defined as products, and the output of products could be measured. Pedagogical effectiveness—which meant cost-effectiveness—

could be determined with "scientific" accuracy. This was the era of the educational efficiency expert. (NCTE even had a Committee on Economy of Time in English.) The combination of positivism, efficiency, and skittishness about correct grammar would have a profound influence on pedagogy and research.

This was the time when workbooks and "practice pads" first became big business. Their success could at least partly be attributed to the fact that they were supported by scientific reasoning. Educational psychologists had demonstrated that simply memorizing rules of grammar and usage had no discernible effect on the quality of student writing. What was needed was application of those rules through practice provided by drills and exercises. The theoretical underpinning was expressed in terms of "habit formation" and "habit strength," the behaviorist equivalent of learning—the resilience of an "acquired response" being dependent on the power and number of reinforcements. The logic was neat: specify a desired linguistic behavior as precisely as possible (e.g., the proper use of the pronouns "he" and "him") and construct opportunities to practice it. The more practice, the more the linguistic habit will take hold. Textbooks as well as workbooks shared this penchant for precision. One textbook for teachers presented a unit on the colon.[2] A text for students devoted seven pages to the use of a capital letter to indicate a proper noun.[3] This was also the time when objective tests—which had been around since 1890—enjoyed a sudden rebirth as "new type" tests. And they, of course, were precision incarnate. The tests generated great enthusiasm among educators who saw in them a scientific means accurately and fairly to assess student achievement in language arts as well as in social studies and mathematics. Ellwood Cubberley, the dean of the School of Education at Stanford, called the development of these "new type" tests "one of the most significant movements in all our educational history."[4] Cubberley and his colleagues felt they were on the threshold of a new era.

Research too focused on the particulars of language, especially on listing and tabulating error.

One rarely finds consideration of the social context of error, or of its cognitive-developmental meaning—that is, no interpretation of its significance in the growth of the writer. Instead one finds W. S. Guiler tallying the percentages of 350 students who, in misspelling "mortgage," erred by omitting the "t" vs. those who dropped the initial "g."[5] And one reads Grace Ransom's study of students' "vocabularies of errors"—a popular notion that any given student has a more or less stable set of errors he or she commits. Ransom showed that with drill and practice, students ceased making many of the errors that appeared on pretests (though, unfortunately for the theory, a large number of new errors appeared in their post-tests).[6] One also reads Luella Cole Pressey's assertion that "everything needed for about 90 per cent of the writing students do . . . appears to involve only some 44 different rules of English composition." And therefore, if mastery of the rules is divided up and allocated to grades 2 through 12, "there is an average of 4.4 rules to be mastered per year."[7]

Such research and pedagogy was enacted to good purpose, a purpose stated well by H. J. Arnold, Director of Special Schools at Wittenberg College:

> [Students'] disabilities are specific. The more exactly they can be located, the more promptly they can be removed. . . . It seems reasonably safe to predict that the elimination of the above mentioned disabilities through adequate remedial drill will do much to remove students' handicaps in certain college courses. ("Diagnostic and Remedial Techniques for College Freshmen," *Association of American Colleges Bulletin,* 16[1930], pp. 271–272)

The trouble, of course, is that such work is built on a set of highly questionable assumptions: that a writer has a relatively fixed repository of linguistic blunders that can be pinpointed and then corrected through drill, that repetitive drill on specific linguistic features represented in isolated sentences will result in mastery of linguistic (or stylistic or rhetorical) principles, that bits of discourse bereft of rhetorical or conceptual context can form the basis of curriculum and assessment, that good writing

is correct writing, and that correctness has to do with pronoun choice, verb forms, and the like.

Despite the fact that such assumptions began to be challenged by the late 30s,[8] the paraphernalia and the approach of the scientific era were destined to remain with us. I think this trend has the staying power it does for a number of reasons, the ones we saw illustrated in our brief historical overview. It gives a method—a putatively objective one—to the strong desire of our society to maintain correct language use. It is very American in its seeming efficiency. And it offers a simple, understandable view of complex linguistic problems. The trend seems to reemerge with most potency in times of crisis: when budgets crunch and accountability looms or, particularly, when "nontraditional" students flood our institutions.[9] A reduction of complexity has great appeal in institutional decision making, especially in difficult times: a scientific-atomistic approach to language, with its attendant tallies and charts, nicely fits an economic/political decision-making model. When in doubt or when scared or when pressed, count.

And something else happens. When student writing is viewed in this particularistic, pseudo-scientific way, it gets defined in very limited terms as a narrow band of inadequate behavior separate from the vastly complex composing that faculty members engage in for a living and delve into for work and for play. And such perception yields what it intends: a behavior that is stripped of its rich cognitive and rhetorical complexity. A behavior that, in fact, looks and feels basic, fundamental, atomistic. A behavior that certainly does not belong in the university.

ENGLISH AS A SKILL

As English, a relatively new course of study, moved into the second and third decades of this century, it was challenged by efficiency-obsessed administrators and legislators. Since the teaching of writing required tremendous resources, English teachers had to defend their work in utilitarian terms. One very successful defense was their characterization of English as a "skill" or "tool subject" that all students had to master in order to achieve in almost any subject and to function as productive citizens. The defense worked, and the utility of English in schooling and in adult life was confirmed for the era.

The way this defense played itself out, however, had interesting ramifications. Though a utilitarian defense of English included for many the rhetorical/conceptual as well as the mechanical/grammatical dimensions of language, the overwhelming focus of discussion in the committee reports and the journals of the 1920s and 1930s was on grammatical and mechanical error. The narrow focus was made even more narrow by a fetish for "scientific" tabulation. One could measure the degree to which students mastered their writing skill by tallying their mistakes.

We no longer use the phrase "tool subject," and we have gone a long way in the last three decades from error tabulation toward revitalizing the rhetorical dimension of writing. But the notion of writing as a skill is still central to our discussions and our defenses: we have writing skills hierarchies, writing skills assessments, and writing skills centers. And necessary as such a notion may seem to be, I think it carries with it a tremendous liability. Perhaps the problem is nowhere more clearly illustrated than in this excerpt from the UCLA academic senate's definition of a university course:

> A university course should set forth an integrated body of knowledge with primary emphasis on presenting principles and theories rather than on developing skills and techniques.

If "skills and techniques" are included, they must be taught "primarily as a means to learning, analyzing, and criticizing theories and principles." There is a lot to question in this definition, but for now let us limit ourselves to the distinction it establishes between a skill and a body of knowledge. The distinction highlights a fundamental tension in the American university: between what Laurence Veysey labels the practical-utilitarian dimension (applied, vocational, educationalist) and both the liberal culture and the research dimensions—the latter two, each in different ways, ele-

vating appreciation and pure inquiry over application (*The Emergence of the American University* [Chicago: University of Chicago Press, 1965]). To discuss writing as a skill, then, is to place it in the realm of the technical, and in the current, research-ascendant American university, that is a kiss of death.

Now it is true that we commonly use the word *skill* in ways that suggest a complex interweaving of sophisticated activity and rich knowledge. We praise the interpretive skills of the literary critic, the diagnostic skills of the physician, the interpersonal skills of the clinical psychologist. Applied, yes, but implying a kind of competence that is more in line with obsolete definitions that equate skill with reason and understanding than with this more common definition (that of the *American Heritage Dictionary*): "An art, trade, or technique, particularly one requiring use of the hands or body." A skill, particularly in the university setting, is, well, a tool, something one develops and refines and completes in order to take on the higher-order demands of purer thought. Everyone may acknowledge the value of the skill (our senate praised our course to the skies as it removed its credit), but it is valuable as the ability to multiply or titrate a solution or use an index or draw a map is valuable. It is absolutely necessary but remains second-class. It is not "an integrated body of knowledge" but a technique, something acquired differently from the way one acquires knowledge—from drill, from practice, from procedures that conjure up the hand and the eye but not the mind. Skills are discussed as separable, distinct, circumscribable activities; thus we talk of subskills, levels of skills, sets of skills. Again writing is defined by abilities one can quantify and connect as opposed to the dynamism and organic vitality one associates with thought.

Because skills are fundamental tools, basic procedures, there is the strong expectation that they be mastered at various preparatory junctures in one's educational career and in the places where such tools are properly crafted. In the case of writing, the skills should be mastered before one enters college and takes on higher-order endeavors. And the place for such instruction—before or after entering college—is the English class. Yes, the skill can be refined, but its fundamental development is over, completed via a series of elementary and secondary school courses and perhaps one or two college courses, often designated remedial. Thus it is that so many faculty consider upper-division and especially graduate-level writing courses as de jure remedial. To view writing as a skill in the university context reduces the possibility of perceiving it as a complex ability that is continually developing as one engages in new tasks with new materials for new audiences.

If the foregoing seems a bit extreme, consider this passage from our Academic Senate's review of UCLA Writing Programs:

> . . . it seems difficult to see how *composition*—whose distinctive aspect seems to be the transformation of language from thought or speech to hard copy—represents a distinct further step in shaping cogitation. There don't seem to be persuasive grounds for abandoning the view that composition is still a *skill* attendant to the attainment of overall linguistic competence.

The author of the report, a chemist, was reacting to some of our faculty's assertions about the interweaving of thinking and writing; writing for him is more or less a transcription skill.

So to reduce writing to second-class intellectual status is to influence the way faculty, students, and society view the teaching of writing. This is a bitter pill, but we in writing may have little choice but to swallow it. For, after all, is not writing simply different from "integrated bodies of knowledge" like sociology or biology? Is it? Well, yes and no. There are aspects of writing that would fit a skills model (the graphemic aspects especially). But much current theory and research are moving us to see that writing is not simply a transcribing skill mastered in early development. Writing seems central to the shaping and directing of certain modes of cognition, is integrally involved in learning, is a means of defining the self and defining reality, is a means of representing and contextualizing information (which has enormous political as well as conceptual and archival importance), and is an activity that develops over one's lifetime. Indeed it is worth pondering whether many of the "integrated bodies of knowledge" we study, the disciplines we practice, would have ever developed in the way they did and reveal the knowledge they do if writing did not exist. Would history or philosophy or economics exist as we know them? It is not simply that the work of such disciplines is recorded in writing, but that writing is intimately involved in the nature of their inquiry. Writing is not just a skill with which one can present or analyze knowledge. It is essential to the very existence of certain kinds of knowledge.

REMEDIATION

Since the middle of the last century, American colleges have been establishing various kinds of preparatory programs and classes within their halls to maintain enrollments while bringing their entering students up to curricular par.[10] One fairly modern incarnation of this activity is the "remedial class," a designation that appears frequently in the education and language arts journals of the 1920s.[11] Since that time remedial courses have remained very much with us: we have remedial programs, remedial sections, remedial textbooks, and, of course, remedial students. Other terms with different twists (like "developmental" and "compensatory") come and go, but "remedial" has staying power. Exactly what the adjective "remedial" means, however, has never quite been clear. To remediate seems to mean to correct errors or fill in gaps in a person's knowledge. The implication is that the material being studied should have been learned during prior education but was not. Now the reasons why it was not could vary tremendously: they could rest with the student (physical impairment, motivational problems, intelligence), the family (socio-economic status, stability, the support of reading-writing activities), the school (location, sophistication of the curriculum, adequacy of elementary or secondary instruction), the culture or subculture (priority of schooling, competing expectations and demands), or some combination of such factors. What "remedial" means in terms of curriculum and pedagogy is not clear either. What is remedial for a school like UCLA might well be standard for other state or community colleges, and what is considered standard during one era might well be tagged remedial in the next.

It is hard to define such a term. The best definition of remedial I can arrive at is a highly dynamic, contextual one: The function of labelling certain material remedial in higher education is to keep in place the hard fought for, if historically and conceptually problematic and highly fluid, distinction between college and secondary work. "Remedial" gains its meaning, then, in a political more than a pedagogical universe.

And the political dimension is powerful—to be remedial is to be substandard, inadequate, and, because of the origins of the term, the inadequacy is metaphorically connected to disease and mental defect. It has been difficult to trace the educational etymology of the word "remedial," but what I have uncovered suggests this: Its origins are in law and medicine, and by the late nineteenth century the term fell pretty much in the medical domain and was soon applied to education. "Remedial" quickly generalized beyond the description of students who might have had neurological problems to those with broader, though special, educational problems and then to those normal learners who are not up to a particular set of standards in a particular era at particular institutions. Here is some history.

Most of the enlightened work in the nineteenth century with the training of special populations (the deaf, the blind, the mentally retarded) was conducted by medical people, often in medical settings. And when young people who could hear and see and were of normal intelligence but had unusual—though perhaps not devastating—difficulties began to seek help, they too were examined within a medical framework. Their difficulties had to do with reading and writing—though mostly reading—and would today be classified as learning disabilities. One of the first such difficulties to be studied was dyslexia, then labelled "congenital word blindness."

In 1896 a physician named Morgan reported in the pages of *The British Medical Journal* the case of a "bright and intelligent boy" who was having great difficulty learning to read. Though he knew the alphabet, he would spell some words in pretty unusual ways. He would reverse letters or drop them or write odd combinations of consonants and vowels. Dr. Morgan examined the boy and had him read and write. The only diagnosis that made sense was one he had to borrow and analogize from the cases of stroke victims, "word blindness," but since the child had no history of cerebral trauma, Morgan labelled his condition "*congenital* word blindness" (W. Pringle Morgan, "A Case of Congenital Word Blindness," *The British Medical Journal,* 6, Part 2 [1896], 1378). Within the next two decades a number of such cases surfaced; in fact another English physician, James Hinshelwood, published several books on congenital word blindness.[12] The explanations were for the most part strictly medical, and, it should be noted, were analogized from detectable cerebral pathology in adults to conditions with no detectable pathology in children.

In the 1920s other medical men began to advance explanations a bit different from Morgan's and Hinshelwood's. Dr. Samuel Orton, an American physician, posed what he called a "cerebral physiological" theory that directed thinking away from trauma analogues and toward functional explanations. Certain areas of the brain were not defective but underdeveloped and could be corrected through "remedial effort." But though he posed a basically educational model for dyslexia, Dr. Orton's language should not be overlooked. He spoke of "brain habit" and the "handicap" of his "physiological deviates."[13] Though his theory was different from that of his forerunners, his language, significantly, was still medical.

As increasing access to education brought more and more children into the schools, they were met by progressive teachers and testing experts interested in assessing and responding to individual differences. Other sorts of reading and writing problems, not just dyslexia, were surfacing, and increasing numbers of teachers, not just medical people, were working with the special students. But the medical vocabulary—with its implied medical model—remained dominant. People tried to *diagnose* various *disabilities, defects, deficits, deficiencies,* and *handicaps,* and then tried to *remedy* them.[14] So one starts to see all sorts of reading/writing problems clustered together and addressed with this language. For example, William S. Gray's important monograph, *Remedial Cases in Reading: Their Diagnosis and Treatment* (Chicago: University of Chicago Press, 1922), listed as "specific causes of failure in reading" inferior learning capacity, congenital word blindness, poor auditory memory, defective vision, a narrow span of recognition, ineffective eye movements, inadequate training in phonetics, inadequate attention to the content, an inadequate speaking vocabulary, a small meaning vocabulary, speech defects, lack of interest, and timidity. The remedial paradigm was beginning to include those who had troubles as varied as bad eyes, second language interference, and shyness.[15]

It is likely that the appeal of medical-remedial language had much to do with its associations with scientific objectivity and accuracy—powerful currency in the efficiency-minded 1920s and 30s. A nice illustration of this interaction of influences appeared in Albert Lang's 1930 textbook, *Modern Methods in Written Examinations* (Boston: Houghton Mifflin, 1930). The medical model is quite explicit:

> teaching bears a resemblance to the practice of medicine. Like a successful physician, the good teacher must be something of a diagnostician. The physician by means of a general examination singles out the individuals whose physical defects require a more thorough testing. He critically scrutinizes the special cases until he recognizes the specific troubles. After a careful diagnosis he is able to prescribe intelligently the best remedial or corrective measures. (p. 38)

By the 1930s the language of remediation could be found throughout the pages of publications like *English Journal,* applied now to writing (as well as reading and mathematics) and to high school and college students who had in fact learned to write but were doing so with a degree of error thought unacceptable. These were students—large numbers of them—who were not unlike the students who currently populate our "remedial" courses: students from backgrounds that did not provide optimal environmental and educational opportunities, students who erred as they tried to write the prose they thought the academy required, second-language students. The semantic net of "remedial" was expanding and expanding.

There was much to applaud in this focus on writing. It came from a progressive era desire to help *all* students progress through the educational system. But the theoretical and pedagogical model that was available for "corrective teaching" led educators to view writing problems within a medical-remedial paradigm. Thus they set out to diagnose as precisely as possible the errors (defects) in a student's paper—which they saw as symptomatic of equally isolable defects in the student's linguistic capacity—and devise drills and exercises to remedy them. (One of the 1930s nicknames for remedial sections was "sick sections." During the next decade they would be tagged "hospital sections.") Such corrective teaching was, in the words of H. J. Arnold, "the most logical as well as the most scientific method" ("Diagnostic and Remedial Techniques for College Freshmen," p. 276).

These then are the origins of the term, remediation. And though we have, over the last fifty years, moved very far away from the conditions of its origins and have developed a richer understanding of reading and writing difficulties, the term is still with us. A recent letter from the senate of a local liberal arts college is sitting on my desk. It discusses a "program in remedial writing for . . . [those] entering freshmen suffering from severe writing handicaps." We seem entrapped by this language, this view of students and learning. Dr. Morgan has long since left his office, but we still talk of writers as suffering from specifiable, locatable defects, deficits, and handicaps that can be localized, circumscribed, and remedied. Such talk reveals an atomistic, mechanistic-medical model of language that few contemporary students of the use of language, from educators to literary theorists, would support. Furthermore, the notion of remediation, carrying with it as it does the etymological wisps and traces of disease, serves to exclude from the academic community those who are so labelled. They sit in scholastic quarantine until their disease can be diagnosed and remedied.

ILLITERACY

In a recent meeting on graduation requirements, a UCLA dean referred to students in remedial English as "the truly illiterate among us." Another administrator, in a memorandum on the potential benefits of increasing the number of composition offerings, concluded sadly that the increase "would not provide any assurance of universal literacy at UCLA." This sort of talk about illiteracy is common. We hear it from college presidents, educational foundations, pop grammarians, and scores of college professors like the one who cried to me after a recent senate meeting, "All I want is a student who can write a simple declarative sentence!" We in the academy like to talk this way.[16] It is dramatic and urgent, and, given the current concerns about illiteracy in the United States, it is topical. The trouble is, it is wrong. Perhaps we can better understand the problems with such labelling if we leave our colleagues momentarily and consider what it is that literacy means.

To be literate means to be acquainted with letters or writings. But exactly how such acquaintance translates into behavior varies a good deal over time and place. During the last century this country's Census Bureau defined as literate anyone who could write his or her name. These days the government requires that one be able to read and write at a sixth-grade level to be *functionally* literate: that is, to be able to meet—to a minimal degree— society's reading and writing demands. Things get a bit more complex if we consider the other meanings "literacy" has acquired. There are some specialized uses of the term, all fairly new: computer literacy, mathematical literacy, visual literacy, and so on. Literacy here refers to an acquaintance with the "letters" or elements of a particular field or domain. And there are also some very general uses of the term. Cultural literacy, another new construction, is hard to define because it is so broad and so

variously used, but it most often refers to an acquaintance with the humanistic, scientific, and social scientific achievements of one's dominant culture. Another general use of the term, a more traditional one, refers to the attainment of a liberal education, particularly in belles-lettres. Such literacy, of course, is quite advanced and involves not only an acquaintance with a literary tradition but interpretive sophistication as well.

Going back over these definitions, we can begin by dismissing the newer, specialized uses of "literacy." Computer literacy and other such literacies are usually not the focus of the general outcries we have been considering. How about the fundamental definition as it is currently established? This does not seem applicable either, for though many of the students entering American universities write prose that is grammatically and organizationally flawed, with very few exceptions they can read and write at a sixth-grade level. A sixth-grade proficiency is, of course, absurdly inadequate to do the work of higher education, but the definition still stands. By the most common measure the vast majority of students in college are literate. When academics talk about illiteracy they are saying that our students are "without letters" and cannot "write a simple declarative sentence." And such talk, for most students in most segments of higher education, is inaccurate and misleading.

One could argue that though our students are literate by common definition, a significant percentage of them might not be if we shift to the cultural and belletristic definitions of literacy or to a truly functional-contextual definition: that is, given the sophisticated, specialized reading and writing demands of the university—and the general knowledge they require—then it might be appropriate to talk of a kind of cultural illiteracy among some percentage of the student body. These students lack knowledge of the achievements of a tradition and are not at home with the ways we academics write about them. Perhaps this use of illiteracy is more warranted than the earlier talk about simple declarative sentences, but I would still advise caution. It is my experience that American college students tend to have learned more about western culture through their twelve years of schooling than their papers or pressured classroom responses demonstrate. (And, of course, our immigrant students bring with them a different cultural knowledge that we might not tap at all.) The problem is that the knowledge these students possess is often incomplete and fragmented and is not organized in ways that they can readily use in academic writing situations. But to say this is not to say that their minds are cultural blank slates.

There is another reason to be concerned about inappropriate claims of illiteracy. The term illiteracy comes to us with a good deal of semantic baggage, so that while an appropriately modified use of the term may accurately denote, it can still misrepresent by what it suggests, by the traces it carries from earlier eras. The social historian and anthropologist Shirley Brice Heath points out that from the mid-nineteenth century on, American school-based literacy was identified with "character, intellect, morality, and good taste . . . literacy skills co-occurred with moral patriotic character."[17] To be literate is to be honorable and intelligent. Tag some group illiterate, and you've gone beyond letters; you've judged their morals and their minds.

Please understand, it is not my purpose here to whitewash the very real limitations a disheartening number of our students bring with them. I dearly wish that more of them were more at home with composing and could write critically better than they do. I wish they enjoyed struggling for graceful written language more than many seem to. I wish they possessed more knowledge about humanities and the sciences so they could write with more authority than they usually do. And I wish to God that more of them read novels and poems for pleasure. But it is simply wrong to leap from these unrequited desires to claims of illiteracy. Reading and writing, as any ethnographic study would show, are woven throughout our students' lives. They write letters; some keep diaries. They read about what interests them, and those interests range from rock and roll to computer graphics to black holes. Reading, for many, is part of religious observation. They carry out a number of reading and writing acts in

their jobs and in their interactions with various segments of society. Their college preparatory curriculum in high school, admittedly to widely varying degrees, is built on reading, and even the most beleaguered schools require some kind of writing. And many of these students read and even write in languages other than English. No, these students are not illiterate, by common definition, and if the more sophisticated definitions apply, they sacrifice their accuracy by all they imply.

Illiteracy is a problematic term. I suppose that academics use it because it is rhetorically effective (evoking the specter of illiteracy to an audience of peers, legislators, or taxpayers can be awfully persuasive) or because it is emotionally satisfying. It gives expression to the frustration and disappointment in teaching students who do not share one's passions. As well, it affirms the faculty's membership in the society of the literate. One reader of this essay suggested to me that academics realize the hyperbole in their illiteracy talk, do not really mean it to be taken, well, literally. Were this invariably true, I would still voice concern over such exaggeration, for, as with any emotionally propelled utterance, it might well be revealing deeply held attitudes and beliefs, perhaps not unlike those discussed by Heath. And, deeply felt or not, such talk in certain political and decision-making settings can dramatically influence the outcomes of deliberation.

The fact remains that cries of illiteracy substitute a fast quip for careful analysis. Definitional accuracy here is important, for if our students are in fact adult illiterates, then a particular, very special curriculum is needed. If they are literate but do not read much for pleasure, or lack general knowledge that is central to academic inquiry, or need to write more than they do and pay more attention to it than they are inclined to, well, then these are very different problems. They bring with them quite different institutional commitments and pedagogies, and they locate the student in a very different place in the social-political makeup of the academy. Determining that place is crucial, for where but in the academy would being "without letters" be so stigmatizing?

THE MYTH OF TRANSIENCE

I have before me a report from the California Postsecondary Education Commission called *Promises to Keep*. It is a comprehensive and fair-minded assessment of remedial instruction in the three segments of California's public college and university system. As all such reports do, *Promises to Keep* presents data on instruction and expenses, discusses the implications of the data, and calls for reform. What makes the report unusual is its inclusion of an historical overview of preparatory instruction in the United States. It acknowledges the fact that such instruction in some guise has always been with us. In spite of its acknowledgement, the report ends on a note of optimism characteristic of similar documents with less historical wisdom. It calls for all three segments of the higher education system to "implement . . . plans to reduce remediation" within five years and voices the hope that if secondary education can be improved, "within a very few years, the state and its institutions should be rewarded by . . . lower costs for remediation as the need for remediation declines." This optimism in the face of a disconfirming historical survey attests to the power of what I will call the myth of transience. Despite the accretion of crisis reports, the belief persists in the American university that if we can just do *x* or *y*, the problem will be solved—in five years, ten years, or a generation—and higher education will be able to return to its real work. But entertain with me the possibility that such peaceful reform is a chimera.

Each generation of academicians facing the characteristic American shifts in demographics and accessibility sees the problem anew, laments it in the terms of the era, and optimistically notes its impermanence. No one seems to say that this scenario has gone on for so long that it might not be temporary. That, in fact, there will probably *always* be a significant percentage of students who do not meet some standard. (It was in 1841, not 1985 that the president of Brown complained, "Students frequently enter college almost wholly unacquainted with English grammar . . ." [Frederick Rudolph, *Curriculum: A History of the American Undergraduate Course of Study* (San Francisco: Jossey-Bass, 1978), p. 88].) The American higher educational system is constantly under pressure to expand, to redefine its boundaries, admitting, in turn, the sons of the middle class, and later the daughters, and then the American poor, the immigrant poor, veterans, the racially segregated, the disenfranchised. Because of the social and educational conditions these groups experienced, their preparation for college will, of course, be varied. Add to this the fact that disciplines change and society's needs change, and the ways society determines what it means to be educated change.

All this works itself rather slowly into the precollegiate curriculum. Thus there will always be a percentage of students who will be tagged substandard. And though many insist that this continued opening of doors will sacrifice excellence in the name of democracy, there are too many economic, political, and ethical drives in American culture to restrict higher education to a select minority. (And, make no mistake, the history of the American college and university from the early nineteenth century on could also be read as a history of changes in admissions, curriculum, and public image in order to keep enrollments high and institutions solvent.[18] The research institution as we know it is made possible by robust undergraduate enrollments.) Like it or not, the story of American education has been and will in all likelihood continue to be a story of increasing access. University of Nashville President Philip Lindsley's 1825 call echoes back and forth across our history: "The farmer, the mechanic, the manufacturer, the merchant, the sailor, the soldier . . . must be educated" (Frederick Rudolph, *The American College and University: A History* [New York: Vintage, 1962], p. 117).

Why begrudge academics their transience myth? After all, each generation's problems are new to those who face them, and people faced with a problem need some sense that they can solve it. Fair enough. But it seems to me that this myth brings with it a powerful liability. It blinds faculty members to historical reality and to the dynamic and fluid nature of the educational system that employs them. Like any golden age or utopian myth, the myth of transience assures its believers that the past was better or that the future will be.[19] The turmoil they are currently in will pass. The source of the problem is elsewhere; thus it can be ignored or temporarily dealt with until the tutors or academies or grammar schools or high schools or families make the changes they must make. The myth, then, serves to keep certain fundamental recognitions and thus certain fundamental changes at bay. It is ultimately a conservative gesture, a way of preserving administrative and curricular status quo.

And the myth plays itself out against complex social-political dynamics. One force in these dynamics is the ongoing struggle to establish admissions requirements that would protect the college curriculum, that would, in fact, define its difference from the high school course of study. Another is the related struggle to influence, even determine, the nature of the high school curriculum, "academize" it, shape it to the needs of the college (and the converse struggle of the high school to declare its multiplicity of purposes, college preparation being only one of its mandates). Yet another is the tension between the undergraduate, general education function of the university vs. its graduate, research function. To challenge the myth is to vibrate these complex dynamics; thus it is that it is so hard to dispel. But I would suggest that it must be challenged, for though some temporary "remedial" measures are excellent and generously funded, the presence of the myth does not allow them to be thought through in terms of the whole curriculum and does not allow the information they reveal to reciprocally influence the curriculum. Basic modifications in educational philosophy, institutional purpose, and professional training are rarely considered. They do not need to be if the problem is temporary. The myth allows the final exclusionary gesture: The problem is not ours in any fundamental way; we can embrace it if we must, but with surgical gloves on our hands.

There may be little anyone can do to change the fundamental tension in the American university between the general educational mission and the research mission, or to remove the stigma attached to application. But there is something those of us involved in writing can do about the language that has formed the field on which institutional discussions of writing and its teaching take place.

We can begin by affirming a rich model of written language development and production. The model we advance must honor the cognitive and emotional and situational dimensions of language, by psycholinguistic as well as literary and rhetorical in its focus, and aid us in understanding what we can observe as well as what we can only infer. When discussions and debates reveal a more reductive model of language, we must call time out and reestablish the terms of the argument. But we must also rigorously examine our own teaching and see what model of language lies beneath it. What linguistic assumptions are cued when we face freshman writers? Are they compatible with the assumptions that are cued when we think about our own writing or the writing of those we read for pleasure? Do we too operate with the bifurcated mind that for too long characterized the teaching of "remedial" students and that is still reflected in the language of our institutions?

Remediation. It is time to abandon this troublesome metaphor. To do so will not blind us to the fact that many entering students are not adequately prepared to take on the demands of university work. In fact, it will help us perceive these young people and the work they do in ways that foster appropriate notions about language development and use, that establish a framework for more rigorous and comprehensive analysis of their difficulties, and that do not perpetuate the rare show of allowing them entrance to the academy while, in various symbolic ways, denying them full participation.

Mina Shaughnessy got us to see that even the most error-ridden prose arises from the confrontation of inexperienced student writers with the complex linguistic and rhetorical expectations of the academy. She reminded us that to properly teach writing to such students is to understand "the intelligence of their mistakes."[20] She told us to interpret errors rather than circle them, and to guide these students, gradually and with wisdom, to be more capable participants within the world of these conventions. If we fully appreciate her message, we see how inadequate and limiting the remedial model is. Instead we need to define our work as transitional or as initiatory, orienting, or socializing to what David Bartholomae and Patricia Bizzell call the academic discourse community.[21] This redefinition is not just semantic sleight-of-hand. If truly adopted, it would require us to reject a medical-deficit model of language, to acknowledge the rightful place of all freshmen in the academy, and once and for all to replace loose talk about illiteracy with more precise and pedagogically fruitful analysis. We would move from a mechanistic focus on error toward a demanding curriculum that encourages the full play of language activity and that opens out onto the academic community rather than sequestering students from it.

A much harder issue to address is the common designation of writing as a skill. We might begin by considering more fitting terms. Jerome Bruner's "enabling discipline" comes to mind. It does not separate skill from discipline and implies something more than a "tool subject" in that to enable means to make possible. But such changes in diction might be little more than cosmetic.

If the skills designation proves to be resistant to change, then we must insist that writing is a very unique skill, not really a tool but an ability fundamental to academic inquiry, an ability whose development is not fixed but ongoing. If it is possible to go beyond the skills model, we could see a contesting of the fundamental academic distinction between integrated bodies of knowledge and skills and techniques. While that distinction makes sense in many cases, it may blur where writing is concerned. Do students really *know* history when they learn a "body" of facts, even theories, or when they act like historians, thinking in certain ways with those facts and theories? Most historians would say the latter. And the academic historian (vs. the chronicler or the balladeer) conducts inquiry through writing; it is not just an implement but is part of the very way of doing history.

It is in this context that we should ponder the myth of transience. The myth's liability is that it limits the faculty's ability to consider the writing problems of their students in dynamic and historical terms. Each academic generation considers standards and assesses the preparation of its students but seems to do this in ways that do not call the nature of the curriculum of the time into question. The problem ultimately lies outside the academy. But might not these difficulties with writing suggest the need for possible far-ranging changes within the curriculum as well, changes that *are* the proper concern of the university? One of the things I think the myth of transience currently does is to keep faculty from seeing the multiple possibilities that exist for incorporating writing throughout their courses of study. Profound reform could occur in the much-criticized lower-division curriculum if writing were not seen as only a technique and the teaching of it as by and large a remedial enterprise.

The transmission of a discipline, especially on the lower-division level, has become very much a matter of comprehending information, committing it to memory, recalling it, and displaying it in various kinds of "objective" or short-answer tests. When essay exams are required, the prose all too often becomes nothing more than a net in which the catch of individual bits of knowledge lie. Graders pick through the essay and tally up the presence of key phrases. Such activity trivializes a discipline; it reduces its methodology, grounds it in a limited theory of knowledge, and encourages students to operate with a restricted range of their cognitive abilities. Writing, on the other hand, assumes a richer epistemology and demands fuller participation. It requires a complete, active, struggling engagement with the facts and principles of a discipline, an encounter with the discipline's texts and the incorporation of them into one's own work, the framing of one's knowledge within the myriad conventions that help define a discipline, the persuading of other investigators that one's knowledge is legitimate. So to consider the relationship between writing and disciplinary inquiry may help us decide what is central to a discipline and how best to teach it. The university's research and educational missions would intersect.

Such reform will be difficult. True, there is growing interest in writing adjuncts and discipline-specific writing courses, and those involved in writing-across-the-curriculum are continually encouraging faculty members to evaluate the place of writing in their individual curricula. But wide-ranging change will occur only if the academy redefines writing for itself, changes the terms of the argument, sees instruction in writing as one of its central concerns.

Academic senates often defend the labelling of a writing course as remedial by saying that they are defending the integrity of the baccalaureate, and they are sending a message to the high schools. The schools, of course, are so beleaguered that they can barely hear those few units ping into the bucket. Consider, though, the message that would be sent to the schools and to the society at large if the university embraced—not just financially but conceptually—the teaching of writing: if we gave it full status, championed its rich relationship with inquiry, insisted on the importance of craft and grace, incorporated it into the heart of our curriculum. What an extraordinary message that would be. It would affect the teaching of writing as no other message could.[22]

Notes

1. Quoted in Lawrence A. Cremin, *The Transformation of the School: Progressivism in American Education* (New York: Alfred A. Knopf, 1961), p. 185.

2. Arthur N. Applebee, *Tradition and Reform in the Teaching of English: A History* (Urbana, Ill.: National Council of Teachers of English, 1974), pp. 93–94.

3. P. G. Perrin, "The Remedial Racket," *English Journal,* 22 (1933), 383.

4. From Cubberley's introduction to Albert R. Lang, *Modern Methods in Written Examinations* (Boston: Houghton Mifflin, 1930), p. vii.

5. "Background Deficiencies," *Journal of Higher Education,* 3 (1932), 371.

6. "Remedial Methods in English Composition," *English Journal,* 22 (1933), 749–754.

7. "Freshmen Needs in Written English," *English Journal,* 19 (1930), 706.

8. I would mislead if I did not point out that there were cautionary voices being raised all along, though until the late 1930s they were very much in the minority. For two early appraisals, see R. L. Lyman, *Summary of Investigations Relating to Grammar, Language, and Composition* (Chicago: University of Chicago Press, 1924), and especially P. G. Perrin, "The Remedial Racket," *English Journal,* 22 (1933), 382–388.

9. Two quotations. The first offers the sort of humanist battle cry that often accompanies reductive drill, and the second documents the results of such an approach. Both are from NCTE publications.

   "I think . . . that the chief objective of freshman English (at least for the first semester and low or middle—but not high—sections) should be ceaseless, brutal drill on mechanics, with exercises and themes. Never mind imagination, the soul, literature, for at least one semester, but pray for literacy and fight for it" (A University of Nebraska professor quoted with approval in Oscar James Campbell, *The Teaching of College English* [New York: Appleton-Century, 1934], pp. 36–37).

   "Members of the Task Force saw in many classes extensive work in traditional schoolroom grammar and traditional formal English usage. They commonly found students with poor reading skills being taught the difference between *shall* and *will* or pupils with serious difficulties in speech diagraming sentences. Interestingly, observations by the Task Force reveal far more extensive teaching of traditional grammar in this study of language programs for the disadvantaged than observers saw in the National Study of High School English Programs, a survey of comprehensive high schools known to be achieving important results in English with college-bound students able to comprehend the abstractions of such grammar" (Richard Corbin and Muriel Crosby, *Language Programs for the Disadvantaged* [Urbana, Ill.: NCTE, 1965], pp. 121–122).

10. In 1894, for example, over 40% of entering freshmen came from the preparatory divisions of the institutions that enrolled them. And as late as 1915—a time when the quantity and quality of secondary schools had risen sufficiently to make preparatory divisions less necessary—350 American colleges still maintained their programs. See John S. Brubacher and Willis Rudy, *Higher Education in Transition: A History of American Colleges and Universities, 1636–1976,* 3rd ed. (New York: Harper and Row, 1976), pp. 241 ff., and Arthur Levine, *Handbook on Undergraduate Curriculum* (San Francisco: Jossey-Bass, 1981), pp. 54 ff.

11. Several writers point to a study habits course initiated at Wellesley in 1894 as the first modern remedial course in higher education (K. Patricia Cross, *Accent on Learning* [San Francisco: Jossey-Bass, 1979], and Arthur Levine, *Handbook on Undergraduate Curriculum*). In fact, the word "remedial" did not appear in the course's title and the course was different in kind from the courses actually designated "remedial" that would emerge in the 1920s and 30s. (See Cross, pp. 24–25, for a brief discussion of early study skills courses.) The first use of the term "remedial" in the context I am discussing was most likely in a 1916 article on the use of reading tests to plan "remedial work" (Nila Banton Smith, *American Reading Instruction* [Newark, Delaware: International Reading Association, 1965], p. 191). The first elementary and secondary level remedial courses in reading were offered in the early 1920s; remedial courses in college would not appear until the late 20s.

12. *Letter, Word, and Mind-Blindness* (London: Lewis, 1902); *Congenital Word-Blindness* (London: Lewis, 1917).

13. "The 'Sight Reading' Method of Teaching Reading, as a Source of Reading Disability," *Journal of Educational Psychology*, 20 (1929), 135–143.

14. There were, of course, some theorists and practitioners who questioned medical-physiological models, Arthur Gates of Columbia Teacher's College foremost among them. But even those who questioned such models—with the exception of Gates—tended to retain medical language.

15. There is another layer to this terminological and conceptual confusion. At the same time that remediation language was being used ever more broadly by some educators, it maintained its strictly medical usage in other educational fields. For example, Annie Dolman Inskeep has only one discussion of "remedial work" in her book *Teaching Dull and Retarded Children* (New York: Macmillan, 1926), and that discussion has to do with treatment for children needing health care: "Children who have poor teeth, who do not hear well, or who hold a book when reading nearer than eight inches to the eyes or further away than sixteen. . . . Nervous children, those showing continuous fatigue symptoms, those under weight, and those who are making no apparent bodily growth" (p. 271).

16. For a sometimes humorous but more often distressing catalogue of such outcries, see Harvey A. Daniels, *Famous Last Words* (Carbondale: Southern Illinois University Press, 1983), especially pp. 31–58.

17. "Toward an Ethnohistory of Writing in American Education," in Marcia Farr Whiteman, ed. *Writing: The Nature, Development, and Teaching of Written Communication,* Vol. 1 (Hillsdale, N.J.: Erlbaum, 1981), 35–36.

18. Of turn-of-the-century institutions, Laurence Veysey writes: "Everywhere the size of enrollments was closely tied to admission standards. In order to assure themselves of enough students to make a notable "splash," new institutions often opened with a welcome to nearly all comers, no matter how ill prepared; this occurred at Cornell, Stanford, and (to a lesser degree) at Chicago" (*The Emergence of the American University*, p. 357).

19. An appropriate observation here comes from Daniel P. and Lauren B. Resnick's critical survey of reading instruction and standards of literacy: "there is little to go back to in terms of pedagogical method, curriculum, or school organization. The old tried and true approaches, which nostalgia prompts us to believe might solve current problems, were designed neither to achieve the literacy standard sought today nor to assure successful literacy for everyone . . . there is no simple past to which we can return" ("The Nature of Literacy: An Historical Exploration." *Harvard Educational Review*, 47 [1977], 385).

20. *Errors and Expectations* (New York: Oxford University Press, 1977), p. 11.

21. David Bartholomae, "Inventing the University," in Mike Rose, ed., *When a Writer Can't Write: Studies in Writer's Block and Other Composing Process Problems* (New York: Guilford, 1985); Patricia Bizzell, "College Composition: Initiation into the Academic Discourse Community," *Curriculum Inquiry*, 12 (1982), 191–207.

22. I wish to thank Arthur Applebee, Robert Connors, Carol Hartzog, and William Schaefer for reading and generously commenting on an earlier version of this essay. Connors and Hartzog also helped me revise that version. Bill Richey provided research assistance of remarkably high caliber, and Tom Bean, Kenyon Chan, Patricia Donahue, Jack Kolb, and Bob Schwegler offered advice and encouragement. Finally, a word of thanks to Richard Lanham for urging me to think of our current problem in broader contexts.

Inventing the University

David Bartholomae

Bartholomae's essay is taken from When a Writer Can't Write: Studies in Writer's Block and Other Composing-Process Problems. *Ed. Mike Rose. New York: Guilford Press, 1985. 134–65. It was also reprinted in* Perspectives on Literacy. *Eds. Eugene Kintgen, Barry Kroll, and Mike Rose, 1988. 273–85. Another version of the essay was printed in the* Journal of Basic Writing 5 (1986): 4–23.

Education may well be, as of right, the instrument whereby every individual, in a society like our own, can gain access to any kind of discourse. But we well know that in its distribution, in what it permits and in what it prevents, it follows the well-trodden battle-lines of social conflict. Every educational system is a political means of maintaining or of modifying the appropriation of discourse, with the knowledge and the powers it carries with it.—FOUCAULT, *THE DISCOURSE ON LANGUAGE*

. . . the text is the form of the social relationships made visible, palpable, material.—BERNSTEIN, *CODES, MODALITIES AND THE PROCESS OF CULTURAL REPRODUCTION: A MODEL*

I.

Every time a student sits down to write for us, he has to invent the university for the occasion—invent the university, that is, or a branch of it, like history or anthropology or economics or English. The student has to learn to speak our language, to speak as we do, to try on the peculiar ways of knowing, selecting, evaluating, reporting, concluding, and arguing that define the discourse of our community. Or perhaps I should say the *various* discourses of our community, since it is in the nature of a liberal arts education that a student, after the first year or two, must learn to try on a variety of voices and interpretive schemes—to write, for example, as a literary critic one day and as an experimental psychologist the next; to work within fields where the rules governing the presentation of examples or the development of an argument are both distinct and, even to a professional mysterious.

The student has to appropriate (or be appropriated by) a specialized discourse, and he has to do this as though he were easily and comfortably one with his audience, as though he were a member of the academy or an historian or an anthropologist or an economist; he has to invent the university by assembling and mimicking its language while finding some compromise between idiosyncracy, a personal history, on the one hand, and the requirements of convention, the history of a discipline, on the other. He must learn to speak our language. Or he must dare to speak it or to carry off the bluff, since speaking and writing will most certainly be required long before the skill is "learned." And this, understandably, causes problems.

Let me look quickly at an example. Here is an essay written by a college freshman.

In the past time I thought that an incident was creative was when I had to make a clay model of the earth, but not of the classical or your everyday model of the earth which consists of the two cores, the mantle and the crust. I thought of these things in a dimension of which it would be unique, but easy to comprehend. Of course, your materials to work with were basic and limited at the same time, but thought help to put this limit into a right attitude or frame of mind to work with the clay.

In the beginning of the clay model, I had to research and learn the different dimensions of the earth (in magnitude, quantity, state of matter, etc.) After this, I learned how to put this into the clay and come up with something different than any other person in my class at the time. In my opinion, color coordination and shape was the key to my creativity of the clay model of the earth.

Creativity is the venture of the mind at work with the mechanics relay to the limbs from the cranium, which stores and triggers this action. It can be a burst of energy released at a precise time a thought is being transmitted. This can cause a frenzy of the human body, but it depends on the characteristics of the individual and how they can relay the message clearly enough through mechanics of the body to us as an observer. Then we must determine if it is creative or a learned process varied by the individuals thought process. Creativity is indeed a tool which has to exist, or our world will not succeed into the future and progress like it should.

I am continually impressed by the patience and goodwill of our students. This student was writing a placement essay during freshman orientation. (The problem set to him was: "Describe a time when you did something you felt to be creative. Then, on the basis of the incident you have described, go on to draw some general conclusions about 'creativity.'") He knew that university faculty would be reading and evaluating his essay, and so he wrote for them.

In some ways it is a remarkable performance. He is trying on the discourse even though he doesn't have the knowledge that would make the discourse more than a routine, a set of conventional rituals and gestures. And he is doing this, I think, even though he *knows* he doesn't have the knowledge that would make the discourse more than a routine. He defines himself as a researcher working systematically, and not as a kid in a high school class: "I thought of these things in a dimen-

sion of . . ."; "I had to research and learn the different dimensions of the earth (in magnitude, quantity, state of matter, etc.)." He moves quickly into a specialized language (his approximation of our jargon) and draws both a general, textbook-like conclusion—"Creativity is the venture of the mind at work . . ."—and a resounding peroration—"Creativity is indeed a tool which has to exist, or our world will not succeed into the future and progress like it should." The writer has even picked up the rhythm of our prose with that last "indeed" and with the qualifications and the parenthetical expressions of the opening paragraphs. And through it all he speaks with an impressive air of authority.

There is an elaborate but, I will argue, a necessary and enabling fiction at work here as the student dramatizes his experience in a "setting"—the setting required by the discourse—where he can speak to us as a companion, a fellow researcher. As I read the essay, there is only one moment when the fiction is broken, when we are addressed differently. The student says, "Of course, your materials to work with were basic and limited at the same time, but thought help to put this limit into a right attitude or frame of mind to work with the clay." At this point, I think, we become students and he the teacher giving us a lesson (as in, "You take your pencil in your right hand and put your paper in front of you"). This is, however, one of the most characteristic slips of basic writers. (I use the term "basic writers" to refer to university students traditionally placed in remedial composition courses.) It is very hard for them to take on the role—the voice, the persona—of an authority whose authority is rooted in scholarship, analysis, or research. They slip, then, into a more immediately available and realizable voice of authority, the voice of a teacher giving a lesson or the voice of a parent lecturing at the dinner table. They offer advice or homilies rather than "academic" conclusions. There is a similar break in the final paragraph, where the conclusion that pushes for a definition ("Creativity is the venture of the mind at work with the mechanics relay to the limbs from the cranium") is replaced by a conclusion that speaks in the voice of an elder ("Creativity is indeed a tool which has to exist, or our world will not succeed into the future and progress like it should").

It is not uncommon, then, to find such breaks in the concluding sections of essays written by basic writers. Here is the concluding section of an essay written by a student about his work as a mechanic. He had been asked to generalize about work after reviewing an on-the-job experience or incident that "stuck in his mind" as somehow significant.

> How could two repairmen miss a leak? Lack of pride? No incentive? Lazy? I don't know.

At this point the writer is in a perfect position to speculate, to move from the problem to an analysis of the problem. Here is how the paragraph continues, however (and notice the change in pronoun reference).

> From this point on, I take *my* time, do it right, and don't let customers get under *your* skin. If they have a complaint, tell them to call your boss and he'll be more than glad to handle it. Most important, worry about yourself, and keep a clear eye on everyone, for there's always someone trying to take advantage of you, anytime and anyplace. (Emphasis added)

We get neither a technical discussion nor an "academic" discussion but a Lesson on Life.[1] This is the language he uses to address the general question, "How could two repairmen miss a leak?" The other brand of conclusion, the more academic one, would have required him to speak of his experience in our terms; it would, that is, have required a special vocabulary, a special system of presentation, and an interpretive scheme (or a set of commonplaces) he could have used to identify and talk about the mystery of human error. The writer certainly had access to the range of acceptable commonplaces for such an explanation: "lack of pride," "no incentive," "lazy." Each commonplace would dictate its own set of phrases, examples, and conclusions; and we, his teachers, would know how to write out each argument, just as we know how to write out more specialized arguments of our own. A "commonplace," then, is a culturally or institutionally authorized concept or statement that car-

ries with it its own necessary elaboration. We all use commonplaces to orient ourselves in the world; they provide points of reference and a set of "prearticulated" explanations that are readily available to organize and interpret experience. The phrase "lack of pride" carries with it its own account of the repairman's error, just as at another point in time a reference to "original sin" would have provided an explanation, or just as in certain university classrooms a reference to "alienation" would enable writers to continue and complete the discussion. While there is a way in which these terms are interchangeable, they are not all permissible: A student in a composition class would most likely be turned away from a discussion of original sin. Commonplaces are the "controlling ideas" of our composition textbooks, textbooks that not only insist on a set form for expository writing but a set view of public life.[2]

When the writer says, "I don't know," then, he is not saying that he has nothing to say. He is saying that he is not in a position to carry on this discussion. And so we are addressed as apprentices rather than as teachers or scholars. In order to speak as a person of status or privilege, the writer can either speak to us in our terms—in the privileged language of university discourse—or, in default (or in defiance) of that, he can speak to us as though we were children, offering us the wisdom of experience.

I think it is possible to say that the language of the "Clay Model" paper has come *through* the writer and not from the writer. The writer has located himself (more precisely, he has located the self that is represented by the "I" on the page) in a context that is finally beyond him, not his own and not available to his immediate procedures for inventing and arranging text. I would not, that is, call this essay an example of "writer-based" prose. I would not say that it is egocentric or that it represents the "interior monologue or a writer thinking and talking to himself" (Flower, 1981, p. 63). It is, rather, the record of a writer who has lost himself in the discourse of his readers. There is a context beyond the intended reader that is not the world but a way of talking about the world, a way of talking that determines the use of examples, the possible conclusions, acceptable commonplaces, and key words for an essay on the construction of a clay model of the earth. This writer has entered the discourse without successfully approximating it.

Linda Flower (1981) has argued that the difficulty inexperienced writers have with writing can be understood as a difficulty in negotiating the transition between "writer-based" and "reader-based" prose. Expert writers, in other words, can better imagine how a reader will respond to a text and can transform or restructure what they have to say around a goal shared with a reader. Teaching students to revise for readers, then, will better prepare them to write initially with a reader in mind. The success of this pedagogy depends on the degree to which a writer can imagine and conform to a reader's goals. The difficulty of this act of imagination and the burden of such conformity are so much at the heart of the problem that a teacher must pause and take stock before offering revision as a solution. A student like the one who wrote the "Clay Model" paper is not so much trapped in a private language as he is shut out from one of the privileged languages of public life, a language he is aware of but cannot control.

II.

Our students, I've said, have to appropriate (or be appropriated by) a specialized discourse, and they have to do this as though they were easily or comfortably one with their audience. If you look at the situation this way, suddenly the problem of audience awareness becomes enormously complicated. One of the common assumptions of both composition research and composition teaching is that at some "stage" in the process of composing an essay a writer's ideas or his motives must be tailored to the needs and expectations of his audience. Writers have to "build bridges" between their point of view and the reader's. They have to anticipate and acknowledge the reader's assumptions and biases. They must begin with "common points of departure" before introducing new or controversial arguments. Here is what one of the most popular college textbooks says to students.

Once you have your purpose clearly in mind, your next task is to define and analyze your audience. A sure sense of your audience—knowing who it is and what assumptions you can reasonably make about it—is crucial to the success of your rhetoric. (Hairston, 1978, p. 107)

It is difficult to imagine, however, how writers can have a purpose before they are located in a discourse, since it is the discourse with its projects and agendas that determines what writers can and will do. The writer who can successfully manipulate an audience (or, to use a less pointed language, the writer who can accommodate her motives to her reader's expectations) is a writer who can both imagine and write from a position of privilege. She must, that is, see herself within a privileged discourse, one that already includes and excludes groups of readers. She must be either equal to or more powerful than those she would address. The writing, then, must somehow transform the political and social relationships between students and teachers.

If my students are going to write for me by knowing who I am—and if this means more than knowing my prejudices, psyching me out—it means knowing what I know; it means having the knowledge of a professor of English. They have, then, to know what I know and how I know what I know (the interpretive schemes that define the way I would work out the problems I set for them); they have to learn to write what I would write or to offer up some approximation of that discourse. The problem of audience awareness, then, is a problem of power and finesse. It cannot be addressed, as it is in most classroom exercises, by giving students privilege and denying the situation of the classroom—usually, that is, by having students write to an outsider, someone excluded from their privileged circle: "Write about 'To His Coy Mistress,' not for your teacher but for the students in your class"; "Describe Pittsburgh to someone who has never been there"; "Explain to a high school senior how best to prepare for college"; "Describe baseball to an Eskimo." Exercises such as these allow students to imagine the needs and goals of a reader, and they bring those needs and goals forward as a dominant constraint in the construction of an essay. And they argue, implicitly, what is generally true about writing—that it is an act of aggression disguised as an act of charity. What these assignments fail to address is the central problem of academic writing, where a student must assume the right of speaking to someone who knows more about baseball or "To His Coy Mistress" than the student does, a reader for whom the general commonplaces and the readily available utterances about a subject are inadequate.

Linda Flower and John Hayes, in an often quoted article (1981), reported on a study of a protocol of an expert writer (an English teacher) writing about his job for readers of *Seventeen* magazine. The key moment for this writer, who seems to have been having trouble getting started, came when he decided that teenage girls read *Seventeen;* that some teenage girls like English because it is tidy ("some of them will have wrong reasons in that English is good because it's tidy—can be a neat tidy little girl"); that some don't like it because it is "prim" and that, "By God, I can change that notion for them." Flower and Hayes's conclusion is that this effort of "exploration and consolidation" gave the writer "a new, relatively complex, rhetorically sophisticated working goal, one which encompasses plans for a topic, a persona, and the audience" (p. 383).[3]

Flower and Hayes give us a picture of a writer solving a problem, and the problem as they present it is a cognitive one. It is rooted in the way the writer's knowledge is represented in the writer's mind. The problem resides there, not in the nature of knowledge or in the nature of discourse but in a mental state prior to writing. It is possible, however, to see the problem as (perhaps simultaneously) a problem in the way subjects are located in a field of discourse.

Flower and Hayes divide up the composing process into three distinct activities: "planning or goal-setting," "translating," and "reviewing." The last of these, reviewing (which is further divided into two subprocesses, "evaluating" and "revising"), is particularly powerful, for as a writer continually reviews his goals, plans, and the text he is producing, and as he continually generates new goals, plans, and text, he is engaging in a process of learning and discovery. Let me quote Flower and Hayes's conclusion at length.

> If one studies the process by which a writer uses a goal to generate ideas, then consolidates those ideas and uses them to revise or regenerate new, more complex goals, one can see this learning process in action. Furthermore, one sees why the process of revising and clarifying goals has such a broad effect, since it is through setting these new goals that the fruits of discovery come back to inform the continuing process of writing. In this instance, some of our most complex and imaginative acts can depend on the elegant simplicity of a few powerful thinking processes. We feel that a cognitive process explanation of discovery, toward which this theory is only a start, will have another special strength. By placing emphasis on the inventive power of the writer, who is able to explore ideas, to develop, act on, test, and regenerate his or her own goals, we are putting an important part of creativity where it belongs—in the hands of the working, thinking writer. (1981, p. 386)

While this conclusion is inspiring, the references to invention and creativity seem to refer to something other than an act of writing—if writing is, finally, words on a page. Flower and Hayes locate the act of writing solely within the mind of the writer. The act of writing, here, has a personal, cognitive history but not a history as a text, as a text that is made possible by prior texts. When located in the perspective afforded by prior texts, writing is seen to exist separate from the writer and his intentions; it is seen in the context of other articles in *Seventeen,* of all articles written for or about women, of all articles written about English teaching, and so on. Reading research has made it possible to say that these prior texts, or a reader's experience with these prior texts, have bearing on how the text is read. Intentions, then, are part of the history of the language itself. I am arguing that these prior texts determine not only how a text like the *Seventeen* article will be read but also how it will be written. Flower and Hayes show us what happens in the writer's mind but not what happens to the writer as his motives are located within our language, a language with its own requirements and agendas, a language that limits what we might say and that makes us write and sound, finally, also like someone else. If you think of other accounts of the composing process—and I'm thinking of accounts as diverse as Richard Rodriguez's *Hunger or Memory* (1983) and Edward Said's *Beginnings* (1975)—you get a very different account of what happens when private motive enters into public discourse, when a personal history becomes a public account. These accounts place the writer in a history that is not of the writer's own invention; and they are chronicles of loss, violence, and compromise.

It is one thing to see the *Seventeen* writer making and revising his plans for a topic, a persona, and an audience; it is another thing to talk about discovery, invention, and creativity. Whatever plans the writer had must finally have been located in language and, it is possible to argue, in a language that is persistently conventional and formulaic. We do not, after all, get to see the *Seventeen* article. We see only the elaborate mental procedures that accompanied the writing of the essay. We see a writer's plans for a persona; we don't see that persona in action. If writing is a process, it is also a product; and it is the product, and not the plan for writing, that locates a writer on the page, that locates him in a text and a style and the codes or conventions that make both of them readable.

Contemporary rhetorical theory has been concerned with the "codes" that constitute discourse (or specialized forms of discourse). These codes determine not only what might be said but also who might be speaking or reading. Barthes (1974), for example, has argued that the moment of writing, where private goals and plans become subject to a public language, is the moment when the writer becomes subject to a language he can neither command nor control. A text, he says, in being written passes through the codes that govern writing and becomes "de-originated," becomes a fragment of something that has "always been *already* read, seen, done, experienced" (p. 21). Alongside a text we have always the presence of "off-stage voices," the

oversound of all that has been said (e.g., about girls, about English). These voices, the presence of the "already written," stand in defiance of a writer's desire for originality and determine what might be said. A writer does not write (and this is Barthes's famous paradox) but is, himself, written by the languages available to him.

It is possible to see the writer of the *Seventeen* article solving his problem of where to begin by appropriating an available discourse. Perhaps what enabled that writer to write was the moment he located himself as a writer in a familiar field of stereotypes: Readers of *Seventeen* are teenage girls; teenage girls think of English (and English teachers) as "tidy" and "prim," and, "By God, I can change that notion for them." The moment of eureka was not simply a moment of breaking through a cognitive jumble in that individual writer's mind but a moment of breaking into a familiar and established territory—one with insiders and outsiders; one with set phrases, examples, and conclusions.

I'm not offering a criticism of the morals or manners of the teacher who wrote the *Seventeen* article. I think that all writers, in order to write, must imagine for themselves the privilege of being "insiders"—that is, the privilege both of being inside an established and powerful discourse and of being granted a special right to speak. But I think that right to speak is seldom conferred on us—on any of us, teachers or students—by virtue of that fact that we have invented or discovered an original idea. Leading students to believe that they are responsible for something new or original, unless they understand what those words mean with regard to writing, is a dangerous and counterproductive practice. We do have the right to expect students to be active and engaged, but that is a matter of continually and stylistically working against the inevitable presence of conventional language; it is not a matter of inventing a language that is new.

When a student is writing for a teacher, writing becomes more problematic than it was for the *Seventeen* writer (who was writing a version of the "Describe baseball to an Eskimo" exercise). The student, in effect, has to assume privilege without having any. And since students assumes privilege by locating themselves within the discourse of a particular community—within a set of specifically acceptable gestures and commonplaces—learning, at least as it is defined in the liberal arts curriculum, becomes more a matter of imitation or parody than a matter of invention and discovery.

To argue that writing problems are also social and political problems is not to break faith with the enterprise of cognitive science. In a recent paper reviewing the tremendous range of research directed at identifying general cognitive skills, David Perkins (in press) has argued that "the higher the level of competence concerned," as in the case of adult learning, "the fewer *general* cognitive control strategies there are." There comes a point, that is, where "field-specific" or "domain-specific" schemata (what I have called "interpretive strategies") become more important than general problem-solving processes. Thinking, learning, writing—all these become bound to the context of a particular discourse. And Perkins concludes:

> Instruction in cognitive control strategies tends to be organized around problem-solving tasks. However, the isolated problem is a creature largely of the classroom. The nonstudent, whether operating in scholarly or more everyday contexts, is likely to find himself or herself involved in what might be called "projects"—which might be anything from writing a novel to designing a shoe to starting a business.

It is interesting to note that Perkins defines the classroom as the place of artificial tasks and, as a consequence, has to place scholarly projects outside the classroom, where they are carried out by the "nonstudent." It is true, I think, that education has failed to involve students in scholarly projects, projects that allow students to act as though they were colleagues in an academic enterprise. Much of the written work that students do is test-taking, report or summary—work that places them outside the official discourse of the academic community, where they are expected to admire and report on what we do, rather than inside that discourse, where they can do its work and participate in a common enterprise.[4] This, however, is a failure of

teachers and curriculum designers, who speak of writing as a mode of learning but all too often represent writing as a "tool" to be used by an (hopefully) educated mind.

It could be said, then, that there is a bastard discourse peculiar to the writing most often required of students. Carl Bereiter and Marlene Scardamalia (in press) have written about this discourse (they call it "knowledge-telling"; students who are good at it have learned to cope with academic tasks by developing a "knowledge-telling strategy"), and they have argued that insistence on knowledge-telling discourse undermines educational efforts to extend the variety of discourse schemata available to students.[5] What they actually say is this:

> When we think of knowledge stored in memory we tend these days to think of it as situated in three-dimensional space, with vertical and horizontal connections between sites. Learning is thought to add not only new elements to memory but also new connections, and it is the richness and structure of these connections that would seem . . . to spell the difference between inert and usable knowledge. On this account, the knowledge-telling strategy is educationally faulty because it specifically avoids the forming of connections between previously separated knowledge sites.

It should be clear by now that when I think of "knowledge" I think of it as situated in the discourse that constitutes "knowledge" in a particular discourse community, rather than as situated in mental "knowledge sites." One can remember a discourse, just as one can remember an essay or the movement of a professor's lecture; but this discourse, in effect, also has a memory of its own, its own rich network of structures and connections beyond the deliberate control of any individual imagination.

There is, to be sure, an important distinction to be made between learning history, say, and learning to write as an historian. A student can learn to command and reproduce a set of names, dates, places, and canonical interpretations (to "tell" somebody else's knowledge); but this is not the same thing as learning to "think" (by learning to write) as an historian. The former requires efforts of memory; the latter requires a student to compose a text out of the texts that represent the primary materials of history and in accordance with the texts that define history as an act of report and interpretation.

Let me draw on an example from my own teaching. I don't expect my students to *be* literary critics when they write about *Bleak House*. If a literary critic is a person who wins publication in a professional journal (or if he or she is one who could), the students aren't critics. I do, however, expect my students to be, themselves, invented as literary critics by approximating the language of a literary critic writing about *Bleak House*. My students, then, don't invent the language of literary criticism (they don't, that is, act on their own) but they are, themselves, invented by it. Their papers don't begin with a moment of insight, a "by God" moment that is outside of language. They begin with a moment of appropriation, a moment when they can offer up a sentence that is not theirs as though it were their own. (I can remember when, as a graduate student, I would begin papers by sitting down to write literally in the voice—with the syntax and the key words—of the strongest teacher I had met.)

What I am saying about my students' essays is that they are approximate, not that they are wrong or invalid. They are evidence of a discourse that lies between what I might call the students' primary discourse (what the students might write about *Bleak House* were they not in my class or in any class, and were they not imagining that they were in my class or in any class—if you can imagine any student doing any such thing) and standard, official literary criticism (which is imaginable but impossible to find). The students' essays are evidence of a discourse that lies between these two hypothetical poles. The writing is limited as much by a student's ability to imagine "what might be said" as it is by cognitive control strategies.[6] The act of writing takes the student away from where he is and what he knows and allows him to imagine something else. The approximate discourse, therefore, is evidence of a change, a change that, because we are teachers, we call "development." What our beginning students need to learn is to extend themselves, by successive approximations, into the commonplaces, set phrases, rituals and gestures, habits of mind, tricks of persuasion, obligatory conclusions and necessary connections that determine the "what might be said" and constitute knowledge within the various branches of our academic community.[7]

Pat Bizzell is, I think, one of the most important scholars writing now on "basic writers" (and this is the common name we use for students who are refused unrestrained access to the academic community) and on the special characteristics of academic discourse. In a recent essay, "Cognition, Convention, and Certainty: What We Need to Know about Writing" (1982a), she looks at two schools of composition research and the way they represent the problems that writing poses for writers.[8] For one group, the "inner-directed theorists," the problems are internal, cognitive, rooted in the way the mind represents knowledge to itself. These researchers are concerned with discovering the "universal, fundamental structures of thought and language" and with developing pedagogies to teach or facilitate both basic, general cognitive skills and specific cognitive strategies, or heuristics, directed to serve more specialized needs. Of the second group, the "outer-directed theorists," she says that they are "more interested in the social processes whereby language-learning and thinking capacities are shaped and used in particular communities."

> The staple activity of outer-directed writing instruction will be analysis of the conventions of particular discourse communities. For example, a main focus of writing-across-the-curriculum programs is to demystify the conventions of the academic discourse community. (1982a, p. 218)

The essay offers a detailed analysis of the way the two theoretical camps can best serve the general enterprise of composition research and composition teaching. Its agenda, however, seems to be to counter the influence of the cognitivists and to provide bibliography and encouragement to those interested in the social dimension of language learning.

As far as basic writers are concerned, Bizzell argues that the cognitivists' failure to acknowledge the primary, shaping role of convention in the act of composing makes them "particularly insensitive to the problems of poor writers." She argues that some of those problems, like the problem of establishing and monitoring overall goals for a piece of writing, can be

> better understood in terms of their unfamiliarity with the academic discourse community, combined, perhaps, with such limited experience outside their native discourse communities that they are unaware that there is such a thing as a discourse community with conventions to be mastered. What is underdeveloped is their knowledge both of the ways experience is constituted and interpreted in the academic discourse community and of the fact that all discourse communities constitute and interpret experience. (1982a, p. 230)

One response to the problems of basic writers, then, would be to determine just what the community's conventions are, so that those conventions could be written out, "demystified" and taught in our classrooms. Teachers, as a result, could be more precise and helpful when they ask students to "think," "argue," "describe," or "define." Another response would be to examine the essays written by basic writers—their approximations of academic discourse—to determine more clearly where the problems lie. If we look at their writing, and if we look at it in the context of other student writing, we can better see the points of discord that arise when students try to write their way into the university.

The purpose of the remainder of this chapter will be to examine some of the most striking and characteristic of these problems as they are presented in the expository essays of first-year college students. I will be concerned, then, with university discourse in its most generalized form—as it is represented by introductory courses—and not with the special conventions required by advanced work in the various disciplines. And I will be concerned with the difficult, and often violent accommodations that occur when students locate themselves in a discourse that is not "naturally" or immediately theirs.

III.

I have reviewed 500 essays written, as the "Clay Model" essay was, in response to a question used during one of our placement exams at the University of Pittsburgh: "Describe a time when you did something you felt to be creative. Then, on the basis of the incident you have described, go on to draw some general conclusions about 'creativity.'" Some of the essays were written by basic writers (or, more properly, those essays led readers to identify the writers as basic writers); some were written by students who "passed" (who were granted immediate access to the community of writers at the university). As I read these essays, I was looking to determine the stylistic resources that enabled writers to locate themselves within an "academic" discourse. My bias as a reader should be clear by now. I was not looking to see how a writer might represent the skills demanded by a neutral language (a language whose key features were paragraphs, topic sentences, transitions, and the like—features of a clear and orderly mind). I was looking to see what happened when a writer entered into a language to locate himself (a textual self) and his subject; and I was looking to see how, once entered, that language made or unmade the writer.

Here is one essay. Its writer was classified as a basic writer and, since the essay is relatively free of sentence level errors, that decision must have been rooted in some perceived failure of the discourse itself.

> I am very interested in music, and I try to be creative in my interpretation of music. While in highschool, I was a member of a jazz ensemble. The members of the ensemble were given chances to improvise and be creative in various songs. I feel that this was a great experience for me, as well as the other members. I was proud to know that I could use my imagination and feelings to create music other than what was written.
>
> Creativity to me, means being free to express yourself in a way that is unique to you, not having to conform to certain rules and guidelines. Music is only one of the many areas in which people are given

opportunities to show their creativity. Sculpting, carving, building, art, and acting are just a few more areas where people can show their creativity.

Through my music I conveyed feelings and thoughts which were important to me. Music was my means of showing creativity. In whatever form creativity takes, whether it be music, art, or science, it is an important aspect of our lives because it enables us to be individuals.

Notice the key gesture in this essay, one that appears in all but a few of the essays I read. The student defines as his own that which is a commonplace. "Creativity, *to me,* means being free to express yourself in a way that is unique to you, not having to conform to certain rules and guidelines." This act of appropriation constitutes his authority; it constitutes his authority as a writer and not just as a musician (that is, as someone with a story to tell). There were many essays in the set that told only a story—where the writer established his presence as a musician or a skier or someone who painted designs on a van, but not as a person at a remove from that experience interpreting it, treating it as a metaphor for something else (creativity). Unless those stories were long, detailed, and very well told—unless the writer was doing more than saying, "I am a skier" or a musician or a van-painter—those writers were all given low ratings.

Notice also that the writer of the "Jazz" paper locates himself and his experience in relation to the commonplace (creativity is unique expression; it is not having to conform to rules or guidelines) regardless of whether the commonplace is true or not. Anyone who improvises "knows" that improvisation follows rules and guidelines. It is the power of the commonplace—its truth as a recognizable and, the writer believes, as a final statement—that justifies the example and completes the essay. The example, in other words, has value because it stands within the field of the commonplace.[9] It is not the occasion for what one might call an "objective" analysis or a "close" reading. It could also be said that the essay stops with the articulation of the commonplace. The following sections speak only to the power of that statement. The reference to

"sculpting, carving, building, art, and acting" attest to the universality of the commonplace (and it attests the writer's nervousness with the status he has appropriated for himself—he is saying, "Now, I'm not the only one here who has done something unique"). The commonplace stands by itself. For this writer, it does not need to be elaborated. By virtue of having written it, he has completed the essay and established the contract by which we may be spoken to as equals: "In whatever form creativity takes, whether it be music, art, or science, it is an important aspect of *our* lives because it enables *us* to be individuals." (For me to break that contract, to argue that *my* life is not represented in that essay, is one way for me to begin as a teacher with that student in that essay.)

All of the papers I read were built around one of three commonplaces: (1) creativity is self-expression, (2) creativity is doing something new or unique, and (3) creativity is using old things in new ways. These are clearly, then, key phrases from the storehouse of things to say about creativity. I've listed them in the order of the students' ratings: A student with the highest rating was more likely to use number three than number one, although each commonplace ran across the range of possible ratings. One could argue that some standard assertions are more powerful than others, but I think the ranking simply represents the power of assertions within our community of readers. Every student was able to offer up an experience that was meant as an example of "creativity"; the lowest range of writers, then, was not represented by students who could not imagine themselves as creative people.[10]

I said that the writer of the "Jazz" paper offered up a commonplace regardless of whether it was true or not; and this, I said, was an instance of the power of a commonplace to determine the meaning of an example. A commonplace determines a system of interpretation that can be used to "place" an example within a standard system of belief. You can see a similar process at work in this essay.

During the football season, the team was supposed to wear the same type of cleats and the same type socks, I figured that I would change this a little by wearing my white shoes instead of black and to cover up the team socks with a pair of my own white ones. I thought that this looked better than what we were wearing, and I told a few of the other people on the team to change too. They agreed that it did look better and they changed there combination to go along with mine. After the game people came up to us and said that it looked very good the way we wore our socks, and they wanted to know why we changed from the rest of the team.

I feel that creativity comes from when a person lets his imagination come up with ideas and he is not afraid to express them. Once you create something to do it will be original and unique because it came about from your own imagination and if any one else tries to copy it, it won't be the same because you thought of it first from your own ideas.

This is not an elegant paper, but it seems seamless, tidy. If the paper on the clay model of the earth showed an ill fit between the writer and his project, here the discourse seems natural, smooth. You could reproduce this paper and hand it out to a class, and it would take a lot of prompting before the students sensed something fishy and one of the more aggressive ones said something like, "Sure he came up with the idea of wearing white shoes and white socks. Him and Billy 'White-Shoes' Johnson. Come on. He copied the very thing he said was his own idea, `original and unique.'"

The "I" of this text—the "I" who "figured," "thought," and "felt"—is located in a conventional rhetoric of the self that turns imagination into origination (I made it), that argues an ethic of production (I made it and it is mine), and that argues a tight scheme of intention (I made it because I decided to make it). The rhetoric seems invisible because it is so common. This "I" (the maker) is also located in a version of history that dominates classrooms, the "great man" theory: History is rolling along (the English novel is dominated by a central, intrusive narrative presence; America is in the throes of a Great Depression; during football season the team was supposed to wear the same kind of cleats and socks) until a figure appears, one who can shape history (Henry James, FDR, the writer of

the "White Shoes" paper), and everything is changed. In the argument of the "White Shoes" paper, the history goes "I figured . . . I thought . . . I told . . . They agreed . . ." and, as a consequence, "I feel that creativity *comes from when* a person lets his imagination come up with ideas and he is not afraid to express them." The act of appropriation becomes a narrative of courage and conquest. The writer was able to write that story when he was able to imagine himself in that discourse. Getting him out of it will be a difficult matter indeed.

There are ways, I think, that a writer can shape history in the very act of writing it. Some students are able to enter into a discourse but, by stylistic maneuvers, to take possession of it at the same time. They don't originate a discourse, but they locate themselves within it aggressively, self-consciously. Here is another essay on jazz, which for sake of convenience I've shortened. It received a higher rating than the first essay on jazz.

> Jazz has always been thought of as a very original creative field in music. Improvisation, the spontaneous creation of original melodies in a piece of music, makes up a large part of jazz as a musical style. I had the opportunity to be a member of my high school's jazz ensemble for three years, and became an improvisation soloist this year. Throughout the years, I have seen and heard many jazz players, both professional and amateur. The solos performed by these artists were each flavored with that particular individual's style and ideas, along with some of the conventional premises behind improvisation. This particular type of solo work is creative because it is, done on the spur of the moment and blends the performer's ideas with basic guidelines.
>
> I realized my own creative potential when I began soloing. . . .
>
> My solos, just as all the solos generated by others, were original because I combined and shaped other's ideas with mine to create something completely new. Creativity is combining the practical knowledge and guidelines of a discipline with one's original ideas to bring about a new, original end result, one that is different from everyone else's. Creativity is based on the individual. Two artists can interpret the same scene

differently. Each person who creates something does so by bringing out something individual in himself.

The essay is different in some important ways from the first essay on jazz. The writer of the second is more easily able to place himself in the context of an "academic" discussion. The second essay contains an "I" who realized his "creative potential" by soloing; the first contained an "I" who had "a great experience." In the second essay, before the phrase, "I had the opportunity to be a member of my high school's jazz ensemble," there is an introduction that offers a general definition of improvisation and an acknowledgment that other people have thought about jazz and creativity. In fact, throughout the essay the writer offers definitions and counterdefinitions. He is placing himself in the context of what has been said and what might be said. In the first paper, before a similar statement about being a member of a jazz ensemble, there was in introduction that locates jazz solely in the context of this individual's experience: "I am very interested in music." The writer of this first paper was authorized by who he is, a musician, rather than by what he can say about music in the context of what is generally said. The writer of the second essay uses a more specialized vocabulary; he talks about "conventional premises," "creative potential," "musical style," and "practical knowledge." And this is not just a matter of using bigger words, since these terms locate the experience in the context of a recognizable interpretive scheme—on the one hand there is tradition and, on the other, individual talent.

It could be said, then, that this essay is also framed and completed by a commonplace: "Creativity is combining the practical knowledge and guidelines of a discipline with one's original ideas to bring about a new, original end result, one that is different from everyone else's." Here, however, the argument is a more powerful one; and I mean "powerful" in the political sense, since it is an argument that complicates a "naive" assumption (it makes scholarly work possible, in other words), and it does so in terms that come close to those used in current academic debates (over the relation

between convention and idiosyncracy or between rules and creativity). The assertion is almost consumed by the pleas for originality at the end of the sentence; but the point remains that the terms "original" and "different," as they are used at the end of the essay, are problematic, since they must be thought of in the context of "practical knowledge and guidelines of a discipline."

The key distinguishing gesture of this essay, that which makes it "better" than the other, is the way the writer works against a conventional point of view, one that is represented within the essay by conventional phrases that the writer must then work against. In his practice he demonstrates that a writer, and not just a musician, works within "conventional premises." The "I" who comments in this paper (not the "I" of the narrative about a time when he soloed) places himself self consciously within the context of a coconventional discourse about the subject, even as he struggles against the language of that conventional discourse. The opening definition of improvisation, where improvisation is defined as spontaneous creation, is rejected when the writer begins talking about "the conventional premises behind improvisation." The earlier definition is part of the conventional language of those who "have always thought" of jazz as a "very original creative field in music." The paper begins with what "has been said" and then works itself out against the force and logic of what has been said, of what is not only an argument but also a collection of phrases, examples, and definitions.

I had a teacher who once told us that whenever we were stuck for something to say, we should use the following as a "machine" for producing a paper: "While most readers of _____ have said _____, a close and careful reading shows that _____." The writer of the second paper on jazz is using a standard opening gambit, even if it is not announced with flourish. The essay becomes possible when he sets himself against what must become a "naive" assumption—what "most people think." He has defined a closed circle for himself. In fact, you could say that he has laid the ground work for a discipline with its own key terms ("practical knowledge," "disciplinary guidelines," and "original ideas"), with its own agenda and with its own investigative procedures (looking for common features in the work of individual soloists).

The history represented by this student's essay, then, is not the history of a musician and it is not the history of a thought being worked out within an individual mind; it is the history of work being done within and against conventional systems.

In general, as I reviewed the essays for this study, I found that the more successful writers set themselves in their essays against what they defined as some more naive way of talking about their subject—against "those who think that . . ."—or against earlier, more naive versions of themselves—"once I thought that. . . ." By trading in one set of commonplaces at the expense of another, they could win themselves status as members of what is taken to be some more privileged group. The ability to imagine privilege enabled writing. Here is one particularly successful essay. Notice the specialized vocabulary, but notice also the way in which the text continually refers to its own language and to the language of others.

> Throughout my life, I have been interested and intrigued by music. My mother has often told me of the times, before I went to school, when I would "conduct" the orchestra on her records. I continued to listen to music and eventually started to play the guitar and the clarinet. Finally, at about the age of twelve, I started to sit down and try to write songs. Even though my instrumental skills were far from my own high standards, I would spend much of my spare time during the day with a guitar around my neck, trying to produce a piece of music.

> Each of these sessions, as I remember them, had a rather set format. I would sit in my bedroom, strumming different combinations of the five or six chords I could play, until I heard a series of which sounded particularly good to me. After this, I set the music to a suitable rhythm, (usually dependent on my mood at the time), and ran through the tune until I could play it fairly easily. Only after this section was complete did I go on to writing lyrics, which generally followed along the lines of the current popular songs on the radio.

> At the time of the writing, I felt that my songs were, in themselves, an original creation of my own; that is, I, alone, made them. However, I now see that, in this sense of the word, I was not creative. The songs themselves seem to be an oversimplified form of the music I listed to at the time.

> In a more fitting sense, however, I was being creative. Since I did not purposely copy my favorite songs, I was, effectively, originating my songs from my own "process of creativity." To achieve my goal, I needed what a composer would call "inspiration" for my piece. In this case the inspiration was the current hit on the radio. Perhaps, with my present point of view, I feel that I used too much "inspiration" in my songs, but, at that time, I did not.

> Creativity, therefore, is a process which, in my case, involved a certain series of "small creations" if you like. As well, it is something, the appreciation of which varies with one's point of view, that point of view being set by the person's experience, tastes, and his own personal view of creativity. The less experienced tend to allow for less originality, while the more experienced demand real originality to classify something a "creation." Either way, a term as abstract as this is perfectly correct, and open to interpretation.

This writer is consistently and dramatically conscious of herself forming something to say out of what has been said *and* out of what she has been saying in the act of writing this paper. "Creativity" begins in this paper as "original creation." What she thought was "creativity," however, she now says was imitation; and, as she says, "in this sense of the word" she was not "creative." In another sense, however, she says that she *was* creative, since she didn't purposefully copy the songs but used them as "inspiration."

While the elaborate stylistic display—the pauses, qualifications, and the use of quotation marks—is in part a performance for our benefit, at a more obvious level we as readers are directly addressed in the first sentence of the last paragraph: "Creativity, therefore, is a process which, in my case, involved a certain series of 'small creations' if you like." We are addressed here as adults who can share her perspective on what she has said and who can be expected to understand her terms. If she gets into trouble after this sentence, and I think she does, it is because she doesn't have the courage to generalize from her assertion. Since she has rhetorically separated herself from her younger "self," and since she argues that she has gotten smarter, she assumes that there is some developmental sequence at work here and that, in the world of adults (which must be more complete than the world of children) there must be something like "real creativity." If her world is imperfect (if she can only talk about creation by putting the word in quotation marks), it must be because she is young. When she looks beyond herself to us, she cannot see our work as an extension of her project. She cannot assume that we too will be concerned with the problem of creativity and originality. At least she is not willing to challenge us on those grounds, to generalize her argument, and to argue that even for adults creations are really only "small creations." The sense of privilege that has allowed her to expose her own language cannot be extended to expose ours.

The writing in this piece—that is, the work of the writer within the essay—goes on in spite of, or against, the language that keeps pressing to give another name to her experience as a songwriter and to bring the discussion to closure. (In comparison, think of the quick closure of the "White Shoes" paper.) Its style is difficult, highly qualified. It relies on quotation marks and parody to set off the language and attitudes that belong to the discourse (or the discourses) that it would reject, that it would not take as its own proper location.

David Olson (1981) has argued that the key difference between oral language and written language is that written language separates both the producer and the receiver from the text. For my student writers, this means that they had to learn that what they said (the code) was more important than what they meant (the intention). A writer, in other words, loses his primacy at the moment of writing and must begin to attend to his and his words' conventional, even physical presence on the page. And, Olson says, the writer must learn that his authority is not established through his presence but through his absence—through his ability, that is, to speak as a god-like source beyond the limitations of any particular social or historical moment; to speak by means of the wisdom of convention, through the oversounds of official or authoritative utterance, as the voice of logic or the voice of the community. He concludes:

> The child's growing competence with this distinctive register of language in which both the meaning and the authority are displaced from the intentions of the speaker and lodged "in the text" may contribute to the similarly specialized and distinctive mode of thought we have come to associate with literacy and formal education. (1918, p. 110)

Olson is writing about children. His generalizations, I think I've shown, can be extended to students writing their way into the academic community. These are educated and literate individuals, to be sure, but they are individuals still outside the peculiar boundaries of the academic community. In the papers I've examined in this chapter, the writers have shown an increasing awareness of the codes (or the competing codes) that operate within a discourse. To speak with authority they have to speak not only in another's voice but through another's code; and they not only have to do this, they have to speak in the voice and through the codes of those of us with power and wisdom; and they not only have to do this, they have to do it before they know what they are doing, before they have a project to participate in, and before, at least in terms of our disciplines, they have anything to say. Our students may be able to enter into a conventional discourse and speak, not as themselves, but through the voice of the community; the university, however, is the place where "common" wisdom is only of negative values—it is something to work against. The movement toward a more specialized discourse begins (or, perhaps, best begins) both when a student can define a position of privilege, a position that sets him against a "common" discourse, and when he or she can work self-consciously, critically, against not only the "common" code but his or her own.

IV.

Pat Bizzell, you will recall, argues that the problems of poor writers can be attributed both to their unfamiliarity with the conventions of academic discourse and to their ignorance that there are such things as discourse communities with conventions to be mastered. If the latter is true, I think it is true only in rare cases. All the student writers I've discussed (and, in fact, most of the student writers whose work I've seen) have shown an awareness that something special or something different is required when one writes for an academic classroom. The essays that I have presented in this chapter all, I think, give evidence of writers trying to write their way into a new community. To some degree, however, all of them can be said to be unfamiliar with the conventions of academic discourse.

Problems of convention are both problems of finish and problems of substance. The most substantial academic tasks for students, learning history or sociology or literary criticism, are matters of many courses, much reading and writing, and several years of education. Our students, however, must have a place to begin. They cannot sit through lectures and read textbooks and, as a consequence, write as sociologists or write literary criticism. There must be steps along the way. Some of these steps will be marked by drafts and revisions. Some will be marked by courses, and in an ideal curriculum the preliminary courses would be writing courses, whether housed in an English department or not. For some students, students we call "basic writers," these courses will be in a sense the most basic introduction to the language and methods of academic writing.

Our students, as I've said, must have a place to begin. If the problem of a beginning is the problem of establishing authority, of defining rhetorically or stylistically a position from which one may speak, then the papers I have examined show characteristic student responses to that problem and show levels of approximation or stages in the development of writers who are writing their way into a position of privilege.

As I look over the papers I've discussed, I would arrange them in the following order: the "White Shoes" paper; the first "Jazz" essay; the "Clay Model" paper; the second "Jazz" essay; and, as the most successful paper, the essay on "Composing Songs." The more advanced essay for me, then, are those that are set against the "naive" codes of "everyday" life. (I put the terms "naive" and "everyday" in quotation marks because they are, of course, arbitrary terms.) In the advanced essays one can see a writer claiming an "inside" position of privilege by rejecting the language and commonplaces of a "naive" discourse, the language of "outsiders." The "I" of those essays locates itself against one discourse (what it claims to be a naive discourse) and approximates the specialized language of what is presumed to be a more powerful and more privileged community. There are two gestures present, then—one imitative and one critical. The writer continually audits and pushes against a language that would render him "like everyone else" and mimics the language and interpretive systems of the privileged community.

At a first level, then, a student might establish his authority by simply stating his own presence within the field of a subject. A student, for example, writes about creativity by telling a story about a time he went skiing. Nothing more. The "I" on the page is a skier, and skiing stands as a representation of a creative act. Neither the skier nor skiing are available for interpretation; they cannot be located in an essay that is not a narrative essay (where skiing might serve metaphorically as an example of, say, a sport where set movements also allow for a personal style). Or a student, as did the one who wrote the "White Shoes" paper, locates a narrative in an unconnected rehearsal of commonplaces about creativity. In both cases, the writers have finessed the requirement to set themselves against the available utterances of the world outside the closed world of the academy. And, again, in the first "Jazz" paper, we have the example of a writer who locates himself within an available commonplace and carries out only rudimentary procedures for elaboration, procedures driven by the commonplace itself and not set against it. Elaboration, in this latter case, is not the opening up of a system but a justification of it.

At a next level I would place student writers who establish their authority by mimicking the rhythm and texture, the "sound," of academic prose, without there being any recognizable interpretive or academic project under way. I'm thinking, here, of the "Clay Model" essay. At an advanced stage, I would place students who establish their authority as *writers;* they claim their authority, not by simply claiming that they are skiers or that they have done something creative, but by placing themselves both within and against a discourse, or within and against competing discourses, and working self-consciously to claim an interpretive project of their own, one that grants them their privilege to speak. This is true, I think, in the case of the second "Jazz" paper and, to a greater degree, in the case of the "Composing Songs" paper.

The levels of development that I've suggested are not marked by corresponding levels in the type or frequency of error, at least not by the type or frequency of sentence-level error. I am arguing, then, that a basic writer is not necessarily a writer who makes a lot of mistakes. In fact, one of the problems with curricula designed to aid basic writers is that they too often begin with the assumption that the key distinguishing feature of a basic writer is the presence of sentence-level error. Students are placed in courses because their placement essays show a high frequency of such errors, and those courses are designed with the goal of making those errors go away. This approach to the problems of the basic writer ignores the degree to which error is less often a constant feature than a marker in the development of a writer. A student who can write a reasonably correct narrative may fall to pieces when faced with a more unfamiliar assignment. More important, however, such courses fail to serve the rest of the curriculum. On every campus there is a significant number of college freshmen who require a course to introduce them to the kinds of writing that are required for a university education. Some of these students can write correct sentences and some cannot; but, as a group, they lack the fa-cility other freshmen possess when they are faced with an academic writing task.

The "White Shoes" essay, for example, shows fewer sentence-level errors than the "Clay Model" paper. This may well be due to the fact that the writer of the "White Shoes" paper stayed well within safe, familiar territory. He kept himself out of trouble by doing what he could easily do. The tortuous syntax of the more advanced papers on my list is a syntax that represents a writer's struggle with a difficult and unfamiliar language, and it is a syntax that can quickly lead an inexperienced writer into trouble. The syntax and punctuation of the "Composing Songs" essay, for example, shows the effort that is required when a writer works against the pressure of conventional discourse. If the prose is inelegant (although I confess I admire those dense sentences) it is still correct. This writer has a command of the linguistic and stylistic resources—the highly embedded sentences, the use of parentheses and quotation marks—required to complete the act of writing. It is easy to imagine the possible pitfalls for a writer working without this facility.

There was no camera trained on the "Clay Model" writer while he was writing, and I have no protocol of what was going through his mind, but it is possible to speculate on the syntactic difficulties of sentences like these: "In the past time I thought that an incident was creative was when I had to make a clay model of the earth, but not of the classical or your everyday model of the earth which consists of the two cores, the mantle and the crust. I thought of these things in a dimension of which it would be unique, but easy to comprehend." The syntactic difficulties appear to be the result of the writer's attempt to use an unusual vocabulary and to extend his sentences beyond the boundaries of what would have been "normal" in his speech or writing. There is reason to believe, that is, that the problem was with *this* kind of sentence, in this context. If the problem of the last sentence is that of holding together the units "I thought," "dimension," "unique" and "easy to comprehend," then the linguistic problem was not a simple matter of sentence construction. I am arguing, then, that such sentences fall apart not because the writer lacked the necessary syntax to glue the pieces together but because he lacked the full statement within which these key words were already operating. While writing, and in the thrust of his need to complete the sentence, he had the key words but not the utterance. (And to recover the utterance, I suspect, he would need to do more than revise the sentence.) The invisible conventions, the prepared phrases remained too distant for the statement to be completed. The writer would have needed to get inside of a discourse that he could in fact only partially imagine. The act of constructing a sentence, then, became something like an act of transcription in which the voice on the tape unexpectedly faded away and became inaudible.

Shaughnessy (1977) speaks of the advanced writer as one who often has a more facile but still incomplete possession of this prior discourse. In the case of the advanced writer, the evidence of a problem is the presence of dissonant, redundant, or imprecise language, as in a sentence such as this: "No education can be *total,* it must be *continuous.*" Such a student, Shaughnessy says, could be said to hear the "melody of formal English" while still unable to make precise or exact distinctions. And, she says,

> the pre-packaging feature of language, the possibility of taking over phrases and whole sentences without much thought about them, threatens the writer now as before. The writer, as we have said, inherits the language out of which he must fabricate his own messages. He is therefore in a constant tangle with the language, obliged to recognize its public, communal nature and yet driven to invent out of this language his own statements. (1977, pp. 207–208)

For the unskilled writer, the problem is different in degree and not in kind. The inexperienced writer is left with a more fragmentary record of the comings and goings of academic discourse. Or, as I said above, he or she often has the key words without the complete statements within which they are already operating.

Let me provide one final example of this kind of syntactic difficulty in another piece of student writing. The writer of this paper seems to be able to sustain a discussion only by continually repeating his first step, producing a litany of strong, general, authoritative assertions that trail quickly into confusion. Notice how the writer seems to stabilize his movement through the paper by returning again and again to recognizable and available commonplace utterances. When he has to move away from them, however, away from the familiar to statements that would extend those utterances, where he, too, must speak, the writing—that is, both the syntax and the structure of the discourse—falls to pieces.

> Many times the times drives a person's life depends on how he uses it. I would like to think about if time is twenty-five hours a day rather than twenty-four hours. Some people think it's the boaring or some people might say it's the pleasure to take one more hour for their life. But I think the time is passing and coming, still we are standing on same position. We should use time as best as we can use about the good way in our life. Everything we do, such as sleep, eat, study, play and doing something for ourselves. These take the time to do and we could find the individual ability and may process own. It is the important for us and our society. As time going on the world changes therefor we are changing, too. When these situation changes we should follow the suitable case of own. But many times we should decide what's the better way to do so by using time. Sometimes like this kind of situation can cause the success of our lives or ruin. I think every individual of his own thought drive how to use time. These affect are done from environmental causes. So we should work on the better way of our life recognizing the importance of time.

There is a general pattern of disintegration when the writer moves off from standard phrases. This sentence, for example, starts out coherently and then falls apart: *"We should use time as best as we can use about the good way in our life."* The difficulty seems to be one of extending those standard phrases or of connecting them to the main subject reference, "time" (or "the time," a construction that causes many of the problems in the paper). Here is an example of a sentence that shows, in miniature, this problem of connection: *"I think every individual of his own thought drive how to use time."*

One of the remarkable things about this paper is that, in spite of all the synatic confusion, there is the hint of an academic project here. The writer sets out to discuss how to creatively use one's time. The text seems to allude to examples and to stages in an argument, even if in the end it is all pretty incoherent. The gestures of academic authority, however, are clearly present, and present in a form that echoes the procedures in other, more successful papers. The writer sets himself against what "some people think"; he speaks with the air of authority: "But I think. . . . Everything we do. . . . When these situation changes. . . ." And he speaks as though there were a project underway, one where he proposes what he thinks, turns to evidence, and offers a conclusion: "These affect are done from enviornmental causes. So we should work. . . ." This is the case of a student with the ability to imagine the general outline and rhythm of academic prose but without the ability to carry it out, to complete the sentences. And when he gets lost in the new, in the unknown, in the responsibility of his own commitment to speak, he returns again to the familiar ground of the commonplace.

The challenge to researchers, it seems to me, is to turn their attention again to products, to student writing, since the drama in a student's essay, as he or she struggles with and against the languages of our contemporary life, is as intense and telling as the drama of an essay's mental preparation or physical production. A written text, too, can be a compelling model of the "composing process" once we conceive of a writer as at work within a text and simultaneously, then, within a society, a history, and a culture.

It may very well be that some students will need to learn to crudely mimic the "distinctive register" of academic discourse before they are prepared to actually and legitimately do the work of the discourse, and before they are sophisticated enough with the refinements of tone and gesture to do it with grace or elegance. To say this, however, is to say that our students must be our students. Their initial progress will be marked by their abilities to take on the role of privilege, by their abilities to establish authority. From this point of view, the student who wrote about constructing the clay model of the earth is better prepared for his education than the student who wrote about playing football in white shoes, even though the "White Shoes" paper is relatively error-free and the "Clay Model" paper is not. It will be hard to pry loose the writer of the "White Shoes" paper from the tidy, pat discourse that allows him to dispose of the question of creativity in such a quick and efficient manner. He will have to be convinced that it is better to write sentences he might not so easily control, and he will have to be convinced that it is better to write muddier and more confusing prose (in order that it may sound like ours), and this will be harder than convincing the "Clay Model" writer to continue what he has already begun.

ACKNOWLEDGMENTS

Preparation of this chapter was supported by the Learning Research and Development Center of the University of Pittsburgh, which is supported in part by the National Institute of Education.

Notes

1. David Olson (1981) has made a similar observation about school-related problems of language learning in younger children. Here is his conclusion: "Hence, depending upon whether children assumed language was primarily suitable for making assertions and conjectures or primarily for making direct or indirect commands, they will either find school texts easy or difficult" (p. 107).

2. For Aristotle, there were both general and specific commonplaces. A speaker, says Aristotle, has a "stock of arguments to which he may turn for a particular need."

   If he knows the *topoi* (regions, places, lines or argument)—and a skilled speaker will know them—he will know where to find what he wants for a special case. The general topics, or *common-*places, are regions containing arguments that are common to all branches of knowledge. . . . But there are also special topics (regions, places, *loci*) in which one looks for arguments appertaining to particular branches of knowledge, special sciences, such as ethics or politics. (1932, pp. 154–155)

And, he says, "the topics or places, then, may be indifferently thought of as in the science that is concerned, or in the mind of the speaker." But the question of location is "indifferent" *only* if the mind of the speaker is in line with set opinion, general assumption. For the speaker (or writer) who is not situated so comfortably in the privileged public realm, this is indeed not an indifferent matter at all. If he does not have the commonplace at hand, he will not, in Aristotle's terms, know where to go at all.

3. Pat Bizzell has argued that the *Seventeen* writer's process of goal-setting

> can be better understood if we see it in terms of writing for a discourse community. His initial problem . . . is to find a way to include these readers in a discourse community for which he is comfortable writing. He places them in the academic discourse community by imagining the girls as students. . . . Once he has included them in a familiar discourse community, he can find a way to address them that is common in the community: he will argue with them, putting a new interpretation on information they possess in order to correct misconceptions. (1982a, p. 228)

4. See Bartholomae (1979, 1983) and Rose (1983) for articles on curricula designed to move students into university discourse. The movement to extend writing "across the curriculum" is evidence of a general concern for locating students within the work of the university; see Bizzell (1982a) and Maimon *et al.* (1981). For longer works directed specifically at basic writing, see Ponsot and Deen (1982) and Shaughnessy (1977). For a book describing a course for more advanced students, see Coles (1978).

5. In spite of my misgivings about Bereiter and Scardamalia's interpretation of the cognitive nature of the problem of "inert knowledge," this is an essay I regularly recommend to teachers. It has much to say about the dangers of what seem to be "neutral" forms of classroom discourse and provides, in its final section, a set of recommendations on how a teacher might undo discourse conventions that have become part of the institution of teaching.

6. Stanley Fish (1980) argues that the basis for distinguishing novice from expert readings is the persuasiveness of the discourse used to present and defend a given reading. In particular, see the chapter, "Demonstration vs. Persuasion: Two Models of Critical Activity" (pp. 356–373).

7. Some students, when they come to the university, can do this better than others. When Jonathan Culler says, "the possibility of bringing someone to see that a particular interpretation is a good one assumes shared points of departure and common notions of how to read," he is acknowledging that teaching, at least in English classes, has had to assume that students, to be students, were already to some degree participating in the structures of reading and writing that constitute English studies (quoted in Fish, 1980, p. 366).

Stanley Fish tells us "not to worry" that students will violate our enterprise by offering idiosyncratic readings of standard texts:

> The fear of solipsism, of the imposition by the unconstrained self of its own prejudices, is unfounded because the self does not exist apart from the communal or conventional categories of thought that enable its operations (of thinking, seeing, reading). Once we realize that the conceptions that fill consciousness, including any conception of its own status, are culturally derived, the very notion of an unconstrained self, of a consciousness wholly and dangerously free, becomes incomprehensible. (1980, p. 335)

He, too, is assuming that students, to be students (and not "dangerously free"), must be members in good standing of the community whose immediate head is the English teacher. It is interesting that his parenthetical catalogue of the "operations" of thought, "thinking, seeing, reading," excludes writing, since it is only through written records that we have any real indication of how a student thinks, sees, and reads. (Perhaps "real" is an inappropriate word to use here, since there is certainly a "real" intellectual life that goes on, independent of writing. Let me say that thinking, seeing, and reading are valued in the academic community *only* as they are represented by extended, elaborated written records.) Writing, I presume, is a given for Fish. It is the card of entry into this closed community that constrains and excludes dangerous characters. Students who are excluded from this community are students who do poorly on written placement exams or in freshman composition. They do not, that is, move easily into the privileged discourse of the community, represented by the English literature class.

8. My debt to Bizzell's work should be evident everywhere in this essay. See also Bizzell (1978, 1982b) and Bizzell and Herzberg (1980).

9. Fish says the following about the relationship between student and an object under study:

We are not to imagine a moment when my students "simply see" a physical configuration of atoms and *then* assign that configuration a significance, according to the situation they happen to be in. To be in the situation (this or any other) is to "see" with the eyes of its interests, its goals, its understood practices, values, and norms, and so to be conferring significance *by* seeing, not after it. The categories of my students' vision are the categories by which they understand themselves to be functioning as students . . . and objects will appear to them in forms related to that way of functioning rather than in some objective or preinterpretive form. (1980, p. 334)

10. I am aware that the papers given the highest rankings offer arguments about creativity and originality similar to my own. If there is a conspiracy here, that is one of the points of my chapter. I should add that my reading of the "content" of basic writers' essays is quite different from Lunsford's (1980).

Works Cited

Aristotle. (1932). *The Rhetoric of Aristotle* (L. Cooper, Trans.). Englewood Cliffs, NJ: Prentice-Hall.

Barthes, R. (1974). *S/Z* (R. Howard, Trans.). New York: Hill & Wang.

Bartholomae, D. (1979). Teaching basic writing: An alternative to basic skills. *Journal of Basic Writing, 2,* 85–109.

Bartholomae, D. (1983). Writing assignments: Where writing begins. In P. Stock (Ed.), *Forum* (pp. 300–312). Montclair, NJ: Boynton/Cook.

Bereiter, C., & Scardamalia, M. (in press). Cognitive coping strategies and the problem of "inert knowledge." In S. S. Chipman, J. W. Segal, & R. Glaser (Eds.), *Thinking and learning skills: Research and open questions* (Vol. 2). Hillsdale, NJ: Erlbaum.

Bizzell, P. (1978). The ethos of academic discourse. *College Composition and Communication, 29,* 351–355.

Bizzell, P. (1982a). Cognition, convention, and certainty: What we need to know about writing. *Pre/text, 3,* 213–244.

Bizzell, P. (1982b). College composition: Initiation into the academic discourse community. *Curriculum Inquiry, 12,* 191–207.

Bizzell, P., & Herzberg, B. (1980). "Inherent" ideology, "universal" history, "empirical" evidence, and "context-free" writing: Some problems with E. D. Hirsch's *The Philosophy of Composition. Modern Language Notes, 95,* 1181–1202.

Coles, W. E., Jr. (1978). *The plural I.* New York: Holt, Rinehart & Winston.

Fish, S. (1980). *Is there a text in this class? The authority of interpretive communities.* Cambridge, MA: Harvard University Press.

Flower, L. S. (1981). Revising writer-based prose. *Journal of Basic Writing, 3,* 62–74.

Flower, L., & Hayes, J. (1981). A cognitive process theory of writing. *College Composition and Communication, 32,* 365–387.

Hairston, M. (1978). *A contemporary rhetoric.* Boston: Houghton Mifflin.

Lunsford, A. A. (1980). The content of basic writers' essays. *College Composition and Communication, 31,* 278–290.

Maimon, E. P., Belcher, G. L., Hearn, G. W., Nodine, B. F., & O'Connor, F. X. (1981). *Writing in the arts and sciences.* Cambridge, MA: Winthrop.

Olson, D. R. (1981). Writing. The divorce of the author from the text. In B. M. Kroll & R. J. Vann (Eds.), *Exploring speaking-writing relationships: Connections and contrasts.* Urbana, IL: National Council of Teachers of English.

Perkins, D. N. (in press). General cognitive skills: Why not? In S. S. Chipman, J. W. Segal, & R. Glaser (Eds.), *Thinking and learning skills: Research and open questions* (Vol. 2). Hillsdale, NJ: Earlbaum.

Ponsot, M., & Deen, R. (1982). *Beat not the poor desk.* Montclair, NJ: Boynton/Cook.

Rodriquez, R. (1983). *Hunger of memory.* New York: Bantam.

Rose, M. (1983). Remedial writing courses: A critique and a proposal. *College English, 45,* 109–128.

Said, E. W. (1975). *Beginnings: Intention and method.* Baltimore: The Johns Hopkins University Press.

Shaughnessy, M. (1977). *Errors and expectations.* New York: Oxford University Press.

Toward a National Public Policy
on Language

Geneva Smitherman-Donaldson

This essay appeared in College English *49 (1987): 29–36.*

Darlene tryin to teach me how to talk. . . . Every time I say something the way I say it, she correct me until I say it some other way. Pretty soon it feel like I can't think. My mind run up on a thought, git confuse, run back and sort of lay down. You sure this worth it? I ast. She say, yeah, bring me a bunch of books. Whitefolks all over them, talking bout apples and dogs. What I care bout dogs I think. . . . But I let Darlene worry on. Sometimes I think bout the apples and the dogs, sometimes I don't. Look like to me only a fool would want you to talk in a way that feel peculiar to your mind. (*The Color Purple* 222–23)

With Celie's profound philosophical statement as backdrop, I am here issuing a challenge to speech, language, and composition professionals to take the leadership role in working toward a national public policy on language. The immediate impetus for this call to action comes from the precipitously declining rates of literacy and educational achievement in Afro-American communities. For example, school drop-out rates are running about 65 percent in Chicago and 66.5 percent in Detroit, both urban school districts with overwhelmingly large Black student populations. However, the policy would govern language teaching and language use throughout the U.S. and ultimately would be beneficial to all communities. Thus, as has always been the case throughout U.S. history, whenever Blacks have pioneered social

change, the result has been change and betterment throughout the American social reality. Recall, for instance, how the movement for Black Power ushered in calls for Brown Power, Red Power, Female Power, Student Power, Counterculture Power, Grey Power, and on and on—the Black struggle in the 1960s and 1970s opened up the economic and social structure for everybody.

It is time to call the children in and teach them the lessons of the Blood.

In 1974, the Conference on College Composition and Communication passed a policy resolution, "The Students' Right to Their Own Language." I am honored to have been a part of the movement behind this resolution and later a member of the committee that wrote the expanded document accompanying the resolution (Butler). Our goal at that time was the promotion of such a policy throughout the profession of speech, language, and composition scholars and educators. Unfortunately, that goal was not realized.

In 1977, I wrote that "ultimately teachers should struggle for a national public policy on language which would reassert the legitimacy of languages other than English, and American dialects other than standard" (*Talkin and Testifyin* 240–41). Unfortunately, that goal was not realized.

In 1979, in *King v. Ann Arbor* Judge Charles C. Joiner issued a ruling reaffirming the legitimacy of Black English and the existence of its African substratum and mandated that the Ann Arbor School District "take into account" Black English in the educational process of teaching Black children to "read in the standard English of the school, the commercial world, the arts, science, and professions." Thus, the *King* decision laid the basis for instituting a language policy for the Black community that would have had far-reaching implications for other communities. Unfortunately, that goal was not realized.

Although linguist Wayne Williams applauded my work and that of my colleagues in *King,* he nonetheless argued that from a policy standpoint, the "Black English Case" may have been "premature." However, I say to my fellow linguist, Brother Williams, that recent movements against linguistic minorities and the alarming school drop-out rate among the Black English speaking underclass serve to remind us that the motion of history does not wait for political maturity.

Because we failed to act, now we must re-act. The aborted movement, spearheaded by the Conference on College Composition and Communication, to establish a national public policy on language would have addressed the mother tongue and language crises of *all* Americans—not just Blacks, Browns, Reds. The "Students' Right to Their Own Language," after all, reaffirmed the language rights of White Appalachian students, female students, Arab students, Polish students, White counterculture students, middle-class students—in short, *all* students. For you see, no one escapes the tentacles of the self-appointed guardians and preservers of the national tongue (as spoken by themselves, I remind you). Witness, for example, the castigation of President Reagan when he said in his 1985 Inaugural Address, "If not us, who?" meaning, "If *we* do not make the hard decision, then who will?" (in which case, according to the long arm of the linguistic law, Reagan should have said, "If not *we,* who?"). In his *New York Times* language column, William Safire defended Reagan's right to his own language and took the President's detractors to task for insisting on such formal and "laughably stilted" usage. While the powerful, such as Reagan and others of his ilk, don't need linguistic sanctu-

ary, the less powerful among us do. Thus a policy affirming the mother tongue language and dialect of ALL would have the effect of protecting the many from the linguistic imperialism of the few.

All that is required for oppression to take hold is for good and well-meaning folk to do nothing. A language leadership vacuum has been created by the absence of national policy action from the professions and from political progressives. Into that vacuum has stepped reactionary and counterprogressive forces and movements. An illustrative case is "U.S. English." Some may dismiss this movement as the folly of an erring and aging self-hating Japanese semanticist. But that would be folly, for Hayakawa's campaign to amend the U.S. Constitution to make English the official language has succeeded in creating a burgeoning, highly effective and increasingly mass movement, a linguistic corollary to the reactionary mood of conservatism reemerging across America. U.S. English is a national, well-financed organization, headquartered in Washington, D.C., which distributes a newsletter-journal, called *Update.* The Constitutional amendment that Hayakawa introduced into the U.S. Senate is currently being refined in a Senate committee which has done a significant amount of work on the proposed amendment already. Undoubtedly, U.S. English is primarily responsible for the proposal in California to overturn the tradition of printing election ballots in languages other than English. Such a proposal, if successful, would, of course, effectively disenfranchise large numbers of Spanish-speaking voters who are on the verge of becoming the dominant population in that state. Moreover, a movement like U.S. English provides yet another justification for cut-backs in Federal funding for the language-based educational programs for Blacks and other minorities struggling against functional illiteracy in school districts across this country.

It is time to call the children in and teach them the lessons of the Blood.

I am proposing that speech, language, and composition professionals take up the unfinished business of the Committee on the Students' Right to Their Own Language, bring to fruition the implications of the *King* decision, and move quickly to counteract those reactionary sociolinguistic forces that would take us back to where some folk ain't never left from. In calling for a national public policy on language, I take as theoretical framework the policy and planning models of Fishman, LePage, Bamgbose, and Alleyne. I shall use the terminology proposed by Fishman, the "language of wider communication," to refer to standard American English.

I propose a three-prong policy—a 360° Trinity that constitutes an inseparable whole.

1. Reinforce the Need for and Teaching of the Language of Wider Communication

The teaching of the language of wider communication has never been an issue (though I for one have erroneously been accused of rejecting its teaching). It has never been an issue, *if* and *when* it has been promoted as an integral part of a policy which includes recognition, use, and acceptance of the native tongue.

Among speech, language, and composition professionals, there is plenty of evidence that this has not been the case. For example, in our analysis of the essays of Black students from the National Assessment of Educational Progress (Smitherman and Wright), we found significant correlations between the frequency of Black English and the rater's scores, that is, the more Black English, the lower the score. This correlation existed even in the body of essays in which raters were instructed to look only at rhetorical features, that is, to use primary trait scoring to assess how well the student writer had mastered the rhetorical modality under evaluation. Yet many of the essays rated high were deplorably devoid of content, meaning and message, and further, the frequency of Black English was generally quite low—generally less than 20 percent Black English forms in any given linguistic category. Quite apart from the distribution of Black English in the essays, the writers experienced difficulty in coping with the demands of the assignment and writing towards the topic. For example, some students, in very edited American English

syntax, would shift topic and focus right in the middle of an essay.

It must be stressed, then, that emphasis on the language of wider communication is toward the use of language as power, not mere "correctness" but the use of language to "make the impossible possible."

The language of wider communication is the language of literacy and technology, as well as the medium in which even the historical experiences and lessons of the Blood have been captured. Thus there is no question, nor has there ever been any, about the need for linguistic competence in this language. If today's speakers of non-mainstream languages and dialects are rejecting the teaching of standard English, if indeed, as Labov has suggested from his recent Philadelphia study. Black English is diverging from the language of wider communication, particularly among the Black underclass, it may be, in large measure, because educational institutions have never seriously accepted the mother tongue of the speech community. They've paid lip service to it, but they have not really accepted it. As Baldwin said in his *New York Times* article, "If Black English Isn't a Language, Then Tell Me What Is?", published two weeks after the *King* decision:

> Now, no one can eat his cake, and have it too, and it is late in the day to attempt to penalize black people for having created a language that permits the nation its only glimpse of reality, a language without which the nation would be even more *whipped* than it is. . . . It is not the black child's language that is in question; it is not his language that is despised; it is his experience. A child cannot be taught by anyone who despises him, and a child cannot afford to be fooled. A child cannot be taught by anyone whose demand, essentially, is that the child repudiate his experience, and all that gives him sustenance, and enter a limbo in which he will no longer be black and in which he knows that he can never become white. Black people have lost too many black children that way. (392)

It is time to call the children in and teach them the lessons of the Blood.

2. *Reinforce and Reaffirm the Legitimacy of Non-Mainstream Languages and Dialects and Promote Mother Tongue Instruction as a Co-Equal Language of Instruction Along with the Language of Wider Communication*

The mother tongue language or dialect, of course, will vary according to the speech community. The point is that the indigenous language is the authentic voice of the speech community, and, as such, can establish the firm foundation upon which to build and expand the learner's linguistic repertoire. What Williams termed the "language conscious hypothesis" has been shown to have a great deal of validity. In Williams' own research in the Seattle Black community, he demonstrated that Blacks who were conscious of their own language as a legitimate system were more receptive to learning the language of wider communication. As Bamgbose and other non-Western scholars have taught us, the mother tongue may be the only "passport to literacy" for the great majority of Third World schoolchildren. Certainly this appears to be the case for many speakers of Black American English. For example, Pearson's work indicated that Blacks more fluent in Black speech acts, such as sounding and the Dozens, tended to be more fluent in the figurative, literary forms of the language of wider communication (see Taylor-Delain). Similarly, Simpkins, Holt and Simpkins' research with the *Bridge* materials demonstrated the feasibility and success of using Black English as a bridge to understanding and reading the language of wider communication: some of the students in their experimental research program advanced as much as two years in reading level after one semester's exposure to the "bridge approach."

Finally, reaffirming the legitimacy of non-mainstream languages and dialects is critical if we are to bridge the developing divide between the "have's" and "have-not's" in Black and minority communities and between those minorities and Whites.

3. *Promote the Acquisition of One or More Foreign Languages, Preferably a Language Spoken by Persons in the Third World, Such as Spanish, Because of its Widespread Use in this Hemisphere*

The educational benefits to be derived from foreign language study have to do with sharpening critical thinking and heightening verbal skills. In times past, one was not considered truly educated unless he or she commanded a foreign language. The excruciating and embarrassing narrowness of the American populace in language matters is illustrated in the following joke:

What do you call a person who speaks three languages?

Answer: Trilingual.

What do you call a person who speaks two languages?

Answer: Bilingual.

What do you call a person who speaks one language?

Answer: American.

Most important, it is imperative that Americans —of whatever color, race or sex—be enlightened about world cultures; sensitivity through language is one way to achieve such enlightenment. Contemporary history is rife with the sordid remains of narrow provincialism emanating from a world superpower (e.g., the Viet Nam War). Our students, the citizens of the future, must be capable of understanding and carrying on dialogue with non-Western peoples—the majority population in today's world.

There are several pragmatic moves necessary to make the policy outlined here a workable reality.

First, speech, language, and composition professionals must work on the political front, in whatever way they can, to insure that, for instance, jobs and services are available for all, and especially for those we are teaching in our ebony and ivory towers. Acquisition of the language of wider communication, as Fishman tells us, must provide entree to power and resources, or there is little reason for indigenous populations to adopt it. Further, as Alleyne cautions us, we should try to profit from the tragic history of several newly-independent countries that have undergone linguistic and cultural transformation but have not achieved modernization of the means of production or economic self-sufficiency—in short, they are still poor. And thus, in many Third and First World countries, the masses are rejecting technology and literacy campaigns.

Similar circumstances prevail in this country. For instance, in Black communities, intuition and logic suggest—if Labov's methodology, which some have labelled flawed, does not—that Black underclass communities are becoming speech communities whose language is increasingly diverging from the language of wider communication, as spoken by *both Whites and Blacks*. Of what benefit, one may well ask, is the language of wider communication, to a community in which, for example, 75 percent of its youth, from 16-24 years of age, are unemployed—and unemployable, without some kind of massive economic intervention? Given the poverty and class powerlessness of such a community, linguistic differences are easily predictable.

To insure rewards from language and literacy for America's working and UNWORKING classes, speech, language, and composition professionals should align with political progressives in demanding the restoration of budget cuts from education and other domestic programs and in opposing the military build-up and its gross and offensive budget. In general, then, we as professionals should take an active role in the political affairs of the country.

Second, we should work with other professions and organizations to promote the call for a language policy and to garner the political support for it in the public domain. Groups like foreign language teachers' associations, psychologists' associations. Children's Defense Fund, and others all have a stake in a national public policy on language.

As a third step, speech, language, and composition professionals are the ideal group to conduct the language awareness campaigns needed to accompany the movement for a language policy. These campaigns would be geared toward combating the myths about language use. Campaigns would be conducted through newspapers, television and radio programs, magazines, and in other popular media, in community forums, churches,

and throughout the general public domain. The objective would be to combat the myths and misconceptions about both non-mainstream languages and the language of wider communication. Language standards do change, and attitudes about language change also. While Safire's approval of Reagan's "If not us, who?" is a dramatic example, it is only one of many such changes in attitudes about usage. In the case of Black English, for example, Linn has suggested that attitudes toward Black English are more positive than a decade ago. Intelligent speculation suggests that this may be the legacy of the Black Pride Movement of the 1960s and 1970s that ushered in the widespread adoption of language, dance, music, and other cultural forms from the Black speech community. We should capitalize on this healthy transformation of American language standards and extend it further.

Finally, we should work with the public schools to develop uniform standards and guidelines for linguistic performance. This kind of institutional collaboration is vital not only to the promotion of a language policy but also for the general education of our students. At least two states are currently involved in this kind of educational collaboration: California through its focus on the educational underachievement of the state's linguistic minorities; Ohio through its Urban Initiatives Action Program for Language Education spearheaded by Central State University. Speech, language, and composition professionals should all work collectively from preschool through graduate school on matters of language, literacy, and standards of effective and successful uses of language. A vivid illustration of the need for this kind of educational cooperation is presented in a recent Georgia court case. Professor Jan Kemp filed suit against the University of Georgia after she was fired for protesting the University's lowering of academic standards for its athletes and wealthy donors' sons. Reacting to the court ruling in Kemp's favor, John Thompson, basketball superstar Patrick Ewing's former coach at Georgetown, put it best:

> Of course there are things wrong with athletics . . . but if you want to look at the real scandal, look at the

entire educational system. . . . It wasn't a coach who passed these kids from grades one through six when he wasn't able to read. . . . What about all these kids who can't read who AREN'T playing basketball and football? (Wilbon 12)

To summarize, the language policy proposed here has three inextricable parts: 1) reinforce the language of wider communication; 2) promote and extend the legitimacy of mother tongue languages and dialects; and 3) promote the acquisition of one or more foreign languages, preferably those spoken in the Third World. Such a policy is not only concomitant with the emerging pedagogy that language is the foundation stone of education, this kind of policy is also a basis for participation and leadership in world affairs.

It is time to call the children in and teach them the lessons of the Blood.

Works Cited

Alleyne, Mervyn C. *Theoretical Issues in Caribbean Linguistics.* Mona: U of the West Indies, 1982.

Baldwin, James. "If Black English Isn't a Language, Then Tell Me What Is?" Smitherman, *Black English* 390–92.

Bamgbose, Ayo. "Introduction: The Changing Role of the Mother Tongue in Education." *Mother Tongue Education: The West African Experience.* Ed. Ayo Bamgbose. Paris: Unesco, 1976. 9–26.

Butler, Melvin, ed. *Students' Right to Their Own Language.* Urbana: NCTE, 1974.

Fishman, Joshua A. *Language and Nationalism.* Rowley, MA: Newbury, 1972.

———. "Bilingual Education, Language Planning and English." *English Varieties World-Wide* 1.1 (1980): 11–24.

Joiner, Charles C. *Memorandum and Opinion: 7-71861. Black English and the Education of Black Children and Youth.* Ed. Geneva Smitherman. Detroit: Center for Black Studies, 1981.

Labov, William. *The Increasing Divergence of Black and White Vernaculars.* National Science Foundation, 1981–84. Complete report available from the author: William Labov, Director, Linguistics Laboratory, U of Pennsylvania, Philadelphia, PA.

LePage, Robert B. *The National Language Question: Linguistic Problems of Newly Independent States.* London: Oxford UP, 1964.

Linn, Michael. "Black and White Adolescent and Pre-Adolescent Attitudes toward Black English." *Research in the Teaching of English* 16 (1982): 53–69.

Safire, William. "The Case of the President's Case." *New York Times Magazine* 10 March 1985: 18+.

Simpkins, Gary. *Cross-Cultural Approach to Reading.* Diss. U of Massachusetts. Ann Arbor: UMI, 1976. DCJ77-06404.

Simpkins, Gary, Grace Holt, and Charlesetta Simpkins. *Bridge.* Boston: Houghton, 1976.

Smitherman, Geneva, ed. *Black English and the Education of Black Children and Youth.* Detroit: Center for Black Studies, 1981.

———. *Talkin and Testifyin: The Language of Black America.* 1977, Detroit: Wayne State UP, 1986.

Smitherman, Geneva, and Sandra Wright. "Black Student Writers, Storks, and Familiar Places: What Can We Learn from the National Assessment of Educational Progress?" Final Research Report. NCTE Research Foundation, Urbana, IL. Also available from Geneva Smitherman, Center for Black Studies, Wayne State University, Detroit, MI.

Taylor-Delain, J., P. D. Pearson, and R. C. Anderson. "Reading Comprehension and Creativity in Black-Language Use: You Stand to Gain by Playing the Sounding Game." *American Educational Research Journal* 22 (1985): 155–74.

Walker, Alice. *The Color Purple.* New York: Pocket, 1983.

Wilbon, Michael. "Thompson: Education a Problem." *Washington Post* 21 Feb. 1986: 10–12.

Williams, Wayne. "Language Consciousness and Cultural Liberation in Black America." Paper delivered at the Sixth Annual Conference of the National Council for Black Studies. Chicago, March, 1982. Available from the author: Center for Afro-American Studies, University of Washington, Seattle, WA.

The Wyoming Conference Resolution Opposing Unfair Salaries and Working Conditions for Post-Secondary Teachers of Writing

Linda R. Robertson, Sharon Crowley, and Frank Lentricchia

This statement appeared in College English *49 (1987): 274–80.*

Members who attend this year's Conference on College Communication and Composition will have an opportunity to vote on the Wyoming Conference Resolution, which has been proposed by participants attending the Wyoming Conference on English this June. The resolution calls upon the Executive Committee to establish grievance procedures for post-secondary writing teachers seeking to redress unfair working conditions and salaries. The resolution reflects a remarkable and spontaneous consensus that emerged during this year's conference. Participants felt it should be called the Wyoming Conference Resolution to indicate the co-operation and conviction that gave rise to it. Tilly Warnock, the conference director, readily agreed.

So remarkable was the spirit of the Wyoming Conference that this discussion would be incomplete without some effort to describe how the resolution arose. The conference began on a Monday and ended Friday afternoon. The topic this year was "Language and the Social Context." By midweek, many of us had become persuaded that we ought to consider how the topic applied to our own profession: "What is the social context for writing teachers?" Some stark polarities gave rise to

this question. James Moffett, one of the major consultants to the conference, spoke of his conviction that teachers of writing ought to enable students to discover the freedom of self-expression. Some of us were struck with the irony that those of us charged with this significant responsibility often feel unable to speak freely about the fundamentally unfair conditions under which we labor.

From the stories we tell one another, it is clear that many of us regard ourselves as victimized by our institutions, relegated to marginal positions and tenuous employment with no benefits. Conference participants told of the repression and exploitation they experienced at their home institutions. Graduate students told of feeling coerced to teach courses without pay; teachers at community colleges told of heavy, unreasonable course loads; part-time and adjunct instructors at major private and public universities told of the demeaning status and inequitable salaries they were forced to accept as conditions of employment; full-time faculty members with a primary commitment to teaching writing told of unfair tenure review proceedings; and literature faculty members who are sometimes called upon to teach writing expressed their unease at the inequitable treatment handed out to their part-time or full-time and adjunct colleagues in composition.

Those stories were told over breakfast in the dining hall, during coffee-breaks between sessions, and in late-night talks after the honky-tonk bands playing at Laramie's night spots had finished the last set. We hear such stories whenever teachers of writing gather. But there was a harder edge to them at Laramie, a greater insistence in the telling, a deeper silence in the listening. Perhaps this was because of the natural intimacy that comes when 200 people meet for a week, live together in dorms, and eat together in the cafeteria, while surrounded by a spectacular and harmonious natural world, one which needs neither social context nor language to endure. Certainly the greater intensity of our concern was due in part to the way James Slevin chose to address the conference topic. He hammered home to us just how endemic are the local conditions we described.

Reporting on studies conducted by the Association of Departments of English (ADE), Slevin told us that only forty percent of new English PhDs now find tenure-track positions. We have been told this disheartening reality is the result of economic forces beyond the control of English departments. Plaintive cries against economic hardships were first uttered twelve to fifteen years ago amid predictions that enrollments in the late 1970s and early 1980s would plummet. Contrary to these predictions, enrollments in colleges and universities increased by twenty to thirty percent between 1974 and 1984. About one-third of the English departments recently surveyed by ADE report growth in the undergraduate literature major, while one-fourth to one-third of the graduate programs report growth. Of those institutions offering undergraduate technical communication programs, eighty percent report growth. Three-fourths of those schools offering graduate degrees in rhetoric report growth in their programs. But despite the reasonable health of literature programs and the robust health of rhetoric and technical communications programs, English departments are the departments most likely to employ part-time faculty members, and they almost always hire them to teach writing.

Slevin's talk clarified how disenfranchised are teachers of writing. It also suggested to some of us that there are larger issues of academic freedom inherent in hiring policies which rely heavily on part-time or temporary positions. Since sixty percent of new PhDs in English cannot find full-time, tenure-track employment, many of them must accept part-time or temporary full-time employment if they wish to participate in academic life at all. And since the salaries offered for such positions are usually low, they are often filled by women; that is, by those who constitute an underclass in the economy generally. Indeed, the decline in the number of full-time, secure positions and the increase in part-time or temporary full-time positions in higher education reflect national employment trends. There has been a decline in the number of full-time jobs typically held by women, and an increase in part-time positions, a strategy that allows employers to save money on benefits while at the same time meeting their traditional labor needs.

Slevin heightened our awareness of the polarity between the freedom we are asked to promote in the classroom and the threats to academic freedom and absence of job security faced by many teachers of writing. He also heightened our awareness of the polarity that divided the privileged from the underprivileged in English departments. Many participants expressed bitterness and frustration that their demeaning status is visited upon them, or at least abetted, by their tenured colleagues. At many of our colleges and universities—even those enjoying great prestige—teachers of writing hold the same degrees as their tenured counterparts; yet they are excluded from participating in academic life, prohibited from teaching courses in their fields of academic preparation, denied the traditional support for research, and denied even basic benefits. Sometimes their numbers exceed those of the tenured faculty in English. They often carry heavier teaching loads even though they are designated as "part-time" faculty. Most demoralizing is the lack of respect accorded those who teach writing. Composition is regarded as something "anyone can do," as one professor said when he read a copy of the resolution circulated in his department after the conference.

The bitterness toward tenured English faculty surprised some of those attending the conference who enjoy this privileged status. English professors are unused to thinking of themselves as privileged in any sense. Some genuinely believed that such conditions were not prevalent, or at least did not prevail at their home institutions. Motivated by the concerns raised at the conference, some of them have since made inquiries and have found that indeed composition teachers at their colleges or universities are exploited, denied privileges, and, in one case, are earning less than those employed by the physical plant. Others honestly expressed their fear that if the conditions for teachers of writing were improved, tenured faculty members would have to carry a heavier burden in teaching composition.

With these realizations, we met the enemy, and discovered they are us.

This polarity—and the bitterness it inspired—threatened to pull the conference apart. Fortunately, James Sledd's talk galvanized us. He spoke on the global issues of language instruction in the context of class power and exploitation. As part of this larger concern, he chastened teachers of writing by pointing out that we condemned the unfair and exploitative attitudes that have resulted from the creation of a privileged and protected class, while at the same time we sought that same status ourselves. He chastened English faculty with the remark that, if we sought evidence to disprove the notion that the study of the humanities promoted more humane conduct, we need look no further than the way we treated graduate students and part-time faculty in our own departments. During the question and answer session, many of us sought to avoid the issues Sledd raised by asking safe "academic" questions of the other panelists. Then suddenly the top blew off. A graduate student rose to speak. So conditioned was she to keeping silent that her voice broke as she spoke; so frustrated was she by the conditions she had felt compelled to endure in order to seek a degree in English that she wept. She challenged our silence

and apathy; she asked us why we had not spoken to the issues Sledd charged us with addressing.

It probably is not possible to convey the galvanizing effect her challenge had on those who heard her. After this session, an unusually large number of participants came to the room set aside for writing comments on each day's sessions, comments that are then published the following day. One of the responses to this session is representative of the general reaction:

> Well, I'll say the obvious—it's about time someone stood up and did what the last speaker of the session did. There's nothing wrong with talking about what have been called "local" concerns. But the fear—perhaps the fear that "there's nothing to be done"—about trying to deal with the global issues needs to be brought into the open and dealt with. We listen to someone like Sledd. We laugh at his wonderful humor. We nod our heads as he talks about the state of education within the context of our world. We give him the biggest round of applause of the evening. Then, damn it, we run as fast as we can from what he's saying, and we do it by almost ignoring it. We don't want to face *our own roles* in the problem, and how we—as people, as teachers, as "professionals"—are implicated in the very problems we're trying to solve. Perhaps there is no solution. Perhaps nothing we do as individuals, or even as a group, can do anything to mitigate the frightening direction that some of us see us going. But to ignore it—no. Not if we take ourselves seriously when we speak so glibly about making things better.

Another kind of response was made later that evening when two conference participants met, not really by chance. One of them was male, a tenured faculty member at a state school, well-known in the profession, who had been maintaining during the conference that the predatory conditions described by many participants were not necessarily reflective of the profession as a whole. The other was female, untenured, changing jobs, and certainly not at the top of the professional hierarchy. She had been arguing throughout the conference that the unfair conditions were so endemic to the profession that the professional organizations ought to take action to correct them. Following the emotion-charged session, he guided her to a quiet spot and asked, Luther-like, "Are you really ready to lead the revolution?" She said, Erasmus-like, "It is not a revolution we need. It is a resolution of conflict within the existing structures." From this colloquy, there emerged a mutual sense of what action we might take, and the foundation was laid for the Wyoming Conference Resolution.

The results of the late-night conversation were circulated the next day as a draft resolution, and conference participants were invited to discuss it later that afternoon. They filled the dormitory lounge to overflowing. James Sledd sat quietly on the floor, perhaps contemplating what he had wrought. The two who offered to incorporate these suggestions in a final draft were seen collaborating on it during a session on collaborative writing. A typed copy of the revised version was circulated at a reception later that evening and edited. The final version was presented as a petition at the final session Friday morning. More than enough signatures were gathered to enter it as a resolution at the CCCC this spring. Conference participants were nonetheless urged to carry the resolution to their home institutions and to seek more support.

We urge you to join us in the spirit of the Wyoming Conference Resolution. We do not offer it—nor was it proposed—as the only anodyne to our problems. But it does provide those who seek change one way to do so. The provisions of the resolution are:

> WHEREAS, the salaries and working conditions of post-secondary teachers with primary responsibility for the teaching of writing are fundamentally unfair as judged by any reasonable professional standards (e.g., unfair in excessive teaching loads, unreasonably large class sizes, salary inequities, lack of benefits and professional status, and barriers to professional advancement) . . .

The wording of this provision is intended to indicate concern for all ranks in our profession: graduate teaching assistants, teachers at community colleges, part-time or temporary teachers in colleges and universities, and those on tenure-track

lines whose work is often considered less worthy than that done by faculty members teaching literature or linguistics.

> AND WHEREAS, as a consequence of these unreasonable working conditions, highly dedicated teachers are often frustrated in their desire to provide students the time and attention which students both deserve and need . . .

This provision is included to remind us that the unfair conditions under which teachers of writing labor have profound implications for educating the next generation. We are aware of the deep concern expressed by the public at large and their elected representatives about the apparent decline in students' ability to articulate their interests and hopes. This concern is one we share.

> THEREFORE, BE IT RESOLVED that the Executive Committee of College Composition and Communication be charged with the following:

The resolution is addressed to College Composition and Communication as the professional organization most immediately and exclusively concerned with the teaching of writing. Participants discussed the desirability of seeking further endorsement from other professional organizations—such as MLA, NCTE (as the umbrella organization for CCC), NEA, and others—after it was approved by CCC.

> 1. To formulate, after appropriate consultations with post-secondary teachers of writing, professional standards and expectations for salary levels and working conditions of post-secondary teachers of writing.

We felt it was important to provide those who have feared to speak on their own behalf an opportunity to do so. We also felt it would be pointless to try formulating professional standards without detailed information about working conditions and salaries at diverse institutions. We also hoped that one result of gathering such detailed information would be that the knowledge would inspire other proposals and initiatives for change.

The wording "working conditions of post-secondary teachers of writing" was carefully chosen, so that those full-time faculty members in English who teach composition only occasionally will feel included. The resolution as a whole is worded so that enlightened English faculty members, even those who never teach composition, can feel encouraged to participate in helping to alleviate the unfair conditions under which some of their colleagues labor.

2. To establish a procedure for hearing grievances brought by post-secondary teachers of writing— either singly or collectively—against apparent institutional non-compliance with these standards and expectations.

This provision is included as a way of empowering those who feel most disenfranchised. We wanted to avoid imposing Draconian solutions. This might result if our professional leadership attempted to provide generic solutions to unfair practices that vary widely from institution to institution. We were also impressed by the irony that those who teach self-expression to students feel themselves coerced into silence as a condition of employment. We felt the healthiest approach was for them to have an opportunity to demonstrate to themselves and their institutions that we can, through the language of petition and complaint, promote peaceful change. Finally, we recognized that some among us are content with their lot, and that, given this complacency, a professional organization seeking to impose change could make little headway. We felt that change can come only if those who wish it take action on their own behalf.

We also recognize that implementing formal grievance procedures will be costly. We assume that if members of CCC feel the procedure will benefit the profession as a whole, they will be ready to spend a bit more on dues.

3. To establish a procedure for acting upon a finding of non-compliance; specifically, to issue a letter of censure to an individual institution's administration, Board of Regents or Trustees, State legislators (where pertinent), and to publicize the finding to the public-at-large, the educational community in general, and to our membership.

In proposing this provision, we were alert to the widespread attention given nationally to a perceived decline in communication skills among students. We felt it was timely to make common cause with those calling for reform. There are those who will argue that some institutions will not feel particularly threatened by the possibility of being criticized in public. This may be true, and speaks again to our sense that no single solution will resolve our problems. But certainly publicizing detrimental conditions of employment will not hinder the efforts of those who seek change at such an institution.

On the other hand, we are aware that many administrators will seek to avoid detrimental publicity because it might bring in its train inquiries from members of boards of trustees, or state governors, or state legislators.

We also hoped that by publicizing the unfair conditions we might discourage candidates from applying for positions at institutions found in non-compliance. Job candidates ought to know that, at a given institution, conditions have become so unbearable that faculty members have formally protested them to their professional organization. It takes little genius to realize that unfair labor practices are often alleviated when the labor pool diminishes or evaporates.

We ask you to consider carefully whether it is not now time to seek ways of redressing the shabby and exploitative circumstances in which many of our colleagues find themselves. These conditions are unlikely to change, even though, as we read in the *Chronicle of Higher Education,* many institutions are now preparing to hire "promising young scholars" to replace retiring faculty. Some may believe that this signals automatic change as we move into an era of labor shortage and seller's market. But the current shabby conditions for teachers of writing are not the product of economic conditions. They are the result of short-sighted policies formulated in response to anticipated economic trends. Not only were the policies short-sighted, but the economic predictions that inspired them never materialized. Moreover, teachers at community colleges will not be helped by any rush to hire new faculty in colleges and universities. Nor will graduate teaching assistants be less exploited even given changes in the job market. And the sad truth is that in seeking "promising young scholars," institutions may well overlook those who have been laboring in their very own vineyards because part-time and adjunct faculty members holding advanced degrees are inhibited by their conditions of employment from developing their scholarly talents.

No other professional organization has come forward with any proposal that would allow teachers of writing to take direct action at their own institutions against unfair practices that are now endemic. If you wish to join in the spirit of the Wyoming Conference, pay your membership dues and come to the CCCC conference to vote in favor of the Wyoming Conference Resolution. Urge your colleagues to do the same. We look forward to voting with you to pass this resolution.

The Feminization of Composition

Susan Miller

Miller's essay was published in The Politics of Writing Instruction: Postsecondary. *Eds. Richard Bullock and John Trimbur. Portsmouth: Boynton/Cook, 1991. 39–54.*

I realize that my title may unintentionally fail to frame my purpose, for it easily leads in two directions. "Feminization" calls to mind both positive new moves in composition to gender-balance research and teaching and negative associations with the actual "feminization" of a field that collects, like bugs in a web, women whose persistently marginalized status demands political action. But I have chosen this potentially slippery term precisely, to point a new reading of composition studies that places both the political action that we obviously need, and many new intellectual and practical movements toward gender balance in composition studies, against a prevailing negative cultural identity that "the feminization of composition" implies. Paradoxically, positive internal desires to gender-balance our field are contained by a negative, insistent external feminization in the phallocentric community where it was born. Much of the field's past, its continuing actual experience, and its usually overlooked but important symbolic associations result from a defining, specifically from a gendered, cultural call to identity.

By using the phrase "call to identity," I mean to bring to mind a group of related leftist political and feminist theories that explain identity formation as a result from a cultural context. Identities do not, in these views, result from the preexisting or essential qualities of a person, or of an area of social action, itself. Instead, they come into being through a cultural context of which we are already a part. This context is partially made up of a framework of assumptions and approaches, a superstructure, that places both individuals and certain kinds of social action in fairly well-enclosed cultural spaces, where they have names and identifiable discursive practices. These identifying spaces are hierarchically disposed, but cultural invitations to inhabit them are not simple edicts from on high. We tacitly accept these identities to maintain the superstructure that we live in, in a process of hegemonic consensus. The "low" is contained by its implied participation in a total system.

In regard to gender and the "low" situation of females, this reasoning emphasizes that categories of identity, or "subjectivities," map both individuals and groups (see Eagleton, "Subject" 95). For instance, a female may be constituted as "a mother," and therefore as a person who will sacrifice her personal separateness to attend to the frequent and private bodily needs of young children—elimination, cleanliness, and nurturance. But the culture also produces "motherhood," a symbolic domain that places a particular woman's self-sacrifice in an acceptable image of *the* Mother, a figure who occupies an idealized space of veneration. For many feminist theorists, it is well understood that no matter what range of individual biological, intellectual, social, economic, class, or other qualities people of the female sex may exhibit, this and other female identities (e.g., "wife," "whore," "girl") participate in similar cultural calls to "womanhood." This "hood" effectively cloaks differences to assure that females (and males) are socially identified by imaginary relations to their actual situations.

Many feminists also point out that within this process, the identity of the female person was specifically differentiated as "woman" to supplement, complement, oppose, and extend male identity. This separation of genders first organized cultures for their biological, economic, and social survival. A female's particularity or her ignorance of such category formation could not at first excuse her and has not later excused her from the cultural identity devised to ensure the continuity of traditions that regulate property, power, and status within and among communities.

I outline these theories and some of their corollaries because I want to argue that this view of lower-status female identity—including both its critique of dominance and submission and its view of historical requirements imposed for the sake of survival and tradition is embodied by composition studies. A similar cultural call acting on composition has, that is, created the field's unentitled "place" in its surroundings and has limited both its old and its new self-definitions. This call and responses to it maintain the regular range of results that follow from the field's most common, as well as its most innovative, practices. Recent reactions to this call often attempt to overcome the field's feminization, but composition remains largely the distaff partner in a socially important "masculine" enterprise, the cultural maintenance of linguistic dispositions of power and enfranchisement.

To support this claim, I want to review "facts," a history, and relevant symbolic associations that negatively feminize composition, despite (and in concert with) some of our best efforts to overcome this identity. Making my case depends, I realize, on persuasively joining information we already know and accept about the status of composition to both a historical context and a larger symbolic domain that is usually preserved to explain purposes, practices, and status in more entitled cultural sites. We habitually, at least among ourselves, quote statistics and tell personal tales about the professional situation of the field and its members, but we rarely account for and evaluate these (quite accurate) perceptions from a theoretical perspective, to show

how they arise from, and contribute to, the superstructure they maintain.

We can, then, begin uncovering the feminization of composition by reviewing some concrete bad news we already know. In fact, in the actual life-world of anyone who teaches English, the field is largely the province of women. As Sue Ellen Holbrook has so carefully shown in her essay "Women's Work," the sexual division of labor that characterizes all jobs has equally characterized composition. Holbrook points out that in decades when women have "risen" in the academy, at least in numbers, they have concurrently assumed lower ranks in subject areas associated with feminine pursuits—home economics, physical education, humanities, social sciences, and education. They have, on average, been paid 18 percent less than men; as late as 1986, they earned but 85 percent of what men in the humanities earned. In addition, women hold the part-time appointments in academic institutions. In 1976, women occupied 25 percent of full-time positions, but 38 percent of the part-time positions.

As we know, a large proportion of this part-time work force are housed in departments of English, where composition is usually taught. These paraprofessionals, to use Holbrook's term, occupy the lowest hierarchical status by virtue of their association with composition teaching itself, typically characterized as *elementary* teaching that is a *service* tied to *pedagogy* rather than theory (9). Holbrook estimates that two-thirds of all who teach composition are female. Two-thirds of the NCTE College section membership are women. In 1986, 65 percent of the program participants at the Conference on College Composition and Communication were female; in 1987, 58 percent were female. (In 1986, 45 percent of the participants at the MLA convention were female.)

Holbrook also points out that the gendered hierarchy these figures represent is repeated within composition as a sub-field of English Studies. In composition research, for instance, the hierarchy that subordinates women is maintained: Men appear to publish a greater percentage of articles submitted to *College English* (65 percent); books by men dominate in selective bibliographies (approximately 70 percent); male authors overwhelmingly dominate in "theoretical" (as against nurturant, pedagogical) publication categories (12–13). Holbrook's analyses of these demonstrable proportions and of the historical position of women as faculty in universities give her good grounds for inferring that "men develop knowledge and have higher status; women teach, applying knowledge and serving the needs of others, and have lower status" (7–8). Her inference is further supported by other concrete facts: according to her 1981 count of unambiguous first names, 71 percent of the members of the Association of Writing Program Administrators are men (13), and 73 percent of the programs Carol Hartzog described in her *Composition in the Academy* are administered by men who outrank the female majority of teachers they supervise (23).

These and other ways that the field of composition mirrors traditional "women's roles" are such normalized parts of our daily experience that we may overlook the seemingly contradictory self-images they force us to accept. That is, we are on the one hand so well persuaded that composition is, as Holbrook says, nonintellectual, pedagogical, service-oriented work that we hardly wonder that it is given over to women. We can, no matter how quickly we would deny our nobility in doing so, easily accept that composition is a field for "women and children," teachers and students whom we expect to be tentative about their commitments to "real" education, that which we (again, easily) assume will chronologically follow writing courses. But we also retain equally deep cultural images that thoroughly convince us that composition teaching is the "important" mission that English studies as a whole was constituted to perform. We see it as the locus for the best sense of the cultural literacy that is the imagined important mission of a university as a whole. Learning to read and write, we easily acknowledge, assures the continuation of our civilization. Our most "civilized" and powerful citizens—college graduates—must be confident, fluent producers and equally skilled analysts of discourse. But we are also accustomed to confessions that composition teaching, and composition research, are not something that "regular" (meaning powerful, entitled, male-coded, theoretical) faculty do. This apparent contradiction in the social text around composition studies deserves a great deal of attention, for it is here that the female identity of composition, clear in the facts I have just cited, becomes a larger "feminized" identity that is situated in a specific history that has its own cultural implications.

To get at this history, we can notice that the low status of composition (which is curiously seen as both the cause and the effect of the statistics Holbrook compiled) has always tied composition to "work" in a specific pairing with literary study, the "play" of English. As Richard Ohmann has pointed out, "Writing and Reading: Work and Leisure" describes the totality of English Studies (*Politics* 26–41). That is, the judgmental manual labor of composition opposes entitlements that females in the academy only rarely claim: relaxed mental contemplation, reflection, and most recently a more powerful "theory" of literary study. Consequently, to understand the well-established contradiction between the low-status and inverted female majorities in composition and its importance as "civilizing work," we need to look at the field's original and still most prevalent institutional position. It is the counterpart, the handmaiden, and low order basement attached to vernacular literary study.

We can reasonably infer that this relationship is a product of the first disposition of composition instruction in new departments of English established in the late nineteenth century, both in England and in America. We have a great deal of historical evidence that the entirety of English, because it was comprised of vernacular language and literature, not the mystified classics, was at first associated with dilettantish, womanish images of belles lettres. It was, that is, letters for belles, identified as a "pink sunsets" tradition of teacups and limp wrists. But this symbolically gender-coded vernacular subject was also, in fact, taught by women in the mechanics and industrial institutes where its advanced courses first appeared, pointedly to address the imagined greater need for "civilizing" students in these institutions. Women taught English even in more elitist schools after its spread (Doyle 23). But not withstanding an elitist imprimatur, "English" was perceived as a "soft," not rigorous or difficult subject, an extension of the popular extracurriculum of polite learning into privileged educational institutions.

Nonetheless, English quite quickly assumed academic centrality, arguably because it was seen as a way to establish national unity among those who were not already entitled to a classical education, but who were being newly admitted to postprimary education. Terry Eagleton's *Literary Theory: An Introduction* argues forcefully that vernacular literature and language study became both the content and the idiom of the modern "parent" country because it included precisely the "poor man's classics," a nationalist substitute for religion. He cites George Gordon, an early professor of English at Oxford: "England is sick," Gordon said in his inaugural address, "and English literature must save it. The Churches (as I understand) having failed, and social remedies being slow, English literature has now a triple function, still, I suppose, to delight and instruct us, but also, and above all, to save our souls and heal the State" (quoted in Eagleton, *Literary Theory* 23). Lest we think this agenda supported only new British English studies, we must remember that similar ideas flourished even more readily in America. There they had been prepared for by an early Puritan morality that had led the *New England Primer* to rhyme "Thy life to mend/This book attend" (Tchudi 4–5). Lindley Murray's infamous *English Grammar, Adapted to the Different Classes of Learners* (1795) taught parsing to "discipline the mind" and to help students write "with propriety" (Tchudi 6). Arthur Appplebee, in *Tradition and Reform in the Teaching of English,* quotes one mid-nineteenth-century teacher/reformer who demonstrates American continuities of this tone in an equally moralistic and chauvinistic justification for vernacular literary study: "The first great aim in the literature course is a training for citizenship by a study of *national* ideals embodied in the writings of American authors, our *race* ideals as set forth by the great writers of Anglo-Saxon origin, our *universal* ideals as we find

them in any great work of literary art" (my emphasis; Applebee 69).

Consequently, the entire complex of activities associated with "English" began its competition for a place among established academic subjects with a gendered, but blurred, spiritual identity. And this identity applied equally to the grammatical instruction that for Hegel was "the alphabet of the Spirit itself" (Graff 29). English originally had *actual* associations with a distaff, "soft" study of vernacular language and literature, which had formerly trained children of both sexes in the preliminaries to the rigorous classical education pursued further only by boys. But in establishing English Studies as a university-level discipline competing against the classics and against an equally plausible scientific center for the curriculum, promoters of English Studies asserted its *imagined,* or symbolic, manly associations with religious and nationalistic ideals.

Charles Eliot, the president of Harvard most often identified as the inspiration for the "new university" in which this blurred identity of English studies was to flourish in America, clarified how these contradictory associations were to become systematic practice in his 1869 inaugural address. There he announced that "English" would be the center of the new curriculum. This subject would ensure something like the unity that men educated in the earlier classical colleges had necessarily shared, despite the newly practical and more fragmented curriculum that characterized more "relevant" effort. But, Eliot qualified, this new Harvard education would be bestowed on two sorts of potential recipients—those already entitled, from "refined" homes, and the "new" student, the person whose hold on good character and correct values was only tentative, and who needed to receive both principles and a test (Douglas 129).

The principles—national, race, and universal—were to be learned in vernacular literary study. But the moral test, which would necessarily precede exposure to these principles, was the "test" of English composition. It became embodied only four years later, in both the well-documented Harvard Entrance Exam and "the" course in composition. This course was supervised by Adams Sherman

Hill, the journalist and former classmate of Eliot's who was recruited to supervise it. It was thereby defined as a device for winnowing and sifting within the newly elevated, central, field of English. Composition was, then, established to be a place where Harvard could assure the worthiness, moral probity, and fitness of those who might otherwise slip through the newly woven net that would now take in additional, *but only tentatively entitled,* students. In this form, as Ohmann has said of its speedy national adoption, "it spread like kudzu" (33).

The actual establishment of university-level departments of English required a further professional implementation of this educational agenda, a "base" cooperating with this new superstructure. To inculcate literary principles, it was necessary to overcome the "nonserious," gender-coded, image of English by emphasizing its new departments' attachments to philology and to traditional methods of teaching classical language and literature, in order that the subject's work, and its professionals, would be perceived as "hard" (Graff 38). To compete against science and other subjects like traditional rhetoric, which had always been learned and taught in combative, exclusively male contexts, these departments had to overcome traditional, feminine, negative images of vernacular literary study. But they also had to implement Eliot's "test." To organize the discriminations and reassurances about social entitlement that Eliot's new vision of postsecondary curricula meant to maintain, the course in composition had to be a place to house those who studied and taught subjects that were now preliminary in a new sense. Divorced from the old college curriculum in classics, "composition" was defined for the first time as preliterary (or preprincipled), not as a part of rhetorical education for those already entitled eventually to "speak."

Even discounting the economic or survival needs that are often cited to explain composition's importance in the origins of English departments, composition conveniently, and precisely, contained within English the negative, nonserious connotations that the entire field might otherwise have had to combat. In mutuality with literary study, it en-

closed those who might not "belong," even as it subsumed the soft, nonserious connotations of vernacular study. It became a place that the "best men" escape from, as we learn both from elaborate placement testing systems and from the frequency with which histories of English and of rhetoric describe Francis Child's release from teaching rhetoric courses at Harvard. But composition was nonetheless the symbolically essential way to verify the social and moral credentials of those admitted to the new university. Given an original societal demand in this cultural call to an identity for composition, we can explain the seeming contradiction between its status as women's work and its ceremonial cultural importance as the essence of an elegantly cooperative pair. Actual "woman's work" filled a necessary symbolic (and often actual) "basement" of literary studies in an easily understood process of identity formation.

The objects of this cooperation, composition students, of course have another subjectivity, or category of identity, that follows from the feminization I am describing. They took an entrance examination whose results were often made public to humiliate them, attended classes that enrolled one hundred or more students in their earliest, introductory exposure to "English," and were taught by ancillary help who were "supervised" rather than admitted to collegial academic freedom. The new pecking order in English departments connected these students to concrete manifestations of the "work" of composition described by Ohmann. For them and their teachers, composition was in fact, as it was in the newly established sustaining mythology of "English," work of a menial, backbreaking sort. "Daily themes" required daily writing and marking (Kitzhaber 169). But since the purpose of assigning these themes was to reveal the fitness of a new student "body"—the unentitled new student's spirit manifest in the physical surface of his language—this heavy, corrective workload was perfectly arranged to accomplish the introductory course's goals. This backbreaking (or more accurately, mind-boggling) work was fit, that is, for tentatively entitled employees of the academy, like women, just as the work of producing correct essays on inconsequential subjects was and remains with few exceptions a task for students whose verbal propriety is in question. It is work required of "new" students in any era, imposed on the majority who are taken to be only tentatively entitled to belong in higher education (Miller, Chapter 3).

But this new educational culture also supplied an acceptable covering mythology that accommodates both the work of composition teaching and its corrective treatment of students' linguistic bodies. Composition teaching, that is, took place in a historically well-established symbolic domain that invited cooperation with distasteful but necessary cultural work. The call to "work" was overlaid on already accepted religious images of grammatical correctness, Hegel's "alphabet of the Spirit." Just as the taxing demands of motherhood give mothers an imaginary relation to a venerable image of the Mother, the corrective task of dealing with writing by students who were now identified as only tentatively suitable for the social rewards of university enrollment provided its workers with a covering myth of the "English teacher." This particular cover story endows the composition teacher of whatever disposition, experience, or relation to status with qualities much like those of the mythologized mother: self-sacrifice, "dedication," "caring," and enormous capacities for untheorized attention to detail. But this figure is ambivalent. It also symbolizes authority, precision, and eternally validated, impeccable linguistic taste, qualities that prompt those who meet composition teachers to expect censure and disapproval.

As this duality suggests, composition teaching is not simply "motherhood," a service to father texts. The social identity of the composition teacher is intricately blurred, in a matrix of functions that we can understand through the instructive example of Freud's description of the "feminine," which was formed at about the same time that composition courses and their teaching first achieved presence in the new university. Despite the problematics feminists point out in his work, Freud's description of associations that contain ambivalently situated women can be seen as a reliable historical account of nineteenth-century sexual mythologies. His de-

scription of the Mother/Maid, a blurred dream figure whom he revised over time, suggests why our resistance to changes in the cultural image of composition teaching is so deep.

Freud first dreamed of his family nurse, a common member of the nineteenth-century bourgeois household, whom he later transformed into "mother." The nurse in his dream "initiated the young Freud in sexual matters" (Stallybrass and White 157). But later, in Freud's writing about "femininity," "the nurse has been displaced by the mother" (157). In various writings, Freud by turns associated seduction and bodily hygiene with motherhood and with the maid, at one time calling the maid the most intimate participant in his initiations and fantasies, and at another thinking of these matters in relation to perfect motherhood. In *The Politics and Poetics of Transgression,* Peter Stallybrass and Alloy White infer that because the nineteenth-century bourgeois family relegated child care to nurses, the maid both performed intimate educational functions and had power over the child. "Because of his seize, his dependency, his fumbling attempts at language, his inability to control his bodily functions" (158), the child could be shamed and humiliated by the maid. But paradoxically, it is more developmentally "natural" to desire the mother than the maid, who is "hired help," so actual interactions with a nurse/maid might be fantasized as having occurred with the mother for whom the maid stood in.

It is fair to suggest that analogous symbolic blurrings still encode teachers of composition, even if we set aside comparisons between the "low" work of composition teaching and this representation of intimate work that at once corrects, educates, and seduces the young initiate. This analogy explains some otherwise troubling contradictions in the ways we habitually conceive of composition teachers, if nothing else. The bourgeois mother and maid, that is, each represent comfort and power, the contradictory endowments required of the service-oriented teacher of students who are, despite their actual maturity, sentimentalized as preeconomic, presexual, prepolitical children (Ohmann, *English* 149). The mother (a "pure" Victorian symbol) was the source Freud turned to for explanatory information about the maid. The mother was also, with the father, an authority. He displaced these associations of comfort and power onto the maid, but she was also given actual "dirty" work. Thus the maid was an ambivalently perceived site for dealing with low, unruly, even anarchic, desires and as yet uncontrolled personal development, the qualities of freshman writing highlighted in much composition pedagogy.

The Wolfman in Freud's writings developed great anxiety about his formal lessons in Latin, the public, formal, consequential language about which his comforting yet ambivalently perceived nursery maid knew nothing. The requirement, that is, to " 'forget' the baby-talk of the body" (Stallybrass and White 166) created great ambivalence about his own body's functions, just as the process of forgoing "home" vernacular language for formal, publicly criticized English compositions displaces the vernacular linguistic confidence of most students. But the composition student is learning a "home," vernacular language *again,* as a formal system that now has public consequences, and is taught in that situation by the maid who is also a designated mother/ power figure, not the new schoolmaster whom Wolfman encountered. Again, the cultural "importance" of composition is overlaid on its demeaned place in the family romance of English Studies.

Consequently, the potential identification between the low-status composition teacher and tentatively entitled "young" students creates yet another blurring. Students in their "practice" composition courses expect both infantile freedom from the embarrassment that the mother/power figure in the "real" family causes *and* those same embarrassments, in the form of corrections and information about propriety and "appropriateness" in a formerly familiar language. This at once comforting and powerful, but public and displaced, figure becomes a blurred point of transference for the student's anxieties over the maturation that inevitably accompanies developmental moves toward public language.

Consequently, the figure of a composition teacher is overloaded with symbolic as well as actual functions. These functions include the dual (or even triple) roles that are washed together in these teachers: the teacher is a nurse who cares for and tempts her young charge toward "adult" uses of language that will not "count" because they are, for now, engaged only with hired help; she is, no matter what her gender, the "mother" (tongue) that is an ideal/idol and can humiliate, regulate, and suppress the child's desires. But she is also the disciplinarian, not a father figure but a sadomasochistic Barbarella version of either mother or maid.

These are deeply held images, whose power is evident in their appearance as humorous stereotypes even among the people whose characteristics and practices contradict them. These images from nineteenth-century bourgeois culture had their own historical precedents, which ironically clarify the readily accepted view that the individual composition teacher is a culturally designated "initiator," similar to a temple priest or priestess who functions to pass along secret knowledge, but not to participate freely in a culture that depends on that knowledge. Strict regulations, similar to those devised to keep "hired help" in its place, prevent those who introduce the young to the culture's religious values and rites from leaving their particular and special status. These mediators between natural and regulated impulses are tied to vows, enclosed living spaces, and/or certain kinds of dress, the categories we might compare with composition teachers' self-sacrificing acceptance of work without time for contemplating its implications, their traditionally windowless offices, and the prissiness expected, at least in the past, in their personal presentations (Lerner 123–141).

This blurred initiating role, whether it is described as a religious/sexual initiation or as the groundwork now symbolically placed "under" an educated public's discursive practices, has been unstable in any context. Cultures never codified it even in ancient times, when socially separated *grammaticus* and *rhetor* competed, as Quintilian noted, over who should initiate students into rhetorical composition (*Institutes,* II.1). Consequently, the teacher of composition is assigned not only these roles, which might involve the initiating care, pedagogic seduction, and practice for adult-hood provided by nurses in bourgeois homes. In addition, this teacher must withhold unquestioned acceptance, represent established means of dis-criminating among and evaluating students, and embody primary ideals/idols of language. This initiator, who traditionally has a great deal at stake in the model-correctness of his and her own language, must also *be* the goddess, *the* mother tongue, the discursive culture to which the student is introduced.

It might be countered that this complex call to identity contains any teacher of any introductory course claiming to initiate students into "essential" cultural knowledge. But the composition teacher consciously and unconsciously introduces students to the culture's discourse on *language,* which is al-ways at one with action, emotion, and regulatory establishments. This teacher is always engaged in initiations into the textual fabric of society, and thus will always be in a particular and difficult rela-tion to the superstructural regulation of that soci-ety. We see this difficulty daily, in the experience of those who are both demeaned by their continuing *ad hoc* relation to status, security, and financial re-wards, yet are given overwhelming authority by students, institutions, and the public, who expect even the most inexperienced "English teacher" to criticize and correct them, even in settings entirely removed from the academy. In these and many other ways, the complexly feminized cultural call to identity imposed on teachers of composition is maintained, even after they themselves censure early mechanistic teaching and its obviously regu-latory practices.

This censure signifies positive moves to redefine composition as a discipline, i.e., "composition studies" (see North 9–17), and to establish it as an academically equal partner in English departments. Such obvious, normal reactions from members of a marginalized culture unquestionably bode well for the fully theorized approach to writing and its instruction that could change the cultural expecta-tion that its teachers be only initiating, service-ori-ented, self-sacrificing, practical people. But in view of the feminized identity I have established, the

motives behind actions to "change" composition need cautious critiques. As statistics about who writes composition theory and who administers composition programs tell us, neither describing composition as a discipline nor asserting its equal-ity has "worked" on the actually gender-coded pro-fessional circumstances of those who teach writing. These motives have not resulted in acknowledging the gender-coded call to identity that marks the field's cultural history, or in offering alternatives to the deep but blurred structures of identity I have described. Our continuing tacit cooperation with hegemonic superstructural values cannot be under-estimated, nor can the hegemonic compromise that continues to constrain the field be "overcome," or "combated," with male-coded fortitude.

We have examples of such fortitude in attempts to follow the formative counterpart of composition, literary study, into an entrenched, privileged, "equal" academic position. The problem with such attempts at equality is that they contribute, no mat-ter how inadvertently, to an improved status that continues the patriarchal hierarchy in which they begin. Despite their perfectly understandable moti-vations and the positive results for both the theory and practice they have created, "equalizing" privi-leges between composition and literature, or be-tween composition and any other established field, signifies acceptance of values that ignore the begin-nings and contradict the purposes of current com-position teaching and research.

For instance, neoclassical histories of composi-tion that insist on its intellectual continuity with ancient rhetoric create both a content and a form for composition history that should give us pause. These histories do not normally focus on composi-tion as a discrete product of American discourse education, whose connection to rhetorical instruc-tion was ruptured, not merely interrupted, by Francis Child's 1875 negotiated defection from Harvard's Boylston Chair of Rhetoric to concen-trated literary research. Nor do they consider other historical events, some of which I have described, in which the test-hungry National Committee of Ten, Eliot at Harvard, and his henchman Adams Sherman Hill began a mechanistic, corrective course without even honorific connections to rhetorical education. Neoclassical histories do not, that is, point out the hegemonic significance of establishing a *freshman* writing course to winnow and sift students in place of—not as a version of—traditionally later, upper-class instruction for postgraduate public discourse.

In an otherwise admirable attempt to give composition a history and thus allow it (as many have said of needed women's history) to participate as an agent rather than an overlooked object in its own system of significance, neoclassical histories inadvertently approve of traditional academic privileges embedded in the fabric of hegemonic "traditions" and their overbearing "common sense." Focusing on a limited "intellectual" history of composition to the exclusion of its material circumstances implicitly places composition in academic "Big" history, where it will accrue entitlements from "authority and the ancients." But this tactic also sustains the hierarchies and privileging mechanisms that those in the field complain of so often.

Similarly, inevitable desires to demonstrate that composition is a research field have in some forms assumed that "research" must be empirical and scientific. This attitude, by no means universal among composition researchers, values "hard" data, "rigorous" methods, and what are taken to be generative "results" that will spawn further study. The intellectual contributions of this form of research are not at issue, but it is politically important to notice that claims for its powerful, masculine academic position imitate quite closely the "scientific" spirit that motivated and legitimized literary New Criticism earlier in this century. The "purified" (ahistorical, intransitive, theorized) "processes" of writers, and newly "objective," disinterested methods of studying them allow composition to claim, as literary studies did under New Criticism, that it has an object of study and that it can discover self-contained "meaning" in the act of writing apart from its contexts—in the "act itself."

This particular way to code composition as academically male, like neoclassical historicism, indicates a felt need to overcome its feminized cultural identity. But displacing either the symbolically "soft" or the actually marginalized status of the field and its female majority will not be accomplished by "combating" that identity, to achieve a success designed to imitate the totalizing effects of New Criticism's reign. And neither research that creates a male identity for composition studies nor historiography that links it to a Big picture actually fulfills this disguised desire. Both, that is, potentially alienate composition from consequential status among those who have historically had all the "principles" endowed to English. One adopts methods and vocabularies that ring false among many who already resent "science" as a field with which they have always competed, and the other focuses on a rhetorical educational history from which literary studies purposefully sets about to estrange itself.

My reasoning implies, I know, that no movement from within composition studies could ever do more than reform the basic structure of its identity, and that we should all at this point perform the intellectual/sexual submission we were culturally called to, to "lie back and think of England." As Althusser (following Marx) wrote about the cooperation of seemingly "new" and "traditional" ideologies (before he acted out his personally held ideological privileges by murdering his wife), "every child knows that a social formation which did not reproduce the conditions of production at the same time as it [was] produced would not last a year" (quoted in Macdonnel 28). But going beyond Marx, he also argued that attempts to overcome what we take to be hierarchical dominance often sustain the hierarchy, the "means of production," in which ideologies install us. Althusser's argument clearly applies to specific "new" moves in composition like those with which I have taken issue. These and many other intellectual and "practical" moves toward equality for composition reproduce the hegemonic superstructure by implying that bourgeois social climbing and successful competition for intellectual "clout" are legitimate signs of improvement. Although they take many seemingly unrelated forms, they are *politically* unified attempts to become equal in, and to sustain, a hierarchy that their supporters often claim to be overturning.

Nonetheless, the negative feminization of composition need not last forever.

The field might, that is, enjoy a different, if not a "new," identity, precisely as a culturally designated space for political action. Composition studies has always had the process available to it that active feminists and African-Americans have employed to transform their marginalized cultures into sites were cultural superstructures and their privileging results are visibly put into question. Composition professionals can also uncover and describe what is at stake for larger cultural maintenance in the marginalized status of their field. By raising a different voice in an active conversation about the feminized actual, historical, and symbolic status of composition professionals and their students, we can, that is, begin to reveal existing counterhegemonic structures in the field's existing practices and intellectual positions. An *actually* improved status depends on openly consolidating the field's resistances to the cultural superstructure that first defined it.

My primary purpose has been to accomplish part of the first, conversational goal, but the second process of intellectual redefinition would rerepresent the negatively "feminine" field as irrefutably counterhegemonic, not as a victim stuck in webs of compromise. For instance, composition might be redefined as a site culturally designated to teach *all* students, not an elite group. It therefore already is an encompassing site for empowering, not for repressing or "correcting," the discursive power of the majority. In addition, the field might highlight (as many have recently done) the status of its female majorities and the constructed marginal identity of its always "new" students. By drawing concrete attention to the ways in which political issues are played out in a contemporary academic situation that was first constructed on antifeminist principles, it would ask neocolonial administrators to recognize, and to be accountable for, the political implications of their enduring definitions of "composition" as the central institutional site for colonizing and regulating otherwise questionable, nontraditional entrants to the academy.

Other frequently noted characteristics of composition equally define it as an already-designated place for counterhegemonic intellectual politics. The field addresses writing-in-progress (and writing as process), not writing as an immutable textual product. It thereby overtly claims that categories of "high" and "low" texts are social, not essential, categories. "Good" writing, as composition must define it, is the result of established cultural privileging mechanisms, not of pure "taste." The field thus vividly demonstrates, in practice and in theory, that a mixture of ideas, timing, entitlements, and luck have designated some rather than others as "important" writer/thinkers. The field's most productive methods of evaluation also judge writing by situational rather than by universal standards, and thus insist on the arbitrariness of evaluations and their relativity to particular power structures. Additionally, the field's research opens rather than closes borders among established fields, thereby arguing that making new knowledge is a shared rather than isolated process, a matter of cooperation rather than of disciplined competition.

Each of these often stated but persistently unpoliticized practices and insights in the field have positioned it to transform its negatively feminized identity by engaging intellectual as well as practical political actions. As the institutional site designated as a passive enclosure for "unauthorized" discourse, composition has simultaneously been designated as a marginalizing power. But this enormous power to contain the discourse of the majority can be, if its professionals wish to claim it, the strength that re-represents the field's negative feminization. Composition is *also,* that is, an active existing site for dismantling particularly troublesome versions of hegemonic discursive "common sense"—particularly the exclusivity, humiliation, repression, and injustice hidden in nineteenth-century bourgeois moralities.

We have frequently translated these counterhegemonic implications of the field's practices and intellectual positions into signs of an undifferentiated "vitality" or "energy." But this abstract "energy" can be plugged into interventions that would undo concrete political structures that have a great deal at stake in negative images of composition teaching and the writing of students. Composition is not, that is, a modern place to celebrate a liberal "healthy pluralism" that reforms systems around it. It contains active resistance to the exhausted social situations that produced both its negative feminization and "traditions" that should have become cultural embarrassments long ago. As Kristeva has said in resisting traditional definitions of females, we can transform our own negative identity by understanding the implications of composition as "that which is marginalized by the patriarchal symbolic order" (quoted in Moi 166).

Works Cited

Applebee, Arthur. *Tradition and Reform in the Teaching of English: A History.* Urbana, IL: NCTE, 1974.

Douglas, Wallace. "Rhetoric for the Meritocracy." In Richard Ohmann, *English in America.* New York: Oxford University Press, 1976, 97–132.

Doyle, Brian. "The Hidden History of English Studies." In *Rereading English.* Ed. Peter Widdowson. New York: Methuen, 1982, 17–31.

Eagleton, Terry. "The Subject of Literature." *Cultural Critique,* No. 2 (Winter 1985–1986): 95–104.

———. *Literary Theory: An Introduction.* Minneapolis: University of Minnesota Press, 1983.

Graff, Gerald. *Professing Literature: An Instructional History.* Chicago: University of Chicago Press, 1987.

Hartzog, Carol. *Composition in the Academy: A Study of Writing Program Administration,* New York: MLA, 1987.

Holbrook, Sue Ellen. "Women's Work: The Feminizing of Composition." Unpublished ms. of 1988 presentation at CCCC, St. Louis, MO.

Kitzhaber, Albert. "Rhetoric in American Colleges: 1850–1900." Unpublished Diss. University of Washington, 1953.

Lerner, Gerda. "Veiling the Woman." In *The Creation of Patriarchy.* New York: Oxford University Press, 1986.

Macdonnel, Diane. *Theories of Discourse: An Introduction.* Oxford: Basil Blackwell, 1986.

Miller, Susan. *Textual Carnivals: The Politics of Composition.* Carbondale, IL: Southern Illinois University Press, 1991.

Moi, Toril. *Sexual/Textual Politics.* New York and London: Methuen, 1985.

North, Stephen. *The Making of Knowledge in Composition: Portrait of an Emerging Field.* Portsmouth, NH: Boynton/Cook, 1987.

Ohmann, Richard. *English in America.* New York: Oxford University Press, 1976.

———. "Writing and Reading: Work and Leisure." In *The Politics of Letters.* Middletown, CT: Wesleyan University Press, 1987. (Chapter 3).

Stallybrass, Peter, and Allon White. *The Politics and Poetics of Transgression.* Ithaca: Cornell University Press, 1986.

Tchudi, Stephen N. *Explorations in the Teaching of Secondary English: A Sourcebook for Experimental Teaching.* New York: Dodd, Mead, 1975.

Inglés in the Colleges

Victor Villanueva, Jr.

"Inglés in the Colleges" is chapter five of Villanueva, Jr.'s autobiography, Bootstraps: From an American Academic of Color. *Urbana: NCTE, 1993. 65–90. Note that "Dr. V" refers to Villanueva, who writes about himself in the third person.*

It was said to be the oldest apartment house in the city of Seattle: from nineteenth-century loggers' quarters to whorehouse to tenement. It stood on a hill at the gateway to the south side. Nights would be filled with the sounds of foghorns coming in from the Puget Sound and the sounds of gunfire from within the neighborhood.

There were other sounds as well. There was the whirring of a sewing machine long into the night: the Vietnamese family doing piecework for a company that made baseball caps. There were the clucks of chickens or honks of geese from the Cambodian family, the crack of a rock when fowl were slaughtered for food. The whoops of joy from the Nigerian fellow the day he was served with deportation papers (couldn't have afforded to return to his home otherwise). The screams of anguish from the panhandler a few doors down the day the government worker took her children away. The long talks about Latin American coffee from the retired merchant marine with the game leg. There was the occasional shout through the kitchen window: "If you can't beat 'em, join 'em." Angry talk about American academics from the apartment manager: a man from India who had recently gotten his Ph.D. in history from the prestigious university but couldn't land a job. There were the family sounds: children at play; the clickings of a 1941 Remington typewriter long enough into the night to know of the whirring sewing machine next door; the nightly screeching and scratching of rats crawling within the walls; the crunching on cockroach carcasses the day the exterminator came by. These were the sounds that came from and came to the one-bedroom apartment of Victor and Carol and their children. And there was the friendly chatter when all gathered by the mailboxes on the eighth of each month, anticipating the mailman and food stamps, discussing different versions of what that great meal would be that night, enjoying a few days' balm after long sorenesses.

Summer mornings, Carol would walk down to the free-bus zone to get to her job in telemarketing, bothering people in their homes for minimum wage. Victor would go with his daughter to the food bank on Empire Way—mainstreet in the heart of the ghetto, the location of the Welfare office, the empire's way—then to the food bank at the Freemont District, then the food bank at the local Catholic Church. Some bags would contain frozen juices or frozen burritos or frozen turnovers, but the apartment had no working freezer and no working oven. Miles for meals. Carol would return, and Victor would walk the five miles to the University to teach his basic-writing class. Pride at teaching; humiliation at food-bank lines, free government cheese and butter lines, welfare lines. He had known greater affluence as a sergeant in the Army. Dr. V, the college professor, can still make that claim, the difference between then and now, matters of degree rather than kind. But he had made a choice, had opted out of the army.

The morality of war, the morality of military occupation, the morality of forced separation from family, all had become unignorable. Memories of Dad speaking about the Americans who would be in charge of the virtually all Puerto Rican American forces in Puerto Rico, of the resentment Dad heard about from the Panamanians when he had served as an American soldier in Panama; Dad's discharge papers reading "WPR," White Puerto Rican; Dad's dissertations on the large American corporations' profiting by being located in Puerto Rico but not passing on the profits to the majority of Puerto Ricans on the Island—all such memories had come flooding back as he thought of his experiences in the Army, especially in Korea, the similarities unignorable. And there were the officers the sergeant from *el bloque* had served under, particularly those whose sole qualification for leadership seemed to be their college degrees, those who seemed no brighter than he, no more competent. And there was Walter Myles, a peer, from the block, even if in Palo Alto; Walter, of color—and a college graduate. It was time to move on, away from the Army.

I wanted to try my hand at college, go beyond the GED. But college scared me. I had been told long ago that college wasn't my lot.

He drives by the University District of Seattle during his last days in the military and sees the college kids, long hair and sandals, baggy short pants on the men, long, flowing dresses on the women, some men in suits, some women in high heels, all carrying backpacks over one shoulder. There is both purpose and contentment in the air. Storefronts carry names like Dr. Feelgood and Magus Bookstore, reflecting the good feelings and magic he senses. A block away is the University, red tiles and green grass, rolling hills and tall pines, apple and cherry blossoms, the trees shading modern monoliths of gray concrete and gothic, church-like buildings of red brick. And he says to himself, "Maybe in the next life."

He must be content with escaping a life at menial labor, at being able to bank on the skills in personnel management he had acquired in the Army. But there are only two takers. The large department-store chain would hire him as a management

trainee—a shoe salesman on commission, no set income, but a trainee could qualify for GI Bill benefits as well as the commissions. Not good enough, not getting paid beyond the GI Bill; and a sales career wasn't good enough either, the thought of his mother's years as a saleslady, years lost, still in memory. A finance corporation offers him a job: management trainee. The title: Assistant Manager. The job: bill collector, with low wage, but as a trainee, qualified to supplement with the GI Bill. The combined pay would be good, but he would surely lose his job in time, would be unable to be righteously indignant like the bill collectors he has too often had to face too often are, unable to bother people like Mom and Dad, knowing that being unable to meet bills isn't usually a moral shortcoming but most often an economic condition.

The GI Bill had come up again, however, setting the "gettinover" wheels in motion. The nearby community college charges ninety dollars a quarter tuition, would accept him on the strength of his GED scores. That would mean nearly four hundred dollars a month from the GI Bill, with only thirty dollars a month for schooling ("forgetting" to account for books and supplies). What a get-over! There would be immediate profit in simply going to school. And if he failed, there would be nothing lost. And if he succeeded, an Associate degree in something. He'd be better equipped to brave the job market again.

So he walks onto the community college campus in the summer of 1976. It's not the campus of the University of Washington. It's more like Dominguez High School in California. But it is a college. Chemistry: a clumsiness at the lab, but relative grace at mathematical equations and memorization. French is listening to audiotapes and filling out workbooks. History is enjoyable stories, local lore from a retired newsman, easy memorization for the grade.

Then there is English. There are the stories, the taste he had always had for reading, now peppered with talk of philosophy and psychology and tensions and textures. Writing is 200 words on anything, preceded by a sentence outline. He'd write about Korea and why *The Rolling Stone* could write about conspiracies of silence, or he'd write about the problems in trying to get a son to understand that he is Puerto Rican when the only Puerto Ricans he knows are his grandparents; he'd write about whatever seemed to be on his mind at the time. The night before a paper would be due, he'd gather pen and pad, and stare. Clean the dishes. Stare. Watch an "I Love Lucy" rerun. Stare. Then sometime in the night the words would come. He'd write; scratch something out; draw arrows shifting paragraphs around; add a phrase or two. Then he'd pull out the erasable bond, making changes even as he typed, frantic to be done before school. Then he'd use the completed essay to type out an outline, feeling a little guilty about having cheated in not having produced the outline first.

The guilt showed one day when Mrs. Ray, the Indian woman in traditional dress with a Ph.D. in English from Oxford, part-time instructor at the community college, said there was a problem with his writing. She must have been able to tell somehow that he was discovering what to write while writing, no prior thesis statement, no outline, just a vague notion that would materialize, magically, while writing. In her stark, small office she hands him a sheet with three familiar sayings mimeoed on it; instructs him to write on one, right there, right then. He writes on "a bird in the hand is worth two in the bush." No memory of what he had written, probably forgotten during the writing. Thirty minutes or so later, she takes the four or five pages he had written; she reads; she smiles; then she explains that she had suspected plagiarism in his previous writings. She apologizes, saying she found his writing "too serious," too abstract, not typical of her students. He is not insulted; he is flattered. He knew he could read; now he knew he could write well enough for college.

English 102, Mr. Lukens devotes a portion of the quarter to Afro-American literature. Victor reads Ishmael Reed, "I'm a Cowboy in the Boat of Ra." It begins,

> I am a cowboy in the boat of Ra,
> sidewinders in the saloons of fools
> bit my forehead like   O
> the untrustworthiness of Egyptologists
> Who do not know their trips. Who was that

> dog faced man? they asked, the day I rode
> from town.

> School marms with halitosis cannot see
> the Nefertitti fake chipped on the run by slick
> germans, the hawk behind Sonny Rollins' head or
> the ritual beard of his axe; a longhorn winding
> its bells thru the Field of Reeds.

There was more, but by this point he was already entranced and excited. Poetry has meaning, more than the drama of Mark Antony's speech years back.

Mr. Lukens says that here is an instance of poetry more for effect (or maybe *affect*) than for meaning, citing a line from Archibald MacLeish: "A poem should not mean / But be." But there *was* meaning in this poem. Victor writes about it. In the second stanza, the chipped Nefertitti, a reference to a false black history, with images from "The Maltese Falcon" and war movies. The "School marms" Reed mentions are like the schoolmasters at Hamilton, unknowing and seeming not to know of being unknowing. Sonny Rollins' axe and the Field of Reeds: a saxophone, a reed instrument, the African American's links to Egypt, a history whitewashed by "Egyptologists / Who do not know their trips." He understood the allusions, appreciated the wordplay. The poem had the politics of Bracy, the language of the block, TV of the fifties, together in the medium Mr. D had introduced to Victor, Papi, but now more powerful. This was fun; this was politics. This was Victor's history, his life with language play.

Years later, Victor is on a special two-man panel at a conference of the Modern Language Association. He shares the podium with Ishmael Reed. Victor gives a talk on "Teaching as Social Action," receives applause, turns to see Ishmael Reed looking him in the eye, applauding loudly. He tries to convey how instrumental this "colleague" had been in his life.

He'll be an English major. Mr. Lukens is his advisor, sets up the community college curriculum in such a way as to have all but the major's requirements for a BA from the University of Washington out of the way. The University of Washington is the only choice: it's relatively nearby, tuition for Vietnam veterans is $176 a quarter. "Maybe in this life."

His AA degree in his back pocket, his heart beating audibly with exhilaration and fear, he walks up the campus of the University of Washington, more excited than at Disneyland when he was sixteen. He's proud: a regular transfer student, no special minority waivers. The summer of 1977.

But the community is not college in the same way the University is. The community college is torn between vocational training and preparing the unprepared for traditional university work. And it seems unable to resolve the conflict (see Cohen and Brawer). His high community-college GPA is no measure of what he is prepared to undertake at the University. He fails at French 103, unable to carry the French conversations, unable to do the reading, unable to do the writing, dropping the course before the failure becomes a matter of record. He starts again. French 101, only to find he is still not really competitive with the white kids who had had high school French. But he cannot fail, and he does not fail, thanks to hour after hour with French tapes after his son's in bed.

English 301, the literature survey, is fun. Chaucer is a ghetto boy, poking fun at folks, the rhyming reminding him of when he did the dozens on the block; Chaucer telling bawdy jokes: "And at the wyndow out she putte hir hole . . . 'A berd, a berd!,' quod hende Nicholas." So this is literature. Chaucer surely ain't white. At least he doesn't sound white, "the first to write poetry in the vernacular," he's told. Spenser is exciting: images of knights and damsels distressing, magic and dragons, the *Lord of the Rings* that he had read in Korea paling in the comparison. Donne is a kick: trying to get laid when he's Jack Donne, with a rap the boys from the block could never imagine; building church floors with words on a page when he's Dr. John Donne. Every reading is an adventure, never a nod, no matter how late into the night the reading. For his first paper, Victor, the 3.8 at Tacoma Community College, gets 36 out of a possible 100—"for your imagination," written alongside the grade.

I was both devastated and determined, my not belonging was verified but I was not ready to be shut down, not so quickly. So to the library to look up what the Professor himself had published: *Proceedings of the Spenser Society.* I had no idea what the Professor was going on about in his paper, but I could see the pattern: an introduction that said something about what others had said, what he was going to be writing about, in what order, and what all this would prove; details about what he said he was going to be writing about, complete with quotes, mainly from the poetry, not much from other writers on Spenser; and a "therefore." It wasn't the five-paragraph paper Mr. Lukens had insisted on, not just three points, not just repetition of the opening in the close, but the pattern was essentially the same. The next paper: 62 out of 100 and a "Much better." Course grade: B. Charity.

I never vindicated myself with that professor. I did try, tried to show that I didn't need academic charity. Economic charity was hard enough. I took my first graduate course from him. This time I got an "All well and good, but what's the point?" alongside a "B" for a paper. I had worked on that paper all summer long.

I have had to face that same professor, now a Director of Freshman Writing, at conferences. And with every contact, feelings of insecurity well up from within, the feeling that I'm seen as the minority (a literal term in academics for those of us of color), the feeling of being perceived as having gotten through *because* I am a minority, an insecurity I face often. But though I never got over the stigma with that professor (whether real or imagined), I did get some idea on how to write for the University.

Professorial Discourse Analysis became a standard practice: go to the library; see what the course's professor had published; try to discern a pattern to her writing; try to mimic the pattern. Some would begin with anecdotes. Some would have no personal pronouns. Some would cite others' research. Some would cite different literary works to make assertions about one literary work. Whatever they did, I would do too. And it worked, for the most part, so that I could continue the joy of time travel and mind travel with those, and within those, who wrote about things I had discovered I liked to think about: Shakespeare and work versus pleasure, religion and the day-to-day world, racism, black Othello and the Jewish Merchant of Venice; Dickens and the impossibility of really getting into the middle class (which I read as "race," getting into the white world, at the time), pokes at white folks (though the Podsnaps were more likely jabs at the middle class); Milton and social responsibility versus religious mandates; Yeats and being assimilated and yet other (critically conscious with a cultural literacy, I'd say now); others and other themes. And soon I was writing like I had written in the community college: some secondary reading beforehand, but composing the night before a paper was due, a combination of fear that nothing will come and faith that something would eventually develop, then revising to fit the pattern discovered in the Professorial Discourse Analysis, getting "A's" and "B's," and getting comments like "I never saw that before."

There were failures, of course. One professor said my writing was too formulaic. One professor said it was too novel. Another wrote only one word for the one paper required of the course: "nonsense." But while I was on the campus I could escape and not. I could think about the things that troubled me or intrigued me, but through others' eyes in other times and other places. I couldn't get enough, despite the pain and the insecurity.

School becomes his obsession. There is the education. But the obsession is as much, if not more, in getting a degree, not with a job in mind, just the degree, just because he thinks he can, despite all that has said he could not. His marriage withers away, not with rancor, just melting into a dew. The daily routine has him taking the kid to a daycare/school at 6:00 a.m., then himself to school, from school to work as a groundskeeper for a large apartment complex; later, a maintenance man, then a garbage man, then a plumber, sometimes coupled with other jobs: shipping clerk for the library, test proctor. From work to pick up the kid from school, prepare dinner, maybe watch a TV show with the kid, tuck him into bed, read. There are some girlfriends along the

way, and he studies them too: the English major who won constant approval from the same professor who had given him the 36 for being imaginative; the art major who had traveled to France (French practice); the fisheries major whose father was an executive vice president for IBM (practice at being middle class). Victor was going to learn—quite consciously—what it means to be white, middle class. He didn't see the exploitation; not then; he was obsessed. There were things going on in his classes that he did not understand and that the others did. He didn't know what the things were that he didn't understand, but he knew that even those who didn't do as well as he did, somehow did not act as foreign as he felt. He was the only colored kid in every one of those classes. And he hadn't the time nor the racial affiliation to join the Black Student Union or Mecha. He was on his own, an individual pulling on his bootstraps, looking out for number one. He's not proud of the sensibility, but isolation—and, likely, exploitation of others—are the stuff of racelessness.

There were two male friends, Mickey, a friend to this day, and Luis el Loco. Luis was a *puertoriceño*, from Puerto Rico, who had found his way to Washington by having been imprisoned in the federal penitentiary at MacNeal Island, attending school on a prison-release program. Together, they would enjoy talking in Spanglish, listening to *salsa*. But Luis was a Modern Languages major, Spanish literature. Nothing there to exploit. It's a short-lived friendship. Mickey was the other older student in Victor's French 101 course, white, middle class, yet somehow other, one who had left the country during Vietnam, a disc jockey in Amsterdam. The friendship begins with simply being the two older men in the class, longer away from adolescence than the rest; the friendship grows with conversations about politics, perceptions about American from abroad, literature. But Victor would not be honest with his friend about feeling foreign until years later, a literary bravado. Mickey was well read in the literary figures Victor was coming to know. Mickey would be a testing ground for how Victor was reading, another contact to be exploited. Eventually, Mickey and his wife would introduce Victor to their friend, a co-worker at the post office. This is Carol. She comes from a life of affluence, and from a life of poverty, a traveler within the class system, not a journey anyone would volunteer for, but one which provides a unique education, a path not unlike Paulo Freire's. From her, there is the physical and the things he would know of the middle class, discussed explicitly, and there is their mutual isolation. There is love and friendship, still his closest friend, still his lover.

But before Carol, there is simply the outsider obsessed. He manages the BA. He cannot stop, even as the GI Bill reaches its end. He will continue to gather credentials until he is kicked out. Takes the GRE, does not do well, but gets into the graduate program with the help of references from within the faculty—and with the help of minority status in a program decidedly low in numbers of minorities. "Minority," or something like that, is typed on the GRE test results in his file, to be seen while scanning the file for the references. His pride is hurt, but he remembers All Saints, begins to believe in the biases of standardized tests: back in the eighth grade, a failure top student; now a near-failure, despite a 3.67 at the competitive Big University of State. Not all his grades, he knew, were matters of charity. He had earned his GPA, for the most part. Nevertheless, he is shaken.

More insecure than ever, there are no more overnight papers. Papers are written over days, weeks, paragraphs literally cut and laid out on the floor to be pasted. One comment appears in paper after paper: "Logic?" He thinks, "Yes." He does not understand. Carol cannot explain the problem. Neither can Mickey. He does not even consider asking the professors. To ask would be an admission of ignorance, "stupid spic" still resounding within. This is his problem.

Then by chance (exactly how is now forgotten), he hears a tape of a conference paper delivered by the applied linguist Robert Kaplan. Kaplan describes contrastive rhetoric. Kaplan describes a research study conducted in New York City among Puerto Ricans who are bilingual and Puerto Ricans who are monolingual in English, and he says that the discourse patterns, the rhetorical patterns which include the logic, of monolingual Puerto Ricans are like those of Puerto Rican bilinguals and different from Whites, more Greek than the Latin-like prose of American written English. Discourse analysis takes on a new intensity. At this point, what this means is that he will have to go beyond patterns in his writing, become more analytical of the connections between ideas. The implications of Kaplan's talk, for him at least, will take on historical and political significance as he learns more of rhetoric.

About the same time as that now lost tape on Kaplan's New York research (a study that was never published, evidently), Victor stumbles into his first rhetoric course.

The preview of course offerings announces a course titled "Theories of Invention," to be taught by Anne Ruggles Gere. His GRE had made it clear that he was deficient in Early American Literature. Somewhere in his mind he recalls reading that Benjamin Franklin had identified himself as an inventor; so somehow, Victor interprets "Theories of Invention" as "Theories of Inventors," an American lit course. What he discovers is Rhetoric.

Not all at once, not just in that first class on rhetoric, I discover some things about writing, my own, and about the teaching of writing. I find some of modern composition's insights are modern hindsights. I don't mind the repetition. Some things bear repeating. The repetitions take on new significance and are elaborated upon in a new context, a new time. Besides, not everyone who teaches writing knows of rhetoric, though I believe everyone should.

I read Cicero's *de Inventione*. It's a major influence in rhetoric for centuries. The strategies he describes on how to argue a court case bears a remarkable resemblance to current academic discourse, the pattern I first discovered when I first tried to figure out what I had not done in that first English course at the University.

Janet Emig looks to depth psychology and studies on creativity and even neurophysiology, the workings of the brain's two hemispheres, to pose the case that writing is a mode of learning. She explains what I had been doing with my first attempts at college writing, neither magic nor a perversion. Cicero had said much the same in his *de Oratore* in the first century BCE (Before the Common Era, the modern way of saying BC):

> *Writing* is said to be *the best and most excellent modeler and teacher of oratory;* and not without reason; for if what is meditated and considered easily surpasses sudden and extemporary speech, a constant and diligent habit of writing will surely be of more effect than meditation and consideration itself; since all the arguments relating to the subject on which we write, whether they are suggested by art, or by a certain power of genius and understanding, will present themselves, and occur to us, while we examine and contemplate it in the full light of our intellect and all the thoughts and words, which are the most expressive of their kind, must of necessity come under and submit to the keenness of our judgment while writing; and a fair arrangement and collocation of the words is effected by writing, in a certain rhythm and measure, not poetical, but oratorical. (*de Oratore* I.cxxxiv)

Writing is a way of discovering, of learning, of thinking. Cicero is arguing the case for literacy in ways we still argue or are arguing anew.

David Bartholomae and Anthony Petrosky discuss literary theorists like Jonathan Culler and the pedagogical theorist Paulo Freire to come up with a curriculum in which reading is used to introduce basic writers, those students who come into the colleges not quite prepared for college work, to the ways of academic discourse. Quintilian, like others of his time, the first century CE, and like others before his time, advocates reading as a way to come to discover the ways of language and the ways of writing and the ways to broaden the range of experience.

Kenneth Bruffee, Peter Elbow, and others, see the hope of democratizing the classroom through peer-group learning. So did Quintilian:

> But as emulation is of use to those who have made some advancement of learning, so, to those who are but beginning and still of tender age, to imitate their schoolfellows is more pleasant than to imitate their master, for the very reason that it is more easy; for they who are learning the first rudiments will scarcely dare to exalt themselves to the hope of attaining that eloquence which they regard as the highest; they will rather fix on what is nearest to them, as vines attached to trees fain the top by taking hold of the lower branches first (23–24).

Quintilian describes commenting on student papers in ways we consider new:

> [T]he powers of boys sometimes sink under too great severity in correction; for they despond, and grieve, and at last hate their work; and what is most prejudicial, while they fear everything, they cease to attempt anything. . . . A teacher ought, therefore, to be as agreeable as possible, that remedies, which are rough in their nature, may be rendered soothing by gentleness of hand; he ought to praise some parts of his pupils' performances, tolerate some, and to alter others, giving his reasons why the alterations are made. (100)

Richard Haswell recommends minimal scoring of student papers, sticking to one or two items in need of correction per paper. Nancy Sommers warns against rubber-stamp comments on student papers, comments like "awk"; she says comments ought to explain. Both have more to say than Quintilian on such matters, but in essence both are Quintilian revisited.

Edward P. J. Corbett looks to Quintilian, Cicero, and others from among the ancients, especially Aristotle, to write *Classical Rhetoric for the Modern Student.* In some ways, the book says little that is different from other books on student writing. But the book is special in its explicit connections to ancient rhetorical traditions.

Without a knowledge of history and traditions, we risk running in circles while seeking new paths. Without knowing the traditions, there is no way of knowing which traditions to hold dear and which to discard. Self evident? Maybe. Yet the circles exist.

For all the wonders I had found in literature—and still find—literature seemed to me self-enveloping. What I would do is read and enjoy. And, when it was time to write, what I would write about would be an explanation of what I had enjoyed, using words like *Oedipal complex* or *polyvocal* or *anxiety* or *unpacking,* depending on what I had found in my discourse-analytical journeys, but essentially saying "this is what I saw" or "this is how what I read took on a special meaning for me" (sometimes being told that what I had seen or experienced was nonsense). I could imagine teaching literature—and often I do, within the context of composition—but I knew that at best I'd be imparting or imposing one view: the what I saw or the meaning for me. The reader-response theorists I would come to read, Rosenblatt, Fish, Culler, and others, would make sense to me, that what matters most is what the reader finds. Bakhtin's cultural and political dimension would make even more sense: that all language is an approximation, generated and understood based on what one has experienced with language. In teaching literature, I thought, there would be those among students I would face who would come to take on reading, perhaps; likely some who would appreciate more fully what they had read. But it did not seem to me that I could somehow make someone enjoy. Enjoyment would be a personal matter: from the self, for the self.

And what if I did manage a Ph.D. and did get a job as a professor? I would have to publish. A guest lecturer in a medieval lit course spoke of one of the important findings in his new book: medieval scribes were conscious of the thickness of the lozenge, the medieval version of the comma. He found that thinner lozenges would indicate a slight pause in reading; thicker lozenges, longer pauses. Interesting, I reckon. Surely of interest to a select few. But so what, in some larger sense? What would I write about?

Then I stumbled onto rhetoric. Here was all that language had been to me. There were the practical matters of writing and teaching writing. There were the stylistic devices, the tricks of language use that most people think about when they hear the word *rhetoric;* "Let's cut through the rhetoric." It's nice to have those devices at one's disposal—nice, even

important, to know when those devices are operating. But there is more. Rhetoric's classic definition as the art of persuasion suggests a power. So much of what we do when we speak or write is suasive in intent. So much of what we receive from others—from family and friends to thirty-second blurbs on TV—is intended to persuade. Recognizing how this is done gives greater power to choose. But rhetoric is still more.

Rhetoric is the conscious use of language: "observing in any given case the available means of persuasion," to quote Aristotle (I.ii). As the conscious use of language, rhetoric would include everything that is conveyed through language: philosophy, history, anthropology, psychology, sociology, literature, politics—"the use of language as a symbolic means of inducing cooperation in beings that by nature respond to symbols," according to modern rhetorician Kenneth Burke (46). The definition says something about an essentially human characteristic: our predilection to use symbols. Language is our primary symbol system. The ability to learn language is biologically transmitted. Burke's definition points to language as ontological, part of our being. And his definition suggests that it is epistemological, part of our thinking, an idea others say more about (see Leff).

So to study rhetoric becomes a way of studying humans. Rhetoric becomes for me the complete study of language, the study of the ways in which peoples have accomplished all that has been accomplished beyond the instinctual. There were the ancient greats saying that there was political import to the use of language. There were the modern greats saying that how one comes to know is at least mediated by language, maybe even constituted in language. There were the pragmatic applications. There was the possibility that in teaching writing and in teaching rhetoric as conscious considerations of language use I could help others like myself: players with language, victims of the language of failure.

In rhetoric, there is history and culture and language with political and personal implications. From Plato I could speculate on why, perhaps, plurality receives so much resistance in our society, even when it is espoused. Plato saw a plurality of the senses as somehow base, good only insofar as the senses could lead to the supersensible, to the one unifying principle of another plane of existence, the ideal, the Idea of the Good. In his *Republic* he argues the case for censorship, in the name of the moral good of young minds. And I know that this continues, despite freedoms of the press. He argues against democracy, as a kind of government that would have everyone running after sensual self-interest, a kind of anarchy. And I think of James Madison's *Federalist Paper #10,* arguing against what he terms "pure democracy" when trying to get the Constitution ratified in New York. Plato was an influence on Cicero; Cicero was an influence on the Founding Fathers (Hirsch, *Cultural Literacy* 109).

In Plato's works on rhetoric, he lambasts the group of rhetoricians known as the sophists for speaking in pluralistic terms, reducing, in *Gorgias,* the sophists to those who simply make the worse case appear the better. There was more to the sophists, as I'll outline below. Plato's ideal rhetoric becomes one that deals in abstractions, the supersensible, a use of language to liberate the mind. And I think of *e pluribus unum,* and how the emphasis seems to be on the *unum,* as in current attempts at English Only legislation, as in the 100 percent Americanism propaganda campaigns earlier this century. "From many, one" is pretty abstract, able to be interpreted as a phrase of conformity or one of pluralism. I think of the guarantees that are not granted by the Constitution, as great as that document may be, the lack of the sensorial, the physical, the lack of guarantees to the right to live, in a very basic sense; no guarantees of health or hearth, homelessness and hunger, in a country of affluence, dismissed through the ideology of individualism: "Well, if they'd stop being so lazy, picked themselves up by the bootstraps. . . ." And I think of teaching ideas to liberate minds, a liberal education, something divorced from education as political, from a liberatory education. Liberating lives is more concrete than liberating minds. I remember, mainly through studies in English literary history, the power-

ful influence of Neoplatonism, Plato adopted to Christianity in a Christian nation with a long Christian heritage, and I know that Plato is very much with us all.

Cicero demonstrates the potential political power in rhetoric. He was a major political figure in the Roman Republic, one who saw and was distressed by what he believed was a change in the government, from representative government to rule by those who held military power. His oratory was geared at preventing those changes, first through public speaking, later by speaking among the senators, and still later by political intrigue. He takes part in the plot to assassinate Julius Caesar, then Caesar's successor. His plottings are discovered; he is himself assassinated. His hands and head, the tools of the public speaker, are nailed to the Roman rostrum, the stage from which public speaking took place. There would be no more oratory of his sort: imperial Rome was coming to the fore. Rhetoric must have been seen as powerful— and dangerous.

Quintilian comes from Spain, a colony of Rome. He is educated in the language and the rhetoric of the Empire. He works for the governor of Spain; Galba, the governor, becomes Emperor of Rome. Quintilian has already become a famous lawyer, the principal occupation of orators now removed from the kinds of political power they might have enjoyed in more democratic times. He becomes a teacher of rhetoric, paid with government funds, the first chair of rhetoric, teaching rhetoric to the sons of the elite of Rome. And I see the parallels to my own new life, my life now: from the colony, teaching the language and ways of the colonizers who can afford college educations, my pay coming from the government. But more importantly, I see the power of rhetoric, no longer to be fully exercised on the rostrum, being moved to the classroom.

There are other figures from classical rhetoric who affected me, and continue to do so. But the figures just mentioned were the ones who most had me thinking in historical terms. The historical brought considerations of the cultural and the political. These particular figures, and others—the sophists, Aristotle—when placed in historical context, helped to explain what Kaplan might have been referring to when he described the rhetoric of schools as Latin and the rhetoric of New York Puerto Ricans as more Greek.

Athens, around the fifth century BCE. The sophists. They are a popular group of orators, in particular among those seeking entertainment, though unpopular in certain important circles. Among the best known, to us at least, are Protagoras and Gorgias, neither of whom is native to Athens. They are *metics,* one reason, perhaps, why they are not well liked among those special circles. *Metics,* aliens, are legislatively second class, not quite enjoying the full benefits of citizenship. Protagoras comes from Abderah, in Northern Greece, and Gorgias from Leontini, in Sicily. Though they cannot take more active parts in the politics of Athens, they serve a vital function in maintaining Athenian democracy: they train those likely to take on important roles in Athenian life, using as one of their principal themes *aretê,* rhetoric in the cause of active participation in domestic, social, and political life.

Protagoras, probably the first of the paid traveling teachers, is something of a problem in his time in that his way of seeing things poses a challenge to the dominant ideology in Athens, Ionian natural philosophy, in which things are as they are because they are in the nature of things, meant to be. Protagoras says that "man is the measure of all things." So if the human is the measure, then rulers are not specially imbued by nature to rule. If the human is the measure, then there are few natural laws; there can be equally valid truths. It was likely Protagoras who first taught that there can be opposing and, in some senses, equally valid arguments to any given case—two sides (at least) to any argument. Not only are there two sides to any argument, but anyone can be taught to present, effectively, the opposing arguments. Anyone can learn to be a rhetor, not just the select few with natural speaking abilities. Protagoras, and the sophists generally, introduced a humanistic, a subjective, ideology: humanity as ul-

timately responsible, able to be taught the ways in which to take on responsibility.

But a subjective and relativistic ideology could cause problems. The aristocracy could not claim a natural superiority; laws and knowledge could not claim to be absolute; everything could become subject to challenge. This relativism would find its most articulate challenge from Plato. Today, the only thing cheaper than "mere rhetoric" is "sheer sophistry," a Platonic legacy.

Democrats also had an argument against the sophists. The democrats complained that what the sophists had to offer, they could, but did not, offer to everyone. Since sophists charged fees for their services, only the wealthy were able to gain access to those services and the potential inherent in acquiring what they had to offer. The way to humanism was a commodity.

In their quest to gain customers, the sophists performed public exhibitions of their skills. These were popular, well attended. Since the public demonstrations were intended to gather students, sophistic orators were about showing off their own unique skills, not just the potential powers of rhetoric. Their speeches, then, seemed less concerned with content than with displaying artistry with language and thereby their proficiency with language.

The most popular sophist of the time was Gorgias. Among his demonstrations, one still available to us is the *Encomium to Helen,* a speech in praise of Helen. The Athenians knew the "truth" of Helen's betrayal. But Gorgias would demonstrate how he could argue skillfully that despite what the Athenians "knew" to be the case, historic Helen was not guilty of betraying Menelaus, her Attic husband, even if she did go off with the Trojan Paris. Gorgias argued that Helen was either a victim of fate, or a victim of the will of the gods, a victim of love, a victim of forcible abduction, or a victim of language. Gorgias argued that there is a kind of magic to language, stronger than individual will, that Paris might have rhetorically seduced her away in such a way that she could not have resisted.

For Gorgias, words and language are obsessions. And his demonstration reflects the attention he placed on the language. The *Helen* is replete with rhyming words and echoing rhythms, with parallelism and antithetical structures, with parallels that are even careful to contain identical numbers of syllables. This consciousness of demonstrating the rhetorical, stylistic skills of the orator, and this consciousness of the sound of the oration, even over the sense, become the marks of the sophist.

Centuries later, in the Roman Republic, Cicero is accused of being "Asiatic" in his rhetorical practices. To be Asiatic is to employ the rhetoric of Asia Minor and Greece. Its opposite, the Attic, might refer to Athens, but it is the plain, precise ways of the Latin. Cicero's writing and oratory have a flair for amplification, a stylistic device in which a certain point is repeated several times in succession, though using different words. His writing displays sophistic tendencies: parallelism, antithetical structures, amplification in order to assure a certain sound to the structure.

But because the sophists were considered morally suspect in working for money, and were surely ideologically and theologically dangerous, they were successfully squelched from Western rhetorical history (or put down) for centuries. Isocrates, a sophist, one to whom Cicero gives credit, writes *Against the Sophists;* Aristotle pits the dialectician against sophists in his *Rhetoric;* and there is Plato. Cicero himself claims not to be Asiatic because the Asiatic is philosophically empty. Yet the Ciceronian, and its sophistic ways with words, dominate Western oratorical style until the eighteenth century, when Peter Ramus redefines rhetoric in line with the new modern ways of thinking. Rhetoric is style; ideas are matters of logic. Aristotle's clarity and logic adopted to the rhetorical takes precedence over the Ciceronian (Crowley).

Then the history is gone as well as the style itself, a reference to the sophists showing up in the writing of Hegel but really only arising again during the last two decades or so.

Sophistry does arise again in the East, however. By the fourth century CE, the Roman Empire is virtually destroyed by the Visigoths, German invaders.

The seat of the empire moves to Constantinople, New Rome, ruled by Constantine. This is the birth of the Byzantine Empire. By 395 CE, Christianity is adopted as the religion of the empire. Greek is the language, even though the Byzantines refer to themselves as Romans (Arnott). And the sophistic is the formal way with the language.

Philostratus calls this rebirth of florid rhetoric the Second Sophistic. Like the sophists of old, the second sophists traveled the empire giving demonstrations, celebrating the greatness of Greece and its reflection in the greatness of Rome. Maybe as early as the second century CE, the second sophistic enjoyed significant influence, even though Christians were critical because of the second sophistic's celebration of pagan mythology, and—like the old sophists—because of the second sophistic's self-indulgent attention to the speaker's skills, its emphasis on language for its own sake. But by the end of the fourth century, the second sophistic's ways were evident in the homilies and orations of Christian patristics like Gregory of Nazianzus, Basil the Great, and his brother Gregory. In 392 CE, the Byzantine Emperor Theodosius forbids pagan worship. St. John Chrysostom (John Golden-Tongued), patriarch of Constantinople, is regarded as the finest of all Christian orators in Greek, trained by the sophist Libanius (Arnott; Kennedy).

Byzantium, and thereby Byzantine rhetoric, remains relatively constant for over a thousand years, finally falling to Turkish invaders in 1453. Rome knows no such consistency, even during the Holy Roman Empire, losing to the Visigoths, retaken by Byzantium, falling to the Ostrogoths, taken and retaken for centuries. But more important for what I am presenting here, is Byzantium's relations to the Arabs and to Spain.

Byzantium had an uneasy relation with the Arabs, frequently fighting, mainly along the long border along the Caucuses and the desert, occasional attempts by Arabs at Constantinople itself. But the Byzantines and Arabs both faced a common threat from the Slavs and the Goths. So from about 395 to 636 there is an alliance between the Byzantine Empire and an Arab federation, the *foederati.*

These Arabs learn enough of Constantinople's Greek ways to act as something like border mediators between Byzantium and the Arab peninsula. There are also the Rhomaic Arabs who take residence in Byzantium (Shahid). Add Byzantium's possession of Syria and Persia, later taken by the Saracens, Moslem Arabs, and there remains a relatively strong Byzantine influence to Arab rhetoric.

During these early centuries of the Byzantine Empire, the Visigoths move into Spain. There, they share the peninsula with the Suevi, another Germanic peoples. Northern Africa is taken by yet another group of Germans, the Vandals, who had settled first in southern Spain, sharing that part of the peninsula with another wandering group, the Alans. Except for the Ostrogoths in Italy, the Germanic conquerors are content to exploit, without regard to converting the native populations. We still speak of vandals as despoilers. The Byzantine Empire, however, had its sense of "Roman-ness," an historical right to rule, now joined with the Christian sense of mission. Byzantium could not allow this blow to the empire's historically proven legacy and to the empire's moral mission. By the mid-sixth century, the Byzantine Empire retakes northern Africa and southern Spain (Jenkins). A continuity from the old Roman Empire is reestablished in Spain, now more visibly bearing something of the older Greek ways. Eventually, Spain is again taken by the Visigoths, but there is nothing to suggest any attempts by the Germans to remove the Greek ways of New Rome in the ancient colony of Old Rome (Jenkins).

Mohammad enters the picture in the seventh century. Beginning in 622, Mohammad is gathering a following, having moved to Medina. It is at this time that the Byzantine emperor Heraclius is on a campaign to regain Persia for the empire, a campaign which is to succeed six years later, establishing the True Cross in Persia, the Orthodox Christianity of the Byzantines. Persia is again part of what Heraclius sees as the Roman Empire, Heraclius himself hailed as the new Scipio, Persians having to take on Christianity, the Hellenistic language of the empire, and Greco-Roman rule generally. But Orthodox Christianity had its problems,

nearly two hundred years of debate over the nature or natures of Jesus. Officially, Jesus was to be regarded as having two natures, the Father and the Son. The dominant "heresy" was that Jesus had one divine nature. This was known as *monophysite*. Heraclius tries to bring the factions together, declaring in 639 that whether two natures or one, Jesus was possessed by a single energy or will. The orthodox patriarch of Jerusalem, Sophronius, condemns the idea. Pope Honarium disavows it. And Mohammad offers the Arabs, Persia, Syria, Egypt, poor and once again subject to Greco-Roman rule, an alternative, likely drawn from the Christian, the Jewish, and the Persian creeds which had been implanted in Yemen during Persian rule there: there is but one God, and Mohammad is His prophet. By 628, the same time as Heraclius's retaking of Persia, Mohammad with powerful followers, generals and caliphs, occupies Mecca, only a thousand miles south of Byzantium, formally expelling Mecca's idols. Four years later, Mohammad dies, but the wheels have been set in motion. By 639 the Saracens are in Syria and taking Egypt. Within a few decades, Islam, the "Surrender to God," is established in Persia and most of the southern and eastern parts of the New Roman Empire (Jenkins).

In 711 the Saracen Tariq ibn Ziyad, accompanied by north African Berber volunteers, sails the nine miles which divide the Pillars of Hercules and takes Spain from the Visigoth Roderic. Within the year Spain is under the control of Moslem Arabs. These are the Moors, likely getting their name in having come from Morocco. The Pillars of Hercules are eventually renamed to Jabal Musa on the African side and Jabal Tariq, Gibraltar, on the Spanish. In 732 the Saracens cross the Pyrenees, but are stopped by Charles Martel. In 756 Prince Abdal-Rahman runs to Spain when Syria overthrows the Saracen capital. The new capital is established at Cordoba. Within 150 years Cordoba is established as the largest city in western Europe, a cultural rival to Baghdad and Constantinople. The *mezquita*, the mosque at Cordoba, remains today, displaying its Arabic calligraphy—and its Byzantine mosaics. Spain had been Byzantine and so had the Arabs. The Arabs remained (though not without conflict, like Charlemagne or the Crusades) until 1492, when Ferdinand and Isabela finally oust the Saracens, the Moors. Later in the same year Isabela commissions Christopher Columbus (Abercrombie). The Spaniard conquerors of the New World brought the Arab and the Byzantine, the sophistic, with them.

Now, I have taken this rather long-winded route because I believe it is interesting, and because a special perspective is gained in understanding the historical, as Freire and others make clear. The particular perspective gained here is that the Latino's ways with words could not help but be influenced by the 400 years in which Spain dominated so much of the New World, and that those ways would have been influenced by the 700 years of Arab domination over Spain, and by the 200 years of Byzantium, with its rhetorical heritage going back yet another 700 years. Nearly two thousand years of certain rhetorical ways, albeit in different languages, are not likely to be overcome in the hundred years and less of English domination, especially when we consider that the rhetorical history of English, though through another route, mainly Cicero, also gave a kind of sophistry special privilege up to the eighteenth century.

This gives an historical perspective to contrastive rhetoric, which has had a troubled record among linguists concerned with second language acquisition since it was first introduced by Robert Kaplan in 1966. Part of the problem with accepting the concept was Kaplan's claim in that 1966 article that different discourse patterns reflected different thought patterns, a psychological perspective that wouldn't trouble rhetoricians but would fall outside the purview of linguistics. A related problem would be that claims concerning the psychological and how rhetorical patterns might reflect different nuances of meaning would be difficult to prove empirically. Linguistics is squarely within the scientific paradigm, not given to the speculative.

But since Kaplan's first introduction, there have been empirical studies that have passed the tests of scientific rigor. These have tended to complement the historical. Shirley Ostler, comparing English and Arabic prose, found that modern Arabic prose is essentially unchanged from its Classical origins. The prose tends to have longer sentences than English prose, given to coordinate rather than to subordinate clauses. There is a tendency to balance the subject and the predicate: equal numbers of words on each side of the sentence or else a rhythmical balance. Paragraphs are longer than in English, given to long elaboration, even when there is no evidence of an attempt at being decidedly ornate. The discourse generally tends toward the global, leaning heavily on proverb-like phrases, what English would consider clichés (but what Milton or others prior to the eighteenth century would have called "commonplaces"). Another study of Arabic prose by Sa'Adeddin showed a heightened use of first- and second-person personal pronouns, indicating an attempt at close reader-writer interaction (Lux and Grabe). Ostler's research had students writing papers on personal topics, so she was not able to draw any conclusions along those lines. What she did find, however, was that the Arabic students she studied displayed features of Arabic prose in their writing in English: a greater attention to the sound of the discourse than to the sense, the language more than the logic; in short, the sophistic.

These same tendencies showed up in studies concerning the written prose of Spanish speakers. Paul Lux and William Grabe studied a large number of texts written by Ecuadorians. They found the tendency for longer sentences, greater reader-writer interaction, and a tendency among the Latin American writers to deal in the abstract. Sister Olga Santana-Seda found these same tendencies among Spanish-speaking New York Puerto Ricans, finding also that these writers tended toward non-sequential sentences, that the logical connections between sentences were not always apparent. And María Montaño-Harmon, looking at written Mexican Spanish, found the same thing, noting that the digressions were conscious, using phrases like *"Volvamos a lo que había dicho antes,"* "We'll return to what's been said later." She also found that the Spanish writers tended to what she termed hyperbole, sentences that repeated a point several times, each time using different words, each more ornate than the previous. This is a kind of amplification, the same Asiatic, sophistic tendency found in Cicero. In a side comment, Montaño-Harmon mentions that five of the Anglo-American students she studied showed rhetorical patterns more like the Spanish than the other forty-five Anglo-American writers. These five lived in a border town in southern Arizona, grew up among Chicanos, considered themselves relatively bilingual. She only makes note. But since I am not a linguist, not constrained by the empirically valid and reliable, I can speculate that these students, having come in contact with the sophistic, found it easy to take on the Spanish ways because those ways for English discourse are more deeply embedded than the less elaborated, more clearly linear, idea-centered discourse of modern English.

Nor is this idea that there is something like a linguistic memory idle speculation. Mikhail Bakhtin's theory of language as dialogic suggests something like a historical linkage to language. For Bakhtin there is no objective language "out there" waiting to be appropriated by a listener-speaker, much less a speaker-writer. We come to know the meanings in language by having heard them from others. Our own experiences add a nuance or a special turn of meaning to what we have heard, which we, in turn, pass on to others. This means that those who have passed language on to us have gathered it from others before them, each passing on the language with a newer nuance. Language, then, is social; insofar as it is social, it is also ideological, carrying various worldviews; and insofar as it is social and ideological, it is also historical. The Russian psychologist Lev Vygotsky, seeing much the same thing as Burke or Bakhtin, sees language as essentially epistemological, as the means by which we come to know, seeing the word as "a microcosm of human consciousness" (Schuster).

James McConnell suggests that memory may be biochemically transmitted through RNA (ribonucleic acid). In a series of experiments, McConnell and his associates trained a flatworm to go through a maze. The planarian was then chopped up, and the pieces were injected into other flatworms. The untrained flatworms who had received the pieces of the earlier learned to navigate the maze at a sig-

nificantly faster rate than those who hadn't. Memory as physical, a body chemical biologically transmitted. Maybe. We know that language is an inherent biological quality in humans. There is at least the possibility that particular linguistic ways may be carried through RNA in something like Carl Jung's archaic imprints.

Steven, my son, was born into a monolingual household. Grandma and Grandpa spoke to him solely in English. When he first began to speak, he would say "walk-side" instead of sidewalk. No one says "walk-side." But in Spanish, nouns come before adjectives.

Steven would not get the word *toes,* a mighty simple word. He'd insist on calling toes "the fingers of the feet," a literal translation of the Spanish for toes. It was he, back then, that reminded me of the Spanish expression for toes. Where did he get this?

Whether biologically transmitted beyond the basic ability to learn language or not (to return from the flight of speculation and to skirt the possibility of being read as somehow advocating something like biological determinacy, of being an Arthur Jensen), it is clear that language is passed on by people. People would pass language on in particular ways. Those ways would reflect social and historical preferences, traditions, conventions—rhetorics.

Nor would the differences between speaking and writing, although real, alter socio-historical and culturally influenced rhetorics significantly, except consciously. At bottom, speaking and writing stem from the same source—language, the differences between speaking and writing amounting to little more than the different conventions which arise out of particular forms following particular functions, the needs for the written that can't be met by the spoken (like transmitting information to many over time, and the demands that become imposed on the language producer in not having the benefits of face-to-face interaction, as well as other things (Vachek). Both historical and empirical research suggest that for Spanish-speakers, or for those exposed to the ways of the Spanish-speaker, those preferred rhetorical ways are fundamentally sophistic.

My problems with logic in those graduate courses stemmed from my not having been exposed to a language that had as its primary focus logic. My exposure to written discourse prior to graduate school was never of the academic variety. Literature is deemed such, in part, because of the imaginative ways in which it plays with or even consciously disregards convention. Even the nonfiction I would have been exposed to in college consisted of things written when Cicero thrived, like Milton's Prolusions. When I didn't understand what was being argued in my Professorial Discourse Analyses, I did not attempt to puzzle out the logic; my concerns were with *patterns,* the sounds. I would even throw in the word *however* into my writing, without intending "on the contrary." It just sounded right. I got called on it only once, in graduate school, after three years of writing papers.

That I was able to get through undergraduate school in this way tells me that teachers have different expectations of undergraduates than of graduates. They might have been satisfied simply to see one who enjoyed playing with language, one willing to take what they perceived as chances, predisposed to being "serious," abstract, likely the only sophist in those classes, surely the only Latino, though with the fluency of the native English speaker, long ago well trained in matters of grammatical correctness and proper spelling, thereby not given the special focus of the foreign-language speaker's rhetoric by the teachers.

With graduate school, however, style must have taken a back seat to concept for many. If my writing was "too formulaic," it was likely in my using contemporary commonplaces, mimicking the formulas of psychological interpretations of texts or Harold Bloom's anxiety of influence or even deconstruction. If it was "too novel," it was likely too speculative, that global tendency of Spanish-speakers, of Arabs, of sophists; or maybe it was stylistically novel, long sentences, digressions which would prove to be relevant, but only for the patient reader.

It was surely these things that prompted one professor to give me the gift for my imagination and later prompted him to ask what my point had been.

Donald Murray says "writing is revising" ("Internal Revision" 85). This is excruciatingly clear to me. If I am to discover my thinking in the writing, I must give vent to my sophistic tendencies. This is not Peter Elbow's freewriting. I agonize over word choices or sentence constructions. I deliberate over opening sentences to paragraphs, over transitions. I backtrack and redirect. I correct. But I also know that I will have to go back when I am done to reconsider the logical predispositions of my audience, make connections explicit, relegate some things to footnotes, delete others, even if they are significant to me. The more theoretical portions of this book display that consciousness. Scientific discourse is never quite in my grasp to this day, proffering drafts to those who are good at grantsmanship and the like, always receiving long "advice" on how I might revise. My writing is always subject to rhetorical "translation."

I speak of such things in courses I teach, not only for the sake of those from Latino backgrounds, but for all. There can be no telling of the linguistic backgrounds of the students. Most have not been exposed to the writing of academics. Some will—or do—teach in schools where the majority of their students will come from, or do come from, linguistic backgrounds other than English. I speak of the imperial conquests and the rhetoric that traveled with the conquerors. I introduce Averroës, the Arab Ibn Rushd, who wrote commentaries on Aristotle, and the class becomes eleventh-century Toledo (Spain, not Ohio), where Christians, Jews, and Muslims translated Averroës and thereby Aristotle into Latin.

Aristotle's ways are presented. After some talk about Aristotle's logic and rhetoric—the essential definition, induction and deduction, the syllogism, and the enthymeme, a kind of syllogism still used in argumentation—we work on the logic and language of a student's text, suggesting ways for a rhetorical translation. We test those translations by consciously seeking to use cohesive devices, words like *however* or *consequently* at the sentence level; word repetitions between sentences; transitions among paragraphs. I supply a relatively short list of such devices (see Halliday and Hasan; Markels; Witte and Faigley). We try to find cohesive devices that fit, discuss it when none does. Sometimes none should, and it's okay. Often new ways of seeing what is being attempted present themselves, revisions. "Tighter" papers result most often, closer to revision than to correction. Ways of seeing, worldviews, and rhetorical predispositions are allowed expression; logic is not reduced to right and wrong, or even propriety; logic is explicitly discussed as yet another convention. Discussion of the historical and the rhetorical so as to be conscious of the mandates of those who rule, especially in classrooms, becomes one way to meet Freire's concern that the liberatory teacher provide a process for the development of critical consciousness without being what he terms *laissez-faire,* without denying the technical training required for academic success.

Victor the graduate student is walking to Safeway one day when one of his professors jumps out of a car to ask if he would be willing to take an academic job. The job is to be a "reader," grading papers for an undergraduate course. The requirements are that the course must have more than fifty students enrolled and that the reader be recommended by the professor teaching the course. He accepts.

Poverty has him living with his family in Mickey's unfinished, unheated basement. Victor wears his sister's down vest and his own gloves, vapor steaming from his nostrils, grading papers in line with his professor's way of seeing, not his own, all literature a reflection of archetypes, Carl Jung and Northrop Frye. Carol computes his real wages: twenty-five cents an hour. And he is grateful.

He earns a reputation as a reader, needs only to hang around the graduate student lounge the first few days of every quarter to get a job. He knows the exploitation. But it's okay somehow. One quarter he is forced to sell his *Riverside Shakespeare* for a dozen eggs, a quart of milk, and a quarter pound of coffee. He loved that book. The next quarter he is asked to be a reader for an undergraduate Shakespeare course. He receives a new copy of the *River-*

side Shakespeare. He has found a more tangible rationalization for being a reader than "good experience." The reward is the book, a symbol for the love he does not yet understand, the love of learning, the love of teaching.

The next year he is granted a teaching assistantship. It's an awkward job, given his mixed successes at writing. He follows the text and borrows classroom strategies from more experienced TAs. There is success. He is well liked. But he knows that he doesn't know what he is doing.

The local Thriftway. Pays for groceries with food stamps. The checker is a former student who throws him a set of keys: "Take a look at my new BMW." Victor steals the grocery cart to get food and diapers home. There is envy, a sense that something isn't right, but he knows he'd rather teach than check groceries.

In his class, a Mexican American student, dressed in an ROTC uniform, writes about his grandmother's gibberish. "Gibberish" is the word he used to define a language the student doesn't understand. The student writes another paper about the deterrent necessity of nuclear stockpiling. Another student, after reading *Catch-22,* explains how Yossarian is simply a coward. There's something "off" about the student's writing, apart from his sensibility. The sensibility troubles Victor, but not inordinately: Victor knows about the headlong drive to assimilate. That isn't the wrong that he can't pin down. Victor can't pin down what's off about the writing itself.

Another Mexican American, in another class, approaches Victor after class, carrying his copy of *Fahrenheit 451,* required reading for the course. The student doesn't understand the reference to a *salon.* Victor explains that this is just another word for the living room. No understanding in the student's eyes. He tries Spanish: *la sala.* Still nothing. The student had grown up as a migrant worker. And Victor remembers the white student who had been in his class a quarter ago, who had written about not understanding racism, that there was none where he had grown up, in Wennatchee, that he had played with the children of his father's migrant workers without there being any hostility. His father's workers. Property. Property that doesn't know of living rooms. And Victor thought of what the man from Wennatchee knew, what the ROTC Mexican American knew, what the migrant worker knew. And he thought of getting up the next morning to go with Serena to St. Mary's for cheese and butter. And he knew there was something he was not doing in his composition classrooms.

Works Cited

Abercrombie, Thomas J. "When the Moors Ruled Spain." *National Geographic* 174:1 (1988): 87–119.

Arnott, Peter. *The Byzantines and Their World.* New York: St. Martin's, 1973.

Bartholomae, David and Anthony Petrosky. *Facts, Artifacts, and Counterfacts: A Theory and Method for a Reading and Writing Course.* Upper Montclair, NJ: Boynton/Cook, 1986.

———. *Ways of Reading: An Anthology for Writers.* New York: St. Martin's, 1987.

Burke, Kenneth. *A Rhetoric of Motives.* Berkeley: U of California P, 1969.

Cohen, Arthur M. and Florence B. Brawer. *The American Community College.* 2nd ed. San Francisco: Jossey-Bass, 1989.

Crowley, Sharon. Personal communication.

Emig, Janet. "Writing as a Mode of Learning." *College Composition and Communication* 28 (1977): 122–28.

Freire, Paulo. *Cultural Action for Freedom.* Cambridge, MA: Harvard Educational Review and Center for the Study of Development and Social Change, 1970.

———. *Pedagogy of the Oppressed.* Trans. Myra Bergman Ramos. New York: Herder and Herder, 1970.

Haswell, Richard H. "Minimal Marking." *College English* 45 (1983): 600–604.

Hirsch, E.D., Jr. *Cultural Literacy: What Every American Needs to Know.* Boston: Houghton Mifflin, 1987.

Jenkins, Romilly. *Byzantium: The Imperial Centuries, AD 610–1071.* Toronto: U of Toronto P, 1966.

Jensen, Arthur R. "The Differences Are Real." *Psychology Today* 7 (1973): 80–82, 84, 86.

———. "How Much Can We Boost IQ and Scholastic Achievement?" *Harvard Education Review* 39 (1969): 1–123.

Kaplan, Robert B. "Cultural Thought Patterns and Intercultural Education." *Language Learning* 16 (1966): 1–20.

Kennedy, George. *Classical Rhetoric and Its Christian and Secular Tradition from Ancient to Modern Times.* Chapel Hill: U of North Carolina P, 1980.

Leff, Michael C. "In Search of Ariadne's Thread: A Review of the Recent Literature on Rhetorical Theory." *Central States Speech Journal* 29 (1978): 73–91.

Lux, Paul and William Grabe. "Multivariate Approaches to Contrastive Rhetoric." *Linguas Modernas* 18 (1991): 133–60.

Markels, Robin Bell. *A New Perspective on Cohesion in Expository Paragraphs.* Carbondale: Southern Illinois UP, 1984.

McConnell, James V. "Confessions of a Scientific Humorist." *Impact* 19 (1969): 3–9.

Murray, Donald M. "Internal Revision: A Process of Discovery." In *Research on Composing: Points of Departure.* Eds. Charles R. Cooper and Lee Odell. Urbana, IL: NCTE, 1978.

Ostler, Shirley E. "English in Parallels: A Comparison of English and Arabic Prose." In *Writing Across Languages: Analysis of L2 Text.* Eds. Ulla Connor and Robert B. Kaplan. Reading, MA: Addison-Wesley, 1987.

Schuster, Charles I. "Mikhail Bakhtin as Rhetorical Theorist." *College English* 47 (1985): 594–607.

Shahid, Irfan. *Byzantium and the Arabs in the Fifth Century.* Washington, DC: Dumbarton Oaks, 1989.

Vachek, Josef. *Written Language: General Problems and Problems of English.* The Hague: Mouton, 1973.

Witte, Stephen P. and Lester Faigley. "Coherence, Cohesion, and Writing Quality." *College Composition and Communication* 32 (1981): 189–204.

Arguing about Literacy

Patricia Bizzell

This essay is taken from College English *50 (1988): 141–53. A slightly longer version appears in Bizzell's collection of essays entitled* Academic Discourse and Critical Consciousness. *Pittsburgh: U of Pittsburgh, 1992. 238–55.*

I

Arguments about literacy typically take the same form. One kind of literacy holds a commanding position, that which comprises the ways of using language valued by the academy and the upper social classes with which it is associated. The dominance of this academic literacy is challenged by people who have made their way into the schools but whose native tongues are at a relatively greater remove from the academic dialect, whose preferred modes of developing ideas conflict with the linear logic and impersonal posture of academic debate, and whose cultural treasures are not included in the academic canon. These challenges of academic literacy typically come from social groups at some remove from the upper classes—that is, from the lower classes, foreign born, non-white, and/or female.

Although they have won some battles, these oppositional forces seem to have lost the war. For example, on the college level they have effected change in isolated instances: perhaps through instituting a pluralistic method of holistic essay exam scoring that avoids penalizing nonstandard dialect writers; perhaps through getting selections from "minority" artists included in reading anthologies. But the requirement that students master academic literacy in order to continue their educations is still institutionalized in the great majority of writing-programs in this country (see Applebee; Baron; Finegan).

Yet this view of the monolithic power of academic literacy is misleading, and itself politically oppressive. I suspect that historical study of academic literacy would show the steady influence of oppositional forces for change. The academic literacy that is now required of American college students is, I suspect, more pluralistic than that enforced at the turn of the century. It is not my purpose to prove this here; because I think of myself professionally as a supporter of the opposition, I certainly do not mean to suggest that no further change is needed. I simply wish to suggest that change is possible; indeed, this possibility is implied by the argumentative tack typically taken by defenders of the status quo, of academic literacy as it is presently constituted.

Typically, people arguing this position have sought to draw attention away from the social class basis of academic literacy. Rather, they have sought arguments that rest on some supposedly transcendent standards, standards preserved above the merely political. Such "foundationalist" arguments, as contemporary philosophers and literary theorists have taught us to call them, aim to end debate, and with it, the embarrassing questions about who holds the political power to decide what constitutes good language use.

In this essay I examine some of these apolitical arguments for the academic status quo. First I discuss arguments adduced from social science research in what I might call literal literacy, that is, the study of what happens when people who were previously completely illiterate learn elementary reading and writing. We rarely see such people in American colleges. Then I look at work on so-called cultural literacy, most notably that of E. D. Hirsch, Jr., which seeks to be more responsive to the actual situation in our colleges by posing the "literacy problem" in terms of competing bodies of knowledge, but which nevertheless attempts to resolve debate in a way that conceals political implications. Finally I argue for a view of literacy—and thus implicitly defend a way of arguing about literacy—that is based on a properly rhetorical understanding of history and knowledge.

II

Social science research in literacy assumes that some kind of decisive change takes place when individuals and societies acquire literacy. Jack Goody summarizes these changes as:

> the move from myth to history, from magic to science, status to contract, cold to hot [an allusion to Lévi-Strauss's "raw/cooked" distinction], concrete to abstract, collective to individual, ritual to rationality. (3)

Yet the social science approach to literacy is not as dichotomizing as Goody's characterization suggests. Social science research tends to focus on how these changes occur within individuals, changes in the ways they think and interact with the world, but also to consider these cognitive changes as conditioned by the social contexts in which literacy is used. Hence there is no monolithic concept of what happens when any individual or society, regardless of the historical circumstances, acquires literacy. Social science research in literacy is moving toward a more pluralistic view of "multiple literacies" (Scribner and Cole) or a "continuum of orality and literacy" (Tannen; see also Heath).

Research on literacy, however, has come into the debate on college reading and writing by way of the work of humanists who study literacy, such as classical philologist Eric Havelock and literary critic Walter Ong. In examining changes attendant upon literacy, humanists tend to focus on the changes occurring within discourse—stylistic changes and

to infer from the discourse the cognitive and cultural changes accompanying it. Humanists tend to dichotomize non-literate and literate states of being, and to reify the two states into all-embracing conceptual universes of orality and literacy (see Ong).

Among literacy scholars, the humanist position is called the "Great Cognitive Divide" theory of literacy. According to this theory, an oral culture, in which speech is the sole medium of verbal exchange, is characterized in its verbal style and in its thinking by parataxis, the simple juxtaposition of ideas; by concrete imagery that appeals to the senses and the emotions; by ritualized references to authority in the form of proverbs, epithets, incantations, and other formulae; and by an agonistic posture in disputation.

According to the humanists, this "orality" can be changed only through mastery of alphabetic literacy, in which symbols are assigned to phonemes rather than to syllables or whole concepts. Alphabetic literacy is more "efficient" than non-alphabetic systems because a much smaller number of symbols represents a much greater number of words, with much less ambiguity, thus enabling more people to master the system more quickly, and allowing textual content to be more varied without the need to codify it in orthodox formulae for easy recognition. Hence alphabetic literacy gives rise to the following characteristics of style and thinking: hypotaxis, the subordination of one idea to another in logical hierarchies; generalizations that appeal to reason and text-assisted memory for validation; and a dialectical relation to authority, encouraging the on-going, disinterested criticism of ideas.

Humanists argue that the single set of changes they see as characteristic of all literacy is always attendant upon the acquisition of literacy and is independent of social variables. They assert that the change from oral thinking to literate thinking can be achieved only through acquisition of alphabetic literacy, and that it is always achieved when alphabetic literacy has been acquired. These two assertions, however, have not been confirmed among variously literate contemporary peoples. Social scientists describe a wider variety of changes than do humanists and link particular changes to features of the particular social situation in which literacy is used. Some forms of alphabetic literacy do not convey all the cognitive changes associated with "Great Divide" literate thinking (see Heath); and some forms of non-alphabetic literacy do encourage some aspects of literate thinking (see Scribner and Cole).

This is not to say that social science scholarship on literacy has disproved the humanist "Great Divide" idea. Rather, the conflict between social scientists' and humanists' findings suggests that they are not looking at the same data. Specifically, social science research has found that the changes accompanying literacy most closely conform to the humanists' expectations when the literacy has been learned in a Western-type secular school. This match suggests that the orality/literacy dichotomy of the humanists has been derived from studying a subset of all possible literate texts, namely those texts that reflect the kinds of thinking induced by academic literacy.

Typically, however, humanist literacy scholars do not acknowledge their conflation of literacy and academic literacy. Thus not only do they reduce all possible cognitive gains attendant upon literacy acquired in various social circumstances to the narrow set of abilities associated with academic literacy, but they also foster arguments that any cognitive gains to be had from any kind of literacy are available only from mastery of academic literacy.

Such arguments have been used in aid of requiring students to learn Standard English because this dialect is preferred in academic literacy. Thomas J. Farrell argues native speakers of Black English score lower than whites on I.Q. tests and do poorly in school because Black English is essentially an oral, not a literate, language. These students' difficulties would be remedied, he claims, by teaching them Standard English; mastering the copula and other elements in the grammatical "alphabet" of Standard English would automatically enable them to think "literately"—that is, in ways sanctioned by academic literacy. In making this argument, Farrell

ignores the fact that the Black English-speaking students he is discussing are not in fact totally illiterate—for example, they read well enough to take the tests upon whose results Farrell's case depends so heavily. Farrell does not recognize the existence of any literate abilities here because the students have not mastered the literate abilities that count for him, namely those associated with academic literacy.

III

The concept of "cultural literacy" has emerged as a corrective to "Great Divide" literacy theories. This concept suggests that all literacy is in fact cultural literacy—that is, that no symbol system in and of itself induces cognitive changes. A cultural context is necessary to invest the features of the system with meaning, to give them the significance that then induces changes in thinking. An alphabet, or a standard grammar, does not somehow structurally force changes in the user's mental apparatus. Rather, such changes flow from the cultural significance attached to mastering the alphabet or the grammar—the kinds of knowledge and social roles open to those who have achieved mastery and so on.

The development of E. D. Hirsch's thought on literacy illustrates how the need for a concept of cultural literacy arises. Hirsch's first major contribution is *The Philosophy of Composition* (1977). Here, like other defenders of the status quo, he attempts to resolve the debate over what should constitute academic literacy by establishing a definition that transcends social contexts and the local ideological agendas to which they give rise. "An authentic ideology of literacy," Hirsch claims, "inheres in the subject itself, and should guide our teaching of it" (xiii).

Hirsch deduces his "privileged ideology" of literacy from psycholinguistic research on memory and information processing, which he interprets as describing the characteristics of an ideally efficient language. He asserts that these characteristics may largely be found in formal written Standard English. Hirsch thus suppresses ideology both in the reasons he gives for teaching Standard English and in the results he hopes to gain from such teaching. He argues in favor of requiring all students to master Standard English because of its cognitive status as the most "communicatively efficient" form of the language. And his predictions of cognitive gains from mastery, like the arguments of humanist literacy scholars for alphabetic literacy, attribute these gains to the formal structure of the symbol system—like the alphabet, Standard English is more "efficient"—rather than to any contextual influences.

Moreover, Hirsch seeks to require mastery not merely of Standard English, but of a particular style of writing Standard English, a style encapsulated in the maxims of Strunk and White's well-known manual, which he recommends. His argument for the cognitive superiority of a clear, concise style of Standard English, like the humanists' argument for the cognitive characteristics of literate style, fails to notice that this style is socially situated. Hirsch's preferred verbal style, and the humanists' literate style, both appear upon further analysis to be the preferred style and thought patterns of academics, not necessarily of all literate people. In short, Hirsch's candidate for privileged ideology of literacy is not as context-free as he claims: it is an academic ideology of literacy.

Many critics have noted problems with the theory of literacy Hirsch defends in *The Philosophy of Composition* (see Bizzell and Herzberg). So has Hirsch. In this book, Hirsch defines a concept of "relative readability" that, he claims, enables him to measure the communicative efficiency of any text. He received a grant from the National Endowment for the Humanities to test the applicability of this concept. His experiments changed his mind. Hirsch and his associates at the University of Virginia "systematically degraded" academic texts (selections from Will and Ariel Durant, Bruce Catton, and others) to render them more difficult according to the standards of relative readability (Hirsch, "Culture and Literacy" 38–42). They then asked different groups ("literate adults" [38], community college basic writing students and others) to read either the degraded text or the original and to answer some comprehension questions.

Hirsch expected to find, of course, that the original texts, those that rated higher in relative readability, would generate better comprehension scores than the degraded texts. Instead, test results were unpredictable—until Hirsch realized the comprehension scores were tied more closely to the readers' prior knowledge of the subject discussed in the reading selection than to the stylistic features of the selection. If prior knowledge, which is conditioned by the reader's social background, affects readability, then social context in general must affect literacy in general much more than Hirsch had thought when he wrote *The Philosophy of Composition*.

Hirsch has explicitly rejected what he calls the "formalist" bias of his book in his essay "Cultural Literacy" (161). He abandons a "Great Divide" approach to literacy in defining "cultural literacy" as "the translinguistic knowledge on which linguistic literacy depends. You can't have one without the other" (165). He argues that "without appropriate, tacitly shared background knowledge" no audience can understand a text, whether the text is an astrophysics journal or a daily newspaper (165). Hirsch uses the term "canonical" to refer to this necessary knowledge, thus suggesting it is essential not only to reading comprehension, but also to membership in the social group that constitutes the audience for the text that the knowledge renders intelligible. Any audience, whether for an astrophysics journal or a daily newspaper, will have its canonical knowledge that, as a common possession of the group, helps the group to cohere, to distinguish itself from others, and to exclude or initiate outsiders.

To this point, Hirsch's "cultural literacy" position sorts well with the social-science approach to literacy. Hirsch suggests that different audiences have different bodies of shared knowledge that enable them to read the texts of their group. In other words, he is describing multiple literacies, and his notion of canonical knowledge helps to explain where multiple literacies come from. The understanding that prior knowledge conditions language use is of the utmost importance. This insight goes far to prevent the "diagnosis" of unsuccessful college writers as cognitively deficient (see

Bizzell; Rose). Instead, as David Bartholomae has shown, we can see them as beginners in academic discourse, trying to find a way to use language for their own purposes in a community whose knowledge they do not yet fully share.

But when Hirsch turns to pedagogy, he begins once again to argue prescriptively. He begins his "Cultural Literacy" essay with this implied causal statement: "The national decline in our literacy has accompanied a decline in our use of common, nationwide materials in the subject most closely connected with literacy, 'English'" (159). Hirsch then invokes the turn-of-the-century practice of teaching from lists of authors, first established (although Hirsch does not say so) by Harvard University. While he names them at length. Hirsch denies he wants to recommend a return to the particular texts that made up these lists (159–60). But he returns to the idea of uniform lists in his recommendation for the formation of a "National Curriculum Board" that could establish new lists for contemporary schools (167–68). Indeed, Hirsch has recently established a Cultural Literacy Foundation with the avowed purpose of designing standardized tests of students' knowledge, tests intended to be used to shape school curricula.

What exactly is wrong with defining cultural literacy in terms of a common list? Opponents question the social and political biases that would inform the process of choosing works for the list (see Warnock). But Hirsch claims that his list is fair and representative (he developed a list, recently published in book form, with the aid of grants from Exxon and the National Endowment for the Humanities; note that Hirsch's continued success in receiving financial support for his work suggests its potential broad influence). In addition to canonical literature, Hirsch includes non-literary references such as the Declaration of Independence, minority figures such as Frederick Douglass, and popular culture items such as Pinocchio. By and large, however, the concessions to popular and minority cultures appear to be few. The core of the list is the core of Western high culture.

Hirsch does not deny that "choosing the contents of cultural literacy" requires a "difficult politi-

cal decision" (167). Moreover, he seems to rule out any transcendent principles for deciding what works belong on the list—a departure from his habitual practice—admitting instead that selection will proceed by "discussion, argument, and compromise" (167). He does not want to require that every American school teach every work on the list—local selectivity and addition would be allowed, within some limits, presumably. He thus attempts to forestall critics who would argue that his dream for a national curriculum is totalitarian, racist, sexist, and laden with social class prejudice.

Nevertheless, the function of history in Hirsch's argument points to the argument's crucial weakness: his idea of how canonical knowledge gets established. One cannot argue with Hirsch's choices of items for his list without tackling this issue first. Hirsch justifies his concentration on Western high or academic culture on grounds that this is our tradition: "no culture exists that is ignorant of its own traditions" (167). At this point Hirsch turns from the question of how this particular tradition got to be *the* tradition, concentrating instead on the need for *some* tradition to unite an increasingly fragmented society. He hopes that we Americans will decide we want "a broadly literate culture that unites our cultural fragments enough to allow us to write to one another and read what our fellow citizens have written" (167). To want this, as Hirsch himself points out, is to adopt the traditional point of view, "Our traditional, Jeffersonian answer" (167).

History functions at this crucial point in the argument in several ways. First, history is depicted as presenting us with the core curriculum of Western academic culture, essentially as a *fait accompli*. We are not now in a position to argue about the canonical status of most of the works on Hirsch's putative list, for they have been established by the impersonal force of history. Hirsch does not depict modern people as completely powerless before the force of history. We can add works to the canon, for instance. But no matter how unfair we now think the processes of history to have been, when we see how history has systematically excluded certain social groups from representation in the high culture, we can do nothing about those injustices now.

More importantly, history blocks our examining the attitudes that compel us to submit to it. One such attitude is that those cultural subgroups not presently represented in the academic canon are "fragmentary" and in need of unification. In short, the academic canon is now performing for Hirsch exactly the same function that Standard English did in *The Philosophy of Composition:* he imagines that it has been granted by history the power to transcend and hence to control local cultural canons. Hirsch detaches the academic canon from its own social origins, which are systematically suppressed—for example, in his forgetting to mention that the turn-of-the-century lists he admires were first promulgated by Harvard, a highly race-, sex-, and class-determined institution.

Moreover, Hirsch assumes that history has granted the academic canon the right to exercise this power over other cultures, through establishing canonical ways of thinking and of using language, canonical values, verbal styles, and mindsets as the "most important" to our national culture. This kind of valorizing of the canon resembles the process whereby humanist literacy scholars establish the importance of literate ways of thinking and of using language. Hirsch links the two arguments when he says: "Estimable cultures exist that are ignorant of Shakespeare and the First Amendment. Indeed, estimable cultures exist that are entirely ignorant of reading and writing" (167). Humanist literacy scholars frequently protest, as Hirsch does here, that their oral/literate dichotomy is not meant to imply any absolute inferiority of oral culture. They simply claim that the cognitive abilities fostered by literate culture are necessary now, the world over. Similarly, Hirsch does not wish to claim that everyone ignorant of his academic canon is inferior. But everyone ignorant of this canon in America is inferior because knowledge of this canon is necessary to enter the national literate forums—as defined by Hirsch.

Hence, "history" in Hirsch's argument becomes a cover term, concealing not only the process whereby certain texts achieve canonical status but also the process whereby attitudes towards the very existence of any canon, and its function in society, become ingrained. Hirsch adopts a determinist view of the power of history. He seems to say that both the content of the academic canon and our attitudes about the rightness of its dominance have been fixed by the past life of the society that has formed us. We may be able to make minor changes, but basically, we must submit. If one believes this, then there is no objection to teaching in the most indoctrinating fashion possible. What students lack is canonical knowledge: let's give it to them.

IV

How can we avoid the "foundationalism" of humanist literacy work and of cultural literacy work such as Hirsch's when we argue about literacy? I would like to suggest a rhetorical view that offers both a better understanding of how to argue and a better understanding of literacy itself. First how to argue: from a rhetorical point of view, one is never able to prove an opponent wrong absolutely, to present evidence that demonstrates the opponent's error and one's own correctness for all times and places. This is the kind of proof sought in "foundationalist" arguments. Rather, from a rhetorical point of view, what one does when arguing is to seek to persuade a particular audience, in a particular time and place. An argument is provisionally correct if it carries the day, but is always subject to dialectical revision.

This rhetorical view of argument means that in framing an argument, what one needs is not absolute truth or unimpeachable evidence, but rather means of persuasion that will move this particular audience. Rhetoric has traditionally been defined as the study of the means of persuasion. "Means" of persuasion can vary from enthymemes to gestures that express a speaker's ethos to tropes that are presumed to have some affect built into them structurally. The study of these means of persuasion has two ends: first, to call them to the communicator's attention, and second, to investigate *what* they mean in a given rhetorical situation. Aristotle notes, for example, that appeals to prudence will move old men, but not young ones. To understand how to use the means of persuasion effectively the rhetorician needs to know the audience well. This can mean knowing the audience's age and social condition, the audience's personal interests, and more, the audience's values.

I would argue that this focus on the means of persuasion implies not only a notion of the provisionality of all arguments but also a view of literacy as something local, something shared in a social context. The rhetorical investigation of audience entails attempting to share the canonical knowledge that constitutes the group as an audience. In other words, it is research into the group's cultural literacy. In classical times, such study appeared to be the study of universal human nature because rhetoricians typically had to do with a single, homogeneous audience. Increasingly since the Renaissance, however, rhetoric has sought to deal with the pluralism of the modern condition. Rhetoricians may very well have to deal with audiences whose shared knowledge seems quite alien at first. Thus the study of contemporary audiences has come to seem like comparative anthropology, while tracing the development of shared knowledge over time calls for discursively sophisticated historical study. In other words, rhetoric's commitment to understanding the means of persuasion has led, especially in modern, pluralistic times, into the historical and comparative study of ideologies.

I do not intend to suggest, however, that such study raises rhetoric above ideology. That would leave me open to a charge rhetoricians have faced ever since Plato, namely that they are fundamentally dishonest because they try to be in a community without being of it—to use some of its shared knowledge to achieve their own purposes while preserving a cynical distance on the world-view implied by the knowledge. The best answer to this charge was suggested by the Sophists, namely that rhetoric itself creates all knowledge (see Gronbeck; Engnell). Knowledge is not a content conveyed by rhetoric; knowledge is what ensues when rhetoric is successful, when rhetorician and audience reach agreement. If this is true, then by the same token,

rhetoricians cannot share a community's knowledge while remaining unchanged. Rhetoricians' own world-views will be influenced to the extent that they assimilate the community's knowledge to their own discourse.

In other words, when you argue with someone, your own thinking is inevitably influenced by what you have to do to persuade the other person. All arguments are not only ideological, but dialectical. Hirsch's approach to the "problem of canon formation" is weakened by ignoring this aspect of argumentation. For him canon formation entails simply figuring out what texts (in the broadest sense) are in fact the most influential. Hirsch rules out any "merely ideological" attack on a work's canonical status. If it is in the canon now, it can be dislodged only if one can "prove" that it has not in fact had such influence. But current debates among literary critics over canon formation have been much more ideological than this. For example, feminist critics have argued that works by women writers should be moved into the canon in order to change the ideological bent of scholarship, to correct its male chauvinism. At the same time, many of these feminist arguments are couched in an argumentative style sanctioned by the male-dominated literary-critical tradition and designed explicitly to appeal to such readers. The feminists have been influenced by the audience with whom they are arguing—as some feminists, in turn, have noted and deplored!

Fundamentally, Hirsch sees ignorance of the canon in terms of a problem in deciphering literary allusions. He does not do justice to the value of his own insight concerning the crucial importance of knowledge to participation in discourse, for he does not consider the possibility that the very ability to count allusions depends on the canonical knowledge one already has. The researchers compiling the common list will be guided in their perceptions of what is frequently cited by what they can recognize on the basis of their own education. The researchers' own cultural assumptions will predetermine what will be perceived as "important." An example of this kind of circular reasoning about influence can be found in Hirsch's "Cultural

Literacy" essay, in which, as I noted earlier, he cites Thomas Jefferson as an authority to support his view that a canon including Jefferson's Declaration of Independence should be imposed on all American schools.

If we see the production of literacy as a collaborative effort—if we adopt a rhetorical perspective on literacy, which dialectically relates means of persuasion to audience's canonical knowledge—then we need a pedagogy much less prescriptive than Hirsch's or Farrell's. Teaching academic literacy becomes a process of constructing academic literacy, creating it anew in each class through the interaction of the professor's and the students' cultural resources. I would argue that this is in fact what happens, very slowly—hence the increasing pluralism in academic literacy noted earlier.

But if one wishes to foster this process, to support oppositional forces as I said I did, then the problem with this model of the dialectical formation of academic literacy is that professor and students do not appear to be equal partners in the collaboration. The professor automatically has more persuasive power for what he or she wants to include in academic literacy, simply by virtue of the social power his or her position provides over the students. A larger version of this problem has emerged in connection with the concept of "interpretive communities" in reader-response literary criticism and writing across the curriculum work: when the professor initiates students into currently acceptable methods of responding to texts—or into the practices of any other academic discipline— isn't he or she simply forcing conformity to these practices? Even if we understand disciplinary practices to be developed by human beings, the master practitioners in the field, rather than to be discovered in some absolute form, independent of human agency, isn't the result for the student the same, namely submission? Can change occur only when the material world erupts into the academic community and forces an adjustment—but not as a result of the initiatives of any human newcomers?

I do not know that anyone has yet articulated a truly collaborative pedagogy of academic literacy, one that successfully integrates the professor's tra-ditional canonical knowledge and the students' non-canonical cultural resources. Certainly I cannot do so. It is extremely difficult to abrogate in the classroom, by a collective act of will, the social arrangements that separate professors and students outside the classroom. Integration has not been achieved if students are simply allowed to express affective responses to canonical knowledge as conveyed by the professor; or if the professor simply abdicates the role of guide to tradition and encourages the students to define a course agenda from their own interests. For example, we might expect Richard Rorty to favor a pedagogy that raises questions about canonical knowledge and opens the academy to new cultural resources. This has been his project in his own scholarly work. Yet in discussing pedagogy, even Rorty can find no way around an unequal relation between professor and students.

Rorty argues that we should "give students a chance for intellectual hero-worship" by depicting the "great men" of traditional intellectual history not as geniuses in touch with transcendent truth, but as "fighters against their time" who "were taking on the problems which the community around them had inherited" and "inventing new forms of communal life by inventing new songs, new discourses, new polities" (10). To be sure, this approach historicizes intellectual work and emphasizes its discursive basis. But students are cast very much in a subordinate role, as worshippers, and whom they are worshipping is made clearer later in the same essay, in which Rorty notes with approval: "In practice, the content of core curricula is whatever books the most influential members of the faculty of a given institution all happen to have liked, or all like to teach—the books which give them the greatest pleasure" (12).

In other words, students are to be seduced into cultural literacy by their admiration, first, for the master practitioners who are directing their lives in the classroom, and second, for their masters' intimate friends to be found in great books. Rorty uses the term "eroticism" to characterize the teacher-student relationship he desires. Of course, this is meant as an ironic commentary on Plato, but

Rorty's version of cultural literacy itself evokes the homoeroticism of the *Phaedrus*. It seems quite appropriate that throughout his essay, Rorty uses the masculine pronoun exclusively to refer to the masters and their worshippers.

It's not that I wish to inveigh against any pleasure resulting from reciprocal acts of teaching and learning, or, more important, against Plato's vision in the *Phaedrus* of an education that reaches the whole person, not intellect alone. Rather, I simply wish to show how difficult it can be to make education truly reciprocal, and not something done to one person by another. Rorty's model inevitably takes on these instrumental overtones, and typically, they are accompanied by elitist implications such as attend Platonic homoeroticism. The masters, too, learned to love their favorites from their own teachers.

Such a closed system would indeed seem to support the view that only a radical change in historical circumstances, an eruption of the material world, can force changes in the academic canon. Once change has been initiated by impersonal forces, students may find the opportunity to act on their own cultural agendas—some newcomers may find that they are better equipped to deal with the crisis, precisely because they have not yet learned to view the world in the currently traditional academic ways, than are the convention-bound masters. If we are forced to this conclusion about the possibility of change, must we give up trying to be actively oppositional? Must we simply passively await an opportunity that may never come?

We have to be careful here not to fall back into a "foundationalist" way of arguing about change. If the power of an individual to effect change is qualified, if opportunities for oppositionally motivated change are contingent upon historical circumstances "erupting" into the academic community, this does not mean that change is now out of human hands. Rather, we should understand that change is always immanent but becomes evident when the time is right—and when those who wish to effect change are willing and able to engage in the rhetorical processes that make change happen. That is, those who support change must persuade other members of the academic community that the prevailing notion of academic literacy needs revision. We should not expect those with a critical perspective on prevailing notions to be any more able to transcend historical circumstances than the supporters of the dominant culture are—to wish for this power is to fantasize avoiding the rhetorical process.

We also have to be careful not to resurrect a determinist view. The opportunities historical circumstances present for cultural change may be very difficult of access for individuals—but not for groups. You can't act alone, perhaps, but you can act with others with whom you make common cause. Again, this view is congenial to the rhetorical perspective—persuasion is not based on idiosyncratic values but on what is shared. A truism worth repeating is that only through collective effort have changes been effected in the academic canon so far—whether we speak of theoretical shifts such as the rise and fall of New Criticism, or changes in the subject of study such as feminist-motivated revision of the textual canon. I need not advocate, then, the creation of oppositional discourses within the academy—people working out their relations to the changing historical circumstances are creating them all the time. I do advocate, however, the recognition that this process constitutes "normal" intellectual life. The crucial moment in the inculcation of cultural literacy will be finding ways to persuade our students to participate in this life with us.

Works Cited

Applebee, Arthur N. *Tradition and Reform in the Teaching of English: A History.* Urbana: NCTE, 1974.

Baron, Dennis. *Grammar and Good Taste: Reforming the American Language.* New Haven: Yale UP, 1982.

Bartholomae, David. "Inventing the University." *When a Writer Can't Write: Studies in Writer's Block and Other Composing Process Problems.* Ed. Mike Rose. New York: Guilford, 1985. 134–65.

Bizzell, Patricia. "Cognition, Convention, and Certainty: What We Need to Know about Writing." *PRE/TEXT* 3 (1982): 213–44.

Bizzell, Patricia, and Bruce Herzberg. " 'Inherent' Ideology, 'Universal' History, 'Empirical' Evidence, and 'Context-Free' Writing: Some Problems in E. D. Hirsch's *The Philosophy of Composition,*" MLN 95 (1980): 1181–1202.

Engnell, Richard A. "Implications for Communication of the Rhetorical Theory of Gorgias of Leontini." *Western Speech* 37 (1973): 175–84.

Farrell, Thomas J. "I.Q. and Standard English." *College Composition and Communication* 34 (1985): 470–84.

Finegan, Edward. *Attitudes Toward English Usage.* New York: Teacher's College, 1980.

Goody, Jack. *The Domestication of the Savage Mind.* Cambridge: Cambridge UP, 1977.

Gronbeck, Bruce. "Gorgias on Rhetoric and Poetic: A Rehabilitation." *Southern Speech Communication Journal* 38 (1972): 27–38.

Havelock, Eric. *The Literate Revolution in Greece and Its Cultural Consequences.* Princeton: Princeton UP, 1982.

Heath, Shirley Brice. *Ways With Words: Language, Life, and Work in Communities and Classrooms.* Cambridge: Cambridge UP, 1983.

Heller, Scott. "Author Sets Up Foundation to Create 'Cultural Literacy' Tests." *The Chronicle of Higher Education* 5 Aug. 1987: 2.

Hirsch, E. D., Jr. "Cultural Literacy." *American Scholar* 52 (1982–83): 159–69.

———. "Culture and Literacy." *Journal of Basic Writing* 3 (Fall/Winter 1980): 27–47.

———. *The Philosophy of Composition.* Chicago: U of Chicago P, 1977.

Hirsch, E. D., Jr., Joseph Kett, and James Trefil. *Cultural Literacy: What Every American Needs to Know.* Boston: Houghton, 1987.

Ong, Walter J. *Orality and Literacy: The Technologizing of the Word.* New York: Methuen, 1982.

Rorty, Richard. "Hermeneutics, General Studies, and Teaching." *Synergos: Selected Papers from the Synergos Seminars* 2 (1982): 1–15.

Rose, Mike. "The Language of Exclusion: Writing Instruction at the University." *College English* 47 (1985): 341–59.

Scribner, Sylvia, and Michael Cole. *The Psychology of Literacy.* Cambridge: Harvard UP, 1981.

Tannen, Deborah. "The Oral/Literate Continuum of Discourse." *Spoken and Written Languages: Exploring Orality and Literacy.* Ed. Deborah Tannen. Norwood, NJ: Ablex, 1982. 1–16.

Warnock, John. "Cultural Literacy: A Worm in the Bud?" *ADE Bulletin* 82 (Winter 1985): 1–7.

Diversity, Ideology, and Teaching Writing

Maxine Hairston

Hairston's essay is from College Composition and Communication *43 (1992): 179–93. It has recently been reprinted in* The Writing Teacher's Sourcebook. *Eds. Gary Tate, Edward P. J. Corbett, and Nancy Myers. 3rd ed. New York: Oxford UP, 1994. 22–34*

WHERE HAVE WE COME FROM

In 1985, when I was chair of CCCC, as my chair's address I gave what might be called my own State of the Profession Report. On the whole it was a positive report. I rejoiced in the progress we had made in the previous fifteen years in establishing our work as a discipline and I pointed out that we were creating a new paradigm for the teaching of writing, one that focused on process and on writing as a way of learning. I asserted that we teach writing for its own sake, as a primary intellectual activity that is at the heart of a college education. I insisted that writing courses must not be viewed as service courses. Writing courses, especially required freshman courses, should not be *for* anything or *about* anything other than writing itself, and how one uses it to learn and think and communicate.

I also warned in my Chair's address that if we hoped to flourish as a profession, we would have to establish our psychological and intellectual independence from the literary critics who are at the center of power in most English departments; that we could not develop our potential and become fully autonomous scholars and teachers as long as we allowed our sense of self worth to depend on the approval of those who define English departments as departments of literary criticism.

We've continued to make important strides since 1985. We have more graduate programs in rhetoric and composition, more tenure track positions in composition created each year, more and larger conferences, and so many new journals that one can scarcely keep up with them. In those years, I've stayed optimistic about the profession and gratified by the role I've played in its growth.

WHERE WE SEEM TO BE HEADING

Now, however, I see a new model emerging for freshman writing programs, a model that disturbs me greatly. It's a model that puts dogma before diversity, politics before craft, ideology before critical thinking, and the social goals of the teacher before the educational needs of the student. It's a regressive model that undermines the progress we've made in teaching writing, one that threatens to silence student voices and jeopardize the process-oriented, low-risk, student-centered classroom we've worked so hard to establish as the norm. It's a model that doesn't take freshman English seriously in its own right but conceives of it as a tool, something to be used. The new model envisions required writing courses as vehicles for social reform rather than as student-centered workshops designed to build students' confidence and competence as writers. It is a vision that echoes that old patronizing rationalization we've heard so many times before: students don't have anything to write about so we have to give them topics. Those topics used to be literary; now they're political.

I don't suggest that all or even most freshman writing courses are turning this way. I have to believe that most writing teachers have too much common sense and are too concerned with their students' growth as writers to buy into this new philosophy. Nevertheless, everywhere I turn I find composition faculty, both leaders in the profession and new voices, asserting that they have not only the right, but the duty, to put ideology and radical politics at the center of their teaching.

Here are four revealing quotations from recent publications. For instance, here is James Laditka in the *Journal of Advanced Composition:*

> All teaching supposes ideology; there simply is no value free pedagogy. For these reasons, my paradigm of composition is changing to one of critical literacy, a literacy of political consciousness and social action. (361)

Here is Charles Paine in a lead article in *College English:*

> Teachers need to recognize that methodology alone will not ensure radical visions of the world. An appropriate course content is necessary as well. . . . [E]quality and democracy are not transcendent values that inevitably emerge when one learns to seek the truth through critical thinking. Rather, if those are the desired values, the teacher must recognize that he or she must influence (perhaps manipulate is the more accurate word) students' values through charisma or power—he or she must accept the role as manipulator. Therefore it is of course reasonable to try to inculcate into our students the conviction that the dominant order is repressive. (563–64)

Here is Patricia Bizzell:

> We must help our students . . . to engage in a rhetorical process that can collectively generate . . . knowledge and beliefs to displace the repressive ideologies an unjust social order would prescribe. . . . I suggest that we must be forthright in avowing the ideologies that motivate our teaching and research. For instance, [in an experimental composition course he teaches at Purdue] James Berlin might stop trying to be value-neutral and anti-authoritarian in the class-room. Berlin tells his students he is a Marxist but disavows any intention of persuading them to his point of view. Instead, he might openly state that this course aims to promote values of sexual equality and left-oriented labor relations and that this course will challenge students' values insofar as they conflict with these aims. Berlin and his colleagues might openly exert their authority as teachers to try to persuade students to agree with their values instead of pretending that they are merely investigating the nature of sexism and capitalism and leaving students to draw their own conclusions. (670)

Here is C. H. Knoblauch:

> We are, ultimately, compelled to choose, to make, express, and act upon our commitments, to denounce the world, as Freire says, and above all oppression and whatever arguments have been called upon to validate it. Moreover our speech may well have to be boldly denunciative at times if it is to affect its hearers in the midst of their intellectual and political comfort. . . . We are obliged to announce ourselves so that, through the very process of self-assertion, we grow more conscious of our axioms . . . . The quality of our lives as teachers depends on our willingness to discover through struggle ever more fruitful means of doing our work. The quality of our students' lives depends on [it]. ("Rhetorical" 139)

These quotations do not represent just a few instances that I ferreted out to suit my thesis; you will find similar sentiments if you leaf through only a few of the recent issues of *College English, Rhetoric Review, College Composition and Communication, Journal of Advanced Composition, Focuses,* and others. Some names that you might look for in addition to the ones I've quoted are James Berlin, John Trimbur, Lester Faigley, Richard Ohmann, and Linda Brodkey. At least forty percent of the essays in *The Right to Literacy,* the proceedings of a 1988 conference sponsored by the Modern Language Association in Columbus, Ohio, echo such sentiments, and a glance at the program for the 1991 CCCC convention would confirm how popular such ideas were among the speakers. For that same convention, the publisher HarperCollins sponsored a contest to award grants to graduate students to attend; the topic they were asked to write on was "Describe the kind of freshman writing course you would design." Nearly all of the contestants described a politically-focused course. All ten essays in the 1991 MLA publication *Contending with Words* recommend turning writing courses in this direction.

Distressingly often, those who advocate such courses show open contempt for their students' values, preferences, or interests. For example, in an article in *College English,* Ronald Strickland says, "The teacher can best facilitate the production of knowledge by adapting a confrontational stance toward the student. . . . Above all, the teacher should avoid the pretense of detachment, objectivity, and autonomy." He admits that his position "conflicts with the expectations of some students [and] these students make it difficult for me to pursue my political/intellectual agenda" (293).

David Bleich dismisses his students' resistance with equal ease:

> There is reason to think that students want to write about what they say they don't want to write about. They want a chance to write about racism, classism, and homophobia even though it makes them uncomfortable. But what I think makes them most uncomfortable is to surrender the paradigm of individualism and to see that paradigm in its sexist dimensions.

He cites his students' religion as one of the chief obstacles to their enlightenment:

> Religious views collaborate with the ideology of individualism and with sexism to censor the full capability of what people can say and write. . . . By "religious values" I mean belief in the savability of the individual human soul. The ideal of the nuclear family, as opposed to the extended or communal family, permits the overvaluation of the individual child and the individual soul. (167)

And here is Dale Bauer in an article from *College English:*

> I would argue that political commitment—especially feminist commitment—is a legitimate classroom

strategy and rhetorical imperative. The feminist agenda offers a goal toward our students' conversions to emancipatory critical action. . . . In teaching identification and teaching feminism, I overcome a vehement insistence on pluralistic relativism or on individualism.

Bauer acknowledges that her students resist her political agenda. She says,

> There is an often overwhelming insistence on individualism and isolation . . . [They] labor at developing a critical distance to avoid participating in "the dialectic of resistance and identification."

Bauer quotes one of her students as saying in an evaluation,

> "The teacher consistently channels class discussions around feminism and does not spend time discussing the comments that oppose her beliefs. In fact, she usually twists them around to support her beliefs."

Bauer dismisses such objections, however, claiming she has to accept her authority as rhetor because "anything less ends up being an expressivist model, one which reinforces . . . the dominant patriarchal culture" (389).

Often these advocates are contemptuous of other teachers' approaches to teaching or the goals those teachers set for their students. For example, Lester Faigley assails the advice given about writing a job application letter in a standard business writing text:

> In the terms of [the Marxist philosopher] Althusser, [the applicant who writes such a letter] has voluntarily assented his subjectivity within the dominant ideology and thus has reaffirmed relations of power. By presenting himself as a commodity rather than as a person, he has not only made an initial gesture of subservience like a dog presenting its neck, but he has also signaled his willingness to continue to be subservient. (251)

In discussing Linda Flower's cognitive, problem-solving approach to teaching writing, James Berlin calls it, "the rationalization of economic activity. The pursuit of self-evident and unquestioned goals in the composing process parallels the pursuit of self-evident and unquestioned profit-making goals in the corporate market place." (What a facile non-logical leap!) He continues in the same article to deride Donald Murray's and Peter Elbow's approaches to writing because of their focus on the individual, saying

> Expressionist rhetoric is inherently and debilitatingly divisive of political protest. . . . Beyond that, expressionist rhetoric is easily co-opted by the very capitalist forces it opposes. After all, this rhetoric can be used to reinforce the entrepreneurial virtues capitalism values most: individualism, private initiative, the confidence for risk taking, the right to be contentious with authority (especially the state). (491)

HOW WE GOT HERE

But how did all this happen? Why has the cultural left suddenly claimed writing courses as their political territory?

There's no simple answer, of course. Major issues about social change and national priorities are involved, and I cannot digress into those concerns in this essay. But my first response is, "You see what happens when we allow writing programs to be run by English departments?" I'm convinced that the push to change freshman composition into a political platform for the teacher has come about primarily because the course is housed in English departments.

As the linguistics scholar John Searle pointed out in a detailed and informative article in *The New York Review of Books,* the recent surge of the cultural left on major American campuses has centered almost entirely in English departments. He says,

> The most congenial home left for Marxism, now that it has been largely discredited as a theory of economics and politics, is in departments of literary criticism. And [because] many professors of literature no longer care about literature in ways that seemed satisfactory to earlier generations . . . they teach it as a means of achieving left-wing political goals or as an occasion for exercises in deconstruction, etc. (38)

I theorize that the critical literary theories of deconstruction, post-structuralism (both declining by now), and Marxist critical theory have trickled down to the lower floors of English departments where freshman English dwells. Just as they have been losing their impact with faculty above stairs, they have taken fresh root with those dwelling below.

Deconstructionists claim that the privileged texts of the canon are only reflections of power relations and the dominant class structures of their eras. Thus the job of the literary critic is to dissect Shakespeare or Milton or Eliot or Joyce to show how language reflects and supports the "cultural hegemony" of the time. They also claim that all meaning is indeterminate and socially constructed; there is no objective reality nor truth that can be agreed on.

Marxist criticism echoes these sentiments. For example, Ronald Strickland writes in *College English:*

> Marxist critics have demonstrated that conventional literary studies have been more complicitous . . . than any other academic discipline in the reproduction of the dominant ideology. . . . Traditional English studies helps to maintain liberal humanism through its emphasis on authorial genius. . . . [Thus] there is a political imperative to resist the privileging of individualism in this practice, for, as Terry Eagleton has demonstrated, it amounts to a form of coercion in the interests of conservative, elitist politics. (293)

All these claims strike me as silly, simplistic, and quite undemonstrable. Nevertheless, if one endorses these intellectual positions—and sympathizes with the politics behind them—it's easy to go to the next step and equate conventional writing instruction with conventional literary studies. Then one can say that because standard English is the dialect of the dominant class, writing instruction that tries to help students master that dialect merely reinforces the status quo and serves the interest of the dominant class. An instructor who wants to teach students to write clearly becomes part of a capitalistic plot to control the workforce. What nonsense!

It seems to me that one could argue with more force that the instructor who fails to help students master the standard dialect conspires against the working class.

How easy for theorists who, by the nature of the discipline they have chosen, already have a facile command of the prestige dialect to denigrate teaching that dialect to students. Have they asked those students what *they* want to learn? And how easy for these same theorists to set up straw men arguments that attack a mechanistic, structuralist, literature-based model of composition and call it "conservative, regressive, deterministic, and elitist" (Knoblauch, "Literacy" 76) when they know such models have long been discredited in the professional literature.

But I think this is what happens when composition theorists remain psychologically tied to the English departments that are their base. Partly out of genuine interest, I'm sure, but also out of a need to belong to and be approved by the power structure, they immerse themselves in currently fashionable critical theories, read the authors that are chic—Foucault, Bahktin, Giroux, Eagleton, and Cixous, for example—then look for ways those theories can be incorporated into their own specialty, teaching writing.

This, according to Searle's article, means that they subscribe to a view of the role of the humanities in universities that is

> . . . based on two primary assumptions. 1. They believe that Western civilization in general, and the United States in particular, are in large part oppressive, patriarchal, hegemonic, and in need of replacement or at least transformation. 2. The primary function of teaching the humanities is political; they [the cultural left] do not really believe the humanities are valuable in their own right except as a means of achieving social transformation. (38)

Searle goes on to point out that this debate about what is "hegemonic," "patriarchal," or "exclusionary" has been focused almost entirely in English departments.

I find it hard to believe that most English professors seriously hold these opinions or that they are ready to jettison their lifelong commitment to the humanities, but evidently significant numbers do. News releases and many professional articles suggest that these attitudes have permeated the Modern Language Association, and the associate chair of the English Department at the University of Texas recently said in a colloquium of the College of Liberal Arts that the "mission of English departments is always to oppose the dominant culture."

For those who agree, how natural to turn to the freshman writing courses. With a huge captive enrollment of largely unsophisticated students, what a fertile field to cultivate to bring about political and social change. Rhetoric scholars who go along will also get new respect now that they have joined the ideological fray and formed alliances with literature faculty who have been transforming their own courses.

Composition faculty who support such change can bring fresh respectability and attention to those often despised introductory English courses now that they can be used for "higher purposes." They may even find some regular faculty who will volunteer to teach freshman writing when they can use it for a political forum. Five years ago the regular faculty in our department at Texas tried to get rid of freshman English altogether by having it taught entirely in extension or at the local community college; this past year, many of those who had previously advocated abandoning the course were in the forefront of the battle to turn it into a course about racism and sexism. Now the course was suddenly worth their time.

The opportunity to make freshman English a vehicle for such social crusades is particularly rich: in many universities, graduate students in English teach virtually all of the sections, graduate students who are already steeped in post-structuralism and deconstruction theory, in the works of Foucault, Raymond Williams, Terry Eagleton, and Stanley Fish, and in feminist theory. Too often they haven't been well trained in how to teach writing and are at a loss about what they should be doing with their students. How easy then to focus the course on their own interests, which are often highly political. Unfortunately, when they try to teach an introductory composition course by concentrating on issues rather than on craft and critical thinking, large numbers of their students end up feeling confused, angry—and cheated.

I also believe that two major social forces outside the liberal arts are contributing to creating the environment that has given rise to this new model.

The first is the tremendous increase in diversity of our student population, especially in states like California and Texas and in all our major cities. With changing demographics, we face an ethnic and social mix of students in our classes that previews for us what our institutions are going to be like in the year 2000. These students bring with them a kaleidoscope of experiences, values, dialects, and cultural backgrounds that we want to respond to positively and productively, using every resource we can to help them adapt to the academic world and become active participants in it. The code words for our attempts to build the kind of inclusive curriculum that we need have become "multiculturalism" and "cultural diversity." They're good terms, of course. Any informed and concerned educator endorses them in the abstract. The crucial question, however, is how one finds concrete ways to put them into practice, and also how one guards against their becoming what Richard Weaver called "god terms" that can be twisted to mean anything an ideologue wants them to mean.

As writing teachers, I think all of us are looking for ways to promote genuine diversity in our classes and yet keep two elements that are essential for any state-of-the-art composition course.

First, students' own writing must be the center of the course. Students need to write to find out how much they know and to gain confidence in their ability to express themselves effectively. They do not need to be assigned essays to read so they will have something to write about—they bring their subjects with them. The writing of others, except for that of their fellow students, should be supplementary, used to illustrate or reinforce.

Second, as writing teachers we should stay within our area of professional expertise: helping students to learn to write in order to learn, to explore, to communicate, to gain control over their lives. That's a large responsibility, and all that most of us can manage. We have no business getting into areas where we may have passion and conviction but no scholarly base from which to operate. When classes focus on complex issues such as racial discrimination, economic injustices, and inequities of class and gender, they should be taught by qualified faculty who have the depth of information and historical competence that such critical social issues warrant. Our society's deep and tangled cultural conflicts can neither be explained nor resolved by simplistic ideological formulas.

But one can run a culturally diverse writing course without sacrificing any of its integrity as a writing course. Any writing course, required or not, can be wonderfully diverse, an exciting experience in which people of different cultures and experience learn about difference first-hand. More about that shortly.

FORCES FROM OUTSIDE

The second major force I see at work is directly political. There's no question in my mind that this new radical stance of many composition faculty is in some ways a corollary of the angry response many intellectuals have to the excesses of right-wing, conservative forces that have dominated American politics for the past decade. Faculty in the liberal arts tend to be liberals who are concerned about social problems and dislike the trends we've seen in cutting funds for human services and for education. We're sick over the condition of our country: one child in five living in poverty; one person in eight hungry; 33 million people with no health insurance; a scandalous infant mortality rate; hundreds of thousands homeless. Yet we see our government spend billions on a dubious war. No need to go on—we all know the terrible inequities and contradictions of our society.

As educators of good will, we shouldn't even have to mention our anger about racism and sexism in our society—that's a given, as is our commitment to work to overcome it. I, for one, refuse to be put on the defensive on such matters of personal conscience or to be silenced by the fear that someone will pin a label on me if I don't share his or her vision of the world or agree on how to improve it. *Ad hominem* arguments don't impress me.

But it's entirely understandable that academics who are traditional liberals sympathize at first with those who preach reform, even when they sound more radical than we'd like. On the surface we share common ground: we'd all like to bring about a fairer, more compassionate society. But I fear that we are in real danger of being co-opted by the radical left, coerced into acquiescing to methods that we abhor because, in the abstract, we have some mutual goals. Some faculty may also fear being labeled "right-wing" if they oppose programs that are represented as being "liberating." But we shouldn't be duped. Authoritarian methods are still authoritarian methods, no matter in what cause they're invoked. And the current battle is *not* one between liberals and conservatives. Those who attempt to make it so—columnists like George Will—either do not understand the agenda of the cultural left, or they make the association in order to discredit liberal goals. Make no mistake—those on the cultural left are not in the least liberal; in fact, they despise liberals as compromising humanists. They're happy, however, to stir up traditional liberal guilt and use it for their purposes.

WHAT'S WRONG WITH THEIR GOALS

Why do I object so strongly to the agenda that these self-styled radical teachers want to establish for composition courses and freshman English in particular?

First, I vigorously object to the contention that they have a right—even a *duty*—to use their classrooms as platforms for their own political views. Such claims violate all academic traditions about the university being a forum for the free exchange of ideas, a place where students can examine different points of view in an atmosphere of honest and open discussion, and, in the process, learn to think critically. It is a teacher's obligation to encourage diversity and exploration, but diversity and ideology will not flourish together. By definition, they're incompatible.

By the logic of the cultural left, any teacher should be free to use his or her classroom to promote any ideology. Why not facism? Racial superiority? Religious fundamentalism? Anti-abortion beliefs? Can't any professor claim the right to indoctrinate students simply because he or she is right? The argument is no different from that of any true believers who are convinced that they own the truth and thus have the right to force it on others. My colleague John Ruszkiewicz compares them to Milton's "the new forcers of conscience." We don't have to look far to see how frightening such arguments really are. They represent precisely the kind of thinking that leads to "re-education camps" in totalitarian governments, to putting art in the service of propaganda, and to making education always the instrument of the state.

Those who want to bring their ideology into the classroom argue that since any classroom is necessarily political, the teacher might as well make it openly political and ideological. He or she should be direct and honest about his or her political beliefs; then the students will know where they stand and everyone can talk freely. Is any experienced teacher really so naive as to believe that? Such claims are no more than self-serving rationalizations that allow a professor total freedom to indulge personal prejudices and avoid any responsibility to be fair. By the same reasoning, couldn't one claim that since we know it is impossible to find absolute, objective truths, we might just as well abandon the search for truth and settle for opinion, superstition and conjecture? Would that advance our students' education? Couldn't one also say that since one can never be completely fair with one's children, one might as well quit trying and freely indulge one's biases and favoritism? It's astonishing that people who purport to be scholars can make such specious arguments.

The real political truth about classrooms is that the teacher has all the power; she sets the agenda, she controls the discussion, and she gives the grades. She also knows more and can argue more skillfully. Such a situation is ripe for intellectual intimidation, especially in required freshman composition classes, and although I think it is unprofessional for teachers to bring their ideology into any classroom, it is those freshman courses that I am especially concerned about.

THE THREAT TO FRESHMAN COURSES

I believe that the movement to make freshman English into courses in which students must write about specific social issues threatens all the gains we have made in teaching writing in the last fifteen years. I also think that rather than promoting diversity and a genuine multicultural environment, such courses actually work against those goals. Here are my reasons.

First, we know that students develop best as writers when they can write about something they care about and want to know more about. Only then will they be motivated to invest real effort in their work; only then can we hope they will avoid the canned, clichéd prose that neither they nor we take seriously. Few students, however, will do their best when they are compelled to write on a topic they perceive as politically charged and about which they feel uninformed, no matter how thought-provoking and important the instructor assumes that topic to be. If freshmen choose to write about issues involving race, class, and gender, that's fine. They should have every encouragement. I believe all topics in a writing class should be serious ones that push students to think and to say something substantial. But the topic should be their choice, a careful and thoughtful choice, to be sure, but not what someone else thinks is good for them.

Second, we know that young writers develop best as writers when teachers are able to create a low-risk environment that encourages students to take chances. We also know that novice writers can virtually freeze in the writing classroom when they see it as an extremely high-risk situation. Apprehensive about their grades in this new college situation, they nervously test their teachers to see what is expected of them, and they venture opinions only timidly. It is always hard to get students to write seriously and honestly, but when they find themselves in a classroom where they suspect there is a correct way to think, they are likely to take refuge in generalities and responses that please the teacher. Such fake discourse is a kind of silence, the silence we have so often deplored when it is forced on the disadvantaged. But when we stifle creative impulse and make students opt for survival over honesty, we have done the same thing. In too many instances, the first lesson they will learn as college students is that hypocrisy pays—so don't try to think for yourself.

My third objection to injecting prescribed political content into a required freshman course is that such action severely limits freedom of expression for both students and instructors. In my view, the freshman course on racism and sexism proposed at the University of Texas at Austin in the spring of 1990 would have enforced conformity in both directions. Students would have had no choice of what to write about, and the instructors who were graduate students would have had no choice about what to teach. Even if they felt unqualified to teach the material—and many did—or believed that the prescribed curriculum would work against their students' learning to write—and many did—they had to conform to a syllabus that contradicted their professional judgment and, often, their personal feelings. That course has since been revised and the freshman course in place since the fall of 1991 offers choices to both students and teachers.

NEW POSSIBILITIES FOR FRESHMAN COURSES

I believe we can make freshman English—or any other writing course—a truly multicultural course that gives students the opportunity to develop their critical and creative abilities and do it in an intellectually and ethically responsible context that preserves the heart of what we have learned about teaching writing in the past two decades.

First, I resist the effort to put any specific multi-cultural content at the center of a writing course, particularly a freshman course, and particularly a required course. Multicultural issues are too complex and diverse to be dealt with fully and responsibly in an English course, much less a course in which the focus should be on writing, not reading. Too often attempts to focus on such issues encourage stereotyping and superficial thinking. For instance, what English teacher wouldn't feel presumptuous and foolish trying to introduce Asian culture into a course when he or she can quickly think of at least ten different Asian cultures, all of which differ from each other drastically in important ways? What about Hispanic culture? Can the teacher who knows something of Mexico generalize about traditions of other Hispanic cultures? Can anyone teach the "black experience"? Do black men and women whose forebears come from Haiti and Nigeria and Jamaica share the experiences and heritage of African-Americans? Is Southern culture a valid topic for study? Many people think so. What about Jewish culture? But I don't need to labor the point. I only want to highlight the concerns any of us should have when the push for so-called multicultural courses threatens the integrity of our discipline and the quality of our teaching.

I believe, however, that we can create a culturally inclusive curriculum in our writing classes by focusing on the experiences of our students. *They* are our greatest multicultural resource, one that is authentic, rich, and truly diverse. Every student brings to class a picture of the world in his or her mind that is constructed out of his or her cultural background and unique and complex experience. As writing teachers, we can help students articulate and understand that experience, but we also have the important job of helping every writer to understand that each of us sees the world through our own particular lens, one shaped by unique experiences. In order to communicate with others, we must learn to see through their lenses as well as try to explain to them what we see through ours. In an interactive classroom where students collaborate with other writers, this process of decentering so

one can understand the "other" can foster genuine multicultural growth.

Imagine, for example, the breadth of experience and range of difference students would be exposed to in a class made up of students I have had in recent years.

One student would be from Malawi. The ivory bracelet he wears was put on his arm at birth and cannot be removed; he writes about his tribal legends. Another student is a young Vietnamese man who came to America when he was eight; he writes about the fear he felt his first day in an American school because there were no walls to keep out bullets. Another is a young Greek woman whose parents brought her to America to escape poverty; she writes about her first conscious brush with sexism in the Greek orthodox church. One student is the son of illegal aliens who followed the harvests in Texas; he writes with passion about the need for young Hispanics to get their education. A young black man writes about college basketball, a culture about which he is highly knowledgeable. A young man from the Texas panhandle writes about the traditions of cowboy boots and the ethical dimensions of barbed wire fences. Another young black man writes about the conflicts he feels between what he is learning in astronomy, a subject that fascinates him, and the teachings of his church.

It's worth noting here that religion plays an important role in the lives of many of our students—and many of us, I'm sure—but it's a dimension almost never mentioned by those who talk about cultural diversity and difference. In most classrooms in which there is an obvious political agenda, students—even graduate students—are very reluctant to reveal their religious beliefs, sensing they may get a hostile reception. And with reason—remember the quotation from David Bleich. But a teacher who believes in diversity must pay attention to and respect students with deep religious convictions, not force them too into silence.

Real diversity emerges from the students themselves and flourishes in a collaborative classroom in which they work together to develop their ideas and test them out on each other. They can discuss and examine their experiences, their assumptions, their values, and their questions. They can tell their stories to each other in a nurturant writing community. As they are increasingly exposed to the unique views and experiences of others, they will begin to appreciate differences and understand the rich tapestry of cultures that their individual stories make up. But they will also see unified motifs and common human concerns in that tapestry.

In this kind of classroom not all writing should be personal, expressive writing. Students need a broader range of discourse as their introduction to writing in college. The teacher can easily design the kinds of writing assignments that involve argument and exposition and suggest options that encourage cross-cultural awareness. For instance, some suggested themes for development might be these: family or community rituals; power relationships at all levels; the student's role in his or her family or group; their roles as men and women; the myths they live by; cultural tensions within groups. There are dozens more rich possibilities that could be worked out with the cooperation of colleagues in other departments and within the class itself.

The strength of all the themes I've mentioned is that they're both individual and communal, giving students the opportunity to write something unique to them as individuals yet something that will resonate with others in their writing community. The beauty of such an approach is that it's *organic*. It grows out of resources available in each classroom, and it allows students to make choices, then discover more about others and themselves through those choices. This approach makes the teacher a midwife, an agent for change rather than a transmitter of fixed knowledge. It promotes a student-centered classroom in which the teacher doesn't assume, as our would-be forcers of conscience do, that he or she owns the truth. Rather the students bring their own truths, and the teacher's role is to nurture change and growth as students encounter individual differences. Gradually their truths will change, but so will ours because in such a classroom one continually learns from one's students.

This is the kind of freshman English class from which students can emerge with confidence in their ability to think, to generate ideas, and to present themselves effectively to the university and the community. It is a class built on the scholarship, research, and experience that has enabled us to achieve so much growth in our profession in the last fifteen years. It is the kind of classroom we can be proud of as a discipline. I don't think we necessarily have to take freshman English out of English departments in order to establish this model, but we do have to assert our authority as writing professionals within our departments and fiercely resist letting freshman English be used for anyone else's goals. We must hold on to the gains we have made and teach writing in the ways we know best. Above all, we must teach it for the *students'* benefit, not in the service of politics or anything else.

Freshman English is a course particularly vulnerable to takeover because English departments in so many universities and colleges refuse to take it seriously and thus don't pay much attention to what happens in it. They can wake up, however, to find that some political zealots take the course very seriously indeed and will gladly put it to their own uses. The scores of us who have been studying, writing, speaking, and publishing for two decades to make freshman English the solid intellectual enterprise that it now is must speak out to protect it from this kind of exploitation. It is time to resist, time to speak up, time to reclaim freshman composition from those who want to politicize it.

What is at stake is control of a vital element in our students' education by a radical few. We can't afford to let that control stand.

Works Cited

Bauer, Dale. "The Other 'F' Word: Feminist in the Classroom." *College English* 52 (Apr. 1990): 385–96.

Berlin, James A. "Rhetoric and Ideology in the Writing Class." *College English* 50 (Sep. 1988): 477–94.

Bizzell, Patricia. "Beyond Anti-Foundationalism to Rhetorical Authority: Problems in Defining 'Cultural Literacy.' " *College English* 52 (Oct. 1990): 661–75.

Bleich, David. "Literacy and Citizenship: Resisting Social Issues." Lunsford, Moglen, and Slevin 163–69.

Faigley, Lester. "The Study of Writing and the Study of Language." *Rhetoric Review* 7 (Spring 1989): 240–56.

Harkin, Patricia, and John Schilb. *Contending with Words: Composition and Rhetoric in a Postmodern Age.* New York: MLA, 1991.

Knoblauch, C. H. "Literacy and the Politics of Education." Lunsford, Moglen, and Slevin 74–80.

———. "Rhetorical Constructions: Dialogue and Commitment." *College English* 50 (Feb. 1988): 125–40.

Laditka, James N. "Semiology, Ideology, Praxis: Responsible Authority in the Composition Classroom." *Journal of Advanced Composition* 10.2 (Fall 1990): 357–73.

Lunsford, Andrea A, Helen Moglen, and James Slevin, eds. *The Right to Literacy.* New York: MLA and NCTE, 1990.

Paine, Charles. "Relativism, Radical Pedagogy, and the Ideology of Paralysis." *College English* 51 (Oct. 1989): 557–70.

Searle, John. "The Storm Over the University." Rev. of *Tenured Radicals,* by Roger Kimball; *The Politics of Liberal Education,* ed. by Darryl L. Gless and Barbara Hernstein Smith; and *The Voice of Liberal Learning: Michael Oakeshott on Education,* ed. by Timothy Fuller. *The New York Review of Books* 6 Dec. 1990: 34–42.

Strickland, Ronald. "Confrontational Pedagogy and Traditional Literary Studies." *College English* 52 (Mar. 1990): 291–300.

Weaver, Richard M. *The Ethics of Rhetoric.* Chicago: Henry Regnery, 1953.

Part Five

Alternative Maps

Map Making

MARK WILEY

. . . Let us go back to the map and the territory and ask: "What is in the territory that gets onto the map?" We know the territory does not get onto the map. . . . Now, if the territory were uniform, nothing would get onto the map except its boundaries, which are the points at which it ceases to be uniform against some larger matrix. What gets onto the map, in fact, is *difference,* be it a difference in altitude, a difference in vegetation, a difference in population structure, difference in surface, or whatever. Differences are the things that get onto a map. . . . (451)

The territory never gets in at all. . . . Always the process of representation will filter it out so that the mental world is only maps of maps of maps, ad infinitum. All "phenomenon" are literally "appearances." (454—55)

—GREGORY BATESON from *Steps to an Ecology of Mind*

Throughout the interpretive process of using this book, we have asked readers to dwell within a particular key in order to hypothesize the content of the field from that perspective. We have also asked you to be mindful of this map, of what it reveals and conceals. Although initially it may have felt a little strange and awkward, we imagine that this map quickly became familiar—at least that has been the experience of other readers. It is hard, even for us, to stay tuned in to the "constructed" nature of this scheme. But we hope you have become reflective about its fictive status. A map like this one can then function in the same way the myth of Oedipus functions in Freudian psychoanalysis. The myth articulates what isn't real, but nevertheless finds intelligible patterns that make sense of certain human experiences.

In adapting the semanticist Alfred Korzybski's famous statement that "the map is not the territory," Bateson reminds us that all maps gauge differences in information. If differences cannot be identified, there is no information and probably no map, or, at the least, not one very helpful. What Bateson implies, however, is that each map *maps* differences differently. The danger of mapping is to forget that the map is not the territory, that the differences represented are only a subset of an indefinite set of possible ones.

A map guides the traveler to a desired destination. As editors, we have assumed that our readers' destinations have generally been greater understanding of the field of composition and rhetoric. Yet the roads traveled have no doubt varied because each reader has been inventing his or her own journey by interpreting the keys and following the leads found along the way. Though any map is valuable to the degree it gets people to where they want to go with the least amount of confusion, no map can tell (or should tell) what specific route to take and what to find. As editors—but also as teachers—we have been walking a fine line between telling you what each key means, telling you our views of the articles and how they fit in each chapter, telling you what the relationships are between and among the keys, and guiding you to make those discoveries on your own.

Have we been completely successful in this tightrope act?

It seems that it is much easier for academics to tell others what we know than to tell what we don't. As scholars, we are trained to produce knowledge, and when we write, we learn how to be strategic in avoiding areas where our knowledge is uncertain. In seeking your destination, you may have intentionally avoided areas you did not understand. You may have been tempted to forget that each key is a heuristic fiction and instead tried to cling fast and make each into an uncomplicated, clearly defined category. These are very real intellectual temptations that scholars wrestle with; sometimes lost among our schemes, our categories, and our theories is the realization that each construct represents a different way to illuminate a tiny portion in an immense dark room.

We have suggested that you create a wildcard category as a sort of placeholder for articles you have found that do not fit this map. When you are dealt a joker in five-card draw, you can create a number of possible "winning" combinations by filling gaps in an otherwise limited hand. Your wildcards might lead you to ask how the boundaries these four keys articulate obscure other significant work in composition and rhetoric. Perhaps formerly prominent scholarship has been forgotten because some theories have become more fashionable. Perhaps the field has constructed its own unofficial canon of texts—that is, those texts most often cited so that they become touchstones for "what everybody should know." Considering what is in and out of favor might provoke you to question how canon formation occurs.

Other wildcards could draw on traditions never recognized as viable for pursuing answers to what was then, or now, articulated as the "important" disciplinary questions. Some of these "misfits" may borrow from American transcendentalism and pragmatism, from Native American cultures, or from traditions outside the Anglo-European. Some of James Moffett's work on yoga and meditation is a case in point of the latter (see his "Writing, Inner Speech, and Meditation"). You might even discern a new key emerging in the possible pattern formed by your collection of wildcards.

Bear in mind that we have never claimed these keys to be four discrete parts to a puzzle, with each part representing 25 percent of composition and rhetoric. That is, the four parts don't add up. Rather, the four keys index salient perspectives that appear to dominate at certain times in the field's literature. The test for this map is whether or not these keys portray the reality of the field from the inside, the reality as it was conceived by those doing work directly in composition during the time we have framed. Do these keys reflect what many scholars and researchers were saying and doing?

1. By mapping the field with these keys, you have also been raising questions about their pragmatic validity. Can you now stand back and reflect more critically on mapping itself as a rhetorical activity? Can you invent representations that might show different relationships between and among keys? Some of Louise Phelps's students created the following illustrations:

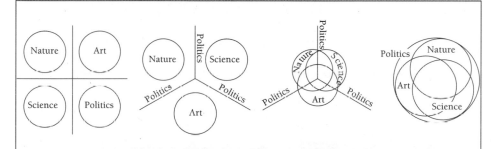

We would like to thank Todd Felton, Suzanne Gittleman, Ellen Lees, and Ken Lindblom for permission to reprint their diagrams. They called their sequence the S.P.A.N. of composition.

Like Louise's students, you may have already toyed with alternative representations. Try to step outside the frame of these keys and create nonverbal depictions. It is perhaps easier to begin "stepping out" by extending the map you are familiar with: You could begin, for instance, by finding other metaphoric associations with keys (doors and locks, each key as a legend on a map, or keys as formulas—for example: Nature = voice + authenticity + intellectual and moral development?).

You might also brainstorm other metaphors for categories and categorizing. Stephen North, for example, describes teacher lore in architectural terms, as "a rambling . . . delightful old manse, wing branching off from wing, addition tacked to addition, in all sorts of materials . . ." (27). Could you substitute types of buildings or even architectural or artistic styles as categories? What about genres and styles from music? In order to really step out, let your imagination go wild. Circles, triangles, and

(continued)

(*continued*)

other geometric figures can be augmented and animated using computer graphics. Or try painting or making a video or writing a poem. Janet Emig asked her students to build a three-dimensional model and to "dance a theory." How do these imaginative constructions reflect your emerging vision? Do they modify what you thought you had learned? How do the representations of others in your group suddenly change your understanding, maybe deepen it, or even reverse it?

2. You might reflect on how your work with this book has proceeded. Have you tried to define what you know at regular intervals and at the same time tried to articulate what you don't know? In what ways has this tension been dramatized in the forms of your own writing produced so far?

You may want to reread our introductions and note places where we, as editors, have traded in our role as guides for one as "tour directors." Perhaps you could try to rewrite parts (or all) of one or more of our introductions.

3. Examine your wildcards to discover the limits of these four keys. Try to explain why specific articles might be difficult to classify. Could one article fit into two or more keys? Why is it that some work might have been ignored—or even suppressed? Was there a paradigm operating, in Kuhn's terms, as some have argued about process theory (see Maxine Hairston, for instance)? Do your misfits form an intelligible category in themselves, or do they break up into several categories? Could they form a new key?

The alternative maps in this chapter provide grounds for comparing how other schemes articulate the field. The selections included here represent a historical range of possibilities for framing composition and rhetoric (we identify some other maps in a later Inquiry). As you examine these alternatives, try to understand the principles on which each is conceived. As editors, we have made certain claims regarding the construction and validity of this map and have asked you to test our claims. We also recommend that you do the same with these other maps. You can use the questions listed next to guide you in evaluating them.

4. What principles underlie the construction of these maps, and how explicitly do these map makers state their premises? Are they aware of the "constructedness" of their own maps, and do they acknowledge where their categories come from and justify their use? Do they argue that their schemes are exhaustive?

5. For what purposes do these authors claim their maps are useful? What is each author using the mapping process to accomplish, rhetorically? To argue for or against a specific view of the field? To create a hierarchy of positions? Do any of these map makers privilege one or more of their keys or categories?

6. For what purposes do *you*, individually, or as a group, find useful one or another of these alternative maps? What light does it cast on the one you have been using? Is it helpful to distinguish between categories that are logical and based on essential features and categories that are pragmatic and rhetorical? Can one map be both? What are the advantages for each type of map?

7. By asking that you scrutinize how these alternative maps are constructed, we are encouraging a progression from analysis to meta-analysis. Now that you have experimented with the four keys as a mapping system and have had a chance to consider alternatives, we ask that you extend your thinking about the activity of mapping itself. In addition to the few selections presented in this chapter, examine other sources that propose or employ schemes of analysis applicable to language, symbols, rhetoric, and to rhetoric and composition as a field. Here is a list of attempts by scholars to propose, synthesize, critique, or defend various schemes.

Philip Arrington. "Tropes of the Composing Process." *College English* 48 (1986): 325–38.

Patricia Bizzell. "Composing Process: An Overview." *The Teaching of Writing: Eighty-fifth Yearbook of the National Society for the Study of Education.* Eds. Anthony Petrosky and David Bartholomae. Chicago: The National Society for the Study of Education, 1986. 49–70.

James Britton et al. *The Development of Writing Abilities (11–18).* London: Macmillan, 1975.

Kenneth Burke. *A Grammar of Motives.* Berkeley: U of California P, 1969.

Michael Carter. "Problem Solving Reconsidered: A Pluralistic Theory of Problems." *College English* 50 (1988): 551–65.

Frank D'Angelo. *A Conceptual Theory of Rhetoric.* Cambridge: Winthrop, 1975.

Lester Faigley. "Competing Theories of Process: A Critique and a Proposal." *College English* 48 (1986): 527–42.

David Foster. *A Primer for Writing Teachers: Theories, Theorists, Issues, Problems.* Upper Montclair: Boynton/Cook, 1983.

Ann Ruggles Gere. "Teaching Writing: The Major Theories." *The Teaching of Writing.* Eds. Anthony Petrosky and David Bartholomae, 1986. 30–48.

George Hillocks, Jr. *Research on Written Composition: New Directions for Teaching.* Urbana: ERIC Clearinghouse on Reading and Communication, 1986.

Roman Jakobson. "Closing Statement: Linguistics and Poetics." *Semiotics: An Introductory Anthology.* Ed. Robert Innis. Bloomington: Indiana UP, 1985. 147–75. Originally published as "Linguistics and Poetics" in *Style in Language.* Ed. Thomas Sebeok. Cambridge: The MIT Press, 1960. 350–77.

(continued)

(continued)

James Kinneavy. *A Theory of Discourse.* New York: Norton, 1980.

————. "A Pluralistic Synthesis of Four Contemporary Models for Teaching Composition." *Reinventing the Rhetorical Tradition.* Eds. Aviva Freedman and Ian Pringle. Ottawa: Canadian Council of Teachers of English, 1980. 37–52.

James Moffett, *Teaching the Universe of Discourse.* Boston: Houghton Mifflin, 1968.

8. Some maps can serve as historical indicators of where the field saw (or sees) itself going. Maps change as their makers are influenced by ideas, cultural events or shifts, trends in other fields, and as their own work evolves, reflecting intellectual development and dialogue with the field as *it* changes. For example, compare Fulkerson's and Berlin's essays in this volume to these later essays that modify their original schemes.

Richard Fulkerson. "Communication Theories in the Eighties: Axiological Consensus and Paradigmatic Diversity." *College Composition and Communication* 41 (1990): 409–29.

James Berlin. "Rhetoric and Ideology in the Writing Class." *College English* 50 (1988): 477–94.

9. Another dimension to consider in mapping is the aesthetic, specifically, the number of categories created for a given scheme. Maps generally appear to have at least two categories (for obvious reasons), yet beyond two the optimal number is an open question. Three categories seem to be a fairly regular occurrence. Compare the well-known discourse triangle, which may persist as much because of its "threeness" as for its validity and utility as a map. Ann Berthoff, who draws on the work of C. S. Peirce, is a prime exponent of threeness (see her essay on "A Curious Triangle and the Double-Entry Notebook" in this volume). A third element can often function as a mediator between two seemingly opposed positions. Louise Phelps invokes this principle in order to mediate dialectically between competing methodologies (see "The Third Way: Paul Ricoeur and the Problem of Method").

Since maps are intended in part to simplify, contain, and order messy realities for human beings, there may also be a maximum number of categories beyond which any map becomes unhelpful because too many categories cause overcomplexity and confusion. Roman Jakobson's model of discourse contains six elements, and I am unaware of any maps that use more than six. There may be a biological and psychological explanation for this limit. George Miller argues in his well-known article, "The Magical Number Seven, Plus or Minus Two: Some Limits on Our Capacity for Processing Information," that short-term memory can handle chunks of information efficiently up to seven, plus or minus two.

We began with three keys but added a fourth. We wondered whether five would be too unwieldy to be useful. It may be that if keys start to proliferate, the human tendency will be to reduce them to two, to erase distinctions and to notice similarities rather than differences. Do you think such reduction occurs because it is the nature of argument to polarize issues (and those supporting them) into two opposing positions? (Again see Berthoff on "Killer Dichotomies," but also see other offerings in the anthology *Farther Along*; in addition, see Kenneth Gergen on the rhetoric of critique.) Do twos eventually merge into each other and become something else again (see Burke for transformations of oppositions, particularly the Introduction to *A Grammar of Rhetoric*)? Or does the inherent conflict between twos cause a third category to emerge?

10. The aesthetics of mapping brings us far from the pragmatic, rough-and-ready qualities of these four keys. But as Burke reminds us in his *Grammar*, the logical schematic of any classificatory system takes on its own logical life because it is essentialized and removed from the temporal flow of ongoing events. We can go up and down this ladder of abstraction and generalization—downward to the molten mass at the center where all distinctions blur or upward to the ethereal heights of pure logic and symmetry. What we gain in clarity from the heights, we lose in the concrete reality of the quotidian. When we go up, we change our perspective, and when we go down, we change it again. The point, I think, is that we cannot stand still, lest like Narcissus we mistake our reflections for reality.

By this time, we hope that you've become subversives, not only fine-tuning this map, but also imagining and arguing for entire new schemes. Follow the trail of your own reading: Look to see where you have been and where you might go next.

Look backward to the wildcards or to what one reader wonderfully called "the caboose" category to identify what got lost, what needs to be restored, or what simply needs to be filed away for further reflection. You may, on the other hand, have identified new distinctions while cataloguing the misfits and opened up new territory in attempting to rationalize this category.

Yet look forward, too—after all, we primarily stopped in the 1980s and ventured only slightly into the 1990s. This leaves you with a tantalizing array of developments in this decade to grapple with now that you have a handle on the history and context for these new directions. Search out recent anthologies, bibliographies, bibliographic essays, conference proceedings, and even current courses and course proposals in order to see where the field might be moving.

Tell us what's happening now. In what direction are we going? Toward what destinations do you want to go—and what maps will you make to guide us?

WORKS CITED

Bateson, Gregory. *Steps to an Ecology of Mind.* New York: Ballantine Books, 1972.

Hairston, Maxine. "The Winds of Change: Thomas Kuhn and the Revolution in the Teaching of Writing." *College Composition and Communication* 33 (1982): 76–88.

Moffett, James. "Writing, Inner Speech, and Meditation." *Coming on Center: English Education in Evolution.* Upper Montclair: Boynton/Cook, 1981. 133–81.

North, Stephen. *The Making of Knowledge in Composition: Portrait of an Emerging Field.* Upper Montclair: Boynton/Cook, 1987.

SUGGESTED READINGS

Berthoff, Ann. "Killer Dichotomies: Reading In/Reading Out." *Farther Along: Transforming Dichotomies in Rhetoric and Composition.* Eds. Kate Ronald and Hephzibah Roskelly. Portsmouth: Boynton/Cook, 1990. 12–24.

Gergen, Kenneth J. "The Limits of Pure Critique." *After Postmodernism: Reconstructing Ideology Critique.* Eds. Herbert Simons and Michael Billig. London: SAGE Publications, 1994. 58–78.

Kenneth Burke. *A Grammar of Motives.* Berkeley: U of California P, 1969.

Miller, George A. *The Psychology of Communication: Seven Essays.* New York: Basic Books, 1967.

Phelps, Louise Wetherbee. "The Third Way: Paul Ricoeur and the Problem of Method." *Composition as a Human Science: Contributions to the Self-Understanding of a Discipline.* New York: Oxford UP, 1988. 183–201.

Four Philosophies of Composition

Richard Fulkerson

This essay was first published in College Composition and Communication *30 (1979): 343–48. It has recently been republished in* The Writing Teacher's Sourcebook. *Eds. Gary Tate, Edward P. J. Corbett, and Nancy Myers. 3rd ed. New York: Oxford UP, 1994. 3–8.*

My research interest in philosophies of composition and their curricular and pedagogical implications had two immediate causes.[1] The first was my reading of Charles Silberman's *Crisis in the Classroom* (1970). Although the book is primarily about elementary and high schools and although I am not persuaded of the soundness of Silberman's proposals, I found the book valuable in two ways. First, it highlighted the existence of serious problems in American education. Second and more important, Silberman said the problems were the result more of mindlessness than of maliciousness. The problem was not, he said, that evil or incompetent people were in charge but that educators exhibited a consistent mindlessness about relating means to desired ends. The second precipitating event was my rereading of M. H. Abrams's *The Mirror and the Lamp* (1953). Abrams analyzes four overriding theories of literature and literary criticism, each emphasizing one of the four elements in an artistic transaction.[2] Since the elements in an artistic transaction are the same as those in any communication, it seemed that Abrams's four theories might also be relevant to composition.

Any theory making the reader primary and judging literature by its effect, Abrams labels *pragmatic.* When the universe shared by artist and auditor becomes the primary element and measure of success, then, Abrams says, we have a *mimetic* theory, such as that of Pope and the Neo-Classical period. Emphasis on the personal views of the artist, such as in the Romantic period, Abrams labels the *expressive* position. And finally, theories emphasizing only the internal relationships within the artifact, Abrams calls *objective* criticism.

Abrams's analysis made me wonder whether a parallel set of four philosophies of composition might exist, each one stressing a different element in the communicative transaction. If so, each would provide—as do the philosophies Abrams outlined—both a description of the composition process and a method of evaluating the composed product. Furthermore, the existence of four such philosophies might help to explain both the widely recognized variations in English teachers' evaluations and (perhaps) what Kitzhaber in *Themes, Theories, and Therapy* referred to as the "bewildering variety" of freshman composition courses.

For application to composition, I prefer to make two shifts in Abrams's terminology. I will keep the term *expressive* for philosophies of composition emphasizing the writer, and the term *mimetic* for philosophies emphasizing correspondence with "reality." But philosophies emphasizing the effect on a reader I will call *rhetorical,* and philosophies emphasizing traits internal to the work I will call *formalist.*

My thesis is that this four-part perspective helps give a coherent view of what goes on in composition classes. All four philosophies exist in practice. They give rise to vastly different ways of judging student writing, vastly different courses to lead students to produce such writing, vastly different textbooks and journal articles. Moreover, the perspective helps to clarify, though not to resolve, a number of the major controversies in the field, including the "back-to-the-basics" cry and the propriety of dialectal variations in student writing.

Let me clarify each of these four philosophies and simultaneously attempt to classify a number of major theorists according to the value philosophies implicit in their writings.

Adherents of formalist theories judge student work primarily by whether it shows certain internal forms. Some teachers, for example, judge a paper a failure if it contains one comma splice or five spelling errors. Those are judgments based purely on form. Indeed, the most common type of formalist value theory is a grammatical one: good writing is "correct" writing at the sentence level. In the classroom, one studies errors of form—in order to avoid them. But forms other than grammatical can also be the teacher's key values. I have heard of metaphorical formalists, sentence-length formalists, and topic-sentence formalists, to name a few. And Janet Emig in *The Composing Processes of Twelfth Graders* (1971) concluded that "most of the criteria by which students' school-sponsored writing is evaluated concern the accidents rather than the essences of discourse—that is, spelling, punctuation, penmanship, and length" (p. 93), four formalist criteria.

Few major writers accept formalist values, but two seem to me to do so. Francis Christensen elevated the form he designated as the cumulative sentence to primacy in value. He wanted "sentence acrobats." Similarly in his provocative and provoking *The Philosophy of Composition* (1977), E. D. Hirsch builds an elaborate argument for what he calls "relative readability." Such a phrase has its origins in a reader-centered value theory, but Hirsch elevates such sentences to goods in themselves rather than goods because they communicate to the reader. He says that "relative readability is an intrinsic and truly universal norm of writing" (p. 89) and that "there are ways of making quite objective comparisons between passages . . . on the criterion of communicative efficiency" (p. 61). In

other words, we can take a pair of passages and determine which is the better embodiment of "semantic intent"—without reference to a reader, or to the writer using them, or to the reality they reflect. This is a formalist philosophy of composition. And one assumes that Hirsch is designing a program to teach students at the University of Virginia how to produce relatively readable sentences. One's value theory shapes his or her pedagogy.

Although formalists are hard to find these days, adherents of the other three positions and of courses built around them are not.

Expressionism as a philosophy about what writing is good for and what makes for good writing became quite common in the late sixties and early seventies, perhaps gaining its chief emphasis with the famous Dartmouth Conference in 1967. Expressionists cover a wide range, from totally accepting and non-directive teachers, some of whom insist that one neither can nor should evaluate writing, to much more directive, experiential teachers who design classroom activities to maximize student self-discovery. The names most commonly associated with the expressive value-position are John Dixon (in England), Ken Macrorie, and Lou Kelly—the latter two of whom have written textbooks about their courses.[3] There were, in fact, quite a few expressive textbooks, including James Miller and Stephen Judy's *Writing in Reality* (1978) and a fascinating book by Dick Friedrich and David Kuester called *It's Mine and I'll Write It That Way* (1972). Half of this book consists of suggestions for classroom activities, while the alternating chapters are a journal kept by one of the authors about a class he taught using those materials. Expressivists value writing that is about personal subjects, and such journal-keeping is an absolute essential. Another keynote for expressivists is the desire to have writing contain an interesting, credible, honest, and personal voice; hence the title of Donald C. Stewart's text, *The Authentic Voice* (1972).

Expressive views even show up in some surprising places. Ross Winterowd remarks early in *The Contemporary Writer* (1975) that "most people in the real world outside of school do not need to write very much" (p. 4). Consequently, he tells the student reader, "There's a very good chance that learning to do self-expressive writing will constitute the greatest benefit that you gain from *The Contemporary Writer*" (p. 8). Using Jung's comments on the function of dreams, Winterowd says that the purpose of such writing is "to restore our psychological balance" by reestablishing "the total psychic equilibrium" (p. 8). Taking "psychic equilibrium" as the major goal of writing leads to quite a different evaluative position from taking, say, "changes in audience opinion" as the prime goal.

The most common presentation of the third philosophy of composition, the mimetic, says that a clear connection exists between good writing and good thinking. The major problem with student writing is that it is not solidly thought out. Hence, we should either teach students how to think or help them learn enough about various topics to have something worth saying, or we should do both. Thus the first mimetic approach emphasizes logic and reasoning, sometimes formal logic as in Monroe Beardsley's *Writing with Reason* (1976), sometimes less formal logic as in Ray Kytle's *Clear Thinking for Composition* (2nd ed. 1973). Sometimes the mimetic-logical emphasis is on propaganda analysis—the detecting of hidden assumptions, emotional appeals, and fallacies in reasoning. All discourse does contain unstated assumptions; the problem with such assumptions arises only if they are also unacceptable assumptions, and usually, they are unacceptable because they violate reality as we know it. That is, an unstated or hidden assumption may be a writing weakness if writing is viewed from a mimetic perspective. Similarly, a fallacy is fallacious precisely because it contradicts what we accept as truth. Hastiness is not the problem with a hasty generalization; the problem is that reality as we know it rarely squares with such generalizations. Thus the teaching of sound reasoning as a basis for good writing is an essentially mimetic practice.

The other major mimetic approach says that students do not write well on significant matters because they do not know enough. One resulting methodology is to emphasize research during the prewriting stages; another is to emphasize heuristic

systems. Still another is the use of a topically arranged anthology of readings. If a student reads four essays taking both sides on a controversial issue—say, capital punishment—then he or she supposedly will know enough to be able to write about that topic; that is, the writing will be closer to the "real situation" and thus better—from a mimetic perspective.

In almost any issue of *College Composition and Communication,* several writers espouse the fourth philosophy, the rhetorical one. Such a philosophy says, in essence, good writing is writing adapted to achieve the desired effect on the desired audience. If the same verbal construct is directed to a different audience, then it may have to be evaluated differently.

Leading adherents of this view are E. P. J. Corbett, Richard Larson, and most other theorists who emphasize an adaptation of classical rhetoric. This group also includes the textbook writers who emphasize a writer's commitment to his or her reader as shaping discourse: Robert Gorrell and Charlton Laird in the *Modern English Handbook* (6th ed. 1976), Michael Adelstein and Jean Pival in *The Writing Commitment* (1976), and James McCrimmon in *Writing with a Purpose* (6th ed. 1976).

Given this four-part perspective, I was much intrigued by one of Peter Elbow's articles.[4] I had already read his *Writing without Teachers* (1973) and had had some trouble classifying him. But in this article, Elbow explained that his theories of free writing, collaborative criticism, and audience adaptation are really classical theories masquerading as modern theories. That is, he said that although most teachers judge student writing either on the basis of its truth or its formal correctness, his courses are built on judging student writing by its effect on an audience. Aristotle in modern dress.

Classifying Elbow as a rhetoricist illustrates an important point. As I said, teaching procedures have to harmonize with evaluative theories. More precisely, one's philosophy about what writing is for leads to a theory of what constitutes good writing. That philosophy, in turn, leads to a concept of pedagogical goals, and the goals lead, in turn, to classroom procedures. But the relationship between goals and procedures is complex, because handled in certain ways, procedures that might usually be associated with one value position can be used to reach quite another end. Elbow's techniques *seem* to put him with the expressivists, but at least in 1968, Elbow saw himself, accurately I think, as a rhetoricist.

Similarly, I mentioned previously the expressivist penchant for student journals, but I also use journals, and I use them most often in the service of a quite different goal: critical thinking about reading assignments. To the extent that I use journals to teach writing, I am using them in the service of a mimetic set of values.

A reasonable response to this model might be, "Yes, those are four positions; they exist, but they are not mutually exclusive. Nor are they a problem. One can either hold to all of them simultaneously or pick and choose among them, depending on which one seems appropriate for a given piece of writing." James Kinneavy's very impressive *A Theory of Discourse* (1971), in fact, proposes that there are four types of writing growing from the four elements in a communicative act: reference discourse, expressive discourse, persuasive discourse, and literary discourse, each to be judged on its own terms. Moreover, the National Assessment of Educational Progress uses three types of writing growing out of three of the communicative elements: expressive (self-centered), expository (world-centered), and persuasive (reader-centered).

That a separate type of writing arises from an emphasis on each communicative element is certainly an attractive position, one that might provide an elegant basis for designing comprehensive composition courses. But such a view leads to both theoretical and practical problems, not the least of which is that it gives us no direction in selecting which writing types merit greater emphasis in our courses. Furthermore, when used as an approach to evaluating writing, such a classification runs into all the problems inherent in determining intent in a text. Most teachers have seen student writing that was impossible to classify as one of Kinneavy's four types of discourse and that would be evaluated

quite differently depending upon which of the four philosophies one applied.

My research has convinced me that in many cases composition teachers either fail to have a consistent value theory or fail to let that philosophy shape pedagogy. In Silberman's terms, they are guilty of mindlessness. A fairly common writing assignment, for example, directs the student to "state and explain clearly your opinion about X" (censorship, abortion, the Dallas Cowboys). There is nothing wrong with such an assignment. But if a student does state his or her opinion and if the opinion happens to be based on gross ignorance or to contain major contradictions, the teacher must, to be consistent, ignore such matters. The topic as stated asks for opinion; it does not ask for good opinion, judged by whatever philosophy. In short, the assignment implies an expressive value-theory. It does not say, "Express your opinion to persuade a reader" (which would imply a rhetorical theory), or "Express your opinion so that it makes sense" (which would imply a mimetic theory), or even "Express your opinion correctly" (implying a formalist theory). To give the bald assignment and then judge it from any of the perspectives not implied is to be guilty of value-mode confusion.

Modal confusion is not easy to locate, since one almost has to be inside a classroom to see it. A few instances, however, have been reported in the literature. Walker Gibson has told the story of visiting a high school class in which the teacher was emphasizing the idea of a *persona* within a piece of literature. She then shifted to composition and had a boy read aloud a paper he had written. She next asked the class, "Now what's the trouble here? What voice did you hear in that paper? Is it Jimmy's voice? Is that Jimmy speaking or is it some artificial, insincere voice?" To this, the student responded, "I don't *have* to sound like *me*." Gibson notes that he agreed with the student; the teacher had failed to relate her appreciation of the author-speaker distinction in literature to the student's writing.[5] For me, she had shown in her evaluation that she was at least momentarily committed to an expressive philosophy: "Good writing is sincere writing; it sounds like the real author." There is nothing wrong with an expressive philosophy, but there is something seriously wrong with classroom methodology which implies one variety of value judgment when another will actually be employed. That is modal confusion, mindlessness.

The worst instance of modal confusion I have come across was reported by Lawrence Langer in a *Chronicle of Higher Education* article entitled "The Human Use of Language: Insensitive Ears Can't Hear Honest Prose" (January 24, 1977). He tells the story of a forty-year-old student who in childhood had been in a Nazi concentration camp in which her parents had been killed. She had never been able to talk about the experience except to other former inmates, not even to her husband and children. Her first assignment in freshman composition was to write a paper on something that was of great importance to her. She resolved to handle her childhood trauma on paper in an essay called "People I Have Forgotten." Langer quotes the entire paper of eight paragraphs and about three hundred words, calling it "not a confrontation, only a prelude." It is a moving and painful piece with a one-sentence opening paragraph, "Can you forget your own Father and Mother? If so—how or why?" The paper was returned with a large D-minus on the last page, emphatically circled. The only comment was "Your theme is not clear—you should have developed your first paragraph. You talk around your subject."

From the perspective of my four-part model, there was a conflict of evaluative modes at work here. The assignment seemed to call for writing that would be judged expressively, but the teacher's brief comment was *not* written from an expressivist point of view. It may imply a formalist perspective (good writing requires directness and development). Or it may rest on an unstated rhetorical perspective (for a reader's benefit this paper needs more directness and development). It is scarcely adequate in either case, and in either case, this sort of judgment was not what the student had been led to expect. There was once more a mindless failure to relate the outcome valued to the means adopted. My hope is that the four-part paradigm I have adopted from Abrams may reduce such mindlessness in the future.

Notes

1. The research upon which this article is based was supported by a grant from the East Texas State University Office of Organized Research in the summer of 1976. The author wishes to thank Professor H. M. Lafferty, Chairman, and the Committee on Organized Research for their support.

2. M. H. Abrams, *The Mirror and the Lamp: Romantic Theory and the Critical Tradition* (New York: Norton, 1953), pp. 2–29.

3. Ken Macrorie, *Telling Writing* (New York: Hayden, 1970), and Lou Kelly, *From Dialogue to Discourse: An Open Approach* (Glenview, IL: Scott, Foresman, 1972).

4. Peter Elbow, "A Method for Teaching Writing," *College English*, 30 (Nov., 1968), 123ff.

5. Quoted in McCrimmon, *Writing with a Purpose*, 6th ed., p. 181.

Contemporary Composition:
The Major Pedagogical Theories

James A. Berlin

Berlin's often cited and reprinted essay originally appeared in College English 44 *(1982): 765–77. It has been reprinted in* The Writing Teacher's Sourcebook. *Eds. Gary Tate and Edward P. J. Corbett. 2nd ed. New York: Oxford UP, 1988. 47–59. It also appears in the third edition, 1994. 9–21.*

A number of articles attempting to make sense of the various approaches to teaching composition have recently appeared. While all are worth considering, some promote a common assumption that I am convinced is erroneous.[1] Since all pedagogical approaches, it is argued, share a concern for the elements of the composing process—that is, for writer, reality, reader, and language—their only area of disagreement must involve the element or elements that ought to be given the most attention. From this point of view, the composing process is always and everywhere the same because writer, reality, reader, and language are always and everywhere the same. Differences in teaching theories, then, are mere cavils about which of these features to emphasize in the classroom.

I would like to say at the start that I have no quarrel with the elements that these investigators isolate as forming the composing process, and I plan to use them myself. While it is established practice today to speak of the composing process as a recursive activity involving prewriting, writing, and rewriting, it is not difficult to see the writer-reality-audience-language relationship as underlying, at a deeper structural level, each of these three stages. In fact, as I will later show, this deeper structure determines the shape that instruction in prewriting, writing, and rewriting as-

sumes—or does not assume, as it sometimes the case.

I do, however, strongly disagree with the contention that the differences in approaches to teaching writing can be explained by attending to the degree of emphasis given to universally defined elements of a universally defined composing process. The differences in these teaching approaches should instead be located in diverging definitions of the composing process itself—that is, in the way the elements that make up the process—writer, reality, audience, and language—are envisioned. Pedagogical theories in writing courses are grounded in rhetorical theories, and rhetorical theories do not differ in the simple undue emphasis of writer or audience or reality or language or some combination of these. Rhetorical theories differ from each other in the way writer, reality, audience, and language are conceived—both as separate units and in the way the units relate to each other. In the case of distinct pedagogical approaches, these four elements are likewise defined and related so as to describe a different composing process, which is to say a different world with different rules about what can be known, how it can be known, and how it can be communicated. To teach writing is to argue for a version of reality and the best way of knowing and communicating it—to deal, as Paul

Kameen has pointed out, in the metarhetorical realm of epistemology and linguistics.[2] And all composition teachers are ineluctably operating in this realm, whether or not they consciously choose to do so.

Considering pedagogical theories along these lines has led me to see groupings sometimes similar, sometimes at variance, with the schemes of others. The terms chosen for these categories are intended to prevent confusion and to be self-explanatory. The four dominant groups I will discuss are the Neo-Aristotelians or Classicists, the Positivists or Current-Traditionalists, the Neo-Platonists or Expressionists, and the New Rhetoricians. As I have said, I will be concerned in each case with the way that writer, reality, audience, and language have been defined and related so as to form a distinct world construct with distinct rules for discovering and communicating knowledge. I will then show how this epistemic complex makes for specific directives about invention, arrangement, and style (or prewriting, writing, and rewriting). Finally, as the names for the groups suggest, I will briefly trace the historical precedents of each, pointing to their roots in order to better understand their modern manifestations.

My reasons for presenting this analysis are not altogether disinterested. I am convinced that the pedagogical approach of the New Rhetoricians is the most intelligent and most practical alternative available, serving in every way the best interests of our students. I am also concerned, however, that writing teachers become more aware of the full significance of their pedagogical strategies. Not doing so can have disastrous consequences, ranging from momentarily confusing students to sending them away with faulty and even harmful information. The dismay students display about writing is, I am convinced, at least occasionally the result of teachers unconsciously offering contradictory advice about composing—guidance grounded in assumptions that simply do not square with each other. More important, as I have already indicated and as I plan to explain in detail later on, in teaching writing we are tacitly teaching a version of reality and the student's place and mode of operation in it. Yet many teachers (and I suspect most) look upon their vocations as the imparting of a largely mechanical skill, important only because it serves students in getting them through school and in advancing them in their professions. This essay will argue that writing teachers are perforce given a responsibility that far exceeds this merely instrumental task.[3]

I begin with revivals of Aristotelian rhetoric not because they are a dominant force today—far from it. My main purpose in starting with them is to show that many who say that they are followers of Aristotle are in truth opposed to his system in every sense. There is also the consideration that Aristotle has provided the technical language most often used in discussing rhetoric—so much so that it is all but impossible to talk intelligently about the subject without knowing him.

In the Aristotelian scheme of things, the material world exists independently of the observer and is knowable through sense impressions. Since sense impressions in themselves reveal nothing, however, to arrive at true knowledge it is necessary for the mind to perform an operation upon sense data. This operation is a function of reason and amounts to the appropriate use of syllogistic reasoning, the system of logic that Aristotle himself developed and refined. Providing the method for analyzing the material of any discipline, this logic offers, as Marjorie Grene explains, "a set of general rules for scientists (as Aristotle understood science) working each in his appropriate material. The rules are rules of validity, not psychological rules" (*A Portrait of Aristotle* [London: Faber and Faber, 1963], p. 69). Truth exists in conformance with the rules of logic, and logic is so thoroughly deductive that even induction is regarded as an imperfect form of the syllogism. The strictures imposed by logic, moreover, naturally arise out of the very structure of the mind and of the universe. In other words, there is a happy correspondence between the mind and the universe, so that, to cite Grene once again, "As the world is, finally, so is the mind that knows it" (p. 234).

Reality for Aristotle can thus be known and communicated, with language serving as the unproblematic medium of discourse. There is an uncomplicated correspondence between the sign and the thing, and—once again emphasizing the rational—the process whereby sign and thing are united is considered a mental act: words are not a part of the external world, but both word and thing are a part of thought.[4]

Rhetoric is of course central to Aristotle's system. Like dialectic—the method of discovering and communicating truth in learned discourse—rhetoric deals with the realm of the probable, with truth as discovered in the areas of law, politics, and what might be called public virtue. Unlike scientific discoveries, truth in these realms can never be stated with absolute certainty. Still, approximations to truth are possible. The business of rhetoric then is to enable the speaker—Aristotle's rhetoric is preeminently oral—to find the means necessary to persuade the audience of the truth. Thus rhetoric is primarily concerned with the provision of inventional devices whereby the speaker may discover his or her argument, with these devices naturally falling into three categories: the rational, the emotional, and the ethical. Since truth is rational, the first is paramount and is derived from the rules of logic, albeit applied in the relaxed form of the enthymeme and example. Realizing that individuals are not always ruled by reason, however, Aristotle provides advice on appealing to the emotions of the audience and on presenting one's own character in the most favorable light, each considered with special regard for the audience and the occasion of the speech.

Aristotle's emphasis on invention leads to the neglect of commentary on arrangement and style. The treatment of arrangement is at best sketchy, but it does display Aristotle's reliance on the logical in its commitment to rational development. The section on style is more extensive and deserves special mention because it highlights Aristotle's rationalistic view of language, a view no longer considered defensible. As R. H. Robins explains:

> The word for Aristotle is thus the minimal meaningful unit. He further distinguishes the meaning of a word as an isolate from the meaning of a sentence: a word by itself "stands for" or "indicates" . . . something, but a sentence affirms or denies a predicate of its subject, or says that its subject exists or does not exist. One cannot now defend this doctrine of meaning. It is based on the formal logic that Aristotle codified and, we might say, sterilized for generations. The notion that words have meaning just by standing for or indicating something, whether in the world at large or in the human mind (both views are stated or suggested by Aristotle), leads to difficulties that have worried philosophers in many ages, and seriously distorts linguistic and grammatical studies.[5]

It should be noted, however, that despite this unfavorable estimate, Robins goes on to praise Aristotle as in some ways anticipating later developments in linguistics.

Examples of Aristotelian rhetoric in the textbooks of today are few indeed. Edward P. J. Corbett's *Classical Rhetoric for the Modern Student* (1971) and Richard Hughes and Albert Duhamel's *Principles of Rhetoric* (1967) revive the tradition. Most textbooks that claim to be Aristotelian are operating within the paradigm of what has come to be known as Current-Traditional Rhetoric, a category that might also be called the Positivist.

The Positivist or Current-Traditional group clearly dominates thinking about writing instruction today. The evidence is the staggering number of textbooks that yearly espouse its principles. The origins of Current-Traditional Rhetoric, as Albert Kitzhaber showed in his dissertation (University of Washington, 1953) on "Rhetoric in American Colleges," can be found in the late nineteenth-century rhetoric texts of A. S. Hill, Barrett Wendell, and John F. Genung. But its epistemological stance can be found in eighteenth-century Scottish Common Sense Realism as expressed in the philosophy of Thomas Reid and James Beattie, and in the rhetorical treatises of George Campbell, Hugh Blair, and to a lesser extent, Richard Whately.

For Common Sense Realism, the certain existence of the material world is indisputable. All knowledge is founded on the simple correspondence between sense impressions and the faculties of the mind. This so far sounds like the Aristotelian world view, but is in fact a conscious departure from it. Common Sense Realism denies the value of the deductive method—syllogistic reasoning—in arriving at knowledge. Truth is instead discovered through induction alone. It is the individual sense impression that provides the basis on which all knowledge can be built. Thus the new scientific logic of Locke replaces the old deductive logic of Aristotle as the method for understanding experience. The world is still rational, but its system is to be discovered through the experimental method, not through logical categories grounded in a mental faculty. The state of affairs characterizing the emergence of the new epistemology is succinctly summarized by Wilbur Samuel Howell:

> The old science, as the disciples of Aristotle conceived of it at the end of the seventeenth century, had considered its function to be that of subjecting traditional truths to syllogistic examination, and of accepting as new truth only what could be proved to be consistent with the old. Under that kind of arrangement, traditional logic had taught the methods of deductive analysis, had perfected itself in the machinery of testing propositions for consistency, and had served at the same time as the instrument by which truths could be arranged so as to become intelligible and convincing to other learned men. . . . The new science, as envisioned by its founder, Francis Bacon, considered its function to be that of subjecting physical and human facts to observation and experiment, and of accepting as new truth only what could be shown to conform to the realities behind it.[6]

The rhetoric based on the new logic can be seen most clearly in George Campbell's *Philosophy of Rhetoric* (1776) and Hugh Blair's *Lectures on Rhetoric and Belles Letters* (1783). The old distinction between dialectic as the discipline of learned discourse and rhetoric as the discipline of popular discourse is destroyed. Rhetoric becomes the study of all forms of communication: scientific, philosophical, historical, political, legal, and even poetic. An equally significant departure in this new rhetoric is that it contains no inventional system. Truth is to be discovered outside the rhetorical enterprise—through the method, usually the scientific method, of the appropriate

discipline, or, as in poetry and oratory, through genius.

The aim of rhetoric is to teach how to adapt the discourse to its hearers—and here the uncomplicated correspondence of the faculties and the world is emphasized. When the individual is freed from the biases of language, society, or history, the senses provide the mental faculties with a clear and distinct image of the world. The world readily surrenders its meaning to anyone who observes it properly, and no operation of the mind—logical or otherwise—is needed to arrive at truth. To communicate, the speaker or writer—both now included—need only provide the language which corresponds either to the objects in the external world or to the ideas in his or her own mind—both are essentially the same—in such a way that it reproduces the objects and the experience of them in the minds of the hearers (Cohen, pp. 38–42). As Campbell explains, "Thus language and thought, like body and soul, are made to correspond, and the qualities of the one exactly to co-operate with those of the other."[7] The emphasis in this rhetoric is on adapting what has been discovered outside the rhetorical enterprise to the minds of the hearers. The study of rhetoric thus focuses on developing skill in arrangement and style.

Given this epistemological field in a rhetoric that takes all communication as its province, discourse tends to be organized according to the faculties to which it appeals. A scheme that is at once relevant to current composition theory and typical in its emulation of Campbell, Blair, and Whately can be found in John Francis Genung's *The Practical Elements of Rhetoric* (1886).[8] For Genung the branches of discourse fall into four categories. The most "fundamental" mode appeals to understanding and is concerned with transmitting truth, examples of which are "history, biography, fiction, essays, treatises, criticism." The second and third groups are description and narration, appealing again to the understanding, but leading the reader to "feel the thought as well as think it." For Genung "the purest outcome" of this kind of writing is poetry. The fourth kind of discourse, "the most complex literary type," is oratory. This kind is concerned with persuasion and makes its special appeal to the will, but in so doing involves all the faculties. Genung goes on to create a further distinction that contributed to the departmentalization of English and Speech and the division of English into literature and composition. Persuasion is restricted to considerations of experts in the spoken language and poetry to discussions of literature teachers, now first appearing. College writing courses, on the other hand, are to focus on discourse that appeals to the understanding—exposition, narration, description, and argumentation (distinct now from persuasion). It is significant, moreover, that college rhetoric is to be concerned solely with the communication of truth that is certain and empirically verifiable—in other words, not probabilistic.

Genung, along with his contemporaries A. S. Hill and Barrett Wendell, sets the pattern for most modern composition textbooks, and their works show striking similarities to the vast majority of texts published today.[9] It is discouraging that generations after Freud and Einstein, college students are encouraged to embrace a view of reality based on a mechanistic physics and a naive faculty psychology—and all in the name of a convenient pedagogy.

The next theory of composition instruction to be considered arose as a reaction to current-traditional rhetoric. Its clearest statements are located in the work of Ken Macrorie, William Coles, Jr., James E. Miller and Stephen Judy, and the so-called "Pre-Writing School" of D. Gordon Rohman, Albert O. Wlecke, Clinton S. Burhans, and Donald Stewart (see Harrington, et al., pp. 645–647). Frequent assertions of this view, however, have appeared in American public schools in the twentieth century under the veil of including "creative expression" in the English curriculum.[10] The roots of this view of rhetoric in America can be traced to Emerson and the Transcendentalists, and its ultimate source is to be found in Plato.

In the Platonic scheme, truth is not based on sensory experience since the material world is always in flux and thus unreliable. Truth is instead discovered through an internal apprehension, a private vision of a world that transcends the physical. As Robert Cushman explains in *Therepeia* (Chapel Hill: University of North Carolina Press, 1958), "The central theme of Platonism regarding knowledge is that truth is not brought to man, but man to the truth" (p. 213). A striking corollary of this view is that ultimate truth can be discovered by the individual, but cannot be communicated. Truth can be learned but not taught. The purpose of rhetoric then becomes not the transmission of truth, but the correction of error, the removal of that which obstructs the personal apprehension of the truth. And the method is dialectic, the interaction of two interlocutors of good will intent on arriving at knowledge. Because the respondents are encouraged to break out of their ordinary perceptual set, to become free of the material world and of past error, the dialectic is often disruptive, requiring the abandonment of long held conventions and opinions. Preparing the soul to discover truth is often painful.

Plato's epistemology leads to a unique view of language. Because ultimate truths cannot be communicated, language can only deal with the realm of error, the world of flux, and act, as Gerald L. Bruns explains, as "a preliminary exercise which must engage the soul before the encounter with 'the knowable and truly real being' is possible" (p. 16). Truth is finally inexpressible, is beyond the resources of language. Yet Plato allows for the possibility that language may be used to communicate essential realities. In the *Republic* he speaks of using analogy to express ultimate truth, and in the *Phaedrus,* even as rhetoric is called into question, he employs an analogical method in his discussion of the soul and love. Language, it would appear, can be of some use in trying to communicate the absolute, or at least to approximate the experience of it.

The major tenets of this Platonic rhetoric form the center of what are commonly called "Expressionist" textbooks. Truth is conceived as the result of a private vision that must be constantly consulted in writing. These textbooks thus emphasize writing as a "personal" activity, as an expression of one's unique voice. In *Writing and Reality* (New

York: Harper and Row, 1978), James Miller and Stephen Judy argue that "all good writing is *personal,* whether it be an abstract essay or a private letter," and that an important justification for writing is "to sound the depths, to explore, and to discover." The reason is simple: "Form in language grows from content—something the writer has to say—and that something, in turn, comes directly from the self" (pp. 12, 15). Ken Macrorie constantly emphasizes "Telling Truths," by which he means a writer must be "true to the feeling of his experience." His thrust throughout is on speaking in "an authentic voice" (also in Donald Stewart's *The Authentic Voice: A PreWriting Approach to Student Writing,* based on the work of Rohman and Wlecke), indicating by this the writer's private sense of things.[11] This placement of the self at the center of communication is also, of course, everywhere present in Coles' *The Plural I* (New York: Holt, Rinehart, and Winston, 1978).

One obvious objection to my reading of these expressionist theories is that their conception of truth can in no way be seen as comparable to Plato's transcendent world of ideas. While this cannot be questioned, it should also be noted that no member of this school is a relativist intent on denying the possibility of any certain truth whatever. All believe in the existence of verifiable truths and find them, as does Plato, in private experience, divorced from the impersonal data of sense experience. All also urge the interaction between writer and reader, a feature that leads to another point of similarity with Platonic rhetoric—the dialectic.

Most expressionist theories rely on classroom procedures that encourage the writer to interact in dialogue with the members of the class. The purpose is to get rid of what is untrue to the private vision of the writer, what is, in a word, inauthentic. Coles, for example, conceives of writing as an unteachable act, a kind of behavior that can be learned but not taught. (See especially the preface to *The Plural I.*) His response to this denial of his pedagogical role is to provide a classroom environment in which the student learns to write—although he or she is not taught to write—through dialectic. *The Plural I,* in fact, reveals Coles and his

students engaging in a dialogue designed to lead both teacher and class—Coles admits that he always learns in his courses—to the discovery of what can be known but not communicated. This view of truth as it applies to writing is the basis of Coles' classroom activity. Dialogue can remove error, but it is up to the individual to discover ultimate knowledge. The same emphasis on dialectic can also be found in the texts of Macrorie and of Miller and Judy. Despite their insistence on the self as the source of all content, for example, Miller and Judy include "making connections with others in dialogue and discussion" (p. 5), and Macrorie makes the discussion of student papers the central activity of his classroom.

This emphasis on dialectic, it should be noted, is not an attempt to adjust the message to the audience, since doing so would clearly constitute a violation of the self. Instead the writer is trying to use others to get rid of what is false to the self, what is insincere and untrue to the individual's own sense of things, as evidenced by the use of language—the theory of which constitutes the final point of concurrence between modern Expressionist and Platonic rhetorics.

Most Expressionist textbooks emphasize the use of metaphor either directly or by implication. Coles, for example, sees the major task of the writer to be avoiding the imitation of conventional expressions because they limit what the writer can say. The fresh, personal vision demands an original use of language. Rohman and Wlecke, as well as the textbook by Donald Stewart based on their research, are more explicit. They specifically recommend the cultivation of the ability to make analogies (along with meditation and journal writing) as an inventional device. Macrorie makes metaphor one of the prime features of "good writing" (p. 21) and in one form or another takes it up again and again in *Telling Writing.* The reason for this emphasis is not hard to discover. In communicating, language does not have as its referent the object in the external world or an idea of this object in the mind. Instead, to present truth language must rely on original metaphors in order to capture what is unique in each personal vision. The private apprehension of the real relies on the metaphoric appeal from the known to the unknown, from the public and accessible world of the senses to the inner and privileged immaterial realm, in order to be made available to others. As in Plato, the analogical method offers the only avenue to expressing the true.

The clearest pedagogical expression of the New Rhetoric—or what might be called Epistemic Rhetoric—is found in Ann E. Berthoff's *Forming/Thinking/Writing: The Composing Imagination* (Rochelle Park, N.J.: Hayden, 1978) and Richard L. Young, Alton L. Becker, and Kenneth L. Pike's *Rhetoric: Discovery and Change* (New York: Harcourt Brace Jovanovich, 1970). These books have behind them the rhetorics of such figures as I. A. Richards and Kenneth Burke and the philosophical statements of Susanne K. Langer, Ernst Cassirer, and John Dewey. Closely related to the work of Berthoff and Young, Becker, and Pike are the cognitive-developmental approaches of such figures as James Moffett, Linda Flower, Andrea Lunsford, and Barry Kroll. While their roots are different— located in the realm of cognitive psychology and empirical linguistics—their methods are strikingly similar. In this discussion, however, I intend to call exclusively upon the textbooks of Berthoff and of Young, Becker, and Pike to make my case, acknowledging at the start that there are others that could serve as well. Despite differences, their approaches most comprehensively display a view of rhetoric as epistemic, as a means of arriving at truth.

Classical Rhetoric considers truth to be located in the rational operation of the mind, Positivist Rhetoric in the correct perception of sense impressions, and Neo-Platonic Rhetoric within the individual, attainable only through an internal apprehension. In each case knowledge is a commodity situated in a permanent location, a repository to which the individual goes to be enlightened.

For the New Rhetoric, knowledge is not simply a static entity available for retrieval. Truth is dynamic and dialectical, the result of a process involving the interaction of opposing elements. It is a relation that is created, not pre-existent and waiting to be discovered. The basic elements of the dialectic are the elements that make up the communication process—writer (speaker), audience, reality, language. Communication is always basic to the epistemology underlying the New Rhetoric because truth is always truth for someone standing in relation to others in a linguistically circumscribed situation. The elements of the communication process thus do not simply provide a convenient way of talking about rhetoric. They form the elements that go into the very shaping of knowledge.

It is this dialectical notion of rhetoric—and of rhetoric as the determiner of reality—that underlies the textbooks of Berthoff and of Young, Becker, and Pike. In demonstrating this thesis I will consider the elements of the dialectic alone or in pairs, simply because they are more easily handled this way in discussion. It should not be forgotten, however, that in operation they are always simultaneously in a relationship of one to all, constantly modifying their values in response to each other.

The New Rhetoric denies that truth is discoverable in sense impression since this data must always be interpreted—structured and organized— in order to have meaning. The perceiver is of course the interpreter, but she is likewise unable by herself to provide truth since meaning cannot be made apart from the data of experience. Thus Berthoff cites Kant's "Percepts without concepts are empty: concepts without percepts are blind" (p. 13). Later she explains: "The brain puts things together, composing the percepts by which we can make sense of the world. We don't just 'have' a visual experience and then by thinking 'have' a mental experience: the mutual dependence of seeing and knowing is what a modern psychologist has in mind when he speaks of 'the intelligent eye'" (p. 44). Young, Becker, and Pike state the same notion:

> Constantly changing, bafflingly complex, the external world is not a neat, well-ordered place replete with meaning, but an enigma requiring interpretation. This interpretation is the result of a transaction between events in the external world and the mind of the individual—between the world "out there" and the individual's previous experience, knowledge,

values, attitudes, and desires. Thus the mirrored world is not just the sum total of eardrum rattles, retinal excitations, and so on: it is a creation that reflects the peculiarities of the perceiver as well as the peculiarities of what is perceived. (p. 25)

Language is at the center of this dialectical interplay between the individual and the world. For Neo-Aristotelians, Positivists, and Neo-Platonists, truth exists prior to language so that the difficulty of the writer or speaker is to find the appropriate words to communicate knowledge. For the New Rhetoric truth is impossible without language since it is language that embodies and generates truth. Young, Becker, and Pike explain:

Language provides a way of unitizing experience: a set of symbols that label recurring chunks of experience. . . . Language depends on our seeing certain experiences as constant or repeatable. And seeing the world as repeatable depends, in part at least, on language. A language is, in a sense, a theory of the universe, a way of selecting and grouping experience in a fairly consistent and predictable way. (p. 27)

Berthoff agrees: "The relationship between thought and language is dialectical: ideas are conceived by language: language is generated by thought" (p. 47). Rather than truth being prior to language, language is prior to truth and determines what shapes truth can take. Language does not correspond to the "real world." It creates the "real world" by organizing it, by determining what will be perceived and not perceived, by indicating what has meaning and what is meaningless.

The audience of course enters into this play of language. Current-Traditional Rhetoric demands that the audience be as "objective" as the writer; both shed personal and social concerns in the interests of the unobstructed perception of empirical reality. For Neo-Platonic Rhetoric the audience is a check to the false note of the inauthentic and helps to detect error, but it is not involved in the actual discovery of truth—a purely personal matter. Neo-Aristotelians take the audience seriously as a force to be considered in shaping the message. Still, for all its discussion of the emotional and ethical appeals, Classical Rhetoric emphasizes rational structures, and the concern for the audience is only a concession to the imperfection of human nature. In the New Rhetoric the message arises out of the interaction of the writer, language, reality, and the audience. Truths are operative only within a given universe of discourse, and this universe is shaped by all of these elements, including the audience. As Young, Becker, and Pike explain:

The writer must first understand the nature of his own interpretation and how it differs from the interpretations of others. Since each man segments experience into discrete, repeatable units, the writer can begin by asking how his way of segmenting and ordering experience differs from his reader's. How do units of time, space, the visible world, social organization, and so on differ? . . .

Human differences are the raw material of writing—differences in experiences and ways of segmenting them, differences in values, purposes, and goals. They are our reason for wishing to communicate. Through communication we create community, the basic value underlying rhetoric. To do so, we must overcome the barriers to communication that are, paradoxically, the motive for communication. (p. 30)

Ann E. Berthoff also includes this idea in her emphasis on meaning as a function of relationship.

Meanings are relationships. Seeing means "seeing relationships," whether we're talking about seeing as *perception* or seeing as *understanding.* "I see what you mean" means "I understand how you put that together so that it makes sense." The way we make sense of the world is to see something *with respect to, in terms of, in relation to* something else. We can't make sense of one thing by itself: it must be seen as being *like* another thing: or *next to, across from, coming after* another thing: or as a repetition of another thing. *Something* makes sense—is meaningful—only if it is taken with *something else.* (p. 44)

The dialectical view of reality, language, and the audience redefines the writer. In Current-Traditional Rhetoric the writer must efface himself;

stated differently, the writer must focus on experience in a way that makes possible the discovery of certain kinds of information—the empirical and rational—and the neglect of others—psychological and social concerns. In Neo-Platonic Rhetoric the writer is at the center of the rhetorical act, but is finally isolated, cut off from community, and left to the lonely business of discovering truth alone. Neo-Aristotelian Rhetoric exalts the writer, but circumscribes her effort by its emphasis on the rational—the enthymeme and example. The New Rhetoric sees the writer as a creator of meaning, a shaper of reality, rather than a passive receptor of the immutably given. "When you write," explains Berthoff, "you don't follow somebody else's scheme: you design your own. As a writer, you learn to make words behave the way you want them to. . . . Learning to write is not a matter of learning the rules that govern the use of the semicolon or the names of sentence structures, nor is it a matter of manipulating words; it is a matter of making meanings, and that is the work of the active mind" (p. 11). Young, Becker, and Pike concur: "We have sought to develop a rhetoric that implies that we are all citizens of an extraordinarily diverse and disturbed world, that the 'truths' we live by are tentative and subject to change, that we must be discoverers of new truths as well as preservers and transmitters of old, and that enlightened cooperation is the preeminent ethical goal of communication" (p. 9).

This version of the composing process leads to a view of what can be taught in the writing class that rivals Aristotelian rhetoric in its comprehensiveness. Current-Traditional and Neo-Platonic Rhetoric deny the place of invention in rhetoric because for both truth is considered external and self-evident, accessible to anyone who seeks it in the proper spirit. Like Neo-Aristotelian Rhetoric, the New Rhetoric sees truth as probabilistic, and it provides students with techniques—heuristics—for discovering it, or what might more accurately be called creating it. This does not mean, however, that arrangement and style are regarded as unimportant, as in Neo-Platonic Rhetoric. In fact, the attention paid to these matters in the New Rhetoric

rivals that paid in Current-Traditional Rhetoric, but not because they are the only teachable part of the process. Structure and language are a part of the formation of meaning, are at the center of the discovery of truth, not simply the dress of thought. From the point of view of pedagogy, New Rhetoric thus treats in depth all the offices of classical rhetoric that apply to written language—invention, arrangement, and style—and does so by calling upon the best that has been thought and said about them by contemporary observers.

In talking and writing about the matters that form the substance of this essay, at my back I always hear the nagging (albeit legitimate) query of the overworked writing teacher: But what does all this have to do with the teaching of freshman composition? My answer is that it is more relevant than most of us are prepared to admit. In teaching writing, we are not simply offering training in a useful technical skill that is meant as a simple complement to the more important studies of other areas. We are teaching a way of experiencing the world, a way of ordering and making sense of it. As I have shown, subtly informing our statements about invention, arrangement, and even style are assumptions about the nature of reality. If the textbooks that sell the most copies tell us anything, they make abundantly clear that most writing teachers accept the assumptions of Current-Traditional Rhetoric, the view that arose contemporaneously with the positivistic position of modern science. Yet most of those who use these texts would readily admit that the scientific world view has demonstrated its inability to solve the problems that most concern us, problems that are often themselves the result of scientific "breakthroughs." And even many scientists concur with them in this view—Oppenheimer and Einstein, for example. In our writing classrooms, however, we continue to offer a view of composing that insists on a version of reality that is sure to place students at a disadvantage in addressing the problems that will confront them in both their professional and private experience.

Neo-Platonic, Neo-Aristotelian, and what I have called New Rhetoric are reactions to the inadequacy of Current-Traditional Rhetoric to teach students a notion of the composing process that will enable them to become effective persons as they become effective writers. While my sympathies are obviously with the last of these reactions, the three can be considered as one in their efforts to establish new directions for a modern rhetoric. Viewed in this way, the difference between them and Current-Traditional Rhetoric is analogous to the difference Richard Rorty has found in what he calls, in *Philosophy and the Mirror of Nature* (Princeton, N.J.: Princeton University Press, 1979), hermeneutic and epistemological philosophy. The hermeneutic approach to rhetoric bases the discipline on establishing an open dialogue in the hopes of reaching agreement about the truth of the matter at hand. Current-Traditional Rhetoric views the rhetorical situation as an arena where the truth is incontrovertibly established by a speaker or writer more enlightened than her audience. For the hermeneuticist truth is never fixed finally on unshakable grounds. Instead it emerges only after false starts and failures, and it can only represent a tentative point of rest in a continuing conversation. Whatever truth is arrived at, moreover, is always the product of individuals calling on the full range of their humanity, with esthetic and moral considerations given at least as much importance as any others. For Current-Traditional Rhetoric truth is empirically based and can only be achieved through subverting a part of the human response to experience. Truth then stands forever, a tribute to its method, triumphant over what most of us consider important in life, successful through subserving writer, audience, and language to the myth of an objective reality.

One conclusion should now be incontestable. The numerous recommendations of the "process"-centered approaches to writing instruction as superior to the "product"-centered approaches are not very useful. Everyone teaches the process of writing, but everyone does not teach the *same* process. The test of one's competence as a composition instructor, it seems to me, resides in being able to recognize and justify the version of the process being taught, complete with all of its significance for the student.

Notes

1. I have in mind Richard Fulkerson. "Four Philosophies of Composition," *College Composition and Communication,* 30 (1979), 343–48: David V. Harrington, et. al., "A Critical Survey of Resources for Teaching Rhetorical Invention," *College English,* 40 (1979), 641–61: William F. Woods, "Composition Textbooks and Pedagogical Theory 1960–80," *CE,* 43 (1981), 393–409.

2. "Rewording the Rhetoric of Composition," *PRETEXT* I (1980), 39. I am indebted to Professor Kameen's classification of pedagogical theories for the suggestiveness of his method: my conclusions, however, are substantially different.

3. There is still another reason for pursuing the method I recommend, one that explains why rhetorical principles are now at the center of discussions in so many different disciplines. When taken together, writer, reality, audience, and language identify an epistemic field—the basic conditions that determine what knowledge will be knowable, what not knowable, and how the knowable will be communicated. This epistemic field is the point of departure for numerous studies, although the language used to describe it varies from thinker to thinker. Examples are readily available. In *Science and the Modern World* (New York: Macmillan, 1926), A. N. Whitehead sees this field as a product of the "fundamental assumptions which adherents of all variant systems within the epoch unconsciously presuppose" (p. 71). Susanne Langer, in *Philosophy in a New Key* (Cambridge, Mass.: Harvard University Press, 1979), calls it the "tacit, fundamental way of seeing things" (p. 6). Michael Polanyi uses the terms "tacit knowledge" in *Personal Knowledge* (Chicago: University of Chicago Press, 1962). Michel Foucault, in *The Order of Things* (1971: rpt. New York: Vintage Books, 1973), speaks of the "episteme," and Thomas Kuhn, in *Structure of Scientific Revolutions* (Chicago: University of Chicago Press, 1970), discusses at length the "paradigm" that underlies a scientific discipline. The historian Hayden White, in *Metahistory: The Historical Imagination in Nineteenth-Century Europe* (Baltimore: Johns Hopkins University Press, 1973), has translated the elements of the composing process into terms appropriate to the writing of history, seeing the historical field as being made up of the historian, the historical record, the historical accounts, and an audience. One compelling reason for studying composition theory is that it so readily reveals its epistemic field, thus indicating, for example, a great deal about the way a particular historical period defines itself—a fact convincingly demonstrated in Murray Cohen's *Sensible Words: Linguistic Practice in England*

1640–1785 (Baltimore: Johns Hopkins University Press, 1977), a detailed study of English grammars.

4. See Gerald L. Bruns, *Modern Poetry and the Idea of Language* (New Haven, Ct.: Yale University Press, 1974), p. 34.

5. *Ancient and Mediaeval Grammatical Theory in Europe* (London: G. Bell and Sons, 1951), pp. 20–21.

6. *Eighteenth-Century British Logic and Rhetoric* (Princeton, N.J.: Princeton University Press, 1971), pp. 5–6.

7. *The Philosophy of Rhetoric,* ed. Lloyd F. Bitzer (Carbondale: Southern Illinois University Press, 1963), p. 215.

8. For a more detailed discussion of Genung see my "John Genung and Contemporary Composition Theory: The Triumph of the Eighteenth Century," *Rhetoric Society Quarterly,* 11 (1981), 74–84.

9. For an analysis of modern composition textbooks, see James A. Berlin and Robert P. Inkster, "Current-Traditional Rhetoric: Paradigm and Practice." *Freshman English News,* 8 (1980), 1–4, 13–14.

10. Kenneth J. Kantor, "Creative Expression in the English Curriculum: A Historical Perspective." *Research in the Teaching of English,* 9 (1975), 5–29.

11. *Telling Writing* (Rochelle Park, N.J.: Hayden Book Company, 1978), p. 13.

From *The Making of Knowledge in Composition: Portrait of an Emerging Field*

Stephen North

Excerpts are taken from The Making of Knowledge in Composition: Portrait of an Emerging Field. *Upper Montclair: Boynton/Cook, 1987. 15–17, 21–27, 59–65, 135–40.*

1: A HISTORICAL CONTEXT

. . . We can therefore date the birth of modern Composition, capital C, to 1963. And what marks its emergence as a nascent academic field more than anything else is this need to replace practice as the field's dominant mode of inquiry. The same was true to some extent, of course, for all of the "reformed" English; granting priority to knowledge generated by the methods of the academy necessarily threatened to undermine the authority of the practitioner. This wasn't always a matter of frontal assault. For example, in his Introduction to the Proceedings of the 1962 conference on "Needed Research in the Teaching of English," Erwin Steinberg tries to temper what he fears will be construed as the ruthlessness of the collection's papers in this regard:

> Amid the profusion of questions raised at the conference and the flood of recommended research, some of the conferees, understandably, began to feel that nothing was known about the teaching of English, that, as one conferee put it, "it is all gap." The reader of this report, unless forewarned, may feel the same. Actually, much is known about the teaching of language, literature, and composition. Teaching, as a profession, goes back several thousand years, and the experiences and, more recently, the research accumulated during that time have been widely published. . . . One need not be a research specialist to discover good teachers; one need only be a student (p. 2).

For Steinberg, the "many questions and recommended research projects, therefore, do not indicate a lack of knowledge," nor does he want to admit there is anything inimical to practical knowledge in the proposed inquiries:

> Sometimes they indicate a desire to buttress an art with science, to analyze and define the techniques of the skillful English teacher and the contents and patterns of good English courses and curriculums. With more exact knowledge available, colleges will be better able to prepare prospective teachers, and administrators and interested citizens will with more confidence be able to distinguish the better from the poorer programs (pp. 2–3).

But this assessment was more diplomatic than prophetic. The reform of English *would* be a top-down affair. Practitioner knowledge, however ancient or hard-won, would have to be supplanted. J. N. Hook, the first director of Project English, probably reflects the spirit of the times more accurately when he argues, in his address to the very same conference, that "in English teaching we have relied too long on our best guesses" (p. 7).

And in the new Composition, this stance would turn out to be, if anything, even more extreme. In that same year, 1962, the NCTE Executive Council formed an ad hoc Committee on the State of Knowledge about Composition, the purpose of which was " 'to review what is known and what is not known about the teaching and learning of composition and the conditions under which it is taught, for the purpose of preparing for publication a special scientifically based report on what is known in this area.' "[1] The document which resulted, *Research in Written Composition,* reflects nothing of Steinberg's optimism about how much is already known:

> Today's research in Composition, taken as a whole, may be compared to chemical research as it emerged from the period of alchemy: some terms are being defined usefully, a number of procedures are being refined, but the field as a whole is laced with dreams, prejudices, and makeshift operations. Not enough investigators are really informing themselves about the procedures and results of previous research before embarking on their own. Too few of them conduct pilot experiments and validate their measuring instruments before undertaking an investigation. Too many seem to be bent more on obtaining an advanced degree or another publication than on making a genuine contribution to knowledge, and a fair measure of the blame goes to the faculty adviser or journal editor who permits or publishes such irresponsible work. And far too few of those who have conducted an initial piece of research follow it with further exploration or replicate the investigations of others (p. 5).

The explicit argument is clear enough. For these authors, the authority of an emerging Composition will derive from inquiry—"research"—modeled in method and rigor on research in the sciences. Measured against that standard, as the analogy suggests, the work of the first six decades of the century have been pathetic indeed. However, the implicit argument seems equally clear, and is even more important here. First, then, practical knowledge, the stuff of teachers' rooms, how-to articles, textbooks, and the like, doesn't count as research— at any rate, it is nowhere considered among the

504 studies Braddock et al. list, is not a portion of "what is known and what is not known about the teaching and learning of composition." Instead, the authors seem to imply, practice needs to be based on research. If that is true, though, then practice is in serious trouble indeed: If Composition research is to scientific inquiry what alchemy was to chemistry, then presumably current practice must be to "scientific" practice what "real" medicine is to witch doctoring. A practice based on "dreams, prejudices, and makeshift operations" is quite capable of doing as much harm as good.

It would be no great exaggeration to call *Research in Written Composition* the charter of modern Composition. With the image it fosters—of a sort of ur-discipline blindly groping its way out of the darkness toward the bright light of a "scientific" certainty—it sets the stage for what I have already characterized as the field's methodological land rush. Composition is declared to be essentially virgin territory; little is known, and even that little is of questionable value, the result of blundering or careless work. If old composition is to become new Composition; if the "profession," as its membership seemed ready to call it, is to take its rightful place in the academy, the dominance of practice and sloppy research would have to end. This was to be a new era, and it would demand new kinds of knowledge produced by new kinds of inquiry.

2: THE PRACTITIONERS

It may seem odd, given the account of modern Composition's origins offered in the previous chapter, to turn immediately to a consideration of Practitioners as knowledge-makers. After all, the whole thrust of the academic reform movement was to remove authority over knowledge from the hands of those whose main source of such authority was their practice. And in Composition, where that authority had at any rate been exercised pretty much by default, the removal was effected quite successfully—so successfully, in fact, that we are by now, some twenty years later, largely unaccustomed to entertaining the notion of practice as a mode of inquiry at all, as involving a series of steps that result in a contribution to a field of knowledge. The more common conception of Practitioners has come to be rather more in keeping with the "emerging science" image Braddock et al. offer. In those terms, Practitioners are regarded essentially as technicians: Scholars and especially Researchers *make* knowledge; Practitioners apply it.

But this latter conception of practice has not come about overnight. However bald the declarations of ignorance about Composition made by people caught up in the fervor of those reform-oriented committees and conferences, the vast majority of the field's members were then, and remain now, Practitioners. Calling for new kinds of knowledge made in new ways was one thing; getting them was quite another. It takes time to identify new modes of inquiry, to acquire expertise in them, and then to find or create outlets in which to publish their results. They have emerged very slowly. Moreover, even as these alternate brands of knowledge have found their way into Composition, they have not brought practice-as-inquiry to a grinding halt. The effect is better understood as a devaluation. Knowledge gained via practice hasn't disappeared. Instead, its credibility, its power vis-à-vis other kinds of knowledge, has gradually, steadily, diminished.

Thus, practice clearly was then, and remains now, not only a distinguishable mode of inquiry, but the one most widely pursued in the field. And in fact, some few Practitioners have always managed to maintain a certain extraordinary visibility and authority, usually by virtue of their power as writers within a Practitioner culture that is, as we shall see, primarily oral. These people can serve here as points of reference, emblems of Practitioner inquiry at its most visible. Some of the names from 1963 are still familiar now, though not always in the same role: Robert Gorrell, Walker Gibson, Priscilla Tyler, Harold Allen, Ken Macrorie, John Gerber, Josephine Miles, Richard Braddock, Paul Roberts, A. M. Tibbetts, Hans Guth, James Mc-Crimmon. And there has been a steady line of new names since: Roger Sale, Donald Hall, Elizabeth Cowan, Donald Murray, William Coles, Mina Shaughnessy, John Schultz, Elaine Maimon, Peter Elbow, Muriel Harris, Toby Fulwiler—all Practitioners who, by virtue of some combination of eloquence and influence, attract a considerable following.

But these people also represent the exception, not the rule. Nor does visibility necessarily equal quality: these are the best known, not necessarily the best, Practitioners. Practitioners are for the most part not highly visible in this way. They are rather, one might say, Composition's rank and file.[2] Day in and day out, thousands upon thousands of them work at Composition. They do so in a variety of settings: classrooms at all levels, some devoted exclusively to writing, some not; in writing labs and centers; as hired graders; as consultants in both academic and non-academic situations, and so on. In these settings, they are faced over and over again with variations on the problem of what to *do* about teaching writing: what sort of syllabus to construct for a seventh-grade class; what kind of writing to assign as a prelude to reading Poe; how to talk to a frightened college sophomore about a philosophy paper; how to respond to research papers on "The Maginot Line"; how to teach middle management people about readability. In the process, they draw on, and contribute to, a body of knowledge that I have come to call *lore:* the accumulated body of traditions, practices, and beliefs in terms of which Practitioners understand how writing is done, learned, and taught.

Eventually, it will be of considerable importance to this study to deal with the circumstances under which Practitioner inquiry has come to be devalued: to consider how this vast majority of Composition's membership should have come to be effectively disenfranchised as knowledge-makers, and what the implications of that devaluation might be. But that is getting ahead of the game. In this chapter I want simply to examine what lore is, and to account for how practice as inquiry works.

The Nature of Practitioner Knowledge: Lore

For some readers, perhaps, the term "lore" will have negative, even denigrative connotations. Lore is what witches know, or herbal healers, or wizards in fantasy fiction. It's exactly the sort of stuff, in fact, that the alchemy metaphor in *Research in Written Composition* warns us about, stuff that "scientific" inquiry would show to be a muddled combination of half-truths, myths, and superstitions. In that sense, lores in general would seem to be out of fashion in our time. On the other hand, Composition's lore is a body of knowledge very much like those accumulated among practitioners of other arts—art here being broadly conceived—like painting or parenting, to offer an unlikely pair. These bodies of knowledge are not "scientifically" rigorous, either. And while they can, like lore, be informed by other kinds of inquiry, including those of the various sciences, they cannot be supplanted by them. For example, analyses of ocular function can help inform us about how we "see" paintings, but they cannot tell a Picasso what to do with his brush; and while careful psychological studies might lead to a developmental model for children—Piaget comes to mind, of course—they cannot produce a formula for parental discipline, nor provide any substitute for an adeptness at reading a child's moods derived from affection and experience.

This is not to say that Practitioners' lore is without logic or form. Not at all. It is driven, first, by a pragmatic logic: It is concerned with what has worked, is working, or might work in teaching, doing, or learning writing. Second, its structure is essentially experiential. That is, the traditions, practices, and beliefs of which it is constituted are best understood as being organized within an experience-based framework: I will create my version of lore out of what has worked or might work—either in my own experience or in that of others—and I will understand and order it in terms of the circumstances under which it did so. In some of its more public manifestations—textbooks, syllabi, and the like—this structure tends to be obscured, usually in favor of some loosely topical organization (prewriting, writing, revision, editing; words, sentences, paragraphs, etc.). But, as we shall see below, such documents do not provide a very accurate image of lore. And indeed, textbook

writers who are able to preserve some measure of this experiential structure in their work—Ken Macrorie or John Schultz, for instance—gain enormous popularity with Practitioners for precisely that reason. However quirky they may seem to other readers, to Practitioners they are operating within a clearly recognizable experiential framework, and so making perfect sense.

Lore's pragmatic logic and experience-based structure account for three of its most important functional properties. The first is that literally anything can become a part of lore. The only requirement for entry is that the idea, notion, practice, or whatever be nominated: some member of the community must claim that it worked, or seemed to work, or might work. Once this nomination is made—by formal publication, in a handout, or just in a hallway conversation—the item becomes a part of lore. No matter whether the nomination seems common-sensical, obvious, insightful, ludicrous—that children should write often, say, or that someone should read that writing, that it should be published, or that errors in it should be met with canings. The nature of a pragmatic logic makes disposition simple: once somebody says that it has worked or is working or might work, it is part of lore.

Lore's second functional property is just as important as this open-door policy, and no doubt equally curious to outsiders. It goes like this: While anything can become a part of lore, nothing can ever be dropped from it, either. There is simply no mechanism for it. Lore's various elements are not pitted against one another within the framework of some lore-specific dialectic, or checked and re-checked by Practitioner experiments, so that the weakest or least useful are eliminated. Indeed, lore can—and does—contain plenty of items that would, were they part of some other system, be contradictory: "Know what you want to say before you begin to write." "Write in order to find out what you want to say." "Never use the first person." "It's perfectly all right to use the first person." All Practitioners are aware, at some level, that what they know is chock full of such seeming contraries. What makes them acceptable, of course, is lore's experiential structure.

Practitioners do not find themselves operating in the Experimentalist's neat world of dependent and independent variables, nor the Philosopher's dialectical oppositions. This place is messier; cause and effect are the objects of intuition, and shadowy at best. And in this messier world, experience regularly affirms seemingly contrary truths: What worked yesterday doesn't work today; what works in one class flops in another. That's how it is with arts, and there is never any accounting for exactly why. So it makes sense to keep around everything that *might* work, just in case. Indeed, for a pragmatic body of knowledge organized in terms of experience, the surprise would be that it did not embody such seeming contraries, not that it does.

The third functional property of lore has to do with the form of contributions to it—those made by Practitioners, but more importantly perhaps, those taken from other kinds of inquirers, from Researchers and Scholars. Because lore is fundamentally pragmatic, contributions to it have to be framed in practical terms, as knowledge about what to do; if they aren't, they will be changed. In effect, then, once a particular nomination is made the contributor gives up control over it: Practitioners can and will make it over in a way that suits their needs in a particular time and place. And not just once. Practitioners are always tinkering with things, seeing if they can't be made to work better.

Such tinkering with the contributions made by other Practitioners seldom seems terribly disturbing. Freewriting provides a good example. Peter Elbow's version of it in *Writing Without Teachers* is probably most familiar. For him, it is an absolutely non-stop activity, thinking on paper. At those junctures where the writer would ordinarily pause—stopping to reread what has been said, say—she is bound to keep writing, even just nonsense. Also, these writings are seen as part of a cycle. One reads the first such draft looking for a "center of gravity" that becomes the starting point for a second draft, which provides a basis for the third, and so on. In the model Elbow describes, the four hours that might produce a single finished paper by more conventional means here produces four drafts in succession.

But in practice, of course, this technique gets changed all the time: people will write more or less freely, but stop to reread what they have written; or they will insist on making careful sense, and so write very slowly; or they will use it only as a kind of journal writing, so that it never involves the cycle of successive drafts. In short, they will change what Elbow has offered to suit their needs. It may be that some Practitioners are purists in such matters, and so might object to such tinkering; but more of them, I think, being themselves rather used to the same sorts of transformations, would not.

Things are not so simple, however, when the contributions come from outside the Practitioner community. As I indicated in the Introduction, neither Scholarly nor Researcher inquiry is instrumental: neither is equipped to tell anyone what to do but only, to put it in epigrammatic form again, to suggest what things mean or what happens, respectively. Thus, even when (as we shall see is most often the case) the contributing Scholars or Researchers propose some practical implications for their offering, what tends to happen is that some or all of the contextual constraints that define the "imported" knowledge in its home community are ignored when Practitioners translate it into knowledge about what to do. A single example will serve to illustrate. In *The Development of Writing Abilities (11–18)*, James Britton and his colleagues devise two classificatory schemes for assessing the 2122 student texts that constitute the data for their study. The first deals with audience, the apparent relationship between writer and reader. They developed four major categories: Self, Teacher, Wider Audience (known), and Unknown Audience. The second scheme delineates what they call "function categories," and its purpose is to distinguish "the principal functions of written utterances." Here they develop three major categories: the expressive (language close to the self); poetic (language as artifact); and transactional (language for doing business in the world).

Now, the purpose of the study was to describe the kinds of writing children do in school between the ages of eleven and eighteen, with an eye toward discovering some developmental pattern. In short, they wanted to know, as Researchers, what happens during those years. The rating schemes, then, were a device created to help with the description; specifically, they provided a set of "bins" into which a team of trained raters could sort those 2122 texts. For that purpose, they seemed to have worked fairly well, even though most of what the investigators learned as a result of the sorting did not necessarily confirm their expectations.[3]

The point here, in any case, is that although they are derived from an interesting and useful theory about the nature of language, these audience and function categories, as presented, constitute rating schemes, and nothing more: ways of sorting out a pile of papers, not kinds or genres of writing, readily identifiable because they contain universally recognizable features. When Britton and his team trained their "assessors," the people who did the sortings, they worked toward getting them to agree that when they were faced with certain textual features, or combinations thereof, they would classify a script in a certain category. That's all. And indeed, the length and specificity of their coding guides, and the relatively low inter-rater reliabilities their scorers managed (.682 and .635 for audience and function, respectively), suggest just how un-universal or non-generic those categories turned out, in practice, to be.[4]

But Practitioners have little need to do this kind of sorting. As a pair of rating scales, the audience and function categories are of little practical use: they don't tell anyone anything particularly useful about what to do. From a Practitioner's point of view, though, it isn't much of a jump from a rating scale to a curriculum guide—from a *de*-scriptive scheme to a set of *pre*-scriptions. Without any particular concern for the schemes' validities, then, or for the fact that in Britton et al.'s sample, anyway, school writing turned out to be far narrower in its range than the investigators had hoped, so that most of the descriptors went little used, Practitioners have begun to assign "expressive" writing in their courses, or "poetic," or "transactional," and to assign these functions-cum-genres to be written for different audiences.

It is hard to say how much Britton and his colleagues are to be implicated in this development. Their last chapter ("Some Implications") rather suggests that schools would do well to conform more closely to the expectations embodied in their rating schemes, although of course they can offer no new arguments as to why that should be so. And I don't mean to suggest that this transformation is any great disaster, anyway. It has already shaken school curricula up some, and maybe that's a useful thing. Still, it is clearly a transmutation of the schemes as they were developed, and a good example of what can happen to Researcher or Scholarly knowledge when it becomes a part of lore . . .

3: THE SCHOLARS

In retrospect, it was probably inevitable that the knowledge-makers quickest off the mark to supplant lore as Composition's dominant form of knowledge should have been those who advocated the modes of inquiry clustered under this heading. True, the field's charter—*Research in Written Composition,* that is—may have ignored them; so far as I can tell, none of the 504 studies it lists would fit in this section. But the group claiming authority over the new field, you will recall, was primarily the membership of the Conference on College Composition and Communication. In the organization's early years, these were people who taught in and/or administered the freshman communications programs that had been its initial *raison d'etre;* and then, later, moving toward the early 1960s, their association was increasingly likely to be with a more narrowly defined freshman *writing* program. Whatever the nature of their programs, these were people trained in the traditions and methods of Western humanist thought. So despite the widespread faith in "scientific" modes of inquiry, it was only natural that this challenge to produce new kinds of knowledge about how writing is done, taught, and learned should lead some of them to fall back on that training, and turn to the Scholarly tradition and methods.

I have identified three distinct Scholarly modes of inquiry in Composition. The first I shall call Historical, and its users the Historians: those who work to provide a coherent past for the field. The second I shall call Philosophical, and its users the Philosophers, although their full title would have to be Philosophers of Composition. That is, while their effort, as for a philosopher in Philosophy proper, is to examine the nature of inquiry itself, their allegiance is finally to Composition and the nature of its inquiry. Thus, it is the Philosophers' task to examine the philosophical underpinnings of Composition. The third mode of inquiry I will call Hermeneutical, and its users, Critics. This mode, as the label suggests, deals with the interpretation of texts—is to Composition what the theory and practice of literary criticism is to literary studies. Just which texts are to be interpreted, for what purposes, and by what means are themselves among the key issues Hermeneutical inquiry faces.

These three modes belong in the same methodological cluster primarily because they share the humanist tradition's reliance on what can be broadly defined as dialectic—that is, the seeking of knowledge via the deliberate confrontation of opposing points of view. Also in keeping with that tradition, each is essentially text-based, although the kinds of texts they use, and the functions of those texts as part of the inquiry, differ considerably. We usually consider history in general a "first-order" kind of inquiry, defined at least as much by its subject matter as its method. That subject, the past, is sought within a body of texts, which provide a common ground for all Historians. They agree, that is, on the existence of those texts, but not on how they might be interpreted, on their significance. And indeed, to the extent that Historians can be said to offer a description of the empirical world—albeit a version of it as it was—they might be placed somewhere in the community of Researchers, much as History departments within colleges and universities seem to straddle the line between the Humanities and Social Sciences.

Philosophy, by contrast, is clearly a "second-order" inquiry, which has access to the findings of first-order inquiry, but has as its subject matter the activities of the first-order inquirers—in this case, the activities of Practitioners, Historians, Critics, the various kinds of Researchers in Composition and, of course, themselves. However, Philosophy never turns outward to "empirical" evidence to gather or test knowledge; it is, rather, the mind studying its own operations, the rational study of rational practices. For Historians, then, texts play two roles. On the one hand—and in this, they are like Researchers—texts are the raw materials from which they construct a portrait of the past; are, in some sense, the *objects* of study. On the other, texts (and the past they represent) can be, as for a Philosopher, not inquiry's object but its *medium:* various portions of, voices in, the continuing debate (or, for Historians, competing narratives) of which their own inquiries are a contemporary extension.

The Hermeneutical mode falls somewhere in between. It is probably best characterized, like History, as a first-order inquiry. It begins, as does Historical inquiry, with a text or set of texts, usually called a canon, to provide the common starting point for inquiry. And it is important—or has been important in most hermeneutical studies, although it hasn't come up much in Composition yet—to establish the authenticity and accuracy of that text or texts as physical objects. And yet, though one might therefore say that these texts are, as for Historians, the "objects" of study, they are not objects in quite the same sense. For a Historian, a text-as-object is a kind of evidence, a record—like the paleontologist's fossil—of some event in a series of events he wishes to understand. For the Critic, by contrast, it may be simplest to say that the text itself is, in some sense, the "event": that her concern is the relationship between that text and its writer(s), its reader(s), its language(s), and some version of the world (which includes, of course, other texts). Which of these relationships the Critic emphasizes, and by what means, are choices that are themselves part of the inquiry, and subject to later, dialectical scrutiny.

Three features of the methodological communities to which these modes of inquiry give rise are worth noting in advance. The first has to do with their collective size—or, rather, their lack of it. Given Composition's roots in practice, it is no surprise that there should be so many—a majority of—Practitioners; nor, given the relative novelty and scarcity of training in the requisite methods, that there should be proportionately few Researchers. But as I have already suggested, nearly all members of the field were trained, to some extent, *as* scholars, and yet there seem not to be very many more Scholars than Researchers. It may be that the explanation is fairly simple. In part, then, it may be that the traditionally low prestige of composition work in English departments will have encouraged even those who taught exclusively writing courses to spend whatever scholarly energies they might have elsewhere. Or it may be that the proportion of Scholars to Practitioners needs, in some sense, to remain small—that in any given academic society, it takes a great many people concerned about what to do to support even a few concerned about what the doing means, in a Scholarly sense. It may even be that, given the power of the image of composition-as-emerging-science, there is too little prestige attached to Scholarly inquiry to attract many recruits. Or, finally, it may be that most of those trained in that literary tradition, but who teach mostly writing, have translated what they learned about Scholarly method into a form they can use in the language and knowledge communities of their classrooms; that the mode of inquiry they were asked to master—the cycle of textual exegesis and dialectic—has become the basis for their practice. There have been some signs of an increase; as we shall see, the number of Scholarly studies, especially in book form, has grown fairly dramatically in the first half of the 1980s. Nevertheless, for whatever reasons, the Scholarly communities' active membership remains quite small.

The second feature, somewhat more problematic for my purposes, is the peculiar relationship between these communities and the others in Composition, especially the Practitioners. In their more regular academic forms—that is, as the disciplines of History, Philosophy, and Literary Studies (most prominently, although criticism obviously gets practiced elsewhere)—these modes of inquiry operate with a very powerful institutional insularity. Let me put it this way: Whatever role the American public might play in supporting scholarly activities, it does not look to those scholars for wisdom. It's a phenomenon fairly typical in our specialized culture. Historians write mostly to and for other Historians, Philosophers to and for other Philosophers, Critics to and for other Critics. Who but a scholar is likely to read Husserl, say, or Merleau-Ponty? These scholars don't operate entirely in isolation, of course; there is often a fair amount of exchange across disciplinary lines. Some of what they produce may be said to make its way into the larger culture, too: given our system of higher education, they will participate, albeit rather indirectly, in the training of teachers. And most ordinary citizens will study history in school, have a run-in with philosophy (although perhaps not until college), and suffer some exposure, however unwitting, to at least practical criticism. For the most part, though, these contacts can be regarded as incidental.

This has not been the case for the Scholars in Composition. For one thing, the society is on a much smaller scale. The "public" consists of the members of Composition, most of them Practitioners. And, no doubt in part because of that relative intimacy, they *are* willing to look to these Scholars for wisdom, for intellectual leadership, as it were. As a result, Composition's Scholars have never had much insularity, institutional or otherwise. Like their better insulated colleagues in the disciplines proper, they do write for one another; but they also write for, or at least very much aware of, an audience of outsiders, as well. The catch, of course—and what makes this situation problematic here—is that the presence of this second audience tends to affect the way that Scholarly inquiry is conducted and presented. This isn't automatically a bad thing. One might as easily argue that History, Philosophy, and Literary Studies proper have been corrupted by their insularity—have lost touch with reality by hiding in their ivory towers. Just the same, the situation in Composition is a tricky one, and part of my task in describing these communities will be to examine its effects on the nature of methodological authority.

Third and last, I think it important to point out that many of the people I will identify here as belonging to one or the other of these communities would call themselves by still another name: Rhetorician. And indeed, much Scholarly work in Composition—both early on and since—has made its way into the field under the banner of "Rhetoric." The theme of the 1963 meeting of CCCC, for example—that date once again—was "Toward a New Rhetoric." And among the papers later printed (in the October 1963 edition of *College Composition and Communication*) were these, presented by as celebrated a trio as one is likely to find in the annals of Composition Scholarship: Wayne C. Booth's "The Rhetorical Stance"; Francis Christensen's "A Generative Rhetoric of the Sentence"; and Edward P. J. Corbett's "The Usefulness of Classical Rhetoric"—authors who also produced, as most readers will recognize, *The Rhetoric of Fiction, Notes Toward a New Rhetoric,* and *Classical Rhetoric for the Modern Student,* respectively.

That Rhetoric should have been thus present as an influence in CCCC is not surprising. It had, of course, been separated from literary studies as a discipline, and from most English departments institutionally, since 1914, when the "speech teachers" had walked out of NCTE to form their own organization. The communications courses launched in the late 1940s at the State University of Iowa, Michigan State, and elsewhere were an attempt to reintegrate speaking and writing (and listening and reading) pedagogically; and the organization to which they gave rise provided a context in which the reintegration might occur in disciplinary and professional terms, too. Somewhat ironically, the pedagogical connection rather failed. By 1960, the CCCC's Committee on Future Directions, headed by first CCCC president John Gerber, was already officially emphasizing "especially written discourse."[5] But the scholarly rapprochement between Composition and Rhetoric had been made, and it has proved quite durable.

What is particularly significant here, though, are the terms of this rapprochement, and the way the

Scholars who identify themselves with Rhetoric have insisted subtly but steadily on the distinction between the two fields. In common usage, the two terms are sometimes used interchangeably: Rhetoric or Composition; and, even more often, as a pair: Rhetoric and Composition (almost always in that order). But for these self-declared Rhetoricians, that pairing seems to represent a rather uneasy compromise. Difficult as it has been to define Rhetoric in this century (indeed, trying to define it has been its adherents' major preoccupation), and however institutionally diffuse its membership, they generally seem to prefer to have it as their primary professional identification. James Kinneavy's handling of the matter in *The Present State of Scholarship in Historical and Contemporary Rhetoric*—a book which he quite freely admits owes its existence in large part to the momentum of Composition—is representative. Writing on "Contemporary Rhetoric," Kinneavy cites "Rhetoric and the Teaching of Composition" as one of *sixteen* areas of interest among Rhetoricians. Hence, although he and most of the book's other contributors share Composition as a "major professional commitment," the message is clear: These are Rhetoricians specializing in Composition, not Composition specialists with an interest in Rhetoric.

I don't want to make too much of this semantic preference. I have not honored it here—have not, that is, labeled either this section nor a single chapter "The Rhetoricians." This is in part because the preference hasn't been shared widely enough; too many other Scholars—for instance Ann Berthoff and James Moffett, to name two I will feature—have shown either no interest in or even some aversion to it. Even more to the point, it is not much help methodologically. Rhetoric can be defined as an art to be mastered; or, as for these Scholars, the various manifestations of that art as practiced can be conceived as an object or field of study. But there is not, in this latter sense, any inherently Rhetorical mode of inquiry. As with Composition, any number of modes might be brought to bear. The Scholars I include in this section, then, are better understood as Historians, Philosophers, or Critics: those who seek knowledge about how rhetoric has been understood and practiced in the past; or who try to get at the theoretical underpinnings of rhetorical activity; or whose approach to textual interpretation has a rhetorical basis—in all three cases, of course, as such inquiries are relevant for Composition.

Still, I don't want to dismiss the preference altogether. The allegiance of Scholars like Corbett, Booth, Christensen, and Kinneavy; of Walter Ong, Louis Milic, Paul Rodgers, Virginia Burke, Winston Weathers, Donald Stewart, Frank D'Angelo; or, more recently, of Andrea Lunsford, Lisa Ede, S. Michael Halloran, C. H. Knoblauch, Robert Connors, James Berlin, and so on—their allegiance to something outside of Composition called Rhetoric marks a pattern we shall see repeated in other methodological communities. As new modes of inquiry compete for power in Composition, they need to prove themselves, and a chief means for doing so is to demonstrate their ties to some already legitimate academic enterprise. One such enterprise—and one that sells particularly well in English departments, where many of these inquiries have had to worry about their academic survival—is Rhetoric. Whereas Composition is conceived of pretty narrowly, usually as "mere" practice, Rhetoric is not only the crown of the classical trivium, but can arguably claim a tradition as deep and rich, maybe deeper and richer, than poetics. It is also concerned with practice, yes; but here it will more often be called *praxis,* which not only seems to have a broader and deeper intellectual resonance, but—well, to put it at its most cynical, *sounds* better, more scholarly, too. In short, Rhetorical inquiry into Composition may not be exactly mainstream literary studies. It may be hard, in fact, to say just what it is, or what the pairing of Rhetoric and Composition actually represents. No matter: Whatever it is, it stands as a more legitimate intellectual enterprise than just plain Composition.

We will see some form of this power-by-association in nearly all of these methodological communities. Investigators will claim philosophical ties, or hermeneutical, psychological, sociological, anthropological ones, and so on. Most of the time, the association holds benefits for both fields. So even though, in this particular pairing, Rhetoric

may actually stand to gain the most—its current revival stemming in large part from this interest in writing—it has been good for Composition, too. It *does* sell in English departments, and so has provided Composition with some knowledge-making leverage there. At the same time, the kind of reluctance demonstrated by these Rhetoricians, their unwillingness to give up what might be called their dual citizenship—or, perhaps more accurately, their resident-alien-in-Composition-status—suggests a division of loyalty that does not bode well for Composition. . . .

4: THE RESEARCHERS

Influential as the Scholarly modes of inquiry have been in Composition, they have for the most part not been conceived—even, as we have seen, by many of their users—as representing its central line of development. If *Research in Written Composition* was indeed the new field's charter, then it designated as first citizens not the Scholars, but those who adopted modes of inquiry geared to lead them to more "scientific" knowledge; and their special status—one they have assumed, but one which has also been granted to them by the rest of the society's members—seems to me to be reflected in the title under which I have gathered them in this section: the Researchers.

Even with the deference accorded them, though, the rise to power of Researcher modes of inquiry has been a very gradual affair. . . . It's a lot easier to call for new or more careful inquiry than it is to get it—to generate methodological momentum, as it were. A handful of landmarks in particular stand out. One of the most important was the initiation of NCTE's *Research in the Teaching of English* in 1967. It has never been devoted exclusively to research in Composition, but a very substantial portion of its space has been, and its annual bibliographies have played an important part in legitimizing the Researcher enterprise. I think it can safely be called the leading Researcher journal in Composition. Of roughly equal significance, though of shorter duration, was NCTE's Research Report series. Here again, not all of the publications deal with Composition, but many do; and its thirteenth publication, Janet Emig's *The Composing Processes of Twelfth Graders* (1971), is arguably the most influential piece of Researcher work ever published.

By the mid-1970s, the pace of development, and the emergence of a more specialized Composition focus, had quickened, so that important markers are more closely spaced. Though its contributors take a much more eclectic perspective on what constitutes knowledge in the field, Gary Tate's 1976 *Teaching Composition: 10 Bibliographical Essays* extends the work of *Research in Written Composition* by framing possible inquiry in terms of what has been done. Even more directly in line with Researcher methodologies is Charles R. Cooper and Lee Odell's 1978 *Research on Composing: Points of Departure*. Its editors, who explicitly draw comparisons between their volume and *Research in Written Composition,* argue that inquiry must shift from asking "What materials and procedures will improve students' work in written composition?" (p. xi) to wondering what composing is, how it is done, and so on—in short, "to examine, test, and modify our basic assumptions about written composition" (p. xiv). By the early 1980s, there were a number of other collections with similar emphases: Lee Gregg and Erwin Steinberg's *Cognitive Processes in Writing* (1980), for example; the two volume *Writing: The Nature, Development, and Teaching of Written Communication* (1981), edited by Carl H. Frederiksen and Joseph F. Dominic; Richard Beach and Lillian Bridwell's *New Directions in Composition Research* (1984). Most recently, two substantial review/bibliographies have been published: Michael Moran and Ronald Lunsford's *Research in Composition and Rhetoric,* and George Hillocks' *Research on Written Composition: New Directions for Teaching.* And finally, *College Composition and Communication,* especially under the editorship of Richard Larson, has taken on a noticeably more Researcher bent, while new journals like *Visible Language* and *Written Communication* so far seem to have a dominantly Researcher orientation.

These are, you will notice, essentially generic landmarks. Methodological differentiation—in-deed, even methodological self-consciousness—has come to Composition in general only very slowly, and these modes of inquiry have been no exception. The notion of "research" has tended to lump together any and all modes of inquiry grounded in empirical phenomena, however conceived, as opposed to the textual phenomena/dialectical grounding of the Scholars; and which purport to be descriptive, as opposed to the prescriptiveness of the otherwise empirical Practitioners. I will trace the emergence of the particular modes of Researcher inquiry, and any concomitant methodological self-awareness, in the chapters that follow. Here it will be enough to point out that this general naiveté—the notion that research is research is research—turns out to be something of a theme in this Section, coming up again and again.

For now, in any case, I have identified four major modes of inquiry in Composition. The first, in both size and longevity, I call the Experimental, and its users the Experimentalists: in broad terms, those who seek to discover generalizable "laws" which can account for—and, ideally, predict—the ways in which people do, teach, and learn writing. The second I have dubbed Clinical, and its practitioners the Clinicians, borrowing the name from its uses in fields like psychology and reading. Here, the focus is on individual "cases": most commonly, the ways in which a particular subject does, learns, or teaches writing. The third mode will be called Formal inquiry. What Formalists do, to put it simply, is build models or simulations by means of which they attempt to examine the *formal* properties of the phenomena under study. In Composition, they have focused almost exclusively on the composing process so far—Linda Flower and John Hayes are the most prominent—but in theory a Formalist could propose a model for anything: teacher behavior, reading, talk about writing, etc. Finally, I will call the fourth mode Ethnography, and its practitioners Ethnographers. And if the Formalists can be said to make models, then what the Ethnographers make are stories, fictions. Their peculiar concern is with people as members of communities, and their mode of inquiry equips them to produce knowledge in the form of narrative accounts of what happens in those communities.

The first three of these constitute a methodological cluster quite as neat as the three Scholarly modes, sharing as they do the positivist tradition's fundamental faith in the describable orderliness of the universe: that is, the belief that things-in-the-world, including in this case people, operate according to determinable or "lawful" patterns, general tendencies, which exist quite apart from our experience of them, and which are, in addition, accessible to the right kinds of inquiry. Where they differ, as my sketches of them might suggest, is in the kind of access to those patterns they provide. The Experimental method proposes what amounts to a direct assault on them. In keeping with its natural science heritage, it attempts to systematically control and manipulate the phenomena it studies—in short, to *experiment* with it—in order to uncover those lawful patterns. The emphasis in Experimental inquiry has been what Gordon Allport calls nomothetic: the overall goals of inquiry are framed in terms of generalization, not particularization. Data collected is valuable not for what it reveals about any particular individual, but as evidence concerning the sought-after broader patterns.

The Clinical method can be understood as the Experimental's idiographic or holistic complement. Its concern is particularization; data collected is valuable precisely for what it reveals about individuals. Clinicians may thus claim an access to the phenomena they study not merely as direct as, but in many ways richer than, the Experimentalists. For while they can (and usually do) manipulate their subjects—giving them tests, say, or asking them to compose aloud—they are not bound by the restrictions that establishing Experimental control imposes. The standard for Clinical inquiry is Janet Emig's case studies of eight twelfth graders, and it is typical in its efforts to examine a very small number of subjects in considerable depth. What Clinicians sacrifice to gain this depth, of course, is their access to the larger patterns. To make it epigrammatic: What they gain in particularization they lose in generalization.

Formalist inquiry, by contrast, might be described as an extension of the human power to understand things by analogy. If the Clinical method trades off its generalizing power to gain greater access to particulars, we might say that the Formal method goes the other way, swapping direct access to particulars for enhanced powers of general explanation. Rather than dealing directly with the phenomenon they wish to study, then, Formalists attempt to create an analogue for it—a model, a simulation. What they gain is great freedom to construct operative, tautological, convincing wholes: self-contained systems which *by definition* work perfectly. What they give up is their grounding in any particular phenomenon; so while the model may work perfectly, its correspondence to any of the empirical systems for which it might claim to be an analogue—even when there is only one such system—must be demonstrated Experimentally. In practice, as we shall see, such demonstrations present incredible, perhaps insurmountable, difficulties, but that need not seriously diminish Formal inquiry's worth; simply building the models themselves can be valuable. So while we might say, again epigrammatically, that Formalist inquiry produces generalizations in search of particulars to account for, it is the producing and the searching, more than any finding, that matters most.

The Ethnographic method doesn't fit with these other three very well at all. It is "research" in the general sense, of course, or it wouldn't be in this Section: as a "human science," it claims a grounding in empirical phenomena. But if both Clinical and Formalist inquiries represent compromises on the positivist faith in our ability to observe and describe human activities as part of what is "out there" in the world, a faith most fully manifested in the Experimental method, then Ethnographic inquiry is a flat-out rejection of it. From a positivist perspective, then, it may be said to represent a profound skepticism about our power to observe or describe any human phenomenon at all as if we were "separate" from it, as if the inquirer could be "objective," and so discount her presence as either participant or observer. But it derives, in fact, from the very different phenomenological tradition.

From that perspective, Ethnography is anything but a kind of negation—is, rather, a methodological celebration of the individual consciousness as the source of meaning—of "lawful" order—in human experience. And its authority lies not in its objectivity—the "pure" use of language by observer-as-lens—but of a kind of collaboration whereby the life of the community finds articulation via the phenomenal experience, and the words, of a single individual.

The communities to which these modes of inquiry give rise need less by way of preparatory remarks than did their Scholarly counterparts. I have already accounted in general terms for both their size and their perhaps disproportionate influence, and will elaborate on both as we proceed. And, as will become clear enough in each chapter, a Researcher can be as polemical—for much the same reasons and to the same effect—as any Scholar. However, I would like to offer one reminder. In the Introduction to this book, I was careful to borrow Diesing's warning to the effect that neither he nor I could claim to be covering all of the modes of inquiry, he in the social sciences, I in Composi-tion; that both of us had chosen, in his phrase, "prominent locations." That caution applies especially in this Section, where it can be hard to say at what point methodological variations go from producing differences in degree to differences in kind. In the Experimentalist chapter, then, I have included not only true Experimental studies, but so-called pre- and quasi-Experimental studies as well. At the same time, I have for the most part disregarded a mode of inquiry that essentially has grown out of Experimental inquiry, the statistical survey. By my rough count, there have been well over 200 survey studies of one kind or another since 1963. They have varied widely in topic and scope: surveys of classroom practices on a single campus, or a collection of junior colleges, or a particular state; surveys of administrative practices, such as how much of what kind of writing instruction is required, again on everything from a local to a national scale; surveys designed to find out things about how writers work—the kinds of outlines technical writers use,

say, or the influences on children who write successful poetry.[6]

No doubt many of these surveys have had some influence: attempts were made to change teaching practices, new writing requirements were created, textbook dicta were adjusted. A handful that are based in whole or in part on survey work might even be familiar: Joseph Mersand's *Attitudes Toward English Teaching;* Richard Braddock's "The Frequency and Placement of Topic Sentences in Expository Prose"; Stephen Witte and Lester Faigley's *Evaluating College Writing Programs;* even George Hillocks' efforts at meta-analysis in *Research on Written Composition,* where the results of large numbers of experimental studies are, in effect, "surveyed" to generate a kind of profile. My sense, though, is that no community of inquirers, united by their loyalty to this methodology, has emerged. Instead, what might have become a method in that sense has been regarded merely as a tool, a technique—and one to be used, most often, not to make a contribution to a knowledge-making community, but to gain political leverage in a school or district or state. So it's no great surprise, either, that only a very few of these studies demonstrate any particular sophistication with the method.

The upshot, in any case, is that while a method for what might be called Survey research has been around in Composition, its use to date does not warrant full treatment here. And it seems safe to assume that there are other modes of inquiry at work that I have not accounted for—combinations of the methods I have described, or variations, or even methods of which I am simply unaware. All of which is by way of reiterating that opening caution: While I present these as the major modes of Researcher inquiry, they are still only *some,* not *the,* modes of Researcher inquiry in Composition.

Notes

1. Quoted in *Research in Written Composition,* p. 1.
2. Conspicuously missing from this community, of course, is that other sort of "practitioner," writers, people whose primary interest is in the doing, not the teaching, of writing. Paradoxical though it may seem, writers *qua* writers

are not considered members of the Practitioner community, nor members of the larger society of Composition at all. Composition journals, for example, rarely publish work that is not more or less directly related to writing as a subject of study. Obviously, some members of Composition do a good bit of writing that falls outside the boundaries of "composition writing" (e.g., poetry, fiction, literary scholarship) and may even gain some measure of respect by doing so; Donald Murray, for example, is often introduced as a Pulitzer Prize winner. The written work itself, though, is of little interest to those in Composition. What may be of interest is the doing of such writing—the practice, and the writer's reflections about it. These are considered to be potential resources, and to offer possible lines of inquiry. There has come to be an axiom that those who teach writing should do writing, and even that they should write along with their students. But "doing writing" in this sense and "being a writer" mean very different things, and no set of credentials as a writer of prose or poetry has, so far as I know, gained anyone much more than guest speaker status in the Practitioner community. Only classroom duty—and that preferably in teaching the writing of non-fiction prose—has done that.

3. That is, Britton et al. had presumably hoped to find a wide range of audiences represented, but found instead that more than 92% of the texts fell into only two of ten possible audience sub-categories, a result they describe as "something of an anticlimax" (p. 192). And in terms of function, 63% fell into the "transactional" category, with very few—about 5%—in the "expressive" category for which the authors had had much higher expectations.

4. They explain their system for computing the raters' reliability in Appendix II, pp. 206–08. The figures I have given are those for the raters alone, without corrective ratings provided by the investigators.

5. First generation in terms of modern Composition, that is. There was certainly historical inquiry by composition teachers before 1963. Kitzhaber, as we shall see shortly, is perhaps the best known, but the Dec. 1954 issue of CCC, for example, features Karl W. Dykema's "Historical Development of the Concept of Grammatical Proprieties," J. E. Congleton's "Historical Development of the Concept of Rhetorical Proprieties," and James B. McMillan's "Summary of Nineteenth Century Historical and Comparative Linguistics."

6. For examples of each kind of survey suggested in this paragraph, see the following, simply pulled in a cluster from my files: G. W. Redman, Jr., "The Philosophy of Teaching Composition Held by Selected Teachers and Students at the University of Northern Colorado, Winter Quarter, 1973" (DAI, 1974, 35, 932A); B. J. Honeycutt, "An Analysis and Prognosis of the Technical Report Writing Curriculum in Texas Public Junior Colleges" (DAI, 1973, 34, 1587a); P. W. Willis, "A Study of Current Practices in Freshman English in Oklahoma Colleges" (DAI, 1974, 34, 4806A); Ron Smith, "The Composition Requirement Today: A Report on a Nationwide Survey of Four-Year Colleges and Universities" (CCC, 25 [1974] pp. 138–48); B. K. McKee, "Types of Outlines Used by Technical Writers" (Journal of English Teaching Techniques, Winter 1974/1975, pp. 30–36); and Charles Schaefer, "Young Poets on Poetry" (Elementary School Journal, 1973, 74, pp. 24–27).

Works Cited

Allport, Gordon. The Use of Personal Documents in Psychological Science. New York: Social Sciences Research Council, 1942.

Beach, Richard, and Lillian S. Bridwell, eds. New Directions in Composition Research. New York: Guilford, 1984.

Braddock, Richard. "The Frequency and Placement of Topic Sentences in Expository Prose." Research in the Teaching of English, 8 (1975): 287–302.

Braddock, Richard, Richard Lloyd-Jones, and Lowell Schoer. Research in Written Composition. Champaign: NCTE, 1963.

Britton, James, et al. The Development of Writing Abilities (11–18). London (Eng.): Macmillan Education, 1975.

Elbow, Peter. Writing Without Teachers. New York: Oxford UP, 1973.

Frederikson, Carl H., and Joseph F. Dominic, eds. Writing: The Nature, Development, and Teaching of Written Communication. 2 vols. Hillsdale: Erlbaum, 1981.

Hillocks, George. Research on Written Composition. Urbana: NCTE, 1986.

Hook, J. N. "The Importance of the Conference to Project English." Needed Research in the Teaching of English: Proceedings of a Project English Research Conference May 5–7, 1962. Ed. Erwin R. Steinberg. Washington: U.S. Government Printing Office, 1963.

Kinneavy, James L. "Contemporary Rhetoric." The Present State of Scholarship in Historical and Contemporary Rhetoric. Ed. Winifred Bryan Horner. Columbia: U of Missouri P, 1983. 167–213.

Macrorie, Ken. Searching Writing: A Contextbook. Rochelle Park: Hayden, 1980.

————. *Uptaught.* New York: Hayden, 1970.

————. *Writing to Be Read.* New York: Hayden, 1968.

Mersand, Joseph. *Attitudes Toward English Teaching.* Philadelphia: Chilton, 1961.

Moran, Michael G., and Ronald F. Lunsford, eds. *Research in Composition and Rhetoric: A Bibliographic Sourcebook.* Westport: Greenwood, 1984.

Schultz, John. *Writing from Start to Finish: The 'Story Workshop' Basic Forms Rhetoric-Reader.* Montclair: Boynton, 1982.

Tate, Gary. *Teaching Composition: 10 Bibliographical Essays.* Fort Worth: Texas Christian UP, 1976.

Witte, Stephen P., and Lester Faigley. *Evaluating College Writing Programs.* Carbondale: Southern Illinois UP, 1983.

Rhetorical Constructions: Dialogue and Commitment

C. H. Knoblauch

Knoblauch's essay appeared in College English *50 (1988): 125–40.*

In *Pedagogy of the Oppressed* Paulo Freire introduces the concept of "praxis," by which he signifies the two dimensions of authentic discourse, that of reflection and that of action, the process of naming reality and the process of changing reality. Reflection alone, he argues, is insufficient because it is mere verbalism, "an empty word . . . which cannot denounce the world." Action alone is similarly inadequate, mere activism, where the energy for choosing exists apart from critical awareness and direction. In true praxis naming always entails transformation because the process of naming renders the world problematic, an object within history, a choice from among possible choices and therefore a limitation to be challenged. At the same time, action, the process of transforming, always entails a new naming because the emergence of reality is only possible through a struggle to articulate. As expression is achieved, it permits the conscious scrutiny that induces occasions and conditions of further transforming. The ultimate motive for any transformation is, according to Freire, the need to be more fully human, the need to participate more completely and more freely in the world. The instrument of transforming is dialogue, where competing representations of reality dynamically challenge each other to compose alternative forms of action. In the absence of dialogue, with the erasure of anyone's "word," with the prohibition of critical inquiry, with the maintenance of dominating conditions, however subtly validated

as necessity, tradition, or evolution, the possibility of becoming more fully human is curtailed. Erosion of that possibility constitutes the inauthentic discourse—the stagnant reality—of oppression (60 ff.).

Freire has applied his concept of "praxis" with dramatic results to the circumstances of teachers and students in classrooms concerned with literacy, helping the disenfranchised in particular to assert their power to name and transform the world. I want to apply the concept here as well, but as a kind of probe with which to examine some philosophical issues that teaching and thinking about teaching regularly bring to mind: first, the relationship between intellectual argument ("reflection") and teaching practice ("action"); second, the conflict between dialogue (the free, collective examination of choices) and commitment (the decision to act); third, the ideological perversion that attends a privileging of some particular argument and the disturbing but finally inevitable oppositional commitment ("resistance") that emerges to displace that argument's authority. The domain for my investigation will be "rhetorical theory"—which I will define simply as a field of statements pertaining to language, knowledge, and discourse. Rhetorical statements expressed within specific historical circumstances have participated in "naming" the social reality of the "school," though they have not, of course, been wholly responsible for it. Specifically, these statements, emerging from the world of educational practice, have by turns rationalized, validated, and transformed instruction, and continue to do so, both unreflectively in the absence of a true praxis, and consciously where that praxis exists. A centuries-old, persistently reinvigorated dialogue among competing rhetorical assertions has sustained the process of transformation, while equally ancient institutional suspensions of that dialogue have served, in Freire's terms, to create dominating conditions and therefore the oppression of both teachers and students.

Obviously, I intend no causal connection between rhetorical argument and teaching practice. The relationship is properly dialectical, each term conditioning and reshaping the other. Many, if not most, teachers understand their classrooms and make sensible choices with little direct regard for theoretical knowledge. They are influenced, as a rule, less by concern for some abstract consistency than by pragmatic, seemingly self-evident beliefs about educational goals and an experienced, no less practical consciousness of "what works" for them in achieving those goals. Their choices reflect the circumstances of the life-world in which they participate and therefore never derive wholly from deliberate reflection. At the same time, it is inaccurate to say that teaching goes on without theory. Aims, assumptions, beliefs, values, expectations, consciously or unconsciously sustained, are what make teaching purposeful; and they can be represented as "theory," even though the practice that implies them is never adequately reduced to theoretical terms. Naming these "theoretical" features at a level of conscious reflection and revealing their historicity allow them to be analyzed, supported, opposed, and changed, so that teaching itself changes deliberately in accordance with altered judgments of its means and ends. This is the essence of praxis, as Freire defines it, a consciousness, manifested in action, which preserves at once the teacher's free exercise of choice and the teacher's responsiveness to the demands of school reality. Rhetorical theory marks one domain of competing arguments in terms of which—presuming a knowledge of this competition—teachers can maintain critical awareness and validate their deliberate ac-

tion. To the extent that teachers are unaware of those alternative arguments, the struggle among them and the unnecessariness of their existence, they risk giving up their freedom to anyone who would employ a single argument (or indeed the enclosure of any posited range of alternatives) to insist upon a reality, separated from history and from critical dissent, to which teachers must passively accommodate themselves.

For my own argumentative purposes, I will group "rhetorical" statements according to four distinct views of the ground or basis for verbal meaningfulness: the metaphysical ground, the experiential ground, the ground of consciousness, and the dialogical or intersubjective ground.[1] The first kind of rhetorical statement, perhaps the most durable and broadly disseminated of the four, is one that I will call *ontological:* it appears, but not exclusively, in the texts of Aristotle and other "classical" rhetoricians, in much religious (or at least theological) writing through the ages, and in traditional "school rhetoric" past and present. The other three, each posed as an argument against the limitations of its opposites, include the *objectivist* statement, associated, for example, with Descartes, Locke, and the rise of modern science; the *expressionist* statement, associated prominently with Kant and European Romanticism; and the *sociological* or "dialogical" statement, often attributed to Marx and the various permutations of Marxism. These contrasting assertions have arisen from, and been realized in, historically explicit social, economic, and political circumstances including some specifically related to the teaching of reading and writing. Each statement has a characteristic potential, in other words, to help produce, or at least ratify, certain forms of consciousness, certain ideological dispositions. This is not to say, however, that they mechanically cause such dispositions or that they enjoy a spiritual, an acontextual, existence "above" the conditions in which they operate.

Some additional clarifications are important. It is a convention of inquiry to divide the world into two or three of something, or into multiples of two or three. My assertion of four "rhetorical statements" is an interpretive generalization, a response to the question, what does some text or group of texts say? Other readings, at other levels of generality, are not just possible but are in fact inevitable, a larger dialectic contextualizing my own. Moreover, these statements do not circumscribe future formulations, whatever their present adequacy, nor does their evident polarity constrain anyone to a simple choice of one over another (though their interdependencies do create conditions of choice).[2] What some have called "the trap of oppositional thinking" results whenever dialectical terms are afforded an encompassing, absolute, in effect nondialectical significance. At the same time, however, there can be no meaning in the absence of "difference," no dialectic in the absence of opposition, and no reflection, in Freire's sense, without acts of interpretation. (Even the antagonists of "oppositional thinking" are, in effect, championing its opposite, whatever they construe that to be.) The reading I offer, a dispersion of opposing views, is an instrument for speculating and critiquing, a site for dialectic, not a set of containers with which to capture and isolate historical persons or produce an artificial history. Each statement may be associated with signatures from the past—Aristotle, Descartes, Von Humboldt, Marx—but none pretends to account for the complexity of some historical person's thought or action. These statements are poles of a dialectic, the stimulus of which is a dispersion of texts. They offer competing possibilities for naming the world, each responsive to insufficiencies in the others, each indeed beginning from those insufficiencies to further the dialectic. They are also, in a sense, therefore, purely discrete: that is, they differ absolutely at critical junctures, although no individual thinker will absolutely articulate, or embrace, one or another. As statements, they are meaningful precisely in their distinctiveness within a context of related statements. We understand the phonemes of some language by virtue of their differences from each other; in a similar but not precisely identical way, we understand texts by their differences from other texts. If my renderings of competing assertions appear polarized, therefore, it is because they are intended to be polarized, the stuff of a dialectic. If they are also enclosed, it is

because they belong to an interpretive framework, not because they exhaust all possible constructions of the world. The framework sets conditions that are themselves subject to scrutiny.

The ontological statement, well represented in the major texts of classical rhetoric, expresses the most successfully maintained view of language and language teaching that the West has so far produced. Mediated by the conditions of current American life, it is called upon to ratify some of our most cherished educational values, including the importance of "literacy" to personal prestige, intellectual capacity, and civic responsibility, as well as the proper concern of schools to socialize the young by promoting normative political, ethical, aesthetic, and other cultural behaviors through language instruction. It has also articulated some of our most venerable teaching beliefs, the emphasis on verbal skill and decorum, the practicing of various forms of reading and writing as the best means of developing literacy, the need to learn control of the techniques of argument and of style, the need to master "basics" of grammar first (whence the derivation of the "grammar" school) and other precepts later. The emphasis on formal propriety in discourse, a hallmark of this position, reflects assumptions about the nature of language as a "dress" of thought. Philosophically, the ontological argument presumes an absolute distinction between the concept of "language" and the concept of "reality," the second prior to the first and denoting an intrinsically coherent "world" (that is, metaphysical order) to which language "makes reference" so as to enable human communication. Writing and speech, Aristotle says, are "not the same for all races of men. But the mental affections themselves, of which these words are primarily signs, are the same for the whole of mankind, as are also the objects of which those affections are representations or likenesses, images, copies" (115). In this view, language use is largely irrelevant to the substance of knowledge although crucial for its transmission. As Cicero writes in *De oratore,* the graceful and harmonious style of the orator "must inevitably be of no account if the underlying subject matter be not comprehended and mastered by the speaker." Yet assuming this separate understanding, "whatever the theme, from whatever art or whatever branch of knowledge it be taken, the orator . . . will state it better and more gracefully than the actual discoverer and the specialist" (I.xii.51–52). The "underlying" substance of discourse is one thing, its surface characteristics another.

This knowledge to which language refers is not, in its fundamentals, subject to growth or change. Such metaphysical constructs as "being" and "becoming," "causality," or "substance" and "accident," such ethical constructs as "good" and "evil," or the "mean between extremes," such political constructs as hierarchical class structure based on intrinsic or God-given merit, are essentially static, "underlying" and giving meaning to the flux of the phenomenal world. Language acts can be evaluated for truth or falsity with reference to these realities, but they have no power to challenge them. This belief supports Saint Augustine's otherwise inexplicable confidence that hermeneutical questions arising out of figurative statements in the New Testament may be referred ultimately to the canonical texts of the Church fathers, which directly assert the substantial meanings that Biblical figures secretly convey (40, 93). Plainly, the ontological view articulates and defends a conservative reality, emphasizing permanence, certainty, and tradition, the maintenance of a status quo, politically as well as intellectually, which no defiant utterance, no provocative metaphor, no discovery of "new" knowledge, is entitled to reconceive. That conservatism satisfies an important social need, as powerfully felt in our own times as in others. It is not surprising, therefore, that two decades of political and educational liberalism in the U.S. should have given way in the 1980s to an aggressive conservative response, supported in part by the rationalizations of neoAristotelianism.

But if conserving is a virtue in the context of other values, it can easily become reactionism when it gains the political authority to privilege itself. The ideological implications of the ontological argument are troublesome, for one negative tendency has been to validate imaginative timidity, social stratification, and determinism by appeal to ahistorical metaphysical absolutes, with profound consequences for educational theory in general and literacy instruction particularly. A powerful belief animating classical thought is that the world possesses a teleology which necessarily shapes human circumstances and expectations. One implication of this belief is that social, intellectual, and other inequities are somehow rooted, not merely in the institutions that support them, but in the nature of things, so that individuals must resign themselves to conditions necessitated by human imperfection, playing their roles in a cosmic scheme with cheerful diligence and leaving unavoidable injustices to be addressed, if at all, in a fairer afterlife. The political, in particular the educational, consequences of this view are still apparent today, where elitist concepts of literacy continue to oppress disenfranchised social groups, where supposedly natural differences of intelligence justify stultifying classrooms for the least able, where canonical forms, texts, and readings of texts silence "outside" voices, and where order, decorum, and "civic responsibility"—values of the status quo—continue to be enforced in literacy programs over imagination, critical inquiry, and self-determination. Since ontological rhetoric has so long dominated Western thinking, has become in large part the "common sense" of contemporary life (a knowledge therefore largely exempt from scrutiny), it is especially deep-seated, subtly protected from challenge, and extremely difficult to reveal in its ideological limitations even to teachers and students who are at times mutually dominated by it, let alone to privileged groups whose claims to power depend on its maintenance. As a result, historical defiance of its authority—the intellectual as well as political resistance to its self-confident (hence, nonargumentative) hegemony—has been, as a rule, strongly worded and unaccommodating.

One effective assault on the ontological statement occurs in the mid-seventeenth century, when objectivist rhetoric successfully challenged classical metaphysics and asserted the contrasting value of direct observation of "experience" as the starting point for knowledge and discourse. This view is in turn challenged in the late eighteenth century by expressionist rhetoric, a theory that locates the source of knowledge not in sensory experience but in the processes of human imagination. The struggle between these statements, as much opposed to each other as to the ontological argument they call mutually to question, provocatively reconceives the relationship between language and "the world"—emphasizing the roles of discourse in constituting reality rather than merely supporting it as an unchanging metaphysical absolute. In some respects, however, that struggle also prompts a debilitating confrontation between the "objective" and the "subjective," particularly at two extremes—the positivist fallacy and the solipsist fallacy, to which a fourth rhetorical argument eventually responds by attempting to reconcile these terms within a dialogical or intersubjective construction of discourse. I will represent these positions with reference to "Cartesian," "Lockean," "Kantian," and "Marxist" signatures, but they are obviously not to be equated with specific historical individuals.

The objectivist statement locates knowledge in human intellectual activity as it acts upon experiential information. Its challenge to the ontological view is its assertion that knowledge depends upon discourse or language use, on the human search for significance, rather than on an intrinsically rational, "revealed" order of things. The "world" is conceived as a range of sensory data that careful (scientific) scrutiny gathers, categorizes, and interrelates in meaningful wholes. "The senses," Locke writes, "at first let in *particular* ideas," furnishing the "yet empty cabinet" of memory with notions denoted by names. Afterwards, intellectual action "abstracts them, and by degrees learns the use of general names," so that the mind "comes to be furnished with ideas and language, the materials about which to exercise its discursive faculty" (35). Scientific "method" manifests itself in the production of the *discourse* of science, which, according to Descartes for instance, was best modeled on the argumentative tactics of geometry: "those long chains of reasoning, so simple and easy, which enabled the geometricians to reach the most difficult demonstrations, had made me wonder whether all things knowable to men might not fall into a similar logi-

cal sequence" (15). In the objectivist view, empirical discourse is naturally privileged over any other because it depends, in theory, on unbiased observation and rigorous argumentative procedure, thereby supposedly avoiding the beliefs, superstitions, emotional excesses, and prejudices of less disciplined, "subjective" language use. The dramatic success of objectivist rhetoric in composing the texts of modern physical science, and in reading those texts for so much conspicuous social as well as intellectual benefit, have made it a compelling force in contemporary life, a force that promotes images of human progress and perfectability, of evolutionary development toward absolute knowledge and control of the physical world. If the values of an ontological perspective include permanence and certainty grounded on tradition and the achieved stability of the past, those of scientific thought include orderly change and the promise of future completion. Whether or not objectivist rhetoric has achieved the unself-conscious, commonsense acceptance that ontological rhetoric enjoys, it certainly receives the special veneration that an age preoccupied with engineering metaphors of beneficial change has reserved for mysteriously esoteric, technical knowledge.

A limitation of objectivist rhetoric, however, is its persistent tendency to "forget" the human origins of knowledge by enfolding "science" within a mythology that celebrates empirical method, quantification, and uncontextualized experiment while concealing its own story-tellers and their tactics of storytelling. In effect, the objectivist argument, no less than the ontological, fails to remain conscious of the rhetoric of its own rhetorical theory. The consequence, too often, is an altered but no less pervasive elitism justified now by appeal to the gods of the research laboratory rather than the gods of our forefathers. Supporters of objectivist thinking in education will list among its achievements an "advance" in our knowledge of the processes of human learning, including the development of literacy, and a willingness to ground instruction on what we can observe about those processes rather than on unexamined commitments of liberal or conservative ideology. But they will less readily confess its own ideological designs, indeed more commonly encouraging our acquiescence to positivism through uncritical celebration of the glamorous arcana of scientific method. Teachers and researchers accept the least advantageous assumptions of a positivist outlook when they call for supposedly neutral, "objective standards" in schools; when they trust more than scrutinize the promise, not to mention the motives, of placement and competency testing; when they want, and believe they can have, teacher-proof curricula; when they encourage the new knowledge of linguistics and behavioral/cognitive psychology to dictate instructional and learning agendas; and when they expect measurable consequences from rigorously schematized classroom methods. Teachers and researchers who assume that students failing to thrive in scientifically refined environments are themselves responsible for the failure reveal the ideological consequences of reifying knowledge and thereby reducing human beings or their activities to the abstract models and structures intended to "explain" them.

Expressionist rhetoric offers a challenge to the experiential reductionism of the objectivist statement. It situates knowledge in human "consciousness," specifically in the imaginative capacities of language users, insisting that even the "experiential information" from which scientists begin their inquiries is itself a product of human imagination, not an external given which renders the mind merely a reactive rather than fundamentally constitutive power. "We learn all things indeed by occasion of experience." Samuel Coleridge writes, "but the very facts so learnt force us inward on the antecedents, that must be presupposed in order to render experience itself possible" (79). The expressionist argument insists too on the value of all human discourses, religious, artistic, literary, mythic, no less than scientific, each of them a unique mode of knowing with its distinctive human value. Above all, the expressionist view celebrates the power of the human "voice" to organize its experience according to personal needs and to achieve insights—personal knowledge—that can have the effect of revolutionizing the larger societal as well as intellectual realities to which individuals make their unique contributions. Indeed, expressionist rhetoric has frequently been associated with liberalizing political action, for instance in the turbulent later eighteenth and early nineteenth centuries when Western Europe came dramatically under its influence. It opposes monolithically social constructions of reality to the extent that they deny or repress the legitimate authority of personal choice whether by reference to metaphysical necessity, as in the ontological position, or to the impervious processes of history, as in some sociological arguments. Expressionist rhetoric is, up to a point, a comfortable perspective for Americans, including American teachers, since it has so pervasively articulated our political myths and institutions. The values of liberalism, including self-determination, freedom of speech, and the potential for enlightened social change, are usually preserved, as a matter of principle if not always practice, in even the most hierarchically organized American work and school settings. At the same time, however, the expressionist statement in education today is nearly always marginalized as "romantic," given its disposition to challenge the prerogatives of established institutional order. As a result, its articulation has tended to feature moral intensity as a substitute for political power, occasionally provoking the conscience of education but seldom affecting the bases of its authority.

Of course, as a corrective to both ontological and objectivist assertions, expressionist rhetoric has had a salutary impact on schools—especially in the twentieth century. It defends the importance of liberating student imagination, of tolerating the messiness of individual searches for meaning, of authorizing personal voices, of acknowledging the creative potential of all students, including those who have been socially and academically disenfranchised in the past. It forces emphasis away from the degrading and largely delusory preoccupation with standards, measurements, "scientifically" structured curricula, and pseudo-causal relationships between instructional methods and results. It tends to value collaborative learning in place of autocratic lecture formats, contending that the interpretive processes by which human beings compose the world are not the exclusive preserve of a politically vested minority merely because that minority has the standing and will to dominate conversation. In short it humanizes and liberalizes classrooms in a social context that has for centuries sought far more oppressive ends. The expressionist argument, however, also stands accused of a well-meant but potentially harmful naiveté about the status of "individual imagination" and "personal voice" given the nature of language as a social practice and given the power, as well as resistance to change, characteristic of social institutions, the school among others. In *Schooling in Capitalist America,* Samuel Bowles and Herbert Gintis warn of the ease with which an uncritical liberalism can be manipulated in the service of realities it seeks to oppose but fails to understand. They conclude that reform movements over the past century, inspired by progressive educational agendas, can only be viewed "as attempting to broaden the discretion and deepen the involvement of the child while (in fact) maintaining hierarchical control over the ultimate processes and outcomes of the educational encounter. The goal has been to enhance student motivation while withholding effective participation in the setting of priorities" (39). The so-called "open classroom" in which reading and writing are taught must stand as fully implicated as any other in this indictment, although, unlike the lecture classroom's overt hierarchical control, it condemns itself less by its complicity than by its innocence.

This is not to suggest, as some critics wrongly charge, that the expressionist argument ignores the social dimension of language—any more than the ontological or objectivist statement ignores it. The *isolated* individual is a *reductio ad absurdum,* not a feature of the expressionist statement as such, however committed it may be to valuing the personal. According to Wilhelm Von Humboldt, a prominent nineteenth-century Kantian, "language develops only in social intercourse, and humans understand themselves only by having tested the comprehensibility of their words on others" (36). Ernst Cassirer, foremost of the modern neoKantians, insists in *The Philosophy of Symbolic Forms* that, if the linguistic

sign "had merely expressed an individual representation produced in the individual consciousness, it would have remained imprisoned in the individual consciousness, without power to pass beyond it." On the contrary, he concludes, "since language arises not in isolated but in communal action, it possesses from the very start a truly common, `universal' sense" (286). At the same time, however, the tendency of expressionist rhetoric, from such British romantics as Coleridge to contemporary advocates of "expressive writing," has been to privilege imaginative consciousness apart from any explicitly social shaping of its character and also, at the extreme, to individualize (but *not* to isolate) that consciousness in the process of dramatizing the "creativity" of personal utterance. Von Humboldt argues, for instance, that speech "proceeds from the interior of a living creature, consists of the articulated sound of a thinking person, and is received as an unarticulated one by a sensitive fellow human being" (34). Hence, if the objectivist statement, as in structural linguistics for instance, is liable to err in finding language an austere "system" of rules precisely constraining individual language use, the expressionist statement is liable to err in offering the particular user a more or less radical freedom to mean in personal terms—to recreate language as a personal instrument. The tendency in literacy instruction proceeding from expressionist assumptions has been (though only at the extreme) to ignore or reduce the visibility of grammatical, generic, and other massively real social constraints on language use in favor of "expressive" discourse, presumably the signature of the individual language user and presumably associated with a degree of authenticity or sincerity inevitably compromised in more public statements. This conceptual exaggeration can lead to misguided classroom practice, where students (as well as teachers) allow themselves to cultivate notions of self-actualization and personal freedom of choice that the stern, politically intransigent world outside the (usually beleaguered) "romantic" classroom will eventually patronize as impractical or even indict as sentimental or dangerous. Failing to assess objective social conditions, students end up cynical about the manipulating liberalism of their teachers while teachers eventually blunt their energies struggling against institutional realities whose power they have not fully enough come to terms with.

The dialogical or sociological statement rejects at once the metaphysics of an ontological argument, the positivist, reifying tendencies of objectivist rhetoric, and the privileging of "consciousness" (universally or individually conceived), associated with expressionist rhetoric. Language is regarded as a social practice rooted, as are all social practices, in material and historical process. The phenomenal world, the "world of everyday life," is itself a material and historical reality—not less real because it is a product of human energies and therefore subject to continuous change as a result of human action, but also not less capable of alteration because it is an objective social fact. The concept of "society" and the concept of "individual" stand in dialectical relationship to each other. Society is to be sure a human construct, but the individual is also a social construct: one's sense of "self" is made possible through the essentially social identifications—family, home, country, culture, religion, ethical orientation, school—that allow selfhood to define itself. "Individual consciousness," writes V. N. Vološinov, a prominent member of the Bakhtin circle, "is not the architect of the ideological superstructure, but only a tenant lodging in the social edifice of ideological signs" (13). In the same way, the concept of language stands in dialectical relationship with the concept of language user, each conditioning the other within the contexts of material social reality and historical change. As social practice, language is neither an abstracted system of unchanging rules nor a merely individual medium of expression. The life of language, including its normative appearance at given moments, is a function of its users, yet the users are themselves constituted by the processes of language as well as by the other material and historical realities that language objectifies. People are born into languages that they did not themselves create, and they learn, even as they practice language use, the values, world assumptions, images of self and other—all

the social realities that particular languages convey. "Signs," according to Raymond Williams, "can exist only when this active social relationship is posited. . . . The real communicative 'products' which are usable signs are . . . living evidence of a continuing social process, into which individuals are born and within which they are shaped, but to which they then also actively contribute, in a continuing process. This is at once their socialization and their individuation" (37). The "world" that language presents to its users as an objectified condition both appears to be and is profoundly actual, immediate, material, and enveloping. Yet it is also wholly historical and dynamic, a human product upon which human beings make their impact.

Sociological rhetoric shares with expressionism a liberationist concern for language users faced with the actual and sometimes dominating conditions of social life. In other words, it acknowledges the fact of social change as well as the responsibility of individuals to work for change insofar as dominating conditions require. The sociological view does not, however, offer the merely "liberal" concern of a romantic perspective, which tends to ignore the power and necessity of social reality while inciting individuals to hurt themselves catastrophically against it. It recommends instead a self-aware and consciously "critical" concern that understands the tendency in all social institutions to forget their origins in human activity, to forget their historicity and thereby monumentalize themselves at cost to the quality of human life. The motive for liberation is always to be found in a perceived jeopardizing of that quality, which depends upon the free converse of human beings working toward the improvement of their condition. Ideally, language acts are dedicated to that end; ideally, the social realities that emerge from language acts and other means of discourse equally serve that end. Yet we are obliged to recognize and grapply with a very human desire to forget the nature of our participation in life; to perpetuate ourselves and prevail as the "evolved" conclusion of a process that anticipated us from the beginning; to dominate or coerce anyone whose difference from ourselves constitutes a threat to hegemony. Oppression, therefore, in the service of our own continuance is a persistent social condition, which it is in part the concern of a dialogical rhetoric to expose and relieve in order to maintain the quality of human life that dominance always puts at hazard.

A classroom informed by the assumptions of this perspective aims above all to situate students self-consciously within the objective social realities that impinge upon them, cause them to be what and who they are, and, in some circumstances, account for their domination. Freire offers the essential instructional stance in his concept of "problem-posing" education, which aims not to make "deposits" of information in passive student minds (the "banking" concept) but instead to pose questions for critical scrutiny within a collaborative setting intended to lead students to claim authority to speak and be heard in the world. This classroom avoids the structured and stratified pedagogy that has evolved to enforce a status quo, an institutional fidelity, by directing reverent attention toward institutional artifacts (perceived as evident and unassailable) while deflecting attention away from the premises that account for them. For example, it avoids the teaching of "works of literature" as though they were unhistorical, unquestionable cultural monoliths while overlooking the critical arguments that secretly define literature as an object as well as the tactics of writing and reading it. The classroom favors instead the "posing" of literature as a human question, encouraging students to learn about its many definitions and the reasons for their emergence so that they can join freely in the processes of reading and writing without subordinating themselves to entrenched ideas about their proper place or function within the institution of "literacy." At the same time, however, this dialogical classroom also avoids naive assurances that speaking necessarily *entails* being heard, that sincerity untempered by sociopolitical intelligence is sufficient for empowerment, that "personal voice" is achieved apart from participation in the social and historical process of making the world by making meaning. Hence, the literature classroom does not stop with "personal connections" to literary texts but proceeds to a full awareness of the interpretive

communities (themselves endlessly evolving) that shape those connections from the very beginning. It aims at creating a critical consciousness of the institution of literature, including its political manifestations in schools, literary establishments, and the "industry" of literature production and reception. It hopes to make students persuasive by making them knowledgeable, to free them by revealing the means of living dialectically within academic institutions and the other worlds that those institutions serve. "Living dialectically" means recognizing our involvement in social reality while resisting wherever necessary the tendency of that reality to make us or to make others less than fully human.

All to the good in theory. But the sociological perspective has its own inevitable limitations, which render it part of the dialogue of rhetorical statements rather than a transcendent position looking piously down upon an otherwise benighted fray. A peculiar deficiency of the emphasis on dialectic so central to a sociological argument is that the insistence is frequently not itself dialectical; indeed, it is as likely as any other to become theological, though the privileged deity is now neither the god of our forefathers nor the god of the laboratory nor the god of consciousness, but instead the god of history. This deity is a particularly truculent being who necessitates change for the sake of change, a turbulent renunciation of the very idea of tradition—as in the case, for instance, of Mao's Cultural Revolution—all in the interest of ideological purity with little consideration of the effects of radical change on the human beings who must endure it for theory's sake. The tendency of a sociological argument, just opposite that of the expressionist perspective, is to content itself with an impoverished conception of individuality, hazarding in the process a substantial effacement of human agency and personal freedom before inexorable sociohistorical forces. We have plentiful enough evidence of the potential for inhumanity in contemporary socialist political experiments to suggest that Marxist and other presumably dialectical arguments nurture the same oppressive capacity as any intellectual commitment when they divorce themselves from dialogue and reconstitute a hierarchy of voices in their own favor. Marxism in theory argues the necessity for its own replacement; but that necessity is all too soon forgotten as it comes to political dominance.

Ontological, objectivist, expressionist, and sociological statements all distinctively influence or validate current programs of literacy instruction. Or, to put it more carefully, a scheme comprised of these oppositional tensions can be applied to that instruction for purposes of scrutiny and critique (just as other schemes might be), although no actual teacher, program, or even theorist is properly reduced to one pole or another. In the United States today, the dominant scholarly argument appears to be objectivist, although the expressionist continues to prick the educational conscience, while the least self-aware instruction continues, as it has for centuries, to be implicitly ontological. Intersubjective or dialogical statements have only lately begun to assert themselves (as recent issues of *College English* attest), though many of them appear allied with structuralist arguments about fully enclosed, ahistorical "genres" and "discourse communities," suggesting only a slight modification of objectivist assumptions to include "social context" among the other "objective constraints" acting upon discursive practice. Writing-across-the-curriculum theory is a representative instance. The objectivist statement in this domain tends to encourage curricula in which modes of reading and writing are regarded as absolute systems of rules, manifested as genres that precisely regulate the practitioners of disciplines. The task, from this perspective, is to introduce students systematically to the rules of a genre (presuming that those rules are objective and analyzable) so that they can enter a discourse that is otherwise inaccessible to them. The expressionist perspective, by contrast, emphasizes the heuristic potential of language use and encourages reading and writing in different disciplines primarily as a means of learning the concepts and modes of inquiry characteristic of them. The expressionist perspective tends not to emphasize the discrete features of different genres as a goal of instruction, partly from the conviction that personal inquiry usefully precedes professionalization within a discipline; partly also from the knowl-

edge that schools in any case do not fully know the features of non-school genres; and partly from the hope that an expressive focus through the disciplines may serve to enfranchise students who are otherwise excluded from or intimidated by the mysterious and self-important rituals of disciplinary practitioners. Inevitably, each of these curricular tactics has limitations stemming from incomplete representations of language and language use.

The sociological perspective, though to date only modestly influential in writing-intensive programs, might respond eventually to the conceptual limitations of such curricula in the following way. Recognizing the character of language as a social practice, it would wish to isolate neither the concept of normative use nor the concept of individual expression. It would deny the ability to learn a genre by conceiving and "memorizing" it as a structural entity, specifically challenging the "container" metaphors and insider/outsider dichotomies that structuralist renderings self-interestedly encourage. But it would equally critique the adequacy of "expressive writing" without a critical awareness of the normative circumstances of school-sponsored disciplines. It would surely commend an awareness of school discourse as an enveloping practice in its own right, one which may finally preclude the learning of genres extrinsic to that setting. Therefore, it might well value informing students of the methods of inquiry and the processes of composition that schools distinctively enforce, revealing their characteristics in order to enable students to live productively amidst the expectations of the school world. At the same time, the most radical socialist agenda would subject the institutional reality of "school" itself to scrutiny in the context of other social realities, so that the need and struggle for institutional change would by no means be limited to the "safe" dimensions of cross-curricular writing programs. My point in applying these different rhetorical statements to the concept of writing-in-the-disciplines is not, however, to recommend one version of that educational effort over another. It is chiefly to turn my present argument back to its starting point in Freire's concept of "praxis"—by suggesting how the dialogue of rhetorical voices that I have contrived (one version of theoretical reflectiveness) can offer a means of assessing instructional practice from sufficient remove to enable the free exercise of educational choices. The four statements map themselves upon axes of human value, permanence and change, necessity and freedom, tradition and futurity, equality and differential merit, polarities in terms of which intellectual arguments endlessly struggle and reiterate their themes. The practical choices of the classroom, mundane as they may appear, represent both the composing and the construing of these themes, a naming and a transforming of the world. There can be no ultimate reconciling of opposed values, certainly, but there must be an enlightened, continuous, sometimes forceful and even raucous reappraisal of possibilities as concrete social conditions require.

To finish here, however, would be politically as well as intellectually dishonest. A last problem will enable me to deny any misleading closure. It concerns the paradoxical relationship between dialogue and commitment, the openness to possibility and the need to choose, that lies at the heart of Freire's "praxis." Plainly, "choice" does not mean an allegiance to one or another of the rhetorical statements I have posed; it means rather a situating of oneself somewhere within the field of possibilities that the statements dialectically articulate. To be sure, "choice" is also not restricted to this single interpretive domain, an important fact since the domain reflects, not just my own priorities, but also (unavoidably I think), in its very rhetorical depiction, some of my own preferred choices. Ultimately, however, laboring such a point will not take us out of difficulty: for while we may propose endless alternative domains, on endlessly alternating levels of abstraction, we cannot escape the composing of them as a precondition of choice nor can we escape, finally, the necessity of choice insofar as we act in the world. Yet, and this is the puzzle that interests me, what shall our attitude be toward the dialogue sustained in these formulations (or sustained elsewhere) at the moment of action in the world?

A rude version of the question is, how dialogical is Freire about the importance of dialogue? Is his ad-

vocacy of dialogue in effect noncommittal? And does dialogue with an oppressor, assuming it can be established, extend to tolerance of oppression or even to nonjudgmental regard for the oppressor's arguments? The realities of power insure, for Freire, that there can be no free debate about dialogue itself—because voices already assured of their dominant positions do not require the maintenance of conversation: that felt need belongs only to the marginalized, the dispossessed, whose hope of an improved quality of life depends on a nonnegotiable right to speak. Nor, assuming that a dialogue has been (forcibly) established, can the possibility of continued oppression be considered a subject of talk for the very purpose of conversation is to redistribute an otherwise oppressive power. Clearly, one's decision to *act* in the world suspends the nonjudgmental posture of reflection by committing the actor to a choice of premises and a position of advocacy. There is, of course, no resolving the paradox, but how to state its implications is what finally matters. Many teachers, besieged by the complexities of classroom life, wish to reject the uncomfortable oppositions of dialectic, such as those I have been sketching, by imagining they can have the best of everything, can affirm everything while denying nothing, as though the repudiating of distinctions could be a practical response to uncertainty. The trouble with such a tactic is that it simultaneously extinguishes dialogue *and* reasoned commitment by homogenizing the ideas that enable both talk and action. Scholars, in contrast to teachers, too often endorse a different response, settling for dialogue alone (what educational traditionalists sometimes call the Great Conversation), a mythic disengagement from reality characterized by boundless intellectual generosity, which, in the actual political world of the school, masks either a genuine failure of the will or a covert commitment that subtly turns the energetic struggle of true dialogue into bland, "scholastic" caricature. Finally, some scholars as well as some teachers support a third response, commitment in the absence of dialogue, a choice which, however, results only in that ossification of intellect that most people have in mind when they speak disparagingly of ideology. Is there a fourth alternative, a way to express the knowledge that paradoxes engender? The best I can come up with is this: we *are*, ultimately, compelled to choose, to make, express, and act upon our commitments, to denounce the world, as Freire says, above all oppression and whatever arguments have been called upon to validate it. Moreover, since conversations seldom entail equal distributions of power or authority, our speech may well have to be boldly denunciative at times if it is to affect its hearers in the midst of their intellectual and political comfort. At the same time, if we are not, like Pogo, to discover that the enemy is us, we are also compelled to review our choices and monitor our commitments, scrupulously, not in their abstract sufficiency, but in their *consequences* as we exercise them in the world. We are obliged to announce ourselves so that, through the very process of self-assertion, we grow more conscious of our axioms and submit that awareness to public debate. The quality of our lives as teachers depends on our willingness to discover through struggle ever more fruitful means of doing our work. The quality of our students' lives depends on the cogency and the humanity of the decisions we make.[3]

Notes

1. My distinctions closely follow those of Raymond Williams in his chapter on "language" (21–44). But similar oppositions of view abound, from Douglas Ehninger to James Berlin and Lester Faigley. Inevitably, characterizations overlap and diverge: inevitably, disputes arise over appropriate terminology. (Berlin and I both use the term "expressionist," for instance, but differ in our depictions of the perspective we intend it to name.) Rightly perceived, such differences encourage a useful interpretive complexity. They are not rightly perceived, however, when they merely vie for power in a positivist or antiquarian historical discourse.

2. Indeed, these statements would not exhaust the past even in my own scheme. Other statements about language and knowledge could include the argument from magic, for instance, which locates meaningfulness in a supernatural potency within words themselves, or the argument of mysticism, which finds meaning in silence, the suspension of verbal discourse and the clearing away of nominal distraction that it allows. But these statements have had less importance, for better or worse, in educational contexts than those I am emphasizing.

3. This essay began as a paper delivered at the Fourth International Conference on the Teaching of English in Ottawa, Canada, May, 1986. A revised and expanded version was read later at a conference at the University of New Hampshire in October, 1986. Its present form owes much to the advice of colleagues at these meetings and again as much to Ann Berthoff, whose discrimination as a reader is matched only by the generosity with which she has given her time.

Works Cited

Aristotle. *On Interpretation.* Trans. H. P. Cooke and H. Tredennick. Cambridge: Harvard UP, 1973.

Berlin, James. "Contemporary Composition: The Major Pedagogical Theories." *College English* 44 (1982): 765–77.

Bowles, Samuel, and Herbert Gintis. *Schooling in Capitalist America.* New York: Basic, 1976.

Cassirer, Ernst. *Language.* Trans. Ralph Manheim. New Haven: Yale UP, 1955–57. Vol. 1 of *The Philosophy of Symbolic Forms.* 3 vols. 1953–57.

Cicero. *De oratore.* Trans. E. W. Sutton and H. Rackham. 2 Vols. Cambridge: Harvard UP, 1976–77.

Coleridge, Samuel T. *Biographia Literaria.* 1817. London: Dent, 1965.

Descartes, René. *Discourse on Method.* 1637. Trans. Laurence J. Lafleur. Indianapolis: Bobbs, 1960.

Ehninger, Douglas. "On Systems of Rhetoric." *Philosophy and Rhetoric* 1 (1968): 131–44.

Faigley, Lester. "Competing Theories of Process: A Critique and a Proposal." *College English* 48 (1986): 527–42.

Freire, Paulo. *Pedagogy of the Oppressed.* Trans. Myra Bergman Ramos. New York: Seabury, 1968.

Locke, John. *An Essay Concerning Human Understanding.* 1690. New York: Collier, 1965.

St. Augustine. *On Christian Doctrine.* 427. Trans. D. W. Robertson, Jr. Indianapolis: Bobbs, 1958.

Vološinov, V. N. *Marxism and the Philosophy of Language.* Trans. Ladislav Matejka and I. R. Titunik. Cambridge: Harvard UP, 1973.

Von Humboldt, Wilhelm. *Linguistic Variability and Intellectual Development.* 1836. Trans. George C. Buck and Frithjof A. Raven. Philadelphia: U of Pennsylvania P, 1972.

Williams, Raymond. *Marxism and Literature.* London: Oxford UP, 1977.

Acknowledgments

David Bartholomae, "Inventing the University," from *When a Writer Can't Write,* ed. Mike Rose. New York: Guilford Press, 1985: 134–65. Reprinted by permission of the publisher.

Ann E. Berthoff, "The Intelligent Eye and the Thinking Hand," from *The Making of Meaning: Metaphors, Models, and Maxims for Writing Teachers.* Boynton/Cook, a division of Reed Elsevier Inc., Portsmouth, NH, 1981. Reprinted by permission of the author. "A Curious Triangle and the Double-Entry Notebook; or How a Theory (of Language) Can Help Us Teach (Critical) Reading and Writing," from *FOCUS: Teaching English Language Arts,* VII: 2, Winter 1981, Southeastern Ohio Council of Teachers of English. Reprinted with permission.

James A. Berlin, "Contemporary Composition: The Major Pedagogical Theories," *College English,* December 1982. Copyright 1982 by the National Council of Teachers of English. Reprinted with permission.

Glenda A. Bissex, "Growing Writers in the Classroom," *Language Arts,* October 1981. Copyright 1981 by the National Council of Teachers of English. Reprinted with permission.

Patricia Bizzell, "Arguing about Literacy," *College English,* February 1988. Copyright 1988 by the National Council of Teachers of English. Reprinted with permission.

James Britton, "Shaping at the Point of Utterance," from *Reinventing the Rhetorical Tradition,* ed. Freeman and Pringle. Canadian Council of Teachers of English, 1980. Reprinted with permission.

Kenneth A. Bruffee, "Collaborative Learning and the 'Conversation of Mankind,'" *College English,* November 1984. Copyright 1984 by the National Council of Teachers of English. Reprinted with permission.

Richard M. Coe, "An Apology for Form; or, Who Took the Form Out of the Process?" *College English,* January 1987. Copyright 1987 by the National Council of Teachers of English. Reprinted with permission.

Anne Haas Dyson, "Negotiating among Multiple Worlds: The Space/Time Dimensions of Young Children's Composing," *Research in the Teaching of English,* December 1988. Copyright 1988 by the National Council of Teachers of English. Reprinted with permission.

Lisa Ede and Andrea Lunsford, "Audience Addressed/Audience Invoked: The Role of Audience in Composition Theory and Pedagogy," *College Composition and Communication,* May 1984. Copyright 1984 by the National Council of Teachers of English. Reprinted with permission.

Peter Elbow, "The Shifting Relationships between Speech and Writing," *College English,* October 1985. Copyright 1985 by the National Council of Teachers of English. Reprinted with permission.

Janet Emig, "Lynn: Profile of a Twelfth-Grade Writer," from *The Composing Processes of Twelfth Graders.* Copyright 1971 by the National Council of Teachers of English. Reprinted with permission.

Kyle Fiore and Nan Elsasser, "'Strangers No More': A Liberatory Literacy Curriculum," *College English,* February 1982. Copyright 1982 by the National Council of Teachers of English. Reprinted with permission.

Linda Flower and John R. Hayes, "A Cognitive Process Theory of Writing," *College Composition and Communication,* December 1981. Copyright 1981 by the National Council of Teachers of English. Reprinted with permission.

Sarah Warshauer Freedman, "The Registers of Student and Professional Expository Writing: Influences on Teachers' Responses," from *New Directions in Composition Research,* ed. Beach and Bridwell. New York: Guilford Press, 1984: 334–347. Reprinted with permission of the publisher.

Richard Fulkerson, "Four Philosophies of Composition," *College Composition and Communication,* December 1979. Copyright 1979 by the National Council of Teachers of English. Reprinted with permission.

Cheryl Geisler, "Toward a Sociocognitive Model of Literacy: Constructing Mental Models in a Philosophical Conversation," from *Textual Dynamics of the Professions: Historical and Contemporary Studies in Writing in Professional Communities,* ed. Bazerman, Charles and James Paradis. Copyright © University of Wisconsin Press. Reprinted with permission of The University of Wisconsin Press.

Maxine Hairston, "Diversity, Ideology, and Teaching Writing," *College Composition and Communication,* May 1992. Copyright 1992 by the National Council of Teachers of English. Reprinted with permission.

S. Michael Halloran, "Rhetoric in the American College Curriculum: The Decline of Public Discourse," PRE/TEXT 3.3 (1982): 245–269. Reprinted with permission.

Richard H. Haswell, "Textual Research and Coherence: Findings, Intuition, Application," *College English,* March 1989. Copyright 1989 by the National Council of Teachers of English. Reprinted with permission.

Gail E. Hawisher, "Research and Recommendations for Computers and Composition," from *Critical Perspectives on Composition Instruction,* eds. Hawisher and Selfe. Copyright © 1989 Teachers College, Columbia University. Reprinted with permission of Teachers College Press.

George Hillocks, Jr., "The Need for Interdisciplinary Studies on the Teaching of Writing," from *Rhetoric Review* 7 (1989):257–72. Reprinted with permission of the publisher.

James L. Kinneavy, "*Kairos:* A Neglected Concept in Classical Rhetoric," from *Rhetoric and Praxis: The Contributions of Classical Rhetoric to Practical Reasoning,"* ed. Jean Dietz Moss. Reprinted with permission of The Catholic University of America Press, Washington, D.C.

C. H. Knoblauch, "Rhetorical Constructions: Dialogue and Commitment," *College English,* February 1988. Copyright 1988 by the National Council of Teachers of English. Reprinted with permission.

Janice M. Lauer, "Instructional Practices: Toward an Integration," from *Focuses* 1.1(1988):3–10. Reprinted with permission of the publisher.

Susan Miller, "The Feminization of Composition," from *The Politics of Writing Instruction: Post Secondary,* by Richard Bullock and John Timbur. Boynton/Cook, a division of Reed Elsevier Inc.: Portsmouth, NH, 1991. Reprinted with permission of the author.

James Moffett, "I, You, and It," *College Composition and Communication,* 16(1965):243–48. Copyright 1965 by the National Council of Teachers of English. Reprinted with permission.

Beverly J. Moss, "Ethnography and Composition: Studying Language at Home," from *Methods and Methodology in Composition Research,* eds. Kirsch and Sullivan. Carbondale: Southern Illinois University Press, 1992: 153–71. Reprinted with permission.

Donald M. Murray, "Teaching the Other Self: The Writer's First Reader," *College Composition and Communication,* May 1982. Copyright 1982 by the National Council of Teachers of English. Reprinted with permission.

Stephen North, from *The Making of Knowledge in Composition: Portrait of an Emerging Field.* Boynton/Cook, a division of Reed Elsevier Inc.: Portsmouth, NH, 1987. Reprinted with permission of the author.

Louise Wetherbee Phelps, "Rhythm and Pattern in a Composing Life," from *Writers on Writing,* vol. 1, ed. Tom Waldrep. New York: Random House, 1985, 241–57. Reprinted with permission of the author.

James E. Porter, "Intertextuality and the Discourse Community," from *Rhetoric Review* 5 (1986):34–37. Reprinted with permission of the publisher.

Linda R. Robertson, Sharon Crowley, and Frank Lentricchia, "The Wyoming Conference Resolution Opposing Unfair Salaries and Working Conditions for Post-Secondary Teachers of Writing," *College English,* March 1987. Copyright 1987 by the National Council of Teachers of English. Reprinted with permission.

Mike Rose, "The Language of Exclusion: Writing Instruction at the University," *College English,* April 1985. Copyright 1985 by the National Council of Teachers of English. Reprinted with permission.

John Rouse, "The Politics of Composition," *College English,* September 1979. Copyright 1979 by the National Council of Teachers of English. Reprinted with permission of the publisher and author.

Mina P. Shaughnessy, "Some New Approaches toward Teaching," *Journal of Basic Writing,* Spring 1994, volume 13, Number 1. Copyright © 1994 by the *Journal of*

Basic Writing, Instructional Resource Center, Office of Academic Affairs, The City University of New York. Reprinted with permission.

Geneva Smitherman-Donaldson, "Toward a National Public Policy on Language," *College English,* January 1987. Copyright 1987 by the National Council of Teachers of English. Reprinted with permission.

Marilyn S. Sternglass, "Writing Development as Seen through Longitudinal Research: A Case Study Exemplar," from *Written Communication,* vol. 10, 1993:235–61. Copyright © 1993 by Marilyn S. Sternglass. Reprinted with permission of Sage Publications, Inc.

Donald C. Stewart, "Collaborative Learning and Composition: Boon or Bane?" from *Rhetoric Review* 7 (1988): 58–83. Reprinted with permission of the publisher.

Victor Villanueva, Jr., "*Inglés* in the Colleges," from *Bookstraps: From an American Academic of Color,* Copyright 1993 by the National Council of Teachers of English. Reprinted with permission.

Tilly Warnock and John Warnock, "Liberatory Writing Centers: Restoring Authority to Writers," from *Writing Centers: Theory and Administration.* Copyright 1984 by the National Council of Teachers of English. Reprinted with permission.

Joseph M. Williams, "The Phenomenology of Error," *College Composition and Communication,* May 1981. Copyright 1981 by the National Council of Teachers of English. Reprinted with permission.

W. Ross Winterowd, "The Rhetorical Transaction of Reading," *College Composition and Communication,* May 1976. Copyright 1976 by the National Council of Teachers of English. Reprinted with permission.

Richard E. Young, "Concepts of Art and the Teaching of Writing," from *Reinventing the Rhetorical Tradition*, ed. Freemand and Pringle. Canadian Council of Teachers of English, 1980. Reprinted with permission.

Index of Authors and Titles